JEAN-
PAUL
MARAT

SERIES EDITOR
Darrin McMahon, Dartmouth College

After a period of some eclipse, the study of intellectual history has enjoyed a broad resurgence in recent years. The Life of Ideas contributes to this revitalization through the study of ideas as they are produced, disseminated, received, and practiced in different historical contexts. The series aims to embed ideas—those that endured, and those once persuasive but now forgotten—in rich and readable cultural histories. Books in this series draw on the latest methods and theories of intellectual history while being written with elegance and élan for a broad audience of readers.

JEAN-PAUL MARAT

PROPHET OF TERROR

Keith Michael Baker

THE UNIVERSITY OF CHICAGO PRESS
CHICAGO AND LONDON

The University of Chicago Press, Chicago 60637
The University of Chicago Press, Ltd., London

For more information, contact the University of Chicago Press, 1427 E. 60th St., Chicago, IL 60637.
Published 2025
Printed in the United States of America

34 33 32 31 30 29 28 27 26 25   1 2 3 4 5

ISBN-13: 978-0-226-82092-7 (cloth)
ISBN-13: 978-0-226-82093-4 (ebook)
DOI: https://doi.org/10.7208/chicago/9780226820934.001.0001

Library of Congress Cataloging-in-Publication Data

Names: Baker, Keith Michael author
Title: Jean-Paul Marat : prophet of terror / Keith Michael Baker.
Other titles: Life of ideas
Description: Chicago : The University of Chicago Press, 2025. | Series: The life of ideas | Includes bibliographical references and index.
Identifiers: LCCN 2025008186 | ISBN 9780226820927 cloth | ISBN 9780226820934 ebook
Subjects: LCSH: Marat, Jean Paul, 1743–1793 | France—History—Revolution, 1789–1799—Biography | LCGFT: Biographies
Classification: LCC DC146.M3 B25 2025 | DDC 944.04092 $a B—dc23/eng/20250321
LC record available at https://lccn.loc.gov/2025008186

♾ This paper meets the requirements of ANSI/NISO Z39.48-1992 (Permanence of Paper).

Authorized Representative for EU General Product Safety Regulation (GPSR) queries: **Easy Access System Europe**—Mustamäe tee 50, 10621 Tallinn, Estonia, gpsr.requests@easproject.com
Any other queries: https://press.uchicago.edu/press/contact.html

To my sons, Julian, Felix, Nicholas

CONTENTS

THE FIRST MODERN POPULIST

FRONTISPIECE. Octagonal medal, colored plaster, 1793. Private collection of Luca Einaudi, reproduced with generous permission.

INTRODUCTION

"Never forget the sublime words of the prophet-Marat: *Sacrifice two hundred thousand heads*, he said, *and you will save a million*."

This was the mandate laid upon the deputies of the French National Convention by radical Paris activists meeting in the William Tell section in mid-November 1793. Marie Antoinette, execrated as the symbol of a society to be eradicated, had mounted the scaffold a month earlier. The principal Girondins, moderate deputies purged from the bitterly divided Convention as enemies of the people, had followed her two weeks later. The Paris activists called for more. "You have just given a terrifying example made to astonish the universe and strike fear into the most guilty," they declared. "The William Tell section congratulates you. It will congratulate you still more if you maintain fear and terror as the great order of the day, that fear and terror which are the two most powerful levers of revolutionaries. . . . A hecatomb of traitors is necessary to bring healing to all the wounds of the homeland, butchered by unnatural children." A great parade of victims to the guillotine—nobles and commoners, rich and poor, learned and illiterate, scientists and priests, women and men, revolutionaries and counterrevolutionaries—was under way. The Terror was taking form.

This book aims to make sense of those "sublime words of the prophet-Marat," the radical journalist and martyred deputy whose notorious calls for blood gave voice to some of the most frightful impulses of the French Revolution. The idea of writing it took root as I reflected on the intriguing fact that Marat's first political work was written in England, in English, in 1774. It was entitled *The Chains of Slavery, A Work wherein the Clandes-*

tine and Villainous Attempts of Princes to Ruin Liberty are pointed out, and the Dreadful Scenes of Despotism Disclosed, and it came prefaced by "An Address to the Electors of Great Britain, in order to draw their Timely Attention to the Choice of Proper Representatives in the Next Parliament." In 1774, it turns out, Marat was calling upon the British electors to cleanse the House of Commons of placemen and pensioners—men corrupted as representatives by their ties of patronage to the royal court and the ministry. In 1789, strikingly, he used very similar language in revolutionary France to urge the French to purge beneficiaries of the Old Regime from the new National Assembly.

By the end of 1790, he was ready to give numbers. Estimating that it might be necessary to lop off five thousand heads to save the French Revolution, he insisted that "if it requires twenty thousand, we shouldn't hesitate for a moment." The figure was constantly revised thereafter, but with the clear implication that it could never be large enough. "Felling five hundred heads would have sufficed to put things back in order eleven months ago," he proclaimed in May 1791; "today it would take fifty thousand. Perhaps five hundred thousand will have fallen by the end of the year. France will have been inundated in blood, but it will not be free." Whether or not he actually called for two hundred seventy thousand heads before the notorious September Massacres of 1792 is still disputed. But something like this was the tally the Paris activists remembered a year later.

How, I wondered, did a rhetoric of denunciation and distrust of representation that was becoming commonplace in eighteenth-century England take on such a different resonance in revolutionary France? How did the language of English radicalism metamorphose as it crossed the Channel? How did it metastasize into a call for Terror? Could an intellectual biography illuminate the origins and contexts of Marat's words, their meanings for him and those who read or heard them, their significance for the radicalization of the French Revolution, their relevance for modern democratic politics? The chapters that follow offer some responses to these questions.

Jean-Paul Marat was a cosmopolitan, a man of the complex and mobile eighteenth-century European world. Swiss-born, the son of a former Catholic priest from Sardinia and a Calvinist mother from French Huguenot stock, he left his homeland in early adulthood for Paris, then spent a decade or so in London interwoven with travel through Holland, Ireland, and Scotland before settling finally in the French capital. He was never entirely free of thoughts of settling again across the Channel in the land that had given him his formative medical and political experience.

Marat's life, and this book, offers a drama in three acts. The first follows him from Neuchâtel to the London of the late 1760s and 1770s, where he passed crucial years practicing medicine and elaborating his philosophical and political ideas. His medical experience proved to be valuable later, but the most salient aspect of his lengthy stay in London was his exposure to the popular mobilization and political radicalism ignited there when the notorious oppositional journalist John Wilkes was elected to the House of Commons but denied a seat by that body. The decision crystallized a central issue for democratic politics: the threat that parliamentary representation could devolve into despotism as the result of the corruption of the deputies by royal or ministerial paymasters. Confronting this issue, Marat drew on the language of classical republicanism—a tradition dating from the Renaissance known for its adoption of the history of the ancient republics as an analytical model for thinking about modern politics. In this mode, *The Chains of Slavery* signaled the danger of encroaching despotism and the rapidly diminishing chances of securing liberty in the modern age. Fear of despotism, on the one hand, and imperatives of press freedom, crowd politics, and popular sovereignty, on the other, were among the preoccupations he carried away from this turbulent decade in England. He would feed on the lessons of London throughout his later political career.

The second act of Marat's life finds him in prerevolutionary Paris. Armed with a medical degree he had acquired, without residency, from the University of St. Andrews, he moved to the French capital early in 1777. There he maneuvered adroitly to establish a lucrative practice as a fashionable doctor. He was soon assured of wealth, but his goal was glory—the modern glory (since the civic glory of the Ancients was no longer an option) of the kind open to anyone who could rival or refute Newton. He spent a decade in this pursuit, publishing the results of experiments on electricity, light, and heat, and battling in vain for public recognition and the approbation of the most powerful scientific body in Europe, the Paris Academy of Sciences. The influential Paris academicians denied his aspirations, and their hostility eventually ruined his candidacy for the directorship of a new scientific academy in Madrid. He was to publish bitter pages decrying the despotism of academies as he led the charge for their destruction in the French Revolution.

Finally, there comes the third act, the one that earned Marat his enduring notoriety. By 1789, his funds were depleted, his hopes for scientific recognition exhausted, his health undermined. The sudden collapse of the Old Regime offered him new opportunities and inspired in him new energies. He had seen the power of the press in English politics and had exploited it assiduously in efforts to publicize his scientific investigations in France. Now, for much of the four years until his assassination in July 1793, he was the most vigorous and vilified radical journalist of the French Revolution, a hideous thorn in the flesh of revolutionary government, his pen constantly inciting the people to action against counterrevolutionary plots, political corruption, the treasonous intentions of the king and the royal family, and the dangers of impending foreign invasion.

For much of that time he lived in hiding, subject to constant government harassment, publishing eight pages daily with the exception of periods when his paper was silenced by official suppression. Throughout these years, his power lay in his language. It gushed forth, fueled by rage and frustration, megalomania and demophilia, hatred and suspicion, patriotism and despair, love of liberty and horror of tyranny, logorrheic exaltation and revolutionary passion. Bitterly critical of the constitutional monarchy established in 1791, he called for the popular insurrection that destroyed it on 10 August 1792 and the paroxysm of bloodletting in the Paris prisons that ensued a month later.

With the advent of the French Republic, this critic of representation became a representative himself, reviled though he was by many of his fellows within the new Convention. There he pressed for the rapid trial and execution of the king and took a decisive part in the factional struggles between Jacobins and Girondins that resulted in the purge of the Girondins—in effect, the event that initiated the Terror—by the popular insurrection of 2 June 1793. He was assassinated by a Girondin sympathizer, Charlotte Corday, on 13 July 1793. Finding him more malleable in death than in life, the Jacobins made him a martyr, commissioning the great revolutionary artist Jacques-Louis David to organize the unprecedented political pageant of his funeral. His assassination was memorialized by David in a secular *pietà* that has become one of the most iconic paintings of the Western artistic canon. The image still stalks the internet.

Alexis de Tocqueville wrote of the "immoderate, violent, radical, desperate, bold, almost crazed" character of the French revolutionaries as an inexplicable mystery, symptomatic of "a virus of a new and unknown kind." No one fits this characterization more aptly than Jean-Paul Marat. How then to penetrate the mystery of his ideas and actions? Were they indeed the manifestation of a novel political virus or the mutation of an old strain in a new environment? Did they spring from personal compulsions or respond to historical circumstances? Marat has often been characterized as monstrous, evil, or mad, but saying so tells us little. There have been many different ways to be monstrous, evil, or mad; the question for the historian is to understand which of them were imaginable in particular times and places, and which were taken, why, and with what effect. Politics hinges on language. My aim is to make sense of Marat's actions, monstrous or not, by bringing into relief the words he used to express his conception of self, diagnose his world, and frame his goals. The objective is to understand the implications of these words and gauge their force within the momentous political transformation of his time.

In an earlier book, *Inventing the French Revolution*, I was most interested in identifying the conceptual conditions of possibility for thinking the French Revolution by showing how the traditional political culture of the absolute monarchy disaggregated into a set of distinct discourses that could be mobilized by political actors competing to establish a new political order as the old one collapsed. I thought of these discourses as both enabling and constraining what could be said, with their recombination and juxtaposition—and improvisation upon them—fashioning the political language of the French Revolution together with the many strains and contradictions within it that drove the revolutionary dynamic. In following Marat's revolutionary career in this book, I have shifted the focus closer to ground level by exploring more fully how these strains and contradictions were played out in action as political choices led constantly to new dilemmas and opened up unanticipated situations and consequences.

As one of the new breed of political journalists the revolution spawned, Marat published his daily paper, *L'Ami du peuple* (The People's Friend), in an effort to understand, control, and shape the events unleashed in 1789. In his eight pages almost every day, he was engaged in fierce competition with other journalists and political actors scripting the French Revolution. I mean "scripting" here not only as the literal chronicling of ongoing events and actions in a daily newspaper, but also in the more extended sense suggested in *Scripting Revolutions*, the book I coedited with Dan Edelstein in 2016. "Scripting" in this conceptualization encompasses the ways actions and events are given character and meaning in a continuous effort to define their relationship to the past, control their implications for the present, and shape their consequences for the future. A script orders events and generates new ones by defining the situation and the actions that must follow from it; as a result, the competition to shape and impose a master script and act out its implications is at the very heart of politics. Nowhere is this process more evident than in the situation created in the French Revolution, in which everything was suddenly and continuously up for grabs in an unprecedented experiment in political invention.

To make sense of Marat, inevitably, I have had to understand the French Revolution for myself in a fresh way, retelling much of the story. Conventionally, it seems to me, historians have tended to use the great moments of the French Revolution as so many monumental stepping stones across its torrential stream of actions and events. I've aimed instead to follow Marat into midstream, to raft the rapids with him as it were, to catch the torrent of events as it flows from choices made and situations created, and as the revolutionary political actors compete to script its meaning and shape its direction. I've tried to avoid hypostatizing marquee events and externalizing as "circumstances" the contexts in which they occur. I've tried, in other words, to show the ways in which issues and events take form in action and enter into the flow of political consciousness.

Encounters with Marat in London in the 1770s left memories of a restless, sharp-eyed little man with a body in constant motion and an agitated, discontented, rebellious disposition to match. Jacques-Pierre Brissot, the future Girondin leader who became his close friend in Paris in the 1780s, found him as thin, agile, and agitated as an organ grinder's monkey. Thirty years later, political enmity had colored Brissot's recollections: his memoirs portrayed a brilliant and intensely ambitious former comrade initially inspired by a dream of political liberty but arrogant, insecure, touchy, hungry for glory, quick to anger, and something of a braggart, an unstable character destined to be transformed by failure and frustration into a dangerous revolutionary maniac.

Megalomania and paranoia spring readily to the modern mind in thinking about this man. But more ancient categories might be no less revealing. Plato would easily have recognized in Marat the psychological type he characterized as thymotic. The tripartite division of the soul suggested in *The Republic* distinguished a desiring part and a reasoning part, but also an element defined by *thymos*, or spiritedness. In this analysis, the thymotic personality is driven by self-esteem, courage, and pride. It demands recognition and justice in acknowledgment of its worth; denied them, it is explosive, quick to indignation, anger, and rage. For Plato, as commentators from Hegel to Fukuyama have emphasized, this expression of character was essentially aristocratic. In Marat, we might say, it is democratized, even vulgarized, and modernized.

Marat sought glory in science and renown in politics, but he was, above all, a populist, a thinker for whom the people as a body existed as the ultimate and essential political reality. The people embodied, rather than the nation represented, was the ground of his political ontology. In 1789, he found his calling as a journalist committed to speaking to and for the people, claiming a direct relationship to it even as he cursed and derided it for remaining unaware of its powers. In the course of the French Revolution, he took on an absolute identity as "The People's Friend." Claiming recognition for himself, he demanded power for the sovereign body of the people. He was the first modern populist.

Sleep and waking were crucial elements in Marat's populist discourse. He goaded the people relentlessly to rouse itself from its civic slumber, to give force to its political existence, to assert its sovereign will. He had seen it do so momentarily in July 1789, only to fall back into a political stupor as the new regime was colonized by remnants of the old. Summoning it to rise up and shed in torrents the blood of the enemies usurping its rightful power, he excoriated it thereafter for its repeated failures to realize its own force and dignity. Raging against enemies he saw viciously destroying the revolution as they postured as the nation's representatives, he denounced treachery, conspiracy, and counterrevolution everywhere.

Two themes run through this book. One tracks Marat's radical distrust of representation. At a time when the French were still experimenting with practices of parliamentary government entirely new to them, he brought from England an intense suspicion of representation in all its forms. The French Revolution, moreover, gave him an ideological niche by opening up a gap between sovereignty represented (in successive national assemblies) and sovereignty embodied (in the Parisian crowd and expressed by the activist sectional assemblies constantly striving to impose a popular will). He inhabited, exploited, and widened this gap, offering a constantly escalating rhetoric of denunciation and purge. This was the crucible in which political alchemy transformed classical republicanism into the language of Terror.

A second theme explores the possibility of relating Marat's science to his politics. He wanted in his physiological writings to cling to the idea of a physical location for the soul as a sovereign self in the body. He wanted in his experimental physics to render natural forces directly visible rather than representing them abstractly and mathematically. He wanted in his political theory to hold on to a notion of sovereignty directly embodied in the people. This essentialist refusal of mediation set him at odds with the advanced scientific philosophy of the Enlightenment. And it extended from his science to his politics. It made him hostile to the abstractions of a market society whose consequences for the poor and propertyless he deplored even as he used its publicity mechanisms to do so. It left him suspicious of institutional arrangements that sought the expression of sovereignty through the derivations of a system of representation. In this, he stood as an Ancient longing for immediacy in an increasingly abstract, complex, and extended modern world. His call for terror was as reactionary as it was revolutionary.

Did it matter? Any biography must ultimately confront the question of the role of its subject in complex historical contexts and transformations. I've been asked more than once whether the French Revolution would look any different if Marat had moved on from Paris to Madrid in 1783. From a distance the answer might appear to be no. A plausible argument can be made that the revolution necessarily produced a figure like Marat, one required to inhabit the gap and crystallize the tensions between the postulate of an absolute sovereignty now vested in the nation and the legitimacy of representative institutions created to channel popular will. From this perspective, he occupied a position in a political force field created by the conceptual opposition between sovereignty embodied and sovereignty represented. Someone else could have taken his place, and indeed others already shared it.

Shifting the focus, though, one also has to say that concepts do not create or activate themselves nor do ideas find their own realization in the world. They need individuals to express them and agents to realize their implications. These actors have their own social and psychological baggage, their own temperaments, their own voices, their own passions, their own ambitions, loves, and hatreds, their own capacities. Situations seen from a historical distance as structured in advance appear to these actors more immediately as circumstances to be negotiated, possibilities to be grasped, threats to be faced, principles to be pursued, enemies to be destroyed. From this perspective, we will see Marat ratcheting up personal animosities and inflaming collective anxieties, amplifying political tensions, intensifying uncertainties and contradictions inherent in competing definitions of the revolutionary situation. The sheer imaginative force of his language, the power of his polemics, his dogged populist commitment, his relentless calls for blood, shaped and sharpened the revolutionary script as its actors struggled to define it and play it out.

In the end, the claim for this book must be that we can see aspects of the French Revolution better if we look at them for a while through Marat's eyes. One advantage of a complex biography is that it offers a kind of guided tour to a historical world. The itinerary may be tortuous, the guide partisan, the destination unanticipated, but they open pathways to understanding—in this case of the ideas, events, and issues shaping the momentous founding of modern politics.

The world has seen representative institutions profoundly strained and subverted in the dozen or so years I have been researching and writing this book. It has been impossible not to recognize analogies between pathologies of representative government that emerged at the time of France's failed republican experiment and those afflicting democratic states in the present moment. The fundamental political tension played out in the experience of the French Revolution, as it acted as a kind of collective petri dish for modern political life, has resurfaced dangerously. Articles of liberal political faith have been eroded, practices of civic deliberation shredded, and accepted modes of collective decision-making imperiled by conspiracy and bad faith, corrupt mechanisms of communication, the eruption and manipulation of populist sentiments, demagogic leadership, and flagrant efforts at mob rule. The imputed will of a putatively embodied people now threatens the crucial conduct of its representative government. Marat's world has unexpectedly become our own.

Fifty years ago, I followed another route from Enlightenment to Revolution in the company of the marquis de Condorcet, a more amiable figure (though one not without his moods). One of the great Enlightenment thinkers and a notable theorist of representative democracy, Condorcet was also a favored target among Marat's enemies in science, philosophy, and politics. The antipathy was mutual. I have come to see these two revolutionary actors as representing opposite poles within eighteenth-century responses to the shaping of the modern world. The differences between them are profound and revealing. In closing this book with a brief diptych, I hope to show that the contrast between them can illuminate the intellectual contours of Enlightenment and Revolution more generally.

ONE

THE SWISS FAMILY MARA

Jean-Paul Marat came into the world without a final "t" to his name. His father was born Juan Salvador Mara in Cagliari, on the southern coast of Sardinia, still at that point a possession of the Spanish crown. Perhaps Juan Salvador was of Sephardi descent, a possibility virulently exploited by anti-Semitic and reactionary writers of the last century, for whom vilification of his son as "Marat the Jew" (the title of a 1944 book) offered explanation enough of the destructive career of a rootless revolutionary. Whatever the truth about his more distant family origins, however, Juan Salvador Mara was a child of Catholic parents, baptized into the Catholic faith on 9 August 1704.[1] He grew up speaking Catalán.

Knowledge of this language was to stand Juan Salvador in good stead several decades later when he found himself translating advertising copy for one of the great commercial undertakings of the eighteenth century, the Société typographique de Neuchâtel, known throughout Europe as a major publisher for Enlightenment philosophers and an enterprising purveyor of forbidden books. Business of this kind, though, was doubtless still beyond his intellectual horizon when, at age fourteen, he sought a more secure career in the Order of the Blessed Virgin Mary of Mercy, commonly known as the Mercedarians. Accepted by that order in 1718 as a probationer, the father of the future revolutionary was perhaps sent to Spain for a period of further instruction before he was ordained a subdeacon in 1725 and a deacon in 1726. He must have taken full orders as a priest shortly thereafter. With these vows, he joined a religious community founded in the thirteenth century to ransom and recover for the true faith those Christians who had fallen into the hands of the Muslim infidel.

In the eighteenth century, there were still Christians to be rescued by the Mercedarians and other religious orders founded for a similar purpose. No longer Crusaders, these captives were seamen, merchants, and other travelers who had been seized by pirates off the coast of North Africa and sold into slavery across the Middle East.[2] Throughout Europe, solemn processions were organized when they were recovered and returned to their countries of origin. Their memoirs of captivity were a favorite literary genre. But their numbers were dwindling, and their would-be rescuers were turning to other forms of service, including teaching. This latter activity was the primary concern of (now) Father Mara in 1737 when he established a school (and a new Mercedarian house) in the town of Bono in the northern Sardinian diocese of Alghero, overcoming the resistance of competing religious orders in the area by invoking the support of the episcopal and royal authorities.

By this time, though, Spain had lost possession of Sardinia to the duchy of Savoy. Authority now flowed from Turin. Father Mara soon came up against it, in a manner somewhat paradoxical for a member of an order tracing its origins to the ancient struggle against Islam. Papal Bulls dating back to the Crusades had given the Spanish monarchy the right to raise subsidies in support of war against the Moslems. When the duke of Savoy claimed to exercise that same right along with his title to Sardinia, Mara's was one of the voices of protest raised in distant Bono. An investigation of his actions was ordered, and witnesses summoned. They testified that Mara had sworn his school would pay no levy of this kind; that he was prepared to dispute the matter as far as the Vatican itself. They confirmed that he had declared the Papal Bull a worthless piece of paper, no longer valid because the rights it conferred were granted in exchange for a war against the Turks in which the ruler was not now engaged.

When this information reached Turin, the fractious cleric was ordered there to hear his punishment. Instead, he fled to Geneva, where he was listed as a convert to Calvinism in 1740. The legend that he arrived in that city as an unfrocked priest expelled from his order for chasing skirt is without foundation. His indiscretions were political rather than sexual. He was remembered in Bono as "de grande ingenio; pero no firme"—a man of "great intelligence, but not solid."[3] Like father, like son?

AN IMMIGRANT'S TALE

Geneva was a magnet for refugees throughout the eighteenth century, but it was difficult to get legal residence there. Wary of provoking Catholic

France by offering easy asylum to French Protestants, and skeptical of opportunistic conversion, the Genevan pastors subjected would-be converts to careful examination regarding their morals and the state of their religious instruction. Nor did they ignore a potential immigrant's capacity to earn a living. The city needed workers, but skill or the aptitude to acquire it was of the essence. Juan (now known as Jean) Mara passed these tests, renounced "the errors of Papism," and was accepted into his new Calvinist faith in October 1740. A month later, he received a subvention to support his training as a designer. The new immigrant had evidently recognized demand for that skill in the manufacture of the colorful printed cottons known as *Indiennes* that was becoming a growth industry in and around Geneva. The fact that production of these textiles was banned in France made them all the more valuable as a Swiss export.

Within six months of his conversion, "Jean Mara, called Bonfils" had added the more French-sounding surname of his mother's family to his own, acquired a fiancée, and raised sufficient funds to pay the cost of formal residence status as an *habitant* of Geneva. Conferring basic legal rights but denying any active participation in the political life of the republic, this was the lowest rank in a civic order still ruled by a privileged municipal elite—though one whose power was bitterly challenged at regular intervals throughout the century. Constant struggles over political participation made Geneva a seedbed of eighteenth-century arguments over the nature of republican government, Rousseau's being only the most notable. But Genevan politics was not Jean Mara's immediate concern. Described as a "painter and designer," he was accepted as an *habitant* on 10 March 1741 and married fourteen-year-old Louise Cabrol nine days later. The bride came from a family of wigmakers on her father's side—Huguenots from Castres in Languedoc who had themselves taken refuge in Geneva a generation earlier. Immigrants on her mother's side included another wigmaker, also originally from Castres, and merchant drapers from the Dauphiné and, earlier still, from Lombardy. The older branch of the family had enjoyed wealth and status in Geneva before encountering more difficult times. Together, the family represented generations of artisans and merchants.

It took time for the newlyweds to settle. Within months of their marriage, they left Geneva for the spa town of Yverdon near the shores of Lake Neuchâtel, where Jean was allowed to reside and give lessons in design. There, in 1742, the hardy Louise gave birth to the first of the nine children she was to bear over the next fifteen years. Within months the family had moved on to the little town of Boudry in the principality of Neuchâtel, where Jean Mara finally found work as a textile designer for a newly established factory producing *Indiennes*. A second child, Jean-Paul, the future revolutionary, was born in Boudry on 24 May 1743. Two other children were to follow during the decade the family lived there. Town records suggest that the Mara family lived a marginal and precarious existence in this community of some six hundred inhabitants. Several times at risk of expulsion for nonpayment of city taxes, the family suffered a serious setback when Jean Mara lost valuable textile patterns on which he had been working. At least once, its dwelling was targeted by local rowdies. At least once, it was forced to seek charity for its "great indigence."[4] By 1752, the Mara family was again ready to move on.

In the nearby town of Peseux, the family's next stop, Jean Mara began to dip into the practice of medicine. In 1753, he was selling prescriptions and medical advice to a local notable. Five years later, he was suing for payment of a fee another patient had promised but now rejected as outrageous. His initial treatments—or so the patient claimed—had worsened her condition rather than achieving the "radical cure" of which she had been assured. The fee was beyond all reason, the patient protested, particularly when charged by someone "neither recognized as a doctor nor possessed of a degree in this country."[5] The court forced Mara to accept a reduced sum but left him undaunted. He continued the practice of medicine, at least to some degree, for the rest of his life, while also giving lessons of various kinds. Many years later, living in Geneva, he was described as "an old man, teacher of various languages and with a little knowledge of medicine."[6]

Under pressure to provide for a growing family—two more children had arrived by 1754—Mara sought the greater opportunities to be found in a larger city. He was described as a "designer and teacher of the Italian and Spanish languages" in February of that year as he sought permission (not, apparently, for the first time) to reside in the city of Neuchâtel itself. But that city, like many others in the eighteenth century, was in no way eager to risk increasing the number of its poor. Its authorities postponed action on this request until Mara could submit "authentic certificates of his good conduct" from his earlier places of residence, as well as "certain and substantiated assurances from the City and Republic of Geneva that his wife and children will be cared for in the event of his departure or death, so that whatever might happen they will not be a charge upon the City and the Public [of Neuchâtel]."[7] Not one to be frustrated, Mara found another way of proceeding. He acquired a protector, and a weighty one—none other than the governor of the city, Lord George Keith, the direct representative of the Prussian king who was the principality's ruler.

Acceding to the governor's request that Jean Mara "not be interrupted in his work," the Neuchâtel Council of State voted on 6 October

1754—"without being absolutely required to do so"—to set aside its earlier decision and "permit said Mara to remain in this City as long as Milord, our said Lord Governor, finds it good."[8] The exact nature of the occupation involved was unspecified, though it seems reasonable to speculate that Mara was tutoring the governor's children, or those of other high-placed persons. Perhaps he was also extending his medical experience. Whatever the case, Mara remained in Neuchâtel with his family (to which three more children were added over several years), "tolerated" under the protection of the governor but without formal residence status until he was officially received in 1763 as an *habitant* of the city. Unsuccessful in several attempts to gain a position teaching secondary school at the Collège de Neuchâtel, he nevertheless made important contacts in the city, including one of its leading citizens, Frédéric-Samuel Ostervald, and other members of the Ostervald family. Ostervald, a scholar and intellectual entrepreneur, clearly recognized a well-stocked mind when he saw one. Ostervald was happy later, after he had founded one of the powerhouse presses of the eighteenth century, the Société typographique de Neuchâtel, to draw on Mara's talents as a translator. The two men maintained a correspondence for many years after the Mara family had left the city.[9]

Jean Mara was also doing well enough by 1765 to pay the substantial fee necessary to acquire the status conferred by the honorary title of citizen (*bourgeois*) of Boudry. Not that the family ever returned to this town to live. It moved instead to Geneva, and under difficult circumstances. Mara was already exploring the possibility of returning there in 1768 when a bitter tax dispute between the principality of Neuchâtel and its Prussian king sparked a popular riot in which the *avocat-général*, a hated royal official, was killed. It appears that one of the Mara children—Pierre, a hot-headed teenager who had been blinded in one eye in an earlier altercation—was active in the crowd, possibly even a ringleader, or at least accused of being so.[10] Within days, the family had left Neuchâtel for Geneva, only to be pursued by denunciations of a quite vicious kind.

Louise Mara had apparently denied her son's involvement in the murderous riot or tried to shift blame elsewhere. No sooner was the family settled in Geneva than she received a blistering anonymous letter from an aggrieved former neighbor that is well worth quoting at length, not least as a reminder that denunciation was a familiar strategy of vengeance long before Jean-Paul Marat perfected it as a political weapon of the French Revolution:

> Madam, since you are the most diabolic tongue there has ever been in our town, a notorious liar, a notorious slanderer, who never stops

> injuring your neighbor with your tongue, I want to make you known in Geneva and I'm writing to various people to paint you in your true colors, as well as your children who are just the same, your one-eyed son is singularly worthless; he's the one who did most harm to the *avocat-général*. Yes . . . you are worthless, a woman everyone despises and very despicable. Your husband is no better. He's an arrant hypocrite, a bigot. Goodbye, change your conduct. I forgot to tell you that I want to make you known everywhere I can, I've already written anonymously to tell four persons what you are and I have six more letters to write to paint you and your children as you are, without forgetting your scoundrel and hypocrite of a husband. . . . That's not all, there will be many things readied for you.

Nice sentiments! As an afterthought, or just gaining a second wind, the writer offered the judgment that "your whores of daughters are totally fit to be in Geneva. . . . Please God someone will rip out your tongue, just as your scoundrel of a son had his eye ripped out. . . . We want to cause as much trouble for you as we can, you deserve it, goodbye, diabolical bad-mouthing sham, lying, slandering slut, filthy whore, stupid cow, wife of a renegade."[11] It appears that the sense of community in the Swiss Alps was not always as Jean-Jacques Rousseau liked to imagine it.

From Geneva, Jean Mara forwarded the venomous letter to the authorities of Neuchâtel, protesting that "our Religion has always been to fear God and honor the King" and imploring the secretary of state, from "your goodness in my regard and your charity toward the afflicted," to assure his family's protection. "The only crime that could be imputed to us," he pleaded, "is to have spoken against their illegal, unnatural, imprudent action; perhaps this is what has set them against us."[12]

No record of further action in this matter has yet been found, and the Mara family settled into life in Geneva. The older children had by this time left the nest, but there were younger ones still to support, and Jean Mara continued until his death in 1782 (only a few months after his wife's decease) to scrabble for students in Italian, Spanish, and Portuguese, as well as geography and history. He tried on at least one occasion to start a school offering classes in these subjects to young ladies as well as to merchants. But Geneva had a glut of teachers, many of them with better qualifications, as he complained to his friend and patron, Frédéric-Samuel Ostervald.[13] Students were not easy to find, even with a promise of moderate fees.

Fortunately, Ostervald helped with loans, and by giving his friend commissions as a translator, agent, and industrial spy for the Société typographique de Neuchâtel. The letters Mara sent to Ostervald in the 1770s were full of details of this employment in the cutthroat publishing business, including recruitment of sought-after printers and commercial snooping into the activities of competitors in the race to bring out ever cheaper and more profitable editions of the *Encyclopédie* and other "philosophical" works in demand. By such means, the family kept afloat "like cork which always rises above the waves," Mara reassured his patron; "bad fortune has not yet been able to submerge us entirely."[14] Nor did he fail to report other family news, including the successes of his eldest son—now making his father proud under the name Jean-Paul Marat.

In a letter dated 15 November 1775 Mara explained that his son had returned to the name his family had once borne by restoring a final "t" to his surname. Jean-Paul had done this, his father reported, "to avoid being confused with the Irish Mara, for whom he doesn't much care." At least one scholar has interpreted this statement as a possible reference to an Irish branch of the Mara family. But that seems unlikely. "Mara" was a recognizable variation on the common Irish surname "O'Meara," or "O'Mara." It seems more probable that the younger Mara just didn't much care to be taken for an Irishman. The added "t" had a certain French flavor.

The letters Jean Mara wrote to his patron in the final months of his life were shadowed by renewed political conflict in Geneva. "I'm angry that the dissensions I have found here, thinking that I was avoiding those in your city, have interrupted the flow of our correspondence," he wrote to Ostervald early in April 1782. A few days later, he added a Latin note to what was to be his final letter. "Hac inter civicos tumultus et strepitus armorum raptim scribe . . . ," he wrote: "I'm writing rapidly in the midst of civic tumults and the clamor of arms at the eleventh hour before the nocturnal cockcrow. May the God of peace deign to calm them—Amen. Amen." Jean Mara had become more conservative, or at least more prudent, than the rash Juan Salvador who had fled Sardinia four decades earlier. His son was to follow a different political trajectory.

The old man died of an "inflammatory fever" on 26 January 1783, leaving a pitiable estate valued at 520 florins. This included the value of his library, which was sold off by the pound. His 130 pounds of books yielded 41 florins.[15]

MADE IN SWITZERLAND

Jean-Paul Marat—to use, in the interest of clarity, the version of his surname he later preferred—was sixteen when he left his family in Neuchâtel and struck out on his own. What memories and motivations did he take with him? Did he think of the region of his birthplace in Boudry when, publishing *An Essay on the Human Soul* in London in 1772, he recalled the joy imparted by "the prospect of a fine country, illumined by the setting sun, and gilded with his departing rays in the evening of a serene day . . . ; the coolness of the air, the pleasing melody of the birds, the murmur of a gently flowing stream, the odour of flowers and easy motion of the zephyrs . . ."? Did he have the Alps in mind when he explained how "in the Pleasing, as in the Terrible, . . . the irregular assemblage of pleasing and frightful objects, together with the variegation of the whole, forms an engaging prospect which charms the heart, or terrifies the soul by the senses"?[16] If his recollections of the Swiss countryside were colored by the intimations of the sublime infusing literature and philosophy in the last decades of the eighteenth century, his souvenirs of childhood could also take on a Rousseauian hue. "I owe the quality of my soul to nature, but the development of my character I owe to my mother," he informed the readers of his journal many years later. "This respectable woman, whose loss I still lament, watched over my early years; she alone kindled in my heart the precious sentiments of philanthropy, love of justice, and glory; they soon became the sole passions that henceforth fixed my life's destinies. The aid she gave the poor was conveyed by my hand, and the sympathetic tone in which she spoke of them inspired in me the sentiment animating it."[17]

Moral sensibility was remembered as the mother's care in this household. Instruction was the father's. "The true preceptor is the father," Rousseau had written in *Emile*. "By rare good fortune," Marat recalled, "I had the advantage of receiving a very thorough education in the paternal household, of escaping all the vicious habits of childhood that weaken and degrade man, of avoiding all the misdemeanors of youth and of reaching manhood without ever having abandoned myself to impetuous passions; I was a virgin at twenty-one and had already long abandoned myself to the meditation of the study." Exactly what this thorough education comprised we do not know, but we can assume that Jean Mara schooled his son in the languages he taught others, in the history and geography he advertised as among his specialties, and in the elements of the sciences he had acquired in his training as a textile designer and his forays into medical practice. And although Marat claimed "my father never aspired to do anything but to turn me into a savant," it seems likely that other lessons of life were imparted as well, whether explicitly or by example. "The sole passion that devoured my soul was the love of glory," Marat remembered. But it was not easy for a young man with more ambition than means to make his way in the eighteenth-century world. How could he not have learned from his immigrant father the necessity of persistence and adaptability, the importance of a willingness to keep moving on, the value of developing multiple skills and of trying a variety of occupations? How could this father not have conveyed to his son the indispensability of making connections, finding patrons, and deploying their influence whenever possible?[18]

Jean-Paul resorted to all these strategies. Nor was he alone among the Mara children in doing so. The career of his younger brother David offers a valuable parallel when it comes to ways of making it in the eighteenth-century.[19] In 1782, David, then aged twenty-six, found his hopes for entering the Genevan clergy dashed by the fact that he was not a native of that city and had no further prospect of gaining citizenship. After studying philosophy and theology at the University of Geneva, he was urged by his father to seek ordination as a pastor in his natal city of Neuchâtel, and he sought help in doing so from that constant family patron, Frédéric-Samuel Ostervald. His situation was all the more difficult, he explained to Ostervald, in that "the majority of the professors and pastors are *négatifs* and have it in for me."[20] This was not just a matter of personal hostility. To call those blocking his way *négatifs* was to make a political statement. David Mara was using a term popularly applied to the members of the Genevan patriciate who resisted demands for fuller political participation by the larger population of the city. Written shortly after the latest struggle over this matter had led to the "civic tumults" his father had already described to Ostervald, this letter suggests that David may himself have been a visible participant in the most recent disturbances.[21] This might explain why he was twice refused certification upon completion of his studies.[22]

Any help from Ostervald notwithstanding, David Mara was refused ordination by the Neuchâtel pastors on the grounds that he had been unable to furnish academic credentials from Geneva. He had to look elsewhere for a career, and he traveled far afield. By 1784, he was in St. Petersburg working as a tutor in families of the court nobility. But this was not the only way in which he drew on his father's example. He also saw opportunities in the production of textiles. Not content with gilding minds, he started an enterprise manufacturing gold and silver cloth of the kind fashionable in the royal court under Catherine II—a fine idea until the empress's successor banned this extravagance and the factory failed. Finding it prudent not to share his brother's name after 1793, he adopted the surname "Boudry," even adding a particle to hint at nobility. It was as David de Boudry, then, that he was appointed to teach French at the Saint Catherine Institute (a school for young noblewomen) in 1803, and at the St. Petersburg Gymnasium in 1806, the year in which he also obtained "eternal Russian citizenship." Five years later, he was appointed Professor of French Language and Literature in the new Imperial Lycée, subsequently named the Lycée Pushkin after one of his first pupils. His bilingual *First Principles of the French Language, or New Grammar for the Use of Russian Youth*, approved for use in schools and dedicated to Czar Alexander I, was published (at the author's expense) in 1811. It was followed in 1819 by an *Abridged French Grammar*. This time, however, the academic authorities screening the text did not deem it worthy of a dedication to the czar. For all his efforts and achievements, David de Boudry, like his older brother, never entirely satisfied the academicians.

The treatment Marat later received from the savants in the Paris Academy of Sciences was to prove a matter of bitter resentment on his part, with significant implications for their eventual fate in the Revolution. But the sensitivity to injustice this fed was a longstanding one. "My moral sense was already developed at age eight," he later told his readers. "At that age, I could not stand the sight of ill-treatment toward others, to see cruelty filled me with indignation and the spectacle of an injustice agitated my heart as if with the sentiment of a personal affront." Interestingly enough, the injustice he recalled in this context was only to himself:

> Docile and industrious as I was, my teachers obtained everything from me by gentle means. I was only ever punished once and the resentment of an unjust humiliation made such a strong impression on me that it was impossible to put me back under the teacher's rod; I went two whole days without being willing to eat. I was eleven years old at the time, and the firmness of my character at that age can be judged by this sole trait. My parents were unable to make me yield and, parental authority believing itself compromised, I was locked in my room. Unable to resist the indignation that was suffocating me, I opened the casement and threw myself into the street. Fortunately, the window wasn't high, but that didn't stop me from wounding myself violently in the fall; I still bear the scar on my forehead.[23]

To be recalled almost forty years later, this memory of childhood must have carried significant psychological freight. Marat's principal editor, Charlotte Goëtz, has noted the way resentment against unjust treatment by a schoolmaster is here projected upon the parents. She suggests that the memory reveals traces of the anger of an older child displaced by the arrival of younger siblings, as well as a foreshadowing of the manner in which the young man would soon be obliged to wrest himself from the bosom of his family, casting himself upon the world in search of his fortune.[24] But there may be more political resonances to this story. Parental authority appears compromised, in Marat's recollections, not only by the son's refusal to obey but also by the parents' willingness to second his subjection to a schoolmaster's unjust rule. Was he investing memory of this childhood event with a later sense of disappointment in a father who had declined to take a position (with Pierre?) against arbitrary Prussian action in Neuchâtel in 1768 or (with David?) against the tyranny of the patriciate in Geneva in 1782? Marat was not directly involved in the political struggles that swirled around his family in their peregrinations through the Swiss city-states after his departure from Neuchâtel, but he surely followed news of these struggles from afar.

He surely carried with him, too, an image of the contingencies of common life in these Swiss cities, the vicissitudes of their often intimate republican politics, the pattern of resentments and denunciations of which his own family had been victim. Rousseau, that other Swiss exile, imagined an idealized polity from which such features of traditional republican life had been erased. In this regard, we might see Jean-Paul as a Jean-Jacques of another kind, one who would carry the instinct for denunciatory personal politics from a small, traditional polity into the new kind of republic Rousseau's dreams would do much to shape.

"A LITTLE MAN... A QUICK EYE"

TWO

ON THE MOVE

Almost nothing is known of how Marat spent the years immediately following his departure from Switzerland in 1759 or 1760. Much that has been written and repeated on the matter has been speculation shaped by notions of what he must have done to acquire the ideas, interests, and knowledge evident later in his writings. It has been surmised that he passed through Montpellier, learning something by proximity to its celebrated medical school. Some accounts also maintain that he tried as early as 1760 (at age seventeen) to join a scientific expedition being planned to observe the transit of Venus from Tobolsk, but again no specific documentation has been found. He later claimed to have spent two years in Bordeaux, where he is thought to have served for a couple of years as tutor in the family of Pierre-Paul Nairac, a Protestant merchant and ship owner busy making an immense fortune from the colonial sugar trade and as Bordeaux's most active shipper of slaves. These commercial achievements apparently led the intendant of Bordeaux to recommend ennoblement for Nairac and the brother with whom he shared his enterprise, but the privilege was denied them on grounds of their religion. Pierre-Paul Nairac eventually represented the Third Estate of Bordeaux at the Estates General and vigorously defended colonial interests in the National Assembly. Marat, for his part, seems to have shown little sensitivity to the injustices of the Atlantic slave trade before they were illuminated by insurrection in the French colonies in 1791.

No direct record has been found to support the conventional story of Marat's employment by the Nairacs, and there is some reason to doubt it—the ages of Pierre-Paul Nairac's children in the early 1760s suggest greater need for a nursemaid than for a tutor.[1] It is, of course, possible that Marat served some other branch of the extended Nairac family or found a position with another family with their help. Biographers have in any case speculated that he owed employment in Bordeaux to direct acquaintance with the young woman of Swiss origin who became Pierre-Paul Nairac's second wife in 1760 (her family was living in the Provençal city of Orange, but the marriage took place in Nyon, along the lake from Geneva). The arrangement could also have been negotiated through connections back in Castres, the Protestant stronghold from which Marat's maternal grandparents and Nairac's father had emigrated. However (and if) secured, the position of tutor in a prominent family in one of the great commercial cities of the Atlantic world would have exposed Marat to the books, ideas, and examples available in a wealthy, cosmopolitan society. The city that had been the intellectual home of Montesquieu (whom Marat would embrace as an idol) would also have expanded the horizons of the young man's ambition. His desire for glory, he later told his readers, "often changed object in the different periods of my life but never left me for a moment. At five I wanted to be a schoolmaster; at fifteen a professor; at eighteen an author; at twenty a creative genius."[2]

"At eighteen an author." This aspiration might have been enough in itself to propel Marat from Bordeaux to Paris, the center of European intellectual life, in or around 1762. We know nothing definite about how he supported himself or otherwise spent his time once he arrived in the capital. Did he (again?) enter a family as a tutor? Did he attend some of the many public lectures and demonstrations in the sciences that were being offered in the capital by this time? Did he perhaps follow his father's example in offering lessons himself, or by venturing into medicine? This latter does seem possible, since medical works he published in London years later discuss illnesses he claimed to have first encountered in Parisian patients. But beyond this, all that is known of his life during this period comes from another assertion of his own. "I had scarcely attained the age of eighteen when our so-called philosophers made various efforts to attract me to their party," he recalled. "The aversion their principles had inspired in me distanced me from their gatherings and preserved me from their fatal lessons. This aversion only increased as my powers of reasoning grew stronger, and it long fixed the focus of my reflections."[3]

Since this version of events was offered two decades later and intended to provide reassurance regarding Marat's suitability to head an academy of sciences in Catholic Madrid, it can hardly be accepted at face value. Why would the philosophes, or the *salonnières* who hosted their gatherings, court an unknown Swiss scarcely out of his teens? The distance from them Marat reported seems, if anything, to imply the young provincial's failure to break into Parisian society and to suggest the sense of estrangement experienced by a would-be author held back at the margins. But it would have been difficult for an aspiring writer not to begin choosing philosophical sides in Paris at the time of Marat's arrival there in 1762. Literate Parisians were deeply divided in the dark closing years of the Seven Years' War, and France was in need of scapegoats for its worldwide military humiliation. Some found the enemy among the Jesuits, self-proclaimed as the ultimate defenders of the Catholic faith, who were nevertheless driven from the country during these years as agents of a foreign power working to undermine French patriotism. Others (not least the Jesuits themselves) targeted the Jansenists, the dissident Catholic sect whose clandestine publications and political maneuverings were by this time challenging the authority of the entire church hierarchy and unsettling that of the absolute monarchy itself.

Still others (and on this Jesuits and Jansenists could make common cause with the king's magistrates) were eager to point the finger at the secular philosophers of the Enlightenment, those followers of Voltaire eager to spread reason, wipe out superstition, and expose injustice wherever they found it in church or state. The year 1762 saw the execution of Jean Calas, the sexagenarian Protestant shopkeeper from Toulouse wrongly condemned to be broken on the wheel in punishment of the alleged murder of his son. Voltaire took up the cause to establish Calas's innocence, broadening it into a general philosophical campaign to *écraser l'infâme*. That same year, he and other reform-minded intellectuals were pilloried in a satirical play, *Les philosophes*, that targeted them under the appellation by which they are still known. Increasingly, the "philosophes" found themselves the target of a backlash accusing them of conspiracy to promote irreligion, or even of an atheistic materialism that would overthrow throne and altar.

Issues of censorship were frequently at the heart of these struggles. Marat's first stay in Paris coincided with the furor following the appearance of Rousseau's *Emile* in 1762. The book was condemned as subversive of the true religion by the royal magistrates in the Parlement of Paris, who ordered the author arrested and all copies of the work confiscated and burned by the public executioner. The action recalled memories of earlier suppressions of key Enlightenment writings, that of Helvétius's *De l'esprit* in 1758, and of the initial volumes of the *Encyclopédie* of Diderot and d'Alembert in the years before that. Rousseau and Helvétius, in particular, were to provide the young Marat with his initial philosophical exercises.

FIRST TARGETS

In 1765, after several years in the French capital, Marat followed his father's example by moving on. "The desire to educate myself in the sciences and to escape the dangers of dissipation led me to move to England," he later told his champion for the Madrid position. "I became an author, and my first work was intended to combat materialism by showing the influence of the soul on the body and of the body on the soul."[4] It may well be that he crossed the Channel with some version of the manuscript that became this first publication, *An Essay on the Human Soul*. The book didn't appear until 1772, and then in London, but the text offers ample evidence that it was composed in French and subsequently translated into English—by someone with less than perfect mastery of that language. The works it engages most directly—Rousseau's *Discourse on the Origins of Inequality* and Helvétius's *De l'esprit*—were still highly debated during the period of Marat's Parisian stay, and it seems reasonable to assume that they drew his attention and stimulated his philosophical reading and reflection at this time.

The *Essay* begins with the blustering claim to originality that would become a familiar feature of Marat's later scientific writings. "Notwithstanding the many works which have been already published upon the Human Soul," it announces, "this subject is entirely new."[5] The book fails, however, to yield any great novelty. Instead, it reads as an exercise in freshman philosophy, a young author's effort to assert some ideas as his own. Like the ascent to Everest in our own day, the philosophical route to understanding the nature of the soul was already littered with the detritus of earlier expeditions. In the very first volume of the *Encyclopédie*, a daring young theologian soon forced into exile, Claude Yvon, had surveyed their manifold routes, affirming orthodox religious beliefs but lingering suspiciously long on the details of ancient and modern arguments for the materiality of the soul: moving from Epicurus to Hobbes and Spinoza, he drew out the heterodox implications of the more nuanced intimations on the matter offered by Locke and Voltaire. Diderot himself had supplemented this article with a discussion of the disputed hypotheses regarding the physiological location of the soul and the indisputable evidence for the influence of the body on its elusive inhabitant. Marat's first work was a shaky initial attempt to find a foothold on a precarious and already crowded intellectual peak. Its significance is more biographical than philosophical.

The young author was trying in this little book to situate himself in relationship to two of the great issues confronting Enlightenment philosophy. One was the nature of the relationship between the soul and the body. Descartes had declared them radically separate, defining the first as a rational, thinking self and the second as an entirely material machine. Once he had done so, several generations of physiologists (to say nothing of the metaphysicians) had sought to sustain, complicate, or dissolve the Cartesian dualism while exploring the operations of the human body as a kind of animal machine. This issue merged with a second one: the question of the origins of human ideas in physical sensations that had been opened up by Locke's *An Essay Concerning Human Understanding*. Shadowing both questions was the distinct possibility of the materiality of the soul.

Among the many French disciples of Locke, Voltaire had toyed with the idea of the material soul in his *Philosophical Letters*, using Locke's refusal to commit himself in the matter as a pointer toward a tolerant society freed from doctrinal strife over things that were essentially unknowable. More pious, or at least more cautious, Condillac had finessed the entire issue in his *Treatise on the Sensations*, even as he gave the Enlightenment one of its fundamental conceptual tools by inviting his readers to imagine how a statue endowed with the various senses, one by one, could become a thinking self with knowledge of an external world. The openly atheistic La Mettrie had taken a different tack, boldly materializing Locke's philosophy in his *Natural History of the Soul* before he cannibalized Albrecht von Haller's physiology in his scandalous *L'Homme machine*, portraying human beings as biological mechanisms functioning in an entirely physical universe. Helvétius had shown a lighter touch in *De l'esprit* when he played with the idea that self-interest, deriving from our susceptibility to physical pleasures and pains, was the motivation behind all human actions.

Rousseau's *Discourse on the Origins of Inequality* had breathed life into Condillac's statue in a different way: as Natural Man set running with other animals in the woods, there to be led from sensations to needs, from needs to reason, and through reason to the fateful creation of a social order. Reworking the sensationist theme, the deist Savoyard Vicar of Rousseau's *Emile* traced the mind's route from the senses to reason yet again, this time offering the principles of an unorthodox creed that led from sensations to sentiments to conscience, and thence to the truths of a natural religion.

Each of these thinkers offered variations on the Lockean approach the Encyclopedists celebrated as "the experimental physics of the soul." Nor was Marat different. He was happy to describe Locke (as soon as he could find him in error!) as "the first rational metaphysician . . . who rescued the science from that chaos of obscurity in which it was involved in the schools."[6] And in good Enlightenment style, the opening lines of *An Essay on the Human Soul* invoked the great Lockean virtue of epistemological modesty. Having no immediate knowledge of the soul, Marat maintained, we know it only by its effects. But this acknowledgment did not prevent him from stating an absolute conviction. Human beings are "sensible of relations not subject to the senses," he contended; they therefore have "a sensibility distinct from that of the body."[7] From the beginning, Marat insisted on a dualism between the immaterial soul—the conscious self—and the material body.

It quickly becomes evident from *An Essay on the Human Soul* that the young philosopher is taking up his pen with Rousseau's *Discourse on the Origins of Inequality* in mind, though neither that work nor its author is mentioned by name. With Rousseau, Marat proposes to "view man as just escaped from the hand of nature" with "no recourse to miracles . . . and [to] supply by philosophical induction that chronology which is unknown."[8] But Rousseau had imagined natural man as "an animal less strong than some, less agile than others," learning like them to satisfy his needs by eating from the first tree and slaking his thirst at the first brook. Lacking any particular instinct of his own, Rousseau's natural man simply adopts those of other animals and survives by imitating them in their choice of foods.

Marat rejects this account. He insists that we must begin by imagining natural man born weak and without knowledge, still unable to distinguish and compare sensations, and thus to perceive the objects of an external world. This first human being would resemble nothing more than Condillac's stone figure: "an almost insensible automaton, an immoveable statue."[9] How would such a being learn to survive? Would it not perish before it could organize its sensations and make sense of its experience? How would it endure the "long interval" before it could learn enough of its environment and distinguish the animals enough to imitate them? "How many difficulties must have opposed this imitation!" Marat declares, echoing Rousseau's language even as he qualifies his arguments. "And what a concourse of circumstances to be imagined!"[10]

From this analysis, two conclusions followed. First, Marat insists, "the necessity of facts obliges us to believe that man came from the hands of the Creator, of full stature, strong and with all the senses in perfection."[11] Second, only a natural instinct conferred upon human beings in addition to the senses would have kept the species alive during the earliest ages, an instinct prior to reason but obscured in later ages as reason developed. "Who does not see that with this so much boasted reason, the human race had perished, not withstanding all the precautions nature had taken to preserve it?"[12] The weakness of reason as compared with the passions, while scarcely a novelty in Enlightenment epistemology, becomes a recurring motif of *An Essay on the Human Soul.*

But Marat has still not finished working out his ideas in relation to the arguments of the *Discourse on the Origins of Inequality*. Following Rousseau, he endows natural man with "an innate sentiment, prior to all sensation, to all idea, to which nature has united the preservation of human beings; I mean *love of one's self*—that powerful principle which irresistibly directs mankind in all their actions, frequently without being perceived, the source of every passion, and the end to which all our desires are directed." This love, Marat argues, is "unbounded, and infinitely more strong than *the love of others*."[13] Rousseau, though, had made a fundamental point of distinguishing love of self (*amour de soi*) from that self-love (*amour propre*) into which it had degenerated as human beings moved from the natural state into society. Love of self, he maintained, is the natural sentiment that leads every animal to care for its own preservation; in human beings, it becomes benevolence or pity when it is extended to other individuals through sympathetic identification with their joys or sufferings. Self-love, in contrast, is an entirely artificial sentiment inculcated as human beings come to see themselves only in relation one to another in society; it is fed by factitious passions such as pride and envy that occur when individuals have lost moral autonomy and find their worth only in comparison (and competition) with their fellows.

Marat accepts this distinction between love of self and self-love, but with none of the subtlety found in Rousseau's thinking on the matter. He sees self-love—which he wants to call "love of preference"—as simply a version of love of self. "When the love of self acts simply, man not comparing himself to others, it is a sentiment that excites him to be careful of his own preservation, to seek for pleasures and to fly from pain," he argues. "When it acts in opposition to the love of others, it is a sentiment that prompts a man to prefer himself and seek his own good, even at the prejudice of his neighbor." In this second case, Marat maintains, "the love of self annihilates every other sentiment and changes its nature." A bloody set of images serves to make his point.

> It is this [love of self], which changes fraternal affections to hatred, arms rival brothers, and instigates them to mutual murders on the ruins of a father's throne. It is this, which with savages pours fury into the breast of warriors, renders the victor merciless to the vanquished, and prompts him to devour the entrails of the slain, yet palpitating with life. It is this, which in a city preyed on by the enemy without, and by the famine within, transforms the tender nature of females to savage fury, and arms the mother against the fruit of her womb.—It is this, in short, that inspires every cruelty, every barbarous and inhuman action, of which nature shudders at the narration.[14]

The fledgling philosopher does not shrink from such scenes of primal violence, even in his very first work. But it is striking that, as if recoiling from their horror, he is moved immediately to declare parental affection another innate sentiment, "independent of every other, and as blind as instinct itself." A mother's love, not a father's, though, is the one he singles out as "a sentiment impressed on the human heart, by the hands of the Creator."[15]

Motherly love once acknowledged, however, Marat rushes to continue his reflections on Rousseau's arguments. This time he presents "A Refutation of the Opinion of Philosophers Concerning Pity." The opinion at issue holds that pity is a sentiment natural to human beings. For the most part, the passages Marat quotes as examples of this mistaken view paraphrase Rousseau, though with an interesting twist. Bernard de Mandeville, in another sanguinary image, had invited readers of his *Fable of the Bees* to consider the mental state of a prisoner forced to observe, through his bars, the sight of a child attacked by a half-starved, ravenous sow:

> To see her widely open her destructive jaws, and the poor Lamb beat down with greedy haste; to look on the defenceless Posture of tender Limbs first trampled on, then torn asunder; to see the filthy Snout digging in the yet living Entrails suck up the smoking Blood, and now and then to hear the Crackling of the Bones, and the cruel Animal with savage pleasure grunt over the horrid Banquet; to hear and see all this, What Tortures would it give the Soul beyond Expression![16]

Rousseau, pointing to pity as a sentiment recognized even by Mandeville, "the most extreme detractor of human virtues," had presented it as a disposition prior to reason, "so natural that even beasts sometimes give palpable signs of it." As evidence, he had adduced the reluctance of a horse to trample a living being beneath its feet, the disquiet of an animal passing the corpse of one of its own species, "the sad lowing of cattle entering the slaughterhouse" as they encounter the dreadful spectacle awaiting them. And he had elaborated on Mandeville's "pathetic image of an imprisoned man who sees outside a ferocious beast tearing a child from its mother's breast, breaking the feeble limbs between its murderous teeth, tearing with its claws the still palpitating entrails of this child. What dreadful agitation would not be experienced by this witness to an event in which he had no personal interest! What anguish would he not suffer at this sight, and at his powerlessness to bring aid to the fainting mother or the dying child!"[17]

Marat reiterates these examples but remains unconvinced by the argument that pity is a natural sentiment humans share with animals. "What foundation is there for this assertion?" he demands. Who can say whether the lowing cattle are moved by compassion rather than fear, or some other disagreeable sensation? Who knows whether a man who affects compassion is actually feeling it? The slightest reflection suffices, he argues, to understand that "pity is a forged sentiment, acquired from society; it is founded on the idea of pain, and the relations which man forms to himself with sensible beings." Pity, Marat thus postulates, depends on our willingness to imagine ourselves in the same circumstances as the person suffering. But the rich readily insulate themselves from the misery of the poor, for whose sufferings they feel nothing. Compassion, moreover, can be extinguished by long exposure to acts of cruelty. "By a long continuance of them, the soul becomes callous to their impressions, unaffected at the prospect of human miseries, and insensible to every tender emotion. Does not the foregoing prove that pity is not a native of the human breast?"[18]

Given these misanthropic arguments about self-love and pity, one might expect their author to opt for Helvétius over Rousseau. But Marat has a different reason for parting company with the author of *De l'esprit*. "Some one has said, that the passions are only the voice of the body, and a philosopher of the present age has vainly tortured his understanding to explain it," he explains in announcing a "Refutation of a Sophism of Helvétius." Marat is willing to accept that many passions are prompted by physical sensations, but he is no less convinced that some derive only from the mind. And he cares most about one in particular. "Leave to the sophistical author of *De l'esprit* to deduce every passion from physical sensibility," Marat declaims, "but he never will deduce therefrom the love of glory, that vain incense which ignorance and weakness offer to power, to valour, to genius, and of which great minds are so very avidious."[19]

Remarkably, of all the sentiments that might be offered to convince the reader that there are passions not originating in physical sensations, Marat opts for love of glory. "Noble souls," he goes on to say, "souls ardent for glory, the sage and the hero, have been almost always found to flourish in poor countries; and if virtue has ever shone forth with éclat, it was among those nations that had no other rewards than honors."[20] One might think that in such countries glory functions as a substitute for more sensual pleasures. But Marat forecloses this thought by arguing that even in the midst of luxury those who have everything still aspire to glory. Fame is still sought by those who lack nothing else; even the wearers of the royal purple have grasped for the laurels of genius. Why? Because they

> aspired to that glory which is founded on personal merit, and sought it in science. Let us then conclude, that souls avidious of glory are inflamed with the desire for pure glory, and that they love esteem only

> for its sake. . . . Is it not the love of reputation, the desire of having our names pronounced with an elogium, and to see it recorded in the annals of history, that produce in our times so many feats of valour, of constancy, and of courage . . . ? Pleasing delusions! flattering images! fictitious pleasures! what man so unfavoured by nature, as never to have enjoyed you? What soul so rude as not to be sensible to your charms?[21]

And what a revealing choice, to make the search for glory—empty though it might be—the touchstone of the immaterial soul. For the poor immigrant's son from Switzerland, this search becomes, as it were, the defining principle of the self, his exalted version of the Cartesian cogito. I seek glory, therefore I am. If I attain fame, I reign with monarchs in the empire of the mind. We begin to understand how profoundly invested Jean-Paul Marat is in intellectual success. And how agonistic is his conception of glory.

Desire for fame leads the author of *An Essay on the Human Soul* into an extended effort to state his views regarding sensibility, memory, judgment, understanding, reason, and the passions—all master topics of eighteenth-century sensationist philosophy. His thoughts scarcely seem to cohere in a single argument, but they do tend to converge upon two basic claims. One points to the weakness of reason in the face of the passions. "O reason! reason! The so much boasted resource of the wise, what can thy feeble voice prevail against the impetuous violence of the passions?"[22] Even more powerful than the sensuous passions deriving from physical experience, Marat maintains, are the passions he calls "fictitious," those deriving from imagination and the sensibility of the soul. Love of glory is one such sentiment. Marat finds another exemplified in the political virtue of Cato the Younger, that Roman idol of eighteenth-century republicans who sacrificed himself for love of country and of liberty. This passion, alas, could only be mourned in modern times. "The fictitious passions produced all those great actions, where éclat dazzles our imperfect sight, all those great personages, worthy of adoration, whose surprising actions to us appear fabulous, since virtue is no longer esteemed."[23] Marat will soon join the ranks of those nostalgic political philosophers who lament the loss of antique political virtue in their own modern society.

Marat's second basic claim regards the distinction between the soul and the body. Human beings, he insists, are "a compound of two sensible substances, and as each of these substances has its particular object, there are two kinds of pleasing sensations and two kinds of painful, to wit, the sensations of the body, and the sensations of the soul." In his analysis, the thinking self does not exist apart from its bodily frame. It could never perceive, recollect, judge, or choose "unless united to an organized and sensible body." Indeed, "it would not even have the sentiment of its own existence, for it is only by reflecting on its sensations, that it acquires this sentiment." But this should not be taken to mean that soul and body are one and the same. Marat adduces sleepwalking as the most basic proof in this regard. In the case of the sleepwalker, "the soul seems to be detached from the body, and man appears as an automaton in motion." He hammers down his conclusion in a footnote. "This power of the soul to detach itself from the senses, proves it to be distinct from the body, much better than the unintelligible jargon of metaphysicians."[24]

Marat may have fancied himself free of the metaphysicians, but he had yet to uncover empirically, to his own satisfaction, the "laws of this union" between soul and body.[25] His next philosophical work was intended to do exactly that.

THREE

MAKING IT IN LONDON

A decade or so after leaving Paris in 1765 Marat had acquired a medical degree and was practicing medicine in Church Street (now Romilly Street) in Soho. How had he managed this transition? Certainly, no formal training was required. Teeming with doctors, would-be doctors, empirics, and quacks of all kinds—the categories were largely interchangeable—London was an unregulated market for medicine, as for much else.[1] And this freewheeling medical bazaar drew its share of the enterprising and ambitious from abroad. The satirical *Art of Getting into Practice in Physick, Here at present in London* (1722) acknowledged their presence, even as it took pains, tongue-in-cheek, to note that its counsel was not intended for them. Whether Italian, French, or German, the satirist protested, they were best left to find networks of their own countrymen.[2] Forty years later, Oliver Goldsmith offered his own characterization of English medical practice and its attractiveness to foreigners. "The *Chinese* boast their skill in pulses, the *Siamese* their botanical knowledge, but the *English* advertising physicians alone, of being the great restorers of health, the dispensers of youth, and the insurers of longevity," reported his fictional Chinese visitor to London in 1762. "I can never enough admire the sagacity of this country for the encouragement given to the professors of this art; with what indulgence does she foster up those of her own growth, and kindly cherish those that come from abroad. Like a skilful gardener she invites them from every foreign climate to herself. Here every great exotic strikes root as soon as imported, and feels the genial beam of favour; while the mighty metropolis, like one vast dunghill, receives them indiscriminately to her breast, and supplies each with more than native nourishment."[3]

Dunghill or not, there was no better place than Soho for an ambitious French-speaking immigrant to find a network, or the potential patients that would allow him to set up medical shop. Fashionable enough to serve as the home of aristocrats and embassies, it had become one of the principal refuges of French Protestants since their escape from France after Louis XIV's Revocation of the Edict of Nantes in 1685. These Huguenots were skilled tradesmen and their families eager to offer prosperous neighbors their services as silk-weavers, clock-makers, jewelers, wood-carvers, and gunsmiths; as designers, engravers, and printers; and also as teachers and tutors, dancing-masters, and physicians. By 1711, the Soho parish of St. Anne was estimated to be forty percent French; in 1739, a visitor to the area could still find it "an easy Matter for a Stranger to imagine himself in France."[4] Dr. Johnson made a point of visiting a coffee house there to improve his facility with the French language.

Amusing though it might be to imagine Marat in the same space as the prolix English Tory, their age difference makes that unlikely. Precisely when the future revolutionary settled in Soho we don't know; he later recalled spending periods in Edinburgh and Dublin as well as London. In Soho he must, like many immigrants, have been a lodger rather than a householder, for his name fails to show up there in the principal tax rolls. He remains under the archival radar for much of his time in Britain—a fact that has allowed for much fanciful speculation. We know little about his actual medical practice. Though he mentioned conditions in hospitals and workhouses for the poor in his writing, it seems likely from his medical publications that his clientele came from higher up in the social scale. There is indeed recorded evidence that he had become well enough connected in Soho to be admitted to the Masonic Lodge that met there at the King's Head Tavern in Gerard Street on 15 July 1774.[5] In London, as throughout eighteenth-century Europe, Freemasonry offered networking possibilities along with its values of cosmopolitanism and fraternity.

Some secondhand recollections of Marat in Soho were also recorded much later in the diary of the painter Joseph Farington. In 1793, after Marat's assassination and as the Terror was mounting, Farington recorded conversations at the Royal Academy Club with his fellow academicians, the architect Joseph Bonomi and the painter William Hamilton. Both recalled Marat during his London years, remarking especially on his friendship at that time with the neoclassical Italian artist Antonio Zucchi and the more celebrated painter Angelica Kauffmann, who later became Zucchi's wife. They remembered "a little man . . . slender but well made, of a yellow aspect," with "a quick eye," who had a great deal of motion, "seldom keeping his body or limbs still."[6] According to Farington's report of the conversations, Bonomi recalled Marat as lodging in St. Martin's Lane, where he frequented a coffee house that was a gathering place for foreigners as well as the artists who formed the nucleus of the future Royal Academy. "Bonomi said Zucchi became acquainted with Marat at Old Slaughters Coffee House, St. Martin's Lane, where many foreigners were accustomed to assemble. It was about the year 1767 or 68."[7] Bonomi remembered Marat as "about 33 years of age" at that time, but he had either confused the date or misjudged the age. The young Swiss would have been twenty-four or twenty-five in 1767–68.

Both academicians remembered Marat and Zucchi as being close friends. Bonomi recalled that "Zucchi had the highest opinion of [Marat's] abilities. Being a man of extensive classical reading Marat continually proposed Subjects which he had selected for Zucchi to design."[8] Hamilton, the younger man who became a pupil of Zucchi's in 1768, remembered Marat some years later, apparently around 1775 or 1776. By that time, Marat was in the habit of coming to Zucchi's house "in the most familiar Manner, a knife and Fork being laid for him every day. He borrowed from Zucchi at different times abt. £500, which he cd. not repay. . . . This was abt. 18 years ago, when Marat appeared abt. 40 years of age."[9] Again, in Hamilton's report as in Bonomi's, age and date don't match, since Marat would have been in his early thirties in 1775. Both the painter and the architect seem to have remembered this quick little man as about a decade older than he was at the time.

Hamilton also recalled that Zucchi was courting the painter Angelica Kauffman in those years and "frequently took Marat with him in the evenings when He went to visit her." Did Marat draw more than cash from these visits? Jacques-Pierre Brissot, Marat's friend before 1789 and bitter political enemy after, implied as much in his *Mémoires*, reporting that Marat later claimed to have had an intimate affair with the painter.[10] Much as biographers have loved to present this tidbit as fact, it remains a matter of speculation.

According to Bonomi and Hamilton, Marat was already styling himself a doctor by 1767 or 1768. "He was called Doctor Marat, and never professed himself to be in any but the *Physical line*," Bonomi told Farington. "His object appeared to be improving himself by consulting the practise in different Countries."[11] Hamilton also remembered that Marat "professed himself a Physician, and cured Bonomi . . . of severe complaints twice or three times." Marat's methods, though, were far from conventional. "He had an original way of thinking in his professional capacity as was observed by the Apothecary who made up the medicines, and acted against common rules. . . . He was then discontented, and abused the establishments that existed."[12]

A would-be doctor, no matter how disaffected, needed to do more than treat acquaintances if he was to survive financially. To build a clientele it was also a good idea, the author of *The Art of Getting into Practice in Physick* snorted, to "make all the Noise and Bustle you can, to make the whole Town ring of you if possible: So that everyone in it may know, that there is in Being, and here in Town too, such a Physician."[13] Publishing was deemed one good way of attracting attention, perhaps in part because bookshops were also principal points of sale for therapeutic pills and powders. One could get into the business of healing by writing poetry, the satirist observed, or by publishing something (the more obscure the better!) on divinity or politics; if opting to write on medicine, one should pick topics that promised the largest clientele or the greatest profit to the medical practitioner, such as fevers or smallpox (or, one might add, that most profitable of poxes, venereal disease itself).

As if following this advice, Marat was ready in 1775 and 1776 to publish two medical tracts sporting newly acquired credentials as "J. P. Marat, M.D." and advertising an address in Church Street, Soho, where he might be consulted. Each of these pamphlets was devoted to presenting a new (and potentially profitable) cure for conditions associated, directly or indirectly, with that great medical moneymaker, venereal disease. Each offered details of remarkable successes claimed by Marat in the treatment of individuals previously deemed incurable by leading practitioners who had tried lengthy administrations of the prevailing therapy. He still felt it necessary to beg indulgence for the defects in English usage in a foreigner's writing, "the fashioning of the stile being less an object of attention, than the importance of matter to the human health."[14] But he also raised his bid for notice by offering these publications, albeit in somewhat belligerent manner, to members of the establishment he apparently preferred to denounce, first the Company of Surgeons, then the Royal Society.

The first of these publications, *An Essay on Gleets; Wherein the Defects of the Actual Method of treating those Complaints of the Urethra are pointed out and An Effectual Way of Curing them indicated*, dated 21 November 1775, prescribed a treatment for the virulent genital sores caused by gonorrhea. The treatment itself, involving the insertion of medicated tapers into the urethra, was a refinement of procedures developed in Paris by the notable doctor Jacques Daran. But Marat's pamphlet emphasized the superiority of his own version of the therapy.

An Essay on Gleets came with a prefatory address to "The Worshipful

Company of Surgeons in London" that sounded an aggressive note. "Long since Surgeons both in *London* and *Paris* have assumed to themselves the treatment of Venereal Diseases, and Physicians generally decline it. I cannot conceive what makes it your exclusive province the treatment of these diseases, since in most case the whole frame of the body is affected, and in very few the hand of an operator is wanted." Nonetheless, Dr. Marat declared himself disinclined to "strive against the torrent" when he could provide the entire company of surgeons with a cure for many more patients than he could reach himself. "A man of mercenary principles would, no doubt, keep it a secret; but a liberal mind is above such interested procedures. To promote the good of society is the duty of all its members; besides, what an exquisite pleasure it is for a benevolent heart to lessen, as much as possible, the number of those unfortunate victims, who, without hope of relief, labour under the many evils to which human nature is subject."[15] Such high-minded principles, combined with an attack on monopoly, made for good advertising copy in Georgian England. Prospective patients now knew where to find the excellent Dr. Marat for the treatment of venereal disease—and also, it turns out, of another medical moneymaker, ailments of the eye.[16]

Published a few months later, on 1 January 1776, a second medical pamphlet followed a similar strategy. Titled *An Enquiry into the Nature, Cause and Cure of a Singular Disease of the Eyes, Hitherto Unknown and yet Common, Produced by the Use of Certain Mercurial Preparations*, it offered a diagnosis and cure for what Marat identified as "accidental presbytopia." This sudden onset of far-sightedness he attributed to excessive medical use of mercury—a therapy employed extensively in cases of venereal disease among others. Marat's treatment mixed the traditional with the novel: judicious bleeding with mild electrotherapy involving induction of electrical sparks to the eye. He would become an active proponent of the use of electricity in medicine late in his career.

This time, the therapy was offered for the consideration of the prestigious Royal Society, but in a preface that again refused all subservience. "This is not a Dedication: Such a Matter of Form I have ever thought beneath the Dignity of Philosophy," the author insisted. He asked only that the society take note of "a Phaenomenon in the Animal Oeconomy: a Singular Phaenomenon, which has hitherto escaped the attention of Physiologers, and which, I presume, is too curious not to excite your Attention." Should its members try experiments to verify this phenomenon, Marat dared to suggest in scarcely idiomatic English, this would not turn out to be "a regrettable Employ of Time." Failing their interest, there was always the judgment of a wider audience. "If one cannot always be the happy instrument of alleviating the Misery of the Unfortunate, it is, however, a sort of service tendered to them, to prevent their being made worse. On this Consideration I claim the indulgence of the Public."[17] Appeal to the public as the authority beyond any academy was also to become a familiar tactic for him in later years.

The advertising ploy these pamphlets represented did not go entirely unnoticed in the London press. The *Essay on Gleets* was reviewed, though somewhat skeptically, in the monthly catalog of *The Critical Review, or Annals of Literature* for December 1775, and again a year later in *The Monthly Review, or Literary Journal* for December 1776. In the latter case, the reviewer gave Marat little credit as a theorist while commenting acidly on the commercial interest motivating his publication. "The Author displays his success in the cure of several gleets unsuccessfully treated by M. Daran himself; and gives an account of the principles on which his method of care is founded, with the avowed liberal view of promoting the good of society;—not forgetting, however, in a *kind* of dedication to the worshipful company of surgeons in London, to give the Reader a hint of where he may be spoke with." Not to be outdone, *The Critical Review* embellished a similar observation the very next month. The cures Marat was touting might well have been successful, that journal observed, "but they probably would have met with greater credit, had he not mentioned the place where he may be spoke with; an innuendo not usually considered as favourable to the idea of a regular practitioner."[18]

But how did Dr. Marat get his medical degree? The question has been much debated. We know he received it from the University of St. Andrews with a diploma dated 30 June 1775.[19] Hostile writers, invoking Dr. Johnson's gibe that the University of St. Andrews would get rich by degrees, have insisted that he simply bought it. Others have pointed out that the degree, even if paid for, was conferred on the recommendation of two Edinburgh physicians who attested to the recipient's medical knowledge and experience. One of them, Hugh James, seems to have left little trace of his activities. Not so the other, William Buchan, the author of one of the great medical bestsellers of the period, *Domestic Medicine, or A Treatise on the Prevention and Cure of Diseases by Regimen and Simple Medicines.* First published in 1769 as a handbook of medical advice for a general audience, *Domestic Medicine* went through scores of editions in a number of languages well into the nineteenth century, making it the most popular health manual published before the twentieth century.[20]

That Marat had the opportunity to impress these Edinburgh physicians in person seems clear. Bonomi remembered that Marat went to Edinburgh in 1774 and returned in 1775, and "there took a degree or said He did."[21]

In fact, though, Marat seems to have left London first for Holland. He signed the visitor's book at the Amsterdam Lodge "La Bien-Aimée" in mid-October 1774 and was still in Holland (or perhaps there again) in late February 1775.[22] He met at that time with Isaac de Pinto, a pillar of the Dutch Jewish community and a notable figure in the European republic of letters. Merchant, investor, and speculator, Pinto had defended the Jews against Voltaire, engaged Hume and others in the international debates over credit, luxury, and the public debt, and offered a *Précis des arguments contre les matérialistes*, published in 1774. It was doubtless this latter work, with its defense of the immaterial and immortal soul, that attracted Marat to him. Pinto, for his part, welcomed a visitor who had been recommended as "a person of irreproachable character," introducing him to a close friend in turn as "a man of letters and of taste, a connoisseur of the fine arts."[23]

Perhaps Marat's intimacy with artists in London now helped him appreciate the art to be found in Pinto's fine mansion. The two men shared a greater bond, though, in their expressed aversion to materialism. Marat showed his host some parts of a forthcoming book, which must have been the manuscript of the enlarged French edition of *A Philosophical Essay on Man*. It was published in Amsterdam later that year, under the title *De l'homme*, by the intrepid international publisher Marc-Michel Rey, with whom Marat must have been negotiating during this stay. Encouragingly, Pinto found Marat's work full of "excellent things, well understood and profoundly analyzed, though his principles do not always coincide with my own."[24]

Marat may have visited Dublin, too, during this period of travel, contracting the animadversion toward the Irish that prompted the change in his spelling of his name. But he was soon in Edinburgh. There, as he reported in his pamphlet *A Singular Disease of the Eyes*, he treated a patient from America during several weeks of August 1775.[25] It seems reasonable to conclude that he was in the city long enough to convince the Scots physicians of his medical expertise. William Buchan, though, may also have been motivated to recommend him for the St. Andrews degree by more than any judgment regarding his medical experience. If, as Hamilton reported, Marat was already inclined to denounce established institutions, he would have found Buchan of like mind. Committed to the popularization of medical knowledge, the author of *Domestic Medicine* was a radical critic of the self-interested obfuscations of the medical establishment. He was ready to diagnose sickness as a consequence of the conditions of modern life—of luxury and lavish consumption on the part of the rich and of the degradation of social conditions that was the lot of the working poor. Buchan became a firm supporter of the American Revolution and eventually of the French Revolution. Fellow of the Royal Society of Medicine in Edinburgh though he was, he called, in his later work *Observations Concerning the Prevention and Cure of the Venereal Disease* (1796), for a democratic medicine for a revolutionary age. "It is no more necessary that a patient should be ignorant of the medicine he takes to be cured by it," he proclaimed, "than that the business of government should be conducted with secrecy in order to insure obedience to just laws."[26]

Upon the recommendations of Buchan and James, in any case, Marat was awarded the St. Andrews degree in 1775 on the grounds that "the distinguished Jean-Paul Marat, Master of Arts, has devoted all his attention to medicine for many years and has acquired great skill in all branches of this science."[27]

A SCIENCE OF MAN

By the time *An Essay on the Human Soul* was published in 1772, Marat was already prepared to promise its readers a fuller explanation of its subject, "should this small essay meet with approbation."[28] There is little to confirm that the *Essay* did indeed garner much approval. The only review of the book found so far was initially disposed toward "lenity and indulgence" regarding "a first and laudable effort of youth, for the attainment of literary reputation," but the tone changed once it became clear that the author was threatening the public with a more substantial sequel. Mistaking badly anglicized French for ludicrous attempts at neologism, the reviewer panned Marat's book for the way words were "thrown together without any precise and determinate ideas." The argument was declared inconsistent, the style "stiff and turgid, not to say . . . unintelligible and obscure." For good measure, the author was reproved for descriptions of the sexual act bordering on indecency. "It is not necessary, in explaining the sentiments and passions of the human nature," the reviewer sniffed, "to disclose their more secret operations, or to stain the page with glowing expressions that tend to excite unchaste and impure ideas."[29]

Marat was not deterred. Perhaps he only took in the reviewer's grudging acknowledgment that "this essay is not altogether without merit, and the Author has talents which admit of cultivation and improvement." Within a year of its initial publication, he had reformatted and embedded *An Essay on the Human Soul* in a substantial second work, now rendered in considerably improved English. This new book was offered to the public in two volumes in 1773 as *A Philosophical Essay on Man, being an Attempt to Investigate the Principles and Laws of the Reciprocal Influence of the Soul and Body.*[30]

Conscious of the weaknesses of his first philosophical effort, Marat sought advice regarding the second. One resource seems to have been a French military officer in London called de La Rochette, who since 1760 had been placed in charge of negotiations for the exchange of prisoners of war between England and France. The dossier Marat later prepared for his friend Roume de Saint-Laurent included copies of two letters, dated January 1773, in which La Rochette offered comments on the manuscript Marat had sent him anonymously. Lamenting his lack of scientific knowledge, La Rochette praised the physiological part of the manuscript as "one of the expositions of this kind that has most made me regret my ignorance." He felt more at home with the part discussing the influence of the soul on the body, which struck him as "well thought out and well written . . . full of new ideas, discriminating judgments, profound details." In such a work, La Rochette opined, failures of expression could only be "spots on a fine face." Above all, he praised the boldness of a text that had taken as its epigraph "the motto of genius," the phrase *impatiens freni* ("unwilling to bear the reins" or, more loosely, "resisting constraint").[31] His second letter was equally enthusiastic: it congratulated the author on avoiding the obscurity of most metaphysical works and returning matters to their original simplicity: "here we appear as we are, beings whose springs are very simple, though the Eternal workman will never reveal their secret."[32]

Marat later reported that "M. de La Rochette, who knew the malign influence of the cabal of the philosophes, and desired the success of this work, advised me to publish it anonymously and in English." Anxious about the accuracy of the translation, though, he first submitted the manuscript, again anonymously, to some English readers "as distinguished by their virtues as by their talents."[33] Two responses from these readers were included in the materials Marat later sent his friend Saint-Laurent. The first came from Lord Lyttelton, a Whig politician pious to a fault, and an earnest author on a variety of subjects (Gibbon quipped of Lyttelton's *Life of Henry II* that the writer's "sense and learning were not illuminated by a single ray of genius").[34] Lyttelton had been a significant patron of other men of letters, including Pope and Fielding (who dedicated *Tom Jones* to him). In a letter dated 19 November 1772, he expressed admiration for the knowledge and talents displayed in Marat's manuscript and offered to provide advice on matters of style and substance if the author would forgo anonymity and call upon him in person. Marat may indeed have accepted this invitation; one way or another, he made enough of an impression that Lyttelton apparently persuaded the Russian ambassador to offer him a post in St. Petersburg.[35]

A second response came from Charles Collignon, professor of anatomy at Cambridge, a prominent physician in that city, and a fellow of the Royal Society.[36] Described by a contemporary as emaciated to a degree that rendered him a walking illustration of his subject, Collignon was known for his dissections. Readers of *A Tale of Two Cities* will recall the activities of the London "resurrection men" who raided graveyards for bodies to be sold as specimens for dissection. One such group apparently provided Collignon with a corpse in 1768 that turned out to be the body of the late Laurence Sterne, author of *Tristram Shandy* (an appropriate end, perhaps, to the author of that tale of comic surprises). In addition to his anatomical researches, though, Collignon was interested in philosophical questions regarding the relationship between the mind and the body. This must have made him a desirable reader of Marat's manuscript. But his own *Enquiry into the Structure of the Human Body, relative to its Supposed Influence on the Morals of Mankind*, published in 1764, had little of the experimentalism of Marat's physiology. Drawing more on classical reading than on observation at the dissecting table, it offered a neo-Hippocratic philosophy that advocated tempering bodily effects on the passions by application of reason, Christian fortitude, and cheerfulness—at least two of which Marat could hardly claim to possess. Having argued that, as with blood and bodily fibres, "the different state of the nerves in different men, is no inconsiderable source of that variety of characters to be met with in the world," Collignon was quick to forestall any misunderstanding, "as if I meant hereby to make man a meer machine. For if Reason were capable of holding her peace at such an assertion, Religion would certainly cry out."[37]

Collignon found Marat's work more daring than his own. In a letter dated 1 May 1773 (shortly after the *Essay* had, in fact, been published) he congratulated the young author on "an interesting book in which, in my opinion, you have shown much brilliance and brought as much judgment to bear on its subject as is probably achievable. If all your observations are not strictly true, they are certainly very probable." Comparing Marat's work with his, Collignon was moved to "confess that fear of being misunderstood, in subjecting a great part of the moral to the influence of the corporal, made me treat this subject in a very superficial manner in my researches. But you have expressed yourself generally in such a wise manner that I think you have nothing to fear in this regard."[38] Professor Collignon, it appears, had played it safe, lest Religion cry out. After all, he had had more to lose than did his as yet unknown correspondent.

With this encouragement, probably in April 1773, Marat published *A Philosophical Essay on Man* in two volumes with a third intended. No longer the effort of a freshman philosopher to decide his views, it drew less on the thought experiments of the philosophers than on the observations of the physiologists and the knowledge the author had gained from his own medical practice. This time, Marat had scientific authorities to invoke for further reference. He suggested two works in particular. The *Neurographia universalis*, published in 1684 by the seventeenth-century Montpellier doctor Raymond Vieussens, could still be recommended for its intricately engraved atlas of the brain and the nervous system. More recently minted, Charles Nicholas Jenty's *Course of Anatomico-Physiological Lectures on the Human Structure and Animal Oeconomy* (1767) offered a history of the progress of anatomy since ancient times, along with a digest of "Whatever is most valuable in the WORKS of all the eminent Professors on these Subjects," followed by "TWO ESSAYS on the ARTS of Dissecting, Injecting and Making ANATOMICAL PREPARATIONS." Wielding these authorities, Marat presented himself as a master of the microscope, as of the dissecting knife. He had joined that legion of mid-eighteenth-century thinkers convinced that physiology and medicine would open the avenue toward the true citadel of a "science of man."

Not that this medical practitioner and experimental anatomist declared himself satisfied with the state of his topic. His readers were subjected to a polemical introductory account of the progress of the "science of man" intended to show that little had been achieved. "How many systems have been invented! How many volumes written upon this subject! And what a multitude of absurdities involve the few truths that have been published thereon!"[39] Marat's survey treats the history of the topic from the Greeks to modern times, passing from ancient confusion via priestly obscurantism to the dawning of a philosophical age. Finally, at this point, it acknowledges some genuine contributions. Locke (in his *Essay Concerning Human Understanding*) had effectively opened up investigation of the operations of the mind. La Rochefoucauld (the disenchanted seventeenth-century moralist whose *Maximes* incited a century-long excavation of the vices underlying all apparent virtues) had "examined the passions of the human heart, and . . . displayed their nature and principles indifferently well."[40] And Jacques-Bénigne Winslow (the Paris academician whose work on the anatomical structure of the human body appeared in 1732) had laid the basis for physiological understanding.

These separate achievements, Marat maintained, had nevertheless fallen far short of an integrated science of man revealing the reciprocal influence of the moral and the physical. Treated by "metaphysicians who were not anatomists, and by anatomists who were not metaphysicians,"[41] the subject still consisted of scattered ideas or fanciful theories extrapolated from fragmentary information. Among the philosophers, Descartes's "anatomical knowledge was very imperfect, and his metaphysical notions erroneous." He had left only "idle dreams" and "empty notions." La Mettrie, "so highly commended by atheists," had produced nothing more than "a sorry collection of trivial observations, and of false metaphysical reasonings." Helvétius, whose ignorance of anatomy was matched by his "erroneous and superficial understanding," had offered "only a series of sophisms, elaborately adorned with a pompous display of useless erudition." Montesquieu alone had "despised the unintelligible Jargon of Psycologists, and reduced the study of Man to that of nature."[42]

The term *psycologie* had recently been coined by the Genevan naturalist Charles Bonnet in his attempt to develop a physiology of sensations and ideas without compromising the idea of the immateriality of the soul. But Marat would have nothing positive to say about Bonnet's work. Nor would he offer a much more favorable judgment upon the physiologists from whom Bonnet had drawn. The celebrated Swiss scientist Albrecht von Haller, Marat argued, "having no clear knowledge of metaphysics," had confused the faculties of the mind with the properties of the body; "his ideas are a chaos as dark as the subject he undertook to clear up appears to have been to himself." Haller's dogged rival, the Rouennais surgeon Claude Nicolas Le Cat (whose many works culminated in a three-volume *Traité des sensations et des passions en general, et des sens en particulier*, published in 1767–68), had offered "some good observations, and some scattered rays of light," and "even an appearance of something like principles." But lacking "the manly force of a close reasoner," a virtue on which Marat prided himself, Le Cat had abandoned himself to the greatest sin known to Enlightenment thinkers, "the frenzy of systems."[43]

Beyond these authors, Marat saw only confusion, pompous inanity, and the empty speculations of those who "looked upon the knowledge of Man as an enigma, as an impenetrable mystery, a labyrinth whence there was no issue." A sweeping footnote, breathtaking in its arrogance, invited the reader, "for proofs of this, [to] read the works of Hume, Voltaire, Bonnet, Racine, Pascal, &c." One can only imagine how many others were indicted by that etcetera! To Marat, the result of all this philosophical babble was clear: a few fragmentary facts aside, "the science of Man," that Holy Grail of eighteenth-century philosophy, remained "entirely unknown."[44] Lost amid the systems of the "vain and presumptuous" and the "perpetual ecstasy" of the "timid and credulous," its secrets remained to be revealed, not by advancing any "vague and arbitrary hypothesis," but by "attentive examination of the phenomena."[45] As a simple observer, Marat promised, he would offer no system to which he was not obliged by the necessity of the facts. These were good Enlightenment slogans. In keeping with them, Marat's object of inquiry was to be "Man in general, of all countries, of all climates, and of every age; an immense undertaking; a profound abyss for the mind to attempt to fathom."[46] He would not count his labor lost, he assured his readers, "should my success hold any proportion to the dignity of my subject."[47]

FOUR

LOCATING THE SOUL

With mandatory Enlightenment declarations of epistemological modesty behind him, Marat stated the fundamental claim of *A Philosophical Essay on Man* categorically. "Man, in common with all animals, is composed of two distinct parts, soul and body." It was unnecessary, he thought, to prove this proposition. "I shall not stay here to prove so established a truth," he declared in an emphatically starred note; "should any of my readers entertain the least doubt, he may dispense with reading my work: it is not for such that I write."[1] The way to the soul, he was convinced nonetheless, was through the body. Eluding the senses, it could only be detected indirectly. It was necessary "to penetrate to the soul through the integuments of the body, and observe the influence of the material substance upon the spiritual, to be able to distinguish the properties peculiar to it, from such as are dependent on a foreign principle."[2] Marat aimed, in effect, to push physiological explanation to the limit, confident that there would be something left over to attribute to the soul.

But this was a hazardous path. What if physiology left nothing for the defender of the soul to explain? Was Marat putting the soul at risk even as he sought to demonstrate its existence? Diderot's reading of his work is interesting in this respect. Annoyed by the categorical assertion of the distinction between soul and body when he read the French version of *A Philosophical Essay on Man* a few years later, he almost accepted Marat's invitation to stop reading. "I thought about closing the book. Eh! Ridiculous writer, if I once admit these two distinct substances, you have nothing more to teach me. You don't know what it is that you call soul, even less how they are united, and not at all how they act reciprocally one upon another."[3] But Diderot didn't close the book; instead he pored over it in search of physiological evidence for his own materialistic philosophy. He found much he could use or reinterpret. A recent analysis of the sources for his *Eléments de physiologie* has shown in detail that, apart from the mighty Haller, Marat was among the most consistent.[4]

The immortal and immaterial soul, Marat saw, was in danger of vanishing from eighteenth-century physiology. In *A Philosophical Essay on Man* he aimed to locate it and make it secure. Le Cat's is the work he engages most directly, adopting its basic physiological approach even as he jettisons some of its metaphysical assumptions. Following Le Cat, and beyond him Boerhaave, he analyzes the human body as a system of tubes, vessels, membranes, and fluids, "an admirable machine on hydraulic principles."[5] With Le Cat, he addresses the most fundamental problem of mid-eighteenth-century physiology: the relationship of the nervous system to the functioning of bodily motion, on the one hand, and to the operations of the mind or soul, on the other.

Haller had posed the essential terms of this problem in 1753 when he published a key "Dissertation on the Sensible and Irritable Parts of Animals" that reported the results of hundreds of animal experiments. Offering a radical conceptual clarification, he defined "irritability" as the propensity of bodily tissue to react when stimulated by a foreign body, distinguishing it from "sensibility," the property that causes such stimulation to be accompanied by sensation in human beings or evident pain in animals. An amputated bodily part (or an eel cut into many pieces) will continue for a while to move or respond to stimulation. A muscle paralyzed by tying or severing the related nerve can be made to move by poking it with a needle, without this producing any sensation in the animal concerned. Such results led Haller to regard irritability as a basic property of bodily tissue, responsible for most vital functions through involuntary, unconscious motion. Even more fundamentally, they allowed him to separate the ongoing mechanism of involuntary motion from the operation of the nervous system that communicated sensation to the brain and will to those parts of the body moved by voluntary action. Delimiting the operation of sensibility in this manner was Haller's way of saving it from materialistic accounts. He aimed to sustain a view of the soul as a spiritual entity that remained distinct from the body even as it received sensory information from the body via the nerves and the brain, and in turn gave conscious direction to voluntary physical motion.[6]

Like any dualism, Haller's distinction between irritability and sensibility invited subversion. By 1753, La Mettrie had already used results of

Haller's earlier work to collapse sensibility into irritability, thus reducing the operations of the soul to the material functioning of the body. Haller could only insist in his "Dissertation on the Sensible and Irritable Parts of Animals" that his research had nothing in common with the "impious system" of *L'Homme machine.*[7] Le Cat, however, sought to subvert the Swiss physiologist's dualism from the other direction. A leading proponent of the vitalist approach advanced by the medical school of the University of Montpellier, he set the motion of the human body within a kind of spiritualized hydraulics of the universe. In his philosophy, the world and everything it contains are imprinted by God through the action of a first, most subtle fluid or "universal spirit." Le Cat imagines this fluid as "Minister of the Supreme Being," the agent through which the Almighty has brought order from chaos, giving life to the universe, and consequently to all the animals that are part of it. The solids and liquids of the human body, like those of other animals, are made of earthly materials of different degrees of density, but they all owe their operation to the infusion within them of subtler, invisible fluids penetrated in turn by the universal spirit that is the moving force of the universe.[8] Given these vitalist convictions, it is not surprising that Le Cat was determined to counter Haller's arguments and to restore the operation of the immaterial soul throughout the entire body. He could only do so by restating the primacy of the sensibility operating through the nervous system over the muscular motion Haller had attributed solely to the operation of the material property of irritability.

Motivated by the conviction that "the material principle is without energy unless it is animated by the true sensitive principle that is the soul,"[9] Le Cat offered an extended repudiation of Haller's physiology in his *Traité de l'existance, de la nature et des propriétés du fluide des nerfs, et principalement de son action dans le mouvement musculaire*, published in 1765. The theories advanced by Haller and his disciples, Le Cat contended, were not only "abstract and incomprehensible" but "revolting." Returning to the mechanistic systems of the seventeenth century, they still relied on a notion of irritability as a kind of "occult virtue"—an eighteenth-century code word that could be used to impugn descriptions of effects offered without rational explanation of causes (as in rationalist attacks on Newton's theory of gravity) or, conversely, to attack the kind of scholastic obfuscation Newton himself had famously sought to avoid.[10] Even worse, Le Cat charged, the denial that sensibility operated in most bodily motion turned human beings into automata. Against Haller, he insisted that the brain communicates with the muscles by means of a fluid circulating through the network of the nervous system. This fluid, "the instrument of our sensations," is a kind of "amphibious entity" composed of a material part ("a mucilaginous lymph") and a more spiritual part (a "*nuance supérieure*") that links it with the immaterial soul.[11]

Le Cat did not explain why his own theory relied less on an occult force than Haller's. But he was willing to consider an objection he ascribed to Haller's disciples: that if there is no irritability without sensibility, then sensibility must remain in severed bodily parts that continue to move or respond to stimulation. This would mean, in turn, that an animal has a sensitive soul; that this soul is still somehow present in its severed bodily parts; and that the soul itself is therefore divisible indefinitely. Le Cat responded to this reasoning by allowing that since animals experience sensations, they must indeed have a true immaterial soul (though not, he hastened to add, an immortal one). But he disallowed the further conclusion that the soul is indefinitely divisible. An immaterial substance occupies no place, he argued; it cannot therefore be said to occupy several places at the same time. The material fluid through which the soul acts can indeed be divided, but "the immaterial substance, the true soul," cannot. While not itself being separated, the soul exercises its influence on the separated parts, presumably through the operation of a fluid more subtle than human senses can detect, a fluid deriving its action from the thinking, immaterial entity Le Cat called "the sensitive soul."[12]

This is the point on which Marat first engages Le Cat directly in *A Philosophical Essay on Man*. Addressing the vitalist's claim that the soul is not material and does not occupy any place in the same manner as a material substance, Marat responds that "it does not follow from thence, that it has no determinate seat, whence it extends its influence."[13] In fact, Marat argues, the soul is located in the meninges of the brain:

> for, if we trace the nerves to their entrance into the membranes of the brain, we shall find they confound themselves with the *meninges*, and form one simple uniform substance with them. Hence if the nerves only are sensible, and if the sensations are not continued to the soul but by these organs, we plainly perceive, that the meninges must be esteemed the seat of the soul.[14]

This proposition is not in itself a significant departure from Le Cat's view. He too had found the seat of the soul in "the envelopes of the brain, the dura mater and the pia mater."[15] But in emphasizing the specific location of the seat of the soul at this specific point of his argument, Marat is nonetheless moving away from Le Cat's vitalism. He follows the Rouennais surgeon in giving primacy to the nervous system ("the nerves only, and the nervous productions, are the seat and organs of motion")[16] but reduces the role of the soul by ruling out the notion that it acts throughout the body. Citing the fact that severed limbs continue to move for a while, he concludes that the soul is neither the immediate source of movement in the body nor in any way diffused through it. Sensation, he argues, is produced by the operation of the nervous fibers in response to stimulation; sensations are communicated to the soul by the nerves. It follows that "the body is therefore sensible of itself independently of the soul, since irritability is a property of nervous fibres."[17]

It is important to note (as Diderot did) that Marat is explicit here in making sensibility a function of the irritability of the nervous fibers. He is even prepared to speculate that "sensibility probably belongs to matter, as a property dependent on its organization. Moreover, he argues, sensibility extends itself to every part of the body, in the same manner as life, and animates these parts no longer than while the fluid of the nerves remains . . . and while the combination of the organs continues unchanged."[18] In effect, Marat is abandoning Le Cat's vitalist arguments for the immediate action of the soul throughout the body, while at the same time muddying Haller's distinction between irritability and sensibility. In his analysis, sensations are communicated to the soul by the nervous fluid, and the soul acts upon this fluid to produce voluntary motion. How can a material substance act on an immaterial one, or vice versa? Marat acknowledges that such a thing is impossible to explain, given that "we are entirely ignorant of the essence of things."[19] But he does advance a theory as to how the irritability of the nervous fibers produces sensation. Again, this proves more mechanistic than Le Cat's.

If, having tied the nerve above a muscle, one presses upon the nerve with the fingers while sliding them toward the muscle, then the muscle will contract. From this well-established fact Marat concludes that the soul produces movement through impulsive motion in the nervous fluid and that, conversely, the flow of nervous fluid back to the brain communicates sensation to the soul. It follows from this argument, in his view, that "the nervous fluid is the band which unites the soul and the body."[20] Flowing through the minute channels in the coating of the nerves, it is the organ of sensation; flowing through the cavities within the nerves, it is the principle of motion. It operates as the instrument of the soul in the case of voluntary movement, and independently of the soul in the production of involuntary motion. Marat's description of the composition of this fluid remains essentially the same as Le Cat's. He too thinks of it as a twofold substance comprising "a spirituous and extremely subtil part, called *animal spirits*" and "a gelatinous juice, distinguished by the name of the *nervous lymph*."[21]

But he makes no effort to link these *animal spirits* to a universal spirit of the universe understood as the moving force of all that is. Even though he retains much of Le Cat's physiology, he despiritualizes it in significant ways. He substitutes mechanical explanations for vitalistic ones as far as he can without appearing to fall into materialism. Closer to Haller's thinking than to Le Cat's in this regard, he contains the soul within a specific site while still affirming its existence as an immaterial entity.

Although he proclaimed his opposition to materialism, Marat's research clearly propelled him in that direction. Diderot was to take its implications to a logical extreme in developing what Caroline Warman has described as his "materialist vitalism."[22]

A PHYSIOLOGY OF MIND

The second volume of *A Philosophical Essay on Man* is devoted to exploring (in substantial detail) the reciprocal influence of the soul and the body. The force of the latter nevertheless emerges as considerably more powerful than that of the former. A fever can induce us to dream that we are dying of thirst; a wound can render us delirious; an acute illness can weaken our memory and understanding. "To behold the manner in which the soul partakes of the affections of the body," Marat concludes from such phenomena, "we should almost be induced to believe it material."[23] Indeed, atmospheric changes and differences in climate so obviously affect the mind and spirit that "seeing that the soul is subject to physical laws, and is under the influence of the heavens and earth, we might be induced to believe that Man is wholly material."[24]

Marat hastens to counterbalance such an inference by asserting that the influence of the soul on the body is no less immediate. He reminds his reader that friendship, love, and joy express themselves in physical symptoms, as can "terror, that painful emotion excited in the soul by fearful exclamations, the cries of fury or the sight of imminent danger, and always compounded of dread of the object terrifying us."[25] Nonetheless, he allows, the power of the soul over the body is less complete and less continuous; many of the ongoing functions of life proceed independently of the soul or are affected by it only occasionally or indirectly. "The influence of the body on the soul is permanent; the influence of the soul on the body only momentary."[26] Diderot's judgment of this conclusion was severe. "Marat doesn't know what he's saying when he talks of the action of the soul on the body," he wrote. "If he had looked closer, he would have seen that the action of the soul on the body is the action of a part of the body on another, and the action of the body on the soul is the action of another part of the body on another. He is as clear, firm, precise in his chapter on the action of the body on the soul as he is vague, feeble in the following one" (on the action of the soul on the body).[27]

When it comes to explanation of these phenomena, Marat acknowledges that he is entering hazardous territory littered "by the vain efforts of so many great geniuses." Yet "notwithstanding so great a combination of prejudices, and the ridicule inseparable from such an undertaking," he is ready to "attempt the explanation of these mysteries, enter this dark labyrinth, sound this immense abyss, and carry light into those regions of darkness . . . ; in a word, reduce to fixed principles a science, wherein every thing is yet hypothetic, obscure and mysterious."[28] He insists that the interaction of soul and body, mind and matter, must ultimately remain "a mystery impenetrable to human understanding."[29] He nevertheless promises, by proceeding empirically from effects to cause, to uncover the principles underlying their reciprocal relations.

To this end, the question of the mechanics of the soul's influence on the body is resolved relatively quickly, since Marat has already shown that the interaction is effected entirely by the nervous fluid. Bodily expressions of emotions, he argues, depend entirely on variations in the intensity and volume of the flow of this fluid into the nervous fibers and the muscles, and particularly to such organs as the heart, the plexus nervosi, and the diaphragm. Exactly how emotional variation produces changes in the action of the nervous fluid, he does not claim to explain. He is more engaged in showing how emotions themselves are produced by bodily sensations.

Marat repudiates as too materialistic any effort to relate emotional dispositions, or intellectual powers, to specific physiological structures of the brain. This, he maintains, would be to attribute to the body the properties of the soul. At the same time, he is eager to show that the sensibility of the soul is affected by the sensibility of the body, which in turn derives from its physical organization. Emotions arise in response to sensations, which vary with the physical propensity of the body to receive them. It follows that the more delicate the body, and the more intense its sensibility, the more vivid the emotions and the greater the subjection of the soul to the body. In Marat's analysis, the same logic applies to thinking as to feeling. Individuals will be rational or imaginative, sane or mad, depending on the sensibility of their physical organization. "Organization alone causes almost* every difference which is observed between souls. . . . Thus everything in nature is influenced by physical laws."[30]

This consideration underlies a statement of a kind of physiology of intellectuality. Thinking—"this perpetual fermentation of reason" (note the materialist resonances of the metaphor)—is activated by the passions, which emerge as functions of bodily responsiveness to sensation. "*Men therefore are more or less ingenious, as they possess greater or less sensibility.*"[31] Too delicate a sensibility, Marat maintains, will lead to a chaos of indistinct ideas. To yield clarity and profundity, the mind must be united to organs composed of strong and elastic fibers. This is not to say that all those endowed with a vigorous constitution are profound. Without further training, such people cannot attain "that sublime knowledge, which is derived from the constant study of Nature . . . their minds may be congenial with the minds of Pope and Voltaire, but will never rise to the dignity of Newton's or de Montesquieu's; they may be called men of wit and learning, but never men of depth."[32] Whether this passing slight caught Voltaire's eye before he wrote a review that ripped into the later French translation of *A Philosophical Essay on Man* we are unlikely ever to know.

Marat remained faithful in his judgment of Montesquieu, but Newton (as we shall see) was to be his next scientific target. His rating of intellects reminds us, though, that Marat was constant in measuring himself against the Greats. He could not close this work without again casting his intellectual endeavors in the agonistic mode. "Whatever the object may be, the passions ever actuate the mind; by their activity its faculties unfold and rise to perfection. To arrive at excellence of any kind, Man must be animated by some passion; and the more violent his eagerness to succeed, the more efficacious are his efforts for that purpose. For only the violent passions produce illustrious, heroic and great men: he who is animated by no passion, does nothing to render himself illustrious, and is wholly insignificant."[33] Marat is determined to avoid the latter fate.

From a defense of the vanishing immaterial soul, Marat had shifted toward a physiology of the agonistic intellect. He had started his book in face of the danger notoriously represented by La Mettrie's *L'Homme machine*—the danger that the immaterial soul could be banished, or simply disappear, from eighteenth-century physiology. Vitalism, toward which Le Cat pointed him, offered an obvious alternative to materialism. As his thinking developed, though, he also moved away from Le Cat's notion of the soul as everywhere infusing the body. He wanted to save the immortal soul by giving it a firm physiological location and mode of action. But this effort brought him closer than he would acknowledge to the materialism he was aiming to refute. In effect, he was left caught between a vitalist physiology that found the soul everywhere in the body and a materialist physiology that found it nowhere. Both threatened to distribute being and consciousness. But Marat wanted to concentrate being and consciousness, not to distribute them. He fell back on a physiology of great souls motivated by intense passions.

Despite his claims to originality, Marat scarcely revolutionized the science of man. But his inquiries lay well within the bounds of what counted for normal science in this field in the mid-eighteenth century. He would not abandon the idea of the soul, or replace it explicitly with a physiology of the brain, as the celebrated doctor Cabanis was to do a couple of decades later (perhaps with some inspiration from Diderot's still unpublished *Eléments de physiologie*).[34] Nevertheless, by stressing the importance of physical organization in the development of mental perception and emotional sensibility, he participated in the broad movement toward the physiological treatment of the relationship between the moral and the physical that Cabanis finally turned into a research program for the Class of Moral and Political Sciences of the Institut de France when it was established in 1795. By that time, of course, Marat was dead, remembered (among other things) as a declared enemy of any kind of scientific academy. But he was destined to make several further attempts to secure academic glory before coming to this view.

FIRST FIRE

Citing the evidence of a review that appeared in *The Westminster Magazine* in May 1773, Marat claimed later that the appearance of *A Philosophical Essay on Man* caused a sensation. That review pleased its author enough that he sent a copy to his father in Geneva, who eventually passed it on to the worthy Frédéric-Samuel Ostervald.[35]

If this relatively brief account of the book was positive, it scarcely announced a sensation. "This is a singular book," the reviewer had written. "The great and occult study of man has engaged the best philosophers throughout all ages . . . ," he had observed, rehearsing Marat's account, "but the path which our Author has chosen has remained hitherto in a great degree unexplored. The faculties of the soul, and the mechanism of the body, were known; but not the whole Man, as compounded of both. No one has yet accounted for the singular relations between the two substances which compose his being. It is in this curious track our philosopher succeeds. . . . He advances many singular propositions, but does not often forget the important necessity of establishing them upon facts. He treats his subject always with perspicuity, often with conviction: and it is seldom that he is so dogmatic as he appears to be in the first sentence of his book."[36]

An earlier London review of *A Philosophical Essay on Man*, in *The Gentleman's Magazine* for April 1773, had been more restrained. It pointed without comment to the author's disdain for systems, his determination to refuse "vague and arbitrary hypothesis," and his commitment to "an attentive examination of the phaenomenon" of the reciprocal influence of soul and body. But the reviewer seems to have missed the fact that the work was intended as a defense of the immaterial soul. The author, he reported, proceeds "to account for every phaenomenon from known physical laws; and, by an attentive examination of them, attempts to draw sufficient natural explanation of their relations; that is, he endeavours to replace, in the class of simple effects, those phaenomena which have occasioned such wonder among philosophers."[37]

A Philosophical Essay on Man received more extended attention when it reached the Belgian city of Bouillon, home of a thriving publishing trade aimed at the French market. The *Journal encyclopédique* published there declared Marat's topic "an eternal subject of disputes, systems, and vain investigations" regarding which the philosopher could only try to discover laws from observed effects. It saw nothing new in his conclusions regarding the reciprocal relationship of body and soul, though it found them "based on very detailed proofs," which it deigned to summarize at some length.[38] Three years later, the same journal offered a lengthier review of the French version of the work that Marat had now expanded to three volumes for publication in Amsterdam under the title *De l'homme ou Des principes et des lois de l'influence de l'âme sur le corps, et du corps sur l'âme*. This time Marat dropped the shield of anonymity, entering the field of philosophical contestation as "J. P. Marat, Docteur en Médicine." The book's French title also conveyed a particular challenge. If "*De l'homme*" was an obvious choice for rendering the earlier English title, it was doubtless made more attractive to Marat and his publisher, the enterprising Marc-Michel Rey, by the fact that it had been used to package the slick materialism of the posthumous book by Helvétius that appeared in 1772. Marat was escalating his bid for attention by reclaiming the title for his own work.

This time the *Journal encyclopédique* began with a caveat. It was a mistake, it insisted, "to imagine that one can, on the basis of a vague and underdeveloped idea, establish plausible systems, propose new conceptions, reject those of others, and dismiss their ideas and even their manner of observing." If this was offered as a general observation, its application to Marat's work was soon made evident. In the lengthy account of *De l'homme* that followed, the magnitude of Marat's ambitions and his pretentions to originality were adroitly ridiculed, along with his cavalier dismissal of earlier thinkers. "We strongly doubt that the public will adopt M. Marat's severe judgments," the review snidely noted, "even after having read all his work."

Substantial excerpts from Marat's text followed, ostensibly to compensate for the reviewer's failure to grasp much of the argument. The final verdict was grave. "[The author's] way of proceeding is so vague, his manner of defining and presenting his ideas so far from precise, so lacking in method, that it is not easy to follow it and to grasp its reasoning. He analyses nothing, discusses little. . . . He refutes vaguely the opinions he attacks emphatically. He resolves few questions, proposes many, and too often offers phrases rather than proofs. For the rest, his style is sometimes vigorous; he succeeds in depicting the movements of the human heart and elegantly describing the external symptoms of its passions. His book, despite its weaknesses, announces a range of knowledge and leaves readers with the best opinion of his mind and heart."[39]

The closing dose of faint praise scarcely took the sting out of a damning overall assessment. From Geneva, Jean Mara anxiously solicited Ostervald's opinion of this review of his son's work. In March 1776, he was finally able to send his patron a copy of the book itself. Pleading a father's partiality, he asked the more enlightened Ostervald to decide whether the dismissive review was justified. He also declared himself eager to know the judgment of Ostervald's son-in-law and business partner Jean-Elie Bertrand, the "enlightened and knowledgeable" pastor who had taught Jean-Paul as a youth at the Collège de Neuchâtel. *De l'homme*, after all, was the work "not of a Socrates, but of one of his former students."[40] Regrettably, the verdict of neither man shows up in the surviving correspondence.

Two months later, however, Marat himself was back in Switzerland to spend some time with his family after an absence of a decade and a half, "before returning to London to settle there." From Geneva he wrote his own letter to Ostervald about *De l'homme* and its reception. Respectful in expressing his hope that his "little work" might meet with Ostervald's approval, he was nonetheless smarting from its treatment in the Bouillon journal.

> A little too much liberty in judging others, or rather, too great a frankness in saying what I think of them, has made me enemies. Some of them (who are not unknown to me) have, brave souls, entrusted their vengeance to the manufacturers of the Journal De Bouillon. I don't know how far they will be able to congratulate themselves on their success, but they could not have done better in setting about to prejudice the reader against my book: vague insinuations, false imputations, a feigned silence on the essential points, bits of praise conferred with an air of mockery, in effect everything one could expect from malign ignorance, was put to work.[41]

Dr. Marat had apparently expected better, and claimed he had received it in the English press. "I had the right to expect more impartiality, more justice, more candor from men who set themselves up as public censors and pretend to hold the balance of merit in the literary world," he complained to Ostervald. "This is not the way the English journalists received my work. I don't claim to decide whether they have merely appreciated its true worth; but if I could rely on the judgment of those taken to be the most enlightened 'I would have undertaken to reduce a new science to its principles and would not have failed in my goal.' In any case, I have only given the public a part of the work: four other volumes are ready for the press; in these I apply the principles laid out in the others and consider Man in relation to the animals, the species, the sexes, temperaments, constitutions, climates, etc."[42]

Perhaps because of the negative reception of the initial three volumes of *De l'homme*, the remaining four never sprang from the press. But who were the unnamed enemies Marat had in mind? Several years later, he was to maintain that "some of our modern philosophers," recognizing the danger of *De l'homme* for their materialistic principles, had conspired to prevent the work's shipment into France, causing it to be held up in customs at Rouen for thirteen months, and arranging for the book to be prohibited.[43] None of these charges can be confirmed. Diderot, as we have seen, found Marat's book infuriating but fed on it nevertheless for his materialist speculations. One other philosophe did indeed respond to the work, and waspishly, though he was scarcely a convinced materialist. For the book was soon reviewed (anonymously) by Voltaire.

The wind from Ferney blew cold. Ironically, given his own track record in this regard, Voltaire was severe in condemnation of Marat's expressions of disdain for his predecessors. "It would have been wise and useful to show us new truths without belittling those announced to us by MM. Buffon, Haller, Le Cat and so many others," he insisted in the *Journal de politique et de littérature* in May 1777. "One must begin by doing justice to all those who have tried to make man known to us, at least in order to win the goodwill of the being of whom one is speaking, and when one has nothing new to say, except that the seat of the soul is in the meninges, one should not be lavish with disdain for others and esteem for oneself to a point that revolts all the readers one wants to please." There followed a series of lectures demonstrating that the author, in denigrating his predecessors among the Ancients, had merely revealed his ignorance of them. And to what end? Marat claimed to have demonstrated that the fluid of the nerves was the link between the body and the soul. This would have been a great discovery, Voltaire retorted, if anyone had ever seen this fluid. Bad-mouthing one's predecessors was no substitute for a demonstration. "No one will find it good that the Lockes, the Malebranches, the Condillacs, the Tilladets are arrogantly called ignorant. One can establish the nervous fluid without insulting them; insults are not reasons, either in physics or in metaphysics."

And what of the "specious arguments" of Le Cat to the effect that the soul is immaterial and dispersed throughout the body? Voltaire agreed with Marat that it did not follow from Le Cat's reasoning that the soul has no specific seat in the body. But neither was he convinced by Marat's claim that the soul lives in the nerve-lined meninges of the brain. "Trust me, leave this to God; he alone has prepared his hostelry and he hasn't put you in charge of it."

Nor did Voltaire think much of Dr. Marat's attempted refutation of Helvétius, "a generous man who paid his physicians well." Marat's arguments for the importance of the love of literary glory were dismissed as simply ridiculous, along with his attempts at a physiology of mind and temperament. In the end, Voltaire warned readers against "this long declamation in three volumes announcing the perfect knowledge of man." It offered only "what has been repeated for three thousand years in so many different languages." As for Marat's efforts at literary embellishment, or his appeals to Rousseau for inspiration, the old man of Ferney found them merely pathetic. "It is amusing that a doctor cites two novels, one named *Eloise* and the other *Emile*, instead of citing Boerhave and Hippocrates. But this is also the way people too often write these days. All the genres and styles are mixed up. It becomes an affectation to be bombastic in a physical dissertation and to write about medicine in epigrams. Everyone tries to surprise his readers. Everywhere one sees Harlequin clowning to amuse the parterre."[44]

Welcome, Jean-Paul Marat, to the literary life.

FIVE

WILKES AND LIBERTY

New to London, Marat was soon to be found in one of the city's favorite institutions, the coffee house. The architect Joseph Bonomi remembered him as a frequent visitor to Old Slaughter's Coffee House by 1767 or 1768, a couple of years or so after he had first crossed the Channel. It remained his habitual resort. He found friends there, as Bonomi recalled, and he was still in 1774 using Old Slaughter's as a return address to pick up his mail. He doubtless used it also to get his political news, both directly in conversation and in the readily available collection of newspapers offered (and eagerly shared) in any coffee house in the capital worthy of the name. Newspaper publication exploded in London during this period, and with it the production of events to satisfy the growing taste for politics that explosion created. One coffee house habitué of the time, fatigued by going through as many as ten morning and evening newspapers, reflected on "the raging thirst for news, which is excited by the very multiplication of the means of satiating us with occurrences."[1]

And plenty of news there was, eagerly sought by an urban population that was becoming strikingly more literate, vocal, and active in political matters during this, one of the crucial periods of popular political mobilization in British history. For Marat's stay in England coincided with years that resounded, in the capital and throughout the country, with popular demonstrations and protests in the name of "Wilkes and Liberty." These were the years of Marat's political education, raising issues regarding liberty, popular will, and parliamentary representation that would engage him for the rest of his life. They culminated with the publication, in 1774, of his most fundamental work, *The Chains of Slavery*. Cast as an intervention into British politics, this lodestar book laid out a conception of political existence that would define his understanding of the French Revolution and dramatically structure the choices he would face within it.

By the time the young Swiss crossed the Channel in 1765, the first act in the Wilkes drama had already been played.[2] John Wilkes, the squint-eyed Member of Parliament for Aylesbury, was ugly, dissolute, profane, profligate, and reckless. He was also a brilliant journalist, a shrewd polemicist, politically an improvisational genius, and a magnetic public personality with a popular touch. In 1763, moving against a new ministry that had replaced his own political allies among the party of William Pitt, he had published a sulfurous issue (no. 45) of his journal, *The North Briton*. It blasted the peace proposals to end the Seven Years' War that were floated in the traditional King's Speech at the opening of Parliament that year.

Though the royal speech was conventionally understood as presenting the ministers' program for the new parliamentary session, it could nevertheless be claimed that Wilkes's criticism of its proposals was an insult to the monarch himself. On these grounds, his papers were seized and he was arrested for libel on the basis of a "General Warrant" dubious in its legality in that, identifying no one by name, it authorized detention of any persons responsible for the production of the now notorious issue of the journal.[3] When he was brought into court, cheered by a noisy crowd in the galleries, Wilkes linked his fate to that of the nation. The judges' decision, he proclaimed, would determine "whether English Liberty shall be a reality or a shadow." Declared exempt from prosecution as a Member of Parliament, he was escorted home in triumph by a crowd of thousands—as Marat was to be after a similar trial in 1793. From that day, "Wilkes and Liberty" became the new public cry.

Wilkes soon tossed his enemies an opportunity to retaliate. He came out with a reprint edition of *The North Briton*. Worse, he had his printers run off a proof of an obscene *Essay on Woman*, a blasphemous poem in parody of Pope's *Essay on Man* that somehow found its way into the government's hands. The poem was denounced in the House of Lords, while the House of Commons ordered *The North Briton*, no. 45, publicly burned. With further action threatened, and his personal affairs in disorder, Wilkes found it prudent to leave for Paris at the end of 1763. He traveled the Continent for several years. In the meantime, he was expelled from Parliament early in 1764, and a grand jury condemned his latest publications and ordered his arrest. Failing to appear before the court, he was formally declared an outlaw for evading detention.

Marat doubtless heard all this recounted as recent history around the tables of Old Slaughter's Coffee House. He would have learned, too, of growing discontent with the English system of parliamentary representation, its rotten boroughs and inequitable franchise, its opportunities for hawking of votes at the hustings, and its corruption of deliberations in the House of Commons by the extensive presence of placemen and pensioners beholden to the court and the ministers. He was in London himself when Wilkes, pressed by his Paris creditors and eager to return somehow to the House of Commons, was allowed by a new ministry to return in 1768. The result was a rapid escalation of political contestation in the name of English liberty. In the bitter winter of that year, with prices and popular unrest on the rise, Wilkes declared himself a candidate for election to Parliament by the City of London, resting his campaign on issues with which he had been identified since 1763, "the two important questions of public liberty, respecting *General Warrants* and the *Seizure of Papers*."[4]

Wilkes lost this election badly to court and city insiders, but he still had options. He immediately declared his candidacy for a parliamentary seat to represent the county of Middlesex, where he was elected as resoundingly as he had been defeated in the city. Marat may well have seen for himself the widespread London rioting that celebrated this triumph, since an excited mob smashing windows in its exhilaration marched across Soho where he lived. Whether or not he witnessed them directly, he would certainly have heard (or read) of the popular outbursts reported in *The Annual Register*:

> At night likewise the rabble were very tumultuous; some persons, who had voted in favour of Mr. Wilkes, having put out lights, the mob paraded the whole town from east to west, obliging every body to illuminate [their windows], and breaking the windows of such as did not do it immediately. The windows of the mansion-house, in particular, were demolished all to pieces. . . . They demolished all the windows of L[or]d Bute . . . and many other gentlemen and tradesmen in most of the public streets of both cities, London and Westminster. . . . At Charing-cross, at the Duke of Northumberland's, the mob also broke a few panes; but his Grace had the address to get rid of them by ordering up lights immediately into his windows, and opening the Ship alehouse, which soon drew them to that side.[5]

More intense unrest was to follow. Buoyed by electoral success, Wilkes appeared before the Court of King's Bench to appeal the 1764 declaration of his outlawry. Hoping for a decision that would remove any obstacle to his being seated in Parliament, his supporters were in for a surprise. Initially allowed to go free, he was detained a week later. His arrest ignited many more days of demonstrations, this time more menacing. Marat was there to witness the protests in St. George's Fields, the open space facing the King's Court prison. "In the riots that occurred in London over Wilkes, who was regarded by the nation as a victim of the Court, I saw twenty thousand men assembled in front of the King's Bench prison, where Wilkes was being held," he recalled.

> Rushing to the scene with their constables, several Justices of the Peace attempted to dissipate the crowd, and were mocked at. The regiment of guards arrived and assumed battle order. A Justice of the Peace read the Riot Act and the people remained assembled. When the Justice ordered the soldiers to fire, they put down their arms. Why? Because they regarded the cause of the people as the cause of liberty and the magistrates and officers therefore seemed to them to be unjustly applying the law, before which every Englishman bows the knee. When the soldiers were berated by the officers who had sold themselves to the prince, in England as everywhere else, they replied that the people was defending its rights and they would not budge.[6]

Marat offered this recollection in October 1790 as a lesson to Lafayette regarding the use of the National Guard to impose order in Paris. On that occasion, he invoked a general rule: "Commanders can never demand obedience except in matters pertaining to army matters, military exercises, the bearing of arms; in everything else, the soldiers only recognize the law of the state."[7] But Marat himself must have drawn a different conclusion when he witnessed these events in 1768: a conclusion regarding the power of the crowd to shape the course of events.

The protests in London culminated on 10 May 1768, the first day of the new Parliament. This time, soldiers lost control of a demonstration held in support of Wilkes. They opened fire on a crowd in St. George's Fields, killing a dozen or so among the thousands of protesters. The event sparked further unrest as the capital descended into "a daily scene of lawless riot and confusion" with "mobs patrolling the streets at noonday, some knocking all down that will not roar for Wilkes and Liberty" (the description is Benjamin Franklin's).[8] The political damage to the government was far greater than the body count might suggest. Historians of the French Revolution can easily recognize the similarity between this "Massacre of St. George's Fields" in London and the panicky suppression of popular activism by city officials in the "Champ de Mars Massacre" in Paris almost a quarter-century later. Marat lived to do the same. In both cases, a popular cause had found its martyrs.

Meanwhile, Wilkes was sentenced to twenty-two months' imprisonment. A "Society of the Supporters of the Bill of Rights" sprang into existence to uphold "the legal, constitutional liberty of the subject" and to mobilize support for his cause. The ministry, for its part, organized a parliamentary vote expelling him from the House of Commons. Twice again he was elected unopposed by the Middlesex electors; twice again the House of Commons refused to seat him. When he was reelected unopposed a third time, a candidate was found to oppose him in yet another election. Still the Middlesex electors declared themselves for Wilkes, choosing once more to send him to Westminster as their Member of Parliament. In response, the House of Commons simply declared that his opponent "ought to have been" elected. Despite widespread popular protests, he was formally seated on 8 May 1769.

In the popular political mobilization that followed, petitions condemning this action and calling for its reversal were directed to Westminster from counties and cities across the country. Within a year, tens of thousands of signatures had been collected to protest the arbitrary power of a corrupt and unrepresentative House of Commons to decide its membership against the will of the electors.[9] Nor were signatures alone circulating. An explosive commercialization of politics, as John Brewer has brilliantly shown, sent portraits of Wilkes and symbols associated with him swirling through the country, not only as engraved prints but on such artifacts as "coffee and tea pots, spoons, jugs, figurines, snuff-boxes, pipes, tobacco papers, buttons, and . . . coins and medals."[10] The petitions themselves were only one expression of the sentiments developing among those who felt themselves "out of doors," at once excluded from the closed circuits of parliamentary government and drawn to express their anger through more open, extra-institutional channels.

In this flurry of political contestation, demands were raised for more frequent elections (triennial or even annual, rather than at intervals of up to seven years, as allowed by the Septennial Act of 1716), for exclusion of placemen from the House of Commons, and for more equitable distribution of the suffrage.[11] They were notable, for example, in the *Observations on a pamphlet, entitled, Thoughts on the Present Discontents*, the sally against Burke that Catharine Macaulay published in 1770. A radical historian and a Wilkesite herself, Macaulay was closely associated with the Society of the Supporters of the Bill of Rights. True to her republican inspiration, she decried a system of corruption that had been growing in England since the revolutionary settlement of 1689. She saw a huge public debt, a standing army, and legions of placemen and pensioners hollowing out the fabric of freedom. She denounced the cabals that had been formed in Parliament between the ministers and the nation's representatives to plunder a credulous people. From her perspective, "parliaments, the great barriers of our much boasted constitution, while they preserved its forms, [had] annihilated its spirit; and, from a countrouling power over the executive parts of government, [had become] a mere instrument of regal administration." With the nation's liberties thus expiring, Macaulay insisted, the need was desperate for "an independent parliament, the true parliament of the people . . . intrusted with sufficient powers to keep the executive in a subordination, which must prevent any possible infringement either of the form or the spirit of the constitution."[12]

Macaulay's indictment drew much of its authority from her *History of England from the Accession of James I to that of the Brunswick Line*. By 1769, four of its (eventual eight) volumes had appeared to keep the history of despotism and the ever-present threats to liberty before the public mind, and they were brought out in a new edition in that year. The work was cast as a celebration of the seventeenth-century struggle against the tyranny of the Stuarts. But it opened by shouting a warning against the threats to liberty still remaining in the 1760s. The English constitution as it had been reformed after the Glorious Revolution, Macaulay held, was still far from perfect. She saw that corruption, "that undermining mischief," had sapped the foundations of a political fabric "cemented with the blood of our best citizens." She warned of conspiratorial factions ready to "remove the limitations necessary to render monarchy consistent with liberty." They were lying in wait "for the first opportunity that the imperfections of this government may give them, to destroy those rights, which have been purchased by the toil and blood of the most exalted individuals that ever adorned humanity."[13] This anxious view of the English constitution was to make Macaulay's *History* one of Marat's favorite works.

Protests, petitions, prints, and pamphlets notwithstanding (to say nothing of other artifacts), the government stood firm against the Wilkesite cause as it spread in the capital and throughout the country. Wilkes remained imprisoned and excluded from the House of Commons. But with the authority of Parliament so profoundly contested in his name, and that of the people, a related issue quickly came to the fore: the power of Parliament to prevent unauthorized disclosure of the debates held within its walls. One of the effects of the struggle over the disputed Middlesex elections was to put into question a longstanding prohibition against newspaper publication of parliamentary debates. An aroused public confronted by arbitrary decisions now wanted to know how these decisions had been reached, by whom, and on what grounds. Suddenly there was a market opportunity for printers ready to break the taboo against reporting parliamentary debates. John Almon, a radical printer and bookseller and an active associate of Wilkes, had begun to do so in the *London Evening Post* as early as 1768. By 1771, so many newspapers were following his lead that the House of Commons started summoning the offending printers to appear before it, subsequently ordering the arrest of those who remained defiant. These actions brought it into full-scale confrontation with elected officials of the City of London who supported the printers' cause. To add to the political drama, these officials suddenly included none other than John Wilkes!

His sentence completed, Wilkes had been released in April 1770, immediately assuming a seat as an alderman in the City of London, to which he had been elected while still imprisoned. The following year, he was in session with the Lord Mayor of London and another alderman at just the right moment to declare illegal a printer's arrest ordered by the House of Commons. The House, in its turn, summoned offending city officials to appear before it. Wisely choosing not to include Wilkes in this summons, it denied him the opportunity for further troublemaking that would have been afforded by his appearance in a chamber from which he had been formally excluded. Nonetheless, he was again at the center of resistance as the capital exploded in protest once more, this time when the House of Commons ordered the offending Lord Mayor dispatched to the Tower of London. Demonstrations again sprang up, windows were again smashed, and pro-government figures were executed in effigy.

To some, the whiff of revolution was in the air. "The ferment now raised is certainly symptomatic of a disease much more dangerous," worried one supporter of the ministry; "[it] must be subdued or we shall live to see the country without a King or Parliament."[14] But the moment for repression was allowed to pass. A month later, a triumphant procession of city officials accompanied the still defiant Lord Mayor and his fellow prisoner to the city following their release from the Tower. The city was again illuminated in celebration, though a few more windows were smashed for good measure. Messages of congratulation flowed to the capital from elsewhere in the nation. The tyrannical House of Commons had in this case been routed. Reports of parliamentary debates continued to flow from the presses.

Three years later, in 1774, Wilkes won a prolonged struggle for election as Lord Mayor of London. He also returned, finally, to the House of Commons as MP for Middlesex. There, in 1776, he rose to propose the introduction of a reform bill that would include universal male suffrage. The idea had little support in a House of Commons now overwhelmingly concerned with events in America, and Wilkes's star, in any case, was on the wane. Over a decade, nonetheless, he had incited a campaign for reform of parliamentary representation that had long-term ramifications in Britain. Not surprisingly, he had also become a hero across the Atlantic. For the aggrieved Americans, his treatment by the House of Commons exemplified the tyranny of a corrupt and unrepresentative assembly ready to ride roughshod over the will of the people. Remarkably, Marat left no trace of his views regarding American discontents during this period. But he, too, had learned much from the Wilkes Affair about the risks to liberty inherent in the practice of parliamentary representation. He offered his conclusions in a work published in 1774, his first political publication, and the one that set the direction of his political ideas throughout his subsequent career. It bore the title *The Chains of Slavery. A Work Wherein the Clandestine and Villainous Attempts of Princes to Ruin Liberty are Pointed Out, and the Dreadful Scenes of Despotism Disclosed.*

TO THE ELECTORS OF GREAT BRITAIN

Marat later recalled that *The Chains of Slavery* had been in his files for years before he took it out and readied it for publication in England in 1774. The occasion for doing so was clear. A new Parliament was to be elected, and Marat saw an opportunity to enter his work into the public debate over parliamentary representation that had been escalating since John Wilkes had been denied admittance to the House of Commons. To ensure its relevance, he prefaced the book with an address "To the Electors of Great Britain" that defined the political stakes of the forthcoming election in dramatic terms. He would be the happiest of men, he assured readers, "if by collecting into one point of view under your eyes the villainous measures planned by Princes to attain absolute empire, and the dismal scenes ever attendant on despotism, I could inspire you with horror against tyranny, and revive in your breasts the holy flame of liberty which burnt in those of our forefathers." His goal was to announce a fateful moment of choice between virtue and despotism, the time for a critical political decision that could either leave the nation moving ever closer to slavery or turn it back toward freedom. "Your most sacred rights have been flagrantly violated by your representatives . . . ," he warned the electors, "your complaints silenced by pursuing the same conduct which raised them. Such is your condition, and if such it continues, the little liberty which is yet left you, must soon be extinguished."[15]

The British electors, Marat declared, still retained "a power to secure the liberty of the people, or enslave the nation." Election day would make them again (though only momentarily, as Rousseau had emphasized) the "arbiters of the state." But to recover liberty, the voters had to restore the freedom of Parliament, "to revive that august assembly, which, in the last century, humbled the pride of a tyrant, and broke your fetters." They had to purge Parliament of the corruption that was undermining the balance between royal prerogative and threatening to enslave the nation to an absolute prince sharing his spoils with "a band of disguised traitors, who, under the name of guardians, traffic away the national interests, and the rights of a free-born people."[16]

To end parliamentary corruption, Marat warned, the electors had to find "men whom an independent fortune secures from the temptations of poverty . . . men who have not been corrupted by the smiles of a court, men whose venerable mature age crowns a spotless life; men who have ever appeared zealous for the public cause, and have had in view only the welfare of their country, and the observance of the laws." They had to reject "mercenary suitors" seeking to buy their votes; placemen and pensioners; men of "pompous titles"; "the insolent opulent." They had to spurn the untrustworthy young, inexperienced or prone as these latter were to the dissipation and debauchery that rendered them vulnerable to the seductions of the ministers. Above all, they had to deny themselves the easy temptations of the hustings, repudiating the "fawning caresses" and "alluring baits of corruption" that would lead them to hawk their votes. "When your great common interest ought to direct you, shall the selfish passions dare to raise their voice?" he demanded.

> Are they worthy to be indulged at such a price? Behold the dismal scenes arising from the neglect of national interest; behold your senators busy in making, altering, and amending acts for securing the property of their dogs, whilst half of the subjects, lingering in misery from the villainy of monopolizers, cry to them for bread. . . . What are the bribes taken for votes, to the losses suffered by a neglect of your interests, to the advantages you would reap from being represented with ability and fidelity? . . . With virtue and courage a people may ever maintain their liberty: but when once this inestimable treasure is lost, it is almost impossible to recover it; and it is very near being so, when electors set a price on their votes.[17]

Electors in England's complaisant counties and rotten boroughs, men who were the last, corrupt remnant of a once free people, had in the past proven all too eager to reap a profit from the uneven patchwork of the right to vote, Marat lamented. Would they now overcome their selfishness in order to recover the liberty of the nation? The outcome had to be far from clear. The charms of corruption, and the ease with which a people could slip ever more deeply into political lethargy, was a prevailing theme of *The Chains of Slavery*. Marat's suspicion of the people went as deep as his distrust of its representatives.

Claims for the relevance of this book to the concerns of the British electors notwithstanding, the match between the text and the moment was not perfect. "I am sensible that many things in this work have no relation to our own actual situation," Marat acknowledged in the English voice he now adopted, "and in this we are to be accounted happy: how much more so should we be, had we not so great a concern in the rest!"[18] To make *The Chains of Slavery* speak more directly to a British audience, he later recalled, he had to stuff it with notes and additional passages of material from English history, working to the point of exhaustion for twenty-one hours a day over three months as he poured over "thirty deadly volumes, making extracts from them, adapting them to the work, translating it and getting it printed."[19] The process of revision hardly made the work more coherent. While its theme remained broadly consistent, the sequence of chapters became choppier, and the trajectory of the book more erratic. The book became baggier, and more disjointed, as further iterations and more extended examples were stuffed into it.

That this first of Marat's political works was indeed revised and adapted for an English audience rather than originally drafted for it is abundantly evident from the text. James Burgh's *Political Disquisitions*, the bible of British radicalism in the later 1770s, supplies an illuminating point of comparison in this regard.[20] That book was published the same year as *The Chains of Slavery*, to address the same abuses of parliamentary government; and, like *The Chains of Slavery*, it was rushed into print to influence the general election of 1774. Though the two authors shared many sources of inspiration and offered very similar criticisms of the corruption of English parliamentary politics, the list of titles Burgh cited in his first volume serves as a reminder of some of the most obvious English writings Marat fails to reference, at least directly: works in the classical republican tradition like James Harrington's *Oceana*, Algernon Sidney's *Discourses on Government*, John Trenchard's *Cato's Letters*, the various tracts of Richard Gordon, and Bolingbroke's *Remarks on British History* and *Dissertation on Parties*, as well as such obvious other authorities as Blackstone's *Commentaries* or Locke's *Second Treatise*. Both Burgh and Marat draw on their classical sources. But compared with Burgh, who moves more directly toward a discussion of the British situation, Marat lingers on the continental political experience of the sixteenth and seventeenth centuries.

Compared with *Political Disquisitions*, too, which directed its denunciation of taxation without representation as much to the American context in 1774 as to the English, *The Chains of Slavery* reveals no concern at all about events across the Atlantic. Nor, indeed, do the chains in its title appear to suggest any reference at all to the scandalous shackles of plantation slavery. At a moment when the evils of the Atlantic slave trade were being brought into clear sight, Marat's attention lay elsewhere.

Instead, Marat opens his account of the insidious rise of despotism in the most general terms, infused with the spirit of Tacitus, Machiavelli, and especially Rousseau's *Discourse on the Arts and Sciences*. He draws his initial evidence from ancient Rome, but more particularly from histories of Spain, France, and Italy. Cosimo de' Medici and treacherous doges of Venice, Ferdinand of Aragon, Philip II, Charles V and other kings of Spain, together with Richelieu and Louis XIII, make early appearances as conspirators against liberty, to be joined eventually by Mazarin, Louis XIV, and the more notorious Roman emperors. The kings of England enter the scene only gradually, with references to their depredations introduced occasionally or in footnotes before they take a more conspicuous place in the text. Increasingly, though, as Marat adapts his work to the English situation, the nefarious Tudors and Stuarts are made to play starring and more substantially documented roles. Bringing the story up to date, footnotes are added on Wilkes's stand against ministerial and parliamentary despotism, on the activities of the Society of Supporters of the Bill of Rights in his cause, and on the fundamental importance of the freedom of the press in Britain. A long note warns of the dangerous potential of parliamentary representation to usurp the sovereignty of the people unless the power of the representatives is clearly fixed within constitutional limits. Eventually, an extended chapter is inserted to anatomize the defects of the British constitution. Marat did indeed bring his arguments to bear on English politics in forceful ways, but broad reflection on continental experience seems to underpin them.

If England did not provide the original context for *The Chains of Slavery*, what did? The suppression of the French parlements by Chancellor Maupeou in 1771 suggests itself as an obvious possibility, and may indeed have been a significant factor. But Marat's text, while copious in examples of abuses of power, is remarkable for its omission of any explicit reference to this action so immediately denounced in France as an expression of ministerial despotism. Nor does *The Chains of Slavery* allude to the bitter propaganda battles that continued there until the old courts were restored in 1774 upon Louis XVI's accession. France supplies frequent examples of the ruses of monarchical power throughout the book, and Marat devotes some substantial pages to the despotic machinations of Louis XIV. But while he several times discusses the way kings destroy justice by replacing virtuous judges with corrupt ones—a theme that would naturally invite reference to the Maupeou coup against the parlement—he takes no opportunity to signal the most recent French political developments.[21] When indeed he does refer directly to political events in France "in recent years," these date from the mid-1760s rather than the early 1770s.

This evidence suggests that Marat wrote an early draft of *The Chains of Slavery* before the Maupeou Revolution in 1770, rather than in response to it. Talk of impending despotism was growing in France in the 1760s as Jansenist resistance became more overtly political and the parlements battled with the crown and its ministers during the years of Marat's initial stay there, and this may well have prompted him to begin writing on this theme. Rousseau's premonitions of social collapse and political enslavement, and behind them a classical republican tradition stemming from Machiavelli, were also clearly a stimulus to his thinking on the subject. Nor should we forget that Marat was Swiss, not French; that he was schooled in a city republic chafing under its distant Prussian overlord; that he was born of a family built on memories of a father's flight from royal power and of a mother's descent from Huguenots uprooted by a tyrannical Louis XIV. This Swiss republican had more than enough reasons for beginning "A Work wherein the clandestine and villainous Attempts of Princes to ruin Liberty are pointed out, and the dreadful Scenes of Despotism disclosed." But whenever he started *The Chains of Slavery*, wherever he found the deepest springs of the work, and whatever the specific reasons that initially motivated him to undertake it, Marat's observations of English politics caused him to revise and complete it in dramatic ways—and to sharpen the political views that were to compel his later revolutionary career. "I came to the Revolution with my ideas fully formed," he later recalled. Nowhere do we see these ideas taking shape more clearly than in London in 1774. There Marat learned directly the power of the crowd and the menace of representation.

SIX

THE CHAINS OF SLAVERY

The Chains of Slavery came armed with an epigraph, *vitam impendere vero*—"to stake one's life on the truth." The phrase carried a rich freight. It derived from the fourth of Juvenal's *Satires*, a brilliantly acid portrayal of a discussion between the despotic emperor Domitian and his fawning councilors that became necessary when the emperor was presented with a gigantic turbot of a size never before seen. "Hasten to fill out thy belly with fat fare, and devour a turbot that has been preserved to grace thy reign," begs the obsequious fisherman as he offers the scaled tribute to the ruler. For good measure, he even assures the emperor that "the fish himself wanted to be caught." "Could flattery be more gross?" the poet interjects. "Yet the Monarch's comb began to rise: there is nothing that divine Majesty will not believe concerning itself when lauded to the skies."[1] The supersized fish is too big for any cooking pot, though, and the emperor hastily summons his advisors to consider the problem. Among the first to arrive is the pliant Crispus, remarkable for his longevity in a court where lives are frequently abbreviated at the ruler's whim. How has Crispus managed to survive? He has long recognized the danger of offering a tyrant honest counsel. Crispus, the poet says, is not a man "to speak freely the thoughts of his heart, and stake his life for the truth."[2]

But the author of *The Chains of Slavery* declares himself such a man, even though he prefers to remain anonymous in doing so. He makes *vitam impendere vero* his motto, declaring his willingness to dedicate his life to the truth, even to become a martyr for it. Doing so in a century better schooled in the classics than our own, he could expect the phrase to evoke Juvenal's indignation at the base flattery and rampant corruption of an imperial court, the loss of civic virtue in a republic that had succumbed to despotism, the corruption of public morality in a world of luxury and excess. And Marat must have anticipated, too, that readers would know that he was not alone in echoing Juvenal's cry. Jean-Jacques Rousseau had made the phrase his own in justifying his condemnation of the world around him. "*Vitam impendere vero*: this is the motto I have chosen and of which I feel worthy," Jean-Jacques had declared in his *Letter to d'Alembert on the Theater* in 1762. "Love of the public good is the only passion which causes me to speak to the public."[3] Two years later, the phrase appeared as an epigraph on the title page of the *Letters Written from the Mountain*, at once a seething protest at the suppression of his recent works by the Genevan authorities and a defense of the sovereignty of the citizens of that city against the growing tyranny of the oligarchical elite. Rousseau even had a seal made so that his correspondence could go forth with this inscription.

For Marat, then, *vitam impendere vero* was more than a decorative flourish on a title page. It activated a kind of hyperlink to an entire discourse of nostalgia for the lost civic virtue of the Ancients, of indignation at the disappearance of political freedom in the modern age, of indictment of the excesses of consumption and corruption in modern commercial society. Behind Juvenal, Marat felt the inspiration of Tacitus, the greatest annalist of Rome's descent into despotism and debauchery, frequently cited in *The Chains of Slavery*. He owed no less to the thinking of Machiavelli, at once the theorist of civic virtue and the strategist of princely power, the writer who had made the rise and fall of the classical republics an indispensable reference for early modern political thought. And he drew profoundly from Rousseau, that quintessential Enlightenment outsider whose reworking of the classical republican tradition offered the greatest eighteenth-century indictment of the new forms of political despotism and social dependence encroaching within modern life.

If Tacitus, Machiavelli, and Rousseau offered the principal inspiration for Marat's political analysis, he looked widely for historical evidence to support it. To minds steeped in the classical republican tradition, the dissolution of civic virtue and the advance of impending despotism were to be found on a European scale rather than in any single country; nor were these phenomena restricted to a single period. Like other writers in this tradition, Marat moved readily from the classics through a wide range of sources detailing the political histories of the European states from medieval to modern times. Among the roughly one hundred works mentioned in *The Chains of Slavery*, the most frequently cited was the five-volume

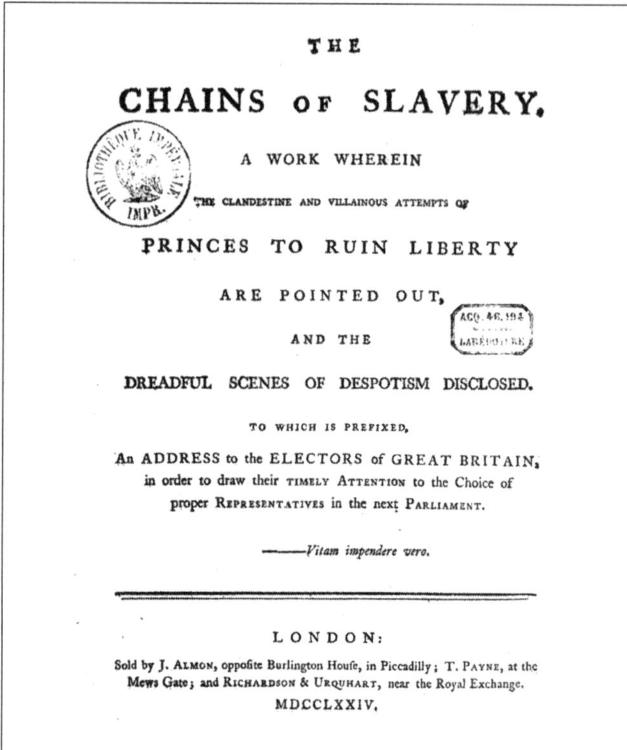

THE

CHAINS OF SLAVERY.

A WORK WHEREIN

THE CLANDESTINE AND VILLAINOUS ATTEMPTS OF

PRINCES TO RUIN LIBERTY

ARE POINTED OUT,

AND THE

DREADFUL SCENES OF DESPOTISM DISCLOSED.

TO WHICH IS PREFIXED,

An ADDRESS to the ELECTORS of GREAT BRITAIN,
in order to draw their TIMELY ATTENTION to the Choice of
proper REPRESENTATIVES in the next PARLIAMENT.

——*Vitam impendere vero.*

LONDON:

Sold by J. ALMON, oppoſite Burlington Houſe, in Piccadilly; T. PAYNE, at the Mews Gate; and RICHARDSON & URQUHART, near the Royal Exchange.

MDCCLXXIV.

FIGURE 6.1. Title page, *The Chains of Slavery*, published anonymously by Marat in 1774.

Abregé chronologique de l'Histoire d'Espagne published in France by Joseph Louis Ripault-Desormeaux in 1759. Marat supplemented it with references to Sandoval's *The Civil Wars of Spain in the Reign of Charles V*, which he cited in the 1655 translation offered to the English as a work "wherein our late unhappie differences are paralel'd in many particulars." References to the mid-seventeenth-century European revolutions and their outcomes came also from Giannone's account of the Neapolitan revolt against the Spanish crown in *Istoria civile de Regno di Napoli*, from the *Mémoires* of the duc de Guise, and from the *Histoire du ministère du cardinal Mazarin sous le règne de Louis XIV* translated from the Italian of Gualdo Priorato, Count Galeazzo. Despite the very different perspectives of these works, Marat also found illustrations of the ruses of power to destroy liberty in Richelieu's *Testament politique* and the *Histoire du gouvernement de Venise* compiled by the Tacitean Amelot de la Houssaye, the seventeenth-century French translator of Machiavelli's *Prince*.

For British history, Marat preferred his references to come from the standard eighteenth-century account by the Huguenot refugee (and veteran of William III's army in 1688) Rapin de Thoyras, or from the more recent work of Catharine Macaulay, rather than from Hume's more conservative *History of England*. Rapin's work, in particular, seems to have shaped his views. First published in French in 1723, but frequently republished in English as well throughout the century, its narrative was cast in terms of the constant struggles of the English people to preserve from monarchical infringement the liberties originally brought to their shores by the Saxons and most recently rescued from Stuart absolutism by the Glorious Revolution. Marat reinforced references to Rapin by citing sources from some of the folios he later blamed for sleepless nights he spent adapting his original French text for English publication: Rymer's *Foedera* (the great collection upon which Rapin had been the first to rely for materials up to the reign of Charles I), Rushworth's *Historical Collections of Private Passages of State*, and the standard *Parliamentary or Constitutional History of England . . . from the Earliest Times*.[4] Nor did he neglect the account of recent parliamentary history by the Wilkesite publisher John Almon, *The History of the Late Minority*. This reading left him considerably less sanguine than Rapin had been about the future of British liberty. He was writing at a time when parliamentary representation seemed as likely to usher in despotism as to preserve liberty.[5]

Not that Marat put much trust in historians. With few exceptions—notably Rapin and Mrs. Macaulay, whose names he deemed worthy of mention in the same breath as "the respectable one of Tacitus"—he found them all too willing to praise the enemies of liberty. "Abased by fear, seduced by hope, or corrupted by avarice, those who write history inculcate no aversion to absolute power, excite in us no horror against tyranny," he complained. They "basely insinuate the maxims of slavery" and lavish encomiums on those "the voice of all ages should brand with infamy." They present monarchies as happy families protected by beneficent fathers while portraying free peoples as misguided, restless, and seditious. Above all, they "never give to things the real names." In the historian's lexicon, spreading terror and desolation becomes "the art of governing"; usurpations are redescribed as "extension of power, addition of privileges, and new prerogatives acquired by the crown." Individuals who try to throw off the yoke are termed "rebels, or revolted slaves, who ought to be again put into fetters"; efforts of a people to throw off its oppressor appear as "a rebellion, a guilty revolt."[6]

By means of such language, Marat protested, historians had made "democracy" synonymous with "discord." "We are told of the frequent factions, seditions, and rebellions, in popular governments; but has a people ever took arms but to secure their liberty, to oppose the pernicious designs of ambitious men?" Marat took a very different view from the "pensioned sophists" who churned out apologias for power packaged as histories. With Machiavelli, he saw political conflict as the seedbed and guarantee of liberty. "We are terrified at public dissensions," he wrote, assuming an English voice. "From the fires of discord, however, all those laws, which were made formerly at Rome in favour of liberty, took their origin; and from the fires of discord liberty has arisen among us." In this view of politics, clamor signified liberty, silence meant death. "Men are too easily imposed upon by the noise of civil discords. . . . What mischiefs were ever caused at Rome by the dissensions of the Forum, to be compared with the horrors of the calm reigns of Tiberius, Nero, Caligula? What evils were ever suffered by any people under popular government to be compared with those we suffered under Henry VII, Mary, Charles I and James II? And that calm of monarchical states so much extolled, what is it, but the sad silence of an unfortunate people, who dare not vent their griefs?"[7]

Marat offers a very different kind of historical account from the panegyrics of monarchy he pillories. His is an anatomy of despotism, a story of "the slow and gradual efforts of policy which by degrees subjects the necks of the people to the yoke, depriving them at the same time both of the means and desire of shaking it off." There is no cause for celebration to be found in the pages of *The Chains of Slavery*. This is a profoundly pessimistic work. "It appears the common lot of mankind not to be allowed the enjoyment of liberty," its author announces on the very first page. "Princes every where are aspiring to despotism, and the people sinking to servitude." As in Rousseau's *Second Discourse*, the reader is offered a kind of universal history of the loss of liberty. Paying "less regard [to] the order of time than the connection of the subject," *The Chains of Slavery* promises to link examples from many different periods and places into a generic political history more true than any particular one. It undertakes to reveal the hidden maneuvers by which "the Magistrate usurps the title of Master, and substitutes his will for the law." It offers to detail "the multiplicity of machines, which the sacrilegious audacity of Princes has recourse to, in order to sap the foundation of liberty." It will expose "their dark projects, their crafty proceedings, their secret plots," and "reduce to one point of view the various attacks that have been made upon Public Freedom."[8] Machiavelli's *Prince* is to be rewritten here from the republican perspective of Rousseau's *Discourses*.

THE POWER OF TIME

Not surprisingly, then, the starting point of Marat's analysis is formulated in Machiavellian terms. "No constitution maintains itself unaltered but by virtue," he maintains. "If this spring be long unbent, adieu liberty. Instead of concurring to the public welfare, every one seeks his own interests only; the laws fall into contempt, and the magistrates themselves are the first in violating them. Thus the people being abased, an attempt is made to corrupt them." In "a state newly founded or reformed," the people remains still jealous of its liberty and the new ruler cannot openly and immediately enslave his subjects. He must allow time for the people to relax its guard, thinking its liberty assured. But time can be aided surreptitiously by crafty efforts. "To enchain their subjects, [princes] begin by setting them asleep."[9] Thus announced, the theme of political slumber will run throughout Marat's political writing and dominate his later revolutionary career. He sees the fate of nations acted out in the struggle to wrest political vigilance from the fatal ease of civic repose.

Plays, feasts, dances, and songs are among the first seductions offered by rulers—"the entrance of despotism is sometimes pleasing and joyous"; only the wise see "the chains concealed with flowers." War and public works follow, as do public entertainments, shows of generosity, displays of kindness, the pomp of glory. But this is just the beginning. "Vigilance, frugality, disinterestedness, love of glory and one's patria, are the virtues by which people preserve their liberty." To attain absolute power, princes must undermine these virtues by spreading artifice, dissipation, and debauchery. They encourage the theater, "the most fatal school of servitude." They foster the arts and sciences, herding their subjects toward slavery "by ways strewed with flowers." They advance industry and commerce, which in turn give rise to opulence and luxury, and their offspring, corruption and effeminacy. "The arts which luxury maintains, and the pleasures it promises, rendering society delightful," destroy the heroic (and masculine) virtues upon which liberty depends.

"By concealing with flowers the chains which are prepared for us"—Marat again adopts the phrasing of Rousseau's indictment in the *Discourse on the Arts and Sciences*—"they extinguish in our souls the sense of liberty, and make us in love with servitude." Luxury encourages neglect of public interests for private ones, extinguishes love of country. It produces new desires and escalating competition for distinction. There is no longer any proportion between wants and means; eager for wealth, everyone bows to fortune. Novel pleasures sow "new seeds of discord": envy and jealousy, hatred, pride, and contempt. Often nothing more is needed to complete the destruction of liberty. Thus it vanished from Rome as the spoils of vanquished nations dissolved the ancient virtues of the people, goading powerful men to put themselves at the head of the degraded mob, tear the state to pieces, usurp supreme power, and silence the laws. "Thus perished liberty at Sparta, and thus it will perish among us."[10]

But Marat's account of the devices by which rulers corrupt and enslave their subjects is only just beginning. The possibilities for princes appear as inexhaustible as time itself. They can begin by plunging peoples into a state of debauchery that stifles the true idea of liberty as independence. "This idle and lewd life, which the people call liberty, is one of the chief causes of their slavery." They can gather courtiers around them, fill public offices with their creatures, promise rewards to legions of placemen and pensioners. They can invent factitious honors that reward servility, displacing and debasing that true glory earned by generous actions and patriotic deeds. They can divide the people the better to rule over them, fostering inequalities of rank, wealth, and status; sowing religious hatreds; and inciting sectarian conflicts. They can favor evil ministers, empty or take over the offices that should check their power, fill the judiciary with venal placemen, and pervert the course of justice. They can exploit inevitable flaws in the political constitution by introducing innovations that pave the way to tyranny more effectively than extreme measures. "It is not . . . by open and violent attacks that Princes commonly begin to overturn the constitution; they rather undermine it; they innovate by degrees, and make things yield insensibly to their will." Violence has its uses, Marat allows, but princes do better to deploy it strategically. "If sometimes they follow violent measures, it is only in relation to some notorious villain, whose punishment, though arbitrarily inflicted, is always agreeable to the people, more mindful of their own interests than jealous of their liberty, and ever ready to confirm the unjust power which is at last to oppress them."[11]

Consideration of the uses of violence brings Marat, naturally enough, to one of the principal themes of classical republicanism: the threat to liberty represented by a standing army. "Every where," he argues, "mercenaries stand armed by tyranny against liberty." As commerce and industry extend inequality, so they create an "abject populace, destitute of all knowledge, of every virtue, of every principle of honour, without patrimony, and ashamed of their indigence." Drawing their armies from this desperate mass, and reinforcing them with foreign mercenaries, princes are able to disarm their populations and advance more openly to the exercise of absolute power. With standing armies, a new chapter is opened in the history of despotism. Personal acts of protest are blatantly crushed;

the rights of individuals are trampled without hope of redress from courts either cowed or corrupted. Usurpations are transformed into hallowed precedents and sacred prerogatives. Marat adds footnotes citing abundant instances of arbitrary power and the corruption of justice from the reigns of the Tudors and Stuarts before pointing to the prosecution of *The North Briton* no. 45 and the subsequent trial of John Wilkes as prime examples.[12]

But *The Chains of Slavery* is not uncritical of Wilkes. Its author emphasizes that "the subjects, in order to maintain their liberty, ought to watch the motions of the ministry with a jealous eye. Men are never so easily undone, as when they suspect no danger; and too great security in a nation is almost always a forerunner of slavery." The greatest misfortune in a free state is that "no party, no commotion, no faction agitate the minds of the subjects. All is undone, when the people are unconcerned for public affairs; on the contrary, liberty constantly springs up out of the fires of sedition."[13]

Nonetheless, Marat insists, the zeal of the people can be exhausted by false alarms or by ill-considered writings. Wilkes "kept the ministry in perpetual alarm, and made them tremble under the lash of his spirited writings" so long as he focused on abuses of power and the machinations of ministers. He went too far, however, in spreading the smear that the king's mother was mistress to the hated minister and royal favorite Lord Bute. "When he disgraced his pen, by employing it in grossly aspersing the character of a certain Princess . . . he furnished his enemies with weapons to his own destruction."[14]

This somewhat puritanical view of tactics of slander sounds an odd note published in a city that was the capital of personal vilification and already becoming by 1774 a haven for French libelers directing their bile across the Channel. It also comes as a surprise in light of the vitriol that was to flow from Marat's pen in the revolutionary years to come. The future editor of *L'Ami du peuple* seems oddly straitlaced when he condemns "satirical writings" that "attack indeed the tyrant, but not tyranny." But to his civic republican mind, laughter fosters lethargy; counterproductive in their effects, scurrilous libels diffuse the people's resentment rather than focusing it. Marat wants political denunciation to assume "a grave and animated stile." He also wants to avoid squandering it. He fears that the proliferation of (bad) writings drives out the good, wearies the public mind, and exhausts patriotic zeal. "This unfortunately has happened to us in our late dissensions. Plagued with so many writings, and exhausted by our own efforts, we are at present reduced to such an apathy that nothing is able to fix our attention."[15]

Is Marat simply deaf to the irony of publishing another political broadside that condemns the multitude of political broadsides already published? Is he so mesmerized by the advance of despotism that he falls into contradiction and sees no clear way of proceeding? Does he see himself as arriving too late on the scene of liberty's destruction, fearful that his voice will be simply crowded out in the frenzy of freedom's last moments? On the one hand, he emphasizes that liberty needs its sentinels, "men to watch the transactions of the ministers, unveil their ambitious projects, give alarm at the approach of the storm, rouse the people from their lethargy, disclose the abys before them." On the other hand, he fears that the proliferation of protest becomes self-defeating once loss of liberty reaches a certain point.[16]

There's a fatal contradiction here. The very next chapter of *The Chains of Slavery* deplores the "excessive moderation of the people," their "propensity to separate their common interests," their failure to detect and unite in opposition to the initial, insidious steps by which rulers proceed to subvert liberty. "The sacrilegious ambition of Princes prompts them to make attempts upon liberty; but the cowardice of the people alone permits their fetters to be forged." More fearful of disturbing public tranquility than anxious about oppression, "quiet men do not perceive that they gain nothing by their indulgence, but to be oppressed with more impunity; that they encourage tyranny, and that when they at last undertake to stop its progress, it often proves too late." Yet Marat holds out little hope, even for early resistance to the arbitrary exercise of power. The advantages are all on the prince's side. Marat lavishes detail on the many political strategies and manipulations of justice, legal and illegal, available to a cunning ruler intent on preventing redress of grievances and suppressing public outbursts. Since "despotism owes its support greatly to ignorance," he argues, efforts to prevent the acquisition and circulation of knowledge, censorship, and suppression of ideas likely to promote the taste for liberty, and payment for the production of writings that stifle it, are obvious moves for monarchs jealous of their power.[17]

Exploitation of superstition provides yet another means of oppression. And for superstition, read religion. "To stamp on their authority a sacred character, and secure their empire, all Princes cause heaven to interpose," Marat maintains. With this, he warms to an Enlightenment theme, and a classical republican one, too: the insidious alliance between kings and priests to plunge the people into slavery. "Opinion . . . obstructing our sight with the bandage of superstition, subjects our necks to the yoke of priests; and its power Princes make use of in order to enchain us." Marat joins with Montesquieu and Rousseau, and with other admirers of the ancient republics, in allowing the possibility of a civic religion that would help "render men patriots" and become "one of the greatest pillars of liberty." But with them he sees religion more often contributing to the opposite effect, "the most humiliating servitude." And with them he is convinced that, of all religions, Christianity is the most destructive of civic virtue.[18]

"Every religion countenances despotism, but none so much as the Christian." This descendant of Huguenots locates many reasons for such an effect in "the true spirit of the Gospel." Civic liberty, he argues, is essentially local, tied to a particular political system; Christianity is universal, indifferent to political identity. Liberty "depends on the love of the patria," but the Christian's homeland is not of this world. Grounded in the passions, like all human institutions, love of liberty is secular, tied to the desire for earthly well-being; but Christianity condemns earthly passions, preaching indifference to terrestrial enjoyments. Liberty, moreover, is jealous, it requires citizens to be ever suspicious, ever watchful. How, in contrast, can a true Christian "without suspicion, without cunning, without wrath" fail to succumb to the first attempt upon his liberty? How can men urged to turn the other cheek "take up arms against the disturbers of the public peace, how combat the usurpers of their own rights, how repel by force the enemies of liberty, how spill their blood for the sake of their country? To so many dispositions contrary to those of a good patriot, add the express command of *obeying the supreme powers, good or bad, as being established by God*."[19] As if these gospel teachings were not enough to incline subjects to "kiss the rod of power with devotion," priests conspire with princes to make them even "more servile from principle." The rule of the hated Stuarts had shown how princes "borrow the tongue of the divine, to subject the people to despotism," while priests "borrow the arm of the magistrate, to subject them to superstition."[20]

By such means, despotism establishes itself inconspicuously, by slow steps. Sooner or later, nonetheless, its weight becomes palpable and some tyrannical action incites general alarm. But popular indignation rarely turns into effective resistance. The people generally lack leadership and planning; difficult to mobilize and call to arms, they are even harder to keep united. It is easier for rulers to sow discord and factionalism among them, to corrupt or destroy those who would lead them, to defeat them by treachery or force. Popular resistance is momentary and shortsighted; the project of princes is relentless, their horizons long. "*I and Time*, said Charles V, *defy any two others*."[21]

THE FATE OF THE MODERNS

In eighteenth-century histories, Charles V's reach for universal European empire could seem to mark the beginning of the modern world. William

Robertson's *History of the Reign of the Emperor Charles V* was notable for this view. For Marat, too, Charles V, claiming time as his ally, seems to supply a hinge for his historical exposition. From this point on, *The Chains of Slavery* unravels in increasingly rambling and overstuffed chapters that point to ways in which modern rulers, having overcome efforts at resistance, continue the relentless project of subjugation. They learn how to preempt further insurrections, or to crush them ruthlessly. They concentrate their military power and engage in wars, taxing and demanding subsidies to wage them. They secure the loyalty of the army, separate it out from civil society, and inspire the military with contempt for ordinary citizens.

In the whirling catalog of attacks on modern liberty that *The Chains of Slavery* offers, three long-term developments emerge most clearly. One is public finance. Not content with heavy taxes, Marat argues, governments borrow at generous rates from the public at large. The Roman Senate, he remarks, preyed on the people by lending money at usurious rates. The modern prince is craftier: he enchains the people not by lending but by borrowing at high interest. Subjects fearful of losing their investments through a public bankruptcy are less likely to revolt; leaving their funds in the hands of the government, they give princes all the greater means to crush them. At the same time, they render themselves subject to financial manipulation as rulers hold back interest payments, find ways of repaying loans on advantageous terms, or simply cancel the debts completely.

Such steps had never been taken in England, Marat allows, but the peoples of France, Spain, and Naples had too often experienced them. And even in England, "public loans bind us not the less strongly: for by their means the government has intertwined itself with the property of the people, in such a manner that it is impossible to lay the ax to the root of the former without destroying the latter." Marat was one of the many eighteenth-century observers who found an intimate relationship between public debt and the corrosion of freedom. Investors, he believed, were willing to accept any infringement upon liberty to avoid the threat of a state bankruptcy. Monied men, allied with courtiers and in sway to ministers for the sake of lucrative shares in financial contracts, "assist the Prince to enslave their country." Meanwhile, "the locust tribe of subscribers, brokers, ticket-mongers, all those who act or seek to act that dirty part, on all occasions appear the avowed advocates of every corrupt minister . . . , [raise] their clamours against the complaints of true patriots, smother the voice of the nation, and become a dangerous faction in support of tyranny."[22]

A swollen treasury could also be used to enhance the simulacrum of majesty. This consideration suggests a second theme in Marat's analysis of modern statecraft: the gullibility of the people to shows of authority, success, and splendor. In this respect, he maintains, "the inconsideration and folly of the people also prepare the way to tyranny." Over time, and unless the true principles of a free constitution are continually refreshed, subjects lose sight of their rights. They accept the semblance of protection offered by a despot at the cost of their liberty. Forgetting that the only true aim of political association is the happiness of the people, they come to regard the prince's authority as sacred. Rulers and their lieutenants, adorned with marks of success and power, become "like antient idols, stupidly admired and adored." Of all the monarchs recorded in history, and setting aside Alexander, Caesar, Henry VIII, and Charles V, Marat finds the most despicable illustration of this phenomenon of political idiocy in the tyrannical and destructive reign of Louis XIV, "whom courtiers, poets, academicians, and historians have so greatly cried up, whom inconsiderate men have so stupidly admired, but whose memory good men ought to detest."[23]

The shadow of Louis XIV also falls heavily over the discussion of the third modern development to which Marat points: the evasion of the constraints of any legislative assembly representing the sovereign people. Unchecked by dispirited patriots, rulers become adept at corrupting or intimidating the representative body, robbing it of any power of initiative beyond the narrow purpose for which it must be called, or moving to govern without it entirely. Emperor Charles V in Spain, along with the Tudors and Stuarts in Britain, offers ample illustration of these political evasions and incursions, but Marat finds his best evidence in an indictment of the kings of France. Working over centuries to usurp the supreme power that once resided in the hallowed general assemblies of the Frankish nation on the Champ de Mars, he argued, French monarchs had erased the memory that legislative authority once belonged to the people. "At present the idea of this authority having been vested in the crown during every period of the monarchy, is so universal in France, that any assertion to the contrary would be deemed absurd." He failed to mention that invocation of the collective liberty exercised by the Franks on the Champ de Mars was a powerful theme of critics of monarchical absolutism in France in the eighteenth century.[24]

But Marat's consideration of the susceptibility of representative institutions to corruption or intimidation leads him to an opposing thought: the vulnerability of the people to oppression by, or in the name of, the representative body itself. Cromwell, he reminds his readers, rose to power under cover of parliamentary rule. The history of Venice he adduces as offering another instance of oppression of a people by its representatives. Abruptly, though, showing the seams between earlier and later versions of his work, Marat interrupts this discussion to add a lengthy note denouncing the arbitrary power of the British Parliament to fix the duration of its sessions and the period between elections. In this respect, he emphasizes, "the English constitution is extremely defective. Our representatives are the guardians of our rights; they must always defend, never attack them. But no boundaries have been fixed to their authority, in order to secure the constitution against their attempts. They enter into no engagements with their constituents . . . and instead of considering themselves only as the defenders of the constitution, they believe themselves to be the arbiters of it; they have even altered it many times."

From this perspective, Marat claims, reformers are misguided in their campaign against the Septennial Act. Their call for a Triennial Act providing for shorter, more frequently renewed parliaments misses the fundamental point that decision in this matter must necessarily belong to "the people at large, and to the people at large alone." If representatives are allowed to fix the duration of their mandate at three years rather than seven, could they not also extend it to fifteen, twenty, thirty years, or even make it perpetual? Could they not, in effect, claim "a right to render themselves independent, to overturn the constitution, to oppress their constituents, and reduce the nation to slavery?"[25]

It was essential, therefore, that the people recover the power to fix the term for parliamentary renewal. In this, as in "whatever belongs to the fundamental laws of the state," the representatives should have no power to alter the constitution, "not even to render it perfect, without previously taking the advice of the nation. . . . According as this point is gained or lost, we are free or slaves. As long as the power of our representatives is not confined within proper limits, liberty may be enjoyed, but not firmly established; we have no other laws but the decrees of our deputies; thus absolute masters of our birthrights, they may subject us to the yoke, tyrannize over us, and forbid us even to complain."[26]

If Parliament should ever prolong its duration against the will of the nation, Marat argues, "however hard be the act of vindicating liberty by force, the nation ought not to defer a moment to take up arms. This is the case of a just revolt."[27] Well before the French Revolution, the future People's Friend was thinking of ways to bind a national assembly to the people's will or to overthrow by insurrection representatives threatening to usurp popular sovereignty.

This extended note makes clear that ten years in Britain had not turned our Swiss republican into a eulogist of the British constitution. He was not prepared to join that other Swiss exile Jean-Louis Delolme, whose *The Constitution of England* was published in 1770 (and heralded as a classic for a century thereafter), in declaring the English form of government the ideal polity for a modern society. He found the English blind to the defects of a constitution whose virtues they were ever eager to extol. "The constitution of England is, no doubt, a monument of political wisdom, if compared to others," he insisted in his English voice; "yet it is not so perfect as we are pleased to affirm, nor can it be so, considering its origin and its revolutions." Montesquieu had famously traced the lineage of this remarkable system of government back to the woods of ancient Germania. Marat took a more critical view of its distant origins. "If traced to its first principle, it will be found to be very simple, and such as suited uncivilized men; good enough for a people who subsisted by pillaging, but containing a thousand sources of anarchy."[28]

AN ANATOMY OF BRITAIN

To substantiate this judgment, Marat devotes the longest addition he makes to *The Chains of Slavery* in 1774 to a chapter offering an extended account of the deficiencies of the English constitution.[29] At the heart of his analysis is a judgment of English government as shaped by a succession of factional struggles and uneven settlements resulting in a political bricolage, the precarious outcome of partial victories and makeshift remedies that have yet to place public liberty on secure foundations. In a well-constituted government, he insists, the people is the real sovereign and exercises supreme power, but in England remnants of royal prerogative still circumscribe the boundaries of national liberties. The Parliament still acts as if it were the servant of the king rather than vice versa. And the elected representatives of the nation still share legislative power with a hereditary body of peers who remain supreme judges in the realm, "nay, the arbiters of it." To the extensive constitutional powers of the Lords "are annexed high dignities, and many prerogatives equally oppressive and insulting to other subjects. Is it for their sublime virtues and exalted merit, that they are honoured with a coronet? No, the fatal privileges which they claim and arrogate to themselves, are but the inheritance of the plunders, usurpations, and violences of their ancestors."[30] Marat is already declaiming the language of 1789!

As if this were not enough, the future *Ami du peuple* continues, the House of Commons is chosen on the basis of a scandalously small and inequitably distributed suffrage, tainted by all the abuses of rotten boroughs and corrupted county elections. This unreformed, corrupted Parliament, stuffed moreover with placemen and pensioners, is then left virtually untrammeled in its exercise of power. The people has no constitutional authority to limit its representatives to the expression and implementation of its will, or to restrain or disown them if they abuse their trust. It has no power to determine the duration of its representatives' mandate. It does not even have the ultimate right to choose these representatives (as the case of John Wilkes had demonstrated) since "our deputies have arrogated to themselves the essential privilege of judging of returns, nay, of excluding such members as they object to, in spite of their constituents." As a result of these defects in the organization of parliamentary representation, the English people has lost the exercise of supreme power that rightfully belongs to it. "We are reduced to the deplorable situation of seeing our liberties invaded without being able to oppose more than vain murmurs, or reduced to the situation still more deplorable of vindicating our rights with arms in our hands."[31] Thoughts of insurrection arise again.

At this point in his indictment Marat shifts perspective, moving from constitutional to social consequences of unequal suffrage in England. He reminds his readers that eligibility for election has been restricted—again by act of Parliament—to the wealthy, to men of the landed interest. A prudent step this might be, assuming these men of wealth to be reliably persons of merit. But if they are interested only in extending their fortune, if "luxury, extravagance, ignorance, debauchery, and venality, are their only characteristics," the effects upon the disadvantaged classes of the people are disastrous. Beyond onerous taxes laid on the poor, Marat finds more grievous instances of injustice. The power of magistrates to round up for military service idle persons with no source of support is necessarily oppressive in a society "where the strongest and most artful have invaded almost everything," where "poverty is often the consequence of misfortunes, nay, of the injustice of knaves," where education is beyond reach, where "without a proper capital, it is almost impossible to carry on any lucrative business, or even to get an honest livelihood, and where poverty becomes the everlasting lot of the poor." Should indigents reduced to misery be required to shed their blood to protect the property of their usurpers or the power of their tyrants? "What law could be more unjust?"[32]

There are institutions established for the care of the poor, the rich respond. But Marat the doctor has seen these institutions, their scene so shocking as to be indescribable, their conditions not to be witnessed without utter horror. "Dismal places! wherein the needy is kept alive by unwholesome food, lays in nastiness, breathes an infected air, and groans under the severe hand of a warden; wretched habitations! wherein abuses, diseases and hunger reign constantly." Plagued by disease, the poor are rarely given admittance to hospitals. They are more often found in prisons, to which even those found innocent are forcibly returned, cursing the day of their birth, to linger in a dungeon until they can pay their jailor for the cost of their own unjust imprisonment. A very few benevolent members of Parliament, Marat allows, have called for inquiry into the state of the prisons. But legislators remote from the wretched condition of the poor care little about these abuses; they are more concerned to legislate regarding the security of their property in their dogs. "Be it again said, as long as the members that compose the legislature are selected from among one particular class of people, it must never be expected so see them applying themselves to promote common welfare."[33]

But wait. The author feels his ostensible subject slipping away from him. He needs to "draw, with indignation, a veil over these mysteries of iniquity, to continue our examination." He needs to remind himself, and his audience, that the British, "while at the mercy of [their] representatives . . . have much more to dread from [their] Princes." To this purpose, Marat reviews the dangerous prerogatives of the monarch in matters of legislation and the resources accruing to the king as commander of the army. But he cannot resist turning yet again to the threat that derives from the king's power to corrupt a Parliament, bend it to his criminal purposes, and transform the people's representatives into "a band of disguised traitors, who, under the name of guardians, traffic away the national interest and the rights of a free-born people." His conclusion is bleak. "A King of England will ever endeavour to make his progress to absolute empire by a pensionary parliament."[34]

With this excursus on the defects of the English constitution and the precariousness of English liberty completed, Marat seems finally ready to return to his original text (though he continues to bolster it with examples from British history) and bring it to a close. Here, as in Rousseau's *Second Discourse*, the pace of subjugation to despotism accelerates as the work reaches its culmination. Heedless peoples gradually give themselves up to tyranny; vile authors (Hobbes not least among them) proclaim princes sole sovereigns; frightened nations rush to forge their own chains by offering themselves to an absolute master. Princes, having spared no crimes to usurp supreme power, now spare none to maintain it. Grasping despotic power, they terrorize their subjects, reducing them to a state of superstition, ignorance, and servility. Abandoning all pretense to provide protection, they prey openly on their peoples at will. As *The Chains of Slavery* ends, Tiberius, Caligula, and Nero come into their own. Tacitus is given the last footnote. The conclusion of the work is profoundly pessimistic.

> Such are commonly the steps by which Princes advance to despotism. Thus Liberty has the fate of all other things: It yields to Time, which destroys every thing, to Vice which corrupts every thing, to Ignorance which confounds every thing, and Force which crushes every thing.[35]

Marat had started with a manuscript denouncing the political menace of kings, but his English experience left him with a book more keenly attuned to the threat of parliaments. The sovereignty inherent in the body of the people can be neither alienated nor represented, Rousseau had warned in *The Social Contract*. Of this, Marat was now convinced. Within his global attack on monarchy through the ages, he came to inscribe a critique of a more specifically modern alienation of the people's sovereignty, the practice of representation rendered dangerous and potentially despotic in a society where money corrodes civic virtue and selfishness corrupts electors and elected alike. The gap thus defined, between sovereignty embodied in the people and sovereignty entrusted to representatives, was to become the obsession of his later political career.

FAILURE

Sometime in 1774, probably in April or May, Marat penned a letter to John Wilkes. Writing (in French) as "the author of the book entitled, *The Chains of Slavery*," he gave his address as "Old Slaughter Coffee House." The earliest of his letters yet known, and the only one of substance from the period of his English stay, it would merit quoting in full even if it were not addressed to so pivotal a figure.

> I must let the veil fall, Monsieur, I can no longer hold on to it with you. Your language resists my pen and betrays the foreigner; perhaps you have already guessed this.
>
> I am not English by birth but I am at heart; I chose England as my country and have since then regarded myself as one of its children.
>
> As a passionate friend of liberty, I have closely followed your disputes with the ministry and its creatures. I've seen with admiration your generous efforts for the public cause, and with sorrow the triumph of your enemies. Outraged at the violation of the most sacred rights of the Nation, I dared form a plan to add my feeble voice to that of some good patriots, and to attack the unjust exercise of power, in a work destined to expose the dark plots of the tyrants. This plan I executed; perhaps I would have done better to gauge my powers in advance, and to learn that zeal alone is not enough to offer a worthy sacrifice on the altar of Liberty, but I counted on the indulgence of a public always inclined in such a case to forgive the zealous citizen the faults of the author.
>
> A hundred times, pen in hand, I wanted to be able to ignite in my readers' souls the sacred flame that devoured my own. I was conscious

that the mediocrity of my talents did not allow me to hope for much from my efforts. But I never imagined that tyranny would find a new way to render them totally useless and confound my best intentions. Unable to suppress my book by force, the public enemies of liberty have done it by trickery, condemning it to oblivion the moment it saw the light of day. A strange means of oppression, a hundred times more deadly than open acts of authority, and one that amounts to nothing less than silently annihilating the liberty of the press.

Lose from sight for a moment, Monsieur, the cause of an individual, to see only that of the public so closely linked to it.

Recognizing all the value of your time, I will not make myself tiresome; but should love of country ever fire your heart, I beg you to tell me how to thwart these cowardly measures of the Cabinet. To help me with your good advice would be to continue serving the Nation from which you have merited so much in so many regards. I am eager to receive that advice at the day and time you would be willing to set.

I have the honor of being with a perfect respect, Monsieur, your very humble and very obedient servant.

The author of the book entitled, *The Chains of Slavery*

Old Slaughter Coffee house
Sint-Martin's Lane [*sic*][36]

It appears that Marat had not met Wilkes, though there is no reason to doubt his avowal that he had closely followed his hero's political struggles. But this letter was more than the effort of an obscure author obsequiously seeking the patronage of a media figure. It was a bitter acknowledgment that *The Chains of Slavery* was failing to realize its author's hopes to "ignite in my readers' souls the sacred flame that devoured my own." The work, in other words, was a failure, "condemned to oblivion the moment it saw the light of day." But why? Marat was convinced that his book had been scuttled by a ministerial conspiracy to suppress it. Who better to approach for help in foiling this plot than Britain's greatest opponent of arbitrary power and loudest defender of the liberty of the press? Sadly, in this case Wilkes falls silent to us, if not to Marat; no direct record that he responded has come to light, though we shall find probable grounds for thinking that he must have done so.

Did the ministry really maneuver to suppress the circulation of *The Chains of Slavery*, or was this just the paranoia of a despondent author? There is scant evidence relating to the conspiracy that Marat was denouncing. But he did claim to offer further details, almost twenty years later, regarding "the silent persecution" his book had earned him from "the cabinet of Saint-James." Writing in 1793 to introduce a French edition of the work—somewhat belatedly for a people that had just killed its king—he recalled that his efforts to bring the book out in 1774 had left him in a state of mental collapse. Upon delivering it to the publishers, he recalled, "I fell into a kind of exhaustion bordering on unconsciousness; all my mental faculties were stunned, I lost my memory, I was in a stupor and remained all of thirteen days in that pitiable state, from which I emerged only with the help of music and rest." Upon his recovery, Marat told the readers of his journal, he found that his publishers had neglected to arrange announcements of the book's publication to the public. Rushing to various newspaper editors, he offered to pay the usual cost of such an announcement. They all refused, without offering any reason. Only one, Henry Sampson Woodfall, the printer of the *Public Advertiser*, was willing to intimate that the "Discourse to the Electors of Great Britain" might be the cause. Suspecting that the editors had been bought off, Marat recounted, he offered Woodfall twenty times the usual price for an announcement, but without success. He could no longer doubt that his efforts had been preempted by someone with a fatter purse than his own.[37]

But by whom? In Marat's account, he was pointed toward the truth by the fact that one of the publishers of *The Chains of Slavery* quickly disappeared from the book's title page. That publisher was discovered to be the Prince of Wales's bookseller, hence connected to the court and the ministry. Too late, Marat recalled, he understood that the ministry, fearing that the appearance of the work would stymie its efforts to assure a majority in the next Parliament, had bought off the printer, the publishers, and the journalists. Learning that his printer was attached to Lord North, he began to suspect that pages had been passed to the minister as they came off the press. A few words the printer dropped in conversation one day apprised him of this connection, warning him that the book's "excessive energy" would prevent its acceptance and could cause him trouble. With the treatment of Wilkes following the publication of *The North Briton*, no. 45, in mind, he claimed, he kept a pair of pistols under his bed for six weeks, determined to deal appropriately with the agent he expected to arrive to confiscate his papers. But the agent never came. "The ministry, informed of my character," Marat concluded in typically self-inflating fashion, "had decided to use ruse rather than force." A few years later, he added, he learned from a patient that the ministry had spent more than eight thousand guineas to delay the appearance of *The Chains of Slavery* until the 1774 election was over.[38]

Outraged at the obstacles being raised to his book's publication, Marat continued in this 1793 account, he finally sent almost the entire edition to the "popular societies" in the North of England, those "reputed to be the purest in the realm." But the ministry got wind of this maneuver, he recounted. Government agents began to shadow him, and his landlord and servant were pressured to intercept all his letters. Finding his correspondence interrupted, and certain he was surrounded by spies, he decided to leave for Holland. Returning to London by way of the North of England, he recalled, he visited the local societies to which he had sent the copies of his book, staying three weeks in Carlisle, Berwick, and Newcastle. In each he was fêted and given the keys to the city. There, too, he learned that these societies had sent him letters of affiliation "in a golden box," which had been forwarded in his absence to his publishers and picked up from them by the agents of the ministry. The Newcastle society in particular, Marat contended, not only reimbursed him for the cost of the edition of *The Chains of Slavery* he had presented to them but made a new one it circulated throughout the three kingdoms. "My triumph was complete, but it was late. I had the pain of seeing that by spreading handfuls of gold the minister had succeeded in stifling my work until the elections were finished, only allowing it to circulate freely once there was nothing to fear from the arousal of the electors."[39]

Can this be true? How much of it can be confirmed independently? We know that an initial version of *The Chains of Slavery* did show the book as "*printed for T. Becket, corner of the Adelphi, in the Strand, T. Payne at the Mews Gate and Richardson & Urqhart, near the Royal Exchange.*" We also know that a new title page quickly appeared, advertising the work instead as "*Sold by J. ALMON, opposite Burlington House, in Piccadilly, T. PAYNE, at the Mews Gate; and Richardson & Urquhart, near the Royal Exchange.*" While no independent evidence exists regarding Becket's motivation in the matter, this change does argue in favor of Marat's suspicion that Becket was pressured to withdraw responsibility for the book for political reasons. In Almon, Marat certainly found a publisher more sympathetic to the book's arguments. Given the close association between Almon and Wilkes, moreover, there is a strong possibility that Almon stepped in to underwrite the book's publication at Wilkes's suggestion, and that Wilkes had urged him to do so in response to Marat's plea for help. It may also be that Marat's admission to a Masonic lodge in mid-July 1774 was connected in some way to support from Wilkesite quarters. The lodges were well known to be active centers of support for that cause.

Whatever efforts may have been made to kill the book in advance of the 1774 elections, however, *The Chains of Slavery* was indeed brought to the public's attention well before the vote took place in October. Its publication was briefly noted in the *Public Advertiser* on 3 May and in the *Gentleman's Magazine* later that same month. *Scot's Magazine* provided a similar announcement, adding that the work was "executed in a manner that will reflect honour on the author's abilities." In June, *The London Magazine* offered a substantial review, praising the book as "truly a patriotic performance, by an intelligent and spirited writer." The journal singled out the "many excellent sentiments" of the "Address to the Electors of Great Britain," much of which it reprinted verbatim ("for the entertainment and profit of our readers, and as a specimen of the author's style and spirit"). It concluded with a summary of the arguments by which the author had "both forcibly illustrated and proved his melancholy doctrine by numerous examples from ancient and modern history."[40]

The appraisal of *The Monthly Review*, also appearing in June 1774, was significantly more critical. It found "many important observations" in the work and recognized that "this performance is intended as an alarm-bell, to rouse and terrify us." Nonetheless, the journal found the alarm too raucous and the book unlikely to find success. "The person who pulls the rope, tugs it in all his might, and puts himself into a violent heat; like a fiery, ill-broken steed, who prances, choses [*sic*] and frets, without much progress on the road. In plain language, the Author, though he possesses a considerable fund of knowledge relative to the subject, writes with too much intemperance and too little regard to decency, to effect any great good." Little was to be gained, from this loyal reviewer's perspective, in quoting at length "a publication, the very title page of which is enough to prejudice all but the lowest of the vulgar against him: and we may, indeed, refer to it as a sufficient specimen of the writer's manner of treating the lord's anointed and the rulers of the people."[41]

As for the "popular societies" of northern England, there is evidence that Marat did indeed look to tradesmen's associations there to bolster his book's fortunes. The *Newcastle Chronicle* reported on 28 May 1774 that the city's Bricklayers' Company, its Goldsmiths' Company, and its "Lumber Troop" (a political club) had each received, by coach, two copies of *The Chains of Slavery*. "The work is spirited," it announced, "and appears through the whole a masterly execution."[42] Copies inscribed with the date 1774 still remain in the archives of the Company of Bricklayers, Wallers, and Plasterers, as well as those of two other Newcastle guilds, the Company of Cordwainers and the Company of Butchers. The records of the Newcastle Company of House Carpenters reveal that it too had received the book and was making it available for loan.[43]

That these copies of *The Chains of Slavery* were sent to Newcastle by

Marat himself is evident from a letter transcribed inside the volume presented to the Bricklayers' Company. Dated 20 May 1774, it explains this gift (in language reminiscent of Marat's appeal to Wilkes) as an effort to outmaneuver the ministry in its attempt to strangle the work at birth. "Not daring to suppress my book by force, they have employed artifice to prevent its being divulged. A strange method of apprehension this, a thousand times worse than open acts of authority and attended with the silent but intire destruction of the liberty of the press unless their clandestine measures be baffled by the influence of true patriots. To make these oppressive dealings miscarry, I know of no other means but the dispersing my work among the real Sons of Liberty. I beg therefore you would acquaint me with the names of Companies as sincerely addicted to its cause as you are."[44]

It appears, then, that Marat had initially contacted the Bricklayers' Company, sending it his book and asking it for names of other tradesmen's companies fervent in the cause of liberty, and that the Bricklayers' Company responded with a list of other Newcastle guilds to which he could send copies of his endangered work. How he came to approach the Bricklayers' Company in the first place remains a matter of speculation, but a Wilkesite connection again seems more than likely. The city of Newcastle had been a hotbed of support for John Wilkes during his earlier struggles over the disputed Middlesex election, and enthusiasm for the Wilkesite program of parliamentary reform was still playing a powerful role in its local politics in the run-up to the 1774 election. During this same period, Serjeant John Glynn, the radical lawyer celebrated as Wilkes's defender, was also actively engaged in a legal case over the rights of the city's freemen to decide the use of common land.[45] Wilkes himself, or Almon or Glynn at his request, could well have urged Marat to look to the patriots of the North for the means of frustrating the machinations of Whitehall.

Almon, in any case, must have had some part in an effort to relaunch *The Chains of Slavery* from Newcastle a year after the 1774 election it had been intended to shape. The *Newcastle Chronicle*, on 21 October 1775, printed a notice to the effect that "next week, will be published, price 10s. 6d. and sold by the booksellers in Newcastle, THE CHAINS OF SLAVERY, written by Dr. MARIOT [*sic*]. A work well worth the attention of the public." In the two weeks following, the actual publication of the work was announced and the book listed as for sale by Almon in London, by three booksellers in Newcastle, and by one in each of the northern towns of Sunderland, Stockton, Durham, Hexham, and Alwick.[46] In all probability, this "edition" was a reissue, with yet another revised title page, of the stock of the London edition that Marat had sent north before he left the country for Holland in 1774. The work remained in circulation in northern England, at least in a manner of speaking, for a century. Pages were reported still being used in 1887 as a wrapper for groceries. A sad fate for a book that had been handsomely produced with fine print on paper of excellent quality, offered at a price that may have rendered it unsaleable.[47]

SEVEN

DOCTOR TO THE INCURABLE

Marat left England abruptly in 1776. The reason is obscure. Perhaps government harassment had indeed taken its toll. Perhaps there were financial difficulties. Most likely, as he later maintained, he had to rush to Paris to overcome obstacles to the distribution of *De l'homme*. The only direct evidence is a curt note written from Dover to an unknown creditor on 11 April. "A few days before my setting out from London, I called on you to set[tle] our account, but did not find you at home. Affairs of great concern call me for a while in the continent. I shall return to London on the beginning of next October, at which time I'll take care of discharging my little bill."[1] The creditor's patience may have been sorely tested: years passed rather than months, and circumstances changed dramatically, before Marat returned briefly to England. After spending time in Geneva with his family, he went instead to Paris. His plan to establish himself permanently across the Channel was shelved. The French capital offered more.

Within a year, the Swiss arrival had been named doctor to the corps of guardsmen serving the king's youngest brother, the twenty-year-old comte d'Artois, destined after the French Revolution to become the reactionary King Charles X. By the act of appointment dated 24 June 1777, Marat was favored with "all the honors, prerogatives and advantages" this court position accorded, and authorized to use its title in all public and personal matters.[2] A place of this kind was typically purchased from the previous holder by a kind of private contract, but Marat was the first person to be named to this particular post. It could have been created specifically for him at a patron's request, as one biographer has speculated, or simply have become available at an opportune time. The young prince was expanding his household and fashioning new plans for the housing of his retinue. That same year Louis XVI gave him undeveloped land along the rue du Faubourg Saint-Honoré on which he intended—emulating the development of the Palais Royal by his enterprising and commercially minded relative, the duc d'Orléans—to lay out a new city district to be called "Nouvelle Amérique." Stables to accommodate his 150 guards were projected, one of which was completed in 1781 on the site now occupied by the residence of the Canadian ambassador to France.[3]

It has been thought that the post carried a comfortable annual stipend of 2,000 livres, along with other perquisites, but that figure is surely exaggerated.[4] A stipend, in any case, would only have been the beginning of the benefits an appointment of this kind conferred. It offered status, visibility, and, above all, significant commercial advantage.

Officially, medical practice in Paris was policed by the Faculty of Medicine and restricted to Catholics holding a degree from a French medical school—neither of which conditions Marat could fulfill. But in France, as in Britain, the medical marketplace was growing rapidly in the latter part of the eighteenth century—and growing rapidly more entrepreneurial. Health was emerging as the mantra of the day, with demand for medical services fostered by an expanding medical and general press, and their supply ensured by a dramatically increasing mass of practitioners. The old Faculty of Medicine and the new Royal Society of Medicine, corporate institutions of the Old Regime, still fought for their own authority (and against one another) to police the competitive new world of commercial medicine, but their efforts were becoming more desperate and less effective. Often they were undermined by the market practices of individual members of these same established institutions. Denunciations of charlatanry abounded as licensed and unlicensed practitioners competed to offer their medical services and to hawk their own proprietary medications. Medicine had become a central commodity in the "Great Chain of Buying" that marked the Old Regime in its final decades.[5]

In this entrepreneurial free-for-all, physicians with court appointments enjoyed considerable advantages. They were free to practice medicine without the requirement of any formal authorization by the Faculty of Medicine. They were also listed, with their addresses, in the annual *Almanach royal*—advertised, in effect, as preferred suppliers to royalty. As a result, they could command fees substantially higher than average. Marat appeared in the *Almanach royal* under the listing of *Médecins de Monseigneur Comte d'Artois*, his address given as the rue de Bourgogne, faubourg

Saint-Germain.[6] This was a fashionable location indeed, and an ideal one to attract a wealthy clientele.

How had this come about? Since positions in a royal household were rarely bestowed on the basis of merit alone, it would seem sensible to look for a source of patronage. That probably resulted from a remarkable cure that soon had fashionable Paris talking.

HEALING THE RICH

The cure in question was announced to the world in a letter published in the newly founded *Gazette de santé* on 16 October 1777 by the abbé Filassier, "member of several Academies of the realm," soon to be revealed as Marat's close associate. According to this account, the patient, the marquise de l'Aubespine, a niece of the powerful royal minister Choiseul, had been suffering for five years from consumption or some other form of pulmonary disease. Under the futile and fleeting ministrations of a series of doctors her condition had only deteriorated. Her cough had become convulsive, her expectoration purulent, her fever incessant, her insomnia obstinate, her weight loss severe, her condition extreme. Fearing for her life, her parents had called yet another doctor, "English by nationality," reputed to have saved other patients whose condition had been declared hopeless. Under this new physician's care, the marquise had rapidly recovered her health, and with it her energy, color, gaiety, and charm. One could scarcely believe that she had ever been ill. Restored to life, Filassier reported, Mme de l'Aubespine had encouraged him to make known her miraculous cure. He was sure that the *Gazette de santé* would want to ask this remarkable doctor to make public his treatment of a disease "as cruel as it is common."[7]

The editors of the *Gazette de santé* were in no doubt of the value of this story. They immediately called upon the unknown practitioner to describe, "as a service to humanity," his treatment of a condition still regarded as incurable. A response was published a month later, on 13 November 1777. It was signed by "Marat, Doctor of Medicine and Doctor to the Bodyguard of Monseigneur the comte d'Artois." A decade before, finding himself isolated and unable to make his way in the French capital, the young Swiss émigré had left that world with little in his bags but a few manuscripts. Now he was managing a triumphant return as an English physician.

The goal of their journal was so noble, Marat wrote in reply to the editors of the *Gazette de santé,* that one would have to be lacking in all humanity to refuse to support it. He would respond with pleasure to their request for a description of his cure for pulmonary disease. But it was important, he emphasized, to recognize that the malady stemmed from such different causes and had such diverse and complicated symptoms that no one treatment could fit all cases. His own success in treating this cruel illness derived from the care he had taken to match any treatment to the particular state of the individual patient. In the case of the marquise de l'Aubespine, he had found her so weak that it had been unthinkable to bleed her. Instead, he had administered an emulsion of sweet almonds and nitrate salts to clear the inflammation in her chest, followed by a potion of his own devising that resembled the waters of Harrogate, the famous English spa. This latter reduced the purulence of the patient's expectoration, relieved her wracking cough, and alleviated the tightness in her chest. Continuing its administration, he had also purged her several times. As her chest cleared, he had offered various herbal infusions, finally settling on fifty drops of ambergris in goat's milk each morning. The patient's health was soon so soundly reestablished that she no longer needed treatment of any kind.[8]

It seems more than likely from these letters that Marat's appointment to the household of the comte d'Artois was arranged through the wealthy and well-connected marquise de l'Aubespine and her compliant husband. "Several persons of distinguished rank, patients I had restored to health after they had been abandoned by doctors, joined with my friends and put everything into motion to get me settled in the capital," Marat later recalled. "I yielded to their insistence."[9] In addition to providing patronage, the marquise de l'Aubespine was also clearly willing to advance her new doctor's career in Paris in other ways. To this end, she allowed publication of the intimate details of her illness and its treatment, and even of the vicissitudes of her menstrual cycle. She gave Marat lodging in her fashionable residence in the rue de Bourgogne. She may well have taken him to her bed. The accounts of her remarkable recovery under Marat's care were heralded as a generous service to humanity, but they were also a service to Marat himself, part of a media campaign orchestrated to jump-start his medical practice in the French capital. The *Gazette de santé* needed copy, Marat needed publicity; this exchange was to their mutual benefit. Marat promised the editors that he would follow up with a description of his treatment for other pulmonary conditions. The editors expressed eagerness to receive the new information. And they begged Dr. Marat's permission to offer some reflections on the marquise's treatment and to invite others to comment on a cure that had been the talk of Paris.

Meanwhile, the publicity dance continued to another tune. Readers who found Marat's description of Mme de l'Aubespine's treatment in the 13 November issue of the *Gazette de santé* would also have seen a letter to the editors inquiring about a case, "as important as it is singular," that raised questions about the possible importance of mercury treatments in damaging a patient's sight. How remarkable that this was the exact subject of one of Marat's publications! The letter could only have been planted on his behalf. It gave him the opportunity, a week later, to draw attention to his dissertation on *A Singular Disease of the Eyes*, the first work to identify "this singular malady . . . always the disastrous result of badly administered mercury." There followed a lengthy technical discussion of the physiology of the eye and of the effects upon it of the mercury dosage customary for venereal disease. Treatment of eye conditions had become a specific branch of medicine requiring knowledge of both optics and physiology, Marat emphasized, but it was still sometimes left to practitioners "who often know nothing about the function of the different parts of the eye and are even ignorant of the structure of this admirable organ." He had explained the nature of this singular disease, but it remained for him to describe its cure. But alas! Time was short and Dr. Marat was too busy to do this now. He promised to return to the task at his first moment of leisure.[10]

The editors of the *Gazette de santé* published Marat's letter somewhat apologetically. They had in this case broken their policy not to publish "entirely theoretical pieces, usually more seductive than instructive," but they hoped that M. Marat would indeed communicate his treatment for this unnamed condition of the eye as soon as possible. He eventually did so (along the lines of *A Singular Disease of the Eyes*) for the issue of the journal published on 4 December.[11] In the meantime, the essential purpose had been served. Readers had already learned that Dr. Marat was skilled in the care of pulmonary conditions. They were aware now that he was also an expert in the field of eye disease, and knowledgeable too regarding the dangers of the mercury treatments universally prescribed for victims of venereal disease. Maladies of the lungs, the eyes, the genitalia: these three constituted an ample portfolio for a practitioner offering medical care to the rich and powerful. And these latter now knew where they could consult him in Paris, as they had in London.

The celebrated cure of Mme de l'Aubespine nevertheless found its critics. A letter to the editors of the *Gazette de santé* from a Dr. Levi, published on 27 November 1777, expressed doubts regarding the precise diagnosis of the marquise's malady. Censuring Marat's loose use of medical terminology, Levi speculated that the patient's symptoms had stemmed from a nervous condition rather than a true pulmonary infection.[12] A week later, in a haughty response from none other than the patient's spouse, the marquis de l'Aubespine himself, this idea was repudiated as absurd. The aristocrat's demand for immediate publication of his communication in its entirety drew a prickly protest from the editors. "Even in states where one is accustomed to subordination," they huffed, "opinion is not subject to command." Resentment of the presumptions of rank was never far from the surface of the Old Regime, but the journalists hastened to comply. The marquis insisted in his letter that his wife had for five years been treated as a chest case ("poitrinaire") by the doctors who had attended her, and that "one of the most celebrated doctors of the Paris Faculty [of Medicine] declared to me, some days before M. Marat was called in, that Madame de l'Aubespine was coughing up pus and was beyond help."

The same issue of the journal published a letter arriving late from one Côme, a former army surgeon writing from Poitiers. He claimed twenty-five years' experience in treating pulmonary disease successfully and without harsh therapies, and offered to demonstrate his ability to do so at the very first opportunity Paris could afford him.[13]

Marat's reply, on 11 December, was testy. He was outraged that his diagnosis was being challenged. He deeply resented being lectured on the correct use of medical terms. He upbraided the editors of the *Gazette de santé* for their betrayal in publishing Levi's criticism. In the face of Côme's letter, he belligerently renounced his intention to describe his other cures of pulmonary disease, deeming it useless to do so "since there exists a new Aesculapius before whom I avow that I am nothing." The editors were no less irritable in their response. They retorted that their publication of the details of Marat's treatment of his aristocratic patient, far from constituting an endorsement, had simply opened the topic to public discussion. And they peppered Marat's answer to Levi with critical comments of their own.[14]

Relations between Marat and the editors of the *Gazette de santé* were souring. They soon grew worse. In the following issue, the editors found themselves charged by Marat and the marquis de l'Aubespine with cutting Marat's previous letter to the journal. Protesting that they were under an obligation to save their readers from empty verbosity, they grumpily restored the letter's truncated ending with its full dose of acid thrown in the face of the presumptuous Côme.[15]

Soon, though, the *Gazette de santé* was able to publish a report of the analysis of Marat's patent medicine carried out by the abbé Tessier, regent doctor of the Faculty of Medicine and member of the Royal Society of Medicine, two institutions ever on the watch against charlatans outside their ranks. Famous for an earlier exposé of medical chicanery that had earned him few friends, Tessier had abandoned the fight against that "hydra constantly reborn," declaring himself determined "to leave the charlatans to profit from their exclusive privilege of persuading whomever they could." Nonetheless, he had now been compelled to reenter the fray by the appearance on the market of the "eau anti-pulmonique" Marat had administered to Mme de l'Aubespine and was currently offering for sale to the general public. Analyzing this product with some help from the chemists, Tessier had found the precious remedy to be no more complex than "limewater partially precipitated by fixed alkali."[16]

The editors of the *Gazette de santé* took a certain pleasure in this discovery. "It results from the chemical analysis . . . of the *eau antipulmonique* used by M. Marat, [that] this artificial and so precious mineral water similar to that of Harrogate is nothing other than limewater, and probably limewater pure and simple," they reported in the following issue of their journal. "In this regard, we cannot avoid reproaching M. Marat a little for enveloping in mystery and offering at such high price a substance so simple and so easy to procure." The editors acknowledged the value of limewater to treat pulmonary conditions in rare cases but felt obliged to report a long list of its harmful side effects. Cattle, they added, citing an account published by the Paris Academy of Sciences, had even perished upon drinking it! These facts warranted an Enlightenment lecture on epistemological modesty: "One must be careful, more than is usually the case, to distinguish and identify the cases for which any given remedy is appropriate. Systematic ideas, and the notion of the universality of the virtues often ascribed to the same remedy, are the great causes constantly opposing the progress and the perfection of the healing art."[17]

Despite these criticisms, Marat's marketing strategy appears to have worked. Soon he was receiving wealthy patients, charging elevated fees, and selling his patent medicine at a high price. "Word of my outstanding cures drew a prodigious crowd of the sick to me," he later boasted; "my door was continually assailed by the carriages of people who came from all parts to consult me. In the exercise of my art as a physician, knowledge of nature gave me great advantages: rapidity of eye and sureness of touch. Multiple triumphs earned me the appellation *doctor of the incurable*." The language was inflated, and the facts remain unverifiable, but it seems that Marat was indeed a talented diagnostician and clinical practitioner. If the letters he later submitted to his friend Philippe Rose Roume de Saint-Laurent are to be believed, high-placed persons from Paris and the provinces were soon begging for his attention and celebrating his successes; he was even recommended by minister Choiseul to the intendant of Tours. In gratitude, the intendant praised this "very brilliant man who, with a quick eye, recognized in a moment what all the Faculty [of Medicine] together had not found after many observations."[18]

At first, it appears, Marat was as punctilious in his practice as he was demanding with his bill. A lawyer from Lyon seeking care for his wife in March 1779 was sent, along with an interim prescription, a detailed questionnaire to complete regarding the patient's condition. The intermediary in this case—the lawyer's younger brother, a medical student in Paris—was unimpressed by the flashy doctor he had been charged to contact and uncomfortable with the idea of medical treatment at a distance, common practice though it was. Even more did he dislike those "system-minded physicians who apply mathematics to medicine, and medicine based not on principles but on ideas." Such doctors, he warned his sibling, "heal few and kill many." Besides, he advised, "Dr. Marat seems a bit expensive to me; he charges 24 livres for a consultation and the little sheet of paper I'm sending you cost twelve."[19]

This may have been a bargain. Jacques-Pierre Brissot later recalled that Marat claimed 36 livres a consultation; the days were not long enough, he recounted, to accommodate all those seeking his one-time friend's ministrations.[20] Under daily pressure, though, the popular doctor appears to have become less committed to the higher calling of his profession. An undated note (if authentic) reveals him thanking an aristocratic patron for a referral he was too busy to accept: "I am full of gratitude," he wrote, "but I beg you to reserve your good offices for less difficult cases. I love only those illnesses where there is little to do and much to gain; and when one can choose, why not do so?"[21]

If the medical student from Lyon advised caution, other critical evaluations of Marat's medical practice were less restrained. In one case, they led to fisticuffs. The scene was worthy of Beaumarchais. Arriving the day after Christmas 1777 to treat one Mme Courtin, a patient he had been attending for nine weeks, Dr. Marat found his path to her bedroom barred by some of her acquaintance, a Polish aristocrat by the name of Count Zabielo and two of his henchmen. Zabielo and company escorted Marat to a nearby room, where the count proceeded to complain of the patient's lack of progress and the doctor's high fees. Complaints led to insults, insults to ripostes, ripostes to blows. In self-defense, Marat drew his sword—only to have its blade broken by his three assailants—and shouted to his lackey that he was being assassinated. When the lackey forced his way into the room to free his master, the two of them, master and servant together, were chased into the street. There the good doctor found his face and hands battered and bloodied, his lip split, and some of his hair torn out. Taking to his bed, he called physicians to examine and confirm his condition.

All this was detailed in the official complaint Marat lodged the following day, demanding that the judicial authorities give him redress and the assurance of security in the exercise of his profession. In later testimony, he charged that Zabielo and accomplices had been bad-mouthing him to all his patients, spreading rumors that Mme Courtin had died, and claiming that the fraudulent doctor had been thrown down the stairs. In a separate affidavit, Marat's lackey (he could now well afford one!) supported his master's story.[22]

We don't know how the Zabielo case was settled, but events like this could well have tempered Marat's zeal for his lucrative calling. And there were more subtle developments, he sensed, to discourage him from practicing medicine in the capital. "The doctors of the Faculty had taken umbrage at my success and they calculated the extent of my gains with dismay," he reported later. "To console themselves, they organized to dry up my revenue at its source. I would prove, if necessary, that they met frequently to devise the most effective ways to defame me. From then on, calumny flew everywhere and anonymous letters were sent to my patients from all over to alarm them regarding me. It is true that many people whose friendship for me was founded on respect took my defense; but their voices were drowned out by the clamors of my adversaries."[23]

It would be easy to see more paranoia than proof in these claims, and we can already begin to recognize that Marat's sense of victimization grew dramatically during these years following his return to Paris. But there is a shred of evidence to support his claims. The Paris police chief, Alexandre Lenoir, had Marat tagged as a "bold charlatan," noting in his papers that "M. Vicq d'Azyr asks, in the name of the Royal Society of Medicine, that he be run out of Paris. He is from Neuchâtel in Switzerland. Many sick persons have died at his hands, but he has a medical diploma that was purchased for him."[24] Vicq d'Azyr was a member of the Faculty of Medicine and of the Paris Academy of Sciences, a noted anatomist, and himself a consulting doctor to the comte d'Artois. He was also a founder of the Royal Society of Medicine, a body that claimed the authority to vet patent medicines and license mineral waters (but whose members were not above engaging in that trade themselves).[25] Vicq d'Azyr counted as someone in the Old Regime.

But Marat, in any case, was beginning to lose interest in everyday medical practice. He must have kept it up for a while, peddling his tonic water and earning the ample revenue he could derive from the easy cases he asked his friends to refer. But his passion was shifting to experimental research. More focused medical applications of electricity became one of his passions: for years he subjected patients experimentally to a range of electrical treatments, while also exploring electrical effects on animal tissue, living and dead. His search for scientific glory also grew broader and more ambitious. "The aggravations inseparable from the exercise of medicine had made me sigh more than once for the solitude of my study," he recalled for Roume de Saint-Laurent in 1783; "there I devoted myself entirely to my favorite subjects. Should I have expected that I would be creating a new source of envy?"[26]

PLEADING FOR THE POOR

Marat still yearned for literary and philosophical renown. Healing the rich, he thought also of the poor, whose miserable condition in English workhouses and prisons he had denounced in *The Chains of Slavery*. The two concerns came together in a work he soon composed in response to an announcement in the *Gazette de Berne* on 15 February 1777. The journal advertised that "a friend of humanity, content to do good but wishing to avoid public recognition by concealing his name," had given the Economic Society of Berne the sum of 50 louis d'or to be awarded for the best essay submitted to it on the topic of reform of criminal legislation. The terms of the contest were precise. Essays were to be received by July 1779, though the deadline was later extended to 1782. Contestants were required to offer a complete and detailed plan of criminal law encompassing the variety of crimes and the penalties proportionate to them; the nature and evidentiary weight of proofs and presumptions; methods of criminal procedure that would reconcile mild and just penalties with the certainty of prompt and exemplary punishment ensuring that society achieves the greatest security possible for liberty and humanity. An Enlightenment project if there ever was one.

This language made clear the line of thinking that submissions were expected to follow. Its inspiration came from Cesare Beccaria's *On Crimes and Punishments*, the philosophical manifesto for reform of criminal law that had rocked enlightened Europe when it appeared in 1764. Rapidly translated from Italian into French in 1766, the book had been enthusiastically welcomed the same year both by Voltaire, that great enemy of the French law courts, and by one of the courts' most enlightened jurists, Joseph-Michel-Antoine Servan. This was only the beginning. Beccaria's treatise unleashed intense discussion of criminal law reform, which became an obsession throughout Europe in the decades following its publication. The highly visible essay contest sponsored by the Economic Society of Berne was intended to focus and advance that debate. Its initial funder was a celebrated Parisian barrister, Elie de Beaumont, but Voltaire, the patriarch of Enlightenment in his last year of life, soon gave another 50 louis anonymously to double the prize money. While making it his mission to urge the crowned heads of Europe to come up with additional contributions, he also published a kind of handbook for prospective contestants under the title *Prix de la justice et de l'humanité*.[27]

Marat offered his essay as a disciple of Montesquieu, whose thinking he would analyze at length a few years later for another literary contest. That piece he deemed inadequate and wished never to see published, though it was dredged up a century later. In contrast, he remained enormously proud of his *Plan de législation en matière criminelle* ("perhaps the least imperfect of all those that have come from my pen").[28] True to the *Spirit of Laws*, he began it by criticizing the formulation of the essay question as too general, on the grounds that it failed to specify the people for which the proposed law code was intended. Criminal law is necessarily related to the political system, he emphasized; it must never clash with the nature of the government. A single code of law can never suit all nations, or even the same one at different stages of its history. Laws appropriate for a small or primitive people can never be right for a populous or long civilized one. Justice, nonetheless, was too often sacrificed in the search for appropriate local arrangements. "Having heard its voice," he warned readers, "I am writing for free men."[29]

Details were important in this endeavor, Marat acknowledged, because there could be "nothing obscure, uncertain, or arbitrary in ideas about crimes and punishments." Claiming that his essay could offer only "an exposition of basic principles, the spirit of criminal laws, to put it that way," he did, however, consider an impressive range of crimes (real or purported) and their proportionate penalties. Curiously, he also made a case for discretion in the enumeration of possible infractions. "To forbid a crime is almost always to give birth to the idea," he cautioned. A plan intended for men innocent of vice would leave the government discretion to conceal what need not be known.[30]

Did such men exist? An attentive reader would have to doubt it. "To cast an eye over the criminal law of different peoples is to be outraged at the sight of justice plunged in a dark chaos," Marat expostulated. "What am I saying! Seeing men everywhere subject to unjust laws and abandoned to the tyrant's blade, one shudders in awe at the power of superstition." Times had changed, he allowed, the philosophical spirit was piercing the darkness. But humanity would long lament its lot before wise men would have the power to bring change. "Let them continue nonetheless to enlighten the world: to the degree that enlightenment spreads it will change public opinion: gradually men come to know their rights, at last they want to enjoy them; then, only then, impatient at their chains, do they seek to break them."[31] Writing, Reform, Revolt were here the three Rs of Marat's Enlightenment.

After Montesquieu, there was Beccaria, another close reader of *The Spirit of Laws*. Following the program laid out by the Italian reformer,

Marat called for the publicity and transparency of criminal legislation; for principles of legality requiring equal treatment of individuals before the law without consideration of differential social status; for the presumption of innocence; for severe constraints upon judicial interpretation. He emphasized the need to eliminate barbarous penalties, arbitrarily inflicted, in favor of a rational economy of punishment proportionate to the nature of the crime. He urged prevention over punishment. He advocated the decriminalization of actions that had been penalized through centuries of ignorance and superstition. These propositions were becoming chapter and verse of the reform gospel by the time he came to it.

At the same time, Marat wrote in a tone very different from Beccaria's. *On Crimes and Punishments* was a clinical brief for administrative reform offered in the spirit of enlightened absolutism. Marat's pen had a sharper political edge. Turning, with Rousseau, to the annals of history, he saw only tyranny and servitude, usurpation, illegality, and abuse of power. All states there had been founded on violence, murder, brigandage; they had no title to authority beyond force. To render this force less odious, he acknowledged, efforts were being made to make it less tyrannical. Perhaps, he conceded, there would come a time when power would be used solely for the people's good. But with Rousseau, too, he remained nostalgic for the Ancients, among whom justice had held the sword in one hand, laurels in the other. Ancient legislators, he reminisced, had sought above all to inculcate virtue. Modern legislators, in contrast, had aimed only to repress the atrocious crimes that threatened to destroy the bonds of society. They brandished only the blade, staying the criminal's hand but neglecting the citizen's heart. They had no thought for the civic virtue of the Ancients. "But let's leave these sublime institutions that are no longer made for us; and since we cannot hope to make man good, let's at least prevent him from being wicked."[32]

For Marat, as for Rousseau and Beccaria, the obligation to obey the law followed imperatively from the logic of the social contract. Beccaria had made mildness of the laws a further consequence of the principle of consent. But Marat was more radical in asking, with Rousseau, whether the obligation to obey outlasted the terms of a contract that was no longer respected. "Equal rights, reciprocal advantages, mutual support," he insisted, were necessarily the true foundations of social order; "justice, peace, concord, happiness" were necessarily its fruits. The only legitimate foundation of society was the happiness of those composing it. Men had united only for their common interest; they had established government only to assure the enjoyment of their rights. They had renounced personal vengeance in favor of public vengeance, natural liberty in favor of civil liberty, community of property in favor of individual ownership.[33]

But what if the laws had become arbitrary? What if they now served only a small minority? What if population growth and differentiation in talents, ambition, and industry had led to unequal accumulation of wealth and the appearance of "a multitude of ruined subjects leaving their descendants in poverty?" The poor now found themselves "on an earth already covered with others' possessions"; nothing was left for them to appropriate; sharing only in society's disadvantages, they were dying of misery. Were they obliged, then, to respect the laws? Marat's answer was clear. "Certainly not. If society abandons them they return to the state of nature, and are authorized to claim, by force of arms, the rights they could only have alienated to secure greater benefits. Any authority that opposes this is tyrannical; and the judge who condemns them to death is only a cowardly assassin." To maintain itself, society had therefore to free men from the temptations of need. "It owes them an assured subsistence, appropriate clothing, complete protection, assistance in sickness, care in old age. Only after having fulfilled these obligations toward all members of the state does the government have the right to punish infractions of the society's laws."[34]

With this argument, as Marat veered toward a program of social reform, his case for changes in the criminal law became a brief for the dispossessed. Charged by the terms of the Berne essay contest to categorize crimes and punishments, he immediately set aside the logic of classification to "fix the reader's ideas on a very common offense by which the others are often complicated: an offense that, more than any other, seems to destroy civil society, but whose punishment in the present state of things should almost always revolt nature."[35] He meant theft. It was the crime of the poor, above all, its punishment notorious for the exaction of heinously disproportionate penalties.

"Let's begin with theft, the most common of transgressions," Voltaire had counseled in the *Prix de la justice et de l'humanité*.[36] Marat followed this counsel. But while the patriarch pleaded for more humanitarian punishment, Marat interrogated the very right of property from which the notion of theft derived. What was its basis? The usurper appealed to the right of the strongest, the possessor to the claim of the first occupier, the heir to the legitimacy of testament, the cultivator to the logic of labor. Each of these justifications Marat dismissed. "By what right do you appropriate a corner of this earth that was given to all its inhabitants in common?" he demanded of the cultivator. "Do you not see that you can only receive your share after an equal distribution of the whole? Even after this division, you have right to the land you cultivate only to the extent absolutely necessary for your existence. . . . The right to possess necessarily derives from the right to life: thus everything is ours that is absolutely essential for our existence, and nothing superfluous should belong to us while others lack necessities. This is the legitimate foundation for all property, in the civil state as in the state of nature."[37] Marat did not advocate redistribution of property or of its fruits, as proposed by some other critics of modern society. But here, as in his revolutionary writings, he followed Rousseau in arguing for limitation of property rights as a condition of republican freedom.

To demonstrate that incarceration was a more effective deterrent than capital punishment, Beccaria had imagined a soliloquy in the mind of a hardened criminal weighing the costs and benefits of defying laws imposed on the poor by the rich and powerful. Marat went further, projecting an extended and passionate defense into the mouth of a destitute thief standing before rich and powerful judges. "Self preservation is the first duty," he would have the accused say. "The man who steals in order to live . . . only makes use of his rights. . . . What do I owe society, I who know only its horrors . . . ? What have you done to be so happy at my expense?" While the lot of the poor is fixed, while they are irrevocably condemned to misery, the thief would continue, the rich enjoy the exclusive privilege to pillage the state. Liberal and lucrative arts are for the wealthy; degrading, dangerous, and disgusting occupations are left for the poor. Reduced to indigence by sickness and injustice, they beg in vain from those who turn their heads and cross to the other side.

Where, then, can the wretched go? Marat was far from sharing Locke's vision of still unpeopled lands awaiting cultivation. "Isn't the earth covered everywhere by possessions the rich have usurped from the poor?" he had the poor thief exclaim. "If there were still some desert left, could I get myself there? Pressed by hunger and reduced to despair, I've profited from the darkness of night to wrest from a passer-by some aid his hardness refused me. Because I have used the rights of nature, you drag me to punishment. Iniquitous judges! Remember that humanity is the first of virtues and justice the first of laws. You pretend to be human but cannibals would shudder in horror at an account of your cruelties. Barbarians! Bathe in my blood, because that is necessary to assure your unjust domains. In the midst of the torments I am going to endure, my sole consolation will be to reproach the heavens for giving me birth among you."[38]

That the poor could legitimately reclaim their sacred rights by force Marat had no doubt. What did the destruction of society matter if it sacrificed the multitude to the few? But he had a better idea: the creation of free schools, paid for by the rich, to instruct the poor in the useful arts. With productive members restored to the homeland, he reasoned, land would be better cultivated, manufactures expanded. Abundance would reign, foreign commerce grow, the strength of the nation increase, and the state shine with a new luster. "I know that the establishment I propose would face many obstacles, and I dare not hope to see the disappearance of all the abuses it could remedy. I repeat that it is only for free men that I write. But so long as princes want to command only slaves they will always need rich subjects corrupted by pleasures and poor ones degraded by misery."[39]

It is scarcely surprising, given these contentions, that Marat's submission for the Berne contest failed to win the prize. It was nevertheless published in 1782 in a vast repertory of writings on the reform of criminal law edited by Brissot. "Perhaps the principles of liberty forming its basis frightened some of those timid censors who are found in republics as well as in monarchies," Brissot speculated in his editorial introduction to the work. "[They] fear the effect of enlightening the people too much, as if the most enlightened people is not the most peaceful and the happiest."[40]

As its editor, Brissot had to explain away the presence in this essay of "radical ideas accepted in republics but rejected in monarchies for good reason." The anonymous author, he emphasized, had long been "nourished in the principles of the English constitution" and had adapted its spirit in a program intended for "an entirely free and new people." It would be slanderous to apply this plan to any other form of government or to a people already corrupted. Brissot was less concerned at the discussion of theft in his friend's work than he was at its analysis of regicide, which he endeavored to excuse by representing the author as an inhabitant of Pennsylvania! But Marat had no need to relocate that far away. In fact, his treatment of king-killing rehearsed many of the radical themes of *The Chains of Slavery*. So-called "crimes against the state" had proliferated, he contended, as rulers became absolute masters of their peoples. Men wanting to destroy liberty feared anything that could maintain it. Those courageous enough to oppose this dark design had to be found guilty and eliminated. For this purpose, crimes were invented. Love of the homeland was criminalized, along with appeals to the rights of humanity, examination of the king's conduct, refusal to obey unjust orders, discussion of governmental affairs, protests by the oppressed. Once the prince alone counted in the state, anything that offended him was designated an act of lèse-majesté. Tyranny thus dug an abyss beneath the citizens' feet. Wanting to reign without resistance, the despot also turned to superstition and ignorance. After debasing hearts, he debased minds.[41]

Happily times had changed, Marat prudently declared. The torch of philosophy had dispelled the thick darkness into which peoples had been plunged by tyranny. For Marat reform of criminal law was meant to reopen the path to freedom. It was necessary, in order to "re-establish the true idea of things, to beware of erecting into law those barbarous ordinances created to uphold an unjust power."[42]

Among the most barbarous of these ordinances Marat found the suppression of free speech. Few princes are fit to govern, he insisted; many fear the light. Monitoring their conduct is the prerogative of a free people and the precious possession of each individual. It often serves to prevent abuse of power, even where public liberty has not yet been secured. "Monarchs themselves are subject to the empire of opinion. What then will be the organ of public opinion if no one dares to raise his voice?" Unrestrained by it, and encouraged by wicked courtiers to abuse his power, the prince will sacrifice everything to his destructive impulses. He will lop off the heads of those most threatening to tyranny. No longer having to fear the voice of the people, he will soon free himself from that of conscience.

To prevent this outcome, Marat concluded, the law must permit any writing in which, without lacking decency, the conduct of government is examined, its projects analyzed, its actions weighed, its pretensions discussed, its illicit innovations denounced. Traditional arguments against press freedom he quickly brushed aside, though (in this work published anonymously) he countenanced the repression of anonymous writings. He saw the liberty to monitor government conduct as "the boulevard of public security." It had to be protected by law. No good prince need fear it.[43]

This discussion led, finally, to the question of regicide. Was it rightfully a crime against the state? Marat thought not. In any legitimate government, he argued, the prince is only the first minister of the law. In monarchies, where the order of succession is established, the death of the ruler does not threaten the state. But wasn't an attack on the prince an attack on the sovereign people itself, in the person of its minister? No more than an attack on any other magistrate, Marat retorted. (Brissot quickly interjected, in an editorial note, that "despite his penchant for republican ideas, the author of this essay should have acknowledged a very great difference in this regard.") But wasn't the death of a prince who was a worthy minister of the law a loss for the state? Certainly so, Marat acknowledged, as would be the murder of a man of genius who consecrates his talents to the public good. Should this latter, then, also be deemed a crime of state? This invocation of the force of intellect led to an evident conclusion. Regicide was murder, to be punished as such, neither more nor less, but without any of the hideous spectacular punishments with which despotism had constantly surrounded itself. For Marat, the only crime of lèse-majesté truly worthy of the name was attempting to destroy the constitution.[44]

Brissot claimed in his *Mémoires* that he had asked his friend at the time whether he wished this audacious work to appear under his own name. He reported the answer as emphatically negative: "The Bastille is there, and I have no desire to see the inside." Remarking acidly that it was he who had taken the risk of publication, Brissot added that Marat had remained resistant to active political engagement as revolution approached.[45] His radicalism was to lie dormant until after the Bastille had fallen.

Science may have seemed safer for a while, but would it yield renown?

AGONISTIC SCIENCE

EIGHT

BIG GAME

Set up in a laboratory in the de l'Aubespine residence by 1778, Marat turned to the business of natural philosophy. In his writings on the soul and the body, he had dismissed as fanciful the works of a veritable galaxy of Enlightenment thinkers. He now decided to take on the leading scientists of his age, including Isaac Newton. What greater glory could there be than in going beyond Newton, or even proving the great Sir Isaac wrong? For a decade, he devoted himself obsessively to this endeavor, abandoning his medical practice, eventually forfeiting his position in the household of the comte d'Artois, and ultimately beggaring himself in the search for knowledge and glory.

Newtonian science had two broad sites of exploration in the eighteenth century. One derived from the *Principia*, the other from the *Opticks*. The latter work established the gold standard for eighteenth-century experimentalism: as celebrated by Joseph Priestley in his *History and Present State of Discoveries relating to Vision, Light, and Colours*, it offered "a specimen of the most perfect analysis that was ever exhibited, and which is justly considered as the best model for all future inquiries into the powers of nature."[1] No less important, the *Opticks*—especially in the celebrated Queries with which the work concluded—laid out an entire field of physical phenomena for further investigation, seeding it with an array of speculative explanations. While mathematicians soared from the pages of the *Principia* into an ever more abstract universe in which equations stood in for physical relations, experimentalists were scrutinizing the world laid out in the *Opticks* to disclose the hidden material forces and fluids, aethers and exhalations, upon which Newton had, after all, allowed himself to hypothesize.[2]

The spirit of excitement and promise of this endeavor was well brought out by Priestley, one of its great proponents, in another of his works with which Marat was well acquainted. "Hitherto philosophy has been chiefly conversant about the more sensible properties of bodies," Priestley declared in his *History and Present State of Electricity*. "Electricity, together with chymistry, and the doctrine of light and colours, seems to be giving us an inlet into their internal structure, on which all their sensible properties depend. By pursuing this new light, therefore, the bounds of natural science may possibly be extended, beyond what we can now form an idea of. New worlds may open to our view, and the glory of the great Sir Isaac Newton himself, and all his contemporaries, be eclipsed, by a new set of philosophers, in quite a new field of speculation."[3]

The promise of penetrating beyond the appearance of sensible phenomena into their internal structure was a huge one. Here, in this still open site for experimentalists—replete with unanswered questions about heat, light, and electricity—Jean-Paul Marat now sought fame. But the mathematicians and those they inspired were making inroads into this ground. They were also the dominant group in the Paris Academy of Sciences, which was by this time the most powerful and prestigious scientific body in Europe. The academicians were watchful of any challenge to their authority, or to Newton's.

In his experiments, Marat used an instrument of his own devising that he called a helioscope. In essence, it was an adaptation of the so-called solar microscope, itself a refinement of the magic lantern and precursor of the modern slide projector, that had become a prominent feature in popular science demonstrations since its invention in the middle of the century. The solar microscope was installed in the window shutter of a darkened room. A mirror on the outside of the shutter (necessarily adjustable at frequent intervals to match the sun's movement) reflected sunlight onto a convex lens that focused the beam through a narrow aperture into the darkroom. Inside the room, the light was passed through a microscope to project the image from a transparent object or slide onto a screen or an opposite wall. In creating his helioscope, Marat typically replaced the microscope assembly with a single lens, using this instrument to project onto the screen the magnified shadow cast by opaque objects placed at varying intervals along the path of the resulting cone of light. As duplicated by a modern historian of technology, the effects have been found quite striking.[4]

Marat could well have encountered the solar microscope during his first

FIGURE 8.1. Solar microscope, Dollond, London, c. 1775–1800. Courtesy of Collection of Historical Scientific Instruments, Harvard University.

FIGURE 8.2. Martin Frobenius Ledermüller, *Amusemens microscopiques, Troisième Cinquantaine* (Nuremberg: Winterschmidt, 1768). Bibliothèque nationale de France, Gallica Digital Library.

stay in Paris, where it was used in physics demonstrations by the famous abbé Jean-Antoine Nollet, or in London, where it became a favorite device of scientific showmen in a city addicted to revelations in natural philosophy. Once reestablished in Paris, however, and installed in his own laboratory, he developed his helioscope as an instrument to unlock new truths rather than demonstrating established ones or entertaining an audience with spectacular effects. Over the course of a decade, he performed hundreds of painstaking experiments addressed to still basic problems of eighteenth-century physics and chemistry: the natures of the so-called "imponderable fluids" that were manifested in the phenomena of electricity, fire, and light. "I shut myself in my darkened room," he recounted:

> I resort to my method of observation, I make the electric fluid visible, I compare it to the fluid of fire and to that of light, with which it has been confused; I observe its properties, its modes of action, the phenomena that result from the contributions of air, light, and fire to its action; then, no more hypotheses, no more conjectures, no more probabilities; everything becomes intuitive, knowledge takes form.[5]

The helioscope, Marat was convinced, could illuminate a path to discoveries that would equal and correct Newton's. Its inventor would be empowered to rewrite the *Opticks*. "This mode of observation is absolutely novel," he proclaimed, "and I urge physicists to try it. Its application to certain branches of physics would, I think, open a source of new knowledge."[6]

BEHOLD THE FLUID OF FIRE

The initial results of this experimentation were published in 1779 as *Découvertes de M. Marat, Docteur en Médecine & Médecin des Gardes du Corps de Monseigneur le comte d'Artois, sur le feu, l'électricité et la lumière, constatées par une suite d'expériences nouvelles*. The book was short, a mere thirty-eight pages, but its ambition was immense. Its principal goal was to achieve for the study of fire what Newton had accomplished in his crucial prism experiments for the study of light and color. "It seems to me," Marat announced, "that the theory of fire is today in the same state as that of color before Newton. Fire is taken to be matter, whereas it is only a modification of a particular fluid, just as color is only the modification of the light that bodies reflect."[7] As Newton had used the prism to reveal the properties of light, so Marat, in turn, would use his helioscope to make visible the properties of the "igneous fluid" that was the hidden source of heat and combustion.

The basic experiment on the igneous fluid projected onto the screen the shadow of a lighted candle that showed shimmering undulations around and especially above the flame. Similar but less brilliant emanations could also be seen surrounding the shadows of a variety of heated or incandescent objects observed in the same manner. We would today attribute this phenomenon to the movement of heated air—and so, indeed, did one contemporary critic—but this explanation Marat rejected in advance on the grounds that the same emanations were observed when heated objects were placed in a vacuum (presumably an incomplete one) produced by an air pump he frequently incorporated into these experiments. He was convinced that the helioscope made visible the movement of the otherwise imperceptible igneous fluid escaping from the burning or heated bodies. This fluid penetrated all matter, he argued, and his experiments showed it to be distinguishable from both the fluid of light and that of electricity with which it was often confused. Variations on the basic experiment allowed him to demonstrate that its properties included transparency, tensile strength, weight, mobility, and extreme hardness.

Marat claimed to show that heat, fire, and flame were all products of the movement of this fluid's particles. The temperatures of bodies put in contact converged toward a mean as the igneous fluid flowed from one to another. Heat was produced when the motion of its particles was excited (for example, by rubbing or by rays of light from the sun). Combustion occurred when that excitation reached the more extreme point at which the fluid, expanding as the result of the dynamic attraction and repulsion of these particles, was rapidly forced from the body into the surrounding air. Air was necessary for combustion because it both permitted and limited the expansibility of the igneous fluid. It was also necessary in that it allowed the phlogiston within combustible bodies to be brought to the surface and feed the flame.

This latter contention brought Marat's observations into line with the still prevailing chemical theory that explained combustion as an effect of the movement of phlogiston out of combustible substances. These substances, he reasoned, contained an abundance of phlogiston; noncombustible ones contained little or none. The igneous fluid attached itself to combustible bodies because of the particular affinity of its particles for the phlogiston with which such bodies were saturated. "Thus phlogiston is the food of fire insomuch as it fixes the action of the igneous fluid by virtue of a particular affinity."[8]

With its author's status as doctor in a royal household emblazoned on the title page, the *Découvertes . . . sur le feu* also boasted that its discoveries had been verified by a committee of the Paris Academy of Sciences. In another act of aristocratic patronage, Marat's research had been brought to the attention of the Academy by one of its noble honorary members, the comte de Maillebois, an amateur of scientific novelty and later an enthusiastic supporter of Mesmerism. Maillebois requested that a committee be charged to investigate this new researcher's claims. In addition to himself, the committee included three other regular members of the academy: Balthazar-Georges Sage, Jean-Baptiste Le Roy, and Etienne Mignot de Montigny. Sage, a chemist with good connections but scant scientific talent, enjoyed little respect among the academicians. He was to remain adamant in defending the phlogiston theory against Lavoisier's new chemistry throughout his life. Le Roy was a physicist and an expert on scientific instruments, a friend and strong ally of Franklin, for whose electrical theories he offered experimental support. Montigny was an engineer and geographer, interested in technical innovation, who had participated in the preparation of the famous Cassini map of France. Given their scientific interests and experimental approach, the three were appropriate choices to judge Marat's work, but they were not among the most respected in a body where power and prestige were enjoyed, above all, by the mathematicians and more theoretical physicists. Marat's discoveries were to fall along a fault line within the Academy that was separating and creating tensions between the more empirical experimentalists and the mathematicizers.

The report the committee submitted on 17 April 1779 gave Marat credit for employing the solar microscope for the first time as an instrument of research, and for using it to reveal emanations not perceptible otherwise or in as clear and distinct a manner. It noted his claim that his experiments revealed an igneous fluid leaving heated bodies. And it acknowledged that his conclusions, if solidly established through critical examination of the facts and experiments on which they were based, would hold "important and numerous consequences for physics." But the committee members were not yet ready to declare themselves convinced that they had actually been shown the operation of an igneous fluid. "We do not undertake to determine here to what degree the author has succeeded in proving what he advances regarding this fluid," they stressed; "this would lead us into too lengthy discussions." They confirmed that many of the experiments on which Marat based his theory had been repeated in their presence, that they found them "very exact, and that they had verified them all as much as is possible in an examination of this kind." They also declared his work "very interesting in its subject and containing a series of new and exact experiments carried out in an equally ingenious manner, and fit . . . to open a vast field of research for physicists." But they did so "without pronouncing definitively on what the author undertakes to establish . . . regarding the igneous fluid."[9]

In short, the committee praised Marat's experimental ingenuity and confirmed a number of his empirical results but declined to judge the plausibility of his theoretical arguments. It justified this evasion further on the grounds that the author had indicated in any case that he was particularly requesting the Academy's assessment of his empirical findings. A note added by Marat at the end of the report when it was printed in the *Découvertes . . . sur le feu* confirmed that he had asked the committee to evaluate only the precision and novelty of his experiments. The facts underlying his theory were completely unknown hitherto, he argued, and many of them were hard to confirm given the difficulty of acquiring the appropriate apparatus. Accordingly, he had thought it important that these facts first be substantiated by the Academy of Sciences. Once they were confirmed, he maintained, the conclusions to be drawn from them could be grasped by all enlightened physicists.

Why had Marat taken this position? Why had he not wanted the Academy's full endorsement of a theory he so clearly saw as revolutionary in its implications? He later claimed that he wanted essentially to protect his work from plagiarism, a goal only requiring confirmation of his empirical findings. Reading between the lines, though, one modern researcher has seen a rearguard action on his part, perhaps even a compromise reached with the committee as he began to realize that its review of his theories was going badly.[10] Evidence that Marat had tried preemptively to add Benjamin Franklin's authority to the scale against any negative judgment seems to support this view. Posing as an agent for the author, he had sent an anonymous English version of his work to Franklin (then resident in France as the ambassador of the young United States) toward the end of 1778, at about the same time he had entrusted its academic fate to the comte de Maillebois. "It seems to be well written, and is in English, with a little tincture of French idiom," Franklin noted in his journal on 13 December 1779, adding that he would like to see the experiments, "without which I cannot well judge of it."[11] Shortly thereafter, still writing anonymously as "the author's representative," Marat invited Franklin to observe the experiments the committee was beginning to investigate. "In an age where envy obstructs the way to truth, ingenious and candid men are much wanted to support it," Franklin was exhorted. To sharpen his interest, he was promised that "new experiments on the electrical fluid will be performed."[12]

As the committee's examination was concluding toward the end of March 1779, Marat intensified his efforts to get the sage of Philadelphia to observe his experiments. Those relating to electricity were "imagined for you alone," the gouty Franklin was assured; "the darkroom is very comfortable, the apparatus very complete, and all the instruments function readily." Le Roy, a close friend of Franklin's, also encouraged him to observe the experiments of this "unknown or anonymous Monsieur."[13] A series of polite excuses notwithstanding, Franklin did eventually witness the experiments at least once. Indeed, he even participated in them. The committee's report verified that the screen had displayed emanations escaping from Franklin's bald crown into the colder air surrounding it (as indeed they did from any other body warmer than its environment). Years later, Sage still likened these oscillations to the plumes of genius.[14]

Finally, as the moment for the presentation of the committee's report to the academy approached, Marat begged Franklin to attend the meeting and to offer his opinion, "which will be requested by M. le comte de Maillebois." Marat and his patron were clearly preparing to bring the weight of Franklin's authority to bear against anticipated resistance from within the Academy. "Was it not now so material a point to the Author, that a candid judgement should be pass'd upon his work, we would trust to time alone," Marat implored in his still halting English. "But he is certain that many a Accademical gentleman do not look with pleasure upon his discoveries, & will do their utmost to prejudice the whole body. Let the cabal be ever so warm, it certainly will be silenced by the sanction of such a Man as Doctor Franklin; and how far judgement passed by himself & the Royal Academy can influence public opinion is well known. If I appear troublesome, Sir, my consciousness of your benevolence, and my respect for your candour and understanding are my apology."[15]

Franklin did not attend the meeting of the Academy on 17 April at which the committee's report was presented, and we don't know whether his opinion entered in any way into the judgment of Marat's work. It seems clear, though, that the committee's report prompted a number of the academicians to take a keen interest in the experiments the *Découvertes . . . sur le feu* described. A letter sent by Le Roy a few days later informed Marat that "extreme desire to see his experiments" had led several members of the Academy to visit his laboratory despite warnings that lack of sun made his apparatus inoperable. Those who showed up had been disappointed by the weather; others, heeding the warning, had stayed away. Le Roy asked to reschedule a demonstration, hopefully for a better day.

More significantly, though, the academician went on to counsel Marat about a particularly touchy matter: his reluctance to have Lavoisier included among those viewing his experiments. Considering ill-advised any effort to deny the increasingly powerful chemist access to his laboratory, Le Roy encouraged Marat to schedule a visit by Lavoisier. "If one gives the impression of excluding him," he reasoned, "that could also give the impression of fearing him, and it seems to me that the experiments [you have] performed for us need fear no one."[16]

Le Roy was wrong. Paranoid though Marat may have been, there were good reasons (and more than he knew) for him to be wary of Lavoisier's attention. He must already have imagined Lavoisier as a dangerous competitor and was probably aware that the chemist's work threatened his own ideas in serious ways. Born in the same year, the two were exact contemporaries. But by the time Marat had established himself in Paris and begun his own experiments, Lavoisier was an academic star. He had already published, in his 1774 *Opuscules physiques et chimiques*, his discovery of the role of atmospheric air in combustion and calcination, and he was much on display to present new research at the Academy's twice-yearly formal public sessions. He was also the talk of the Paris establishment for the wealth he was accruing as a partner in the lucrative tax-collecting business of the Company of Farmers-General, for his prominent administrative position as a director of the Gunpowder Administration, and for the state-of-the-art laboratory he was fitting out in the lavish official quarters that position afforded him at the Arsenal (to say nothing of his charming wife and research partner, who built loyalty for him by entertaining academicians in these same luxurious quarters).

Fiercely ambitious and competitive, constantly bombarding the Academy's secretary with the sealed and dated envelopes used in its system to safeguard the priority of discoveries, Lavoisier kept close watch on competitors and was notable for his ability to seize on the implications of their experimental results. One visiting researcher reported that he was "eager for renown and ready to purloin ideas from others . . . jealous of them, longing to have discovered everything himself." Another recalled his bragging that "those who start the hare do not always catch it."[17] Seizing in 1774 on a dinner-table hint from his great rival Joseph Priestley, he had rushed to confirm the British experimentalist's discovery of "dephlogisticated air" (the gas he was later to call "oxygen"), and had begun making more precise claims for it as a specific agent acting in processes of respiration and combustion.[18] By 1777, he was embarking, together with the mathematician Laplace, on a first round of experiments on the phenomenon of vaporization that would change the face of chemistry. Over the following years, working in close collaboration, the two carried out experiments using the ice-calorimeter they invented to quantify the measurement of heat. Their results empowered Lavoisier to transform the study of combustion and discredit the theory of phlogiston, incidentally rendering ridiculous the notion of a visible igneous fluid.

Marat would not have been alone at this moment in beginning to fear such a result. "M. Lavoisier was scaring me for a long time for a great discovery that he was keeping secret, and that would do nothing less than overthrow entirely the theory of phlogiston and fixed fire," the chemist Macquer wrote in January 1778 to his disciple Guyton de Morveau; "his air of confidence was frightening me to death. Where would we have been with our old chemistry if we'd had to rebuild it from scratch."[19] Macquer was actually expressing relief that the paper Lavoisier had read to the public session of the Academy on 12 November 1777 appeared less threatening than he had anticipated. But his reaction was shortsighted. This "Memoir on Combustion in General," drawing on results of Lavoisier's initial collaboration with Laplace, was only an opening assault on the theory that explained combustion in terms of the movement of phlogiston out of combustible bodies.

Exactly what Lavoisier said in speaking at this public session in 1777 was not recorded; we know only the version of the paper that was read again to the Academy in December 1779 and rushed into print the following year in its annual publication of *Mémoires* for 1777. That version (and possibly the earlier one) opened with a bold methodological declaration. "Facts, observations, experiments are the material for a great edifice," it argued, "but in gathering them we must beware of producing an encumbrance to knowledge; we must, on the contrary, classify them, distinguish the ones that belong to each order, to each part of the whole to which they belong." Denouncing a mere experimentalism that encumbered science by mindlessly accumulating observations, this paper now insisted on the need for an analytical method modeled on the practice of the mathematical physicists. "Systems in physics considered from this point of view are no more than instruments fit to alleviate the feebleness of our organs," it argued; "strictly speaking, they are methods of approximation that put us on the way toward a solution of the problem; they are hypotheses that, as they are successively modified, corrected, and changed to the degree they are belied by experience, must lead us ineluctably one day, by force of exclusion and elimination, to knowledge of the true laws of nature."[20]

Phlogiston, Lavoisier was suggesting, was exactly such a hypothesis ripe for elimination. It could be said to account for some of the phenomena of combustion and calcination. But if these phenomena were explicable just as readily "without supposing the existence of matter of fire or phlogiston in materials called *combustible*," then the phlogistic theories deriving from Stahl "would be found overthrown to [their] very foundations."[21]

Lavoisier acknowledged that as yet he had no rigorously demonstrated theory but "only a hypothesis that seems to me more probable, more conformable to the laws of nature, and involving less forced explanations and fewer contradictions,"[22] which may explain Macquer's relief upon hearing the initial version of this paper at the public session of November 1777. He still retained the notion of a "matter of fire or light," declaring "with Franklin, Boerhaave, and some of the philosophers of antiquity" that it was "a very subtle, very elastic fluid that surrounds all parts of the planet we inhabit and penetrates with greater or lesser facility the bodies that compose it, tending when it is free to put it itself into equilibrium in all of them." But he went on to suggest the possibility that "pure air" (his interim name for Priestley's "dephlogisticated air") is "the true combustible body, and perhaps the only one in nature, and that to explain the phenomena of combustion one sees no more need for an immense quantity of fire fixed in all the bodies we call *combustible*."[23]

This theory was soon elaborated in a paper Lavoisier read before the Academy on 18 July 1778 (but artfully published in the volume of the Academy's *Mémoires* for 1777). The "igneous fluid, the matter of fire, of heat and of light," he now argued, penetrated all bodies without exception, reaching a state of equilibrium in all of them but not penetrating them equally. It existed in both free and fixed forms, vaporization being the result of the combination of its free form with the evaporable fluid. Heat was thus generated in this analysis by the absorption of the igneous fluid, not by its expulsion (as supposed by Marat) or that of phlogiston.[24]

By May 1779, then, as Marat published his initial *Découvertes . . . sur le feu*, Lavoisier was taking research on combustion in a very different direction. For the moment, the two researchers shared the still conventional language of an "igneous fluid" and of the "matter of fire or light." Marat claimed to be able to make the igneous fluid visible in the darkroom and to manipulate images on his screen in ways that could differentiate it from the fluids of light and of electricity. But Lavoisier, crucially, was not showing that fluid at all; he was inferring its action from the quantifiable phenomenon of heat loss in the process of vaporization. Moreover, he was moving to replace phlogiston as the putative agent of combustion with "dephlogisticated" or "pure air" and to reverse the directionality of its action. Combustion, he was now beginning to suggest, occurred not with the expulsion of the "fixed matter of fire" (phlogiston) from combustible bodies but with their absorption of the "free matter of fire," the "pure air" that he would soon call "oxygen." We can understand, then, why he reacted so emphatically in 1780 when Marat published a fuller account of his own experiments on the igneous fluid and their implications.

FANNING THE FLAME

This second volume, published as *Recherches physiques sur le feu*, increased the number of experiments reported, complicated them, buttressed them with notes and discussions of earlier views, and extended the discussion of their meaning. While still emphasizing the importance of the greater or lesser presence of phlogiston in making bodies more or less combustible, Marat expanded his account of the igneous fluid as the essential agent in the production of fire and heat. His conclusion now argued more explicitly for a mechanical explanation of the phenomena associated with combustion as "effects of the internal movement of a particular fluid, considered in its relations with some other fluids of the universe. This principle once established in an incontestable manner, everything is carefully related to physical knowledge, and the explanation of phenomena is taken only from the laws of rational mechanics."[25] He was intimating, in effect, that his discoveries would realize a Newtonian dream of a unified theory linking macroscopic and microscopic phenomena of the universe.

Handsomely produced by a publisher with court ties (paid one knows not how!), the *Recherches . . . sur le feu* provided dramatic illustrations of the effects achieved by the helioscope, more practical information regarding the apparatus required, and the name and address of the instrument maker who could sell helioscopes inspected and warranted by the author himself. Marat was now more openly dismissive of traditional views "so consecrated that one renders oneself ridiculous in undertaking to destroy them." It was hardly his fault, he insisted by way of introduction, that these notions had worn thin after so many centuries. In the case of a subject so long treated speciously by authors carrying authority, one had to destroy before one could build. "So what if the prejudiced do not read me? I will always be read only by the small number of people who think, the only ones whose judgment interests me."[26]

The disingenuousness of this statement scarcely needs remarking. Its author was very much interested in a larger audience. He had asked for the privilege of the approbation of the Academy of Sciences for this book, too, though that had not been forthcoming.[27] Even before official permission for its publication had been registered, public demonstrations of the experiments it described were being offered in the *Journal de Paris* by Marat's friend and ally the abbé Filassier, who had served as publicist for his earlier medical cures. "The beauty and novelty of the spectacle they offer in making visible an entity that plays so great a role in nature would be enough to excite curiosity," the advertisement promised; "but they have a more important object, that of extending the knowledge of the human mind." To

RECHERCHES
PHYSIQUES
SUR LE FEU.

PAR M. MARAT, Docteur en Médecine & Médecin des Gardes du Corps de Monſeigneur LE COMTE *D'ARTOIS.*

A PARIS, RUE DAUPHINE;

Chez CL. ANT. JOMBERT, fils ainé,
Libraire du Roi pour le Génie & l'Artillerie.

M. DCC. LXXX.
Avec Approbation & Privilege du Roi.

FIGURE 8.3. Title page, Marat, *Recherches physiques sur le feu* (Paris: Cl. Ant. Jombert, *fils aîné*, 1780). Courtesy of Huntington Library, San Marino, CA.

allow for variations in sunlight that would affect the operation of the helioscope, two series of eight lectures were scheduled for different times in a fashionable location at the Hôtel d'Aligre, rue Saint-Honoré. Subscription was open chez M. Jombert, *fils aîné*, Bookseller to the King, rue Dauphine, where a copy of "the author's great book on fire" could be purchased, as

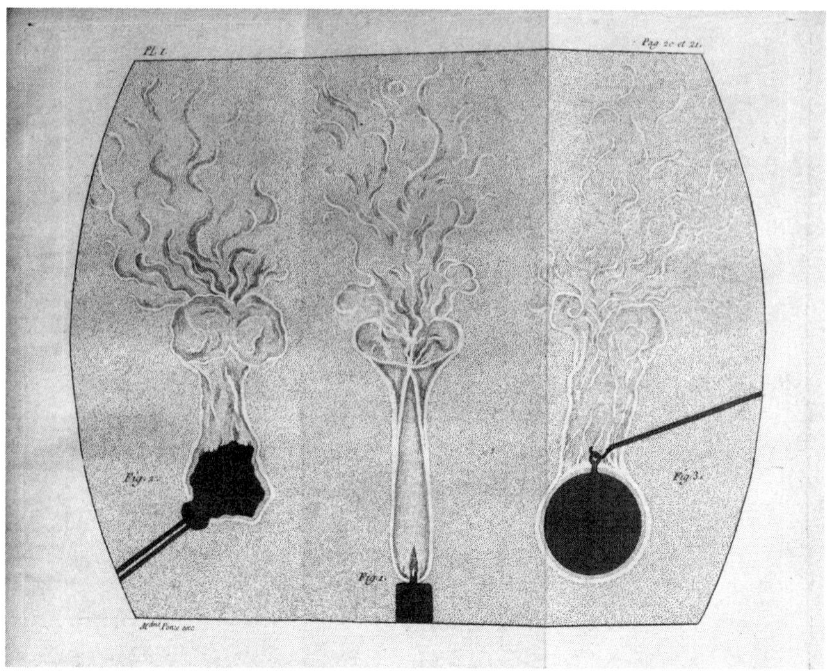

FIGURE 8.4. Plate I, Marat, *Recherches physiques sur le feu* (Paris: Cl. Ant. Jombert, *fils aîné*, 1780). Courtesy of Huntington Library, San Marino, CA.

well as chez M. Sikes, Optician to the King, place du Palais Royal, the maker and purveyor of the author's apparatus. No subscription price was mentioned, but the addresses of the publisher and instrument maker, and their court appointments, suggest an appeal to a toney audience.[28]

Subscriptions for the lectures may have lagged, however. Readers of the *Journal de Paris* were reminded again of their availability on 9 June 1780, this time as part of a more formal announcement of the publication of Marat's book. The experiments reported in the *Recherches . . . sur le feu*, the public was informed, had "by a simple and novel method, that merited the approbation of the Academy of Sciences . . . made visible the igneous fluid at the moment it escaped from combustible bodies or those it penetrated. All the properties of the igneous fluid are set forth with the same exactitude, and this work must be regarded as the most complete and best written treatise on the topic."[29]

Lavoisier would have none of this. At the Academy's session the following day—coincidentally, the session at which he completed a second reading of the paper in which he introduced the term "oxygen"—he moved quickly to protest the assertion that the academicians had endorsed Marat's claims. "M. Lavoisier read an article in the *Journal de Paris* representing as approved by the Academy the observations by which M. Marat claimed to make visible the element of fire," recorded the minutes for 10 June. "As he finds nothing of the kind in the report, M. Le Roy undertook to respond to this assertion."[30] Thus charged to correct Filassier's announcement, Le Roy followed up promptly in a letter to the journal published on 20 June. Transcribing several passages from his committee's original report on the *Découvertes . . . sur le feu*, he emphasized that the Academy had rendered no judgment at all on Marat's claims to have shown the igneous fluid. "Though always inclined to favor and encourage the savants whose experiments announce new ideas and opinions," he professed, the Academy was "uniquely guided by the truth." It could "only accept as certain matters that are sufficiently proven and established." Filassier's rejoinder on 30 June acknowledged that Marat had not requested the Academy's judgment of his theoretical claim but was no less adamant in reiterating that the committee report had confirmed the precision and veracity of his findings.[31]

Lavoisier's action on 10 June sparked an enduring resentment that Marat nursed for a decade as he watched the ever more renowned chemist elbow rivals aside. From resentment grew enmity; from enmity erupted outright public denunciation. Of all the "modern charlatans" Marat caricatured in 1791 when he denounced the despotism of the privileged royal academies, Lavoisier was targeted for the most extreme vilification. "Lavoisier, putative father of all the discoveries that make so much noise," Marat sneered. "Since he has no ideas of his own, he makes do with those of others. But almost never knowing how to appreciate them, he abandons them as thoughtlessly as he has taken them up and changes systems like slippers." What were this man's claims to immortality? He had made a vast fortune for himself as a Farmer General plotting to turn Paris into one great prison by erecting customs barriers around it (an indictment that eventually cost the chemist his life). He had come up with a battery of new chemical terms. He was, nonetheless, a plagiarist. "There is nothing more convenient for the academic plagiarist than the *Mémoires* of the academy," Marat roared in indicting Lavoisier. "The moment he gets wind of a discovery he likes, he snatches what he can from the often erroneous and always incomplete accounts. Then he dashes off a paper . . . , rushes to read it at a particular session to get a date on it. Then, when the original work appears, he reworks his paper; and since the volume in which it is inserted bears a date several years prior to its publication, he has the effrontery to come, this volume in hand, to dispute the honor of the discovery with its inventor."[32]

Lavoisier's opposition may have embittered Marat, but it left him determined not to quit the field. He countered instead with a publicity campaign. His efforts to spread word of his discoveries on fire had already begun well before his initial *Découvertes . . . sur le feu* had reached the printer. "To ensure that credit for it not be snatched from me," he noted later, an abstract had been circulated to each of the principal academies of Europe in December 1778. Encouraging responses had been received from at least some of them. Copies of the manuscript were also sent to other individuals; friends were mobilized to give advance notice to the periodical press.[33] One early reader was the chemist Macquer, who must have been asked to serve as royal censor for this book. Marat wrote on 31 January 1779 to assure him that passages to which he had objected had been removed from the manuscript. "There is therefore no further reason to make difficulties," he insisted, threatening to appeal over Macquer's head to the minister responsible for the book trade. "I await your approval with impatience. If you refuse it, I beg you to return the manuscript to me; I will show it to M. le Garde de Sceaux, and he will judge the reasons for refusal."[34] One wonders about Marat's confidence that he could bring his work directly to the attention of the Keeper of the Seals—perhaps a patient or the friend of one? But there can be no doubt regarding our researcher's readiness to do battle for his work!

Once the *Découvertes . . . sur le feu* was published in May 1779 (with a second edition later in the year), the push for publicity escalated. A copy was quickly sent to the Accademia dei Georgofili in Florence urging repetition of the experiments in that sunny clime.[35] The *Journal de Paris* published an enthusiastic notice on the very first page of its issue for 4 August 1779, striking themes that would become so familiar in subsequent reviews that it is difficult not to suspect a process of orchestration behind the scene. After centuries of vague and unfounded notions regarding the nature of fire, the review proclaimed, a skillful physicist had opened a new path by inventing a method of rendering visible and differentiating the igneous fluid, the electric fluid, and air itself! "One hundred and sixteen experiments, each more interesting than the others, support this ingenious system. M. Marat has recognized the necessity of supporting it with the facts, for in a century as enlightened as our own there is no future for theory, even at its most beautiful, if it does not proceed in step with experiment." One could not fail to see the vast field this research opened to physicists, "as the Royal Academy of Sciences had judged," or its potential to "bring light to the operations of chemistry." With what impatience, the reviewer concluded, must savants await the work from which this little book was merely an extract.[36]

That this notice was fed to the *Journal de Paris* by Filassier, or even Marat himself, seems quite likely. Filassier was in any case using similar terms in a letter to the *Journal de Paris* in October that lamented the failure of other journals to take notice of an experimental procedure that could "open a vast field for the physicists' research, as the Academy of Sciences has judged," and prove of particular benefit to chemistry. To these benefits he now added (thus preparing the ground for his friend's new research and marketing project) the potential contributions to the science of optics that could derive from use of the solar microscope, "an instrument too modest in price for any optician jealous of his reputation not to make this use of it." Marat's discoveries were "of the kind that mark an epoch in the history of science," proclaimed Filassier, but he found periodicals these days too filled with puerilities to notice them. There was no longer space, he lamented, to review the really important books.[37]

Generally speaking, the accounts of Marat's initial publication on fire were positive. Some of the reviews could well have been authored by his close friends and allies, or perhaps by himself—far from an unusual practice at this time. Others appear to have been more independent. An approach had clearly been made to the editor of the *Année littéraire*, who reported that he had been invited by Marat to view his experiments but had not yet been able to do so. He was ready, however, to say that Marat's discoveries "seem as real as they are important, according to the experiments described in his memoir, and the exactitude of these experiments cannot be doubted since it is guaranteed by four of the most distinguished members of the Academy of Sciences."[38]

One of the earliest reviews to appear, that in *The London Review of English and Foreign Literature* in August 1779, also suggests that Marat had contacts eager to publicize his ideas in England. The review was careful to point out that this publication was "only the extract or abridgement of a more extensive work, which we hear Mr. Marat is preparing for the press" and that the journal would "take the first opportunity of entering more largely upon Mr. Marat's very interesting discoveries." In the meantime, readers were reminded that volumes had been devoted over the centuries to the question of the nature of fire, none of them providing satisfactory answers. "Although we do not presume to advance that Mr. Marat has entirely removed every doubt and difficulty," the review continued, "yet we may venture to say that he has proved more successful. And that his discoveries seem best calculated to rectify our notions of that element." His work, after all, had the weight conferred by repeated experimentation. "This is no time to give unsupported opinions. Credulity is by no means the vice of the age, and Mr. Marat's arguments would have very little weight, and might pass with many for a philosophical dream, had he no other proof to give us than his *ipse dixit*; but his doctrine is supported by repeated and successful trials, and the test of one hundred and sixteen different experiments. . . . [I]t opens a very extensive field to new discoveries in natural history and may serve to cast the greatest light on the operations of chymistry."[39]

Other reviews appeared in much the same vein. The *Découvertes* was given a long, appreciative though not uncritical review in the *Journal encyclopédique* of Bouillon in October 1779. The *Mercure de France* praised it the following month for turning the solar microscope into a universal instrument for physics and establishing fundamental facts that ran contrary to common opinion. These latter were discoveries that could "mark an epoch in the history of science," the journal concluded in a familiar phrase; it was up to the physicists, and time itself, to decide. The *Journal de physique*, that same month, was one of the few publications to express serious skepticism, speculating as it did that Marat had merely seen warm air swirling from the heated bodies. More open-minded was the substantial article appearing in February 1780 in the *Journal helvétique* published in his native city by the Société typographique de Neuchâtel, with whose director his family was linked. While admitting little or no knowledge of the subject, the writer praised the *Découvertes . . . sur le feu* as the work of a courageous young man offering a series of ingenious experiments and new discoveries that, wrong or not, would open new routes to the truth. Even the *Journal des savants*, the periodical published under the auspices of the Academy of Sciences, praised the book in April for a new and ingenious method opening a large field for new research. It warned, though, that there would be disagreement with Marat's conclusions regarding the visibility of the matter of fire or the role of phlogiston.[40]

From London, *The Monthly Review, or, Literary Journal* for June 1780 also mixed enthusiasm for Marat's experimental approach with caution regarding his conclusions. It gave the *Découvertes* credit for expanding the use of the solar microscope in "curious, new, and well-conducted experiments"; for going beyond the "ingenious conjectures and hypotheses" that had for so long characterized the study of fire; and for "improv[ing], by important discoveries, this useful and entertaining branch of natural philosophy." These were the accomplishments of "a sagacious and acute observer of nature" possessing "all the knowledge and qualities that are requisite to make important discoveries in natural science." But obscurity in Marat's reasoning and account of his actual experiments nevertheless led the reviewer to suspend judgment pending "still more irresistible light."[41] A very brief notice in *The Critical Review, or, Annals of Literature* a few months later was rather more dismissive. Judging the experiments ingenious, it declared that "the inferences drawn by the author seem to be liable to a variety of objections."[42]

By the time *The Monthly Review* called for more evidence, the expanded *Recherches physiques sur le feu* had already appeared, gilded with an official "privilège du Roi." Filassier, as described earlier, began advertising a series of lectures on it in April 1780, and others were soon expressing interest in teaching and demonstrating the experiments it reported—including Pilâtre de Rozier, the ill-fated ballooning pioneer.[43] The *Recherches*, too, got largely favorable coverage in the press. In May–June 1780 the *Journal de littérature, des sciences et des arts* published a long account, stuffed with excerpts. Its writer judged that the book had established "with all the success imaginable" the properties of the igneous fluid, "this physical agent whose existence we have not suspected until now and that M. Marat makes us touch, as it were, with our fingers and eyes." The claim that Marat was making hidden forces of nature almost palpable struck a strongly experimentalist note. These researches, the notice concluded, would certainly "mark an epoch in the history of physics and place Marat's name alongside those of Franklin, Matran, Muschenbroek, Priestley, etc."[44] Lavoisier was notably absent from this list!

The *Journal de physique* still remained guarded in its evaluation. In July 1780, it noted the claims of the *Recherches* to offer new principles and singular ideas on the nature of fire, observing only that physicists needed to repeat the experiments to establish their truth and utility. The following January, though, it was once more the turn of the *Journal encyclopédique* of Bouillon to voice admiration of Marat's achievements. Its notice declared that the *Recherches* could not fail to become a classic work. Physicists had been unable for two thousand years to study fire in isolation, it argued. As a result, they had been condemned to consult imagination rather than experience. Marat had finally surmounted this problem with a simple and ingenious method that had to be "adopted by all physicists" and utilized immediately in educating the young. His work, moreover, offered a model of scientific writing: "No heavy-handed preliminaries in his writings, no verbiage, no digressions: always simple, clear, decisive facts, from which he almost invariably derives only the immediate consequences; exactness, lucidity and originality of ideas always go along with clarity and fidelity of style."[45] A year later, this entire review reappeared almost verbatim in the *Année littéraire*, its friendly editor pausing only to lament that the journal did not allow the space for an even more detailed account of such an important work.[46] It was recycled yet again, after another six months, by the *Esprit des journaux*, in combination with material from the earlier notice in the *Journal de littérature, des sciences et des arts*.[47]

By that time, the *Recherches* had also appeared in German translation.[48] The book had clearly made a ripple in the scientific world. But attention in the press was already turning to Marat's new and even more ambitious work, the research in which he offered a frontal challenge to Newton's theory of optics. He did not return to his research on combustion, which must have seemed increasingly irrelevant as Lavoisier's theories upended the field of chemistry in the course of the 1780s. It was Marat's misfortune to be swept aside by the paradigm shift we now know as the Chemical Revolution: as Lavoisier advanced by redefining the very terms of chemical research, Marat was left behind. It now seems ridiculous even to discuss them together. At times their language still overlapped. But the contrast between their scientific approaches offers a clue to Marat's intellectual temperament that may prove valuable as we follow the further development of his thinking.

Lavoisier's analytical approach to chemistry (as to society and politics more generally) has been characterized as resting on the metaphor of the "balance sheet." He weighed and measured as a "decompositionist" understanding chemical substances as elements or combinations of elements; his method of investigation aimed to discover processes of decomposition and recomposition that could be analyzed quantitatively. Marat is better described, in contrast, as a "principlist" whose aim was to reveal the very nature of fire as a material entity.[49] In his later caricature of *Les Charlatans modernes* he ridiculed the decompositional method in chemistry as proliferating agents and shuffling names. "They take as simple principles the results of the resolution of compounds," he remarked of the chemists, "and since these results vary with the substances producing them, they make them into different elements. To what prodigious number have they not carried the acids and are carrying the aeriform gases?"[50] His own approach was closer to that of the physicists he described as aiming to relate all the phenomena of nature to a single agent. It was more essentialist than reductive, more qualitative then quantitative, more holistic than combinatorial, more empirical than analytical. Weight, for him, could be shown to be one of the attributes of the igneous fluid, but it offered him no investigative or analytical purchase beyond that. He wished to make visible a fundamental principle, to display the essential properties of a material entity active in the world, one that had for centuries been hidden from view, even from the greatest philosophers. Above all, he wanted to disclose and reveal.

NINE

A NEW NEWTON?

"There is much talk of a new Newton who is the son of M. Marat of Geneva," the mountaineer Marc Théodore Bourrit wrote to his fellow Genevan and Alpine explorer Horace Benedict Saussure in November 1779, expressing a measure of local pride at news presumably making the rounds of Genevan expatriates in Paris. "This physicist has invented a new method of seeing the secrets of nature; at first he had the whole Academy against him, but he has contrived to force them to witness his experiments and to sign them. This extraordinary physicist started as a doctor in London, then in Paris where by knowledgeable cures he has attracted an astonishing following, then wealth and with it the envy and hatred of all the Aesclepiuses of this city, who are not reputed to be the most tolerant of men." Bourrit was impressed by the story of Marat's achievements to date, but even more astounded by word of those about to come. "By his new experiments, he has reduced Newton's seven colors to three, and he has had the audacity to place the sun and consequently all the stars among the planets in taking away its blazing matter and giving it to the igneous fluid, etc. His experiments and proofs will be seen in works to appear shortly. If this is the case, Monsieur, don't you think that many authors will find themselves forced to toss their works into the fire?"[1] Things were to work out differently than Bourrit imagined in his rather garbled account. Few works would be cast into the flames as a result of Marat's next round of experiments. But it would indeed generate much heat.

The avid experimenter had sent the comte de Maillebois a copy of his *Découvertes . . . sur le feu* in mid-June 1779 for presentation to the Academy of Sciences as "a little offering I place by your hand on the altar of the sciences." In the accompanying letter, he informed his patron that he had also used his apparatus to decompose light without the help of a prism. As a result, he had arrived at "absolutely new discoveries" enabling him to "strip nature of its secret" and "perfect Newton's doctrine on colors, not to say establish a new one." It was not without regret, Marat postured, that in studying nature he had been forced to abandon the ideas of this great man, "but if I invalidate his doctrine of colors, I render indubitable in return his doctrine on the cause of refractions, and I demonstrate this cause in plain sight . . . , drawing conclusions I will use one day to perfect optical and astronomical instruments."[2]

REDIRECTING LIGHT

Using his helioscope, Marat had observed two phenomena. The first was a bright fringe (divided by dark bands into three colors) appearing around the edges of the shadow of an object placed in the path of the light's beam. He explained this fringe as the effect of the gravitational attraction of the light by the mass of the object it had passed on its way to the screen. The resulting deviation of the light's rays toward the body they were passing thus brightened (and differentiated) the light immediately surrounding its shadow, at the expense of dimming the light that passed it farther away. The second phenomenon was produced when a card with a small hole at its center was placed in the light's beam. In this case, a bright fringe was observed at the circumference of the circle of light projected onto the screen through the hole in the card, and a darker space observed at its center. Marat inferred that the brighter outer fringe (and the fainter center) was produced by the gravitational pull of the material around the hole in the card.

Observations of such phenomena were far from unprecedented. Francesco Grimaldi had first described the basic effect as "diffraction" in a work published posthumously in 1665. Other investigators had followed, Newton among them. Newton used the term "inflexion" in the third part of his *Opticks* when he described the procedures by which he had replicated and refined Grimaldi's experiments. But this third part of the *Opticks* was left incomplete. Newton had imagined that a theory of diffraction would provide crucial evidence for a corpuscular theory of light by demonstrating how light corpuscles passing very close to an edge of a body would be deflected by the force of the corpuscles of the body. After carrying out an experiment that convinced him this theory could not possibly be correct, however, he had removed his discussion of refraction from the *Opticks* until he could carry out further investigation that, in the event, he was never able to perform. "When I made the foregoing Observations," he wrote, "I design'd to repeat most of them with more care and exactness, and to make some new ones for determining the manner how the Rays of Light are bent in their passage by Bodies, for making the Fringes of Colours with the dark lines between them. But I was then interrupted, and cannot now think of taking these things into farther Consideration. And since I have not finish'd this part of my Design, I shall conclude with proposing only some Queries, in order to a farther search to be made by others."[3]

The celebrated Queries that brought the *Opticks* to a close therefore began precisely with the problem of examining the phenomena of diffraction/inflexion to which Marat now turned his attention. "Do not bodies act upon Light at a distance, and by their action bend its Rays; and is not this action (*ceteris paribus*) strongest at the least distance?" the first Query asked. "Do not the Rays which differ in Refrangibility differ also in Flexibility; and are they not by their different Inflexions separated from one another, so as after separation to make the Colours in the three Fringes above described?" continued the second. "Do not the Rays of Light which fall upon Bodies, and are reflected or refracted, begin to bend before they arrive at the Bodies; and are they not reflected, refracted, and inflected, by one and the same Principle, acting variously in various Circumstances?" posed the fourth. All these queries Marat implicitly answered in the affirmative. The effect was to direct Newton's own speculations against the optical discoveries for which he was most renowned, those resulting from his crucial experiments with the prism.

The incomplete *Opticks* had thus left open the question of the relationship between refraction and diffraction—between, on the one hand, the bending of light and its decomposition into seven colors as it passed through the prism and, on the other hand, the bending of light and its separation into three colors as it passed bodies closely. Into this breach the ambitious Dr. Marat rushed. The bending of light and its decomposition into separate colors was not, in his view, the effect of differential refrangibility of the light rays as they passed through the prism. Instead, this behavior was the result of the differential gravitational attraction exercised upon the light rays by the body of the prism before they entered it. Already inflected by gravitation, the rays entered the prism at different angles; the resulting color separation was thus a consequence of their differential diffractibility, not of their differential refrangibility. It followed too, in Marat's judgment, that there were only three primary colors—yellow, red, and blue—rather than the seven Newton had identified. In "the mingling of dependence and hostility" toward Newton upon which one historian has rightly remarked, Marat had turned Newton against himself.[4]

The argument had potentially significant technological implications for the manufacture of optical devices, as Marat emphasized in sending the *Recherches* to Maillebois. The principal challenge for makers of lenses, especially those for telescopes, was elimination of the chromatic aberration attributed to the differential refraction of the light rays passing through the glass. John Dolland, the great London optician, had achieved fame by perfecting (and fortune by patenting) a method of fitting two types of glass together to create the achromatic doublet, a lens designed to solve precisely this problem by bringing differentially refracting light rays into a common focus. Other opticians had aimed for the same result by varying the colors of their lenses. But what if the phenomenon of differential refraction was just illusory? It would follow that the whole practice of making lenses could be transformed. Marat devoted considerable time and energy to experiments that showed decisively, in his estimation, that differential refraction simply did not occur. "Light never decomposes in traversing a homogeneous glass that is of good quality and well polished, whatever its shape," he insisted.[5] In this regard, Newton's experiments were thus declared specious and the technology based on them misdirected.

This was the claim, supported in his own view by the evidence of more than a hundred painstaking experiments and reinforced by pointed criticism of some of Newton's optical investigations, that Marat now proposed to submit to the scrutiny of the Academy of Sciences in June 1779. Maillebois responded with alacrity, presenting Marat's letter to the Academy on 19 June, along with the presentation copy of the *Découvertes . . . sur le feu*. The Academy immediately charged the same committee members to consider that book's sequel on light and color. Maillebois reported to Marat in turn that the astronomer Lalande had been added to the committee and that all the physicists in the Academy had been encouraged to witness the experiments, only one of them having expressed doubts about their promise. The committee's verification of the new series of experiments began a few days later and continued through the summer. By mid-July, though, Lalande had secured his replacement on the committee by the more imposing and tougher minded Cousin, a significant exponent of mathematical physics—not, perhaps, a promising sign for the author![6]

Marat, for his part, continued as best he could to keep Franklin in the loop. He had invited the great man to dinner in early June, together with Maillebois and other members of the committee who had evaluated his fire experiments. We don't know whether the invitation was accepted, but Franklin was encouraged to bring his grandson along ("if the time [i.e., *temps*, meaning weather] keeps clear; it will be to him an opportunity to see the experiments") and also implored to return, "with your judgement," the manuscript on fire Marat had previously sent him. Franklin was solicited again on 22 August, this time to dine with the new committee for Marat's work on light and to witness "new, interesting, and curious experiments." But he was soon advised that the committee had postponed its visit for two days.[7]

This postponement may well have signaled growing reluctance on the committee's part to proceed with the investigation of the new experiments. Marat later asserted that the committee members had been daunted from the outset by the number of experiments they were obliged to watch and had wanted to see only the most important ones. Sage, pleading his unavailability for yet another meeting on account of business in the country, informed Marat in early October that he would defer to his colleagues' judgment. Other excuses were received from Maillebois and Montigny. This left Le Roy and Cousin still actively engaged, but Marat complained that he had been obliged to beg them for additional sessions before verification of the experiments was concluded in January 1780. His evident desperation makes it highly unlikely that he ever threw the committee members out "with a kick up the ass," as he later bragged.[8]

The committee report still had to be written, and that was not to be done quickly or easily. The dossier Marat kept describing his encounters included correspondence (with annotations, emphases, and analyses added) that suggests his increasingly frantic demands for information about the committee's progress.[9] Unfortunately, we know these letters to and from Marat only as he recorded (and highlighted) them, which means that their precise wording cannot be independently ascertained. In some cases, the veracity of the specific language is of particular importance. Marat was building an indictment here.

At first, the replies came from Le Roy who wrote in early January 1780 that the report would be written the following week, "without delay or interruption, at least for my part." Marat was already anxious: Le Roy, urging calm, had to reassure him that a report rumored to have been refused by the Academy was not the one relating to his own research. Ten days later, though, Le Roy wrote that his own draft was still not completed, excusing his tardiness on the grounds that "M. Marat must recognize himself that the report *is not an ordinary report and demands much attention.*" (The emphasis, here and later, was added by Marat himself.) This same excuse was reiterated after another ten days, and Le Roy was apologizing yet again after two more weeks. "*There is such a spirit of chicanery in the Academy* that this obliges me to pay even more attention to what is read there," he informed Marat on 13 February; "but in God's name be calm and believe that I am very sorry for this delay." Yet another ten days later, on 23 February, Le Roy was stressing that "the matter is very delicate, as you know, and consequently demands careful examination; and, as *you are too good a physicist* not to know, there are many experiments that are not so simple that it is a matter only of pronouncing on a matter of fact. . . . Your report is finished, though, and I will occupy myself only with you from now on."

Le Roy's assurances were growing thin. It was Cousin's turn to write, almost two months later, that presentation of the report was now finally scheduled for 15 April. Cousin added, though, that "we cannot promise *to finish the same day*; that will depend on the amount of attention the Academy will wish to grant us" (a caveat Marat later made much of). He was soon obliged to say that there had not even been time for the Academy to hear the report on that date and that its reading had again been postponed. In the meantime, Cousin asked for the return, by the same messenger, of the translation of Newton's *Opticks* Marat had borrowed from him. Did he just want to be sure of getting a borrowed book back before delivery of the bad news, or were there passages relevant to Marat's work that had to be revisited and argued over? All one can say is that the anxious and doubtless exasperated author escalated his complaints about the committee's continued delays ten days later—by writing directly to the academy's permanent secretary, the marquis de Condorcet.

In all probability, this was the first sustained encounter between these two men who shared (with Lavoisier) a birth year and eventual annihilation within months of one another, each a victim in his own way of the ravages of the French Revolution. Destined to act out diametrically opposed visions within the Revolution, Condorcet and Marat were already dramatically contrasting figures within the scientific milieu of the Old Regime. One was an aristocrat, an accomplished mathematician and theoretician, an ornament of the Old Regime (in Sainte-Beuve's words), the friend and disciple of such leading Enlightenment thinkers as Voltaire, d'Alembert, and Turgot, and charged with directing the academic business of the most powerful scientific body in Europe. The other was an immigrant with no scientific pedigree, author of works professing admiration for Rousseau and horror at the materialism of Enlightenment thinkers, an outsider brought by persistence and patronage to the Academy's threshold, an amateur claiming to unseat Newton with experiments improvised on an apparatus adapted from an instrument for popular amusement. Condorcet was soon to dub Marat a charlatan and doubtless played a part in wrecking his hopes for academic preferment and scientific glory. For the moment, however, academic civility prevailed in their exchange.

Marat's principal concern, as he informed the permanent secretary in his letter of 26 April, was that the experiments the academicians had been pondering for so long had in the meantime been seen by many other people curious about them. Still lacking formal authentication that would assure him the fruit of this work, he was thus "reduced to the sad necessity of laying claim to my discoveries against those who might be tempted to appropriate them." The account of his discoveries had been turned over to the committee, he insisted, but two parts had gone astray and he was now learning that other researchers were working incessantly to adapt his experiments in support of a different theory. "To believe those privy to this secret," he lamented, "the refutation of my doctrine could well appear before the work containing it." He could thus afford to lose no more time before publishing his discoveries. If the report on his work could not be considered at the Academy's very next meeting, he urged, "I pride myself that my new experiments (all of which have been verified by the committee members) may be immediately published, with their sanction declared, since I have gained that right."[10]

Condorcet could hardly have relished this declaration of right from a resentful, pushy outsider with no scientific standing, but he did read Marat's letter to the Academy that same day, confirming that the description of some of the experiments had been lost and stating the committee's promise, "this loss notwithstanding," to present the report at its next meeting, 29 April.[11] Marat was so informed, but the presentation still did not occur. Thereafter, Condorcet was subjected after each academic session to a pressing inquiry from Marat about the status of the report and a demand for an immediate reply, by return of messenger.

As Marat recorded these exchanges, the word from Condorcet on 30 April was that presentation of the report had been preempted by other business and postponed until 3 May. On 4 May, the news was that the report had indeed finally been presented the previous day, but the Academy "*did not have the time to hear it read in its entirety*."[12] It is important to note, however, that this is not quite what Condorcet's draft minutes of the Academy's sessions (the *plumitif*) had recorded. They say only that "MM. Le Roy __ et Cousin" (the dash possibly indicating another name to be inserted) "rendered account of the new experiments of M. Marat. Postponed to the next session."[13] This could mean that the presentation of the report was not completed (as Marat suggested) or that it was completed and only the discussion was postponed. On 7 May, in any case, Condorcet informed Marat that "the report was not made yesterday" because Le Roy had been absent from the session. Two days later, Le Roy himself wrote to ask for the return of the French version of the *Opticks* he had lent Marat "last summer" (and that of the English version, too) because "he would like to verify something." Le Roy also asked for "*the signed verifications of the experiments he had witnessed with M. Cousin, to establish an authoritative record.*"[14]

Finally, on 10 May 1780, the committee submitted its final judgment. According to the Academy's official minutes, a report was presented by Maillebois, Sage, and Cousin (Le Roy was not mentioned in this case, though he was listed as attending the session). It consisted of two utterly devastating paragraphs. The first summarized without comment Marat's claims that light bent as it approached bodies and that its decomposition into separate colors therefore resulted from bending of the rays before they entered the prism rather than from their differential refraction as they passed through it. The second declared the Academy categorically unwilling to approve such claims or even to acknowledge with a description the experiments purporting to support them. It was as if these experiments were to be deemed never to have occurred.

> Since these experiments are in very great number . . . and we have not been able for that reason to verify them all with the necessary precision (despite all the attention we have paid to them), and since moreover they do not appear to prove what the author imagines they establish, and since they are contrary in general to what is most fully known in optics, we believe it would be useless to enter into any detail to make them known because, for the reasons we have just stated, we do not regard them as of the kind to which the Academy can give its sanction or recognition.[15]

It had been eleven months in all since the committee had begun its evaluation of Marat's new experiments and five months since Le Roy had declared the report almost finished. What had gone on? Marat surmised that the report had originally been much lengthier—too long to be read at a single session of the Academy, as the phrasing he underscored in the letters from Cousin and Condorcet suggested. He was convinced that a more substantial evaluation of his work had been suppressed by a cabal determined to deny him recognition. As evidence of the pressure to discredit his experiments, he pointed to Le Roy's confession of a "spirit of chicanery" in the Academy, to the latter's protestations of the delicacy of the issues raised by the report, and to his expectations of increased scrutiny. And to Roume de Saint-Laurent he later retailed an account of a conversation in which Le Roy had been criticized by an acquaintance for producing so risible a document. "What do you want . . . , it's not my fault," Le Roy was quoted as saying. "I wrote a report forty-five pages in 4°, in which I took pride in making M. Marat's work known; but at my every statement of an experiment contrary to Newton's system, the mathematicians gave me the lie, and asserted to our faces, my colleague and me, that we hadn't seen the fact to which we were attesting. When we insisted, they replied 'That's impossible, we've done our calculations.' Their shouting reduced us to silence. In the end, dominated by the strongest party, the Academy badgered me into stitching together the report with which you're reproaching me."[16]

While it cannot be fully confirmed, Marat's suspicion that a longer evaluation had been suppressed seems plausible. There may not have been a cabal against him, exactly, but the lengthy delay in completing the report does seem to suggest protracted disagreement about his work—both within the committee and among the academicians more generally. That the initial reading of the report to the Academy could not be completed in a single session when it did occur on 3 May (as Marat claimed), or was at least postponed for further discussion, makes it plausible that the document presented that day could have consisted of more than the mere two paragraphs that were eventually submitted on 10 May. And the week intervening before the Academy returned to discussion of the matter could well have allowed Le Roy, Cousin, and Sage to cobble together a brief substitute text. It is striking, too, that the report finally conveyed to Marat was signed only by these three academicians. The signature of Maillebois, Marat's previously stalwart patron, was notably missing, as was that of Montigny.

Marat, nonetheless, decided to brave it out. The *Découvertes . . . sur la lumière*, when it appeared, displayed London as its place of publication while announcing its availability in Paris, "Chez Jombert, *fils aîné*, rue Dauphine"—a conventional fig leaf for a work printed in France without formal permission. Defiantly, the title page declared that the experiments upon which the work was based had been "performed a very great number of times under the eyes of Messieurs the members of a committee of the Academy of Sciences." Marat had apparently chosen simply to assert the right to make this statement he had earlier solicited from Condorcet. Even more obstinately, he not only printed the text of the harsh committee report as a preface to the work but followed it with a rebuttal of his own. Only two members of the committee had played an active part in verifying his experiments, he protested. Moreover, he insisted, having requested that the committee limit its inquiry to verifying the truth of the experiments, he had never flattered himself that the Academy would confirm the conclusions he had deduced from this "long series of surprising and unknown facts." It was nonetheless his right, he contended, to expect a verdict on their precision and originality.

As to the reasons that had reduced the committee to silence, Marat reiterated that the experiments had been repeated in the presence of the academicians many times. Whether or not the facts appeared to prove the theoretical conclusions he drew from them was not the issue, he emphasized; there had never been any question of the committee's examining these conclusions in any case. And if the conclusions were now judged "contrary in general to what is most fully known in optics," this was exactly the claim to originality upon which he prided himself—and to which the academicians had been alerted in advance. His rebuttal ended with a challenge. No learned society in the world, he proclaimed, could render true what was false and false what was true. There was a higher authority in these matters.

> In refusing me its sanction the Academy of Sciences cannot change the nature of things. If one has to be judged, then let it be by an enlightened and impartial public: I appeal with confidence to its tribunal, this supreme tribunal whose decrees scientific bodies themselves are forced to respect.[17]

Marat apparently thought better of this final challenge. Later, when he was preparing a substantially revised edition of the *Découvertes . . . sur la lumière*, he eliminated the defiant final appeal to public opinion.[18] He nevertheless spent much of the next decade in efforts to find—or fabricate—the enlightened and impartial public that would (as a criterion of its enlightenment!) accept his views on diffraction and color theory. In the meantime, he had yet to complete the immensely ambitious project announced in his *Découvertes . . . sur le feu, l'électricité et la lumière*: to resolve fundamental questions regarding forces and fluids of the universe left still unanswered by Newton. He had entered the lists with Lavoisier to reveal the nature of fire, and he had challenged Newton's account of the behavior of light. It remained for him to engage Franklin on the theory of electricity.

TEN

FOLLOWING FRANKLIN

Electricity, as old as amber, was suddenly made new in the eighteenth century. The unexpected discovery of the Leyden jar in 1746, an apparatus allowing an experimenter or demonstrator to store and discharge electricity, made it an irresistible topic of conversation and entertainment. The public flocked to see the novel device, to witness the phenomena it displayed, and to feel the shock delivered from the electricity it stored. Demonstrators sprang up everywhere to gratify popular curiosity. At Versailles 180 guards held hands to be electrified together for the edification of Louis XV and his court. In Paris an entire Carthusian monastery, linked by iron rods to form a two-mile chain, was shocked into a new form of communion. "While the vulgar of every age, sex, and rank were viewing the prodigy of nature and philosophy with wonder and amazement . . . ," wrote Joseph Priestley of the Leyden discovery, "all the electricians of Europe [were] immediately employed in repeating the great experiment, and attending to the circumstances of it."[1] The most startling contributions, though, came not from Europe but from Philadelphia, in the form of Franklin's *Experiments and Observations on Electricity*, first published in 1751 and expanded incrementally until its fifth English edition appeared in 1774. The work had seen three French editions by 1773.

Enthusiastically pushed in France by the naturalist Buffon and his followers, who relished their vitalist implications, Franklin's theories were no less energetically opposed by the abbé Nollet in one of the dramatic scientific struggles of the century. By the time Marat took up the subject, the

Franklinian paradigm was in the ascendant in France as elsewhere, pushed as it was by Priestley's *History* (translated into French in 1771) and by Franklin's most strenuous French supporter within the Paris Academy—and Marat's brief ally—Jean-Baptiste Le Roy.[2] The discoveries in Philadelphia nonetheless left a host of questions unanswered and created as many new ones. Priestley acknowledged as much with enthusiasm in a section of his *History* identifying problems for further research. Physicists throughout Europe—Beccaria, Boscovich, and Volta in Italy; Aepinus in Russia; Wilcke in Sweden; Symmer and Canton in Britain, to name only the most prominent—raced to perform new experiments and publicize new theories. Attuned to new developments, Marat eagerly perused the literature in an attempt to join these researchers. The field, he characteristically declared in 1782, citing Priestley's account in evidence, was still in a state of chaos. He set out to remake it, following methods he had used in his research on fire. "Not a single hypothesis, not a single reasoning offered at random," was his claim: "theory always marches in step with experiment; and everything is deduced with rigor from constant facts as I permit myself to draw only their immediate implications."[3]

This time the engagement with a founding figure was more direct. In optics, Newton was long dead; in the physics of fire, the haughty, conniving Lavoisier kept his distance from a man he deemed a charlatan. In electricity, though, Marat could hope to touch Franklin's hem. "I know your taste for the sciences and your love of truth," he wrote to the renowned Philadelphian on 18 November 1780. "My high opinion of your sagacity and impartiality allow me to submit to your judgment, without fear, some new experiments diametrically opposed to received ideas." Sagacity and impartiality were indeed required in this case: ideas Marat challenged were held by Franklin himself.

Among his experiments, he divulged, were "those demonstrating that the electric fluid is not endowed with a repulsive force essential to its globules. There are also others proving that all bodies conduct the electric fluid. Finally, there are some establishing the method of charging the Leyden jar even if it is isolated. The instruments I have invented include a new electrometer that forms a true electric repetition; a discharger appropriate for liquids; a Leyden jar that charges itself even when isolated, &c &c." Franklin was invited, "if these novelties can pique your interest," to choose a day later that month to visit the laboratory on the rue de Bourgogne. "I flatter myself, Monsieur, that you will look kindly on my approach to you today as the most respectful token I can give you of the great value I place on your knowledge and candor."[4]

Does the fulsome tone of this gesture hint also at a note of anticipated condescension toward the man who had (in Turgot's words) "snatched lightning from the sky and the scepter from tyrants"? Was a modern idol about to be cast down? "I hate the polemical genre," Marat would note somewhat disingenuously when engaging Franklin's views in the book on electricity he published eighteen months later. "Let one judge of my regrets when it comes to refuting an opinion of an author whose genius I know and whose virtues I respect. . . . I hope the reader will do me the justice of believing that I would not have allowed myself any discussion if it had not seemed necessary for the triumph of truth."[5] Franklin, in any case, seemed unperturbed. He was laid up with gout, as he soon responded in November 1780, and saw no early prospect of traveling to Paris from his home on the outskirts of the capital. He expressed interest, though, in seeing an account of the experiments if Marat had one.[6]

The intrepid experimenter did indeed have an account ready to hand. It appeared in the form of a letter published in the *Journal de littérature, des sciences et des arts* that same month. "I don't know which is more astonishing," the letter read, "the ardor with which M. *Marat* gives himself to the study of nature or the brilliant success that always crowns his endeavor. Not content with having (in the space of two years) enriched physics with important discoveries relating to fire and light, he has now enriched it with discoveries on electricity that are no less important."[7] Marat's results were already being circulated and discussed in the scientific circles of the capital, the letter reported; the manuscript describing them having fallen into the writer's hands, they could now be summarized for all those interested in this branch of physics.

Thus launched yet another campaign by Marat's media team, this time to promote his research on electricity. In the year before his book on the subject finally appeared in March 1782, its findings were being spread in advance not only in the *Journal de littérature, des sciences et des arts* but in lengthy and often virtually identical reports appearing in the *Mercure de France*, the *Esprit des journaux*, the *Journal de physique*, and the *Journal encyclopédique de Bouillon*. In a second wave of publicity, expanded accounts and extracts in the *Journal de littérature, des sciences et des arts* and the *Journal encyclopédique de Bouillon* also preceded the book's publication.[8] They were taken up in mid-March by the *Courier de l'Europe*, which printed extravagant praise of the book in early May.[9] Even after the *Recherches physiques sur l'électricité* finally appeared, the media blitz continued. Further accounts and extracts, often echoing one another, came out in the *Journal helvétique*, the *Journal de littérature, des sciences et des arts*, the *Esprit des journaux*, and the *Journal encyclopédique de Bouillon*. The Bouillon publishers also inserted lengthy extracts from the book in their *Calendrier intéressant ou Almanach physic-économique pour l'année 1783*.[10] Against this wave of hype, only the *Journal de physique* continued to sound a skeptical note. "Savants already know the work and discoveries of M. Marat on fire and light," it reported; "today he offers . . . his new principles and new theory on electricity. . . . Much reform in the principles generally adopted by the physicists studying electricity; new explanations, new apparatuses, and consequently new experiments; in short, a new system: such is the work of M. Marat. It will be in reading it, and in repeating its experiments, that one will be able to judge it."[11]

Marat made at least one more effort to get Franklin's judgment before his electrical research was published. "If you are curious to see a series of new electrical experiments, directed to establish many a principle hitherto unknown, I shall do myself the pleasure of summiting [*sic*] them to your judgment," he wrote to Franklin on 14 February 1782. This time the sage agreed to attend, assuming "nothing will happen to prevent me, and the weather will be good." He was apparently expecting to see experiments carried out with the solar microscope, but Marat now had other instruments of his own invention to display. In response, he assured Franklin that "the shinning [*sic*] of the sun is by no means necessary to the experiments I intend to show you. Thus I flatter myself to have pleasure to see you on Monday next, let the weather be what it may."[12] Whether it occurred or not, we learn no more of this planned visit or of any further interest on Franklin's part. No copy of Marat's handsomely produced *Recherches physiques sur l'électricité* has been found in Franklin's library.[13]

Presenting arguments and conclusions based on several hundred often ingenious experiments devised to address the findings of other practitioners in the field, Marat placed himself stolidly in the Philadelphian's camp.[14] Franklin, he wrote, had been "the first to consider [the science of electricity] from broad perspectives; he multiplied the facts, generalized the results, illuminated the phenomena, and gave it some principles and laws." Franklin, too, had been the first to demonstrate the identity between electricity and lightning. "The grand scene he opened to our eyes made better known the matter that had escaped observation for so long. A subtle fluid spread everywhere over the surface of the globe, it lies peacefully hidden inside bodies as long as it is proportionally distributed among them. But if, after being accumulated in the clouds, it abruptly returns to the space it has abandoned, it often becomes one of the most irresistible agents of nature." Discoveries of such magnitude could not remain sterile in the hands of their author. "Beneficent genius, he thought of turning them to the advantage of society; bold genius, he undertook to disarm the sky."[15]

Franklin's discoveries did not winnow the field of competitors, however. It still remained true, in Marat's analysis, that the great majority of works published on the topic of electricity offered little beyond "puerile observations, badly executed experiments, false inductions, rash hypotheses, and contradictory opinions." A science studying such diverse phenomena required "an active mind that would proscribe the random facts and trivial observations, analyze the complicated experiments, generalize the results, subject the received laws to examination, verify the principles, link the consequences, and reduce the effects to their causes."[16] One need hardly add that Marat prided himself on such a mind. It was time, he thought, to bring new order to this branch of physics.

His most radical move—to which he had wanted to direct Franklin's immediate attention personally in 1780—was to eliminate repulsion as an essential attribute of the electrical fluid. To capture the significance of this claim it must be noted that Franklin's key innovation had been to replace a theory initially offered by the French academician Charles François de Cisternay du Fay that postulated the existence of two different kinds of electricity called *vitreous* (typically produced by friction on glass) and *resinous* (typically produced by friction on amber). In this theory, bodies exhibiting the same kind of electricity repelled one another, while those exhibiting different kinds were mutually attractive. Nollet, Du Fay's disciple, had reworked this dualistic approach by explaining electrical attraction and repulsion (and the sometimes-rapid shift from one to the other) in terms of an alternation or interaction between affluent and effluent flows of the electrical matter.

Franklin, more simply, made the case for a single electrical fluid normally existing in a state of equilibrium in every material. Bodies were electrified, he argued, when this neutral state of equilibrium was disturbed. He then explained the phenomena of electrical attraction and repulsion in terms of the flow of this single fluid between bodies with more or less of the fluid than in their normal (neutral) state. Two bodies were mutually attractive when one charged with an excess of the electrical fluid (hence called "plus" or "positive") was brought into proximity with one that had a deficit of it (hence called "minus" or "negative"); they were mutually repellent when each had an excess or a deficit. Bodies in their normal or "neutral" state were also attracted by those that were electrified, whether positively or negatively.

Accepting Franklin's views regarding the existence of a single electrical fluid that could be positively or negatively charged (and insisting that the electrical fluid was quite distinct from those of fire, light, and magnetism), Marat hazarded an even more radical simplification. He did not deny the fact of electrical repulsion in the ordinary sense. At issue was the existence of repulsion as an attribute of electricity at the globular or corpuscular level. In the physics of the time, fluids flowed because their corpuscles were mutually repulsive, thus rendering them expansive. Since electricity was seen as a fluid, its globules were therefore held to be repellent one to another at the same time as they attracted (and were attractive to) the globules of other matter. Marat interpreted his experiments as confirming the fact of attraction at this level but disconfirming that of repulsion.

Franklin himself had hesitated on this point, opting finally to retain both repulsion and attraction as attributes of the electrical fluid at the globular level, despite the arguments to the contrary urged upon him by Ebeneezer Kinnersley in correspondence published in the 1769 edition of the *Experiments and Observations on Electricity*.[17] Marat was convinced of Franklin's error in this regard. He aimed, in effect, to achieve for the study of electricity what he thought he had accomplished for the study of light: to clarify and simplify understanding by reducing the phenomena ultimately to the operation of the single (Newtonian) principle of attraction. This force, he maintained, was adequate to explain all known electrical effects. "Thus the attractive force having become the great principle to which it is reserved to illuminate the phenomena, the theory of electricity will become simpler, clearer, more luminous."[18]

One implication of this argument was to deny electrical fluid the elasticity (resulting from corpuscular repulsion) that made all fluids flow. The force of attraction, Marat contended, was instead aided by the pressure of the ambient air. He used this consideration to interpret one of Franklin's central discoveries (and the key to the operation of the lightning rod), the tendency of electricity to seek out pointed objects. The explanation for this so-called "power of points" had been up for debate since Franklin had first identified the phenomenon. Marat claimed to have solved the problem by reasoning that the air pressure required to aid the passage of electricity from one body to another was less to the degree that the column of air already separating the two bodies was narrower. The more sharply pointed the receiving body, therefore, the greater the likelihood that the electric charge would find it.

It remained to explain the central mystery of electricity: how some bodies conducted it and others did not. To answer this question, Marat chose in good Enlightenment fashion (as Lavoisier was doing for chemistry) to redefine conventional terms. "I have begun by proscribing the vicious nomenclature devoted to this branch of physics: for what greater obstacle is there to the progress of science than the multitude of names differently given to a single thing?"[19] The language was indeed confusing: materials sometimes called "non-conductors" were at the time called *electrics* (because electricity could be excited on their surface by friction), while those called "conductors" (because they were not seen to be electrified as the result of friction) were also called *non-electrics*. Marat instead offered a distinction between *déférens* and *indéférens*, from a Latin root meaning "yielding" or "carrying."

We might think that the only advantage of this new terminology was that it was Marat's own, but he imagined otherwise. "Having rectified words," he proclaimed in good Condillac fashion, "I have rectified things." His purpose was to replace an absolute distinction between conductors and non-conductors with a more nuanced differentiation between bodies that "immediately transmit the excess quantity of [electrical] fluid necessary to give a shock" (*déférens*) and those that "transmit this quantity only gradually" (*indéférens*), this differentiation depending not only on the material of the bodies involved but also on their texture and shape.[20] The relevant consideration here was the nature of insulating materials, and especially that of glass, which Franklin and many others had declared impermeable to electricity.

Marat offered "new and decisive experiments" intended to demonstrate that no insulators were completely impermeable. Among his inventions to advance this research was an instrument designed to measure degrees of permeability, which he called a "permeometer." The permeability of glass was a critical issue for understanding the operation of the Leyden jar, an improved version of which was another of the inventions Marat claimed, along with "the simplest, most exact, and best adapted electrometer to compare the force of different electrical machines." This latter instrument, he declared, was "the most convenient" and "only true one known. . . . If there is a science where an instrument to measure a force is necessary it is surely Electricity, where so many of the effects attributed to different causes often come from the differential energy of the same cause."[21]

Using this apparatus, Marat offered his solutions to several key problems. One was to discover accurate methods of differentiating positive from negative electricity ("I have given infallible ones"). Le Roy had suggested that a positive discharge was shaped like a plume, while a negative discharge was shaped like a star. Marat thought he could do better by developing a method that would display the direction of the flow from positively to negatively charged bodies. Returning to his darkroom, he developed experiments that would show the direction of the flow of the electrical fluid (which he deemed not itself visible to the naked eye) from the movement of the igneous fluid it always pushed before it. "With the aid of our method of observation in the darkroom, one always sees the electrical fluid, which emanates from a body that is positively electrified and armed with a point, chase before it the igneous emanations of an incandescent body inalterable by fire."[22] Rendering hidden forces visible (if only indirectly) remained an obsession for Marat the scientist. It would become no less a compulsion for Marat the revolutionary journalist.

In science as in politics, too, knowledge had to be offered in service of the public. Aiming at a theory of electricity "as solid as it is illuminating," Marat hoped also to show its utility. Concluding sections of the *Recherches . . . sur l'électricité* turned accordingly to "the uses to which the electrical fluid is destined" in its role as "a general agent . . . in nature." His discussion of this issue seems surprisingly cautious. Beyond offering a general rhapsody to electricity as a source of fertility in the universe, Marat was skeptical of claims hitherto made for the utility of its effects and applications. Two applications of electrical knowledge interested Marat—and his contemporaries—in particular. One, its use in medical practice, he reserved for discussion elsewhere. The second, adoption of the lightning rod, formed the topic of the final section of the *Recherches . . . sur l'électricité*. His description of lightning's effects was dramatic. It is worth reproducing because the phenomenon was destined to become a powerful metaphor for revolution.

> Lightning ignites the inflammable vapors the earth exhales; it enflames the combustible matter it strikes; it powerfully forces its way through bodies it penetrates; it shatters, melts, or pulverizes those it penetrates too brutally; it rips the trees it overthrows; it strips the paint from gilded panels; it magnetizes susceptible bodies; it always gives violent shocks to the unfortunates it strikes; it often paralyzes animals; it often also dissolves their bones; sometimes it blinds them; and sometimes it executes them—phenomena replicable at will by means of the explosions of a strong electric battery.[23]

Comparable phenomena would be replicable at will within a few years, too, by the power of popular sovereignty.

FIRE BROUGHT DOWN FROM THE SKY?

For the moment, though, there were horrors from which men rendered prostrate by fear might be protected. What a great spectacle, Marat proclaimed, to see nature disarmed by Franklin's lightning rod and fire brought down peacefully from the sky! "Oh you, who formed this great design, beneficent Genius! You whom Renown so justly celebrates, receive the homage of our hearts."[24] He was nonetheless critical of Franklin's theories regarding the formation of lightning and the means of preventing it. The sage of Philadelphia had originally thought that the primary use of lightning rods could be to draw atmospheric electricity steadily and silently from the clouds and return it to the earth, thus reducing the likelihood of electrical storms rather than just guarding against them as they occurred. This conception depended on a notion of electrical fields that Marat rejected. He thought, in any case, that the distance between a lightning rod and the clouds was generally too great for Franklin's idea to be theoretically plausible. He invoked instances of buildings armed with lightning rods being destroyed by violent discharges as empirical evidence against it.

Marat did allow, though, that lightning rods could be useful, especially if improved by addition of several points facing in different directions and grounded by thick wires sinking deep enough in the earth to reach subterranean water. He deemed them far superior, indeed, to the age-old (and frequently fatal) practice of rushing to ring the church bells to divert lightning and dispel a storm! But he doubted the power of reason to persuade a benighted populace to abandon this suicidal custom and rejected as tyrannical any use of violence to compel it to do so. Preferring deceit to save the people from its prejudices, he advocated a ruse, "the only convenient way of preventing so many useful subjects from going foolishly to their deaths."[25] Local clergy, he thought, could allow the bell-ringing practice to continue while covertly installing a lightning rod on the church steeple.

That Marat considered this alternative safe spoke indirectly to arguments in a much-publicized trial—one of the *causes célèbres* of the century—then under way in the little northern town of Saint-Omer. There the young Maximilien Robespierre was about to make a dramatic legal debut in defense of a homeowner forced by a terrified neighbor's protest to dismantle the lightning rod he had recently installed.[26] Though Marat's views on the matter were garbled when invoked in his absence in the course of that trial (and have been frequently misrepresented by historians since), he clearly maintained that a house armed with a lightning rod did not endanger adjacent property. His main proposal, though, was an ambitious one to preserve whole towns by creating an integrated urban grid connecting lightning rods at the ends of each and every street. Adoption of this plan being unlikely, he fell back on the idea of prohibiting useless towers on new buildings. This, he thought, would at least offer "the double advantage of diminishing dangers and restoring good taste to architecture."[27]

Discussion of the lightning rod did not quite bring the *Recherches* . . .

sur l'électricité to a close. Its final pages offered a withering dismissal of the idea of sinking similar rods into the ground to prevent the disasters produced by earthquakes and volcanoes. Marat found ridiculous the notion that these phenomena were precipitated by electricity and did not hesitate to say so. That a particular venom tinged his arguments in this case is easily explicable: their target, the proponent of the theory of the earthquake and volcano rods, was none other than a well-known electrical theorist and champion of medical electricity, the abbé Pierre Bertholon. It was against Bertholon, a rival in this latter field destined to become a bitter personal enemy, that Marat would soon launch his critique of this second great application of electrical knowledge.

In the meantime, Bertholon was not amused by the attention paid to him in the *Recherches . . . sur l'électricité*. "Nothing is said of [Marat] in Paris, or in the provinces, or even abroad," he reported to Antoine Buissart, an acquaintance in Arras who was also Robespierre's closest friend in his hometown there. "This is a madman who has believed he could grab fame by attacking many great men and by offering paradoxes that seduce no one because experience is the true touchstone. Who is this man to dare measure himself against the immortal Newton who carried out experiments on optics for forty years?"

Marat had used defective prisms to generate defective results, Bertholon charged; he had feigned ignorance of elementary truths in optics established by earlier research. What could reveal greater ignorance than Marat's earlier claims to render visible the matter of fire? As for his notions about the lightning rod, they had been received with the sovereign disdain they deserved. He had been obliged to send journals fake letters from "the chevalier . . . or the marquis . . ." to get the reviews no one wanted to write! "What enrages this man is that no one discusses or refutes him; he longs to be refuted by someone well known." Bertholon was determined not to reply in print to the diatribes of a man he deemed so entirely ignorant of electricity. "I believe I will punish this man more in not refuting him," he pompously assured his friend; "he only wants a refutation to rescue his works momentarily from the oblivion to which they have been returned."[28] Resolute words! But the good abbé was soon goaded into eating them.

MEDICAL SHOCKS, THERAPEUTIC SPARKS

There was something intuitive about the idea that a jolt of electricity might provide a cure for paralysis. No sooner had the Leyden jar been discovered than its power to deliver shocks more powerful than hitherto possible was put to the test for this purpose. Believing that electricity was a vitalizing agent capable of increasing the flow of fluids through narrow vessels, Nollet had already used a frictional generating machine to show that electricity improved growth in vegetables and respiration in animals. By early 1746, within weeks of his learning from Leyden about the new device, he tried it out as a means of curing paralysis, apparently concluding that the effort was premature. News spread in 1748, however, of an electrical cure effected by Jean Jallabert, professor of mathematics and experimental philosophy in Geneva. Jallabert had hooked up to a Leyden jar a worker who had been left by a workplace accident with a paralyzed arm. The shocks restored limited mobility, though at the cost of traumatizing the injured worker even further.

Not to be outdone, Nollet rushed to quiz Jallabert on his methods and results—and to get government permission to conduct his own experiments on paralytics at the Hôpital des Invalides in Paris. Of the four patients chosen, one died as the treatment got under way and the remaining three received little benefit from their experimental treatment. Nollet salved his pride, and regained his scientific authority, by rushing to Italy to denounce as quackery the celebrated but very different medical applications utilized there to volatilize medicaments in a kind of aromatherapy. Attitudes to medical electricity remained skeptical.[29]

The situation was very different by the time Marat opened his medical practice in Paris a generation later. Integrated into physiological theory as an agent acting upon the nervous fluid, electricity had been adapted to medical treatment in the 1750s at the famous medical school of Montpellier. Despite charges of charlatanism, electrotherapy was finding vociferous new advocates by the 1770s—among them the pugnacious founder of the *Gazette de santé* in 1773—and was being gradually taken up more generally by practitioners. Case histories began to circulate, like those published by a roaming cleric from Perpignan, abbé Sans, in his *Guérison de la paralysie par l'électricité ou cette expérience physique, employé avec succès dans le traitement de cette maladie regardée jusques à present comme incurable* (1772). In response, evaluation and standardization of electrical treatments became a special mission of the new Royal Society of Medicine (and an assertion of its claims to authority over medical practice) from the very moment of its creation in 1778. The society's principal investigator in this domain, Mauduyt de la Varenne, had already warned readers of the *Journal de médicine* in 1778 against exaggerated enthusiasm for electrical treatments that could be as potentially dangerous as they could be beneficial.[30] His official assessment of eighty-two such cases was first published in 1779. It was followed in 1784 by his *Mémoire sur les différentes manières d'administrer l'électricité et observations sur les effets que ces divers moyens ont produit*. Each of these publications was offered to a broad public.[31]

While the Royal Society of Medicine was sponsoring Mauduyt, its rival institution, the Paris Faculty of Medicine, took up the cause of Nicolas-Philippe Ledru, *alias* Comus, a popular entertainer whose shows included dramatic demonstrations of electrical cures. In 1783, Ledru was offered a professorship and accepted the Faculty's invitation to leave the streets for the lecture hall. Later the same year, he and his son, already named "His Majesty's physicians for the electrical treatment of epilepsy and other illnesses of the same nature," opened a new "hospice-médico-électrique" in premises provided by the government. The inaugural ceremony celebrated its official sponsorship in the presence of Benjamin Franklin. A year later it was being advertised as "treating with all possible zeal and disinterest, under the surveillance of commissioners named by the Faculty of Medicine, all persons suffering from epilepsy, catalepsy, madness, and maladies of the nerves." This official support for electrotherapy contrasted dramatically—perhaps intentionally—to treatment the government meted out to the more notorious competing cure in the popular medical marketplace, the magnetic baths brought to Paris from Vienna by Franz Anton Mesmer in 1778.[32] Seen increasingly as a threat to public order, Mesmerism was condemned by a prestigious royal commission in 1784.

Ledru, *alias* Comus, was a thorn in Marat's flesh even before his elevation to the Faculty of Medicine. His son had already written a substantial letter to the *Journal de physique* in 1781 charging that electrical discoveries claimed by Marat had actually been made and published several years previously.[33] Bertholon's instinct had been shrewd in disparaging Marat by lumping him, as a charlatan, with this successful but still disreputable showman. But that had been a private jab. Marat, ever smoldering, erupted immediately, early in 1783, when he was openly compared to Comus in a popular course of lectures delivered by another rival, the experimental physicist (and ballooning expert) Jacques-Alexandre-César Charles. Feeling ridiculed and offended by the comparison, he rushed to confront this new critic at his lodging, only to be received with disdain. As he turned to leave, he was set upon by Charles and other members of his household, relieved of his sword, which was broken in the process, and dispatched with a black eye and bashed-up face. This, at least, was the account Marat gave in the formal deposition he immediately submitted to the police. Charles, for his part, told a different story, according to which the furious Marat, denied an apology and ordered to leave, had begun hurling insults and drawing his sword—at which point Charles had overpowered him and broken the sword, keeping as evidence a piece "judged by everyone to be a most dangerous and bloody weapon."

Whatever the truth, Marat had not only lodged a formal complaint in response to this humiliation but summoned Charles to a duel. It is hardly metaphorical to say that he was willing to fight for the personal honor he equated with scientific glory. "You will find me a generous enemy who would blush to take an adversary unawares and want to deprive him of part of his superiority," he declaimed. "To convince yourself, choose a witness and I will have another. The bearer of this letter will tell you the rest." Dueling had long been illegal in France and plans for this encounter were soon brought to the attention of the lieutenant of police. It appears, in any case, that Charles had no taste for such an encounter. "Who is the aggressor, the man who would force you to take up a sword over simple opinions, or the one who, when assailed at home by an unknown person, seeks to evade uncertain intentions?" he asked, probably in response to an inquiry from the lieutenant of police, Lenoir. "If I allowed myself the slightest personal insult against M. Marat, let him prove it, and I am ready to make him a public apology. I have attacked his systems and I promise him to do so again; but if it's necessary to fight over that, then all of Europe must be armed against him."[34] The duel was soon quashed by Lenoir's order. Marat, doctor of the bodyguard of Monseigneur le comte d'Artois and irascible researcher, had been brought to heel.

This was the context, hardly serene, in which Marat prepared his own *Mémoire sur l'électricité médicale*. His views on the topic had remained notably absent from the *Recherches . . . sur l'électricité* in 1782, perhaps because he was already planning to submit them as a response to a prize-essay competition proposed by the Academy of Rouen. The question, "to what extent, and under what conditions, can one count on magnetism or on electricity, whether positive or negative, in the treatment of illness?" had been announced in 1781 for a prize to be awarded in 1782, but the deadline for submissions had been extended for lack of responses. Even then, the competition only attracted two entries, of which Marat's was eventually declared the winner. A recent historian has suggested that the paucity of submissions may have been a sign that medical electricity was no longer controversial enough to make the essay competition interesting.[35] If that was indeed the situation, Marat had certainly set out to change it. His essay barely mentioned the medical application of magnetism, dismissing it as still devoid of any systematic theoretical or empirical basis while allowing the possibility that it could ease pain caused by engorged organs. Nor did he show any inclination to enter into extended debate over Mesmerism, from which he had prudently kept his distance.[36] But he launched into a lengthy and savage critique of Bertholon's *De l'électricité du corps humain dans l'état de santé et de maladie*, a work published in 1780 as the recipient of a prize awarded by the Academy of Lyon.

The wording of the Rouen Academy's competition, with its specific interrogation of the medical role of electricity "whether positive or negative," was an implicit invitation to respond to Bertholon's book, which had placed distinctive emphasis on the therapeutic use of the "negative" electricity the author claimed as his own discovery. Perhaps the Academy's tactic misfired, discouraging potential competitors rather than attracting them. The five hundred pages of Bertholon's *De l'électricité du corps humain*, stuffed with observations and results taken from some two hundred and fifty savants, national and international, were touted by the publisher as "the first complete exposition of the Electrico-animal economy and of electrical medicine."[37] This was the magnum opus of a prize-winning author honored by many academies, a darling of the provincial Enlightenment. It offered a global theory regarding the effects of atmospheric electricity on the human body, a classification of illnesses in relation to those effects, and an analysis of the various methods of electrical treatment appropriate to these illnesses. Other researchers were apparently reluctant to take it on. Not so Jean-Paul Marat.

Submitted anonymously to the Académie de Rouen in May 1783 by a friend, the baron de Feldenfeld, Marat's response to the prize-essay question was declared the winner despite the Academy's disapproval of the aggressive tone he had adopted against Bertholon, one of its members, whom it now defended as "an estimable man, accepted by nine learned societies that have almost unanimously crowned his efforts." Never easy to deal with, Marat then tussled with the Academy (with Feldenfeld as the intermediary) over maintaining his anonymity and reclaiming the manuscript he had submitted too hastily to make a second copy. As we shall see, he now had other plans for the publication of this work. He was nonetheless obliged to reveal his name to the academicians and prove his authorship before he could receive the cash prize and accompanying medal.

At that juncture, he also took the opportunity to send the Academy's secretary a handsomely bound set of his books on fire, light, and electricity—"a little offering that I place by your hand upon the altar of the sciences."[38] This show of modesty was effective—the Academy, bending its rules, responded by providing a copy of his manuscript gratis—but it only went so far. Marat made it a point to rebut the academicians' criticism of his essay's tone when it was published anonymously a year later as *Mémoire sur l'électricité médicale, couronné le 6 août 1783, par l'Académie des belles lettres, sciences et arts de Rouen*. "I read my essay carefully and found not a single term that should be avoided by a self-respecting author," his preface insisted. "It would have been lacking in zeal for humanity to soften the refutation of a system that could become dangerous as a result of the ill-considered praise it has received."[39]

Bertholon's notion, broadly speaking, was to imagine living beings in the same way that Franklin imagined physical bodies. The atmosphere, he thought, was an immense reservoir of electrical fluid: human bodies were plunged into it as fish into a lake. They absorbed this atmospheric electricity through every pore and with every breath. They also generated spontaneous electricity of their own, as a result of the friction of fluids and solids within them. Health, that "most precious of goods,"[40] depended on the maintenance of a certain electrical equilibrium appropriate to a person's age, sex, or temperament; illness resulted from the disruption of this equilibrium as a result of too much electricity, or too little. The balance could be affected by the body's internal capacity to generate spontaneous electricity of its own. More important, it could also be disturbed as changing external conditions produced variation in atmospheric electricity that would, in turn, render the body more positively or more negatively charged. Bertholon's particular claim was that he could generate negative electricity artificially to provide a therapy that would draw excess electricity from a patient's body, thereby restoring health.

Marat thought all this was nonsense and did not hesitate to say so. He decried "negative electricity" as a meaningless term and declared nonexistent the capacity of the body to produce spontaneous electricity. Above all, he considered the notion of the bodily effects of atmospheric electricity confused and absurd, a return to ancient chimeras in the face of the empirical complexities of actual medical practice. "A modern author has made [electricity] the universal medicine," he wrote in announcing his quarry; "not content to regard it as the sole remedy for our ills, he makes it also the sole preservative of our health."[41]

The *Mémoire sur l'électricité médicale* was a merciless dissection of Bertholon's work as typifying current procedures and pretensions in a field dominated by "uncertain, exaggerated, or false facts, ridiculous hypotheses, improbable conjectures, puerile reasoning, vague rules, absurd methods of administering electricity, pretended marvelous cures, etc."[42] Such practices undercut the potential benefits of medical electricity, Marat insisted, rendering it more dangerous than therapeutic and bringing it entirely into disrepute. In effect, the field did not yet exist, he argued; its potential could have been realized only in "the hands of a true doctor who had thoroughly studied the nature of the electrical fluid and its effects on the animal economy. Occupied in gathering facts and observations, or rather in establishing, multiplying, and varying them, he alone would have been able to show the cases in which application of this new remedy can become efficacious or dangerous."[43] That Marat was proclaiming himself such a doctor is evident. That he considered demolition of Bertholon's work an effective means of doing so is no less clear. Critical examination of the abbé's book was indispensable, he contended, because it brought together all that had been published on the topic, had been honored by a learned society, and had been publicized widely in the European periodicals. In its hodgepodge of assertions and claims, he found a perfect target.

As one might expect, Marat drew heavily on the arguments of his own *Recherches . . . sur l'électricité* in refuting Bertholon's theories. "I often cite this work and that is not surprising," he acknowledged, unable to suppress the obviously specious assertion that "it is the only one that contains the first known theory of electricity: a theory already adopted throughout Europe by the best physicists."[44] But the more striking fact about this violently pugilistic *Mémoire* is that it offers a window into Marat's own medical experimentation. Many of his arguments against the confused abbé Bertholon adverted to his clinical experience or to the evidence of direct medical investigation carried out in his laboratory.

In response to Bertholon's claims for the medical effects of atmospheric electricity, for example, Doctor Marat cited his own case. "Called by profession to cultivate medical electricity," he claimed, "I have passed several years in my cabinet carrying out experiments, which is to say living fifteen hours out of twenty-four in air always very impregnated with electrical fluid, and though I am of a very irritable temper and affected by a spasmatic illness in addition, I have experienced no marked effect from this way of living. Although the spasmatic outbursts from which I suffered were very regular, I did not perceive that my discomfort increased in prolonging this work, or diminished when I took the air."[45]

He could, he added, "report here observations made during six years of practice on a great number of sick persons, who passed several hours each day in a room where the air was strongly electrified." But he refrained from doing so on the grounds that these observations, though exact, were not specifically intended for this purpose. Instead, he offered the results of a carefully controlled experiment on three patients about the same age but with difficult medical conditions. "To a delicate constitution, they joined difficulties in respiration, irritation of the nerves, great sensibility to atmospheric variations." Their symptoms were recorded, all their other therapies were discontinued, and they were subjected to "the mildest means of administering electricity." Three hours a day for fifteen days, the room in which they were seated was "saturated with electricity" from a conductor hooked to a generator. (To control psychological effects, the generator was hidden in the next room to avoid stimulating their imaginations. Someone with wit was also recruited to amuse them and prevent any effects of boredom.) Asked daily if they had experienced any change in their condition, the patients responded negatively. Carefully examined at the end of the experiment, they displayed no effects. Experiments of this kind left Marat convinced, beyond any doubt, that electrical fluid in the atmosphere had no observable effect on the economy of the human body. "The influence of atmospheric electricity is nil, and the existence of spontaneous electricity chimerical: these are truths we have just established on the basis of invincible proofs. If contrary opinions have prevailed and still prevail, that simply proves that their authors know very little about the matters they undertake to treat."[46]

So much for Bertholon's theoretical claims. The second part of the *Mémoire sur l'électricité médicale* offered a painstaking analysis of the conventional procedures the good abbé recommended. Of these, the two extremes were the so-called electrical bath and the electrical shock. The bath treatment was so named because the patient (isolated, insulated, and hooked up to the conductor of an electrical generator) was presumed to be immersed in an electrical atmosphere. This was supposed to restore sensation and movement to paralyzed limbs and to heal a multitude of illnesses. In addition, a variety of beneficial effects (on circulation, respiration, and strength) had been attributed to it by experts from the abbé Nollet on. Marat's analysis of Bertholon's ideas about atmospheric electricity had, in effect, already shown the assumptions underlying this treatment to be gratuitous. He reported further experiments to bolster his utterly dismissive conclusions and to render even more ridiculous Bertholon's version of a bath circulating putative negative electricity. A passing comment on the power of the imagination also offered him an opportunity to refer the reader to his discussion of the subject in *De l'homme*, "a work far beyond everything else that has issued from my pen, and which a number of authors have put to use without citing it."[47]

At the other therapeutic extreme lay the electric shock treatment. Without condemning its use entirely, Marat emphasized the danger of this practice and denounced its ignorant, excessive, and frequently fatal use. To consider its effects, he drew on evidence from extensive laboratory experiments he had performed on animals in procedures he now hastened to justify to delicate readers. Dissection, he insisted, was the only path to truth in medicine. "Be very sure of one thing," he had written to an old friend from England (or Ireland), probably in December 1782; "one can only acquire skill or renown in this art . . . in making numerous and daily experiments directly from life." Writing in English so that his letter could be more widely circulated to other friends who knew only that language, he reported that he had found ways to secure bodies cheaply from hospitals in any quantity he desired. To experiment with living animals, he had even made an arrangement with a local butcher, "who provides me with lambs, calves, pigs, and even cattle if I need them. Since he takes them all back, I pay only for the damage to the meat." No wonder he claimed that Paris offered him great conditions for his research and urged his friend to join him there to help with his work.

The friend, apparently more tender-hearted, had expressed reluctance to see innocent animals under the knife. But Marat had learned to set his initial repugnance at vivisection aside. "It would be impossible to understand the secret, astonishing, and inexplicable marvels of the human body if one did not try to seize upon nature at work," he reasoned, "and this goal can't be achieved without doing a little evil for the sake of much good: this is the only way one can become a benefactor of humanity. Observation of the muscles and the different properties of blood have enabled me to make important discoveries I would never have achieved without severing the head and limbs of a multitude of animals." Combining his interests in criminal legislation and physiological research, he was even willing to imagine ("if I were a legislator . . . for the good of my country and of the entire world") the possibility of offering those condemned to death the option to submit to life-threatening surgical investigation in exchange for their freedom if the procedure were successful.[48]

Returning to the *Mémoire sur l'électricité médicale*, we soon find reiterated this same argument against the sway of sentiment. "Perhaps one will find that it is to pay very dearly for physiological knowledge to acquire it at the expense of pity," he acknowledged in continuing that work. "But could one resolve to torment animals without the strongest desire to be useful to men? Sensitive readers, draw the curtain over the cruelties exercised in the details that follow and see only my desire for humanity."[49] With this appeal to enlightened consciences, he launched into a description of experiments, some carried out in October 1781 and March 1782 on pigeons, a frog, a cat, and a dog, others repeated frequently over a period of ten years on sparrows, chickens, and rats, in which the animals were subjected to electrocution by shocks of varying strength, dissected, and then examined for the extent of the damage to their organs. This account was followed, first, by a report of post-mortems on humans struck by lightning and, second, by an analysis of experiments on animal flesh designed to discover the degrees to which various bodily parts and fluids transmit electricity. These latter investigations had been carried out over a period of ten years, Marat assured his readers, and always performed "on fresh animal substances at a constant air temperature of 9 degrees Réaumur."[50]

Between the electrical bath and shock treatment there was a range of more targeted electrical therapies to be analyzed. Marat considered only two of them to be potentially efficacious. One was the friction method favored in a study by Masars de Cazeles that had been published under the seal of the Royal Society of Medicine.[51] In this procedure, the affected part of the body was wrapped in flannel, then gently rubbed with an electrified metallic ring. The second was the method of drawing sparks from the affected part by moving a conductor toward it. Marat himself had reported use of this technique for treating a disease of the eye in one of his early medical pamphlets. The virtue of sparks, in his view, was that their application was strictly localized in relation to a specific part of the body (unlike the bath and the shock) and entailed no risk of doing harm, even to the most delicate patients. "They gently excite the fibres to stronger oscillations," he advised, "favor the movement of liquids, and aid organs to disgorge and de-obstruct."[52]

Having established friction, sparks, and mild-to-moderate shock treatments as the only acceptable medical uses of electricity, Marat proceeded in the final part of his *Mémoire* to consider, in great detail, the application of these methods to specific maladies. The discussion is lengthy and complex, and also cautious and nuanced, repudiating any notion of electricity as a universal remedy. "Electricity has had the fortune of all other fashionable remedies, one has believed it fit for everything," he argued. "As if electrical treatment could cure pneumonia, hydropsy, dysentry, diarrhea, putrid and bilious fevers, epidemics, plague, anthrax, smallpox, venereal and verminous diseases, cancer, aggravations of the liver or spleen, ascites, tympanitis, urinary gravel, calculi. As if it could cure illnesses arising from the plethora, exhaustion, or dissolution of fluids; from the drying out of solids, the ossification of the muscular fibers of the heart, the contraction of the nerves caused by corrosive poisons. As if it could cure illnesses arising from unnatural deformities, or the destruction of organs."[53]

The principles with which the *Mémoire sur l'électricité médicale* concludes are notable for their insistence on the vast range of maladies for which electrical treatment is at best ineffective or at worst harmful or even fatal if ignorantly or recklessly utilized. They recommend moderate, targeted treatments applying only progressively stronger doses of electricity, precisely measured and for carefully monitored periods of time, and always as part of a broader treatment of the patient. Above all, they include strong warnings against indiscriminate, ill-informed, and excessive use of shock treatment. In this they run parallel to the most enlightened medical thinking of the time, as represented by Mauduyt's *Mémoire sur les différentes manières d'administrer l'électricité* (published the same year) and Tiberius Cavallo's *Essay on the Theory and Practice of Medical Electricity* (1781) from which Mauduyt had borrowed.[54]

Against Marat's brutal, impassioned, and self-promoting critique of Bertholon's rhapsodies, we must therefore set his careful analysis of conventional electrical treatments and his cautious practical recommendations. Far from being the work of a charlatan, these suggest the reasoning of an experienced medical man suspicious of the dangers of theoretical extravagance and aggressive therapeutic practice. Not that Bertholon was prepared to yield to reason doused in vitriol. He responded violently, again and again.

JOUSTING WITH BERTHOLON

Sans was the first to attack, and quickly. His open letter in the *Année littéraire*, dated 9 May 1785, charged that Marat's rejection of conventional therapies had "returned us to the state of ignorance in which we began to apply electricity to the human body." Speaking in the name of "suffering humanity" and invoking his years of successful practice, he defended his identification of the nervous fluid with the electrical fluid as the basis for the use of the positive electrical bath in the treatment of paralysis, as of the negative in the treatment of childhood convulsions.[55] His assumptions were demolished by Marat the following month in a scathing work, *Observations de M. l'amateur Avec à M. l'Abbé Sans, sur la nécessité indispensable d'avoir une théorie solide et lumineuse, avant d'ouvrir boutique d'électricité médicale*. Its acidly ironic opening salutation, "My respect for your virtues is equaled only by my admiration for your talents," set the tone for a contemptuous critique of the dangerous and confused assumptions he found wrapped by Sans in a cloud of sentimentality.[56]

Invoked by the flailing Sans to answer for himself, Bertholon held to his vow of public silence regarding Marat for no more than a few months. A notice printed in the *Journal de médicine* in April 1785 must have offered a provocation, especially when it was republished in the *Esprit des journaux* in June and reproduced again with some revisions in the July issue of the *Journal encyclopédique de Bouillon*. It was evidently produced by someone well acquainted with Marat's work. It cited his *De l'homme* and his *Recherches . . . sur l'électricité* as proof of his mastery of the physics and physiology equally necessary to bring theoretical understanding to a subject that had grown by fits and starts only to yield vague, uncertain, and dangerous notions. It explained the nature and necessity of Marat's refutation of Bertholon's vain system, laid out his careful critique of accepted therapies, and endorsed his skepticism regarding animal magnetism. Expressing regret only that the author had failed to provide more precise descriptions of his therapeutic techniques and instruments (perhaps a teaser for another publication Marat had in mind), it justified its lengthy discussion of his book by the desire "to shed light on a branch of medicine that empiricism has abused so much and still can."[57]

A publisher's blurb for the *Mémoire sur l'électricité médicale* and the *Notions élémentaires d'optique* ("the précis of the big work M. Marat is preparing on optics, a science that he has enriched") may have strained Bertholon's forbearance to the breaking point when it appeared in the *Journal de physique* in September 1785.[58] In a letter exploding in the *Journal encyclopédique de Bouillon* in October and November, and soon reprinted in the *Esprit des journaux*, he restated his views at length, hurling in their defense a volley of citations from contemporary authorities on the subject. Marat's acerbic tone he dismissed as "the effect of an inveterate habit" his enemy had customarily exhibited "in attempting to refute Newton, Franklin, Wilke, Nollet, Le Roy, Sigaud de la Fond, and all savants in general." How, he demanded, could one take seriously the views of a man who had dismissed the research of Newton, "the finest genius of the universe, the most mathematical mind ever to exist, who had his treatise on optics printed only after forty years of experiments"? How could one take seriously the views of a man whose experiments had been dismissed by a committee of the Academy of Sciences as failing to prove what their author had imagined and as "contrary in general to what is most fully known in optics"? A coded reference to Marat's fight with Charles warned him that there were weapons of derision still remaining in Bertholon's arsenal against a man he despised as not only ignorant but mad.[59]

December brought another exasperated letter from Bertholon to the editors of the *Journal encyclopédique de Bouillon*, this one published by that journal in January 1786. It laid down an indictment of the falsifications introduced into passages from his own book that had been quoted in the account of Marat's *Mémoire sur l'électricité médicale* that the Bouillon journal had published in July. The editors excused themselves by acknowledging that the review was not their work, having been "sent to us in manuscript last June by a man no longer alive, who we are certain had not composed it and who left us ignorant of the name of the author." But Bertholon's letter pressed the point further by demonstrating that the same falsifications occurred in the text as it had been published previously in the *Journal de médicine*.

In effect, the editors had accepted not only a fraudulent text but a secondhand one at that! Its tone and the inflated claims made for the importance of Marat's research left Bertholon in no doubt that Marat himself was the author of the piece, which he had succeeded "by means it is useless to discuss, in getting into your journal after having employed the same ruses for another journal where the same extract appears . . . with the same exaggerated encomiums he gives himself, his empiricist style, his favorite and frequently repeated expressions, a certain singular turn of phrase, and the numerous alterations in citations easily recognized as his signature." This notice was Marat's alone, Bertholon insisted, because "he alone had an interest in promoting his erroneous opinions in opposition to the general doctrine; he alone was capable of altering the citations; he alone covered himself with exaggerated encomiums." Was it for Marat alone "to strip away the veil that covers the truth"? Bertholon's ideas may have been illusory, but he had caught Marat at an underhand and fraudulent game against which readers needed to be warned. "One has to be profoundly convinced of the weakness of one's case to use such devices."[60]

ELEVEN

THE FIGHT FOR GLORY

"If one has to be judged, then let it be by an enlightened and impartial public," Marat had declared in response to the dismissal of his *Découvertes . . . sur la lumière* by the Academy of Sciences. "I appeal with confidence to its tribunal, this supreme tribunal whose decrees scientific bodies themselves are forced to respect."[1] We cannot know the views of this public to which our stubborn researcher declared himself willing to submit. It was a rhetorical abstraction, an imagined authority, a public populated in Marat's own mind by those ready to endorse his arguments. It was more an effect to be created than a tribunal whose judgment could be declared.

How might an injured author give force to such a claim? What support could he find once his discoveries had been so decisively dismissed by the most prestigious scientific body in Europe? What resources could he deploy in his continuing fight for glory? He had his pen above all—that would rarely lie at rest! The true thinker, as his then friend Jacques-Pierre Brissot would tell him, had to direct public opinion, not subject himself to it. "It is by the constancy of his work and the conviction of his opinions that the philosopher eventually succeeds in mastering public opinion; then he enjoys a greater empire than the most despotic sovereign. He commands public opinion and public opinion commands the entire universe."[2] But the pen alone was not enough for this purpose. Friends and patrons had to be mobilized, personal connections activated. The manifold sites and situations of a densely variegated social, institutional, and commercial world had to be exploited. And in 1782, though no one yet knew it, Marat still had seven years to do this before the entire web of that world imploded.

Among the companions the maligned researcher could call upon, the faithful Filassier had already given a public lecture course in Paris to publicize the results of Marat's experiments on fire. Another friend, the abbé Miollan, would resort to the same method to popularize Marat's theories of optics.[3] Allies elsewhere were also eager to spread the teaching of his ideas. The pioneering balloonist Pilâtre de Rozier had claimed some proselytes and promised more if Marat would send apparatus to demonstrate his experiments on fire.[4] Paté, a physics teacher from Châlons sur Marne, traveled to Paris for the principal purpose of discussing his ideas with the master. More significantly, Pahin de La Blancherie, the intellectual entrepreneur behind a new-model public salon taken up in the creation of so-called *musées* in the 1780s, invited him to present his ideas to this novel weekly assembly for the promotion of science, literature, and the arts.[5]

This invitation to speak may have been prompted by Jacques-Pierre Brissot, who probably made La Blancherie's acquaintance in late 1779 when he was introduced into the circle of the geographer Edmé Mentelle, professor at the Ecole Militaire. Like Marat a member of the extended household of the comte d'Artois, whom he served as official historian, Mentelle was a key figure in a network around Artois and his cousin, the duc de Chartres (later duc d'Orléans), with which Brissot remained closely associated in the years preceding the French Revolution. Brissot gave the impression in his *Mémoires* that he had introduced Marat to Mentelle and his group, though it is possible, given the Artois connection, that Marat was already moving in that circle. In any case, Brissot's papers make clear that he and Marat bonded within that group until he left Paris for England in November 1782.[6]

One of the efforts to spread word of Marat's research on optics seems indeed to have originated from within the Mentelle circle. Appearing in the *Nouvelles de la république des lettres et des arts*, a journal edited by Pahin de La Blancherie as the organ of his "general assembly," it opened with an article on 21 November 1781 announcing that "of so many authors who have attacked Newton's theory of colors, M. Marat alone has taken the true route, the only one that could be successful." As a result of Marat's experiments ("a spectacle as striking as it is enchanting"), this notice explained, the effect of gravity on light had been made visible, a new law of optics had been revealed, the different refrangibility of light rays had been rendered chimerical, and the way had been opened to the manufacture of achromatic lenses toward which he planned to direct future research. A brief preview of Marat's *Recherches physiques sur l'électricité* followed.[7]

"And wouldn't you know, now they're trying to shout us down," the *Nouvelles* expostulated on 1 December. The initial article praising Marat had clearly incited some pushback. "Whatever your motives," the unnamed critics were answered, "whether to find a quarrel with us or start one with M. Marat, we can't silence everything relating to the sciences and the arts that will get publicity or need it." The fact that the Academy of Sciences had dismissed Marat's experiments on light must have been raised at a meeting of Pahin's group, prompting a statement by Pahin on the role of academies. The substance of these remarks remains unclear, but, given the dependence of Pahin's assembly on the Paris Academy's approval, they were doubtless respectful of that body's authority. Endorsed in the journal but without being repeated, his statement was countered in effect by a declaration of independence. "We will always be ready to serve, with all our zeal, individuals who may mistake the truth in their research but consecrate their fortune and youth to it, thereby meriting the esteem and the praise of the Republic [of Letters]. And is it not the case that errors have often led us to the truth?" Walking this tightrope, the *Nouvelles* reprinted the Academy's judgment of Marat's work, but it countered on 30 January 1782 with a lengthy article on his research on combustion and, again, on 20 March 1782 with a report of a demonstration of his electrical experiments and an account of the conclusions he had drawn from them. An even longer summary of the *Recherches . . . sur l'électricité* appeared on 15 May 1782.[8]

The authorship of these articles is uncertain, though Brissot seems likely to have had some responsibility for them. Marat doubtless pressed other friends, allies, and patrons into service during the early years of the 1780s and could well have done so here. But of all the support he received during this period the most energetic came from the ambitious intellectual ten years his junior who would eventually become the principal Girondin leader. Brissot's memoirs offer the fullest contemporary account of Marat's situation and personality at this time. They need to be read with suspicion, but they do offer a glimpse of an intense intimacy, even if evoked later in the light of bitter estrangement.

The two men had much in common. Both were deeply inspired by Rousseau. Both dreamed of glory; both were passionate about legal reform; both saw England as a land of opportunity where one could be useful to the human race; both contemplated returning there. Sharing a knowledge of English, they talked of collaborating on a translation of Milton, a project Brissot had picked up but one scarcely to their taste. It was eventually dropped, to their mutual irritation.

Revealing himself to be "a fervent apostle of liberty," Brissot recalled, Marat regaled the younger man in their first meetings with stories of the sensation caused by publication of *The Chains of Slavery* and the civic honors accorded him thereafter by several English cities. He also bragged about his financial success as a fashionable Parisian physician, a career he was now sacrificing to the search for scientific truth. In addition, he intimated his adventure with Angelica Kauffman in London (or so Brissot says) and the complaisance with which Mme de l'Aubespine had welcomed him in Paris to her home and her bed. The latter relationship appeared improbable to Brissot. How, he recollected maliciously, could this little man so resembling an organ grinder's monkey have attracted a woman of such delicacy and charm? He could only explain the liaison by portraying as abandoned, betrayed, and infected by a perfidious husband this aristocratic lady so "sweet, lovable, good, [while] there was nothing so rough, so violent, so savage in domestic life as Marat."[9]

Brissot was nonetheless taken with the older man. In excuse, he subsequently declared himself "always credulous." Only later, however, reflecting on his dealings with this "odious man" over the longer term, did he become convinced of the "charlatanism that has, his whole life, directed and concealed his actions and his writings."[10]

Brissot's commitment to proselytizing Marat's theories is evident from a letter he sent him from Lyon in June 1782. He was circulating copies of a prospectus to persons and institutions that could afford to buy the apparatus necessary to demonstrate Marat's experiments, he wrote, and he was doing the rounds of the booksellers, though presumably on his own account as well as Marat's. But the going was rough. "You have enemies in the provinces, my dear, as you do in the capital." One target, the professor of physics at the Collège de l'Oratoire, was "an old papa who gives demonstrations very badly, and is two hundred leagues from your ideas. I am preaching nonetheless that your books will become classics and I will get information here about all the correspondents with the other college." A piece intended for the *Journal de Paris* had apparently misfired, but Brissot assured his friend that he was pressing his cause. "I am dining these days with a big bookseller and will do what I can to make arrangements. In your case, they object that in the provinces books on physics don't sell like novels."[11] Marat had challenges like this in mind when he prepared a brief text, *Notions élémentaires d'optique*, published in 1784, to summarize his theories and describe the nature and availability of the apparatus necessary to replicate his experiments. This booklet, he avowed, appeared thanks to "a distinguished Amateur whose enlightened zeal for the propagation of useful knowledge is well known."[12]

When he wrote this letter, Brissot was returning to Paris after a provincial circuit with a few pieces of writing accomplished, many projects in mind, and growing contacts with the publishers at the mighty Société typographique de Neuchâtel for which Marat's father had once spied. Smarting from the legal profession's hostile reaction to his book on the reform of criminal law, he was abandoning his plan to train for the bar and striving instead to make up for his ignorance of the natural sciences by following public lecture courses in anatomy, chemistry, and physics and networking with the scientists around Mentelle. Exhilarated though he was by Fourcroy's chemical researches, Marat's very different experiments piqued his curiosity, and he was impressed by the researcher's proud resolve.

Full of enthusiasm in 1782, he rushed to bring acquaintances to Marat's laboratory and talk up the latter's discoveries in the intellectual circle surrounding Mentelle. Neither of these strategies seems to have worked. He would later say that visitors to the laboratory were as offended by the researcher as they were interested in the research. According to this later Brissot, Marat expressed himself with difficulty, his ideas were confused, and he was so touchy that he fell into a rage at the least hint of indifference or disagreement, thus losing the thread of his thought in the process. Among the visitors he brought to the laboratory Brissot recalled the celebrated Alessandro Volta, eager to see experiments that purportedly negated Franklin's electrical theories but offered insults rather than reasons by their author in response to critical questions. There was Mercier, too, he of the famous *Tableau de Paris* first published in 1781; he met Marat once, only to hide thereafter at the very sight of him.[13] But there were others among the visitors Brissot claimed to have introduced to Marat who did become his friends and admirers, among them the abbé Louis-Antoine Miollan and the mysterious baron Etienne Claude de Marivetz, whose strange works on the *Physique du monde* were subsequently filled with laudatory references to Marat's research.[14]

The chief result of Brissot's canvassing for Marat among the Mentelle circle was a "long and too vehement argument" with the mathematician Laplace (also Lavoisier's collaborator, as we have seen) that Brissot would quickly make public—eventually to his own regret. "To the mathematician, my panegyric of a man endowed with talent whom I found it unjust to treat as an imbecile made me look like a fanatic who understood nothing of logic or the sciences. We didn't talk for several years."[15]

Brissot was struck, above all, by Marat's singleness of purpose. Hard on others, he remembered, his new friend was no less demanding of himself. He devoted all his resources to his physical experiments, repeating them day and night, content to subsist on bread and water for the sake of humiliating the Academy of Sciences. He dreamed of avenging himself against the academicians; he burned only with the desire to overthrow their most revered idol, Newton.

Brissot was convinced, too, that Marat was indeed being treated unjustly by the academicians in reaction to his antisocial behavior, his "immoderate pride" and "scandalous diatribes." He saw them as relentless in attacking Marat's work, never granting it the least novelty; they didn't even want his name pronounced, "so afraid were they to contribute by their criticism to his repute."[16] New to the world of scientific competition, Brissot believed one owed at least some measure of esteem to a man who had buried himself in his darkroom for several years to push back the frontiers of knowledge. Not that this was really Marat's intention, the future Girondin eventually concluded. To combat and destroy the reputation of famous men, he decided, was instead the dominant passion at work here. Marat's sole concern was for his own glory; he wanted only to make a reputation for himself that would outrank all others; he was entirely occupied with himself, his discoveries, and the celebrity he imagined was his due.[17] But this acid judgment Brissot reserved for the future. In 1782, he made Marat's defense a central element in a book he quickly published, *De la vérité, ou Méditations sur les moyens de parvenir à la vérité dans toutes les connaissances humaines*. Among the most successful publications of the Société typographique de Neuchâtel, at least in Paris, it offered a powerful early version of the diatribes against the despotism of the academies that would eventually prepare their destruction by the French Revolution a decade later.[18]

THE MARCH OF REASON? MARAT AS VICTIM

With its title an implicit rejoinder to the rational system-building of Malebranche's *De la recherché de la vérité*, Brissot's manifesto offered itself as a kind of handbook for the would-be philosophe, with recommendations regarding how he should live in public, private, and political life. Not that the book went much beyond a hodgepodge of Enlightenment themes regarding the search for truth, the desire to be useful, and the love of humanity as the marks of the true philosopher. Observation, analysis, and epistemological modesty were its philosophical mantras. As had d'Alembert in the *Discours préliminaire* of the *Encyclopédie*, and Diderot in the article defining the goal of that great work, Brissot imagined a universal system of knowledge that would place man at the center of all that is. "The totality of human knowledge can be conceived as a perfect system of ramifications multiplied to infinity, all emanating from a common center. Place an individual at this center, give him senses numerous and good enough to grasp all its links instantaneously: that will be the universal savant." But this ideal, Brissot emphasized, was also an impossibility; humans could not aspire to the holistic divine perspective envied by the rationalists. Human senses were too limited, human reasoning too weak, human passions too strong. Even the Baconian project of collective investigation could lead only to the massive accumulation of error. "Universal knowledge is thus a chimera."[19]

These considerations led Brissot to a skeptical view of claims that his own century was the dawn of a new age. "Academic speeches have predicted the birth of the happy day when truth will govern all minds; the academies have been congratulated for accelerating the approach of this brilliant epoch through their work. . . . This is the philosophical century: the enthusiasts have said so, and a thousand echoes have repeated it."[20] When he wrote these words, Brissot may well have had in mind the paean to progress Condorcet had given that same year in his reception speech at the Académie française. *De la vérité* was, in any case, a vehement repudiation of the official culture of the academies that Condorcet represented. It was also a passionate embrace of Rousseau, the great heretic of the Enlightenment denounced by the philosophes—in a litany Brissot bitterly intoned—as a liar, defamer, hypocrite, villain, and madman. "I have the misfortune to love, to adore this madman, and I share this affliction with a host of sensitive and virtuous souls," he proclaimed; "this is not for his style, it's for his virtue."[21]

With this declaration, Brissot launched into a Rousseauian attack on the cultural phenomena of modern society: the explosion in the number of published books ("harmful to the progress of knowledge"); the proliferation of dictionaries and journals ("the two most fatal scourges that have desolated the empire of letters"); the expansion of public lecture courses ("a conduit of error") that enriched lecturers while spreading an incomprehensible jumble of scientific knowledge.[22] Distrust of the commercialization of modern society lay at the heart of this critique: it had meant the rise of charlatanry and the dissemination of ignorance. This was not the progress of knowledge, Brissot protested, but its systematic corruption. And at the heart of this nefarious system, brandishing Rousseau's *Emile*, he found the academies. "It is undeniable, said a great man whose works I will never stop reading and citing, that the learned societies of Europe are only public schools of lies; and there are certainly more errors in the Academy of Sciences than among the entire Huron people."[23]

The conviction that the proliferation of academies subverts the search for truth lay at the very heart of *De la vérité*. And it was expressed in a language surely meant to evoke the tones of Rousseau's *Discourse on the Origins of Inequality*. "The first man who, to perfect the sciences, imagined the idea of gathering together those who cultivated them, knew little of human nature and the scientific spirit," Brissot announced. "He did not know that the first degree of corruption was not exactly the establishment of societies but the gathering of men into cities. He did not know that the more human beings are united in great masses the more they are corrupted, and that this vice inherent in large societies reappears also in particular ones." The merest glance should have revealed separate bodies within each state "all agitated by the same spirit of intrigue, baseness, and cabal . . . [and] the useful man, the superior man, everywhere crushed by the crowd of useless and mediocre beings." It should have made obvious that crowding savants together into corporate bodies enfeebled and corrupted science just as crowding individuals into urban ant hills robbed them of their vigor.[24]

Corporate bodies, Brissot therefore insisted, could only undermine the progress of knowledge by increasing mediocrity and oppressing true originality. The Ancients had known no such institutions. They had understood that true genius was rare and mediocrity common; that men of genius had no need of official institutions to attract followers who made no claim to be their equals. Only the moderns had introduced into the empire of the sciences "a kind of elective aristocracy, which supposes that each century produces a certain quantity of perfectly equal minds [and] that these electors are constantly guided by the spirit of justice and of truth." To do this was a double absurdity. "The empire of the sciences must know neither despots nor aristocrats nor electors. It presents the image of a perfect republic, where usefulness confers the only title to honor. To admit a despot, or aristocrats, or electors, who put their official seal on the productions of genius, violates the nature of things and the liberty of the human mind. It is an assault on public opinion, which alone has the right to crown genius; it introduces a revolting despotism . . . delays the progress of the sciences and harms the search for truth."[25]

Make your way through the modern capital cities, Brissot urged his readers, frequent the academies, attend their official functions, watch their working committees. Shadow the academicians in their social lives and public appearances; don't be taken in by the ceremonial speeches, the praise showered on them by society women and repeated by a thousand ignorant echoes. Do all this and "you will see adroit charlatans who know how to impose upon the public by means of their brilliant veneer, after having been themselves imposed upon; you will see them run after glory, after fortune. But what of the simple man who seeks the truth in good faith and without ostentation? Where is he?"[26] Such a man was nowhere to be found in the academies, Brissot insisted, whether those of the great modern capitals or in the provincial backwaters upon which Brissot poured even more of the acid of disdain.

For Brissot, academies meant intellectual despotism and its consequences: scientific sterility, the death of innovation, the tyranny of conformity. To his mind, nothing exemplified this fact more clearly than the trajectory of Newtonianism in France's leading scientific body, the Paris Academy of Sciences. Long resisted by the Cartesians, Newton's ideas had now become the new orthodoxy. "Today the name of Newton has become, as was Aristotle's in times past, the signal of persecution."[27] Errors this great man would retract if he were alive were now defended as a matter of esprit de corps. Adopting Newton's doctrine as furiously as they once resisted it, the Paris academicians now persecuted anyone who dared repeat his experiments, disconfirm them, and refute the theory they were held to support.

To make his case, Brissot apostrophized with the familiar "tu" (soon to be the democratic revolutionary form of address) the man who had dared to challenge their authority: "Thou whom nature has endowed with the genius of observation and an indefatigable ardor for the search for truth; thou who, believing only in experiment and not in names or prescription, has courageously overthrown the idol of the academic cult and substituted a system of well proven, well explained facts for Newton's errors regarding light! If the scientific Sanhedrin, enslaved to ancient belief, has condemned thee, posterity will not ratify its shaky judgment; await all justice from its judgment. The truth can be combated by corporate bodies; but the ephemeral publications of these sadly immortal bodies disappear, and the truth remains." The identity of this persecuted genius can easily be guessed. Brissot, in any case, was not reticent in mentioning his name. "I only cite here the story of this celebrated physicist, M. Marat, to whose philosophy and investigations I am pleased to render justice. I could cite a hundred others, but this one is enough for me to conclude that in fact academies rise up against innovations, and consequently their spirit is contrary to the search for truth, because only the taste for innovation can bring the man of talent to it."[28]

Condorcet would respond to Brissot a couple of years later, in a letter prompted by statements in the periodical the latter was then editing from London, the *Journal de la Lycée de Londres*. "You seem to me to be a bit prejudiced against the academies," wrote the secretary of the Academy of Sciences; "you believe them animated by a corporate spirit that renders them difficult. I would reproach them rather with being too easy. The business of M. Marat is a proof of that. The academy's only mistake was to have given the impression of welcoming experiments that were presented as new but were known, their only novelty being the systematic jargon in which the author had wrapped them." Academies served as a constant barrier to charlatanism of every kind, Condorcet maintained, and they rendered their members independent of popular opinion. "A member of an academy has no need to play the charlatan to enjoy a reputation as a savant among the ignorant. It is then up to his works to earn him fame or glory."[29]

But Brissot had already made up his mind to the contrary in 1782. It could not be claimed that academies protected merit, he charged in *De la vérité*; to the contrary, they destroyed merit by shielding it from attack. For Brissot as for Marat, science was inherently agonistic. Genius achieved force only in proportion to the resistance it encountered; the spirit of independence and the need for glory were its two most powerful springs. The academician, by contrast, was a sluggish slave impervious to the spur of true glory. Why should one be surprised that it was impossible to cite a single useful book, or a single useful invention, produced by an academy? Nor, fortunately, could it really be said that academies functioned to govern public opinion. Quite to the contrary, it was the enlightened public that presented academies with the men they must welcome; it was the disinterested public that assessed new theories, ranked them after long deliberation, and forced their acceptance upon academies that were, like all corporate bodies, motivated by the competition of petty interests. Multiplication of academies and academic prizes did not produce geniuses; it merely created "a host of mediocre men of letters, rampant insects, that destroy fertility while appearing to support it."[30]

In this diagnosis, the harm done by official academies went beyond the realm of the sciences. It was telling, Brissot thought, that monarchies teemed with these noxious institutions while England—where liberty flourished along with scientific innovation—had only a couple. It was telling that the Académie française had been Richelieu's creation. That adroit minister had understood the value of academies in tranquilizing inquiring minds and diverting them from dangerous political truths; he saw their uses for the mastery of public opinion; he saw in their institution "a new spring for his despotism."[31]

Of all the academicians, Brissot pilloried the mathematicians as most presumptuous and dogmatic in making everything in Newton an article of faith. To clinch his case, he reported a version of his earlier debate with Laplace, now represented as an encounter between "a skeptic" and a mathematician dismissing as an imbecile a physicist whose experiments on light had contradicted Newton's. It is worth quoting at length, not only for its disgust at academic despotism but for its distrust of the mathematicizing spirit.

THE SKEPTIC: Newton was a *man*, and *subject to error*. . . . Descartes was mistaken . . . why could Newton not be mistaken? Were all the academicians imbeciles in 1710 because they persecuted the Newtonians?

THE MATHEMATICIAN: But Newton's errors were soon recognized.

THE SKEPTIC: Only after they had been defended for fifty years. . . .

THE MATHEMATICIAN: But [Newton's] detractors are obscure, and Newton enjoys universal support.

THE SKEPTIC: Were not Newton and Descartes obscure before they became famous? . . .

THE MATHEMATICIAN: But if I prove to you mathematically that his system is true, are you not forced to agree that his detractors are imbeciles?

THE SKEPTIC: But these detractors also inherit their mathematical books. What to do in this chaos of figures? Return to nature, observe the fact, because the fact is the basis for the calculation. If the fundamental fact is false, all the calculations fall; and if the calculations prove the truth of this false fact what then do you want to call mathematics? I'd rather believe my senses and nature than your volumes of figures.

THE MATHEMATICIAN: So you also doubt mathematical certainty?

THE SKEPTIC: This is not the place to proffer my opinion; but I believe that when the calculations rest on the facts it is necessary, before accepting the calculations, to verify the fact. . . . Whether the experiments of the modern physicist are true, whether he has reduced seven primary colors to three, whether the solar spectrum is composed of three colors, whether it is formed simply by the decomposition of light at the borders of the hole through which the ray passes; whether the prism decomposes, whether the rays are all equally refrangible: these are the facts in question. Now the modern physicist bases his new opinions on a host of direct experiments. He has a conclusive one proving, for example, that light does not decompose as it passes from one medium to another because with a prism it produces a bundle of white rays impossible to decompose. These facts are false, absurd, impossible.

You're like the sixteenth-century theologians who believe that by multiplying words they are piling up reasons. But have you seen these experiments . . . ?

THE MATHEMATICIAN: I have no need to see, to read, or to hear.

These ideas contradict Newton, the academy, my calculations: thus they are absurd and I have no need to examine them. . . .

THE SKEPTIC: This was exactly the reasoning of the Aristotelians against Descartes. . . . Newton's name must not dispense one from examining. Before judging you have to see, read, and hear.

THE MATHEMATICIAN: My God! What will become of us if everything has to be examined!

THE SKEPTIC: I agree that the task is burdensome. But if, as you say so extravagantly, the academy is the sovereign tribunal consecrated to judging the progress of human knowledge, recognizing new truths, and setting error aside; if you its members are the judges of writers, should you not hear them before you condemn them? . . . In a word, you owe the people enlightenment. Your doctrine is attacked from all sides; how do you not enter the lists; how do you not destroy these experiments, these new theories? What should the public think, in seeing you refuse combat and maintain a cowardly silence? You drag yourself from your mind-numbing sleep only to command a blind faith. Is that the march of reason?[32]

By his own admission, Brissot was a scientific neophyte. But his rhetoric turned Marat into the perfect Rousseauian victim. He found the corruption of humanity as it was herded into the great cities of modern civilization exemplified by the institutionalization of academies in a society where the pursuit of truth had been sacrificed to the greed for power, prestige, and profit. He found in the academicians' persecution of his friend the proof that genius had been overwhelmed by mediocrity, virtue undermined by conformity, and the agonistic struggle for glory nullified in the name of enlightenment. Marat, like Rousseau, was declared a victim of modern society as it was emerging in the perverted form of the Old Regime.

WORKING THE PRESS

Not surprisingly, Marat was delighted with *De la vérité*. Reading it only after "a long and cruel illness"—a harbinger, perhaps, of the notorious affliction he suffered in later years—he declared himself entertained by the dialogue between the skeptic and the mathematician, but even more gratified by the way his friend had conducted his defense. "You know, my dear one, the place you occupy in my heart," he wrote to Brissot, by then in London. "If any praise can flatter, it's that given by an enlightened friend. After your friendship, your esteem is the most flattering thing for me, if there can be one without the other. Accept, my very dear one, my sincere thanks for the obliging efforts you have been willing to make in support of my works, and continue your good offices; one needs a friend's zeal when one has so powerful a faction to combat."

His affairs were taking a turn for the better, Marat reported, though he would make the decision to return to London unless that trend continued. In the meantime, he pressed Brissot to scout out English journals that could publish favorable reviews of his research and to spread news of his discoveries in other ways. "Maty's journal, the *Westminster Magazine*, and the other English journals are not to be scorned," Marat urged. "I have written to Wirchaux, who has asked me for extracts. Repeat my experiments well. If you can place a certain number of copies of my books with Elmsley, let me know and I will send them to the address you indicate. Write to me often and see if some Englishman would like to translate my research on fire and electricity; I will send you corrected copies."[33]

Brissot published this letter in his *Mémoires* as an illustration of how tiresomely self-centered and exploitative his former friend became. Marat had bombarded him (unsuccessfully) for introductions to Fourcroy and Lavoisier, Brissot complained, even as he was passing along an article denouncing the latter as a plagiarist. Conscious of his difficulties in expressing himself, he had begged Brissot to become his ghost writer. This Brissot had refused, but he had nevertheless served Marat frequently as a kind of publicist.

> Marat had very clearly grasped that the journalists were the privileged distributors of reputations, but his arrogance, his insolence, his pretentions left him shunned by all who sought him out. He knew that I was acquainted with some of them, and I believe I owe to this circumstance rather than to his esteem the kind of attachment he showed me for a number of years. He constantly sent me extracts, panegyrics of his works written by himself. I could not conceive of someone having the impudence to sing his own praises in this way; but thinking only of the injustice of which I thought him the victim, I used all my zeal to give his works publicity, and I often succeeded. . . . I allowed myself to pare down his exaggerations, especially in the praise.[34]

So, the campaign for Marat's theories on light (as for his other works) also comprised a systematic effort to work the periodical press by feeding it extracts and reviews. Journalists, those "privileged distributors of reputations," were eager to receive copy that they often reproduced from journal to journal. Among the first notices of the *Découvertes . . . sur la lumière* was a substantial article in the issue of the *Journal de littérature, des sciences et des arts* for September–October 1780. It praised the work in lavish terms as "destined to produce a striking revolution in the most sublime of the exact sciences and to illuminate the majority of the great phenomena of nature astronomers still seek to understand." After years in which physicists had merely repeated Newton's experiments while adding nothing to his theory of color, readers were told, Marat's unusual sagacity and indefatigable activity had transformed optics into a fundamentally new science. "By returning to the truth a matter regarding which, following Newton, all physicists have gone wrong," the journal predicted, "M. Marat will have the glory of lifting the greatest obstacle to the perfection of dioptric instruments; the work this profound physicist announces on this subject can only be awaited with extreme impatience."[35]

Not to be outdone in spreading enthusiasm for Marat's work, the *Journal encyclopédique de Bouillon* offered another lengthy review in December 1780 to celebrate his discovery of "a new law of optics of which we had not the faintest idea." "A method that renders intuitive truths whose existence was never even suspected must change the face of physics," the writer insisted. "Thus the majority of those who cultivate this science have rushed to adopt the method of observation in the dark room that Marat has invented." Never had a theory seemed better founded than on Newton's optical discoveries, the writer opined, but the intrepid Marat had shown them to be illusory. In this account, he was claimed as the very model of the enlightened researcher. He had turned to nature rather than to books that perpetuate erroneous opinions "until the arrival of some original author who opens the eyes of the servile multitude." At the same time, he was far from being a mindless empiricist thoughtlessly piling experiment upon experiment. "The facts, although the only source of all our knowledge, always become a fertile source of errors when one doesn't know the art of analyzing them: Marat possesses this art to the highest degree, thus he achieves the most brilliant successes."[36]

The language of this Bouillon review was close enough at some points to that in the *Journal de littérature, des sciences et des arts* that the two might well have come from the same source. Its similarity to the notice published by the *Mercure de France* on 17 March 1781 is even more striking: the two reviews were almost identical.[37] (They were destined to be recycled again, in any case, in the July 1782 issue of the *Esprit des journaux*.)[38] Yet even the *Journal de physique*, which had been critical of Marat's fire experiments, now swelled the chorus of praise for his optical research. "With the aid of an apparatus astonishing in its simplicity, Marat has found the art of making light a spectacle as striking as it is enchanting," it reported in January 1781 after declaring in its turn that Marat had rendered Newton's views on refraction chimerical. "These discoveries, for a long time under the eyes of Messieurs of the Academy of Sciences, have just been made public in print. From the favorable response to the author's first discoveries one can judge the curiosity they must excite."[39]

Apparent evidence of that curiosity—or perhaps it was simply an effort to keep Marat's research in the public eye—emerged when a letter to the *Journal de littérature, des sciences et des arts* "from your subscribers" called publicly on Marat in April 1781 to carry out further experimentation to extend his analyses. "The revolution that M. Marat has just produced in optics has made such a great sensation among the physicists who cultivate this science that they have not yet recovered from their astonishment," the letter proclaimed. "Even those least persuaded by innovations cannot deny that since the publication of his *Lumière* Newton has lost the finest jewel in his crown." There followed a further letter from a vicomte de Montigni, apparently an early supporter, pointing to the possibilities for producing aesthetic objects opened up by Marat's optical research.[40]

Further urging of Marat to advance his research, especially in a way that would make possible the construction of achromatic lenses, soon came from the *Année littéraire* in June 1781. "Under the pen of this ingenious physicist, optics has become a new science," this journal declared. "The greatest part of Newton's optics is intended to establish the different refrangibility of heterogeneous rays and never has a theory appeared to be established on the basis of more complete proofs; but our skillful physicist analyses the experiments of the English philosopher and shows that they are defective, complicated and illusory. . . . After demonstrating that in the Newtonian experiments light is not decomposed by the prism and that it is never decomposed when refracted in a good quality and well polished glass, the author shows that the aberration of refractibility is an opinion without foundation; thus the construction of achromatic lenses would require another theory. Having lifted the greatest obstacle to the perfection of dioptric instruments, M. Marat offers us hope of a work directly on this important object. We urge him to publish it as soon as possible; it can only be favorably received."[41]

The barrage of notices of the *Découvertes . . . sur la lumière* was already ebbing by October 1782 when *The Monthly Review*—perhaps thanks to Brissot—turned British attention toward a second edition of this work. It had sold out almost immediately upon publication, remarked the author of this lengthy review, not surprisingly since it announced "a new revolution in optics and an attempt to dispossess our immortal NEWTON of one of his most brilliant acquisitions in the field of science." The reviewer deemed this challenge a serious one: what the boldest and best-armed Cartesians had failed to achieve in the course of a thirty-year contest was now being attempted again "with a fresh legion of experiments and observations to renew the combat and establish a new standard." Marat's claims to prove the Newtonian theory of differential refraction illusory held immense theoretical and technological implications, the review emphasized. "The adversary is bold even to temerity; yet his experiments are specious and alluring, and his observations are subtle and ingenious." Experimenters could indeed deceive; the value of experiments themselves could be undermined by their thoughtless accumulation in the absence of "the momentous art of analyzing them" (a consideration apparently borrowed from the *Journal encyclopédique de Bouillon* review). Nonetheless, the review concluded, "we think, that the experiments of M. MARAT have a peculiar title to a free trial."[42]

PROVINCIAL FORAYS

Marat thought so, too. But beyond the press, there was another court of appeal. A potential audience could be found in the network of provincial academies that had spread throughout France in the eighteenth century—a veritable archipelago of enlightenment dedicated to cultivating the arts and sciences, spreading useful truths, and stimulating public discussion. As we have seen, the signature device of these local academies was the prize-essay contest—best remembered today for the questions (first on the utility of the arts and sciences, then on the origins of inequality) that elicited from Jean-Jacques Rousseau the denunciations of modern civilization that launched his career and condemned him (so he thought) to a literary life bringing fame, persecution, and misery in equal proportions.

Marat was less ambivalent about prize-essay competitions. He did not hesitate to seek in the provincial arenas the recognition denied him in the capital. He explained his strategy later, in a volume bringing together essays on optics he had submitted to provincial academies in the years following the appearance of the *Découvertes . . . sur la lumière*. Convinced that the results of his experiments were destined to "change the face of optics" and eager to demonstrate them rigorously, he explained that "I made them the subject of several [prize-essay] programs, incorporated them into specific essays, and provoked their examination by learned companies." To do this required the help of "some friends of the truth who took an interest in the progress of the sciences, and they chose the academies where I could not flatter myself that I would find many supporters."[43]

Anonymity was a necessary element of this strategy. Marat's entries were written pseudonymously and submitted by others on his behalf.

"Such is the empire of outmoded opinions that an innovator without intrigue, without a party, without extravagant eulogists, is often reduced to hiding to escape persecution: but this is not the place to expose the hidden intrigues of my adversaries." That being said, he could not resist another paranoid outburst: "They are agitating more and more to close the journals to me. . . . In the meantime, let them not flatter themselves that they will wear me down: one is not made to be the apostle of the truth if one lacks the courage to be its martyr."[44] *Vitam impendere vero!*

This was Marat's defiant stance in 1788, five years after he had begun his campaign for recognition of his research by the provincial academies. Earlier, he had submitted his plan for the reform of criminal law to the Economic Society of Berne, and he appears soon to have sent an *Eloge de Montesquieu* to the Academy of Bordeaux.[45] Neither of these would meet with success. But the initial responses to his scientific writings were more encouraging. In 1783, responding to a prize-essay contest on the medical uses of electricity and magnetism announced by the Academy of Rouen, he had submitted anonymously (through the good offices of another friend, the baron de Feldenfeld) the lengthy study of medical electricity discussed in the previous chapter. His was declared the winning submission despite the Academy's disapproval of the aggressive tone it adopted against one of its own members, the abbé Bertholon. Once identified as its author, Marat claimed the prize and an accompanying medal; he also took the opportunity to send the Academy's secretary (with a show of modesty we have seen before) a handsomely bound set of his books on fire, light, and electricity—"a little offering that I place by your hand upon the altar of the sciences."[46] As already seen, however, he did not fail to rebut the Academy's criticism of the tone of his essay when it was published anonymously in 1784 as *Mémoire sur l'électricité médicale, couronné le 6 août 1783, par l'Académie des belles lettres, sciences et arts de Rouen*. "I read my essay carefully and found not a single term that should be avoided by a self-respecting author," he insisted. "It would have been lacking in zeal for humanity to soften the refutation of a system that could become dangerous as a result of the ill-considered praise it has received."[47] Characteristically, Marat did not mince his words.

His foray into the provincial scene made a bitter enemy for Marat in the person of Bertholon, with whom he carried on an intellectual feud for several years. It also found him a friend and intellectual ally in Dom François-Philippe Gourdin, a Benedictine monk and man of letters who played a leading role among the Rouen academicians. A protégé of Le Cat, the academy's most illustrious member, Gourdin had, like Marat, written an essay on the nervous fluid while remaining fervent in his repudiation of materialism. Gourdin fought hard if unsuccessfully, in 1784, to award Marat the prize (or at least an honorable mention) for an essay in another Rouen competition on the means of bringing the *Encyclopédie* to its highest possible point of perfection. (The essay, savage as one might expect, advocated eviscerating Diderot and d'Alembert's text.) More important, he financed another prize-essay contest specifically tailored to give Marat "the opportunity to develop his system against Newton's optics."[48] The topic, announced on 3 August 1785, was to determine the true causes of the colors appearing in plates of glass, soap bubbles, and other diaphanous materials, phenomena hitherto explained by the Newtonian doctrine of differential refrangibility that had now been "brought into question." Contestants were warned that the Academy would "reject all hypotheses without exception and accept as proof of their assertions only simple and unvarying facts."[49]

With his friend financing the prize, serving on the evaluation committee, and writing the report, it is scarcely surprising that Marat was declared the winner of the competition on 2 August 1786. (He turned back the medal, thus allowing Gourdin to underwrite yet another essay contest, this time on the adequacy of the experimental basis for the modern theory of latent heat, a topic that was possibly tilted against Lavoisier. Marat's entry, now lost, won that contest too!) Gourdin's report acknowledged that Marat's theory of color was "absolutely opposed to Newton's and not yet proven demonstratively." It stated nonetheless that the theory appeared to be "based on numerous and varied facts," which the committee had verified in thirty-two of the experiments described. Marat's conclusions might remain open to challenge, the report hazarded, "but what theory invented by men has attained mathematical certainty?" In awarding the prize, Gourdin reassured his colleagues, the Academy was not adopting the author's opinion as its own. "But if the revolution that seems to be approaching in the science of optics succeeds, if a new doctrine does replace Newton's . . . , it will be glorious, I think, Gentlemen, that the Academy of Rouen will have crowned the efforts of whoever will have contributed to effect this revolution that is more important than one imagines for the perfection of dioptrics and catoptrics."[50]

When, in 1788, Marat eventually published this essay on the theory of color in his volume of *Mémoires académiques*, he also charged Gourdin to publicize the appearance of that work in the *Journal de Normandie*. Gourdin complied with a long, enthusiastic letter that also condemned other provincial academies for their failure to recognize his friend's achievement.[51] But he was already becoming exasperated that Marat's arrogance and rancor were making as many enemies as the novelty of his theories.

Their friendship—undermined further, Gourdin later recalled, by petty dishonesty on Marat's part—did not survive the shock of 1789.[52]

In the meantime, a new front had opened in the campaign to secure Marat's recognition in the provinces. His next target was the prestigious Academy of Sciences in Lyon, the second-largest city in the realm. There the offensive was launched by none other than Gabriel Louis François de Neufville, duc de Villeroy, military governor of the region, and a grand figure of the Old Regime whose forebears had held this same powerful position since the beginning of the seventeenth century. How on earth had Marat come to the weighty Villeroy's attention? The details are unknown, but they probably involved court connections of some kind. His cause may have been pleaded by members of the circle around Mentelle and the comte d'Artois, by the marquise de l'Aubespine or her husband in the circle around the former minister Choiseul, or by the duc de Maillebois or some other aristocratic patron or former patient. It's quite possible that Marat had treated Villeroy personally. Whatever the case, Villeroy's expression of interest was emphatic. "I am unable to refuse the entreaties made to me by persons to whom I am strongly attached," declared his letter to the Lyon academicians dated 28 February 1784. These persons, the letter continued, "desire that I urge you to propose, as subject of the prize to be awarded in 1785, a question that seems extremely interesting to me, and no one is better positioned than you to judge its utility for the progress of the arts and sciences."[53]

The issue the duke identified as so pressing was the validity of Newton's theory of differential refractibility, which (as he wrote) had "changed the face of optics" and laid the foundations for the construction of optical instruments of every kind. "This theory has recently been attacked with force and it is important to know whether this is on valid grounds," his letter stressed; "for as long as we are not enlightened by sure principles, its productions can only depend on blind routine and must be always imperfect." The Lyon academicians were thus invited to oblige their protector by adopting as the subject of their 1785 physics prize contest the question: "Are the experiments upon which Newton established the differential refraction of heterogeneous rays decisive or illusory? The authors' examination must be probing and their assertions based on simple experiments yielding uniform and unvarying results."

The formulation of this question seems unlikely to have been Villeroy's. Clearly intended to serve Marat's purposes, the entire argument for it might well have been drafted by Marat himself, or at least by someone well acquainted with his claims. But the authority at issue was now the duke's, and the proposal was closer to a command—as the academicians recognized in voting immediately to accept it. There was a complication, however. The topic of the academy's 1785 prize-essay question for physics had already been announced. Given the academy's institutional calendar and limited resources, the contest Villeroy wanted could not occur until 1788.[54]

This was not soon enough, as the duke soon made clear. "The goal in view would be missed if examination of this interesting question were deferred until 1788," he informed the Academy. "The solution of this problem must decide the matter of an expensive establishment, and I see with true satisfaction that your vote will determine it." The academicians were instructed to take action at their very next meeting by adopting Villeroy's question as the subject for an "extraordinary prize in Physics to be awarded in 1785." To provide the prize, the duke sent a gold medal worth 300 livres that had been "passed on" to him as the award for the eventual winner.

The first historian to consider this evidence speculated that the gold medal was the one Marat had recently received from the Rouen Academy for his essay on medical electricity and that the "expensive establishment" under consideration involved a project on Marat's part to manufacture new optical instruments based on his theories. The first speculation seems unlikely because the medal turned out to have been originally awarded by the Académie française. The second seems very plausible; we shall see later that Marat was eager to realize the practical benefits of his work by developing a method for the production of achromatic lenses. There can be little doubt in any case that the Lyon Academy was effectively being ordered to mount a prize-essay contest on his behalf.

This time, Villeroy was even more direct than before: "I hope, Gentlemen, given the importance of the subject, and the keen interest with which I express my request, that you give me this mark of your sentiments toward me, and I beg you to believe that I will appreciate it more than I can express to you. I have the honor of being, with true consideration, Gentlemen, your very humble and very obedient servant."[55] There was iron behind the Old Regime courtesies. The Lyon Academy hastened to comply. The competition was announced with great solemnity on 4 August 1784 as the express wish of "M. le duc de Villeroy, pair de France, gouverneur général de Lyon et des provinces de Lyonnais, Forez et Beaujolais." An early and strict deadline was set for receipt of the essays by 1 August 1785.[56]

There may nonetheless have been some lingering suspicion among the Lyonnais academicians as they announced the prize and awaited submissions. The existence of Marat's work attacking Newton, though never mentioned by Villeroy, must have been known to some of them, if only brought to their attention by Marat's determined adversary, their colleague Bertholon. One of them, De Villers, took an initiative in March 1785: he asked for an open reading of the preface to Marat's book aiming to correct Newton's color theory and of "the report that the Paris Academy of Sciences gave M. Marat on this subject." That report, of course, had been brutally dismissive. Its reading was apparently enough to prompt the Academy to create a committee, even before submissions had been received, to "repeat the experiments that would appear a necessary basis for an enlightened judgment" on the subject of the prize. De Villers was designated to proceed with these experiments in the presence of other colleagues, even though no entries had yet been received. In the event, the strict deadline had to be extended until 1 April 1786 for lack of submissions. By that date, eight essays had been submitted, including two by Marat (though they were copied in different hands to conceal their common origin).[57] One aimed to prove Newton's principles powerless to explain the phenomena; the other he described as identifying "a multitude of facts, unknown before me, but simple and invariable, [and] diametrically opposed to these principles."[58]

With the Lyon prize committee beginning its evaluation, it was time, once again, for the wily Dom Gourdin to spring into action on his friend's behalf. He soon informed the secretary of the Lyon Academy, the extravagantly named Marc-Antoine-Louis Claret de Fleurieu de La Tourrette, that he had been charged to write the committee report for the Rouen prize on color phenomena in thin materials. (This was the contest that would be won by Marat, though that had not yet been formally decided. Gourdin left his friend unmentioned in his letter.) Promising to send a copy of the report once it had been completed, Gourdin forwarded "in the meantime" a brief account of the experiments he had carried out as a member of the Rouen prize committee, experiments he now invited La Tourrette to share with his Lyon colleagues. Each of these experiments he presented as arguing against Newton's color theory. "I don't yet draw any conclusions from these experiments," he wrote somewhat disingenuously, "but I believe they throw doubt on the theory of differential refrangibility."

With this overture played, Gourdin relayed the startling news from London (via Rouen) that Newton's theory of optics was already being abandoned by the leading English physicists. "One of our colleagues has assured us of this in a full meeting of our Academy, and he has it according to the most skillful Englishmen he visited. I see that in France we want at least, if we abandon it, to do so after mature examination, and we have good reason to do so. . . . As it is, whether mistaken or not, Newton will not be any the less an immortal." For Gourdin, the fate of Newtonianism was still bound up with national pride.[59]

It seems obvious that this letter was an effort by Gourdin to tilt the Lyon prize competition in Marat's favor at the same time as he was working simultaneously to secure his friend's success in the Rouen competition.[60] But Villers's committee had performed its own experiments. Rendering its decision on 8 August, it reported that half of the eight submissions received had argued for Newton, half against. The decision had come down to a choice between (Marat's) two essays attacking Newton and two defending him. When the winner and runner-up were identified, Marat's was not among them. The winning entry had impressed the judges, in fact, precisely because it culminated in a thorough "refutation of M. Marat's system." The author, Villers explained in the committee's written report on 22 August, "goes through everything Marat has written against the number of primary colors and the different refrangibility of the heterogeneous rays. He repeats the same experiments, brings them back to Newton's theory, explains why the image of the hole is surrounded by different colors, applies mathematical analysis to the most interesting cases, and demonstrates by a calculation that is both rigorous and warranted by experience that the dimensions of the colored bands in one of Marat's most victorious experiments are as they must be from the superimposition of unequally refrangible rays." Citing its own experiments as additional confirmation, the committee concluded that "the experiments included in the immortal work of the great Newton, far from being illusory, have the double advantage of joining mathematical and physical certainty."[61]

The results of the competition were formally revealed at a public session of the Academy of Lyon on 29 August 1786. The language of the announcement was at once emphatic, celebratory, and self-congratulatory. In effect, it declared Newton the victor by proxy. "All the experiments have been rigorously repeated, with instruments furnished by the zeal of a number of academicians; the Committee added new ones; the results were invariably in favor of the celebrated English physicist, and the Academy congratulates itself on crowning two defenders of his doctrine who are truly worthy of this great man."[62] The Academy ordered the winning submissions and its committee's report published as soon as possible. It was a bitter defeat for Marat.

The two essays Marat had submitted for the Lyon contest were included in his *Mémoires académiques* in 1788, as were his objections to the procedures the Academy had followed in denying him the prize. The committee's report should have been printed immediately, he protested, along with all four of the final contending papers, so that the public could judge for itself. Knowledgeable readers would find, he was sure, that the committee had resorted merely to counting pages; they would recognize, too, that the Academy had undermined its claim to impartiality in congratulating itself on its vindication of Newton. As for the assertion that the experiments repeated by the committee invariably confirmed Newton's results, this amounted in Marat's view to a confession that his own investigations had not even been put to the test. Readers who did take the trouble to repeat them, he promised, would be surprised at the conclusion the Lyon Academy had reached.[63]

One informed reader did, indeed, express surprise, though it was another of Marat's friends, the crystallographer Romé de Lisle, who reported to the secretary of the Lyon Academy in January 1788 that the *Mémoires académiques* were already causing a sensation. Romé acknowledged that Marat's response to the Academy was "doubtless too energetic," but he registered astonishment at a judgment favoring a theory "demonstrated false forty years ago by Père Castel in his comparison of the systems of Descartes and Newton." The Lyon academicians could have distinguished themselves as the first to endorse "a fact that is easy to demonstrate and finally spreading everywhere despite the prestige of Newton's calculations. Newton has for him, I accept, the astronomers, the mathematicians, the calculators, but what physicist would today want to defend the English philosopher? In a word, Sir, since truth is one and M. Marat's experiments on light are totally destructive of the Newtonian theory, it is necessary either to prove these latter experiments false or to accept in good faith that Newton was wrong."[64]

So far, the outcome of Marat's provincial strategy had been a wash. Victorious in Rouen, he had been trounced in Lyon. But there was yet another battle to be fought. No sooner were the results of the Lyon contest revealed than the prestigious Royal Society of Sciences of Montpellier announced its own competition for the best essay on the question: "Whether Newton's explanation of the rainbow is based on incontestable principles; and is it well demonstrated that the heterogeneous rays supposedly emerging from an infinite number of raindrops falling from the clouds must form separate arcs?"[65] Since Newton had analyzed the rainbow as an effect of the differential refraction of light rays through the drops of rain, this question invited yet another debate over the validity of his color theory.

How this question came to be posed by the Montpellier Academy is unclear. Its wording seems to invite so much skepticism regarding Newtonian doctrine that the anonymous donor funding the prize could well have intended to promote Marat's views. Earlier historians have suspected the naturalist baron Philippe-Laurent de Joubert, owner of a fine laboratory Marat had praised in his *Notions élémentaires d'optique*, as the Maecenas who had paid for its publication. Baron Joubert was a less imposing personage than the duke de Villeroy in Lyon, but he was nonetheless a notable figure in Montpellier society, a member of its Royal Society of Sciences, and a corresponding member of the Paris Academy of Sciences. If he was indeed promoting Marat behind the scenes, however, he was quickly outmaneuvered.

Marat submitted an essay for the Montpellier contest and published it later in the *Mémoires académiques*. But the prize, announced on 9 January 1787, quickly went to the astronomer Pierre-Gilles-Antoine-Honoré Flaugergues, one of the academy's corresponding members, the cousin of its permanent secretary—and none other than the author who had won the Lyon contest! "He has rigorously demonstrated Newton's theory," the Academy declared, "which he had defended with equal force in a work on the differential refrangibility of heterogeneous rays to which this new dissertation can serve as a sequel, and which has been crowned by the Academy . . . of Lyon." Manuscripts left by Flaugergues show clearly that he had made refutation of Marat a central goal before the prize-essay question had been announced and would do so again after Marat published his unsuccessful essay in the *Mémoires académiques*. Perhaps the prize-essay question had been proposed precisely for this purpose. Perhaps Marat had been hoisted by his own petard.

TWELVE

DESTINATION MADRID?

Two new friends appear in Marat's correspondence in 1783. One of them, Abraham-Louis Breguet, was the brilliantly innovative horologist still building the business that would make him the greatest watchmaker of his age. His timepieces, progressively more astonishing in the ingenuity of their mechanism and the beauty of their design, would become costly objects of desire among the greatest figures in courtly (and, later, revolutionary and postrevolutionary) Europe. They remain collectors' pieces today. Marat, though he offered a striking contrast to the more typical customers, would eventually carry one himself. The two Swiss émigrés, acquainted perhaps since 1777, shared memories of their birthplace in Neuchâtel and experience in the practice of medicine—and doubtless their hunger for renown in the capitals of Europe. They remained close friends until Marat's death, furnishing mutual aid and support through the turmoil of the French Revolution. It was to Breguet that Marat entrusted his testament and scientific apparatus when he thought himself on his deathbed in 1788. Typically, though, he soon fretted that the watchmaker, in catering to the high and mighty, could inadvertently betray his scientific secrets. He had the testament and apparatus transferred instead to the care of a notary.[1]

Breguet was mentioned faithfully as a member of Marat's intimate circle in his correspondence from 1783. But the most important letters that year were directed to a new friend, Philippe Rose Roume de Saint-Laurent. Born on the island of Grenada, Roume (who added the "de Saint-Laurent") was a third-generation colonial from a German family that had migrated to

France and thence to the Antilles. His grandfather had served in the royal administration of Martinique, his father in the judiciary of Grenada. He himself cultivated natural history, remaining in Grenada for that purpose when the French lost it to the British in 1763. Meanwhile, he began taking an interest in Spanish efforts to exploit the agricultural and commercial potential of the relatively untouched neighboring island of Trinidad, to which he moved in 1781. There, in concert with a fresh civil administration, he developed ideas for a constitutional charter that would give the island a new status and institutions. In the face of resistance to these plans by the military authorities, he set out for Madrid to lobby for them. En route, he spent several months in Paris, cultivating the Spanish diplomats there and awaiting signs of favor from the Spanish court. During this period, he and Marat bonded in friendship.[2]

By the time he was summoned to Madrid in May 1783, Roume had a second project in mind. In addition to his plans for Trinidad, he had formed the ambition to secure his new friend's appointment as director of an academy of sciences that King Charles III was being urged to create there by his first minister, José Moñino, Count Florida-Blanca. The minister, one of the great proponents of enlightened despotism and a key figure in achieving the destruction of the Society of Jesus in 1773, now faced the problem of building an educational system in Spain to replace the Jesuits' schools. The establishment of a scientific academy was an important element in his program of reform, one meant also to achieve a new stature for Spain within enlightened Europe. Could it also offer Marat the possibility of a new life?

A NEW LIFE?

During Roume de Saint-Laurent's stay in Paris, Marat revealed that he had been offered a position by a "Northern power" that would provide a generous annual salary and an assured pension at retirement. The two men had decided to use this offer as a basis for securing a more agreeable position for Marat in Spain. Roume broached the matter with the Spanish authorities as soon as he arrived in Madrid, leaving Marat in Paris to work on his Spanish.[3]

By mid-June Marat was desperately eager for news of his suit. It would be another month before he could report back to Roume that he had met with a diplomat in the Spanish embassy, Viscount de La Herreria, to discuss arrangements for his departure for Madrid. He was concerned that he could lose his current position in the household of the comte d'Artois if word of these negotiations was leaked. At the same time, while he had agreed not to accept any other offer until the negotiations with the Spanish government had been concluded, he was surprised at the measures taken to make sure he held to this promise. "Those acquainted with me personally know well that few precautions are necessary with a man who has always respected the government, the laws, the customs of the countries he has passed through, who wants only to instruct the young, and will never do anything to tarnish a reputation to which he has sacrificed everything."[4]

Other anxieties were to follow. Marat was soon telling Roume of his concern that the Spanish ambassador, in checking his credentials, might listen to the wrong people, hearing only "the clamors of our philosophers for whom it is a crime to believe in God. You know their attitude towards those like me who have refused to enlarge their criminal sect and have dared to combat courageously their pernicious errors. And you also know how skillful they can be in denigrating their adversaries." He was hopeful, nonetheless, that Florida-Blanca, in order to learn about "a man of letters who has passed his life in his study and frequented only friends distinguished by their piety and their virtue," would be seeking information from persons of that ilk. "How many respectable ecclesiastics could I give as guarantors!"[5]

This more pious persona is not one seen before. It soon gave way to one more familiar, able to offer Roume proof of his devotion to Spain in that he had refused another career opportunity. Members of the Royal Society eager to follow a course on his experiments had conveyed an offer from London, Marat reported. The Board of Longitudes was ready to pay him 24,000 livres for a method of making a good flint glass. "They know my research has led me to happy results; in consequence they have invited me to spend a few weeks in London. You know well that I have been deaf to their proposition." In the meantime, he was awaiting news from Madrid before making a decision. "My heart is drawing me to Spain, as you know, because independently of the reasons drawn from my natural inclination, it is sweet to cultivate men whose rich nature is capable of the finest productions of the human spirit."[6]

A firm offer from Madrid was nonetheless slow to materialize. Promised in mid-July that it would be sent shortly, a discouraged Marat was still awaiting it on 8 September. Congratulating Roume on the positive reception of his colonial project—"you will be the creator of a large and new colony"—he imagined that the domain his friend would receive for his service might include "a little corner" for "a philosopher who loves the countryside." In the meantime, he reported, he was keeping himself busily at work perfecting a method to manufacture achromatic lenses. "I am at my furnaces morning to night. I'm slipping away from my crucibles for a moment to converse with you."[7]

Finally, a letter from Florida-Blanca and a summons to meet did come from the Spanish ambassador to France, Count Aranda, who honored the candidate that same morning by also visiting his laboratory. Marat thought the meeting had gone well and the experiments had been found satisfactory. Asked by the ambassador to submit a letter describing his ideas and plans for Spain, he hastened to comply that very afternoon in a letter dated 17 September. "The project of consecrating to Spain the fruits of my physical discoveries is not mine but M. [Roume de] Saint-Laurent's, formed in appreciation of the revolution I have begun in the sciences," he modestly informed Aranda. Roume, learning of Marat's offer from the North (and his disinclination to take it), had asked him if he would be prepared to move to Spain under appropriate conditions. To this question Marat had replied that he would find nothing more agreeable than "to be called to work for the progress of the sciences amidst a nation whose natural beauty I knew." Roume, he explained, understood something of the sacrifices he had made to advance the sciences and recognized that his research was now stalled for lack of funds. Accordingly, he had led Marat also to understand that "the munificence of the King of Spain would restore my fortune and that the personal treatment accorded me would be worthy of the greatness of a monarch and of the services I would render to the nation."[8]

First, then, to the money. Since Roume had asked him to fix upon an amount, Marat informed the ambassador, he had revealed that the offer from the northern power had comprised 24,000 livres in annual salary and a pension of 12,000 livres a year at retirement. He had intimated to Roume that he would be satisfied with this same amount but that (since money was not his principal goal) he would accept any sum that Roume might negotiate on his behalf. Fearing that this degree of flexibility had not been conveyed adequately to the Spanish minister, Marat hastened to reiterate it. "I set no condition . . . I know the fairness of the Spanish government . . . and I will accept the price it deems fit to place on my services."[9]

What then could the candidate offer Spain in exchange for anything approaching so handsome a sum? Marat's letter exploded with ambitious ideas and grandiose projects. His principal goal, he assured Aranda, would be to cultivate the talents of young Spaniards destined for the sciences while saving them years of "harsh, fastidious, and sterile study." He would train a new generation that would become the admiration of scientific Europe. For this purpose, he would prepare a "complete course of national study in the exact sciences," to which he would add the sure method of bringing astronomical and marine glasses, and optical instruments in general, to the highest point of perfection. Such a move, Marat implied, would have significant consequences by allowing a humbled Spain an opportunity to improve its competitive position in international trade. "It is thus in Spain's power at the present moment to take over a considerable branch of commerce that England has been forced to renounce for lack of lenses suitable for optics since the death of the artisan who was making them."[10]

There was still more Marat could offer the ambassador. He had in his portfolio many other objects from which commerce and agriculture could profit equally, "without speaking of the advantages that would result from medical electricity, which is almost everywhere abandoned to empirics [*l'empiricisme*] and which only a doctor who is also a physicist can truly exploit in applying it to the cure of various maladies." To all these pursuits Marat promised to devote the entirety of his time, "so much honor will I take in being attached to [the nation's] service and resolved to consecrate to its glory the few more years of strength it will please Providence to grant me. However considerable this sacrifice may appear, it will not surprise Your Excellency on the part of a man who has sacrificed fortune, youth, pleasure, and repose to his reputation and to the ambition to extend human knowledge. These facts are a matter of public knowledge; they will be the guarantee of my zeal and of the purity of my intentions."[11]

A copy of this letter to Aranda was sent to Roume de Saint-Laurent in Madrid the following day—by which time Marat had come up with ideas to expand his projects even further. His memoir on medical electricity had just been crowned by the Academy of Rouen, he informed his friend in an accompanying missive; the provincial Academy was now eager to identify the author and proceed to publication. But Marat had other ideas. "Wouldn't it be glorious for the true theory of medical electricity to see the light of day in Spain?" To tie the appearance of his work more closely to his future homeland, he would associate with it the most distinguished doctors of Madrid. In addition, he would ask Florida-Blanca to give it government approval and accept a dedication as if from the medical faculty of the Spanish capital. Few authors would make such a sacrifice of *amour propre* for the honor of their country, he reminded Roume. "But you know my soul, which is above such pettiness, and as for my heart it has long been Spanish. Goodbye, my tender friend. I am entirely yours for life."[12]

Two days later, still giddy from his success at Rouen, Marat fired off another letter to Roume that madly reiterated his ideas for signaling to enlightened Europe the importance of his move to Madrid. Giving Spain the glory for his work on medical electricity was the way to achieve this. The subject was all the rage, and in the hands of dangerous empirics. Doctors were ignorant of physics; physicians knew nothing of medicine. He alone could bring the two together. His Rouen memoir had destroyed Bertholon's system and all others, he insisted. Nonetheless, and to the astonishment of his friends in Paris, he was still determined to preserve his anonymity, refrain from collecting the prize medal, and refuse the Rouen Academy permission to publish his work.

All this he was prepared to do, Marat wrote, in order to give Spain the glory of revealing to the world the first sound theory of medical electricity. And he now had an additional idea for achieving this purpose. A number of patients could be selected in Madrid for treatment according to his methods, thus demonstrating the validity of his therapy. If he wanted to return to medical practice as a star and repair his fortune at the same time, he assured Roume, this would be the most auspicious moment for him to do so. But he was counting on Florida-Blanca's word and hoping he would not regret this sacrifice of his pride.[13]

As if all this were not enough, Marat had yet another idea to convey—about ballooning! After all, 1783 was the year of the balloon in Paris. The Montgolfier brothers had given the first public demonstration of the hot-air balloon in June. Marat's enemy Jacques Charles had launched the first hydrogen balloon from the Champ de Mars on 27 August. On 17 September, scarcely a week before Marat wrote this new letter, the Montgolfier brothers had sent a hot-air balloon aloft from the palace of Versailles bearing a sheep, a duck, and a rooster. Before the end of the year, humans had soared from earth in both the Montgolfier and Charles inventions. Ballooning was the talk of Paris and Versailles, Marat wrote, but it was being treated as if it were a children's game. He had more serious ideas in mind to make the technology useful, and he wanted, yet again, to unveil them first in Spain, showing Florida-Blanca the great role the balloon could play in his theory of air. "Perhaps I will be able to make it an infallible means of forever preserving from hail Spain's fields and vineyards."[14] Marat, it seems, was dreaming of making Spain a new Eden!

The passion behind these letters is almost palpable. They must have been written in a high state of emotional excitation. Academic status, financial security, and assured research funding were suddenly within Marat's grasp. He would have power and prestige, a position to rival that of the Condorcets and Lavoisiers and Franklins of the world, an entire nation awaiting experimentation and transformation at his hands. His dream of glory would come true. Any academic dean today would recognize in these letters the symptoms of the fantasy of "the right offer."

Escalation of demands and expectations is often one of these symptoms, and Marat had little resistance in such matters. A week later, fretting that he had heard nothing from Madrid, he was reporting to his friend that he had received yet another offer from London. He had achieved great success with the method of fabricating lenses upon which he was working, he maintained, and Roume must know that he could not spend his life waiting. Already regarding himself in the service of Spain, he needed to move forward. Once the information about him the Spanish government was seeking had arrived and his fate had thus been definitively decided, it would be important to inform Florida-Blanca that his new appointee had dismantled his *cabinet* two years previously and could not pursue his research without the necessary scientific instruments. "To procure the ones that are indispensable and bring some skillful workers in brass and glass with me, a month in London and a sum of 15,000 to 20,000 livres would suffice."[15] Marat needed the minister to authorize him to acquire the appropriate instruments for the king's cabinet and arrange payment to the merchants supplying them.

In the meantime, Marat could tell his friend that he was doing good works. He was using electrical therapy to restore sight to Romé de l'Isle after thirty-three years of blindness, and he was employing the same means to treat Roume's brother-in-law for impending paralysis. "But it is in Spain that I want to deploy all the resources of the admirable remedy when it is administered by a doctor-physicist." He was also making progress in Spanish, which would be his fourth modern language.[16] In addition, he was having a coat of arms prepared that would be appropriate to the status of a person in such a distinguished position!

Roume's business in Madrid was coming to an end; he needed to move more actively in his friend's cause. On 1 October he sent Count Florida-Blanca copies of Marat's letters of 17 September (to Aranda) and 18 September (to himself). Declaring himself delighted to have found means by which Spain could "impress by its enlightenment the rest of an astonished Europe," he expressed concern in his cover letter that he had not been explicit enough in earlier discussions about the terms Marat should be offered. "I beg Your Excellency to forgive me and to recall again that I am completely unfamiliar with the practices in Europe." Perhaps demonstrating this fact better than he knew, Roume now allowed himself the liberty to inform the minister that Marat was ready to make a serious commitment to Spain but would find it impossible to live honorably on 24,000 livres a year. To fulfill his goals as director of the new Academy, he would have to travel several times a year to appear before the minister at various sites and also to inspect the royal glass factories in San Ildefonso. These costs, of which the candidate was not yet even aware, would add at least 10,000 livres to his annual expenditures.

"Money is unfortunately indispensable for great men, as it is for common souls," Roume reminded the minister. Even so, it was not enough. "Honors alone can reward their noble ambition. . . . The Order of Charles III exists to reward transcendent merit; Monsieur de Marat has a sure right to it, and I know how much this favor from the Sovereign is coveted by all those who believe they merit it." Embellishing Marat's name with the notorious little particle used to convey a *soupçon* of nobility, Roume respectfully insinuated that his friend had all the qualities necessary in the director of the proposed Academy. He urged Florida-Blanca to consider these qualities before making a commitment to any other candidate.[17]

Having opened the negotiations with too light a touch, Roume may now have been too heavy-handed in trying to complete them. Florida-Blanca had, in any case, already seen Marat's 17 September letter to Aranda describing his plans and expectations. It had been immediately forwarded from Paris by the ambassador. Moreover, it had been accompanied by a highly skeptical assessment. Aranda had been less satisfied with their meeting than the candidate had imagined. Marat struck him as "one of those little Frenchies that do marvels with their pen and start a fire even under water when it comes to their interests." If the man were to be believed, the ambassador acidly remarked, he would be worth even more than he was angling for! He was capable and had a lot of talent, Aranda opined, but his knowledge was uneven. It would be better to bring in one of his competitors as well, so that the Spanish could learn from disputes between the two. The ambassador was no scientist, but he was a practical man, a man of the world who knew the value of disagreement. "Controversy is the true school, the one that forms men. With books alone, without response or discussion, ideas are accumulated but not purified; the same thing happens when one follows a single oracle, especially in systematic matters."[18]

As for the proposed salary and eventual pension, Aranda considered the amounts Marat had mentioned inflated, given that the more reputable and popular Paris lecturers never earned more than 12,000 livres a year, from which they still had to deduct their business expenses and ward themselves against the uncertainties of illness and insecure retirement. A sum of 18,000 livres in annual salary and an eventual pension of 6,000 livres would make the candidate more than happy, Aranda opined. The salary would be ample, given the difference in the cost of living between Spain and France, and reducing the eventual pension to one-third of the salary amount would create a better incentive structure. The ambassador, though, put it in more folksy terms: "If he turns out to be a pumpkin [the pension] would be more than he deserves; and if he is a good melon then he would think less about retiring on a third than he would on a half."[19]

Meanwhile, Florida-Blanca's inquiries had begun to bear sour fruit. A report sent from Paris on 21 September had brought news that did not bode well for the candidate. It came from one Bernardo Belluga, signing himself "a minor subaltern" of the minister, probably as an employee in the Spanish embassy. "The interest of the nation and love for Your Excellency oblige me to write to you in particular about Marat," he declared. "I am the creature of Your Excellency whose glory I serve and I feel that equivocation in a report that should serve the advancement of the sciences would only set them back." He had cultivated the sciences since childhood, he added, and deserved to be a member of the Royal Society. His reliability in the matter thus established, if not his modesty, he went straight to the point. "I must tell Your Excellency that Marat is a notorious charlatan; that I am ready to prove it at length; that he only knows something about light and fire; that his electrical experiments are juggling tricks; that his theory of light is at most a hypothesis that serves for nothing; that he is greatly scorned by the true savants, and that his disciple Miollan who gives the course because of his own bad presentation has not found more than three people to take it."[20]

Even if there were another true physicist to join Marat in debate, Belluga demanded—presumably in response to Aranda's idea of appointing a team of two—who would follow the charlatan? What mockery would there not be when Europe learned that a researcher repudiated by the Academies of Paris, London, and St. Petersburg was being paid 24,000 livres in Madrid?

Belluga begged the minister to await a further report from another informant, one Solano, who eventually met with Marat several times in Paris.[21] Marat, lacking social antennae, again came away with a favorable impression of the encounters, believing that Solano had formed no objection to his experiments and was in any case convinced of Newton's errors in optics. The Spaniard was "as reserved as he is amiable," he had decided. "Perhaps he will be more open to me when we are more closely linked," he told his friend, "and don't doubt that I will do everything in my power for the triumph of truth."[22] We don't know the inscrutable Solano's verdict, but it seems unlikely to have been positive. Belluga, in any case, was writing to Florida-Blanca again on 10 October to reiterate his judgment that Marat was a charlatan. "If the matter comes up again," he assured the minister, apparently in the conviction that the issue had been decided, "I will speak clearly and prove by A minus B what I said to the count [Aranda] . . . we have no need of mediocrity."[23]

A few days later, another sneering report was added to the Marat dossier. This one came from the painter and academician Antonio Ponz, a favorite in the Spanish capital. Famous for his *Voyage Around Spain*, a multivolume work deriving from a commission he had received to travel the country compiling an inventory of artistic works left behind by the Jesuits, Ponz was touring Europe in 1785 on a similar journey of cultural and philosophical exploration. While there he had learned of Marat's negotiations with Aranda and Herreria, but also of his contestations with the Academy of Sciences. He also claimed to have run into Marat in London with one of the latter's brothers (a Toledo merchant?) who had paid all the bills. Seeing that Marat had all doors closed to him, Ponz recalled, he had advised him to be "as quiet as a mute" and to take more care around other savants ("his brothers of the order").[24]

Roume, meanwhile, had been raising warning flags from Madrid. "You tell me there are more reports," an astounded Marat replied to him on 6 November. "I can't imagine what they are about. Whatever it may be, I flatter myself that I can withstand the most severe examination. I would have thought myself in any case well-enough known to the public to be dispensed from this." Florida-Blanca, he complained, had said that the entire business would be concluded by 15 November, but they were already at 6 November and he had heard nothing. "You exhort me to patience, my dear friend, in consideration of the importance of the matter for Spain's glory and my own. As for my own triumph, it will come without fail. But I have set my happiness on bringing the exact and useful sciences to the highest point they can attain. To succeed, I need the protection of a great King and I would be at the pinnacle of my desires if I could devote my talents to the good of a nation I love and respect."[25] Persevere, he urged his ever-patient ally; don't leave the task unfinished.

Roume, perseverant though he may have been, was losing traction in this matter at the Spanish court, and Marat was ready to explode when he heard the latest from Madrid. "It's true then, my friend, that calumny has flown from Paris to the Escurial to blacken me in the mind of a great King and an illustrious Maecenas. Twenty letters, you say, have painted me in the darkest colors." Who, then, were his detractors? "Envious cowards, the numerous horde of whom never cease striving for my ruin; the modern philosophers who hide under anonymity or false names to defame me. Shall I always be their target for having renounced academic honors for the love of truth, for having advanced useful knowledge, for having recalled to life a great number of my fellows who had been declared incurable, for having defended the cause of virtue? My heart is revolted at this idea. But no, I will not murmur against the sacred decrees of Providence; whatever the excesses of my enemies, they will never force me to repent for being a good man."[26]

With these cries of outrage against his victimization, Marat opened the longest personal letter of his life still known, and the one most revealing of his character. Forty pages in length—some 15,000 words—it was bolstered by a dossier of roughly equal size placing copies of some forty personal documents in evidence of the conduct of his life to date. "I could have enlarged the list if the majority of my acquaintances were not still in the countryside," he pleaded. "But I hope it will be judged more than sufficient to demonstrate that I am a good man in the most rigorous sense of the term."[27]

A VICTIM'S PLEA

This letter of 20 November 1783, together with its attachments, constitutes by far the greater part of the body of Marat's personal correspondence that has been preserved. The dossier, held in Madrid and thus not destroyed with many of Marat's personal papers after his death, remains indispensable for understanding the prerevolutionary period of his life. One has to acknowledge, though, that its documentation was compiled by Marat himself to serve a particular purpose and to make a very specific case for his appointment in Spain. Doubtless selective in its presentation of facts in a situation that had brought him to a frenzy of despair, it is nonetheless revelatory in the portrait he now drew for himself, for Saint-Laurent, for the Spanish court—and by extension for the historian.

From start to finish, this life story is framed in terms of the persecution Jean-Paul Marat has endured from the modern philosophers and academicians. "I have combatted the principles of the modern philosophy," he writes. "That's the origin of the implacable hatred its apostles have vowed against me. It couldn't humiliate me in the views of the knowledgeable, but you will soon see that I was destined to attract their persecutions on more than one account. Since they neglected nothing to extend their evil empire they multiplied in every form. Our Faculties, our Academies are full of them and, powerless to avoid them, I've had to deal with them in all my undertakings."

Strikingly, Marat portrays his early intellectual motivations in entirely negative and reactive terms. Aversion to the principles of "our pretended philosophers long fixed the object of my reflections," he recalls. This antipathy had led him to compose his early works to combat materialism—"the starting point of my misfortunes" (to strike a Rousseauian pose). "My work finally appeared and made a sensation," he crows, citing an enthusiastic review in *The Westminster Magazine*. "I will say nothing of the praise [the review] lavished upon it, but I cannot pass over in silence the censure [it received] for the disdainful manner in which I treated our pretended philosophes." The latter's machinations had almost prevented the initial importation of *De l'homme* into France, Marat reminds Roume, but a revised version of that book is now ready to appear "with the approbation of the Sorbonne," one even more vehement against materialism. He is postponing the appearance of this book too, he claims, "for the glory of Spain." Of course, this account of Marat's early works in England entirely omits mention of his sturdily radical *The Chains of Slavery*. That anatomy of the inevitable advance of despotism would not have gone down well in Bourbon Spain.

Tracing his steps back to Paris, Marat then passes to his successes as "doctor to the incurables," the consequent hostility of the Faculty of Medicine, and his decision to abandon medical practice for scientific research. There follows the painful history of his efforts, under cover of anonymity, to secure recognition of his initial experiments by the Academy of Sciences. His grudging treatment by the academicians is contrasted with descriptions of the prodigious sensation his work caused throughout Europe ("all the public papers mentioned it. For six months I had the court and the city at my doorstep"), testimony to the more positive reception by academies beyond Paris, and the success of Filassier's course presenting his experiments ("among his subscribers he counted princes of the blood and the most eminent personages of the State").

With fame like this, Marat contended, anonymity was no longer possible. The daring researcher felt himself even further exposed to his enemies. "While the curious flocked to my disciple to see my fire experiments, I submitted my discoveries on light to the Academy's examination. No longer able to remain incognito, I counted less on the impartiality of my judges, almost all extreme partisans of Newton." Against the inevitably harsh treatment that work received, Marat set other claims: three of the academicians had asked if he wished to enter the Academy ("The academy, recognizing that it could not stifle my discoveries, sought to have them spring from within its ranks"), and one had come to the point of risking expulsion by refusing to accept the majority opinion. "It took seven months to confirm my experiments on light; three months to draft the report; and five months of my solicitation to get it. The result was a denial of justice." How could the academicians have decided otherwise?

> To admit the truth of my experiments was to recognize that they had worked on the basis of false principles for forty years, an avowal implicating in particular the class of mathematicians and astronomers, which formed a terrible cabal against me. After denying facts they had

> not seen, they all cried out: "*If this man is right, what's to be done with the Mémoires de l'Académie.*" The Academy, convinced by this fine argument, closed its eyes to the evidence. All this will become clear from my correspondence with this Society (see the supporting documents).

Thereafter, Marat insists, his persecution by the cabal of Paris academicians became clandestine. Decrying him in their circles without bothering to refute him, they recruited journalists to suppress his work or undermine his reputation even as much of the European press celebrated his achievements and as public interest in his experiments continued to grow. Their harassment could not deter him from pressing on with his researches on electricity, abundant public success for which Marat now cites. Nor could they prevent his success in demolishing Bertholon's claims in his winning essay for the Rouen competition. "You see again from this little success that the academicians themselves know how to do justice to me when I maintain my anonymity."

All this is rehearsed to rebut the charges now circulating in Madrid. There are imputations of *ignorance, incapacity, charlatanism*, but they are belied by the unanimous testimony of a multitude of distinguished men of letters, the decisions of learned societies, and the voice of the public. Motivated by bad faith, they are also self-contradictory. "If I were without intelligence in [my adversaries'] eyes why would they want so desperately to defame me? . . . Why has none of them dared descend with me into the arena? It's because they recognize their feebleness; they are afraid I will reveal their incompetence; they know the public they are trying to abuse would soon do justice to them."

Another imputation: "they accuse me of being *a man who promises great things and is incapable of fulfilling any of his commitments*. This is the portrait of an ambitious intriguer. But it is widely known that I have passed almost my whole life in my study, that I have never aimed for wealth, that I have never pursued even the least lucrative scheme." For six years, Marat protests, he has renounced wealth to pursue useful knowledge, carrying out his costly experiments at his own expense. Why has he not accepted the offers he has received from the North, or from London? Why has he asked Spain for no more than he has already been proffered elsewhere, when he could easily get a larger offer from England or make more by returning to the practice of medicine? He is now accused of promising great things. Doesn't this just show that his negotiations with Spain have been leaked to his enemies who everywhere contrive to secure secret intelligence?

This thought incites another violent outburst against the dark conspiracies of the modern philosophers. They are corrupting the youth, creating proselytes in great numbers. "Daily they multiply; thus spread across the face of the earth, what a fearsome confederation will they not form? A confederation all the more formidable in that it would be invisible because, having no external sign to distinguish them, they can, without being known, fill all the orders of society: learned societies, universities, tribunals, royal councils." Already, Marat insists, these madmen have formed the project of destroying all religious orders, of annihilating religion itself. To succeed, they poison the springs of all useful knowledge and seek to fill with their sectaries all the positions established for public instruction. "What evils have they not already committed? What evils will they not still do? If one day they come to conceive ambitious projects, to turn their views to political matters by means of their creatures who will soon discover everything that goes on in the cabinets, who will prevent them from shaking governments, overthrowing states?" He saw only one way of preventing these misfortunes: to mobilize all the great writers of the age to cover these apostles of modern philosophy with ridicule.

"I come back to me." With fantasies of philosophical Armageddon receding, Marat returns to the charges against him. *A man who promises great things and is incapable of fulfilling any of his commitments?* "To this, I have a trenchant reply: I have sometimes executed great things, and always without promising them." There follows an extensive accounting:

The solar microscope: "I have invented an observational method in the darkroom that is very capable of opening a vast field of physical researches and of bringing the torch into the labyrinths of nature. . . . The majority of European physicists have adopted it."

Fire: "I have used [my method] to make the igneous fluid visible, that entity unknown before me, which plays so great a role in the works of the Creator. . . . After 2000 years passed in useless research into the nature of fire . . . I disengage the theory of fire from all hypothesis, all conjecture, all convoluted reasoning; I purge it of errors, I render it intuitive and put it into a little volume. Would it be from the pen of an ignoramus that one would see emerge this little volume that would condemn to oblivion all that the learned societies had ever published on this matter?"

Optics: "Attempting to snatch from Newton the finest jewel in his crown must seem like a rash enterprise. But his devoted disciples don't know what I can do. . . . Soon the members of the Academy rush to me to demand to see. . . . Resorting to my observational method in the darkroom, I show them a multitude of unknown phenomena; they are mute with astonishment. . . . I show them the numerous contradictions of the Newtonian theory they blindly admire. . . . Finally, I put my discoveries into a little book. Is it from the pen of an ignoramus that would come the little volume that condemns to oblivion so many sublime speculations comprising the enormous mass of academic collections?"

Electricity: "Before me, everything that had appeared on electricity was reduced to a mass of isolated, complicated experiments, contending against one another and dispersed over five hundred volumes. It was a question of deriving knowledge from this hideous chaos; I close myself in my dark room, follow my observational method, and render the electrical fluid visible . . . ; I observe its properties, its mode of action, the phenomena resulting from its interaction with air, light, fire; everything becomes intuitive, knowledge is formed. Would it be an ignoramus, again, who has brought to light the only methodical work, the only known theory of electricity?"

And, finally, *Medical Electricity*, rescued from the confusions and dangers of rampant empiricism: "My judges were members of an Academy; they were overwhelmed by the force of my proofs. Would it be an ignoramus like me who would force a learned society to crown my work and grant me a triumph over the member upon whom it rested most of its glory?"

One last charge: *The greatest misfortune that could occur in Spain would be for it to accept me.* "To be viewed as such, one would have to be a frightful rebel conspiring against the government or a clever hypocrite corrupting the morals of the nation. In these two regards, the imputation of my adversaries is the most ridiculous of all."

What is one to make of this truly remarkable letter? What must Roume, Aranda, and Florida-Blanca have made of it? Was Marat unhinged? Paranoia sharpened by megalomania might have been expected. But were these religious sentiments sincere? What of the melodramatic denunciations of philosophical conspiracy and frightful anticipations of global cultural conflict? Were these elements of a rhetorical strategy slipping into fantasies beyond their author's control? Were they anticipations of rhetorical obsessions and compulsions to come? They must, in any case, have been quite inappropriate to the situation Marat faced. Roume's religious convictions may have run toward the conservative (there had been tensions between the two friends over this matter), but it is unlikely that Florida-Blanca, enlightened minister and hammer of the Jesuits, would have warmed to denunciations of philosophical attacks on religious orders.

Roume held on to this explosive document for quite some time. He may not have known what to do with it. He finally sent a copy to Florida-Blanca on 14 February 1784, entitling it "A very interesting letter in which M. Marat provides me with a recapitulation of what has happened to him since he entered into the career of the sciences."[28] One could scarcely have been more noncommittal.

No more was heard of Marat's departure for Spain. He must have found the humiliation and disappointment stemming from this episode crushing, the collapse of his financial hopes no less so. Whether as a direct result of disclosure of his Spanish flirtation or not, Dr. Marat's appointment in the household of the comte d'Artois ended in late 1783 or 1784, plunging him further toward penury. We find him pleading in 1785 to be relieved from payment of the capitation tax, first as a foreigner and second as a man of letters without formal position since he had long ago renounced the title of doctor to the bodyguard of the comte d'Artois. Having in this position once enriched the French public with works costing all his time and great expenditures, he contended, he now found himself in the situation of "all foreigners who travel and spend to instruct themselves."[29] The outcome of this request remains unknown, along with the precise state of Marat's finances in the later 1780s. Brissot described him at this time as "poor and living miserably," but his works continued to appear in handsome, expensive editions suggesting wealthy patrons.[30]

A SECRET TRIUMPH

Like the cork his father had been before him, Marat continued somehow to bob in troubled waters. One undoubted triumph was reserved for him during these prerevolutionary years, though it was mitigated by the fact that it remained anonymous. His most enduring scientific achievement—the object, indeed, of his most secret satisfaction—was a translation of Newton's *Optics* upon which he relied in his later scientific works. "I've used a new translation of Newton's *Optics*," he wrote, "a clear and faithful translation that has earned the approval of the Royal Academy of Sciences."[31] The work was his own, but it had been submitted to the Paris Academy in 1785, without mention of his name, by a prestigious man of letters, Nicolas Beauzée. A member of the Académie française and numerous other academies, and an authority on translation to whom the editors of the *Encyclopédie* had turned for their article on the subject, Beauzée was also the "secretary-interpreter" of the comte d'Artois—and in that capacity a figure earlier in the same royal household as Marat. Court connections had again proved their value.

Once received by the Paris Academy, this new translation of the *Optics* had been referred to a committee for immediate examination. That the committee included not only the astronomer Jean-Sylvain Bailly but the abbé Alexis-Marie de Rochon—an expert in optics and the official in charge of optical technology for the French Navy—underlines the practical importance of Newton's text as the basis for optical instrumentation in an age of maritime warfare, geopolitical expansion, competitive research, and commercial struggle. That Condorcet, the Academy's permanent secretary and principal spokesman for the mathematical physicists, also became himself a committee member indicates the work's scientific, symbolic, and institutional importance within the Academy's walls.

Rochon may have carried the principal burden of vetting the accuracy of the translation, as one historian has suggested.[32] But Condorcet himself presented the committee's report on 4 May 1785. It noted with regret that the initial translator of the work (Pierre Coste, one of the greatest cultural intermediaries among the Huguenot exiles, and the translator also of Locke's *Essay Concerning Human Understanding*) had lacked knowledge of mathematics and physics. It expressed satisfaction that the new translator had taken particular care to "present in a more illuminating manner the extremely difficult and often obscure passages of Newton's *Optics* . . . [and had] enriched the translation with important notes in which he shows the progress made in optics since Newton." It even observed that these notes had necessarily entered into a measure of detail in discussing achromatic lenses "because the achromaticism produced in some Newtonian experiments is diametrically opposed to the fundamental experiments of this illustrious mathematician."[33] It did not hurt, of course, that the notes to this translation drew substantially on Rochon's own work and would have been of considerable interest to him for their consideration of the problem of producing an achromatic lens.

The judgment was, in any case, enthusiastic. Declaring the impossibility of encouraging too greatly the translators of a work "of such importance, and which does so much honor to the human mind," the committee did not hesitate to endorse its publication with the Academy's official sanction.[34] With this ringing endorsement, the book was offered for purchase by subscription (with no down payment required) in April 1786. Potential subscribers were promised the most perfect translation possible of this sublime work in a version of the text they would find purged of the barbarous infidelities and servile obscurities of the earlier French translation, pruned of burdensome repetitions, and rendered all the more intelligible by notes tracing the history of optics since Newton's time. In addition to its formal dedication to the king and approbation by the Academy of Sciences, bibliophiles were assured, the beauty and magnificence of the work's production would command a place in any library.

Appear the translation did in 1787, in full typographical dress, as *Optique de Newton, Traduction Nouvelle, Faite par M*** sur la dernière Édition originale, ornée de vingt-une Planches, & approuvée par l'Académie royale des Sciences; Dédiée au Roi, par M. Beauzée, Éditeur de cet ouvrage, l'un des Quarante de l'Académie Françoise; de l'Académie* della Crusca; *des Académies royales de Rouen, de Metz, & d'Arras; Professeur émérite de l'École royale militaire, & Secrétaire-Interprète de Monseigneur Comte d'Artois.* Beauzée's dedication to Louis XVI, "the greatest of Kings," of this "masterpiece of one of the greatest geniuses that Heaven has ever granted the earth" was appropriately fulsome in its appreciation of royal favors showered upon him. It was also profoundly disingenuous, at least in its declaration that he was only "the simple editor of this translation, whose author is unknown to me."[35]

Beauzée's dedication was followed by an editor's preface more surely Marat's work than his own. It was rhapsodic in its appreciation of the radiance of light, "this subtle fluid that fills the universe . . . and spreads an indescribable charm over all of Nature." It was grandiloquent in its celebration of the elegance and the utility of the science to which Newton had devoted his "sublime work." But it was savage in its excoriation of Coste's translation, which it declared "unfaithful and obscure . . . servile and barbarous," the work of someone "ignorant of the subject, little versed in languages, and still less in the art of writing." How precious then was this moment, the preface declaimed, when a travesty of Newton's sublime ideas could finally be replaced by the version offered by "a savant equally versed in the art of writing and familiar with Newton's experiments."[36] How precious, too, to this secret author, must have been the trick he had managed to play on the academicians he so hated! How sweet must have been the praise the Academy had poured upon a researcher they had persecuted as a charlatan!

What delight, too, Marat must have taken in the favor now lavished upon his translation in the press—for some of which he might well have been responsible! A piece sent for publication in the *Année littéraire* in February 1787, for example, was extravagant in its praise of a translation that had, in effect, refashioned Newton's work for him. "It illuminates, it prunes, it transposes, it links more tightly the different parts of the original; everywhere it separates the gold from the dross . . . the *Opticks* becomes a finished work, such, in a word, as it would have left the pen of Newton himself if this great man had taken the trouble to put the last touches to it." The fact that this paean of praise closed with a reminder to subscribers to pick up the copies they had ordered from the publisher suggests that it was far from offering a disinterested judgment.[37]

But there were other reviews. With the Paris academicians' endorsement trumpeted on its title page, the work scarcely needed further praise, as a review in the *Journal encyclopédique de Bouillon* noted in March 1787. The Bouillon journal, ever a favorable conduit for Marat and this time ecstatic, heralded a translation it declared long necessary and now delivered by the hand of a master, reprinted the introduction, and offered a comparison of passages from the old and new versions of the text.[38] In December, the Academy again offered its imprimatur in the form of a review by Lalande, published in the semi-official *Journal des savants*, that lauded the translation and legitimated reconsideration of Newton's views of gravitational effects on light by reporting Boscovich's new investigations into the matter.[39]

Modern scholars have followed the Academy of Sciences in praising Marat's translation of the *Optics*. It was reprinted in 1989 as still the best French version available.

STILL FIGHTING

In the meantime, Marat was gathering into an anti-Newtonian manifesto the papers on light he had submitted to the Rouen, Lyon, and Montpellier Academies. Sumptuously produced with hand-colored plates, and with the half-title *Oeuvres de Marat* suggesting a collected edition of his scientific writings in preparation, this volume of *Mémoires académiques ou Nouvelles découvertes sur la lumière, relatives aux points les plus importants de l'optique* was the last of Marat's scientific publications, the one of which he declared himself the proudest. Clearly intended to launch his scientific comeback, it was published in January 1788. But an advance campaign had already been undertaken for it.

In early December 1787 the *Journal général de France* had published two leaked extracts from Marat's Rouen essay on the phenomenon of color in soap bubbles, which were followed up by letters to the editor calling for the publication of the piece in its entirety. A month later, the journal identified Marat as the author. In late December it had also accepted from a "Newtonian reader" two extracts from Marat's Lyon essay on differential refrangibility. These were succeeded in early January by a letter, fed to the journal in the name of one Lagranges, that claimed confirmation of Marat's investigations of this phenomenon. What were the Lyon academicians thinking when they rejected Marat's essay? the writer demanded. Were the laws of nature different in Lyon than in Paris? The academicians needed to justify their decision.[40]

Beyond that, the writer went on to put the entire academic prize system in question. Learned societies relied on their committees for an initial judgment of work submitted to them, he pointed out, but petty politics and ingrained prejudices distorted these committee evaluations. As the academies simply accepted these flawed valuations, the progress of truth was hampered and error propagated. This tendency was all the more regrettable in the case of investigations relevant to the construction of optical instruments whose importance would certainly justify a review of this case by the Paris Academy of Sciences![41]

In January, too, the Lyon academicians were challenged to reconsider their verdict. A letter from Romé de Lisle, a loyal friend, demanded that they either demonstrate the falsity of Marat's experiments or acknowledge that Newton was wrong. This call prompted a procedural tussle in the Academy over questions of access to the committee report Villers had declared confidential.[42] From Normandy, Gourdin's announcement of the appearance of the *Mémoires académiques* also rehearsed the story of Marat's earlier victimization. The academies, he declared, could no longer suppress the truth of these anti-Newtonian essays.[43]

In continuation of this campaign, the *Journal général de France* added an extended and enthusiastic notice of the *Mémoires académiques* to its issue of 22 January 1788. Its account of the book began by emphasizing the significance of the question of the differential refrangibility of light rays for the construction of optical instruments, and most particularly of achromatic lenses. At a point when savants appeared unable to go further, it declared, Marat's darkroom experiments had transformed the entire science of optics. His correction of the doctrine of differential refrangibility ("regarding which the physicists and mathematicians had all gone astray under Newton's influence") rested on proofs that could not be contradicted. "This striking revolution effected in optics will not be less advantageous than glorious to the Nation, but one can only appreciate its importance in considering the prodigious influence it will have on the construction of optical, astronomical, and maritime instruments the progress of which is so profoundly significant for society." No longer offered to Spain, the glory of the new optics could be reclaimed by France! The article closed with fighting words. "The author seems to fear that his adversaries have succeeded in closing the journals to him. We can assure him that we will always make it our duty to do him justice, and we dare to assure him also that there is no journalist so craven that he would sacrifice to the views of a despicable cabal a man of merit whose nights have been constantly consecrated to the progress of useful knowledge."[44]

This rapturous appreciation of Marat's research was echoed a month later (and perhaps from the same source) in a lengthy letter to the editor of the *Année littéraire* again signed by one Lagranges, "professor of mathematics, etc." It is possible that the writer existed under this name, though one might well doubt it. The language of this communication suggests that it came (like its predecessor) from someone close to Marat, if not himself. It was clearly fashioned to publicize the *Mémoires académiques* as the triumphal comeback and vindication of a sadly victimized researcher. "Misfortune is good for some things," the letter pronounced, "for it is to the kind of denial of justice the author experienced in 1780 on the subject of his initial discoveries on light that the public owes the important work I announce to you." That judgment had not fallen upon one of those modern charlatans skimming the surface of the sciences for money's sake, but upon "a true savant obsessed by the desire for knowledge and willing to defer gratification, developing his ideas in the silence of retreat and endowed with an energy and enduring resolve."

Instead of seeking attention, the author of this letter wrote, "M. *Marat*, forgetting himself in a way and postponing his triumph to better assure it, has shut himself in his study for several years and devoted himself to the study of nature, carefully observing the phenomena of light, investigating their causes by means of precise and delicate experiments, skillfully analyzed, establishing luminous principles, combating accredited errors, and pruning, simplifying and extending knowledge. He has thus opened up a new path for himself, and has finally achieved in optics a striking revolution upon which he has long reflected."

The truth, of course, was rather different. Marat had hardly retreated quietly to his study. He had spent several years energetically engaged in the prize-essay politics of the provincial academies. This the writer in the *Année littéraire* implicitly allowed. "Persuaded of the importance of his discoveries, and jealous to establish them in an authentic manner, he has made them the subject of several programs and has himself provoked the severe examination of the learned societies. These are the titles under which this celebrated physicist presents himself to the public today, and it must be agreed that it would be difficult to have more honorable ones."

There followed in the letter to the *Année littéraire* a description of the four papers on light that Marat had submitted to the provincial academies, papers tending (in the now familiar phrase) to "change the face of Optics, which they reduce to its elements," to reveal the doctrine of differential refractibility as a tissue of errors, and to transform the construction of optical, astronomical, and naval instruments. How desirable it would be then, the writer concluded, for the Academy of Sciences to hasten to recognize these new discoveries, imprinting upon them the mark of confidence they merited.[45]

Despite these calls in the journals, the opportunity the *Mémoires académiques* now offered the Parisian academicians to reconsider an injustice they had inflicted years before was not taken up. The Academy of Sciences preferred to keep its counsel.

The campaign to rebuild Marat's scientific reputation was nonetheless a remarkable effort. If the reviews and notices planted in his favor now seem egregious, one must remember that working the press was no easy task. In one fascinating letter, Marat castigated an editor for an account of the *Mémoires académiques* that "so greatly attenuated the importance of my work . . . that your readers can only form an unfavorable view of it." To counter these negative impressions, he had written a rejoinder for the editor to insert in his next issue. "Perhaps I would have the right to demand this grace from you as an act of justice, but I expect it from your heart, and with all the more confidence in that it will not compromise you," he wrote. Easy sentimentality aside, his correspondent should know that if this request was disregarded, the matter would not end there. "If my expectation proves wrong, I must not leave you ignorant of the fact that I will have the honor of addressing you in other journals, where I will certainly not keep silent regarding the despicable persecution I have experienced. In so vaunted a century of philosophy, does truth no longer have friends, and are there no longer men courageous enough to espouse its cause openly against the powerful cabal?"[46]

It seems likely that this challenge was addressed to Jean-Claude de La Métherie, who had taken over the editorship of the *Journal de physique*. His February review of the *Mémoires académiques* had provided an informative discussion of the arguments at issue between Marat and Newton without taking a definitive position in favor of either side. "Achromatic lenses have proven that the great Newton was mistaken regarding the refractions of light," the article concluded; "is he equally mistaken on the points M. Marat attacks? It's up to the savants to pronounce."[47]

Incensed by this show of impartiality, Marat shot off a letter, dated 10 March 1788, expressing his surprise at this refusal to endorse the positions he had demonstrated, offering a lengthy summary of them, and calling for a final repudiation of Newton's errors. "Let us no longer be afraid to say it. Consecrated by learned Europe, these errors fetter genius, set back knowledge of the marvels of vision, block the progress of optics, and halt the advance of the arts and sciences that depend on it. It is time that their reign come to an end, and may all savants who love truth soon unite to precipitate their fall."[48]

La Métherie must have responded that it was not up to him to decide for the public. "No, Monsieur," Marat retorted in a second letter, "I have never thought that your judgment of my works could determine that of the public, but I believed that you could present it in a manner that would stimulate some interest." When journalists prostituted themselves to lavish praise on miserable productions, he complained, was it surprising that original works offering important discoveries were not much sought after when they were presented to the public in an unfavorable light? There followed a rant on journalistic ethics. "It is for the pitiless way you have mutilated the extract I sent you, the deliberate care you have taken to strip from it all my claims to the benevolence of readers, that I reproach you, and the bias you have shown against me alone that I make your crime. Stop objecting that the truth must be presented naked in the Areopagus, that encomia do nothing for the public, which judges only on the basis of the book itself. You are little persuaded by these fine maxims, since you belie them on every page of your issues."

He would not remind the journalist of the exaggerated praise he had lavished on a thousand mediocre works (including Priestley's *Mémoires*), Marat wrote, but he could not suppress a particular reference to "the ridiculous encomia you conferred (in your August 1787 issue) on a book you didn't even take the time to read. I mean the illustrious Bertholon's *Electricité des météores*." To an exasperated Marat, for whom any favorable mention of Bertholon served as a red flag to a bull, La Métherie's ethic of journalistic impartiality seemed mere timidity posturing as philosophy. "Let's agree that you were afraid to do me justice because I have powerful adversaries. For my part, I am ready to pity you for not being in fortunate enough circumstances to consult only the love of truth."[49]

Were there other moves beyond this desperate press campaign that Marat could make to improve his situation? As early as May 1786, he had used Romé de Lisle as a messenger to deliver copies of his works to a distinguished savant who was a subject of "the greatest of kings, the Maecenas of the artists and men of letters of his states." This correspondent was begged, assuming he found Marat's publications worthy, to lay them at his monarch's feet with a volume bound and decorated with the monarch's coat of arms. "His Majesty will deign to receive them with favor. He is pleased to encourage the sciences and protect those who cultivate them; would he refuse one of his subjects a benevolence he accords so often to foreigners?"[50] The ruler in question was undoubtedly Frederick the Great, still for a few months king of Prussia, whose subject Marat remained by virtue of his birth in Neuchâtel. Unsuccessful in Madrid, the persecuted scientist could perhaps find grace in Berlin.

Two years later, Marat wrote again to the Prussian capital. This time he addressed Samuel Formey, the secretary of the Berlin Academy, sending a copy of his *Mémoires académiques* for the Academy's consideration. A committee had been created for this purpose, Formey told him in response, but it had soon discovered that Marat had omitted to send the *Notions élémentaires* declared in the *Mémoires* to be indispensable to the latter's comprehension. Lacking this evidence, the committee could not proceed. Formey wondered whether Marat could call on members of the Berlin Academy currently in Paris for advice on how to get the committee the copy of the work it needed. He also expressed puzzlement that Marat claimed to be a subject of the Prussian king. He and his colleagues had no idea how that might be the case. Nor had they been helped by consulting *France littéraire*, a standard directory of French writers. Not surprisingly, given its date of publication in 1769, that compendium had offered them no entry under Marat's name.[51]

The frustrated petitioner responded immediately in early May with the information that the *Notions élémentaires* would be found included with the copies of the *Mémoires académiques* he had sent to his earlier Berlin correspondent (whom he now identified as baron Heiniz) and with a copy of a baptismal certificate documenting his status as a Prussian subject. "I could add that if my admiration for a monarch who is truly father of his peoples could extend the bonds of the social state, I would be doubly the subject of Frederick William II."[52] This effusive language apparently yielding no response, he wrote to Formey again, probably toward the end of June, to state more explicitly his desire to be admitted to the Berlin Academy. "Deign, Monsieur, to extend to this illustrious society the homage of my works on physics and to state on my behalf that if I have served the sciences well I will regard the honor of being admitted to the number of its members as a flattering recompense for my work. Dare I await your indulgence for the Academy's judgment of my discoveries when it is pronounced, and the return of the baptismal certificate included in my previous letter?"[53] Sadly, we know nothing more of this initiative.

Nothing came, either, from a letter addressed to the president of the "Académie de Boston et Américaine" on 8 February 1788, along with a copy of the *Mémoires académiques*, a work containing "useful truths . . . of the greatest importance, for their influence on the construction of optical, astronomical, and naval instruments, and for the study of the science that they render shorter and easier." The Academy was requested to appoint a committee to examine the book "with rigor," repeat its experiments, confirm its author's conclusions, and "consecrate the theory flowing from them"—on the assumption, of course, that it had "lifted a corner of Nature's veil." A committee was indeed appointed to this task on 12 November, but no further activity was reported. Nature's veil was apparently left untouched.[54]

If not Berlin or Boston, then what about London? A plea could also be sent to the mighty naturalist Sir Joseph Banks, president of the Royal Society. To Banks Marat turned in March 1788 to request that institution's approbation of his *Mémoires académiques*. The Royal Society did not customarily pronounce its judgment on works submitted to it, he acknowledged in an effusive letter of 27 March. But it had done so in the case of Franklin's kite experiments, he insisted, and again in considering the great American's ideas regarding the construction of lightning rods.

His own new experiments he proffered to Banks as surely no less important, no less worthy of an exceptional review. The truths deriving from them would simplify the study of optics and transform the manufacture of astronomical and naval instruments. "In marking them with the degree of confidence they merit, the Royal Society will thus contribute to the progress of science; it will save young persons destined for that science from the disgust of long and sterile study as well as from the irreparable loss of precious time; and it will show opticians the way to perfect their art, for, as long as it is based on an erroneous theory, as it now is, it will only ever amount to a blind routine." Banks was asked to support this request in putting it before the Royal Society and deploying for the progress of the most sublime of the exact sciences the enlightened zeal he had so often displayed for the advance of natural history.[55]

Unmoved by this appeal, Sir Joseph drafted a blunt response. The Royal Society was too busy advancing knowledge itself to examine "works already submitted to the tribunal of the Public," he maintained; indeed, it had never even expressed a judgment on the works of Newton. The special treatment for which Marat was pleading was simply not possible. Besides, came the final barb, "your Royal Academy of Sciences has already made known its judgment of your work."[56] A door was being firmly closed.

Marat's response was so furiously written that the letters threatened to skid off the manuscript page. Politesse was now abandoned. If Banks had taken the trouble to open the work sent to him, the injured author exclaimed, he would have seen that it had nothing in common with the one that had been submitted to the judgment of the Paris Academy of Sciences eight years before. If he had taken the trouble to page through the work, he would have been so struck by the experiments it described that he would have rushed to repeat them himself, he would have recognized their exactitude, and he would surely have drawn from them the same conclusions as the author himself. But no! "No, Sir, I am not unaware of how difficult it is for new truths to come to light when they collide with an accepted system, how numerous is the crowd of people who agitate to snuff them out, how few are the number of those who agree to accept them, and how little these truths have to expect from the zeal of so many societies instituted to propagate them. But I had thought obliged to make an honorable exception in favor of the body you preside, and it is in consequence of this manner of thinking that I renew my appeal."

The outburst over, and respectful once more, Marat again rehearsed for Banks the importance of his research and its practical implications. Again he begged that the Royal Society give his experiments the exceptional review he thought they deserved, one that would "confirm my discoveries and consecrate them in its bosom." But this tone could not be sustained. The passive voice soon gave way once more to the aggressive, to the threat of a final judgment expressed by a higher authority. "If my prayer is finally rejected without appeal, one day the public will know of my unceasing efforts to proscribe error and it will learn with astonishment that the truth found neither friend nor defender even in your Society."[57]

One day, indeed, the world would know. One day the world would change. One day soon. But not in any way Jean-Paul Marat had anticipated.

THYMOTIC POLITICS

THIRTEEN

REVOLUTIONARY REBIRTH

Marat fell gravely ill toward the end of 1788. Fearing death, he briefly entrusted his friend Breguet with his papers and scientific instruments. The latter were to be conveyed at his demise, in a posthumous act of defiance, to the Academy of Sciences. In later years he saw this bout of illness as symbolizing a passage toward transformation. An open letter he addressed to the president of the revolutionary National Assembly in May 1790 likened his travails under the Old Regime to those of the French nation. The critical engagement in radical politics to which he had been drawn in England had been too dangerous to continue in France, he now claimed. He had turned instead to a career in the sciences—only to encounter persecution by multiple enemies. He saw his own victimization reflecting that of the French nation. Abuses of all kinds had been reaching their height, the people had been growing increasingly wretched, the wealthy had been discovering the expropriation of their fortunes to pay for court excesses, and enlightened minds had been longing for a new order of things. As the French barely escaped annihilation, so did he. "Long groaning at the ills of my country, I was on my deathbed when a friend, the only one I had wished to witness my final moments, informed me of the calling of the Estates General. This news made a strong impression on me, I experienced a salutary crisis, my courage revived, and the first use I made of it was to give my fellow citizens proof of my devotion. I wrote *L'Offrande à la patrie*."[1]

Alerted by Breguet in this telling, Marat wrote his way back to health—as he would eventually write his way to his death. The persecuted scientist was delivered to persecute in his turn, the "apostle and martyr of liberty" was born.

In January 1793, again under particular fire for his radical views, Marat once more recounted the story of his deliverance from the injustices of the Old Regime. This time, he emphasized the "ten years of disgraceful persecution" he had received from the likes of "the d'Alemberts, the Caritats [de Condorcet], the Le Roys, the Meuniers, the Lalandes, the Laplaces, the Monges, the Cousins, the Lavoisiers," those charlatans of the Academy of Sciences who wanted to remain at the top of the heap, orchestrating the trumpets of renown. "I was groaning for five years under this cowardly oppression when the revolution was announced by the convocation of the Estates General," he declared. "I soon saw the way things were going and I began to breathe again in the hope of seeing humanity finally avenged, of helping break its chains, and of achieving my place. This was still only a fine dream about to vanish; a cruel illness threatened that I would finish it in the tomb. Not wishing to end my life without doing something for the cause of liberty, I composed *L'Offrande à la patrie* on a bed of pain. This little work had much success . . . the pleasure I felt was the principal cause of my recovery. Restored to life, I only occupied myself thereafter with the means of serving the cause of liberty."[2]

Thus "restored to life," Marat seized a moment of opportunity for yet another career. He became a political pamphleteer and then a revolutionary journalist. His very existence would henceforth be utterly bound up with the Revolution. It is striking that illness, recovery, and the passage to political resurrection were so closely related in his accounts of this rebirth. Thanks to Jacques-Louis David's painting immortalizing him at the moment of his assassination in his medicinal bath, Marat is remembered as the most dramatically afflicted among the revolutionaries. Though we have no way of ascertaining this, the grave illnesses from which he suffered in 1782 and 1788 may well have sprung from the same underlying condition that would incapacitate him by 1793. We can only guess at its nature, and many retrospective diagnoses have been hazarded. It seems likely that he suffered from some kind of itching, burning, purulent skin disease spreading from the anogenital area. A recent analysis of DNA from a bloodstain on an issue of his journal cast doubt on contemporary diagnoses such as syphilis and leprosy, hypothesizing "a fungal infection (seborrheic dermatitis), possibly superinfected with bacterial opportunistic pathogens."[3] It could well have been an inflammatory bowel disease or acute celiac disease, or similar chronic condition that can flare up during periods of stress. The years 1782 and 1788 saw particular despair and frustration of Marat's hopes for scientific recognition. Months of privation subsequently spent in hiding during the revolutionary period, culminating in exhaustion from intense political engagement, could only have exacerbated the seriousness of his symptoms to the point of forcing his confinement to a curative bath in 1793. He was widely rumored to be again on his deathbed at the time of Charlotte Corday's fateful visit in July 1793.

AN OFFERING TO THE NATION

L'Offrande à la patrie, the pamphlet that brought Marat back to life, bore the inscription, "From the Temple of Liberty, 1789." Addressing "my fellow citizens" and "my fellow countrymen," he apostrophized France as "my homeland." Reborn, he was no longer seeking patronage and recognition in Paris, Madrid, Berlin, or London. Claiming the rights of citizenship for the French, he was also arrogating this new status to himself. Together with them, he would become a citizen rather than a subject. The constitution of 1791 would eventually confer formal citizenship on him, as on all descendants of the Huguenots driven from the country a century earlier.

This *Offering to the Nation, or Address to the Third Estate of France*, his first revolutionary pamphlet, was among the thousands unleashed in Paris in the months following the French government's decision to accede to public demands for a meeting of the Estates General, the antique representative assembly of the traditional three orders of the realm—clergy, nobility, and commoners of the "Third Estate." Louis XVI's ministers had not made this decision willingly. A half-century of global competition against the British, culminating in French intervention in the American War of Independence, had proved ruinous to crown finances. Necker, the Genevan banker who had overseen the French treasury for five years before he was forced from office in 1781, had kept the government afloat by amassing loans negotiated on the international market. In the years that followed, as borrowing became harder and the threat of government bankruptcy increased, his successors had been forced to formulate plans to reform a tax system that sheltered the incomes of the privileged and laid a heavy but still inadequate burden on the commoners of the so-called Third Estate. Recognizing that matters were reaching a point of crisis, a new finance minister, Calonne, had summoned the elite of the realm to an Assembly of Notables in 1787. The participants were invited to approve two radical reforms: the introduction of an indefinite tax on all landowners that would replace the complex exemptions and particularistic arrangements of privileged persons, corporate bodies, and provincial jurisdictions that constrained the powers of the monarchy to raise revenues; and the creation of provincial assemblies, representing all three Estates together, to participate in tax assessment and local administration.

Calonne's plan had been resolutely resisted by the Notables as contrary to the fundamental constitution of a realm that was—by its very legal and historical nature as a monarchy comprising provinces, orders, and Estates—multiple, differentiated, and particularistic. As a result, the minister had been forced to resign. His replacement, Archbishop Brienne, had brought a version of these same reform initiatives before the parlements, the high courts of justice that had contested royal authority on many occasions throughout the century. This time, Brienne's heavy-handed government pressure had been resisted by the privileged magistrates of these courts, led by the Parlement of Paris and with increasingly vociferous public support. Efforts at compromise had been destroyed by inflamed political opinions on all sides. The result had been a full-blown constitutional crisis in the spring of 1788: the Paris magistrates had thundered against royal despotism and issued a declaration of the fundamental rights of the nation; the ministers had denounced parlementary resistance as a defense of aristocratic privilege and restructured the entire legal system to reduce the courts to submission. The contestation triggered widespread popular protest and scattered outbursts of insurrection in support of the parlements.

Throughout this period, demands for the calling of the Estates General had grown louder. First the Assembly of Notables, then the judicial magistrates, and finally the Assembly of the Clergy had declared this traditional gathering the only representative body that could agree to new taxation. With the government's political and financial credit entirely evaporating, Brienne had seen no choice but to yield to these demands. He had announced on 8 August that the Estates General would meet on 1 May 1789. His resignation had followed shortly thereafter, presaging a meltdown of the French state.

The Estates General had not been convened since 1614. How exactly would it be organized in 1789? Acknowledging publicly in July 1788 that it could not answer this question, the government had called for research into the nation's archives to recover the historical precedents for a "truly national assembly." This amazing announcement was doubtless a tactic to play for time and to sow division from which the government might eventually profit. But it also brought into the open a fundamental political problem. The Estates General was now being called to represent the nation, but in what form? What exactly was the nature and composition of the nation to be represented? With this problem abruptly posed, the political debate suddenly shifted.

The enormity of the issue might be suggested by a somewhat far-fetched counterfactual comparison. Imagine that for some improbable reason it became necessary in the United States today to recall the Constitutional Convention of 1787. Many questions would have to be addressed to make that body, or the constitution it might produce, reflect the social and political evolution of American society over the past two hundred years. Twelve of the thirteen initial states had sent delegations to that convention, each delegation exercising an equal vote. Should that number now be increased to fifty? Should Washington, DC, now be added? What about US territories? More fundamentally, should each state delegation now have an equal vote, or should votes be allocated to them differentially in proportion to the size of the population they represent? Beyond this issue of whether representation should be by state or by population, further questions would be raised about the nature of representation within state delegations. How should Native Americans now be represented, or women, or the descendants of former slaves, or those of immigrants? Why should differential representation not be demanded to compensate for earlier injustices? How should electoral districts be drawn? Should weighted representation be demanded for great cities, or for unprivileged suburbs? One can readily see that questions like these would prompt an intense and divisive public debate. How would they be decided? By constitutional bodies suddenly rendered provisional? How else? The entire character and composition of the nation would be up for grabs.[4]

Analogous questions faced the French at the end of 1788. How should a body that had not assembled for 175 years now be convoked to represent a society that had profoundly changed its character in the interim? By what definition of the body politic would this gathering be made a "national" assembly? How would the matter be decided? The Parlement of Paris gave its answer toward the end of September 1788: it declared that the Estates General should meet according to the forms observed in 1614. This was taken to mean that there would be three chambers separately elected to represent the clergy, the nobility, and the Third Estate, with the members of each chamber meeting separately to vote "by order" (as a distinct body, or "Estate") rather than "by head" (as individuals, without regard to social status). The effect of this decision would be a tricameral assembly in which, whatever the numbers of individual deputies within each chamber and however they were chosen, the privileged orders of the clergy and the nobility could always outvote, by two to one, the commoners in the Third Estate.

The parlement's proclamation ignited an immense conflagration of protests, petitions, and pamphlets that was rendered all the more furious by the fact that the government had now abandoned efforts to enforce traditional limitations on the press. From this explosion of claims and counterclaims there emerged widespread sentiment in favor of "doubling" the Third Estate and instituting vote "by head." This would mean that commoners would have a number of representatives in the Estates General equal to those of the clergy and nobility combined, and that (to give this doubling of its numbers political force) decisions would be made collectively by a vote of the entire body of the representatives regardless of any division by Estate. It was the arrangement introduced by Necker in earlier provincial assemblies and now favored by him for the Estates General as he was called back to Versailles as finance minister in August 1788. To achieve it, he convened his own Assembly of Notables in November.

Despite his broad popularity, Necker fared little better with this second Assembly of Notables than had Brienne with the first. The Notables voted overwhelmingly against the doubling of the Third Estate and insisted that the matter of the vote by head be left for the Estates General itself to decide when it eventually convened. With local conflicts over representation now breaking out across the realm, Necker issued a decision of the Council of State on 27 December. It ordered the doubling of the representation of the Third Estate but left open whether the Estates General would be required to vote by head or by order. This absolutely crucial question, the one upon which the significance of the doubling of the Third Estate would depend, remained for the deputies themselves to decide when they arrived in Versailles at a date still not firmly fixed. The stage was set for confrontation.

It was the declaration of 27 December that aroused Marat to pen the *Offrande à la patrie*. This pamphlet is so febrile that one can easily imagine it written from a sickbed. Nonetheless, it suggests the confusion of the political situation in France at the very beginning of 1789 and the uncertainty regarding available options. One minute it fantasizes the people's revenge against privileged oppressors, the next it is hoping for the rapprochement of the three Estates in pursuit of the common good. One minute it threatens a refusal of taxes that would incite civil war and invite foreign invasion, the next it applauds a generous king and wise ministers ready to preside over the transformation of a divided nation. It lacks the incisive logic, the clear analytical vision, and the sheer rhetorical virtuosity of the most celebrated pamphlet to appear at the same time, *What Is the Third Estate?* by the abbé Sieyès. It also reveals a very different historical and political sensibility.

Sieyès repudiated entirely the arguments resting on historical precedent or constitutional claims that filled many of the contemporaneous pamphlets. He did not plead for rights of the nation as historically constituted; he articulated in the most radical terms the principle of entire, unconstrained, and inalienable national sovereignty essential to the very nature of the nation as a political body. In effect, he announced a new political ontology that made the nation the ultimate ground of politics: the nation could never be less than one and indivisible; it could never alienate the exercise of its sovereignty; nothing could constrain the exercise of its common will. To answer the question posed by its title *What Is the Third Estate?* proceeded according to a logic of excision. Analyzing the nation in economic terms as a modern society based on relations of production and exchange, Sieyès excluded the privileged from it by the very act of definition: they were parasites living in idleness from the labor of the productive Third Estate. Defining the nation politically as an association of citizens sharing equal status and a common law, he excluded the privileged from it on the grounds that their claims to particular statuses automatically rendered them an alien body within it, an *imperium in imperio*. By this logic, the Third Estate constituted the nation in its entirety; its representatives, once elected, had necessarily to declare themselves a national assembly. Only as a unitary body could they represent the sovereign, common will of a nation one and indivisible.

Sieyès had moved beyond the politics of protest against ministerial despotism; he had as much contempt for the English model of liberty inherited from earlier times as he did for the tradition of French absolutism. There was nothing of the English Commonwealth Man in *What Is the Third Estate?* Marat, in contrast, saw the French situation through the political lens he had fashioned for himself in *The Chains of Slavery*. Ministerial despotism was his target. *L'Offrande à la patrie* began with an evocation of corrupt and despotic ministers ravaging the nation in the name of absolute monarchs ruling by virtue of conquest and divine right. Indeed, much of the pamphlet was taken up by denunciation of the succession of ministers that had brought France to such a disastrous plight over the previous quarter-century. It showed a people punished for its blind obedience to kings by being delivered over to the depredations of "inept, crazed, and destructive" ministers.[5]

But the time was past, Marat now declared, when stupefied subjects believed themselves slaves. Enlightened men were telling monarchs everywhere "that the sovereign power resides in the body of the nation, from which emanates all legitimate authority, that princes have been established to enforce the laws to which they are themselves subject, that they reign through justice and owe it to the very least of their subjects." In this analysis, the despairing cries of a tormented people had finally reached the ears of a monarch outraged at the abuse of his authority. At last there was a moment of choice, an opportunity to grasp freedom through the exercise of a determined political will. "Oh Frenchmen, your ills are over if you are tired of enduring them; you are free if you have the courage to be so."[6]

This was the language of classical republicanism, deployed in definition of a moment of political crisis in which liberty could either be regained or once more lost. "Know for once the price of liberty, know for once the price of a moment," Marat urged the French people; "refuse everything . . . until your rights have been fixed irrevocably." It was necessary above all, he argued, for the Third Estate to refuse the offer of the privileged orders to pay off the government debt. "Beware of the trap they're setting for you," he warned. "They agree to pay once without limit in order not to have to pay for life; acting once for everyone, they would remain in control of the field of battle; they would hold you down for ever, they would weigh on your chains and continue to fatten themselves on your sweat while gorging themselves on your blood." Forced to choose between the Third Estate and the privileged orders, Marat anticipated, Louis XVI could not but opt for the former. "You are the force and the wealth of the state. At your head, the king will be the most powerful monarch in the universe. Without you, at the head of the nobility and the clergy, he would only ever be a simple lord among his vassals; like the little princes of the Empire, he would be forced to beg protection from a powerful neighbor; afraid of being crushed by it, he would soon cease to be counted among the potentates."[7]

Sieyès, an economist who saw himself as the rival of Adam Smith, wanted the freedom of the market to provide for social needs. Marat wanted economic justice too, but political liberty above all. Demand what you need to feed, lodge, and clothe yourselves and to raise your children, he warned the Third Estate, but "assure the liberty of your persons against the assaults of ministerial despotism, your innocence against iniquitous judges, the honor of your wives and children against the maneuvers of the titled, your reputation against the attacks of favored calumniators; obtain justice against the powerful oppressors and procure for yourself the facilities to develop your talent and cultivate your happiness. . . . This is the only way to render the nation flourishing, respected, and feared, and to bring the honor of the French name to the height of glory."[8]

For Marat, as for Sieyès, the unity of the Third Estate was thus a crucial principle of action. But Sieyès wanted to establish that unity by way of exclusion, eliminating from his conception of the nation all those who did not contribute productively or accept equal status in it. Marat, in contrast, insisted that the Third Estate maintain its unity by inclusion—by resisting efforts to shave off some of its varied components: the wealthy financiers, the newly ennobled, the royal and urban officials, lawyers and lower magistrates, the lower clergy, the men of letters, scientists, and philosophers. His Third Estate comprised the servants, laborers, workers, artisans, merchants, bankers, farmers, untitled property owners and *rentiers*, teachers, artists, surgeons, doctors, writers, savants, lawyers, magistrates of the lower courts, priests, soldiers, sailors, and so on, "an innumerable and invincible legion that contains knowledge, talents, force, and the virtues." At its head would be placed those nobles, magistrates, seigneurs, prelates, and magnanimous royal princes who could forget their prerogatives and be content to remain simple citizens.[9]

This strategy required strict attention to the choice of representatives. In this regard, Marat drew his advice to the Third Estate, almost verbatim, from the address he had offered the English nation in *The Chains of Slavery*. "Remove from the arena rash and fiery young men, men reputed for their superficiality and frivolity, men given over to dissipation, luxury, debauch, greed, ambition," he urged. The Third Estate had to choose right-minded men of recognized probity and clear talents, men zealous for the public good, experienced men with interests inseparable from those electing them, grave and mature men beyond reproach. It needed deputies impervious to the temptations of corruption, men freed from necessity by their fortune or their work, independent men whose positions did not depend on the favor of the great or of a minister. "Your happiness, your salvation, depends on your choice of representatives. . . . Tremble that in disdaining the counsels of wisdom and yielding to the lures of seduction, your own hands do not dig an abyss beneath your feet. Tremble that your children do not one day reproach you for having riveted their chains, that in deploring the bitter fruit of servitude and moaning under their ills they do not curse their fathers' venality."[10]

To avoid this fate required that the French monarchy finally be given a fixed constitution. All would be lost, Marat declared, if an assembly of the nation did not assert its sovereignty to impose fundamental laws. It would have to be established that the Estates General meet regularly at least every three years, setting its own agenda and procedures, and consenting to taxation only for a three-year period at a time. A corruption-proof committee would have to remain in existence in the interim between these meetings to watch over the constitution and prevent abuses. Other fundamental laws would abolish *lettres de cachet* and arbitrary acts of authority, reform criminal procedure following the example of England, and guarantee the principle of proportional taxation.

No less crucially for Marat, complete freedom of the press would become a fundamental law. It was necessary to prevent clandestine works of denunciation and libel, intrigue and fraud, the despotism of academies, persecution of talent, perpetuation of error and ignorance, and all the evils brought about by royal censors—these latter serving as instruments "invented to stifle the cries of liberty against tyranny, innocence against oppression, reason against fanaticism, merit against charlatanism, to prevent minds from soaring, talents from developing, and genius from deploying its powers." Liberty of the press had prevented all these abuses in England, he announced—the personal experience he had claimed to the contrary notwithstanding. But the fundamental laws that France could soon boast would also surpass the British example. "It is not a matter of obtaining a Magna Carta from the King but of a legitimate government that the nation must establish. In this, the French constitution will be superior to the English because, in every well-ordered state, the nation doesn't hold its rights from the prince, but the prince holds his prerogatives from the nation."[11]

Only fundamental laws such as these could return French government to its primitive constitution and destroy its radical vices, maintained the *Offrande à la patrie*. That said, the pamphlet concluded with a touching vision still meant perhaps as a possible last testament from the author's sickbed. "Dear homeland, I see your children united in a sweet society of brothers, securely resting under the sacred empire of the laws, living in abundance and peace, animated by love of the public good and happy in your honor. I see them forming an enlightened, judicious, brilliant, redoubtable, invincible nation, their adored head at the pinnacle of glory." Achievement of this vision required wisdom and courage. "If you lack them, it will disappear like a dream; a hideous awakening will find you in misery and enchained. May the divine fire of liberty, which always burned in my breast, flare up in yours!"[12]

Little of this utopia would be found in Marat's subsequent appeals to the French nation. He would soon find the French sadly in need of wisdom, courage, constancy, and the divine fire of liberty. His dream of unity was destined to disappear; his hopes would soon give way to despair. It would become his obsession to goad the people to that *hideous awakening* that would bring it to political consciousness of its misery and oppression. Warnings that *all will be lost* without immediate action, admonitions to *tremble* before the political *abyss*, revelations of *traps* set for a *stupefied and mindless* people: these would become keywords in his political arsenal. From this first revolutionary pamphlet to the last issue of his journal more than three years later, Marat would make outrage, denunciation, denigration, exposure, urgency, despair, fear, and trembling the order of the day.

AN OFFER TO THE KING

L'Offrande à la patrie did not go unnoticed amid the flood of writings that opened 1789. In his own estimation, Marat had "uncovered the abyss and sounded its depths," but he feared his pamphlet would be washed away in the "deluge of futile works inundating the public." Feeble works, he thought now, as he had in England a decade and a half earlier, would crowd out the bold. Nonetheless, *L'Offrande* was favored with particular condemnation by the former finance minister Calonne, who warned Louis XVI against it in a pamphlet of his own dated 9 February. For the disgraced minister, it exemplified the "incendiary writings that . . . all seem coordinated to lead the nation to the most boundless pretensions."[13]

Marat, meanwhile, was beginning to bring his ideas into clearer focus, particularly after 24 January when more specific electoral regulations for the Estates General were published. How eager he had been to read these long-awaited letters of convocation, he declared; how sad he was in doing so. He had looked for "the simple, true tone of a tender father who desires only the good for his children, who is moved at the sight of their miseries and outraged against the guilty authors of their ills, who is preparing to rescue them from oppression and restore them to liberty and peace." He had found "only the banal language of an imperious prince whose affairs are disordered and who is quite willing to accept the supplications of his subjects provided they give him in return the means of escaping his difficulties." The result was a new publication, a *Supplément à L'Offrande à la patrie* that parsed the January regulations in considerable detail. The nation had been too long caught in misery between the contending powers of despotic ministers and oppressive magistrates, the pamphlet proclaimed. "It's time for it finally to open its eyes . . . , to recognize all its resources are in its hands, and courageously reclaim its sacred and imprescriptible rights."[14]

How to provoke this awakening, if not by activating and exploiting the meaning of terms? This new broadside began, as would so many others in the war of words shaping the revolutionary struggle, with definitions of "terms continually abused." Dictionaries were to become revolutionary armaments, and counterrevolutionary ones too. In the lexicon Marat now offered, *sovereign* meant the nation itself, assembled in a body or represented by its deputies. *Constitution* signified the body of fundamental laws governing the different powers within the political body and the rights of its subjects. *Legislator* designated the sovereign exercising its legislative power. *Government* referred to the body entrusted with executive power, comprising the king, his ministers, and councilors. *Administration* signified the exercise of government functions. *Tribunals* were the bodies charged with judicial power. It followed from these definitions that in a well-constituted state the legislative, executive, and judicial powers had to be placed in different hands, each separate from the other and all subject to the power of the sovereign nation. "Thus a nation is only free in as much as it retains sovereignty, can repress the government, and keeps watch on it. Since the rights of nations are no less sacred or imprescriptible than the rights of man, it can always reclaim them or rather it never loses them, usurpation never becoming a valid title, even after ten thousand centuries of possession." There followed a familiar series of Commonwealth arguments for mixed government as the best means of slowing the inevitable drift of liberty toward despotism.[15]

From this perspective, there was little to like in Necker's January announcement. In Marat's analysis, it offered no more than a vague project to reinstate order and repair the poor state of government finances. He saw through grandiloquent ministerial phrases promising the reform of abuses and eternal public happiness, to be effected by the establishment of a constant and invariable administrative order. These promises, he thought, would be realized only as far and as long as particular ministers saw fit. They fell far short of relieving the people's misery and assuring the nation's happiness. The ministers, having abused the king's authority to plunge the state into the abyss, allowed Louis XVI no recognition of "the public calamities, the sad lamentations of his subjects reduced to despair."

Nor did the announcement grant the king's subjects any acknowledgment of their rights. It filled Marat with fury that the order of convocation summoned deputies to arrive at Versailles carrying the traditional *cahiers de doléances*: declarations of grievances, and mandates for action, drawn up in their constituencies. This vicious mode of proceeding, he predicted, would constrain the liberty of the Estates General to decide matters, divide the assembly, undermine its deliberations, and leave the government supreme arbitrator of the demands and rights of the citizens. "It's not *complaints* but cries of indignation that we'll raise against the authors of our misery. *Hopes* are not what we'll express, but claims of the rights of man and of the citizen. The nation isn't begging a favor, it's demanding justice and expecting it. Father of the people, reinstate us in those sacred rights that nature gave us. Help us break our chains, give us back our liberty and then demand our blood."[16]

From this appeal followed a series of challenges addressed more or less directly to the monarch. In Marat's analysis, the time for petty palliatives was past. The king had to relieve the nation of its misery by sweeping away the entire apparatus of the baroque state. "At the sight of an entire nation in movement and of these immense preparations to do good, I ask myself: is the good so difficult to accomplish when one wants it sincerely? The public treasury has been ransacked, I would tell the prince; make a terrible example of the plunderers. . . . The temple of justice is inhabited by oppressors; reform the criminal laws and the tribunals. . . . Perhaps I'm wrong, but it seems to me that the depository of the public force needs only the right conviction, good will, and firmness to reform all the crying abuses and give the government the direction it must have."

A reforming king, Marat promised in his turn, would have the support of an entire nation. "As for the numerous vicious men with interests in the bad state of things, what can they do when one has the mass of the people, the body of the nation, behind one? Show the nation by action, and not by words, that you really want its good. Begin by reforming this empty ostentation, this vain pomp that adds nothing to the majesty of the throne and the dignity of the monarch while exhausting the provinces. Cut deep. Take back that multitude of pensions grabbed through intrigue or snatched through favoritism. Trim the excessive ones, even if they are deserved. Make the tax farmers, the extortionists, the men on the take, and the plunderers of the state disgorge their gains. Turn them over to the public indignation."[17]

Cut deep! This was Dr. Marat's prescription. In effect, he was inviting an alliance between the monarch and the Third Estate against the privileged, the placeholders, and the pensioners. But he did not call for the respectful subordination to the royal will preached by some advocates of such an alliance. "No liberty without order, no order without subordination, no subordination without authority, no authority without a provisional legislator," one of its propagandists had declared.[18] Marat would have none of this. His plans for the people were not timid, he allowed; they could cause disruption in the political order. But he would not see the nation advance unprepared toward the fateful day that would decide its history. He would not have it shrink, that day, from actions in the name of liberty that others would call revolt. "No, my dear compatriots, that day will not find you lulled in sleep, but prepared for combat, armed with courage, and sacrificing to nature, justice, and liberty on the altars of wisdom."[19]

A national assembly free from royal control, voting by head, and making common decisions in a single chamber: these conditions alone, Marat maintained, could open the way to liberty and the institution of fundamental laws. The assembly should neither vote taxes nor accept dissolution until such laws had been achieved through a confrontation and renewed negotiation between the people and the king. The result could be a constitutional regime resting on the principle of national sovereignty, the institution of a standing representative assembly, a secure separation of powers, and the abandonment of royal claims to prerogatives of arbitrary rule the monarch had never been granted. "The only sacrifice the nation demands of the monarch is to renounce rights that he does not and cannot have. This new order of things will in no way diminish the prerogatives of the crown and, in cementing public happiness, it will assure forever the authority, the peace, and the happiness of the king."[20] Here was a challenge Necker might have welcomed, but not one Louis XVI and the majority of his ministers were ready to accept.

Political struggles lay ahead. Marat did not fail to assure the nation that it would find guidance in a work upon which the *Supplément* explicitly drew, "an English work entitled *The Chains of Slavery*, a work as remarkable for its energy as for its profundity. I hear that a patriotic society is currently busy on a translation to put the nation in a position to profit from the great lessons it contains." It would be several years before any full translation of this book would appear. In the meantime, its author would continue to draw on it as he scripted a path through a new kind of revolution. "In times of disorder and confusion, it's the duty of friends of the homeland to devote all their thoughts to it," he promised. "My dear fellow countrymen, the desire to see you free and happy inflames my breast and, like a devouring fire, consumes it night and day."[21]

These were passionate words, in a pamphlet radical enough to arouse the suspicion of the authorities. On 12 March, the lieutenant general of police ordered all available copies of the *Supplément* seized, together with the matrices from the print shop that had produced it.[22]

UNCERTAIN DAYS

How did Marat respond during the succeeding weeks, as residents of the sixty electoral districts created in Paris began the extraordinary experiment of naming the delegates who would choose the city's deputies to the Estates General? How did he react as political excitement inflamed tensions over wage levels and the price of bread, causing working areas of the capital to explode into riots? In fact, we know very little of his actions during this period, though it appears that he participated in the electoral body of his locality, the district des Carmes-Déchaussés, and was actively engaged in its choice of delegates to the electoral assembly of the municipality. From the vantage point of this district committee, he must have followed closely the news from Versailles once the Estates General convened on 5 May 1789. Could he not have applauded the determination of the Third Estate deputies in refusing to verify their status as members of a distinct chamber separate from those of the clergy and nobility? Could he not have relished the weeks-long political struggle that ensued as the three Estates fought, in effect, to decide the great issue Necker had left unresolved: would they deliberate by order or by head? Could he not have hailed the decisive vote taken on 17 June by the Third Estate deputies (now joined by a few renegades from among the clergy and the nobility) to declare themselves a National Assembly representing a unitary and sovereign people? Could he not have rejoiced at this Assembly's obstinacy three days later, when its defiant members bound themselves by the Tennis Court Oath not to disband "until the constitution of the realm is established and strengthened on solid foundations"?[23]

The decisive assertion of a national political will for which Marat had called in his pamphlets had been conjured up, though not perhaps in quite the manner he had anticipated. There would be no alliance between the king and his people. Deep divisions had been opened, both in and around what would henceforth be called the National Assembly. Given his later views, it seems unlikely that he welcomed reports that deputies of the clergy and the nobility were now moving over to join the Assembly in significant numbers. Nor could he have been enthusiastic at the news, on 27 June, that the king had ordered the remaining and most recalcitrant deputies of the privileged orders to quit their separate assemblies and do the same. The presence of these beneficiaries of the Old Regime, many of them increasingly embittered by the course of events, would rapidly pollute and pervert the National Assembly in his eyes. Could such a body, corrupted from within, actually sustain its claim to represent the unitary will of the people? Marat would soon begin calling for a purge.

If the first momentous act of the French Revolution was the revolt of the deputies played out in Versailles in June 1789, the second was the insurrection of the people in Paris the following month. Marat was no stranger to popular mobilization. He had witnessed it in London at the time of the Wilkes Affair. He would now observe it in Paris. Doubtless he took note as crowds numbering in the thousands began gathering daily at the Palais Royal. This site, the eighteenth-century version of a shopping mall—part park, public garden, pleasure den, commercial center, and luxury residences—had been developed by the duc d'Orléans in the very center of the city, a stone's throw from the palaces of the Louvre and the Tuileries. It now became a hypersensitive political node of the capital. Its bookstores were loaded with hundreds of the latest pamphlets, its spaces resounded with speeches, proclamations, and plans. Reports from Versailles were quickly relayed to its crowds. Ten thousand people were there to celebrate news of the Tennis Court Oath. But the political mood soon changed. Joy turned into anxiety in the following days as royal troops began moving to encircle the city. And anxiety flared into panic as the dismissal of the still popular Necker from the ministry on 11 July was interpreted as a prelude to military repression in the capital and the forced dispersion of the National Assembly from Versailles. In the days that followed, the Parisian populace sought desperately for arms, and for bread. Customs barriers and gatehouses bordering the city were already burning by the night of 13 July; suspected arsenals were being invaded in a hunt for weapons.

The next day, the crowd turned its search toward the royal fortress of the Bastille, long since identified as a bastion of arbitrary power. This time, the mob was reinforced by mutinous French guards. The prudent decision of the prison's governor, Bernard-René de Launay, to surrender this symbol of royal despotism did not save him from being hacked to pieces. His head was paraded around the city on a pike, accompanied by that of Jacques Flesselles, the municipal official suspected of impeding the efforts of an enraged people to arm itself. A week later the intendant of Paris, accused of attempting to starve the city into submission, was strung up and dismembered together with his father-in-law, the two of them caught as they tried to escape the city.

"Was this blood so pure?" it was asked. Marat scarcely had to wonder at the question, but he condemned the disorderly manner in which the guilty blood had been shed. Not for the last time, he called upon the National Assembly to create a special tribunal to try crimes against the state. "To the atrocious scenes the people's vengeance has produced there must succeed regular judgments," he wrote. "Let the punishment be capital and shameful for traitors to the nation who want to bathe in its blood or make it die of hunger . . . but let it be lawful." Marat wanted the harshest penalties for abuse of power, but penalties imposed by strict legal process. "Punish crime without violating justice" had been the watchword of the treatise on criminal law he had written a decade earlier.[24]

We know little beyond this of Marat's actions in this revolutionary moment. Decades later, the counterrevolutionary author Mallet du Pan was cited as hearing him preach the doctrine of *The Social Contract* in the streets, but there seems no way of knowing when, or whether, this was true.[25] Marat himself later claimed to have been horrified at the stupidity of the people's blind faith in Necker, even though he confessed to supporting the minister's recall the very day the Bastille fell. He also confided to Brissot, for publication in the latter's journal, that he had played a heroic part on the evening of 14 July in turning back a detachment of dragoons heading into the city. In this telling, the commanding officer harangued the crowd, promising that the troops would be there to fight alongside the citizens. But Marat turned his fellow Parisians against the soldiers, denouncing them as agents of an aristocratic plot to murder the patriots in the middle of the night. The reluctant officer was convinced to order a retreat. "It is known," Marat later wrote, "that at nightfall on 14 July I aborted the project to take Paris by surprise by treasonously introducing several regiments of dragoons and German cavalry, a numerous detachment of whom had already been received with acclamations."[26] Perhaps this did happen.

Following this patriotic act, Marat recalled, he spent the next three days without interruption at the former electoral assembly of des Carmes that was now, like other district assemblies of the capital, declaring itself a section of the people in permanent session. With the Bastille's fall, the entire municipal government of Paris was abruptly reorganized in accordance with new principles of representation. A people was energized. A citizen militia took the form—and soon the uniform—of a National Guard. Pamphlets proclaimed a revolution that had taken place; they would soon mutate into periodicals pushing forward a revolution to be continued. "Revolution" had once meant a sudden and unexpected turn of events that had occurred in human affairs. Revolution experienced in this old sense as fact would now give birth to revolution in a new sense as a collective act. This profound shift, in turn, would spawn "revolutionaries" struggling over a script for conscious political transformation. A French Revolution, the idea of a new kind of transformation, would enter the collective imagination.[27]

Marat was eager to swell the ranks of the new revolutionary journalists. Returning to his district assembly once the immediate crisis was over, he later recounted, he proposed that it acquire a printing press that would enable him, under its auspices, to "serve the homeland by writing the history of the revolution, preparing the plan of the organization of the municipalities, and following the work of the Estates-General." This proposition receiving no support, and "convinced of my utter inaptitude for anything else," he chose to quit the assembly. "I know that, in the eyes of many honest citizens who speculate in the honor of serving the homeland, my withdrawal must appear pure stupidity," he acknowledged, "but my proposition was not that of a man whose pen was for sale. The plan I had proposed to the Carmes committee I executed in my study at my own expense. My friends did their damnedest to stop me writing about daily events, but I let them protest and was not afraid to lose them."[28] Throughout the summer months of 1789, Marat would follow the debates and decisions of the National Assembly obsessively. He later claimed to have sent it a score of communications during that period.

AN IMPATIENT OBSERVER

At the beginning of August, pursuing his journalistic ambitions, Marat put out (anonymously, and without the name of a publisher) the first issue of a journal entitled *Le Moniteur patriote*. Undertaking to monitor events—to watch and warn on behalf of the nation—it reclaimed the Rousseauian motto *Vitam impendere vero* that he had emblazoned earlier on the title page of *The Chains of Slavery*. Marat directed that slogan now against a new power, the National Assembly, promising particularly to examine the work of its constitutional committee, to dissect each and every article that committee would draft, and to demonstrate for its enlightenment the true principles that would assure the nation's happiness. This, he wrote, was "the task that we impose upon ourselves in these moments of alarm when the enemies of the homeland are still afoot, when each day sees the appearance of some new perfidy, when a thousand false patriots seek to plunge it into a fatal security."[29]

This opening number of the *Moniteur patriote* lamented, above all, the inability of the deputies to arrive at a declaration of the rights of man and of the citizen. They had been arguing over this issue for weeks, virtually from the beginning of the National Assembly's existence. They had resolved to fix the French constitution, but they remained deeply divided over what that meant, and over whether it was necessary for them first to draft a declaration of rights. Some, particularly those wanting a constitution to be written anew, argued for the crucial importance of a declaration that would lay down principles to guide the legislators writing the constitution and enlighten the people awaiting it. Others, particularly those who aimed to regenerate an ancient constitution rather than creating a new one, insisted, to the contrary, that any abstract declaration of rights would undermine authority and fan the flames of social conflict in a country that was slipping from its historical foundations into disorder and violence.

In effect, these disagreements spoke to a profound uncertainty as to the meaning of the French Revolution and how it should proceed. How could a body of some twelve hundred deputies, radically divided and still improvising its deliberative procedures, begin to address such questions? Little had been accomplished to resolve them by the end of July. Scattered draft versions of a declaration of rights were beginning to emerge from some of the assembly's leading figures, but Marat found little in them beyond disjointed maxims and convoluted metaphysical abstractions. He looked in vain for "the grand views of the philosopher who long meditated on the rights of man and of the citizen, closely observed the operations of the political machine, made a particular study of the different governments of the earth, and detected their essential defects and organizational vices, which have brought misery to humankind for so many centuries."[30] Perhaps he meant Rousseau, though Montesquieu is more likely. The description seems highly approximate in either case.

Against such a standard, nonetheless, the author of the *Moniteur patriote* found wanting the early draft declarations offered by emerging leaders of the National Assembly. In his judgment, their texts not only failed to lay down a fundamental basis for society but also neglected to assert "the rights of humanity in favor of that numerous class of unfortunates disdained, rejected, mistreated, and oppressed everywhere." Marat called on Sieyès, in particular, to help save the assembly from "a revolting omission that would tarnish in the eyes of the wise the eternal monument it is going to raise to the honor of human nature and the happiness of France." In the meantime, he leveled an acid critique of the prerogatives of monarchy upheld in the moderate and conciliatory summary of the principles of French monarchical government offered by the Constitutional Committee's spokesman, Jean-Joseph Mounier. The committee, he was convinced, was "endeavoring to reface this odious monument of barbarism while retaining all its defects that so many tyrants have abused in oppressing us since the beginning of the monarchy."[31]

The first issue of *Le Moniteur patriote* was also the last. Its fate was apparently decided indirectly, along with a fundamental inflection of the revolutionary script, by two major events occurring in the National Assembly on 4 August 1789. That morning, in a stormy argument over the desirability of a declaration of rights to precede the constitution, the deliberation took a dramatic turn. The more conservative speakers insisted, with strong and noisy support from the clerical deputies, that any enunciation of rights should also include a statement of the duties necessarily paralleling and limiting these rights. Otherwise, they cried, the assembly would dissolve social bonds by legitimating egoism and pride. The dissension was heated enough to require a roll-call vote, rather than the usual procedure of standing or sitting. In the event, rights trumped; the vote was overwhelmingly against a declaration of duties. Before the morning was over, the Assembly had decided, almost to a man, that the constitution would indeed be preceded by a Declaration of the Rights of Man and of the Citizen. It was beginning to feel pressure to act.

The second momentous event of 4 August is better known. The National Assembly's evening session that day, extending far into the night, resulted in its dramatic choice to abolish every vestige of the "feudal regime." The context was as clear as the decision itself was surprising. In the weeks deputies had spent debating the question of rights and duties, châteaux were being put to the torch across France; seigneurial archives recording peasant obligations to their lords were being ransacked; payment of taxes, tithes, and dues was being refused; grain convoys were being attacked; towns and communities were organizing to protect themselves against the fear of brigands mobilized in the pay of vengeful aristocrats. Somehow, property had to be defended in the face of this social and political meltdown; somehow, violence protesting misery and oppression had to be repressed or appeased.

A response was offered on the evening of 4 August when some liberal nobles among the deputies proposed the abolition of most seigneurial rights, subject to redemption, and the outright suppression of others—the former being, in effect, those that could be construed as subject to modern principles of individual property and exchange, the latter those deemed vestiges of barbaric forms of personal subjection and enserfment. Presented to a National Assembly that had finally committed itself to a declaration of rights but remained frustrated by divisions and delays, an assembly acutely conscious that the political and social situation of the country was spinning out of control, an assembly desperate to take action before it was too late, these proposals unleashed an emotional tsunami.

In a psychodrama of political sacrifice, lords secular and ecclesiastical shed their hunting rights, their seigneurial courts, their labor dues; clergy yielded their tithes and parochial fees; towns and provinces abandoned their traditional liberties and particularistic statuses, magistrates their venal offices, courtiers their places and pensions. By the end of the session, deputies overwhelmed by emotion found their vests drenched with tears. In a veritable "holocaust of privileges" the encrustation of an entire society of orders and Estates had been stripped away. At least by implication, nothing was to be left but a society of free individuals equal before the law. The Assembly took the time, before dispersing, to order the singing of a *Te Deum* throughout the kingdom and to proclaim Louis XVI "Restorer of French Liberty." As if the monarch were already an afterthought!

Awakening on 5 August, the deputies marveled at what they had done. They spent most of the next week codifying and qualifying their decisions. Exactions seen as illegitimate remnants of serfdom were eliminated outright; other seigneurial dues, conceived as legitimate forms of property, were abolished subject to compensation to be paid as part of the public debt. The privileges of particularistic corporate bodies, particularly those of the church, were redescribed as antiquated ways of fulfilling social obligations that would now be better assumed as public functions supported by the nation. Venality of judicial and administrative offices was suppressed; justice made free; public employments opened to the talents. Declaring the "feudal regime" entirely destroyed—but meaning by that the entire corporate and particularistic structure that would quickly come to be called the *ancien régime*—the legislation of 11 August was celebrated as clearing a path toward "a national constitution and public liberty." The way ahead was nonetheless cluttered by debris not easily or cheaply removed.

Historians have come to see the Night of Fourth August as a fundamental moment in the French Revolution.[32] Property was saved, in effect, by a radical redefinition that disengaged it from privileged personal status and implicitly made it a corollary of the rights of individuals; the National Assembly acted to exercise its claim to express the sovereign will of the nation. But none of this was good enough for Jean-Paul Marat. He was impatient. He wanted direct and immediate action to eliminate public oppression and popular misery. Where others saw the Night of Fourth August as a moment of political transformation, he saw prevarication and manipulation. Where others saw a collective act of conversion, he saw a rearguard action by an already compromised assembly in the face of popular insurrection. Where some saw a miracle of altruism, he detected a ruse, a snare, and a delusion.

Quickly, he drafted a denunciation of *A Project Uncovered to Delude the People and Prevent the Constitution* that revealed his deep and growing suspicion of the deputies. "Let's be careful not to insult virtue, but let's not be anyone's dupes," he admonished. "If benevolence dictated these sacrifices, we have to agree that it was a little late in raising its voice. What! It's in the glow of their burning châteaux that they have the magnanimity to renounce the privilege of holding in chains men who have recovered their liberty by force of arms. It's at the sight of the agony of the plunderers, the extortionists, and the satellites of despotism that they have the generosity to renounce seigneurial dues and demand nothing more from the unfortunate beings who have scarcely enough to live!"[33]

Marat saw through an abolition of privileges made subject to compensation. As for the elimination of servitude and other burdens deriving from disparities of personal status, "those monstrous abuses embellished by the name of rights," he thought they must necessarily fall with the promulgation of a fundamental law establishing individual liberty. He wanted positive legislation assuring each citizen the right to his property and the proportional assessment of taxes, not the piecemeal paring of abuses like hunting rights, rabbit warrens, and dovecotes. The establishment of civil liberty would get rid of seigneurial justice, he maintained; privileges would be erased by the enactment of general laws. Why provoke endless debates over the details of particular concessions, none of which would relieve the misery of the people or remedy the defects of the state? Why let fragmentary legislation delay the great work of the constitution, the sole means of restoring peace, confidence, and credit, of restoring security and liberty, and of cementing public happiness?

Seen from this perspective, the deputies of the Third Estate had been duped; they had succumbed to political manipulation camouflaged by a show of patriotism. They had taken a false turn, destroying piecemeal without first thinking about constructing a new edifice. Failing on the one hand to establish fundamental laws based on general principles, they had neglected, on the other, to address the most urgent issues, such as the lack of bread, or indiscipline and desertion among the troops. These disorders were reaching a point at which there would no longer be an army, and the people would be on the brink of expiring from hunger. "Let's not trust them. They are trying to postpone the great work of the constitution until some way has been found to oppose it. They are trying to put us to sleep, they are trying to delude us."[34]

This denunciation of the National Assembly may have been intended for publication as a second issue of the *Moniteur patriote*, to appear in the second week of August. It never materialized in that form and was only printed a few weeks later as part of Marat's second attempt to publish a journal. He blamed the delay on the "pusillanimity" of printers and booksellers in the face of new police regulations, and it may have been in response to publishers' uncertainty about their legal situation that he went to the police committee on 12 August for authorization to print a journal. The visit ended in an altercation when the functionary responsible told him no specific authorization was necessary. He was then summoned to appear before the entire municipal council on 13 August to account for his "indecent words." There he excused himself on the grounds that he "had been moved only by the desire to make public the sentiment of patriotism and liberty animating him." The municipal assembly was unimpressed by this posture of political enthusiasm. Free to publish, as it insisted, he neither needed—nor would he receive—any special permission to do so. The police committee was not required to provide any such authorization to a prospective journalist, nor could it compel printers to print against their will.[35] To secure this latter may well have been Marat's aim in the first place.

There followed a lecture on civic comportment and respect for the principle of representation by the National Assembly. "We praise the zeal that drives you to sacrifice everything for what you believe is in the public interest," intoned the president of the municipal assembly; "but we cannot restrain ourselves from condemning, as at least indiscreet, the pretension of a citizen who tries to make his opinion and his will prevail against that of an assembly the homeland has especially honored with its confidence and charged to watch over its most sacred interests." An attitude like this, the president admonished, would become a crime if it led to denunciations subjecting to violence people of modest education, citizens devoted by desire and duty to maintaining the laws and the happiness of their homeland. "We hope, Monsieur, that you will act in accordance with principles, and we exhort you not to allow yourself to seduce by the appearance of good. Remember, in all your undertakings, that public happiness rests on the bases of wisdom, always moderated, and the subordination of every individual to the general will, which is the sole law in all places and at all times."[36]

This was not advice Marat would care long to remember. The tenor of his attack on the decisions of the Night of Fourth August and the urgency with which he sought to publish it reveal the extent of his disaffection toward the representative body. He made clear in later years how profoundly he resented Louis XVI's decision to order uncompromising members of the First and Second Estates to join the National Assembly after the fall of the Bastille. This contamination of the National Assembly by the forced admission of the privileged became, for him, the original sin of the Revolution, the fatal flaw that would ensure the corruption and compromises to which representation was always vulnerable. His protests against the sleight of hand by which the National Assembly was appearing to destroy privilege while prolonging misery and oppression in the name of property proved how out of step he already was with the nation's representatives. The disparity was to become even more evident as the Assembly finally moved, in the latter part of August, to produce a definitive text of the Declaration of the Rights of Man and of the Citizen.

A DECLARATION OF RIGHTS

The deputies returned to the matter of a declaration of rights in mid-August by naming a committee to derive a text for discussion from the several dozen drafts in circulation by this time. The resulting Committee of Five, led by the renegade noble Honoré-Gabriel Riqueti, comte de Mirabeau, found it impossible to synthesize the competing formulations and arrived, perhaps somewhat cynically, at a text of its own. The draft was presented on 18 August, only to be rapidly set aside by the Assembly (though its preamble would resurface in the text that was ultimately adopted). Instead, the deputies opted to base their deliberation on a much earlier draft declaration drawn up weeks before. This version had the initial advantage of being brief, conservative, and the collective work of a group of deputies representing each of the three orders. Over a week of intensive daily debate, nevertheless, it was utterly transformed into the document with which we are now familiar as the founding text of modern politics—so familiar, in fact, that we often overlook the disagreements, compromises, and omissions involved in its fabrication.[37]

Among the omissions was any elaboration of the theoretical, metaphysical, religious, or historical bases for the rights the National Assembly declared. The Declaration of the Rights of Man and of the Citizen was a laconic text, stripped to the bare-bone formulations that alone could secure agreement within a deeply divided Assembly. The deputies had rejected extended expositions of social and political theory earlier in the summer as too abstract—hence too dangerous—for a declaration intended to reach the people. Such reasoning they judged too likely to incite the further destruction of the existing order before institutional form could be given to a new one. After weeks of debate they had been forced to recognize that agreement could be achieved only by linguistic restraint. Proposed invocations of religious principles were excluded; appeals to nature were reduced to rudimentary form. Remarkably, while asserting in its preamble that the aim of all political association is the preservation of the natural and imprescriptible rights of man, the final declaration steered far away from any discussion of a state of nature and subsequent transition to the state of society. So, by and large, had the majority of the several dozen draft declarations that circulated during the summer of 1789. Those that had touched on the topic assumed a more or less seamless development of society as an expression of the natural tendency of human beings toward self-preservation and the search for happiness; only a few mentioned the potentiality for conflict in the state of nature as a motivation for leaving it. Human sociability was largely assumed. Rights of man in society were asserted; the origin of such rights in nature was postulated but left unexamined in the interest of reaching agreement.

Marat had something very different in mind when he issued his own draft declaration of rights toward the end of August 1789. Its publication had been delayed for several weeks, he said, by "pusillanimous fears the new police regulations have inspired among printers."[38] The text appeared much too late to have any impact on the National Assembly's statement of rights. It was, in any case, written in an entirely different register, and in a language that would have filled a majority of the deputies with dread.

A strange concoction of Hobbes, Mandeville, and Rousseau, it was redolent of the disenchantment of the seventeenth-century moralists. Closer in tone to Babeuf than to Locke, it was delivered with an almost Sadean relish. It offered a lengthy, explicit, and horrifyingly violent picture of man's natural state and the vulnerable fabric of society that had been laid over it. It was meant to be brutal.

Marat assured his readers that he had not feared to disclose great truths that were being "studiously concealed." Long stifled by tyranny, disfigured by paid sophists, and unknown to the people, these truths would finally be made public. Nature had engraved them in every heart; a lone voice raised among the multitude would suffice to make them triumph. "May our feeble efforts engage the legislature to consider them in its wisdom and prevent the terrible commotions the State would suffer from forgetting the justice society owes its unfortunate members."[39] There was a threat of popular violence in these words.

"Rights derive solely from men's needs," Marat stipulated. "The latter are always clearly perceived, but not the former. To discover them, they have to be sought, a search so difficult that the best-trained minds rarely arrive at the same results." He himself found no difficulty, however, in meeting this challenge. In his analysis, each individual is born with needs, the capacities to provide for them, and the drive to reproduce. These characteristics fuel "the constant desire to be happy and a boundless love for oneself, an imperious sentiment to which is attached the preservation of the human race, but a fertile source of quarrels, conflicts, aggression, attacks, murders, in a word all the disorders that seem to trouble the order of nature and that, in fact, trouble the order of society."[40]

Why do these struggles only *seem* to trouble the order of nature? For Marat, the answer—strongly and unconsciously masculinist though it was—could be made clear for all to see. Nature is fundamentally violent. "Whatever aggression a man commits, whatever outrage he wreaks upon his fellow beings, he troubles the order of nature no more than does a wolf devouring a sheep." Human beings receive with life the irresistible inclination to preserve and defend it and to render it enjoyable. Charged by nature with his own conservation and well-being, a man has the right to do anything to defend himself and to appropriate everything that is necessary for his nourishment, maintenance, security, and happiness. Absolute master of all his actions, he thus enjoys a limitless freedom. This being the case, all is well as long as nature offers men an abundance of things with which to nourish and clothe themselves. Peace can reign on earth. But as soon as any individual lacks for anything, he has the right to wrest from another the superfluity that other has in abundance. "What am I saying? He has the right to wrest from him what he needs and, rather than dying of hunger, he has the right to cut his throat and devour his still palpitating flesh. Let's draw the curtain on this horrible image, let's silence for a moment the voice of prejudice, and let ourselves be told what might be set against these consequences, the source of which is incontestable."

For self-preservation, Marat explains, an individual has the right to attack the property, liberty, and life of his fellows. To escape oppression, he has the right to oppress, enchain, massacre. To assure his happiness, he has the right to take any action, whatever harm he may do to others. In relating everything to himself, then, he is only yielding to an irresistible inclination implanted in his soul by the author of his being.[41]

These, Marat declares, are "the limits of the natural rights of man, incontestable rights, but equal for all individuals, whatever differences nature may have established among them." But where exactly are the limits? He seems to suggest only one. He adds a note to make a tender point about the right to reproduce, the only right that cannot be exercised by force. Sexual violence, he wants to say, occurs often in society, where imagination heightens the power of the senses. In the state of nature, such a thing is impossible: "a gentle inclination moves the sexes to unite, and even among the most ferocious animals the male always tries to win over the female."[42] Is there a plaintive Rousseauian note here amid this cacophony of violence so different from the picture drawn by Jean-Jacques himself?

In this agonistic world, nonetheless, Marat sees no natural limits but only consequences. The preferential love each man has for himself leads him to sacrifice the entire universe to his happiness. Exercise of limitless rights necessarily results in war and the innumerable evils accompanying it: violence, revenge, oppression, treason, conflict, murders, carnage. These, Marat concludes, are the frightful ills men have wished to escape in uniting together. To do so, each had to commit himself to refrain from harming others, to remit to society his personal vengeance and the care of his defense and protection, to renounce common possession of all the productions of the earth in favor of individual ownership of a part, and to sacrifice some of the advantages deriving from his natural independence in order to enjoy the advantages of a common association.[43]

With this reasoning, Marat arrives at the moment of the social compact. But he immediately swerves into another political language, a language of political association more Machiavellian than Hobbesian in its account of collective life. History, he asserts, "shows that in all ages free men have bonded together to pillage, massacre and enslave others." He cites the Romans, the Gauls, the Germans, the Franks, the Scythians, the Normans, the Saxons, the Huns, "and all those brigands who devastated the world in earlier times." No less constantly does history show that tyranny has pushed peoples to rise up and that the fear of a just vengeance has often led oppressors to make terms with the oppressed. It also reveals that some peoples have overthrown the yoke and joined together to form a government assuring their liberty, fortune, peace, and happiness. Witness the union of the Swiss, the Batavians, the English, the Anglo-Americans, among others.[44] Alliances for the sake of pillage, pacts between oppressor and oppressed, insurrections in the name of liberty: these, it seems, are all forms of the social compact. From whatever circumstances they arise, their sole impetus is the common advantage. Marat sets a republican political history within the frame of an agonistic theory of the social contract.

Seen from this perspective, the social contract seems more like the aggressive bonding of a warband than rational participation in a moral pact. Union derives from a collective appropriation and shared deployment of violence in the name of liberty and the common advantage. Violence is constitutive of society and the undergirding of liberty. We must keep these assumptions in mind as we consider Marat's later calls for terror to save the French Revolution in the name of the people.

Returning to a more conventional language of rights, however, Marat goes on to emphasize that the legitimate goal of every political association is the happiness of its members. But since each individual citizen may carry his claims too far, it is up to the collectivity to regulate the respective rights of all. As derived from nature, these rights are without limit and authorize each individual to sacrifice the interests of others to his own. It is therefore indispensable that the members of the association agree to abstain from anything that would dissolve their union, any act of violence, wickedness, oppression, personal vengeance, any means of harming another. "It is essential that they submit their differences to the decision of the laws, in a word, that they renounce their natural rights to enjoy their civil rights."[45]

To assure the peaceful enjoyment of his own rights in society, each individual imposes upon himself the obligation to respect the rights of others. "Thus by the social pact natural rights take on a sacred character." Marat reduces these (now) civil rights to a familiar trinity: personal security, which implies the feeling of safety from all oppression; individual freedom, which includes the just exercise of all one's physical and moral faculties; property, which means the peaceful enjoyment of all one possesses.

To talk property is to think inequality. Having received the same rights from nature, however, men must preserve equal rights in society. In a well-organized state, its members must enjoy approximately the same advantages—"approximately," because rigorous equality is impossible in society, as it is in nature. Individuals have different attributes and hence unequal means of working for their happiness. Nonetheless, the law must prevent too much inequality. Without a certain proportion among fortunes, the benefits of the social pact become next to nothing for the man without property. He is reduced to the meanest, most disgusting, most dangerous occupations; to pain, servitude, disdain. "Liberty itself, which consoles us for so many ills, becomes nothing for him."[46]

This reasoning leads Marat to formulate a scale of inequality and oppression within states. In some, disparities of wealth arise naturally from differences in occupations, industry, and talents, but nothing has been done to limit them. In these cases, society owes an assured subsistence to those without property, or whose work scarcely provides for their needs. It owes them the means of nourishing, clothing, and lodging themselves comfortably, of caring for their illnesses, of providing for their old age, and of raising their children. "This is the price of the sacrifice they have made of their common right to the productions of the earth and their engagement to respect the property of their fellow citizens." It had to be said, however, that if society owes this support to every man who respects the established order and seeks to make himself useful, it owes nothing to the idler who refuses to work.[47]

There are societies, too, where fortunes are very unequal and the greatest disparities in wealth are almost all the fruit of intrigue, charlatanism, favor, embezzlement, harassment, and plunder. In these circumstances, the wealthy must be required to subsidize those who lack necessities. There are societies still worse, though, those where certain privileged persons enjoy in idleness, splendor, and pleasure the goods of the poor, the widow, and the orphan. Justice and wisdom demand that, in these cases, "at least a part of these goods finally return to their proper destination as the result of a judicious distribution among the citizens who lack everything." The consequences of doing otherwise are self-evident. "The honest citizen whom society abandons to his misery and despair returns to the state of nature and has the right to reclaim by force of arms the advantages that he could only have given up to acquire greater ones. Any authority that opposes this action is tyrannical and the judge who condemns him to death is no more than a cowardly assassin."[48] Marat is already building a case here for extending rights talk to the claims of the poor against social oppression.

A CONSTITUTION IN SIGHT?

The history of the French Revolution offers a constant reminder that politics is about the meaning of words. By the end of August the National Assembly had agreed on language declaring the rights of man and of the citizen. No sooner had it done so than it was forced into new debates over the implication of the terms upon which it had just agreed. Men were declared free and equal in rights, but who was to be regarded as a man, who a citizen? The source of all sovereignty was located in the nation, but was that sovereignty an active or a residual power, was it to be exercised directly or indirectly? The law was declared the expression of the general will, but how was its generality to be defined, achieved, and maintained? Separation of powers was deemed an indispensable feature of any true constitution, but what were these powers, by whom would they be exercised, and how would they be clearly separated?

It would take two convulsive years for the National Assembly to decide such questions (and only a few more months for the resulting constitutional structure to come unstuck). But the deputies were eager to begin. On 28 August, the day after they had decided on the text of a declaration of rights, they opened debate on the opening clauses of a proposed constitution. It had been clear for weeks that the leaders of the Constitutional Committee were determined to salvage the foundations of a French monarchical constitution, proceeding from there to build a more stable structure along the lines of the English model. They wanted a hereditary monarchy to serve as the executive power and elected representatives, separated into upper and lower houses, to exercise legislative power—though with the institution of a royal veto also functioning as the key to balancing powers while limiting the dangers of popular sovereignty.

By his account, Marat had prepared to contest this program by translating into French a substantial section of *The Chains of Slavery* devoted to the vices of the English constitution. Submitting this analysis to the president of the National Assembly on 23 August as a *Discours adressé aux Anglais le 15 avril 1774, sur les vices de leur Constitution, et les moyens d'y remédier*, he added a list of fundamental laws necessary to secure liberty. They included dilution of the tiny (rotten) boroughs too easily compromised by the crown; the elimination of placemen and pensioners from the representative body; abrogation of the royal privilege to create peers; insistence that Parliament review governments accounts.[49]

An accompanying *Lettre au président des États Généraux* boasted of the knowledge of English politics its author had acquired while residing across the Channel for ten years, the horror of despotism with which he had followed the events of the Wilkes Affair, and his admiration for the public spirit displayed by the English in resisting ministerial oppression. It explained how he had sought, in *The Chains of Slavery*, to rekindle among his English readers the consciousness of their rights by disclosing "the odious artifices princes employ to reduce peoples to servitude and the fearful ills that despotism always brings in its wake." Boasting in an improbable claim for its influence that the book's publication had been followed by "general fermentation" in support of measures favored by the popular societies to ensure a more equal representation of the people, he reiterated (with minor variations) the list of reforms he had added to the *Discours*. This time he presented them as bills he had proposed and claimed credit for a subsequent Place Bill that had limited the power of the British monarch and his ministers to manipulate the choices of voters and corrupt parliamentary procedures by handing out pensions and places.[50]

To avoid the importation of the vices of English government into France, Marat offered a constitutional plan to accompany his proposed declaration of the rights of man and of the citizen. He regarded few members of the Estates General as well enough versed in politics to decide the best organization of the monarchy, to gauge the right degree of power to be safely entrusted to the prince, and to arrive at a form of government equally distant from despotism and anarchy. "Politics is a science like any other; it has its principles, its laws, its infinitely varied combinations requiring attentive study, profound reflection, and long meditation. But we have only just been born to liberty: for ten months we have taught ourselves from day to day; we've scarcely thought for a few moments about the rights of man and of the citizen, the rights of peoples and the duties of their ministers, the organization of the political body, the balancing of powers, the reciprocal relations between the sovereign and his subjects, etc."[51]

Marat began his own exposition of constitutional principles by invoking Montesquieu and Rousseau. Had these thinkers still been living, he maintained, the nation would have needed only to beg them for a constitution that would have possessed "all that genius, wisdom, and virtue could perfect." In effect, they would have served the role of the great legislators of antiquity who figured so prominently in their writings. Marat lavished particular praise on Montesquieu, "the greatest man of a century that has made France illustrious." Mounier and his monarchist allies saw the author of *The Spirit of the Laws* as the theorist of the English model of balanced government they were hoping to implement in France. In more radical circles, he was already being denounced as a defender of aristocratic privilege who had sided with the parlements against a reforming monarchy. But Marat was determined to save this great man from portrayal as a reactionary. He pointed to the latter's love of humanity, his hatred of despotism, his zeal for the public good, his devotion to the homeland. "He was the first among us to dare disarm superstition, wrench the dagger from fanaticism, reclaim the rights of man, attack tyranny. And when? When no one in France dared raise a voice against a minister, at a time when the French were slaves on principle."

In a monarchy trending toward despotism and a nation lapsing into slavery, Marat insisted, Montesquieu had understood that any dike was good to hinder the torrent of evils inflicted on humanity by despotic power. He could scarcely be condemned for upholding the parlements as the best available defense against the caprices of absolute authority, this disciple argued. Criticized for his moderation, he had indeed been compared unfavorably to Rousseau. "But Rousseau had nothing to lose from persecution, he carried his genius and celebrity with him, and his glory could only gain from it." Montesquieu, with his landed fortune, his distinguished family name, his wife and children, had risked much more in attacking arbitrary authority, the vices of the government, and the extravagances of the prince.[52]

Marat dared not compare himself to such great men, he assured his readers, "but I am far from being a complete novice in these matters and I can vouch for the integrity of my views and the purity of my heart." Alarmed at the proposals of the Constitutional Committee, he ventured to offer his own plan for a "just, wise, and free constitution," one necessarily derived (as Montesquieu had taught) from "the nature of things."[53]

Like Montesquieu, and indeed like the members of the Constitutional Committee and most of his contemporaries, Marat still believed that a large state required a monarchical government. "This is the only government suitable for France. It has arisen from a fortuitous combination of events, but the extent, position, and complexity of the realm require it, and many powerful reasons would make it necessary even when the character of its peoples permitted another choice." The task facing the French in 1789, therefore, was to establish the principles of a "well constituted monarchy."[54]

The very first of these principles, for Marat, was essentially Rousseauian. Sovereignty inheres not in the monarch but in the entire body of the citizens. "Since the sovereign is composed of all the members of the state," he argued, "it is the absolute master of the empire. Supreme authority belongs essentially to it alone, and from it alone emanates all the powers, all the privileges, all the prerogatives." A people can have no other representatives, chiefs, ministers, or officers than those it chooses to give itself, and their power remains provisional. The nation retains the right to confer the scepter upon another family. Its representatives must only have short terms. Magistrates and other officers holding lifetime appointments must remain revocable in the case of misconduct.[55]

It followed from this reasoning that "the sovereign is independent of all human power and enjoys a liberty without limits, by virtue of the unlimited liberty that each of its members receives from nature. . . . The absolute independence of the nation must therefore be the fundamental law of the state." To preserve that independence, the nation must retain sovereign power over the organization and periodicity of its assemblies, their manner of deliberation, and the promulgation of their decisions. If laws pass unanimously, the authority of the sovereign has no limits since each individual has decided for himself. If laws pass by a majority, however, they are limited by the rights of citizens, "more sacred even than the fundamental laws of the state."[56]

In a small state, Marat acknowledged, the members of the sovereign body can assemble within the same walls. But he offered France no prescription for direct democracy. "The agreement of everyone on everything would always be extremely impracticable, sometimes impossible, and often dangerous." In his analysis, public affairs were scarcely within the purview of the most common of men; it was better on many occasions that the wise alone decide. The fact that the people were too often seduced by seditious and self-interested speakers left the state vulnerable to factionalism and instability. This being the case in a small state, how much greater would the danger be in a larger one? It was therefore necessary that the people act through its elected representatives.[57]

Representation, however, carried its own dangers. It would be an enormous defect in the constitution, Marat maintained, to allow the people's representatives unlimited power. "The absolute and unlimited sovereign power can only ever reside in the body of the people, because it is the result of the general will and the people taken collectively can never will what is harmful to it, sell itself, or betray itself. As for its representatives, their authority must always be limited; otherwise, absolute masters of the empire, they could, at will, abrogate the rights of the citizens, attack the fundamental laws of the State, overthrow the constitution and reduce the people to servitude."[58]

Marat did not, however, follow Rousseau in favoring imperative mandates as a device for limiting the power of representatives. Considering them too constraining except on absolutely essential points, he doubtless feared their invocation by reactionary members of the National Assembly still claiming to be constrained by their *cahiers*. He insisted, though, that once the constitution had been achieved, the decrees of the representative body should have only provisional force pending their formal sanction by the people.

It would be three years before the revolutionaries instituted universal male suffrage. Marat was ahead of his contemporaries in this respect: he assigned the right to vote to all French men by birth. He was less radical when it came to women. Females, like the young, he deemed simply incapable of exercising such a function. In this regard he retained the prejudices of his time. While he believed that representatives themselves had to be drawn from all orders of citizens, he also thought it best, assuming equal enlightenment and virtue, that they be drawn from among the rich to render them less susceptible to corruption. For the same reason, with his English experience doubtless in mind, he held it necessary to declare representatives ineligible to possess any position depending on the prince, to receive any court distinction, or especially to hold any ministerial appointment within ten years of their service as a deputy. No placemen, no pensioners, remained his watchword.

Beyond the legislative power, Marat saw two others as essential: the power to execute the laws, and the power to defend the empire. It was critically important, he insisted, that these three powers be separated. Otherwise, tyranny and annihilation of liberty would result. This much was clear from the examples of Rome, Venice, England, Spain, France—indeed, of almost all the governments on earth. England's history, in particular, demonstrated that tyranny invariably resulted from an incomplete separation of these powers. It showed, above all, that royal approval of legislation should never be seen as a formal action required for the consecration of the laws, but only as an act of loyalty by which the prince subscribed solemnly to the laws he must never violate. There could be no royal veto.[59]

"Separating and limiting the different powers," Marat reasoned, was thus "the height of wisdom in politics." Judicial and military power had to be separated to avoid the terrible evils exemplified in Rome after the destruction of the republic. Ministers had to be chosen by the executive power only after consulting the public. The army had to take a vow of fidelity to the nation before taking one to the prince. The power of the standing army had also to be counterbalanced by that of a civic militia. In the repression of disorder, soldiers had to obey the municipal magistrates.[60]

Since attacks on public liberty come always from the government, it was necessary to be constantly on guard against its dealings and to deny it pretexts for abusing its power. Ministers and magistrates had to be accountable to the legislature. The state had to have a supreme tribunal charged with judging the schemes of ministers, the prevarications of magistrates, public crimes, and acts of lèse-nation. Because the crimes of ministers were often carried out in secret, the press had to be free to expose their abuses and to publicize the complaints of their victims. "To prevent license, though, every denunciation must be signed by its author."[61]

Freedom of religion Marat regarded as a civil right. No citizen should be troubled in religious matters, he emphasized, except for having disturbed an established cult (a defense of an established religion the National Assembly had refused to admit into its Declaration of the Rights of Man and of the Citizen). Society must tolerate all religions, he insisted, except those that sap it. But Christianity, in preaching blind obedience, tended only to make slaves. Its priests had found the secret of turning the people's credulity into a rich patrimony, living in idleness, abundance, and pleasure, and consuming the goods of the poor in the midst of splendor and indulgence. "The veil is sundered. The light of reason has dispersed the mystical darkness in which they have enveloped themselves; their conduct has succeeded in destroying the illusion and today the profane eye of the vulgar sees them as they are." It was time to reform the scandal of the church hierarchy, to return to the poor the property the higher clergy had so shamefully dissipated, to suppress useless religious communities, and to allow the faithful to name their pastors in accordance with the practice of the early church and the dictates of reason.[62] Marat was already prepared in 1789 to embrace a civil constitution of the clergy.

These considerations, he concluded, amounted to a description of "the only form of monarchical government appropriate to a great nation instructed in its rights and jealous of its liberty." They required radical transformation of the present form of government, "inevitable reforms that would be resisted by the creatures of the court, the crooks, the intriguers, the ambitious, the timid, or the insiders." They went far beyond any proposals that could be expected from Mounier and his allies in the Constitutional Committee. These latter had taken care to stress that they were not undertaking their constitutional task *de novo*. "The French," Mounier had declared, "are not a new people that has just left the forests to form an association, but a vast society of men that wishes to tighten the bonds uniting all its parts and to regenerate the realm, a society for whom the principles of the true monarchy will always be sacred."

Marat placed no trust in these "vague, obscure, and specious words." Did they mean that the true principles of monarchy consisted in leaving the crown in possession of prerogatives it had usurped in order to oppress the nation for the past fifteen centuries? "Thank heavens that we are *no longer a new people that has just left the forests to form an association* . . . ," he declared. "We are an enlightened, powerful, formidable nation that wishes to give itself a government appropriate to ensure its happiness forever. . . . Are they trying to privilege a stupid respect for the institutions of our fathers, for the antique customs of the realm? What! We should be bound by barbarous practices! The power our forebears had to make certain laws we possess to abolish them. Their power to found a government is ours to perfect, modify, refound it. When we can reconstruct anew, why should we amuse ourselves to rebuild an edifice that threatens to crush us in its fall and bury us in its ruins?"[63]

The French had learned much since the convocation of the Estates General, Marat argued. Realizing the full extent of their rights, they were ready to extirpate all the vices of the government and give it the best possible form. They now understood that supreme power belonged solely to the nation, that the legislative power entrusted to its representatives was limited, that it alone had the right to revise the work of the deputies and sanction the laws they had made. They now knew that the king was only the nation's first minister, and that the disorders of the administration had no other source than the supposed independence of the government. They had learned that the only means of preventing abuse of authority was to surround it with insuperable barriers, to remind the king at each moment that his authority derived from his people, and to make it impossible for him ever to contravene his duties.

To do all this was the nation's desire, its unshakeable resolution. "Let the enemies of the homeland lose the hope of preventing the revolution from being consummated," Marat shouted. "All the obstacles have been removed, prejudices are falling silent before the laws of eternal truth, the swollen torrent of power has returned within its banks. . . . Never has a moment been more favorable to the establishment of public liberty on its true foundations and giving it an unshakeable base!" The nation expected its representatives to seize this opportunity by working with ardor on the constitution. Hence, this grave warning for them. "If they neglect to respond to its wishes, or to fulfill its expectations, it will demand an account from them of this abuse of confidence and will see in them only its cruelest enemies."[64] Jean-Paul Marat, in particular, would henceforth make it his responsibility to demand such an accounting from the representatives he so profoundly distrusted. And he would use the power of the periodical press to do so daily.

FOURTEEN

THE PEOPLE'S EYE

The journal that would define Marat's revolutionary career was born, like its author, under another name. It appeared in the early days of September 1789 as *Le Publiciste parisien, Journal politique, libre et impartial, par une société de patriotes, et rédigé par M. Marat, auteur de L'Offrande à la patrie, du Moniteur et du Plan de Constitution, etc.* One of the swarm of new periodicals that sprang up in Paris in the summer and autumn of 1789 as men of letters of the Old Regime retooled for a transformed political situation, it was among the most enduring.[1] Its goal was to monitor the discussions and decisions of the National Assembly. In Marat's definition of the political situation, the French had recovered their liberty by force of arms, despotism had been crushed, troublemakers put to flight, enemies of the fatherland forced to assume a mask; the barriers of prejudice were collapsing before the voice of reason, the rights of man were being consecrated, and France was anticipating the happiness that would come from a free constitution. He saw only one thing, the National Assembly itself, threatening the realization of this dream. "Nothing could oppose the wishes of the Nation but the play of prejudices and passions among its representatives in the Assembly."[2]

It followed from this analysis that the greatest gift the nation could receive in its present state was "a periodical in which one would carefully follow the work of the Estates General." The terminology is important here. Marat was vowing to monitor "the Estates General," not the "National Assembly." Today we can recognize the formation of the National Assembly on 17 June as a grand "performative" in the sense given to that term by speech-act philosophers. A performative, in J. L. Austin's classic analysis, *does something* with words; if successful, it creates a fact on the ground. But its effect can be resisted, it can fail. One historian has compared the 17 June declaration to a theatrical performance as understood in the eighteenth century. The efficacy of the drama required the production and maintenance of a sense of verisimilitude; the audience had to believe in its truth. But that sense of verisimilitude could be punctured, and an entire performance thus destroyed, by a single snicker or hiss.[3]

Many in Paris in 1789 were ready to puncture the political performance of the so-called National Assembly by hooting at its claims to stand for the nation; most of them were counterrevolutionaries in the making. Marat shared their suspicions of this body, though from a radical revolutionary perspective. He could not imagine the will of the people expressed by the problematic assemblage that had been created when Louis XVI ordered recalcitrant deputies of the clergy and nobility to join the representatives of the Third Estate in the self-declared National Assembly. All the more reason, in his analysis, for a journal to "dissect the assembly's decisions impartially, recall it constantly to good principles, avenge the rights of man, establish the rights of the citizen, outline the organization of a wise government, develop ways of nullifying the sources of the state's ills, and bring back union, abundance, and peace." Each article of the journal, he promised, would express his personal convictions. "Liberty without license, energy without violence, wisdom without obfuscation": these would be its goals. *Vitam impendere vero* would be its motto.[4]

Still wary of the uncertain legal situation of the exploding revolutionary press, Marat had again sought explicit permission to circulate his journal from the police committee of the municipality of Paris. He received it on 8 September. Accordingly, *Le Publiciste parisien* began reporting on the Assembly debates occurring from the seventh to the twelfth of that month (though with some delay while the editor scoured material from other journals). This was the moment at which the National Assembly was making its most crucial constitutional choices. In tumultuous debates, the leaders of the Constitutional Committee, supported by many moderate or conservative deputies, argued for the institution of a bicameral assembly along British lines, with an upper house balancing against the dangers of rash decisions in the lower house. They could never strip this idea of its aristocratic tarnish. That vote lost, they wanted to maximize political stability by allowing a legislative assembly to serve lengthy terms before renewal—if not up to seven years as in England, then at least three or four. They lost that vote, too, when the electoral term was eventually set at two years. Above all, they concentrated on assuring the king a share in legislative power by giving him an absolute veto over decrees of the representative body. When this idea was repudiated as incompatible with the principle of national sovereignty, they settled for a suspensive veto—a device also favored by deputies who remembered Rousseau's concerns that an assembly could err in declaring the general will.[5]

At the heart of these decisions, and of Marat's thinking about them, was the question of the relationship between the practice of representation and the principle of the general will, each of which had been endorsed in the Declaration of the Rights of Man. Beyond that issue, however, and complicating it further, was the problem of the convergence between the general and the popular will. Those who argued for a bicameral assembly had learned from their ancient history (and modern commentators on it) that a single legislative body could become too easily subject to the arbitrary, unpredictable, and coercive whims of an ignorant populace. They had cause for concern. The Assembly's deliberations were now subject, after all, to the pressure of constant judgment by a vociferous crowd in its galleries. More threatening still, clerical and aristocratic deputies, together with "ignorant and corrupt members of the Commons," had been warned by the crowd at the Palais Royal that there were men in their thousands ready to "light up their *châteaux* and their houses" in the event of a wrong decision.[6] How could the formulation of a unitary general will be imagined under such conditions? How could a democratic, representative politics find a place between monarchical authority, with its power to corrupt, and popular will with its power to coerce and subvert? A bicameral assembly, lengthy legislative terms, and a royal veto were all put forward as bastions against the dangers of democratic politics. Among these, only the suspensive veto was adopted, with dire results.

Conflict over these issues in September 1789 was sharpened by a letter addressed to the National Assembly by the citizens of Rennes that declared any monarchical veto dangerous in placing the monarch above the nation. (It deemed a popular veto no more acceptable.) Marat's *Publiciste parisien* took particular note of the fact that some leading members of the National Assembly bridled at this intervention from outside its chamber. The Rennes protest was denounced by the deputies as the work of the nation's enemies and an attack on the freedom of the legislative assembly. Mirabeau himself raised his voice in condemnation, insisting that the representatives could not be subjected to the absurd opinions of every province, town, or village. These latter were only subjects, he declared, and the legislative body owed no legal deference to their opinions. Marat remarked acidly that the mercurial aristocrat was unlikely to have expressed such views when he was campaigning to represent the Third Estate in Provence. "What! Will it be a crime for constituents to make their views known to their deputies!" he expostulated. "Will defending the cause of the people declare oneself its enemy? Will it be a violation of the liberty of the representatives and an attack on the homeland to threaten with public indignation the cowards who dare to betray the nation's interest? Such odious maxims could only emerge from the mouth of a paid sophist."[7]

Marat offered readers of *Le Publiciste parisien* a clear path through these early constitutional deliberations, carefully stating the nature and implications of the contending arguments while also revealing the agitation of the debates and the National Assembly's confusion over the still uncertain voting procedures. In pedagogical mode, he introduced paragraphs from his earlier constitutional plan to emphasize his two fundamental principles. Absolute sovereign power, he reiterated, could reside only in the body of the people; the power of the people's representatives must always be constrained. "Thus it is an enormous vice in a constitution to allow the representatives of the people an unlimited power."[8]

Le Publiciste parisien nonetheless rejected the constitutional devices that had so far been offered to limit the power of a representative body or stabilize its discussions. A bicameral assembly, an extended term between elections, a royal veto on legislative decisions: all these, the journal contended, would leave the legislature less immediately responsive to the will of the people. Marat saw the decision in favor of a suspensive veto, in particular, as a monstrous mistake, subversive of the sovereignty of the people. Nor did he favor reviving the ancient practice of a binding mandate that, in constraining the action of the deputies, would also deprive the people of the benefits of their enlightenment. This left him only two constitutional options to restrain the power of the representative body and ensure the exercise of the sovereign popular will.

One option was to make legislation provisional until it had received the formal sanction of the people (implementing, in effect, an absolute popular veto exercised by referendum). Another was to secure the representatives against corruption. To this end, deputies could be declared ineligible for any distinction or place deriving from the crown, and especially for ministerial positions. Betrayal of the people on their part could also be punishable by revocation of their powers by their constituents. The organization of primary assemblies to elect the people's representatives, to determine the extent of the latter's power, and to establish the means of disavowing and sanctioning them: this, Marat maintained, was the most fundamental part of the constitution, the one upon which all the others depended. It should have been the first concern of the National Assembly. "That the supreme power of the constituents be misunderstood by their delegates is too greatly to be feared."[9]

Neither of the constraints on representation Marat favored was yet on the agenda of the National Assembly. What remained to fill the gap between the people's will and that of its representatives? He saw only public opinion, necessarily informed by a free press. "Let us conclude, then, that in every point relating to the fundamental laws of the state, and the rights of the nation, the deputies are only the organs of their electors, whose wish they must follow. For lack of positive mandates, this wish can only be formed by public opinion; it is therefore important to allow the free flow of discussion." In this formulation, public opinion took on the character of a popular political will authorized in the name of popular sovereignty. The tribunal of public opinion, its enlightenment guaranteed by "the free flow of discussion," stood in for binding mandates, bringing the voice of reason to the expression of a sovereign popular will. But it did so at the price of allowing denunciation free rein. "The safety of the people being the supreme law, and the obligation to watch over it being the first duty of the citizen, to denounce to the homeland as traitors all those who attack the rights of the people and endanger the public liberty is not only the right of the inhabitants of each village, each town, each city, each province, but the right of each individual."[10]

This sentence, as Colin Lucas has emphasized, marks a decisive moment in Marat's thinking. It made denunciation not only a duty but a right of each individual citizen, as a member of the sovereign body of the people, to alert that body publicly to threats against its freedom. Crucial to this claim was the implicit distinction between denunciation and delation, the work of the denouncer and the informer. Delation was the hidden action of the informer in the service of power, a characteristic feature of the policing of the Old Regime perpetuated, in effect, by the *comités de recherches* created by the National Assembly in July 1789 and the municipality of Paris the following October. Denunciation, the hallmark of the new revolutionary politics in Marat's conception, was to be public action in the service of the sovereign, the effort of a virtuous citizen to ensure the transparency and responsibility of the exercise of power on behalf of the nation.[11]

Into the space between representation and popular sovereignty Marat thus thrust two elements: the force of public opinion and the power of denunciation to alert and enlighten it. Firm in this conviction, he was about to find his distinctive revolutionary voice.

L'AMI DU PEUPLE

On 16 September 1789, after five initial issues, *Le Publiciste parisien* assumed a new title and proclaimed the name of its writer, who would adopt its identity as his very own. It became *L'Ami du peuple, ou Le Publiciste parisien, Journal politique, libre et impartial, par une société de patriotes, et rédigé par M. Marat, auteur de L'Offrande à la patrie, du Moniteur et du Plan de Constitution, etc.* Twenty-two numbers appeared within barely four weeks before the journal was forced underground, but in that brief period elements of the character it would exhibit in following years were already becoming evident. It would be an organ of divulgation and denunciation, incessantly vilified in its turn, constantly subject to censure by the revolutionary authorities it condemned. Its presses would be targeted for confiscation or destruction, its printers and peddlers harassed, its circulation networks disrupted, its publication intermittently halted, its author driven from the country, or underground, for lengthy periods. Its author would welcome martyrdom, revealing truth "at the price of his life."

In these early weeks of its existence the journal operated as if it were showing a split screen, with one side reporting from Versailles, the other from Paris. On the first screen, readers could follow the debates of the "Estates-General" in Versailles as the National Assembly proceeded with the work of framing the initial articles of the new constitution, waited impatiently as Louis XVI temporized over his acceptance of these articles along with the text of the Declaration of the Rights of Man and of the Citizen, and drifted into discussion of the nation's finances and issues of taxation—this latter development immediately denounced by Marat as contrary to the nation's declared wish that no tax matters be addressed before a constitution had been completed. As portrayed by *L'Ami du peuple* from the very first, the Assembly had no coherent plan; moving from one thing to another, it reacted to practical details and immediate issues rather than laying down fundamental laws. This had been the burden of Marat's critique of the decisions taken on the Night of Fourth August, which he now took the opportunity to bring to the public's attention. There was a powerful reactionary faction hidden within the Assembly, he was convinced, one that was conspiring to prevent the regeneration of the realm.

Whose fault would it be, Marat asked, if the enemies of the state recovered the upper hand? The blame would fall to those deputies of the Third Estate who had been too frightened by the bloodshed that had followed the fall of the Bastille. "Scared by the tragic end of a few criminals, traitors to the country, they were too eager to end bloody scenes." Instead of pressing for a supreme tribunal to judge the nation's enemies, they had let the miscreants slip away. At the same time, they had allowed the government to suppress the right of public assembly. The effect was to deny the most zealous citizens the possibility of popular action that could precipitate "those salutary crises that alone could make the enemies of the homeland tremble, force the national senate to purge itself, hasten the constitution, assure liberty, and cement public happiness."[12]

There followed, in installments, an "Address to the People," the first of Marat's many efforts to goad the French into arousing themselves to assert their will. "Oh Frenchmen! Vain and frivolous people, will you never grasp the ills that threaten you, will you always fall asleep like this at the edge of the abyss?" he expostulated. Failing to see that its freedom was more the result of circumstances than of any act of concerted national will, blinded by a false sense of its triumph, the people was permitting its foes to reweave their odious web. Far from being relentless in punishing public enemies, it was allowing feeble and corrupt men to shelter the guilty. "Let's stop complaining. The cruel ills that make us groan are our own work, the bitter fruits of our depravation. What is to be expected of a people of egoists who act only from interest, consult only their passions, and are motivated only by vanity?" A nation without enlightenment or virtue was not made for liberty, Marat fretted. It could break its chains momentarily, but could it avoid reassuming them? The French were no longer fettered by force, but were they destined to be enslaved by deceit? "Demented as we are, we close our ears to the sages who try to rouse us from our lethargy and open them to the scoundrels who try to lull us to sleep. Ah! If there remains any hope for us, let's escape, escape from our fatal security, recognize the abyss yawning beneath our feet, sound its depth, and work to close it before it has swallowed us up."[13]

It need hardly be remarked that this warning against lethargy and somnolence echoed the language of *The Chains of Slavery*. Redolent of the politics of the Wilkes Affair, it led naturally to the denunciation of placemen and pensioners in language Marat now imported into France a decade and a half after encountering it in England. "Reflect carefully," he trumpeted. "The political machine is only ever recharged by violent shocks, just as the air is only purified by storms. Let's take the ax to the root of the tree. The only way to put an end to our ills is to purge our committees of men whose principles are suspect or dangerous, men who hold some place or government pension. Let's require that the national senate purge itself, that its first decree declare ineligible to serve any man who receives a favor from the court or speculates in the glory of serving the homeland."

Every deputy enjoying a place or a pension deriving from the crown should now be "invited" to return it, *L'Ami du peuple* insisted. Each of them should undertake to receive no benefit from the court within ten years of the expiration of the legislature of which they formed part. Deputies who had lost public confidence could be recalled by their constituents if the Assembly itself refused to purge them. "We know who they are; the public names them loudly. Let men of true merit be summoned to replace them."[14]

Marat would have preferred the election of a brand-new legislature to the political monstrosity he saw the French now passively accepting as representative of the nation. Failing that, he called incessantly for political purification. "Today there is only a single order of citizens in the state," he reasoned. Noble and clerical deputies were no longer sitting in the assembly as representatives of privileged classes. Only those who offered proof of patriotic zeal should be permitted to remain. Shedding the others, he estimated, could reduce the legislature to a quarter of its bloated current size, leaving it composed solely of enlightened and virtuous men. "I repeat and will not stop repeating, at peril of my life, that there is only one way to save the state. This is to purge and reform the national assembly by expelling with ignominy its corrupt members, reducing its numbers, and calling to it men distinguished by their enlightenment and their virtues." Months earlier, he had imagined something like a union of orders; now he could think only of excision as clearing the path to unity. Bitterly he denounced "Our Seigneurs, the Estates-General," deploying this sarcastically archaic form of address to highlight the mixture of aristocracy and despotism he saw the putative National Assembly now embodying.[15]

L'Ami du peuple was meant to be disruptive. An "Editor's profession of faith," published on 23 September, rejoiced at reports that the journal was already causing a scandal. It proclaimed extremism no vice in the service of liberty. "The enemies of the homeland shout 'Blasphemy!' and the timid citizens, those who never experience the fervor of liberty or the rhapsody of virtue, grow pale as they read it. They agree that I am right to attack the corrupt faction that dominates the National Assembly, but they wish I would do it with moderation. This is like putting a soldier on trial for fighting desperately against perfidious enemies."

Disillusioned with the National Assembly's actions in the course of 1789, Marat now disclosed to his readers "the criminal design formed by an enemy faction to sacrifice the nation to the prince and public happiness to the cupidity of a handful of ambitious men." To sound the alarm had become his duty, he declared. This was the sole means of preventing the nation from being cast into the abyss. To those "good patriots" already fearing that his journal would be suppressed, he offered reassurance that he had no fear of the supporters of despotism. "I defy them to touch me; they know how little I fear them; and I don't think they are crazy enough to show themselves enemies of the people and threats to the homeland by doing so." The people needed men versed in politics to defend its interests night and day. Marat declared himself up to the task. "I will consecrate to it my every moment," he pledged. "I will attack the scoundrels without restraint, I will unmask the hypocrites, I will denounce the traitors, I will drive from public affairs the greedy men who speculate in false zeal, the cowards and incompetents incapable of serving the homeland, the suspects in whom one can have no confidence." His denunciations, he promised, would always come with a warranty. "I know what I must expect from the crowd of evil men I will provoke against me, but fear has no effect on my soul. I devote myself to the homeland and I'm ready to pour out all my blood for it."[16]

He would find ample opportunity to act upon these claims.

FAMINE PLOT

Among the conspiracies Marat detected as the work of the aristocratic faction lurking within the National Assembly in Versailles was an effort to destroy the spirit of liberty by reducing the people to desperation for lack of bread. The politics of the grain trade and the threat of famine also featured significantly on what we might imagine as the second screen showing in *L'Ami du peuple*, the one presenting reports from Paris. The journal's initial issue under its new title deplored the horrors of scarcity that were being felt anew in the capital as markets were ransacked and bakers' shops besieged by those ravenous for bread. After a particularly rich harvest, and in the midst of abundance, it charged, the people were about to perish from hunger or be poisoned by infected grain. "Can it be doubted that we are surrounded by traitors seeking to achieve our ruin? Do we owe this calamity to public enemies, to the cupidity of monopolists, to the incompetence or infidelity of the administrators? This is a mystery that the communes of all the districts of the capital must make it a duty to illuminate without delay." The call for action was soon repeated in more pointed terms. It was up to the representatives of the city's districts to appoint a special prosecutor to investigate charges of "frightful malversations" by the National Assembly's committee on subsistence. Exemplary punishment was a pressing need. "We need striking examples of justice. If the guilty always escape us, that's the end of liberty. The abyss is open beneath our feet; soon, soon, we will be cast into it."[17]

The notion that famine was the fruit of conspiracy was no new idea in 1789.[18] It was deeply embedded in the popular consciousness of the Old Regime, where the movement of grain and the provisioning of markets had been closely controlled by royal authorities. As supply of bread at a customary price was held to depend on just government rather than on natural conditions, so shortages driving up prices were suspected to be the result of injustice and oppression, an effect of some malevolent will, of sinister agents hoarding and manipulating the market. Revived at every hint of dearth, fear of a "famine plot" had been exacerbated in the prerevolutionary decades by ill-timed and ineffective efforts to remove market controls and stimulate production through the introduction of a free market in grain (a policy the National Assembly continued to support). The same suspicions of conspiracy had become a central element in the "Great Fear," the massive popular panic that had afflicted much of France in the early months of the Revolution. They were revived in late summer and early fall of 1789 as bread supplies dwindled again, prices rose, grain convoys were violently interrupted, and the people of Paris cried out for bread at a tolerable price. Soon these popular convictions would fuel the passions of the rapidly growing mass, largely made up of women, that left the ravaged grain markets for Paris on 5 October to march on Versailles.

Once there, having disrupted the deliberations of the National Assembly to demand bread and vengeance against the nation's enemies, the crowd was diverted by the deputies to the royal palace to present the same demands—and to call for the king's unambiguous acceptance of the constitutional articles so far presented to him. This aggressive popular incursion, henceforth known as the October Days, had a double effect. Louis XVI assented to the constitutional decrees he had been resisting. He also allowed himself and his family to be shepherded by the National Guard from Versailles to the Tuileries palace in Paris, toward which he was followed by a vast crowd and, eventually, by the National Assembly itself. For a second time, and not the last, the course of the French Revolution had been decisively shifted by popular intervention.

Did Marat participate directly in these events? Camille Desmoulins suggested as much many months later. "Marat flies to Versailles, returns like lightning, makes as much noise himself as the four trumpets of the Apocalypse, and cries out to us: Oh You Dead, arise."[19] In all probability, this was just mockery. Marat himself never boasted of active participation in the march to Versailles, though he did soon claim some credit for inspiring it. He had "saved the homeland," he asserted, by "unveiling in advance the dark conspiracy of the aristocrats, of the odious league of the criminal faction of the Estates General, and of the minister and the corrupt members of the municipality of Paris, and by preparing the insurrection that took place."[20]

L'Ami du peuple had indeed called for popular action on 5 October in response to rumors that helped spark the massive march on Versailles. There had been news of a military orgy, a counterrevolutionary celebration held at Versailles by the Flanders Regiment the previous day. Did it presage yet another plot to suppress the capital by force of arms? In anticipation of this possibility, the journal summoned patriots to rise up in search of arms to defend the capital. "There's not a moment to lose. All good citizens must assemble in arms. . . . If the peril becomes imminent, we're done for unless the people names a tribune and arms him with the public force."[21] *A tribune of the people.* This call for a figure empowered to deploy emergency force in defense of the people marked the appearance of a theme with which Marat would soon become strongly identified.

As for "unveiling the dark conspiracy," *L'Ami du peuple* had also continued to denounce the existence of a famine plot in the weeks preceding the October Days. A lengthy article on 2 October, devoted to "France's Disastrous Situation and How to Remedy It," had offered an acid denunciation of the king's declaration sanctioning the National Assembly's decision to maintain the freedom of the grain trade in the face of increasing scarcity. In part, it mocked as "an insult to the majesty of a free people" the traditional protocol of this proclamation of the king's willingness to accede, "of our own certain knowledge, full power, and royal authority," to the Assembly's humble request for royal sanction of its decrees. In part, it protested the exceptional penalties to be imposed on those "disturbers of the peace" who dared to contravene the law. "Extraordinary prosecutions" of this kind Marat declared to be "the terrible weapon of despotism . . . the cruel continuation of a tyrannical administration making itself more keenly felt than ever." Behind this law he once again divined a government plot to amass grain and sell it abroad, a conspiracy to reduce Paris to starvation before moving the encircling troops against it.[22]

What was to be done? This time Marat widened the circle of blame. Behind the criminal faction in the National Assembly he sensed others, notably among the representatives and administrators of the city government of Paris that had been hastily improvised after the municipal revolution of 14 July. This body, he now urged, was the one to be purged above all. "The suspected persons, the royal pensioners, the prosecutors, the lawyers, the academicians, the magistrates of the Châtelet court, the functionaries of the judiciary and of the parlement, the financiers, the speculators, and the dealmongers" had to be swept from City Hall. The municipal assembly had to be reduced to no more than fifty reasonable, independent, and trustworthy men.

Marat was destined to become bitterly entangled with the Parisian municipal government, its assembly, and its committees. He saw it as the tool of the corrupt elite of the Old Regime—old enemies like Condorcet and Lavoisier among them—that was decking itself out in revolutionary colors. It saw him, in return, as a dangerous fanatic preaching anarchy and threatening public order. His pen, expostulated one outraged member of the city assembly, "distilled sedition and calumny."[23] And this rejoinder was in indignant repudiation of Marat's praise!

AGAINST THE MUNICIPALITY OF PARIS

In a lengthy attack on 24 September, *L'Ami du peuple* had declaimed against the organizational vices of the municipal government, its shameful representatives, and its outrageous committees. The journal found scarcely one of the latter without a royal pensioner, some favorite of the prince, some benighted aristocrat, some corrupt agent. How was it possible, Marat demanded, that the mayor of the revolutionary city was none other than Jean-Sylvain Bailly, a member of the Academy of Sciences "weighed down with royal pensions!" How could one believe that there were notorious speculators of grain among the representatives in the city council! How could that body bear the shameful presence of men like the despicable and corrupt playwright and speculator Beaumarchais![24]

Of all the vices of the new municipal government, Marat found most dangerous the secrecy under which its committees operated. Everything at City Hall went on behind closed doors, he told his readers. The building was surrounded by troops, the doors guarded, the people cut off from its delegates. The palace of a tyrant had never offered a more terrible spectacle! "Fellow citizens, open these doors that separate you from us; let the public witness your zeal to serve the homeland . . . let it constantly surround you. Don't offer it any longer, in the days of liberty, the odious spectacle of secret inquisitions that make us regret the days of slavery."[25] In the name of the people, Marat demanded transparency.

Open these doors: to reveal what? The tirade was far from over. The next issue of *L'Ami du peuple* continued the excoriation of the Paris municipal assembly. How could the people bear the lavish use of funds by these its representatives as they showered Bailly and Lafayette (now commander of the Paris National Guard) with remuneration and rewards in a ridiculous show of pomp redolent of the Old Regime! How could they thus open the floodgates to corruption! "Unhappy people, will you be always devoted to your misery?" Marat demanded. "Always vexed, downtrodden, pillaged, will you escape the royal embezzlers only to fall into the hands of the popular embezzlers. Groan, groan at your miserable fate. You deserve it in all its atrocity if you are too cowardly to resort to a remedy: it's in your hands!"

Within the city government, Marat disclosed, the academician-turned-mayor was conniving to capture all executive authority for himself; the police committee was being run by insolent aristocrats daring to decide the fate of prisoners; the subsistence committee was controlled by known hoarders. The municipality's secret procedures, impenetrable operations, lavish use of funds, oppressive militia, support from the corrupt faction within the Estates General, rigid suppression of popular assembly, and subservience to a minister ready to let the people die of hunger: all these elements betrayed a profoundly contrived plot deriving from a single source.[26] The minister indicted was Necker, against whom Marat raged for weeks before launching an incandescent denunciation.

The Paris municipality, he sensed, was at the center of a conspiracy of the Old Regime against the New. An academic, financial, and intellectual elite nurtured in the corridors of the absolute monarchy was now threatening to penetrate, colonize, and dominate the political order instituted in the name of the nation. Against these men, the Revolution had to be revived, reinvigorated, revolutionized. The enemies of the state would be immediately confounded as a result. The invisible strands of their dark plot would be broken forever. The National Assembly would purify itself. Public liberty would be established on an unshakeable base. For this new revolution against the Revolution, a purge was necessary.

"Demented people, will you always be the victim of your own blindness?" *L'Ami du peuple* demanded. "Open your eyes at last, emerge, emerge from your lethargy, purge your committees, preserve their healthy members, sweep away the corrupt ones, those royal pensioners, those cunning aristocrats, those dishonored or suspect men, those false patriots. From them you can only expect servitude, misery, and desolation." In an address to the Parisian district assemblies the following day, *L'Ami du peuple* called on them to carry out the work of regeneration. Their delegations to the municipal assembly had to be cleansed of the now familiar list of suspects: every royal pensioner, every royal official, every parlementary magistrate, every henchman of despotism, every speculator, every monopolist, every hoarder. Their deputies, charged to avoid every clandestine transaction, had to be made subject to recall for abuse of power.[27]

For the moment, the appeal fell short. There was no purge. Instead, Marat was summoned to appear before the Paris city council on 25 September 1789. After waiting five hours to be heard that evening, he was told to reappear the following day, with the same result. "Your business is infinite, no doubt," he protested to the council in an open letter published in *L'Ami du peuple* on 28 September; "mine is no less infinite and matters much more to the public happiness: I am the people's eye, you are at most its little finger." The letter was rounded out with renewed censure of the municipal assembly and reiterated calls for that body to cleanse itself and its committees of corrupt members.[28]

In response, Marat was immediately summoned to reappear before the municipal assembly. He had been denounced to this body, he informed his readers, by one of the wealthiest Paris districts, home of "the brokers, the bankers, the financiers, the speculators, which is to say those who build their fortunes on others' ruin, who drink the people's blood, and whose rapacity is a true scourge of humanity and one of the principal causes of public misery." Appearing before the municipal assembly, he claimed, he had been contemptuous in retort. He had called upon the assembly to purge its corrupt and unpatriotic members, naming names to be investigated. Against attacks from one of the representatives, a minor academician enjoying the privileges of a professorial chair endowed by the crown, his defense had been a bitterly personal declaration of purity, sacrifice, and civic virtue. If it glossed over his earlier years as a paid retainer in a royal household, it nevertheless betrayed the sting of previous academic rejections. "I defy you to find my name on the list of royal pensioners," he yelled back, "although I may perhaps have merited more from the letters and sciences than yourself. I will not answer that, since losing what little wealth I had, I live economically in a modest retreat. I will not answer that for the last nine months I've been reduced to a diet of bread and water in order to cover printing costs that have become exorbitant and to serve the homeland with my pen. What other motive than the purest love for the homeland could oblige a man of good judgment, a man free of intrigue, interest, and ambition . . . to expose himself to the vengeance of the villains he pursues, to sacrifice his existence, to devote himself unto death?"[29]

Marat wanted his readers to know that he had declared himself unable to match the artfulness with which corrupt municipal representatives had masqueraded as good patriots while keeping their places and pensions. Tell us of your patriotism, he had answered the posturing, privileged professor. "But allow us to tell you that in a free country your mere title as a royal pensioner would exclude you from an assembly that should comprise only independent men, men who don't speculate in the public good, men ready to sacrifice everything to the rights of the people as its representatives and defenders." It was time, he editorialized, to force the resignation of Bailly, the grasping academician who had passed his life studying the exact sciences, knew little of public affairs, and was now aiming to assume all power within the municipality. It was time to purify the municipal assembly of its corrupt and suspect members. It was time to attack without mercy its abusers of public authority. The next issue of *L'Ami du peuple* called on honest citizens to submit evidence of abuse by municipal authorities. The war would continue, it promised. "I am the nation's attorney and I'll never back down."[30]

Nor would the municipal assembly do otherwise. On 3 October, it denounced the nine issues of the journal published since 25 September, referring them to the public prosecutor for investigation. (Further numbers were added to the indictment as they appeared.) The next day, it accused Marat of calumny on the grounds that he had wrongly charged one of its members with falsifying documents. This formal denunciation was published, pasted up as a placard, circulated to all the Parisian districts, and brought before the Châtelet court for investigation. Marat soon offered a public retraction, but the case did not go away. Meanwhile, the public prosecutor brought the municipality's original complaint against him before the Châtelet court on 4 October. The indictment declared the self-described "Friend of the People" its most dangerous enemy, "since he abuses his talents and the liberty of the press to rob the people of the sole support remaining to it amid the ills that are oppressing it, since he directs all his efforts toward arousing the people against those it has itself chosen to watch over its preservation, security, and prosperity." It was evident, the prosecutor argued, that "the plan of the author of *L'Ami du peuple* is to prolong and even increase the horrors of anarchy the capital has suffered for so long."[31]

Quick action followed. On 6 October, the publisher and printer of the journal were identified for questioning. In vain, Marat appealed to the administration of his home district of the Cordeliers for protection; in vain, that body cited the Declaration of the Rights of Man in protesting against his treatment and vowed to place under its safeguard any citizen harassed in contradiction of the fundamental laws of the nation. On 6 October, bailiffs were sent to Marat's home with an order for his arrest and interrogation. Too late. The bird had flown. *L'Ami du peuple* did not appear again until 5 November, and then only clandestinely. The publisher quickly moved to compensate its subscribers by sending them issues of the rival *Courier de Paris* instead. The void was filled at the same time by the first of many counterfeit versions to leech upon the journal's popularity throughout its existence.[32]

The arrest order of 8 October 1789 remained formally in effect until 14 September 1791 when Louis XVI, having accepted the belated new constitution, issued a general political amnesty. By that time, Marat had lived more or less clandestinely for 706 days.[33]

BEFORE THE TRIBUNAL OF THE PUBLIC

From a refuge somewhere near Versailles (or so he claimed) Marat appealed to the National Assembly for protection, and to the public for exoneration.

Without success. He also began work on a denunciation of Necker that had been fermenting in his mind throughout the year. The issue of *L'Ami du peuple* he had written before disappearing had already identified the hoarders, along with the majority of municipal administrators, as "merely servile instruments" in the hands of the first minister. Necker himself, he insisted, was "the sole author of the scarcity that we have experienced for so long . . . , the soul of these disastrous speculations in bread that are well fit to figure one day among his fine speculations that have ruined France." The minister's plan was "as clear as day for those who have eyes." Once a popular idol, he had fallen victim to that desire for power to which even the most celebrated of men end up sacrificing their reputation. He had pushed the king to show himself a despot and the people's representatives to set themselves up as petty tyrants.[34] It was time, Marat thought, to settle the score.

The final provocation came from the minister himself, who appeared at a meeting of his district—the plutocratic Paris locality of Filles-Saint-Thomas—to urge his fellow citizens to apprise him of writings directed against him so that he could answer them in public. Marat was unimpressed by this posture of accountability, which he judged to be no more than a Jesuitical ploy. He seized upon it nonetheless as a solemn recognition of the principle he claimed as his own: that "it is before the tribunal of the public alone that the agents of power must justify themselves against accusations." There is irony in this appropriation of the authority of public opinion on Marat's part. He must have forgotten, or perhaps he was simply unwilling to acknowledge, that Necker himself had been the great theorist and invoker of public opinion in the prerevolutionary years. He was, in any case, eager to challenge the enemy to battle before this, his sovereign court. "You have voluntarily submitted to this supreme tribunal," he warned the minister, "and you have committed yourself to recognizing no other."[35]

The engagement Marat offered was couched in the most fantastical gladiatorial terms. "I'm going to descend into the arena," he proclaimed. "I want neither buckler nor breastplate. I forbid myself any ruse, any feint, I will attack you only face-to-face; but allow me the courtesy of an open encounter and place no obstacle against the publicity of my blows. I will conduct myself as a generous enemy. Defend yourself bravely, bring me to your feet, and receive in advance this sacred declaration—that if you emerge the winner in this combat I will be the first to make known my defeat and your triumph."[36]

The resulting *Dénonciation au tribunal du public faite par un simple citoyen contre un agent de la puissance exécutive* offered an early set-piece of revolutionary incrimination. Marat had been planning a history of the

French Revolution for some time. He was not alone: a rival journalist, Elysée Loustalot, editor of the *Révolutions de Paris*, was among those doing the same.[37] But while Loustalot would soon publish a celebratory account of the Revolution as the momentous fruit of a happy conjuncture between Enlightenment philosophy and popular misery, Marat would end up telling a story of conspiracy, stupidity, and betrayal. In essence an indictment of the entire history of the Revolution to that moment, his denunciation of Necker was presented as impartial and impersonal, the truth as offered by an obscure and disadvantaged individual citizen against an opulent public official surrounded by "a crowd of flatterers, partisans, acquaintances, innumerable legions of aristocrats, magistrates, bloodsuckers of the state, enemies of the homeland." This degenerate public man held the people in awe by sounding the trumpets of renown, Marat insisted. He himself, on the other hand, honest private man that he was, could offer only "the purity of my heart, the energy of virtue, and the irresistible force of truth."[38]

There followed an indictment of Necker the opulent banker whose wealth derived from "an impure source . . . speculation, that occupation unworthy of a noble and delicate soul, condemned by probity and proscribed by honor." Under the Old Regime, the minister had been no more than "the satrap of a despot." His one great act, in Marat's estimation, had been to summon the Estates General after so many broken ministerial promises to do so. Thereafter, "adored by the blind multitude," he had increasingly become "an unworthy minister who had cravenly abandoned the interests of the nation for those of the monarch."[39] The truth of his betrayal of the people was now complete. He had to be denounced as a public enemy. Marat proceeded to carry out this task under several heads.

First charge: Necker had turned a blind eye, before the fall of the Bastille, to the plans of the court to surround Paris with troops and reduce the city to obedience by "famine, the sword, and fire." At best, it could be said that he feared losing his position. To his vanity, his ambition, his thirst for power, he had thus sacrificed the safety of the capital, of the provinces, of the realm. "What! The torrents of blood, the pillage of houses, the evils, the calamities, the disasters that accompany the sack of an immense city, seemed too negligible to prevent for the sacrifice of his self-love. And this is the father of the people! The benefactor of humanity! The savior of France! The man whose loss the nation mourned and for whose return it had cried out!" What to conclude from Necker's complicity in remaining silent about such a conspiracy? The nation could choose whether to punish him as a traitor or throw him out as an imbecile. "An imbecile! If only that had been the case! We would not be groaning so long under the weight of our misfortunes."[40]

Second charge: the famine plot. Necker had inherited a troop of government hoarders and grain traders when he entered the ministry. He had allowed them to ship good grain to the Austrian Netherlands at a low price while bringing back to France rotten and infected grain purchased elsewhere at a higher price. Mixed before milling with a modicum of good grain to hide its foul taste, this infected staple produced bread that ravaged the throat and the stomach, weakened the appetite, and sapped bodily strength. "What infamy, Good God! to profit from a speculation that hit the poor still more through the time they lost waiting daily at the baker's door than by the high price of bread. What cruelty to render an infinite number of fathers powerless to feed their children. What barbarism to leave an immense people nothing but an unwholesome food that ruins health and produces epidemics!"[41]

Third charge: Necker had sacrificed the people to the rich, and the rich to the bloodsuckers of the state. What cuts in expenditures he could have made! "Master of the field of battle after our glorious revolution, how could he not have cut to the quick, how could he not have extinguished the source of disorders?" The immense list of targets Marat identified for elimination included the wasteful expenditures of the court; the military households of the king's brothers (which he himself had once served); excessive ministerial, military, ecclesiastical, administrative, and fiscal positions and expenses; and the royal manufactories of fabrics and furnishings. All this was to say nothing of the vast array of pensions and places available to academicians, historiographers, entertainers, police spies, and so on. "Comb through all M. Necker's operations and one will constantly see the perfect Jesuit, the successful juggler, the friend of the great, the enemy of the people."[42]

Necker had made no such economies, choosing instead to burden the nation with new taxes. Why? Because he did not want to create enemies and lose his job. "He thus sacrificed to his cupidity, ambition and vainglory the reestablishment of order, the regeneration of finances, the relief of the people, and the salvation of the realm—a sacrifice unworthy of a man of honor, an act of cowardly circumspection that must lower him in the esteem of good men, an unpardonable crime for a minister whom the nation has honored with its confidence."[43]

Fourth charge: Necker had pushed to restore the full plenitude of executive power to the monarch and rebuild the apparatus of despotism in the form of the National Guard. He had acquiesced in the development of counterrevolutionary sentiment around the king and among the troops surrounding him. He had been complicit in plans for the king to flee Versailles for Metz that had been frustrated only by the forced return of the royal family to Paris in the October Days. He had tried countless times to "return the nation to its chains, to fetter it to the yoke of the hideous despotism under which it has groaned so long."[44]

Fifth charge: Necker had compromised the honor of the king and of his subjects, subjecting them to ridicule before the whole of Europe. Under his leadership, France had been brought to its knees by the lunacy and betrayals of its administrators. If the English had not profited from this moment by stripping the country of its colonies, it was because they did not want to dishonor themselves by delivering the final blow to an already humiliated enemy. "Let's not be in any doubt: respect and fear are the best ramparts of peoples; but the Genevan speculator, blinded by his petty passions, doesn't see that."[45]

Marat's denunciation of Necker was total. The French had been betrayed by a foreign banker, a speculator extraordinaire, an international moneyman who had kept the bankrupt monarchy afloat for a decade on a sea of loans flowing from Amsterdam. "I arraign you before the nation as a public enemy," he charged the minister; "you must exonerate yourself completely or endure the consequences of its just indignation." There was no point recruiting paid hacks to defame him in return, he warned. Purity was his shield, virtue his sword. "My principles, my morals, my way of life are known. I shall not abase myself to combat the cowardly assassins who lurk in the shadows to stab me. . . . It is enough to glance at my writings to be assured that I am perhaps the only author since J.-J. [Rousseau] who must be free of suspicion."[46]

Who, after all, could be paying him, Marat demanded. He had denounced all possible patrons. He held neither place nor pension. Never had he solicited one; never had he accepted one. For whom had he made such a multitude of enemies? "For the people, this poor people exhausted by misery, always humiliated, always crushed, always oppressed, which never has places or pensions to give. It's for espousing its cause that I am the target of the attacks of the scoundrels who persecute me, that I am subject to an order of arrest as a criminal. But I feel no regret. What I have done I would do again if I were about to begin. Vile men, who know no other passion in life than gold, don't ask me what interest has been pushing me. I have avenged humanity, I will leave a name, and yours is made to perish."[47]

I will leave a name! Necker was indicted in the cause of integrity against corruption, courage against connivance, transparency against conspiracy, glory against empty celebrity, and the people against its oppressors. Jean-Paul Marat was offering a thymotic politics of ancient virtue, a politics of paranoia, a politics of disclosure, a politics of persecution, a politics of victimization and sacrifice. He saw it as a politics of purity inspired by the first analyst and victim of modern society, Jean-Jacques Rousseau.

Not everyone perceived it that way. Marat claimed that he offered his denunciation of Necker to as many as ten printers after he finished it on 4 November 1789. None of them had dared bring it out, and it did not appear until mid-January 1790. Among the number of pamphlets eventually published in equally virulent defense of Necker, one took particular exception to Marat's appropriation of the mantle of the citizen of Geneva. It denounced him as one without education, without friends, without fortune, without consolation, without science, without morals, without patriotism. Here, it charged, was a man motivated by vengeance and criminal desires against every association and companion; a misanthrope finding pleasure only in slandering genius, innocence, and virtue; a monster profiting from moments of horror and anarchy to ease a psychological torment and physical compulsion.

To achieve wealth and fame through crimes and madness, the critic continued, Marat was ready to brave public contempt and the rigor of the laws, to sell his pen to a powerful enemy of liberty, to become the disgrace of his century and the scandal of the nation. To seduce the feebleminded, he had declared himself the friend of the people and boldly prostituted the motto of the philosopher of Geneva. "This usurpation is an outrage Master Marat commits against the memory of the author of *Emile*. J. J. Rousseau and Master Marat; My God, what a contrast! Are vice and delirium of mind meant to be associated with virtue and genius? Is the sensitive philosopher who wanted to see peoples and kings united by bonds of perpetual peace to be compared to a seditious man who wants to overthrow empires?"

There's a whiff of intimacy about this denunciation of the denouncer. We don't know whether it came from a former friend or acquaintance, but its tone leaves no doubt that revolutionary politics was already becoming intensely personal. Portraying Marat as a preacher of rebellion, an apostle of falsehood, an apologist of conspiracy, an enemy of all humanity whose deepest desire was to see murders, conflagrations, scaffolds, victims, and executioners everywhere, it called for repression of intellectual delirium and the defense of social order. Liberty of the press fostered genius, the enraged critic allowed, but unbridled press license fostered hatred and discord, extinguished patriotism, and corrupted public morals.[48] Reversion to the distinction between liberty and license was to become a familiar reaction to Marat's writings. No one was to put more radically in question the revolutionaries' hesitant initial commitment to freedom of opinion.

A DENOUNCER'S CREED

The October crackdown on *L'Ami du peuple* left its production and distribution in complete disarray. The journal's previous printer, Jorry, had already been frightened off by an interrogation. With the printing shops of Paris now closed to him by police pressure, Marat found it imperative to have access to a press of his own.[49]

Still in hiding, though he had inched back into the Cordeliers district of Paris near his home on the rue de l'Ancienne Comédie, he may have acquired two hand presses as early as 5 November when the journal resumed publication, this time explicitly under his name alone (thus personalizing the journal by shedding the putative authorship of a "society of patriots"). This new issue of *L'Ami du peuple* railed against the "formidable league of enemies of the homeland" that had driven its author into hiding and was now pushing for reaction in the wake of the October Days. The Revolution, Marat feared, was losing momentum. Returning to the fray, he called for action by the "good citizens" of the Paris districts. To keep their representatives under surveillance, they had to demand public access to the hall of the National Assembly for at least two thousand spectators. They had to "chase mercilessly from all the committees the suspected persons and the citizens known not to have demonstrated patriotism and probity." Otherwise, he urged, "we strive in vain to break our chains. We will groan for an entire century in the convulsions of anarchy or the horrors of civil wars. Liberty cost the English twenty-five battles in a row and sixty years of misfortunes. And we think that we can conquer it in a day, with our arms crossed, while blabbing about city affairs."

If liberty was not the work of a day, least of all had it been the work of 14 July 1789, which had done so little in Marat's view to sweep away the beneficiaries of the Old Regime who were now assuming the mask of patriotism. How could these men be trusted, he demanded. "What! On the morning of 14 July, the nobility, the clergy, the creatures of the court, and the innumerable crowd of lowlifes who live off the disorders of the state and public calamities reveal themselves as our mortal enemies. By the evening, they will have become our best friends! And the taking of the Bastille will have given them a new soul . . . ! And they will never try to undo the concessions forced on them by fear! And they will not conspire constantly against us! Taken with weapons in their hands, they will only have to conceal themselves with the mask of patriotism, and we will believe in their patriotism. And we will let them peacefully renew their perfidious design! How stupid we are! They treat us like imbeciles, but are they wrong?"[50]

Issues of the journal followed daily until 14 November under the imprint of a "Presse Patriotique" (with subscriptions still available from its former publisher, Dufour). Written from hiding several weeks earlier, for the most part, the numbers were thin on news and poorly updated; Marat soon launched into an effort (never completed) to revise and reissue them for subscribers.[51] In addition to renewed calls for purge, the original pages nevertheless contained some passionate statements of themes that had crystallized in his political thinking during his weeks in hiding. Amounting to a manifesto for popular insurrection, on the one hand, and for public denunciation, on the other, they signaled central elements of his developing revolutionary creed.

To repress popular agitation in the wake of the October Days, the National Assembly had adopted a hastily written riot act on 21 October that allowed the imposition of martial law against popular gatherings deemed to be threatening violence. Marat reacted with a passionate defense of crowd action. "Timid citizens, men who love their peace, the bloodsuckers of the State, and the scoundrels that live off public abuses fear nothing more than popular uprisings that tend to destroy their happiness and bring about a new order of things," he declaimed. "They speak out constantly against energetic writings, against vehement speech, in a word against everything that can make the people feel the bitterness of its misery and remind it of its rights."[52]

This attitude, Marat expostulated, merely revealed the ethic of the privileged and the powerful. Blind to abuses of authority and the horrors of tyranny, these men were concerned only to calm the people and prevent it from expressing its rightful fury. They had strong reasons of their own for doing so, and a persuasive pretext. "I speak of the tragic scenes that always accompany insurrections." Acknowledging the terror inspired by popular violence, and the memory of the bloodshed that followed the taking of the Bastille, *L'Ami du peuple* offered several responses. The first was a Lockean reassurance: "The people only rises up when it is pushed to despair by tyranny." The second was a Tacitean question: "Is there a comparison to be made between a small number of victims that the people sacrifices to justice in the course of an insurrection and the innumerable host of subjects a despot reduces to misery, or sacrifices to his fury, his cupidity, his glory, his whims?" What were the drops of blood now shed by the people to recover its liberty as compared with the torrents unleashed by a Tiberius, a Caligula, a Caracalla, or a Commodus, by the mystical frenzy of a Charles IX, or by the shameful ambitions of Louis XIV? What were a few individuals ruined, as compared with the thousands stripped bare by financiers, vampires, and embezzlers?[53]

It was incontestable that philosophy had prepared, sparked, and favored the present revolution, Marat acknowledged. "But writings are not sufficient; actions are necessary." There followed a list of popular protests that had restored French liberty in the course of 1789. "Follow the work of the National Assembly and you will find that it has only acted or passed good laws after some popular uprising, and that in times of calm and security this odious faction has never missed an opportunity to rouse itself to place obstacles in the way of the constitution or get disastrous laws passed. Thus we owe everything to insurrection, both the fall of our tyrants and that of their favorites, their creatures, their satellites; both the abasement of the great and the elevation of the little people; both the return of liberty and the good laws that will maintain it by assuring our peace and happiness."[54]

Squeamish souls saw only the misfortunes of a few individuals who were the victims of transitory violence, Marat argued. They were touched only by the punishment of a few criminals. He viewed things differently. "I see only the misfortunes, the calamities, the disasters of a great nation at the mercy of tyrants, enchained, pillaged, harassed, downtrodden, oppressed, massacred for entire centuries. Which of us has more reason, humanity, or patriotism? They strive to lull the people to sleep, I to awaken it. They give it opium, I pour acid on its wounds and will continue to do so until it has entered fully into its rights, until it is free and happy." "Opium to the people": a notion destined to reap a rich harvest. Under an established constitution upheld by virtuous authorities, Marat allowed, martial law might serve as a rampart of liberty against treasonous manipulation of the people. But for a nation still struggling to break its chains, one still threatened by public enemies throughout government who were trying to reduce it to anarchy and servitude, such a law could only become a wall of iron enclosing the abyss into which the people had been thrown.[55]

Denunciation was also a crucial weapon against those faithless enemies of the nation everywhere entrenched in power. An independent public tribunal was necessary, Marat now argued, to protect accusers from oppression and the accused from calumny. In effect, this body would institutionalize the court of public opinion. Its proceedings would necessarily be open to ensure that "truth, having no fear of being stifled by intrigue, artifice, or violence, can show itself in all its purity because the public is the first judge of matters concerning it and can best assess the morals of accuser and accused and the grounds for the denunciation." This consideration led to a kind of denunciatory manifesto, the expression of Marat's fundamental convictions. It was essential for the safety of the state, he insisted, that the management of public affairs not be entrusted to criminal hands. Anyone in authority who was corrupt, or suspected of being so, had to be publicly unmasked. It was therefore up to public opinion, in a kind of self-institution, to lay down the principles upon which its authority must rest. "Let opinion consecrate these great maxims, so proper to disconcert the ambitious, the scoundrels, the traitors, and to deter those tempted to become so."

L'Ami du peuple thus set them forth.

> Every citizen is allowed to denounce men in place, from the first minister to the lowest clerk, and to bring them before the state tribunal.
> When a denunciation contains several counts of indictment, it must be deemed well founded even though all the charges are not proved.
> Every well-founded denunciation will be a title to public esteem for its author.
> No denunciation that is unfounded but motivated by love of the homeland will expose its author to any punishment because, man not being infallible, an error does not make him a criminal.
> Any man denounced unjustly will be honorably acquitted and any denouncer in good faith will be obliged only to extend his hand in peace.
> A calumnious denouncer will be branded by public opinion and the good man denounced without justification will receive a mark of honor as a token of the esteem of his fellow citizens, though he will be deprived of it if he proves unworthy.
> Two tables will be displayed in the courtroom of the tribunal, one containing the names of agents of authority who have offended, the other of denouncers guilty of calumny.
> Who would want to denounce wrongdoers if a simple error could render an honest man victim of his zeal for the homeland? No one.
> Who would want to serve the homeland if one were ceaselessly exposed to informers? The good man.[56]

LIBERTY OR LICENSE?

Though Marat managed to bring out sporadic issues of *L'Ami du peuple* in late November and again in early December, his new presses were soon seized by one district committee and copies of the journal confiscated by another. He also fell into a dispute over subscription lists with his publisher Dufour that led to a definitive break in their association by the end of the year.[57] In the meantime, his hiding place in the Cordeliers district was discovered. On 12 December he was arrested and brought before the investigative committee (*comité des recherches*) of the municipality. The hearing led to a chance encounter and extended conversation with Lafayette, Marat's first, and the only one that was amicable by his account; his relations with the commandant of the National Guard would soon deteriorate. Cordially dismissed by the investigative committee without further action, he was left free to recover his presses and put them to work.[58]

Why this indulgent treatment? Brissot's influential presence as a member of the *comité des recherches* may have helped. Like Marat, indeed before him, he had become a revolutionary journalist, though his *Patriote français* was more supportive of the National Assembly and of the municipality than was *L'Ami du peuple*. The bitterly divergent paths the two friends would follow through the Revolution were already prefigured, in a way, by the difference in the titles of their journals. Though he was becoming more critical of Marat's radicalism during this period, Brissot may not have wanted to endanger the principle of the liberty of the press before a law had been passed to govern its practice. The weeks following the October Days had, in any case, seen a reactionary shift in the National Assembly that favored the influence of Marat's preferred target: the aristocratic faction of nobles and clergy eager to slow or reverse the course of the Revolution. Lafayette and the members of the city's investigatory committee may not have wanted Marat's attacks on these recalcitrant elements within the Assembly to be silenced at this particular moment. In the complex politics unfolding within the French Revolution over the next few years, The People's Friend was often a pariah but never entirely without usefulness to one group or another.

Publication of *L'Ami du peuple* resumed on 19 December and continued without interruption until 22 January. The shift toward repression of popular political action during this period, efforts to constrain the freedom of the press, jostling between and within overlapping institutions of the new regime and the old, rivalries among ambitious political leaders, and some notable political trials: these developments produced a period of political uncertainty regarding the character and direction of the Revolution.[59] They also offered rich opportunities for denunciation. Marat took them.

The deputies of the divided National Assembly, and particularly the retrograde elements within it, remained a favorite target. They were leaving the nation "more enslaved than ever." In an affront to national sovereignty that would make the legislature sovereign, they were requiring the National Guard to take a civic oath to uphold the laws, whether just or not. In Marat's analysis, everything went back to the error of allowing noble and clerical deputies to remain within the National Assembly. The Revolution would have been achieved if, on 15 July, ten thousand Parisians had marched to Versailles to cleanse the Assembly of the nobles and prelates who had no right to be sitting there. Liberty would have been consolidated without the slightest violence if, on 6 October, aristocrats who were ready to quit the Assembly had been allowed to do so. Instead of profiting from such moments of terror to exclude enemies of the nation forever, the more moderate revolutionary leaders had given these enemies time to recover their nerve—and to dominate the Assembly in their turn.[60]

In this political conjuncture the people, too, was at fault. It had acted blindly and sporadically, Marat insisted; its passing bouts of fury had been followed by inaction. Since it lacked any planning or consistent goals, it had constantly fallen victim to the "cupidity, greed, and venality of the intriguers who want to lead it in order to enchain it and strip it bare." There had been no revolutionary script for it to follow. "History offers no example of a revolution like the one that has occurred among us," lamented *L'Ami du peuple*. The natural and necessary consequence of administrative excesses and the universal corruption of manners, this revolution had nonetheless resulted from stupidity and accident rather than from conscious political action. "The wisdom and courage of the Parisians, which have been so much honored, have played almost no part in it. Heaven may have seemed miserly in doling out distinct opportunities for us to break our chains, but we have done everything in our power to let them pass without profiting from them." There followed a renewed call for popular vigilance and political purge.

"Oh, my fellow citizens!" Marat exhorted. "Redouble your vigilance, be on your guard, and if some unforeseen event leads to a new insurrection of the people, profit from it to expel the nobles and prelates from the Assembly. Representatives of orders that no longer exist, not of the people, they have no right to sit there." But the winnowing of the Assembly for which he called could not stop at former members of the privileged orders. "Purge it too of all the inept and corrupt plebeians," he urged. "Purge as well the municipality and the district committees. Deal with all the public administrators who have professed antipatriotic principles."[61]

Hence another favorite target: the mayor and the municipality of Paris. To Marat's mind, the office of mayor was worse than useless, its sumptuous trappings not only expensive but a powerful trough for corruption. Bailly commanded like a king in the capital while remaining blindly obedient to Necker. In the hands of this former academician, moreover, the power of this mayor was particularly dangerous. "The maxims of submission to royal authority upon which he has sucked since childhood, his lifelong habit of seeking places and pensions, his daily dealings with the creatures of the court, along with his needs and interest, can only extinguish in his heart the love of independence that alone characterizes true patriots, while the numerous favors he has received from the king puts him into dependence upon the minister."[62]

Marat blamed Bailly for the crackdown on the radical press effected by the decision of the municipality to limit the number of book peddlers in Paris to three hundred and to require their official registration, thus returning to the practice of the Old Regime. This regulation he denounced as "the most adroit of the attacks against the liberty of the press because that liberty is nothing without the publicity given to the writers' productions. And in every case where the publicity must be prompt, the cry of the book peddlers is indispensable. If the districts apply themselves to the execution of this destructive regulation . . . liberty is forever done for."[63]

The municipality was castigated, as well, for agreeing (at Necker's insistence) to lend its enforcement power to assist officers of commercial courts in the arrest and imprisonment of persons accused of civil debt. This ordinance Marat denounced as an instrument of tyranny "as unconstitutional as it is impolitic, vexatious, and barbarous." It offered new possibilities for oppression at a moment of economic misery and commercial collapse. Contrary to natural rights, it would divide citizens even further in "a time of troubles, anarchy and confusion." The municipality, moreover, had no right to pass regulations without consulting the city's district assemblies, just as the National Assembly had no right to make laws not sanctioned by the nation.[64] Marat wanted popular sovereignty all the way down.

Lurking behind Bailly and the municipality, too—indeed, behind everything that threatened the people's advance toward liberty—Marat detected Necker, the ultimate source of political evils. The mayor was "an automaton" in the hands of the minister, "the most adroit and most dangerous supporter of arbitrary power, the cruelest adversary of liberty, the firmest bastion of the aristocracy." Marat saw the minister's hand behind the riot act decreed by the National Assembly; he saw it behind the decision of the municipality to enforce arrest and imprisonment for civil debt; he saw it still behind manipulation of the grain trade. Issues of the scarcity and price of bread continued to play out in outbreaks of popular riot, as in the trial of the chevalier James Rutledge accused of working behind the scenes to bribe Parisian bakers not to bake their bread.[65] Was the imprisoned Rutledge a victim of tyranny or one of its underlings? Either way, his case could be made to serve Marat's purposes.

Rutledge had been brought before the Châtelet court, a pillar of the judicial system of the Old Regime that had so far survived into the new order. The court was at the same time hearing evidence in two other high-profile cases. The first, the trial of the baron de Besenval, a royal military commander who had been captured fleeing Paris after the fall of the Bastille, had reactivated questions about the Revolution's founding moment. The second, that of the marquis de Favras, accused as an agent of a conspiracy to bring troops into Paris, kill the leaders of the Revolution, and wrest the monarch from the capital, raised anxieties about the readiness of court circles to accept the Revolution's achievements. The implication in this conspiracy of the king's brother (comte de Provence and future Louis XVIII), though widely suspected, was officially covered up in the court proceedings.

By the beginning of 1790, as a result, the Châtelet had become a focus of political tensions in Paris. It was also a particular target for Marat. This was, after all, the court that had ordered his arrest on 8 October. It was also the tribunal to which the National Assembly had temporarily assigned jurisdiction over political crimes of lèse-nation on 21 October 1789. In Marat's view, the continued existence of this antiquated body symptomized the colonization of the Revolution by the Old Regime; its jurisdiction now blocked the creation of the independent revolutionary tribunal for which he had been clamoring. "In the pretended tribunal of state sit men ennobled for cash and devoted to the minister, creatures of the prince, henchmen of despotism, cowardly agents of injustice eager to manipulate all the artifices of the courts to save the traitors of the homeland," pronounced *L'Ami du peuple* on 7 January 1790. "Thus, as a result of some antique formulas, some perfidious equivocations, some shady maneuvers, the people sees its guilty enemies escape and, gradually losing the fruit of its efforts, its combats, its victories, it finishes by succumbing, by being put back into chains."[66]

This attack was offered on 7 January. There followed, the next day, a proclamation of the need for decisive popular action—and a denunciation of the people that was unready to take it. Earlier, Marat had talked of purge; now he invoked acts of slaughter. "Consider the history of nations: none of them has succeeded in breaking its chains without choking its oppressors in their own blood, without putting them to the sword on a day of battle, without felling them on a day of insurrection. Instead of resorting to means imperative for the security of the state, we have the stupidity to want to reintegrate [the oppressors], we leave them peacefully among us, and each day they spin some new web. If only we would make use of the means fortune presents us!"

The National Assembly had to be cleansed, then, the mayor's office abolished, and the Châtelet stripped of jurisdiction over crimes against the state. "Almost entirely composed of subordinates of the parlement, men infatuated by judicial maxims, officers of the crown, gangrened aristocrats, insolent oppressors, how could [this court] inspire the confidence of good citizens?" The answer was clear, but so was the consequence. "To take vigorous action like this, virtue is necessary. I say it with bitterness. Liberty doesn't appear to be made for us. Slaves because of our ignorance, our needs, and our vices, our vanity, our luxury, our greed, our ambition, we belong to the first ready buyer, and we claim to enjoy the advantages of a free and just government, which is impossible."[67]

For the magistrates of the Châtelet, this outburst was one provocation too many. On 9 January, while *L'Ami du peuple* was floating ideas for the formation of a patriotic society to resist the people's enemies—the model was the English Society for the Rights of Man—the court readied plans for its author's arrest. That evening, a detachment of the National Guard drawn from various districts within the city was dispatched to search his hiding place and print shop at 39 rue de l'Ancienne Comédie, which happened to be in the same building as the guard post of the Cordeliers district! Thence, finding him nowhere there, the soldiers proceeded to the residence on the nearby rue du Vieux Colombier he had been forced to avoid for weeks. This location, too, they left without their intended prisoner.[68]

"The poor Friend of the People is so exhausted by weariness, anxiety, and lack of sleep that he hasn't the strength for his work," Marat wailed to his readers after this attempted arrest. But he promised them an issue the following day that would again display the "purity of his zeal and the integrity of his sentiments." It came in the form of a blistering attack on the Châtelet that called for the reorganization or total abolition of the oppressive court. How, he demanded, could this body that had "grown old under despotism, sucking the maxims of despotism with its milk . . . not be a secret enemy of the revolution?" The following day, he launched appeals for his protection to the National Assembly and to Lafayette as commander of the National Guard. A more immediate retort came, however, from a power now rapidly emerging onto the scene of the Revolution, the assembly of the Cordeliers district under the leadership of Danton. On 11 January, following Marat's call to extend the principle of popular sovereignty to the local level, this assembly prohibited troops drawn from beyond the district from executing any orders for the arrest of citizens within it.[69]

By this time, it was clear, Marat had managed to turn liberty of the press into an urgent issue. Number 83 of *L'Ami du peuple* had been indicted by the assembly of the Sorbonne district on 31 December for slanderous remarks against Necker and Bailly. A second Parisian district, that of Sainte-Marguerite, had repudiated the journal's claim to speak for the people by demanding on 8 January that its title be changed. It was denounced in the National Assembly on 12 January. A resolution of the Assembly that same day called for immediate consideration of a press law, prompting Sieyès's controversial and unsuccessful proposal on 20 January for a repressive temporary decree.[70] Marat saw this latter as "a criminal, political, civil, moral, typographical and theatrical hodge-podge," the work of a paid sophist that, if passed, would "destroy public liberty in a day under the pretext of preventing license and preventing disorders." There were deputies in the meantime who demanded a committee to monitor journals like *L'Ami du peuple* and its rival *Les Révolutions de Paris*.[71]

Summoned to appear before the police tribunal of the Paris municipality on 11 January to answer the charges of the Sorbonne district, Marat declined on the grounds that his journal complied with existing legal requirements. This refusal prompted a lengthy consideration by the tribunal the following day. No law had yet been passed by the National Assembly to govern freedom of the press. Censorship had been one of the most offensive aspects of the Old Regime, liberty of the press one of the most hard fought of the rights enumerated in the Declaration of the Rights of Man and the Citizen. But the declaration had left still undefined the "abuse of this liberty" that the law could not permit. What was to be done to safeguard liberty from license? Marat was forcing the issue. The authorities needed to decide.[72]

Decide they did, at least for the moment. "The time has passed," the police tribunal announced, "when, to follow Montesquieu's phrase, one could be covered at one and the same time with infamy and dignity. Under the reign of liberty and the surveillance of public opinion, great positions are only the reward for great virtues or the price of great talents." An esteemed journalist could exercise a kind of censorship over an entire society, the officials reasoned, but would lose all credit by ceasing to be circumspect, impartial, and true. All the more scandalous, then, was it that journalists like Marat had breached the limits on the liberty of the press prescribed by morality, reason, and even public interest. These writers were eroding their own credit and undermining the legitimacy of press freedom in the process. "Liberty of the press is considered a rampart of the constitution in England," the police officials acknowledged. "But was there no other way of naturalizing this strange plant among us than by showing us its such bitter fruits?"

The police tribunal looked forward to the passage of a law that would make "wisely limited" press freedom the safeguard of general liberty without its becoming the scourge of individuals. Admitting that individuals could seek recourse against slander in the courts, it declared itself hesitant to proceed against Marat. But there were laws still on the books, and fears apparently justifiable. The officials found him subject to judgment under an ancient *ordonnance* declaring slanderers punishable as "breakers of the peace and disturbers of public tranquility." To clinch the matter, they also noted that another longstanding regulation denied him the right to possess his own press since he was not among the thirty registered printers of Paris. Bad old laws these might be, they implicitly acknowledged. But it was better to have bad laws than none. On 13 January, they ordered Marat's presses halted and referred his case to the Châtelet court for judgment.[73]

Two days later it was the turn of Antoine-Gaspard Boucher d'Argis, honored under the Old Regime as a prolific Encyclopedist, noted jurist, and magistrate of the Châtelet, to open another front in the war against untrammeled press freedom. Boucher d'Argis had been subjected to vicious attacks in *L'Ami du peuple* for his conduct as prosecutor of Besenval and his accumulation of positions in the new order. The municipal assembly, after hearing the magistrate defend himself and his court for two hours, declaimed against the atrocities visited upon this irreproachable citizen. Liberty, it held, would be impossible without rapid repression of the "unbridled license with which some periodical publications, and notably that entitled *L'Ami du peuple*, rail against the most respectable citizens." These were "incendiary writings" intended to plunge the capital into anarchy by "exciting the people to violate the sanctity of the laws, profane the sanctuary of justice, and go to extremes against its organs and its ministers." A salutary freedom of the press, the assembly laid down, was far from conferring the dangerous right to slander with impunity. Even among the English, until now the freest people of Europe, authors and printers were held responsible for their publications. Moreover, the Declaration of the Rights of Man and of the Citizen was far from authorizing writings that breathed only sedition, revolt, and calumny. The assembly had no hesitation in ordering the municipal prosecutor to indict the author of *L'Ami du peuple* before the Châtelet court. The decision was printed, posted, sent to all the districts of Paris, and ordered read at every pulpit in the city. The following day, in response to yet another denunciation of *L'Ami du peuple*, the assembly urged officers of the National Guard to crack down on the hawkers of the journal and incendiary writings like it.[74]

"It's all bad faith, trickery, hypocrisy, prevarication and outrage," was Marat's response to the announcement of his indictment before the Châtelet court. It spoke "the language of despots, the language of tyrants." Fearing any disturbance that might threaten their authority, the "provisional mandataries" of the Commune were treating as incendiary writings destined to awaken the people from its lethargy and to recall it to the defense of its rights. They preached "the deceptive tranquility and apparent calm commanded by fear and terror, the image of the sleep of death." Their aim was to sap the foundations of liberty, set themselves up as absolute masters, strip the people of its rights, and gorge on its blood. Their invocation of the English example was disingenuous. In England, Marat insisted, citing the famous *Letters of Junius*, "a writer speaking for the homeland can drag any public man in the mud, no matter how elevated his rank." In that happy island across the Channel, he avowed, the Parisian administrators would have met the fate of Warren Hastings (the colonial administrator impeached for corruption in 1787). There, first minister Necker himself, along with the mayor and the entire municipal government of Paris, would have retraced the steps of Charles I to the scaffold. As if to make the point, the same issue of *L'Ami du peuple* advertised the actual publication, at last, of Marat's seething *Dénonciation . . . contre M. Necker*. It, too, was soon liberally denounced in the press.[75]

POWER TO THE PEOPLE?

A response to the municipal representatives came also from the popular assembly of the Cordeliers district, by now fully committed to protecting its most infamous resident from arrest. On 19 January, it warned against the judgments of "men attached to the principles of the old regime and imbued with prejudices and false maxims of the old financial magistracy." Their aim was "to stifle the voice of patriotic writers whose zeal, even if supposed exaggerated, can only contribute to the triumph of truth and the consolidation of a constitution superior to that of peoples whom we regarded as truly free only because we were plunged in the most shameful slavery." In effect placing Marat and other radical writers under its direct protection, the district then created a committee of five "Conservators of Liberty" without whose permission no citizen within its bounds could be deprived of freedom. The local battalion of the National Guard was ordered to stand ready to enforce this decree.[76]

The scene was set for a dramatic confrontation offering a kaleidoscopic view of political power within the city. Necker may have watched from afar, but Bailly, Lafayette, the National Assembly, the Châtelet court, the municipality of Paris, the National Guard, and the officers and citizens of the Cordeliers district, with Danton emerging at their head, were all thrust into motion on 21 January when the Châtelet court finally ordered Marat arrested and his printing equipment confiscated.

Early on 22 January, a detachment of the National Guard drawn from outside the Cordeliers district, together with officers and bailiffs of the court, arrived at the Hôtel de la Feutrière to enforce the execution of this order. The agents of the court were immediately confronted by local guardsmen, who directed them to the district headquarters to seek the prior approval, now required, from the new "Conservators of Liberty." There they were met with hostility as Danton protested loudly against Lafayette's provocation in authorizing the intrusion of guardsmen from outside the district without its prior consent. An implicit threat underlay his observation that his fellow citizens "had only to sound the tocsin and beat the general alarm to get the entire faubourg Saint-Antoine and more than 20,000 men before whom all these troops would blanch." Nonetheless, three of the Conservators had given their consent before Danton, scrutinizing the warrant, suddenly declared it invalid. Issued on 8 October, he objected, the order no longer followed the form required by subsequent legislation of the National Assembly. The result was a standoff as agitated local citizens crowded into the meeting room ready to protect The People's Friend from arbitrary arrest.[77]

Eventually, an emergency meeting of the district assembly was convoked, and citizens were summoned to attend it bearing arms. A delegation was sent to Lafayette, warning him of the heated situation, inviting him to withdraw the National Guard troops brought from outside the district, and offering to replace them with guardsmen from within the locality. Receiving this deputation with disdain, the general ordered his troops to execute their orders by force.

Meanwhile, the district assembly had approved an address to the National Assembly in explanation of its actions. It expressed respect for the representatives' decrees and for their immediate enforcement, as well as for the stipulation of the Declaration of the Rights of Man that "no man may be accused, arrested, or detained except in cases determined by the law and *according to the forms it has prescribed*." Obedience to the letter of the law was all the more important, the district emphasized, at a moment of uncertainty in which the distribution of public authority remained provisional. "At a time when the execution of new laws is still referred to ancient tribunals imbued with ancient prejudices; at a time when all elements of authority are not yet coordinated; at a time, finally, when citizens must be on guard against enemies of the public good who detect any occasion to abuse authority," the address declared, it was incumbent upon the district to "take measures to safeguard citizens from arbitrary authority and ensure their enjoyment of the advantages of your decrees." A delegation was chosen to convey these sentiments to the National Assembly. Another was mandated to beg Lafayette to come to the district himself to resolve the issue directly and personally. Refusing to comply or to give the order for the withdrawal of the troops, the haughty general summarily referred the delegation to Mayor Bailly.

With the Cordeliers district on the verge of insurrection, and the Châtelet now urging prudence upon its officials, the National Guard hesitated to act for fear of "provoking a revolution." But agitation extended around the Hôtel de la Feutrière where a face-off continued all day between the troops of the National Guard and a crowd of local citizens. The impasse was only broken at the end of the afternoon, perhaps by a firm decision on Bailly's part to see the arrest warrant enforced, perhaps by a resolution of the National Assembly that declared the resistance of the Cordeliers district illegal. Proceeding to Marat's quarters to execute their orders, the officials discovered his presses and other printing equipment, interrogated his assistant, and confiscated papers before putting an official seal around the premises.[78] The author of *L'Ami du peuple*, yet again, was nowhere to be found. After hiding elsewhere in Paris for a few more days, he headed for the comparative safety of London.

FIFTEEN

ENEMIES OF THE PEOPLE

It was not long before Marat was addressing the French nation from London, "the shore where the tempest has thrown me, naked, crushed, covered with bruises, exhausted by my efforts, and dying of fatigue." He declared himself full of dread in face of the stormy political waters upon which his blind fellow citizens were now sailing with such a false sense of security. "I shiver with horror at the sight of the dangers threatening them; I lament that I am no longer able to offer them a sustaining hand." Instead, he found himself "rendered powerless by cruel destiny, left only with futile charges against the perfidious and barbarous pilots who expose the ship to destruction after tossing me overboard in the pretense that they want to calm the storm." In all probability, he himself had washed up in London before he readied this pamphlet for the printer. Its publication opened a time of reckoning for him, as well as a moment of prophetic despair.[1]

FROM ANOTHER SHORE

This renewed *Appeal to the Nation* began by setting aside any hope for responsible action by the corrupted National Assembly. Marat was addressing the nation now, he announced, not its purported representatives. "Let's not beat about the bush. Martyr to my zeal for the safety of the fatherland, I will no longer bring my complaints before the National Assembly. The haughty and vain men who deck themselves out in the spoils of the people, the hypocrites who mislead it, the lawyers who sell it justice, the intriguers who attempt to subject it, the scoundrels who try to starve it, the criminals who strive to plunge it back into the abyss, and—in a word—the public enemies who dominate the legislature rear up at the very sound of my name. Blinded by their passions and deaf to the voices of duty, they immolate piteously the man of integrity who dares to unveil their dark plans and to defend the cause of liberty against them. Let them enjoy their false triumph, I won't tire them further with my complaints. It's to the nation that I dare address them, it's on behalf of the nation I have fought, for the nation that I have made myself execrated."[2]

In this prophetic, self-immolatory mode, Marat offered yet another flashback of his struggle to save the Revolution since it had been left fatefully incomplete on 14 July 1789. He saw a mindless people that had allowed its enemies to seize leadership of institutions hastily improvised in its name. The results had been disastrous. Necker, speculator extraordinaire, still had to be hounded from the ministry (a *Nouvelle dénonciation contre Necker* would soon volley forth); the corrupt municipal government of Paris still had to be purged (and with it Bailly, the despicable and imperious academician serving as mayor); and the Châtelet court, that relic of the Old Regime now given inquisitorial power, still had to be dismantled. Against all these enemies of the people, the denunciations of *L'Ami du peuple* had so far proved of no avail.

It was time, Marat announced, for the French to face the reality that a true revolutionary transformation had yet to occur. In his diagnosis, a chance combination of circumstances had been enough to allow an ignorant and corrupt people to throw off momentarily the yoke of despotism. But the recovery of liberty called for more than mere conjuncture. Enlightenment and virtue were indispensable if a vicious political cycle was to be escaped. "Without them, the people passes rapidly from servitude to anarchy, from anarchy to license, from license to oppression, and from oppression to servitude, the inevitable circle that we have just traversed. Thus, after several months passed in the daze of hunger and the delirium of a false triumph, here we are finally returned to our chains by the same hands we armed to support our independence."[3]

By this point, this exile's notion of enlightenment was a cruel and disenchanted one. He thought it a fantasy to assume that the people's deputies were incorruptible, its judicial officials upright, its public administrators faithful. Men could not be expected to renounce their prejudices and their passions, their love of power, their honors, their love of pleasure and worldly vanities. He considered it wishful thinking to suppose that dull souls and base hearts might sacrifice everything to virtue. Reality taught a different lesson. "Let's not disregard nature," he counseled. "Nothing worthy must be expected from those in authority; they must be nailed to their duties. We don't have to demand that they be good; we have to prevent them from being evil."[4] The actions, machinations, and plots of men in power had to be constantly revealed and openly denounced. Machiavellian realism had to be channeled here into the service of the people, not that of the prince.

Denunciation, then, was to be the order of the day. But Marat no longer deemed it sufficient. A nation recovering its liberty had also to repress and punish. Its vengeance could be entrusted only to proven patriots as wise as they were firm and incorruptible. There had to be a state tribunal filled with such men, a court before which public censors would indict agents of the people who had abused their authority. And finally, when corruption had gone so far as to pervade all branches of the administration, the sole means of putting things back in order was "to name a supreme dictator for a very short time, to arm him with the public force and charge him with punishing the guilty. A few heads suitably felled can put a stop to public enemies for a long time, safeguarding a great nation for entire centuries from the evils of misery, the horrors of civil wars."[5]

"*A few heads suitably felled. . . .*" The People's Friend had talked before about purging those enemies of the people who had managed to insinuate themselves into hastily improvised revolutionary institutions. He had made clear his view that blood had been too sparingly shed in the days following the fall of the Bastille. Now he turned the pruning of heads from a missed opportunity into a political program. To save liberty, he called for blood.

The dictatorship he had in mind in advocating such a purge was modeled on a feature of the classical Roman constitution providing for the appointment of a dictator granted emergency powers for a limited period (typically no more than six months) to defend the republic against internal or external enemies. Emphasis on the essential importance of this institution was a key element of classical republicanism as a corollary of its driving conviction that freedom was constantly at risk of an urgent threat against it. Machiavelli's insistence that "all republics . . . should have some institution of this kind to fly to, in cases of extreme necessity" was taken up by Algernon Sidney, John Trenchard, Thomas Gordon, and James Burgh in England, as by Montesquieu (in his discussion of aristocratic republics), Rousseau, and Mably in France. It seems clear that Marat followed Rousseau in conceiving of the dictatorship as exercised on behalf of the people, as an emergency mechanism for the protection of popular sovereignty rather than as a replacement for it. But Rousseau, along with others in the classical republican tradition, was keenly aware of the risk that constitutionally appointed dictators could turn into tyrants by arbitrarily extending their power beyond the strict limits set for it. Sulla and Caesar stood as examples of the way dictatorship could destroy democracy and lead to unbridled personal rule. Accusations (or denials) of aspirations to dictatorship in this latter sense became a dominant theme in the political conflicts of the French Revolution. Marat was virtually alone in his insistence on the classical Roman model.[6]

A dictatorship and a few heads suitable felled: these, Marat acknowledged, were "maxims very far from our destructive prejudices." There followed a condemnation of the French character as destining the nation to its chains, "delivering it, bound hand and foot, to the power of its agents and servants." Ignorance, vanity, presumption, and blind confidence were among the elements of this Rousseauian indictment. "Without understanding, without customs, without character, we are only a tissue of frivolities, weaknesses, and contradictions. We prostitute sensibility and discount sentiment; we don't know how to love and we are idolators; we want to judge everything and can appreciate nothing; we caress our enemies and neglect our friends; we celebrate the adroit scoundrels who conspire against us and disgust the sages who enlighten us; we adore the hypocrites who work to destroy us and abandon the virtuous men who make themselves anathema to save us."[7]

In the absence of salutary institutions, Marat recalled, a patriotic militia had once seemed to offer a rampart against oppression. But the example of the Paris National Guard now afforded little grounds for hope in this regard. This improvised civic force had soon sloughed off the poor among its volunteers, reinforced its ranks with regular troops, and become a uniformed and organized army of the prosperous in the service of oppression. In the wake of the events of 22 January 1790, General Lafayette, the architect of this militarization, was about to be added to Marat's list of the people's enemies.

"Public censure, a state tribunal, a tribune of the people, and a temporary dictator could alone end our misfortunes, deliver us from the enemies of the fatherland, establish liberty and cement public happiness," Marat reiterated in this pamphlet. Though he was to repeat the prescription endlessly in the months and years to come, his analysis offered little hope of seeing these institutions adopted. "Oh Parisians!" he chided. "You are nothing but children, you close your eyes to the misfortunes that await you, thoughtlessness keeps you feeling secure, vanity consoles you for all your ills. . . . You're happy with your chains, so keep them! The intriguers who deceive you, the scoundrels who despoil you, the criminals who enslave you are the men you deserve. Continue to adore the divine Necker, the heroic Lafayette, the immortal Bailly. Prostrate yourselves before these models of civic behavior, impartiality, and virtue. Run around from café to café, chatter in the newspapers, gather over a jug or around a table, recount your exploits, and bear your chains."[8]

Paris looked lost from this vantage point across the Channel. The return of despotism appeared inevitable. Disenchanted, Marat seemed to be bidding the hapless French a melodramatic farewell. "The People's Friend, saddened at your blindness, your sense of security, your depravity, will thus have seen the dawn of liberty only to deplore its loss. Holding within the depths of his heart his alarm, his regrets, his despair, he will lament your fate for the rest of his life, as a tender father laments the fate of an unnatural child."[9]

Dismal farewells notwithstanding, he was back in the French capital within three months. Little is known about how he had passed his days in London in the meantime. He later proclaimed to the National Assembly that he had participated in meetings of the city's patriotic societies, where he "several times witnessed the favorable dispositions of the English in our regard." It can be assumed that he frequented the cafés and bookstores familiar to him from his earlier life in the city. Perhaps he rejoined fellow Freemasons in the Grand Lodge. It's possible that he met there with the duc d'Orléans, from whom he was widely accused (despite frequent denials) of receiving payment. Only the barest hints about his English acquaintances show up in a personal letter he sent, soon after his return, to Breguet, who was then in London on business. He had enjoyed the company of Breguet's great friend, the celebrated English watchmaker (and great talker) John Arnold, he wrote, together with the latter's son and "charming daughter." He also sent warm greetings to the "amiable sisters" of a Mr. Charlon (perhaps Charlton?), whom Breguet was asked to assure that "I have not forgotten about him, but I am in the greatest difficulties myself and beg him to be patient until the situation becomes clear." Marat apparently had another debt to pay and, as usual, needed money. Among the personal errands he begged Breguet to perform on his behalf was the sale of some "little jewels."[10]

Whatever other distractions he may have found in the English capital, one can be certain that Marat's attention remained directed largely across the Channel. The *Appel à la Nation* was followed by a lengthy *Nouvelle dénonciation de M. Marat, l'Ami du peuple, contre M. Necker* that extended his attacks on the French first minister. Soon thereafter appeared a *Lettre de M. Marat, l'Ami du peuple, contenant quelques réflexions sur l'ordre judiciaire*. Expressing satisfaction at the suppression of the French parlements, "these courts of iniquity, these tribunals of blood where gold gave the right to sit," he took this opportunity to call for a sound criminal code and a true state tribunal ("two powerful ramparts of public liberty") and to warn, even more fundamentally, against ongoing efforts by the National Assembly and its allies in the municipal government to wrest sovereignty from the people, this time by shredding the power of the city districts. He also announced that he had developed a plan for a reformed criminal legislation.[11]

He was referring to a version of the *Plan de législation en matière criminelle* he had written for the Economic Society of Berne a decade earlier. Taking out that piece in London, he must have spent many hours revising and restructuring it. Sections were moved, recombined, retitled; paragraphs were broken up, chapters reorganized, many minor changes made. Most notably, the discussions of the principles of social order, property, and theft were highlighted at the very beginning of the text: Marat's loquacious thief would now speak for the poor before the nation and its legislators. The section classifying crimes and punishments then proceeded by recategorizing actions once erroneously considered crimes against the state: publications attacking governments and public officials, resistance to unjust royal orders, regicide. In a state where sovereign majesty had been transferred to the nation, Marat insisted in this vein, transgressions against the prince were no longer to be considered crimes of lèse-majesté. This reorganization of the text also brought into clearer view the need for laws that would foster a reformation of corrupted manners and morals inherited from the aristocratic society of the Old Regime. Revised and retitled, this *Plan de législation criminelle* was soon ready for publication and presentation to the National Assembly.[12]

THE FRENCH JUNIUS

Back in Paris by mid-May, Marat struggled to resurrect *L'Ami du peuple* and fight off the counterfeit journals that had in his absence usurped his journal's title and competed to fill its space before the public. "The People's Friend, whose ardent zeal for liberty is well known, has returned from London, where he had been forced to seek asylum by his enemies' persecution," he trumpeted in a letter to the National Assembly he had so recently sworn to ignore. "Can the apostle and martyr of liberty find no support within an assembly that has solemnly consecrated its principles and whose every moment must be employed in giving wise laws to a nation that wishes to be free?" He wanted to affirm his patriotism, distance himself from his counterfeiting competitors, and get the Châtelet's longstanding order for his arrest lifted, though he received no help from the Assembly in this latter regard. *L'Ami du peuple* resumed publication illegally, nonetheless, on 18 May 1790. Two weeks later, its author was even starting a second journal "to fight for the homeland with two hands."[13]

Titled *Le Junius français* in tribute to the fearsome Wilkesite virtuoso of English radical journalism, Marat's new sheet may, in part, have been a move in his ongoing battle against the counterfeiters who had put the authenticity of *L'Ami du peuple* into question. While pressing constantly for police action to close these competitors down, he was perhaps readying this second weapon in case the first had suffered irreparable damage. Though he launched *Le Junius français* under cover of anonymity, he claimed it as his own after three issues and insisted repeatedly thereafter upon his personal authorship of both journals.

Clearly, though, this decision to create a second journal was more than a tactic against the counterfeiters. It grew from reflections on political strategy that must have preoccupied him during the months of his London exile. The first number of *Le Junius français* opened with a full-bore indictment of the people of Paris that amplified the charges of popular blindness and superficiality leveled against the French in the *Appeal to the Nation*. The Parisians were again condemned as frivolous, feeble, and pusillanimous. They carried love of novelty to extremes while their passion for serious matters was only fleeting. Lacking knowledge, plans, or principles, they were as skittish about liberty as they were about fashion. They preferred skillful sycophants to severe counselors, misjudged their defenders, and were suckered by their enemies. Constantly following their most immediate impulse, they showed themselves incapable of sustained effort and immune to love of glory. Were they always to be treated as children?

Apparently so, for the French Junius went on to lament the erosion of serious political language he saw threatening the Revolution. "The lessons of wisdom and counsels of prudence no longer work for you," he charged the populace. "Legions of half-starved journalistic hacks have dulled you with their stupidities and atrocities; good arguments wash over you without effect. Already, you only take pleasure in extreme views, destructive notions, crude invectives. Already, the strongest terms appear to have no force for you. Soon you will only open your ears to cries of alarm, murder, treason."

Such a diagnosis required a change in journalistic strategy. "How to fix your attention when you have been agitated so many times over nothing, how to keep you on guard against every blow, how to keep you constantly alert? Only one means remains to me, which is to follow your tastes and vary my tone. Oh Parisians, no matter how bizarre this role appears in the eyes of the sage, your old friend will not disdain taking it, his only care is to save you. To prevent you falling back into the abyss, there are no efforts he will disdain. *Le Junius français* will be your incorruptible defender, your intrepid defender."[14]

The philosopher stooped to conquer in this reversal of the relationship between the journalist and his public. The shift announced by *Le Junius français* found several manifestations. Denunciation was now declared the journal's first selling point: it was "particularly intended to follow the secret maneuvers of the enemies of the revolution, unveil their relations with foreign cabinets, expose traitors' plots against the homeland, shout cries of alarm, and confound their evil plans." The work of the National Assembly would be reported, this new Junius went on to promise, but more briefly so. Accounts of the Assembly's sessions would be slimmer, and followed by "suitable reflections, portraits of the authors of the most important motions, and those of the ministers and most remarkable persons in the history of the revolution." Finally, there would be reports of new events likely to pique public curiosity.

This language differed noticeably from that Marat had used in launching *L'Ami du peuple* in September 1789. He had promised then to scrutinize the deliberations of the National Assembly, combing through each and every article of its legislation to ensure the establishment of a wise government that would bring union, abundance, and peace. For the first months of the journal's existence, it had been dedicated overwhelmingly to reports on the sessions of the National Assembly, often with extended discussion of constitutional options and choices. Only gradually was more space made for the war of denunciations into which Marat was drawn against the municipality, the ministry, and the Châtelet court. A revised prospectus published in late December marked this development by adding that the journal would "monitor the agents of power, probe their intrigues, their wrongdoings, and their assaults, and espouse the defense of the oppressed."[15]

This was the task to which The People's Friend now committed himself on his return to Paris in May 1790. Political engagements had become sharper, in the capital and beyond; ambitions, rivalries, and suspicions were vexing constitutional deliberation and administrative reorganization; revolutionary sentiments were becoming more intense; counterrevolutionary reactions were flaring; the boundaries between the Assembly and the people were exploding. Union, abundance, and peace were fading into more distant horizons. After a few issues, *Le Junius français* dropped its separate section designated "National Assembly." Scanning for enemies, its pages became more kaleidoscopic.

The new journal folded after thirteen issues. Producing two daily publications proved too great a challenge, even for Marat's manic energy. *L'Ami du peuple* was, in any case, making headway in eliminating its counterfeiters. It also began to follow the more varied strategy pioneered in *Le Junius français*. It, too, soon dropped its formal separate section designated for the National Assembly. As the earnest constitutional expositions of its early months eased up, it became more furious, more brutal, more virulent, more hyperventilated in its calls for violence. Its punctuation screamed at the reader. Marat had opted for shock treatment to blast a mindless people back from the edge of the abyss. A marginal note written on a later issue of the journal acknowledged that cultivated readers would reproach him for the crudeness of his denunciations. "Let them open my works on physics and philosophy," he pleaded; "they will see that a noble and elevated style is not foreign to me. But it's for the people, not for savants and sophisticates, that I write. My first goal is to be well understood."[16]

Two years later, he would defend this choice to Robespierre in the only face-to-face conversation he said the two ever held. By Marat's account, the Incorruptible reproached him for undercutting the "prodigious influence of my journal on the revolution by drenching my pen in the blood of the enemies of liberty, by talking about gibbets and daggers, doubtless against my heart, because he liked to tell himself that these were only words in the air, dictated by circumstances." Marat's response was frank.

> Understand, I responded immediately, that my journal's influence over the revolution didn't derive, as you imagine, from those dense analyses in which I methodically laid out the vices of the frightful decrees drawn up by the committees of the Constituent Assembly. It came instead from the hideous scandal the journal spread among the public when I tore away the veil covering the eternal plots against public liberty contrived by the enemies of the homeland conspiring with the monarch, the legislature and the principal holders of authority. It came from the audacity with which I crushed every destructive prejudice, from the outpouring of my soul, the fervor of my heart, my protests against oppression, my impetuous outbursts against the oppressors, my painful tones, my cries of indignation, fury, and despair against the criminals abusing the confidence and power of the people in order to deceive it, despoil it, enchain it, and cast it into the abyss.

These sounds of alarm and fury were no mere words adapted to circumstances, Marat assured Robespierre. They were authentic, personal, and immediate, "the purest expressions agitating my heart."[17]

The thymotic pages of the renewed *L'Ami du peuple* were also significantly more open to correspondence from readers. Letters now tumbled into them from across France, praising the author or excoriating him, feeding him news and illuminating in the process the geography and sociology of perceptions of counterrevolutionary threat. It is unnecessary to ask how many of these letters were fabricated by Marat himself; he later acknowledged that many were. The point is that Marat engaged them in direct replies or trampolined off them in commentary that made his journal more interactive, more dynamic, more personal.[18] By this time, the identification of the author with his sheet was complete. Marat *was* "*L'Ami du peuple*," "The People's Friend." His "I" had become a "We," his "Us" had become "the People"—except when the members of this putative body were being castigated for their superficiality, gullibility, or stupidity. By turns a victim, a prophet, a scold, a clairvoyant, a martyr, Jean-Paul Marat offered himself as at once a fervent patriot and a brutal political realist with an eye for corruption, an ear for conspiracy, a nose for despotism, a thirst for violence. In the omnipresence of its author and the immediacy of his voice, in the intensity of its communicative effect, in the implied intimacy it created between writer and reader, his journal, seen from today's perspective, is most easily imaginable as a kind of hyperactive blog.[19]

But a blog is not necessarily scrupulous with its information. Camille Desmoulins later criticized the use of correspondence in *L'Ami du peuple* on these grounds. Marat's journal was useful, he granted, but it was too often filled with falsehoods, not least "because certain correspondents affected to be passing on to him notes that were grossly untruthful in order to defend truths that he alone was publishing."[20] Marat was quick to rebut the charge. An accusation like this would be a serious matter in a news sheet like Desmoulins's, he argued, but not at all in a political journal like his own. "How do you know that what you take to be fake news isn't a text I needed to ward off some fatal blow and reach my goal?" he countered. "To judge men, you always need positive facts, very clear and very precise; for me, their inaction or their silence on great occasions is often enough. To believe in the existence of a conspiracy, you need judicial proofs; I only need the general direction of affairs, the relationships among enemies of liberty, the comings and goings of certain agents of power."[21] His method, in effect, was often to float rumors and falsehoods to see which ones would stick.

COUNTERREVOLUTION IN VIEW

Much had been happening in France during the months of Marat's absence. Order was everywhere being imposed—and contested. The transformation of provinces into departments had been carried out; municipal government had been standardized and strengthened with emergency police powers across the country. In Paris, where the reorganization of city government had been delayed by administrative complexities, bitter tensions had emerged over reducing the sixty former districts to forty-eight new sections, thus eliminating the noisy electoral assemblies of the districts that had assumed a permanent existence as centers of popular activism. Popular protests had multiplied against these changes, and against the stringent property requirements for active citizenship and eligibility for electoral office the National Assembly was establishing as it drafted the new constitution.

Ideological differences had sharpened, too. Personal rivalries had intensified, warring political clubs had crystallized. As Necker's influence waned, Mirabeau, Lafayette, and (from London) the duc d'Orléans, among others, vied for power in the arena between the court and the National Assembly. The Jacobin Club, earliest and most successful of the new political organizations, was well on its way to building a provincial network of affiliated societies while forming a powerful antechamber for the advanced revolutionary deputies in the National Assembly. The more radical, egalitarian, and populist Cordelier Club had emerged in late April under Danton's leadership. A reactionary monarchist club was taking embryonic form in meetings of deputies at the former monastery of the Capuchins before bursting into political prominence by the end of the year. Fearing extremes, more moderate conservatives were clustering in the Club des Impartiaux while the financial, philosophical, and technocratic elite of the Old Regime sought to direct affairs from the haughty assemblies of the Société de 1789. Only the Cordelier Club would escape Marat's withering attacks.

Across France, too, disorder had been growing. Anger against former seigneurial dues that were still being levied by owners awaiting the passage of legislation providing indemnification was flaring again. Aristocrats were emigrating in greater numbers and gathering around the nation's borders, even before the National Assembly formally abolished nobility in June. Counterrevolutionary insurrections were erupting in major cities. Conflicts between Catholics and Protestants were surfacing, a reminder that monarchical absolutism had found its raison d'être in the suppression of religious wars—and a challenge to revolutionary government to do the same. Calls for a national French church mounted, fissuring the National Assembly and provoking the violent debates that would soon produce the Civil Constitution of the Clergy—the legislation destined, above all others, to drive the country to the extremes of civil war. That crucial decree was passed 12 July 1790.

Most immediately, though, the prospect and potential political implications of external warfare began to impinge upon the consciousness of revolutionary France. Discipline in the army was seen to be eroding in the spring of 1790, just as conflict between Spain and Britain in the Pacific waters of Nootka Sound raised the possibility that the country would be dragged into war by its obligations under the Family Compact sworn between the two branches of the Bourbons. Unwilling to honor a dynastic alliance outmoded in the new era of national sovereignty, the National Assembly found itself nonetheless facing the question of where the power to declare war would now lie. A compromise authorized the king to propose war and the National Assembly to declare it, but did so at the cost of stretching thinner the putative bond between the nation and its monarch. Revolutionary France renounced wars of conquest, though fears of hostile foreign encroachment were soon awakened by threats that Habsburg troops would traverse its borders to suppress a revolution in Belgium. Demands for reform of the regular army followed in response to these threats, as did calls to restructure and unify the National Guard as a fighting force across the country.

On all these issues Marat soon joined battle. It was to avert French military engagement in support of Spain against England, he claimed, that he had rushed back to Paris at news of the Nootka Sound incidents. He had to warn against "a ministerial plot to drag the nation into war in support of Spain as a way of bringing about a counterrevolution." The latter term was a new one in the pages of *L'Ami du peuple*, but the threat it designated was never far from Marat's mind. "What's the Family Pact to us, or the loss of the alliance with Spain," he cried as his journal resumed circulation. "Our great, our only concern is to give ourselves a free and wise constitution, to establish our liberty, and to assure our happiness. . . . The right to make war and peace must belong solely to the nation. It must renounce all wars of aggression." Though it appeared to achieve these goals, the decree on war and peace eventually adopted by the National Assembly filled him with alarm. It placed the "terrible right" to declare war and peace formally in the hands of the nation, he granted, but the legislative details had been crafted by the wily and corrupt Mirabeau to serve the purposes of the ministry. It preserved for the monarch the power to initiate hostilities that, once engaged, would be difficult for the nation to abandon, and it allowed the executive power a responsibility to conduct war that would be easily and inevitably abused.[22]

In Marat's analysis, peoples always have the greatest interest in enjoying the benefits of peace, princes the greatest interest in dragging them into war. Military engagement furnishes "eternal pretexts for demanding subsidies and overburdening subjects with taxes." For this classical republican thinker, Roman history offered the definitive demonstration of the power of war to make citizen soldiers "forget the homeland amidst the tumult and license of the camps, to accustom them to all the crimes, to murder, rape, and pillage, to turn them into hardened villains, to attach them by the hope of booty, by the love of debauch." The effect was "to tear the nation away from the care for public affairs, to occupy it with news, to impoverish it, and oppose to it numerous legions of veterans and followers ready to undertake everything for experienced leaders." In evidence: the legions that followed Caesar to Gaul. "A few years under the command of this ambitious man were enough to stifle in their hearts the cries of duty and nature, enough to make them brave hell and cross the Rubicon."[23]

Marat (declaring himself aligned with "the wise Robespierre") was thus among the first to see war as the great threat to the Revolution. He viewed it as offering an invitation to the executive power to corrupt and destroy liberty and an opportunity for generals to bring their armies back from the front to impose tyranny. On 4 June, *L'Ami du peuple* headlined "the hideous evils" that would result from war against England, "the annihilation of the constitution, the ruin of the state, the loss of liberty, the triumph of the aristocracy, the massacre and the servitude of the people." The journal would point to the danger of this counterrevolutionary scenario frequently in the weeks and months to come.[24]

It would point, also, to the disorders spreading across the country, all of which it saw as produced in one way or another by enemies of the Revolution. In Marat's diagnosis, trouble in the army was being provoked (as, already, in Nancy and elsewhere) by the tyranny of counterrevolutionary officers; unrest in the National Guard stemmed from patriotic resentment against its militarization; conflicts between Catholics and Protestants (as in Nîmes) were fanned by the ploys of reactionary municipal leaders; agitation in Paris was flaring against restrictions to the suffrage and efforts to reorganize municipal government in ways that would suppress popular activism. Taken together, these phenomena could only mean one thing. "The hideous plot to put the realm to fire and sword has erupted at the same time in all the provinces with troubles and seditions," the journal reported on 2 June. "Let's be careful not to fall asleep. Dangers still surround us. The blade still hangs over our heads. They conspire against us more than ever."[25]

Marat saw few institutions upon which patriots could now rely to counter these dangers. "The just fury of the people could contain them," he argued, but even the "salutary remedy" of popular protest had been prohibited by the riot act passed after the October Days. The mistaken decision to save a few heads back then could make it necessary, one day soon, "to make rivers of blood flow." This call for blood was justified in a lengthy note. "Will you accuse me of being cruel, I who can't bear to see an insect suffer? When I think that sparing a few drops of blood risks shedding it in great waves I'm outraged, despite myself, at our false maxims of humanity and our stupid procedures against our cruel enemies. Imbeciles that we are, we're scared to give them a scratch, we're content to disperse them, and we inanely leave them standing against us. Let them be masters for a day and soon we'll see them spreading across the provinces, sword and fire in their hands, felling all those who offer resistance, massacring the friends of the homeland, slaughtering women and children, and reducing our cities to ashes."[26]

L'Ami du peuple offered another omnibus denunciation on 13 June, with lengthy enumeration of the enemies of the homeland to be found anywhere and everywhere. It declared the National Assembly filled with representatives of orders now abolished, with warriors always ready to gather around the throne of tyrants, with scandalous prelates gorged with the goods of the poor, with arbitrary judges, merchants of iniquities, eternal talkers, abettors of chicanery. Every moment of every day, Marat knew, these purported representatives were cursing the Revolution and liberty. To oppose the defenders of the homeland, they had been uniquely occupied with reckless motions and specious, illusory, and dangerous decrees that were sapping the bases of the constitution and subverting the principles upon which the edifice of liberty rested. They'll take over, these enemies, The People's Friend warned, they'll destroy the Revolution, they'll return the people to its chains. This amounted to saying that the National Assembly was moving France back to a ground zero of politics, a state of war from which the nation could be rescued only by the terror of popular insurrection. "In the state of war we now find ourselves, only the people, the little people, the people so despised and so little to be despised, can face down the enemies of the revolution, restrict them to their duty, force them into silence, reduce them to that state of salutary terror so indispensable to consummate the great work of the constitution, wisely organize the state, and impress movement upon the new political machine."[27]

The issue of 24 June, in contrast, brought respite from talk of terror. The journal could now rejoice at the abolition of nobility five days earlier. "Like the magician's wand," it rhapsodized, "the celebrated decree which has restored political equality is going to produce the greatest changes in the realm. Those emblazoned insignia, those enormous coats of arms surmounting haughty porticos, all those monuments of pride and domination are going to disappear, and with them the miserable hovels and untended fields surrounding them. Everywhere, industry and work will open new sources of fertility. The soil will offer no more barren wastes. Carefully cultivated countryside, covered with comfortable and pleasing dwellings, will offer a vision of happiness."

Nor would these be the most striking results. "Justice and liberty triumphant, vices punished, virtues rewarded, the restoration of manners, the regeneration of the species, men feeling the dignity of their existence and consecrating their labor to the good of society, in a word, a people happy in the most beautiful climate of the world and under the empire of the laws: this, this, is the object most worthy to enchant the human heart."[28]

The euphoria of this vision was soon punctured. Its promise could be no more than provisional. To enjoy these precious advantages, Marat insisted, the Revolution had to be completed. "Oh Frenchmen! All the barriers are razed, nothing appears any longer to block your happiness. But all your efforts will have served for nought if you don't return to its banks the unchecked torrent of royal power. Despotism will soon re-emerge above its ruins and, far from being the freest of peoples, you will be forever the most enslaved. The ramparts of servitude have been leveled but I don't yet see the temple of liberty, and your virtue alone can raise it."[29]

Marat's mood darkened that very same day as he wrote an article intended for publication in Camille Desmoulins's journal, *Les Révolutions de France et de Brabant*. It dismissed the National Assembly as a fraud, "this momentary organism [*embryon d'un jour*] that the people hasn't created, this posthumous child of despotism, this shamefully concocted body containing so many enemies of the revolution and so few friends of the homeland, this illegitimate assembly that the nation has tolerated rather than constituted." It declared the deputies' decrees entirely provisional until ratified by the consent of the people, whose sovereignty required its exercise of an absolute veto over legislation. More crucially at this point, it offered the draft of a petition making clear that the popular veto might have to take extra-constitutional form. It amplified the threat of insurrection made imminent by the despair of "the little people," those whom revolutionary legislation was leaving behind.[30]

This new "Petition to the Conscript Fathers, or Very Serious Protests of Those who have Nothing against Those who have Everything" offered a bitter indictment. "Conscript Fathers"—or *pères conscrits*—was a recapitulation of *patres conscripti*, the Latin designation traditionally applied to the Roman Senate, whose members were named by magistrates (the Censors) rather than chosen by the people.[31] The implication of this choice of term in the context of 1790 was clear: it emphasized the illegitimacy of the National Assembly as a putative representative body that had not been elected as such by those it claimed to represent. The antique designation became Marat's favorite expression of derision for the usurpers of popular sovereignty he now saw claiming inviolability for themselves as deputies of the nation.

In this impeachment, the political pretenders had done everything for the rich and nothing for the poor. "What good is political liberty for us, we who have never known it and never will know it?" he expostulated on behalf of the two-thirds of the nation being "humiliated, vexed and oppressed" by the Assembly's decrees. The people that had actively made the Revolution had been reduced to the role of spectators, he protested. Incoherent reforms and repressive legislation had left it a hundred times more vulnerable to oppression than under the yoke of despotism. "We once had five hundred little tyrants; today we have a million oppressors." False maxims of liberty, grand slogans about equality of conditions, had done little for those who labored. "The lot awaiting us is an eternal servitude. Nailed to our work the entire day, whether as laborers or valets, we can only be at the orders of a hard and imperious master. . . . The inestimable liberty you are going to enjoy is not made for us. In this regard we are as much foreigners to the revolution as if we were not members of the state."[32]

Church property, protested The People's Friend, could have been used to create charitable workhouses (along lines he had already proposed in his plans for reform of criminal legislation). Instead, this patrimony of the poor had been diverted to pay off government debt. Paupers remained burdened with taxes, while the rich slathered themselves with gains. The Declaration of the Rights of Man had claimed for all the title to enjoy the benefits of society, participating in its activities with no other distinctions than those of their talents and virtues. But the censitary restrictions now placed on the active exercise of citizenship rendered the poor "incapable of possessing any of the employments to which you called us by virtue of our natural rights." The National Assembly, in effect, had rendered the entire Revolution illusory for the great majority of the nation. "Your famous declaration of rights was thus only a derisory trap to distract the stupid while you dread their wrath, since it comes down in the last analysis to giving the rich all the advantages, all the honors, of the new regime. This glorious revolution will end up serving the lucky ones of the century."[33]

Marat was pushing here toward a rhetoric of social revolution. There's a fascinating coincidence in the fact that he was at this same time defending from prosecution Gracchus Babeuf, the future instigator of the Conspiracy of Equals and avatar of revolutionary socialism for much of the nineteenth century. Their disciples would end up on very different wavelengths.

The rambling "Supplique aux pères conscrits," with its implicit threat of populist insurrection, made for a brew Camille Desmoulins deemed too bitter for his readers. Marat published a more coherent and corrosive version in *L'Ami du peuple* on 30 June 1790. Now addressed disarmingly to the "Fathers of the Homeland," but on behalf of eighteen million unfortunates, it nonetheless reinforced protests against the injustice of the restricted suffrage with more direct threats against the social order. "What! At a time when the homeland most needs forces to repel the numerous enemies hidden within its breast, you work to increase their number by the most hideous injustice! Remember that, in every revolution, he who is not for the homeland is against it. What motive would still attach to the good of the polity men who can no longer participate in it? They must therefore become its enemies."

The menace was clear. "Tremble that in refusing us the right of citizenship on grounds of our poverty we will recover it by relieving you of your excess. . . . Tremble at reducing us to despair and leaving us no alternative but to avenge ourselves against you by giving ourselves over to every kind of excess, or rather by abandoning you to yourselves, because we need only to stand with arms crossed to put you in your place. Thus reduced to serving yourselves with your own hands, and to working your own fields, you will again become our equals. Less numerous than we, will you be sure of collecting the fruit of your work? You can still prevent this revolution to which our despair would inevitably lead. Return to justice and don't punish us any longer with the harm you've done us."[34]

By framing, sharpening, and exploiting social cleavages that would become increasingly fraught, Marat was writing a new social dimension into the revolutionary script.

A VAST PARALYZED MACHINE

By the beginning of July, *L'Ami du peuple* was declaring revolutionary France a "vast paralyzed machine." In another image, it likened the country to a dying man, calm about his condition, congratulating himself on his good health. Marat saw anarchy everywhere, the laws violated by the very agents of authority, tribunals active only against the friends of freedom, a National Assembly declaring its members inviolable the better to destroy liberty. Praising the few patriotic deputies he found in the Assembly—men like Adrien Duport, Antoine Barnave, Robespierre, and the former nobles Armand Aiguillon and the brothers Alexandre and Charles de Lameth—he hurled lengthy and contemptuous accusations against the leaders he portrayed as conspirators betraying the nation. Necker, "the great hoarder," was still the object of his harshest contempt: "Necker, Necker, the infernal Necker, this hypocrite, this double-dealer, this traitor who has made us glimpse liberty the better to make us feel its loss when he takes it away: here, citizens, is the soul of all the conspiracies against the homeland." Behind Necker were Bailly, Lafayette, and Mirabeau, "the principal instruments this satrap is using to subject us again to the yoke of a despot. . . . But let the blade come down an instant on the criminal head of the vizier and all the links in this formidable league will soon be broken."[35]

It was time, again, for Marat to foreground the classical republican scenario from which his political thinking never strayed, the long cruel history of the people's servitude punctuated by outbursts of liberty ever doomed to destruction. "Never does love of liberty reign more powerfully and never is its triumph less assured than among a people that has just broken its chains," he lectured his readers. "It scarcely escapes from servitude before its oppressors, recovering from their shock, look for means to put it back under the yoke. The despot indignantly protests his devotion to his faithful subjects. He invites them to rely on the protection of his paternal love. He speaks to them of his eagerness to address their grievances. He flatters them, deceives them, soothes them, and lulls them to sleep. Cunning scoundrels, fanning the fires of discord, work to divide and corrupt them. Promising reform of abuses, they establish principles whose implications the people cannot perceive and put forward plans whose consequences it cannot foresee. Other scoundrels work to get these plans adopted. And in the new order of things that gradually emerges, the people's hopes evaporate and it finds itself finally returned to the yoke by the very men it has charged to complete the task of breaking its chains."[36]

This was the cycle in which Marat saw the French now trapped. It had been inevitable, he argued, that an unenlightened people, barely liberated, would misplace its trust in casting around for leaders. Misled by a show of revolutionary zeal, it had put Bailly at the head of the municipality of Paris. Now it was witnessing his efforts to hang on to power. With the support of the corrupt National Assembly, the former academician was gerrymandering the city's representation to destroy the districts in which the people had been exercising its sovereign right to assemble at will. He was manipulating plans for forthcoming city elections and suborning future voters with Necker's cash.[37]

Marat's denunciations of Bailly's plots against liberty, his grasping for power and his luxuriating in municipal loot, had been unrelenting for months, and continued to be so. Now, too, The People's Friend turned his censure, full bore, against Lafayette. He had already published a "Denunciation of Lafayette" on 28 June, a personal declaration of war, promising battle to the death. Lafayette, Marat charged, had conspired with the ministry and worked to undermine the people's right to revolution, protect the royal family, and buttress the monarch's power. Above all, he had transformed the volunteer force of the Paris National Guard into a militarized and disciplined instrument of tyranny. In this analysis, Lafayette the consummate courtier had long since displaced Lafayette the putative patriot. "I know the dangers to which I expose myself by standing up against you in this way," Marat assured the general. "Don't hope to reduce me to silence. I vow eternal hate to you for as long as you scheme against liberty. Stoop to the most cowardly vengeance to punish me . . . , come with the henchmen still devoted to you, attack my latest refuge. If I can't escape their fury, I'll face their rage head on. Felled by their blows and bathed in my own blood, my failing voice will not cease to reproach you for your attacks, and my last breath will be to denounce you as one of our most dangerous enemies."[38]

With these words, the fantasy of martyrdom continued to pulse through Marat's rhetoric. But the prophet was not to be silenced. "Yes, rage, indignation, despair suffocate me. But no, they will not stifle my voice. Though a hundred thousand daggers are leveled at my chest, I will call vengeance and death down upon them. Oh citizens, may the holy fury that rips my breast pass into yours, may you soon drag to the altar the guilty victims that justice has branded, may you soon sacrifice them to the safety of the homeland, and to your liberty."[39]

Lafayette was pilloried again, alongside Bailly, on 11 July. In the general's case, Marat sniped, the still gullible people had been seduced by a reputation built on "a few rifle campaigns among insurgents fighting their masters" (so much for the American War of Independence!). "This great-hearted hero, this blazing patriot, this incorruptible defender of liberty," so-called, had remained at heart a courtier. Accepting the honor of serving the homeland, he had plotted with the cabinet to use the nation's own defenders to enchain it.[40]

In a revised account of the early days of the French Revolution Marat now offered, a general insurrection against a common enemy had left the entire people in arms. "That immense crowd of unfortunates the insolent rich call the rabble, that healthiest part of the nation which never gains from changing masters and is always the first to brave the dangers of overthrowing the yoke of tyrants, had shown an incredible ardor to punish traitors to the homeland." But the rich had soon claimed, and curtailed, the Revolution as their own. In panic, these enemies of the public good had purged the poor from the National Guard by requiring volunteers to wear uniforms beyond the means of a majority of citizens. The Guard had been transformed by Lafayette into an army of the opulent, "men least formed for liberty, well-off citizens whose fear of misfortune rendered them enemies of all revolution, merchants and luxury workers attached by love of gold to the fortunes of the grandees, young men made forgetful of their duty by a uniform, henchmen of the old regime who had hidden in their caves during the days of crisis only to emerge to seize command." Units of the regular army had then been appended to this citizen army and the whole had been subjected to military discipline and organization. A civic militia had been transformed into a praetorian guard.

It was essential, Marat concluded, that the National Guard be returned to the spirit of its initial institution, that it be reopened to all honest residents ready to defend the common cause, that it be given the right to choose its own officers. Without these changes, "the Parisian army will soon succeed in losing the liberty that the National Assembly silently undermines, that the ministers audaciously attack, that the general has so many times imperiled, and whose mortal enemies are the creatures of the court and the lackeys of the old regime."[41]

The People's Friend was to continue a running battle against Lafayette and his agents for many months. For the moment, though, he was spitting into the wind. He was about to witness the general's greatest moment of triumph.

14 JULY 1790: FEDERATION AS FARCE

First-time observers of the Bastille Day festivities in Paris frequently express surprise that the celebrations in the streets are preceded by a military parade that seems endless. The tradition harks back to the Festival of Federation, the very first 14 July celebration in 1790. Under torrential skies that day—the weather was dubbed "aristocratic"—some 50,000 men in arms marched from the demolition site of the Bastille across the Seine into the Champ de Mars (now the home of the Eiffel Tower) to be received by a crowd of more than 300,000 of their fellow citizens. Thousands of these marchers, so-called *fédérés*, had been summoned to Paris as representatives of local National Guard and regular army units throughout France, a majority of them traversing the country for the first time to receive the fraternal embrace of the members of the National Guard of the capital. Preceded by a large delegation of Parisian and provincial clergy, the guardsmen were followed into the arena by members of the National Assembly—led by Lafayette on a white charger. Once all the marchers had taken their place, and after rowdy acclamations of fraternity, an artillery salute announced the arrival of the king.

The open ground of the Champ de Mars, at that time well outside the city of Paris, had been readied for this great national festival by the enthusiastic work of thousands of citizens, rich and poor, notable and obscure, all working to the strains of the new revolutionary song "Ça ira!" An altar had been set up at the center of the space, a ceremonial throne raised for the monarch at one end, a triumphal arch at the other, and places designated for members of the clergy from Paris and the provinces and for the deputies of the National Assembly. Oaths had been rehearsed, but before their swearing came the celebration of a mass by some three hundred priests directed by the former comte Charles de Talleyrand, bishop of Autun, a man destined for a long and sinuous political career. Then Lafayette, having laid his sword upon the patriotic altar, intoned the oath prescribed for the National Guard. "We swear to be faithful to the Nation, the Law and to the King; to maintain with all our power the Constitution decreed by the National Assembly and accepted by the King; to protect, in keeping with the Laws, the safety of persons and property, the circulation of grain and of other supplies within the realm, and the collection of public taxes in whatever form they may take; and to remain united with all Frenchmen by the indissoluble bonds of brotherhood." As the guardsmen in their thousands cried "I swear!" cannon sounded in celebration, the crowd exalted, and communities assembled throughout France took oaths of their own in a gesture of simultaneity, solidarity, and fraternity.

The cheers finally dying down, members of the National Assembly duly took their own oath "to be faithful to the Nation, the Law, and the King, and to maintain with all my might the Constitution decreed by the National Assembly and the King." Then, after transports of patriotic joy had again subsided, it was time for Louis XVI to play his part. Some said the rain stopped and the sun came out as the monarch, accepting rather awkwardly his new designation as "King of the French," swore "to employ all the power delegated to me by the constitutional law of the state, to maintain the constitution decreed by the National Assembly and accepted by me, and to attend to the execution of the laws." The crowd erupted in renewed cheers and tears of joy before the celebration could be concluded with the singing of a *Te Deum*. Thereafter, feasts and festivities continued in Paris for several days before the *fédérés* left the capital to tell all to their fellow citizens in distant provinces.

To many contemporaries, as well as subsequent historians, this event symbolized, and indeed effected, the transformation of the French into a nation bonded in a spirit of fraternity and ready to exercise its common sovereignty through representative institutions under the protection of a patriotic, constitutional monarch. The constitution had yet to be completed in its entirety, they thought, but its principal branches had taken form and its roots had now been firmly implanted. Louis-Sébastien Mercier, portraitist of Paris under the Old Regime, later wanted to recall for posterity this remarkable emotional generation of the new order. He likened it to one of the great electrical demonstrations popularized with the advent of the Leyden jar. "On this solemn day," he wrote, "there was something like an electrical experiment. Everyone who touched the chain had to feel the charge: it was great, it was universal, making its memory fit to rally all the French if outside enemies, jealous of our liberty, come to attack us."[42]

Rhapsodic though it may have proven, this first comprehensively planned national festival of the French Revolution had been shaped to serve immediate political purposes. Celebrating unity, it also summoned France to order. The National Assembly had grown uneasy at the confusion spreading across the country, as well as the potential for disunity inherent in the spontaneous regional alliances and local "federations" that had been reshaping the particularistic political culture of the provinces over the preceding months. It needed to assert central authority and control. Bailly and his city government had been concerned, in promoting the idea of a great national festival in the capital, to secure and glorify the position of Paris—and their own—as the very heart of the Revolution. Lafayette, ready to celebrate the fashioning of the National Guard as a force in which regular troops and volunteer militia units could share a common ethos and discipline, was no less eager to foster the appeal of a constitutional monarchy at its head. He also welcomed the opportunities the festival provided him for influence with the court and political advantage over his rivals, notably Mirabeau and the returning duc d'Orléans, soon self-proclaimed Philippe Egalité.

All these strategic considerations were eclipsed, however, by the enthusiasm generated by the event itself. The day of 14 July 1790 turned into the great shining moment of the French Revolution, an exhilarating affirmation of fraternity in a nation now truly one and indivisible in spirit as well as in law, a spontaneous communion of sentiment, a celebratory performance of a Revolution cleansed of bloodshed. Erupting into enthusiasm for a transformative ideal of fraternity, the Festival of Federation was thus also a triumph for law and order, for a project of pacification, for a king hesitatingly posing as a constitutional monarch, for the National Assembly, the municipality of Paris, and the National Guard—and for Marat's principal enemies in the capital, Bailly and Lafayette. The event left him ballistic.

L'Ami du peuple had welcomed the celebration of a great patriotic confederation when it was initially broached by the Paris districts and endorsed by the municipal assembly toward the end of May. Indeed, Marat had imagined nothing better to consolidate the Revolution than to have articles of the constitution ratified by deputies sent from all the departments at a ceremony on the Champ de Mars marking the anniversary of the storming of the Bastille. "This pact of union, which will soon make all good Frenchmen children of the same family by joining their hearts and merging their dearest interests, will form a new spectacle, hitherto unknown, and the most beautiful upon which the sun has shined," he exalted on 23 May. "May it soon be presented to our eyes! Only then will the nation sense all its strength, all its resources. What energy these bonds of fraternity will give to the state! What an inexhaustible source of repose, peace, and happiness."[43]

This vision of the enactment of a new social contract soon faded, however, as the project for the ceremony of federation was appropriated for their own purposes by the mayor, the general, and the National Assembly. An address proposed for the occasion at a gathering of the sections filled Marat with scorn at its unctuous references to "the sage who governs us" (Bailly) and "the hero who commands us" (Lafayette). He was spurred to express more serious reservations by the plans presented to the National Assembly on 8 June in a report by Talleyrand on behalf of the committee on the constitution. The original idea had been to bring to Paris representatives from the National Guard, the regular army, and the newly reorganized municipalities throughout the realm. But Talleyrand's report, quickly accepted, was emphatic in proposing an exclusively military gathering without the political representation of the municipalities. "It is France armed that is going to gather together," the bishop insisted, "not France deliberating."[44]

Marat was convinced that the decision to exclude representatives of the municipalities was a maneuver to preempt any possibility that they might use the opportunity of their presence in Paris to push to reopen debate over the National Assembly's ill-considered constitutional decisions. His anger increased as the National Assembly voted to expand military representation in the festival to include ever more units and grades of the army, even those among the foreign regiments and household troops serving the royal family. This expansive militarization, he protested, would nullify the whole idea of a civic festival. "What's a federation if it's not restricted to men brought together by their common interests, as if everyone is allowed in? If it doesn't change relations, interests, principles, or hearts, it leaves men as it finds them; it's reduced to nothing, or it becomes an empty ceremony made to impress simpletons."[45]

In this analysis, no festival could cover up the deep enmities threatening the nation. There could be a federation in defense of the homeland only among friends of the homeland, a federation in defense of liberty only among friends of liberty, a federation in support of the constitution only among friends of the constitution. "What can one make of a patriotic federation that extends to citizens indifferent to the homeland, cowards who have abandoned it, traitors that never stop conspiring against it, atrocious men who work ceaselessly to ruin it?" How could this gathering credibly include an officer corps riddled with placemen and pensioners of various stripes, regular troops and mercenary units comprising men only recently ready to cut patriotic throats, and a general staff full of the Revolution's most implacable enemies? "What! These are the men who are going to swear to fight only under the banners of liberty, to shed their blood to the last drop for the constitution, to live or die for the defense of the homeland?" *L'Ami du peuple* expostulated. "Idiots! Are you hoping that the civic oath will silence their passions, extinguish their rage, shackle their arms, transform them into new men? What can an oath do to men steeped in filth? Fear will place it on their lips but their heart will immediately deny it. Vowing to defend you, they will swear to your destruction and make every effort to accomplish it."

Torrents of rage swept through subsequent issues of *L'Ami du peuple* as Marat continued to rail against the "ridiculous farce" of this "military confederation" and the blindness of the people in accepting the plans for it. Pretty soon he was renewing his call to "the little people" to rise up in insurrection.[46]

The National Assembly's adoption of the official wording of the federative oath on 7 July unleashed yet another outburst from *L'Ami du peuple* against the unfaithful deputies, their vicious constitutional decisions, their dangerous claims to inviolability. It was essential, the journal now maintained, that the *fédérés* refuse to take "this criminal oath" to uphold the vicious decisions of a tainted legislature. In promising fidelity to the nation, they had to swear that they would defend to their last breath the sacred rights of the citizen and punish the villains who attacked them. "Far from you this false respect for the decrees destructive of your rights and your liberty," Marat declaimed. "Far from you that stupid veneration for faithless mandataries, for this phantasm of a legislature almost entirely composed of your cruelest enemies. Far from you the fatal inviolability that has emboldened perfidious legislators to plot in silence against the nation and forge new chains for it in security."[47]

To that nation, The People's Friend now offered warnings of terrible disasters about to befall it as the ministers prepared for war. "We're done for," he predicted, castigating a dormant people for its failure to recognize a harsh truth. "Blind citizens, continue to sleep at the edge of the abyss. Empty spectacles console you for everything. Intoxicate yourselves with the window dressing of this ridiculous festival in which your implacable enemies will swear fraternal friendship to you, turn your eyes from the traps they are laying for you, rest confidently on their breast, and wait stupidly for the death they are preparing for you." Could his words not wake his compatriots from their lethargy and make them see the dangers threatening them? Marat demanded. Could he not convince them that they had been reduced to a state of war in which cowardly enemies constantly conspired against them? "Learn that resistance to oppression is a sacred duty, that the people threatened with slavery has the right to take up arms. Don't let unworthy representatives strip you of your rights to hand them over to a despot." Should war break out, he urged, let the blade of justice immolate on the altar of liberty the atrocious ministers who had contrived it. "Wash in their blood the traces of their black crimes."[48]

Would this "pompous spectacle" of the federation restore France to abundance? *L'Ami du peuple* clamored a few days later. Would its "empty vows of fraternity" assure peace? Would a pact of federation bring liberty? "Why rush from the far reaches of the realm to swear, on an altar decked out at such expense, to live and die for the homeland? This vow dwells in the heart or it is nowhere. It must be always there, or never. But what do I say, live or die for the homeland? Credulous people, it's not with your rights that your deputies concern themselves, it's with their interests, their preeminence, the means of assuring their rule." The *fédérés*, Marat warned, would march to Paris "under banners more royalist than national."[49]

Finally, on 13 July, the very eve of the great event, after a full day of ceremonial embraces with which the marchers had been welcomed to Paris by the king and the political establishment of the capital, Marat had another pamphlet ready for them. This *Infernal projet des ennemis de la Révolution* warned of a plot to dismiss Necker and replace him with someone worse. There would be a ministry of reaction, it predicted, a ministry headed by Lafayette, "this traitor to the homeland who wanted to make the monarch an absolute dictator and works ceaselessly to bring back despotism," and Mirabeau, "this villain covered with crimes and opprobrium, for whom nothing is sacred . . . , this cowardly voluptuary who would exhaust the treasure of France in its entirety, reduce the nation to mendacity, and finish by putting the realm up for auction to satisfy his filthy appetites."

Was it for this, Marat demanded, that the marchers had left their homes and abandoned their own affairs? Had the soldiers of the National Guard taken up arms to become the nation's cruel oppressors, arbiters of the state instituting a cruel tyranny? "No! No! Whatever the depravity of the century, we have not yet reached that degree of mindlessness, stupidity, and degradation. Our brothers in arms have not rushed from all corners of the realm to bring us chains; they know the reputations of the base men it is proposed to call to the helm of affairs . . . , they know how desperate public safety would become in these men's hands." A threat like this made insurrection more imperative than celebration, preached The People's Friend. The patriots in the National Guard had to seize control of its officers. The people had to awaken from its lethargy, eviscerate its despoilers, relieve dangerous men from their posts, and proscribe forever the corrupt men being proposed for the new government. It had to do it now.[50]

This call for insurrection was circulated among the tents of the *fédérés* camping on the Champ de Mars as they kept watch during the night of 13 July. A letter to *L'Ami du peuple*, purportedly from a guardsman there at the time, subsequently described the pamphlet's warm reception by his comrades, quickly followed by the fracas that erupted a few hours later as Lafayette's agents spread through the camp to neutralize its impact by denouncing the denouncer. These agents must have worked effectively. The "hero of two worlds" found all was well in the morning.

Not so Marat. "Why this unfettered joy?" he howled. "Why this mad applause? Why these stupid declarations of joy? The revolution is still only a sad dream for the people." The Festival of Federation had been initiated to unite all the friends of liberty against its enemies, he protested. Instead, the ministerial party had turned it into a military demonstration of support for the government. One more instrument of oppression, its fateful results would soon become evident. "I was the first and am still the only one who has seen it from this perspective. My fears will be only too soon justified in the event, but until that moment I'll share Cassandra's fate, as I have so many times since the revolution began."[51]

SIXTEEN

HOW MANY HEADS?

An Infernal Project was only the first of a series of incendiary pamphlets Marat circulated in the heat of summer 1790. It was followed on 26 July by the notorious *C'en est fait de nous* (*We're Done For*). Writing in hiding, he embraced the increasingly familiar theme of martyrdom. "I know, there's a price set on my head by the scoundrels at the helm of state," he began. "Five hundred spies are searching for me day and night. So what! If they catch me and hold me, they'll slit my throat and I'll die a martyr of liberty. It won't be said that The People's Friend kept a cowardly silence as the homeland perished."[1]

This time, The People's Friend revealed details of a new "counterrevolutionary project" aiming to spirit the king and the royal family to Metz, bring Austrian and other foreign armies down upon Paris, and force the nation to return to its so-called senses. A version of this script would haunt the Revolution in the following years. "Citizens," the pamphlet warned, "the enemies are at your gates. . . . We're forever done for if you don't rush to arms and rediscover the heroic valor that, on 14 July and 5 October, twice saved France." There followed a script for a preemptive popular uprising. Fly to the royal palace of Saint-Cloud, the people was urged; bring back the king and the dauphin; lock up the Austrian woman, Queen Marie Antoinette. Seize all the ministers and their agents, and put them in chains (a revised version would have said "lop off their heads!"). Assure yourselves of the mayor and his lieutenants; keep an eye on the general; arrest the general staff; occupy all the arsenals and gunpowder factories, distribute cannon across the city; reestablish the districts and make them permanent; have them revoke disastrous decrees. "Rush, rush, if there is still time, or numerous legions will soon descend upon you. Soon you will see the privileged orders arise again and despotism, hideous despotism, reappear more formidable than ever." Yet again, there was not a moment to lose.

In the meantime, on 25 July, Marat had offered the people of Paris a passionate denunciation, in advance of municipal elections, of the fiscal requirements the National Assembly had instituted for the exercise of active citizenship. The Assembly's mission as a representative body, he argued, was to consecrate the rights of the people, secure it abundance and peace, and work to establish its liberty, repose, and happiness. "How then would it be authorized to violate the rights of citizens, attack them, destroy them . . . ? The people being the true sovereign of the state, the sole source from which all powers emanate, certainly has the power to annul decrees that harm its rights and those of its members."

A call for poorer citizens of the capital to exercise their right of resistance by assembling, marching to their district administrations, and compelling their own enrollment as electors, went nowhere. But Marat renewed his attack on the restrictions on active citizenship a few days later, insisting in any case that the imprescriptible rights of the people required that the constitution be ratified by the people before its adoption. Savaging the deputies and ministers on 30 July, he was ready to declare respect for the law a "prejudice destructive of nascent liberty in every state emerging from slavery." "Let's recognize that we are in a state of war," he exhorted, "that the safety of the people is the supreme law and that every means is licit when it works to get rid of perfidious enemies who have put themselves above the laws and never cease conspiring against the public happiness."[2]

The constitution would be abortive, Marat reiterated, as long as former beneficiaries of the Old Regime were allowed to plot against liberty. Patriots had been mistaken in 1789 in not erecting a state tribunal to judge conspirators. They should also have instituted the office of "a dictator to be elected by the people in moments of crisis, given authority that would only need to last three days, to fulfill the charge to punish under military justice the bad citizens threatening public safety." It was the height of folly, he insisted, "to think that men empowered for ten centuries to devour, pillage, and oppress us with impunity would resolve in good grace to become our equals. They'll scheme against us eternally until they're exterminated."[3]

All this was striking enough, but in concluding *We're Done For*, The People's Friend broke new political ground in his call for bloodshed. "Felling five or six hundred heads would have assured your repose, liberty and happiness," he insisted; "a false sense of humanity has restrained your arms and held back your blows. Let your enemies triumph for a moment and blood will flow in torrents. They'll slaughter you without pity and rip open your women. To extinguish forever the love of liberty among you, their bloody hands will rummage for your children's hearts amid their entrails."[4]

The reaction was immediate. These words made Marat notorious; his endless future variations upon them marked him forever as a bloodthirsty monster. There was quibbling in the press over the fact of his authorship of them, but little real doubt. The Paris police descended in force on the residence of one Mme Meunier, distributor of his publications, scouring her premises for evidence of her involvement in the pamphlet's circulation (which proved to be ample), interrogating her about her operatives, and hauling her before Mayor Bailly for questioning. Scandalized reports of the pamphlet, avidly reprinting the infamous passage nonetheless, soon began to ripple through the Parisian and provincial press. Camille Desmoulins himself took his distance. "You're the dramatist among journalists," he rebuked Marat, comparing *L'Ami du peuple* to the most bloodthirsty of ancient tragedies. "You kill off everybody in the play, even down to the prompter. You don't know that tragedy when exaggerated goes cold." Dubbed "attorney of the lynching post" since the time he had famously called for heads at the Palais Royal in July 1789, Desmoulins declared that he had long renounced this sobriquet. Now he called for moderation. Fearing that Marat was compromising all patriotic journalists, he pointed to the threat that they would turn against him.[5]

LIBERTY OR LICENSE?

Amid this brouhaha, Pierre Victor Malouet, plantation owner, former royal intendant, and fervent defender of monarchical authority as the foundation of public order, rose in the National Assembly to interrupt the day's business for an emergency decree. "There's no agenda more pressing than to reveal atrocious plots and ensure their authors' punishment," he lectured the deputies on 31 July. "You would shudder to be told that there is a plot to arrest the king, imprison the queen, the royal family, and the principal magistrates, and cut the throats of five or six hundred persons. Well, here before your eyes, at your door, villains are plotting and publishing all these atrocities, arousing the people to fury and the spilling of blood, debasing morals, and attacking the Constitution and liberty at their very foundation." Whom did Malouet denounce for treasonous writings provoking the people to bloodshed and revolt? Marat, of course. But also Desmoulins, an old personal enemy whom Malouet now castigated for an article in *Les Révolutions de France et de Brabant* that had been critical of Louis XVI's conduct at the Festival of Federation.[6]

The Assembly erupted as the apoplectic monarchist read out the inflammatory passages of *We're Done For.* Some deputies called for an expansion of the list of publications to be condemned, others tried to limit the damage that would be done to that "palladium of liberty, liberty of the press." Eventually adopting Malouet's draft decree, the Assembly ordered the criminal prosecution of Marat and Desmoulins, as well as that of "all authors, printers, and hawkers of writings that incite the people to insurrection, bloodshed, and the destruction of the constitution."[7]

Second thoughts in defense of press freedom soon followed. Jean-Paul Rabaut, the voice of beleaguered French Protestantism under the Old Regime and a fervent defender of individual rights since, sprang to the tribune the following day to demand that the list of works to be prosecuted include "all writings that would invite foreign princes to invade the realm." His amendment, a stick in the eye of the monarchists, was immediately accepted. That accomplished, Rabaut pointed adroitly to the danger that expanding the decree would give the courts inquisitorial power, particularly when the Assembly had yet to organize a reformed and uniform system of criminal procedure. His call for the interim appointment of a special jury to lay down criteria for the judgment of incendiary works found some support but went nowhere.[8]

Was it as a barb rather than in putative homage to the deputies that Marat solemnly presented to the National Assembly, on 2 August, a copy of his newly published *Plan de législation criminelle?* What chutzpah for a man in hiding! The work came embellished with a finely engraved likeness of "Jean Paul Marat, The People's Friend" that was much commented upon. The portrait also bore a proclamation. "People! See your friend who, for the sake of your liberty, tells you the truth at risk of his life." This defiant gesture of presentation was followed by the Assembly president's reading of a letter from Desmoulins. Protesting that the Assembly had condemned his publication without any direct evidence from the text, Desmoulins "respectfully requested" that a committee be charged to read and report on the relevant issue. The reading of this letter was interrupted by competing shouts of approbation and protest, before the deputies were called to order and the crowd in the galleries urged to silence. Malouet was quick now to defend his decree of 31 July. "Is Camille Desmoulins innocent?" he demanded. "Let him justify himself if he dare." The challenge was abruptly answered as a voice from the hall shouted, "Yes, I dare!" The riposte incited the deputies to further tumult. Desmoulins was not a member of the Assembly, hence not authorized to speak. Deeming his response an indecent outburst within the sanctuary of the laws, the president ordered his arrest. While this decision was being challenged, Desmoulins vanished from the chamber.[9]

In the lengthy debate that followed, Malouet's decree was attacked from the left as at once vague in its language and arbitrary in its retroactive character. Did this measure apply to everything published since the beginning of the Revolution? Pétion demanded. Did it apply to the call to arms on 14 July 1789? In the absence of a law defining treason against the nation, did it not invite arbitrary application by the courts? Alexandre de Lameth joined the fray to insist that the decree's very vagueness revealed its hidden purpose: to silence all patriotic writers. Marat's pamphlet was "criminal . . . extremely criminal," Lameth allowed. "If there were prior laws regarding this matter, I would be the first to call upon you loudly for the most severe prosecution of this work." The point was that there were no such prior laws, but Lameth's acknowledgment of Marat's putative criminality was telling. The deputies went on to suspend application of the punitive decree to any writings so far published—with the single exception of *We're Done For*![10]

Malouet was disgusted. In a white-hot pamphlet, he immediately cast this whole debate over the press as a decisive moment in the history of the Revolution. Either the Revolution was accomplished, he contended, or it was not. In the first case, its achievements had to be consolidated by peace, moderation, and security for the citizenry; in the second, there would be utter folly in resorting to calumny, insurrection, and violence to advance its progress. Embracing these latter means would turn the Revolution over to the mob. "What! It's enough to call oneself a patriotic writer, a patriotic citizen, to get applause or at least defenders for the most disgusting cynicism, the most foul-mouthed ferocity! Pathetic declamations regarding liberty and despotism never cease to have the same empire over the misguided multitude, the feeble men who accept the yoke of tyranny as long as their subjection is decked out with the symbols and language of liberty."[11]

Malouet knew his history, both ancient and modern. Among men destined to change the face of empires, he observed, some had chosen the methods of Solon, others those of Cromwell. Whether these men were known for their great virtues or their beneficent crimes, they had directed all their energies toward the imposition of their new regime. Why then, in Paris, were there legislators now more eager to undermine the laws founding a new order than to strengthen them? It was shocking to Malouet that Desmoulins's "Yes, I dare!" had been applauded by some members of the Assembly. Posterity, he predicted, would seize on these words as epitomizing the moment at which the Revolution was collapsing. "We hear constantly about counterrevolutions!" he reminded his fellow deputies. Agitators were multiplying and sharpening resentments, while millions of anxious citizens were begging only for peace and security in their homes, their commerce, their social relations. Yet the deputies were abandoning these defenseless citizens to all the disorders of anarchy. "We're abandoning the peace of France to the most seditious writers," he declaimed. "We're concealing to ourselves that these men are aiming to carry out a counterrevolution. It's obvious that they want no other laws or authority than that of the lowest class of the people they keep riled up; that they mean to direct this force at will against the laws, the magistrates, the monarch and the legislative body; and that, to push the people into this stance, they perpetually denounce to it, as its enemies, as men sold out to despotism, those who want a king and a monarchical government."[12]

Malouet's purpose was to turn Marat's charge of "counterrevolution" against him. The term had begun to seep into National Assembly discussion during the spring of 1790; it took on a sharper edge in the debates provoked by *We're Done For.* "What's a counterrevolution if not the dissolution of all the constituted powers?" Malouet declared. "I ask, then, whether in all the writings one dares to defend as favorable to liberty there is a single authority that is respected, that one does not want to destabilize?" What stability could there be, he demanded, in a government where "friends of the people" could write with impunity to incite violence against men unwilling to follow popular passions, where they could call at any time for five or six hundred heads? Political actors in a free society could expect personal denunciation from an open press, Malouet acknowledged, though they needed legally guaranteed means to defend their honor against calumny. But calls to murder and insurrection were a different matter. "It's not the same with these bloody-minded proclamations that incite the people to murder, that invest it with the effective exercise of absolute power . . . such offenses have nothing in common with liberty of the press, they're its violation, for there's no kind of legitimate liberty that can ally itself with an act of tyranny."[13]

Marat, in turn, exploded with rage. "What!" he protested. "What! It's Malouet, the reactionary Malouet, mortal enemy of the revolution, vile slave of the court, fanatical persecutor of the friends of liberty, who has the effrontery to play the patriot and invoke the laws preventing the overthrow of the constitution. This is really something new . . . he uses the safety of the homeland and the cause of liberty as pretexts to eviscerate the defenders of the people. This is the devil turning himself into a hermit to devour the shepherds."[14] Marat could scarcely leave Malouet's attack on "exterminatory patriotism" unchallenged. "Liberty is done for if fear succeeds in closing every mouth," he had written in the *Plan de législation criminelle* he had just presented to the Assembly. But this work already seemed a relic of the Old Regime; it offered no sustained defense of press freedom of the kind necessary in the political situation of 1790. Marat responded to the decree against him with a brief but passionate pamphlet, *Denunciation of the Nation Against Malouet*, that presented a fervent defense of press freedom as essential to the preservation of liberty.

Was it not the height of stupidity, this pamphlet declaimed, to declare it treasonous to counsel the people to look to its own safety, punish unfaithful public servants, and exterminate its enemies? Was it not the height of tyranny to criminalize mere opinions? Error reigns only because truth is prevented from confronting it, Marat insisted. Prevent the free circulation of ideas, and the field of politics will soon be overgrown with the poisonous weeds the tyrants are pleased to let grow there. Give all opinions an open field, however, and truth will gradually take root amid these weeds, springing forth as a "majestic queen" reigning with the irresistible power of reason. Marat found treason in acts, not in words. In his view, the most indecent speech and writings, the most unrestrained, the most violent, the most atrocious, the most scandalous, could never rise to the level of the new crime of lèse-nation. Treason consisted in acting against the nation, working to strip it of its sovereignty, ruin its interests, attack its liberty, or imperil its safety. It was to be found not in the works of patriotic writers but at the court, in the ministries, in the National Assembly, in the places where the criminals showed themselves with insolence and impunity. The true criminals, he charged, were those who wanted to criminalize free speech. In opposing the right to say anything, they were grasping for the power to do everything.[15]

In the weeks that followed, arguments over the scandalous language of *We're Done For*, the identity of its clandestine author, and the grounds for its suppression continued to roil the press.[16] Thousands of copies of the pamphlet were confiscated from distributors and hawkers. Agents of justice and surveillance competed to police the press in the absence of any coherent legislation governing its activities. Malouet, for his part, continued to push for a general press law—to no avail. Adding fuel to the fire, Marat answered with a series of pamphlets that denounced faithless deputies and warned the sovereign people repeatedly that it was sleeping on the edge of a political abyss. *They're Lulling Us to Sleep, Let's Watch Out*, was followed by *It's a Fine Dream, Beware of the Awakening*. Soon *The Hideous Awakening* arrived to spread news of a mutiny of army units in the Nancy garrison.

It was succeeded in turn by a story of a crucial act of repression, *A Faithful Account of the Unfortunate Events in Nancy.*

CARNAGE IN NANCY

Scattered mutinies had occurred across France throughout the summer of 1790 as revolutionary enthusiasm spread among the troops and resentment against reactionary officers was sharpened by lengthy delays in pay. Everywhere these acts of insubordination were suppressed, but nowhere more ruthlessly than in the eastern city of Nancy. In early August, mutinous sentiments had sparked defiance among the three regiments stationed there, gathering support among members of the local National Guard and the civic population. On 16 August, the National Assembly decided that it was time for exemplary repression, brutal responsibility for which was entrusted by the king to General François-Claude-Amour de Bouillé, commander of the eastern armies (and also Lafayette's cousin). By the time the general reached Nancy with some four thousand troops on 30 August, the situation had deteriorated badly. His assault on the city left hundreds of casualties on the streets. Victorious, Bouillé imposed extreme punishments, especially on the leaders of the resistance among the Swiss mercenaries of the Châteauvieux regiment. One of them was broken on the wheel, a score were hanged, some forty sentenced to thirty years in the galleys, and more than seventy subjected to punishment at the regimental level. The two French regiments involved were disbanded, along with the city's National Guard.[17]

For Marat, this was a defining moment. He reported for weeks on the Nancy affair. "Remember Nancy" became his mantra. The "hideous carnage" Bouillé had inflicted on soldiers and citizens alike left him in little doubt that the counterrevolution had begun and civil war would follow. "Counterrevolution started by the government," shouted the hawkers of *L'Ami du peuple* on 4 September 1791.[18]

To save France and the Revolution, Marat proclaimed, more heads had to fall. "Without the severed heads of Launay and Flesselles, of Berthier and Foulon, would we today have a Declaration of the Rights of Man?" he had demanded on 26 July, reminding his readers of dramatic events a year earlier. These savage acts had advanced the Revolution, Marat was convinced, but they had not been sufficient to secure it indefinitely.

We're Done For had claimed, notoriously, that five or six hundred heads would once have been enough. This, in effect, became Marat's benchmark figure, the number of heads he thought should have fallen with the Bastille in the first place. "Sacrificing 600 heads to save 3,300,000 is a very simple calculation dictated by wisdom and philosophy," he explained on 3 August 1790. "This is what all sensible citizens think and all courageous citizens avow." A few days later, the ratio of criminal heads to be felled to patriotic heads that would be saved had been revised. "It would be better to lop off 600 heads than to see 5 or 6 million citizens slaughtered," he reasoned on 13 August. On 16 August, his estimation was that the severing of five or six hundred heads could still ensure the people's peace, liberty, and happiness, while sparing that number out of a false sentiment of humanity would expose "several million innocents" to the risk of massacre.[19]

The Nancy events changed this calculation. To Marat they revealed a nation about to be torn apart by legions of conspirators and devoured by the fires of a civil war ignited by enemies of the Revolution led by the ministers. "Five or six hundred heads leveled the day the Bastille was taken would have given us peace, liberty, and happiness forever," he asserted on 17 September. But the enemies of the Revolution had been given time to join forces across the realm, to form powerful factions at home and abroad, and to seize control of the National Guard and the army. "Today ten thousand heads lopped off would scarcely be sufficient to save the homeland. Remember my prediction: the nation is ready to be reduced to servitude or torrents of blood will flow to ensure its liberty."[20]

By the end of 1790, however, Marat saw counterrevolution advancing too fast for the sacrifice of another ten thousand heads to remain adequate. "Citizens!" *L'Ami du peuple* admonished on 17 December, "if you let the winter pass without having dealt with the counterrevolutionary, Mottié [Lafayette], the general staff, the reactionaries and the ministerial faction in the assembly; if you don't force the repeal of shameful decrees; if you don't get yourselves back to 14 July 1789, you're forever done for." Notwithstanding that "the paid scribblers scream bloody murder when I tell you to forestall the monsters that want to slaughter you," Marat again ran the numbers. Five or six hundred heads would have sufficed a year ago; ten thousand heads would be enough at this moment; but ten times that many would be required unless immediate action were taken in the Revolution's defense. "There will be no peace for you until you have exterminated, down to the very last remnants, the implacable enemies of the homeland."[21]

The following day offered an even more dramatic accounting. The People's Friend reduced the target number of heads but accelerated the time frame and intensified the summons to action. Now there could be nothing less than *a general insurrection and popular executions.* "Begin by laying hold of the king, the dauphin and the royal family," he urged the people. "Lock them up and let their heads stand as surety. . . . Then, without hesitation, lop off the heads of the general [Lafayette] and the counter-revolutionary ministers and ex-ministers, and those of the mayor and the anti-revolutionary municipal government. Put to the sword the entire Parisian general staff, all the reactionaries and the ministerial faction in the national assembly, and all the known henchmen of despotism." The reasoning was made clear:

> Six months ago, five or six hundred heads would have been enough to draw you back from the abyss. Today, now that you have stupidly let your implacable enemies conspire and gain strength, perhaps it will be necessary to lop off five thousand. But if it requires twenty thousand, we shouldn't hesitate for a moment. If you don't prevent them, they will slaughter you barbarously to ensure their domination. Remember the Nancy massacre. Let the perfidious men lulling you to sleep cry *barbarism*. No, no, [the barbarian] isn't the man who counsels you to slaughter the implacable enemies preparing to massacre you to quench their criminal passions; it's the traitors who want to plunge you into a fatal sense of security in order to deliver you, defenseless, into the chains of your tyrants' underlings.[22]

Similar wild computations continued throughout the early months of 1791. "You shouted against barbarism when I cried that the only way to avoid civil war and firm up liberty was to fell five or six hundred heads of the leaders, the conspirators; already more than thirty thousand have been slaughtered since the taking of the Bastille and that's still only a prelude: let the king, the dauphin and the Austrian woman escape and you will be drowned in torrents of blood." This on 22 February. There was more of the same a few months later. "I was called bloodthirsty when I proposed lopping off five hundred heads to secure liberty," Marat insisted on 8 May 1791. "On the contrary, it was a counsel of humanity and justice. If this wise advice had been followed before our cowardly enemies had united and gathered force, how much innocent blood would have been spared! Twenty thousand patriots would not have been massacred and five hundred thousand more would not be threatened with the same fate at any moment." Three weeks later, his estimate of necessary bloodletting had been significantly revised. "Felling five hundred heads would have sufficed to put things back in order eleven months ago," he declared on 27 May. "Today it would take fifty thousand."[23]

The number of heads to be severed soared even higher on 8 September 1791, as the Constituent Assembly was drawing to a close. By then, *L'Ami du peuple* was calling for "a general insurrection throughout the empire, a general massacre of the enemies of the revolution." This "horrifying but indispensable execution of two or three hundred thousand rebels" could once have been prevented by extinguishing five or six hundred counter-revolutionary conspirators. But the time had passed to assure public liberty and felicity by such minimal means. The "idiotic people" had stupidly let that opportunity slip. "Through an act of barbarous pity, it [had] placed itself under the frightful necessity of shedding blood in torrents."[24]

Five hundred, six hundred, five thousand, ten thousand, twenty thousand, fifty thousand, a hundred thousand, two hundred thousand, three hundred thousand: these numbers, at once gratuitously vague and chillingly labile, heralded notoriety for Marat and a new script for the French Revolution. By the time of his death, his bloody calculations had become legendary. They inspired the popular activists of the William Tell section in November 1793 as they called for a reign of terror. "Never forget the sublime words of the prophet, Marat," they declared. "Sacrifice 200,000 heads, and you will save a million."[25]

Should these computations be taken at face value? Were they just a manner of speaking? Were they meant to be taken literally, or were they issued as a kind of bloody metaphorical index of the intensity of political crisis? Was Marat actually advocating mass slaughter or wielding the numbers to convey his estimation of the gravity of a rapidly deteriorating situation? This latter is the conclusion reached by the most recent editors of his political writings, who support their judgment by noting that Marat tweaked Malouet over liberty of the press by offering him a little lecture on journalistic license. Malouet had responded in horror at a hyperventilating passage of *L'Ami du peuple* that had conjured up an image of eight hundred gallows erected in the Tuileries Gardens, together with a vast pyre to punish faithless deputies and incinerate corrupt ministers. Marat, in response, had imagined how this language would have been treated in an English courtroom, where press freedom and the arts of political speech were more readily understood. "Between us, M. Malouet . . . ," the justice of the peace would say, "there is no need of your intelligence to recognize that these 800 gallows and this vast bonfire are only a little maneuver on the author's part . . . to focus your compatriots' attention . . . , to ignite their just indignation and prevent the sort of terrible misfortunes that often befall your fellow citizens when they allow themselves to be deluded by their virtuous representatives. We English savor frankness and know a bit about one another in politics."[26]

But these calls to violence were more than mere *jeux de mots*. Marat was in no doubt that the popular executions of July 1789 had been necessary and justifiable, and that there should have been more of them. Moreover, as his numbers of potential victims swelled, some individuals were specifically targeted. He called for popular insurrection, anticipated civil war, and did not shrink from its logic. In his view, the Nancy massacre had changed the political situation radically. Bloodshed would have to be met by bloodshed. Today, we might call his numbers flamboyant messaging, but they came to be taken literally by at least some who invoked his inspiration. Populist politics necessarily carries this risk.

The language of purge, moreover, had deep roots in Marat's thinking. It sprang from profound anxieties regarding the alienation of popular sovereignty through representation that were already evident in *The Chains of Slavery* in 1774.[27] Opposing calls for a Triennial Act, he had maintained that allowing representatives the authority to shorten the term of their mandate implied their right to lengthen it at will. The nightmare scenario he evoked then was a move by the House of Commons to usurp the sovereignty of the people by freeing itself from any restrictions regarding the duration of its powers. But this, in effect, was what the National Assembly had done in 1789. Not only had deputies simply declared themselves a National Assembly; they had also sworn to remain in place until they had completed a constitution of their choice. Pending that moment, which they alone were in a position to determine, no constitutional or legal political mechanisms existed to bring their rule to an end. They had, in effect, arrogated the sovereignty of the nation to themselves until they were ready to declare the constitution completed.

A year later, the end of their task was still nowhere in sight. Claiming inviolability, they remained in power indefinitely, sustaining in turn the authority of other institutions like the municipality of Paris, the Châtelet court, the National Guard, and even the monarchy, that had been improvised or remodeled in the name of the nation. In short, Marat reasoned, the people was being oppressed by institutions arbitrarily enforcing order on its behalf. In a situation like this, he had argued in 1774, "however hard be the act of vindicating liberty by force, the nation ought not to defer a moment to take up arms. This is the case of a just revolt." By 1790, the call to throw out placemen and pensioners had metastasized into incitements to insurrection and the lopping off of heads.

Between popular sovereignty and representative government the divide was absolute: no middle ground was possible. In this classical republican vision, purge could reset the clock, political storms could clear the air, but only for a time. Violence was necessary. Sovereign will, ever on the defensive, could act only through radical negation.

SEVENTEEN

REMEMBER NANCY

A good massacre, like the proverbial firing squad, concentrates the political mind. If Marat remained haunted by the confrontation at Nancy, so did the enemies he blamed for it. Among them were the leaders and majority within the National Assembly, now even more determined to impose civil order and military discipline. There was Lafayette, suddenly less certain of his National Guard but eager to maintain control of the capital along with Bailly, whose Parisian government was growing ever more fearful of popular agitation. There too was Bouillé, epitome of reactionary officers in the regular army, who was soon bent on a plot to spirit the royal family from the capital to head an invasion of counterrevolutionary forces. And most dramatically, there was Louis XVI himself, and behind him the malign conspiratorial figures of his traitorous wife, the counselors in her so-called Austrian Committee, and the panicky royal court. These were Marat's principal targets in the months that separated the bloodshed at Nancy from the massacre awaiting popular protest on the Champ de Mars a crucial year later.

In Marat's analysis, the king revealed himself an open enemy of the people on 2 September by addressing a striking letter to the National Assembly. It lamented the necessity for bloodshed in Nancy but lauded Bouillé and his loyal troops for their imposition of order in that traumatized city. "We owe it to the firmness and good conduct of M. de Bouillé, to the fidelity of the national guards and the troops who, under his orders, have shown themselves obedient to their oath and to the law," declared the monarch. "I am sadly touched that order could not be re-established without bloodshed; but I hope that this will be the last time, and that henceforth no regiment will evade the military discipline without which an army would become a scourge to the state." Marat did not take long to condemn this royal gesture of regret. He saw it as an empty show of sentiment dictated by the ministers. "The king advertises in vain the sadness his ministers whisper to him. A modicum of feeling would have made him blush at the shameful role they are making him play," he protested on 4 September. "Good God! Is it left to fools to govern the earth? Is it up to the likes of Tiberius, Caligula and Nero to determine the destinies of the human race? Take a look at the abominations of this executive power under which we groan, that drinks our blood and makes a sport of slaughtering us."[1]

A proclamation of the National Assembly followed the king's declaration. It too lauded "the patriotism and civic bravery" of the guardsmen (from Metz) who had marched against their fellows in Nancy under Bouillé's orders. It too congratulated the ruthless general and his troops on "gloriously fulfilling their duty." In retort, the Assembly was besieged by an angry crowd demanding the dismissal of the general staffs of all army units, the right of soldiers to nominate their officers, and the immediate arrest of the ministers. Lafayette's National Guard was there to clear the streets.[2]

Necker soon became collateral damage of the Nancy affair. Weakened for months, fearful of popular agitation, and outmaneuvered politically by Mirabeau and Lafayette, he announced his departure on 4 September. Popular demand had brought him back after the fall of the Bastille; public disdain now dismissed him for good. The news gave Marat the chance for a farewell blast against this old enemy. More important, it allowed him a final opportunity to dramatize the misery and uncertainty of his own patriotic existence as contrasted with "the pleasures, honors, and dignities" awaiting his fellow Swiss immigrant.

"You blame destiny for the singularity of your life's events," he wrote of Necker's parting declaration.

> But what if, like The People's Friend, you were the plaything of men and the victim of your own patriotism! What if, afflicted by a mortal illness, you had, like him, renounced self-preservation to enlighten the people regarding its rights and the means of recovering them! What if, the instant you were cured, you had sacrificed to the people your repose, your waking hours, your liberty! What if you had been reduced to bread and water in devoting everything you possessed to the public good! What if, to defend the people, you had declared war on all its enemies! What if, to save the class of the wretched, you had broken with

> the whole universe, without allowing yourself a single place of asylum under the sun . . . ! What if, hounded by a crowd of assassins armed to take your life, you had chosen to live underground to rescue a feckless, blind, ungrateful people!

With this remarkable display of self-promotion as victim and martyr, Marat pledged the departing minister a vow of eternal silence, though one he never fully kept. "I've worked for your fall with uncommon zeal," he bragged; "but the moment you are no longer a dangerous public person you become for me, once again, a person of no importance."[3]

If Necker could outrun Marat's disdain, other enemies remained in place. Not least Lafayette, still head of the Parisian militia "thanks to his fame and the stupidity of the people." In the wake of the Nancy massacre, *L'Ami du peuple* portrayed the general as a desperate imposter, "finally unmasked and fearing the consequences of public indignation." Courting the Jacobin Club in the hope of refreshing his political credentials, Lafayette was promised no quarter. "Here's the devil hiding in the font," the journal warned. "One more bottle of ink, goddamned Lafayette, and you won't dare show yourself. Remember goddamned Necker."[4] That bottle of ink held a generous admixture of bile.

ONE MORE BOTTLE OF INK . . .

A choice opportunity for ridicule soon arrived. Lafayette, having failed to persuade his Parisian National Guard to issue a formal declaration of gratitude to Bouillé and his bloodstained legions, joined Bailly in organizing a solemn ceremony on the Champ de Mars to honor the soldiers who had sacrificed their lives to impose order in Nancy. This pathetic replay of the Festival of Federation was lampooned in *L'Ami du peuple* for the sententiously patriotic inscriptions placed on the symbolic sarcophagus at the center of the event—and for its revelation of a sudden shift in popular attitude toward the vainglorious general. "How times have changed," Marat mocked. "The eyes of the public have been opened; it takes a malign pleasure in this new spectacle. The hero, unmasked, is beyond himself. He runs to the altar, rage exploding from his face, grinding his teeth, strangled accents erupting from his foaming mouth. . . . He hears a chorus of ten thousand voices repeating: *look at his face, how enraged he is at not being applauded!*"[5]

There was a large measure of satisfaction on Marat's part to be found in this portrayal of Lafayette's sudden loss of popularity, but also a large dose of wish fulfillment. The self-aggrandizing general did not disappear from the scene, despite a passing gesture of willingness to resign his position. He remained to push for more effective imposition of law and order, to press for stronger military discipline, and to maintain his personal control of the Paris National Guard. *L'Ami du peuple* pilloried him constantly throughout the following months. Prompted by the appearance of an official report on the October Days of 1789, the journal portrayed him as "the leader of the counterrevolutionaries," "the soul of the conspirators, still under the mask," an enemy of the people already plotting the king's escape. Derisively shorn of his noble title, this mere *Motier*—no longer Marie-Joseph-Paul-Yves-Roch-Gilbert Motier, marquis de Lafayette—was now to be outed as a monster of "bad faith and perfidy," "the buttress of the royalist faction," "an enemy of the revolution, a perfidious courtier, treacherous and cruel." "Can it be doubted any longer that the great general, the hero of two worlds, is *the leader of the counterrevolutionaries, the soul of all the conspiracies* against the homeland," the journal demanded on 12 October; "can it be doubted that the intriguer Motier holds all the threads of their perfidious web in his hands?"

By Marat's measure, this puffed-up hero of two worlds had been a mere instrument of the foreign policy of the Old Regime. As a former noble, a marquis, a courtier, he could only be regarded as a mortal enemy of the Revolution, a "dyed-in-the-wool royalist," a "generalissimo of the conspirators, a hypocritical charlatan." He was turning the National Guard into an instrument of a military dictatorship in the service of a despot. "Citizens, I repeat, you delude yourselves," Marat warned; "the political machine won't work, or it will work only under the despot's orders, until the avenging blade has lopped off the leading conspirators' heads, beginning with the shameful general's."[6]

"Just one more bottle of ink, petty intriguer, I told you two months ago, and you'll be put in your place. I dare to hope that you will have disappeared before the bottle is empty," Marat assured Lafayette on 10 November. A few days later, he was sensing victory. "Thanks to the liberty of the press, [Motier's] reign is finished and, despite his trickery, his false protestations of civic loyalty, all the venal trumpeting of renown, he's seen as no more than a dangerous public enemy covered in a hypocrite's mask," proclaimed *L'Ami du peuple*. "Soon he will be forced to seek safety in flight and, like all the other court valets, he will depart covered with opprobrium and infamy, parading his shame and despair in a foreign land." This rejoicing at Lafayette's imminent fall had been fueled by a popular riot on 13 November, unchecked by the watching National Guard, that had resulted in the sacking of the mansion of the reactionary duc de Castries on the rue de Varenne. But celebration was premature. Lafayette responded by urging the National Assembly to hasten a reorganization of the National Guard to ensure enforcement of public order. Marat, dubbing this action a demand for "a second Nancy decree," called on the people to take up arms in protest. To no effect. Within days, Rabaut was presenting to the National Assembly, on behalf of the Constitutional Committee, the draft of a new law on military organization.[7]

The decree Rabaut proposed for debate on 5 December 1790 began by asserting a number of constitutional principles. Defining the public force as the union of the forces of all the citizens, it distinguished two elements: the regular army established for defense against external enemies, and the National Guard organized against "perturbers of order and peace" at home. This lapidary formula at once characterized the function of the National Guard as suppression of public disorder (that is, popular agitation) and assimilated it to the broader organization of military force. It declared active citizens obliged to bear arms when public order was disturbed or the homeland attacked. They could not refuse service when legally summoned to do so; they and their adult sons were required to register for the National Guard in acknowledgment of this obligation. Passive citizens were thus excluded, by definition, from bearing arms. The armed force, moreover, was held to be "essentially obedient": its units had no right to deliberate regarding their orders; its members were ineligible to vote in any political assembly if they were armed or in uniform. The nation being one, so was the National Guard; it was necessarily subject, throughout the realm, to the same rules, the same discipline, the same uniform.[8]

In Marat's analysis, this legislation was being foisted upon the Constitutional Committee by Lafayette. It was the counterrevolutionary general's underhand attempt to complete his longstanding project to militarize the National Guard and make it the blind instrument of executive power. The People's Friend derided the monarchists in the National Assembly who protested that the draft did not explicitly name the king as the head of the nation's forces; he hailed Robespierre for a powerful speech that exposed the text's antidemocratic provisions and upheld the right of all citizens to bear arms; he decried the rapidity with which the proposal was accepted by the National Assembly. Dubbing this law the "Motier decree," he denounced its terms as vague and dangerous enough to annihilate liberty forever. "These words *order and peace* can mean the regime established by despotism and the calm inspired by fear," he protested. Were they not just the odious names that despots leveled at the just and courageous men who dared challenge their tyrannical orders? Were they not applied in servile states to all the friends of liberty? Had they not been deployed against "all the authors of the blessed revolution, all the conquerors of the Bastille, all the defenders of the rights of man?" Had the corrupt National Assembly not utilized them in its barbarous decree against the garrison and citizens of Nancy, against every patriotic soldier and citizen who did not want to be oppressed? "Learn then, Frenchmen, that it is solely against the friends of liberty that your shameful legislators, sold out to the infamous Motier, author of the decree, intend to mobilize the national guards throughout the realm."[9]

No less absurd and dangerous, seen from this perspective, were the claims that the National Guard, like the regular army, was "essentially obedient" and had no right to deliberate regarding its orders. For Marat, these were maxims of tyranny. An oppressed nation had no obligation to resist an invader offering a better fate, he emphasized in addressing the troops; a free one had no duty to follow an ambitious monarch or corrupt representatives into a disastrous war, or to engage in a war of conquest to oppress another people. As for the right to deliberate, "it is essential that you know whether the citizens against whom you are ordered to march have really violated the laws, and whether the laws they have violated are just." To grasp this principle, it was necessary only to remember (yet again) the bloody decree against Nancy. "Soldiers of the homeland, I repeat, you escape the misfortune and crime of serving as instruments of tyranny only by examining and reasoning about the orders you receive; this is a law imposed on you equally by the duties of man and of the citizen."[10]

The net effect of this Motier Law, in Marat's eyes, was to enlarge the forces the king could use to crush the nation. "The revolution would then have done nothing but rivet our chains instead of breaking them." French citizens had to recognize that their chief enemy was not the foreign troops but "the agents and henchmen of your king, this good king, the implacable, eternal adversary of the revolution." They had to awaken to "the truth that the king is the most fearsome of your enemies." The ability to deliberate regarding leaders' plans and to disobey their orders—in a word, "open revolt against the established order"—had produced the "blessed revolution" and created the National Assembly. By what criminal audacity did the legislature now criminalize the means that had saved the nation from the abyss?[11]

Against attacks like this Lafayette thrust back. Working with Bailly throughout the fall of 1790, he had seeded streets, cafés, and popular assemblies with agents and spies, while his propagandists kept the presses busy. Marat became a prime target of these *mouchards*, the derogatory popular term already favored under the Old Regime for police agents, spies, and informers; he reciprocated their attentions, outing them in increasingly hostile denunciations as the year advanced. At the same time, official attempts to locate his hiding place, intimidate and shut down printers of his journal, and harass its hawkers continued. Still unable to show his face in Paris, he had treated his readers to a melodramatic account of raids on his printers and confiscations of his publication carried out on 15 September by three hundred "ass-pushers" from the National Guard. The police inquisitors of the Old Regime, he protested, would never have permitted themselves the revolting vexations now being ordered by Bailly and Lafayette, "these friends of the fatherland, these defenders of the citizens, these restorers of liberty!"[12]

Three months later, in an action instigated by a *mouchard* named Estienne who had been savagely denounced by Marat as Lafayette's principal spy and propagandist, police targeted the print shop of a Mlle Anne-Félicité Colombe. There they ripped proof sheets of *L'Ami du peuple* from the press. There, too, they discovered and confiscated issues of another journal, *L'Orateur du peuple*, whose editor, Stanislas Fréron, had become Marat's close ally in the literary and political guerrilla war against the general and his agents. Derided by reactionary journalists, Fréron was soon dubbed "Marat's monkey."[13] His publication in effect replaced the ill-fated *Junius français*, the secondary sheet Marat had been unable to keep producing alone earlier in the year. *L'Ami du peuple* and *L'Orateur du peuple* were to be twinned during the coming months. Sharing Marat's printer, Fréron now partook of his persecution.

The raid on 14 December gave rise to a series of sensational court cases of fiendish complexity.[14] Estienne sued Colombe for printing the two journals, accusing them both of defaming him. He was quickly joined in the case by a dozen other individuals denounced as *mouchards* by the offending journalists. When Colombe failed to appear in court on 18 December, she was condemned by the police tribunal, prohibited from printing or distributing the two journals, and ordered to pay damages to Estienne and his cohort. The latter, in response, were purged as police spies from an association of political activists calling themselves "Conquerors of the Bastille," to whom Marat had fingered them. A bitter pamphlet war of denunciation and counter-denunciation flared until meetings of the Conquerors of the Bastille were suppressed by order of the Paris municipality. The group soon reemerged as the Club of Enemies of Despotism.

In a seething denunciation of the mayor and the general on 19 December, Marat declared Lafayette a mortal enemy. "I won't rest until he has paid for his crimes with an ignominious punishment," he swore. "Every day I'll reveal his traps, his intrigues, his plots, his attacks. Every day I'll expose his lies, his impostures, his deceits, his roguery, his baseness. Every day I'll drag him in the mud, to the point that . . . he will seek safety in flight or have me assassinated by his thugs." The indictment continued a week later, to the effect that "The Hero of Two Worlds" had nothing to offer the Old World but "platitudes, villainy, lies, baseness, attacks and treason." In the heat of the conflict, The People's Friend forgot his commitment to press freedom, insisting that the only presses that should be allowed to function were those enlightening the people as to its rights, unmasking the conspiracies of traitors to the homeland, and wrecking their plots. To defend from "typographical treasons," he urged patriots to smash into pieces every press found serving the enemies of the people.[15]

Colombe, in the meantime, was not intimidated. Marat had found her an able lawyer, Claude Rémy Buirette Verrières, destined for leadership in the radical Cordelier Club and a busy career representing other targets accused by the authorities over the coming months. Before the end of the year, she appealed the judgment against her and sued for damages, charging abuse of the liberty of the press. Marat called on all patriots to show up at the hearing of the case scheduled on 5 January. It attracted a large and boisterous crowd, augmented first by the arrival of several score members of the now illegal Conquerors of the Bastille and then by a deputation of the conservative Notre Dame section, suborned by Lafayette and Bailly in Marat's account, and bearing a fervent excoriation of a highly inflammatory issue of *L'Ami du peuple*. Violent hostility of the audience toward this deputation and abuse against Estienne himself forced an adjournment of the proceedings. The *mouchard* declined to appear before the tribunal again.

The trial resumed nonetheless on 10 January before an audience further enlarged by Marat's call upon popular activists to crowd the benches. This time Mayor Bailly himself chose to preside—an indication of the importance he attached to a decision in this case. Among the already overheated audience was a young firebrand, Théophile Mandar, member of the former Conquerors of the Bastille and author of *De la souveraineté du peuple*, an adaptation to the French revolutionary situation of the seventeenth-century tract *On the Excellency of a Free State* by the English republican Marchamont Nedham.[16] Taking it upon himself to speak for the people, Mandar challenged the legality of Bailly's action in presiding over the trial. The mayor was himself implicated in the case, the young radical claimed, and hence ineligible to conduct it. Losing face but still denying any grounds for his recusal, Bailly agreed to step down. The tribunal vacated the earlier judgment against Colombe and imposed the payment of damages on the absent Estienne, but it prevaricated by declaring its incompetence, as a police court, to decide the question of the liberty of the press.

There was yet another act to this court drama. As Paris sections began sounding support for Colombe and slinging their own anathemas against the *mouchards*, a group of the latter sued Fréron for defamation and hired a notable attorney to plead their case. Marat responded by declaring his own responsibility for Fréron's denunciations, urging him not to appear before the tribunal, and calling upon the Conquerors of the Bastille to mobilize in protest. Extravagant arguments, noisy hearings, repeated postponements, and warring declarations fanned public interest in the disputes until the end of January, when the police tribunal again found the matter of calumny beyond its legal competence and directed the parties toward civil courts.

Though they ended inconclusively, these warring suits had clear implications. In effect, they served as show trials revealing the repressive tendencies and sheer confusion over liberty of the press that had afflicted revolutionary policies throughout 1790. They also brought Lafayette's agents out of the shadows, exposing them dramatically to public view. Fréron declared the entire episode a triumph—to the annoyance of The People's Friend, who had wanted the hearings to end in more decisive judgments. But Fréron was right in claiming victory. Again and again, Marat had called on popular activists to show up in strength at the extended hearings in the cases. Each delay he had turned into an incitement to political mobilization. When, at Mandar's urging, the resulting crowd prevented Bailly from presiding over the tribunal, Marat counted that a personal success. Progressively, his coverage of the cases projected a view of himself as a kind of unindicted conspirator, the true target of the prosecution. Generating a cloud of pamphlets and a surge of radical popular support, the battle against the *mouchards* showed his campaign to incite a populist public spirit beginning to take hold.

"Public spirit is forming," rejoiced *L'Ami du peuple* on 10 February 1791, in the wake of these trials. "The French want to be free, even those who sell themselves today will abandon their corruptors tomorrow. As soon as public opinion is formed, the people will order the reform of all the deadly decrees that are the shame of the legislator and will infallibly be the ruin of the nation." And public opinion, Marat now emphasized, was the opinion of the people, not that communicated by an enlightened elite.

In this, he was countering the deputy Antoine Balthazar Joachim d'André who had argued for locating a new high court outside the capital by distinguishing the dispersed "public opinion" of the nation from the concentrated and embodied popular opinion of the Paris crowd. The first, d'André imagined, assured the integrity of judicial and administrative institutions; the second (in Marat's rendering of the argument) triggered "all the commotions that ceaselessly compromise the liberty and peace of the empire, and are always stronger because of the greater mass of the people gathered together in the same location." D'André had invoked basic principles of the Enlightenment: respect for rational deliberation and distrust of popular will. For Marat, the deputy's distinction between public judgment and popular heft had become reactionary. "There is no public opinion other than that of the mass of the people."[17]

KING OR DESPOT?

An army requires a uniform, a uniform a button, a button a motto. Such was the logic of the National Assembly's decision on 5 September to emblazon the buttons of the new National Guard uniform with the words, *The Law and the King*. Marat was outraged. "In this button that seems so unimportant to you, dear fellow citizens," he insisted, "you will soon find the heaviest of chains." Supporters of the chosen formula could offer the argument that the law is the nation and the nation the law, he acknowledged, but this reasoning was palpably specious if the law was made not by the nation itself but by its mortal enemies in an assembly that had betrayed its interests in manifold ways. With this motto adopted under present circumstances, "the law and the king would soon be reduced to the king and the disastrous decrees he would execute. . . . You would bear the signs of servitude on your coats." It was time for The People's Friend to insist yet again on the true nature of things: that the king was no more than the first servant of the nation; that the current Assembly, composed almost entirely of the nation's enemies, had no authority to attack the rights of the people and the citizens. "There must be no question of the king or the law on your buttons. The only motto they must bear is the word PATRIE."[18]

Discussion of this matter was revived a month later when Desmoulins and others argued for replacing Marat's proposed "PATRIE" with "NATION" on the buttons because this word "conveyed a majestic idea, an idea of grandeur." Again, Marat was incensed. The substitution, he argued, would "sacrifice a cherished name, so fit to awaken in the soul the idea of the sacred bonds uniting citizens, for a vague term applying equally to enslaved and free peoples, and this for the pathetic advantage of flattering French vanity."[19]

Patrie was an emphatic and cherished designation for a political entity constituting a civic bond among citizens. For lack of a better English word, the French term has been rendered as "homeland" throughout this book, a translation that elides the gendered implications of the more literal "fatherland," while falling far short of the term's deep political resonances. Marat could not let go of this name that still carried values of ancient republicanism, civic virtue, and active and engaged political participation by the entire body of (male) citizens.[20] In comparison to it, *nation* seemed too weak and loose. He could not imagine liberty existing in the absence of public spirit. He saw it as the duty of radical journalists to foster that spirit, to instruct the people as to its rights, "to keep it in a constant state of agitation, to make all minds ferment until the government is founded on laws that are truly just." For this, the principle of liberty of the press guaranteed the medium of liberty; it was the sole rampart of civil and political freedom. "So long as liberty of the press exists, we are sure to overcome." For this, too, great truths informed the message. They were gradually becoming evident. Among them: "Every prince born on the throne is the base enemy of peoples, and his ministers can only be villains."[21]

In face of the *patrie* loomed the prince. In another dramatic consequence of the Nancy affair, Louis XVI now fell more personally and directly under Marat's critical eye. Earlier in August, *L'Ami du peuple* had deemed the monarch precisely the person for the job in the current circumstances. A man "without projects, without artifice, without tricks, without finesse, and not much of a threat to public liberty," it had concluded, he could be a good prince if he had enough sense to choose wise advisers. "But alas! His atrocious ministers are making his reign as hideous as a tyrant's." After the Nancy bloodletting, however, and with no one of political stature replacing Necker as first minister, the convention of blaming evil counselors for the king's conduct became less plausible. With the appearance in mid-September of Louis de Lavicomterie's premonitory pamphlet *Du peuple et des rois*—soon followed by François Robert's *Le Républicanisme adapté à la France*—republican sentiments began to rumble around the capital. Embracing this moment, Marat now openly professed his hatred for kings as the eternal enemies of nations. He saw Louis XVI, along with the reactionaries in the National Assembly, as "covered with the blood of the unfortunate Nancy patriots whose executioners they applaud. This hideous image haunts me night and day, and for as long as I live I won't stop making it their crime."[22]

This hostility to Louis XVI intensified a month later when The People's Friend heard news that counterrevolutionary gestures by officers in the Belfort garrison were being punished less harshly than the patriotic insurrection at Nancy. "And you take the title of restorer of French liberty!" Marat railed against the monarch. "And you claim to be the defender of the revolution! And you are called minister of the laws, dispenser of justice, father of the people! Cease to adorn yourself with the glorious title of king, you will never know the sacred duties it imposes. When you were exalted you abandoned the reins of state to inept ministers, forgetting the august cares of empire in the hunt, at table, and in the sheets. Today you abandon the helm of affairs to atrocious ministers who think only of machinations against the state and will end up causing your downfall."[23]

Nature had not fashioned Louis XVI to rule, Marat now declared; put in place by fortune, this king could be discarded along with his office if he no longer served the public good. "Thanks to philosophy, the National Assembly could dismiss the monarch and annihilate the crown without the least commotion in the state. . . . It is a gross error to believe that French government could never be anything but monarchical, that it even needs to be monarchical today. In the name of common sense, what good is a monarch incapable of holding the reins of the state?" To the impartial eye, it seemed clear, "the king of the French is less than a fifth wheel on a carriage since he can only disrupt the working of the political machine." Patriotic writers, concluded The People's Friend, should hasten to convince the nation that "the best means to assure its peace, liberty and happiness is to do without the crown."[24] Marat had arrived at a republican moment.

Left to themselves by a neglectful prince, Marat reasoned, ministers would become an oligarchy, a handful of petty despots. With each minister isolated as a sovereign in his department, all would work "to pillage or oppress the people and render their master absolute the better to abuse his power." Against these dangers, he floated the idea of a general executive council composed of informed, wise, and trustworthy men sharing decisions and their execution under strict conditions of accountability to the legislature and the public. Such an administration would achieve the happiness of the nation, he argued, even at the cost of speed in the conduct of affairs. This latter he thought no great loss; slowness in government was to be considered a virtue in a well-constituted state. "If the activity of the government is necessary in a great empire, it is only when it is despotic, which is to say exposed to the undertakings of numerous enemies provoked by the ambitious projects of the despot. This extreme rapidity in the execution of the orders necessitated by the defense of the state is thus useless when the nation, renouncing conquests, wants to live in peace with all the peoples of the world, when it has consecrated justice and moderation as constitutional principles. Not only is this extreme activity useless, but it is dangerous because it results in rash and irreparable decisions."[25]

The ideal of slow government motivated by a spirit of justice and moderation may come as a surprise in the thinking of a prophet of terror, but its appearance must remind us that Marat was a professed disciple of Montesquieu, the great eighteenth-century theorist of moderate government. It also explains the paradox that his anxiety about Louis XVI's rule was now aggravated by the decrees of the National Assembly finally abolishing the parlements and other "gothic and dreaded" high courts of the Old Regime in early September 1790. His initial fear was that the institutions replacing these privileged tribunals might prove no better than the old. In this great transformation, he warned, "nothing will have changed but the name." To avert the danger of filling the new courts with remnants of the Old Regime, he called for the active public posting of lists of proscription that would allow voters to winnow these men out.[26]

As the year advanced, however, this reader of *The Spirit of the Laws* came to the realization of a more terrible truth. Something fundamental had indeed changed. "I've been saying for thirteen months that the cabinet, reactionaries, partisans of the ministry, committees of inquiry, the mayor and the general have been conspiring to reestablish despotism," he was insisting on 9 October. "It's a mistake still to blame the aristocrats for our problems. Far from being masters to crush us, they don't even have the strength to defend themselves." The clergy had been powerless to prevent the sale of church property, the defunct ancient nobility to oppose the abolition of its privileges, the judicial robe nobility to stop its own annihilation. "The ones in command are the atrocious ministers, the royalist and corrupted deputies of the people . . . cowardly deserters of the homeland who have joined with the courtiers, municipal administrators, and Parisian general staff in rallying around the monarch, to make executive power triumph and sacrifice the nation to its servant."[27]

The point was made even more directly on 13 October. "Let's keep repeating it. The constitution is a complete failure; the political machine won't work or it will only work at the orders of the prince, in whose hands our faithless representatives have placed all the reins of power. The privileged orders no longer exist; the corporate judicial bodies no longer exist; all the barriers have been overthrown, the people itself, whose sovereignty should have been guaranteed, has been sacrificed to the executive power. Soon, soon, the despot will be more absolute than ever." Only one hope was left: the creation of a high national court composed of "judicious and zealous patriots." But this was not to be expected from a legislature that had already sold out to the monarch. "If it succeeds in extirpating the last vestiges of feudalism, that's for the sake of establishing pure despotism."[28]

Bitterly critical of the constitutional decisions being made by the National Assembly, Marat was convinced that the nation had been betrayed by corrupt deputies paid by the court. "The damage is done," he insisted in early October, "the constitution is a complete misfire. Apart from the decree regarding the declaration of rights and a few others the people has wrenched for itself in moments of crisis, there isn't one that shouldn't be annulled by the next legislature." The Assembly's fundamental error was its failure to respect the principle of the separation of powers. "Show me a single example where the traitorous assembly has neglected to put the king into the mix of public affairs," he demanded of his readers two weeks later. The deputies were boasting of being the first legislators in the universe to know how to fix the limits of the different powers of the political body. In effect, though, rather than radically separating powers, they had intruded the executive power into every aspect of government. They had allocated the king a share in legislation through the royal veto; they had made him supreme military commander with the right to initiate war; they had entrusted him with supreme executive power, with responsibility for public subsistence, with control over the system of justice, with the administration of finances, with direction over the postal system. All these functions could readily be made instruments of despotism.[29]

Even now, Marat contended, the legislators were allowing the monarch to name judges to a newly created supreme tribunal (from a list established by the Assembly) rather than creating the independent body he had long demanded, "a high national court composed of true patriots to take cognizance of all the crimes of lèse-nation and punish the enemies of the homeland, the traitors, the conspirators, to prevent plots against liberty and repress the corrupt practices of ministers and their agents." Who could doubt that an assembly sold to the court would choose candidates most likely to please it? The sole goal of the prince, "this born enemy of liberty," was to enchain the people in order to pillage and crush it with impunity. "See him free now to make the laws speak or fall silent at his pleasure through the action of his creatures, see him now with the power to overthrow all the dikes raised to oppose excesses of his power. What more obvious proof could there be that the shameful constitutional committee has prostituted itself to the court . . . ? Oh perfidy! Oh treason!"[30]

The much-vaunted constitution the National Assembly was erecting was thus already, in Marat's analysis, a masterpiece of stupidity, a complete farce. Its vices could not be remedied without a profound redistribution of the powers within the political machine. Since redress could no longer be expected from the present legislature, it would have to be left to the next one to restrict monarchical power. Or, infinitely better, that new legislature could "organize the government in such a way that the crown, whose eternal plots we will always have to fear, will be proscribed. These views are beginning to take hold. But whether through timidity or thoughtlessness, they are everywhere grasped from false points of view."[31]

A few weeks later, *L'Ami du peuple* was calling for more immediate action against the crown. There was a plan for counterrevolution, the journal warned. The court would never abandon that plan, even down to the tenth generation. To pretend otherwise was to imagine that a river could flow backward toward its source. (Montesquieu, of course, had concluded that monarchies flow into despotism as rivers to the sea.) It was to assume that the love of splendor, honors, and pleasures, the thirst for power, and the compulsion to command could remain dormant in the hearts of princes, that *amour propre* could be extinguished forever within their souls. The legislators having refused to restrain the king's prerogatives within their true limits, the only remedy remaining was "to abolish the crown. Shall we wait until the monarch has achieved our ruin before taking the only means left to us to put an end to our ills?"[32]

Before year's end, Marat was stating this challenge in tones even more explicitly resonant of Montesquieu. In destroying privilege, he argued, the Revolution had eliminated the Old Regime ramparts against tyranny. "The privileged orders have been brought down, the parlements are destroyed, all the barriers are overthrown, the monarch, master of all the gold in the kingdom, will shower it on the troops. More powerful than ever, he will destroy the constitution, he will lay hold of all the wealth of the church which will be shared out among the valets of the court. A new despot, he will extend an iron scepter over an enslaved people and reign as a tyrant over devastated states. Cowardly citizens, you'll be subjected to all the horrors of tyranny if you don't crush its henchmen and choke them in their own blood."[33]

A lengthy diagnosis, developed a few days later, offered an extended analysis of the ways in which barriers against despotism, raised under the Old Regime in defense of privilege and corporatism, had now been destroyed by the Revolution in the name of national sovereignty. Traditional limitations on absolute royal power had been replaced by constitutional authorizations of it. "Thanks to the National Assembly, the king has become constitutionally the supreme arbiter, the absolute master of the nation, though he is only its mandatary." Louis XVI could now "tyrannize the nation in the name of the nation itself." The new French constitution was giving form to "an absolute monarchical government under the veil of a popular legislation, a shameful monument of ignorance, trickery, perfidy, anarchy and tyranny, a government a hundred times worse than the one it has replaced unless we hope to correct its vices." Montesquieu, in a memorable passage, had declared the English constitution to be a republic in the guise of a monarchy. In revolutionary France Marat now saw precisely the opposite. The French were erecting a new, more powerful despotism in the guise of a constitutional monarchy, purportedly founded on the principle of national sovereignty.[34]

The swerve toward despotism Marat perceived in the closing months of 1790 gave him all the more reason to make "Remember Nancy!" a continuing watchword. His fury over the massacre reignited by a justificatory official report on its events, he was calling in mid-December for Louis XVI and the National Assembly to suffer the punishment of an *amende honorable*, the penitential ritual of public humiliation imposed on criminals under the Old Regime. In a radical inversion of traditional royal justice, he imagined that this penalty previously inflicted in the king's name would now be imposed on the king himself in the name of the people. The "monarch unworthy of the throne, perfidious conspirator against the homeland, cowardly executioner of your fellow citizens," would march at the head of the procession, wearing sackcloth and ashes, barefoot, a rope around his neck. He would demand pardon from heaven and earth for his evil attacks; he would efface with tears the crimes with which he was covered.[35]

A MIRROR FOR A PRINCE

Marat leveled another indictment against Louis XVI as 1790 drew to a close. He became incensed by the monarch's reluctance to sanction the decree authorizing punishment of priests who refused to swear the mandatory oath to accept the Civil Constitution of the Clergy. In his analysis, the king's delay amounted to an open revolt against the Revolution, a tactic to stir up civil war while waiting for a counterrevolutionary invasion. Outraged, The People's Friend summoned the Paris sections into the streets to demand immediate royal acceptance of the decree. That acceptance eventually came, but in a manner that Marat nonetheless found infuriating. The monarch had deigned, in a disingenuous letter to the National Assembly, to elucidate the grounds for the deferral of his decision "openly and frankly, as befits my character," achieving thereby "a mode of communication with the assembly that would strengthen the bonds of mutual confidence so necessary to the happiness of France." He had hoped that mild measures could avert the need for severe ones, he explained, reasoning that time would calm troubled minds. Nonetheless, he was willing to give his consent now in order to dispel suspicions regarding his true intentions and the confidence he placed in the nation's representatives. "There are no means surer or more appropriate to calm agitation and conquer all resistance than the reciprocity of this sentiment [of mutual confidence] between the National Assembly and myself," Louis assured the deputies. "It is necessary, I merit it, and I count on it."[36]

Marat published an astonishing response to this royal explanation. He had addressed Louis XVI somewhat less directly in 1789 with his *Supplément à L'Offrande à la patrie*. Now he fired off a frontal condemnation of the monarch, an *Address of J. P. Marat, Friend of the People, to Louis XVI, King of the French.* It put a hypocritical king on trial in the court of public opinion two years before he faced the denunciations of Robespierre and Saint-Just in the tribunal of the National Assembly. And it did so in a remarkably personal, even intimate, tone. This was Jean-Paul Marat, The People's Friend, addressing one Louis Capet, victim of centuries of monarchical indoctrination and now challenged to recognize new truths of personal and political conduct.

"Sire, if you were born a simple citizen you might perhaps deserve to be believed on the basis of your word," Marat scolded the monarch. "But born to the throne, with all the vices of your education and after thirty-six years spent in the most corrupt court of Europe, constantly pandered to by the lackeys that surround you, pushed into crimes by atrocious ministers or perfidious courtiers, and continually dragged by your family into revolt against your duties, what confidence could you inspire by your protestations of attachment and fidelity to the homeland?" Don't flatter yourself that you can pull the wool over the eyes of clear-sighted patriots, The People's Friend warned the King of the French. In their eyes, the monarch could only appear a despot.

There followed a vitriolic denunciation of kings and kingship. The inherent stupidity of kings, Marat insisted, is to believe themselves superior beings by nature. They are mad enough to claim that heaven has called them to command, while spending their days in idleness, luxury, and pleasure. Told they are absolute masters of the earth, they finish by believing it. Soon they regard their compatriots as slaves born to serve their pleasures, vile beings they can sacrifice to their whims with impunity. Inevitably, the thirst for boundless authority stifles all other sentiments in their heart. "Who is ignorant of the fact that the morality of kings makes cunning, lying, imposture, perfidy, treason, assassination, poisoning and parricide a duty for them in order to maintain or recover the empire they have usurped? History is filled with the crimes of kings and the abject state of almost all the peoples of the world is graphic proof of these hideous truths."[37]

"Answer, Louis XVI," Marat commanded his monarch. "What have you done so far to merit that Heaven perform a miracle in your favor by shielding your soul from the contagion of the criminals who surround and obsess you ceaselessly, by inspiring you with the enlightenment and virtues necessary to triumph over their fatal lessons? Don't assume in any case that I rely on these infallible principles that are sufficient alone for the philosopher to judge kings. No, I judge you by your past conduct, I judge you by yourself." In this indictment, the hypocrisies and betrayals committed by Louis XVI since the calling of the Estates General could only be described as perfidious or imbecilic. "Could we believe you without being taken for imbeciles ourselves, without betraying our duties as men and citizens, without renouncing our liberty, our peace, our happiness, without sacrificing our friends, our brothers, our parents, our children, our wives, without sacrificing ourselves? Sire, you are the *friend of liberty* in the same way your spouse is *the friend of the French*. Your very tone invites suspicion. What! Would it be appropriate to the dignity of a king unaccustomed to dissimulation to say to us, 'I will speak *openly and frankly*.' I'll tell you the truth you owe us and are hiding from us. Have the courage to hear it and try to profit from it."[38]

This truth, Marat insisted, was that the current ministers were knaves and perfidious traitors, weaving a hideous plot to massacre patriotic citizens and reestablish despotism by force. The corrupt majority of the National Assembly, the chiefs of the army and of the Paris municipality, the commanders of the troops of the line and royal agents throughout the realm: all were complicit in this conspiracy. The kings of Europe were massing troops at French frontiers to support it. Fugitive Capets were poised to return to the country at the head of disaffected conspirators.

> And you, Sire, seeking a pretext to ignite civil war, make blood flow and reverse the constitution you have sworn to maintain, have fixed on the one offered by the revolt of the clergy . . . , hoping that the maneuvers of these fractious priests will set the state on fire and that the conspirators will flood it with the blood of the friends of liberty. Heaven has defeated this hideous project and only after seeing it everywhere frustrated do you finally consent to accept the decree to repress these fractious priests. And you color your stubborn refusal to accept it under the ridiculous pretext of wanting to wait until tempers calmed down, as if it were not the real means of bringing them to the point of despair and igniting the torch of war.[39]

"These, Sire, are the hideous truths that dared not leave your mouth," Marat declared in summation. "In revealing these impostures to the outraged eyes of the public, I'm fulfilling the holiest of obligations." But the nation, he acknowledged, wasn't yet ready to decide. It would trust the monarch's word yet again, judging his good faith by his zeal in ensuring the punishment of priests who were refusing or violating the oath of adherence to the Civil Constitution of the Clergy.

> If a single one of them escapes judgment as a result of your negligence in having them arrested or turned over to the tribunals, you will be seen, Sire, as an enemy of public liberty, a perfidious conspirator, the most cowardly of traitors, a prince without honor, without decency, the least of men. May the fear of being covered with opprobrium throughout Europe strengthen your heart against the counsels of the criminals who surround you. . . . Never forget that it is on this new test that you will be judged by the present generation and future races.[40]

This admonition to the monarch erupted amid a protracted volley of denunciations of conspiracy and betrayal—and accompanying calls for insurrection and purge—that *L'Ami du peuple* blasted throughout Paris in the closing days of 1790. In his analysis, the Revolution was being transformed into a nightmare version of the vicious modern politics against which he had warned the English in *The Chains of Slavery*: a king at the head of a professional army ready to enforce his will; venal ministers corrupted by the court and corrupting in their turn; crooked politicians posturing in the name of the people; a polluted legislature selling to the highest bidder its illegitimate claims to represent the nation. To this picture could now be added threats of counterrevolutionary conspiracy within and invasion from without—and the growing risk that Louis XVI would flee the country.

The issue of *L'Ami du peuple* for 22 December offered a design for Christmas lights. Let the entire capital be illuminated for two nights before and after Christmas Eve, it urged. Let the churches be empty, or filled only with children and old folks. Let citizens, both men and women, be out in the streets fulfilling the first of all human duties, that of self-preservation. "To watch over public safety is to honor the divinity," intoned the journal. "During these stormy nights, let Paris be up in arms. . . . Until the royal family is brought within your walls, let the mayor and the general be held under guard as hostages in City Hall."[41]

In the coming months, the prospect of the king's escape from Paris would become Marat's greatest obsession. He saw the fatal moment approaching. The king was being pressured by his family to leave the country against his better judgment; he had been reduced to tears by reminders of the last moments of Charles I; his decision could throw the nation instantly into civil war. "I'm tired of repeating to you, mindless Parisians," Marat warned. "Bring the king and the dauphin within your walls, guard them with care, lock up the Austrian Woman, her brother-in-law and the rest of the family. The loss of a single day can be fatal to the nation and dig the grave of three million Frenchmen."[42]

L'Ami du peuple thus ended its year in a paroxysm of denunciation and a frantic call for courage and determination. "No, nations don't win liberty in a day," Marat preached. "It took the English twenty-five battles, five hundred thousand men laid out on the battlefield, and sixty years of misery and disaster, and they don't believe the price too high. If you are continually on your guard and don't lose heart, it will only cost you a few years of agitation and some lengths of rope."[43]

EIGHTEEN

MOBILIZING THE PEOPLE

1 January 1791. The calendar, to say nothing of his inner compulsions, gave Marat no respite. He had to publish his eight pages a day, even while finding cover from "the virtuous Lafayette's assassins." Often, he informed readers, he was so burdened with correspondence that he had scarcely two hours to produce his copy; sometimes there was no time to reread it before it went to the printer. *L'Ami du peuple* nonetheless opened its initial issue of 1791 on a relentlessly familiar note. "You're sleeping, citizens, free of suspicion, in the arms of your perfidious agents. Already the implacable enemies of your liberty are hatching new plots to destroy you."[1]

For Marat, this was an opportune moment. Popular politics in the capital veered dramatically in his direction in the first six months of 1791. He was not alone in pushing a radical definition of the situation. There were other voices in the press and on the streets eager to denounce the revolutionary authorities as despotic in their arrogation of the sovereignty of the people, antidemocratic in their constitutional policies, and repressive in their resort to police powers.[2] But few went to his thymotic extremes in articulating these judgments. Political and social circumstances were also shifting in ways that amplified the political resonance of his language. Recent research into the evolution of Parisian political culture in the first half of this new year has revealed a city on the brink of conflagration. Popular mistrust of the authorities was becoming endemic in a capital burdened with indigence, unemployment, food crises, and currency fluctuation. Tempers flared, crowd protests erupted, political altercations proliferated. Clubs and political societies multiplied.[3]

The streets during these months were loud with rumors of famine plots, counterrevolutionary conspiracies, and betrayals of the Revolution by the National Assembly, the municipal government still led by Bailly, and the National Guard still commanded by Lafayette. The city remained saturated by police spies as popular volatility, social instability, and economic uncertainty kept government officials in a state of anxiety. In fear of popular agitation, authorities resorted to increasingly aggressive policing, with growing numbers of arrests, interrogations, and imprisonments. Their repressive impulses offered The People's Friend fertile ground and enhanced credibility for his fulminations. Letters of complaint and protest from outraged citizens pulsed throughout his journal during the early months of 1791. Offering accounts of oppression, petty tyranny, and hideous conspiracy, they served to etch out the details of Marat's dystopic political vision.[4]

The new year thus saw *L'Ami du peuple* pounding the public with its core denunciations. In its pages, Lafayette and Bailly, "these base valets of the prince, these consummate hypocrites, true models of deceit, spewed up from hell to complete your ruin," still featured at the head of the vast conspiracy against the people. They had to be brought to the foot of the scaffold. The National Guard, militarized by Lafayette as an obstacle to the establishment of a truly democratic new order, still had to be purged—as did the traitorous National Assembly dedicated to easing the monarch back into the exercise of sovereign power by means of its ever more vicious constitution. The risk was still mounting that the king would flee the realm; threats of counterrevolution and civil war were continuing to escalate; criminals and spies were pullulating in the capital, massacres were being planned, weapons stockpiled. To Marat's eyes, Paris appeared increasingly to mirror Rome under the Tarquins. Even worse, it was becoming viler than the degenerate seat of empire in the reign of Nero; it was "a cesspool of all the vices" where gambling dens and houses of prostitution were mushrooming in the stench of corruption.[5] In this portrayal, as in all classical republican narratives, expiring liberty was being reflected in the degradation of morals.

His response was to redouble his efforts to arouse, mobilize, and direct the people. He had opened the year by warning of actions by the municipal leaders to prohibit political association. Bailly and Lafayette he now targeted as heads of a new conspiracy to stifle the rights of citizens. "To destroy love of the homeland, to destroy the homeland itself and reestablish hideous despotism, they have to destroy all civic association and isolate citizens one from another." They were purportedly shutting down the Monarchical Club, Marat charged, but only as a cover for suppressing patriotic popular assemblies. Not that this reactionary club should be allowed to exist, he added. As an assembly of citizens, it could not legitimately be dissolved by an arbitrary act of authority. But its members were "evil citizens, enemies of the revolution, traitors to the homeland, and conspirators." Their meetings could be rightfully terminated by any patriotic friend of liberty, even to the extent of torching their meeting place.[6] For Marat, as for his enemies, freedom of assembly went only so far.

In the January spy trials, *L'Ami du peuple* had begun to sound the call for all good citizens to band together for their common defense by forming "a holy federation admitting only true friends of the homeland." Soon, it was urging the creation of a society of "Avengers of the Law." There were plenty of babbling societies in existence, the journal insisted. It was time now for action by a punitive association pledged to "pursue the punishment of all crimes attacking public or individual security and compromising the people's safety." Three patriotic deputies, Robespierre, Edmond-Louis-Alexis Dubois-Crancé, and Jean-François Rewbell, could be its founders, Marat thought, heading up a kind of inner directory of no more than twenty-five members required to present authentic proof of "enlightenment and civic spirit" and sign a written commitment to "pursue to the very extreme and without exception (apart from the king) every public functionary and subaltern agent who has twisted, flouted, subverted, or violated the laws." In effect, this new organization was to be a machine for the production and diffusion of denunciations. Led by wise, eloquent, independent men capable of facing up to wrongdoers, Marat predicted, it would soon earn the people's veneration as "an infallible guide" and "guardian angel." The nation would empower it against all the enemies of liberty. "The mere terror of its name would dissipate the legions of wrongdoers, traitors, and conspirators." It would constrain the agents of authority within the bounds of their duty, give force to the laws, and save the homeland.[7]

Despite Marat's repeated calls for the formation of this society of vigilantes, the idea went nowhere. Robespierre, for one, seems to have shown no sign of interest. In the meantime, The People's Friend was pushing a more effective plan for political mobilization. The prototype was the Cordelier Club, a transformation of the earlier district assembly that had sprung to his defense a year earlier. The municipal reform introduced by Jean-Nicolas Démeunier in May 1790 had been framed to break the power of the district assemblies by redistributing them into sections whose organization and activities were made subject to administrative surveillance and control. The former Cordeliers responded by reconstituting themselves as a radical political club, the Society of the Friends of the Rights of Man and of the Citizen, open to all citizens, active or passive, men or women, and eventually throughout the capital.

This was the model The People's Friend now proclaimed as a means of advancing populist politics, subverting the influence of those sections that had taken more conservative positions, and opening up the possibility of concerted popular action across the city. "Honor and glory, dear Marat," applauded a letter to *L'Ami du peuple* on 7 February 1791, signed "Garin, active citizen of the Champs-Elysées Section"; "you have restored life to the sections paralyzed by the deadly plan the infamous Démeunier got decreed, and by the traitorous regime of their committees. . . . Today almost all the sections of the capital have clubs formed by the elite of their citizens in the way you communicated to them. . . . These clubs can convoke the general assemblies in less than three hours, and the majority of them have called for permanent sessions to watch out for public safety in these days of danger when the enemies of the revolution seem determined to complete the destruction of the homeland."[8]

L'Orateur du peuple sounded the same note a few days later. "The fraternal societies of the sections, whose father you are, are multiplying every day," Fréron assured his collaborator. "The citizens are instructing themselves in their rights, their interests, and their duties. The rage of the enemies of liberty against these associations only proves their utility." Marat's response made clear that he saw these clubs as a kind of revolutionary avant-garde. "These fraternal societies formed of the elite of the citizens of each section will have all the advantages of the permanent districts that our municipal and national mandators stupidly flattered themselves on having destroyed forever," he declared. "I have resuscitated them." United, determined, and energetic, he promised, these agglutinations of activists would be free of quarrels, disputes, and chicanery. They would be "a school of continual instruction for all citizens." Passing from their club to their section, members would no longer be ignorant or duped. They would bring "views and an already formed opinion on the questions debated and push them necessarily in the direction of the general good." These happy effects were already evident in most of the sections of the capital, he maintained, "although it's scarcely a fortnight since the fraternal societies have been formed." To sustain this dynamic, he declared it essential that the societies consist only of good patriots, men untainted by association with the municipality or the old order, and that they be continually subject to public scrutiny ensuring the purity of their members. Tables of denunciation, publicly posted, would be the best means to achieve this result.[9]

The Cordeliers soon weighed in with their own salutation to their club's most notorious member, prompted apparently by word of his discouragement at the dismal prospect of ever securing liberty. Considering how much all patriots would lose if "he who has alone borne the glorious weight of defending the public . . . despaired of our liberty or stopped upholding it," they were convinced that his silence would be "a public calamity . . . , a universal bereavement and the most certain harbinger of the ruin of the empire." Accordingly, they determined on 12 February to offer The People's Friend "the testimony of their feelings, the expression of their sincere devotion, and their affectionate encouragement to hope better for the public good and continue to support its cause with the same zeal, energy and firmness." To this they added their assurance that all members of the club would "contribute by all their means, and with all their strength, even at risk of their life, to the security of his person, the propagation of his principles, and the spread of his patriotism."[10]

Marat responded in kind. If ever his patriotism should cool, he assured his fellow Cordeliers, he would hasten to rekindle it in their company. Martyrdom he again declared himself ready to embrace. "If I have to sacrifice to the salvation of the homeland a life whose every moment I consecrate to it, I am ready to seal with my blood the sincerity of my profession of faith."[11]

The Cordeliers' declaration of solidarity signaled a boost in Marat's popular recognition as he rode the wave of unrest in the early months of 1791. He was not averse to promoting his own popularity by avowals of his persecution and suffering, exaltation of his influence, protestations of his incorruptibility, and the publication of letters saluting or beseeching his aid against oppression. These flowed endlessly through the pages of *L'Ami du peuple*. Fréron's journal also maintained a constant barrage of praise for "Marat, our brother the prophet." "My compliments, dear Friend of the People, you have set the pace for patriotic writers, you have done more, you have thwarted a host of conspiracies, you have raised a great number of citizens to the level of the revolution," rhapsodized *L'Orateur du peuple* in one issue. "Honor and glory to you, our dear Marat," Fréron intoned. "You are the terror of the enemies of the homeland. Judge by their rage against you."[12]

Brandishing such testimonials, The People's Friend was ready to place himself at the head of the popular movement. By mid-March he was advertising the availability of entire collections of the four hundred issues of *L'Ami du peuple* published since its founding. They were now offered at a twenty-five percent discount from the original subscription price. "Liberty of the press is the sole safeguard of the people," he broadcast; "it can't be infringed without betraying the people. To me alone must wrongly accused citizens address themselves; my printer publishes nothing I don't guarantee. I am and must be responsible only to the tribunal of the public for the errors I may have innocently committed. I renew here my confession of faith, that I will not recognize, nor ever have, the competence of any other tribunal."[13]

DISCONTENTS AND DISORDERS

Fréron was not wrong in celebrating the rage directed against his ally. If the pace of radical journalism accelerated, so did the denunciations of "the incendiary Marat," this "cannibal," this "tiger turned to carnage," "this goddamned scoundrel." So, indeed, did official efforts to prevent the circulation of *L'Ami du peuple* and arrest those invoking it. The monarchist Montlosier may have been joking on 8 February when he suggested that the National Assembly forward for circulation in *L'Ami du peuple* a citizens' address supporting election of priests. Nonetheless, the authorities were unnerved by mounting popular disorder and their perception of Marat's role in inciting it. The pattern had become clear as the year began. Altercations between smugglers and customs guards at the barriers surrounding Paris were far from new, but in the early weeks of 1791 they had begun to take on a sharper political edge. News of bloodshed in the outlying village of La Chapelle on 24 January had resounded throughout the capital. Several people had been killed in this altercation, either by the customs police or the National Guard or some combination thereof.[14] Marat, among others, made much of this event, blaming the violence on thugs receiving payment the Monarchical Club offered in the guise of handouts for the hungry and unemployed. Resentments flamed against the monarchists as a result, and especially against the president of their club, the former comte de Clermont-Tonnerre, whose house a crowd soon placed under siege. The attack unnerved many among the conservative deputies, whose speeches began to betray fears for their own personal safety.

The morning of 27 January thus found Bailly careening around Paris in fear of crowd agitation. Accompanied by a cavalry detachment, he headed first to the Sèvres customs barrier on the news that officials were being overwhelmed there by smugglers. Order had been restored by the time of his arrival. Learning on his return into the city that people were gathering outside Clermont-Tonnerre's house, he chose the better part of valor and decided not to show up—his anxiety that his appearance would aggravate the crowd a telling acknowledgment of popular animus against him. Before long, though, even as he was also hearing reports of trouble in the ever-simmering faubourg Saint-Antoine, he was informed of the National Assembly's concern for Clermont-Tonnerre's property and opted to give that location priority after all. Finding the situation there calm, he reversed course, rushing instead to the faubourg Saint-Antoine in time to discover a large National Guard contingent struggling to save from an angry crowd "a man denounced in the pages of *L'Ami du peuple*." The victim was one Kabers, fingered by The People's Friend as a Lafayette spy. The man had been cruelly treated and was close to death, Bailly informed the deputies, and it had taken all the courage and firmness of the municipal officers to rescue him from the popular fury. The mayor's report prompted renewed demand for a decree against incendiary writings and all the abuses held to result from the liberty of the press.[15]

Not to be outdone in attacking freedom of speech, Marat's old enemy Malouet weighed in at the Assembly the following day to reiterate his own call for press repression. This time, he was impassioned by a heated debate over the reciprocal relationship between the nation's external and internal security. Presenting the draft of a decree to reinforce national defenses, Alexandre de Lameth had stressed that popular agitation was being fueled by rumors of impending counterrevolutionary invasion. Mirabeau had deployed his immense influence in the same vein. "Popular alarms" were being ignited by ambitious and fractious men for their own purposes, the stentorian orator had acknowledged. But were they not fueled also by "the exaggerated distrust that has long agitated minds, that delays the moment of peace, aggravates evils, and becomes a source of anarchy when it ceases to be useful to liberty?" We fear external enemies and forget the one that ravages the interior of the realm, Mirabeau had continued; it was time to constrain popular unrest. "Almost everywhere the public functionaries chosen by the people are at their posts; its rights are thus being exercised; it remains for it to fulfill its duties. Let it keep up its surveillance of its mandataries while honoring them with its confidence, and let the turbulent force of the multitude yield to the calmer power of the law."[16]

Malouet seized on these remarks. Before the proposed defense legislation could be brought to a vote, he demanded immediate action to safeguard public order from "the tumultuous influence of the multitude on public functions, on the deliberations of administrative bodies, or on those of the people's mandataries." Mirabeau, he contended, had wisely said that the people, having chosen its delegates and placed them in all the positions of public authority, should now let them peaceably exercise their functions. Popular surveillance of the authorities was necessary, Malouet conceded in response to heckling, but only by constitutional means. Otherwise, "the result of this pretended surveillance, exercised individually and tumultuously, is the anarchy we are now seeing."[17]

As a storm erupted from the left of the Assembly at this comment,

Malouet was shouted down. In the spirit of Lameth's proposal for enhanced national defense, the deputies proceeded to decree the formation of additional military reserve units and increased production of muskets to equip them. Unwilling to be silenced on this matter, though, Malouet countered immediately with a pamphlet condemning popular agitation. By Marat's account, 300,000 copies of this *Continuation of M. Malouet's Opinion on the Causes of Internal Disorders and of General Agitation* were delivered free to the peddlers, who were given an additional 12 livres gross to sell them. (Each peddler was also assigned an escort to ensure that these precious pages were not dumped wholesale, ending up in the bakers' shops as wrapping paper!) Two issues of *L'Ami du peuple* were needed to rebut this rabid attack on popular activism. Not for the first time, an exchange between Marat and Malouet revealed the symbiotic relationship between these political enemies bent on mutually assured denunciation.[18]

"Why this furious multitude that accuses, that tears to pieces the innocent and the guilty?" Malouet demanded of the National Assembly in his extended rant against the Revolution. "Why are properties and persons in danger as soon as it pleases an assassin to provoke a crowd . . . ? Why do you let each section of the people exercise all the public powers, when you have defined, divided, and distributed all the powers?" Having smashed what was merely defective, Malouet argued, the deputies had acquiesced in the continuation of something more monstrous. They had mistakenly delayed firm action against popular disorder, forgetting that no one was free or secure without the clear presence of force for the law. As a result, he warned, the arbitrary authority of the Old Regime was being replicated and directed, with greater excess and fury than ever, against suspected enemies of the new. Brigands styling themselves patriots were acting with impunity. How could the deputies accept an order of things offering continual anxiety and a blade suspended over their heads? "You're waiting . . . to put a stop to discontents and disorders until they are no longer happening, until Marat and company have no one left to have slaughtered, until the multitude has become more enlightened and circumspect in its judgments and ends its encroachments itself, until the clubs notify us that crimes are no longer necessary, and the dove bearing the green branch emerges from the ark of the Revolution!"[19]

This was a fine dream, Malouet lamented, or rather an appalling one. In the meantime, he saw anxiety universal and evils multiplying throughout a troubled realm. "No one is free, no one secure, no one sure of the morrow, neither the oppressors nor the oppressed, because no legal force constrains those who can only be contained by force." People had been safe under the old order from brigandage, arson, and assassination, he maintained; no paid scribbler could then calumniate his victims and hand them over to the fury of the populace. One could be vexed by a powerful man but didn't have to fear the proscription of ten thousand clubs, to say nothing of all the cafés and motion-makers of sections throughout France. There had been only one Bastille in the old days, not many, and *lettres de cachet* had been beyond the power of all the municipalities of the realm. Now unconstitutional assemblies of the Paris sections convened in daily session; they deliberated, decreed, denounced, governed. While honest men awaited the summons of the law, intriguers were anticipating and outbidding it, mobilizing the unemployed, the starving, and "that class of men the Romans wisely called the proletarians." For 6 francs, in Malouet's estimate, anyone could now be set upon by a crowd of assassins.[20]

Marat responded in passionate kind, with a denunciation of an unrepresentative National Assembly, a defense of popular insurrection, and his own pop history of "the mysteries of the revolution." King and people had united to destroy the privileged orders, he contended in this thumbnail account of events since 1789, but while the people had sought thereafter to recover its rights, the monarch had dreamed only of placing it again under the yoke. To this end, Louis XVI had corrupted the people's representatives, who had conspired with him to render illusory the Declaration of Rights and eviscerate the work of the constitution. Philosophers, zealous defenders of the people, had now sounded the alarm against the attacks of these traitorous and conspiratorial deputies, prompting the present resistance to the latter's dark designs and the frequent uprisings against their tyrannical orders.

In this history, The People's Friend himself figured large. It was his own fury, he claimed, that had woken the capital to the dangers represented by the spies and assassins in the pay of Bailly and Lafayette. At his summons, societies infiltrated by these villains had roused themselves to purge them, and the audacious maneuvers of the authorities to retaliate against his printer had stirred the people from its lethargy. The efforts of the general's hirelings to terrorize the citizens had opened the public's eyes. Their repressive massacres of the population had spread general alarm, awakening the people to the dangers threatening it. Finally, the clubs formed from the sections, composed at his urging from the elite of the citizens, had quickened the municipality to political life. Their activity, zeal, and energy had at last disrupted the insidious designs of the Revolution's enemies. Malouet's jeremiad was the response. Marat deemed it worth answering precisely because it expressed all the specious arguments the enemies of the Revolution were deploying to delude the people and lull it to sleep.

In this indictment, then, Malouet was nothing but a "perfidious hypocrite," silent about counterrevolutionary excesses (witness Nancy), railing against the just fury of a people tired of the eternal machinations of its enemies, and avid for vengeance against the populace he had deserted and betrayed. "Why spread alarm like this, sighing for the re-establishment of despotism?" Marat demanded. "What are a few drops of blood distilled to save the people when compared with the torrents shed by a despot's caprice?" What of the rivers of blood unleashed for centuries by so many villains disputing the throne, or in the disastrous conflicts ignited by the mad ambition of a monstrous oppressor? What of the insane wars undertaken by rulers long glorified—the Charlemagnes, the Louis IXs, the Louis XIIs, these evil princes who laid waste the earth so many times, filling the world with their sound and fury? What! All could be well when a despot sends half a million underlings to ravage provinces and slaughter inhabitants, but all is lost and a land is criminally sullied when an entire people does away with a few villains to establish the reign of justice and liberty? "Vile slave, grasp then that if the nation must assure its happiness by the bloody sacrifice of all the formerly privileged castes, that wouldn't be too great a price. It would only ever be a small evil for a great good." Did Malouet long to have nothing to fear from the people? The secret was simple. "Be a patriot and urge your accomplices to do the same."[21] The threat of popular retribution was Marat's counterpoint to Malouet's fearmongering.

Paris saw more dramatic agitation a few weeks later. On 28 February it was General Lafayette's turn to fishtail between incidents of popular disorder. Mobilized by news that an additional prison was being constructed at the château of Vincennes, several hundred inhabitants of the activist faubourg Saint-Antoine marched there to demolish this new Bastille. Their action was already under way by the time the National Guard arrived to make arrests. In the meantime, Lafayette learned that another altercation had broken out at the Tuileries palace. He raced back there to find a group of former aristocrats intending to help the king escape engaged, along with the palace guards protecting them, in a violent face-off against a crowd determined to prevent them from doing so. More arrests were made before the National Guard imposed order. By Marat's account, the march to Versailles had been provoked by Mirabeau and Lafayette to divert popular attention from the issue of preventing the flight of the royal family, while the confrontation at the Tuileries had been a triumph of the citizens in preventing such a flight from occurring. His principles were vindicated in this affair, he maintained. Even so, he warned, a perfidious deputy, Isaac-René-Guillaume Le Chapelier, was struggling in the National Assembly that very same day "to close all ears to the voice of *L'Ami du peuple*, to make it possible to betray the nation without fear of popular indignation, to paralyze and dissolve all the patriotic associations."[22]

LE CHAPELIER STRIKES BACK

From Marat's catalog of the people's enemies, Le Chapelier now leaped to the fore. The legislation this lion of the Constitutional Committee presented over the following months offered a hardcore vision of the democratic principles of propertied individualism enunciated in 1789. It modeled a society of men acting individually and a nation of citizens represented collectively, their interactions mediated by the impartial mechanisms of the constitution, the law, the ballot, and the market. It opened a campaign to eliminate collective social movements and partial political associations from a civic landscape in which citizens properly pursued their interests as individuals, subject to laws made by and for them as a nation through the institution of a representative body alone capable of expressing their sovereign will. It opposed sovereignty represented to sovereignty particularized, popularized, and embodied.

Thus Le Chapelier, like Sieyès, was an apostle of radical representation in a Hobbesian sense. In his conception, the nation truly became one and sovereign only as transformed by representation from a multiplicity of individuals into a unitary body. Its political identity was constituted, and its sovereign will expressed, only in and by the collective person of its assembled deputies (as it had once been constituted from heterogeneous elements only in and by the individual person of the king). As a result, the successive decrees he presented to the National Assembly aimed at the institution of a political world uncluttered by popular noise, an abstract space in which the deliberations of the National Assembly could proceed, and its sovereign decisions be made, without contamination from populist intervention.

Consistent with these views, the first draft decree Le Chapelier presented on behalf of the Constitutional Committee on 28 February was a declaration of war against popular politics. He opened his remarks that day by taking up a theme already familiar from earlier debates, one that would reverberate throughout the deliberations of this Constituent Assembly to its very last days. Disorders were inevitable in the stormy passage from political servitude to a free constitution, he allowed, but with the advent of liberty must come order and peace. It was time to teach the people that the noblest and happiest being on earth is "a free man who resists all men's arbitrary wills and never resists the law; who is the more compliant with its salutary decrees in that they preserve him from oppression by subjecting him to the sole rules of reason and justice." This free man understands "that he can have no liberty where the law does not reign with undivided sway and is not religiously observed . . . ; that the need for peace becoming one day the most imperious of sentiments, he must resolve to choose between slavery groveling under the tyranny of the strongest and free submission to the general will."

The ensuing elaboration of this idea was striking in the way it forged the soft iron of physiocratic reason into the hard steel of Rousseauian political will. "Despotism was right to say that society can only be maintained by obedience . . . ," Le Chapelier hazarded; "but its ferocious pride distorted its application of this maxim. It wanted the people to bend a servile head beneath the yoke of violence and caprice, and it is to the law alone that the people must submit a free, proud head." Upholding respect for the law as a necessary condition of freedom, he set forth as fundamental that the sovereignty inhering in the nation as a whole was exercised only through its representatives; that since this sovereignty was inalienable, unitary, and indivisible no particular body or section of the people shared in its exercise; that every citizen without exception was subject to it. In accordance with these principles, the legislation he proposed required that order and respectful silence be maintained in all public tribunals, and that disruption of the deliberations of municipal administrative assemblies, resistance against the execution of the law, and violence or incitement of popular agitation against public officials be declared offenses subject to rigorous punishment.[23]

Deputies on the left of the assembly, Pétion and Robespierre in particular, were quick to challenge this parsing of the principle of national sovereignty. Since the general will is composed of all the particular wills, Pétion reasoned, each section of the nation expressing its particular will thereby participates in the exercise of sovereignty. There followed a confused debate, in effect a reprise of 1789 deliberations over sovereignty and representation, leading the majority of the deputies to conclude that statements of abstract general principle could only mystify and disorient the people. In the meantime, Démeunier offered an alternative formulation, denying participation in the exercise of sovereignty to any section of the nation while allowing the right of petition to "each citizen individually." This last phrase was then recast in the course of debate to confer on "each citizen . . . the right to petition, to be employed in accordance with the forms that are or will be decreed."[24]

The People's Friend greeted this legislation with derision. How, he demanded, could a contemptible majority of trumped-up and overwhelmingly corrupt deputies dare to command respect in tribunals and popular assemblies? "Hearing them bickering, applauding, holding one another in contempt, booing, jumping from their seats, stamping their feet, running to the middle of the chamber, grinding their teeth, thrashing about, shouting abuse, threatening one another, sticking it to one another, talking of sabers and pistols, what sensible man wouldn't think himself in a bar or a guardhouse?" Mocking these clowns, The People's Friend dressed them down. "Gentlemen! You expect poor artisans, poor workers, poor laborers without practice, knowledge, or education, to conduct themselves more decently than fine lords like you, so knowledgeable, so well raised, so well born, who know all the fine points of Gallic civility, the refinements of court decorum, and because a poor devil indignant at the sight of public functionaries committing atrocities is unable to suppress the feelings of an honest and sensitive soul, you send him to prison to calm down. You don't even think about this unless it's to claim the privilege of acting indecently as a prerogative of sovereignty."[25]

It was no more than a linguistic trick, in Marat's view, to characterize the collective declarations, decisions, addresses, and protests of popular societies as sectional infringements on a unitary sovereign will that could be exercised only through representation. The aim was just to paralyze and destroy the patriotic societies that were rallying against the Revolution's enemies. These associations were not claiming a share in the exercise of sovereignty, he insisted, *pace* Pétion and Robespierre. They were asserting an incontestable right of surveillance over representatives enacting laws that were in any case subject to eventual ratification by the nation as a whole. They could properly assemble to deliberate, propose, advise, and call for action. But the conviction that sovereignty was embodied in the people left him unwilling at this point to allow it to be shared by particular bodies, even those claiming the right to speak for the people.

More to the point, Marat emphasized, when it came to moments of political crisis popular societies could exercise the right to resist oppression sanctioned by the Declaration of the Rights of Man and of the Citizen. Faced with attacks against liberty and public security, the machinations of the Revolution's enemies, and the threat of conspirators scheming to destroy the homeland, they had the right to be "not only deliberating societies but acting, repressing, punishing, massacring societies." And they could do so as soon as they had exhausted all legal ways to repress the public enemies and contain authorities uniting to trick the people, lull it to sleep at the edge of the abyss, and achieve its ruin. This was "just the pure and simple exercise of the right to resist oppression and look out for one's security, a right that nature has given all men at birth, all governments have recognized, and the Assembly itself has solemnly consecrated."[26]

As for individual petitions, what a charming resource, what a fine privilege the deputies were now conferring upon the citizenry! The people had possessed this privilege under the most absolute of despots, Marat protested. Had so many sacrifices been made over the past two years just to retain it? At least, the enemies of liberty had not then formed, as they did now, "a chain of conspirators sworn to restore despotism and tyrannize us." At least, those in search of justice were not then, as they were now, sent back to their oppressors.

The argument, alas, was soon moot. Within weeks, at Le Chapelier's urging, the National Assembly would move to place more radical restrictions on the right to petition it had just so ambivalently upheld.[27]

TAINTED GLORY

On 16 April, Marat addressed a letter to his watchmaker friend Breguet, then living in London. It expressed deep discouragement. "All is lost, my good friend, the gawking Parisians are only made for slavery. . . . We're on the eve of a catastrophe and flight to a foreign land will be all that's left to the friends of liberty. Happy will be those who can get to the country where you are, and where you are bored. God knows how! How true it is that men can never be happy and life is just a tissue of griefs and sorrows. But I'm not preaching here. To hell with that occupation. I should never have dreamed of it."[28]

The People's Friend had cause for despondency at that moment, both political and personal. The preceding issues of *L'Ami du peuple* had been filled with his angry analyses of the militarization of the National Guard conceived by Lafayette and now being pushed through the National Assembly by "the Huguenot hypocrite," Rabaut. Section by section, clause by clause, Marat reiterated his attacks upon legislation he saw as transforming a citizen militia into a standing army of active citizens conscripted to impose order upon a disarmed and disenfranchised populace. This "essentially obedient public force" could not fail to become an instrument of despotism, he warned a mindless people. "Employing the very instruments of liberty to reestablish despotism is the masterpiece of politics."[29]

Personally, too, Marat was worried about money. He had entrusted Breguet with some valuables—his own Breguet watch and a precious box of some kind—to sell on his behalf in England. Had these items been peddled, he wondered in his letter. Could the proceeds, up to 200 louis or more, be conveyed to him in Paris by an indirect arrangement (between their common English friend, the watchmaker John Arnold, and Breguet's Paris agent) that would permit disbursement in the vanishing specie? This could save the nine, ten, even twelve percent that discount bankers could demand for paying out in assignats. "We're on the eve of the most hideous depreciation," he reminded Breguet, "one no longer sees a silver crown in circulation."[30]

What if the valuables had not yet found a buyer? It would be better to leave them with Arnold in London, Marat opined, since it would be pointless to return them to Paris only for him to carry them back to London, "where I must be in less than three weeks." What is this? To London in three weeks? Why this abrupt resolve to quit the scene of the French Revolution after so many sacrifices to it? The letter suggests an immediate cause. The Parisians, Marat laments, "are flying to meet their chains: their extravagances at the death of Mirabeau have made the friends of liberty lose the least glimmer of hope."[31]

Mirabeau's death was a crucial factor here. Marat had been pushed from discouragement to despair by the dramatic public response to news of that event on 2 April. His own sheer joy at this sudden demise was initially heightened by the rumor that Mirabeau had been poisoned by his own accomplices. But elation had turned to dismay as expressions of loss seeped through the sections. "You are lamenting him as a hero who sacrificed himself for you, as the savior of the homeland," Marat reproached the people. "Will you then always be deaf to the voice of prudence, and will you always forfeit the public good as a result of your blindness? Riqueti's life was stained by a thousand crimes. . . . Beware of prostituting your incense; save your tears for your honest defenders."[32]

Marat's dismay turned into outright disgust as the National Assembly voted to commemorate the achievements of this, its most treacherous member, by authorizing transformation of the still uncompleted church of Sainte-Geneviève into a temple of secular immortality to hold his remains. *Aux grands hommes, la patrie reconnaissante!* Under this banner, it was decreed, Mirabeau would lie first and foremost among the great men henceforth to be deemed worthy of the nation's gratitude.

Marat was beside himself at this news. "I won't dwell here on the ridiculousness of an assembly of base, sycophantic, vile and inept men constituting themselves judges of immortality . . . ," he protested. "How do persons covered with opprobrium have the effrontery to declare themselves dispensers of glory!" They would only open their temple of civic virtue to men like themselves. "Judge by the way they've started. Here's a double-dealer, a fraud, a traitor, a conspirator placed ahead of benefactors of humanity, defenders of the oppressed citizen, martyrs of liberty. What man of goodwill would want his ashes to rest in the same place?" This tainted honor could only belong to a Le Chapelier, a Démeunier, a Voidel, a Malouet, a Bouillé, a Motier, and other villains of that ilk! "May the propitious heaven answer my prayers in putting them there at the earliest moment!"[33]

All this was intensely personal. It was about glory—glory accorded, of course, but also glory denied. How painful the moment must have been for a man so long desperate for renown. He had felt himself cheated of recognition he had claimed in the scientific sphere by charlatans wielding spurious authority as academicians. Now he had to witness glory accorded in the political realm—to one he deemed least worthy of it—by contemptible charlatans posturing as legitimate representatives of the nation. "Today the treasonous Assembly is profiting skillfully from the death of one of its most gangrenous members to mislead public opinion . . . and to cover with the glitzy honors conferred on him the fatal decrees he got passed," Marat wrote on 6 April. "Take a look at the conscript fathers shamelessly constituting themselves arbiters of renown and distributors of certificates of immortality. Not content to have usurped the rights of the present generation, they are also usurping those of future ones."[34]

The consequences could be predicted, Marat was sure. "To deserve well of the homeland is to consecrate to it one's intellect, one's works, one's waking hours, one's liberty, one's life. It's to make great sacrifices for it, to seek no recompense but the pleasure and glory of serving it." Corrupt deputies, it was now clear, could not be expected to honor such service! Instead of true benefactors of the homeland, the likes of Descartes ("famous dreamer") and Voltaire ("adroit plagiarist") had already been proposed to join Mirabeau in the new Pantheon. Soon this temple to patriotism would become a monument of "national ostentation." There would be tired busts of all the illustrious personages of the age of Louis XIV, the Corneilles, the Racines, the Boileaus, the La Fontaines, the Turennes, the Vendômes, the Vaubans, and so on. These would be followed, in turn, by stolid academicians, public functionaries, and valets of the court such as Lafayette, Bailly, and Bouillé. Eventually places in the national temple would be acquired by the kind of corruption and clandestine dealing that had governed access to place and position under the Old Regime. This would usher in the senatorial and academic rabble. Villains gorged on the blood of the people—men like Le Chapelier, Target, Thouret, Condorcet, Démeunier, and others—would be raised to the rank of its benefactors. What honest person would want his ashes to lie alongside men of such kind? "Rousseau and Montesquieu would blush to see themselves in such bad company, and the Friend of the People would be inconsolable at it."

The point was clear. With his pride lacerated and his passion for glory frustrated, Marat saw the Pantheon as a monument to his own personal defeat. "If ever liberty was established in France and some legislature, remembering what I have done for the homeland, was tempted to grant me a place in Saint-Geneviève, I would protest here at the top of my voice against this bloody insult. Yes, never to die would be a hundred times better than having to dread so cruel an outrage." No wonder his letter urged Breguet to establish himself in England, where he could make a good marriage and amass great wealth. "As for your friend, he has nothing left to hope for but to vegetate in obscurity."[35]

The trip to England evaporated when the political situation in Paris changed unexpectedly. But Camille Desmoulins apparently got wind of the plan, broadcasting in his *Révolutions de France et de Brabant* that "the intrepid Marat . . . , seeing the excessive honors raining on Mirabeau's coffin, is succumbing to discouragement and requesting a passport to exercise the apostasy of liberty in a less corrupt nation. After leading so troubled and laborious a life underground, he is leaving, penniless and poor, which is the best response to his enemies." *Apostasy?* This was undoubtedly a typographical error for *apostolate* (and it was revised to that effect in some late printings of Desmoulins's journal), but Marat was incensed. His response severed a relationship that had been deteriorating for months as Desmoulins had shown increasing ambivalence toward the inflammatory political style and radical positions forged in *L'Ami du peuple*. It was easy to be extravagant in one's radicalism when one was hidden away in a cellar, Desmoulins had sniped, even as he protested that Marat was his hero. The People's Friend offered "great truths, observations of an astonishing exactitude," Desmoulins had allowed, but to reach them one had to set aside "the exaggerations, the fake facts for which one would normally reproach him." Marat was without a doubt the journalist who had best served the Revolution, Desmoulins had observed, "despite the falsifications with which [his] journal is too often filled."[36]

Marat's rejoinder, when it came, was furious. With this loose talk about a passport, he charged, Desmoulins was irresponsibly alerting the authorities to his potential plans and escalating the risk of his capture. "You can imagine the fate they're reserving for me. What can I expect from them but to be thrown into a burning oven if they catch me secretly, and chopped into pieces by their henchmen if they arrest me publicly?" There followed a cascade of Desmoulins's slights toward him over the years, culminating in the implication of his cowardice in hiding underground. "O Camille! I knew you as thoughtless, superficial, and frivolous; but how to imagine that in a moment of pique you would renounce all decency?"

How could The People's Friend be smeared with apostasy, he demanded, he who had never varied for a moment in his principles, had sacrificed his health, his peace, and his liberty to the homeland for twenty-eight months, burying himself alive and defending the rights of the people for a year with his head on the block? "Young man, learn that, after truth and justice, liberty has always been my favorite goddess, that I have always sacrificed at her altars, even under the reign of despotism, and that I had already suffered for her before you even knew her name. Open the work I published in London in 1774 under the title, *The Chains of Slavery*, read the preface, and you'll see that I played the same role in England sixteen years ago that I have been playing in France since the revolution. . . . One day, you'll learn the results of that bold undertaking. Let it be enough for you today to see that, in whatever country I find myself, humanity, justice and liberty will always have in me an apostle and a martyr."[37]

Never one to let go easily, Marat returned to the charge in the following issue of *L'Ami du peuple*, this time to rebut Desmoulins's accusation that the journal was proliferating fake news. "For a journal of news like yours, Camille, an accusation like this would surely be serious," he explained; "but for mine, a political journal, it amounts to nothing. How do you know that what you take to be false news isn't a text I needed in order to ward off some fatal blow and reach my goal? Is it for you, devoid of ideas, to claim to get me back into line with your petty conceptions? To judge men, you always need positive facts, very clear and very precise; for me, their inaction or their silence on great occasions is often enough. To believe in the existence of a conspiracy, you need judicial proofs; I only need the general direction of affairs, the relationships among enemies of liberty, the comings and goings of certain agents of power." Desmoulins aimed to please, Marat castigated him; he constantly changed his mind, now praising Lafayette or "Saint Mirabeau," now blaming them. "My poor Camille, the obsession to be witty torments you so powerfully that you sacrifice even the fear of appearing crazy to the pleasure of appearing amusing, and you prefer being liberty's clown to being its apostle."[38]

More fundamentally, Marat emphasized, Desmoulins had to understand that the point of press freedom was not to enlighten public functionaries, convert the henchmen of despotism into patriots, reform the committees of the National Assembly, or regenerate corrupt agents of the old regime. To the contrary, it was destined to instruct citizens in their rights, and to inspire the desire to enjoy them, the courage to defend them, the daring to avenge them. It existed to expose the crimes of the people's representatives and bring them to justice; to teach citizens to resist tyrannical laws and troops to disobey arbitrary orders; to break all the sinews of despotism; to rescue the victims of oppression. "This is how I have used it to this day," Marat insisted, "and I dare to believe that I have not wasted my time. There are very few great events since the fall of the Bastille that I have not prepared, and how many have I not provoked myself?" The French were not free yet, he acknowledged, nor could they expect to be so soon, since they had not begun the Revolution by wisely exterminating the guiltiest accomplices of the old regime and constraining the others by terror. Nonetheless, without liberty of the press, "the bloody scenes of St. Bartholomew's Day" would have been renewed and "the gore of slaughtered victims would still be steaming in our public squares. So, stop insulting the liberty of the press, feckless man, you don't understand its benefits." Desmoulins was being cut down to size here. "For heaven's sake, Camille, content yourself with being unable to serve the homeland, and don't try to destroy the good I'm working to do for it."[39]

HOLY RESISTANCE, RESOUNDING ACTIONS

The discouragement so palpable in Marat's letter to Breguet was rapidly and unexpectedly alleviated by striking popular action. The very day after the letter was written—Palm Sunday, 17 April—the Cordeliers issued an outspoken *Decision of the Cordeliers Club Regarding the King's Communion*. It disclosed that Louis XVI had participated that very morning in a Mass celebrated by priests harbored in the Tuileries palace who were refusing to swear the oath to the Civil Constitution of the Clergy, even going so far as to receive communion from the hands of one of them in the presence of Lafayette and Bailly. It charged the monarch, as "the first functionary of the state," with breaking the constitutional law he had sworn to maintain, with justifying rebellion, and with exposing the nation to the horrors of discord and civil war. It condemned the mayor and the general for complicity in unconstitutional acts they were charged to repress. It summoned all good citizens to unite against this new effort of a cabal hostile to the nation's rights and happiness.[40]

Posted on walls all over Paris and widely reprinted, this call to political arms ricocheted around the city producing remarkable results. The very next day, a crowd rallied in the courtyard of the Tuileries palace to halt the king's carriage as he was leaving for the château of Saint-Cloud. Ostensibly the royal trip was to observe Easter there (though, in effect, it saved the king from taking a public Paschal communion in the capital from a priest who had sworn allegiance to the newly nationalized church). But many Parisians had been drawn to suspect, in line with Marat's warnings, that this departure from the capital would be the first leg in a flight that would take the rebellious monarch out of the country. Ordered by Lafayette to disperse the crowd, men of the National Guard mutinied in refusal. Despite the general's insistence that Louis was at liberty to leave, the king and the royal family were forced by the crowd to return to what had now clearly become their prison. Lafayette responded by announcing his resignation, perhaps in embarrassment but possibly, as Marat charged, in a ruse to regain the support of his troops.

The People's Friend was quick to applaud this crowd action. "Oh Parisians! You would have been the executioners of three million of your brothers if you had been foolish enough to let him flee your walls," he rejoiced on 20 April. "This hypocritical prince in revolt against his sovereign, shamelessly and remorselessly declaring himself its most mortal enemy," would have been back with an army to massacre the friends of liberty and return the nation to its chains. By his own deed, the monarch had exposed the lies his defenders had deployed to mislead the nation for fifteen months. Mindless citizens were now obliged to recognize the truth of charges that had been deemed criminal as they came from Marat's pen. But vindication was less than sweet. How long it had taken, he growled. "How long will you insult the only one of your defenders who knew how to judge your mandataries, your agents, the only one who never for an instant stopped watching out for you, the only one who has immolated himself for your safety?"[41]

In the more detailed account of this event that followed, *L'Ami du peuple* broadcast the humiliation inflicted on Lafayette by his troops' refusal to obey the order to let the king pass. The journal also congratulated the people on finally recognizing the logic of its political diagnoses. "Citizens, you have thus understood that the representatives of the nation, the king, the general, and the head of the municipality have been rendered unworthy of your confidence by their treason, and that you remain sole judges of what your safety demands." The crowd had done well in preventing the king's departure, it proclaimed, and so had the National Guard. But (by a logic now well established) Marat's praise for the people quickly turned into his own self-acclaim as its prophet. "Oh Frenchmen! If ever I have deserved well of you, it is for having been the first to unmask your unworthy representatives and to have covered them with opprobrium in unmasking their turpitude . . . , the first to destroy the superstitious respect you had for the monarch's orders and his person . . . , the first to preach resistance to fateful decrees. Behold holy resistance to legal repression now being consecrated by resounding actions. It has just covered with glory the soldiers of liberty whose blind obedience rendered them until today the alguazils of the despot."[42]

As if stung by Marat's praise, though, the National Guard quickly returned to the path of political obedience. Urging its commander to withdraw his resignation, it resumed the task of repressing popular activism that Lafayette demanded of it. Marat, for his part, returned to the task of denouncing Lafayette, urging the guardsmen to resist the authoritarianism of this new Cromwell. "My bottle of ink is not yet used up," he warned the general on 25 April before devoting several issues of his journal to a lengthy denunciation of this false patriot who continued to celebrate the sovereignty of the people while doing all he could to destroy it. Convinced at this point that Lafayette was part of the conspiracy to spirit Louis XVI from the capital, he maintained his unsparing attacks on the general throughout the following weeks, fueling political crisis from his apparently bottomless inkwell. "O Marat, our friend, our prophet, no you're not a man, you're an angel, a god, the savior of the homeland," proclaimed one letter to *L'Ami du peuple* in appreciation of these denunciations.[43]

Louis XVI spent the next few days trying to convince the National Assembly that his exercise of executive power required a demonstration of his freedom to leave the city as he pleased. Jean-Paul Marat spent them insisting that the king remain in his palace as the people demanded. Things had changed, he warned the monarch on 22 April. "Refrain from talk of agitators, or of the misguided multitude. Learn at last, as a rule of your conduct, that when the inhabitants of a city as immense as Paris unite against the prince, and his own lackeys are reduced to silence, the will of these inhabitants is the will of the nation itself. It's your sovereign, Sire, who forbids you to quit the city's walls."[44] Marat had earlier insisted that no particular body of the people could claim to express the sovereign national will. He was beginning to change his mind.

To buttress the point, *L'Ami du peuple* summoned citizens the following day to surround the Tuileries palace indefinitely to prevent the royal family from leaving. "They say the king wants to leave tomorrow morning and that all the conspirators have taken their measures to carry him off by force . . . if the people opposes his departure again," the journal reported on 24 April. "Empty dreams! The king would deserve to be treated as a madman if he exposed himself to new troubles. Let him be assured that we will not let him flee. . . . The king is the declared enemy of the nation; care for the public safety and our own preservation imposes upon us an imperious law to keep the royal family hostage." As for the accomplices conspiring on the monarch's behalf, the journal invited them to remember the unhappy fates of Launay, Bertier, and Foulon, infamous victims of popular rage in July 1789.[45]

With the king denied permission to leave the city, his advisers changed tactics. To ease the political crisis and pacify the deputies while plans for royal flight were being finalized, they allowed his foreign minister, the former comte de Montmorin, to share with the National Assembly a communiqué sent to French ambassadors throughout Europe. The letter charged the diplomats to reassure foreign courts that the king had freely accepted the Revolution and sworn to uphold a constitution that annihilated abuses, regenerated royal power, and left him free and happy among his fellow citizens. The National Assembly responded by sending a deputation to the palace to express unctuous gratitude. *L'Ami du peuple* reacted by denouncing the letter as a sham (which, indeed, it was: word soon leaked out that surreptitious counter-letters repudiating its contents were sent simultaneously to foreign governments). The king was ready to leave, the journal blared on April 30, troops were at the ready to support his exit, carnage would result if it were opposed, civil war was imminent. "Sleep, sleep at the edge of the abyss, stupid Parisians, and wait to snap out of your lethargy until the sound of trumpets announces the despot Louis XVI's manifesto and the murdering cannon arrives to batter your walls. A few more days and the fatal bomb will detonate the machinery of death."[46]

A BATTLE FOR THE STREETS

The drama of the Easter crisis opened weeks of political agitation in the streets of Paris. Protestations of popular societies, ongoing conflicts over the posting of competing placards, and rumors of radical plots and counter-revolutionary conspiracies were met by unremitting efforts at repression.[47] Fearing the loss of their authority to maintain public order, panicky departmental and city administrators called on the National Assembly on 26 April to take urgent action. It was essential in their view to prevent postings emanating from "audacious men whose public provocations excite violence against persons or properties, and who preach, with factious enthusiasm, disobedience to the laws and revolt against the constitutional authorities." In the administrators' definition of the situation, enemies of the constitution were counting on an oppressed people's distrust and the inflammation of its patriotism to create anarchy. Time and enlightenment would doubtless dissipate these frightful agitations, they allowed, but the effect might well come too late.

The administrative authorities disclaimed any desire to infringe upon the liberty of expression, this "sacred fire that must be religiously preserved." They acknowledged that its "salutary flame must purify all ideas, all opinions, all sentiments." But they decried abuse of this liberty to incite citizens to criminal action. "One of the most powerful causes of our ills," it had to be punished. A cacophony of addresses, declarations, and proclamations was polluting public space and confounding administrative order, they protested. The right of petition could not be construed as allowing toleration of conflicting claims to power. Official communications of the constitutionally established authorities had to possess a clearly recognizable character to distinguish them from "those alien to the public order." Actions or opinions of individuals, clubs, or other particular associations could not be allowed to mimic the typographical form or discursive majesty of the law.[48]

It took the Constitutional Committee a couple of weeks to draft legislation intended to eradicate popular protest. Le Chapelier presented it to the National Assembly on 9 May, trumpeting the urgent necessity of measures to rescue freedom of the press from abuse and deliver liberty of opinion from anarchic calls to assassination, arson, and revolt. Pronouncing repression the essential condition of liberty, he offered a stark vision of a public space purged of political dissonance and collective action. In this conception, he reiterated, the state saw only individuals. Collective bodies existed as private associations or to serve specific public functions delegated to them by the nation as a whole; in neither case did they possess an essential identity beyond that of the individual citizens composing them. It followed that exercise of the right of petition had necessarily to be restricted to individual citizens—and indeed, in Le Chapelier's logic, to active citizens alone. Individuals could lodge complaints, he allowed, but only active citizens could express a political will. The right of petition was "the right of every active citizen to present to the legislative body, to the king, to administrators, his views on matters of legislation, public order, and administration." But it was a right to be invoked directly and individually, "in accordance with the sacred maxim that the people can only delegate the powers it cannot itself exercise."[49]

By this reasoning, public bodies—be they administrative, judicial, electoral, municipal, or sectional—exercised functions specifically delegated to them; they could not go beyond the limits of their designated tasks without usurping the rights of the people. In expressing views regarding public issues beyond their specific purview, they would be claiming capacities of representation not constitutionally conferred upon them. Summoned to exercise specific responsibilities, they could not extend the purview or duration of their meeting once their expressly designated business had been completed. Petitions or collective addresses produced in their name could carry no more authority than the individual opinions of those individuals actually signing them.

The same was all the more true of voluntary political associations. The political clubs and societies created by the Revolution had been born with liberty and very useful to it, Le Chapelier again acknowledged, but they would soon threaten that liberty if they were permitted to publish deliberations, decrees, addresses, and petitions implying their legal identity as corporate bodies. "They must be invisible to society," he insisted; "they must exist only for those who compose them." If they produced petitions collectively, they would usurp the rights of individuals both within them and beyond. A club that did so "would soon become a corporation vitiated by all the spirit, all the passions, all the despotism that have always accompanied corporate bodies and are incompatible with a free government where there are only two kinds of rights, those of the citizens and those of the nation."[50]

Collective petitions once banned, it followed that city walls had also to be stripped of placards circulating them, streets freed from the violence of struggles to post or efface them, and air cleared of the pollution of their public proclamation. The right to display posters in public places "can belong to no individual, no association, no section of a commune," Le Chapelier stipulated. "A separate section is nothing, it forms part of the elective body, it exists only with it. The streets, the public squares are common property: belonging to no one, they belong to all. It follows that society has the right to control them without infringing on any individual right." Posters, or pronouncements heralded by the trumpet and the tambour, were prompt and efficient ways of communicating official decisions; they had to be reserved for this purpose.

But what of the argument that city walls had the potential to educate and instruct? For this claim Le Chapelier had little patience. To his mind, instruction wasn't acquired on street corners. It came from calm and enlightened discussion of peaceful associations free from passions and partisanship. It came from books, from laws dictated by sane philosophy. Posters could serve "only the turbulent fellow or the despicable intriguer who wants to create a party or excite a dangerous movement." Allowing them incited disorders and bloody brawls over the wall space for them. It invited the danger that proliferation of competing addresses bearing simulacra of authority would crowd out official publications, thus subverting respect for the powers constitutionally delegated by the people. It followed that the right to post placards must never belong to a section or society: "to a section . . . that is nothing in isolation, that is only the part of a whole . . . ; to a society that has no public existence and cannot assume one without usurping the power of the people and the individual rights of citizens."[51]

With this reasoning, Le Chapelier presented the Assembly on 9 May with eighteen articles of legislation radically restricting popular political action and reclaiming the streets for the display of public authority. They provoked powerful reactions among the deputies in a lengthy debate that became increasingly confrontational. From the left, Robespierre and others insisted on granting the right of petition to all citizens, Grégoire called for opening the walls to the free expression of political opinion, Buzot for allowing sections and communal bodies free right of assembly. In response, to some derision, the reactionary Maury claimed the right of petition for public bodies.

In the end, the deputies upheld the right of petition as belonging inalienably to every individual, whether active citizen or not. They nonetheless accepted Le Chapelier's core demand that exercise of this individual right be denied to electoral, judicial, administrative, and municipal bodies, as well as to sections and societies. Collective petitions, they insisted, had to be signed individually by each and every citizen endorsing them; they could represent no others' views. Meetings of municipal and sectional assemblies had to be restricted to the specific business for which they had received explicit authorization, their consideration of matters beyond this purview being declared null and void. Sections, as Le Chapelier could not stop reiterating, were to remain as nothing, fractions of a whole that could themselves have no separate existence.

As for Le Chapelier's call to strip the streets entirely of battling posters, the deputies were less convinced. They ordered cities and districts to establish special sites reserved for the display of official pronouncements. They prohibited imitation of the forms and imperative address of such pronouncements in unauthorized publications. But they left to the walls the power of the word—open to the free expression of speech by individuals, though subject to strict repression of its abuses.[52]

Marat, for his part, was not taken in by pieties regarding the freedom of speech he believed "anti-revolutionary" deputies were desperate to destroy. In his assessment, Le Chapelier was leading an effort to deny friends of the people any means of enlightening public opinion or mobilizing it against unjust, oppressive, and disastrous laws. He saw this decree restricting the right of petition as a masterpiece of deception framed by a notorious gambler, a legislative trickster, a card shark loading the deck against liberty. Its "stupid preamble" aimed only to deny assemblies of citizens the right to participate in the management of public affairs. Its claim that sections and societies had no true political existence and served only to interfere with the exercise of sovereignty by delegates of the people was entirely specious. To the contrary, he insisted, these bodies were acting only to resist oppression by opposing the derelictions of the people's mandataries and recalling to their public duty the former henchmen of the Old Regime suborned by the monarch to reestablish despotism. The National Assembly had no more right to prohibit the deliberations of free assemblies and the publication or placarding of their decisions than to stop citizens in the streets shouting "Thief!" or "Assassin!" A decree to this effect would be null and void, fit to be trampled to the ground, good only for wiping patriotic asses.[53]

Could the arguments of patriotic deputies prevent enemies of the Revolution from fooling the public and depriving the people of its rights? Reporting on the ensuing debate, Marat gave vent to mounting outrage at the hostility directed by an "assembly almost entirely prostituted to Louis XVI" against those opposing the decree—Grégoire, Buzot, Pétion, and most notably "the worthy Robespierre . . . the incorruptible Robespierre." Despite the valiant efforts of this minority on the left, the treacherous Assembly had voted to add one more chapter to a constitution he deemed almost entirely a work of "trickery, infamy, servitude, venality and perfidy."

The right to petition, *L'Ami du peuple* reiterated, is a natural right. To restrict it to individuals is "to declare that associations of workers, artisans, merchants, savants, etc. can have no particular branch of industry to uphold, no common interest to defend, no common wrong to be remedied. It's to claim that no lawyer, no informed or courageous person can be legally charged to pursue their grievances, interests, and advantages. It's to pretend that abuse, harassment, malfeasance, prevarication, extortion, betrayal, conspiracy—in a word, all the machinations directed against the public good by the agents of the people—attack only individuals, pertain only to isolated persons, do not concern the nation, and can be of no matter to assembled citizens, to the united citizens of the empire." The restrictions this decree placed on the deliberations of municipal assemblies, on their right—and that of sections—to gather at will, and on the right to post petitions, stripped the nation of its right to engage in its own affairs. For The People's Friend, it was the most hideous of the attacks to date on the rights of the citizen and of the nation. It left "*patrie* an empty word . . . public liberty forever done for."[54]

A BARBAROUS DECREE

More was to come. Le Chapelier had not yet emptied the legislative arsenal against popular mobilization. Rising to speak for the Constitutional Committee on 14 June, he offered the National Assembly a further decree, this time specifically targeting collective action by workers agitating for higher pay.

Economic conditions in Paris had worsened through the spring of 1791, not least as assignats (against which Marat fulminated almost daily) drove out coin and inflated prices. At the same time, workplace relations had been disrupted by the passage of the d'Allarde law abolishing Old Regime guilds and corporations as of 1 April. Marat was troubled by this legislation on the grounds that it undermined traditions of apprenticeship and occupational training that ensured craft values and the quality of work. He was wary of the argument that emulation, the companion of liberty, would encourage the arts to flourish. "There is doubtless nothing better than to emancipate citizens from the obstacles hindering the development of talents and keeping the unfortunate in a state of indigence," he granted. "But I don't know whether this entire liberty, this dispensing with all apprenticeship or any initiation into the exercise of a given trade or occupation is a good idea for policy."

The People's Friend was no economist. At base, he was profoundly suspicious of the operation of a free market. Individual greed, he feared, would erode the desire to establish a reputation; good faith would yield to intrigue and villainy. When workers could work for themselves, they would no longer want to work for others. Soon there would be no workshops, no manufactures, no commerce. Free to pursue many occupations, workers would be masters of none. Cheap shoddy goods would drive out better ones, harming poor consumers and driving the rich toward foreign markets. "Follow the unlimited development of the desire for gain that torments the classes of people in the large towns, and you'll be convinced of these sad truths. . . . It's in the capitals especially that this decay of the useful arts, this annihilation of good faith, this uprooted and scheming worker's life, the indigence besetting all professions, the public misery causing the ruin of commerce will be felt. I may be wrong, but I wouldn't be surprised to discover in twenty years that there wasn't a single worker in Paris who knew how to make a hat or a pair of shoes."[55]

A dramatic effect of the d'Allarde law became more immediately evident, however, as journeymen now released from guild constraints organized to demand higher wages from masters and employers equally free to lower them. Paris carpenters—urging their fellows in other cities to follow their lead—began campaigning for higher pay as early as April, refusing to work themselves and blocking the labor of others in often violent confrontations. In the ensuing weeks, members of other trades followed suit. Drawing on practices of association and mutual support embedded in long-established and semi-clandestine practices of *compagnonnage* rooted in the Old Regime, these traditional collective actions of workers now gained new justification in revolutionary notions of natural rights and popular sovereignty propagated by the Cordelier Club and other "fraternal societies."[56]

A letter to *L'Ami du peuple* published 12 June placed Marat at the center of these newly politicized labor disputes. Addressing The People's Friend as a "dear prophet, true defender of the class of the indigents," it was signed by "all the workers of the new church of Sainte-Geneviève, 340 in number." Denouncing the rapacity of the masters in general, and identifying some of the most scandalous among them by name, these laborers on the future Pantheon condemned the pitiless efforts of their oppressors to drive down wages. The masters had profited from the Revolution while risking nothing for it, the letter charged; vampires gorged in luxury, they were trying to bend workers to the yoke, crushing them without pity or remorse. They were even calling on the National Assembly for "a barbarous decree" that would reduce journeymen to starvation. "Hear our complaints, dear Friend of the People, and give voice to our just demands in these moments of despair when we see our hopes misplaced, because we had counted on participating in the advantages of the new order of things and seeing our lot alleviated."[57]

Marat found this situation shameful but offered little hope that it could be remedied by debates within the National Assembly. In fact, as he expected, the legislation for which the masters called was every bit as barbarous as the workers feared. Le Chapelier was stern in condemnation of worksite disruption when he brought the proposed decree before the deputies on 14 June. He saw workers' coalitions as a contravention of constitutional principles and a threat to public order. In his judgment, they amounted to a recrudescence of the corporations that had blighted the Old Regime. Members of specific professions or occupations had no right to assemble in pursuit of their "supposed common interests," even to engage in activities purportedly devoted to organizing mutual aid for the sick and unemployed (functions that were now the sole responsibility of public officials). "There are no longer corporations in the state," he reminded the Assembly; "there is only the particular interest of each individual and the general interest. No one is permitted to inspire in citizens an intermediary interest, to separate them from the public good by a spirit of corporation." He was suspicious, too, that these workers' movements had been promoted "less in the goal of getting an augmentation of the daily wage . . . than in the secret intention of fomenting disturbances." Prepared to admit (in the face of protests within the chamber) that wages were too low, he nonetheless insisted on the principle that "the daily wage for each worker must be set by free agreements between individuals; it is then up to the worker to maintain the agreement he has made with the person employing him."[58]

The deputies were in no mood to delay passage of the legislation they were now offered. They readily passed the decree that became notorious as the Le Chapelier law. "Annihilation of all kinds of corporations of citizens of the same condition and profession being one of the fundamental bases of the French Constitution," the Assembly declared, "it is forbidden to reestablish them in practice under any pretext or form whatsoever." Le Chapelier was careful to note that this ban on collective organization applied to employers as well as workers, and its provisions did indeed shape antitrust law as well as labor law in France throughout the nineteenth century.[59] But in 1791 it was more directly targeted at troublesome coalitions of workers. Gatherings of citizens sharing the same profession or occupation were not themselves forbidden, but they could not name officers, keep minutes, take collective decisions, or institute regulations regarding their purported common interests. Administrative bodies were prohibited from receiving addresses or petitions emanating from such groupings and were required to declare their deliberations null and void.

Collective action to determine wages was thus declared unconstitutional, injurious to liberty, and contrary to the Declaration of the Rights of Man. Its instigators were made subject to fines and the loss of the rights of active citizenship, with penalties increasing to imprisonment for those threatening employers or workers who resisted strikes. Violence at the workplace was criminalized; crowds disturbing the freedom of economic activity were declared "seditious gatherings, to be dispersed as such by the forces of public order . . . and punished according to the full rigor of the law."[60]

Marat was in no doubt about the political motivation of this legislation. He condemned it as the culmination of the attacks by corrupt representatives on popular societies and public protest. "To prevent numerous gatherings of the people they fear so mightily, they have deprived the innumerable class of laborers and workers of the right to assemble to deliberate regarding their interests," he declared. The claim that these assemblies could resuscitate the abolished corporations of the Old Regime was, in his eyes, no more than a pretext. "They want only to isolate the citizens and prevent them from concerning themselves in common with public matters. Thus by means of a few crude sophisms and the abuse of a few words the infamous representatives of the nation have stripped it of its rights."[61]

Throughout the debate on the Le Chapelier law, there had been calls to extend its prohibitions explicitly to meetings of clubs and societies. On this, perhaps not surprisingly, Malouet had the last word. "Let them be, let them be," he crowed to applause from the right of the assembly and mutterings from the left; "they're in their final agony." He could not have been more wrong. Popular societies exploded in anger a week later at news that the king and the royal family had been stopped at Varennes as they headed toward the northeastern French border. The flight Marat had so long predicted had finally occurred. In this regard, at least, the prophet was vindicated.

NINETEEN

SALUS POPULI

Throughout May and into June 1791, Marat had warned of an impending flight of the royal family that would detonate a full-scale counterrevolutionary intervention. "Everything is ready to satisfy the desires of the king and his henchmen to eviscerate the good citizens, cement the return of the old regime with their blood, and rivet their chains forever," he had reported on May 21. Two weeks later, on 4 June, he was exposing a putative plan by Lafayette to provoke a National Guard massacre of the most patriotic citizens in one part of the city while Guard units in another spirited the royals away. "Redouble the efforts to keep watch on the Tuileries Palace and prevent the royal family from taking flight," he urged on 6 June.[1] To no avail. Louis XVI was on his way to the frontier within the fortnight.

By then not only the capital but the whole country was in a state of unrest. As popular disaffection had spread across Paris and the resulting crackdown there had grown more severe, a cycle of disorder and repression had mounted in the provinces. In early May, The People's Friend had signaled a new crisis by calling again for heads. "I was called bloodthirsty when I proposed lopping off five hundred heads to assure liberty," he cried out on 8 May. "To the contrary, it was a counsel of humanity and justice. How much innocent blood would have been spared if this wise counsel had been followed before our cowardly enemies had united and gained force! Twenty thousand patriots would not have been massacred and five hundred thousand others would not be threatened with the same fate at any moment." A few weeks later, he was running the numbers. "Felling five hundred heads would have sufficed to put things back in order eleven months ago, today it would take fifty thousand. Perhaps five hundred thousand will have fallen by the end of the year. France will have been inundated in blood, but it will not be freer as a result. Let those who accuse me of barbarity for proposing this expedient meditate a little on these alarming truths and let them finally learn to judge better my head and my heart."[2]

With this renewed head count, the need for emergency powers now moved more powerfully to the fore of Marat's thinking. He began to write more insistently about the need for a tribune of the people, even a dictator, who would exercise emergency authority on the Roman model. "Lynching! Lynching! my dear friends, is the only way to make your faithless agents get a hold on themselves and inspire in them the salutary fear of not doing their duty," he had insisted the previous December. "Far from relying on the tribunals, wisdom would require beginning almost always by doing justice to them."

This was about *doing* justice, inflicting it, not seeking it. The time for courts was over, the hour for revolutionary dictatorship at hand. This thought triggered bitter reflections about emergency action The People's Friend could have taken had he been tribune of the people earlier in the Revolution. He would have expelled clerical and noble deputies from the National Assembly after 14 July 1789; he would have decimated the Assembly in response to its disastrous decrees on the suspensive veto, martial law, and the right to declare war. A fantasy of supreme emergency power followed. "If I had been tribune of the people, I would have had nothing to do after an initial order. At the sound of my name, public enemies would have buried themselves alive and one wouldn't have found in the whole realm a scoundrel who had hesitated to fall headlong."[3]

The mirage of an all-powerful tribunate reappeared on 31 May as Marat attacked deputies he accused of still declaring themselves arbiters of a nation whose liberty they had stifled at birth. "They owe much to their inviolability," he growled. "If I were tribune of the people, I would make them wear a certificate of their good conduct on their shoulder. . . . I'd dismiss the speechifiers in breeches, ordering them never to show up on the benches again, and I'd give the civic crown to Pétion, and especially to Robespierre."

All praise, then, to the people's few friends in the Assembly. But the would-be tribune soon imagined himself inflicting a more severe punishment upon the people's enemies. "When the nation's representatives degrade the august functions of the legislator to such a degree, it's up to the people to relieve the faithless deputies of their powers and punish them for their treachery," he pronounced on 15 June. He saw the moment approaching when the people would find a tribunate or temporary dictatorship indispensable. "If ever I were judged worthy of that honor," he promised, "my first order would be to have the conscript fathers who had betrayed the homeland hanged, each at his seat, except for the ones to be resurrected as worthy of their inviolability." Virtue, above all, was required in the exercise of such extreme power. It was up to the people to confer that power only upon "a citizen whose virtue has emerged pure from all ordeals."[4]

A PREDICTION FULFILLED

Everything was ready for the king's departure, *L'Ami du peuple* clamored on the morning of 21 June. The dangers to the lethargic people had never been more obvious, the need to fire it up for its self-preservation never more urgent. A terrible moment was at hand. Louis XVI was expected to attend a council of crowned heads of Europe in Brussels on the twenty-sixth, the journal revealed, together with the Capet princes heading the conspiracy of counterrevolutionary exiles. The royal family was waiting only to see the people at sleep before taking off for the frontier. "Friends of the homeland, remember that you are marked for carnage like sheep at the slaughterhouse; remember that in the face of implacable enemies it would be the height of madness not to forestall them." In the event of the king's escape, Marat warned his readers, they should instantly "lay hand indiscriminately" on all the known supporters of despotism, beginning with the traitors in the National Assembly, the general staff, the municipal government, the departmental administration, the Monarchical Club, the sections, the agents of the old police. "They're all known; let their entire species be annihilated forever. The only principle to direct your conduct from now on must be that there's nothing sacred under the sun except *the people's safety*."[5]

This time, though, the call for purge extended beyond the usual checklist of corrupt deputies and reactionary government officials to a broader swath of the population. "So that the putrid members of the nation can be excised from the healthy parts, let each city close its gates at the news of the royal flight and slaughter the antirevolutionary conspirators," urged *L'Ami du peuple*. Behind the medical terms of Dr. Marat's prescription were echoes of St. Bartholomew's Night. "Public security" was becoming the code for slaughter.

The royals' coach was trundling from Paris as this call fell from the press. Finally, on 22 June, The People's Friend could publish, in a paroxysm of denunciation, the news of the event he had long anticipated. The royal family had escaped its gilded prison in the Tuileries palace on the night of the twentieth to the twenty-first, leaving behind a manifesto in which the monarch disavowed the Revolution and all its works, denouncing most notably the agitation and disorder provoked by the popular clubs and the growing tyranny of the mob. Marat's claim to political prophecy had finally been vindicated.

After departing in ignominy, The People's Friend went on to predict, Louis XVI would soon return at the head of an army to slaughter those of his fellow citizens refusing his tyrannical yoke. So much then, he raged, for the fidelity of kings to their oaths! So much for the honor of revolutionary leaders like Lafayette and Bailly, without whose complicity the king's flight would have been impossible! So much for the people's reliance on deputies whose repressive policies had cleared the ground for foreign invasion by waging war on patriotism throughout the land and filling the nation's officer corps with reactionaries! "Citizens, friends of the homeland, the moment of your ruin is at hand. I won't lose time heaping useless recriminations on you for the misfortunes you have brought down on your heads by your blind confidence and fatal sense of security. Let's think only of your salvation."[6]

Salus populi suprema lex. This was the primal creed. Nonetheless, the carnage for which *L'Ami du peuple* had called in the event of Louis XVI's flight failed to materialize. The capital remained largely sullen as Parisian authorities mobilized the National Guard to preempt disorder in the streets. The only option the people had left, the journal reiterated, was to name immediately "a military tribune, a supreme dictator, to lay hold of the principal traitors." Who might that tribune be? The answer was obvious. "Let your choice fall on the citizen who has to this day shown you the most enlightenment, zeal, and fidelity. Swear unbreakable devotion to him and obey him religiously in everything he will order to rid you of your mortal enemies." This, yet again, was the moment of crisis. It was the moment to lop off the heads of the ministers and their subordinates, of Lafayette, of the criminals of the general staff, and of the commanders of antipatriotic battalions, of Bailly and all the counterrevolutionaries in the municipal government. It was the moment to shatter the organization of a National Guard rendered repressive by its militarization, to call on the provinces for aid, occupy the Arsenal, seize weapons, disarm police agents. In a word, it was the moment for bloodshed, for the people to avenge its rights, defend its liberty, and exterminate its enemies.[7]

"A tribune, a military tribune, or you are lost irremediably," Marat again exhorted the people. "Until now I've done everything within human powers to save you. If you neglect my salutary counsel, the only advice left for me to give you . . . , I'll take my leave of you forever." There followed a portrayal of the hideous scene of repression that would play out as

Louis XVI reclaimed his capital at the head of an army of exiles, counter-revolutionary malcontents, and Austrian legions. Fervent patriots would be rounded up, populist journalists dragged to the dungeon. The People's Friend, calling for liberty until his last breath, would turn his tomb into a fiery oven. "Just a few more days of indecision and there will be no more time to emerge from your lethargy," he cajoled. "Death will overcome you in the arms of sleep."[8]

"The Parisians' Sleep of Death" headlined the journal the following day. The issue derided a pantomime of feigned confusion and sham regret at the king's flight being played out by perfidious leaders, compromised ministers, and tainted deputies. He would not go back on his word, Marat assured his fellow citizens. Unless they named a military tribune that very day to march at their head and target the traitors to be brought down, he vowed, "I have nothing to say to you." The unique characteristics indispensable in this tribune were by now familiar. He could only be "the man of the people most distinguished by his enlightenment, his foresight, his devotion to the homeland, his firmness in times of crisis." But alas, that man, "entrails torn with grief as I wait until you've reduced me to silence by your invincible apathy," may also have been suffering more literally.[9] As at earlier moments of personal and political crisis, nervous strain may have inflamed the illness afflicting his physical existence. His publisher had to announce on 24 June that the journal was dispensing copy from issues prepared earlier. The prophet, in a torment of despair, physical or emotional, had put down his pen.

A PROBLEMATIC RETURN

Not for long. *L'Ami du peuple* was back on the streets three days later, on 25 June, to herald the news that disaster had been averted. The royal party had been recognized and its flight aborted not far from the northeastern border, at the town of Varennes. "Our revolution is a continual web of miracles," Marat now exulted. "It's true, then, that heaven looks out for us and some unforeseen event always stops us on the verge of the abyss into which we are about to be hurtled." Let immortal gratitude be rendered, he implored, to those citizens who had halted the royal renegade and frustrated the barbarian hordes readying to return alongside him to bathe in the people's blood. Let the traitors who had plotted to deliver the realm to fire and sword be subjected to public execration as they awaited the avenging blade. Let the people be transported with joy, as it must be, at so fortunate and unanticipated an event. "But let it be fearful of abandoning its security. The dangers are not over, our most fearsome enemies are still within our walls, they are humbling themselves for a moment to regain favor by a feigned popularity. As long as they are not exterminated, we will have their frightful machinations to dread."[10]

If the moment was indeed providential, it still demanded a fateful choice. Joy at an unexpected return rapidly gave way to anxiety about its implications. What, now, to do with this monarch so ignominiously freighted back to the capital of the Revolution he had repudiated? Marat was in no doubt as to the proper course of action. Louis XVI had shown himself too unworthy of the throne not to be deposed. "Who doesn't see that the king, having not only taken flight but protested against the constitution and, even worse, against the nation whose sovereignty he refuses to recognize . . . , *is deprived by this act of rebellion of all right to the throne*," insisted a second issue of *L'Ami du peuple* rushed from the press on 25 June. In its analysis, the reluctance of the National Assembly leaders to grasp and act upon this imperative simply confirmed their complicity in the king's escape. By doing nothing, they were already insinuating that the king had been abducted by counterrevolutionary enemies. The People's Friend wanted immediate action instead! Lafayette and Bailly, responsible for Louis XVI's custody but denounced by Marat as principal instigators of his flight, deserved to be removed as inept imbeciles or punished as despicable criminals. The ignominious ministers, too, had to be dismissed. Bouillé had to be put to the rack as a traitorous conspirator.[11]

None of this would be decreed, Marat acknowledged. Who today could doubt that the National Assembly was almost entirely composed of counterrevolutionaries? The deputies were vile slaves of the court, paid to bring back despotism. Instead of deposing the unworthy monarch, they were already looking for ways to exonerate him, harbor him from public indignation, assure him of impunity, maintain him in his dignities, and force the people to respect him. This was "insanity on a scale never seen before." As for the Parisians, The People's Friend had more harsh words for these "eternal gawkers." The current turn of events, he charged, stemmed from their cowardice and lack of political consciousness. "With a people of your character, how could you not be eternally the dupes and victims of the scoundrels . . . to whom you have blindly abandoned the reins of the state? Are you waiting to be continually hammered by the most hideous anarchy until some audacious criminal captures you and returns you to the yoke?"[12]

Marat's intuition was correct. In shock at the news of the king's departure and terrified of popular reaction, the deputies soon seized on a notion put forward by Lafayette and Bailly to counter accusations of complicity or incompetence leveled against them. Louis XVI, they lamented, had been kidnapped, stolen from the nation, spirited away from his watchful guard. Upon his forced return to the capital, however, the Assembly's joy and relief quickly gave way to the realization that his recapture was even more problematic than his initial departure. Fleeing the country entirely, the monarch would merely have left the throne vacant. His return to the capital, albeit forced, left his personal culpability to be determined and his constitutional status unclear. More crucially, it placed the very function of the throne in question and the entire constitution at risk. Could a king declared inviolable now be deposed or placed on trial? Could he be deemed to have abdicated, thus replaceable by constitutional means? Could an untrustworthy monarch now be restored to executive power, or should that power be exercised by an elected national council? Should a tainted monarchy give way to a republic? Could these issues be resolved, or perhaps even evaded, and the constitutional work of two years saved? Suspending Louis XVI for the moment from the exercise of his functions as executive power, the National Assembly insisted on the need to maintain respect due to his royal person. In fear of the potential for popular mobilization that primary assemblies might provide, it also suspended the elections for the legislative assembly meant to succeed it. Beyond that, profoundly divided, it writhed over its political options.

As it did so, *L'Ami du peuple* continued to demonize the general and the mayor while lacerating faithless representatives. The latter were clinging to power in sparsely attended sessions, it declaimed; they were fabricating futile laws to contain popular protest while plotting to restore a king revealed to the universe as a traitor, a conspirator, the enemy of the people, the most hideous of tyrants. The Assembly's decree of 23 June had declared traitors to the nation and the king "those who counseled, aided and executed the kidnapping of the king," ordered the arrest of all who failed to respect the monarch's dignity or threatened those accompanying him back to Paris, and commanded authorities to "prosecute vigorously and immediately" anyone threatening the tranquility of the capital. "Frenchmen, trample this sacrilegious decree underfoot, recover your rights, feel your force and your dignity," thundered the journal in response on 26 June. "Today it's from you that your perfidious mandataries must receive orders, it's for you to dictate laws to them. Seduced or seducer, Louis XVI has shown himself forever unworthy of the august functions with which you have honored him. What confidence could you have in a vile criminal who wanted to bathe in your blood or return you to your chains. If he has deserted his post once, he will do it ten thousand times. . . . Let him descend a throne he has sullied so many times, and let him at last expiate his evil crimes in a prison." In a last-minute news flash the same day, the journal reported that a counterrevolutionary army of émigrés and Austrian forces were already bringing fire and sword to Metz. "Citizens, deal immediately with Bailly and Motier, the general staff, the traitors in the Assembly; and let the avenging blade rid you finally of the infamous race of these tyrants under whom you have groaned for so many centuries."[13]

"Hey, brother, have you got today's Marat?" a group of women were heard demanding of a man in the crowded Palais Royal that same evening. It was no accident that the person accosted, one Siméon Vallée, had a copy of *L'Ami du peuple* in his pocket—he had been linked to distribution of the journal before. He pulled the issue out and read from it for half an hour before being mauled by anxious citizens and handed over to the National Guard. The incident was not unique. As political tensions rose, Lafayette's troops remained on high alert for radicals carrying Marat's message. "Every day the hawkers of Marat, of *L'Orateur du peuple*, are arrested and their journals shredded by Lafayette's satellites," Mme Roland reported to her correspondent Bancal on 25 June.[14]

This was scarcely surprising. Marat was becoming increasingly unhinged in his demands for wholesale slaughter. On 7 July, in a counsel of despair, he warned against empty talk of a republic. "Let's set aside empty dreams, let's work to make our position bearable; if we can't work to make it happy, let's think of our safety. Never has the homeland been in more danger. Never will it find itself in a more violent crisis, despite the torpor in which the citizens are plunged." What, then, did he want? For the moment, he could think only of purge. On 8 July, he was calling down ancient savagery on deputies like Sieyès, Le Chapelier, Duport, Target, Démeunier, and Barnave, men he saw selling out to despotism. "Impale them alive," he urged, "and let them be exposed on the battlements of the senate building for three days in sight of the people. . . . Brand with a hot iron the cheeks of all the other rogues who have supported these dreadful decrees. . . . And don't forget to award the crown of glory to Robespierre." These were the measures, he admonished the people, that would have been taken by a patriotic military tribune, "if you had had the good sense to name one. But what sensible man who had not lost his mind would today agree to march at the head of an imbecilic people without character, without discipline, a people that would massacre in the evening the idol it had adored in the morning?"[15]

By 12 July, eve of the presentation of the crucial report on the king's fate prepared jointly by nine of the National Assembly's committees, *L'Ami du peuple* was demanding that Louis XVI suffer the ultimate penalty. "His crime is indisputable, his punishment must be exemplary," it declared. "That he should be cast from the throne is insufficient, his head must fall under the executioner's axe." Instead, the journal disclosed, the Assembly was expected to prolong the dishonored monarch's fake arrest until the constitution was revised and completed, at which point he would be invited to accept its provisions and resume the exercise of executive power. This, Marat warned, would be the most fatal blow the Assembly had ever inflicted on public liberty. The effect would be to destroy the principle of national sovereignty by turning the constitution into a contractual arrangement between king and people. To prevent this outcome, the king's death or lifelong imprisonment were the only possible responses. "By his crimes, Louis XVI has irretrievably lost the confidence of the nation. He is no more than a vile criminal unworthy of any public employment. If he is not eliminated from the number of the living, let him forever lose his liberty."[16]

These tirades, though, were flecked with hints of illness. Declaring himself "tormented by a violent migraine," Marat filled the 9 July issue of *L'Ami du peuple* with a speech of Robespierre's to the Jacobin Club that had dissected Louis XVI's proclamation on leaving Paris. The following day, he failed to publish. On the next, he "rose from his bed of pain" to demand pardon for the soldiers of the Châteauvieux regiment imprisoned after the Nancy affair (a pardon suddenly rendered thinkable by recognition of Bouillé's indisputable treachery in organizing the king's flight). On the twelfth, he held at bay "the pain tearing me apart" to rage against news that the National Assembly was planning simply to reinstate the king. On the thirteenth, he fell silent again. Here, as on other occasions, a crisis in the life of the Revolution coincided with one in his health. "Marat is dying," Mme Roland wrote to Bancal on 15 July, adding word of a rumor that he had been poisoned like Elisée Loustalot, another patriotic journalist said to have met this fate.[17]

In all probability, Marat was experiencing a flare-up of the disease that afflicted him at intervals throughout his life. But this malady could also be spun as a token of patriotism. So thought a faithful friend reporting to *L'Orateur du peuple*. "The empty-headed men who claim love of the homeland is not a passion and regard it as an expression of pride, of the fury to distinguish oneself, would soon change their language if they were at the bedside of The People's Friend," reported this Blondel, declaring himself citizen of the Mauconseil section. They had only to witness him "on a bed of pain tormented by a hideous migraine, devoured by a burning fever, his head swollen like a barrel, an unbearable discharge down his entire left side, poultices on his legs, unable to change his posture for several days." They had only to see him "deploring his situation only because he could not attend assiduously to the public safety," or hear him "talking in his sleep only about political affairs," or "using the slightest respite to dictate to a friend some articles for his journal." If only there were thousands like him in Paris, this Blondel lamented to *L'Orateur du peuple*. "Offer him as a model to the cowardly citizens who desert their sections out of timidity or prefer to run to the theaters or houses of pleasure."[18]

ABDUCTION OR ABDICATION?

In the meantime, as the National Assembly churned in uncertainty following the king's return, Paris suffered a veritable canicule of opinions, debates, placards, and demonstrations. Quick to act, the Cordeliers issued three manifestos within hours of news of the king's departure. The first, a petition equating monarchy with enslavement, maintained that Louis XVI had returned the French to their situation on 14 July 1789, leaving them *free and without a king*. "Louis has abdicated the throne," it asserted; "henceforth, he is nothing for us unless he becomes our enemy." Printed, placarded, and circulated to political clubs throughout the nation, this protestation demanded that the deputies proclaim France a republic, or at least wait until primary assemblies throughout the nation had decided the king's fate.[19]

The Cordeliers' second pronouncement, printed and placarded in its turn, urged resistance against the disarming of individual citizens by the National Guard "at the moment the homeland and public existence are in the direst danger." This incitement to action was quickly denounced by sections supporting Lafayette and condemned as seditious and incendiary by the department of Paris, which demanded prosecution of its authors, signatories, and disseminators. A third Cordelier proclamation followed the second a day later. Prefaced by doctored stanzas from Voltaire's play *Brutus* that called down death at the Champ de Mars upon a perfidious, lying tyrant, it attested that the "free Frenchmen" comprising the club included "as many tyrannicides as members . . . all sworn *individually* to stab the tyrants who dare attack our frontiers or violate our liberty and our Constitution in any manner whatsoever." A *Journal du Club des Cordeliers* soon appeared to continue the drumbeat against the perfidious monarch and treacherous National Assembly.[20]

The National Guard was not slow to rough up and arrest persons caught posting these publications in the streets. One such incident, widely reported, was encountered in the Palais Royal on the afternoon of 22 June by the journalist François Robert, a Cordelier activist, agitator for a fraternal association of the popular political societies, and author also of *Républicanisme adapté à la France*. Passing by as part of a Cordelier delegation to the Jacobin Club, he had intervened against arbitrary treatment of citizens posting petitions, only to be harassed and arrested himself by local officials. Protests by the Cordeliers, the Jacobins, and several other popular societies eventually secured his release, as he gratefully informed the Jacobin Club that same evening. But in thanking the Jacobins he threw them into turmoil by announcing that his original mission had been to present them with the Cordeliers' petition calling for the destruction of the monarchy. In the uproar that followed, one member called upon the society to refuse any further deputation from the Cordeliers until the latter retracted their proclamation against monarchy. Another protested the indulgence that was being shown toward "writings like Marat's." The name had clearly become a code for radical extremism. "He only denounces the greatest patriots and only counsels carnage," one member had complained earlier in the session. But another objected, asserting that he had consulted the people in recent days only to hear "Monsieur, if we hadn't believed this man we wouldn't be where we are." A thousand voices were raised in affirmation of this judgment. "They were right!"[21]

The three Cordelier manifestos opened a republican moment. During these weeks, the reissue of Robert's *Républicanisme adapté à la France* was joined by Louis de Lavicomterie's *Crimes des rois de France depuis Clovis jusqu'à Louis XVI*. Théophile Mandar's adaptation of Marchamont Nedham's seventeenth-century republican tract *On the Excellency of a Free State* was now boosted in an enthusiastic review by the *Journal du Club des Cordeliers* as "the most eloquent and profound of all the works that have appeared to date before the *Social Contract*, and superior to it in citations" (the latter judgment being perhaps unsurprising since the title promised enrichment by notes from Rousseau, Mably, Bossuet, Condillac, Montesquieu, Letrône, Raynal, etc. etc. etc.). Mandar borrowed as an epigraph a maxim from Rousseau's *Gouvernement de Pologne*: "The circumstance of the present event must be seized to raise souls to the pitch of the souls of the ancients." The sentiment was shared by the future terrorist Jacques-Nicolas Billaud-Varenne, who also joined this chorus in classical republican mode. Despotism was inherent in monarchy, Billaud insisted in his *L'Acéphocratie, ou le gouvernement fédératif*. In his view, the corrupt National Assembly had merely given its twelve hundred members a share in the arbitrary power previously exercised by the king and his council. France at its origins was republican, he knew, as Mably's history had shown him. Billaud-Varenne called upon the nation to seize the moment to become so again.[22]

New republican voices also emerged from the intellectuals and politicians meeting as the Cercle Social. Their press had printed the Cordeliers' manifestos in the first place, and they also played a leading role in the political radicalization of the larger and hitherto more moderate society known as the Confédération des Amis de la Vérité. Among this band Nicolas Bonneville, the editor of the society's journal, *La Bouche de fer*, began taking a sharper tone against monarchy. Thomas Paine and Condorcet followed suit by launching a series of issues of *Le Républicain, ou Le Défenseur du gouvernement représentatif*, a journal intended to "enlighten minds regarding the republicanism that is made an object of *calumny* because it is not known, and the uselessness, vices and abuses of royalty that prejudice is determined to defend even when they are known." Theirs was a republicanism of the moderns, "a government based on the great republican principles of electoral representation and the rights of man," or, as Paine put it later in the second part of his *Rights of Man*, "a representative system [that] takes society and civilization as its basis; nature, reason, and experience as its guide."[23] These men, at least, were far from embracing the model of the Ancients.

In addition to offering Paine's republican credo, the first issue of *Le Républicain* summarized the case for the deposition of Louis XVI, whose flight, it insisted, had necessarily reduced him to the status of "an individual in the crowd," a mere M. Louis Bourbon. Condorcet spiced a later issue with a satirical proposal to replace the monarch with a robot to carry out the ceremonial duties of royalty, then followed it with a more elaborate blueprint for the institution of a nationally elected council to exercise executive power instead. The speech the academician delivered to the Cercle Social on 8 July under the title "The Republic, or whether a king is necessary for the preservation of liberty?" shocked his friends among the liberal former nobility, splintered the ranks of moderate constitutionalists, and horrified the king's defenders. Brissot was more explicit when he insisted at the Jacobin Club on 10 July that Louis XVI could and should stand trial. His lengthy address ignited fury among defenders of the crown by declaring that the principle of absolute royal inviolability was "prejudicial to the sovereignty of the nation and of the law, and subversive of the constitution."[24]

In calling for an elected executive council to displace the king, however, Brissot dismissed "the ridiculous charge of republicanism" as a maneuver on the part of those still hoping to benefit from the handouts of a despised monarch or his feeble successor. Like Paine and Condorcet, he advocated a representative democracy but wanted this modern form of government freed from the taint of anarchy and mob rule associated with democratic rule since the ancient republics. What did those denouncing republicanism fear, he demanded, if not the anarchy they saw in the tumultuous assemblies of Greece and Rome? What did their opponents fear, if not the very same tumult? Unity was to be found, he dared wager, in face of the mob.[25]

Brissot's appeal was urgent. There was reason to fear tumultuous assemblies. On 23 June, a citywide celebration of the Feast of Corpus Christi had mutated into an evening procession of another kind as tens of thousands of the citizens marched through the National Assembly. With some of them brandishing a variety of weapons, others carrying barriers bearing the slogan "Live Free or Die," the marchers reminded the deputies of the presence of the people and its potential for violence.

The following day, in an even more dramatic moment of political mobilization, some thirty thousand members of the popular societies, their families, and other individuals from across the city had headed to the Place Vendôme with the intention of marching from there to carry a petition to the National Assembly. Stopped by Lafayette and the National Guard, the marchers agreed to choose a delegation to deliver their message. "We haven't all signed," their petition avowed, cocking a snoot at Le Chapelier's law requiring petitions to bear individual signatures. "Time hasn't permitted that, the homeland has never been in more imminent danger." The king had fled, it continued; he had fled as an enemy, "and he will be judged." Had he crossed the frontier, he would have joined all the traitors who had emigrated "*and blood would have flowed*." "If France were here, it would tell you what is to be done," the petitioners attested. "But we are here. . . ." In an act of political embodiment, they demanded in the name of the entire nation that judgment of Louis XVI be postponed until the eighty-three departments had weighed all the consequences of any decision regarding him. When the petition was presented, the president of the Assembly declined to read it before ending that day's session. Mandar, who had headed the deputation, protested this treatment the following day. "The time has passed when one can disdain the people," he warned, "and it would be disrespectful for the assembly to silence its just demands."[26]

The Cordeliers smoldered for days over the mangled reading this text eventually received. By 12 July, following the dismissal of yet another of its petitions by the National Assembly's president, the club was ready to appeal beyond the deputies to the nation as a whole. The "Address to the Nation" it adopted that day called, in effect, for a suspension of the National Assembly and its replacement by an emergency executive body. It demanded an end to the "abusive and arbitrary prolongation" of the Assembly's existence and the reactivation of elections to transfer the people's mandate to the "purer hands" of a new legislature in a vote unrestricted by property discriminations. At the same time, it appeared to call for the selection of an individual from each department to join a provisional "national directorate," in effect an emergency council that would exercise executive power strong enough to maintain order until a decision had been made regarding the fate of "the former king" and the eventual form of government. In conclusion, claiming that experience had demonstrated that deputies could exceed or elude their mandates, it pledged the Cordeliers' constant surveillance of any future assembly to prevent such an occurrence.[27]

TO JUDGE A KING?

Was Louis XVI a counterrevolutionary abscess to be lanced from the body politic or a constitutional head upon whose vigor that body still depended for its survival? A decision could not be postponed indefinitely. On 13 July, at last, a deputy from Franche-Comté, Hyacinthe-François-Félix Muguet de Nanthou, rose in the National Assembly to present a weighty report on behalf of no fewer than seven of its committees. Marat commented two days later—as problems with printers left issues of *L'Ami du peuple* lagging continuously behind events—that the date had been chosen in the expectation that the people would be diverted by 14 July celebrations. In his analysis, the infamous Assembly was flattering itself that it could "sacrifice the interests of the nation to the ex-monarch, wipe clean his crimes, his perjuries, his treasons and even put him in a position to machinate anew against the homeland until he had consummated his flight and the ruin of liberty."[28]

Pilloried by Marat as a spokesman for the Assembly's "perfidious committees," Muguet presented their unambiguous verdict that the royal family had indeed been abducted by an audacious conspiracy masterminded by Bouillé. His report gave details of this criminal plot, tracking its long and careful preparation, its bungled execution, its abrupt termination at Varennes as a result of the vigilance of patriotic citizens, the energy of the National Guard, the refusal of regular troops to follow treasonous orders, and Bouillé's hasty departure across the frontier. Scrutinizing the actions of many individuals high and low, whether intentionally complicit or merely caught up in these events, it concluded with the recommendation that those suspected of treason be sent for judgment before the new high court in Orléans.[29]

The question of the king's culpability nonetheless lay, inescapably, at the heart of this report. Had Louis XVI not committed a crime in fleeing the capital? Had he not left a declaration denouncing the course the Revolution had taken from the very beginning? Were these actions not tantamount to abdication or grounds for deposition? Should he not be indicted by the National Assembly or brought before a court of law? In answer to these questions, Muguet offered two assertions. First, there was no legal basis for finding the king guilty. Second, and in any case, his constitutional inviolability precluded his being brought to judgment.

That the king's actions were unwise Muguet acknowledged and deplored. But he allowed no grounds for declaring them illegal. There were draft constitutional articles requiring that the monarch reside within 20 leagues of the National Assembly when it was in session and that he be deemed to have abdicated if he left the country and refused to return. But Louis XVI had not left the country, the committees had reasoned, and legislation regarding other possible justifications for deposition was still lacking. Moreover, the National Assembly had in April explicitly declined to limit the king's freedom to travel as a matter of law, merely "urging" him instead to remain in Paris for his own safety.

As for the declaration Louis XVI had left behind on 21 June, Muguet first questioned its authenticity and then dismissed it as selfish and ill-considered, the act of a man alive only to his own interests when those of the nation were at stake. "Uncivic" this royal manifesto may have been, he argued, but it conveyed no explicit statement of abdication on the king's part. The constitutional arrangements it protested remained provisional in any case, pending the completion of the entire constitutional document. Only then, Muguet contended, would the king be fully constrained by the Assembly's decisions. Only then, "knowing all his duties, able to judge the entirety of the means he would have to fulfill them, free to refuse the eminent position to which the nation is calling him," would he be bound "positively and invariably" by his acceptance.[30] The aim of this reasoning was to render moot the question of Louis XVI's guilt in fleeing the country, thus shelving that issue until it could be effaced entirely by his eventual acceptance of the constitution once it was completed.

These were disingenuous arguments designed to bolster the case against bringing the monarch to judgment, but the main thrust of the committees' reasoning lay elsewhere, in the principle of absolute royal inviolability. "The king is not guilty in the eyes of the law," Muguet assured the deputies, "and even if he were, the inviolability of his person, which you have decreed, would not permit his indictment." To maintain political unity in a vast country faced with centrifugal tendencies, Muguet recalled, and to stifle the spirit of faction, the Assembly had chosen to concentrate executive power in the sole person of a monarch, making that power hereditary to assure its peaceful transmission. By elevating a single individual, it had guaranteed for others "that precious equality, the immutable base of your constitution. Thus it was for the nation, not for the king, that the monarchy has been established."[31]

The same logic had required that the king's person be declared inviolable to ensure the independence of the executive function entrusted to him, Muguet reminded the deputies. The essential principle was that "since the executive power resides in the person of a single individual, his functions are so inherent in his person that they are, in a manner, inseparable from it." From this it followed that "the king is not a citizen but a power in and of himself alone." Because this power had to remain independent, the king himself could not be called to account. Only the ministers obligated to countersign his decisions under the constitution could be held formally responsible. To subject the king to the judgment of the National Assembly would destroy the necessary separation between the executive and the legislative bodies, two inviolable powers upon whose independent existence rested the preservation of liberty. To bring him before a court would open the way to endless accusations, inevitably undermining the authority of the executive power and respect for the royal veto. This was as much the case in personal as in political matters. The immunity of the monarch had to be kept entire.[32]

In this argument, "principles, circumstances, and above all the interests of a nation that wants to finish the Revolution, not restart it," militated against indicting Louis XVI. Charging him would open the way to disorder and civil war, Muguet warned; it would destroy the infant constitution in its cradle. The Assembly had to remain firm in the face of universal agitation. It had to continue resisting agitators who were claiming, in the name of the nation, that the flight of one individual threatened the entire constitution. Conversely, it had also to repudiate those "still slaves in the midst of a free people, always courtiers, never citizens . . . , devoted to an old idolatry," those monarchists still seeing a man where they should be considering the state. It had to defer further discussion of the status of the king, allowing spirits to calm. It had to complete the constitution.

This meant, in short, that the crime had to be Bouillé's. Muguet failed to acknowledge the sinuousness of appealing to some of the Assembly's constitutional decisions as authoritative while declaring others still provisional. The committees for which he was speaking, indeed most of the deputies hearing him, were too eager to see the Assembly complete its task. Barely mentioning the king who had been "lured away," the draft decree they offered simply indicted Bouillé and other possible offenders for plotting to overthrow the constitution. His speech concluded with an appeal to the royal émigrés to seize this moment to return to their homeland, thus playing their own part in bringing the Revolution to a close.[33]

Marat made mincemeat of this report in the pages of *L'Ami du peuple*. He couldn't resist remarking that this same Bouillé now vilified by the deputies as a traitor had been acclaimed by them a year earlier for the repression in Nancy. Ridiculing Muguet's dismissal of the king's manifesto on leaving Paris, he repudiated as an insult to public credulity the denial that Louis XVI was putting himself at the head of fugitives and enemies "to enslave and slaughter us." Louis had to be judged, insisted The People's Friend; he had to be indicted for "violation of his duties and vows, the wickedness of his projects, the atrocity of his plots and the terrible consequences that would have followed from their execution." This monarch was a criminal guilty of lèse-nation, a valet intent on slaughtering, pillaging, or enslaving his master. No law was necessary to tell him that he was revolting against the nation, his sovereign, or that he was sacrificing an immense people to his ambition. Justice demanded that he be immolated for the good of the people. *Salus populi*: this was "the sole law of the state by which he must be judged and under which he must lose his life."

As for the argument that making the king accountable to the courts would lead to endless troubles, *L'Ami du peuple* deemed it more dangerous to refuse the people's call for the monarch's destitution. "Abrogate without fear all the ridiculous laws made for a privileged caste, these laws of the hereditary succession of the crown, these laws regarding personal inviolability," Marat urged the legislators. "The time is over when the French would be ready to engage in bloody wars over the choice of a master; today they see the monarch as a mere public functionary, a useless even dangerous agent. And in Louis XVI they see only an imbecile, a coward, a perjurer, a traitor, a conspirator whom they would watch dragged to the scaffold as coldly as if he were a simple brigand."[34] This was a powerful prophecy, indeed, though one the nation was not yet ready to fulfill.

It was pure gibberish, moreover, Marat held, to claim that the monarch was inviolable, a power not a person. "Everything you say to transform him into a power is just fantasy and absurdity," Marat chided the deputies. "What you say to turn him into an independent power is truly criminal. What, there exists some independent power in the state other than the people, the sovereign arbiter of all . . . !" There were "vile slaves of the court" working to make their old master absolute, he warned. But Louis Capet had already been "proscribed by the voice of the public as inept, an imbecile, a coward, a deadbeat, a hypocrite, a conniver, a betrayer, a perjurer, a traitor, a conspirator, a hideous tyrant." And this was "the monster sullied with crimes" to whom the treacherous Assembly was proposing to return executive power in the name of the nation that had repudiated him.[35]

Let this horrible attack on the sovereignty of the people be the last one, Marat implored. Let the Parisians finally open their eyes and grasp that it was time to "expel ignominiously this infamous assembly that has messed so long with the rights and interests of the nation and seeks only to perpetuate its existence in order to reestablish despotism." Were the Parisians too blind or cowardly to do justice to these traitors? Then "let the provinces break their federative bond with the capital, abandon it to its unhappy fate, and form a just and free government among themselves. Let them have enough virtue to establish a pure democracy."[36] The People's Friend avowed himself ready to abandon Paris for this democratic confederation. But few could have believed this Parisian ready for such an oath.

MONARCHY OR REPUBLIC?

Pétion, intrepid patriot in Marat's eyes, was the first to address the National Assembly at length in response to Muguet's report. Praised by *L'Ami du peuple* for its "thunderous eloquence," his speech condemned the principle of royal inviolability as a fiction permitting a king to "slaughter men like beasts, bringing fire and sword to his country." To proclaim the monarch not a person but a power was no more than a "miserable subtlety" in Pétion's judgment. "The king . . . is not an abstract being," he insisted to roars of applause from deputies on the left of the hall and the crowd in the galleries; "he is not a power; a judge is not justice, a king is not kingship. A king is a man, a citizen, a public servant, a corporeal being upon whom a penalty can be imposed." Persevering in this vein despite constant interruptions, Pétion ridiculed the arguments that Louis was not bound by a constitution that remained unfinished; that there was as yet no legal basis for indicting him; that calling him to judicial account would incite civil war and foreign invasion. What confidence, he asked, could be placed in a monarch whose guilt or innocence would be left undecided? The issue had to be resolved by bringing Louis XVI for judgment before the National Assembly or a special convention called for that purpose.[37]

The atmosphere in the Assembly was electric over the next few days as conflicting responses to Muguet's report ignited ideological hostilities among the deputies and galvanized the crowd in the galleries. The resulting debates were at once a reprise of deliberations over the royal veto that had occurred almost two years earlier and a virtual rehearsal for arguments that would be heard at the king's trial eighteenth months later. Tense and noisy, constantly interrupted by cheers, jeers, applause, protestations, insults, and even personal threats, they decisively shifted the political configuration of the Assembly.

Principal among the victims of this shift were the deputies of the traditionalist monarchical right. They had become largely marginalized since 9 July, when 294 of them had formally protested the king's arrest and the suspension of his exercise of executive power. Swearing to abstain from active participation in the deliberations of an assembly that was "laying an embryonic republic over the debris of the monarchy," they had vowed to take no part in perpetrating "a crime we do not wish to share." Two of their number, the marquis de Ferrières and the irrepressible Malouet, nonetheless still offered their opinions in print. Ferrières called for an end to the dangerous anarchy of ideas that was serving the efforts of enemies of the public good to arouse and mislead the people. It was easy in an immense city, he insisted, to trigger the eruption of a tumultuous, irrational opinion. But this "so-vaunted public opinion" was still only that of a few individuals, imprinted with terror and circulated in speeches, journals, and publications. Malouet, for his part, decried "the truly frightening example of the despotism of errors when they obtain the favor and support of the multitude." Denouncing a new fanaticism that disdained the wisdom and experience of the ages, he warned that liberty could never to be found in the land of republican chimeras.[38]

Political reality, these traditionalists argued, could only be found by going back to 1789, to the *cahiers* the deputies had first carried with them to the Estates General. Honoring the monarchical government France had known for fourteen hundred years, these *cahiers* had been the true mandates the people had laid upon its representatives. The National Assembly had shredded them by asserting its own claims to constituent power. In repudiating binding mandates, it had subjected the minority of the deputies to the will of the majority while simultaneously substituting the particular will of that majority for the general will of the nation. The great crime was not the king's flight; it was the Assembly's arrogation of constituent power. In this conclusion, it might be noted, Malouet and Marat were in large agreement.

To indict the king now for leaving Paris, Malouet cautioned the Assembly, would abolish what was left of monarchical government. His reasoning was simple: make the king removable, and you have a republic. It was madness, Ferrières agreed, that the king's action was now feeding talk of deposition and "the ridiculous chimera of a French republic." The form of representative government necessary in France required a division of powers only achieved when an executive power could secure the unity of the political body while effectively checking the ambitions of a legislature.

Was the Assembly, in a moment of political breakdown, social crisis, and foreign threat, now going to overthrow the constitution it had decreed? How monstrous would be "a republic composed of twenty-five million men equal in rights, equal even in opinion, all authorized to participate individually in the making of the law and the nomination of magistrates because, make no mistake, in a republic the man who is not an active citizen is a subject."

An interesting move this, to portray the king as the representative of those to whom the Assembly was denying active citizenship. Ferrières wanted to warn the deputies that, absent a monarch acting as a guarantor of social hierarchy, a republic would bring the threat of social leveling. Fear of the mob ran as a red thread through the debates on royal inviolability. To many, talk of the republic signaled anarchy and equality, the rule of the multitude. "Let's abandon to idle speculators the mad idea of a French republic," Ferrières begged.[39]

These men were pleading a lost cause, an idea of royal inviolability sacred to a monarchical tradition they traced back fourteen centuries. Pushed to the ideological periphery of the Assembly, however, the traditionalists were being replaced by a new right, former moderate constitutionalists defending inviolability, not now as a sacred inheritance but as a "happy fiction," the very cornerstone of constitutional monarchy. These men, too, took up the refrain that there could be no middle ground between monarchy and republic.

The former duc de La Rochefoucauld-Liancourt, a flower of the liberal nobility Marat denounced for infiltrating the Revolution, made his choice clear on 14 July as he opened the second day of debate on the king's fate. Affirming the dogma of absolute inviolability as essential for the separation of powers and the maintenance of liberty, he was followed in due course by others eager to defend constitutional monarchy as a bulwark against faction, a rampart against anarchy, a dike against radical democracy, a safeguard against the dangers of extremes of social equality. A session like this would have been amusing for an impartial spectator, Marat commented in *L'Ami du peuple*. "What a pleasure to hear all these grand antirevolutionary perorators, transformed into imbeciles and ashamed themselves of their metamorphosis," he joked. These men were talking nonsense as they strained to whitewash Louis Capet and prove that his constitutional inviolability allowed him to "cover himself with crimes with impunity, attack the sovereignty of the people, conspire against the public safety, fleece his fellow citizens, drown the nation in its own blood, insult the laws, defy the courts, yet still not be culpable, especially not accountable to justice."[40]

Liancourt's full-blown arguments for the king's inviolability were directed against "those who want a republic." These men were attacking Louis XVI, he charged, but their real target was the monarchy. Political opportunists grasping for "the sort of tyranny the multitude serves as an instrument," they were ready to incite civil war to serve their personal interests and ambitions. Adrien Duport, another "apostate of liberty" in Marat's book, presented the choice between monarchy and republic in less personal and more powerfully constitutionalist terms harking back to the great debates on the royal veto in September 1789. Inviolability, he recapitulated, was the essential condition for the proper exercise of the royal veto: the constitutional device necessary to bridge the gap in representative government between "the real will of the nation" and its "supposed will" as expressed by the legislature. Without it, the king could not prevent the despotism of the deputies by "enabling the people to declare whether this supposed will is its own, whether it recognizes and accepts it." To refer legislative decisions back to the primary assemblies for confirmation would be an absurdity, Salle added in clarification of this argument. It would be "putting the decision to the parts rather than placing it at the point where the general will is formed and the diverse interests meet and are harmonized." The only alternative to a monarch armed with a royal veto to brake the arbitrary exercise of legislative power would be some other body, a senate, or an executive council. Duport put the point succinctly. "The only question for you, Messieurs, is to choose between a republic and a monarchy."[41]

Was a republic really an option? Was it not almost already in place with the king's power suspended? Or was it a rhetorical snare, a code word for popular rule and the tumult traditionally associated with it, a bogeyman inflated by the deputies on the right, a fearful projection of the uncertainty of deputies navigating uncharted constitutional waters? Certainly, few of the representatives on the left took the ideological bait. "Accuse me of republicanism if you wish," Robespierre proclaimed. "I declare I abhor any kind of government where the factious reign." Would the doctrine of inviolability allow a king to slaughter your son or violate your daughter before your eyes? he demanded of the legislators. Would it allow him to visit upon his homeland all the horrors of civil war? The king might be inviolable by virtue of a constitutional fiction, Robespierre declared, but peoples were inviolable by right of nature. It was time, he held, to restart the elections for a new legislature, ending the long reign of an Assembly that was too vulnerable to corruption and the temptations of oligarchical rule. It was imperative to consult the nation regarding Louis XVI's fate.[42]

Marat praised "the faithful Robespierre" throughout the period of these debates, consistently building the latter's reputation as "the Incorruptible." David Bell, in a recent analysis of political charisma in the revolutionary period, has astutely compared Marat, the megalomaniac who projected himself constantly through his journal, with the strategically anticharismatic Robespierre, who claimed never to speak of himself except in response to calumny and in defense of principles. There was a bond, nonetheless, between the two men. The People's Friend never ceased to promote Robespierre as the epitome of political virtue.

There were other speakers Marat found true to the people. One was Prieur, deputy from the Marne and another future member of the Committee of Public Safety. Prieur, too, evaded the charge of republicanism. "I'm not one of the factious . . . ," he soon declared. "Nor am I a republican if a republican is someone who wants to change the constitution; I've sworn to maintain it and I shall defend it to my death." He meant that he would defend it against the king. To attribute inviolability to a monarch duly exercising his constitutional functions was one thing, he contended. To say that a so-called king could attempt to destroy the constitution by virtue of which he reigned was quite another. Prieur found it inconceivable that a nation would fail to bring to judgment an individual who had betrayed the executive power delegated to him. He waved the king's declaration upon leaving Paris as proof of Louis XVI's abandonment of his post. "If these protestations are not an abdication there's never been one," he insisted, "nor will there ever be one."[43]

Omitting any mention of whether Louis XVI would be judged, Muguet's proposed decree had left vague whether exercise of executive power would be immediately returned to him or not. Was it wise, Prieur now demanded, to restore to the person who wanted to destroy the constitution the command of forces intended to defend and maintain it? The deputies had to decide quickly, he urged, before a decision was forced upon them from the streets. His persistence forced a crucial clarification. There was no question of restoring Louis XVI's executive power immediately, Démeunier shot back on behalf of the Constitutional Committee. The king would be suspended from his functions until the constitution had been completed and other grounds for deposition had been included in it. More specifically, one of these grounds would be refusal to accept the constitution "purely and simply." Once this change was made, Démeunier assured the Assembly, there would be no further question of judging the king who had accepted the constitution. On the matter of deposition, constitutional law would be made clear, its future infractions unambiguous, its sanctions automatic! No trial would be necessary.[44] In effect, Démeunier was saying that the whole matter of indicting Louis XVI could be finessed by revising the constitution around him.

A very different note was sounded by one Marc Vadier, an obscure deputy and future terrorist from Pamiers who mounted the tribune the same day to summon "all the energy that liberty can inspire in just and virtuous souls." Vadier's was a language of the streets, the sections, and the radical clubs, an outburst bespeaking the vigorous patriotism of the Ancients. "A great crime has been committed," he asserted; "you have great criminals to decide on, the universe is watching and posterity awaits you." This was a moment of choice, he told the deputies. "You are going, in an instant, to lose or consolidate forever your work and your renown." Before deciding whether a king could be judged in principle, he argued, a question of fact had to be addressed. It concerned "a perjuring and fugitive king, a king who cowardly deserts his post in order to paralyze the government, deliver you to all the horrors of civil war and anarchy, who carries away with him in his flight the presumptive heir to the throne . . . , who dares to shred your constitution in a perfidious manifesto, who has consequently renounced the throne it has handed him." Could such a man still be described as "King of the French"? Was it not superfluous to debate the "monstrous fiction" of inviolability when Louis had already voluntarily and shamefully abdicated the crown? "Could a crowned brigand . . ." At this point in Vadier's speech the Assembly erupted, bitter objections surging from the right, applause from the left. Vadier found himself threatened with fisticuffs.[45]

Ironically, this interruption offered a moment for the president of the Assembly to dispatch its deputation to a *Te Deum* celebrating the muted festival of 14 July. The selection of the deputation's members (Robespierre among them) was interpreted by Marat, among others, as a move to rid the Assembly of its more radical members for a few hours. But how different, in any case, was this occasion from the celebration of the Festival of Federation a year earlier. Petitions demanding the king's deposition were already being readied for circulation among the crowd assembling on the Champ de Mars.

Vadier, in the meantime, was not to be silenced. He continued to expand on the possibility that "a crowned brigand . . . could with impunity kill, burn, conspire, call foreign henchmen to our frontiers, spread desolation and carnage everywhere." Royal inviolability, he warned, would be a true poison in the laws, a pestilential germ that would give birth to the likes of a Nero, of a Sardanapalus. How could the laws be executed in the name of "a deserter, a perjurer," he demanded. "A proud and generous nation" would not calmly abide "this monstrous reversal"; it would not accept such ignominy. He saw no need to rehearse the story of horrors best covered with a "religious veil": the corrupting gold that flowed from the civil list, the perfidies of the royal council, the buildup of an army, the hoarding aimed at piling famine on top of the miseries of war. "The thread of these machinations," he intimated to the deputies nonetheless, could "throw light on the mysteries of iniquity that remain for you to disentangle."

"*You're talking like Marat*," a voice protested from the right of the hall. "These Gentlemen say I talk like Marat," came the retort; "it's because I love liberty." "I don't appear much at the tribune," he added; "I won't bore you with long speeches." "*So much the better*," was the riposte. But Vadier continued nonetheless, speaking long enough to demand that the Assembly restore activity to the electoral assemblies and charge them immediately to name a national convention to decide on the deposition Louis XVI had incurred by his perjury and his flight.[46]

Vadier did indeed talk like Marat. "I would have liked to be able to reprint his energetic speech," The People's Friend noted on 16 July in praise of its "thunderous eloquence." And he did reprint it several days later, in his 19 July issue of *L'Ami du peuple*, after the debate on inviolability had been concluded with no further action taken against the king. By that time, though, his enthusiasm had soured. The speech had been immediately tagged as pure Marat, he acknowledged; as the text had circulated, readers had demanded how this vigorous orator had so long hidden his light under a bushel, depriving the people of his enlightenment and genius. There, perhaps, was the rub, for Marat was not charmed by Vadier's moment of populist acclaim. "If one takes the trouble to examine this fine speech," he fumed, "one will see that it is a tissue of phrases pillaged from patriotic newspapers, especially from *L'Ami du peuple*, whose doctrine was immediately recognized as such."[47]

The People's Friend must have felt profoundly threatened by this new voice speaking his lines. Now he confided to his readers that Vadier had approached him in advance of the 14 July session, asking him out of vanity to publish the speech. He had contented himself with praising it. But Vadier had ended up giving it the lie by throwing his "most cowardly support" toward the eventual adoption of Muguet's decree. For this reason, Marat explained, he would now publish the text in full. Why this bizarre decision? Because "this coward, instead of protesting against an atrocious decree, had fallen to his knees and presented his head to the yoke like a slave." The People's Friend wanted credulous citizens to grasp that "Vadier had no sooner thundered against Louis the conspirator than the enemies of the court had made him an offer and he had sold himself like a beggar."[48] It was scarcely necessary, though, to reprint the speech if the aim was to denounce the author for selling out to the court. Clearly, Marat wanted also to reclaim his own words from this avatar.

With this justification for printing Vadier's speech, *L'Ami du peuple* could also repeat a more general indictment: that the majority of the deputies were still in it for the money. They had suspended elections for a new legislature because they were jealous of those leaders among them who had already made a fortune from the corruption that flowed from the court. They were greedily hanging on to power until they could do the same. "Yes, they'll be gorged," Marat warned, "and they won't give up until the court that is buying them attains the height of its desires and they have decreed the establishment of despotism."[49] Court corruption and parliamentary betrayal went together in this analysis. He still held to the etiology of political evil he had offered in *The Chains of Slavery.*

THE KING ABSOLVED

Vadier, in the meantime, had been back in the spotlight on 15 July, this time reading, as Assembly secretary, a petition presented by members of popular societies assembled on the Champ de Mars in celebration of 14 July. Drafted by the Cordelier Club the previous day, it was signed "The People" and bore individual signatures, a hundred of them, as required by Le Chapelier's regulations. It was brutally direct in telling the deputies that the French had elected them to write a constitution, not to restore to the throne a perjurer who had betrayed his most sacred oaths and revealed his intention to destroy their great work. It reminded them that the first free people, the Romans, had gathered as a people to dictate to the Senate (and not vice versa) whenever they saw the homeland in danger and the interests of all in question. "The present citizens come then with the character inherited from the Romans," it proclaimed, "the character of liberty, that they will defend to the death."

In this spirit, the crowd gathered on the Champ de Mars demanded that the representatives of the nation decide nothing definitive regarding Louis XVI's fate before the communes had been consulted and the voice of the mass of the people had made itself heard. It called on them to swear a sacred oath to await the pronouncement of the public voice on an issue concerning the entire nation, one to which the powers delegated to them did not extend. Beware, it warned, of condemning the homeland to the horrors of civil war that perfidious enemies hoped to inflict. "Remember that you cannot and must not prejudge anything regarding a question of this nature, and that any decree exceeding the limits imposed on you would be reduced to nullity and take the form of the strangest attack on the rights of the sovereign, The People."[50]

The National Assembly shrugged off this latest denial of its sovereign power as a constituent body, as it had done with others. "What I predicted on 11 October has occurred," reported The People's Friend. "The anti-revolutionary conscript fathers, entrenched in their compound against the people they are betraying, have set aside the will of the eighty-three departments, counted as nothing the supreme will of the nation, and defied public indignation in wiping away the atrocious crimes of the ex-monarch." Threatened by "the weight of the truth and of public opinion" and "alarmed by the people's mood," he continued, the leaders of the Assembly had met with Lafayette on the night of 14 July to assure themselves that the National Guard could repress a general insurrection. The following morning, the general had blocked all the avenues with detachments of troops and surrounded the Assembly with five thousand armed men. "Strong in this support," Marat deplored, "the traitors ran to the senate to sanctify the royal crimes, sacrifice to the despot, and deliver the last blows to public liberty."[51]

As debate reopened on 15 July, Guillaume François Charles Goupil de Préfeln, one of the Assembly's more fervent defenders of royal inviolability, launched a tirade against the "consummately perverse machiavellists" intent on destroying the constitution. "The clubs established in this capital, these clubs that have many times displayed their zeal for liberty, have now become nothing but a machine to be used," Préfeln protested, channeling the spirit of Louis XVI's own manifesto on leaving Paris. They were being deployed "to cast the French nation into the abyss of the horrors of anarchy and disorder." "Clubocrats" versed in the arts of misleading the thoughtless multitude had provoked riots and plotted tumult. Journalists and pamphleteers had been recruited to demand the destruction of monarchy and its replacement by the monstrosity of a republic—men like Condorcet ("covered with a reputation earned one knows not how, and decorated with the title of academician") and Brissot (less of a celebrity, in Préfeln's estimation, but nonetheless willing to traffic in his erudition). The latter's speech to the Jacobin Club on 10 July had been circulated by that body as if "public opinion resides only in [Brissot de] Warville and his followers," Préfeln grumbled. "They say confidently in these clubs that it is the general will of all Paris." The word goes out to the provinces, he objected, then it boomerangs back to the capital to be misrepresented as the putative will of all the departments (by those who don't even know there are eighty-three!).[52]

Outbidding earlier defenders of royal inviolability in "baseness and atrocity," Marat observed, Préfeln wanted Muguet's draft decree to state explicitly the "servile adage" that the person of the king was inviolable and sacred. He was no less eager to slander the popular writers who had demonstrated that absolute inviolability of the prince was incompatible with national sovereignty. To this latter attack Marat responded in a striking personal note. He himself had been the first to establish the principle of popular sovereignty, he insisted, and he should therefore have been at the head of the list of writers Préfeln had denounced. Instead, he had been targeted but not named. Adding insult to this injury, Préfeln had fixed blame on Condorcet, the enduring enemy Marat quickly dismissed as a "mediocre academician and writer in the pay of the court." Readers of *L'Ami du peuple* were invited to "judge whether this intriguer whom Louis Capet named commissioner of the treasury and is enjoying 25,000 livres in court handouts would risk losing his riches by offending his master."[53] The personal pique of *I said it first* was manifest in this note, but perhaps also fear (as in Marat's resentment of Vadier's speech) that the prophet was becoming marginalized as more prominent established figures moved toward radical positions.

Following Préfeln to the tribune, the abbé Grégoire, lauded by Marat for his patriotism, demanded that Muguet's entire report be rejected and a national convention named to judge the king's actions. In this radical priest's view, Louis XVI had abandoned his post as first public functionary of the realm, knowingly exposing the nation to the dangers of civil war. Grégoire rejected the claim that no prior legislation had explicitly prohibited such an action, ridiculing it in light of "the maxim revered by the entire universe, that the people's safety is the supreme law." Finding the arguments for inviolability absurd, he called for the electoral assemblies to be reactivated to name a national convention to judge the king's actions. The law had to be the expression of the common will, he reiterated. "The representatives of the people would outrage the nation if they decided its fate without it and perhaps against it, against its wish!"[54]

L'Ami du peuple judged these arguments devastating, but the debate continued nonetheless until Salle, calling for calm in tones the journal ridiculed as "folksy" and "sanctimonious," stipulated proposed constitutional articles that would henceforth trigger a king's abdication under a revised version of the constitution. His draft decree was adopted immediately, "despite the protests of the faithful Robespierre." The decision was followed by calls to bring the debate to a close.[55]

Deputies to the left, nonetheless, were not ready to call it a day. Demanding the floor, one of their most eloquent speakers, François Buzot, opened a lengthy attack on the principle of inviolability and the accessory notion that the king could only be held accountable for offenses prohibited by a prior law. "Absolute inviolability cannot exist in your decrees," he lectured the deputies. "What! A king-individual would attempt to overthrow the constitution and enslave his fellow citizens, and the French nation could not depose and punish him," he expostulated. In this case, "Nero and Caligula would have been inviolable in France; they could have abandoned themselves with impunity to all the ferocious tastes that have stained their history, bathe at leisure in the blood of the unfortunates the law had subjected to them."

Pausing only to invoke the names of Rousseau, Mably, Pufendorf, and Algernon Sidney, Buzot turned more attentively to an unlikely source, William Blackstone, the legal authority known to many as one of England's firmest supporters of royal prerogative. The silence of the law, Blackstone had maintained in Buzot's account, did not authorize the performance of any action not explicitly prohibited. Nor did deposition require exhaustive prior enumeration of circumstances in which a king could be considered to have abdicated his crown. Future generations had to be free to decide such matters when and as they were forced to do so, "because the natural rights of society can never be destroyed or weakened, either by time or any constitution." To assure the balance between legislative and executive powers, moreover, each had to remain independent of the other; neither could be subjected to the other's judgment.

Following this logic, a decision regarding Louis XVI had to be taken by the nation, not its representatives. Its terms did not have to be spelled out by the constitution in advance or defined by the National Assembly in retrospect. James II had been deposed and replaced in England not by Parliament but by an ad hoc national convention, Buzot reminded his fellow deputies. "I do not believe that, on principle, you can follow any other conduct." For the National Assembly to decide the matter, whether as a legislative body or as a constituent assembly, would violate the people's sovereignty. "The nation alone will judge whether Louis XVI can lay claim to its confidence; whether he can take back the reins of a government difficult to lead after a long Revolution; whether it can at last promise itself, under such a prince, the order and tranquility that must revive from the harmony and confidence among the governed, the representatives, and their rulers."[56]

Buzot's was a serious and sober speech, a decisionist manifesto with radical implications. It was overpowered, nonetheless, by the parliamentary pyrotechnics soon displayed by Antoine Barnave, the Assembly heavyweight who became the last major speaker in this fateful series of debates. One of the deputies chosen to chaperone Louis XVI back from Varennes, Barnave was already a "bribed apostate" in Marat's book. In fact, he had been engaged for weeks in strategic secret discussions with the court, aimed at keeping the monarch in place. The event of the king's flight was solidifying the Revolution, he now assured the Assembly. It was forcing a more profound understanding of "what the crowd had perhaps not yet understood . . . the nature of monarchical government." Decrying political fabulists who were invoking the case of America to demonstrate the possibility of a republic in a vast territory, he cast the nation's choice in more brutal terms. Monarchy or Republic? Monarchy would guarantee stability and liberty; a republic could do nothing but spawn the twin evils of anarchy and tyranny.[57]

Dismissing the American example, Barnave also repudiated the British one. He had little patience for Buzot's resort to Blackstone in support of demands for a national convention to decide the king's fate. With their de facto form of government, he retorted, the British were constantly obliged to derive their laws from circumstances. They had not anticipated possible grounds for deposition because they had no written constitution. In effect, they were condemned to improvise in a context of competing political passions and interests. The French, in contrast, desired order and predictability. They wanted their political laws, like their civil laws, to be fixed in advance. They wanted to eliminate all arbitrariness. They aimed, "in a country more subject to revolutions because it is larger, to lay down a stable base that would anticipate or master events, and to submit even revolutions to constitutional law."[58] With this argument, Barnave in effect offered a reconceptualization, in constitutionalist terms, of the traditional claims for French absolutism as a form of government securing the mastery of time and events—an achievement that had constantly eluded the tumultuous nation across the Channel.

Barnave located the key to mastering political vicissitude in the principle of royal inviolability. Essential to secure the separation and mutual independence of executive and legislative powers, this inviolability was both political and personal. It was protected in regard to the monarch's political conduct by the constitutional requirement that executive decisions bear the countersignature of ministers to be held personally accountable for any infraction of the law. And it had to be maintained in relation to the monarch's personal conduct by ensuring his immunity from any prosecution for offenses under civil and criminal law. The state, Barnave argued, was "evidently not obliged to sacrifice the people's safety and the established government to an individual complaint." Apart from provision for a regency in case of royal insanity, a king was inviolable until he ceased to be king, which could only occur in the event of his deposition for actions explicitly prohibited in the constitution under which he held his authority. Hence the inevitable conclusion: Louis XVI's flight had not been barred by the constitution; he therefore remained inviolable.[59]

The genius of this reasoning was to take the king's individual conduct out of the equation. "We have to choose between attachment to the constitution and resentment against a man," Barnave lectured the deputies. The great virtue of the hereditary principle, he reasoned, was that its mechanism allowed for no personal or moral discriminations. It worked automatically to produce a monarch whose personal conduct had to be irrelevant to the stability of government. If this were not the case, he continued to a wave of applause, "I would see the greatest danger not in the king's faults but in his grand actions; I would distrust his vices less than his virtues." To enemies of Louis XVI leveling "complaints that are perhaps justifiable morally but very puerile in politics" he offered a cynical rejoinder. "You'd be at his feet if you were content with him."[60]

L'Ami du peuple erupted at this comment, invoking the popular disdain that had recently been showered on Barnave as a supporter of colonial slaving interests. "Vile apostate!" Marat spat back. "We'll act in his regard as we have in yours. . . . You saw how rapidly the encomiums we lavished on you gave way to the opprobrium with which you are now covered. In the same way, the blessings that rained on Louis XVI so long as he was believed to be faithful to his vows have yielded to the maledictions now heaped upon him."[61]

In Barnave's analysis, sacrificing the constitution to resentment against one individual risked losing liberty for all. How could those mobilizing the people against Louis XVI not anticipate popular enthusiasm for some great man who might, in turn, overthrow their "absurd Republic"? Believing that the nation could destroy monarchy in a moment of agitation, how could they not recognize that the people could soon reverse itself, not to reestablish a monarchical constitution but to create "the most terrible tyranny, that established against the law, created blindly"? With these questions, Barnave decisively refocused the issue the Assembly faced. Popular agitation was the real threat to France in his analysis, not the looming counterrevolutionary invasion Louis XVI had allegedly intended to ignite by fleeing across the frontier. France could defend itself, if necessary, from foreign powers aiming to incite counterrevolutionary violence. Talk of such "chimerical dangers" served only the purposes of those who wanted to keep the people in a constant state of arousal. "It's not our feebleness I fear," he continued, "but our agitations, the indefinite prolongation of our revolutionary fervor. . . . I don't fear foreign nations. I fear the continuation of the anxieties and agitations that will always be present among us until the revolution is totally and peacefully ended."[62]

The essential issue, then, as Barnave now framed it, was not the fate of the king but the future of the Revolution. "Shall we end the revolution or shall we restart it," he demanded. "Any change is fatal today, any prolongation of the revolution disastrous." In this logic, the revolutionary movement could go no further without danger. Advancing in the direction of liberty would lead to destruction of the monarchy; moving in the direction of equality would lead to an attack on property. The men who want to make revolutions don't do so with abstractions, Barnave warned. They need the multitude, which is mobilized by "realities," by "palpable advantages." He was talking property, which the National Assembly had upheld on 4 August 1789 when it destroyed privilege. Would the deputies now open the way to a new Fourth of August attacking property itself? If the Revolution were to continue, Barnave argued, this would be its only remaining target.[63]

The conclusion was clear: the common interest required that the Revolution be brought to an end. It remained only for the deputies to complete the work to which they had already devoted two years. "Regenerators of the Empire, representatives of the French nation, hold directly to your course," he urged. "You will return to your homes having obtained by your courage the satisfaction and love of the most ardent friends of the revolution, and by new positive actions you will secure blessings on behalf of us all, or at least the silence of calumny." With this peroration, to rapturous applause, Barnave rested the case for the king's absolution. This time, the Assembly declared discussion closed and hastened to adopt Salles's constitutional articles specifying actions that would in future trigger a monarch's deposition. The language of the decree was made definitive the next day: the king would be deemed to have abdicated if he failed to take an oath to maintain the constitution, if he placed himself at the head of an invading army or refused to denounce an invasion in his name, or if he left the country and refused to return. An address explaining all this to the nation was planned but never materialized.[64]

Fanning fears of popular mobilization with anxiety regarding the rights of property, Barnave thus fueled the desire of the majority of the deputies to be done with the Revolution and head home. The king would not now be brought to judgment, either before the National Assembly or before a national convention. Neither convicted nor acquitted, he would be simply held in limbo until a revised constitution had spelled out more explicit conditions for his resumption of a simulacrum of executive power exercised in fact by ministers responsible to the representative body. In effect, Louis XVI had been saved by casting him as an institutional cipher, a symbol of law and order to be regarded as irrelevant in both his political and personal conduct, a kind of empty placeholder not so very different from the crowned automaton Condorcet had recommended in his scorching republican satire. The result was to prove very different. The automaton would turn disruptive.

Marat, in the meantime, was outraged at this outcome. "By this iniquitous, atrocious, infamous decree, Louis Capet is not only shielded from the blade of justice but absolved, whitewashed, declared not guilty of crimes with which he has just covered himself," protested *L'Ami du peuple.* He had been "raised above the empire of the law, invited to satisfy without restraint his brutal appetites and his ferocious tendencies . . . , encouraged to commit his most evil attacks . . . , authorized to flee and conspire without end." What recourse would there be if a king simply appeared at the head of a counterrevolutionary army bringing death and destruction? Deemed to have abdicated the throne, how would he respond? *What me,* would he say, *choosing to abdicate the throne? Don't even think about it, rebellious subjects! I want only to slit your throats if I can't put you back under the yoke.* "He will have already shed rivers of blood and put the nation back in irons before . . . it has dared to defend itself, march against the tyrant, and make him atone for his crimes under the executioner's blade."[65] Where Barnave and company saw a constitutional fiction, Marat saw the threat of tyranny.

As ever, his denunciation of the faithless deputies went along with ridicule of a people calling itself sovereign but allowing itself to be treated as enslaved. This "senseless people" had wanted to be rid of "a prince besmirched by his crimes and covered with opprobrium," but would now recognize him as an august master. It had wanted to repudiate an infamous perjurer but would now accept his vows. It had wanted execution of the laws no longer entrusted to their most audacious violator but would now allow him to direct its tribunals and administrations. Henceforth the responsibilities of government, the fate of the state, and the public safety would depend on a criminal without honor and without shame. "He'll corrupt the representatives, dissipate the treasury, produce ruin," Marat howled, "but you'll watch his villainies in silence and respect his person. It's been ordained *sacred* by the faithless delegates who have sold him your rights for gold. From now on he'll be everything, and you're already nothing."

In the despairing conclusion The People's Friend now offered, the Revolution indeed seemed over. Nascent liberty, conquered in 1789 by a swarm of unarmed indigents, had been stifled in its cradle, under the aegis of the Parisian guard, by the pretended fathers of the homeland charged to secure it. These treasonous deputies had handed the monarch all he would need to effect a counterrevolution with impunity. Should there ever be faithful deputies, they would be bound by their predecessors' decision to transform the constitution into a contract with their master. Any effort to reform the laws would be blocked by the vile monarch on the grounds that he had sworn to maintain the constitution *as it is*. Marat's judgment of the people was acerbic. "Now that, despite my cries, you have cowardly allowed [the king's] henchmen to give him back all the springs of authority, and all the forces of the nation, here you are today enchained by your own hands. Deplore your blindness from now on and bewail the lot that awaits you. But No! Gaily take back your chains, efface by your base actions your vague desires for freedom, prostate yourself at the foot of the despot, topple the altar of the homeland and dance around its debris, as you once danced around the ruins of the Bastille. That's the only role that suits your abasement, and your cowardice."[66]

MASSACRE AT THE CHAMP DE MARS

Was this a bitterly satirical acknowledgment of defeat or a desperate last-minute incitement to popular action? Was a popular insurrection still possible? There were certainly conditions to prepare such an event. Tensions between the National Guard and the Parisian populace had worsened in the weeks following the king's flight. Political uncertainty had been compounded by economic unrest. Recent closing of public workshops had only expanded the numbers and increased the desperation of the unemployed and homeless in the capital. Bailly and Lafayette were widely thought to be plotting to squeeze the indigent out of the city. Conflicts had flared higher in the streets as the National Guard was caught between political dissension and swelling popular protests against the king's treachery, on one hand, and the determination of the majority in the National Assembly to quell resistance and keep the monarch in place, on the other. Protestations, petitions, placards, pamphlets, and prints had swirled through the sweltering summer streets. Competing journals had traded denunciations. Pockets were being searched by the guardsmen, bags opened. Stop-and-frisk had become the order of the day.

The location of sovereignty, too, was patently up for grabs in these weeks. Was it in the clubs and fraternal societies that had sprung up throughout the city? Was it in street gatherings and demonstrations? Was it in the eighty-three departments? Or was it in a tarnished and tattered National Assembly approaching its end and now suddenly struggling to secure the constitution upon which it had labored for so many months? Never more contested, this issue exploded on 15 July as the agitated capital received news of the deputies' decision to shelter Louis XVI from judgment.

Already primed by anger that the site of the National Assembly had been sealed off from the people, the Cordelier Club and members of fraternal societies gathered at the Champ de Mars that evening in a crowd of thousands. A petition was soon sent to warn the legislators of the consequences of their decision to spare the king, but the delegation carrying it was turned away by the people's most trusted deputies, Robespierre and Pétion, on the grounds that the fateful decree was now irrevocable. At this point, frustrated demonstrators raced to the overflowing Palais Royal, where a meeting of Bonneville's Society of the Friends of the Truth soon turned into a huge republican demonstration repudiating the Assembly's decision to absolve the monarch without prior consent of the entire nation in the primary assemblies. Thence, in due course, thousands more protesters marched to the Jacobin Club, whose members were themselves engaged in a contentious effort to frame a petition of their own. As the forced incursion of several hundred demonstrators threw this assembly into chaos with their calls for a republic, a majority of the deputies exited the premises and betook themselves to the nearby former convent of the Feuillants. In a schism that proved irreparable, they quickly formed a rival, more moderate society henceforth known by the name of their new haven. Many saw the irony that yet another revolutionary club had claimed the site, and with it the name, of a religious order the Revolution had destroyed.

The next morning, 16 July, the Jacobins remaining in the club adopted a draft petition that a committee (notably including Danton and Brissot) had fashioned overnight. It demanded that the National Assembly acknowledge on the nation's behalf that Louis XVI had abdicated the throne by taking flight. This phrasing, taken to imply continuation of the monarchy with a minor king under the regency of the deeply mistrusted duc d'Orléans, turned out to be explosive. It was vigorously repudiated when the draft was brought for signature to the crowd at the Champ de Mars—fifty thousand strong in Marat's account[67]—where radical voices were clamoring for a republic. The text was eventually sent back for revision to the Jacobin Club, which voted after much discussion to retain the original formulation. At news that the National Assembly's decision exculpating the king had now been formalized, the entire problematic petition was dropped by the club's leaders.

Meanwhile, Mayor Bailly had been summoned to the National Assembly to face complaints that the municipality had been too lax in its efforts to maintain order. Deputies griped that collective petitions had been permitted despite their prohibition; that dangerous gatherings had been allowed to threaten fire, pillage, and devastation; that they themselves had been threatened as they entered the assembly hall. It was time for more rigorous repression, the most frantic among them insisted; it was time for martial law, for a crackdown on popular societies, for suppression of the press. To Marat, all this was reminiscent of the prelude to reaction and repression in the Nancy affair. He, too, called now for stronger measures. "Inept and cowardly citizens," he raged against the people, "what bulwark have you raised against the torrent of legislative and municipal despotism. . . . What are you going to do to finally punish these cowardly prevaricators, these traitors, these eternal conspirators?" Petitions? What good were these petitions when they were treated with such contempt by an Assembly that scarcely heard them before casting them aside?

"Blows not words are necessary," The People's Friend now shouted, reminding the Cordeliers that "you boast of having among you forty tyrannicides who have vowed to perish for the good of the homeland." What were they waiting for, these tyrannicides? "Until the homeland is no more, and your oppressors have drowned your children in their blood?" One assassination would have sufficed, Marat proclaimed.

> Ah! If there were only a single Scaevola within our walls, liberty would have been secured forever among us long ago. A single stab of the dagger in Motier's heart would have . . . allowed the people to recover power and fell beneath its avenging blade the criminal heads of the leaders of its most mortal enemies. Babbling, stupid people, make motions, draft petitions, exhaust yourself in empty talk, make the air resound with your complaints, your grievances, your empty projects. . . . My poor citizens, it's not with words that you will subdue the hordes of criminals sworn against your happiness, hellbent to destroy you. If they were the strongest, they would slaughter you without pity. So stab them mercilessly.

The list designating immediate victims for bloody sacrifice included many of the most notable revolutionary leaders: Le Chapelier, Rabaut, Duport, Barnave, Démeunier, Malouet, Préfeln, Target, Sieyès, Dupont, Bailly, Lafayette, and a dozen others.[68]

Despite deployment of the National Guard to prevent any mass movement, the crowd reassembled on the Champ de Mars the morning of 17 July. Two men were soon discovered attempting to hide under the altar of the homeland. Suspected of planting a bomb (on Lafayette's orders, Marat charged), they were dragged away, lynched, and decapitated. As news of this act of popular justice ignited calls in the National Assembly for extreme measures to repress disorder, the stalwart republican François Robert took the lead at the Champ de Mars in drawing up yet another petition. This one demanded that the deputies convoke a new constituent body to proceed "in a truly national manner to judge the guilty monarch and decide on the replacement and organization of a new executive power."[69]

Demonstrators in their thousands were lining up to sign this coded call for a republic as Bailly declared a general emergency and marched infantry and cavalry units from City Hall under the red flag of martial law. Reinforced en route by troops under Lafayette's command, the forces of order lost control of the situation upon their arrival at the Champ de Mars, fired on the crowd, scattered and chased demonstrators, and mowed them down as they fled the field. Estimates of the casualties ranged from the tens to the thousands. Marat claimed that four hundred bodies had been thrown into the Seine and allowed to flow into the sea.[70] It seems likely, though, that several score were killed and many more wounded.

The account *L'Ami du peuple* gave of this "*Hideous massacre of peaceable citizens, women and children gathered on the Champ de Mars, barbarously slaughtered by order of the infernal Motier,*" was couched in a language of searing rage. On 20 July, denouncing "*Legislative tyranny shored up by military despotism,*" the journal launched a wholesale attack. "Never before had such a tissue of infamies, crimes and horrors been deployed by tyrants to stifle liberty and destroy its defenders," it screamed. "And these are our mandataries, the men we have honored with our choice, accorded boundless confidence, invested with our powers to defend our rights and interests and guarantee our liberty and happiness. They have covered themselves with the mask of hypocrisy to impose on us, enveloping themselves with sophisms, subtleties, tricks, traps, lies and impostures in order to annul the declaration of rights, the sacred basis of the constitution."

There followed a kind of summary indictment of the crimes of the representative body Marat had been denouncing for months. Under the pretext of enforcing the laws and defending the state, the treacherous deputies had fomented troubles and spread false alarms in order to restore to the monarch who was paying them all the resources of authority and the arbitrary control of the nation's forces. They had stripped the people of its patrimony to gorge the bloodsuckers of the court, the public extortioners, royal agents, and custodians of the shameful secrets of the ministries. They had sold the people's sovereignty and the rights of citizens to the monarch for cash on the barrel, wresting from the blade of justice the minions of the despot and traitors to the homeland. They had whitewashed a monarch a hundred times guilty of lèse-nation, restoring him to his royal functions against the will of the nation, and suppressing the clear-sighted citizens still daring to resist oppression.

Above all, Marat charged, the bloodstained deputies, intent on reigning only over slaves, had now ordered in cold blood the massacre of the friends of the liberty they had the effrontery to say they were restoring. He was convinced the carnage was premeditated. Bailly had confiscated all weapons available for sale across the city to prevent a general insurrection in response, he reported, while Lafayette had assembled his "paid brigands" in the National Guard together with troops from counterrevolutionary districts fired up with cash and liquor. The crowd had been seeded with provocateurs primed to pelt the troops with stones as they arrived, and to fire off a few random pistol shots. These actions became the excuse to slaughter unarmed citizens in cold blood. It was left for Bailly to rush to the National Assembly to deplore the tragic events he had brought about on its orders and to boast of his efforts to maintain public tranquility; for the conspiratorial deputies to applaud these atrocities and applaud its infamous perpetrators for "bathing in the blood of their unfortunate fellow citizens"; and for Lafayette's minions to run through the streets accusing the popular societies of responsibility for this atrocity.[71]

The inevitable sequel to the massacre on the Champ de Mars was the attack against the popular press and freedom of speech that deputies had been demanding for some time and now decreed on 18 July. In the first among several repressive articles, the Assembly declared that "all persons who provoke murder, pillage, arson, and explicitly counsel disobedience to the law, whether in placards or posters, in published or hawked books, or in speeches in public places or assemblies, will be regarded as seditious or disruptive of the public peace" and subject henceforth to immediate arrest and punishment according to the law. Protests from the left decried this measure as grievous for the press, indeed "fatal to Marat, Brissot, Laclos, Danton."

This decree was criminalizing the despair of the oppressed, echoed *L'Ami du peuple*. It was an outrage to the humanity of peaceful citizens crying out in fear, an attack on their natural expression of the right of self-defense. "Infamous legislators, vile criminals, monsters transformed by gold and blood, privileged brigands who traffic with the monarch in our fortunes, our rights, our liberty, our ideas, you believe you can strike the patriotic writers with terror and immobilize them in fright at the prospect of punishment," the journal raged. "As for The People's Friend, you've long known that your decrees contradicting the Declaration of Rights are nothing but ass-wipes for him." Would that he could rally two thousand men, he seethed. He would have them rip out Motier's heart amid his battalions of slaves, burn the monarch in his palace along with his henchmen, skewer the legislators to their seats and bury them beneath the cinders of their chamber. "Just Heaven! Would that he could pass on to the souls of his fellow citizens the fire that devours his own; would that he could leave the tyrants of the world a terrifying example of popular vengeance. Oh, my homeland! Hear the tones of my grief and despair."[72]

In the repression that followed, the distribution network of *L'Orateur du peuple* and *L'Ami du peuple* became a particular target of an order posted by the municipality of Paris on 27 July. All hawkers, sellers, or distributors of these publications, and others that seemed intended "only to encourage crime and overthrow the constitution under the fraudulent veil of fanatical patriotism," were threatened with arrest. It was preferable, the municipality judged, "to prevent all offenses rather than to punish them." This manifesto of preventive censorship was roundly denounced as an abuse of press freedom—not least by Condorcet, one of Marat's favorite targets. But by then the press from which *L'Ami du peuple* had been rolling copy had already been smashed.[73]

TWENTY

REPRESSION, REVISION, DESPAIR

The night of 20 July, police descended on 8 rue de Buci in the faubourg Saint-Germain where, on the second floor, they entered the apartment of Anne-Félicité Colombe. Of the two individuals they encountered, one was correcting proofs that turned out to be number 525 of *L'Ami du peuple* and a manuscript of its projected number 528. Interrogated, he declared himself to be Conrard Redelé, residing at the Café des Étrangers on the rue Saint-Louis, a compositor who had been working for Colombe for several months at a press on the third floor of the building. He attested that he had never seen the journal's author and knew nothing of him. Turning their attention to their second suspect, Colombe herself, the agents found her ready to acknowledge that she was the printer of these papers but unable or unwilling to identify the two individuals, a man and a woman, from whom she received the manuscripts and payment for her work. Search of the apartment disclosed a "considerable quantity" of issues of *L'Ami du peuple* and *L'Orateur du peuple* along with a third publication, *Colère du Père Duchesne*. A further room revealed another resident, one Adrien Deflers, a printer whose desk yielded an additional stash of printed copies and manuscripts of *L'Ami du peuple*. Mounting to the third floor, the agents found the offending press with a tray of type set up to print Marat's number 525. The tray was taken as evidence; the press itself soon followed, broken into fragments.[1]

Eager to track down an entire network, the police hurried to other addresses. Finding no one at home at the lodging of the butcher Legendre in the rue des Boucheries Faubourg Saint-Germain, where Marat had been hiding for some time, they moved on to the site of the Café du Rendez-Vous on rue de Condé. The second floor of that building housed the apartment of the lawyer Claude Rémy Buirette Verrières, identified as a former seigneur around forty years old, whose handwriting Colombe had identified on papers in her possession. This was the lawyer who had defended her so effectively in her earlier lawsuits against Lafayette's spies. Searching Verrières's lodging intensively in his absence, the agents found a quantity of copies of *L'Ami du peuple* and *L'Orateur du peuple*, publications of the Cordelier Club, and other papers and letters, all of which they confiscated. They then compelled the doorman to identify Fréron's apartment, which happened to be connected to Verrières's. A neighboring locksmith was recruited to open it up. "The most exacting search" failed to discover the occupant, but its continuation yielded "at least 20,000 copies of *L'Orateur du peuple*," some of *L'Ami du peuple*, and a bag of other papers, to say nothing of gunpowder and equipment for making ammunition. The agents were about to end their search when Verrières himself arrived, in time to be arrested and taken to police headquarters.

Interrogation during the night explored many aspects and evidence of Verrières's political activities but focused above all on his association with Jean-Paul Marat. Had he not written and had printed a journal entitled *L'Ami du peuple, ou Le Publiciste parisien par Marat? Never.* Had he not written the manuscript of the incriminating number 258 of that journal? *No, he did not recognize that manuscript and it was not in his handwriting.* Had he written a manuscript defending the National Guard officer Santerre against Lafayette's charges? *Yes, he had written it; half of it was in his own hand, the rest in that of a copyist, one [Evrard?] currently living in the rue du Temple.* Did he recognize the handwriting of an address for Marat, and a reply, that appeared on one of this manuscript's pages? *Yes, he had written the address but did not recognize the handwriting of the response.* Had a draft contract for the writing and printing of a journal entitled *L'Ami du peuple* been written by him? *He did not recognize it, it was not in his handwriting, and he had never seen it.* Had it not been found in his apartment? *That was impossible, or perhaps it had been put there.* Did he not recognize as his own the handwriting on the manuscript of number 515 of that journal also found in his apartment? *It could not have been found there and he had never seen it.* What about some manuscripts apparently written in a numerical code? *He knew nothing about them; he had never learned the art of reading or writing in that way; and they could not have been found where he lived.* Did he recognize letters found among his papers and know their authorship? *Yes, they were written by Marat, whom he had known since the previous November when the journalist had charged him to defend Colombe against Estienne and others. He had not seen Colombe since the end of her lawsuit in January when she had paid him two-and-a-half louis d'or to defend her. As for Marat, there had been no other correspondence with him.* Did he know where Marat lived? *No, but he had written to him at the Café Flamand on the rue des Cannettes.* Had he been among the crowd at the Champ de Mars in recent days? *He had been there on the sixteenth to hear the presentation of the abortive Jacobin petition, but not on the following day. And yes, he had been imprisoned for twenty-four hours for a small debt, but charges had been dropped.*

One final question: was it true that he had dumped some papers in the convenience of his buildings a few days earlier, covering them over with some rubble and plaster debris? *Yes, he had disposed of some mouse-eaten legal papers. The plaster was fragments of a bust of Lafayette that had been broken at the house of Camille Desmoulins the previous winter and brought home by Fréron. He did not know why the bust of Lafayette had been broken chez Desmoulins, had not been there, and had only learned about it after Fréron brought the plaster pieces home.*[2]

This inquisition over, Verrières, Deflers, Redelé, and Colombe were taken to the prison in the former abbey of Saint-Germain. Questioned there two days later, Deflers claimed to have been using Colombe's press to print the journal of the Jacobin Club. He denied all responsibility for the manuscripts and printed copies of *L'Ami du peuple* that had been found in his desk, which he reported he frequently left open to the use of others. He had read only two issues of that journal in his life, having found them "too disgusting to read more." These disclaimers apparently satisfied the authorities enough to secure his release.

As for Colombe, she was less fortunate. Marat later published two letters he said she had written to Mayor Bailly (though it's not clear how he would have known about them). The first, from the prison of La Force on 22 July, protested her situation in chains "among criminals and women of the streets," demanding prompt judgment and an early end to her captivity. "I'm claiming the protection of the law," she reminded the mayor; "as for yours, I despise it." The second letter, from the Abbey of Saint-Germain the following week, was no less bitter in decrying the illegality of her imprisonment without formal charges. "Tell me how you square your professed respect for the laws with the audacity you show in infringing upon them," she demanded. "Don't forget that I am innocent, and I am in chains."

Her cries, if heard, must have had little effect. It was left to Marat to report (though he seems later to have had second thoughts about this account) that she went to the scaffold with other victims of the repression that had followed the Champ de Mars Massacre. "The atrocities she endured . . . inspire horror," he mourned in a brief eulogy. "But if the barbarism of her persecutors was extreme, her courage was even greater. The sentiment of her innocence, and of the cause for which she suffered, raised her above that of her misfortunes and the fear of torments. Her energy astonished her tyrants, jailors and judges. She entered a dark prison without blanching and left it without having bent an instant under her oppressors."[3] Scores of other individuals were caught up in this "little Terror," as some historians have dubbed it; many were left imprisoned until they were released by a general amnesty in mid-September. "The cells overflow with patriots thrown into chains," Marat wrote in mid-August. He later estimated their number at five hundred or six hundred—the emblematic figures upon which he had remained strangely fixated as a benchmark for preemptive slaughter.[4] Plausible estimates of arrests during this period are hard to come by, but it seems that the distribution network of *L'Orateur du peuple* and *L'Ami du peuple* had been made a particular target of this repression. Fréron, among other potential targets, had slipped away from the capital in mid-July.[5]

What of The People's Friend himself? Where was he? This was the obvious question, but there were others. Not only where was he, but who. Not only who was he, but if. Word was that Verrières was the real author of *L'Ami du peuple*. Word was, to the contrary, that the journal had been the instrument, all along, of an insidious counterrevolutionary plot to destabilize the Revolution and bring it to a catastrophic end. Word was that the real Marat was being hunted along with clandestine printers and other radical journalists. Word was that he had been arrested. So thought Mme Roland when she reported on 22 July that "Marat, who had been very ill and rumored poisoned, has recovered in time to be imprisoned with many others." More bizarrely, though, word was that he was long dead, assassinated by a counterrevolutionary faction now using his journal to incite anarchy as a means to bring back despotism.[6]

Having made this dramatic claim three weeks earlier, the journalist Gorsas returned to it on 23 July, determined to blame the anonymous criminals who had taken over *L'Ami du peuple* for the entire bloody horror visited upon the nation on the Champ de Mars. But Fréron had already blasted this notion in a bulletin reporting on his ally's health. "How sad it is," *L'Orateur du peuple* had declared, "for the friends of liberty to know that the most alarming illness has as its prey the most intrepid defender of the people's rights, one of the writers most honored by the hatred of all the conspirators he has relentlessly unmasked, a citizen inflamed with the purest and most indefatigable patriotism." Eager to repudiate rumors that The

People's Friend was no longer living, Fréron refuted the "absurd calumny of [Marat's] assassination" by insisting that the alleged victim had surfaced to dine with friends in Versailles a fortnight earlier, "having decided to rise from the tomb where he had remained hidden for fifteen months." The report ended with a pious hope. "May this writer dear to the homeland soon be restored to his vocation."[7]

It was to be some time before Fréron's hope was fulfilled. Several counterfeit versions of *L'Ami du peuple* had invaded its space in the meantime, but it sputtered back to life on 7 August, blasting a draft of the constitution that had been presented in its entirety to the National Assembly for the first time two days earlier.[8] Thereafter, the journal's publication gradually recovered a measure of regularity as Marat followed the deputies' efforts to finalize the language of the text upon which they had been laboring since 1789. He did so without his most energetic ally. Soon after his return to the capital, Fréron left *L'Orateur du peuple* in other hands.

A HISTORY OF AN ILLUSION

Still under threat of repression, *L'Ami du peuple* resumed its clandestine circulation in dark despair. Hidden away during a period of enforced silence, Marat had not stopped reflecting upon "the evils into which the stupid credulity of the people had plunged it." In the account he offered his readers on 14 August, the French Revolution rested on a political illusion. His analysis evokes François Furet's much-debated interpretation (following early Marx) of the "illusion of politics" originating when the absolute monarchy collapsed under the weight of its own contradictions and its destruction was paradoxically claimed as a victory for enlightened public opinion. Strikingly, Marat offered another version of the birth of an illusory democratic politics. The Revolution had occurred accidentally, he claimed, when "an unprecedented conjuncture of circumstances had toppled the ill-defended walls of the Bastille under the pressure of a handful of soldiers and a troop of unarmed wretches, German for the most part and almost all provincials." When the Parisian onlookers arrived at the fortress, "curiosity alone led them to visit its dark dungeons." The garrison had no sooner surrendered than "a treacherous voice cried out to plunge them into a fatal sense of security." "'Citizens,'" this voice called, "'the victory is yours, what more do we have to fear, you have taken the Bastille?'" "Everyone repeated: 'The victory is ours, we have taken the Bastille, what do we have to fear?'" As if with unanimous voice, the people celebrated the chimera of its "empty triumph."[9]

While it was doing so, The People's Friend recounted, a detachment of the Royal-German regiment was reconnoitering in preparation for an effort to retake control of the capital. He alone, he added in a note recycling an earlier claim, had aborted that "dark plot" by convincing the soldiery to declare support for the people. Even as he was declaring the Revolution illusory, he had to place himself at its very inception!

Trickery soon followed in this account, in a scene reminiscent of the duplicitous social contract the rich had offered the poor toward the end of Rousseau's *Discourse on the Origins of Inequality*. "'Citizens, we're all equal; we're all brothers,'" declared the nobles, clergy, magistrates, and financiers, oppressors under whom the people had suffered for centuries. "And the imbecilic people, applauding their perfidious discourses and yielding to their false caresses, rushed to choose them as its leaders in the districts, in the battalions. And who would believe this? It put a crafty courtier, a low valet of the court, at the head of its army."[10] No one reading *L'Ami du peuple* needed Marat to spell out the name "Lafayette."

This history of an illusion deepened when the deputies of the Third Estate were joined in the National Assembly by representatives of the privileged orders with all their pride, insolence, ambition, and greed. Fearing that the people would finally strip them of their unjust prerogatives, the privileged had been quick to make a few superficial sacrifices on the Night of Fourth August, "almost all of them illusory" (as Marat had argued at the time). Instantly, paid fraudsters had waxed ecstatic in praise of these purportedly generous renunciations. Celebrating a return to the laws of justice, they had "vaunted the empire of philosophy that had so spectacularly brought the lucky ones of the century back under the yoke of the common equality that nature imposes on all men. Instantly, our onlookers, deaf to the voices striving to expose this illusion, exhausted themselves in praise of the feigned generosity of their enemies."[11] So much for the glorious alliance of philosophical reason and popular will lauded in other patriotic journals. So much for celebration of the Revolution as the progeny of Enlightenment.

In this bitterly disenchanted analysis, only the Declaration of the Rights of Man and "suppression of the scandalous opulence of the high clergy" could be credited as effects of popular insurrection in the Revolution's early days. Beyond that, Marat's historical rewrite rehearsed a story of tricks, betrayals, deceptions, and repressions imposed on a blind, credulous, and demented people, a story leading eventually to slaughter on the Champ de Mars.[12]

And the result? The constitution the deputies had vowed to establish and were still struggling to fix. It was finally emerging from the putrid labyrinth of its creators, "this FRENCH CONSTITUTION so lauded, the dark work of madness, venality, arrogation and perfidy, save for a few laws that salutary fear extracted initially from our faithless deputies." Exposed to the light of day, it was being revealed as a "shameful monument of turpitude, oppression and enslavement that defiles the sacred base of the rights of nature upon which it has been traitorously raised." Marat scorned this text as the most hideous code of laws ever devised. Substituting legalized despotism for mere usurpation, he charged, it was a hundred times worse than the French constitution it was replacing. As if this were not evil enough, its ignominious authors were now readying it for acceptance—not by the sovereign people but by the people's purported first servant, the traitor whose attempted flight had threatened to plunge the nation into civil war. The corrupting power of gold would soon give Louis XVI the capacity to alter, mutilate, and denature that constitution even further. "Oh turpitude! Oh treason! How, amid a sovereign people and to enslave it, [had] villainous mandataries been able to abuse with such audacity the powers they received to guarantee its rights and cement its liberty?"[13]

The People's Friend saw no hope for salvation from the Legislative Assembly now scheduled for replacement at the end of the summer. He detected a new conspiracy being prepared, a more successful replay of the king's flight to Varennes. At the slightest display of popular opposition, he anticipated, blood would flow in streams. Louis XVI would bolt once again; his corrupt supporters would follow. Reactionary generals would open the frontiers to bloodthirsty émigrés and counterrevolutionary armies. Lafayette would wait in Paris to join with invading Austrians in a massacre of the population. The elections to the new Assembly would be aborted, the hope of liberty forever annihilated. The People's Friend could envision only two actions to avert this outcome: a mutiny of soldiers of the National Guard against orders for their integration into regiments of the line defending the frontiers; an insurrection of friends of liberty throughout the realm to massacre the Revolution's enemies. "Your ruin has been decided," the prophet warned his readers. "It would be madness to let traitors to the homeland take a breath, wisdom to forestall them." Power for the people frustrated, fantasies of wholesale bloodshed erupted yet again in Marat's imagination. Variations on this theme would recur in issues of *L'Ami du peuple* throughout the summer.

A SHAMEFUL MONUMENT

The gloves were off during these last weeks of the Constituent Assembly's existence as it struggled finally to revise and fix the draft constitution Marat found so shameful. The abrupt secession of the Feuillants from the

Jacobins had clarified and polarized the ideological rifts among deputies who were former members of the Society of Friends of the Constitution, leaving the Feuillants in a dominant position over the remaining Jacobins. At the same time, the decision to secure the king from popular judgment had emboldened deputies on the monarchist right. The bloodshed at the Champ de Mars had also exacerbated divisions across the entire political spectrum, intensifying fears, aggravating suspicions, and embittering personal animosities. Fear of the people and hatred of those heard speaking for it ran as a red thread through rowdy, angry exchanges constantly interrupted from the floor and the galleries. The sessions were long, exhausting, and harshly contested, but they generated some of the most impressive speeches in the entire life of the Assembly. The constitutional revisions proved relatively few, but crucial for the future of the Revolution. Marat would report on their emergence—and bewail their implications.

Malouet was quick off the mark when, on 8 August, the deputies prepared to discuss the constitutional draft now finally before them. Thouret, opening debate on behalf of the Constitutional Committee and a newer committee on revision, had emphasized that the initial goal was to review the overall organization of the document rather than the content of any specific articles. Malouet blew up that plan by launching a wholesale attack on the Declaration of the Rights of Man as disastrous for "simple and uneducated men dangerously misled." Wanting to destroy the pride of power, he charged, the deputies risked hacking away the roots of property, sociability, security. If those for whom liberty is no longer sufficient become intoxicated with independence, he asked, what force of repression will be required to constrain them?[14]

Malouet went to the heart of the constitutional project by targeting the contradiction in the reconciliation of popular sovereignty and national representation the Assembly was still attempting to achieve. "You've wished, by going back twenty centuries, to move the people more intimately close to sovereignty, and you continually hold out the temptation of it without conferring the immediate exercise," he assailed the deputies. "But as reason has advanced, you have seen all legislators and celebrated political men separate the exercise of sovereignty from its source in such a way that the people that produces its elements recovers them only in a palpable and imposing representation impressing obedience upon it." It was one thing, he continued, to say that the people is the source of sovereignty to be expressed by delegation. But it was false to proclaim that sovereignty belongs to the people, and dangerous while doing so to assert that the people could only exercise its sovereign power by delegation. Tell a subject constantly that he is sovereign, he reasoned, and "in the impetuosity of his passions he will always seize on the principle in rejecting your consequence."[15]

The principal defect of the constitutional draft, Malouet thus charged, was that it "placed sovereignty in abstraction." To do so weakened supreme powers that could only be efficacious "insofar as they are linked to palpable recognition and sustained by the responsibility of the subject"—in effect, as the expression of social solidarity. Made dependent on an abstraction, the monarchist contended, constituted powers are diminished in the opinion of a people misguided in its pretensions and duties, allowing the aberrations of the disoriented multitude to threaten security and individual tranquility. "It would be different if, wanting to constitute a monarchy after recognizing the source of sovereignty, you had explicitly delegated its exercise to the legislative body and the king. This principle, I declare, appears indispensable."[16]

Malouet was shouted down, but he circulated a complete version of his speech that went on to cite Rousseau's arguments regarding the incompatibility of sovereignty and representation. He found the Declaration of the Rights of Man and the Citizen dangerously flawed in its assertion that law is the expression of the general will. This had given the people the fanciful notion that its will makes the law, thus weakening the legislative power by "constantly raising partial and audacious views to the menacing level of the general will." The general will could be unjust and irrational, often uncertain and difficult to determine. So many minds had already been inflamed by such false notions, he lamented; it would be cruel to perpetuate such madness.[17]

One has to be impressed by Malouet's unflagging perseverance in rearguard action. To the end, he would argue for a constitutional order grounded in palpable social bonds and affective ties of duty expressed most enduringly in the traditional institution of the monarchy. He was at one with the majority among the deputies in fearing the social and political disorder of popular movements claiming the legitimacy of the general will. At the same time, he was far from the conception of political and social order for which Le Chapelier had gained the deputies' support in crucial earlier debates: the model of a society of individual citizens interacting as atoms in a rarefied political space where palpable expression of the general will was denied and sovereignty was given instantiation only by decisions of the representative body.

Seen from this perspective, there was a revealing symmetry between Malouet's constitutional critique and Marat's. Each opposed Le Chapelier in demanding embodiment of the nation's collective political existence, the monarchist ultimately locating it in the person of the king, the populist in the physical presence of the people. To Malouet's mind, the Declaration of the Rights of Man should have stated immediately that national sovereignty was exercised only by delegation. In Marat's analysis, it should have done the opposite. He saw sound principles of the declaration being eroded by the National Assembly's decisions and actions. Who could not be outraged, he demanded, at finding the preamble to the declaration "nailed at the head of an explicit system of oppression and servitude?" The deputies had whittled away the right of free assembly, for example, restricting its exercise in the name of public order while demonstrating that a popular gathering could always be suppressed (as on the Champ de Mars) by the mere act of declaring it seditious. "The right of citizens to assemble where and when they please to concern themselves with public matters belongs inherently to every free people," he insisted. "Without this sacred right, the state is dissolved, and the sovereign annihilated because, once the citizens can no longer show themselves as a body, only isolated individuals remain in the state; the nation no longer exists."[18] Sovereignty embodied remained his fundamental principle.

For The People's Friend, then, the people had to show itself as a body. The general will had to be manifested in the streets. It had also to be made palpable in the electoral assemblies. Marat saw a fundamental constitutional error in the decree that deputies to the Legislative Assembly would represent the entire nation, their actions unconstrained by any mandates from their constituents. He fumed against the provision prohibiting electoral assemblies from extending their political life beyond the act of voting. "Our decree makers, marching from assault to assault, have reached the height of their audacity in ruling that primary assemblies will be limited to election," he protested. "This is to prevent the nation from ever being able to declare its wishes, manifest its will, or even show itself. This is to strip the nation of sovereignty and vest it in those charged with its powers, its agents. What a heinous sacrifice, fully worthy of these vile crooks who have so many crimes to expiate and tremble that their throats will be cut."[19]

The constitutional attack on popular sovereignty was made all the more grave, in Marat's judgment, by the provision that deputies, after swearing collectively at the opening of each legislature to "*Live Free or Die*," would then be required to swear individually an oath "*to maintain with all their power the Constitution of the realm decreed by the National Constituent Assembly in the years 1789, 1790 and 1791*" and "*to propose or consent to nothing in the course of the legislature that could subvert it, and to be entirely faithful to the nation, the law and the king.*" Having no power itself to bind its representatives to its will, the people would thus be compelled to see them shackled by the terms of a constitutional oath foisted upon them. For Marat, this oath was "a shameful monument of oppression and tyranny." It was also an "inconceivable absurdity, because how could one imagine the representatives of the nation swearing fidelity to its premier agent, and the sovereign swearing to its first servant?"[20]

MONARCHY AS REPRESENTATION?

Sovereignty embodied or sovereignty represented? The deputies reached a crossroads on 10 August when they took up discussion of Title III of the draft constitution.[21] Its first article declared "sovereignty is one and indivisible. It belongs to the nation; no section of the people can claim its exercise. The nation from whom all powers emanate can only exercise it by delegation." The second, having stipulated that "The French Constitution is representative," went on to declare that "the representatives are the Legislative Body and the king." The third added that "the legislative power is delegated to a National Assembly, composed of temporary representatives elected by the people, to be exercised by it with the king's sanction, in the manner to be determined below."[22]

The rationale of the constitutional committees was clear: deputies chosen by election were by definition *temporary* representatives of the people; the king was by implication its *permanent* representative, charged as such with a veto power to constrain the momentary and potentially arbitrary will of the elected legislature. The paradox here is that the Assembly had earlier shielded Louis XVI from judgment, at Barnave's urging, on grounds that kingship in a representative constitution could be understood as little more than an institutional device. The deputies were now being prompted to give the monarch back a greater measure of legitimation, not merely as the nation's chief executive but as its hereditary representative sharing in legislative power. In this debate, Barnave himself had to invert the logic of his earlier argument. The king had been declared inviolable like the legislative body, he explained, because the king, like the legislative body, had to will for the people as its representative by giving or withholding his sanction to the laws. "It is necessary for the nation that he who wills on its behalf be inviolable, for without that his will would cease to be free and the interests and liberty of the people would be compromised. Thus inviolability, which you have recognized, is an immediate consequence of the character of representation."[23]

Roederer rejected reasoning like this in a lapidary formulation: "No representation without election," he declared; "thus the ideas of heredity and representation are mutually repugnant; thus a hereditary king is not a representative." The king was not a co-legislator, Roederer insisted, nor did his capacity to grant or withhold his royal sanction to the laws make him one. The suspensive veto was not an act of legislative will, but an appeal to the people to reconsider an action the king would have no power to prohibit in any case after two successive legislatures had continued to support it. Robespierre followed up by calling for the designation of the monarch as "the first public functionary, the head of the executive power," language making clear that legislative power belonged solely to representatives elected by the people.[24] It required some contortion on his part, though, to cite Rousseau to the effect that a nation that delegated its exercise of sovereign will to representatives was no longer free, indeed no longer a nation.

Responding on behalf of the constitutional committees, Thouret resisted the addition of "inalienable" to characterize national sovereignty, offering "imprescriptible" instead. Only after much disagreement were both terms adopted and the nation's sovereignty declared to be "one, indivisible, inalienable, and imprescriptible." The mood became even more tempestuous, though, as Thouret defended the proposal to designate the king as a representative of the nation. "Royalty has a representative character foreign to the domain of the executive power," he reasoned, adding that the king already possessed an indisputable quality as the nation's representative by virtue of the fact that it had conferred upon him the right to negotiate with foreign powers. Even more, "the king is representative further because he is the depositary of all the majesty, all the dignity of the nation; and it is in this respect that the civil list is established, because he is the only individual in the nation who represents the national dignity within and without."[25]

Taking the argument ad absurdum, Thouret concluded that the king had to be deemed a representative because the constitution was by definition representative: since his authority went beyond the exercise of executive power, no other constitutional designation was possible for him. "Royalty would become, in a way, discordant with the representative constitution if it were not one of the modes of representation." As for the claim that it was contradictory to name a king a hereditary representative, Thouret responded that it was no more contradictory than to name a king a hereditary public functionary. "Royalty thus necessarily falls outside the common order," he pleaded; "it's an artificial composition that, regarded as useful to the nation that adopts it, must be accepted in the most useful manner."[26] Mona Ozouf has noted the potential for radicalization of this argument by Saint-Just and Robespierre a year later.[27] Marat would not wait that long.

In the meantime, the Assembly sought to head off the risk of arbitrary exercise of royal power by adding that "no individual," in addition to "no section of the people," could arrogate the exercise of national sovereignty. It also subsequently confirmed articles determining the conditions under which the king would be deemed to have abdicated. The relative ease with which it did so was in striking contrast to the conflicted debates from which these articles had emerged after Louis XVI's flight to Varennes, to say nothing of the importance they would assume at his eventual trial.[28]

Marat would rail against the constitutional articles relating to the monarchy throughout the remaining weeks of the Assembly's life. They combined "two political blasphemies," he wrote on 16 August, the first asserting that the nation, from which all powers emanate, could only exercise them by delegation, the second designating the king, a mere public functionary, as representative of the nation. Having sold out to the court, he protested on 20 August, the deputies had turned a constitution that could have been a precious monument of public liberty into a shameful testament of their infamy, "making the king independent of the nation and absolute master of the legislative body after having placed him explicitly above all the laws." In a fundamental decree "they had furtively inserted the king's name among the representatives of the nation. . . . Thus the prince, declared independent of the legislative body, has become independent of the nation itself, since they have stipulated that it can only speak through the organ of its mandataries." From the abusive privilege of the veto, Marat charged, the traitorous deputies had attempted to deduce the king's right to represent the nation without its delegating him that power, making him its "born representative . . . almost as the henchmen of the monarch had made him the representative of the divinity on earth." "They had invested the prince with the innate right to represent the nation, making him sacred and inviolable." With brutal symbolism, they had ordered that new coins bear the image of this "mortal enemy" of public liberty while entirely omitting mention of "nation" or "*patrie*."[29]

The matter was complicated by other potential implications of upholding the hereditary character of the monarchy. Heredity required a royal family. Could members of that family be refused special status as citizens? Could they be denied privileges and titles? And how far down the tracery of lineage might such titles extend? In short, could there be a hereditary monarchy without a nobility? After fierce debate, the Assembly contained the issue for the moment by allowing heirs to the throne the skeletal title of *prince français*, without any privileges accruing thereby and with restrictions on the admissibility of these individuals to public office. But Marat was not alone in anticipating and deploring the possibility that restoration of noble titles would follow Louis XVI's acceptance of the constitution.[30]

In the meantime, he stood by as the Assembly engaged in fierce and extended battle that resulted in elimination of the detested income requirement for election to the National Assembly (payment in annual direct taxes of a *marc d'argent*, or "silver mark," roughly equivalent to income from fifty-four days' labor) but compensated for this measure of democratization by vastly increasing the income requirement for electors in the secondary assemblies that would choose those deputies. One objection to the *marc d'argent* had been that it would have rendered the great Jean-Jacques ineligible to election as a deputy; it remained the case that he would have been ineligible to join in selecting one. The effect, for Marat, was that it left the choice of deputies to the rich and corrupt, "opulent men, almost all partisans of the court, fully assured that the prince, once master of the electors, will in consequence be master of the elected." He saw this outcome guaranteed even further by decisions denying electoral participation to individuals targeted by official prosecution, on the one hand, and lowering barriers to the corruption of deputies made agents of the crown, on the other.[31]

With the king thus secured in power, Marat prophesied, there would be "A New St. Bartholomew's, a general massacre of the friends of liberty." By late summer, he was beginning to sound like a crazed Burkean. "I never set eyes on the constitutional act without recalling with bitterness how insolently the conscripted fathers insulted the memory of Montesquieu and the English constitution," he cried out on 25 August. They had boasted of readying a model of perfect legislation, the best of all governments that would soon consign the English constitution to oblivion: "A fine undertaking for ignorant lawyers who had rotted all their lives in the slime of the Bar, who had no idea of the great art of governing peoples, of organizing a political body, of wisely separating and balancing powers, of making justice and liberty reign together. A fine undertaking for word merchants habituated to selling their babble and anger to clients, for sophists skilled in misleading the public and deceiving judges, for priests occupied in advancing themselves in the world or scandalizing the church in their pomp and debauchery, for courtiers nourished on all the refinements of perfidy, for military men uniquely versed in the art of killing, or rather intriguers prostituted to authority, all of them valets of the prince, or valets of the valets of the prince."

The constitution these men had contrived, Marat raged, was "a shameful monument of servitude, oppression and opprobrium, a monument all the more hideous in that it founded despotism on the laws, made the person of the despot sacred, enslaved the nation to its representatives and stripped it of the right to examine their conduct and watch out for its own interests, imposed crushing chains on it and, to make them as eternal as the world, placed all the public force in the hands of the prince, the most implacable of the enemies of liberty."[32]

This was to say nothing, the denunciation continued, of the 83 departments, 400 districts, 40,000 municipalities, 100,000 administrators, 600,000 judges, 800,000 ministerial satellites, and 400,000,0000 "ass-pushers and assassins of the nation" that had been "placed under the orders of the despot to force the desolate peoples to obedience and make this horrible machine work." The story could only end badly. The destruction of the parlements, the abasement of the clergy, and the despoliation of the church had overthrown all the barriers opposing a dike to the torrent of ministerial despotism. With the king likely further to insist on the reestablishment of the hereditary nobility, the entire clique of the former privileged, "both gothic and modern," threatened to reappear on the horizon, more radiant than ever. The deputies had appeared heroic in 1789 when they swore the Tennis Court Oath never to disband until a constitution had been established. Now they looked more like a gang of greedy crooks unwilling to let go before they had traded for themselves on the interests of the nation and sold out to the king. Rendered ever worse by daily revisions, Marat predicted, their constitution would end up "a monster patched with all the abuses of the new and the old regimes."

In the meantime, *L'Ami du peuple* warned of counterrevolution being mounted everywhere. "Oh citizens! Two years ago, you made all the cruel enemies of the revolution tremble and THE PEOPLE'S FRIEND counseled you to suppress them and slaughter their leaders in order to escape the horrors of civil war. But you stupidly gave them the means to recover and gain power. Today they crush you pitilessly. Thirty thousand of your brothers, caught in their traps, have fallen under their blows. Their audacity has no limits, they threaten to slaughter all who oppose their criminal projects and drown liberty in the blood of its defenders. Such is your deplorable situation that your sole resource is now civil war, that frightful scourge it was once your sole object to banish."[33]

A RIGHT TO DEFAME?

Language like this was a reminder that renewed debate over constitutional protection of freedom of the press was inevitable. The matter had been taken up again on 22 August when, in the context of delimiting judicial powers, Thouret offered the revised articles on the topic. A key provision stipulated that alleged abuses of press freedom be judged only by a jury—by then a matter of broad consensus within the Assembly. More contentious was the proposal that no one be prosecuted for printing or publishing writings unless they had "deliberately provoked disobedience to the law, denigration of the constituted powers and resistance to their acts, or any actions the law had declared crimes or offenses." This wording differed in some critical respects from that of the decree restricting press freedom passed immediately after the Champ de Mars Massacre. That act had been directed against writers who "explicitly" counseled disobedience to the law; this one targeted those held to be doing so "deliberately," which could also include statements made by indirection or implication. This one, furthermore, added "denigration" of the constituted powers to the list of press offenses. Robespierre was followed by Pétion, Roederer, Buzot, and others in protesting that these changes rendered restrictions on the press vaguer, hence potentially more arbitrary and repressive. In opposition, Le Chapelier stood firm with members of the constitutional committees in support of them. After increasingly testy exchanges, the new restrictions were adopted.[34]

This debate had been tense, but the next one became positively explosive as the deputies considered freedom of the press in relation to the issue of defamation. The constitutional committees had proposed that allegations of slander, whether against public officials in the exercise of their functions or individuals in their private conduct, be brought to the courts by the persons they targeted. There was little disagreement within the Assembly regarding the right of individuals to seek legal redress against attacks on their private conduct that they deemed slanderous. But there was acute dissension over the right of public officials to sue for slander in response to charges of misconduct in the exercise of their public functions.

Pétion unleashed tempers when he denied this right in a remarkably long and eloquent paean to freedom of the press. Printing he celebrated as "the sublime invention that communicates human ideas, makes them everyone's patrimony anywhere on earth; that renders them imperishable and, as it were, material; that has already so prodigiously expanded the sphere of our knowledge and pushed back the barriers to the human spirit, and surely prepares new wonders for posterity." Liberty of the press makes the arts and sciences flourish, and gives new life to all human institutions, he rhapsodized. It dissipates errors and prejudices, purifies opinions, and allows truth to triumph. It elevates the soul, energizes talents, develops greatness of character. It safeguards political and civil liberty, keeping watch when the law slumbers, constraining what the law cannot repress, denouncing to opinion when the law cannot denounce to the courts. It is the enemy of slavery, the scourge of ignorance and the despotism that feeds upon it. With freedom of the press a bad constitution can be improved, a vicious one reformed; without it, the best constitution can be corrupted, the wisest laws can degenerate. No law was thus more important, none more efficacious, Pétion proclaimed, than that establishing "full, entire, indefinite liberty of the press."[35]

"I know what terrifies you," he acknowledged to his fellow deputies: "it's the energy of the ideas, the vehemence of the style; you would prefer there always to be calm explanations, appeals to reason and not to the passions." One wonders whether he had Marat specifically in mind in arguing that writers were like painters, each true to his own manner, more or less passionate, more or less impetuous. It is impossible to legislate in matters of style or to regulate expressions, he maintained. Forbidding a man to express himself as he chooses is tantamount to forbidding him to think and write. "Let's proclaim the most absolute freedom of opinion, on any matter whatsoever; it seems to me that this proposition can meet no contradiction in this assembly."[36]

But it could meet contradiction, as Pétion well knew, and he was eager to anticipate objections. Did he not agree that the press had its abuses? Did he really mean to authorize seditious and incendiary publications that incited the people to unrest and violence, violated honor and defamed individuals? Should liberty really be allowed to degenerate into violence? The press has its abuses, he granted, but perfect institutions are chimerical, and the benefits of a free press outweigh any disadvantages. Under a despotism, so-called seditious writings are an act of virtue. In a well-organized free state, they are inconsequential. During the passage from despotism to liberty it is impossible to prevent them and extravagant to want to punish them. What then to do in the midst of this overthrow of an established regime? Renounce useless laws, Pétion urged, let pass the storm that no one can stop, enlighten the people, inspire it with sentiments of its dignity and duties. A law against seditious writings would be political nonsense amid the convulsions of a state that is regenerating itself. It would open the door to arbitrariness that, once introduced, would be impossible to check. He offered the gradual stifling of the press in England as a salutary tale.[37]

This was a grand speech, a wholesale defense of a liberating tradition of seditious writing. But much of it was a day late. The Assembly had already decided to prohibit publications deemed explicitly or implicitly subversive. It was left to Pétion to engage the question to which the Assembly had now turned: whether public officials could prosecute their critics for libel. On this matter, he had no doubt that the answer was also entirely negative. "One of the great benefits of liberty of the press is to keep constant watch on men in place, shed light on their conduct, unmask their intrigues, warn society of the dangers it runs; it's a vigilant sentinel that guards the state day and night. Sometimes it gives false alarms; but an excess of foresight is preferable to a fatal security." Only the corrupt and perverted man fears the light of publicity, Pétion insisted. In contrast, the "proud and virtuous man, strong in his achievements and his conscience, invokes public opinion rather than fearing it, seeks the light as much as the evildoer flees it, and would desire, to the bottom of his heart, that all men be able to read."[38]

The ensuing debate was electric. There was contestation over the difficulty of distinguishing censure of the actions of a public functionary in execution of his office from willful slander of his motivations and intentions. There were protests that it would be impossible to find enough men throughout France with the courage to accept public office without the right to protect themselves from constant calumny. "Censure of the acts of the constituted powers is permitted," it was decided; "but willful slanders against the probity of public functionaries and the rectitude of their intentions in the exercise of their functions may be prosecuted by those who are their object." In addition, all persons were to be guaranteed the right to seek legal redress for libels against their private conduct.[39]

For Marat, who had made calumny his stock in trade, these decisions were frightful. "Annihilation of Liberty of the Press" headlined *L'Ami du peuple* on 26 August. "The jugglers of these committees, having thrown powder in our eyes by seeming to guarantee individual liberty against arbitrary arrest, have dealt the death blow to liberty of the press," the journal shouted. In vain had Robespierre and Pétion cried out against criminalizing "denigration of the constituted powers" in a clause that was open to a thousand arbitrary interpretations. They should have insisted that inciting disobedience to the law, impugning constituted powers, and resisting their actions were exactly the grounds upon which the most despotic governments and the cruelest tyrants persecuted political writers. Oppressors needed no other pretexts. Indictments in these terms would be used in a purportedly free France to punish any courageous writer working to save the people.[40]

As for the articles against defamation, Marat warned, they were both ridiculous and contradictory; together they made liberty of the press illusory. The first supposed that agents of authority were all saints who transgressed involuntarily or unknowingly; the second that an out-and-out blackguard in his private conduct was always pure in his public behavior. "Stupid legislators, or rather perfidious mandataries, you would fear the whip of censure less if you had fewer crimes to hide," he castigated the deputies. "It's only in exposing the vices of private men that we can exclude them from positions and have upright men. But to ruin the homeland and destroy liberty the prince needs criminals in every position of trust; and it's to fill them with villains devoted to his orders that you have made it a crime for public writers to expose the turpitude of these shameful candidates."[41]

He would not change his tone, The People's Friend swore to his readers. "For me a prince will only ever be a tyrant, his ministers atrocious traitors, his valets who fabricate decrees perfidious criminals, and almost all the public functionaries prostituted villains." One last thing he would never lose from sight. The deputies had been charged to make a just and free constitution; their decrees were almost all oppressive and iniquitous. "Far from submitting to them, we must annihilate them, punish their authors and begin the work again until we have a just and wise government, or all our efforts to free ourselves will have served only to have riveted our chains."[42]

The following issue of the journal was nonetheless bitter in its judgment of the French nation, whom Marat now compared to the Romans under the reign of despotism satirized by Juvenal. "No, liberty is not for us. We're too ignorant, too vain, too presumptuous, too cowardly, too base, too corrupt, too attached to peace and pleasure, too enslaved to wealth, ever to know the price of liberty," he lamented. The rich, cowardly, and corrupt had rushed for places in the new regime, even before the constitution had been completed, while the greedy or inept commoners prayed for the reestablishment of the servitude of the old regime to which the people were being returned piecemeal after two years of agitation and anarchy. The diagnosis came as an image from the laboratory. "Our revolution is like a crystallization disturbed by violent shakings. First, all the crystals distributed through the liquid are agitated, randomly repelling and intermingling; then they start moving more sluggishly, gradually coalescing until they finish by resuming their initial constitution and tightly rebinding."[43] To reverse this process, it seemed, the renewed agitation of civil war now offered the only hope.

A FRAGILE CLOSURE

Begin the work again! This was the last thing the deputies wanted to hear. Indeed, it was the language they most feared as the Assembly to succeed them was being elected toward the end of August. Their constitution was too fragile; it could soon be undone; it needed time to take hold. They had denied themselves eligibility for reelection. How then could they prevent a new Legislative Assembly from mutating into another Constituent Assembly and unraveling their work to start anew? There had to be a way of protecting their constitutional achievement from disaffected factions, from popular pressure, from agitation in the streets.

Appropriately, it was Le Chapelier who proposed such a way on behalf of the constitutional committees on 29 August. The nation had a right to improve its constitution, he granted; every wise constitution had to include a mechanism for it to do so. But this mechanism had to be designed carefully, "for under the pretext of improving a constitution one could destabilize its bases to such an extent that one revolution would succeed another." Several possibilities had been considered, Le Chapelier reported. One was to schedule a future convention that could exercise full constituent power to create a new form of government. This the committees had dismissed as disastrous on the grounds that approach of the scheduled date would precipitate economic disorder, political divisions, and social disorder. A second option, constitutional conventions at fixed intervals, had been judged even more dangerously disruptive. The committees feared it would prolong revolution indefinitely. A third choice was to establish procedures for the convocation of a constitutional convention by popular demand. This had been repudiated as potentially the most catastrophic of all, threatening to perpetuate and aggravate current divisions, increase agitation, disrupt public tranquility, and even lead to the convocation of a new constituent assembly before the work of the old one had been tested by experience. There remained two more possibilities to avoid upheaval: one to restrict the identity of those who could call for a constitutional convention; the other to limit the powers a convention could exercise. The latter was the committees' choice.

The intricate mechanism Le Chapelier laid out was meant to admit the possibility of constitutional change while delaying, restricting, or preventing it for as long as possible. A national "Assembly of Revision," chosen by procedures used to elect a Legislative Assembly, would be scheduled to meet 1 June 1800. This body would have no powers to act on its own initiative. It would disperse as soon as it had considered proposals for specific constitutional revisions submitted by citizens, the legislative body, or the king. To be discussed, these proposals would require majority support in at least half the departments and approval by the Legislative Assembly and the king. Their veto by the legislature or the monarch could delay their submission to the Assembly of Revision for the period of three subsequent Legislative Assemblies, to each of which they would have to be resubmitted for approval. In addition, consideration of any reforms put forward by the legislature could be postponed for the duration of two Legislative

Assemblies by the usual suspensive royal veto; that of reforms proposed by the king would be denied if opposed by three legislatures in succession.[44]

All this was as if the constitution were not already visibly "a monument to servitude and tyranny," exploded *L'Ami du peuple*. Marat found it hard to imagine more onerous impediments to constitutional change than those Le Chapelier proposed. "It's the policy of the jugglers in the corrupt assembly's committees to pay homage to the principles of liberty in their preambles, then trample them underfoot in the body of the decrees," he protested. Never had he seen the treacherous deputies follow this odious policy more faithfully. "What are they proposing? An assembly of revision that will decide on the combined demands of citizens, the legislature, and the king for reform of some part of the constitution, which is to say that it will never decide. . . . Thus the supreme power of the nation to revise, correct, and perfect the constitution would be limited to the rare and precious prerogative to plead and beg, pleadings and supplications that the legislature would have the right to laugh at, that the king would have the right to repudiate"—and would do so continuously "so long as they contravene his projects for absolute domination, which is to say that they don't augment his power and increase the enslavement and misery of the people whose most mortal enemy he will eternally be."[45]

The French had to reject these fake reform mechanisms, insisted *L'Ami du peuple*. The people alone could approve or reject laws made by its mandataries or order their reform. Indeed, these laws could only be considered provisional until they had received the people's sanction. As for the constitution, it was "not simply a failure but manifestly the work of a legislature prostituted to the court." There was only one way to correct and perfect it; any other would be vile and ridiculous. The people had to "order the next legislature to revoke all decrees contrary to the sovereignty of the nation and the rights of its members, while waiting to order subsequent legislatures to reform other decrees in the event that experience reveals their vices."[46] In effect, this meant a return to binding mandates.

Within the Assembly, meanwhile, Le Chapelier's presentation met substantial resistance. It was followed by mammoth speeches from the two extremes of the chamber. Malouet, at the ready again, could not wait to oppose the proposal outright, and with it the Revolution it was meant to close. In his judgment, the scheduling of any future constitutional convention could only extend the agitation and disorder of the moment. Sustained mockery did not deter him from throwing the entire history of the Revolution into question. It had eradicated too much, he protested; its means had been too violent; it had no end. "License has produced too many ravages, the dregs of the nation seethe over our heads." The country would not be afforded the time, stability, and experience necessary to identify and enact necessary constitutional revisions, he argued, as long as "all contrary opinions are subjugated by terror or force; as long as France still expresses itself through the organ of its clubs, as long as the only public functionaries in place today come from these societies or are enslaved to them." What good is the purity of your theory if the practices accompanying it perpetuate the disorders under which we groan? he demanded bitterly. "Have you taken measures so that this multitude of tyrannical societies corrupting and subjugating public opinion, influencing all the elections, dominating all authorities, restore to us the peace they have stolen from us? Have you taken measures to ensure that the multitude of armed men with whom France is covered are invincibly constrained within the limits prescribed by the law?"[47]

The constitution, Malouet asserted, had to be freely and thoughtfully accepted by the king and the nation. But first it would be necessary to roll back all decrees contrary to the principles of individual security and liberty, freedom of conscience, and respect for property. The laws against émigrés, prohibitions of traditional religious observance, the persecution of priests, arbitrary imprisonments, baseless prosecutions, the fanaticism and domination of the clubs: all these had to disappear. Louis XVI would be invited to resume the reins of government, and the constitution would be executed provisionally while he considered any revisions he might wish to propose. The people would then be invited to discuss these revisions peacefully—with political hostilities, denunciations, and acts of violence rigorously suppressed. For Malouet, as for Marat, time was of the essence. He wanted the primary assemblies to be convoked within two years, on 1 June 1793, to approve or reject the revisions proposed by the king, with the results expressed in *cahiers* sent to the legislature by the secondary assemblies. The deputies would then make the changes desired by the nation and submit them to the king, who would have the right to veto any contradicting the nation's will. In effect, then, the monarch would be appealing to the nation, and deciding for it, over the head of the representative body.[48]

There were demands that this proposal be referred to the constitutional committees. One deputy quipped that a committee on counterrevolution would be more appropriate. Though it received no immediate discussion, the potential of its strategy to pit king and people together against the representative body was not lost on deputies sitting on the right. Marat had no comment beyond ridiculing Malouet for again playing the clown, calling for destruction of the clubs and the return of full plenitude of power to the king.[49] He could scarcely acknowledge that his enemy was playing the card of national sovereignty by calling for the king to appeal to the people's will over that of its deputies.

Pétion followed Malouet at the tribune with a long speech in a very different key. He prefaced his remarks with a substantial disquisition on the ideas and practices of conventions in the Anglo-American world. This led him to a truth he found indisputable: that with regular conventions a bad constitution could be improved, without them a bad constitution could only deteriorate. But the conventions had to be periodic and held at regular intervals determined in advance. They could not be convoked at the will of a legislature or their powers appropriated by one. A widely distributed population, still largely uneducated, could not realistically be entrusted to demand one before disorder was at its height, and it would be dangerous to wait for an insurrection to impose one. Regularly scheduled conventions held every twenty years would alone ensure that the nation retain the full plenitude of its sovereignty. Though not without their dangers, they would allow each generation to exercise the constituent power to ratify or revise the constitution for itself. The sequence would begin in 1800, the year Le Chapelier had originally proposed as the earliest date for any constitutional change.[50]

Admirer of Pétion though he was, Marat was cool in reporting his speech. He found the projected date of 1800 for the first convention ridiculous if the goal was to avert insurrections by revising the constitution before administrative disorder reached its height. By that time, he objected, Louis XVI would have had the opportunity to overthrow the political order a hundred times![51]

When the deputies resumed discussion of constitutional revision a day later, it was to the tune of a frantic appeal by the principal architect of the Civil Constitution of the Clergy, Camus, who urged them to resolve the issue more quickly. "We have to recognize that our weakness is increasing daily," he warned, "and that it will grow every hour we postpone the end of our work, because in this situation we have factions developing in the assembly itself." He no longer saw in the Assembly "the fine, grand majority" that had produced the heroic acts of 1789. The deputies were no longer able to find a rallying point; they were tying themselves in knots over details; they were losing arguments in one debate only to revive them in the next. In the meantime, the ministers were dragging their feet. "I only see the most reprehensible inertia among the agents of executive power," he deplored (as Saint-Just would do so much more urgently two years later). They were waiting for the Assembly to destroy itself, waiting for the moment they could call in foreign aid, waiting for the day they would be the masters and nothing would stand in their way.[52]

If that were not peril enough, Camus added, the new Legislative Assembly had already been elected; its deputies were on their way to the capital. How dangerous it would be to have two representative assemblies side by side. The arriving deputies would want to participate in completing the constitution; having once shared in the exercise of constituent power, they would want to continue doing so, turning themselves into a constitutional convention. They might even want to reopen the question of the king's fate. None of this could be allowed to happen. The incoming Legislative Assembly had to "execute a completed constitution, not get involved in discussion of a constitution to be made. The revolution is finished, the revolution must survive no longer, no traces of it must remain." Stick to principles, Camus urged his fellows; decide the basic questions; forget the details.[53]

These anxieties notwithstanding, the deputies plunged into a torrent of debate. Arguments for delaying a constitutional convention for ten, fifteen, twenty, or thirty years met objections that fixing any such term would amount to a violation of the nation's sovereign right to change its constitution whenever it saw fit. Schemes to limit any changes a convention could consider to those proposed in advance by citizens' petitions in the primary assemblies were countered by claims that doing so would amount to a system of binding mandates contradicting the principle of representative government on the one hand, infringing upon the exercise of constituent power on the other. "You're leaving the representative system and throwing yourselves into the democratic system," warned d'André. Regnaud de Saint-Jean-d'Angély was more blunt in calling the question. "Everyone agrees that we are proposing a useless law and we are doing violence to national sovereignty." Hoisted by its own petard, the Assembly could only manage a feeble appeal for suspension of sovereign will and deferral of the exercise of constituent power. "The nation has the right to review its Constitution when it pleases," the deputies decreed, "but the National Assembly declares that it is in the nation's interest to suspend the exercise of this right for thirty years."[54]

Marat, oracle of insurrection, was not impressed. National conventions would never occur, he insisted, "unless the nation, rising up at one and the same time in all the corners of the realm, breaks the shameful yoke imposed upon it by those it has charged with power, or, more likely, unless the troops of the line, revolted at the tyranny of their chiefs, finally immolate them in just fury, giving the patriotic party the means of rising back up and crushing in its turn the enemies of the homeland." His hopes were now in the troops, he told his readers; all the soldiers needed to crush tyranny was a smart and courageous leader, a People's Friend. "I would give one of my fingers for them to know my sentiments and put them to the test. The enemies of the homeland would be buried alive and in three months France would be free and happy."[55]

Still anxious to buttress their work against change, the deputies returned to fundamental questions about the nature of constitutional conventions on 31 August. Again, the argument ground down to basic antinomies long destabilizing revolutionary thinking: between constitution and revolution, between representation and the sovereignty of the general will. Fearing that the constitution might actually be made to last until 1800, partisans of royal authority now began to invoke the general will of the nation against the particular will of the representatives. "I believe, for my part, that insurrection is the only means the nation has to manifest its will," asserted de Croix. He saw no need for further plans since the nation had already indicated the only means to change the constitution. Reminding the Assembly that the royal veto had been instituted to guarantee the rights of the people against the errors of the representative body, he proposed that the constitution be submitted immediately to the king to elicit "the observations that the interest of the people might suggest to him." Challenged that this would destroy the very foundations of the constitution, he retorted that the deputies themselves were the ones destroying these foundations: "you're putting yourselves in place of the nation and you are only representatives." Responding to invocation of the principle that sovereignty inhered in the nation, that it alone, and not the king, could ratify the constitution, he was all too willing to agree. "I recognize the sovereignty of the nation," he declared; "but I also say that you are not the nation; you are only its representatives, and the nation has wanted the king to be your moderator." Don't flatter yourselves that you could not have fallen into errors, he sneered at the majority. Don't refuse to employ the means the nation has indicated to reveal and repair them.[56]

These arguments may have been disingenuous, but they were threatening enough to the principle of representative government to require a forceful response. It came from Nicolas Frochot, who launched what became the crucial proposal for a mechanism placing constitutional revision firmly under the control of the representative body. "I understand the objection of those who recognize, or at least purport to recognize, that the assembly of representatives comprises only particular wills imposing laws on the general will," he declared. "But they're not even worth refuting, they display too profound an ignorance of the principles of representative government, and we're not at the point where we have to repeat an elementary course on the topic with them." Enemies of the constitution feign to misunderstand the existence of national sovereignty, Frochot warned; give them a means of abusing this principle and they will soon deploy it. One such means would be to require popular ratification of the constitution, as Malouet had proposed. This Frochot repudiated as incompatible with the principle of representative government that held the general will expressible only through the deliberations of an elected legislature.[57]

To save the representative system was Frochot's fundamental purpose. He was against any scheme for periodical conventions constraining the legislature, whether at fixed moments or unpredictable ones, such as at the end of a reign. More significantly, he repudiated the notion that convocation of a constitutional convention could be initiated from below. Vague, partial, local demands should not be mistaken for the expression of public opinion, he insisted. "Let's never lose sight of the fact that caprice, passion, or a day's enthusiasm must play no part in reforming or changing the constitution. Substantial reasons are necessary, a clearly pronounced will, a fully formed public opinion." This was the case whether the convention was called to consider specific constitutional changes or to exercise "the imposing but terrible majesty of the constituent power" in the creation of an entirely new form of government.[58]

Consistent with these principles, Frochot developed a plan allowing a Legislative Assembly at any time to determine a need for a "national convention," his term for an assembly to decide on specific proposals for constitutional revision, or a "constituent body" to remake the entire frame of government. Only if the determination of this initial legislature was confirmed by the votes of two further successive assemblies would a third act to transform itself into a national convention by calling for the election of additional deputies to double its number (or into a constituent body by the addition of a somewhat larger group of deputies, chosen in ratio to population). In the process, momentary, ill-considered movements would be replaced by ripe reflection, the risk of losing everything in a single day annihilated. Excluding the reelection of deputies from one of these assemblies to the next would also obviate the risk that a single group could usurp constituent power. There would be no need for other trigger mechanisms that would "suppose the general will where it doesn't exist . . . , place it where it cannot be, because, to repeat, the general will is the necessary product of the common deliberation and *physical* meeting of all the parts composing it." Instead, the purity of representative government would be preserved in its entirety: everything would be determined "by the actual and precise will of the people, nothing by caprice, or by vague and puerile combinations; and, moreover, nothing . . . by the people, but everything by its representatives."[59]

Frochot's speech was acclaimed within the Assembly, but *L'Ami du peuple* castigated its sophistry. "In this project that is so applauded, so vaunted," the journal argued, "one sees the sovereignty of the nation consistently reduced to zero despite all the charlatanism the author has employed to hype it, since it is limited to making demands that the legislatures, mere agents entrusted with powers, will decide on as the supreme arbiter . . . and can repudiate at will."[60]

The ensuing debate was Sisyphean. In an extended speech, Salle insisted on the sovereign right of the nation to change its constitution without restriction, while repudiating monarchist objections that insurrection was all that was needed to secure this right. "A people that needs an insurrection to constitute itself is enslaved," he maintained, "and we don't want to enslave the French people." At the same time, he urged a twenty-year delay before any attempt at constitutional change. "A generation is necessary to purge from this land of liberty the slaves who still crowd it; the breast of the homeland must no longer be torn apart by its enemies in order for it show us all its serenity, all its dignity, all its charms." The plan he presented allowed for a convention convoked by an initiative of the primary assemblies sustained by three-quarters of the popular vote over three electoral cycles, then subject to suspension by the king for a further two years. D'André, never short of words himself, immediately rejected this form of popular initiative as "inadmissible in a representative government." Instead, he urged a simplification of Frochot's scheme that would drop provision for a Constituent Assembly (on the grounds that changing the constitution entirely was beyond the power of the constitution itself to regulate), while authorizing a National Convention to consider specific revisions identified as necessary by three successive Legislative Assemblies.[61]

Marat was appalled. "Note well how skillfully the convocation of national conventions is being pushed back in making the will of the nation pass through three legislatures, in order to allow emissaries and henchmen of the court time to work on the departments to make the demand for revision of the laws disappear," he enlightened his readers. "Note how impudently individual petitions are being rejected after collective petitions have been so loudly repudiated." When it had been a matter of annihilating the fraternal societies, he observed, "the clown d'André had shouted his head off that collective petitions were unconstitutional and only individual petitions were legal. Why? Because he anticipated that [individual petitions] would set up the signatories for persecution by the enemies of liberty. Today, he is rejecting individual petitions furiously as veering too close to democracy. Thus the conscript fathers have neither principles nor fixed maxims, they change them with ease, according to their aims and circumstances; and if it's necessary to avow opposing maxims in the same session in order to deceive the audience, they are always ready to do so, accustomed as they are to no longer blushing."[62]

Robespierre's response to d'André was closer to Marat's convictions. His opposition to proposals that would subject the people to the tyranny of its representatives was immediately seconded by Buzot, who cautioned against the corresponding danger that a constituted power could transform itself into a constituent power to transform the entire political order. But the two radicals were trumped by Barnave, who intervened to defend principles of representation he held necessary in a large country. Tranquility and liberty are the goal of every good government, he preached, but "tranquility is indispensable to common men, liberty is only a superfluity for them; if you take away their tranquility, beware that the people not soon destroy its liberty by its own hands." It was enough for him to remind his fellow deputies of the disorders produced in Rome by tribunes of the people mobilizing the indigent multitude in favor of an agrarian law. Liberty, he laid down, could only be preserved by allowing limited constitutional revision to be decided by successive Legislative Assemblies. This mechanism alone could secure tranquility by saving the nation from the horrors unleashed by the exercise of "constituent powers, eternal cause of revolutions."[63]

"What a fraud," fumed Marat at this speech. "The blackguard has made his pile. He's scared to death of something that could sustain the salutary agitation of minds, lead to a new order of things, and destroy the abuses he sees still promising him so many advantages; today he yearns only for the people's lethargy, which alone can assure him impunity and permit him to enjoy in peace the fruit of his betrayals." In Marat's book, Barnave's insistence that national sovereignty was expressible only by representatives amounted to saying that the people was limited to choosing agents to deceive it constantly—"a convenient maxim for miscreants trembling that they might be targeted for selling out the rights of the nation."[64]

In the wake of Barnave's intervention, nonetheless, momentum in the debate turned toward securing representation against the threat of popular sovereignty and saving the constitution from the danger of renewed revolution unleashed by the exercise of constituent power. It was eventually decreed that if three consecutive legislatures had agreed on the need to reconsider specific constitutional articles, these articles—and these alone—could be submitted for revision to a fourth legislature that would be doubled in size for this purpose. The lengthy debate seemed to be winding down when d'André suddenly proposed that the king be allowed to express an opinion on the constitutional articles as they were designated for revision by the successive legislatures. This idea was only set aside after agitated discussion. At the last minute, however, the deputies decreed that the next two legislative assemblies would be barred from discussing the terms of the constitution, thereby postponing for a further four years the possibility of initiating a revision process already designed to take at least six.[65]

This decided, the deputies prepared for one last read-through of the constitutional text before presenting it to the king. But that reading left them in a quandary: they had initially voted to recommend that the nation defer exercise of its right to change the constitution for thirty years; they had since voted for a process that allowed revision of specific articles after ten years. The first vote had aimed to defer, for as long as seemed plausible, the exercise of the dangerous and unpredictable constituent power to change the form of government in its entirety; the second aimed simply to evade exercise of that frightening power entirely. Skillful editing allowed them to drop the recommendation for a thirty-year postponement of constituent power and mandate the procedure for revision; the people's right to revolution at any time was pared down and operationalized as an elaborate mechanism allowing representatives to revise specific constitutional provisions after extended delay. Thus, with its handiwork at last completed—and hopefully secured against threats from popular action, royal influence, and the tampering of overzealous legislatures—the Constituent Assembly was ready, on 3 September, to submit it that very evening to the king.[66]

Marat warned, caustically, against the danger that there could be two versions of the founding text, one for the nation and another for the king, the latter intercalated with additional clauses affording the monarch absolute power and subjecting the citizens to increased servitude. He followed up with a caricature of the ceremony in which the Assembly's deputation offered Louis XVI a constitution "that consecrates the imprescriptible rights of the French nation, which we have sold to you . . . , that returns to the throne its true dignity, to the monarch full power," and "keeps the nation in chains, at least until it suddenly opens its eyes to our villainy and discovers with a shudder the abyss into which we have plunged it and breaks its yoke by a general insurrection a hundred times more terrible than that of 14 July." This, he had the deputation say, is "an evil we have foreseen and have tried to prevent, for which we can't answer and for which we make no engagement to restore the property of the poor that we have shared with you." In response to which, he ventriloquized, the monarch informed "my dogsbodies" from "the National Assembly, my protector and protégé," that he would examine the text while remaining in Paris, "where I have nothing more to fear since the massacre of the patriot scoundrels at the Champ de Mars." The celebrations that actually followed Louis XVI's eventual decision to accept the constitution on 13 September filled The People's Friend with disgust at the excesses of joy exhibited by "the abused people that believes it has finally reached the end of its misfortunes and arrived at the day it will be able to breathe in peace under the aegis of justice and liberty."[67]

Rapturous they may have been, but these celebrations could not obscure the fragility of the moment. Resentments of a repressed popular movement, inflation escalating threats of social unrest and economic collapse, resistance against the Civil Constitution of the Clergy, insubordination in the ranks of the army, émigrés chafing to return home in expectation that the king would restore their titles and possessions, counterrevolutionary armies waiting to invade, unrest in the colonies as planters repudiated the 15 May decree extending civil rights to free people of color, all of these would tear at the uneven seams of the constitutional monarchy. It would not, could not, last.

A MOMENT OF DESPAIR

The People's Friend seemed ready to give up. On 5 September, he started to talk again of "quitting the pen I've consecrated for three years to the defense of the people and public liberty." On the sixth, he declared futile the hope that the new Legislative Assembly could restore the people's sovereignty. On the eighth, he predicted that Louis XVI would invite the fugitive princes and other counterrevolutionaries to return to the realm, offering a general amnesty to all the traitors and evildoers. Patriots arrested for the cause of liberty would be included, he acknowledged, "but the only one who won't be pardoned for his efforts to avenge oppressed humanity, citizens and the homeland will be The People's Friend, and perhaps his disciple The Orator will be engulfed in his ruin." (When the general amnesty did come, Marat refused to accept it.) Again he signaled that the new order of things could not last, that the king's counselors were planning to overthrow the constitution by force "because it's insupportable for a monarch, recently a despot, to see above him a sovereign master who can at any moment make its ultimate power felt, whatever care the faithless representatives have taken to enchain it." Even if the king had no such intention, he predicted, all the former privileged orders, "the public bloodsuckers and henchmen of the court," would connive incessantly to restore the old regime.[68]

Could one imagine, Marat asked, that a dazzling marquis, a haughty duke, a former *maréchal de France*, a beribboned chevalier—men accustomed to abasing and humiliating plebeians—would ever consent to be the equal of their tailor, their cobbler, their groom, their bootblack, or become the inferior of a former lawyer or agent who had been elevated to public position? Would a scion of a great family, a Crillon or a Montmorency, still a baron or a duke in his own eyes, ever be satisfied with a position as district administrator, municipal official, or section head? "Don't flatter yourselves, they'd prefer death a hundred times more than life under such a regime," he insisted. "As long as they are not destroyed they will conspire with the court forever to reestablish their privileges, their titles, their dignities, their decorations. These so-called sacrifices will be an inexhaustible source of discord, dissension, intrigues and conspiracies that can only end in civil war and plunge us back into the abyss until the nation, exhausted by its ills, will finally decide to exterminate the damned race of these henchmen of iniquity, the only efficacious way to put an end to its woes." A general insurrection would necessarily be the outcome, a "frightful but indispensable execution of 200,000 to 300,000 rebels" that could once have been avoided by lopping off the heads of (yet again!) 500 or 600 criminal conspirators. But it was too late now to assure liberty and happiness by so slight a sacrifice. "The idiotic people stupidly missed the chance for that, and through barbarous pity it has put itself under the hideous necessity to restore order by making blood flow in great torrents." Civil war was necessary, in short, to prevent civil war.[69]

Even so, The People's Friend was losing heart for the fight. On 8 September, too, he sent the deputies a bitter capitulation from the "hotel of lost liberty." On the eleventh, he was denouncing shameful electoral choices for the Legislative Assembly and the shuffling of corrupt elites between the representative body and the administration and judiciary. This system, "the most profound of all those hell could produce," was making popular mobilization or insurrection impossible, no matter how violent public indignation might be. "Our chains are riveted for eternity," he lamented. "The people is dead since the massacre at the Champ de Mars." With no hope of awakening it, "I've given up trying, and probably forever. But I may still amuse myself by playing the prophet."[70]

Prophet or not, the past still weighed on him. On 9 September, *L'Ami du peuple* began advertising publication of *Les Charlatans modernes*, the bitter diatribe against the scientific despotism of the Paris academicians Marat had started to write years before. "Indignation makes for poetry" was the tagline from Juvenal he gave it, but why publish it now? Cast in epistolary form, the attack was supplemented and reinforced with a final letter underlining its relevance to the immediate situation, not least because the National Assembly was about to consider the future of the academies. "Judge now the utility of the academies and the virtue of their members," it urged. "Those of the capital have never done anything for the progress of human knowledge but persecute men of genius. They'll be preserved by the conscript fathers for the sole reason that they are paid for by the nation and are composed of vile henchmen of the despot, gutless champions of despotism."

Announced on 9 September as forthcoming shortly, and as still available on the twentieth, *Les Charlatans modernes* was timed to coincide with Talleyrand's report to the Assembly on the organization of public instruction, which indeed proposed a hierarchical system of instruction topped by an Institut National that would regroup the academicians in a series of more specialized sections. It spoke, too, to the issue of public expenditures the Assembly had to address before it disbanded, and also, less directly, to the elections then going on in Paris to choose the city's deputies to the Legislative Assembly. The Academy of Sciences represented at once the power and privilege of the technocratic elite of the Old Regime and its continuing penetration of the institutions of the Revolution. It was not coincidental that Condorcet, epitome of the double-sided despotism and servility of the academicians in Marat's eyes, was among the list of candidates.[71]

Old embitterments served to intensify more recent ones. On 15 September, *L'Ami du peuple* offered a dismal comparison between the old regime and the new in which traditional barriers against despotism had been overthrown and the monarch freed to control the legislature, corrupt the administration and the judiciary, ransack the public treasury, and use the army to enforce obedience. The king's authority was less respected, Marat judged, because his agents were deploying it against "the torrent of public opinion that was always, in every country, the queen of the world." Even so, the monarch had more power than ever; he could have those who disobeyed his orders massacred while displacing onto the legislature the blame for this atrocity. "Louis XVI the constitutional king," Marat concluded, "is thus no less a despot than was Louis XVI the illegitimate king. . . . They lull us ridiculously with the great words of LIBERTY, but we have never been more enslaved." What then had the French gained from the Revolution? he asked. Certainly not a better life: solid currency had virtually disappeared; bread had become dearer and more putrid; taxes were higher; justice more ruinous and more barbarous; procedures to leave the country complicated to the point of humiliation. "Was it worth taking up arms against our tyrants and spending two years of vigilance, exhaustion, and alarms to be reduced to suffering the cruelest vexations and perishing finally in misery? Was it worth throwing the state into the convulsions of anarchy, stripping the poor of their patrimony, and gorging with their goods the seigneurs of the court and faithless mandataries of the people?"[72] The questions were left unanswered.

Experience of the bureaucratic humiliations to be undergone in order to leave the country may have been fresh in Marat's mind. He was telling a friend on 20 September that he would be in London by the time she read the letter he addressed to her publicly in the journal that day. She was Mlle Fouaisse, a woman who had helped him on occasion by relaying copy for his journal to his printer, but also the abused servant of an engraver with whom he had been lodging for several months before being thrown out. The unfortunate woman now found herself in the middle of a scandal after she had decamped with the help of The People's Friend while carrying off some of her master's furniture for good measure. The aggrieved engraver, one Maquet, had arranged to have Marat denounced at the Jacobin Club for theft of the woman and the furniture.[73] The letter Marat now addressed to her detailed the harassment he had suffered as her brutish master had contrived to drive him from one new hiding place to another, forcing him into the streets in broad daylight at risk of his life, and leaving him to beg a friend for a bed in Paris that night. At this, he declared, he had decided to leave for London. At least, he assured her, his enemies would know that "I'm giving up the pen while defending the oppressed." Her defense, and his complicity in saving her from domestic tyranny, became a theme in subsequent issues of the journal and resurfaced a year later as Marat sought election to the Convention.[74]

The following day, 21 September, *L'Ami du peuple* offered its author's "Last Farewells to the Homeland." They took the form of yet another review of the Revolution and the sacrifices he had made for it. Now he saw the Revolution as an affliction rather than an illusion; it was an accident born of a concatenation of circumstances, condemned from the start to be no more than a momentary crisis, its contingent causes incapable of generating liberty. It could have been otherwise, he added, if the indigent classes that formed the mass of the people had been able to choose an enlightened and upright leader to lop off criminal heads and prevent traitors from leaving, as he had urged so many times. But this chance had been squandered. "The loss of the homeland seeming assured to me, I dreamed only of delaying it in the hope that some unforeseen event could finally open the people's eyes and halt it at the edge of the abyss to which its implacable enemies had striven to drag it." Alone and without support, he had warred against the traitors of the homeland. Outraged at their baseness and revolted by their atrocities, he had torn away their masks, put them in the spotlight, covered them with opprobrium, despised their calumnies, impostures, and defamations, defied their fury, withstood their persecution.[75]

There followed a litany of the sufferings The People's Friend had endured in the name of popular liberty. "Twenty military expeditions directed against me at night, an entire army mobilized to take me from the people, only served to increase my audacity. A price was put on my head. Five hundred spies put on my tail, and two thousand assassins paid to slaughter me, couldn't make me betray my duty for a moment. To escape the assassins, I've been condemned to a life underground disrupted every so often by battalions of police, forced to flee into the streets in the middle of the night, not knowing where to find asylum, pleading the cause of liberty in the midst of chains, defending the oppressed with my head on the block, and becoming even more formidable to the oppressors and public scoundrels." He had led this wretched life for eighteen months without a moment's complaint, he attested, without regretting his loss of peace and enjoyment, taking no account of his health and social condition, without ever blanching at the blade directed at his breast. He had preferred it to all the advantages of corruption, all the delights of wealth, all the glitter of the crown. He would have been protected, caressed, and fêted if he had chosen to remain silent; showered with gold if he had wanted to dishonor his pen. "I repudiated the corrupting metal, lived in poverty, kept my heart pure. I'd be a millionaire today if I had been less scrupulous and had not always forgotten myself." Instead of wealth, he proclaimed, he had only debts inflicted by faithless manipulators to whom he had entrusted his journal's publication. He was abandoning to his creditors the debris that was left.

Now he declared himself overwhelmed by calumny, defamed by the public scoundrels he had unmasked, burdened by the maledictions of all the enemies of the homeland, abhorred by the great, and targeted in every minister's office as a monster to be throttled; he was running, penniless, to vegetate in the only corner of the world where he could breathe in peace, perhaps to be forgotten there by the people to whose salvation he had sacrificed himself. "I have fought without respite until today, and I have not quit the breach until the position has been captured. . . . Citizens, I ask neither regrets nor gratitude of you; don't even preserve the memory of my name; but if ever some unexpected twist of destiny brings you victory, remember to clinch it by profiting from your advantages and, to ensure your triumph, never forget the counsel of a man who lived only to establish the reign of justice and liberty among you."[76]

What a performance! This number 556 of *L'Ami du peuple* has to be one of Marat's most accomplished scripts. A cry of despair, a bitter surrender to defeat, an embrace of sacrifice, a self-abnegating farewell: Rousseauian victimization in the guise of political martyrdom. And all this in the mirror of self-promotion, the projection of an image of self-sacrifice meant to last for eternity. There are two flaws, perhaps, in this pearl of populist pleading. For one: its author, consigning himself to oblivion, couldn't resist intimating that "if the people rises up, I'll come and resume my post." For another, he couldn't actually bring himself to stop writing. "Before quitting the pen," he promised as he declared himself on the eve of heading for England, "I'll share with the public the interesting observations I'll make *en route*."[77]

The result was a series of travel reports, among the most curious issues of the entire run of *L'Ami du peuple*. The first, "sent by the author from Clermont in Beauvais on 15 September 1791" but published a week later, found him in a coach bound for the frontier in the company of a group of would-be émigrés aiming to join counterrevolutionary armies. The experience proved illuminating. On the road he learned that a true patriot could agree with a renegade aristocrat in judging the Revolution a disaster; that the one could indeed pass for the other by staying mum about principles and purposes. He discovered the way that, for a price, aristocratic emigrants could be smuggled out of the country. To his secret joy, he heard word from an officer deserting his post that the entire army was in revolt.[78]

Continuing in the same vein, the second report, "sent from Breteuil," offered news of émigrés heading in droves for the Austrian Low Countries. It also detailed a conversation with a particularly perceptive escapee, a noble keen-eyed enough to have appraised the author of *L'Ami du peuple* as the only one of the revolutionaries true to the spirit of the Revolution, and perhaps the only one not for sale. Nobles, prelates, loyal military officers, and all the partisans of the king would have been done for if Marat's counsels had prevailed, this enemy of the Revolution observed. But the people had been deaf to its friend's voice as "the devious deputies of the Third Estate . . . , carried away by petty resentments," had offered it a fantasy of equality impossible to achieve in society because it did not exist in nature.[79]

With this, the aristocrat's confession of faith blossomed into an extended denunciation of the brutal leveling of the old order. "What do they imagine is to become of the nobility, especially the high nobility, if they have no political existence today?" Marat had him continue. "That we'll vegetate on our lands, insulted by the peasants we'll be feeding; that we'll command rustics in blue uniform; that we'll hang out in a committee of a section, district or department along with our business agents; that we'll sit in a police or judicial tribunal? This might have been good for a while to save us from being slaughtered and hold back the explosion in the early days of the revolution, but we'd rather not live than lead such a life. In depriving us of our political existence, the National Assembly has itself reduced us to the cruel necessity of taking up arms." It was their turn now to take revenge, the incensed noble averred. The people would long be denied the happiness it had been tricked into expecting through the grand words, "equality" and "liberty," trivial illusions that would cost it rivers of blood. And if the aristocrats failed to recover their position and were finally subjected to the law, he promised, they would take what was left of their capital and put it into commerce; they would become monopolists of all kinds, stripping the people everywhere of the fruits of its labor. "We'll turn ourselves into Dutchmen and become [the people's] masters on other terms." This was making derogation a path back to power, the substitution of class for caste, exploitation of civic equality as a form of vengeance![80]

Readers of *L'Ami du peuple* might scarcely have been surprised to hear of such language on the lips of an aristocratic rebel. But would they have anticipated Marat's confession that he had listened to it in silence while applauding it secretly? Would they have been convinced by his claim that he had many times preached the same doctrine? "It was doubtless good to annihilate the privileged orders, and nothing was better than to have stripped them of their prerogatives," he acknowledged, "but they should have been left their decorations and their titles and taxed heavily." Could one doubt that abolition of noble titles had been a scheme to plant an eternal source of discord and sedition within the state? he demanded. The next legislature would surely have to restore these baubles to the nobility before their loss fed the flames of civil war. "So long as I had a hope of seeing an entire liberty established among us, I didn't cease preaching to the friends of liberty the need to keep felling their implacable enemies. Now we're forced today to live with them, wisdom demands that they amuse themselves to prevent their tearing us apart."[81]

Little more than a week earlier, The People's Friend had been calling for a war of extinction against the damned race of aristocrats. Now, it seems, he was ready to accept defeat and opt for accommodation. His third report on his travel, "sent from a hamlet near Amiens," justified this volte-face at substantial length. He had apparently forgotten the fervor with which he had once welcomed abolition of the symbols of aristocratic oppression. It must have been a cruel enemy of the homeland, he now wrote, who first thought of stripping the nobility of their empty titles and decorations. To eliminate oppressive privileges and prerogatives was indeed indispensable to achieve the reign of liberty. But why abolish purely honorific distinctions, dignities without power, and all the baubles of human vanity whose possession gratifies cramped souls, and whose deprivation triggers so many infractions, disorders, and crimes, troubling the state and throwing the homeland into the horrors of civil war?

"Doubtless, the doctrine of perfect equality must be received enthusiastically by the blind multitude, which is always led by words," paradoxically exclaimed this wordsmith extraordinaire! "Judge the intoxication of a water carrier, a tailor, a shoemaker believing himself the equal of a duke or *maréchal de France*! Imagine the influence that jugglers preaching equality must have had over the mind of the people, and the illusion they must have cast over the vulgar among our legislators. I can't conceive that no one in the nation's senate had seen the problems with this doctrine and foreseen its disastrous effects on public security and tranquility."[82]

It had indeed been imperative to destroy feudalism. To this conviction, The People's Friend remained firm. But had it been necessary to strip nobles of the glory of titles transmitted to them by their forbears, criminalizing names that had been illustrious for centuries? How could these acts not have been resented as arbitrary, a tyrannical assault? How could ignorant legislators have expected the descendants of a Montmorency, a Bouillon, a Villar to content themselves with bare-bone names fit for a candle-merchant or local porter. "They will never destroy the relations of nature or of society," Marat now insisted. "A duke will always be a duke to his servants, his agents, his suppliers, his hangers-on, his toadies . . . , the artists, the poets, the writers and lawyers who want his money and his protection . . . , the insolent jurists who have disqualified him, as long as they need him." And what had the poor people gained from this? It had not stopped groveling before the heir of an illustrious predecessor merely to do the same before a parvenu a hundred times less worthy. "Ah! Since it's born for humiliation, better that it abase itself before a *maréchal de France* who has received an education than a money-grubbing lowlife draped with a tricolor sash." In this mood, Marat anticipated little to be gained for the benighted populace in a transition from a hierarchical society of orders to a regime of democratic leveling.[83]

One senses here how deeply this populist despised the people in this moment, how bitterly he resented its failure to grasp its sovereignty, how disenchanted he was with empty forms of equality he saw being offered instead. At the limit, it seems clear, popular liberty was dearer to him than individual equality. "Oh Frenchmen, will you always be empty and frivolous, refusing the obvious and lacking common sense?" he demanded, returning to a favorite trope. "Will you always lend a docile ear to the deceptive talk of scoundrels misleading you? Will you never open your eyes to the abyss into which they want to drag you?" This time, though, Marat called for settling rather than slaughter. Give the former nobles back their empty titles, he admonished. "Hasten to occupy them with these diversions to prevent them from being eternal conspirators; hasten to turn them back into court jesters to prevent them from becoming your assassins."[84]

The finale of this series of travel reports appeared in *L'Ami du peuple* on 27 September, unexpectedly written "upon return to Paris." "An event as disagreeable as it was unanticipated brings me back to the capital," Marat explained. "For how long? I don't know. At least I won't be an impassive spectator of the machinations of the enemies of the homeland, and the extra time I'll spend here will be consecrated to the public good." Why had he come back to the capital? He could barely wait to tell the story. But he had to say first that he had left Paris on 14 September, the day of the king's formal acceptance of the constitution, to avoid benefiting from the general amnesty intended to reestablish "the blind sense of security that tyrants need so much to plunge the peoples back into slavery." This "excess of ministerial philanthropy," he deplored, could only serve the enemies of the Revolution at this point because so many friends of liberty had been massacred.[85]

The story of his unanticipated return to Paris is the stuff of a picaresque novel. Recognized by one of Lafayette's spies and fearing that he was about to be arrested in Amiens as a result, he managed to slip away by mingling in a local youth parade and reach a meadow on the banks of the Somme. There, seated on a mound of stones behind a hedge, he contemplated, as had Marius above the ruins of Carthage, the vicissitudes of human affairs, the play of fortune, the blows of cruel destiny. Helped by a nearby shepherd to locate a guide to get him safely to the road back to Paris, he trusted his fate to a former grenadier of the French guards, withered and emaciated, prematurely aged by misery, and desperately poor. Setting out across a field in the dark, he injured his foot and had to drag himself to the nearest village, where a cart and broken-down horse were found to carry him on. An encounter with the local guard in Clermont, as houses were being torched in the middle of the night by "villains enraged at the civic commitment of the good inhabitants of the countryside," almost resulted in his guide's arrest. But the two made it to Beauvais, whence, exhausted and burning with fever, The People's Friend was returned by cabriolet to Paris to continue his suffering as the people's savior.[86]

Did any of this happen? One cannot forget that Marat had already written one novel. Was this account just another piece of fiction? If so, it was quite an elaborate invention, and it immediately invited skepticism. He had to insist in a later issue of *L'Ami du peuple* that he had indeed written these letters from the road and that the arguments for restoration of noble titles they presented were entirely consistent with his previous views (a disingenuous claim) as well as the needs of the current political situation. How stupid the people had been to rejoice in the suppression of noble titles, he insisted; this had merely allowed the former holders of these titles to shed the marks of their allegiance to the old regime while assuming positions of authority in the new.[87]

The whole story may have been a hoax. It seems plausible, though, that he had decided in despair to leave France for England, as he had on previous occasions. And it is not impossible to imagine that, after hiding in the capital for months while sheltered by like-minded patriots, he had found his ideas complicated by an encounter with real émigrés rather than the faceless ones he had been denouncing for so long. There might be elements of truth embellished here in a much-embroidered tale. Or perhaps it was just a dramatic way of signaling a change of journalistic direction.[88]

He had returned, he announced, with a ray of hope since learning of the entire uprising of the army against its oppressive officers and witnessing the energy of the inhabitants of the countryside. He now thought it possible, if the new legislature was less corrupt than the previous one, that patriots could recover strength and a degree of liberty could be established. "In any case," he informed his readers, "I will follow the progress of the new legislative body until I have penetrated its plans and can foresee the turn of events that public affairs will take." *L'Ami du peuple* would try a different tack in the face of new realities. The people had contemplated with horror the bloody sacrifices necessary for its happiness; it was meek enough to allow its unfortunate members to be slaughtered with impunity. "I won't talk anymore, then, of its just vengeance against the enemies of its repose . . . but I'll continue to bring to light the dark machinations of the scoundrels determined to destroy it, and I'll look for means of foiling them. I'll do more, I'll propose means of bringing back the enemies with whom we are forced to live, amusing them with their baubles after taking from them the power to undo us."[89]

L'Ami du peuple would go on after all. Marat would not lay down his pen. The prophet could not abandon the people. There were new deputies to be watched. "Since the massacre of the Champ de Mars the veil of illusion is torn. The unworthy mandataries promised us an august temple elevated to liberty; instead, they have built a gothic edifice on sand. It's up to the new deputies to sweep it away and to the patriotic writers to prevent our being crushed in its ruins."[90]

THE FIRST MODERN POPULIST

TWENTY-ONE

A MACHINE THAT WOULD NOT WORK

L'Ami du peuple bade the Constituent Assembly good riddance on 3 October 1791, not before excoriating its last-minute efforts to annihilate liberty by harsh decrees constraining press freedom and denying clubs and societies any collective public existence or right to engage as a body in political affairs. If the first effort failed, the second succeeded after pitting Le Chapelier against Robespierre in a bitter debate over the legitimacy of popular political action that foreshadowed the future course of the Revolution.[1] Marat pointed to it as a preface to his description of the popular acclaim lavished on the departing patriotic deputies, "incorruptible defenders of the people and its rights," and the jeers hurled at the shameful majority who had sacrificed the happiness of their fellow citizens to their avarice and ambition. "May you forever be covered with infamy," he screamed at the latter; "may you be reduced to fleeing the light of day, dragging into a desert your shame, your remorse, your despair! The People's Friend was the first to tear away the imposter's mask with which you covered your perfidies. May his book at least pass to posterity to bear witness against you for all time!"[2]

Not that The People's Friend had great hopes for the Legislative Assembly. He was unimpressed by the representatives elected from the provinces, largely consisting of men who had been holding positions in local government since 1789. They were judicial and administrative officials of districts and departments, military and National Guard officers, mayors, judges, and other government agents: people who had committed their future to the Revolution. *L'Ami du peuple* dismissed them all as repositioned lackeys of the Old Regime, cronies of the court brought to Paris by ministerial intrigue to halt the triumph of liberty and promote counterrevolution. As for the choices made by the Parisian electors, Marat found them nothing less than shameful. There had been little question of his own nomination, but he dismissed the new representatives of the capital as mediocrities ready for handouts, intriguers tending to counterrevolution, dangerous careerists, clients of Lafayette and double-dealers like Condorcet. He was more ambivalent about Brissot, whom he now considered tarnished by association with Lafayette. When the city electors had seemed to be passing Brissot over, Marat had urged him publicly to avoid humiliation by withdrawing his name from the list of candidates; Brissot remained a candidate and was elected. The Legislative Assembly had barely met before Marat was detecting "the ascendancy of the villainous deputies from Paris."[3] He would be forced to watch furiously, months later, as Brissot and Condorcet joined in leading France into war.

The new Assembly faced many challenges, not least the constraints of the meeting place inherited from its predecessor. The deficiencies of its locale in the Manège, the former riding school of the Louvre, were well known by now. The keen eye of the architectural theorist Antoine-Chrysostome Quatremère (formerly de Quincy), one of the newcomers, was scarcely required to recognize that the seating arrangement made it impossible for them all to see or hear one another, thus turning the hall into "a gladiatorial arena where everyone fights to talk."[4] Quatremère wanted debate to stop until architects could design a smaller space in which the deputies could engage in orderly discussion and there would be more room for auditors to follow it. Marat went further, calling (again) for the Assembly to find a different location with galleries allowing a popular audience of three thousand.[5]

Ideas like this went nowhere. But The People's Friend was more immediately concerned, in any case, to decry the special galleries the Constituent Assembly had set up in advance for its members to observe their successors' proceedings. He was sure these enclosures had been constructed to allow venal men already prostituted to the ministers to sway discussion and identify potential targets for corruption. These spaces were also symbolic more generally: for many weeks, and with good reason, he sensed former Constituents pulling the strings behind the scenes of the new legislative body whose powers and procedures they had worked so hard to constrain.[6]

Some of the new deputies also protested the heavy presence of the National Guard in and around the Manège, even accusing individual guardsmen of haranguing those with patriotic opinions. "This is how Cromwell, when he had corrupted the army, used it to put parliament under the yoke," Marat warned. "There was never a tyrannical bill proposed when he did not occupy all the avenues of Westminster with a troop of cavalry and post his regiment of red-coated spawn in the corridors of the House of Commons to menace the people's deputies as they passed through."[7]

But the principal constraint Marat saw on the new deputies, of course, was the constitution itself, which barred this Legislative Assembly and its successor from making any changes to it. Continuing to denounce the founding text as profoundly flawed, and insisting that it could indeed be corrected if the nation's representative body so willed, he was appalled by the idolatry displayed on 4 October when the deputies had the document brought solemnly from the archive to be touched as scripture by each of them in turn as they repeated the constitutional oath individually. "Friends of the homeland, this farce is the tomb of nascent liberty," he warned; "the new conscript fathers are no better than the old ones. . . . Don't expect anything but betrayal, misfortune, and desolation until the fugitive Capets come back with sword and fire in hand to throw out our decree makers and rivet our chains forever."[8]

The People's Friend was surprised, nonetheless, by the newcomers' next action, even quipping that they would be suspected of being awakened by his journal. Affronted when the king put off the deputation sent to inform him that the Assembly had now been formally constituted, they retaliated by stripping down the ceremonial protocol established by the Constituent Assembly for receiving him. Louis XVI, they decreed, would be addressed not as "Sire" or "Majesty" but as "King of the French"; they would not await his command to be seated upon his arrival, and the monarch himself would be seated at the same level as the Assembly president, and to his left, on a chair no more splendid.[9] Each of these decisions marked a symbolic diminution of the king's majesty in relation to that of the nation's representatives.

"So that's the king put in his place and the insolence of the ministers repaid in fine manner," trumpeted *L'Ami du peuple*. "It's their stupid counsels that pushed Louis XVI to play the ridiculous role of an absolute monarch in the presence of his masters." The nation's gain was immense, Marat rejoiced; this "immortal session" of 5 October offered him hope for reform of the constitution's vices. If the deputies were ready to set aside rules of etiquette laid down by their predecessors, "why should they show so much respect for the disastrous decrees responsible for the misfortune of the people and opprobrium toward its first representatives?" Redeeming themselves for their constitutional idolatry, he proclaimed, they had upheld the majesty of the nation against an ungrateful and haughty prince who had already forgotten the respect owed to the representatives of his sovereign people. Now they had to go further, repudiating the "political blasphemy" that the prince exercised an independent power equal to their own, and decreeing that he was a mere public functionary in no way the representative of the nation.[10]

The hope was short-lived. The "immortal decree" was killed off the very next day. Marat blamed the influence of former Constituents agitating from their special galleries, and on the ministers' machinations. It had taken less than a week to convince him that the patriotic majority within the Assembly was so ignorant, weak, and blind that it would be manipulated by a handful of "ministerials," the term he began using for scoundrels among the deputies who were willing to follow the lead and serve the interests of the executive power. Louis XVI appeared before the Assembly on 7 October with all due ceremony, to acclamation from the galleries packed with courtiers and sullen silence from the deputies, who stood as he took his gilded, fleur-de-lys-embroidered seat to the right of the Assembly's president. From there, he laid out a law-and-order agenda and urged collaboration between the legislative and the executive powers. The administration "will no longer be troubled by empty terrors," he avowed, "and there will remain no more pretext to leave a country where the laws will be respected." Marat was outraged by the curtness of the address and its imperative tone (and doubtless, also, by its gesture toward the émigrés). This was the performance of "a despot prescribing his officers' duties," he exclaimed; the king's handlers had opted for "the tone of a master solely concerned to give orders, doubtless out of temper against the patriotic deputies responsible for passage of the glorious decree his henchmen had soon got revoked."[11] The speech did not bode well.

Nor, in Marat's analysis, did the political composition of the Assembly itself. By this point, he saw it divided into three groups. One consisted of "fervent patriots" who desired the public good and sought no other reward than the glory of serving it. A second was a more motley assemblage: the "prejudiced men who had not yet been able to shake off the filth of their education," had no idea of the majesty of the nation, and continued to debase themselves before the more fortunate; the reprobates anxious to lull the people to sleep because they feared nothing so much as public unrest; the egoists seeking advancement and always ready to sacrifice duty and honor to it. A third group comprised the "enslaved ministerials infecting the senate, faithless, lawless, shameless men who would prostitute themselves to the will of the court for the least sign of approval and betray their homeland, their friends, and their family for the slightest favor." Among the latter he included almost all the Parisian deputies.[12]

"I will be tracking all the moves of these dastardly enemies of the homeland, exposing all their turpitudes to the light of day," Marat promised his readers. He would "brand their foreheads with the sign of opprobrium and give them over to public execration," as he had with their predecessors. He would be no less attentive to "the false patriots who will be seeking to put themselves up for sale." And he would "make it my sacred duty to do justice to the civic virtues of the true defenders of the homeland and show their generous efforts." This latter he would do, though, without ever placing blind confidence in these men, or showering them with praise. "It's doubtless necessary to show support for their courage as they pursue their onerous career, but we have to wait to the end to crown them." For The People's Friend, it was clear, the political world was a corrupt and fallen one; any approval of its denizens could only ever be provisional. But these were early days for the Legislative Assembly. For the moment, he saw among the patriotic deputies "none of those men of great character destined to lead the multitude."[13]

Over the next few months *L'Ami du peuple* portrayed an assembly divided, outmaneuvered, undermined, and corrupted by ministers and the court as it confronted crises ramifying almost daily. Marat blamed the deputies, in part, for failing to organize their parliamentary business effectively. He was relieved to see them eliminate the dangerous special galleries set up for former members of the Constituent Assembly, though dissatisfied that these spaces remained closed to the public. But he called in vain for the Assembly to reduce the number of its standing committees on the grounds that they invited corruption and manipulation by moving decisions behind closed doors. Instead, the number of committees was increased, largely in response to Condorcet's proposal to proliferate those dealing with financial matters. Seven new committees meant seven new sites for prostitution to the ministers and the court, thus seventy new votes for the ministerials! As evidence of what could still be gained from royal largesse, Marat pointed to the handsome emoluments enjoyed by Condorcet, that "false patriot in the pay of the court."[14]

Convinced since he had published *The Chains of Slavery* that parliamentary representation was inevitably vulnerable to manipulation and corruption, Marat consistently denounced the pressure Louis XVI's ministers were placing on the Legislative Assembly. "Believe The People's Friend," he was already writing on 12 October. "As long as the crown is hereditary, the prince will be the eternal enemy of the nation and his ministers will only ever be scoundrels paid to execute his deadly projects. We put all our hope in our representatives; they could have fulfilled our wishes; they betrayed our expectations. . . . For two years, in cahoots with the court to reestablish despotism, they openly protected all the treasons plotted against the homeland. They annihilated public liberty, destroyed individual security, favored the projects of conspirators, concerted with enemy powers, prepared our ruin, which their successors will perhaps consummate." By early November, he was protesting that every session of the Legislative Assembly was interrupted by messages from the ministers, every discussion derailed by their interventions, and many important debates infiltrated by them despite their lack of constitutional standing to participate. Sessions once over, he added, the ministers were habitually besieged by intriguers seeking favors, thus enabling them to build clientage by gratifying some supplicants and playing others along. He wanted a decree that would prohibit deputies from soliciting like this on pain of destitution and punish them by suspension for personal communication with ministers.[15]

Above all, he pressed the legislators from the very beginning to control and regulate the order of their own debates. Many of the Constituents' most frightful constitutional decisions, he reminded his readers, had emerged from chaotic scenes in which procedures had been disregarded, agendas derailed, and debates constantly disrupted. Recognizing as much only after the damage was done, they had finally adopted regulations for their successors to follow a calmer and more coherent path to decision-making. "Trembling at the prospect that the fatal dissensions that tore the Constituent apart would be revived in the Legislative," the new Assembly accepted these procedures and added to them. Marat had called on 15 October for further rules to require that fixed daily agendas and the texts of proposed decrees be published a week in advance; to prohibit the introduction of extraneous issues into debates; to bar deputations and ministerial or other official communications from interrupting the deliberations; and to prevent abrupt closure of debate before those wanting to speak had been heard. A few days later, he was objecting that the Assembly was spending all its time hearing petitions. Its morning sessions had to be devoted only to legislation, he insisted, and its evening sessions to indictment and punishment of agents of the executive power.[16]

This criticism of the Assembly's procedures and practices continued for months. On 25 October, *L'Ami du peuple* was grousing that the deputies were so distracted by other business that they had been unable to achieve a regular routine or engage in a single discussion in peace. Again, it urged them to reserve their morning sessions, uninterrupted, for legislative matters. Otherwise, it predicted, the Assembly would never consummate its work, remaining the eternal plaything of the scoundrels the ministers were paying to fetter, mislead, and dishonor it. The Assembly secretaries, for their part, had to be watched as prime targets of corruption. As the issues facing the deputies became more crucial, and their disagreements more intense, they also had to take firmer control of the order of speakers. The journal made much of a scene that erupted on 30 October, during the tense debates over emigration, when it was discovered that names in the list of speakers had been inserted out of order, or simply erased and replaced by others. These, Marat lamented, were the tricks played by the ministerials on the friends of the homeland. "When one sees men presumptuous enough to want to govern a great empire unable to regulate the procedures of their collective body, one shrugs one's shoulders in pity." Doing so, he nonetheless went so far as to prescribe that the speakers' list be organized in columns with twenty lines each![17]

Intriguing though it might be to discover Jean-Paul Marat instructing the deputies on minutiae of parliamentary procedure, it seems even more remarkable to find him supporting their decision to impose silence on the public in the galleries. His argument on this point was revealing. It was important for a truly free people to keep its representatives under constant scrutiny by observers ready to recall them to their duty, he acknowledged. To clap or hiss was "the right of every enlightened citizen." Political prudence, though, dictated that this right be denied to "an ignorant, frivolous, and inconsistent public incapable of understanding and fired up by words, driven crazy by charlatans skilled at deceiving it, that ruins the best of causes in abandoning itself to the passions of the moment and turns the most serious matters of life into a comedy, a ridiculous farce." Such, he argued, was the public in Paris, now little inclined to hiss but all too ready to applaud. "Our sad experience of this mania would be more than enough to make us renounce it if we knew how to profit from our mistakes."[18]

Would his readers not accuse him of changing his mind on this matter? His response was direct. "It's not my fault if they don't know how to read." When enlightened patriots had filled the galleries of the National Assembly and formed the audiences of the tribunals, he explained, he had rightly encouraged them to recall the agents of the people to their duty by showing disapproval. Now the galleries were crowded with enemies of the people, he wanted applause forbidden. "To my eyes, liberty must be made only for its friends. I've demanded a hundred times that it be denied to its adversaries who abuse it." There was a bitter reality behind this torturing of principle: the friends of liberty were no longer present in the galleries of the National Assembly. "The people is dead since the Champ de Mars Massacre," he had wailed on 11 September. He was still calling in mid-

November for a new popular movement to support patriotic deputies in their demand for action against émigrés.[19]

He also wanted more powerfully concerted action by friends of the people within the Assembly. By now, he argued, they should have formed a cohort of energetic, civic-minded patriots. They should be pushing for measures of public safety, shouting for decrees to reestablish liberty, blocking the maneuvers of the government, unmasking and punishing miscreants, and facing down the ministerials. Even so, he could only see such efforts as a call for a holding action "until the tyrannized people finally awakes from its lethargy and acts to get rid of its tyrants, for we can no longer hide from ourselves that all our hope lies in civil war."[20]

In an uncharacteristic moment of fancy Marat had imagined civil war in France signaling liberty to all the peoples of the world, but he soon returned to his habitual refrain. The moment of cataclysm was approaching, he assured his readers. How rapidly The People's Friend could pivot from details of parliamentary strategy to visions of violent confrontation and political catastrophe. Caught between the threat of servitude and the delusion of liberty, between massacres and supplications, he proclaimed, the people had only one option. "All that's left to us is to take back our chains in shame unless we have the courage to break the yoke a second time, fight for our rights, and choke our oppressors in their own blood. Perhaps Heaven will give us victory anew; but if we succumb, we'll become more enslaved than ever."[21] Apocalypse was never far from the surface of his thoughts.

THE SCOURGE OF EMIGRATION

By Marat's report, he had fallen in with a group of emigrants among those crowding the road when he left Paris on 14 September, the day Louis XVI took his oath in acceptance of the constitution. The date was not mere coincidence. The completion of the constitution and expectations of the king's decision to accept it had opened the floodgates to a wave of emigration that had been building since his attempted flight. September and October saw thousands of new departures and more intensive efforts at recruitment by fugitives already beyond the frontiers. By then, they were amassing their forces in armed camps. The king's brothers, the comte d'Artois (Marat's former employer, who had led a conspicuous early wave of emigration in July 1789) and the comte de Provence (who had left the country in 1791 as the king headed ineptly toward Varennes) were commanding an army outside Coblentz (Koblenz) in the Rhineland territory of the archbishop-elector of Trier. The king's cousin, the prince de Condé (a hothead who had also emigrated in 1789), was organizing a second force on the border with Alsace. A third band had moved into position near Colmar under the leadership of André Boniface Louis Riqueti, vicomte de Mirabeau (brother of the famous orator, and a reactionary former deputy who had emigrated in July 1790). For months these émigré leaders had been inciting political division and religious conflict in the French provinces, particularly in the south. Now they were preparing to invade.

Their armies and other activities were largely funded surreptitiously by the European powers led by the Austrian emperor, Leopold II, who, when pressed by the French princes for more direct military support, joined somewhat reluctantly with the Prussian king to issue the Declaration of Pillnitz on 27 August 1791. Appealing to the crowned heads of Europe to recognize the French king's situation as a matter of their common interest, the declaration nevertheless remained understated. It expressed the "hope" that sovereigns "would not refuse" to help put Louis XVI "in a position to strengthen, in the most perfect liberty, the foundations of a monarchical government equally suitable to the rights of sovereigns and the well-being of the French." At the same time, it held back from any commitment to immediate military intervention, signaling instead that any action would depend upon a common agreement among the European powers, in anticipation of which the two signatories would ready their troops. Such common agreement among the powers was not yet in sight, as the emperor well knew, but the declaration nonetheless served to energize the émigrés and heighten fears of counterrevolutionary invasion within France.[22]

Facing this threat, the Legislative Assembly found itself without a policy. A decree adopted on 1 August had summoned absentees without legitimate business abroad to return to their homeland within a month or face significant fiscal and other financial penalties. It had been nullified, with other early laws against the emigrants, by the general amnesty issued on 14 September. In declaring his acceptance of the constitution to the French people on 28 September, Louis XVI had called on the departees to repatriate themselves to "render easier and sooner the reestablishment of order and tranquility." This entreaty evoked no apparent response from the emigrants and was widely suspected of being disingenuous. "Why these solicitations when you could be giving orders?" Marat sneered. "All the rebels recognize you as their lord and master." The monarch had only to order his brothers to be ready to leave within twenty-four hours or face his indignation, he complained, and they would return with all their followers. "You're stringing us along with these fine words, but you won't say the one that counts."[23]

By 1 October, the day the Legislative Assembly began its sessions,

L'Ami du peuple had already dismissed reports in the royalist press that Louis XVI had ordered the fugitive princes to rejoin his court. If the king had done so, it observed, the rebels would have returned, and the daily flood of emigrants would no longer be mounting. Instead, "all the henchmen of despotism are running to place themselves under the flags of the fugitive Capets." By spring if not sooner, the journal predicted, Louis XVI would be waiting to greet them in a château far from Paris. A hundred thousand former nobles would have swept into unprotected provinces, putting to the sword the ill-disciplined and poorly armed citizens who refused to submit. The country would have been wracked by famine and the wretched inhabitants reduced to servitude. Only the new legislature could avert these evils, the journal added, "but to judge by the choices made by the capital, there is everything to fear from its composition."[24]

The deputies were still organizing themselves for parliamentary business when they began receiving reports from throughout the country of garrisons abandoned by officers, whole regions deserted by nobles, and weapons and supplies migrating from military depots. On 13 October, they were informed of the almost total emigration of the officers of the line in the department of the Nord. Then 15 October brought them a dramatic letter from the mayor of Sierck, a frontier town in the Moselle, alerting them to the loss of men and theft of matériel the nation was suffering, and the alarm of his community situated close to insecure and ill-defended borders. "You have no idea how many valuable things are being taken elsewhere from France . . . ," complained the mayor; "it's time to get out of your lethargy." Most strikingly, he reported that the town had arrested fugitive soldiers and confiscated a shipment of uniforms and other military accoutrements bearing the king's arms that was addressed to "Vergennes, minister of the king in Coblentz." An inconclusive discussion of this news left the deputies in disagreement over the city's right to confiscate goods that were possibly royal property! But it also ignited demands for strong action to revoke laws that allowed the export of money, property, and men from the country and to punish military men who were abandoning their posts. A proposal for a motion that "these men unworthy of bearing the French name be declared infamous, barred from ever bearing arms for the homeland, and deprived of the rights of active citizens" threw the Assembly into tumult before it decided to table the matter until its committees had been organized.[25]

The discussion continued the following day, nonetheless, until the Assembly received a letter from the acting war minister, Claude-Antoine Valdec de Lessart (or Delessart), reporting that 1,932 officers' posts had been vacant as of 1 August, of which 764 had been filled to date. The minister also predicted that the "madness" of emigration was continuing at a pace likely to require another 1,200 replacements. His letter prompted a discussion of procedures for replacement and ways of expediting them that again issued only in a referral of the matter to a committee. More dramatically, it led to calls from the left for the publication of the names of the officers who had deserted, a measure repudiated in horror by the ministerials as a blunt instrument amounting to a proscription. The scale of desertions reported by Delessart had finally made clear, however, that the issue had to be confronted more decisively. The debate was scheduled for 20 October.[26]

In the meantime, Louis XVI had issued yet another royal proclamation on 14 October pleading with the emigrants to rejoin the nation for the common good and declaring it a matter of honor among officers to resume or remain at their posts. In a sterner appeal to his princely brothers on 16 October, the monarch reiterated his commitment to uphold the constitution and urged their return as "proof of attachment to your brother and of fidelity to your king," thus sparing him the need to take more aggressive action against them.

L'Ami du peuple weighed in on 19 October, drawing on the Assembly debates and other reports to depict emigration and desertion "from every corner of the realm." Characteristically, Marat had to begin by reminding his readers that he alone had warned of all the plots against the homeland since the beginning of the Revolution. His intimate knowledge of the hostile dispositions of all the henchmen of the old regime and his grasp of political situations had almost always been sufficient to uncover the truth, he proclaimed; his personal correspondence network had almost always offered proof. Accordingly, he had been taken for a prophet by the multitude and a bird of ill omen by the enemies of liberty. He had been dismissed as a dreamer, he carped, perhaps in implicit reference to his advocacy in September of a policy of reintegration of the emigrants that might avoid civil war. Now, clearly, he had changed his judgment, or rather reverted to it; he offered proof, alarming proof, of the dangers posed by massive departures of the Revolution's enemies. "But the ministers and the ministerial faction continue to lull to sleep the people that nothing can any longer awake from its fatal lethargy."[27]

Desertion had only increased since September, *L'Ami du peuple* protested; the army could by now be almost entirely denuded of officers. Yet the ministerials had blocked all action in the Assembly against the émigrés, even tabling the demand of patriotic deputies that the deserters be identified by name so their public shaming could discourage others from following their example. All the ministers could offer, Marat charged, was "a model of derision": pathetic pleading with officers remaining, as a matter of honor, not to abandon their king. As if the sentimental values of the monarchical tradition were still in place. If Louis XVI was animated by the sentiments of loyalty he had been professing since the day he accepted the constitution, The People's Friend reiterated, he would have ordered the fugitive princes to rejoin him immediately. He would have done the same in regard to all the courtiers, all the military officers, all the disaffected aristocrats who had fled, fixing a date after which those who had failed to return would be subject to the rigors of the law. This would have been "the honest and loyal conduct of a prince faithful to the nation," conduct the monarch could still pursue but would not. "He'll follow relentlessly the course of the cowardly machinations of his ministers, taking some hypocritical actions from time to time to lull the people to sleep until he has succeeded in consummating its ruin." An "Extract of a Letter from Brussels" printed in *L'Ami du peuple* the next day told of emigrants flooding across the border and amassing funds for war. "It appears that winter won't pass without a violent explosion," the letter concluded. "What surprises us, and must surprise you even more, is the insouciance of your national assembly in the midst of all these alarming preparations."[28]

The Assembly became more souciant that same day. Sixty deputies signed up to speak in the 20 October debate on emigration, though the discussion was not too urgent to be interrupted for a vote to cover the funeral expenses of the great Mirabeau, who had died insolvent. The initial speakers were, in any case, reluctant to support strong action against the fugitives (as Mirabeau had been months earlier). Variously, they dismissed generalized anxieties about the emigration as exaggerated alarms spread by "patriots more zealous than enlightened" or by enemies trying to spread fear, discouragement, and division. They upheld freedom of movement as a fundamental right secured by the Declaration of the Rights of Man and of the Citizen and insisted that attempts to constrain it would be not only despotic but useless and, indeed, counterproductive in provoking more emigrations than it would constrain. To the extent that emigrants were monsters motivated by hatred of the Revolution, they reasoned, the nation was better served by facing these enemies openly across a frontier than forcing them to smolder in disaffection and await a moment of crisis to destroy it from within. "Let them go" was the call; allow a flight that was "only the natural transpiration of the order of liberty." As for the fugitives who were already preparing to turn their arms against the homeland, they had as yet committed no crime; no action could be taken against them until their first shots had been fired. Only those military officers or public functionaries who had deserted their posts could yet be punished by ineligibility for future public functions and deprivation of the rights of active citizenship.

The tone of the debate changed, though, when Brissot took the floor to deliver a marathon speech tinged with the bellicose fury, already nurtured for months, with which he would eventually lead the Legislative Assembly into a fateful declaration of war. He went straight to the point: the Assembly was fixing on the wrong target. "We are hounding the droves of men fanatical for their old parchments, who are seduced by perfidious admonitions into abandoning their homes," he maintained, "and through unpardonable weakness we not only tolerate but spare, and even feed with French blood, the heads of the rebellion who command these baneful emigrations." General laws against emigration would be useless, he declared, as well as contrary to the principles of the Declaration of the Rights of Man and of the Citizen. Punishment had to be directed against military and other deserters abandoning public functions, and more specifically against the principal rebels amassing troops beyond the frontiers, beginning above all with the king's brothers. Was judicial evidence necessary to prove criminal actions already notorious throughout Europe? he demanded. "It's by observing these forms too rigorously that peoples regenerating themselves lose the fruit of their liberty: weakness toward the great offenders encourages and prepares new revolutions."[29]

It followed from this analysis that action had to be taken, too, against the foreign powers harboring and sustaining the forces of the French rebels and fostering the chimerical hopes of the fanatical and the ignorant. It was time, Brissot continued, to break the factitious chain of fraud and seduction by which the foreign powers were fooling the princes, who were fooling the rebels, who were fooling the emigrants. It was time for the deputies "to show yourselves to the universe as free men and French." Time also to examine the outrages and hostile dispositions toward the Revolution displayed (or concealed) more generally by the powers of Europe in acts Brissot inventoried in some detail. Time, finally, to "efface the abasement into which France has been plunged by indifference or pusillanimity, to give it the imposing stance appropriate to a great nation, to return it to the rank it must occupy among the powers . . . , to force these powers to respect the decrees it issues against emigrants and rebels."[30] Brissot was beginning to campaign for war.

The decree Brissot proposed summoned emigrants to return within a month. Public functionaries failing to return were to be stripped of their positions and emoluments, and of the rights of active citizenship. More dramatically, the émigré princes were to be deprived of their rights of succession to the crown and of their allowances. They would be persecuted as criminals if they continued to recruit French citizens to their ranks or incite foreign citizens or powers to act against the homeland. No citizen would be allowed to leave the country without a passport, no functionary without permission from the appropriate minister. Exportation of munitions of any kind would be forbidden. Finally, the French would reserve the right to take measures against foreign powers that harbored French rebels and sustained their preparations for war. Brissot's logic made clear the dynamic by which the threat of emigrants outside France would drive it toward war with its neighbors.[31]

Received enthusiastically by some deputies, this aggressive speech was followed by pushback from others. Marat treated it coolly in reporting on it a few days later; he was less eager to praise it than to note that he himself had been calling for reprisals against the conspiratorial Capets for eighteen months. He was certain the government, the ministerials leading the Assembly, and the functionaries of the deep state were in league with the fugitives to reestablish despotism and undercut any measures against them. The machinations of these conspirators would continue, he warned, until the nation recognized that its representatives and agents were playing with them; until its cowardly enemies appeared in arms; until, victorious, it made those it captured expiate their crimes on the scaffold and put a price on the heads of those who had escaped.[32]

The following day, accusing the Assembly of "wallowing around, doing nothing," Marat offered a more extended expression of his views on the emigration. At the heart of his argument was the assertion that abandoning the homeland at a moment of crisis was a crime only for those who were benefiting from it, which was to say persons in place, functionaries feeding at the public trough, or people aspiring to do so. "These are the only ones obliged to defend the homeland since the constitution is totally made for them. Claiming to prevent others from emigrating would be oppression, punishing them for doing so would be tyranny." It followed that so long as the rights of active citizenship depended on wealth, "all those the constitution has declared non-active citizens, which is to say eight tenths of the French," had every right to leave the realm. There was a cutting edge to this conclusion: if loss of active citizenship was a penalty for a crime, it followed that all those denied it for lack of fortune had been unjustly declared equivalent to criminals, iniquitous judges, public enemies, conspirators, traitors to the homeland. The Constituents' disenfranchisement of the poor rankled him constantly until their work was overthrown.[33]

By this reasoning, to prevent travelers from leaving the country for personal reasons, or emigrants from departing in fear of disorder, would be the height of barbarism. But public functionaries deserting their posts should be denied further public employment if they returned, and active citizens abandoning the homeland should lose their rights of citizenship. More critically, emigrants seeking to incite action by foreign powers or preparing to arm themselves to invade the homeland should be treated as traitors, their property confiscated, a price placed upon their heads, and foreign powers required to deny them asylum.

The list of these traitors was ready, Marat proclaimed; the fugitive Capets were at its head. Not that he thought any such action would be taken. The ministerial faction was leading the Assembly by the nose, the constitution had placed power in the king, the henchmen of despotism were filling all places of authority, three-quarters of the French were tired of liberty, and the remaining patriots were only showing themselves to protest oppression. Severe measures would be vetoed, he anticipated, weaker ones left unexecuted. Such was the machine of state the Constituent Assembly had contrived to support despotism under the appearance of liberty. "Two years ago . . . I predicted that this machine would not work or would do so only to crush the friends of the homeland. Sadly, everything that has happened since has justified my prediction all too much."[34]

L'Ami du peuple scarcely mentioned the continuation of the debate on emigration on 25 October in which Condorcet and Pierre Victurnien Vergniaud, most notably, reached back to the principles of the social contract to arrive at markedly diverging conclusions. Condorcet, setting both indignation and generosity aside in favor of an "inflexible equity" toward the emigrants, even "those dregs of the nation who still dare to call themselves the elite," made the civic oath the principal instrument of his proposed decree. He proposed to allow French citizens abroad to retain their rights of citizenship if they had taken the civic oath before departure, or if they subsequently appeared before a French envoy or consular official to acknowledge the legitimacy of the constitution and declare their willingness to submit to it. Those unwilling to do so would be regarded as aliens, enjoying the rights to property allowed to foreigners in France provided they swore that they would not bear arms against the country or collaborate with foreign powers to do so. Refusal to take this further oath, or subsequent violation of it, would incur sequestration of property until amnesty or death.[35]

Vergniaud, the future Girondin leader, in a speech that gained him the Assembly's attention for the first time, was more aggressive. He offered two draft decrees. The first followed Brissot's lead in requiring French citizens abroad to return within six weeks or face a tripling of their tax burden unless they could justify their absence for personal or business reasons.

Public functionaries who did not meet this deadline would be stripped of their titles, places, emoluments, and other income, as of the rights of active citizenship; military deserters would be prosecuted and punished as criminals under military law. No payments of pensions or other obligations of the national treasury would be made to unauthorized emigrants who failed to return, including the princely leaders. The king would be called upon to demand extradition of deserters from foreign powers. The second decree, targeting the fugitive princes explicitly, required the comte de Provence to return within six weeks or lose his constitutional right to a regency. He and his princely co-conspirators would be made subject to criminal prosecution if they failed to return within the same period or continued their hostile activities. Action against foreign powers would be considered further.[36]

A further battery of draft decrees against the emigrants followed on 28 October in a sequence one deputy declared so agonizing that it would result in the emigration of the Assembly itself. In response, the Assembly decided to choose one draft as a basis for further discussion, fixing after heated debate and repeated votes on an amplified version of Condorcet's proposal. Before a much-contested adjournment, however, it hastily agreed to issue a proclamation to summon the comte de Provence to return or be presumed to have abdicated from the regency. Stipulation of a three-day delay in the application of this measure amounted, in effect, to a challenge to the king and his ministers to act more decisively against Provence before the deputies did so.[37]

The planned debate on Condorcet's draft decree took place on 31 October. It gave The People's Friend a new hero: the future Girondin Henri Maximin Isnard, a deputy from the Var. Their political paths would diverge dramatically, but for the moment Marat praised this new idol as "the only deputy who has so far shown enlightenment and audacity . . . , whose holy zeal announces a pure soul . . . , whom the voice of a grateful nation will one day call the Robespierre of this legislature." Marat was so stirred by Isnard's speech against Condorcet's proposal that he reproduced much of it in *L'Ami du peuple*. He could have written it himself. "We're placed between contempt and respect, courage and feebleness, duty and abasement," Isnard had warned the deputies in Marat's rendition. "Choose, you can be firm with glory or temporize, vacillate, and fall into the precipice. Choose!" Did the deputies want their cowardice to earn the terrible anger of the people? "Yes, the anger of the people; its vengeance is often only the terrible supplement to the silence of the laws. What! How would it remain the stupid and immobile spectator of its ruin, of its enslavement?"[38]

How could Condorcet's legalistic proposal to require the civic oath and other commitments to the constitution compete with language like this? Isnard and other deputies regarded such measures as useless against conspirators who had already shown themselves willing to break their word. Isnard called instead for immediate suspension of payments and pensions to the fugitive princes and other emigrants. This was a speech "radiating wisdom and burning with civic spirit," Marat reported, though supporters of despotism had moved to efface its impact by engaging in their usual ploy of interrupting the flow of crucial debate with a volley of unrelated matters. Returning to the issue nonetheless, the deputies approved Isnard's motion to reject the Condorcet plan. Marat rejoiced at this triumph against "the somnifier Caritat [de Condorcet] . . . , the royal pensioner, the most humble valet of the fugitive Capets." But he remained skeptical that actions against the conspiratorial princes and their supporters would ever be executed by a monarch who had been placed in a position to do only what he wanted. The constitution had made the French hostage to "a prince who will not stop dragging the nation into the abyss until the people becomes outraged at its abjection and stirs in its misery."[39]

The crucial debate on emigration finally took place on 8 November when Jean-Baptiste-Louis Ducastel, deputy from the Seine-Inférieure, mounted the tribune to offer a draft decree on behalf of the Committee on Legislation. The first article, approved by acclamation, categorically declared Frenchmen assembling across the borders suspect of plotting against the homeland. The second, pronouncing that those who had not disbanded by 1 January 1792 would be deemed in "a state of conspiracy," prosecuted, and subject to punishment by death, raised a storm. An amendment was finally passed, over strong opposition, to the effect that the royal princes and public functionaries at the frontiers who had not disbanded by 1 January would be "presumed guilty of attacks and crime against the general security and the constitution, and made subject to accusation." Later provisions ordered confiscation of the revenues of the condemned on behalf of the nation (without prejudice to their families) and immediate sequestration of the revenues of the royal princes. Functionaries who had not returned by 1 January were made liable to forfeiture of their positions and emoluments; officers abandoning their posts were to be treated as deserters; persons carrying off or diverting army supplies were to face punishment for theft; recruiters for the émigré army were assured of execution. Finally, the Assembly mandated the Committee on Legislation to present proposals for action against the foreign powers allowing the emigrants to assemble on their territory and declared null any prior law contradicting its present decree. At its passage, Marat reported, the vast cavern of the Manège resounded with acclamation.[40]

There was jubilation outside the Assembly, too. *L'Ami du peuple* reported that the day had been celebrated as "a triumph for our faithful representatives," a moment raising the people's hopes, filling the friends of the homeland with joy, and leaving its enemies wiped out and ready for death. But Marat himself was less than moved. In his acid judgment, the law was "a skillful trick to calm public anxiety and appease the rightful outrage of the people." He could not abide the fact that reputedly patriotic deputies had played a blind role in passing a decree concocted by the ministers to give the emigrants time to carry out their plots and guarantee them immunity. The crucial point in his indictment was that the law failed to set out clear judicial procedures or legal criteria that could lead to punishment, even leaving uncertain the court in which such matters would be decided. He cited its author, Ducastel himself, as contending that it would be impossible legally to prove the emigrants guilty of criminal assembly, thus admitting the decree's "perfect inutility." He reproached the patriotic Georges-Auguste Couthon for a botched intervention that weakened the chances of the punishment of absent royal princes and public functionaries by declaring them "presumed guilty" of crimes against public safety rather than actually "in a state of conspiracy."[41]

Above all, The People's Friend was certain that the law would have no effect. It could be repudiated as unconstitutional insofar as it claimed to supersede all relevant earlier legislation. The king could veto it; the ministers could simply evade executing it. If dangers escalated to such a point that, *mirabile dictu*, the deputies showed unexpected energy in forcing out the ministers, suspending the king, and instituting a state tribunal to judge the plotters in absentia, still no charges would be provable. It would be "impossible to convict the emigrants of treason so long as they did not enter the realm as an armed force, so long as they had not attacked any inhabitant, so long as they were not captured with weapons in hand." There was no law, moreover, that made desertion by military officers a crime.[42]

Marat was utterly dismissive, too, of the deputies' call for plans for military action against the foreign powers protecting the emigrants. The principal enemies were within, he countered; they were occupying all the positions of authority and influence. Extermination of adversaries at home had to precede effective action against those abroad. "Until then, every action we undertake will be useless." Thoughtless readers would doubtless be scandalized at this judgment, Marat acknowledged. "So be it, it takes enlightenment the common man lacks to perceive the vices behind the semblance of severity needed to impress the multitude. Sound in the people's ears the great words of love of the homeland, preservation of liberty, defense of the rights of man, and sovereignty of the nation: the people applauds like mad. It doesn't matter that the scoundrels mouthing the words are using them to fetter it. Treat its true defenders as agitators, enemies of order and of peace, and it's ready to condemn them in an instant. . . . To subjugate the people, all one needs is words; why then use weapons? They would be useless if the scoundrels who want to enslave it weren't always in too much of a rush to enjoy the fruits of their crimes."[43]

The ministers and corrupt members of the Committee on Legislation had made their play, The People's Friend concluded; the patriots who had accepted this decree had demonstrated their shortsightedness. What should they have done? "Nothing, I've told you, because all my hope for saving the homeland lies in civil war, provided the people has the upper hand." The patriots should have tried to move the Assembly to demand that the king order his brothers, cousins, and courtiers, in the name of the nation, to return by a certain date. They should now publish the list of the emigrants, shaming those whom the law could not reach. "But virtue is needed to employ such means, and we can't dream of it among us." Again, the people was left without redress. "Ignorant, cowardly and base men, subject yourselves then with good grace, since you don't have the courage to break it, to the oppressive yoke the conscript fathers have imposed on you; kiss your chains covered with flowers, you are more enslaved than ever."[44]

On 11 November, as if to prove the point, the minister of justice announced Louis XVI's refusal to sanction the decree against the émigrés. This after Isnard had offered news that 47,000 armed fugitives were gathered in Coblentz, awaiting another 1,200 to join them. In Marat's account, the deputies merely fussed that the king's decision had not been conveyed by a letter bearing his signature. Why had they not immediately sent back a deputation demanding immediate sanction of this emergency decree, he demanded, and, upon a redoubled refusal, declared public safety in danger? Why had they not proclaimed that they had lost all confidence in the executive power, suspended it from its functions, and invited all citizens to rally around them in support? Why were they risking eternal dishonor by failing to force the minister to proclaim the decree against the comte de Provence for which no sanction was necessary? "I hereby summon the patriotic deputies to return to the charge with greater force than ever," cried The People's Friend, "or the representatives of the nation will become the plaything of the ministers and perhaps the first victims of the vengeance of the privileged public functionary."[45]

He heard no response. "What! The legislative body is sleeping while the laws are audaciously trampled underfoot by the agents of the executive power," *L'Ami du peuple* cried out the following day. Marat was outraged that the minister of justice had refused the Assembly any explanation of the veto, even as the ministry published yet another proclamation by Louis XVI in which the monarch justified his decision while calling on the emigrants to disband. "Return; this is the wish of each your fellow citizens; this is your king's will," read the royal proclamation. "But this king, who speaks to you as a father . . . declares to you that he is resolved to defend, with all the means circumstances might require, both the security of the empire entrusted to him and the laws he is irrevocably committed to maintain . . . ; there is no just but vigorous law he is not resolved to adopt, rather than see you any longer sacrifice to a culpable obstinacy the happiness of your fellow citizens and your own, and the tranquility of your country."[46]

Marat recognized this proclamation as an effort by the king and his ministers to outbid the Assembly in the court of public opinion. "They are working to create a split among the people in trying to detach you from the national assembly," he warned his readers; "they'll chase out your representatives, they'll annihilate the legislative body, and the prince will unceremoniously usurp the power to make laws. After which, he'll rifle through your pockets and have dragged to the scaffold those among you who dare to object." Should this attempt miscarry, "having no other hope than civil war to usurp sovereign power by force, they'll make a last-ditch effort to light the torches in every corner of the realm." A nightmare scenario would follow. Dissident priests would be pushed to ignite discord everywhere; alguazils would be deployed to crush resistance to royal hoarders working to create famine; foreign soldiery would be mobilized to slaughter patriots refusing to be slaves. Louis XVI would take flight, "soon to return at the head of the conspiratorial fugitives and their . . . satellites to enchain or massacre you."[47]

What could be done? "It's urgent that all the sections of the capital assemble to rally around the patriotic deputies, surround them with the public force and press the senate for enforcement of the emergency decree against the emigrants, suspend the prince from his functions, and put the ministers on trial," Marat cried on 16 November. He repeated a similar call for concerted popular action a week later. Without effect. On 24 November, *L'Ami du peuple* reported, the Assembly heard an address from the department of Loire et Cher. "What evil will not be produced by this exercise of the king's will in opposition to the general will?" the signatories demanded. They went on to predict frightful events that would occur in consequence of this decision as the realm was devastated by the horde of emigrants across the Rhine and fanatical priests swam in the blood of patriots. "Will he dare also to stop the decree you are going to pass against the sacrilegious priests?"

Though this protest against the royal veto was vigorously applauded by the deputies, Marat reported, the ministerials blocked its publication or any mention of it in the Assembly's minutes. The ministerial faction of the Constituent Assembly had deserved the noose a thousand times, he recalled. "If this lot escapes equally, the nation is lost without resource." His words were telling. Resentment of the king's veto of the decree against the émigrés would become a major factor in the chain of events eventually bringing the Legislative Assembly to its end. "A single individual deciding at will the fate of twenty-four million and sacrificing their liberty and happiness to his ambitious projects" could only leave the nation outraged, he commented on 14 December. He was reporting on the fact that the Assembly had finally welcomed a battery of protests against the veto from the Parisian sections. At least the nation had been woken from its lethargy, he remarked, but it would have been better if the deputies had rejected these addresses, thereby provoking agitation that could lead to a salutary crisis. "What to conclude, if not that this kind of welcome is a soporific shrewdly administered by the ministerials to bind the arms of the friends of liberty!"[48]

"REBELLIOUS FANATICS"

From its earliest sessions, the Legislative Assembly had confronted a second issue that would eventually force its destruction along with the constitutional monarchy: the dramatic violence ignited throughout the country by the Civil Constitution of the Clergy. In the months that followed, religious dissidence and emigration became strands of a political double helix, winding one around another in the Assembly's debates, radicalizing the deputies' political consciousness and indeed that of the whole of France. By the time the Legislative Assembly first met, many regions had been experiencing open conflict between priests ready to swear the civic oath in acceptance of the nationalization of the French church and those who refused it. Jurors and nonjurors, and their followers among the faithful, fought over principles of clerical hierarchy, ecclesiastical organization, and religious practice; they battled for control of churches and the right to conduct services, administer the Mass, or provide for other sacraments within them; they brawled over the right of nonjurors to receive payments from the state; they sundered parishes into rival congregations and divided families, instigating cycles of hatred, hostility, and violence that became ever more intense; they competed to conduct baptisms, burials, and marriages, thus wrestling one another for the longstanding authority of the church to register civil status.

In his proclamation to the nation on 28 September Louis XVI had urged an end to these conflicts. "Let every idea of intolerance be set aside forever . . . ," he had declared; "let religious opinions no longer be a source of persecutions and hatreds. May each individual, in observing the laws, practice as he wishes the religion to which he is attached, and no offense be given, from any side, to those who believe they are obeying their conscience in following different opinions." Marat had exploded at this royal plea. He was not ready for moderation. "Observe that the only goal of this sermon is to make us forget the machinations of the refractory, counterrevolutionary priests, who are constantly occupied in conspiring against the homeland, and at a time when the rebels are assembling in arms on the frontiers to carry sword and fire throughout the whole realm. What! We're being given the opinions of the henchmen of despotism as the voice of conscience, and their servile maxims as religious precepts, while speaking ill of the prince and his family is made into a crime for patriots and they are being punished for suspecting the purity of the public functionaries prostituted to the court."[49]

Marat had been calling for stronger action against refractory priests for months, convinced that the king and his agents were permitting or provoking their agitation to bring about a civil war that would end by reversing the course of the Revolution. For months to come, he watched with a mad fury as he saw the wildfire of resistance to the constitutional church spreading and intensifying throughout the provinces, eventually merging with the threats and incitements of the emigration into a massive counterrevolutionary conflagration that the legislature seemed unable—and the executive and judicial power of the state unwilling—to contain. For months to come, he denounced a plot by the king, his ministers, and his advisers to allow this blaze to grow unchecked as a means to reduce the new constitutional order to civil war and to restore despotism, phoenix-like, from its ashes. For months, too, he embraced the prospect of civil war as pushing an oppressed people to save itself from political extinction.

On 8 October, *L'Ami du peuple* was reporting news from Strasbourg that the Rhineland departments were riven by seditions ignited by refractory priests in which patriots had been massacred. Marat was sure that the policy of the court was to leave these agitators free to foment civil war in the hope that the Assembly would respond by giving the king carte blanche to extinguish them, and with it control of the national forces necessary for him to regain absolute power. Two days later, this time repudiating Louis XVI's reiterated calls for peace in opening the sessions of the Legislative Assembly, the journal was again denouncing tolerance of disorders over religion. Arles was in the grip of civil war ignited by the refractory priests whom Louis XVI had taken under his protection, it reported, and the Rhineland departments were being torn apart by the provocations of "the refractory priests, these men whose machinations are described by the king as religious opinions, whose atrocious crimes are called errors of conscience, these villains for whom the king solicits the fraternal friendship of all Frenchmen instead of requiring the rigor of the law and delivering them over to the blade of justice. Whatever! They're his cherished children."[50]

In the meantime, the Legislative Assembly had been forced to concentrate its collective mind on the convulsions arising from the creation of a national church. On 9 October, it heard the results of an investigation of conditions in the departments of the Vendée and the Deux Sèvres initiated by the Constituent Assembly in July. Presented by one of its authors, Armand Gensonné, deputy from the Gironde, the report anticipated the dechristianizing rhetoric of 1793 in its blistering denunciation of the superstition of the rural inhabitants, their dogmatic religiosity, their utter confidence in priests who had long manipulated their imaginations and controlled their existence. These priests, it found, were now whipping up emotions through seduction and fear, igniting anxiety and alarm among the weaker of mind and emboldening the stronger with hopes of happiness and salvation. Though it acknowledged that some priests might be acting in good faith, the report pointed to evidence of a generalized campaign of opposition and aggression against the revolutionary church, spearheaded by guerrilla missionaries, that was creating profound divisions among the population, disorientation among municipalities, paralysis of the National Guard, and distrust of local administrations.

Applauding Gensonné's report and approving a motion for its publication, the Assembly postponed any discussion of its substance and returned to its preliminary business of organizing standing committees. Refractory priests were pushed off the agenda for twelve days, largely as the deputies confronted the problem of the emigration. News of extended religious violence continued to reach the capital, nonetheless, and Marat continued to report on it and protest failures of repression. His account of the Assembly's session on 17 October spread word that the deputies had been told of massacres of patriots fomented by refractory priests, often with impunity, in Montpellier, Morbihan, and in the Haute-Loire. The minister of justice, he charged, had merely denounced the popular societies that had protested the inaction of local judicial authorities. How could a minister do more, he demanded, when the refractories were under the special protection of the monarch? "Isn't it the favored plan of the Tuileries cabinet to use these incendiaries to light up the whole realm with the torch of civil war?"[51]

Finally confronting the issue in a lengthy debate on 21 October, the deputies found themselves as divided in their opinions over refractories as they were over émigrés. All speakers called for some measure of repression of violence and punishment of the instigators of disorder; almost all called for a new civil system for registering births, marriages, and deaths. But some, seeing the state threatened by fanaticism and rebellion, demanded exclusion of nonjurors (and their followers) from national churches, termination of their state salaries, and their removal from their troubled localities and resettlement in regional capitals. Others called instead for freedom of worship, toleration of competing religious cults, and cohabitation between Catholics accepting the constitutional church and those choosing an alternative supported at public expense or their own. Persecution would foster disorder, they reasoned; tolerance would restore calm.[52]

Interrupted again as the Assembly returned its attention to the threats of the emigration, the debate on refractory priests resumed on 24 October. "These disorders that will finish by convulsing the state, igniting the torches of civil war, and overturning the constitution seem finally to have drawn the national assembly from its lethargy and fixed its attention," Marat reported. In commentary, *L'Ami du peuple* offered lengthy extracts from the intervention of Pierre-Edouard Lemontey, a deputy from Rhône-et-Loire, "inflated and verbose" though he declared it to be. "Is it true, then," Lemontey demanded, "that it has been left to the end of the eighteenth century to see the marvels of philosophy and the horrors of fanaticism, the most beautiful constitution in the universe confronting the most horrible errors?" Waving a document in evidence, he declared refractory priests the "instruments of a criminal enterprise" even more powerful than the report of the Vendée commission had imagined. He pressed for continuing replacement of nonjuring priests and denial of their payments, strict repression of religious disorders, and the establishment of a new system of registration of civil status. But he also wanted the Assembly to issue a declaration to the nation, and especially to those "simple and good men who have been led astray," telling them that they were being manipulated by conspirators for whom religion was merely an excuse. "Their religion is counterrevolution," he wanted the deputies to proclaim. "Their God is not yours; their God is across the Rhine."[53]

Profoundly convinced of this diagnosis bundling refractory priests and criminal emigrants in a single counterrevolutionary conspiracy, The People's Friend nonetheless remained skeptical of the proposed cure. Even if passed, he predicted, the measures Lemontey proposed would be ignored at every level of government, from the Tuileries cabinet to the lowest of local administrations and the officers of the National Guard. In his analysis, the resistance of refractory priests and the provocations of the emigrants were woven into one great counterrevolutionary conspiracy sustained by the king, the court, the ministers, indeed by the whole apparatus of the state. "I say, and I'll say it unceasingly: organized as it is, the machine of government cannot work unless it is to persecute the friends of liberty. The realm will always be prey to the horrors of anarchy and tyranny until the people becomes so exhausted by its agitations that it succumbs to despotism or is finally pushed by despair to arm itself and massacre its oppressors, down to the very last one. Civil war or anarchy, tyranny, and despotism: these cruel scourges are the alternatives the Constituent fathers have left us."[54]

The more intense the debates over religious conflicts, the more convinced Marat became that they could lead nowhere. His journal scarcely mentioned the "labored loquaciousness" of a star of the new constitutional church, Claude Fauchet, one of the founders of the Cercle Social and the Society of the Friends of the Truth, an early republican now constitutional bishop of Calvados. This neglect was remarkable, given the radical character of the bishop's speech on 26 October. "No persecution, Gentlemen," Fauchet cried; "fanaticism is hungry for it; philosophy abhors it; true religion condemns it." He was searing, nonetheless, in his denunciation of fanaticism as the worst scourge in the universe. Refractory priests were avid to swim in the blood of patriots, he declared; compared with them, atheists were angels. His solution was simple: deny payment to these implacable enemies of the Revolution; starve for material resources the now illegitimate dissident rival to the official church. Forced by hunger and penury, the bishop anticipated, most of the refractories would abandon their flocks for other useful occupations or lead them back into the constitutional church. Their followers, initially willing to pay privately to support a separate priesthood and church establishments, would eventually tire of doing so. Disciples of the few fanatics remaining crazed and hungry enough to incite disorders would soon be brought to their senses by the "useful terror" of the laws. And, ultimately, the apparatus of the monarchy they were claiming as their own would grow weary of them, along with all the other "vermin of the crown."[55]

Castigated for its intolerance, calumny, and an incendiary radicalism more worthy of the clubs than the National Assembly, Fauchet's speech was soon countered at length by another gladiator of the revolutionary church, Pierre Anastase Tourné, a philosophically minded theologian eager to save the constitutional church from being identified with Fauchet's position. Religious errors were of no concern to legislators, he insisted, nor were religious differences a matter for penal law, which could apply only to direct acts of disobedience or disorder. The civic oath was not compulsory, and priests had the option to refuse it. Freedom of worship was a right for every religion, to be protected by the law. Cohabitation should therefore be allowed between the nationally funded constitutional church and privately supported Catholic churches, with dissident priests free to say Mass in any church and to administer the sacraments in their own church once a system had been set up for the civil registration of births, marriages, and deaths. Tolerance would bring calm, Tourné reasoned, which would allow for enlightenment; dissident churches would wither away. A storm followed this appeal for calm, and insults were thrown. Fauchet seethed for several days until he was allowed to reply in even more bitter terms.[56]

But Marat was shifting readers' attention from this ongoing debate. He was predicting that its only outcome would be to give seditious priests, secretly supported by public authorities, the facilities and the time they would need to fan the flames of discord and engulf the entire realm in civil war. In evidence for this prediction, his pyromaniacal gaze was shifting toward Avignon and the former papal territories around it, where combustion of religion and political differences was reducing France's newest region to hideous scenes of civil strife.

Inhabitants of these papal enclaves had been intensely divided since 1789 over the prospect of unification with France and adoption of its revolution. By early 1791, an army of radicals from Avignon favoring union with France had invaded Cavaillon and was threatening Carpentras, the neighboring cities that were centers of political allegiance to Rome. In May, invited by the warring factions, the Constituent Assembly had dispatched commissioners backed with French troops to mediate the conflict, pacify the region, and supervise a first modern plebiscite over unification. With the vote favoring union, annexation had finally been approved by the Constituent Assembly in its last weeks, on 14 September. The vote had done little to ease the turmoil in Avignon. To the contrary, division over the institution of the Civil Constitution of the Clergy permeated and profoundly exacerbated the tensions between factions of "papalists" and "patriots" struggling to control the city.

In the issue of *L'Ami du peuple* dismissing Fauchet's speech, Marat published a dispatch from Avignon presented to the National Assembly on 21 October. It recounted a counterrevolutionary insurrection in that city on 16 October, triggered by a rumor that a statue of the Madonna was weeping at the dangers now threatening the Christian religion. One of the patriotic leaders was dragged into the Church of the Cordeliers and butchered on the altar. The response was the Revolution's earliest prison massacre: an immediate act of retribution in which several hundred of the patriotic party dragged some of their leader's assassins from the prison in the former Papal Palace along with several score other prisoners already held there as counterrevolutionaries. The victims were slaughtered and their corpses hurled from the famous Glacière Tower in that building. Marat brandished this episode as clear evidence of the way troubles ignited by refractory priests would multiply until France was entirely engulfed in civil war.[57]

Headlining "Complete Anarchy in the State," *L'Ami du peuple* returned to these events on 31 October. This time it reported the appearance before the National Assembly of Joseph Stanislas Rovère, a special emissary from the Avignon municipal administration, who had launched (on 26 October) a tirade of denunciation against the abbé François-Vincent Mulot, one of the commissioners initially sent to pacify the Venaissin in May. In Rovère's account, Mulot had organized a reign of terror in the region. He had used French troops to massacre a sovereign people. Supporting counterrevolutionary dissidents, he had brought death and devastation, ordered arbitrary arrests, perpetrated attacks on elected representatives, and facilitated the bloody events of 16 October. The outlines of Rovère's account were largely confirmed in a report presented a few days later by the Committee on Petitions for an assessment. (The weeping Madonna's tears, the committee concluded in bitter anticlerical mode, had been effected by "one of those monks' tricks that in the ages of superstition and ignorance almost always succeeded in serving the purposes of the infamous hypocrites who made use of them, and are still in use here, to the shame of our century.") On the committee's recommendation, the Assembly ordered that Mulot be summoned before the Assembly to answer charges. Arguments over whether the minister of the interior could be allowed to enter into the discussion of the abbé's whereabouts resulted in a deliberative meltdown.[58]

L'Ami du peuple rehearsed the events in Avignon again on 6 November, this time publishing a letter from Pierre-Toussaint Durand Maillane, former deputy and co-author of the Civil Constitution of the Clergy, that upheld the indictment of Mulot against contrary accounts circulating in Paris journals. On 15 November, the journal reported that Jacques Le Scène Des Maisons, a second commissioner charged with complicity in Mulot's crimes but ordered to return to Avignon, was preparing to besiege the city and put the patriots there to the sword. Troops had been moved from the frontiers for this purpose, Marat disclosed. "New Nancy massacres are being readied. And soon France will be inundated with blood."[59]

Who was to blame? The minister of justice, Marguerite-Louis-François Duport-Dutertre. "One of the most atrocious valets of the court" in Marat's estimation, this crony of Lafayette's had withheld comment regarding the seditions of the refractory priests and filled reactionary Paris journals with fake news against the Avignonese patriots, all the while maintaining a profound silence regarding the atrocities carried out by the Carpentras papalists (which *L'Ami du peuple* now detailed). Dutertre had vociferously condemned the patriots responsible for the Glacière massacres, whom Marat defended as having resorted to the only means they had left to save themselves after being "abandoned by the ministers of the law, betrayed by royal commissioners, and threatened with death by the enemies of revolution." Was the Legislative Assembly going to allow these atrocities to proceed unchallenged? "Let it beware of becoming complicit in them," shrieked *L'Ami du peuple*, "let it tremble at covering itself with all the blood that's going to flow in waves unless some act of heaven draws our homeland back from the abyss. We're close to some horrible catastrophe, the king is at the point of taking flight, and France will be delivered over to the horrors of civil war."[60]

L'Ami du peuple reported on 19 November that the Assembly had been informed of actions imposing peace on Avignon. Marat reacted with another passionate denunciation of Mulot and Le Scène, and renewed justification of the Avignon patriots. Aghast that the miserable Mulot was now hanging out with soldiery in Paris bars while preparing his defense with the justice minister, The People's Friend was even more disgusted the following day that minister Delessart had paved the way for Mulot's appearance before the deputies by presenting the Assembly with revolting accounts of the Glacière massacre. His speech, Marat protested, had incited the ministerials to denounce as cannibals the patriots who had punished a gang of brigands incited by priests and paid by Mulot to carry out the slaughter. In the minister's calls for brutal repression, Marat heard a replay of the pantomime acted out by the Constituent Assembly at the time of the Nancy massacre. He countered the next day by publishing a lengthy address to the Assembly by Rovère that advanced renewed charges against Mulot and Le Scène, together with a repudiation of lies emanating from the ministry. Presentation of this address had been blocked on 19 November. Mulot was cleared of all charges and seated as a representative in the Assembly, to which he had earlier been elected by the Paris district of the Jardin des Plantes. There he was, then, Marat chafed, this criminal protected by parliamentary inviolability, taking the civic oath to the nation he had betrayed, to the law he had trampled underfoot, and to the king he would serve forever while gorging himself on the goods of the poor. His response was bilious in its bitterness: "Long live the triumph of justice under the reign of liberty!"[61]

In the meantime, as conflicts over the organization of the church exploded throughout the country, the divided deputies continued to grasp for measures upon which they could agree. On 12 November, the Committee on Legislation began a blistering condemnation of refractory priests. Its draft decree, presented to the Assembly two days later, proposed what amounted to a reign of religious terror. It prohibited payment from public funds to anyone who had refused to take the civic oath and denied nonjuring ministers the right to preach or conduct services. It required surveillance of religious services by local administrations and punishment of anyone found guilty of provoking disorders, or discussing political matters, during them. It laid down a penalty of a year's detention for publishers or distributors of writings that might provoke revolt against the laws, and more severe punishments for sedition, murder, and pillage. An accounting of this repression would be submitted to the National Assembly at least every three months, and the minister of war would be called upon immediately to report on the organization of a national gendarmerie. A law would be drawn up immediately to institute a new system of registering civil status.[62]

No sooner was this decree proposed than members of the legislative committee, acknowledging profound division among them, protested that they had not agreed to its language! Voting to ignore it entirely, the deputies were ready to send the matter back to the committee without further debate. But Isnard, still Marat's champion for the moment, insisted on intervening to offer powerful support for the kind of repression the committee had appeared to favor. His speech, the most violent of all those pronounced in these debates, was so bitter in its denunciation of priests and their craft that it was constantly interrupted and immediately decried as a "code of atheism." The Assembly was convulsed over the suitability of its publication and eventually denied it.[63]

Marat so admired Isnard's language that he published an abbreviated version of his speech in *L'Ami du peuple* on 18 November, sharpening it in the process. Could these priests be treated as ordinary criminals, he reported Isnard's demanding, "these pernicious men who have in their hands the most powerful means of slaughtering the people . . . these men of whom Montesquieu said that they could do everything by great threats and great rewards?" A law was necessary to prevent the ministers of a God of peace overthrowing the social order in his name. How? "By purging the realm of them through deportation." Pestiferous, they had to be sent back to the lazarettos of Rome and Italy. Who could forget that all France was defiled by their crimes? Priests could do more harm to the nation than all other enemies combined. Ceasing to be virtuous, they became the most evil men of all. "Bad priests are the plague of society, the executioners of the human race; they sell to crime the heaven that the deity promised to virtue." Rome's lightning had to be snuffed out on the shield of liberty. The triumph of liberty was in no doubt, Isnard had assured his listeners in Marat's account, but it was hard and needed to be watered by blood. "The French Revolution needs a resolution; without provoking it, we must advance toward it with courage. Let's not give crime time to gather force."

At this point, Marat relayed, the Manège resounded with applause that the ministerials tried to obliterate with their howling. Isnard continued nonetheless to repudiate toleration as a trap and to call for one great action to conquer public opinion and make the Assembly invincible. Intending to speak in favor of the decree proposed in the committee's name (and having clearly done so), he acknowledged that he had not prepared an alternative draft of his own; he now left it to the Committee on Legislation to do so. But he insisted for the moment that every individual, without exception, be required to take the civic oath or be sequestered. "My God, this is the law," Marat had him conclude, "it's the public good."

Other versions of this speech had Isnard advocating that priests who refused the civic oath be allowed to remain in the country unless and until complaints were raised against them, at which point they would be deported—as would those (whether they had taken the oath or not) who disturbed public tranquility. Marat was more severe in the version he offered his readers, making "sequestration" a direct and immediate consequence of refusal to swear. It is fascinating that, in summarizing Isnard here, he may have omitted a move (mentioned in other accounts) to assimilate the civic oath to signing the social contract, with failure to do so implying refusal to join with other individuals in accepting the rights and obligations of liberty under the general will. Perhaps he was opting for a variant on the Roman "proscription," preferring punishment on the ancient model of expulsion from the body of the people to that arising, in the modern notion of the social contract, as a consequence of withholding individual consent.[64]

Isnard's speech once over, the deputies were obliged to recognize the obvious fact that the Committee on Legislation was so profoundly riven over the issue of dissident priests that it was dysfunctional. Taking a remarkable step in authorizing division of the committee into four sections, they charged each to produce a draft decree. Two days later, they chose as a basis for detailed discussion the first and most severe of these drafts, the work of François de Neufchâteau, a deputy from the Vosges destined for greatness under Napoleon. Revising and adopting this decree article by article, arguing fiercely down to the very last minute, they reached a final text a fortnight later, on 29 November. Neufchâteau's concluding speech offered a devastating indictment of the practices, pretensions, and privileges of the French church, "this excrescence of the political body" under the Old Regime, along with a bitter condemnation of dissident priests now resisting the provisions of a constitution he defended as grounded on the will of the nation and written in accordance with the principles of the Declaration of the Rights of Man.[65]

The decree at which the deputies had arrived was severe in the extreme. Its preamble, emphasizing that the social contract must bind equally all the members of the state, insisted on the need to "define unambiguously the terms of this engagement so that a confusion in the words not produce one in ideas." It thus made clear that the "purely civic oath" was the guarantee each citizen must make of his fidelity to the law and his attachment to society, and that refusal of this oath on religious grounds should be regarded as no more than a pretext to "spread disorder on earth in the name of heaven." That being the case, the nineteen articles that followed ordered all ecclesiastics who had not yet done so to take the civic oath within a week. Catholic priests who had taken the oath, or would now do so, would retain their emoluments from the state, while those refusing would be denied them; the sum of the payments terminated would be allocated annually to support the poor and disabled. Church buildings maintained at public cost would be reserved exclusively for the practice of the established religion by conforming priests; those no longer needed by the national church could be purchased or rented for the celebration of other cults, but only by ecclesiastics who had sworn the civic oath and under the surveillance of the public authorities.

Loss of payment was far from the only penalty this decree ordered against Catholic priests who refused or retracted the civic oath. In what amounted to an incipient Law of Suspects, it declared nonjuring priests "suspected of revolt against the law and evil intent toward the homeland, and, as such, more particularly subjected to and recommended for the surveillance of all the constituted authorities." In the event of disorders caused by differences of religious opinions (or on the pretext thereof) nonjurors would be exiled from their commune; their failure to comply with this penalty would be punishable by up to a year's imprisonment; actual conviction of provoking civic disobedience would double the period of imprisonment to two years. Communes in which seditions arising from religious conflict required military intervention would be held liable for the cost of that deployment; authorities failing to deploy their lawful power to prevent or repress disorder would be subject to punishment. Local governments would be required to establish separate lists of juring and nonjuring priests, submitting them to their departments with an account of actions taken (and obstacles encountered) in execution of the laws relating to religion. This information would be relayed to the Legislative Assembly in departmental reports that would include details about the conduct of individual nonjurors, "or their seditious coalition one with another, or with French defectors or deserters." The legislative committee, in turn, would examine these communications, report to the Assembly those administrations that had satisfied the terms of the decree, and propose measures to be taken against those that had not yet done so. Finally, popular enlightenment being of the essence, works countering fanaticism would be published and their authors rewarded by the state.[66]

The decree was presented to Louis XVI for his sanction that very same day, 29 November. How could he be expected to approve a law that, in addition to its severity, clearly infringed upon the exercise of executive power? He vetoed it on 19 December, turning one more screw in the machine of the constitution. As for Marat, this second veto would surely have come as no surprise to him, though his immediate reaction to it remains unrecorded. He had suspended publication of *L'Ami du peuple* before it occurred.

A COLONY AFIRE

Together with growing threats of attack from émigrés and resistance by nonjuring priests, the Legislative Assembly faced a third major challenge. It learned in late October that the colony of Saint-Domingue had been convulsed by a slave revolt since 22 August. The time lag is worth emphasizing. Roughly 4,500 miles lay between Paris and Port-au-Prince; communications between them could take as long as two months. The logic of the French Revolution was played out in the French colonies in a kind of time warp that left actors on each side of the Atlantic in a continuous state of ignorance, uncertainty, confusion, agitation, and indecision.

Situated on the western part of the Caribbean island of Hispaniola that France shared with Spain, Saint-Domingue was the nation's most populous and productive possession by far. The eighteenth-century world's largest source of sugar and coffee, it generated immense wealth that funneled back to the metropolis and fertilized its entire economy. Close to a half-million black slaves labored there, a population whose harsh conditions and high mortality required regular replenishment from Africa to the steady profit of French merchants in the slave trade. The slaves vastly outnumbered the roughly 31,000 whites (slave owners and others) as well as some 28,000 free people of color—typically mixed-race descendants of slaves and their owners, but also freed or free-born blacks, many of whom also owned slaves themselves.

News of the French Revolution, when it occurred, had reached a territory already riven by social and political tensions overlying the brutal oppression and endemic terrors of a slave-owning society. Local government bodies representing white planters were constantly at odds with the administrative agents of metropolitan authority they denounced as despotic in regulating their practices and imposing strict French monopolization of their trade. Resentments and inequities set poor whites against rich ones, but also, perhaps even more bitterly, against the prosperous free people of color. The latter, achieving growing wealth and importance within the colonial order, found themselves frustrated at the same time by increasingly racialized discrimination imposed by whites whose authority and status they threatened. By 1789, they owned as much as forty percent of the land and twenty-five percent of the slaves in the colony.[67]

No sooner were the principles of the Revolution declared, however, than they threw the entire colonial system into question. Abolitionists in the prerevolutionary Society of the Friends of the Blacks called almost immediately on the National Assembly to end the slave trade and phase out slavery in accordance with the principles of the Declaration of the Rights of Man. Planters, though initially excluded from the convocation of the Estates General, forced their claims to representation in the National Assembly, where their deputies and commercial and political allies mobilized opposition to the abolitionist program and defended the exploitation of property in persons upon which French power and prosperity so heavily depended.

Campaigning in Paris for the right of colonial assemblies to propose their own constitutions, the planters saw their demand granted by a decree of 8 March 1790. Its execution was immediately complicated, however, by the appearance in Saint-Domingue of an upstart general assembly that challenged the authority of the National Assembly (and the colony's governor general) by asserting the sovereign, constituent power of the colony to decide for itself. This rebellious assertion of independence was finally quashed by a decree of the National Assembly on 12 October 1790 that reiterated the decision of 8 March allowing the colonists to propose constitutional arrangements best suited to their particular situation. More significantly, a preamble to the 12 October degree also declared the National Assembly's firm intention to answer another fundamental concern of the white planters by refraining from any legislation regarding the status of persons in the colony, except in response to a "precise and formal demand" of the colonial assemblies themselves.[68]

This language not only preempted the possibility that the Constituent Assembly would put an end to slavery, it also promised white colonists the authority to decide on the claims to political equality and active citizenship for which leaders of the free people of color had also been lobbying in Paris since the passage of the Declaration of the Rights of Man. The frustration of the free coloreds at this outcome was made evident when one of these leaders, Vincent Ogé, returned to Saint-Domingue that same October to incite a rebellion in the name of equal rights for all free citizens without distinction. The insurrection crushed, Ogé was captured and brutally executed in February 1791. The status of free persons of color in the new order remained a radically contested issue in the colony, as in Paris. White fears that the grievances of the colored could incite a revolt of the blacks were exacerbated by the expanding circulation of abolitionist ideas.

By May 1791, alarmed that social and political collapse in Saint-Domingue might mean the colony's destruction or loss to the ever-predatory English, the National Assembly returned to issues its earlier actions had failed to resolve. By this time, it faced intense agitation and uncertainty among the white colonists; a continuing campaign for equality and citizenship by free people of color, now supported by addresses from Jacobin clubs throughout France; and the contrary pressure from commercial cities and slaving enterprises for firm action to protect their interests. At the heart of this contestation were demands by planters and their allies for the passage of a decree enacting the deputies' intention, clearly signaled on 12 October, to cede to the colonial assemblies the initiative to decide the question of citizenship for free persons of color. The matter was referred not to one committee but jointly to four: the committees on the constitution, on the colonies, on agriculture and the navy, and on commerce—some indication of its deep reach into French society.

The decree Barnave proposed on behalf of these committees on 8 May ignited searing debates. They were haunted by threats that the white colonists would secede (following the American example) and by indications that the free colored were ready to emigrate with their property if their claims to equal citizenship were not recognized. The momentous first article proposed that no law relating to slaves could be passed without a "precise and formal" demand of the colonial assemblies. Deeming explicit mention of "slaves" unworthy of their own status as legislators for a free people, however, the deputies opted for an amended version, passed on 13 May, that established "as a constitutional article, that no law on the status of unfree persons can be made by the legislative body except on the formal and spontaneous demand of the colonial assemblies."[69]

This decision left open the question of the rights of free persons of color, upon which the draft decree proposed to defer legislative action until a uniform recommendation had been reached by a committee drawn for this purpose from delegates of all the colonial assemblies. More bitter division followed as deputies arguing for outright recognition of the political rights of the free persons of color again confronted those demanding fulfillment of the promise that colonial assemblies would have the initiative to decide this question. An amendment offered on 15 May proposed a compromise. Reiterating that the legislative body would never decide the political status of free persons of color without the "prior, free and spontaneous wish of the colonies," it made a crucial exception in the case of those born of two free parents. These latter would henceforth be permitted to vote for, and participate in, all parish and colonial assemblies, provided they met the tax and property qualifications for active citizenship. When the amended article was decreed, the colonial deputies walked out in protest of this betrayal, leaving Barnave to predict that the decision would lead to chaos.

Perhaps for the only time, though from a very different perspective, Marat had shared Barnave's assessment. His report on these debates expressed outrage. "Who would believe it?" he had written on 18 May. "In the senate where man was first reestablished in his rights and liberty proclaimed as his natural prerogative, we have soon after seen consecrated the enslavement of the unfortunate Africans transported to our colonies by the cupidity of Europeans and bound to the soil by the barbarism of the colonists." Praising the eloquence and vigor of the patriotic deputies Bouche, Grégoire, Pétion, and Robespierre, and the powerful arguments of Julien Raimond who had addressed the Assembly as spokesman for the free people of color, The People's Friend could only express disgust at the bad faith displayed by their opponents, Barnave first among them. "We're done for, Gentlemen," he quoted them as crying, "everything is lost if you don't give the colonists the initiative for their new constitution. Hasten to make the whites absolute masters of the mulattoes, or they're ready to secede from the metropole. Beware of provoking a scission that will bring about the loss of French commerce, the ruin of its navy and of a part of its inhabitants." "Oh sordid interest!" The People's Friend exclaimed. "What crimes do you not incite if pure hearts have such difficulty resisting your bait and you succeed in turning the apostles of truth into vile sophists?" The Assembly's decisions, he foresaw, would satisfy no one. Deputies of the whites had already signaled their fury in quitting the Assembly for good. Soon free persons of color not born of free parents, together with enslaved blacks, would arm themselves to reclaim their rights. The horrors of civil war would result.[70]

These predictions soon proved true. News that even some free persons of color had been granted rights of citizenship drove white colonists into a frenzy of opposition as soon as it reached the island. A letter from the governor general to the minister of the marine, dated 3 July, reached Paris on 22 August, eight weeks later. It portrayed violent reactions of whites to a betrayal they saw endangering the very survival of a colony dependent on the legal demarcation of an intermediary class separating slaveowners and enslaved. The governor general declared the decree impossible to enforce without provoking civil war. This message plunged the deputies into harsh recriminatory argument over responsibility for what might be happening in the colony. They could not know, as they exchanged accusations, that a massive slave revolt—the specter that had haunted the colonial Atlantic world—was taking hold in Saint-Domingue that very same day.[71]

Ten days later, its information ever lagging events, the Assembly received a further communication from the governor general, initially dispatched on 16 July. Reiterating that efforts to enforce the 15 May decree would cause bloodshed, he forwarded addresses from the assembly of the northern province of the colony to the National Assembly, to Louis XVI, and to the eighty-three departmental administrations, each protesting the deputies' betrayal of previous commitments to the colony. By this time, arguments for and against a change of policy were everywhere, within the Assembly and beyond. Petitions for the revocation of the decree reached the deputies from the merchants and shippers of the great slaving cities of Nantes, Le Havre, and Bordeaux. Arguments to the contrary followed from the official administration of the Gironde (which repudiated the Bordeaux petition as the product of an illegal assembly) and from representatives of the port of Brest. Insisting that the 15 May decree had been welcomed in their city, as in others whose expressions of support had been buried by the Colonial Committee, the Brestois charged further that the violent reception of the decree in the colonies had been fomented by those responsible for executing it and was in any case being exaggerated as an excuse to revoke it.[72]

These claims sparked a conflagration in the Assembly, a personal firefight between Barnave and "the incorruptible Robespierre" (whose remarks elicited calls to lock him up), and a lengthy tirade by Barnave against Brissot (the latter of which *L'Ami du peuple* entirely passed over in its report). The following day the Colonial Committee presented the deputies with addresses from the cities of Le Havre, Rennes, and Rouen. Marat dismissed them as concocted by the committee to prove the colonies would be lost unless the fatal decree was revoked. He was convinced that the committee's members, and notably Lameth and Barnave, were being paid by the white colonists to achieve this result. Barnave, he insinuated, had pocketed 1,500 livres as his share—an amount he needed to acquire the most beautiful abbeys in his canton. The debate left many deputies perplexed by their ignorance of circumstances several thousand miles distant (and many weeks away) and ready to defer the entire matter to the Assembly about to replace them. Barnave, holding fast, urged them to decide the question now.[73]

By 23 September the committees responsible for the colonies were sounding a high alert. Their report, again presented by Barnave, betrayed utter panic that the Assembly's inconsistent actions to date had destroyed colonists' confidence in its authority, producing a situation in which the planters were on the verge of declaring independence and French prosperity was on the brink of collapse. Barnave offered nothing but harsh realism regarding the situation. A regime in Saint-Domingue subjecting some 450,000 slaves to 30,000 whites (his numbers) was "artificial and beyond nature," he allowed. It depended entirely on maintaining the moral and political distinction between free coloreds and enslaved blacks, on the one hand, and that between colored and whites, on the other. A color barrier, in effect a cordon sanitaire, was indispensable to demonstrate to enslaved blacks that they or their descendants could never be the equals of whites. The colonial system was absurd, he acknowledged, but it was established and could not be suddenly changed without even more disastrous effects; it was oppressive, but it supported the livelihoods of millions in France; it was barbarous, but imprudent action to change it, taken in ignorance of local conditions, would work incalculable harm. A little philosophy in favor of the most modest reforms, he warned, could yield a frightfully disproportionate amount of harm.[74]

The committees' draft decree amounted to a total surrender of the National Assembly's responsibility to decide the status of persons in the colony, black or colored. Authority in the matter was to be handed back to colonial assemblies, their decisions to be executed provisionally with the approval of the governor general and submitted directly to the king for his sanction. The National Assembly was simply to be excluded from this process. It would retain authority to decide on other matters regarding the organization of the colony, but only on the recommendation of the colonial assemblies. In effect, colonists were to be left to decide their own race regime and to fashion constitutional arrangements necessary to uphold it. Bitterly contested on grounds of principle and practicality, this proposal was adopted on 24 September with an amendment limiting the length of time that colonies could execute their laws without royal sanction (one year in the case of Saint-Domingue). The decree was sent to the king on 28 September, along with a measure extending the general amnesty to colonists who had engaged in resistance to the Assembly's prior legislation.[75]

One of the Constituent Assembly's last acts was thus to betray its commitment to free persons of color in Saint-Domingue after having first betrayed its promise to whites.

"At the news of the revocation of the decree regarding persons of color, a general cry of indignation has made itself heard," *L'Ami du peuple* broadcast the following day. "Where is the man of sense who has not been revolted by the audacity with which the conscript fathers are playing with the nation . . . ! With what effrontery have they today upended a part of the empire by annulling decrees passed to maintain peace there, by reducing the people to slavery!" For Marat, this decision was a final demonstration that the Constituents had saved their last moments of power for "the consummation of their greatest villainies." It was as if they had resolved to light the flames of civil war simultaneously in all parts of the empire. "These infamous legislators, trampling justice and humanity underfoot, have just revoked the decree regarding people of color, handing the people of our colonies over to a handful of whites, its avaricious oppressors, pushing it to despair, and leaving it no other means of escaping tyranny but massacring its tyrants."

Such was the infamy of the deputies' action, in Marat's eyes, that he couldn't help tapping his outrage for a moment of self-dramatization. "Perhaps they'll make my zeal and frankness another of my crimes. But how to remain silent? Before forcing it on me, let them begin by extirpating aversion to crime from honest hearts, let them tear from these hearts all sense of indignation against evil tricks, shameful maneuvers, dastardly betrayals, let them stifle every movement of nature, because so long as these perfidies reveal themselves in their true light, it is impossible not to be horrified and for feeling souls to repress the cruel emotions agitating them."[76]

The People's Friend was sure that the king and his ministers, having dragged their feet in executing the decree of 15 May in favor of free persons of color, would be expeditious in enforcing its revocation. "Yes, everything is ready to reduce the people of color to servitude. What am I saying! It's a million to one that the forces destined to subject them have left, and that the ships carrying them set sail before the decree had been passed." The expedition would be a failure, he predicted. The troops could not be counted on to turn against the people at the command of officers sold out to the court. In any case, "the people of color are not as cowardly as the Parisians. . . . In their holy transports of indignation they'll take up arms, put them in the hands of the blacks, and a few days will be enough to see all the white colonists massacred, along with the henchmen of despotism. This hideous massacre, fruit of our legislators' venality, will inevitably be followed by the loss of our colonies."[77]

WHOSE CHAINS?

News of the slave revolt, so long predicted, reached the Legislative Assembly weeks later, on the morning of 27 October. Within hours, the deputies received a communication from the minister of the marine—to the effect that he had just read of the details of this alleged event in the *Journal de Paris*! He had received no news from the colonies since 15 August, he assured the Assembly, at which time everything there was tranquil. "An amusing mode of self-justification," Marat remarked of this receipt of momentous news. While the Assembly awaited further intelligence, Brissot insisted on laying the blame where it belonged. Marat followed his lead. "If it's true, as M. Brissot observed, that the insurrection must be attributed to the decree disarming the people of color by refusing them citizenship, because it's the mulattoes that keep the blacks in line, all the troubles agitating our colonies are the work of the august Constituent Assembly."[78]

By 29 October, there was less room for doubt. A letter from Cap-Français, reinforced by one from an English planter returning from Jamaica, reported more than two hundred plantations burned in the northern region of Saint-Domingue and fifty thousand black rebels in arms, with munitions possibly supplied by the Dutch and the Spaniards. Brissot, Marat relayed, had questioned the reliability of this news and argued against an overhasty response, fearing "a ministerial lure, to have a pretext to send considerable forces to the islands and strike a fatal blow there." The next day, as the Assembly churned out one decree after another, the minister had informed the Assembly that the king had already ordered the embarkment of thirty thousand troops for Saint-Domingue, with plans for more to follow. "So here's the king declaring his independence from the legislature," Marat remarked. "What a surprise, since the legislature has turned him back into a despot!"[79]

Printing this news on 2 November, Marat again denounced the "prostitution of Barnave" and other Constituents who had conspired with the minister to delay the dispatch of troops to the colony to enforce the 15 May decree. This action, he charged, had allowed the white colonists time to exercise their tyranny with impunity, reduce the persons of color and the blacks to despair, and push them to take up arms in their defense. Again, he castigated the leading colonial deputies who had pushed for the revocation of that decree, this time wishing upon them the retribution of finding their own properties among the ashes. The experience, he thought, could teach them how dangerous it was to tyrannize fellow human beings, and what madness it was to count on the gratitude of monarchs.

"I repeat," Marat added: "the entire hope of the friends of liberty rests on the excess of tyranny, which will finally force the desolated peoples to arm themselves in their fury and throw onto their side the very creatures of the court who will be the victims of its madness and perfidy." He now saw a pattern. The counterrevolutionaries, he reasoned, had learned after the Champ de Mars Massacre that the people would stand by as patriots were assassinated. Firm in this conviction, the minister of the marine had ordered his agents to cheer on the white colonialists in their efforts to reduce blacks and people of color to despair. The plan all along had been the incitement of an insurrection that could be suppressed by troops and men of the National Guard, thus habituating them to march to the despotic orders from the palace of the Tuileries.[80]

To Marat at this point, it seems, all the conspiracies against freedom in the world were rolling into one. There would be civil war everywhere: a vast array of disorders secretly encouraged or instigated by Louis XVI to allow his counterrevolutionary henchmen to amass power and reduce the people to misery and servitude. It is striking that Marat appeared almost to welcome this universal cataclysm, as if civil war were a portal to subjection through which the people had to pass before it could be goaded to recover its liberty in a kind of instinctual reflex response. This was revolution understood almost clinically, as a massive crisis to be experienced rather than a radical choice to be made. It was revolution imagined as reaction rather than action, as mechanism rather than movement, as physiological effect rather than political cause. For Marat in this mood, the people had to be propelled to liberty by its enemies more than it could be inspired to it by its friends.

For a moment, there was an illusion of hope: news from Port-au-Prince of a concordat between whites and free people of color making common cause against the rebellious black slaves based on an agreement of the whites to accept the 15 May decree. "You believe perhaps that everything is arranged; wise up," Marat cautioned his readers, "you'll see all the disorders reappear and the sublime assembly plunged back into the same limbo by the executive power, and unable to extricate or orient itself." He was right. Signed on 11 September, the concordat had already fallen apart in Saint-Domingue before the Legislative Assembly even learned of it on 18 November. Oblivious to that fact, the deputies spent much of the next two weeks discussing whether to recognize it or not.[81]

A report was about to be presented by the Colonial Committee on 1 December when a deputation from the port city of Saint-Malo demanded to be heard. Marat identified them as a group of slave traders headed by one of the Constituent Assembly's most active defenders of the planters, Moreau de Saint-Méry. The language of the deputation's spokesman was bitter in deploring the destruction in the colony and the savagery of the rebellious slaves, outraged at the potential loss of livelihood of six million Frenchmen, urgent in its demand for forces to be sent to the island to re-impose order and prosperity. It was contemptuous in contrasting a savage and enslaved Africa, subjected to the despotism of stupidity and fury, with the courage and productivity of planters guided by the principle of humanity, or at least by enlightened self-interest. But its principal target was "the hypocritical philanthropists" the deputation blamed for inciting the insurrection, the "monsters" from outside the colony (and within the National Assembly) who had usurped the language of benevolence and humanity to light the torches of the furies, spreading abstract principles that were false and destructive of all the bases of society.[82]

The Assembly was convulsed by violent condemnation of these calumnies. The invective of this "maniacal" spokesman, Marat made clear in his report, was directed against Pétion, Robespierre, Buzot, Grégoire, Prieur, and even against Brissot. "He had the audacity to accuse the current assembly of fomenting the revolt of the colonies and the stupidity to accuse the friends of liberty of hatching it within the very bosom of the Constituent Assembly." In the uproar that followed, Brissot seized the moment to present a speech he had been itching to give. Marat called it "very scientific, very tortuous, very cold, very long." It was, in fact, a monumental and passionate analysis of the history of the problem of the colonies since the beginning of the Revolution and a blistering denunciation that cast the essential blame for inciting slave revolt on the maneuvers of colonial deputies, disordered planters, and desperate poor whites, all eager to break free from the homeland.

"It's time to tear the veil," Brissot told his fellow deputies. "It's not only a revolt of the blacks you have to punish, it's a revolt of the whites. The revolt of the blacks was only a means, an instrument, in the hands of the whites, who wanted, in freeing themselves from dependence on France, to free themselves from laws that humiliated their vanity and debts that hampered their taste for dissipation." His speech was accompanied by a proposed decree indicting the colonial assembly for attempts to separate the colony from the homeland and turn it over to a foreign power; ordering the arrest of members of this assembly responsible for other arbitrary, illegal, and counterrevolutionary acts; suspending the governor general and returning him to France for trial; and dispatching commissioners to oversee the creation of a new colonial assembly to include all free persons of color.[83]

The days that followed showed the Assembly in a state of near paroxysm over the colonial issue. It could talk at length, but could it act? A vote was needed to authorize spending on troops to impose order on the troubled colony. But exactly what order were these troops intended to impose? No one doubted that they should repress the violence of the slave revolt. But what order might they impose or maintain in the relations between whites and people of color? The concordat had been based on white acceptance of the provision of the 15 May decree that gave citizenship to free people of color born of free parents, and that decree had been accepted by the colonial assembly on 25 September. But the Constituent Assembly's decree of 24 August had already revoked the decree of 15 May that the white colonists were now finding themselves forced to accept. Was this decree of 24 August to be imposed, or withdrawn before official word of it could reach the island and unsettle the entente between whites and colored? Would the troops enforce its revocation of the rights of free people of color; would they be suborned by white colonists to serve the latter's interests? Should the Assembly approve the concordat, not knowing whether it was still in effect? The time lag between Paris and Saint-Domingue made coherent policy virtually impossible.

Meanwhile, troops had to be sent. But the divided Assembly kept seeking postponement of their departure. Awaiting further resolution, the deputies debated whether the king should be merely "invited" to give specific orders to the troops or instructed to do so. They argued over the longstanding question of the right of ministers to participate in debates. Trapped in a state of ignorance, they finally agreed, on 7 December, to invite the king to order that the troops be deployed only to repress the insurrection of the blacks, doing nothing, directly or indirectly, to protect or support any attacks that might be made upon the status of free persons of color "as they had been fixed in Saint-Domingue on 25 September."

A defense of the white colonists, implicitly directed against Brissot's charges against them, came days later from an unexpected source: The People's Friend himself. On 7 December, the Assembly had debated a charge of calumny leveled by one Roustaing, a member of the colonial assembly of Saint-Domingue denounced by Dupont de Nemours for traveling to the United States to negotiate as a plenipotentiary of a prospective independent republic. Roustaing repudiated this accusation, insisting that he had been sent by the colonial assembly only to seek American aid against the slave revolt. But Marat, reporting on 10 December, denied the very grounds for the charge itself. "The inhabitants of the colonies are a people absolutely separate from the inhabitants of France, who can have not the slightest right against them," he insisted. "The foundation of all free government is that no people is subject to the law of another, that it can have no other laws than those it has given itself, that it is sovereign at home, and sovereign independent of all human power. Simple common sense, recognizing these principles, adds that it is absurd and insane for a people to be governed by laws emanating from a legislature two thousand leagues away."

The colonists had been stupid, The People's Friend decided, in sending deputies to the National Assembly in the first place. They had the right to overthrow the metropolitan yoke or declare themselves a republic, following the example of the English in North America. But to say this, he maintained, was not to absolve the white colonists. They were "inexcusable in my eyes to set themselves up as despotic masters of the mulattoes and tyrannical masters of the blacks." These latter had the same right to liberty against the white colonists as the white colonists had against the French nation. "To overthrow the cruel and shameful yoke under which they groan, they are authorized to use all possible means, death itself, if they have to be reduced to massacring their oppressors down to the very last one."

These were the principles the Legislative Assembly should have enunciated regarding Saint-Domingue, Marat concluded. He thought it enough to say that the last decree concerning the status of persons of color was equitable and the one on the blacks was atrocious. Yet if he had no doubts about the right of the enslaved in the colonies to insurrection, he also had in mind an injustice closer to home. "But how could we treat as free beings men who have a black skin while we haven't treated as citizens men who don't pay the state a direct tax of an écu?" he demanded. "We boast of our philosophy and our liberty, but we are no less slaves of our prejudices and our mandataries today than we were ten centuries ago. Ask the families and enlightened friends of the victims slaughtered on the Champ de Mars."[84]

Marat protested the chains of slavery. But is it unfair to conclude that he still weighed some chains more heavily than others?

THINGS FALL APART

"*Complete Anarchy in the Realm—Tyranny Deployed by the Royal Agents against Friends of the Homeland—The National Assembly Paralyzed by the Ministerial Cabinet—The State Burning, Ready to Collapse and Falling Prey to Fire and Famine.*" These were the headlines of the 26 November issue of *L'Ami du peuple*. As the autumn months of 1791 darkened into winter, Marat's outlook turned even bleaker. His prediction of constitutional breakdown was looming larger as crises merged from every direction. He saw counterrevolutionary invasion spearheaded by renegade emigrants drawing closer, its dangers exacerbated by ministerial failures to deploy troops to fortify the frontiers as he had demanded. He saw fires of domestic disorder being fanned by the conspiracies of refractory priests, swallowing the country in flames in the absence of the strict repression for which he had railed. He saw continuing slaughter and devastation in the colonies that could only intensify as troops arrived to end it. These issues, too, were becoming enmeshed in the pages of *L'Ami du peuple*, as in the debates of the Legislative Assembly, with more unsettled daily conditions—a growing subsistence crisis igniting renewed fears of the hoarding of grain and currency, recurrent rumors of a famine plot, outbreaks of popular protest over the price of bread, and steady deterioration in the value of the assignats.

To all these ills was added the prospect of imminent war. Throughout November, Louis XVI and his ministers had indulged in warlike posturing against the Dey of Algiers over the perennial issue of the Barbary pirates, a move Marat interpreted as a plot to destroy the commerce of ultra-revolutionary Marseille and other southern cities. With this charade declared over, The People's Friend predicted on 1 December, Louis XVI would spare no pains to bring about a rupture with the lesser German princes, to be followed by one with the greater powers, blame for which would be cast on the National Assembly. For the court and the cabinet, he was sure, the goal was to trigger an invasion that would bring the revolution to an end. He saw foreign war as inevitable, ending only in civil war.[85]

Not that the deputies were reluctant to engage in war talk. Brissot's belligerent speech of 20 October was echoed throughout the following weeks as deputies called for action against the émigrés and the princes harboring them. Marat was convinced that these resounding words had been paid for by the ministry to trap the Assembly into supporting an ill-advised and disastrous rupture with the European powers. Behind them, he saw a hypocritical effort to divert blame from Louis XVI for vetoing the decree against the emigrants, and to project onto the Assembly the machinations of the ministry to ignite a war that would destroy the Revolution. "I deeply regret not concerning myself earlier with this matter in order to reveal the trap," he confessed. "I fear greatly that the patriots will be caught in it, and I tremble that the assembly, saddled by the prostituted jugglers of the court, will allow itself to drag the nation into the abyss."[86]

Marat's fears that deputies would succumb to war fever were soon realized—by none other than Isnard, who gave a blazingly aggressive speech to the Assembly on 29 November. "If France was intrepid and courageous when enslaved, would it be feeble and cowardly when free?" This was his passionate cry, as *L'Ami du peuple* reported the speech a few days later. "Always ready to die, it will disappear from the globe rather than let itself be enchained. From the height of the tribune we will electrify all the French, suffused as we are by the hatred of tyrants. They will fly into combat, forcing the haughty race beyond the Rhine to suffer the torture of equality. Yes, that equality has become a necessity for us, a sustenance as necessary for us as the air." The deputies would address the king and his ministers with all the pride of a great nation, Isnard continued, offering them the choice between the constitution and public vengeance, between responsibility and death. They would remind the monarch that his crown depended on his fidelity to the constitution, the law, and the sovereign people, "that if he forces us to use the sword we will throw away the sheath, that if there's a possibility of his triumph he will reign only over cadavers. Finally, that if he threatens us with the league of kings and tyrants against the peoples, we will oppose it with the league of the peoples against kings."[87]

Marat was unimpressed by this flamboyant assertion of the nation's revolutionary vigor. "This is a fine dream," he objected. "Handcuffed by the Constituents," in his view, the French were "more enslaved than ever and, to judge by the Parisians, they care very little about liberty; the majority are even asking ignominiously for the return of their former chains." Their wish was about to be granted, he added. "We're about to see an armed counterrevolution in Paris. . . . They say the Parisian army is under orders for the beginning of next week . . . , abundantly supplied with cartridges, whether to support the flight of the royal family or to begin the counterrevolution by massacring the citizens. It remains certain that we're approaching some bloody catastrophe."[88]

With Isnard's speech still ringing in their ears, however, the deputies moved quickly to send a deputation to the king. Their message urged Louis XVI to take measures to compel the German ecclesiastical princes to dispel the émigré gatherings in their territories, prepare France for war against them if they failed to do so, and purge the diplomatic corps of members who had failed to represent the nation effectively in foreign courts. In immediate reply, the monarch responded that he had neglected no measures to establish public tranquility, to maintain the constitution, and to make it respected abroad. This move by the Assembly, Marat commented, was "the emptiest, the most ridiculous, the most impolitic, or rather the most perfidious the enemies of the homeland could counsel." It licensed the king to provoke a rupture with the princes of the Empire and blame the deputies for it. The People's Friend had his own assurances to offer the thoughtless deputies. "Expect an insolent response on the part of the Germanic princes and recognize that you have put yourselves in the cruel position of declaring war on them."[89]

In these circumstances, *L'Ami du peuple* reverted to an earlier, more assertive populist tone. While the deputies were stupidly disputing how to deal with the disorders and disasters incited by the refractory priests, the journal warned on 30 November, "the royal hoarders, the emissaries of the court, the conspirators within and without, and our atrocious ministers are imperturbably following their plan to deliver France to the horrors of misery and hunger and the dissensions of civil war." Marat saw hoarders everywhere robbing the people of grain, as they had of coins. Soldiers and men of the National Guard were without weapons and munitions; those at the frontiers were naked and dying of hunger, the object of derision to the nation's enemies; the few guns they possessed exploded in their hands. Everywhere the country was prey to the furors of fanaticism kindled by factious priests. Everywhere there were new plots, their realization only awaiting the departure of a king whom the constitution had rendered more despotic than ever. The people, in the meantime, had grown indifferent to public affairs. The poor, denied their political and civil rights by the distinction between active and passive citizens, were regarding themselves as no more than aliens within the state.[90]

Once more, Marat desperately concluded, only popular insurrection could restore order in the state. The nation, rising up simultaneously in all corners of the realm, would have to deal with public enemies, wipe out decrees of the corrupt deputies, expel the despot and all his family, arm all the members of the state, and charge someone sane to propose a new constitution based on the Declaration of the Rights of Man. In this constitution, the sovereignty of the people would have to be consecrated, civic assemblies made permanent, citizens authorized to resist every arbitrary order and to hunt down enemies of the homeland. The separation of powers would be perfected, the king's prerogatives restricted, and an oath sworn—not to the constitution but to defend liberty and be faithful to the homeland. But all this was now an empty dream of a distant future. Insurrection, bewailed *L'Ami du peuple*, was "a means no longer in the power of the people, since it has stupidly wasted the crises of 14 July, 5 October, 28 February, 18 April, and 21 June."[91]

In this mood of despair, Marat fell back on counting heads. "This stupid people was afraid to fell 5,000 to 6,000 heads. It preferred to see the realm in flames, suffer centuries of anarchy, allow despotism to rise up again, encourage it to exhaust the nation with misery, destroy it by famine, surrender the friends of liberty to tyranny, expose the state to dissolution—all while waiting to be given over to the horrors of civil war, to become prey to the flames, or to be inundated with blood." A few days later, he was computing 50,000 patriots slaughtered in the past twenty-eight months through the machinations of public functionaries and ministerial agents still in public view. On 7 December, he was thinking that it would be not months but centuries—"centuries of anarchy, oppression, and conspiracies"—before the state would be "torn apart and the monarchy dissolved, or in the midst of civil war some great man would put himself at the helm of affairs to exterminate the tyrant and his henchmen, rebuild the constitution and assure liberty—unless the traitorous conspirators had already succeeded in putting the nation back into its chains."[92]

By mid-December, he was exhausted, dejected, ready to give up. In all probability, he had also been reduced to a state of misery. A news sheet appearing in late November remarked on the failing circulation of all the patriotic journals, including *L'Ami du peuple* and *L'Orateur du peuple*, which "are no longer found almost anywhere." Months later, he claimed that "the court's gold [had] deprived him of all his printers" by the end of 1791.[93] On 12 December, he published a letter (one of the few to appear in the journal since September) from one Bourdon, active citizen of the Louvre section. "Stop, dear Marat," it read. The signature said otherwise, but the sentiments expressed were doubtless his own. "Stop, dear Marat, it's time. What have you gained since you declared yourself the defender of an ignorant and corrupt people, always ready to close its ears to the salutary counsels you have ceaselessly given it regarding the machinations of its infamous mandataries and perfidious agents? Shouldn't your predictions, while sometimes lacking the degree of credibility to force action, have been enough to put it on guard in seeing them all realized?"

The more proofs Marat had accumulated, this letter lamented, the less had he convinced "the imbecilic bourgeois of Paris." "For two years, their constant cry has been that The People's Friend is an incendiary; they'll soon see the torrents of blood that are going to flow because of fear of shedding a few drops, as you told them, to contain the enemies of liberty by terror and assure the public safety. . . . But how to avoid the hideous fate being prepared for us by the criminals to whom we have stupidly left it to plot our ruin when it was so easy to prevent them from doing so? We're done for, let's mourn for liberty. It showed itself to us for a moment only to make us better feel its loss. Or if there is still time, let's rally around its true defenders and yield to our oppressors only after losing our lives."[94]

In this all too familiar trope, liberty was lost—unless there was one last instant to save it! After missing a day, perhaps as a consequence of its author's sickness or despair, *L'Ami du peuple* was back on 14 December to offer a vision of "The Future Unveiled." The prospect it offered was bleak. The ministerials were now in full control of the Assembly, and there was no one among the few patriots clear-sighted, strong of character, or devoted enough to the homeland to resist their sacrilegious attacks on the sovereignty of the nation and the rights of citizens. Who could defend the people against a formidable conspiracy of deputies, the prince, ministers, public functionaries, military leaders, and henchmen of despotism? There was only a crowd of clubbists, talkers, and vain petitioners as quick to hide themselves in moments of crisis while their fellow citizens were being slaughtered as they were to show up at the bar of the Assembly to brag that liberty will pulverize all the tyrants of the universe. "Oh senseless nation! How have you not renounced your empty babbling to follow the counsels of your friend, arm yourself with lengths of rope and daggers, and end the days of those of your defeated enemies bold enough to get back up. Yes, liberty is lost among us, and lost without return." A hideous cycle would play itself out, Marat foresaw. Monarchy would last until its exactions provoked a general insurrection, the realm would be torn apart by factions, and the boldest and most adroit would assume power, subjecting the multitude to a new yoke. "The government would have changed its form, without liberty being re-established."[95]

On 15 December, before the journal fell silent for several months, Marat allowed himself one more issue of *L'Ami du peuple*. "Convinced that the voice of The People's Friend has been lost in the desert since the events on the Champ de Mars," he explained, "I had laid down my pen, to pick it up again only when I saw the people determined finally to get rid of its cowardly and cruel enemies. Some observations important in the current circumstances put it back into my hand today." Anticipating an imminent invasion that the authorities and their forces would be unable or unwilling to turn back, he had imagined a guerrilla war to be waged by a desperate people in defense of liberty. "Little is known of the resources of despair, and the sublime actions it brings forth would sometime pass for fables if the annals of history didn't attest to them," he declared. In this scenario, fired by an outburst of holy fury, and armed with anything at hand, the people would fell its cowardly enemies and drive them back. At the first sound of the cannon, it would close the gates of every city and eliminate seditious priests, counterrevolutionary functionaries, and known plotters. Against cannon, rifles, bayonets, and sabers, it would wield not clumsy pikes but double-sided daggers, well sharpened. Avoiding pitched battles, it would engage the invaders in narrow passes, in woods and marshes, on the march and in their camps. In the towns, it would pull up cobblestones, block avenues, and attack the enemy from barricaded streets or in their barracks. No quarter would be given.

This was not the explosion of a glorious war of peoples against tyrants that orators in the Assembly were beginning to anticipate, for which Brissot and his allies (opposed doggedly by Robespierre) were whipping up enthusiasm in the Jacobin Club, and for which there were now some glimmerings of popular support. It was the grinding struggle for survival by an oppressed and endangered people threatened with political extinction. "This type of warfare, so suited to terrorizing mercenary troops, tyrants, and their henchmen, will put an end in one day and for eternity to all the undertakings of the enemies of the revolution," Marat promised. Multitudes would have to rush from all the departments to overwhelm enemy forces contained within a town or a camp; they would have to refuse any compromise and slaughter the aggressors down to the very last one. Provision would have to be made for the production of strong knives with short blades, well sharpened on both sides, enough for every known friend of the homeland. "The entire art of fighting with this terrible weapon is to make the left arm into a shield wrapped to the armpit with a quilted sleeve of some wool fabric well stuffed with flocks or horsehair, then to pounce on the enemy, the right arm armed with the blade."[96]

Marat had evidently thought this through in some detail. Though he opposed the Brissotins' war cries, it was not for lack of belligerence. He was a man who dreamed of violence all the way down.

TWENTY-TWO

THE PEOPLE'S REVOLUTION

> *1 January 1792*. "The fine qualities of Mlle Simonne Evrard having captured my heart, whose homage she has received, I leave to her, as pledge of my faith during the trip I am forced to make to London, the sacred engagement to give her my hand immediately after my return. If all my tenderness is not enough to assure her of my fidelity, may forgetfulness of this promise cover me with infamy." Paris, 1st January 1791. J. P. Marat, *L'Ami du Peuple*.[1]

This vow, a note inventoried by the authorities at the time of Marat's death in July 1793 and published in a journal shortly thereafter, is his first and perhaps the only known mention on his own part of an intimate relationship that became crucial to his personal existence in the last eighteen months of his life. If it was a promise of formal marriage, it was not kept. But a member of the Jacobin Club, Giraut, who was close enough to The People's Friend to offer his eulogy before the Convention, reported to the public that there had also been another kind of solemnization of the journalist's relationship with this young woman twenty years his junior. "Marat, who did not believe that an empty ceremony formed a commitment to marriage, wanting nonetheless not to offend the modesty of citizeness Evrard, called her one beautiful day to the window of his room. Hand in hand, they prostrated themselves together before the Supreme Being. It's in the vast temple of nature, he told her, that I take the Creator who hears us as witness of the eternal fidelity I swear to you."[2] That the vast temple of nature was seen through an apartment window in the heart of Paris does not seem to have diminished the vow.

The Rousseauian sensibility of this private moment before the Divine offers an intriguing contrast to the more formal language of the note dated 1 January 1792. It seems striking that Marat's declaration of commitment appears addressed more directly to a public than to the object of his love herself. One wonders why it was made, or had to be made, before a trip to England. Was he concerned that there was danger in such a trip? Was he eager to assuage the anxieties about the relationship on the part of Simonne Evrard's family that other evidence suggests? Or was it meant to assert publicly the existence of an arrangement that would authorize Simonne to claim responsibility for his papers at his death, as indeed she so fervently and indefatigably did as "widow Marat" (in the face of virulent defamation) when the time came? That he signed this declaration of personal sentiment in his public persona as "The People's Friend" reveals again how profoundly he had fused his personal with his political identity. Conversely, the note suggests how fully and intimately Simonne Evrard, for her part, must also have embraced that identification. Her espousal of The People's Friend was as much a political as a personal act.

She made this clear in a fierce speech to the Convention on 8 August 1793. "Citizens, you see Marat's widow before you," she announced to the deputies following her introduction by Robespierre. Defying the detractors of "the most intrepid and outraged defender of the people," she condemned "the horrible ferocity with which they are endeavoring to give him a monstrous political existence and a hideous celebrity, with the sole purpose of dishonoring the cause of the people, whom he has faithfully defended." Marat's sister, Albertine, who had rushed to Paris from Switzerland to support Simonne immediately after his death (and remained there with her in what became a lifelong bond cemented by his memory), also celebrated the widow's political commitment in her own *Reply to the Detractors of the People's Friend* in September 1793. Her description of the beginning of the relationship between the couple seems apt to the circumstances Marat faced by the end of 1791. "Finding no recourse among the unfortunate, he had succumbed to his woes," she recounted. "People, your benevolent deity decided matters otherwise. It allowed a divine woman, whose soul resembled his own, to consecrate her fortune and repose to care for your friend. Heroic woman, accept the homage your virtues deserve: yes, we owe it to you. Inflamed with the divine fire of liberty, you wanted to take care of its most ardent defender. You share his lot and his tribulations; nothing can stop your zeal; you sacrifice to The People's Friend both your family's fear and the prejudices of your century."[3]

It seems likely that Simonne and Jean-Paul had grown close during the fall of 1791, after the disruption of Marat's living arrangements with the engraver Maquet and his servant, Mlle Fouaisse. He may well have found lodging with the Evrards at that time. They were three sisters, Simonne, Etiennette, and Catherine, born in the Burgundian city of Tournus in 1764, 1766, and 1769 respectively, who had moved to Paris in search of work sometime after the death of their father, a carpenter specializing in boats. Employed perhaps in a lingerie workshop, they were living together at the time at 243 rue Saint-Honoré. Catherine had married a typesetter who may have worked on the production of *L'Ami du peuple* and may perhaps have introduced Marat to his wife and her sisters. An older half-sister, Philiberte, who had married a certain Persicot (said to be a master at billiards), had died recently in Naples, possibly leaving Simonne a modest inheritance that she used to support her life with The People's Friend and supplement the costs of his publications. Apparently the recipient of a good education at a charitable institution in Tournus, Simonne herself was described by the authorities in 1793 as "1.62 meters in height, with brown hair and eyebrows, an ordinary forehead, round jaw, aquiline nose, brown eyes, large mouth, oval face." Sometime before September 1792, the couple had moved into an apartment on the rue des Cordeliers. Simonne paid the rent.[4]

As for the trip to London, nothing is known of its purpose or duration, or whether it actually occurred. One can imagine that the necessity to make it might have been financial. Perhaps Marat had not yet received the cash from the sale of the watch and jewelry he had consigned to his friend Breguet almost a year earlier. Perhaps he had hopes of raising funds from other acquaintances or political sympathizers. Perhaps he was engaged in pursuing other undertakings, political or literary. So far, the record remains silent. The next available evidence comes from a letter, dated "Paris, 28 February 1792," addressed to the publisher and bookseller Mequignon. Signed "Dr. Marat," it asked for the proceeds from sales of the author's scientific publications over the past three years and an accounting of the copies left unsold.[5]

Hopes for financial success must have been one motive for a project on which Marat began working during these early months of 1792. It was clearly meant, among other goals, to profit from his celebrity as "apostle and martyr of liberty." On 3 March, he addressed a letter to the president of the Cordelier Club invoking the society's commitment to propagate his principles (an obligation now more than a year old). It may have been delivered, along with a similar message to Robespierre intended for the Jacobin Club, by Jacques Roux, the future Enragé soon to be dubbed "the little Marat" by the Cordeliers for the extremism of his social and political program.[6] The letter to the Cordeliers opened with a tale of woe. "Having fought relentlessly for three years against resurgent despotism, I see myself forced finally to give up a career in which I found nothing but fatigue, hardship, grief, misery, danger, peril, tribulation and disgust, and no longer had good to do for the people," Marat confessed. He was less discouraged by attacks from the enemies of the homeland, he lamented, than by the blindness and half-heartedness of its children. No longer on daily duty as one of the people's sentinels, he declared himself determined to serve its interests in a new way by producing a work that would enlighten it, shape public opinion, and reignite the fires of patriotism. He called on the Cordeliers to show their zeal for the public good by circulating a prospectus of this work as widely as possible (while assuring a potential messenger that he would allow the club no authority to judge its contents). It would be entitled *L'Ecole du citoyen—The Citizen's School*.[7]

The Cordelier Club responded with alacrity, eager to recover and display its own political vigor after a debilitating internal struggle in the fall of 1792 (and possibly encouraged also by Marat's willingness to devote a share of the proceeds from sale of the work to its charity toward the poor). In a declaration announced on 18 March, it "seized with zeal the opportunity to give The People's Friend, the apostle and martyr of liberty, a resounding mark of its esteem" by accepting his invitation to give wider dissemination to writings that would have been "enough on their own to consolidate the revolution," had their circulation not been blocked by the forces of despotism. To that effect, the club charged an activist committee to circulate to all the patriotic societies of the realm, with maximum energy, the prospectus of a work so necessary to "reanimate patriotism, form public opinion and enlighten the people as to the vices of the constitution that agents of the executive power are so skillfully exploiting to maintain the disorders of anarchy in the state, fan the flames of discord, ignite civil war, extinguish love of liberty, crush its defenders and drag the state into the abyss." This declaration of support was appended to the prospectus of *L'Ecole du citoyen* when it appeared.

That *Prospectus* rehearsed the record of Marat's denunciations of the betrayals, conspiracies, and other outrages against liberty since the beginning of the Revolution, the persecution he had suffered as a result, and the attacks directed against his printers and distributors, all of these actions already well known to the public. It promised "an indispensable book for all the French who love to instruct themselves in their rights and to know the efforts that have been contrived to mislead the people, enslave it constitutionally, reduce it to misery, torment it with constant famine, crush the friends of liberty, guarantee the conspirators impunity, fan the fires of discord, deliver the realm to the disorders of anarchy, and ignite the flames of civil war at its every point." Intended, in effect, as a distillation of the more than six hundred issues of *L'Ami du peuple* to date, with additional commentary and a list of some three hundred predictions the author had published regarding principal persons and events of the Revolution, the text was projected to fill two octavo volumes, each four hundred pages. To be within the means of citizens less well off, it was offered at a subscription price of 6 livres, 10 sols for Paris delivery and 7 livres, 10 sols for addresses in the departments. It was promised for August 1792.[8]

Work on the project went more slowly than anticipated. A revised *Prospectus* was published in October, this time for circulation by the Jacobin clubs across the country. It now offered two volumes totaling some nine hundred pages, for delivery by February 1793. They never appeared. The inventory taken after Marat's death listed a mixture of printed and manuscript pages in "a bag containing a manuscript work to be entitled *The School of the Citizen, or Secret History of the Machinations of the Court, the Constituent Assembly, the Monarchical Club, the Generals and the Principal Enemies of Liberty who have figured in the Revolution*." Simonne Evrard later advertised its inclusion in an edition of Marat's collected political writings but failed to follow through; the manuscript was lost from sight.[9]

The Cordeliers were active, too, in joining with other popular societies to encourage Marat to resume publication of *L'Ami du peuple*. The journal reappeared on 12 April, prefaced by a declaration of the club a week earlier that lamented its cessation as a "public calamity" and guaranteed a public wary of counterfeiters that it would be the authentic product of the "energetic pen" taken up again by The People's Friend at this time of urgent need. A more emphatic declaration by the club to this same effect on 7 April appeared in successive issues of the journal for several more days.[10]

WAR TALK

By the time *L'Ami du peuple* resurfaced on 12 April, France was eager for battle. Marat had missed many opportunities for denunciation as war fever mounted during the three months since his journal's last appearance. Louis XVI had informed the Legislative Assembly on 14 December that he had issued an ultimatum to the Elector of Trier to disperse the émigré encampments on his territory by 15 January, with failure to do so construed as a hostile act. The elector soon signaled his readiness to comply with this demand, but that scarcely mattered. On 24 December, Delessart, now foreign minister, informed the Assembly that Emperor Leopold, increasingly irritated by bellicose posturing from Paris, had demanded restitution to German princes of their feudal rights in Alsace and Lorraine abolished by the National Assembly following the delirious Night of Fourth August in 1789. This longstanding grievance now served to warn Louis XVI that incalculable damage would be inflicted on France's international standing if it broke its treaties and that a return to the status quo must follow "the cessation of all the innovations undertaken since the month of August 1789."[11] The language was menacing.

In what followed, Delessart treated the deputies to the recitation of a decree of the Imperial Diet that proved particularly aggressive in its protest against works spreading the spirit of disobedience and revolt, its call for punishment of authors threatening the constitution of the Empire and public order, and its commitment to immediate suppression of insurrection within its territories. He concluded by reporting that Louis XVI had renewed the demand that the Elector of Trier disperse the émigrés by 15 January and had warned the emperor of the consequences of his failure to ensure his subject's compliance.[12]

To reinforce this posture, the Assembly was soon invited to approve an emergency budget for military preparations. The resulting debate exploded into a dramatic escalation of war talk, fanned again by Brissot. "The moment has finally arrived when France must show Europe the character appropriate to a free people when it is offended by its neighbors," the accomplished warmonger declared in yet another inflammatory speech on 29 December. "The offenses have been public and continual. The vengeance must be striking, but it must be preceded by a calm and solemn discussion." There was little that was calm and solemn in the debate that followed. "The French Revolution has totally upended diplomacy," Brissot announced. "Although the nations are not yet free, everything is now in the political balance; kings are forced to take their wishes into account." The observation led him to a renewed survey of Europe's political situation, this time intended to demonstrate that its peoples were disinclined to war, the interests of its major powers were unlikely to be served by their engaging in one, and its noisy lesser powers were too debased by despotism to do so effectively. "Despotism is the image of Saturn," Brissot reminded his listeners, "it devours itself after devouring its peoples." The conclusion was obvious. "Governments in every state detest the principles of our revolution, but the nations adore them, understand them, and perhaps are awaiting only an opportunity to realize them; that is the best foundation for our tranquility. The line of demarcation is now drawn between societies and their governments. No people would support its tyrants in putting the French nation in chains." As for a concert of European powers, Brissot deemed it a chimera. He judged the interests of states too conflicting to yield to the general interest of their kings.

All this said, Brissot nevertheless insisted on the need for a show of force powerful enough to drive the émigrés from the German territories harboring them, put an end to the terrors and troubles their activities were producing in France, and establish respect everywhere for the French, their constitution, and their principle of universal liberty. The action had to be compelling enough, too, to serve as a warning to other foreign powers in the event that he had misjudged their interests and capabilities.

More fundamentally, coming to the heart of his case in a performance now punctuated by emphatic applause, Brissot maintained that, above all, France needed war. It needed war to redeem its honor against the émigrés, war to ensure its external security and recover its domestic tranquility, war to restore its finances and public credit. It needed war, finally, "to put an end to terrors, betrayals, anarchy: for there would be no more terrors if the center of the counterrevolution is destroyed, no more betrayals if there is no longer a party to support them." To be free, he continued, "we must ask, like the Spartans, where our enemies are, not how many there are of them. And what power on earth . . . can vaunt its power to enchain six million free soldiers. Thus everything invites us to prepare for war. This war will be a true boon, a national boon; and the sole calamity France has to fear is not having war, thus prolonging the withering and wasting that is exhausting it." All the advantages were on the nation's side, Brissot exalted, "because now every French citizen is a soldier, and a stout-hearted one!"[13]

This address soon gave Hérault de Séchelles the opportunity to demand a declaration that hostilities were imminent and to call for more aggressive diplomacy on Louis XVI's part, more severe sanctions against the émigré princes, and more intense surveillance of internal threats. It was time, he said, invoking Roman example and the words of Montesquieu, to "throw a veil over the statue of liberty."[14] Repression within, in other words, would mirror war without. A powerful recipe.

It was left to Condorcet, true to form, to introduce a more explicitly philosophical tone into the debate. At the core of his speech lay a proposal for a declaration of the National Assembly intended, above all, to free the French from any contradiction between the present call for war and the principle of nonaggression that had been embedded in their constitution. Harboring rebellious émigrés who threatened to invade their own country was already tantamount to an act of war, Condorcet judged. A French attack on these rebels in their foreign enclaves would therefore be a defensive response, to be undertaken with the greatest respect for the rights of the population upon which the émigrés had imposed themselves. This, then, would be a war for peace. France would take up arms with regret, Condorcet's declaration promised, but with ardor too, laying down its weapons as soon as its liberty and equality were secured. Loving peace, it was conscious enough of its powers to embrace the need for war. Free, and armed, it would not be enslaved. Victorious, it would seek neither reparation nor vengeance.[15]

Deputies responded ecstatically. Their "repeated applause and passionate acclamations" prompted immediate decisions that the address be printed and distributed, presented to the executive power for circulation to all the states of Europe and to the eighty-three departments of France, translated into every language, sent to all the regiments of the regular army and of the National Guard. Only objections that the text implied an accompanying declaration of war—a declaration the legislative body had no constitutional power to make—led to second thoughts about the wisdom of distributing it to foreign powers. The Assembly would press harder in subsequent debates against this circumscription of its authority. And it started to do so, notably in reacting to a further Austrian diplomatic note that had been addressed to the French ambassador in Vienna on 21 December and communicated to the deputies by Delessart ten days later.

In that fateful text the Austrian chancellor and veteran diplomat Prince Kaunitz wrote with the "entire frankness" his emperor deemed necessary and appropriate to the important crisis he saw in France. The Elector of Trier had satisfied Louis XVI's demands regarding the émigrés, Kaunitz noted, but fears remained among the elector's subjects that the tranquility of their borders might be disturbed by incursions and violence. Leopold was in no doubt that it was Louis XVI's intention, and France's true interest, to avoid any provocation of sovereign foreign princes, Kaunitz averred. But "daily experience" no longer offered adequate assurance that moderation would prevail in the country and aroused fears that attacks would occur despite the king's intentions and the dangerous consequences that would ensue. The emperor had therefore found it necessary to order the commander of his troops in Belgium to furnish immediate aid to the Elector of Trier if the latter's territory was invaded or threatened with imminent attack. This action, Kaunitz warned, would inevitably trigger the engagement of the crowned heads of Europe "in concert for the maintenance of public tranquillity and the security of thrones."[16]

Kaunitz had not minced words. Louis XVI, expressing his astonishment at this communication, informed the deputies on 31 December that he had been no less firm in response. He had reiterated that France would resort to force if the Elector of Trier had not dispersed the émigrés by 15 January. With this exchange, it was clear, Leopold had significantly raised the stakes by invoking the threat of action by a concert of the crowned heads of Europe, undermined the influence of the Feuillant advisers who had been counseling Louis XVI against aggressive action, and offered Brissot and his allies a momentous opportunity to escalate their bellicose language.[17]

This opportunity the Brissotins took, to dramatic effect. Their offensive began on 14 January 1792, when Gensonné presented the Assembly with the Diplomatic Committee's considered response to the Austrian threat. His report repudiated the once momentous treaty of 1756 between France and Austria, which it now denounced as a one-sided arrangement responsible for a flood of French misfortunes beginning with the disasters of the Seven Years' War. It charged that the treaty had in any case been breached by the emperor in his collaboration with the Prussian king signaled in the Declaration of Pillnitz and by that monarch's support for the French émigrés. It urged an embrace of a salutary crisis that would raise the French people to the height of its destiny, revive its initial energy, uphold public credit, and stifle the seeds of its intestine divisions. Louis XVI had to be told, for his part, that "war is useful, that it is necessary, that public opinion calls for it, and that the safety of the people imposes it as a law." He had to be reminded that his people's loyalty was not unconditional: "the nation expects from its king a firm, frank and loyal conduct, and the confidence and love of all the French will always come at this price."[18]

Accordingly, the committee's draft decree invited the king to demand from the emperor an unambiguous statement, by 10 February, of his attitude to France, his commitment to nonintervention against the French nation, and his respect for its constitution and its full and entire independence in deciding its form of government. It also called for acceleration of military preparations in anticipation of a need for swift engagement. No sooner was this proposed decree scheduled for further discussion than the Assembly's current president, Guadet, stepped down from the chair to repudiate the idea of a congress of European powers that was being mooted by opponents of war as a way to resolve the diplomatic imbroglio. Such a congress, Guadet was sure, would lead inevitably to modification of the French constitution and a reimposition of more absolute monarchical authority. "Let's tell the princes of the Empire that the French nation is determined to maintain its constitution in its entirety," he urged; "we'll die here." At which point, in a moment many found reminiscent of the great moments of the Tennis Court Oath and the Night of Fourth August, the deputies rose as one to cry, "*Yes, we'll swear it!*" In a swell of enthusiasm "penetrating every soul, firing all hearts," the entire gathering was moved to "unite with the representatives of the people, rise up, wave their hats, extend their arms to the president's desk and take the same oath." Cries of *Live free or die! The Constitution or death!* resounded, interspersed with applause.[19]

Guadet was eventually allowed to complete his sentence, declaiming that the deputies would die rather than allow the least threat to the constitution. But "Liberty or Death" meant readiness to kill for liberty as well as willingness to expire for it. "Intriguers, perverse men," those seeking to mislead the people, had to be put on notice, he warned. "In a word, let's mark out in advance a place for traitors, and let this place be the scaffold." This time, cooler heads were not heard. Guadet's cry was immediately translated into a decree pouring infamy on traitors and proclaiming guilty of the crime of lèse-nation any French persons who participated in a congress threatening to modify the French constitution or engaged in any other way with the nation's enemies. The decree was delivered to the king immediately and sanctioned by him that same day.[20]

On 14 January, reporting that the émigré encampments were indeed being dispersed by the German princes, the foreign minister intervened to counsel respect for the nation's constitutional vow to abstain from any war of aggression. Warning of the danger of an ill-considered ultimatum against the emperor, he reminded the deputies that initiative in foreign affairs lay with the king, who was at that moment exploring hopes for a relaxation of tensions. His words had little effect. Brissot had other ideas. The debate once reopened, he was first to the tribune. Deputies fearing a lengthy address were assured he would take no longer than forty-five minutes. At his opening remarks, a number walked out.

With good reason. The confrontation with the German princes over the émigrés apparently resolved, Brissot pitched all the more energetically for a wider war. "The mask has finally fallen," he declaimed. "Our true enemy is known . . . it's the emperor." The German princes had been Leopold's front men, he charged, the French émigrés only his instrument. In truth, the emperor cared only for his throne. "You must not hide from yourselves, Gentlemen, the nature of your enemies' hatred. Our constitution is an eternal anathema to all absolute thrones. All kings must hate our constitution: it puts them on trial, it declares their sentence. To each of them, it seems to say: Tomorrow you will be no more, or you will be king only through the people. . . . We must go straight to the point, we must say to the emperor: 'It's our Constitution you hold in horror; that's what you want to destroy; either renounce these efforts or prepare for war.'"

From this perspective, the language proposed earlier by the Diplomatic Committee was utterly insufficient. The nation now required satisfaction from the emperor, not just explanation. Brissot's alternative formulation invited Louis XVI to address the emperor "in the name of the French nation," informing him that it regarded the treaty of 1756 as null and void, violated by his actions, and inconsistent with the principles of the French constitution—and that it demanded, as a condition of peace, full and entire satisfaction, by 10 February, for his acts of hostility against it.[21] Despite its forms of protocol, this invitation to Louis XVI to speak in the name of the nation offered as great a challenge to the king's authority as to the emperor's.

Over the next several days, counter-arguments for moderation were outbid by aggressive variations on Brissot's proposals, offered notably by Vergniaud, Isnard, Condorcet, and Hérault de Séchelles. The resulting decree, adopted on 25 January, was even more radical than the original in accusing the emperor of threatening the sovereignty and security of the French nation—and in formulating policy for Louis XVI to follow. It invited the king to acknowledge that he could negotiate with a foreign power "only in the name of the French nation and by virtue of the powers delegated to him by the Constitution"; to demand whether the emperor was ready to live in peace with the French nation and renounce any treaty or agreement directed against its sovereignty, independence, and security; and to declare that any response falling short of full and entire satisfaction for French grievances by 1 March would be regarded as a declaration of war. It also called for troops to be readied for instant engagement at the very first command. Louis XVI countered this decree emphatically by reminding the deputies that the constitution empowered him alone to treat of foreign affairs and allowed them to discuss matters of war only upon his initiative. He assured the Assembly that he had already communicated to the emperor sentiments similar to those expressed in its decree, adding that deliberation in negotiating peace had to match rapidity in preparing for war.[22]

The rather different course of these diplomatic efforts became evident on 1 March, however, when the king ordered the foreign minister to disclose the sequence of negotiations between France and Austria since 21 December. The Assembly was shocked to learn of a secret letter the foreign minister had sent on 21 January to the French ambassador in Vienna, intended to be passed confidentially to Kaunitz. Countering the chancellor's earlier complaints of disorder and insubordination in France, Delessart had fallen back on the defense that France was emerging from a great and rapid revolution. Conflict and agitation were inevitable in such an event and a return to order would take time, he pleaded, but the deluge of protest was diminishing. Was the situation of Europe to be troubled by the fulminations of a few incendiary loudmouths? Were they to be honored by a blast of cannon? "To express in a word the king's wish, that of his council and, I have no fear in saying, that of the healthy part of the nation: we want peace," Delessart had written. "We call for an end to the costly state of war into which the fate of circumstances has drawn us; we call for a return to the state of peace. But we have grounds for anxiety that are too rightful not to need full reassurance." This was hardly the forceful reply to the emperor that Louis XVI had led the deputies to expect. Delessart protested that the secret communication had been leaked to discredit him.[23]

Kaunitz had doubled down in response. The dispatch he had addressed to the Austrian ambassador in Paris on 17 February, to be presented to Louis XVI and made public, vigorously justified his orders to his commander to be ready for war; it also substantiated the need for a concert of Europe against the contagion of anarchy and disorder with which France was threatening it. France was not returning to order, he maintained, but showing symptoms of inconsistency and fermentation that were worsening daily. Its condition was sparking anxiety for the safety of its royal family, anticipations of a renewed descent into "popular anarchy, the greatest evil with which a great state can be afflicted," and fears of a contagion that could endanger constitutions throughout Europe. The cause of these symptoms was plain: "the influence and violence of the republican party" (meaning the Brissotins) that was now working to destroy the monarchical constitution, push the Legislative Assembly to claim the essential functions of executive power, and force the king to yield to its will. To fuel the agitation necessary to achieve its goals, this party had provoked the crisis in French relations with other European powers and was now inciting war.[24]

In response to this situation, Kaunitz had concluded, it was the emperor's responsibility to disabuse Louis XVI and the healthy majority of the French nation of the illusions meant to entrap them. But he hadn't stopped there. In an official note to the French ambassador in Vienna on 19 February, he went even further in imputing the French position to the "illegal ascendancy" of "the Jacobin party." The emperor, he added, was authorized by concern for the well-being of France and the whole of Europe to "unmask and publicly denounce this pernicious sect" as the true enemy of the French king and constitution, and the disruptor of the peace of an entire continent. The final document in this series of exchanges, a note to Delessart from the plenipotentiary of the king of Prussia, served to confirm the latter's entire solidarity with the emperor's diplomatic stance.[25] With this hostile new alliance, the arch of a concert of Europe against revolutionary France had been put into place.

It remained for Delessart on 1 March to convey to the Assembly that the king had charged his ambassador to the Austrian court to deplore as unnecessary the formation of a European concert and to call for its cessation. The ambassador had offered the emperor renewed assurance of union and peace, to be answered promptly, openly, and categorically in the same vein. He had proposed a reduction in the buildup of French troops at the frontiers and Austrian troops in Belgium. He had communicated that a failure to respond affirmatively to this initiative would be understood as implying "a desire to prolong a situation in which France cannot and does not wish long to remain." More significantly for the immediate course of events, the ambassador had been charged to inform the Austrian court that the king had "not thought it appropriate to the independence and dignity of the nation to enter into discussion of matters relating only to the internal situation of the realm." If this was a reproach to Kaunitz, it was also an implicit indictment of Delessart for his part in such discussion. With this paragraph, in effect, the foreign minister had been thrown to the wolves.[26]

Brissot soon led the attack. The speech he gave on 10 March was a masterpiece of denunciation and one of the most effective of his entire political career. He excoriated the tissue of lies and misrepresentations by the king, the emperor, and their ministers that had been revealed in the diplomatic documents Delessart had presented: the attacks on the dignity, security, and independence of the French nation from the one side; the pacific protestations, ineffective demands, and intimations of weakness from the other. He charged Delessart with incompetence, negligence, and weakness; with refusing to obey the Assembly's decrees; with betraying it by his secrecy, by withholding communications, by purveying misinformation regarding French internal affairs; with cowardice in calling for peace and a continuation of the Austrian alliance; with lack of foresight in postponing an attack on an enemy still unprepared, thus allowing it time to ready its forces—an act of treachery if intentional, of dangerous ineptitude if not.

After an hour and a half of condemnation, Brissot was ready to propose two decrees. The first invited the king to demand that the emperor state categorically whether he was persisting in a concert of powers against France, with failure to provide a satisfactory answer by a fixed date triggering a vigorous French response to uphold the security, independence, and dignity of the nation. The second was a decree of accusation against Delessart, his alleged offenses listed under thirteen counts. With the Assembly now in a high state of agitation, and over considerable opposition, Brissot's allies demanded an immediate vote. With little further debate, Delessart's indictment was passed overwhelmingly and the executive power charged to order his arrest. He was sent for judgment to the High Court in Orléans the following day. The order amounted to a death warrant. Transferred with other prisoners from Orléans to Paris months later, in the midst of the September Massacres, he was taken instead to Versailles, where he was massacred with forty-three others on 9 September.[27]

Delessart's indictment marked the collapse of a ministry that had become increasingly divided and dysfunctional. Bertrand de Molleville, minister of the navy and the colonies, adamant against war and under fire from the Assembly for incompetence, resigned on 9 March. His principal adversary within the cabinet, the comte de Narbonne, minister of war and ally of Lafayette, was dismissed the following day. With the Brissotins suddenly in ascendancy, the king decided abruptly to clean house entirely, accepting a trio of ministers more to their taste. Within days, Jean-Marie Roland, a provincial government inspector of industry under the Old Regime, contributor to Brissot's *Annales patriotiques*, and better known in Parisian republican circles for his energetic and outspoken young wife, was named minister of the interior. The financier Etienne Clavière, Genevan exile, former adviser to Mirabeau, theorist of the assignat, and a longtime collaborator with Brissot as a pamphleteer pushing ideas for a commercial republic, became finance minister. Charles-François Dumouriez, a soldier and adventurer used by the government before and since the Revolution on various missions, though not without spending some time in the Bastille for insubordination, became foreign minister.

To complete this dramatic turn of events, news reached Paris that Emperor Leopold II had died suddenly on 1 March.[28] His successor to the Austrian throne was a young man whose views were yet unknown; there would be months before a new emperor would be formally elected. The situation was suddenly uncertain. Marat, picking up his pen again, was eager to exploit it.

A DISASTROUS DECREE

When it appeared on 12 April, the very first issue of the revived *L'Ami du peuple* welcomed Leopold's death as a kind of miracle while savoring some of its medical details. But it lamented in advance the people's failure to profit from the opportunity it presented. "Will it always be in vain that Heaven does a hundred new miracles in your favor, that nature puts itself to work to break your chains, that the conjuncture of the most unexpected circumstances foils the traitors hellbent on your ruin?" the journal stormed. "Has cruel destiny ordered that your credulity, your security, your confidence, your blindness, hold you forever suspended over the abyss opened beneath your feet?"[29]

By Marat's account, the emperor's death had left the people's enemies in a state of disorientation. In a tangled swirl of accusations, he saw the Assembly's treatment of Delessart as a response to this circumstance, instigated by a Brissot who had long been speculating on war with Clavière, but played out by the ministerials in a fraudulent pantomime from which they thought the former minister would eventually emerge resuscitated. The change of ministry he dismissed as at once a derisory effort by Louis XVI to play the patriot king, a move by the court to exchange the lion's skin for the fox's, and a plot by Lafayette to discredit the Jacobins by setting up some of their members for failure and inevitable corruption. "The court is trembling, the counterrevolutionary faction is trembling, the venal assembly is trembling," *L'Ami du peuple* assured its readers. The people had to profit from this moment to demand immediate revocation of the decrees leading inevitably to its ruin. "Its mortal enemies are too weak today to oppose it. Look at the legislature backtracking at the voice of the people of color and the blacks. What! A handful of serfs 1,800 leagues away will get the oppressive decree that deprives them of their rights to citizenship revoked and the French wouldn't succeed in getting revocation of the decrees desolating them if they cry *Reform! Reform!* in the middle of the senate!"[30] The People's Friend wanted this to be the moment to force a dismantling of the constitution he continued to denounce as "the cruelest of the calamities that could afflict the state," one that unless reformed "will always turn against the defenders of liberty and . . . will soon consummate the public ruin it's been preparing for so long."[31]

As for the "patriotic" Jacobin ministers, Marat rejected the general view that their appointment augured well for the people. How could they remain uninfected by corruption from the court? Only Dumouriez, whose character and experience of ministerial persecution under the Old Regime vouched for his detestation of despotic government, gave him a measure of hope. Even so, Dumouriez would have to be watched: "were he an angel, surveillance is the first duty of the good citizen." Among the other newcomers to the ministry, he expected Roland to end up as a second Delessart despite his republican pretensions. Clavière was the one he most distrusted. Could a man who had spent his life in speculation to enrich himself by skinning his fellow citizens not end up speculating on the state's finances? Republican or not, he would be a new Necker. "Ruining the state by speculation is one of the cabinet's maneuvers. To consummate this atrocious project, this is the man the court had to have."

The People's Friend would be happy to be proved wrong, he insisted. But if the new ministers were true and incorruptible patriots, he predicted, the court would soon try to force their resignation. In which case, to keep them in place would be the duty of the sections, the municipality, and the faithful members of the Assembly. They would have to catch the court at its own game, crying out that if public opinion had been able to chase perfidious ministers from power, it must be no less powerful to keep faithful ones in place. Let one never forget, though, he warned, that "watchfulness is the surest guarantee of the loyalty of public functionaries." How stupid it was, he soon added, to think that ministers could be good citizens or true patriots.[32]

News of Emperor Leopold's death, it turned out, served only to delay the inevitable a few weeks. Whatever the motives on either side, it was too late to switch postures. "Will war take place? Everyone thinks so," reported *L'Ami du peuple* on 19 April. One could no longer doubt, Marat thought, that Lafayette, aiming to jump-start his career, had persuaded the cabinet to view military engagement as a means to distract the nation from internal dissensions, crush the state under the weight of taxes, and decimate the patriotic ranks of the army and National Guard under the pretext of defending borders. Nor could it be denied that the people, misled by the Brissotins and other scoundrels sold out to the court, seduced by a false picture of the nation's forces, and intoxicated by Gallic conceit, was eager for war as its implacable enemies. "It's been three years since I showed it to be the last resource of counterrevolutionaries and I haven't stopped trying to wreck the various efforts of the cabinet to ignite it," Marat protested. "Since then, I haven't changed my position and [war] remains in my eyes the cruelest of the scourges that can befall the realm."

War would divert public attention, warned The People's Friend, leaving internal enemies free to plot, fan the fires of dissension throughout the realm, foment disorders, and ambush the partisans of liberty. It would destroy national finances. It would wipe out all the good citizens France had left, rob the state of the patriotic youth rushing to its defense without weapons, discipline, training, experienced leaders, or skillful generals. The first campaign would be a disaster, he predicted, the second less so. The third could be glorious, as the nation learned at its own expense and some great man arrived to fulfill his destiny. "But to snatch victory from our enemies, we'll have to suffer a long and disastrous war. And it would be unrealistic to estimate our losses during three campaigns at less than a billion livres and 500,000 combatants." Estimating the cost of what would become "the first total war," The People's Friend had for once not exaggerated; the fatalities incurred in the French Revolutionary and Napoleonic Wars came closer to five million. Nor, of course, was he wrong about the emergence of a charismatic great man to grasp the opportunity it offered to fulfill his destiny.[33]

Marat still conceived of a way, an infallible way, to forestall this tidal wave of blood. He had already proposed one "a hundred times." It was to take the royal family hostage. This once done, the National Assembly could refuse to negotiate with foreign powers and discontinue preparations for war. Louis XVI would be free to negotiate as he wished, but at the first news of an invasion, the deputies would tell him, "Your guilty head will roll at your feet, and your whole race will be extinguished in its own blood." Did The People's Friend think this scenario likely? Not at all. "A senate faithful to the homeland is even less to be found than a patriot king," he said, distilling a sentiment at the very core of his political thinking.

A second possibility was also imaginable, one for which Marat had more frequently called: "a supreme dictator whose powers would be circumscribed so that he would have no authority to dominate but an unlimited one to strike down the leaders of the conspirators designated by the public voice, to force the corrupt legislature to put a price on the heads of the kings, princes, and generals who will come armed against us, to offer their troops sums of money to turn them over to us alive or dead, and to receive them among the number of children of the state." In this case, he anticipated, legions would rush to the flag of liberty, and France would be delivered from its enemies forever.

Fantasies of dictatorship aside, yet another option seemed reserved for the people, "less consoling for the friends of the homeland, but . . . more terrible for its enemies." It was a plan to be adopted in the departments at the first cannon blast across the frontier. The châteaux of the former nobles would be reduced to ashes, public enemies slaughtered. The army would massacre its perfidious leaders and its conspiratorial generals, while the whole nation would rise against unworthy representatives, reclaim the powers that had been stripped from it, and shred the mysterious veil so long thrown over the intrigues of cabinets. "I doubt very much that Louis XVI would be inclined to try anything if he cast his eyes over this terrible scene. May some good man have the courage to put it under his eyes."[34]

This was an empty hope. The declaration of war, long anticipated, finally occurred on 20 April. "Never has the assembly offered more scandalous scenes of delirium, cooption, and prostitution," *L'Ami du peuple* reported four days later. "Never were more fatal blows inflicted on the state. Never has the secret committee of the Tuileries given greater proof of its deceitful politics." In this account, a crowd of barkers and agents had been deployed in the Assembly's hall to pressure hesitant deputies; citizens who had passed the night guarding places in the public galleries had had to watch indignantly as well-coiffed partisans of the despot showed up late to grab preferential seating. Calls to clear the building of intruders had been resisted. Upon the king's arrival, he turned to the minister of war to detail the provocations that had emanated from Vienna. "You have heard the report presented to my council," the monarch then continued; "the result was unanimous approval of the views it contains. They accord with the wish the Assembly has expressed, as well as a very great number of citizens from all parts of the empire. I have adopted them. I had hitherto used all the means in my power to maintain peace. They have been without effect. I come, in accordance with the Constitution, to propose war against the king of Hungary and Bohemia."[35]

Marat saw this language as a ploy on the king's part to appear to yield reluctantly to the counsel of his ministers and the will of the National Assembly, to engage in a war he had long planned and his secret advisers had long manipulated the deputies to demand. Now the plotters only had to hope for the defeat and subsequent invasion that would force revocation of the constitution and the Revolution's end. The deputies put up a show of debate after the king had left the hall, he recounted, but it was no more than an adroit charade of deliberation regarding a decision that had already been made. "Finally, Brissot, the illustrious Brissot, once a spy for the former police, then a paid apologist for Motier's assaults, and today a representative of the French people and a petty scoundrel sold out to the agents of the cabinet," called for the Diplomatic Committee to draft a war decree on the spot. No sooner was it passed (with only seven dissenting votes) than the ministers disappeared to send their dispatches to thirty waiting couriers. Vienna, for its own part, had already also opted for war before any courier arrived from Paris with the news of the French decision.[36]

The fateful session was not yet over. It continued, in Marat's account, as Condorcet pulled from his pocket "a draft manifesto larded with adages and lies" in justification of the representatives' conduct. "'Forced to consent to war by the most imperious necessity,'" he reported the philosopher as saying, the Assembly "'has at least the satisfaction of having neither provoked nor instigated it. . . . It has only followed the direction to which justice pointed the people's representatives.'" To The People's Friend, these were merely the words of a vile rhetorician. The question, he insisted, was not one of the injustice of an attack or the justice of a defense, but whether it was traitorous to squander the nation's resources, spill the blood of its best citizens, threaten the safety of the state, and engage in a war that could only be disastrous—one, moreover, that could easily have been avoided by putting a price on the head of the rebel princes, taking the royal family hostage, and making them responsible for the events they had provoked.[37]

How distressing, *L'Ami du peuple* lamented, to see the best citizens ready not only to pay for a war but to shed their blood to secure their enemies' triumph. It was still worse that the friends of liberty feared the consequences of victory more than those of defeat. The danger, given the French tendency to craziness, was that a general flushed with victory amid an intoxicated army and populace would march his triumphant troops against the capital to ensure the despot's ascendancy. "May heaven grant that . . . the soldiers discover the betrayal in time and finally drown their leaders in their own blood."[38]

This thought led, eventually, to consideration of the aristocratic generals currently heading the French armies. The German count Nicolas Luckner Marat described as a creature of the court and base valet of the monarch; the French count Jean-Baptiste de Rochambeau he dismissed as a vile courtier, decorated with court baubles; Lafayette, ever a favorite target, he denounced as no less well known for his hideous machinations against public liberty than his shameful prostitutions to the palace; Laurent, comte de Gouvion-Saint-Cyr, he condemned as Lafayette's henchman and accomplice in all his crimes; Alexandre, comte de Lameth, he saw covered with opprobrium for his hypocrisy and betrayals; Louis, comte de Narbonne-Lara, he tarred as a child of the court (he was widely thought to be a bastard son of Louis XV) and, expelled from the ministry at public demand, as the most likely of all of them to betray the nation. "And you claim that leaders like this will fight for the homeland and for liberty! . . . That they will not condemn the soldiery to butchery . . . ! That they will not hand over the keys to the kingdom . . . ! That they will not join with our enemies to reestablish despotism, with all its hereditary hangers-on . . . ! To doubt this would show you fit for the madhouse."[39] *Grosso modo*, Marat was clairvoyant. Only Gouvion went on to end his military career with distinction under Napoleon. Luckner, tainted with suspicion following Lafayette's betrayals, was executed in 1794; Lameth went over to the enemy with Lafayette, no longer the hero of two worlds, in August 1792.

All this was in the future. For the moment, Marat was aghast at the popularity of the war that had now been declared. "The war is finally decreed and the blind multitude everywhere applauds the disastrous decree," he moaned. "My dear fellow citizens, we're the most sheep-like people on earth because we're the least sensible and the vainest." With as much derision as despair, he reported the parade of citizens, ranging from wealthy to abjectly poor, who trooped to the Assembly over the next few days to offer patriotic contributions in support of "a disastrous war undertaken solely to put us back in chains." They were "less impatient to make the ultimate sacrifice than jealous to receive the first applause from the conscript fathers ready to fleece it." Manipulated by the court, they were simply piling up loot for greedy deputies to share out among themselves. The Constituents had gobbled up patriotic gifts for themselves in 1789, he recalled. The current deputies, shamefully allowing parents of starving families to turn over their last sous, would do the same. "Run, give them the specie you've amassed and they are demanding," he counseled readers curious to see what the deputies were up to. "No need to fear the insult of a refusal; these gentlemen have a good appetite."[40]

THE PEOPLE STIRS

As *L'Ami du peuple* ceased publication in December 1791, the popular movement was beginning to revive. The months of quiet imposed since the Champ de Mars Massacre were ending. On 11 December, the Legislative Assembly had warmly received petitions from ten of the Parisian sections, some lengthy, all vigorous, in repudiation of an address by departmental administrators urging the king to veto the decree against refractory priests. Marat would have preferred to see the deputies respond more negatively to these petitions. "How much better would rejection of these addresses have served the public cause! It would have outraged the people against the legislature in league with the prince, and it would have excited a fermentation that would finally have led to a salutary crisis. What to conclude, if not that this kind of reception is a soporific shrewdly administered by the ministerials to tie the hands of the friends of liberty?"[41] In retrospect, another conclusion is possible. As the Brissotins gained leadership over the following months, they would conjure the threat of popular agitation against the royal vetoes as a crucial strategy in their struggle to gain political advantage for the Assembly against the crown. It proved a dangerous strategy, eventually provoking the end of the constitutional monarchy and the Legislative Assembly with it.

The political atmosphere in Paris had also changed with the municipal elections occurring toward the end of 1791. In the competition to replace Bailly as mayor in mid-November, Pétion, one of the patriotic former deputies Marat had most admired, defeated the general Lafayette the popular movement had long despised. Pétion was soon joined at the head of the municipality by two other radical patriots, Manuel as the city's prosecutor and Danton as one of the latter's deputies. By mid-February, the General Council elected from the sections and the municipal government chosen from it had also shifted toward the Left. The sharpening of political divisions played out within these bodies became more acute as a result, a phenomenon intensified after 10 March when, at Manuel's insistence, their deliberations were opened to the public. The influx of spectators was evident in stormy sessions during April after Manuel, responding to demands from the more radical sections, proposed the removal of the busts of Bailly and Lafayette displayed in the assembly hall of the General Council. The People's Friend denounced the violence of these "scandalous scenes" produced, he was sure, by a crowd of Lafayette's thugs imported to oppose the change. The effort to oust the stone versions of these icons of moderatism failed for the moment. But their personal political displacement was well under way.[42]

By this time, popular energy was again being more openly expressed. Riots against prices of sugar and coffee (pushed up as insurrection in Saint-Domingue interrupted production), as well as of other commodities, had taken place across Paris in January and February 1792. The following months saw perhaps a doubling of the number of popular societies associated with the sections (along the lines Marat had suggested a year earlier). In January, there were at least eight; by July as many as sixteen. In March, in a spirit of solidarity, they shared a civic banquet on the Champs-Elysées. As war talk grew stronger, more militant clubs began to call for a general distribution of pikes to arm both active and passive citizens against an eventual invasion. That same month, a central organizing committee drawn from the societies began planning a large popular festival in honor of the forty Swiss soldiers of the Châteauvieux Regiment who had been condemned to the galleys for mutiny in Nancy in August 1790. When it occurred on 15 April, its organizers claimed as many as 400,000 participants.[43]

Explicitly excluded from the general amnesty of 14 September, the Châteauvieux prisoners had been freed by a decree of the Legislative Assembly approved on the last day of December and sanctioned by Louis XVI on 12 February. Upon their arrival in Paris, they were received with honor at the Assembly on 12 April, but only after deputies bitterly opposed to acclaiming mutineers had forced a roll-call vote in a failed attempt to prevent it. By the fifteenth, efforts to forestall the popular celebration in their honor had succeeded only in spurring its organizers to ensure that it remained peaceful. "Be content," the journalist writing in *Le Moniteur* congratulated them, "the people you love is worthy of freedom; left to itself in the elation of a contested triumph, it has known how both to abandon and restrain itself. It was there in all its force, which it didn't abuse. There was no weapon to repress excess; no excess to repress; no brawls, even private ones, no disobedience to the general will, which was the happiness and harmony of all."

In the event, this massive ceremonial march took on form and meaning as a Festival of Liberty, a powerful reassertion of popular energy, and a collective repudiation of the oppression in the name of law and order that Bailly's and Lafayette's governance of the city was now seen to typify. Elaborately scripted and performed, the parade became the people's belated response to the Champ de Mars Massacre. The former Swiss prisoners walked at its heart, amid songs, slogans, the beating of drums, the waving of banners, and the procession of floats decorated with symbols of liberty. They wore the Phrygian bonnets that rapidly became the badge of patriotism. Their former chains were borne before them by maidens dressed in white.[44]

This flexing of what might now be called the democratic movement filled Marat with jubilation. It had taken place, he emphasized, despite all the efforts of the court and its henchmen, of Lafayette and his agents, of the leadership of the department of Paris, of the corrupted members of the sections and the cutthroats of the salaried National Guard. Never had a festival displayed more order, tranquility, and decency. "In the midst of an immense crowd, not a flick of the finger given, not a pin stolen, not an insult mouthed. True, not a single mounted guard, not a single police agent, not a single paid ass-pusher showed up to provoke disorder on the pretext of shutting it down. The fraternal union of the citizens, friends of liberty, kept a tight rein and very effectively demonstrated the perfect uselessness of those repressive methods invented by the police to stifle every popular movement and keep the nation under the yoke. Here, then, are the peaceable citizens whom the enemies of the revolution never cease to slander, whom the valets of the court depict as miserable *sans-culottes* greedy for pillage and blood, whom the Constituent Assembly massacred as turbulent insurrectionists . . . and the execrable general had slaughtered like brigands on the Champ de Mars with the support of the criminals of the municipality."

Though not a fan of parades, Marat told his readers, he had witnessed this one with enchantment. "I saw with emotion citizens of every condition mixed pell-mell and united by the bonds of patriotism. I saw the soldiers of the homeland, of all ranks and without their weapons, form long chains of friendship and brotherhood with workers and the poor. I heard with joy the cries of *Long Live Liberty! Long Live the Homeland!* I heard curses heaped everywhere on Bouillé, Bailly and Motier as the primary authors of our ills. Behold then, finally, the hero of two worlds succumbing under the weight of public execration and about to reap opprobrium at the end of his career. May he soon end it in shame and despair!" This eminently peaceful gathering in honor of the Châteauvieux Swiss had also been a celebration of the sacred right of resistance. It was a rare happy day for The People's Friend.

There was a final note to add: the Jardin des Tuileries had been closed throughout the day under the surveillance of the King's Guard, with six hundred cavalry horses kept at the ready, saddled and bridled, at the nearby Ecole Militaire.[45] The space between the crowd in the streets and the guards in the palace grounds would not always be so successfully maintained.

This popular Festival of Liberty cried out for an answer from the Right. Plans were soon being made to counter it with a Festival of the Law. This, too, was to be built around an iconic moment: not an uprising of the people in the cause of liberty but its inversion, a martyrdom in the name of law and order in the face of a savage popular insurrection. On 3 March, the mayor of the town of Étampes not far from Paris, Jacques-Louis Simonneau, had been massacred by a crowd of rioters when he refused their demand for lower bread prices and tried to impose order. Rumors circulated that "all the horrors of cannibals had been inflicted on his disfigured and still palpitating remains." Severe repression followed. The widespread horror at this death not only called for an inquiry by the Legislative Assembly and a monument in the victim's honor; it also quickly inspired plans for a solemn procession in commemoration of his martyrdom.[46]

Marat had seized on the event in one of the earliest issues of the revived *L'Ami du peuple*. On 15 April the journal carried the headline, "Simonneau, Mayor of Étampes, Infamous Ministerial Hoarder Transformed into a Martyr of Virtue by the Court and Its Valets." The journal that day was entirely devoted to excoriation of the victim, vindication of his murderers, and denunciation of "the perfidious plot to pass a notorious hoarder off as a virtuous citizen and the citizens of an entire town as brigands and agitators." What then of the thousands of voices shouting for *the respect due the law*? How futile it was, countered The People's Friend, for the despot and his henchmen, the corrupt magistrates, and the prostituted legislature to preach respect for laws they themselves violated with impunity in order to enslave the people. "No, I'll never stop protesting against the doctrine of superstitious respect for the laws, of blind obedience and provisional submission to public functionaries. We're slaves and remain so forever unless we finally abjure this fatal doctrine that causes all our feebleness and all the force of our oppressors, that perpetuates anarchy among us, calls down on us all the ills that inflict us and will soon consummate our ruin. No, we owe respect only to wise laws and submission only to just ones."[47]

The sacred doctrine of resistance had saved the French in past moments of the Revolution, insisted The People's Friend. It was saving France now by thrusting weapons into the hands of the patriots of Marseille against counterrevolutionaries in the Midi; it was ensuring the triumph of the cause of humanity in the colonies and restoring the honor of the New World. "Cowardly and corrupt Parisians, do slaves have to show you the path to liberty without your having the courage to follow them?" he demanded. "How much longer will you patiently suffer laws that degrade and destroy you?"[48] The reference to Marseille was a crucial one. Radical revolutionary activists there now dominated city government and were sending out armies of militants across the Midi to wrest control from counterrevolutionaries in Aix, Arles, Avignon, and elsewhere. Issues of *L'Ami du peuple* in April were replete with reports and letters detailing what amounted to a war of liberation in the south, undertaken by the indomitable Marseillais. Before long, their revolutionary republican militants would be heading toward Paris to the sound of the song made famous on their march. Marat would be eager to welcome them.

As for the festival being planned to commemorate Simonneau's martyrdom, *L'Ami du peuple* was soon urging good citizens to stay away from an event that would attract the worst enemies of the Revolution the capital could vomit up, the gangrened priests and magistrates, the speculators and public bloodsuckers, the king's armed valets, the whores left unemployed by the departure of the émigrés, and members of the defunct clergy and parlements. On 2 May, he published a bitterly satirical parody of a program for the procession, ridiculing it with the prospect of performances acclaiming the murderers of patriots and banners proclaiming support to the death for the constitution, absolute power, servile submission, tyrannical laws, and counterrevolution. In this imaginary pantomime, *agents provocateurs* would be strategically placed on the Champ de Mars, ready to ignite a massacre of sans-culottes, if necessary, by bombarding the marchers with stones.

In the event, nothing like that happened when the Festival of the Law finally took place on 3 June. Marat was in any case more sober in commenting on the official plan for the festival eventually presented to the Assembly by the Committee on Public Instruction. Its aim, he reflected, apart from reassuring all the royal hoarders who had been terrified at Simonneau's fate, was to keep the people on its knees before the public functionaries harassing, starving, and tyrannizing it in the name of the law. It was an effort to suppress truly popular festivals by monopolizing the Champ de Mars for the king, an amusement to divert the crowd's attention from daily acts of arbitrary authority. As for his judgment of the event when it finally occurred, that went unrecorded: by then, publication of *L'Ami du peuple* was becoming intermittent, and Marat had other battles to fight. Most probably, he would have shared Robespierre's observation that "it wasn't at all a national festival, it was the festival of the public functionaries. . . . How this procession of municipal, administrative and judicial bodies replicated the image of the old regime! Bayonets, swords, uniforms, what ornaments for a free people's festivals!"[49]

A POLITICS OF RECRIMINATION

As political polarization intensified everywhere, the Jacobin Club could scarcely find itself untouched. In April, following the declaration of war, it became a cockpit for bitter personal conflict between Brissot and Guadet, on the one side, and Robespierre, on the other. With seething hostility and vicious innuendo, each accused the other of intrigue, ambition, and grasping for power. The Brissotins resented Robespierre's growing dominance in the Jacobin Club, his idolization by the people, his unwavering opposition to their campaign for war against Austria, and his constant suspicion of their motives. Robespierre, in turn, distrusted the sway the Brissotins had exercised in the Legislative Assembly to start a war he judged insane, feared their power to make and break ministers, and was suspected of encouraging rumors of their putative participation in plots to make Narbonne or Lafayette a dictator under the guise of a protectorate.[50]

The People's Friend watched this struggle closely. He was also intimately implicated in it. Word was out among Robespierre's adversaries that, in arguing the need for a supreme dictator on 19 April, Marat was making a coded call for Robespierre to assume absolute power. Brissot, on the attack in the Jacobin Club on 25 April, accused nameless enemies of spreading talk of a conspiracy for a protectorate that he had nothing to do with. "They want to frighten minds with this word protectorate and familiarize them with the word tribunate," he insisted, doubtless referencing Marat's warnings of this scenario. Guadet went further, intimating that Robespierre had made use of *L'Ami du peuple* precisely to float a bid for dictatorship. The charge was expanded and made more explicit in Brissot's *Patriote français* over the next few days, and soon reverberated through other journals eager to denounce the corrosive ravings of "the bilious Marat." Robespierre, for his part, maneuvered by keeping his distance from his dangerous defender. "Must I be reputed culpable of the extravagance of an extremist," he demanded of the Jacobins, repudiating Marat's journal for preaching cruelty, carnage, and blood, and denying, in any case, that it had promoted him as a potential dictator. "All the illustrious patriots certainly know there's not a word of that in the issue of Marat that is cited."[51]

Marat's defense of the Incorrruptible was insistent, but not unambiguous. He was eager to deny Guadet's accusation that Robespierre had made use of *L'Ami du peuple* to discredit the Legislative Assembly and declare that it was time for a dictator. He had never turned his journal over to Robespierre, he protested, though he had frequently used it to do justice to the latter's patriotism. This was the moment he chose to reveal that the two of them had met in person only once—probably at the end of December 1791, though Marat himself supplied no date. The conversation, he emphasized, had readily revealed the significant differences between them. Robespierre (as mentioned in an earlier chapter) had deplored Marat's talk of blood, of daggers, and of lynching; Marat had responded by defending the unremitting denunciations, the protests against oppression, and the cries of indignation, fury, and despair he had directed against criminals abusing the people's confidence to mislead and despoil it, to encumber it with chains, to cast it into the abyss. "Robespierre listened to me aghast," he recounted. "This interview confirmed me in the opinion I had always had of him: that he combined the enlightenment of a wise senator, the integrity of a truly good man and the zeal of a veritable patriot, but he was equally lacking in both the vision and audacity of the true statesman." There was to be no talk, then, of Robespierre as a dictator. As for Brissot, Marat predicted, there would never be peace within the Jacobin Club until it had purged itself of the Brissot faction, "which is to say, the scoundrels of the deputations of Paris and the Gironde that lead the assembly and serve the cause of the Tuileries cabinet while hiding behind the mask of patriotism."[52]

By the time Marat offered this latest judgment, the Legislative Assembly had ordered his arrest, citing a particularly intemperate issue of *L'Ami du peuple* (number 645, dated 30 April) that had denounced the appointment of an unworthy successor to succeed Robespierre after his brief stint as public prosecutor in the Paris Criminal Tribunal. The electoral body that had made the choice was "completely gangrened with royalism," the journal had charged. "Dreading the cruel consequences of the putrefaction of a political body to which the Constituent Assembly had perfidiously entrusted the destinies of the state," it called on the public to "bring down fire and sword on all the gangrened members in order to stop the virus, save the healthy members and prevent infection of representatives of the people, district and departmental administrators, judges and public functionaries intimately related to the rotten members." Even this measure, it continued, elaborating the medical metaphor, was no more than a simple palliative. "The true remedy would be to separate the healthy members and burn the entire body, and then restore the important functions to the sections. Without that, it's impossible for the political institutions of the state not to be corrupted and the public safety not to be in desperate shape."[53]

Barely a week later, on 6 May, Marat had fixed in no less bloodthirsty terms on another example of "the popular justice that can save the homeland." He had already called several times for the elimination of corrupt, incompetent, or treasonous generals. Now he had a more specific instance of such retribution to celebrate. A detachment of the Army of the North attempting a march on Tournai in the Austrian Netherlands had been led into an ambush by its leader, General Theodore Dillon, a veteran of the American War of Independence and, in Marat's eyes, a darling of the queen and the court. Several hundred men had been left dead before the contingent recovered its momentum, only then to be ordered by its general to retreat to Lille. Infuriated by their perception of a failure of leadership and a cowardly command to withdraw, troops had fallen on Dillon, massacring him and his aide de camp, Dupont-Chaumont, and lynching several prisoners of war (though the reports about Dupont-Chaumont and the prisoners of war were later denied).

Reporting this news in the Assembly, the minister of war had appealed for a decree to tighten procedures of military justice. Marat had little doubt that the Brissotins would support such a decree, still less that it should be resisted. If the Assembly had the temerity to take this disastrous step, he warned, it would not long await the result of its perfidy. "Thank Heaven," he cried, "the time for vengeance has at last arrived, the criminals leading our troops are finally going to expiate their perfidies, like Dillon and Chaumont. May these salutary examples multiply in a way terrifying the court; may the generals soon pay with their blood for the criminal web of their long machinations; may the officers sold out to the despot cover the earth with their bloody cadavers, may the sword of our soldiers soon purge the army of all the traitors to the homeland . . . return[ing] home to exterminate to the very last the henchmen of despotism; may the entire nation, having finally risen up against its external enemies, avenge itself against the tyrants sworn against its liberty, breaking their subjects' chains, and making them free men." The People's Friend was verging at last on imagining a war of liberation, though scarcely a joyful or exalted one. His notion of emancipating the oppressed as an act of vengeance against their despots was far from the Brissotins' sometimes ecstatic conception of the gift of freedom to be conferred by a missionary nation.[54]

The backlash, in any case, was growing. On 2 May, a group of deputies had met with the minister of justice to demand punishment for the language found in number 645 of *L'Ami du peuple*. The minister had apparently been reluctant to act in violation of the constitutional right of freedom of speech, though he had changed his mind that evening and fired off a copy of the offending issue of the journal for the attention of the public prosecutor in the criminal court of the department of Paris. "It is time," he urged, "that the agitators of the people discover that a public order exists and the law has organs to make it respected."

The following day a Feuillant, Jacques-Claude Beugnot, rose in the Assembly to read an extract from an earlier issue of *L'Ami du peuple* calling for the immolation of treasonous generals, and to point to Dillon's massacre as a consequence of these infamous sentiments. "Have no doubt," he exclaimed over noisy interruptions from the left of the hall, "it's the journals of the Carras, the Marats that led Dillon to his death. Let them be known to you as the true traitors, the enemies of the homeland. How will you ever have an army and a government if you put up with writers calling themselves patriots, false friends of the constitution condemning generals to death, the people's representatives to its indignation, the king to its contempt, and when a number of you have been insulted at the entrance to this hall, publicly and with impunity?"

It was time to find out what would prevail, Beugnot continued, "the authority that must protect us or the one that will tear us apart." The nation—not the wasters in Paris usurping that name but the "peaceable and hardworking citizens of the eighty-three departments"—wanted order and peace with and through the constitution. Would the deputies themselves be the next victims in a frightful scenario of total social collapse, he wondered, or would fear be banished, courage and virtue affirmed, extremism silenced or punished, sedition repressed, and every incendiary writer prosecuted? On this note, Beugnot proposed a decree enjoining the minister of justice to require public prosecutors to report in detail on all authors and distributors of writings that advocated or provoked resistance to the laws, violence against their execution, or attacks on generals, magistrates, administrators, and representatives of the nation.[55] Behind all this talk was panic that an ill-prepared army already suffering reverses would be provoked into rebellion.

It was not long before another infamous passage from *L'Ami du peuple* was introduced into the debate, this time a version of lines from number 645 doctored to make the Assembly itself appear the direct target of a call to the people to "bring down fire and sword on the gangrened majority of the representatives of the nation." In addition to violent denunciations, this prompted a demand that any action against Marat also apply to Royou, the editor of *L'Ami du roi*, a royalist journal urging its readers to join the émigrés beyond the frontiers. The two of them, it was soon charged, were being paid from the same conspiratorial purse. The ensuing debate, lengthy and contentious, pitched deputies who demanded a more stringent press law against those, fearing abridgment of the right to free speech, who advocated more vigorous execution of the law already in existence. Speakers claiming that the constitution gave the Assembly itself the right to accuse press offenders were countered by others insisting that such action was limited constitutionally to the agents and institutions of civil or criminal justice. The Assembly finally declared itself ready to call down the vengeance of the law by approving decrees of accusation against both Marat (unanimously) and Royou (with a handful of dissenters), and issuing an order to the executive power to initiate prompt police measures to seal off their premises, effects, and papers.[56]

Marat, for his part, had gone to ground. This was probably the moment at which he took temporary shelter with Jacques Roux, who recalled in July 1793 that The People's Friend had found asylum with him some fifteen months earlier. "I received you with pleasure, you and the number of persons who came to visit M. Legros [Mr. Big!], for that's the name you bore," Roux later reproached his now-alienated friend. "I slept on the floor for six days, I did all the cooking, I even emptied your chamber pot, in a word I did everything for you that a good patriot could." For thanks, Roux recalled, his guest had been base enough to leave 15 livres in assignats on the mantel when he left, as if for a servant. The sum had been repudiated with indignation, as had, eventually, the results of the stay. "Wow, Marat, for the price of my virtue you abused my hospitality, to write not truths but impostures."[57]

Did Roux have in mind the issue of *L'Ami du peuple* Marat published from underground on 14 May, the first to appear since his accusation on 3 May? It offered a highly colored account of the Assembly's debate that day, blaming the Brissotins for instigating a plot to close down his journal before they were unmasked in it. It mocked the fact that Royou had been included in the accusation as a feint, that no further action had been taken against him while five hundred agents had been mobilized to find Marat himself and his editor's printshop had been ransacked. It accused those denouncing him of usurping the functions of a grand jury, brandishing evidence of inflammatory language taken from fake versions published under his name, and refusing to have passages read out by the Assembly secretary to verify the forgeries against his own words. It repudiated as ridiculous the implication that the circulation of incendiary writings had been responsible for the poor performance of the troops, let alone for the decisions of their leaders to lead their men to be slaughtered and forbid them to retaliate.

His accusers had made it a crime for him to predict that the generals would lead their troops to the slaughter, Marat objected. Was it his fault that the only military engagements to occur thus far had proved him right? It had been made a crime for him to call on the public to bring fire and sword to a gangrened political body. "For me," he countered, "the public is the people; to the criminals who betray it, it's the nation itself, it's the sovereign. I not only invite it to remove the gangrened members of the political body by fire and sword, but I beg it to do so on my knees. Will they say that the nation doesn't have this right? It's up to them to prove it. As for me, I'm sure that it not only has the right to excise the rotten members of the electoral body by fire and sword but to torture to the death all its unfaithful representatives." The point of this attack on him, he concluded, was to destroy liberty of the press by taking down the sole journalist devoted to the people. "I will never give myself up to tyrants whose paid followers have doubtless been ordered to massacre me while arresting me or poisoning me in a cell."[58]

It took until 21 May for the Assembly to vote formally to submit charges to the High Court in Orléans that Royou and Marat had violated laws safeguarding general security and the constitution. The deputies had seen little action by the executive power in the meantime. Issues of *L'Ami du peuple* were being sold daily at the door of the Manège, they complained, with language even more incendiary than the numbers that had provoked accusations in the first place. With copies being circulated daily among the troops, it was demanded, how could military discipline be reestablished? The minister of justice was required to report immediately on the measures he had taken to enforce its earlier decrees. He complied at the Assembly's session that evening, offering as major evidence of his activity a report he had received from the justice of the peace for the Notre Dame section. The justice relayed that he had proceeded with the police to the lodging of a printer, one Féret, who had confessed to receiving a manuscript from Marat's messenger that very morning. He had ordered copies of the manuscript printed and confiscated, and the print tray destroyed. A police officer had been posted to wait for Marat's messenger to return, but no one had shown up.[59]

The minister was eager to convey that he had done more. He wanted the deputies to know that he had ordered vigilance against all the incendiary publications that were being circulated in Paris, and among the troops, to provoke resistance, indiscipline, and insubordination. Surprised to receive on 14 May an issue of *L'Ami du peuple* being circulated openly and defiantly in Paris when he thought the journal already dead, he had given instructions that all those peddling this illegal production be arrested and forced to identify their suppliers, this information to be used to locate and arrest the author. He had laid down that it was essential to stop the scandalous distribution of a journal "attacking the authority of the legislative body and all the constituted bodies with a ferocity approaching rage." The offending author had apparently disappeared, the minister acknowledged. Nonetheless, he assured the deputies that all the forces of law and order were being mobilized to execute their decree.[60]

The reach of these measures was limited. On 12 June, the deputy Delfau reiterated the demand for stronger execution of laws restraining the press, complaining that *L'Ami du peuple* was still circulating in the reading clubs in the Palais Royal and throughout Paris, that it was hawked and sold openly even a few steps from the Assembly, that it was distributed to the army and spread everywhere. To make his point, he brandished four or five numbers of the journal and imposed on the deputies an excerpt from the issue dated 16 May that invoked their readiness to assure generals the power to betray the people. Another deputy cited the title of a work he considered even more incendiary, *Têtes à prix*, that put a price on the heads of the king, the generals, and certain members of the Assembly. Summoned to respond, the minister of justice stressed the energy of the actions he had taken to enforce the laws against incendiary writings that were becoming daily more extreme and dangerous, as well as the constitutional limits on his authority to do so. Reminded by the minister that legislation was their responsibility, the deputies referred the matter to the Committee on Legislation, mandating it to report within three days.[61]

Marat clearly expected the worst. He predicted a "fatal decree" that would shield the "atrocious assembly" from all public scrutiny, freeing it to "conspire at will in the shadows and march with giant steps to the fatal epoch when it will decree the counterrevolution." It appears that the committee report the Assembly had demanded was not made. A number of deputies had argued that stricter execution of existing laws was more important at this point than new legislation on the matter. The committee may have agreed. By this time, the Assembly faced more immediate issues.

In all this, The People's Friend had found little support from the journalists on behalf of whose liberty to write he had been claiming martyrdom. On 28 and 29 May he unloaded an extended denunciation against the mainstream patriotic journal *Les Révolutions de Paris*, accusing it of habitual plagiarism of his own views and opinions. He was angry at its repetition of the charge that he had promoted Robespierre for a dictatorship. But he was surely stung more by its scoffing at the Legislative Assembly for wasting time on the "banal exaggerations" habitual in *L'Ami du peuple*—language it discounted as a performance not to be taken seriously, little more than a sustained joke to which the public paid no attention. Perhaps at this point, Marat remembered his observation, a few months earlier, that the multiplication of pretended patriotic journalists endangered the achievement of liberty by offering divergent accounts of events, competing interpretations confusing readers' understanding, and conflicting proposals for action that left the people paralyzed. "To have a great effect and to save the homeland," he had declaimed, "there should be only one political journalist, honest and clear-sighted, responsible for following the work of the assembly and denouncing the principal public functionaries. Enchanted to turn the pen over to one more skillful, I would be the first to set the example."[62] In the event, he had been made an example of a very different kind.

BACK UNDERGROUND

In hiding once more, Marat found it impossible to continue daily publication of *L'Ami du peuple*. He had difficulty finding printers, who either refused to publish the journal at all, delayed its appearance, balked at producing a particularly raw issue, or arbitrarily edited the copy they agreed to print. On 19 May, he was writing to Desmoulins to beg him to publish some letters intended to unmask journalists betraying the cause of liberty, "the enemies of the homeland having put me again under the blade of tyranny." Between 14 May and 9 June, only twelve issues of the journal dribbled onto the streets. The four weeks that followed saw only one fugitive number. Then, from 7 July to 7 August, there were eleven issues in all, a majority of them looking more like a sequence of essays than the more typical daily pages. The revolution of 10 August, when it came, abruptly ended this final period in hiding. "My dear compatriots," he rejoiced that day, "a man who has long been declared anathema for your sake today escapes his underground hiding place."[63]

In the weeks between mid-May and early June, *L'Ami du peuple* painted a fragmentary canvas of defeats, betrayals, assassinations, and repression. It aimed its attacks largely at the early disasters of the war effort, the generals responsible for them, and the Brissotins who had led France into them. On the front with Belgium, into which the Army of the North had been expected to march to broad acclamation, the debacle of Dillon's retreat from Tournai had been paralleled by a panicky fallback of Biron's troops from Quiévran to Valenciennes. Marat counted eight hundred French casualties in these two incidents. General Rochambeau, commandant of the Army of the North, soon resigned. On the northeastern front, around Metz, troops in nearby Tiercelet rose up in insurrection after their leaders were found to be negotiating with émigrés led by Bouillé in a neighboring wood; three-quarters of the regiment deserted to the émigré side. Metz itself, the journal reported, had been left defenseless by Lafayette; the general had been more obsessed with imposing harsh discipline on his troops. In the Rhineland, General Custine resisted orders to take the gorges of Porrentruy. Everywhere, indeed, Marat charged, generals were holding back. Everywhere, troops were undersupplied, without weapons, without food. Everywhere, officers were deserting. Everywhere, the frontiers lacked adequate defense. Everywhere, treason plots were emerging: "we're on the eve of seeing great ones erupting, disastrous events, and soon the god Motier will appear in all his baseness." The Constituents had made a fatal mistake, he argued, in neglecting his advice to purge the aristocratic officer corps and allow the troops to elect their leaders. "We no longer have armies, we no longer have troops, or officers, or generals, and we're on the eve of seeing the state become the prey of external enemies at the same moment it's torn apart by internal ones."[64]

The principal responsibility for all this, in the eyes of The People's Friend, lay with the deputies from Paris and the Gironde, in other words, the Brissotins. Now dominant in the Assembly, Marat warned, they were pushing to assert its power, hence their own, against the king. At the same time, they were threatening to suppress popular societies and stifle the sentiment of liberty in favor of "the despotism of the law, which is to say the despotism of those who make and unmake it at their will." The court was far from blameless in the matter of the poor conduct of the war, he allowed. "How can one believe that the Tuileries cabinet isn't in cahoots with the one in Vienna when our armies stand with their arms crossed and the generals send feeble detachments to attack the enemy on its ground? When one sees our advance troops led into ambushes, retreat in the face of small detachments and abandon their weapons and baggage . . . ? When one sees our ministers forge false accounts of events, imagine fake assassinations, revolts, even the massacre of prisoners of war by the soldiers, to have a pretext to blame these setbacks on the indiscipline of the troops, slander patriotic writers, or wrench out a barbarous decree against soldiers who will not watch their leaders' treason in silence or ease the success of their disastrous projects?" He was referring to "hideous edicts" he saw harshly tightening military discipline to force the troops into "watching their leaders' treasons in silence and consummating the ruin of the people." These laws were as much the work of the Brissotins, he insisted, as of the ministerials in the Assembly. "Whatever the machinations of the Tuileries cabinet against liberty, all the reverses, all the defeats, all the disasters that will accompany the senseless war in which we are engaged will be the work of the corrupt deputations of Paris and the Gironde who got it decreed."[65]

By 25 May, Marat was noticing, the Brissotins were starting to panic. "Beginning to fear the turn taken in the operations of the disastrous war in which they have perfidiously engaged the nation," they found a scapegoat in the so-called Austrian Committee. Imagined as a sinister conspiracy of ministers, deputies, former deputies, generals, and diplomats extending deep into court circles under Marie Antoinette's influence and protection, this shadowy group was held to be working to reverse the course of the Revolution, restore the king to absolute power, and subordinate French policies to Austrian interests. Its putative existence, long rumored, had been pushed particularly by Jean-Louis Carra in his *Annales patriotiques*. Fortunately for the Brissotins, the issue of its hidden influence burst into public view in May when Carra was sued for defamation by two former ministers, Montmorin and Bertrand de Molleville, whom he had targeted as among the Austrian Committee's members. Taken up by a zealous justice of the peace (who ended up the principal casualty in the affair), their case provoked high-frequency debates in the Assembly after Carra claimed that information about their activities had been leaked to him by members of its surveillance committee. Gensonné and Brissot, in particular, took the opportunity to blame this shadow pro-Austrian conspiracy in global terms for "the bizarre character of our particular situation," for provoking the war then opposing it, for blocking or delaying military preparations, for the treasons, setbacks, and atrocities arising from the initial attacks, for the discontent of the troops and the desertions of the officers.[66]

Marat scoffed at all this on 3 June. In his view, talk of an Austrian Committee was banal; it had bounced around in patriotic journals for years. He saw the conspiracy against liberty generalized among the legions supporting despotism rather than concentrated in the hands of a more particular group serving Austrian interests. Belief in the existence of the latter, he suspected, had been deployed in this particular case in a scheme to discredit members of the Assembly's surveillance committee, and hence the representative body more generally. As for Gensonné and Brissot, he saw their denunciations as a ruse to cover their own perfidies with a false show of patriotic virtue; it was in their interest to attribute all the plots that had distressed France for the past three years to a hidden conclave within the ministry.

The speech Brissot should have given (which Marat now concocted for him) would have acknowledged his part in a plan conceived by Lafayette to provoke armed conflict to distract the French from a civil war ignited by refractory priests under the protection of the monarch, and to amuse them with celebrations of minor military actions until the mass of troops had been trained in their camps to slaughter their fellow citizens. At this point, it was anticipated, the king would flee, returning with troops to take the capital. Or, perhaps, the generals would simply wait until foreign armies arrived at the capital instead, leaving foreign regiments to disarm citizens, slaughter leading patriots, dissolve the Assembly, hang the faithful deputies, and kick out the rest. Either way, despotism would be reestablished, and the nation's wealth consecrated to the splendors of the court and the brilliance of a restored, indemnified nobility. "I deeply regret, Gentlemen," Marat would have had his former friend conclude, "that in order to get what was promised me I had to provoke the declaration of war . . . , preach blind confidence in the ministry and servile submission to the generals. But since that's done and I am more than comfortably provided for, I'll try to make up for my errors by spying on all the new plots and bringing them into the light of day."[67]

Disclosure of this shameful scenario (not entirely imaginary) was no more than a prelude to the full-scale denunciation The People's Friend offered the following day as an "Outline Destined for a Portrait of the Jesuit Brissot." It was a scathing character assassination, seething with bitterness against the intrigues and betrayals of an old friend. It stands with Marat's denunciation of Necker as a masterpiece of the genre. "No one has been in a better position than I to see into the depth of his soul," he declared; "I'm going to reveal it today because the dangers to which his gang exposes public safety oblige me to do so." To this effect, he looked back to offer a jaundiced view of a relationship that had once provided him much companionship and support. Brissot, he recounted, was introduced into his laboratory among "the crowd of ignoramuses that besieged me every day," standing out initially as author of a prize-winning essay on the means of ending mendicity in France. It soon became clear that the newcomer was "a schoolboy who had overloaded his memory with sentences taken from several notable philanthropists." Nonetheless, he "appeared to want to do good and that was enough for me to encourage him." In fact, the story that then unfolded seemed to proceed the other way around. "For two years, I had been the object of persecutions by the Academy of Sciences. Having failed to associate itself with the honor of my discoveries, it endeavored to rob me of their fruit, preventing me from announcing even the titles of my works by blocking my access to all the journals." Brissot had undertaken to expose and undo this damage by praising his new friend's discoveries in his *De la vérité*. "Assuredly, I was far from wanting to take pride in the praise he bestowed on me, but those who have read this work must be a bit surprised today to hear the author condemn me in order to laud Condorcet and the other academicians of his ilk he had then decried. If they infer from this that Brissot has always trafficked shamefully in eulogy and defamation, they won't be far from the truth."[68]

There followed an acid inventory of Brissot's readiness to serve whoever was willing to employ him. He had written pornography in Paris for five years; swindled creditors in London with a scheme for a reading room and literary society; cheated Marat himself of proceeds from the sale of his scientific books in England; returned to Paris to spend time in the Bastille; drafted campaign material on behalf of the duc d'Orléans, whom he was soon hired by Lafayette to denounce; and shown himself base and servile, always ready to sell his anger and his talent for calumny to the highest bidder. He had spied for the lieutenant of police for 50 écus a month before the fall of the Bastille, then been blackmailed by Bailly into serving up the plans he and his cronies needed to reorganize municipal government in a way to strip citizens of their rights. All this he had done on the way to becoming a "faithless representative of the people, then agitator for the ministerial faction, then supporter of the despot." Would he now push his villainy as far as to reestablish despotism, Marat asked, or did he merely wish to enrich himself from public spoils and trafficking in the people's interests? "Infamous man! Count your gold, the shameful prize of your base betrayals. It's the only fruit you'll ever gather from so many odious schemes, so many signal deceits. It can doubtless assuage your mad desires, but it can't guarantee you from opprobrium or protect you from the vengeance of the tyrant you'll help to become absolute again. Look at the destiny that awaits you: the hideous truth will come out, the dark web of your perfidies will finally be unveiled. And if the homeland survives its barbarous enemies, your name, abhorred by your fellow citizens, blackened by public opinion, and cursed from age to age, will henceforth serve to characterize a false patriot, a hideous hypocrite, a base conspirator, and the vilest of villains."

One more element remained. "Brissot, you've provoked the new proscription against me that dedicates my head to the blade of tyranny," Marat charged. He was at pains, nonetheless, to deny any base personal motivations in this tirade. "Don't believe that I have lowered myself to vengeance; no petty passion has entered my soul, no personal motive guided my pen. If you were still a private person, I would have kept silent regarding your faults and [been] happy to hold you in contempt. But you are a member of the legislative body, one of the secret agents of the ministerial cabinet, one of the kingpins it is using to annihilate public liberty and reestablish despotism. I've believed it is in the interest of the public to know your life and the depth of your heart."

The challenge that followed surely made clear, though, the deeply personal roots of this passionate denunciation and the profound fusion of the personal and the political in the agonistic politics of the moment.[69] This was a time for settling scores in the name of patriotism and purity. "Do the same to me," Marat taunted Brissot. "Bring my whole life to light, and if there is not enough truth there for you, add all the lies with which the merchants of calumny haven't ceased blackening me since the beginning of the revolution, and be sure that however much you attack my public character, I won't abase myself to repudiate your diatribes. . . . You accuse me stupidly of being the head of a faction, although you're fully convinced that my sole role is to combat them all without exception; and you know full well that the spies and assassins constantly determined to pursue me have forced me to live an underground existence. Ah! If I were leader of a party it would only be the people's. And if the people could have heard me, you would no longer have this reproach to make against me today. The traitors to the homeland and all the villains of your stripe would no longer exist. You accuse me stupidly of selling my pen, just to fend off my charge that you have prostituted yourself to the ministerial cabinet. I have only one word of response. . . . Compare my fortune to yours; you swim in opulence and I'm in poverty."[70]

"If the people could have heard me . . ." There were grounds for despair in this confession of impotence. Four days later, *L'Ami du peuple* bore the headline, "Reasons That Have Finally Decided The People's Friend's Retirement." Brissot, it seemed, would continue rich and corrupt; Marat would retreat poor and pure . . . and angry. "Why persist still in a resistance as vain as it is perilous? All is lost, dear friends of the homeland, all is lost if Louis XVI takes flight, if the people continues to let itself be lulled to slumber by its perfidious mandataries and unless the entire nation rises up together against the henchmen of despotism sworn to return it to its chains. Without a general insurrection, we're forever done for." There followed a litany (continued in a following issue of the journal, its publication delayed until 15 June) of now familiar charges against the conspiracies of the court, the generals, the Assembly, and the Brissotins ("the infamous faction leading the senate"). It continued with a renewed protestation against the muzzling of patriotic writers and the subsidization of hacks willing to defame them, mislead public opinion, and "devote to the triumph of tyranny the very weapons they should be using to protect us from it."[71]

To all this, Marat added some particular indictments. He criticized as beyond the Assembly's powers its decision to dismiss the constitutionally established royal guard and order the arrest of its commander, an action he had previously disparaged as freeing the two thousand royal guards to join the émigrés and return with them to lay Paris to waste. He was particularly outraged, though, by "the latest expression of criminality, covered by the veil of love for the public good and zeal for the triumph of liberty." He meant the proposal of the new Brissotin war minister, Servan, on 4 June, to create an armed camp of twenty thousand soldiers of the

National Guard near Paris for the protection of the capital. The plan had been widely repudiated. It met considerable opposition on the right, from the court and its supporters within the Assembly, and it was denounced on the left by Robespierre in the Jacobin Club. Each side saw it as a profoundly dangerous force to be wielded by its enemies. The general staff of the National Guard, eager to defend its own authority, organized a petition against it, signed by eight thousand of its troops; vigorously decried by the Brissotins, the petition was immediately protested by one delegation of rank-and-file guardsmen, then supported by another, then followed by demands from the sections that the general staff be dismissed for its counterrevolutionary sentiments. "So there's the Parisian guard divided against one another," commented *L'Ami du peuple*; "this was exactly the goal."[72]

To Marat's mind, the plan for an armed camp near the capital amounted to a scheme to bring down on Paris "the dregs of the National Guard, in other words the most hideous enemies of the revolution." It was useless, he insisted, for a city that already included 30,000 active citizens in arms and 150,000 passive citizens capable of bearing them. "How much simpler and more natural to decree that all resident citizens be armed without delay and to order all the armorers of the realm to furnish the necessary supplies immediately to the Paris municipal government?" That such a measure to arm the entire adult male population would contravene the distinction between active and passive citizens already contested in the sections—and that it would have run contrary to the intentions of the court and the counterrevolutionary Assembly—was evident. "Why imagine putting weapons in the hands of a people one wants to decimate, if necessary, to put back under the yoke?" As if the blindness and disloyalty of the Parisian National Guard and the temper of the numerous counterrevolutionaries hiding in the city were not enough, the Assembly leaders' aim was to establish near the capital a camp of twenty thousand men drawn from all corners of the realm. This camp, he had no doubt, was "meant to back up the operations of the counterrevolutionaries of the capital, then those of the national or foreign armies summoned to reestablish despotism."[73] Things turned out very differently.

By the time Marat's issue reporting the debate appeared in print, the decree creating the camp had been adopted by the Assembly on 8 June and sent to Louis XVI for his sanction. The Girondin interior minister Roland had addressed a dramatic open letter to the king two days later, urging him not to delay this approval. It was crucial in this moment of crisis, the minister had written, that the monarch show himself committed "generously and unreservedly" to the constitution. "The Declaration of the Rights of Man has become a political gospel, and the French Constitution a religion for which the people is ready to perish." As enemy forces readied to invade from without, and conspirators waited to join them from within, Roland warned, enthusiasm for the Revolution was mounting. "The state of agitation is extreme in all parts of the empire; there will be a terrific explosion unless a rationally warranted confidence in Your Majesty's intention can finally calm it down." The alternative would be the horrors of civil war. The nation, torn apart, "would develop that dreadful energy that is the mother of virtues and crimes, and always fatal to those who provoked it."

Roland was wagering on the force of truth spoken to the throne. "Just Heaven!" he expostulated. "Could it be that you have struck the powers of the earth with blindness? Will they never have counsels other than those that lead them to their ruin?" Louis XVI responded promptly the following day—by vetoing the creation of the armed camp outside Paris along with a decree of 27 May that had ordered the deportation of refractory priests denounced by as few as twenty active citizens in their locality. Two days later, he ordered the dismissal of the Girondin ministers Roland, Clavière, and Servan, together with their ally in the war effort, Dumouriez.[74] The political landscape had been abruptly transformed.

WHAT IS TO BE DONE?

Outraged by these developments and irritated in addition by news that Lafayette had written a letter to the National Assembly urging suppression of the clubs, members of the most radical sections (Cordeliers notable among them) soon began organizing and publicizing plans for popular protest. On 19 June, a deputation asked the National Assembly for permission to plant a liberty tree at its entrance the following day and to allow demonstrators to march through the hall after doing so. After this request was granted, a thousand sectionnaires met that night to formulate a petition and organize plans for a peaceful show of strength. In the morning of 20 June, thirty thousand marchers converged on the Place Vendôme bearing banners that ranged from "Long Live the National Assembly" to "The Homeland in Danger, Sans Culottes Arise," "Unity, Liberty, Equality," and "Tyrants Tremble." More dramatically, a significant number of the marchers carried crude weapons of various kinds. This was not what the Assembly had been led to expect. Nor did the address presented on behalf of the marchers offer reassurance with its call for the deputies to execute the people's will, its invocation of the right to resist oppression, its assertion that the executive power should be suspended if it blocked the will of the nation, its intimations that blood might have to flow. Only after intense debate and lengthy negotiations over whether armed demonstrators could enter were the marchers allowed to proceed through the hall, "not as 2,000," one thundered for them, "but as 20 million, an entire nation that must arm itself to fight tyrants, its enemies and yours."

Chanting "Ça Ira" and shouting "Down with the Vetoes!" with one of them carrying a calf's head on a pike labeled "Heart of an Aristocrat," another a placard of the Declaration of the Rights of Man, and quite a number of others bearing halberds, pikes, scythes, swords, spits, hatchets, muskets, knives, and pitchforks, the marchers rattled the deputies (particularly those on the right of the hall) by a parade through the Assembly that lasted almost two hours. Leaving the Manège, they turned toward the Tuileries palace, which was now heavily defended by the National Guard. Whether what happened next was planned in advance or improvised in the moment remains uncertain. In any case, as the troops made way for them after some negotiation, the demonstrators flooded into the palace and up the stairs to confront the king, press him back into a window bay, and insist that he withdraw his latest two vetoes and reinstate the Girondin ministers. Forced to wear a liberty cap, Louis XVI nonetheless showed unexpected nerve in refusing to be intimidated into meeting the demonstrators' demands. The crowd was finally persuaded to disperse after two hours.[75]

In the following days, the Legislative Assembly, bitterly divided over what had occurred, was bombarded with letters from across the country protesting or supporting the palace invasion. A petition from Parisians repudiating it claimed twenty thousand signatures. Louis XVI himself issued a defiant proclamation on 22 June that condemned the actions of "a multitude led astray by agitators . . . daringly abusing the name of the nation." He insisted that he would never yield to violence in the exercise of his duties as hereditary representative of the French nation. "To the last moment, the king will give all the constituted authorities the example of the courage and firmness that alone can save the empire," he vowed. "If those who want to overthrow the monarchy need one more crime, they can commit it."

Louis XVI may well have been awaiting liberation by an Austrian or Prussian invasion. He held firm when Lafayette left his army at the front to appear in the capital on 28 June in a spectacularly unsuccessful attempt to intervene on his behalf. After failing to convince the Assembly to prosecute those responsible for instigating the crowd action on 20 June and to suppress the Jacobin Club, the general turned that evening to his former troops in the Paris National Guard. But their loyalty proved weaker than he had anticipated: an improvised plan to rally them in support of the king and against the Jacobins at a military review already scheduled for the following day went awry when the gathering was canceled by Pétion (alerted by Marie Antoinette, who opposed it). That left Lafayette a final option: to spirit the royal family away with him. The offer was declined, and he returned to his army. He was burned in effigy at the Palais Royal the following day.[76]

It would be some time before Marat published his assessment of these events, but when he did so, it was withering. "The Mountain giving birth to a Mouse. General Motier removing His Mask in the Senate and Posturing As a Dictator" headlined *L'Ami du peuple* on 16 July. In essence, Marat deemed the events of 20 June not violent enough. No blood had been shed. The fact that marchers from the radical sections had been armed had saved them from plans by the court and counterrevolutionary elements of the Legislative Assembly to massacre them, he charged. "These citizens had clearly seen this hideous project. After that, can one imagine that they limited themselves to a mere farce?" How, he demanded, could one save from the abyss a people that marched against its enemies with no clear goal; that didn't know what it had to do; that didn't have the common sense to recognize that it could do nothing without leaders, that it could escape the abyss only by ridding itself of traitors to the homeland, that a day would be too short to crush that impious breed?[77]

As for Lafayette's performance, The People's Friend deemed it criminal. A general who abandoned his army in the face of the enemy was a traitor deserving death, he insisted. One as jealous of his reputation as Lafayette had to have been assured by the enemy that no attack would be launched in his absence, which made him a conspirator worthy of the ultimate punishment. Showing up in the Assembly, the general had lifted the constitutionalist mask to speak as master, declare menacingly that he was backed by his troops, threaten the friends of liberty as agitators, and demand the abolition of the patriotic societies and of freedom of the press as a prelude to the reimposition of despotism. He had forewarned the Brissotins of Lafayette's perfidy, Marat claimed. How bitter had to be their regret at making the general all-powerful by declaring war, how deep their humiliation at appearing his playthings if not soon his victims. "The only thing missing in fulfillment of my numerous predictions regarding Motier is to see him bring his army back against the Parisians to annihilate liberty." Everything was ready in Paris for the armed overthrow of the new order, Marat alerted his readers. The entire capital was shot through with counterrevolutionary sentiment; everyone was awaiting the arrival of the Austrians and Prussians to consummate the bloody plans of the court and reestablish despotism in its full force.[78]

What had gone wrong? What was to be done? Between 7 and 16 July,

L'Ami du peuple offered what amounted to an extended reflection on the situation in which the French Revolution now found itself. The style, language, and resonance of some of these pieces make it highly likely that he was engaged in translating *The Chains of Slavery* into French during this period and taking stock of the Revolution against it as he did so. The first, headlined "The Plan of the Revolution Totally Botched by the People," laid down the basic themes. For three years, Marat announced, in now familiar terms, "we have struggled to recover our liberty, yet now we are further from liberty than when we began; we have never been more enslaved." For the people, liberty had become an inexhaustible source of violence, disorder, disasters, and calamities; for the court and its hangers-on, an endless incentive for seduction, swindling, corruption, intrigue, traps, assaults, poisonings, and disastrous conspiracies; for conspirators, a perpetual opportunity for hypocrisy, deceit, intrigue, tricks, venality, baseness, and crimes; for public functionaries, a bountiful field for harassment and oppression; for the legislature, an opportunity for malfeasance, deceit, roguery, perfidy, and tyranny; for the rich and greedy, a chance for illicit gains, monopolies, hoarding, usury, fraud, and plunder, leading to hideous despoliation ruining the people and placing the vast class of the poor between the fear of perishing in misery or the necessity of selling themselves.

How had this disastrous situation come about? At bottom, Marat understood it as a consequence of human nature. "Men have always been tigers toward one another," he wrote, restating his most fundamental conviction. Reflection on the nature of social institutions made it impossible not to recognize that "liberty, like peace, has against it the very inclinations of the human heart, vanity, pride, ambition, avarice, love of advantage and all the vices of self-love," he elaborated. "These vices make men mutual enemies . . . , harassers, oppressors, tyrants . . . , they transform them into tigers one against another. In all times, they have been seen tearing one another apart for bits of gold, for a few corners of the earth. To slaughter one another more ingeniously, they have invented the techniques of combat, glorified their homicidal victories, studied to perfect the rules of mutual destruction. From their differences has come the necessity for laws, from the growth of their ambition the need to give themselves masters to settle their mutual claims. Hence the impossibility of living free and tranquil."[79]

In the French Revolution more specifically, however, The People's Friend also saw several more proximate causes, not least the practice of representation. "Under the old regime, we had as masters the despot, his agents, and his retainers, who despoiled and oppressed us at will, but the law left us our natural defense and allowed us to lodge complaints against them. Under the new regime, the law that should protect us serves only to oppress us. We have no more masters, but we groan under the iron rod of our own mandataries, we're defenseless at the mercy of our own agents. And most horrible of all, they crush us in the name of justice, shackle us in the name of liberty . . . , make our natural defense a crime, prohibit us from protesting, deny us appeal. Thanks to the perfidious institutions of those we've charged with power, we never had so many grounds for complaint against our former tyrants as we have today to cry out against the barbarity of our own delegates." There were echoes of both Montesquieu and Rousseau in this argument. Oppressed under the Old Regime by the king, his agents, and his lackeys, Marat reckoned with Montesquieu, subjects could still find redress by appealing to the justice offered in the courts. In the new regime, he reasoned with Rousseau, citizens were oppressed by laws imposed on them by representatives legislating in the name of a common sovereign will. Liberty had succumbed to the tyranny of representation. "We are further from liberty than ever because we are enslaved in the name of liberty itself." Denunciation of the representatives ran throughout this series of articles.[80]

Cast an eye on the theater of the state, Marat now urged his readers. The scenery had changed, but there were the same actors, the same masks, the same intrigues, the same performances: always a despot surrounded by his henchmen, always vexatious and oppressive ministers, always an iniquitous legislature, always faithless officials, greedy conspiratorial courtiers, petty strivers, shameless intriguers, base hypocrites, adroit rogues, men devoured by lust for gold and deaf to the voice of honor and humanity. While the principal actors were plotting behind the backdrop of this stage, the majority of those out front had already been replaced by others playing the same roles. They too would disappear in their turn to be replaced by others in a sequence of deceit and betrayal that would continue until the people was clear-sighted and courageous enough to end it. "But what could be expected from the people as long as our *moeurs* are unchanged? And what remedy against the chronic contagion infecting all ranks?"[81]

The love of liberty was founded on the love of equality, Marat continued. But that love existed, if at all, in the lowest classes of the people, those disdained and oppressed by all others. What hope was there of achieving or sustaining it in a society like France that was shot through with cupidity and greed, and riddled with egoism, class pretensions, and the lust for power and domination? "The French, of all the peoples in the world, are the least formed to be free," argued the article appearing on 12 July. "Liberty is the privilege of barbarous, rustic, poor peoples," it declared. "It is not made for peoples that are too civilized, for nations corrupted by luxury and pleasure, for men whose only ambition is wealth, power and dignities, who trade their conscience and honor for pounds of gold. How then can one aspire still to summon to liberty an ignorant people degraded by all the vices, grown old in servitude, bent in servitude for thirteen centuries under the yoke of despotism?" Even in nations with customs, character, and energy, there could be no successful revolution unless the people began by naming enlightened, courageous, and virtuous leaders, unless it had a great number of educated and zealous defenders and a multitude of wealthy and patriotic citizens, unless it formed itself as an army, declared eternal war on the enemies of liberty, and rid itself of all the henchmen of despotism. But the French had been stupid enough to listen to false sages, soporificers, charlatans, scoundrels of every kind claiming that the French Revolution was the work of philosophy, that it had to be accomplished and consolidated solely by way of reason. "Instead of crushing the enemies of liberty, we've capitulated to them. . . . We're the only nation in the world to have claimed to consolidate a revolution with empty speeches, parades, festivals and songs."[82]

There was a final reason for the Revolution's failure: "the principal and great reason" deriving from its very character. This had to do with its class basis. Despotism could be overthrown, Marat inferred from the Swiss, Dutch, English, and American cases, when the party opposing the despot was drawn from different social classes. "But this never happens when the plebs, which is to say the lower classes of the nation, are alone in struggling against the higher classes. Crushing everything by its sheer mass at the moment of insurrection, it always succumbs eventually for lack of enlightenment, skills, wealth, weapons, leaders and operational plans because it finds itself defenseless against conspirators possessing . . . all the means that come from education, politics, wealth and authority." Such had been the case in the French Revolution. The nation as a whole had not risen up against the despot; he was still surrounded by his henchmen, the nobility, the clergy, the magistrates, the financiers, the speculators, the savants, the men of letters, and their spawn. Meanwhile, the educated, the better-off, and connivers among the lower classes had turned against the people as soon as they had made use of its force to replace the outlawed privileged orders. "Thus the revolution has been made and supported by the lowest classes of society, the workers, artisans, shopkeepers, farmers, plebeians, by the unfortunates wealthy impudence calls the mob and Roman insolence termed the proletarians. But one would never have imagined its having uniquely served the small landowners, lawyers and operators."[83]

What had gone wrong? Why had the Revolution failed so completely? The deputies should have suspended the despot and his agents from power in 1789, imposed an interregnum until a constitution had been written, and required the king's full acceptance of it on penalty of deposition. Instead, more eager to sell themselves at the highest price, they had proceeded to guarantee the prerogatives of the crown before they had established the rights of the people. Worse, they had returned supreme executive power to the monarch, made him the arbiter of the legislative body, handed him the treasury, and given him command of the military, thus assuring him more effective means of resisting the establishment of liberty and overthrowing the new order. They had stripped the clergy of its property, the nobility of its titles, the financiers of their positions, and the privileged orders of their prerogatives, but allowed these henchmen of the despot to recover position along with him. They had become the buttress of the counterrevolutionaries, the people's mortal enemies.

Had the people known its rights and been able to recognize the perfidy of its representatives, Marat lamented, it would have seen the need to block their misguided actions, arm itself completely, attack its enemies immediately and relentlessly, and reserve to itself the full exercise of its sovereignty by asserting its right to sanction the laws. It was not a mistake to attribute the dire situation of the Revolution in part to the people's ignorance, he allowed. But it was wrong, he now argued, to find reassurance for that situation in the belief that "it is in the nature of things that the march of reason is slow and progressive." (The phrase was Robespierre's, taken out of context from his famous 2 January speech warning against war on the grounds that no one loves armed missionaries.)[84] "There is no progress of reason and enlightenment for the mass of the people. . . . It lacks, and will always lack, the wisdom to uncover the traps set by its enemies. Political deliberations have always been, are, and will remain beyond its capacity. Even supposing the most favorable circumstances, it will never be in a state to analyze a decree, detect what's specious about it, deduce its consequences and anticipate its effects. If an incisive example of this sad truth were necessary, I would say that, despite the eternal speeches of our patriotic societies and the deluge of writings in which we've drowned for the past three years, the people is further from understanding what it takes to resist its oppressors than it was on the first day of the revolution. Then it abandoned itself to its natural instinct, to the simple common sense that led it to the means of bringing its implacable enemies to reason."[85] The plebs could not be enlightened, in Marat's analysis. It had to be aroused, as in the fleeting revolutionary moment of 1789.

Since that day, he insisted, the people had been indoctrinated by a swarm of sophists paid to excuse attacks on its sovereignty in the name of public order, cover assaults on its rights under the mantle of justice, cast measures to destroy it as means of securing its liberty. It had been lulled to sleep by false hopes of liberty, misled by charlatans and conspirators, deceived by public officials, and hoodwinked above all by treacherous representatives. Enchained by the legislators in the name of the law, tyrannized by the authorities in the name of justice, it was "constitutionally enslaved." Renouncing its natural common sense for the perfidious rhetoric of so many imposters, it was now far from recognizing the source of its ills in the fatal decrees that had robbed it of its sovereignty, united all the powers in the hands of the monarch, rendered the Declaration of Rights illusory. It was far from trampling underfoot the monstrous constitution in support of which it was going to be slaughtered on foreign soil. It was far from recognizing that its only means of establishing liberty and ensure its peace was to rid itself pitilessly of traitors to the homeland and drown leading conspirators in their own blood.[86]

What, then, was the last resource of the citizens? Marat asked on 8 July. It was useless to look to the constitution. To assert that it was based on sound principles was like saying that a collapsing building had foundations of marble. Would its unfortunate residents be less likely to be crushed under the ruins? To look to the Declaration of the Rights of Man was fanciful since its principles had already been rendered illusory by a hundred repressive decrees. To imagine a virtuous legislature constraining ministers to execute the law and the monarch to follow the path laid down by the general will of the sovereign was delusory. So was the hope that such a body could lead public opinion toward a better form of government. Where could 750 wise and virtuous representatives be found in a nation debased by subjection and degraded by its vices? As for the call now circulating for a convention to reform the constitution despite its provisions to delay any such change, it was too late for that. It would be as hard to fill a constitutional convention with enlightened men as a legislature, and the crown would surely corrupt it.[87]

Nor, finally, could there be hope for a sustained, ardent, and enlightened civic commitment on the people's part. What did liberty mean for the blind multitude condemned to labor and reduced to a kind of servitude by the fear of starvation? It had to be aroused, not instructed. "From the plebs I only hope for some burst of civic fury like those that have seized it many times." These popular interventions had been constantly repressed by a benighted National Guard, indoctrinated by the rule of blind obedience that some of its members were now beginning to abjure, as in "the glorious scene of 18 April 1791" (when Louis was prevented from leaving Paris for Saint-Cloud). But they had been effective on 14 July and in the October Days of 1789. "So what means are left for us today to put an end to the ills that are crushing us? I repeat, there is only popular executions;

and there will have to be recourse to them after fifty years of anarchy, dissensions and disasters if we resist again at some point the despots sworn against us and wish finally to be free one day. With this difference, that a few drops of blood aptly shed from the beginning would have destroyed the evil at its roots, whereas blood would have to flow in great waves to stop it at last." A variation on Marat's mantra followed: "Taking this salutary step from the beginning would not have cost France a hundred criminal heads. Neglecting it has already cost it more than a hundred thousand innocent heads, the flower of its youth. It would have avoided all internal dissension, all foreign war, the dilapidation of its wealth, the collapse of its trades, the stagnation of its commerce, the loss of its currency, and it would not be threatened today by shameful bankruptcy, the horrors of misery, dearth and civil war, of the general disruption of the state and the subversion of the empire."[88]

The objection was always raised that it would be dangerous to abandon a blind multitude to its fury. But what, The People's Friend countered, was to prevent giving it a clear-sighted, firm, virtuous, incorruptible leader? Where could he be found? "Do you need to ask? You know a man who has been aspiring only to the glory of sacrificing himself to the safety of the homeland. You've long seen his work. But I'd take care to let his disinterestedness be suspected if he could be the object of your choice and if he hadn't himself lost even the hope of serving your cause any longer."[89]

This appeal for power seems at once desperate and defeated. It received no apparent response from the people. With no hope of a tribuneship, Marat had to look elsewhere for decisive intervention to save the endangered homeland. He turned for it to the *fédérés*, the volunteers from the eighty-three departments who had flooded to Paris despite the king's initial veto of the proposal for an armed camp outside the city and as the Assembly summoned them to the capital to celebrate the 14 July Festival.

ON THE BRINK

Marat had become enthusiastic about the arrival of the *fédérés*, as had other Parisian radicals, once it became clear that the contingents called to Paris from the provinces were to be patriotic volunteers from the National Guard rather than deputations chosen by its leadership, and that they intended to remain in the capital to push for decisive political action. He addressed the 18 July issue of *L'Ami du peuple* to them, following it with another two days later. He urged them not to lay down their lives to defend the properties of their oppressors and the privileges of their tyrants, leaving that to the "aristocratic Parisian battalions . . . composed entirely of rich men . . . possessing all the advantages of society and consequently much more interested than you in maintaining the government and repelling the enemy." He denounced Lafayette for his treachery, the generals and ministers for their disastrous conduct of the war, the Legislative Assembly for its failure to overthrow the king, "the principal author of all the disasters about to descend on us," and for awaiting counterrevolution once foreign troops reached the capital they were leaving underdefended. A determined tribune would have made it a priority to round up the despot, the faithless deputies, and the ministers, he argued, confining them by ball and chain and assuring them that their heads would roll at their feet the moment foreign armies crossed the frontiers. Now it was up to the *fédérés* to take action. They had to demand immediate revocation of the most disastrous decrees, including martial law, the distinction between active and passive citizens, the veto, the independence of the deputies, the king's inviolability. They had to arm the people and keep watch on the ministers. But they had one task above all. "Hurry to hold the king, his son, his wife and his ministers hostage. Other measures necessary for the safety of the homeland will follow immediately."[90]

Then, on 22 July, *L'Ami du peuple* again announced "Reasons That Have Determined The People's Friend's Retreat." "Those who have seen me redouble my audacity as the treacherous assembly redoubled its fury against me, as well as the dangers piling up on my head, far from being surprised at my retreat, will be more astonished by my perseverance," Marat now declared. He had sacrificed himself in vain to save his fellow citizens from the abyss, he lamented. "On the triumph of your liberty, it seemed to me, depended that of all the peoples of the world, the happiness of the entire human race. The glory of fighting for so noble a cause inflamed my courage and the grandeur of the interest I had to defend raised me above all fear." His efforts had earned him an ignominious punishment, but he had been more wounded by the base ingratitude of the people and his cowardly abandonment by the patriots. "I don't know what the future holds for me, but all that's left for me today is to flee my enemies, who are also those of the homeland."[91]

Again, though, he was not yet quite ready to put down his pen. He still felt the need to respond to attacks against him. Returning to denunciation of the perfidy of the so-called representatives of the nation, he reiterated that neither the present Assembly nor its predecessor truly represented the body of the people. He invoked the Declaration of the Rights of Man to insist that, since law is only the expression of the general will, the decrees passed by these assemblies had no validity until they had received the sanction of all the members of the state. He protested that the deputies had made it a crime to appeal to the very first of the rights of man, the right of resistance to oppression. What should be done, he demanded, with the current constitution? "Keep its declaration of rights and erase all the rest." And if by some miracle liberty were born amid its ruins, "I have a final offer to make to the homeland, the exposition of all the vices of the constitution and list of all the decrees to reform to assure liberty."[92] Marat always allowed for the possibility of a comeback!

What to make of this latest abrupt announcement that The People's Friend was abandoning his mission? One biographer has suggested the possibility that this 22 July issue of *L'Ami du peuple* might have been intended as a sequel to earlier ones declaring a retreat, its publication delayed for some reason by the printer. There was nothing in this particular issue that tied it to its ostensible date, he has pointed out. And why, he asked, would Marat be ready to give up in this moment of crisis, as so many of the measures he had called for in the course of his journalistic career were being taken?[93]

There are plausible arguments for such a hypothesis. Certainly, Paris was becoming more radicalized by the day. The *fédérés* had been welcomed by the sections and the radical clubs as they came to Paris in early July, and their presence energized the democratic movement throughout the city. By 13 July, they had formed a committee within the Jacobins that denounced Louis XVI. Within four days, they had called (in a petition probably drafted for them by Robespierre) for the king's suspension, a purge of the Paris National Guard, and the indictment of Lafayette. By the end of the month, they had been joined by their most radical contingents, three hundred men from Brest and the five hundred from Marseille who endowed the French Revolution, its armies, and eventually the modern nation with their bloodcurdling marching song. Their arrival increased the total number of *fédérés* to close to five thousand, and their fervor electrified the whole city. They had already formed plans to overthrow the king (postponed at Mayor Pétion's request) before they paraded through the city to enjoy a popular banquet at the Champ de Mars that ended in a riot against men of the National Guard feasting nearby. On 2 August, they petitioned the Legislative Assembly for the king's deposition (and support for their subsistence). On 5 August, they made the Cordelier Club their headquarters.

The sections and the clubs, in the meantime, had become more strenuous in asserting their power and democratizing their membership. Their declarations, petitions, and addresses cascaded over the city and the Assembly in the last weeks of July and into August, though they were far from unanimous in their demands.[94] As early as 28 May the *société fra-*

ternelle had declared itself in permanent session (*en permanence*, generally meaning daily sessions open to the public) and urged the Assembly to decree the same for all sectional assemblies. Its demand was echoed by deputations from a number of sections over the following weeks. On 5 July, the Assembly declared local administrative bodies open to the public permanently but resisted doing the same for the sections until the twenty-fifth. The Gravilliers section had not waited for permission. On 7 July, it used a technicality to begin opening its sessions daily; other sections may have followed suit. On 26 July, the active citizens of the Théâtre-Français section, under Danton's presidency, expressing "repugnance for their former privilege," invited passive citizens resident in the district to participate in its sessions, "share with them the exercise of the portion of sovereignty belonging to the section," and join them as fellow citizens in defending the constitution, the Declaration of Rights, liberty, equality, and all the imprescriptible rights of the people. Other sections were also opened to all male citizens without distinction (and occasionally to women) over the following weeks. By 30 July, the Assembly had authorized passive citizens to join the National Guard (giving them legal access to weapons); on 1 August it had called for mass production of pikes; a day later it had announced that active citizenship would be conferred on all those fighting for the homeland. It had decreed "The Homeland in Danger" on 11 July, the king had issued a proclamation to that effect on 20 July, and the text had been read in public squares the following day. The Revolution needed all its patriotic citizens.

As the active-passive distinction between citizens collapsed, calls for the king's dismissal sharpened. On 22 June, a mass meeting of the Faubourg Saint-Antoine, assembled "without distinction of age, sex or section," drew up a petition for the king's deposition that it plastered on walls throughout the city and circulated among the sections. On 15 July, the Jacobin Club decided on the circulation of an address by Billaud-Varenne on means to save the homeland, the most salient being deportation of the king and the royal family, dismissal of the officer corps, its replacement by nominees of the regiments themselves, and convocation of a National Convention. The latter was to be chosen by direct election in primary assemblies by French men without distinction (the virtues of the poor ensuring elections of Solons and Lycurguses), and its resulting decisions were to be subject to acceptance by two-thirds of the departments to ensure that "the law shall be what it should be . . . the expression of the general will." The same day, the Cordelier Club also resolved to send an address to the *fédérés* urging them to demand that the Assembly call a National Convention, suspend the king and his agents from their functions, strip all members of the ruling dynasty of their pretensions to the crown, and all former nobles of civil and military employment unless granted an exemption on grounds of an exceptional display of patriotic virtue.

The *fédérés* may have been incited by this summons to call two days later for the king's suspension (though Robespierre may have had a hand in the composition of their petition). Robespierre, for his own part, spoke at the Jacobin Club on 29 July in favor of a National Convention elected by all citizens without distinction, though he hedged on the question of suspending or deposing the king and savaged the Assembly with equal contempt. The Mauconseil section, now numbering six hundred citizens after welcoming passive citizens into its ranks, was less hesitant. On 31 July it adopted an address calling on all the other Paris sections and the communes of the Paris department to "forget the law to save the homeland" and unite with it in declaring Louis XVI "no longer king of the French." The address was presented on 4 August to the Legislative Assembly, which annulled it the same day as unconstitutional and contrary to unitary national sovereignty.[95]

By then the threat of invasion had suddenly become more dramatic. An address to the French nation by the duke of Brunswick, commander in chief of the Austrian and Prussian armies now on the borders—the famous Brunswick Manifesto—had been received by Louis XVI on 28 July, with rumors of its arrival already circulating before it was presented to the Legislative Assembly on 1 August and publicized in Paris two days later. It promised an invasion that would reach Paris, demolishing communities that resisted its advance along the way. It required immediate restoration to the king of the full and entire liberty, inviolability, and respect that subjects owed sovereigns by right of nature and of nations. It threatened the guilty with rigorous punishment and the entire population of the city with "exemplary vengeance memorable forever" in the case of the slightest violence against the royal family and its palace.

This manifesto galvanized the city and raised agitation on the streets, already high, to a pitch of intensity. Louis XVI repudiated it as a fake on 3 August, reiterating his commitment to the constitution, the nation, and the war. The reading of this declaration to the Legislative Assembly was soon followed by the appearance of a deputation of a majority of the sections, led by Pétion, that called for deposition of the king, "the first link in the counterrevolutionary chain," and election of a provisional executive council pending the expression of the people's sovereign will by a National Convention. This petition had been drawn up by delegates from the sections who had been meeting daily in City Hall since 25 July. By 3 August, they were acting as a central committee of the sections.[96]

With the *fédérés*, the radicals in the sections had been preparing for an uprising to force the Assembly to take action against the king since the Mauconseil section had proposed it on 31 July. Planned for 5 August, it was held off after Pétion appealed on the evening of 4 August for a postponement until the Assembly had responded to the petition he had presented the day before. It was rescheduled and widely advertised for the night of 9 August. In the meantime, a massive demonstration marched across the city to the Champ de Mars on 6 August to add names to a petition "of a part of the sovereign to its delegates, signed on the altar of the homeland, and presented the day the people will rise up to resist oppression with the sole weapon of its reasons." The signatures filled fifty-five pages. The document itself was long and forceful. "The homeland is in danger," it began; "these terrifying words mean we're betrayed; despotism has only changed form, liberty is still an empty name, the laws are mute and without force; the principles that follow from our declaration of rights are travestied and debased . . . ; the balance of powers is broken, confusion, disorder, criminal impunity, egoism, indifference, and forgetfulness of the virtues threaten us with an impending dissolution of the social body: in this state of things, our sole and unique hope is in resistance to oppression." Three years of perfidies and betrayals had shown a lying, faithless, unpunished king to be the scourge of a free state, the deputies were told. In this final decisive crisis of liberty, "we want to act with you and through you but fulfill the sum of your duties. . . . We have been in a state of revolution for three years; how many conspirators, how many cowards, traitors, perjurers and temporizers we have seen, and the blade of national vengeance has still not fallen."[97]

The Ancients had covered the statues of their gods in times of calamity, the petition concluded. So, now, should a veil be thrown over the Declaration of Rights until grand measures had guaranteed the salvation of the state. Among these measures: a declaration that Louis XVI was deemed to have abdicated the throne; immediate convocation of primary assemblies, elected without further distinction among male citizens, to confirm the king's deposition and choose delegates to a National Convention; a decree of accusation against Lafayette; invigoration of the war effort; recall of the patriotic ministers; purge of the general staffs of the armies and of departmental administrations; loss of civic rights for citizens declared enemies of the public good for failure to take the civic oath; an end to speculation in currency and imposition of severe laws against the "moral assassinations" of hoarding, usury, and monopoly. The deputies had been put on notice.

The following day, 7 August, *L'Ami du peuple* published a third letter to the *fédérés*. Composed on 3 August, it followed Louis XVI in dismissing the Brunswick Manifesto as a fraud (though attributing it to a committee within the Tuileries) but then shredded the rest of the king's declaration to the Assembly that day. "One day, the people will know to render me justice," the king had said. "Oh! it's already rendering you justice in shouting for your destitution and exclusion of your impious dynasty," Marat retorted. "The People's Friend predicted to you ten months ago that you would be cast from the throne within three years. How enchanted I will be to see that he pushed the moment of your fall too far back. Then he suggested making you a big Brie farmer. He's retracting today, ashamed of your hypocrisy and indignant at your crimes." Hold the king hostage, along with his wife, his child, his ministers, all your faithless representatives, all former and current administrators of the Paris department, all the corrupt judges, The People's Friend urged the people: "they are the traitors from whom the nation must demand justice and whom it must first sacrifice to the public good. After that, it will be able to occupy itself with proscription of the shameful Capets and punishment of all the conspirators."[98]

This new timetable was too relaxed. When this issue of the journal was written on 3 August, Marat could not know the immediacy of the plans for insurrection already afoot by the time it appeared in print four days later. Had he in fact been ready to give up entirely and leave the city, as he had announced two weeks earlier? Was his cry of despair on 22 July meant as a declaration of intention or a further dramatization of a critical situation, a strategy to alert the people that a last moment to save liberty was at hand? Perhaps he feared a more calamitous version of the Champ de Mars Massacre—a failed insurrection followed by severe repression of which he could become the victim. Perhaps he was suffering an emotional breakdown. At least one acquaintance, the Marseille radical and future Girondin Charles-Jean-Marie Barbaroux, described him as on the verge of collapse in the weeks preceding the insurrection of 10 August, veering wildly between manic calls for violence and pleas for help in escaping Paris altogether.

Barbaroux recalled in his memoirs that he had studied optics with Marat in the autumn of 1788. In Paris in July 1792 as a special representative of Marseille, he had been invited to visit his former teacher but left their meeting convinced—by the savagery with which Marat expounded the need to slaughter 260,000 men—that he must have "lost his head." They had met on a second occasion, when Marat justified the superiority of daggers over muskets to eliminate the rich, the well-dressed, and theatergoers on the grounds that at least nine out of any ten of them would be aristocrats. This time, Barbaroux recalled, The People's Friend wanted his help to escape Paris for Marseille (disguised as a jockey!). Toward the end of July, he related, Marat had given him the manuscript of an address to print and deliver to the Marseillais; he had found it "abominable . . . a provocation of the Marseillais to exterminate the Legislative Assembly" and had done nothing with it. Throughout the early days of August, even on the evening of 9 August, Barbaroux claimed, Marat was calling on him for help in fleeing Paris for Marseille. The People's Friend was ignorant of the plans for insurrection, Barbaroux sneered, though he later claimed the glory of being its inspiration.[99]

It seems likely nonetheless that Marat learned something of the preparations for the events of 9 August from radical friends who could have kept him informed while he was in hiding, even though he had no direct involvement. Barbaroux reported that he had been led by the Avignon activist Rovère to Marat's hiding place in the home of Jean-Louis-Marie Villain d'Aubigny, who was named to the General Council of the Insurrectionary Commune immediately after 10 August (and subsequently arrested for theft of property looted from the Tuileries palace). He was also invited to meet at the time with Marat's ally Fréron and Etienne-Jean Panis, with whom The People's Friend may also have been in contact via Fréron. Panis was an administrator in the city police department who played an active role in supplying the Marseillais *fédérés* with munitions in the days leading up to 10 August and distributing them to the insurgents more generally on the morning of the actual attack on the Tuileries. Passing immediately to the police department of the Insurrectionary Commune, he reorganized its surveillance committee—to which Marat was added—on 2 September, the very day that began the frightful massacres that stained the history of that month and marked Marat's future career. As for the glory of inspiring the popular insurrection of 10 August, it is suggestive that The People's Friend was honored with a special seat (or *tribune*) from which to observe the proceedings of the General Council of the Insurrectionary Commune, though this honor was only conferred on 23 August for the specific purpose of allowing Marat to produce a journalistic account of that body's decisions.[100]

Barbaroux's memoirs were written several years later. They also seethed with hatred of the monster he had seen Marat revealing himself to be at the time of the September Massacres of 1792 and during the bitter months they had both served in the Convention until the purge of the Girondins forced Barbaroux into hiding. His recollections of Marat in the weeks before 10 August could well be dismissed as a tissue of lies directed against a man he later came to despise. But there are some elements that give them a measure of plausibility. There must have been some talk of flight to Marseille between the two men because Marat, in an exchange of venom in October 1792, claimed that the idea had been proposed to him by Barbaroux rather than vice versa. He had accepted the offer, he related, but had written Barbaroux a letter of reproach when he had heard nothing further from him. Barbaroux had responded with a letter dated 8 August that Marat now printed. He had pleaded too many demands on his time as he struggled to find food for the Marseille battalion of the *fédérés*. "Events are pressing," he had written, "they demand all the activity of men who are devoted to the revolution and hope to preserve liberty in their mountains."[101] This to a man still compelled to remain in hiding.

In the meantime, in the early days of August, as the radicals in the sections planned and petitioned, and the Tuileries palace boosted its defenses with additional troops and aristocratic volunteers, the deeply divided Legislative Assembly had remained indecisive. The Brissotins, having invoked the growing threat of insurrection in a futile effort to pressure the king, now found themselves divided and uncertain over the next step. They dominated the Assembly's so-called Commission of Twelve (expanded to twenty-one in mid-July) to which popular demands had been consistently referred, but found it impossible to reach agreement within that committee on crucial recommendations. A response to popular demands for a decree of accusation against Lafayette misfired on 8 August when the deputies voted 406 to 226 to keep the general in place. The shock in the sections was palpable, but their grounds for anger soared the following day when the Commission of Twelve decided not to decide regarding the king. Arguing the need for extensive further discussion of the complications that would arise from a decision to depose the monarch, the temporizing report Condorcet presented on the committee's behalf was as impeccable in its logic as it was tone-deaf in its politics. All the committee could offer was an address to the people, also composed by Condorcet, laying out the argument that in a representative government no section of the people could assert the sovereignty belonging to the whole.[102] The lecture came too late to reach its intended audience. Closing its session at 7:00 p.m., the Legislative Assembly had run out of time.

INSURRECTION

The tocsin was sounded in the Cordeliers church shortly before midnight on 9 August, and bells were soon tolling in unison across the city. By then the sections had already been in session all evening, with the most radical among them in constant touch as they spurred one another toward concerted action and sent emissaries to motivate the more hesitant or moderate to join them. By 11:00 p.m., apparently at the instigation of the Quinze-Vingts section, it had been decided that each section would send three delegates to City Hall to participate in a central coordinating committee. By midnight, twenty sections had done so. This group set itself up in a room next to the assembly hall from which the elected general council of the municipality was still trying to direct efforts to maintain calm in the face of growing agitation in the streets. Tensions between these two bodies were inevitable. Expanding during the night as more sections sent their delegates, and claiming on their behalf the authority to save the state, the new assembly now surrounded itself with an armed guard. By 6:00 a.m. it had arrested Mandat, the commander of the Paris National Guard who had been reporting to the elected assembly next door on his efforts to mobilize loyal battalions to impose order and defend the Tuileries palace. It then named the radical Santerre to serve in Mandat's stead. That done, announcing that "when the people enters into a state of insurrection, it takes back all powers to resume their exercise itself,"[103] it dispatched the entire constitutionally elected general council of the municipality and took over as an "Insurrectionary Commune." Control of city government and the National Guard was now in insurgent hands. Mayor Pétion was soon placed in custody. Mandat was shot in the head as he was led from the building, the first of many casualties over the next few hours.

By this time, insurgents had already begun breaking into arsenals across the city, distributing weapons over the next hours not only to insurrectionists from the National Guard and the *fédérés* but to the passive citizens joining them who had hitherto been denied the right to bear arms. The radical sectionnaires from the Left Bank, reinforced by the *fédérés* from Brest and Marseille, had also faced down troops defending the bridges across the Seine to reach the place du Carrousel, the open space adjoining the Tuileries palace. There they confronted a force of several thousand gendarmes and guardsmen responding to the call to defend the palace, who were massed in the courtyard with their cannon and reinforced by units of the Swiss Guard. Awaiting comrades from the Right Bank for several hours, the insurgents began to engage with the defenders, eventually convincing most of the gendarmes and guardsmen, and even a few of the Swiss, to leave their positions and change sides.

Inside the palace, negotiations also began between the king and queen and an official of the departmental administration urging them to seek refuge with the Legislative Assembly. Over Marie Antoinette's objections, and only after experiencing an unnervingly mixed reception from some of his defenders when he visited them in the palace courtyard, did a reluctant Louis XVI allow himself and his family to be led surreptitiously through a back door of the palace, across the Tuileries Gardens and into a National Assembly by no means united in eagerness to receive him. Shortly thereafter, Swiss Guards suddenly began firing upon insurgents now in the courtyard, cutting them down and moving into the place du Carrousel to wipe out more. The late arrival of a new contingent of insurgents from the Right Bank served to increase the slaughter on both sides, eventually turning the bloody tide against the Swiss in ferocious hand-to-hand combat, massacring them in the courtyard of the palace and hunting them down through the streets beyond. Over a thousand people died that day, some six hundred of them Swiss Guards, roughly one hundred aristocratic volunteers who had flocked to their king's defense; perhaps as many as four hundred insurgents were killed or wounded.[104]

Before the day was over, with carnage still in the streets and pillage taking place in the Tuileries palace as flames licked at it, the Legislative Assembly issued a decree the Commission of Twelve found finally forced upon it by "events unforeseen by any law." Crucially, it announced that Louis XVI would be suspended from his functions (and kept under guard with his family) until a National Convention had decided the measures necessary to "assure the sovereignty of the people and the reign of liberty and equality." The decree was to be proclaimed immediately in Paris and read in every commune in the country within twenty-four hours of its arrival in the departments. A separate address to the nation, appealing for calm, proclaimed that "today the citizens of Paris have declared to the Legislative body that it is the only authority to retain their confidence."[105] In this, if they actually believed it, the deputies were soon proved wrong.

Marat, for his part, published his own proclamation that day, *The People's Friend to the Patriotic French*. "My dear compatriots, a man who has long made himself anathema for your sake escapes today from his underground hiding place to attempt to secure victory in your hands." He too declared himself worthy of the people's confidence. He had watched out for its safety for the past three years, he insisted, and remained still subject to tyrannical accusations for doing so.[106]

What was Marat's prescription in the meantime, in the wake of the people's triumph on 10 August? More violence. "The glorious day of 10 August can be decisive for the triumph of liberty if you know how to profit from its benefits. A great number of supporters of the despot have bitten the dust, your implacable enemies appear alarmed, but they won't delay in returning to their plots and springing back more terrible than ever." Beware of reaction, he warned. "Give no quarter, then, you're lost without hope of recovery unless you hasten to slaughter the corrupt members of the municipal government, the department, all the antipatriotic judges of the peace and most gangrened members of the national assembly. The National Assembly, I say, and by what destructive prejudice and fatal respect should they be spared?" The call to rally around the deputies, bad though they might be, would be a disaster, The People's Friend predicted. "Consider the assembly your most formidable enemy.... Remember the Champ de Mars."

Other prescriptions followed: declare that the king's head would roll at his feet if the Austrians and Prussian forces had not retreated from French soil within a fortnight; lock up the ex-ministers; punish the counter-revolutionary leaders of the Parisian National Guard and disarm the corrupt battalions; revoke the decree absolving Lafayette; expel the foreign regiments that had supported the king; demand a convention to be elected directly by primary assemblies; put a price on the heads of the fugitive, traitorous Capets. "Tremble, tremble to lose a unique opportunity that France's guardian spirit has arranged for you to get out of the abyss and ensure your liberty."

Above all, though, Marat celebrated 10 August with a familiar refrain. "No one abhors the shedding of blood more than I. But to prevent making it flow in waves, I urge you to shed some drops.... If you hold back, consider that the blood shed today will be a total loss and you will have done nothing for liberty." The people, he was sure, had unfinished business.[107]

TWENTY-THREE

THE MONSTER AND THE MOUNTAIN

The revolution of 10 August left the nation's institutions in disarray. As Marat had predicted, the machine of government fashioned in 1791 had proved unworkable. With the convocation of a National Convention imposed by insurrection, power in France was rendered provisional. Suspending Louis XVI from his functions, the Legislative Assembly transferred executive authority to a provisional executive council. But the Assembly itself, discredited by its failure of political will in response to popular demands, found its own position undermined by the collapse of the constitution under which it existed. Its claim to speak for the entire nation was further weakened among radical Parisians by the fact that its election had been based on the discredited distinction between active and passive citizens. And, above all, its authority as the sole legitimate representation of the sovereignty of the nation was challenged by the emergence of a body claiming a direct warrant to exercise a revolutionary popular will.

In Paris, where the future of the Revolution was for the moment being played out, the new power was the insurrectionary municipal assembly created by the delegates of the sections in the hours preceding the attack on the Tuileries palace. Designating itself initially as "*Commissaires* Meeting at City Hall to Save the Homeland," or "Municipality of Paris. *Commissaires* of the Majority of the Sections Meeting with Plenary Powers to Save the State," this revolutionary body displaced the constitutionally elected municipality and transformed itself on 10 August into an emergency city government. Although the language of its claims was not entirely stable (another document spoke of "representatives of the 48 sections of the capital, with plenary powers"), the preference for *commissaires* over *représentants* was meant to convey that its members were executing the immediate will of the people as expressed in the Paris sections. The deputies of the nation in the Legislative Assembly, selected through indirect processes of election, now faced directly mandated agents of popular will in the General Council of the new Insurrectionary Commune. Institutional struggle, inevitable between these two bodies with competing claims to sovereignty, was further embittered by rivalries and resentments between the Brissotins dominating the Assembly and Robespierre and his allies who soon assumed leadership in the Commune.[1]

The Assembly, while disputing the legitimacy of the Insurrectionary Commune, was nevertheless forced to recognize it as a fact on the ground rendered all the more powerful by a collapse of the administration of the department of Paris on 10 August. Robespierre made the point exquisitely clear on 12 August, speaking on behalf of a deputation from the Commune that challenged the Assembly's intention to re-create the departmental administration. "The people, forced to watch out itself for its own safety, has provided for its security through delegates," he warned. "Since it is obliged to deploy the most vigorous measures to save the state, the magistrates it has chosen must have the entire plenitude of power appropriate to the sovereign. If you create another power that dominates or balances the authority of the direct delegates of the people, then the popular force will no longer be unitary and there will be an eternal source of division in the machine of your government that will foster guilty hopes in the enemies of liberty. It will be necessary for the people to arm itself again in vengeance to save itself from this power destructive of its sovereignty." The Assembly backed down, neither for the first nor last time, in the face of this threat of further popular violence. It had already capitulated, moments earlier, to the demand for the transfer of the royal family to the custody of the Commune, which imprisoned them under the maximum security offered by the medieval fortress known as the Temple.[2]

The deputies of the nation could thus only watch as the Insurrectionary Commune and the sections, meeting in permanent session, assumed police powers in the capital. In the immediate aftermath of the uprising, the Commune directed efforts to reimpose order and clean up the mess. Continuing outbursts of violence had to be ended, prisoners secured, bodies cleared away, pillage stopped, loot from the palace sorted and stored, fallen patriots honored. The city was illuminated by night; movement in and out strictly controlled. But none of these efforts diminished the agitation that continued to surge throughout the city. Demands for immediate vengeance against traitors who had shed the people's blood on 10 August swirled through the streets. Rumors of royalist plots to liberate the imprisoned monarch fed panicky reports of lack of security in prisons teeming with conspirators. Expectations that Lafayette would march troops on the capital to reinstate the monarch resonated with fears of the devastating invasion promised by the duke of Brunswick.

In response, the General Council of the Insurrectionary Commune and its surveillance committee, along with similar committees created in turn by the radical sections, fostered a reign of terror that lasted for weeks. Symbols of monarchy were destroyed or defaced across the capital; statues torn down. Circulation of royalist newspapers was forbidden, "poisoners of public opinion" responsible for them were ordered arrested on 12 August, and their presses confiscated the same day for the use of "patriotic printers." From 14 August, letters of persons suspected of conspiracy were opened and suspicious ones sent for further scrutiny to the Commune's Surveillance Committee. Over the following days, the signatories of the recent "anticivic" petitions—the eight thousand who had opposed the decree of 8 June summoning *fédérés* to defend the city and the twenty thousand who had protested the invasion of the Tuileries palace on 20 June—were declared "unworthy to exercise public functions" along with many other suspects. The Assembly did its part by indicting Feuillants who had served as advisers or ministers of the king. Prisons were visited by committees from the Commune and the sections to release persons who had been incarcerated for offenses against the king, the royal family, and the constitution, replacing them with former officials and other suspects identified as enemies of the people. Refractory priests were rounded up and pressure for their more rigorous punishment increased. On 23 August, by order of the Legislative Assembly, they were required to obtain passports and leave the country within fifteen days; on 26 August, at the urging of the sections, deportation to French Guyana was made the penalty for their failure to comply.[3]

Marat left no doubt as to where he stood in the struggle between the Assembly and the Commune. When *L'Ami du peuple* reappeared on 13 August, he was utterly contemptuous of deputies who had sworn their firm fidelity to Louis XVI at 10:00 a.m. on 10 August and had declared themselves stalwart defenders of the people by noon. And he was among many Paris radicals to denounce the Assembly's decision, in convoking the National Convention, to perpetuate the indirect, two-step electoral process so "fatal to a good choice of deputies." Electoral assemblies were easy to corrupt, he maintained, primary assemblies almost impossible. The homeland would be done for if the delegates to the National Convention were not chosen directly by the body of the people, with former deputies and privileged persons excluded from eligibility.[4]

This issue of *L'Ami du peuple* put the Legislative Assembly on notice. The deputies could not command the people's confidence with "cowardly fawning and jugglers' gimmicks," Marat warned; their acts since 10 August had been almost entirely "new tricks, new treachery." Most egregious among the latter were efforts to dissolve the Insurrectionary Commune and restore the constitutional one along with the judges and the departmental administration. Such an action, "far from permitting the people to deploy its force and exercise its justice against the traitors sworn to destroy it, would repress it and enchain it to have it slaughtered."[5]

There followed, in counterpoint, a paean of praise, and a grave caveat, for the delegates in the Insurrectionary Commune. "Oh You, worthy *commissaires* of the Paris sections, true representatives of the people, beware of the traps offered you by its faithless deputies, beware of their seductions. . . . Rest in place for our peace, for our glory, for the safety of the empire. Don't quit the helm of public authority that has been returned to your hands until the National Convention has rid us of the despot and his despicable race, reformed the monstrous vices of the constitution that have been a never-ending source of anarchy and disasters, and secured public liberty on unshakeable foundations." For that to be achieved, Marat cautioned, the Commune had to get the deadly electoral decree for the Convention revoked. "Enlighten the people, convoke all the sections on this subject, let it deploy its power and dispatch to the tomb the criminals who dare to scheme anew and oppose its happiness."[6] Talk of enlightenment slipped easily here into a call to slaughter.

Two days later, praising the vigor with which the Commune had already secured the royal family, suppressed counterrevolutionary publications, and was tracking down public enemies, *L'Ami du peuple* offered a checklist of additional measures to be taken to secure the people's victory. The Commune had to arm the good citizens of Paris and train them to use their weapons against desperate enemies; hasten the formation of an armed camp to defend the capital; press for justice against the prisoners in the Abbaye prison and the officers of the Swiss Guards; push for the sale of the most luxurious properties of the émigrés, distributing half the proceeds to the disadvantaged who had joined the attack on the Tuileries; urge the troops to demand the right to elect their officers; fire up the administration of food supplies and declare war on hoarders. And it had to keep up its energetic political pace until the National Convention assembled to reform the constitution. This program once achieved, Marat promised, he would regard public safety as assured, sleep soundly at night, and write by day only to contribute to the remaking of the constitution. But again, before that could happen, there was blood to be spilled. The people, once awakened, could not allow itself to relapse into slumber. "The homeland has just been pulled back from the abyss by shedding the blood of the revolution's enemies. If the blade of justice finally strikes the schemers and prevaricators, I won't be heard talking any more about popular executions, the cruel resource that only the law of necessity can impose on a people reduced to despair, and that the deliberate slumber of the laws always justifies."[7]

By 19 August, when *L'Ami du peuple* next hit the streets, one question had become paramount in Paris: the fate of the traitors who had betrayed the nation on 10 August, and especially that of the Swiss Guards who had opened fire on the people in the courtyard of the Tuileries palace that day. "Sovereign people, suspend thy judgment," the Commune had declared on 11 August; "justice lulled to sleep will today recover its rights, all the guilty will perish on the scaffold."[8] But that justice, in the form of a special tribunal, had been slow in coming as the Assembly and the Commune argued over its potential character and scope. Marat was convinced the deputies were dragging their feet on this issue in the hope that Lafayette would return to wipe clean the revolutionary slate. (This threat disappeared the night of 19 August when the general, unable to incite his army to counterrevolution, emigrated with his general staff and was arrested by the Austrians.)

At first the Assembly wanted only a court-martial judging military suspects, the Commune a comprehensive court to try all offenders. Pushed to abandon its plan for a court-martial, the Assembly then moved to institute a tribunal with prosecutors and juries drawn from the sections but presided over by established judges subject to constitutionally established procedures. This decision, in turn, was assailed by Robespierre, speaking again for a deputation from the Commune on 15 August. The scope of the inquiry could not be limited to the events of 10 August, he argued. The people's vengeance had to encompass earlier and broader betrayals that had led to those events. Nor could popular justice be subject to judges in whom there was no longer confidence or to the delays of an appeals process. "The people is resting," the Incorruptible cautioned the deputies, "but it is not asleep. It wants punishment of the guilty, and with reason. You must not give it laws contrary to its unanimous will. . . . We demand that the guilty be judged by *commissaires* of the people, sovereignly and in the last resort."[9]

The threat of a new uprising over this issue was soon made explicit. On 17 August a municipal officer protested on behalf of the Commune that the juries were ready but there were still no judges in whom the people could have confidence. The tocsin would sound that evening at midnight, he warned the Assembly; the people, tired of waiting for vengeance, would administer justice itself. Jurors already chosen by the sections then appeared to urge the deputies to break free of the old jurisprudence. "Rise up, representatives," they cajoled. "Be great like the people in order to deserve its confidence and remember this truth: 'When the schoolboy is bigger than the master, it's too bad for the master.'" Taking the point, the Assembly moved immediately to set up a tribunal with two panels, allowing the sections to choose judges (and other court officials) whose decisions would be final, but requiring that these judges be elected by a two-stage process and have prior judicial or legal experience.[10]

Repudiating these provisions on 19 August, Marat offered advice to the people in a notorious pronouncement that would haunt him for the remainder of his political life. "But what is the duty of the people?" he expostulated. "There are only two options." The first allowed the barest measure of patience: "to press for judgment of the traitors detained at the Abbaye [prison], surround the criminal tribunals, and massacre the traitors if they are acquitted, without regard for the new tribunal and the criminals responsible for the perfidious decree." But the second option, "the surest and wisest," was to take more immediate action: "to march in arms to the Abbaye, drag out the traitors, especially the officers of the Swiss and their accomplices, and put them to the sword." This measure, he reasoned, would simply execute a judgment already delivered. "What madness to want to put them on trial. It's already been done. You took them with their weapons in hand against the homeland, you massacred the soldiers, why spare their officers who are infinitely more guilty? It was stupid to have listened to those who wanted to put you back to sleep and make them prisoners of war. They are traitors who should have been slaughtered on the spot." These words were remembered a few weeks later, after crowds had stormed the prisons and butchered hundreds of inmates. And the argument that the people's judgment on 10 August required no further validation in court would be redeployed by the Jacobins when it came to putting Louis XVI on trial.[11]

Such language must have fallen on receptive ears in the General Council of the Commune because Marat was given a special seat in its assembly from which to report its decisions. His reports never appeared, but that same day, 23 August, armed with an order from the Commune's Surveillance Committee and over the protests of the director of the Imprimerie Nationale, he also took possession of four superb presses and a variety of fonts and printing equipment from that institution housed in the Louvre. The presses were installed in the premises of the Cordeliers, close to the new apartment on the same street that The People's Friend would share with Simonne Evrard. She would continue to use them after his death until they were reclaimed from her by the Convention in 1795.

In the short term, though, The People's Friend needed to pay for the paper and ink necessary for the extensive publishing projects he still had in hand. A possible source was funding for patriotic publications at the disposal of Roland, minister of the interior, to whom Marat applied with support from his ever-faithful local section of the Théâtre-Français, now renamed in honor of the Marseillais. Its effusive endorsement, signed among other noted radicals by Danton, president of the section but also Roland's rival in the Executive Council as minister of justice, failed to loosen the minister's purse-strings. It would be an understatement to say that Marat's brand of patriotism was not to Roland's taste—they would engage in open battle over the following months—or to his wife's. Mme Roland later recalled submission of "a hodgepodge of manuscripts" (including a French version of *The Chains of Slavery*) "the very sight of which inspired fear." The aggrieved author offered a different version of his treatment by the minister when he appealed publicly for similar funding to the duc d'Orléans—with fulsome praise and invoking the cause of the sans-culottes to the prince claiming the title Philippe Egalité—though with little apparent success. In his telling, Roland had terminated the matter by disingenuously requiring that members of the applicant's section offer an evaluation of the manuscripts to be printed. "This was to refer me to the calends of March, or to the Last Judgment, given the magnitude of the works and the multitude of affairs with which my section was burdened."[12]

Marat's appeal to the duc d'Orléans was one of a series of eight placards he had plastered around Paris while he temporarily suspended publication of *L'Ami du peuple*. "Let's hasten to arm ourselves and not let ourselves be surprised by our enemies," the journal had exhorted its readers on 19 August. "Up, Frenchmen who want to be free, Up, Up, and let the blood of the traitors begin to flow." Now, with the Prussians advancing, Marat opted for posters to be pasted up more urgently in the city streets: a medium of communication adapted to gain more immediate attention in what had rapidly become another moment of crisis. The first of the series, *The People's Friend to the Brave Parisians*, had appeared on 26 August, the day the city was struck by alarm at news that the frontier fortress of Longwy had surrendered to the Austrian and Prussian invaders as they marched toward the capital. The bill-poster, making his rounds, was caught in a political brawl as he plastered a copy of the placard on the door of the church of Saint-Germain on 27 August. He was brought before the police somewhat the worse for drink.[13]

In a fervently patriotic call for total mobilization of the citizenry, *The People's Friend to the Brave Parisians* urged citizens of the capital to unite to save their homes from pillage by the despotic foreign hordes, their women from the brutality of a ferocious soldiery, their children from the shame of enslavement, their own lives from the assassins' sword. The city was done for, it cried, if the friends of liberty, the men of the National Guard and the brave sans-culottes trained to handle weapons, did not rush to march against the enemy, if the heights around the capital were not immediately made defensible. Citizens had to be summoned by the Commune that very evening, under pain of death, to turn in any weapons. *Commissaires* had to be named to search the houses of suspects. Armorers and cutlers had to forge pikes and daggers. A special warning for the wealthy urged them to join their fellow citizens in the common defense lest the invaders arrive to pillage their houses first.

Was this, finally, the moment for the dictatorship The People's Friend had so often demanded? Perhaps, this time, there could be a triumvirate of the most enlightened, virtuous, and intrepid men, coordinating all their measures in a council of the most judicious and purest patriots? "Don't be frightened by words," the acrobatic wordsmith now begged, having made a career with his terrifying language! "It's by force alone that one can make liberty triumph and assure public safety." To guarantee their good conduct, an emergency council could have all power necessary to crush the enemies of the Revolution and none to oppress their fellow citizens; their mission would end the moment the enemy ceased to resist. "For so many centuries, you've allowed insolent masters to exercise an arbitrary rule over you to destroy you," Marat now argued. "Will you refuse the most virtuous of your brethren the same rule to save you?"[14] Despotism reclaimed by virtue to secure liberty: this would become a fertile trope for a future Terror.

But panic, not virtue, was the order of the day in Paris following the fall of the fortress of Longwy to the Prussians. Immediately on hearing the news, the Assembly ordered a levy of 30,000 men to march to the frontier. The Commune, responding the next day to fears that this measure would strip the capital of its most energetic defenders against enemies who were biding their time within the city walls, ordered that suspects be identified, disenfranchised, and disarmed by the sections. The house searches Marat had urged for this purpose were probably already under way by the evening of the 28 August, when Danton called on the Assembly as minister of justice for a decree authorizing them. "Everything belongs to the homeland when the homeland is in danger," he declared on behalf of the Executive Council. There were eighty thousand muskets in Paris, he estimated, weapons that had to be sent to the frontier. The decree passed at his instigation required municipalities throughout the country to carry out house-to-house searches to root out weapons. In Paris, the sections were ordered to elect thirty *commissaires* each to begin the searches immediately, confiscate hidden arms for redistribution in defense of liberty and equality, and declare suspect those who had been concealing them. The searches went on for several days, day and night, while the capital's gates remained closed. The yield was in the hundreds of weapons rather than the many thousands Danton had anticipated, but there was a bounty of some four score refractory priests discovered and imprisoned.[15]

At precisely this moment of crisis, vexation at the Commune's perceived abuses of power boiled over in the Legislative Assembly. The deputies had received an increasing number of protests against the tyranny of the General Council, including several from sections opting to withdraw their delegates from that body entirely. Resentment surfaced on 30 August when Roland informed the Assembly that "the provisional representatives" of the Commune had disrupted plans to provide subsistence for Paris by purging the municipal administration. "They disorganize everything, they obstruct everything," complained one deputy, René-Pierre Choudieu, invoking opposition in the sections to the Commune's usurpations. "It's composed of *commissaires* who were charged to coordinate actions relating solely to the events of the Tenth [of August]. On the contrary they set themselves up as a municipality, they've suspended the mayor from his functions, they permit themselves arbitrary acts, they want to upend everything."

Choudieu soon offered a more specific grievance regarding the treatment of Jean-Marie Girey-Dupré, ally of Brissot and editor of *Le Patriote français*, who had been summoned to appear before the General Council to answer a charge of publishing a false report of the Commune's order for house searches. Perhaps remembering the fate of the royalist editor of the *Gazette de Paris* who had been sent to the guillotine on 25 August, Girey-Dupré had refused to appear before the Commune and appealed to the Assembly against a reprisal he denounced as a tyrannical usurpation of authority, an arbitrary attempt by the council to judge in its own cause, an attack on freedom of the press, and an infringement upon his individual rights. When the Assembly responded by summoning the president and secretary of the General Council to explain the Commune's action in this case, their failure to comply provoked some of the deputies to explode against that body's dictatorship. Faint excuses on behalf on the officials who had failed to appear were met with outrage. Why this persecution of an individual citizen when the entire city was plastered with placards "calling for the blade against the National Assembly," objected Reboul. By whom were the posters signed? it was demanded. "They're signed, *Marat*," Reboul retorted. "To those who are fearful of an uprising in the capital I say that there will be a great uprising in the departments that will quash the one in the capital," he exclaimed to applause. "The people knows that its sovereignty is not that of some individuals but of France in its entirety, that the will of France can only be expressed by the assembly of its representatives."[16]

The Assembly proceeded to annul the General Council's summons to Girey-Dupré as a violation of individual liberty and the rights of the press, but in fact the deputies had already decided on a more radical measure against the Commune. Earlier on 30 August, "considering that complaints have been raised against the powers of the provisional *commissaires* of the commune of Paris, and that some sections had already revoked their *commissaires*," they had ordered the sections to elect two delegates each to replace the members of the existing General Council in its entirety, serving provisionally in their stead until new municipal elections had taken place. Sole control of police power in the capital was to be restored to Pétion as mayor, and the municipal body displaced on 9 August was to be reinstated in its functions.[17]

Against this attack, the Insurrectionary Commune remained firm. It had already prohibited sections from withdrawing their delegates without proof of individual negligence or wrongdoing. After an all-night session, resisting Robespierre's call for an appeal to the sections to reassert the people's power more directly, it decided to send a deputation to address the Assembly on the morning of 31 August. Backed by a crowd gathered outside the hall, the deputation's spokesman, Tallien, reasserted the Commune's claim to unlimited powers granted by the people on 9–10 August and invoked the record of the actions it had taken to save the homeland. He demanded that its delegates remain in place until the people had chosen their successors by vote of the primary assemblies in the elections now under way. The president of the Assembly was equally firm in responding that the Commune was illegal, its existence a provisional response to extraordinary and perilous circumstances that no longer obtained. Did the deputation want the spectacle of a commune in rebellion against the general will to discredit the Revolution before the whole world? he declaimed. Would France allow the capital to invest a provisional body with dictatorial authority, thus threatening the nation's unity, evading its law, and rivaling its representative assembly? The deputation departed empty-handed; the crowd was rebuffed. But the General Council held on to its power.[18]

THE SEPTEMBER MASSACRES

The Assembly was still considering further measures to weaken the Commune when news reached Paris late on 1 September that Verdun, the last fortress blocking the way to the capital, was under siege by the invaders. "To arms . . . Citizens . . . to arms, the enemy is at our gates," the General Council thundered the following morning as it sounded the tocsin and decreed emergency measures to mobilize citizens for the front, redistribute weapons from those unable to march, and confiscate arms instantly from suspects or other persons unwilling to share in the common defense. As the delegates to the Commune were spreading out to arouse their home sections to the imminent dangers now faced by the homeland—and to the treasons with which they were more intimately surrounded—Danton was urging the Assembly to transform itself into a war council. "We need audacity, more audacity, audacity always, and France will be saved," was his memorable patriotic cry as he rallied his fellow deputies to direct "this sublime movement of the people." He also demanded death for those citizens who refused to serve or turn over their weapons.[19]

Within the city, audacity turned into terror that same evening as crowds fell on prisoners being transported to the Abbaye prison, then invaded the prison itself and began slaughtering inmates.[20] Frustration had grown among the population as the revolutionary tribunal created on 17 August had proven slow to send the people's enemies to the newly installed guillotine. The accelerating tempo of house visits and the roundups of suspects in the days following the fall of Longwy had fed fears that overcrowded prisons were being primed by conspirators to explode into counterrevolutionary fury. With Verdun now under siege, too, the surge of patriotic energy directed against the invaders found its dark counterpart in a savage impulse to forestall the possibility that prisoners would break out and bring desolation and death to the capital as soon as its most vigorous defenders had left for the front. There was no other way to foster the zeal of those preparing to leave for Verdun than to "get prompt justice, imposed on the spot against all the evildoers and conspirators detained in the prisons," proclaimed the Poissonnière section. Its declaration was immediately circulated to the other forty-seven sections.[21]

Once triggered on the evening of 2 September, paroxysms of popular fury swept through Paris as massacres spread from prison to prison over the next several days, accounting for perhaps as many as thirteen hundred to fourteen hundred deaths (almost half of the total prisoner population). Members of the Assembly and the Commune sent to halt or restrain these executions proved powerless to do so (and may in some cases have ended up

FIGURE 23.1. Anonymous print, "Révolutions de Paris," 1792. Massacres at the Conciergerie and Bicêtre prisons, September 1792. Bibliothèque nationale de France, Gallica Digital Library.

participating themselves in the exercise of revolutionary popular justice). The disorganized National Guard proved unable to intervene as a body, with many of its individual members apparently joining in the slaughter along with *fédérés* from Marseille and Brest remaining in Paris. In some instances, pop-up tribunals interrogated and passed judgment on individuals, in others popular justice was more indiscriminate. The victims included nobles, priests, and other suspected counterrevolutionaries, royal guards, and officers and men of the Swiss regiments who had defended the Tuileries palace on 10 August. Common criminals feared as desperate and dangerous, and as potential fodder for counterrevolutionary mobilization, made up a substantial majority. The popular executions for which Marat had so often called had finally taken the form of the bloodbath that would be remembered as the September Massacres. His name was indelibly tarnished by its memory.

Not without reason, though the exact nature of his implication in these hideous events has long been debated. Early historians of the massacres, replicating recriminations by contemporaries, charged him with direct responsibility for inciting the bloodshed. Later ones have noted that he was not alone in demanding the exercise of popular justice against the people's enemies in the weeks following 10 August, and that no single voice can credibly be blamed for an upsurge of almost instinctual popular anger in a profound moment of crisis. Nonetheless, it is hard to discount the power of Marat's words even as it is impossible to gauge the full force of their influence at this juncture. He bore a moral responsibility, if not a demonstrably immediate one. It is also the case that, though he was never himself present in the prisons as the massacres took place, he ended up endorsing them in dramatic terms.

He did so, remarkably, in his first official position in a revolutionary government—as a member of a new Surveillance Committee of the Commune created after the existing one had been disbanded on 30 August. Threatened by the Assembly, the General Council had apparently decided to tighten its organization by replacing a committee that had become overgrown, chaotic, and dysfunctional. The task of renewal had been assigned to Marat's radical friend Panis, one of the enablers of the assault on the Tuileries palace, who immediately recruited three other police administrators with whom he had served since before 10 August. That core group, now constituted as a "committee of police and surveillance," named adjunct members to share, under their direction, the responsibilities they faced in the critical circumstances of the moment. The most notable of these adjuncts was listed as "Marat, the people's friend." The document, signed at City Hall by the four police administrators, was dated 2 September.[22]

Thus, in a bizarre twist, Marat was added to a committee with police powers the very day the prison massacres began. "A man that the thirst—the inextinguishable thirst—for crimes and blood ceaselessly tormented! What, Marat? Yes, Marat! Yes, to assure the massacre of a greater number of victims, Panis resurrected Marat," howled the Brissotin deputy Louvet when the struggle over an accounting came several weeks later.[23]

The precise nature and purpose of Marat's membership in this Surveillance Committee have been much debated. The fact that his name appeared in a marginal note to the document constituting the committee led one of the earliest (and most hostile) researchers to conclude that The People's Friend must have pushed his way into the group at the last moment with the intention of dominating it and organizing the bloodshed over the next few days. Since the marginal note also included the name of a second adjunct, and at least one other was omitted from the document entirely, it seems more likely to have been a hasty correction of an error of omission than evidence of forced entry. The possibility of prior planning cannot be absolutely precluded. But the committee, though apparently in preparation over several days, was constituted too close to the outbreak of the massacres, in any case, to make convincing the view that Marat had joined it, or had even been recruited by Panis and company, for the explicit purpose of organizing the violence in the prisons. It makes more sense to ask how the committee responded to these dreadful events as they occurred.

Marat later stated that, at first news of the massacres, his instinct, shared with Panis, was to save poor debtors, individuals imprisoned for riot, and petty offenders. By his account, the committee ordered jailors to segregate these prisoners from major criminals and counterrevolutionary traitors, and they were subsequently released as a result of the attentiveness of an acting people's judge—"attentiveness that the despot surely would not have had if he had triumphed on 10 August." This seems to be an admission that the Surveillance Committee attempted to limit the slaughter to some extent, but made no effort to censure it or stop it entirely. Its members were not about to second-guess the summary justice handed down in the name of the people, nor could they hope to arrest a torrent of popular fury. Indeed, a document published in their name went so far on 3 September as to urge the example of the bloodshed in Paris prisons upon municipal authorities throughout the nation. This notorious *Circular of the Committee of Surveillance of the Paris Commune* bore the signatures of "the administrators of the committee of public safety and the adjunct administrators together . . . constituted by the Commune and meeting at City Hall." The title appropriated for the group is worth emphasizing. Jean-Paul Marat, having aspired to exercise the dictatorial authority of a tribune of the people, now signed his name as a member of an official "committee of public safety."[24]

Addressed to "Brothers and Friends" throughout the nation, the *Circular of the Committee of Surveillance* began by rehearsing the story of the month-long conflict for power in the capital. The Insurrectionary Commune, in this account, had been "forced by cruel necessity to seize back the power of the people to save the nation" from a conspiracy involving a great many deputies to the Legislative Assembly. It had nonetheless been suppressed by this same Assembly "for its burning citizenship" at the very moment that new plots were surfacing. Public outbursts having forced the Assembly to withdraw its decree, the Commune would continue to exercise its power until the homeland had nothing more to fear from the ferocious hordes advancing toward the capital. Only at that point would it hasten to resume a status equal to the smallest commune in the state.

This narrative brought the committee's circular to its central purpose: to inform communes throughout the country that "some of the ferocious conspirators detained in the prisons had been put to death by the people in acts of justice it deemed indispensable to constrain by terror the legions of traitors hidden within its walls at the moment that it was going to march against the enemy." There could be no doubt, the circular continued, that other communes would want to follow this example. "Doubtless the entire nation, after a long sequence of betrayals that have brought it to the brink of the abyss, will hasten to adopt this means so necessary for the public safety, and all the French will cry out like the Parisians: we're marching toward the enemy, but we will not leave these brigands behind us to slaughter our children and our wives."[25] Recipients were urged to reprint the message and circulate it to all the municipalities in their district. In effect, this was a summons to mass slaughter.

Few if any of Marat's fellow signatories acknowledged authorship of this document later. Even Panis denied having seen it before publication. Whether or not it had been Marat's idea initially, its language suggests that he took the lead in writing it. Its typography has also been shown to match that of a subsequent issue of *L'Ami du peuple*, making it likely that he was responsible for getting it printed (though Duplain, another committee member, was also a printer by trade). Michelet's speculation that, having composed the circular, The People's Friend arbitrarily inserted the signatures without his colleagues' knowledge or permission seems significantly weakened by the fact that two names were omitted (including that of Guermeur, later imprisoned as a fervent Maratist). One striking fact makes it certain that others were involved, at least in the circulation of the document: it was distributed under the seal of the ministry of justice, hence stamped with official authority and mailed free of charge. There is no further evidence to implicate Danton as minister of justice in this matter, as later charged. The leading historian of the massacres, Pierre Caron, while far from absolving the minister, pointed to the more likely involvement of his secretaries, Camille Desmoulins, François Robert, and most specifically Philippe-François Fabre d'Eglantine. A minister, after all, rarely takes care of the stamps![26]

The circular, Caron also suggests, may have had little immediate impact. How far it radiated in the provinces, how rapidly, and to what effect remains unclear. But its existence became a crucial weapon in the broader struggle over responsibility for the September Massacres that soon followed. It haunted the early days of the National Convention, sharpening the partisan divide that disfigured that assembly from its very beginning.[27]

TOWARD THE CONVENTION

The September Massacres, violent fulcrum of Parisian politics, roiled the Convention from the start. The rivalry between the Brissotins, on the one hand, and Robespierre and his allies, on the other, had been embittered as it played out in the context of the institutional struggle between the Legislative Assembly and the Insurrectionary Commune. It was envenomed irreversibly during the very days of the massacres when Robespierre, responding to the Assembly's attempt to replace the Commune, denounced the Brissotins as traitors in league with the duke of Brunswick. His charges triggered an order by the Surveillance Committee for a search of Brissot's dwelling and met with vehement rebuttals from Brissot and Roland in their turn. They later insisted that there had been orders for their arrest at a moment when casting suspicion amounted to a death threat.[28]

These political divisions played out, too, in the elections to the Convention that were taking place in Paris throughout the period of the September Massacres. Bloodshed and balloting occurred simultaneously, woven into the tapestry of the French Revolution. Largely discredited among voters in Paris, the Brissotins accepted election in the departments. They entered the Convention as representatives of the provinces, soon forming the core leadership of the group of deputies historians conventionally designate as the Girondins, though they were not all from the Gironde region and belonged to several different political networks. Their politics were pitched against the deputies of a Parisian populace they now feared as radical, unruly, and dictatorial. The Parisian electors, in contrast, opted largely for veterans of the Insurrectionary Commune—not surprisingly, since their choices in the unpopular two-stage process required by the Legislative Assembly were made in open view of the public, closely monitored by the Jacobin Club, and subject to veto by the sans-culottes in the sections and primary assemblies. The fatal conflict between Girondins and their Jacobin enemies, each struggling to claim and control expression of the general will in the Convention, took root in this electoral process.[29]

Chosen as an elector by his home section, Marat soon published two lists. The first repudiated as unworthy a score of potential deputies being urged upon the electoral assembly by Louvet on behalf of the Brissotins. In addition to many familiar names (and old enemies) from earlier moments in the Revolution, it utterly rejected "the Brissots or the Guadets . . . , Condorcets . . . , Vergniauds . . . and other faithless deputies" as enemies of the people who had "declared war to serve Lafayette's purposes and dismissed the Commune to usurp supreme authority." The second list, weighted toward members of Marat's section and colleagues on the Surveillance Committee, offered his own favored candidates. In the first rank were "true apostles of liberty," such as Robespierre, Danton, Panis, Billaud-Varenne, and Fréron. Second came "true defenders of liberty" who had upheld the great principles of the Revolution, weapons in hand, including Manuel, the Commune's public prosecutor, and Deforgues, Jourdeuil, Duplain, and Guermeur, all members of its surveillance committee. Third were "excellent patriots who will always march with the intrepid defenders of the homeland," such as Boucher de Saint-Sauveur (the Jacobin friend who had hidden Marat during months of his clandestine existence), Camille Desmoulins and François Robert (most recently Danton's assistants in the justice ministry), and Tallien, secretary of the General Council of the Commune (a nomination soon retracted). Half of the people on this list were eventually elected as deputies of Paris to the Convention. Two other candidates Marat backed later in the voting process were also chosen: one, the painter David, elected deputy, was destined to immortalize him after his assassination; the other, the chemist Fourcroy, elected as an alternate, ended up filling the seat vacated by his death.[30]

Marat mentioned one further name in the placard posting his list of favored candidates. "My Friends," it concluded, "I'll finish by reminding you of The People's Friend; you know what he has done for the homeland, perhaps you don't know what he can yet do for your happiness; the glory of being the first martyr of liberty is enough for him, so much the worse for you if you forget him."[31]

There was good reason for this reminder, as Fabre d'Eglantine made clear in denouncing a campaign under way to mobilize the sections against the election of Marat and Desmoulins. "What, you'll proscribe from the National Convention two men celebrated since 14 July for their inviolable attachment to your cause and their intolerable persecution by Lafayette . . . ?" d'Eglantine expostulated. "Do you have too many pure and incorruptible citizens?" The same concern, though in a different tone, was also expressed by *Les Révolutions de Paris*. "Yes! Marat must be among the first named to the Convention," the journal insisted, castigating the Quinze-Vingts section for omitting him from a list of eligible patriotic journalists. He was among those who had most powerfully influenced public opinion toward a future Convention, it continued. He had foreseen everything and courageously kept silent about nothing. Writing daily for two years, he had provoked the events of 20 June and 10 August. He was as essential to the Convention as yeast was to good bread. "He won't be the wisest or most profound of our legislators, but a place has to be reserved for him among them, if only because he will keep the people's blade suspended above their heads, ready to strike down its traitorous or moderate representatives."[32]

The massacres were still raging when the Paris electoral assembly began its deliberations on 3 September. The tone was set the following day in a fiery speech by Collot d'Herbois urging election of "those who belong among the people . . . , the truly popular men . . . , the ones who have remained firm and always attached to the people's cause." He was chosen as the assembly's president, with Robespierre as its vice president. Marat himself was named one of eight secretaries. On 5 September, when the electors took their first vote, Robespierre won by the required absolute majority to become the first person proclaimed deputy of Paris in the Convention. He was followed in succession over the next three days by Danton and Collot d'Herbois, by Manuel and Billaud-Varenne, and by Camille Desmoulins. Marat's turn came on 9 September, when he became the seventh candidate chosen, by a majority of 420 votes to 338. His closest competitor was Joseph Priestley, a coincidence perhaps reviving the memory of earlier combats over the chemistry of combustion.[33]

The path to election had not been smooth. A nasty face-off on 6 September with Jean-Louis Carra, the journalist whom Marat had badmouthed in his list of undesirable potential candidates, ended in an ostensibly fraternal embrace. A more general confrontation could have occurred the following day when, according to a decidedly hostile account, "the much-touted little Marat crawled to the tribune and, extending at length his atrabiliar expression, provoked at the top of his voice those who had reproaches to make against him." Conflict seems to have been avoided when another elector called successfully for a return to the order of the day, an outcome Marat himself considered a triumph. That same evening, a rival for election, François Chabot, gave a speech in the Jacobin Club urging fervent patriots to send The People's Friend to the Convention.[34]

As votes in favor of Marat rose in successive ballots, the Brissotins in the electoral assembly tried more energetically to deny him the necessary majority. On 8 September Deflers, another elector Marat had dismissed as a potential deputy, targeted him in an extended denunciation alleging details of his ill-treatment of men (notably Boucher de Saint-Sauveur and Macquet, he of the Mlle Fouaisse affair) who had been willing to conceal him during his period in hiding. The People's Friend repudiated the accusations two days later in a placard protesting his patriotic virtue. On 9 September, after a vigorous speech by Robespierre in his favor, a violent rearguard action roiled the assembly. When it failed, and Marat was finally elected, Robespierre was bitterly accused of responsibility for the election of his minion, denigrating the revered Priestley in the process. Answering charges on this score from Louvet in the Convention two months later, the Incorruptible denied he had mentioned Marat explicitly in this speech, protested they had only met once before the electoral assembly, and proclaimed how fundamentally they had disagreed on that occasion over the violence of Marat's journalism. (Marat had performed a similar distancing act the previous April.) The denial carried little weight with a majority of the newly elected members of the Convention. In their eyes, Marat entered the assembly on Robespierre's back.[35] The Incorruptible would find him a troublesome burden.

The Brissotins had one last card to play, by urging the sections to exercise their sovereign right to ratify (or not) the nominations of the deputies the electoral assembly had chosen. "Marat's nomination is the pretext for the suspicion being sown artificially against the twenty-four deputies of Paris," the newly elected Robert reported to his constituents. "I hear that a journal called on the forty-eight sections of Paris to recall Marat, Camille Desmoulins, and Robert." The journal in question was the *Patriote français*, edited by Girey-Dupré for Brissot, which accused Robespierre and company of singing a different song about popular sovereignty now the sections were exercising against them the right of veto upon which they had earlier insisted. But Robespierre was on firm grounds in maintaining before the electoral assembly that its nominations had in any case been upheld by this process of review. Marat himself protested on 15 September that emissaries of the Brissotins had been running from section to section to incite them to revoke his nomination; he later crowed that only one section had voted to do so.[36]

EARLY SKIRMISHES

Throughout the period of the elections and in the days remaining until the Convention assembled, Paris remained in a state of high agitation. Verdun had fallen on 2 September, and anxieties about the course of the war remained acute until news reached the capital of the surprising French victory at Valmy on 20 September, the day the Convention first met in closed session to elect its officers. In the meantime, there had been continuing disorders in the streets, widespread thefts (most dramatically the disappearance from a warehouse of crown jewels confiscated from the Tuileries palace), fears of counterrevolutionary conspiracies, and rumors of pending massacres in prisons that had been refilled by arbitrary arrests since the September Massacres. In response, during its last days, the Legislative Assembly, led by the Brissotins in the Commission of Twelve and Roland in the ministry of justice, had begun to push for measures that would restore law and order, and forestall new episodes of popular violence. Joined by Pétion, who was now eager to recover his authority as mayor after lying low since 10 August, they looked for scapegoats to blame for the horrors that had just occurred. They soon fixed on Jacobins in the General Council of the Insurrectionary Commune, the radicals in its surveillance committee, and that committee's most infamous member, Jean-Paul Marat. Epitomized as the poster boy for slaughter, The People's Friend became a key target in a new round of Brissotin attacks.

A placard dated 8 September, *Marat, The People's Friend, to the Good French*, launched a tirade in response to these hostile authorities. It charged a gangrened majority in the Assembly, still waiting for the enemies of the nation to arrive at the city's gates, with attempting to divide the people from the sections "under the pretext of arresting the course of popular vengeance" while refusing to repudiate monarchy formally. It charged the generals at the front with perfidy, the ministers with favoritism and ineptitude, and Roland for plotting with the Brissot faction and discrediting the Commune in the eyes of the nation. Only Danton, *the patriot Danton*, emerged unscathed from this indictment. Marat urged making him president of the Provisional Executive Committee, with a "preponderant voice," as a prompt and efficacious means of mobilizing a governmental machine that had seized up.[37]

Roland soon struck back with a placard of his own, *The Minister of Interior to the Parisians*, that circulated on 13 September. "I'm accused of plotting with the Brissot faction! . . . I don't believe in this pretended faction," he maintained as he railed against an effort to incite revolt against the National Assembly, blacken the ministry, spread distrust of the generals and all the authorities, and "designate out loud the dictator that France has to be given." These charges were appearing under the name of a man consistently declaring himself the people's friend, now a member of the electoral assembly, and even mentioned as a potential deputy to the Convention. Were they the work of a hidden enemy manipulating the anxieties of an "atrabiliar mind," some secret agent of the duke of Brunswick aiming to weaken France by spreading intestine divisions, or a criminal scheming to overthrow everything and ascend above the ruins? Whatever the case, Roland asserted, "the secret committee of the city" had ordered his arrest on 2 September. "Was this to transfer me to the Abbaye [prison] and have me *released* with the criminals?" In the jargon of the time, he meant released from life, not from jail.

There was a note of panic here, soon amplified in the speech Roland gave before the Legislative Assembly on 17 September and had posted around the capital, protesting inter alia that his placards were being torn down or obliterated by his enemies. The city was filled with extreme agitators, he warned the deputies. The healthy mass of the people wanted order and the execution of the laws, but there were efforts to mislead it. There had been denunciations of the executive committee in the electoral assembly, cries from abused or guilty men that "the axe was still raised; that they had not lost their daggers." There had even been calls for an agrarian law, efforts to destroy respect for property. Conspirators were seeking to tear the nation apart and hold the knife over citizens' heads. "I told the Assembly twelve days ago, and days are centuries in our current situation: measures are necessary to give force to the law." The minister urged the creation of a guard to protect the Assembly itself.[38]

Mayor Pétion weighed in before the Assembly that same evening with his own call for the restoration of law and order. He denounced perverse agitators telling the people that it had no constitution, that a veil covered the law, that its sole will must be its guide. They were inciting insurrection and murder, calling for vengeance against conspirators still in the prisons. They wanted anarchy because it leads to despotism, they wanted France plunged back into slavery. His accusations became more pointed after he was informed that the Assembly had ordered the Commune to provide details of recent arrests and made its members personally responsible for the safety of prisoners. The Commune was not responsible for the arrests, he insisted. They originated from its surveillance committee, about whose activities the Commune itself knew nothing. Reclaiming power within the municipal assembly, the mayor was also seeking to rescue it from ignominy outside.[39]

The move to exonerate the Commune by scapegoating the Surveillance Committee continued, and became more focused, in a meeting of its General Council the following day. There the mayor, expressing approval for the events of 10 August, declared anathema everything that had since occurred. Paris would become a desert, he predicted, the people would die of starvation, the Convention would be forced to leave the city, if the people did not take its revenge on the agitators still misleading it. This time, he singled out for denunciation the adjuncts within the Surveillance Committee, notably "the first adjunct, Marat," whom he denounced as "mad or criminal." Panis sprang to his friend's defense, praising him as "a fervent patriot, a prophet, an enemy of Lafayette," who had spent "six weeks on his ass in a cell." (Between Pétion's "madman" and Panis's "prophet" there was not as much difference as one might think, jibed *Les Révolutions de Paris*. "Wasn't *prophet* once the synonym for *madman*?") The Commune responded by relieving the adjuncts of signature authority within the Surveillance Committee, reducing them to the status of "agents or friends." Panis's offer of resignation was refused.[40]

Roland reiterated the call for law and order that same evening. Shortly thereafter, the Assembly adopted measures to restore security and public peace, thwart conspirators and protect individual liberty, suppress divisions, and assure calm in the capital at the critical moment the Convention began its work. They included mandatory registration of the capital's inhabitants, restriction of authority to order arrests to the mayor and four subordinates, and strict punishment for anyone ordering arbitrary arrests (measures clearly directed against the Surveillance Committee). In addition, the Insurrectionary Commune (and the Surveillance Committee) was to be replaced by a new municipal assembly elected within three days of the decree's publication.[41]

In response to these efforts to constrain extremists, Marat carried out a series of sniper attacks on Roland and his wife, accusing her of spreading the rumor that his writings were the work of an agent of the duke of Brunswick, and of paying to get his posters torn down. But he saved his major salvo for the mayor in another poster dated 20 September, *Marat, The People's Friend, to Maître Jerome Pétion, Mayor of Paris*. A host of excellent citizens had been scandalized to see Pétion denigrate The People's Friend as "*an atrabiliar madman, an enemy of the nation*" at the same time the Brissotins were inciting the sections to exclude him from the Convention, Marat protested. Was it political obtuseness or craven compliance with the faction restoring him to leadership of the Commune that was motivating the mayor to squander what was left of his popularity in defaming the most zealous defender of the nation? There followed a lengthy repudiation of a man who was "indecisive, feeble, cowardly, the declared enemy of the vigorous measures necessitated by the dangers to the homeland, a man without ideas, goals, character." Pétion was a good man, even an honest one, Marat allowed, but he saw nothing, heard nothing, reflected on nothing. Paling at the sight of a drawn saber, he imagined he could save the homeland by crying for peace and unity, for mutual understanding and brotherhood. The "cruel events" of 10 August had revealed the dangerous vacuity of his dreams of political unity. Resign as mayor, this placard urged him. "The Brissotins are leading you by the nose, they're putting a blindfold over your eyes. If the People's Friend doesn't hasten to rip it off, they'll finish by making you call for counterrevolution."

As always, this denunciation of another became a defense of self. "He called me an atrabiliar madman or a cruel enemy of the nation," Marat expostulated. "This is the epithet the Marmontels, the d'Alemberts, the Condorcets and other encyclopedist charlatans gave Jean-Jacques." Was it not strange, he demanded, that his own putative hatred for the nation had led him to sacrifice himself for it while Pétion's so-called civic virtue had not motivated him to take the least risk? Free after three years of life underground surrounded by spies, assassins, misery, and tribulation, The People's Friend was supporting brothers in the Surveillance Committee. And Pétion, without suspecting it, was putting him at risk by painting him as "an atrabiliar madman and the most perfidious enemy of the nation."

In all this, Marat gave voice to the conviction "that all my efforts to save the people will come to nothing without a new insurrection." If the bases of the constitution had not been laid within the Convention's first eight sessions, he warned the people, nothing could be expected from its mediocre representatives. "You're annihilated forever, fifty years of anarchy await you, and you'll only get out of it with a dictator, a true patriot and statesman. Oh babbling people, if you only knew how to act!"[42]

Published the day before Marat entered the Convention for its opening debate, this placard also served as a dramatic final issue of *L'Ami du peuple*. It was a remarkable performance, but an entirely misjudged one. Its most powerful effect must have been to condense, confirm, and broadcast the very image of The People's Friend his enemies wanted to project. He emerged from the final pages of the journal, after three years, as a splenetic madman, the enemy of the nation, the soul of the bloodthirsty Surveillance Committee, ever calling for another insurrection, constantly demanding a dictatorship. In effect, he had offered future fellow deputies an incriminating visiting card. He would be greeted in the Convention as a monster.

An early alert came from a familiar rival paper, *Les Révolutions de Paris*, as it repeated the allegation that Marat was responsible for arbitrary arrests and clandestine incarcerations being carried out in the name of the Commune. "What!" it squawked. "There are magistrates of the people capable of placing the axe and fasces in Marat's hands! His hatreds, his calls for vengeance, his proscription lists have made him too well known." It was deplorable that, to buttress his crumbling reputation, a man who had hidden during moments of peril should now be condemning as factious and criminal those who had stood against despotism during its days of power, the journal reported. It was astonishing that someone who had dedicated his books to the comte d'Artois under the Old Regime was now begging a French prince, in the reign of equality, for 15,000 francs to get three books published. "Think about it, Marat," the journal hectored. "There you are in the National Convention; the people has its eyes on you; you're going to be judged in your turn. Justify its choice, don't denigrate any longer the honorable title of legislator, and work to create good laws rather than provoking assassinations."[43]

A NEW DIRECTION?

Did Marat pay any heed to this less-than-friendly advice? He must have found reason to do so at the very first public session of the Convention on 21 September. It is striking that the issue of dictatorship took precedence in the new assembly's initial deliberations, even over the fate of monarchy. The new deputies now feared dangerous varieties of individual domination beyond kingship. "I've heard talk," Georges Couthon reported, "not without horror, of the creation of a triumvirate, a dictatorship, a protectorate; word is being spread among the public that a party is forming inside the Convention for one or another of these institutions." Absurd though these rumors might be, he reasoned, the deputies had to reassure the people against notions doubtless circulated by its enemies to unsettle it. "OK! Let's all swear to the sovereignty of the people, nothing but its sovereignty, its entire sovereignty. Let's vow equal execration to royalty, dictatorship, a triumvirate, and any kind of individual power whatsoever that tends to modify or restrain that sovereignty."

There was little enthusiasm for an oath, however; too many oaths had been broken by this time. Danton offered an alternative remedy against "the empty phantoms of dictatorships, the extravagant ideas of a triumvirate, all these absurdities invented to scare the people." It lay in the principle of popular sovereignty, which required that any constitution had to be explicitly approved by a majority of the primary assemblies. "Nothing will be constitutional that has not been accepted by the people." No less important was strict imposition of law and order in the protection of property, he added. The laws had to be as terrifying against those who break them as the people had been in striking down tyranny. This intervention was crucial. It led to the Convention's very first decrees, one proclaiming any constitution subject to popular approval, the other placing persons and properties under the protection of the nation. Only after the passage of these measures did the deputies allow themselves the delirious act of abolishing monarchy in France.

None of this appeared in the account of the Convention's early deliberations Marat printed in the opening issue of his new journal, *Journal de la République française par Marat, L'Ami du peuple, Député à la Convention nationale*. He was more concerned to point out the dominance of the Brissotins among the officers the new assembly had chosen. But his principal purpose in this issue was to announce "The Author's New Direction," a declaration intended as a response to "the cowards, the blind, the scoundrels and the traitors who have painted me as *an atrabiliar madman*, an invective with which the encyclopedist charlatans rewarded the author of *The Social Contract*." To destroy confidence in him, Marat charged, the enemies of the homeland had distorted his opinions regarding a military tribune, a dictator, or a triumvirate, absurdly making him the figurehead of an ambitious faction of extremists. But these were his personal opinions, he objected. He had often reproached the most fervent patriots for repudiating "this salutary measure recognized as an indispensable necessity by everyone who knows the history of revolutions, one that can't be taken without costs, limiting its duration to a few days and the mission of its appointee to the custodial punishment of conspirators." No one in the world was more revolted than he at the idea of "an arbitrary authority, even entrusted to the purest hands for some length of time." As for his call for five hundred guilty heads to save five hundred innocent ones, he was convinced this action would have saved a hundred thousand patriots from slaughter and another hundred thousand from the risk of that fate. The countryside would not now be filled with widows and orphans reduced to despair; misery and scarcity would not have desolated the state for four years in a row; and it would be neither overwhelmed by factions nor torn apart by barbarous enemy hordes after being so by its unnatural children.

That was the past. As for the future, Marat declared, his sole ambition entering the Convention was to contribute to saving the people; his only wish that it be free and happy. Supporters of despotism and monarchy still existed; they had to be unmasked and punished wherever they might be found, even in the Convention itself. Nonetheless, he swore, "I'm ready to take the directions judged efficacious by the people's defenders; I must march with them. Sacred love of the homeland . . . , today I sacrifice to you my suspicions, my resentments, my hatred. At the sight of enemies of liberty and their outrages against its children, I'll stifle in my breast, if possible, the movements of indignation that will arise in it. I'll hear, without abandoning myself to fury, the account of the massacre of the old and children slaughtered by cowardly assassins, I'll witness the maneuvers of traitors of the homeland without calling down on their criminal heads the sword of popular vengeance." This stunning declaration of a conversion ended with a prayer, and an oath. "Divinity of pure souls, lend me the strength to fulfill my vow. Never will self-love or obstinacy be opposed in me to measures that wisdom prescribes. Make me triumph over the impulsions of sentiment, and if the transports of indignation drive me beyond the limits and compromise the public safety, may I expire of sadness before committing this error."

The People's Friend, long deeply suspicious of representation, was now signaling his readiness to become a representative himself. This must be why he took a stand, in the very first issue of his new journal, against "the very great number of citizens, even very enlightened ones, [who] claim that the delegates of the people are not representatives, reasoning on the grounds that will is not represented." They could say equally well that will is not delegated, he contended in response. "But this is only a play on words. They themselves agree that every government in which the delegates exercise the sovereign power is representative, thus the delegates of the people are its representatives. This is demonstrated by the simple definition of terms. What is a delegate? Someone entrusted with power to act in the place of his constituents. If he is in their place, he necessarily represents them." It is revealing in this context that Marat's new *Journal de la République française* appeared without the inherently oppositional Rousseauian motto *Vitam impendere vero* that he had cherished for so long. It soon bore a fresh one (from Horace): "May fortune abandon the haughty and return to those in misery" (*Ut redeat miseris, abeat fortuna superbis*).

Marat was promising a new persona, a new program, and a shift toward demands for social justice. He was to find it impossible, however, to shed the bloody stigma with which he now entered the Convention. The Scottish physician John Moore, then in Paris, conjured up a prevailing view of this "little man, of a cadaverous complexion, and a countenance exceedingly expressive of his disposition." "To a painter of massacres Marat's head would be inestimable," he commented. "Such heads are rare in this country [Britain], yet they are sometimes to be met with at the Old Bailey."[44]

AN AMBUSH

A moment of truth came on 25 September, when Marat faced off against his fellow deputies for the first time. This was the occasion, as he later charged, that the Brissotins and their allies in the Marseille deputation chose to "denounce the Paris deputies, crush Robespierre, Panis and Danton, and get Marat slaughtered by the blade of tyranny, or rather by the assassins' dagger." The debate had already turned to the specter of dictatorship as he scrabbled to mount the tribune. Marc David Lasource, deputy from the Tarn, had supercharged a discussion of the need for law and order (and the creation of an armed guard recruited from the provinces to protect the Convention) with a blistering speech. He warned against the threat that the representatives of the nation would be dominated by the brigands and assassins in the capital who claimed to be speaking for the people; against the criminals who had ordered arrests of patriotic (Brissotin) deputies at the height of the September Massacres; and particularly against the party within the Paris deputation that now wanted to "depopularize the National Convention, dominate it and destroy it, and reign under another name by concentrating all the power of the nation in the hands of a few individuals."

Lasource bundled these threats together but gave them no name. One was soon supplied. The party in question was Robespierre's, exclaimed François-Trophime Rebecqui, speaking for himself and his fellow representative from Marseille, Barbaroux. "It's to combat him that we've been sent; I denounce him to you." The accusation was countered by Danton, who rose to the defense of the Paris deputation collectively, and of Robespierre by implication, but declared one of its members guilty as charged. Namely, Jean-Paul Marat. Long accused, himself, of being the author of Marat's writings, Danton complained, he had recently been engaged in a public altercation with him at City Hall. "But I attribute these exaggerations to the vexations this citizen has experienced. I believe that the cellars in which he has been confined have ulcerated his soul." This harsh show of commiseration notwithstanding, Danton went on to call for the death penalty for anyone speaking in favor of dictatorship or a triumvirate.

There followed a too-lengthy self-justification from Robespierre, frequently interrupted, that charged his detractors with the desire to shatter the unity of the nation (under the leadership of the capital) by creating a federal republic. In the ensuing debate, accusations against the tyranny of Paris, the crimes of the Commune and its surveillance committee, and the dictatorship threatened by the Paris deputation swirled together. Barbaroux claimed that Panis had introduced Robespierre to him in July as "the virtuous man who should be dictator of France." Panis denied the assertion and declared himself ready to defend the alleged crimes of the Surveillance Committee. Brissot, for his part, demanded to know why Panis had issued an arrest order that would have led to his slaughter in the Abbaye prison. Panis responded by defending this action of the Surveillance Committee as a response to a state of emergency. Adding to the mix, Cambon testified that he had seen placards in Paris calling for a triumvirate in the name of public safety: they had been signed by Marat. We want the unity of the republic, he cried, but no dictatorship. His denunciations of the tyranny of the Commune, and of the capital, were echoed by deputies from the provinces accusing incendiary emissaries from the Commune of preaching insurrection throughout the country.

In this tempest of bitterness and acrimony, Marat struggled for an opportunity to intervene, if only "to denounce myself." He was shouted down from all sides, and jostled away from the tribune, until Delacroix demanded that he be heard.[45] "I have a great number of personal enemies in this assembly," he was finally able to say. "*All of us, all of us*" came back the reply as a mass of deputies rose in indignation against him. The clamor continued for several minutes as Marat waited for it to abate. He may have been heard in different ways: some accounts had him asking interrogatively whether he had a great number of enemies in the assembly, others had him expressing surprise at the clear fact that he did. Whatever the case, the response was overwhelmingly hostile. "I have a great number of enemies in this assembly," he repeated. "I call on them, for shame, not to level empty clamors, boos or threats against a man who has been devoted to the homeland and their own safety."

Once allowed to speak, Marat maintained that talk of a dictator was his alone, that Robespierre, Danton, and other colleagues had vigorously refused to countenance any idea of a dictatorship, a tribunate, or a triumvirate when he had pressed them to do so. But he launched into a lengthy diatribe defending his call for such an emergency power. "Will you make it a crime for me to propose the only means I believed proper to hold us back from the edge of the abyss that had opened up?" the *Moniteur* reported him as demanding. "When the constituted authorities served only to enchain liberty, slaughter patriots in the name of the law, will you make it a crime for me to have called down the avenging blade of the people on the heads of the traitors? No, if you imputed this to me as a crime, the people would belie you, because in obedience to my voice it realized that the means I proposed to save the homeland was the only one to save it and, having become a dictator itself, it knew how to rid itself of traitors."

A dictatorship of the people? "The people . . . a dictator itself" is what the reporter for the *Moniteur* had heard, though the phrase did not appear explicitly in Marat's own account of what he had said on 25 September. He had called for acts of popular vengeance, he acknowledged, and the people had recognized such acts as its last resource. France had been saved by the bloody scenes of 14 July, 6 October, 10 August, and 2 September. "Dreading, myself, these terrible movements of a savage multitude, distressed to see the axe striking all the guilty without differentiation and mixing petty delinquents with major criminals, and wanting to target it solely on the heads of the principal counterrevolutionaries, I tried to subject these terrible and disorganized movements to the wisdom of a leader, at once an honest patriot and a statesman, who would have sought and executed the principal conspirators, cutting the thread of all the conspiracies at a single blow, spare blood, restore calm and secure liberty." His calls for a dictator, tribune, or vigorous leader by some other name ("titles mean nothing"), then, had been meant as a response to the people's fury and an effort to contain it. The authority he had had in mind was meant to be momentary and limited to "lopping off criminal heads." Abandon scandalous and time-consuming debates over the phantom of dictatorship, he now begged the Convention. Consecrate the Declaration of Rights; create a government in which the safety of the people would no longer be at risk.

For a moment, it seemed that Marat had quelled the storm by invoking the necessary popular violence of 14 July and other revolutionary *journées* upon which the advances of the Revolution had depended—and by assimilating the September Massacres to them. Journalists reported a profound silence in response to his words, a silence explained by his enemies as stupefaction at maxims never before heard in a legislative assembly, and by other commentators as indicating a willingness to move finally to the day's agenda. But the Girondins and their supporters were not ready to desist. Vergniaud now took the floor to read aloud the Surveillance Committee's circular of 3 September urging the provinces to follow the example of the massacres in Paris. He was careful to note in passing that the circular had been preceded, during these terrible days, by a speech of Robespierre's accusing the Brissotins of conspiring to hand France over to the duke of Brunswick, an accusation that could have made himself a victim of the September slaughter. But he was professedly more concerned to protest that the circular had represented the Commune as the center around which France should rally and the Legislative Assembly as a counterrevolutionary enemy.

"What shall I say about an official invitation to murder and assassination?" Vergniaud cried. He saw only an exercise of the right of resistance in the fact that the people, tired of a long sequence of betrayals, had finally risen up (on 10 August) to take dramatic vengeance on its enemies. "The good citizen throws a veil over these partial disorders; he speaks only of the courageous acts of the people, the ardor of the citizens, the glory of a people that knows how to break its chains; and he tries to remove as far as he can the stains that can tarnish the history of so memorable a revolution," he reasoned. "But that men clothed in public authority . . . , charged to speak to the people in the language of the law and constrain it within the limits of justice through the influence of reason, should preach murder and glorify it: this suggests to me a degree of perversity only conceivable at a time when all morality has been banished from the earth."

Though he implied that not all the members of the Surveillance Committee were responsible for this scandalous circular, Vergniaud omitted specific mention of Marat. His accomplice Jacques Boileau, deputy of the Yonne, was less reticent, immediately invoking the evidence of the final issue of *L'Ami du peuple*—printing Marat's placard against Pétion—with its anticipation of the need for another insurrection, its talk of dictatorship, and its denunciation of the babbling people. "Oh Marat. There is more virtue among the people than madness in your head," Boileau cried. His words triggered shouts for Marat's imprisonment ("*To the Abbaye*!"), to which The People's Friend demanded to respond. "And I," Boileau retorted, "I demand that this monster be subject to a decree of accusation."

Allowed a voice, Marat maintained that the attack on Pétion just quoted by Boileau had been written ten days earlier in different circumstances. He asked to read in rebuttal the statement of his current views published in the first issue of his *Journal de la République française*. The assembly's secretary, ordered to do so, read aloud the journal's statement of "The Author's New Direction." He could not retract his earlier convictions, Marat pleaded, but the text that had just been read testified to the purity of his heart. The calls for a decree of accusation against him had been provoked only by the greed of his printer in publishing an outdated text that very day. "This fury is unworthy of free men," he cried, drawing a pistol from his pocket and pointing its barrel against his temple. "There is nothing under the sun I fear, and I must declare that if the decree of accusation had been brought against me, I would have burned my brain at the foot of this tribune. . . . So this is the fruit of three years of hiding places and torments endured to save my homeland! This is the fruit of my vigils and labors, my misery, my suffering, the dangers I have run. Well then, I'll remain among you to face your fury." Upon which, after some mutterings and shouts that he be removed from the tribune, the Convention returned to the day's agenda to declare the principle that the French Republic was one and indivisible. In a final exchange, Couthon demanded the penalty of death for anyone proposing a dictatorship. "And against the conspirator who imagines himself inviolable," was Marat's riposte. "If you raise yourself above the people, the people will shred your decrees."

What a day! It took the Convention a few minutes to affirm the principle of the unity of the republic. It had taken many more for the deputies to step back from a formal indictment of The People's Friend, at least this time. In point of fact, journalists disagreed in describing the moment at which Marat had brandished his pistol. Had he faced down threats of indictment by threatening to blow out his brains rather than face a decree of accusation, or merely flaunted his willingness to do so after the danger had passed? Desmoulins expressed a measure of admiration for the entire performance, though he skipped over the episode with the gun. The attackers had given Marat an opportunity to demonstrate his superiority, he commented in *Les Révolutions de France et de Brabant*: "He took pleasure in listening to their words with *sangfroid*, offering them an example of the way they should have read his less insulting journal." The galleries had applauded, reported the *Thermomètre du jour*, though men of good sense had groaned at having this "atrabiliar madman" as their fellow deputy. The Girondin press was more scathing. Condorcet's *Chronique de Paris* found the gun-brandishing a ridiculous pretense, an empty bid for the celebrity of a Cato or a Brutus by a man guilty of all the crimes that had besmirched the Revolution. Gorsas derided it as "a laughable kind of courage in a weakling who had said just a few minutes ago that he had hidden in a cellar," an antic some viewed as an expression of vigor, others as an object of pity. Brissot's *Le Patriote français* merely dismissed it as a final act of madness in a crazy performance.

From the Left, the *Révolutions de Paris* offered yet another admonition after comparing Marat to an Italian clown posturing with a gun not even fully armed, a show of courage by a man who had boasted of hiding from persecution by Lafayette. "There is work for you to do in the Convention, Marat," it lectured. "You've shown patriotic verve in some of your pamphlets; you've been useful to the revolution, you can be again. But don't abuse the ephemeral ascendance you have over part of the public; be more wary of an equivocal reputation perhaps usurped in a time of trouble, a moment of exhilaration, that is beginning to elude you. . . . Beware of losing in the light of day the kind of success you perhaps owe only to the obscurity of the cellar in which you hid for several months. Charlatanism is no longer in fashion, Marat, give up your conjuring cups."[46]

Marat himself claimed a victory. "The Guadet-Brissot faction was completely unmasked in this stormy session," he boasted in the *Journal de la République française* a few days later. "If I had succumbed in my defense, all would have been over for the Paris deputation, the leaders would have been crushed and I would have been slaughtered by the appointed brigands. . . . I leave the reader to reflect on the villainy of the Guadet-Brissot faction. I'm in the position now to follow all its plots and unmask it completely. . . . As for the leaders, Caritat called Condorcet, Brissot, Lasource, Vergniaud, Guadet, etc., I believe them incapable of repentance and I'll pursue them to the end." By his report, though, he was the one pursued by a couple of roughnecks on the way home from the Convention until he had them chased away by some eager *fédérés*.[47]

Whether he had emerged victorious from rhetorical battle or saved his neck by promising to toe the line, Marat had faced and barely survived a virtual trial before a jury of his new fellow deputies. The Brissotins and their allies had been outmaneuvered for the moment. They had failed to pull off a crucial ambush. But they had no intention of calling a truce against the monster of the September Massacres.

GUERRILLA POLITICS

Over the following months, the Brissotins and their allies seated toward the right side of the Manège struggled against the more radical Montagnards, so-called because they occupied the high benches to the left. At stake was dominance over the mass of provincial representatives in the so-called Plain between them. Historians have estimated the size of the core contending groups at around 50 each, out of a total assembly of 749. Though they were relatively small in numbers, their voices were loud. Personal hatreds, mutual suspicions, and recriminations increasingly marked the assembly debates as men on each side accused those on the other of acting as a sinister faction conspiring to subvert the Revolution.

On the Mountain stood Robespierre, Danton, Desmoulins, Collot d'Herbois, Billaud-Varenne, Panis, and Marat—the radical core of the Paris deputation drawing its support outside the Convention from the Jacobin Club and the sans-culottes in the Paris sections. They were soon joined by Louis Antoine de Saint-Just, the political prodigy barely old enough to meet the minimum age of twenty-five for election to the Convention, and (in a shift of conviction) the more experienced Georges Couthon, already a veteran of the Legislative Assembly. Others gravitated toward them over the course of several months. Against them, on the other side of the hall, the Brissotin leaders—Brissot, Vergniaud, Guadet, Gensonné, and Condorcet—gained support from Pétion and Buzot, former radicals now traumatized by the political events of the previous summer. Finding further support in Barbaroux and the majority of his fellow deputies from the region of Marseille (Bouches du Rhône) they were also abetted consistently by Roland, who chose to remain in office at the ministry of the interior, thus commanding (with his wife) considerable resources for the subvention of propaganda against political enemies. It is convenient to follow the conventional practice of calling this extended grouping the Girondins, though this was not the term used by contemporaries. Marat more accurately called them "the clique of the rolandins, buzotins, gaudétiens, brissotins, barbaroutins, etc." As a group, they were linked by bonds of personal friendship, fear of Parisian radicalism, and a shared hatred of Marat.

This alliance was soon confirmed (by the very act of denial) with the publication of a placard addressed to Marat by the deputies of the Bouches du Rhône at the end of September. It was circulated in twenty thousand copies, subsidized by Roland. Written by Barbaroux, it rehearsed charges that Robespierre had strategized for a dictatorship in August, while the Insurrectionary Commune and its surveillance committee had reached for tyrannical power not only in Paris but over the entire country. "And you, Marat," it continued, replaying the denunciations of 25 September, "haven't you constantly preached dictatorship in your writings . . . ? Your entire defense in that regard was that times had changed, as if there could ever be a time when dictatorship would be good." The People's Friend had done nothing to overthrow Louis XVI on 10 August, this diatribe reasserted; indeed, he had been so fearful at that moment that he had begged

Barbaroux to get him out of the capital. Now he was claiming too much importance for himself in alleging plots to assassinate him, or the readiness of the people to lop off heads if a decree of accusation had been passed against him. "Know that the deputies of the Bouches-du-Rhone have no fear of their heads falling; and, if you were worth spending enough time on a decree of accusation against you, they would vote as tranquilly as if it were a question of draining a pestilential marsh."[48]

The pattern had thus been set on 25 September. In the first four months of the Convention's existence, at a rough count, Marat attempted to address the assembly at least some three dozen times. In as many as fifteen cases, he was prevented from doing so entirely; in another fifteen, he mounted the tribune only with great difficulty. He complained bitterly of the parliamentary maneuvers employed to prevent him from speaking by Brissotins and their allies who dominated the assembly's official leadership positions, citing their refusals to recognize him or acknowledge his place on the list of speakers and their arbitrary use of their power to manipulate the agenda and close off discussion to silence him. He kept readers of his journal informed of the physical hassling he endured in efforts to gain the podium, the protests in the assembly against allowing him to speak, the jeers and insults that interrupted him when he was able to do so. At one point, he reported efforts to lure him from the assembly hall and assassinate him. Hostile speakers expressed physical and political distaste at yielding the podium to him or occupying it after. On occasion, a show was made of perfuming the rostrum after he left it to remove the stench of his presence.[49]

The stench, above all, was symbolic: the reek of violence and blood, the threat of the tyranny of the mob. Marat's reputation as a bloodthirsty agitator calling constantly for slaughter, his incitements to insurrection and massacre, and his calls for a dictatorship made him the perfect target for the Girondins as they sought to blacken the entire Paris deputation. For them, he epitomized the tyranny of the Insurrectionary Commune and its surveillance committee, the slaughter of the September Massacres, the threat of social disorder and popular violence constantly posed by the sans-culottes in the Parisian sections, and the danger of a unitary republic dominated by dictatorship within and by the capital. As a result, he remained largely alone within the assembly, "as isolated in the midst of the Convention" (Desmoulins put it) "as he had been on his ass in his cellar." Robespierre and Danton, in particular, found it difficult to defend him without being tainted themselves by the charges against him. Increasingly, he relied for support on the applause and cheers of the people in the galleries against the jeers and catcalls of the deputies on the benches. There was a reason he had agitated for a meeting place for the Convention that would have offered space for several thousand spectators.[50]

Throughout this period, the Girondins attacked Marat at every opportunity, and vice versa, both within the Convention and in the press. Charges of corruption and conspiracy remained crucial issues in these conflicts. The theme was struck on 1 October when the Surveillance Committee of the Commune, in a move to evade efforts to gain control of its records, sent a deputation to the Convention offering proof of the corruption of members of the preceding national assemblies (some of whom were now seated in the Convention) by agents of the crown. The Jacobin Antoine-Christophe Merlin immediately seized the opportunity to demand the punishment of Louis XVI, which he saw as overdue since 10 August. "It's finally time," he declared, that having decreed the abolition of royalty, the Convention show that a dethroned king is not even a citizen. "He has to fall under the national blade and all those who have conspired with him have to follow him to the scaffold. . . . The Convention must be his jury of accusation and jury of judgment." But the deputies were more concerned with potential charges against the corrupted than the corrupter. Outraged, they instantly demanded a commission to investigate the evidence for these charges, with some of them calling for the Surveillance Committee's papers be handed over to the Convention for immediate inspection.

This latter proposal was resisted strongly by Marat and Panis, who feared a plot to remove evidence that would convict current leaders of the Convention as well as Louis XVI himself. Supporting them, Billaud-Varenne also demanded that the gates of Paris be controlled to prevent the guilty from fleeing. Marat insisted that any commission appointed to investigate the papers work jointly with members of the Surveillance Committee. "One sees how much it would matter to the henchmen of this traitor to get hold of those papers and make them disappear. A criminal conspiracy to strip them from the Surveillance Committee has been hatched in the shadows for some time."[51] His suspicion that the Girondins secretly hoped to save the king's head, and with it their own, was already deeply rooted.

The deputies eventually ordered the Surveillance Committee's papers sealed and named a Commission of Twenty-Four to share with the committee the task of inventorying them. Former deputies and current representatives from Paris were excluded, and the commission was overwhelmingly composed of Girondins and their allies. Within days, it reported that the mountain of material involved would take months to investigate and that, while there was evident and material proof of the conspiracies of the dethroned king, the charges of corruption against former deputies were unproven, hence calumnious. (One member also took pleasure in reporting evidence that victims of the prison massacres were innocent.) Responding in the face of heavy protests and sustained interruptions, Marat ridiculed these conclusions as contradictory. There was a dossier in existence, he insisted, that had to be made public immediately; it proved the treasons of the king and the court (and, by implication, the corruption of deputies in previous legislatures now present in the Convention). His attempt at a further intervention was contested by Buzot, whose violent repudiation of "ridiculous denouncers" now wasting the Convention's time turned the entire discussion, in effect, into yet another hectic debate over Marat's right to speak and, indeed, to sit at all in the representative body.

The People's Friend was defiant when his passionate claim to speak as a deputy was finally accorded grudging procedural acknowledgment. "As for my political opinions, my way of seeing things, my sentiments, I have already declared that I am above your decrees," he proclaimed in the face of the now customary shouts and jeers. "You will never make me see what I don't see, and you won't prevent me from seeing what I do see. No, it's not given to you to prevent a man of genius from casting himself into the future. . . . You put me today under the assassins' blade, you cry calumny. Very well, you'll have proof too late of the crimes your fatal credulity is covering with the mantle of impunity. . . . If you had had the good sense to listen to me, you would not have had so many sufferings, calamities and disasters for four years; you would have spared the blood and wealth of the people."

With this rhetoric of the prophet spurned, Marat launched into an extended denunciation of the Brissotins as the party in the Convention determined to remove evidence that could prove the treasons of the court or the suborning of deputies. Eventually, the assembly ordered the Surveillance Committee's records confiscated pending further investigation. A week later, in retaliation, Marat moved that an accounting be required of all public functionaries, beginning with Roland, whom he accused of taking possession, without issuing any formal receipt, of valuables confiscated by the Commune. This effort failed, but his campaign to discredit the minister he derided as "the god of the Brissot clique" lasted for months. In the meantime, he continued to season his journal with evidence of clandestine court handouts.[52]

This moment in mid-October marked a crystallization of the conflict between Girondins and Jacobins. For several weeks, Brissot had been summoned to answer to the Jacobin Club for his criticisms of the Insurrectionary Commune, the Paris electoral assembly, and the deputation that assembly had sent to the Convention. He had failed to appear.

On 12 October he was formally stricken from the club's list of members (other Girondins soon met the same fate). At the same session, Couthon declared war on the party of subtle and ambitious intriguers who wanted a republic because the public favored it, but only an aristocratic republic in which they would perpetuate their influence; dispose of places, positions, and public resources; and enjoy liberty merely for themselves. These men, Couthon urged, had to be resisted with full force by pure, upright, determined citizens united in the patriotic society that was the birthplace of the Revolution. As if on cue, Marat rose to denounce the criminal faction now dominating the Convention as it had the Legislative Assembly. The charge was less dramatic than the fact that Marat was now making it before the Jacobin Club. This was the first time he had spoken in a society he had avoided since the beginning of the Revolution. Symbolizing this rapprochement, he soon called on the secretaries of the provincial clubs affiliated with the Jacobins to circulate a prospectus for a new edition of his political writings![53]

By this time, Marat charged, the Convention was entirely under the influence of the cabal of former deputies to the Constituent and Legislative Assemblies headed by "the clique of the Gironde and the Bouches du Rhône." At its heart he placed "the pedant Buzot, the formalist Delacroix, the irascible Guadet, the perfidious Brissot, the scoundrel Rabaut." Condorcet, Anthoine, and Basire he set apart, citing rumors that they were distancing themselves from the group. Gorsas and Barbaroux he dismissed as minions peddling the resolutions of the leading conspirators and circulating slogans that served their tricks. The 14 October issue of the *Journal de la République française* was entirely devoted to rehearsing an account of the plots of this "infernal clique." In a few more days, he promised, it would be completely unmasked. "Soon the National Convention will open its eyes and only then will it be able to get to work to save the Republic."[54]

AGAINST THE GENERALS

For the moment, however, military conflicts at the frontiers proved more decisive than political struggles in Paris. The tide of war turned in late September as French troops, joined by thousands of patriotic volunteers, began to push back the Prussian and Austrian invaders and advance against them in an astonishing series of campaigns. An improbable French victory in the massive artillery battle of Valmy on 20 September led, after futile negotiations between the French general Dumouriez and the duke of Brunswick, to the chaotic retreat of the Prussian army toward the Rhine and its eventual evacuation of Verdun and Longwy. The Austrian army, for its part, abandoned its occupation of Lille in early October and began retreating toward Belgium. Meanwhile, French troops in the south under General Montesquiou had invaded Savoy on 22 September and occupied Nice a week later (soon prompting calls by deputations from these territories for their unification with France), while an army to the east under Custine entered the Rhineland on 30 September to occupy Spire and head for Mainz and Frankfurt. Before the end of October, Dumouriez had begun his own invasion of Belgium, reaching Brussels within three weeks and the Dutch border shortly thereafter.

At the news of sudden victories, Marat could only be ambivalent. Profoundly opposed to the French declaration of war in the first place, and subsequently outraged at the resulting ravages of French territories by the Prussian and Austrian invasion, he was more inclined to attribute the collapse of the Prussian army to dysentery than to the skill of the French generals. At the same time, he celebrated the "holy epidemic of liberty" spread by the presence of French troops in Savoy and their support of insurrections in Geneva and Neuchâtel. "What better than the cannon to break the chains of peoples and assure the triumph of the universal liberty that France has conquered and wants to procure for other nations," he enthused uncharacteristically on 5 October. "What ramparts will be provided for her by the grateful peoples she will have made free and happy!"[55]

Nonetheless, The People's Friend remained acutely suspicious of the leadership of the victorious French armies. He had an enduring fear that military success would clear the way for a Cromwell. He could not dismiss the fact that the great majority of the generals and higher officers had been creatures of the court; that many had emigrated (some, like Lafayette, even recently) or remained suspected by their troops of disloyalty to the Revolution; that their possibly treacherous conduct before 10 August had rendered the French military effort ineffective; that their much-touted successes as putative patriots since then had been achieved against a disease-ridden enemy no longer capable of defending itself. "I well believe that today, finding no other salvation than with the people, they will be faithful to the Republic," he reasoned on 5 October. "But it is prudent to wait until they have fulfilled their mission before paying them a just tribute of praise. Much remains for them to do, but all the obstacles have been removed, and they will be regarded as incompetent or treasonous if the rest of the campaign doesn't put an end to offensive war forever."[56]

Judged by this criterion of perpetual peace, the generals' ultimate success was unlikely. But Marat soon found more immediate grounds for indictment, especially against the hero of the hour, Dumouriez. On 9 October, the general wrote to inform the Convention of a report from his subordinate, General Chasot, that the honor of the French army had been besmirched by the conduct of two battalions of volunteers from Paris. Action had accordingly been taken to "repress the license that enemies of French liberty disguised under the respectable uniform of citizen soldiers have just spread in an army full of indignation at these attacks." The volunteer battalions in question, drawn from the Mauconseil and République sections, had been arrested for the summary execution of four Prussian deserters. Stripped of their weapons, Dumouriez insisted, they had now to receive from the Convention the kind of exemplary punishment upon which military discipline, and hence the safety of the entire Republic, must depend.

Already suspicious of misrepresentations by the generals and the ministers, Marat concluded immediately that this episode was contrived by "Roland, the generals, and the infamous faction that wanted to establish the federative republic" as a reprisal against patriotic volunteers intended to discredit the activism of the Paris sections. On 15 October, in an outraged speech to the Jacobin Club, he declared that the charges against the battalions were groundless and called for two delegates from the club to join him in confronting Dumouriez while the general was briefly in Paris basking in accolades. By the time they did so the following day, he was already learning of the possibility that the four Prussian deserters were in fact French émigrés.[57]

The little delegation tracked down Dumouriez, a notorious libertine, at a fashionable *soirée* at the residence of the famous actor Talma. By Marat's account to the Jacobin Club the following day, Paris high society was there in all its splendor, along with "nymphs" from the Paris Opera, officers of the National Guard, and Girondin leaders; the commandant of the Paris National Guard, Santerre, served as the lackey introducing the guests. Marat and his comrades immediately confronted Dumouriez about the facts of the case. The encounter did not go well. The general was defensive from the beginning. He maintained that he had given the relevant documentation to the war ministry. Informed that no such documentation could be found there, he cited the report he had submitted to the Convention. Challenged that the assembly's Surveillance Committee had no evidence to corroborate his charges, he insisted that there were indeed supporting documents. Where, then, were they? The general was not accustomed to such an interrogation; his responses were becoming testy. "I believe, Monsieur," he spluttered, "that I deserve to be believed when I speak." But the four men massacred could have been émigrés, came the reply. "So what if they were émigrés, Monsieur?" "Because the émigrés are rebels against the homeland and your procedures against the battalions are unpardonably violent," was the answer. "Oh, Monsieur Marat, you're too sharp for me to talk to you." With this, the general turned on his heels and walked away, leaving The People's Friend to be hassled by his aides. "Your master will be more frightened of the end of my pen than I am of his scoundrels' sabers," Marat promised in a parting shot. It was not long before an acid portrait of the perfidious general appeared in the *Journal de la République française*.[58]

Slightly different versions of this encounter were retailed by Marat to the readers of his journal over the following days and to the Convention in a stormy session on 18 October. By this time, he had ferreted out a declaration by members of the municipality of Rethel, where the incident had occurred, that the deserters were indeed émigrés. This evidence had been withheld from the Convention by the war minister, along with a paragraph of Chasot's initial report to Dumouriez that disparaged volunteer regiments for lack of the discipline and obedience necessary for the effective execution of military orders. Marat presented his findings to the Convention only after a long wait he ended with a shrewd appeal to its rules that outmaneuvered the objections of the overwhelmingly hostile assembly. His lengthy and impassioned speech was constantly interrupted by demands that he be silenced, and he complained too of threats from fellow deputies to remove him from the assembly forever. Nonetheless, he insisted that the Convention hear the facts supporting his charge that the generals and the ministers had lied and suppressed evidence to secure a harsh decree punishing the volunteer battalions. This was not a charge he was willing to let go. "Small, vain men," he railed in the *Journal de la République française* on 22 October, "or rather presumptuous and corrupt men stupid enough to proclaim yourselves republicans, to dub yourselves Brutus, Socrates, Lycurgus, do justice to yourselves and learn that it's not with former slaves like you that free men will ever be made. Before liberty triumphs among us, the entire generation of men like you will have to be annihilated and the nascent generation will have to replace you with simple honest men."[59]

"A little more patience," Marat had urged upon his readers on 20 October. "The veil will finally be torn despite the efforts of the enemies of the homeland and the artifices of base and corrupt men placed at the helm of affairs." But it was not until two months later, on 18 December, that a report issued jointly by the committees on war and on general security vindicated his protests by annulling the charges against the two battalions, condemning the harsh collective punishment they had received, returning them to service, and declaring Chasot guilty of fraud, Dumouriez of malfeasance, and both motivated by contempt for the volunteers. The triumph was Marat's, though he struggled in vain to mount the tribune that day to claim it. Reporting this decision, he swore in the *Journal de la République française* to continue heaping opprobrium on the "infamous and perfidious valets of the court that the criminal faction maintains at the head of the army . . . until the soldiers of the homeland unite to do justice to the traitors, expel their suspect officers, and choose good ones from among the truly patriotic."[60]

Beyond Marat's enduring distrust of generals and ministers, he saw two issues intersecting in the case of the volunteer battalions. One was contemptuous ill-treatment of volunteer units by the upper ranks of the regular army, making all too obvious "the aim of perfidious generals . . . to rid themselves of volunteer battalions whose surveillance would cause them extreme embarrassment and prevent them from accomplishing their treasons with impunity." In the fall of 1792 and as winter approached, the *Journal de la République française* published constant complaints that volunteer units were underfed, underclothed, undershod, and undersheltered, subject to harsh demands and arbitrary acts of injustice, and "pushed by the generals to acts of insurrection to have an excuse to slaughter them." The goal of this oppressive treatment, he was sure, was "the gradual dissolution of the legions of citizens who had left their homes, their wives and children, rushing to the frontiers to shed their blood for the conquest of liberty . . . ; to disarm the patriotic battalions gradually and arm the crooks, cut-throats, din-makers, valets and henchmen of aristocrats, aristocrats themselves, and the cursed hordes of enemies of the revolution."[61]

The second issue, closely related, was fear of the radicalism of the Parisian populace. The treatment of the two battalions from the Paris sections, Marat declaimed, was "the continuation of a deeply considered system of defamation of the Parisians, the municipality, the surveillance committee, and the Paris deputation, reproduced in every imaginable way." And it was occurring, he charged, in the context of moves by the Girondins to institute an armed force drawn from the provinces to guard the Convention against the threat of disorderly popular movements in the capital. Proposed initially by Roland and energetically supported in the September placard of the Bouches du Rhône deputies, the creation of this guard had been opposed initially by Marat and the Jacobins as the project of proponents of a federal republic to fill Paris with their own armed force while the great mass of its patriots had rushed to the front, a situation that would cause civil war when the Paris fighters returned. But activist volunteers from the provinces had not waited for a formal decree to be summoned. They had flocked to the capital, especially from Marseille, a new wave of *fédérés* ready this time to defend their deputies, and the republic, against Parisian extremism.[62] To win them over became Marat's next cause.

A MOMENT OF TERROR

Convinced that these Marseillais were "true friends of the homeland because they are all brave sans-culottes," as he told the Jacobins, Marat began by inviting some of them to lunch on 24 October. The invitation was declined by men he described as indoctrinated by the aggressive placard of the Bouches du Rhône deputies against him and instructed by their officers to avoid socialization with the notorious champion of dictatorship. Hearing their complaints of ill-treatment, nonetheless, he entered their barracks, finding himself aghast at the filthy conditions, inadequate or nonexistent bedding, and lack of water from which they were suffering. Indignantly, he compared their situation with that of dragoons handsomely equipped and housed in the Ecole Militaire, elite units he denigrated as a nest of counterrevolutionaries, former servants of aristocrats and members of the royal bodyguard, crooks and lowlifes, notorious henchmen of the Old Regime and gangrened royalists.

Within two hours, this visit to the *fédérés* on 24 October was being denounced in the Convention by Barbaroux. A few days earlier, responding to a petition for Marat's removal from the Convention, Barbaroux had quipped that proofs of this enemy's crimes could be found by the cartload. This time, he took from his pocket a slim declaration signed in the name of the *fédérés* from Marseille. It accused Marat of trying to ignite a riot and incite hate between the dragoons and the *fédérés*, pushing credulous volunteers to excesses and disorders. In the outrage that followed, a deputy added an accusation that Marat had declared the need to fell another 270,000 heads before the republic could achieve calm. Overcoming attempts by Guadet, as president, to prevent him from speaking, The People's Friend gave his own account of the visit. He did not deny that he had expressed outrage that the Marseillais troops were being treated worse than former royal guards now parading as well-paid dragoons in their sky-blue uniforms. "If that's a crime, slaughter me. My accusers will know one day that my heart is pure."[63]

As for the 270,000 heads, Marat acknowledged observing that the machine of government was being obstructed by 200,000 enemies of the Revolution shuffled endlessly from department to department, bureau to bureau, court to court. (Saint-Just would mount a similar charge a year later as he called for terror against the bureaucrats in a notorious report on behalf of the Committee of Public Safety.) According to the *Moniteur*, The People's Friend reiterated that there could be no peace until their heads had fallen, though he himself stopped short of that statement when he rehearsed the debate for readers of the *Journal de la République française*.

"We talk constantly of faction," he continued in this account. "There is a violent one among us, Messieurs, it's the one that attacks me bitterly every day. But where's my faction, I'm alone on my side. A proof that I don't have one is that none of you has the courage to speak for me. The atrocious men who are relentless to destroy me know that as well as I do. Ah well, if they need my blood let them slaughter me." Martyrdom was never far from his mind.

After further manipulation of the parliamentary rules by Guadet, Barbaroux's charge was referred to the committees on surveillance and legislation. When Marat returned to his seat, he informed his readers, Desmoulins had congratulated him on a sublime response with the compliment that he was two centuries ahead of his century. His conclusion was acid. "It's a shame that Camille [Desmoulins], who sometimes has bouts of enthusiasm, loses them when he has a pen in his hand, and perhaps for a reason."[64]

By this time, attacks on The People's Friend were becoming even more inflamed. On 27 October a hand-drawn flyer pasted up in the Palais de la Révolution (the former Palais Royal) depicted the hanging of "Marat, the enemy of the people." Its exhortation to this effect was written in a Marseillais patois, along with a threat that the same fate would be met by anyone who tore it down.[65] This turning of Marat's language against himself was widely reported in the press, with the *Courrier français* adding the bad news for Marat that the flyer was applauded by the people. It was also denounced in the Convention (by the younger Robespierre) and in the Commune, which ordered it removed by the National Guard. The same day, in the Convention, Buzot proposed penalties up to death against publications inciting murder, assassination, and sedition.

Two days later, Roland submitted a lengthy assessment on the state of Paris that warned of a continuing threat from the "criminal instigators" of the September Massacres. "Their rage has not yet been quenched because they haven't achieved their goal," he attested. Under a mask of patriotism, these false friends of the people were planning a reversal of the Revolution that would feed their taste for blood, gold, and atrocity.[66] In the battle ignited when Robespierre resisted the clamor to print and circulate this inflammatory report, Danton abruptly called for a halt to partisan divisions in the assembly. He was ready to offer a sacrificial lamb for the purpose, or perhaps a mauled sheep. "These divisions must cease, and if there is a guilty one among us, you must do justice to him," he urged to resounding applause. "I declare to the Convention and to the entire nation that I have no love for the individual, Marat; I say frankly that I have had experience with his temperament; he's not only volcanic and cantankerous but anti-

FIGURE 23.2. Anonymous hand-drawn flyer, "Marat must be hanged," 1792. Archives nationales de France, F/7/4590, plaq. 3.

social."[67] Spurning Marat yet again was his way of saying that he himself belonged to no faction. It was a way, too, for him to deny the existence of a faction around Robespierre. He was declaring, in effect, that there was no Jacobin faction and he didn't belong to it!

This was too much for Louvet, who soon unleashed an extended harangue he must have been saving for the right occasion. It rehearsed months of Girondin grievances against so-called defenders of the people led by the Robespierre he loathed. In this indictment, they had arrogated to themselves the glory of the revolution of 10 August and tarnished it with the slaughter of the September Massacres. They had reduced the Legislative Assembly to impotence and plotted the death of its leaders. Their notorious Surveillance Committee had foisted the example of the massacres on municipalities throughout the country, aiming to create a coalition under the domination of the capital that would destroy not only individuals but the liberty of the nation itself. They had covered the walls of Paris with calumnies of the purest of patriots, circulating ferocious incitements to pillage and massacre, insinuating the need for dictatorship. "This was assuredly their system of conspiracy; you see it still now being pursued."[68]

Though Robespierre was the central target of this tirade, Marat was by no means neglected. "It's time for us to know whether there is a faction comprising seven or eight members of this assembly or the other 730 combatting them," Louvet instructed his audience. "You have to explain to yourselves the reasons for keeping among you this man whom public opinion is beginning to regard with horror. I'm not afraid to say that you must either free us of his presence or insult public reason by a solemn decree proclaiming him innocent." There was more to follow. Louvet was determined to weld Robespierre and Marat together as evil twins conjoined in a bloody factional plot to seize power. "Don't try to pull the wool over our eyes by disavowing this desperado crazy for assassination," he exclaimed. "If he didn't belong to your faction, who emboldened him to emerge alive from the sepulcher to which he was condemned . . . ? If he wasn't one of yours, who then provided the funds necessary for his numerous placards, expenses surely exorbitant for him? If he wasn't initiated into all your projects for oppression . . . , why did you produce him in the electoral assembly you dominated by intrigue and fear . . . you who incite insults against me for having the courage to demand to speak against Marat. . . . Oh God! I've pronounced his name!"[69]

There followed a white-hot denunciation of the "liberticide atrocities" of the September Massacres provoked by "the disruptive faction, accompanied by terror and preceded by the placards of the man of blood." Invoking the example of Sulla, who had begun by striking the most detested men in Rome and ended by destroying the most virtuous, Louvet's attack culminated in a checklist of accusations of Robespierre. "I accuse you, Robespierre . . . ," he repeated at each charge: . . . of calumniating and proscribing the purest patriots, . . . of persecuting and debasing the representative body of the nation, . . . of flaunting popular idolatry of yourself as the only savior of the homeland, . . . of tyrannizing the electoral assembly of Paris, . . . of grasping for supreme power.

Calling for Robespierre's conduct to be brought before a committee of investigation, Louvet saw no need for further investigation of the Incorruptible's evil twin. "Legislators, there's another man among you whose name will not befoul my mouth, a man I don't need to accuse because he has accused himself. He has said himself that in his opinion it was necessary to fell 268,000 heads. He has confessed to you what he could not in any case deny, that he had advocated the subversion of the government, provoked the establishment of the tribunal, of dictatorship, of the triumvirate. . . . I demand a decree of accusation against Marat and that the Committee of General Security be charged to examine the conduct of others." It was time, Louvet concluded, to show strength against mad proponents of anarchy, against intriguers paid by foreign powers to incite disorder and civil war. It was time to halt the mad faction preaching insurrection in the sections, in public spaces, among the Jacobins. "You have to do it; and after passing the decree of accusation against Marat . . . you will pronounce the law against the monsters provoking murder and assassination." Blood, he warned, could not be allowed to flow in the streets of Paris.[70]

Barbaroux and Louvet had done their work. On 1 November, Kersaint was demanding an immediate report from the Committee of General Security regarding the man "whose name is an insult, whose life is a tissue of crimes, and whose presence in this assembly is a scandal." The next day, The People's Friend was writing to the Jacobin Club to beg its help in securing protection. He had been threatened by dragoons, joined by some of the Marseillais volunteers and others, crowding outside his house, wanting to break down the doors, demanding his head. On the following evening, a similar crowd was careening around the city in the hundreds, the dragoons with sabers drawn, invading cafés, drunkenly singing the "Marseillaise," and shouting variations on "*Marat to the Guillotine, Robespierre to the Guillotine, Danton to the Guillotine, Long Live Roland, No Trial for the King*." There were accounts of confrontations in the Palais Royal, where some of the Marseillais had threatened to hack Marat to pieces. The press buzzed with reports of these events, the Commune was invaded by deputations from sections ready to take up arms, the Jacobin Club was inflamed, and the divided Convention merely referred the matter to its Committee of General Security. In the meantime, Marat had gone back into hiding, leaving his journal unpublished for five days.[71]

In consequence, he was not in the Convention on 5 November to hear Robespierre's extended self-justification in response to Louvet, a speech that spectators had waited all night to hear from the gallery. "Citizens, did you want a Revolution without revolution?" the Incorruptible had challenged the deputies in passionately asserting the essential and indissoluble link between the insurrection of 10 August and the slaughter of the September Massacres. It is striking, though, that he began this celebrated speech by repudiating the charge that he had conspired to attain supreme power in the classical guise of a dictatorship, a triumvirate, or a tribuneship. To do so, he had to disencumber himself of The People's Friend. "I won't deny that one of the most terrible reproaches directed against me names Marat. I'll begin then by describing what my relations with him have been." He was careful to recall that the two of them had met only once before they were elected to the Paris electoral assembly and that they had differed strenuously on that occasion over the violent tone of *L'Ami du peuple*. He insisted that as an elector he had declared himself in favor of choosing writers who had fought for the Revolution, but without in any way singling out Marat.

The man had been elected, Robespierre maintained, at a moment of patriotic fervor when his extravagant ideas mattered less than the treasons he had denounced and the evils he had predicted. No one then dreamed that his name would soon serve as a pretext for calumny against the Paris deputation, the electoral assembly, or the primary assemblies themselves (or that efforts would be made to treat the two of them as one at any cost). Had his own combats for liberty not yielded enough cause for hostility, Robespierre demanded, without the need to impute to him excesses he had avoided and opinions he had been the first to condemn? He closed his speech to enthusiastic applause from the galleries, and the assembly instantly voted for its publication and distribution. There followed an intense struggle over whether to return to the order of the day, with Louvet and Barbaroux leading the pack to make an instant response. Eventually overruled, Louvet called for the Committee on Legislation to present its report regarding Marat immediately. The demand was lost in the tumult.[72]

Marat's critics relished Robespierre's act of disengagement from the monster of the Mountain. "Robespierre . . . , whom the people always conjoins with Marat, has just renounced him at the tribune, though it's been proven that he has often defended him in private and in public," rejoiced Dulaure, the editor of the *Thermomètre du jour* on 7 November. "Danton has publicly denounced him, and Camille Desmoulins too. Ah Marat, Marat, your friends are abandoning you!" Not that these efforts by Danton and Robespierre to distance themselves from the monster met with any success. Louvet's extended reply to Robespierre's speech made clear when it was published that he would continue linking Robespierre and Marat as inseparable in their efforts to grasp personal power.[73] The charge of their partnership in crime was too good a weapon for the Girondins to abandon.

Danton and Robespierre had wanted to dissociate themselves from Marat's obsession with the idea of a dictatorship. Desmoulins's denunciation, that of a long-term friend and ally, was personally more wounding. In a gem of character assassination, he had preferred to explain that obsession as a symptom of chronic megalomania. "This Marat whom I've studied ever since he was given importance . . . believes that he has shown physics to the universe, chemistry to the world, medicine to the earth . . . ; no one has ever approached him in diplomacy, in philosophy, and (who would credit it!) even in philanthropy he believes himself the most sensitive of men. He speaks of the massacres for which he has called as bloodlettings necessary to save the great number from the tyranny of the smaller one. He regards himself as the author of the revolution, another Cagliostro who, having prophesied the perfidies of the nobles and the court, seems to say to everyone he meets: if you think, if you reason, if you have been useful to the homeland, if kings are no more, if you are free, you owe it to *Marat*; it's to him you must hand over the reins of government. Such is this being who lives only with himself and has spoken of dictatorship only to make people understand that he alone has the genius, the character and the power to lead and protect it."[74]

It was a brutal analysis, no doubt, but not without some measure of truth.

TWENTY-FOUR

TO KILL A KING?

Though Marat returned to the Convention on 8 November, his attempts to speak were blocked for several weeks. He wrote on 26 November that he had given up trying to present his opinions and was saving his efforts to intervene for moments that offered significant opportunities to "undo the disastrous plots of the criminal faction and defend the rights of the people."[1] By that time, the conflict between Girondins and Jacobins was beginning to find bitter expression in a series of such moments offered by the struggle to determine the king's fate.

Throughout this period, the Girondins had continued to drag their feet in the matter of the king. Their energies were directed toward eliminating from the Convention the men they held responsible for the September Massacres, discrediting the Paris deputation, summoning a provincial guard to defend them from the threat of popular agitation, and mobilizing opinion in the provinces against the tyranny of the capital. They had no desire to rush to judgment against Louis XVI and were uncertain about the implications of doing so; some of them may have preferred to keep their options open indefinitely. The eventual decision to try the king, and the procedures for doing so, were profoundly shaped by the factional struggle within the assembly. Imposing a trial was a triumph for the Girondins; its outcome, though it was not their ultimate defeat, was their crucial one.[2]

Since the Convention's very first days, the Jacobins and the radicals of the popular movement in the sections had been calling for the punishment of "the last king of France" in execution of the judgment they saw already declared by the people on 10 August. A petition from the Gravilliers section on 7 October had urged the deputies to polish the blade of the law, reward anyone striking down known traitors, and make available for scrutiny by the sections the incriminating papers amassed by the Commune's Surveillance Committee. On 16 October, the Jacobin Club of Auxerre had challenged the assembly to explain its delay in executing the people's judgment. Its petition inspired the Jacobin deputy Bourbotte to announce his readiness to vote immediately for the tyrant's death. His call for debate to begin on "the great act of justice . . . demanded from all points of the republic" was answered by Girondins who counseled delay, pending more information and further discussion of procedures to be followed. "The question of the judgment of Louis XVI is endlessly postponed," protested a frustrated member of the Paris Jacobin Club at its meeting of 26 October. "The question has to be pushed relentlessly until we've seen the entire royal family guillotined. Their heads once off their shoulders, we'll have no more troubles."[3]

On 6 November, after weeks of waiting, the Convention finally heard from the Commission of Twenty-Four appointed to investigate the papers collected by the Surveillance Committee of the Commune. The report, presented by Charles-Eléanore Dufriche-Valazé, a former military officer from the department of the Orne, steered well away from the explosive topic of the suborning of former deputies by the crown that Marat and the Jacobins had most wanted to see explored. Instead, it offered abundant evidence of Louis XVI's secret contacts with the émigrés over the past year and his consistent funding of their counterrevolutionary activities. None of this was a great surprise. But on the more contentious question of how the deputies should respond to this evidence, Valazé stumbled over the crucial conundrum offered by the constitution of 1791.

Defenders of the king were claiming by this time that the constitution had declared him inviolable; that he had already suffered deposition, the only penalty against him the constitution had allowed; that he could not be punished further as a private citizen for any actions he had taken before his relegation to that status. The commission reasoned, to the contrary, that royal inviolability had been a fiction, that it was ridiculous to invoke deposition as a punishment now the monarchy had been abolished, that the crimes the former king had committed far exceeded in any case those the constitution had allowed as grounds for enforced abdication.

Valazé concluded, nonetheless, that there was incontestably a contradiction between the particulars of the constitution and the principles of universal reason. The Convention had somehow to resolve this issue, "for never, under any pretext, can the king escape a penalty other than deposition." He declined to consider what that penalty might be; indeed, he declared that his heart recoiled from the task. "Enough and for too long has my mind rested on the crimes of the human race and the punishments appropriate to repress them," he brooded aloud. He could be allowed his ruminations, perhaps, but the Convention could not. As a reminder of the urgency of popular demands for decisive action against Louis Capet, the assembly quickly found itself in renewed argument over the threat of political agitation and social unrest in the capital—along with the now almost customary demands for Marat's head.[4]

The deputies received a more vigorous report on the matter the following day, this time from the Committee on Legislation. The date for this presentation concerning "a man who had exposed 25 million to the risk of becoming victims of tyrants" had been set a week earlier. The very same vote had ordered immediate submission of the results of a second inquiry, by the Committee of General Security. That committee had been charged to investigate another monster: "this man whose name is an insult, whose life is a web of crimes, whose presence in this assembly is a scandal," namely, Jean-Paul Marat. Was this conjunction mere coincidence? Buzot had remarked months earlier that there was a kind of co-dependence between the ever-enraged journalist and the conspiratorial king, such that the former was no longer useful now the latter had been overthrown. It seems true that there had sometimes been an odd sense of intimacy in Marat's effrontery to the monarch he had reproved so often over the years. Were their fates somehow linked in the minds of some of the deputies? Did they indeed need to fall together? Or was the call for one report meant as a tactical answer to the call for the other?[5]

In any case, the report on Marat failed to materialize. The Committee on Legislation, on the other hand, met its deadline. Lucidly presented by a lawyer from Toulouse, Jean-Baptiste Mailhe, this report set the terms of the Convention's deliberations over the king's fate until the final decision was made more than two months later. Could Louis XVI be judged for crimes he had committed while he reigned as a constitutional monarch? By whom could he be judged? Under what procedures? Would it be necessary to submit the judgment to final ratification by the entire body of citizens meeting in their primary assemblies? These were the questions Mailhe posed. At their heart was the nature of royal inviolability, over which the Constituent Assembly had struggled so strenuously. The Committee on Legislation was now ready to resolve the conflict between law and justice so ineffectually addressed by Valazé.

In the analysis Mailhe offered, royal inviolability was not prior to the constitution but an artifact of it, a device established to preserve the separation of powers between the executive and the legislative body (which was also held to be inviolable). As such, he reasoned, Louis XVI's inviolability was subject to the fundamental principle enunciated by the French Revolution from its very origins: the primacy of the sovereign will of the nation, against which no constitution could stand. Since the monarchy had been abolished, the former king no longer enjoyed the constitutional protection his inviolability had afforded him from the judgment of the nation. Moreover, the nation had a right, grounded in principles of nature prior to all institutions, "to avenge itself against the perfidy of an individual who, having accepted the mission to execute its supreme laws and the power necessary to fulfill it, had abused it and made himself its oppressor and murderer." No longer a king, Louis Capet could be judged as an individual according to laws of nature existing in all times and places, laws "as ancient as societies." "He has resumed his original title; he is a man. If he is innocent, let him prove it; if he is guilty, his fate must serve as an example to the world."[6] Innocence was not presumed in this formulation.

Louis XVI could therefore be judged, but by whom? Since he could not be subject to courts created by the constitution, Mailhe reported, the Committee on Legislation had considered only two possibilities for a trial. The Convention had either to sit in judgment on the former monarch itself or create a special tribunal to do so. The committee had preferred the first alternative: that the former king be tried by the Convention according to procedures Mailhe went on to specify. Practical considerations of time and complexity aside, the logic for this choice seemed to rest on the argument that only the representative body could decide on an individual case in the interests of the entire nation. "A society that, in deciding the fate of one of its members, would do so on grounds other than the interests of all, would clearly be moving toward its own destruction; and a political body can never be supposed to desire its own harm." In effect, here, as on many other occasions in the history of the French Revolution, a Rousseauian conception of the general will was being blended awkwardly with a strong theory of representation. The Convention, Mailhe insisted, "entirely and perfectly represents the French Republic."[7] This conclusion, it appeared, left no grounds for considering the final question he had posed at the opening of his speech. Once the representative body had spoken, what need would there be for its decision to be submitted for ratification by the nation in the primary assemblies?

The Convention ordered Mailhe's report printed, translated into many languages, and distributed to the departments, municipalities, and armies. Marat had not been in the Manège to hear it, but he praised it for its solid reasoning in the *Journal de la République française* of 12 November. He emphasized, nonetheless, the need for greater precision regarding the "capital provision" of the procedure Mailhe had proposed, the one requiring that the deputies reach their final decision by a roll-call vote. Unless the votes were delivered aloud and confirmed in writing, he argued, the prospect of public shame or fear of popular execration could not constrain them; secret ballots would be cast to absolve the "ex-king, traitor and conspirator." The point was an essential one. The Convention's eventual decision to adopt this procedure was crucial to the endgame of the king's trial.

In response to Mailhe's reasoning, The People's Friend offered a blunt summary of the position the Jacobins would take for the remainder of the trial debates. To his mind, one consideration alone had to determine the Convention's judgment. "It's that the ex-monarch is a public enemy, captured in arms against the people he wanted to slaughter and put back under the yoke. So it's not a question of paging through the Constitution to discover what kind of penalty he might have incurred given all the means of impunity it contrived for him. Who doesn't see that he must be judged by the imprescriptible right that nations possess to punish their faithless agents, traitors and conspirators?" A warning to the deputies followed. "If the rights of a nation could be restricted by its representatives, it is clear that the French people, restored by the insurrection of the Tenth [of August] to its full plenitude, possesses the power to impose on Louis Capet the penalty all peoples of the world have at hand to punish conspirators."[8]

FIRST RESPONDERS

The deputies did not resume discussion of the Mailhe report until 13 November. Then they heard two fundamentally antithetical responses to it, each arguing against the kind of trial the report had proposed. The first came from Charles-François-Gabriel Morisson, deputy from the Vendée, who had voted consistently with the right in the Constituent Assembly and would survive charges of royalism in 1793 to live through successive political regimes into the Restoration. Shrewdly, whatever his intimate convictions, Morisson did not deny that Louis XVI had committed heinous crimes against the nation. Nor did he contest the principle that "a sovereign people has no other rule than its supreme will." The French nation had declared Louis XVI inviolable, he acknowledged; it could decree that he was so no longer. What it could not do, as a matter of justice, was make that decree retroactive and abrogate the law in effect at the time of the king's crimes. Deposition was the only penalty against Louis XVI the nation had allowed under the constitution of 1792; he had already paid that penalty. No longer a king, he could not legally be subjected as a man to further punishment.

As for rights of vengeance deriving from nature, Morisson insisted that the institution of society depended on limiting the rights of each to maximize the exercise of the rights of all. To do this was the work of the law. "But I have said before, and I repeat with regret, that the law remains silent about this culprit, despite the enormity of his crimes. Louis XVI cannot fall now under the blade of the law; it says nothing in his regard. Consequently, we cannot judge him." Nor indeed, Morrison proceeded to argue, would it be in the interests of the nation to do so. A monstrous and interminable trial could be avoided, the general approbation of Europe earned, and the greatness of the nation demonstrated by a decision to banish the deposed king from the French Republic, making him punishable by death only in the case of his return.[9]

A practiced lawyer before the Revolution and a veteran of the Constituent Assembly, Morisson had thus argued skillfully against putting the former constitutional monarch on trial. In doing so, he eschewed any hint of traditional arguments in favor of royal inviolability, operating instead within the legalistic terms of debate set out by Mailhe on behalf of the Committee on Legislation. The tone changed, though, when Morisson was followed to the tribune by Saint-Just, some thirty years his junior, now making his maiden speech to the Convention with all the passionate conviction of youth. Saint-Just also argued against putting Louis XVI on trial, but he did so in language transcending the legalistic arguments—and amplifying the appeals to natural right—advanced by earlier speakers. The king he denounced was not the constitutional monarch considered by Valazé and Mailhe; the constitution itself had no bearing in his reasoning regarding Louis's guilt. Implicitly, Saint-Just replaced the crown of Louis the Pious upon the head of that ruler's fifteenth namesake, restoring him to the line of his ancestors the better to call for his death.

In this indictment, Louis XVI's guilt went beyond any specific actions to be charged against him as a king or an individual. His crime was kingship itself. "Nothing in the world can legitimate this usurpation, and whatever the illusions, whatever the conventions, with which monarchy cloaks itself, it is an eternal crime against which every man has the right to rise up and to arm himself. It is one of those outrages that even the blindness of an entire people cannot justify; by giving the example a nation transgresses against nature, and all men hold from nature the secret mission to destroy the domination in every land." A trial was unnecessary in such a case. "*No man can reign innocently*. The folly is all too evident. Every king is a rebel and a usurper." Nor, indeed, was a trial possible. "To judge is to apply the law; law supposes a common share in justice; and what justice can be common to humanity and kings?" For Saint-Just, Louis XVI was not a citizen bound to others by the social contract; his throne placed him beyond the common law. He was outside the common body politic, an alien enemy, subject only to the *droit des gens*, the law natural to all humankind. "This man must reign or die" was Saint-Just's verdict. There could be no middle ground.[10]

Saint-Just wanted a decisive act to destroy a king and found a republic. For that he also looked to the Roman example. "There will be astonishment one day that humanity was less advanced in the eighteenth century than in the time of Caesar," he cried. That tyrant had been slain in the Senate "with no other formalities than thirty dagger blows, and no other law than the liberty of Rome." In Paris, by contrast, the deputies were respectfully embarking on a trial for an "assassin of a people, taken *in flagrante*, his hand in blood, his hand in crime." Louis XVI was another Catiline, a murderer who would swear that he had saved his country. "Louis fought against the people: he is defeated. He is a barbarian, an alien prisoner of war . . . ; he was not king of the French, he was king of a band of conspirators." The deputies could seek justice for Louis XVI or found a republic, Saint-Just proclaimed. They could not do both.[11]

In a dramatic shift of tone, Saint-Just thus sanctioned the ancient act of tyrannicide in the name of natural right, the eternal law of nature. In this view, no trial was necessary; a king could be struck down not only as a traitor but as an enemy of the entire human race. Appeals to the right of nature remained a consistent theme as the deputies debated whether the former king could be tried. Dan Edelstein found that some two-thirds of more than a hundred speeches expressing an opinion by 3 December claimed natural right as authorizing the Convention to proceed to judgment against Louis (though only a minority of about one-tenth took the extreme Montagnard view that he could be executed immediately).[12]

That a range of possibilities could nonetheless be derived from an appeal to natural law was already evident in other speeches delivered on 13 November. Claude Fauchet, the constitutional bishop of Calvados who followed Saint-Just to the tribune, invoked the law of nature against any imposition of the death penalty. François Robert, one of the first revolutionaries to call himself a republican, denied Louis any claim to immunity under the constitution of 1791, which had neither been submitted to the people for approval nor accepted in good faith by Louis XVI. The king had to be judged, Robert concluded. He deferred his opinion regarding an eventual punishment.[13]

By this time, it was becoming evident that the argument over the ex-king's fate could be a long one. At Pétion's suggestion, the Convention decided on 13 November to clarify and advance discussion by focusing initially on the very first question addressed by Mailhe: whether Louis could indeed be judged. This effort to move the discussion forward was short-lived. Two days later, the assembly reversed itself at Buzot's urging on the grounds that the issues to be confronted were inextricably linked (hence indefinitely debatable). As if to prove the point, the deputies were immediately subjected to a lengthy speech by an obscure deputy concluding only that the entire matter of the king's fate should be postponed until a new constitution had been written. In response, the abbé Grégoire argued vigorously at similar length that Louis could and must be judged but suggested deferring a definite decision on that matter until the former king had been allowed to speak against it. Different in style and tenor, the two speeches betrayed a widely shared hesitation to advance toward a point of decision.[14]

Marat's own speech on the matter was never delivered to the Convention *viva voce*. It was published by order of the Convention in early December, along with scores of others, after the assembly decided that it could not afford the time to hear any more of them. It also appeared in the *Journal de la République française* on 4–5 December. One of its most notable aspects is that it failed to follow Saint-Just in repudiating entirely the notion of a formal trial. "The crimes of Louis XVI are unhappily all too real, they are sustained, they are notorious," he planned to argue in opening this speech. There could be no doubt that "a despot, stained with every crime, a monster still smothered with the blood of those friends of France he has had slaughtered, can be brought to judgment and condemned to death."[15] But the criminal ruler whose death Marat demanded was not the anointed successor of Clovis whom Saint-Just wanted struck down for the very crime of kingship itself. He was the constitutional monarch of 1791, appointed by the nation and now accountable to it for his contravention of the terms of his office as a public functionary.

In fact, much of Marat's condemnation was leveled against the Constituent Assembly. Too cowardly to overthrow the despot in 1789, he charged, it had created a monstrous constitution designating a mere public functionary as hereditary representative of the nation, placing all power again in the monarch's hands, and allowing him a thousand opportunities to ruin the people with impunity and destroy liberty by force. This monstrosity, Marat protested, was now being used to defend Louis Capet from the nation he had betrayed. The bulk of his speech was therefore devoted to a textual argument. "Throughout this speech I've carefully avoided anything that could inflame the imagination, the pride, and the passions of the Assembly . . . ," he emphasized in a final note. "It's not a question of motivating the friends of liberty to punish the perfidious ex-monarch . . . , but of reducing to silence the friends of monarchy who might protest his slaughter by the sword of the law."[16]

Poring over the crucial constitutional articles that restricted potential punishment of the king to a specifically defined set of actions, Marat detected a crucial fault in the constitutional dike meant to protect the monarch's inviolability. The Constituent Assembly had barely escaped the trauma of putting a king on trial after Louis XVI's flight to Varennes. To avoid that possibility in future, it had laid down in the constitution that the king would be "deemed to have abdicated" by virtue of the very fact of his taking one of several specific actions designated. Punishment was thus made an automatic consequence of the crime: by taking any of the actions stipulated in the text, the king was deemed to have dethroned himself. He thereby assumed the status of a mere citizen and could, according to another article of the constitution, be held legally accountable in that capacity for any subsequent crime. Since one of the specific actions triggering automatic abdication was the king's retraction of his oath to maintain the constitution, Marat argued that Louis could be held accountable for his actions from the very moment he began to conspire to undermine it. More convincing, because the chronology was clearer, was the case of the king's failure to oppose by a formal act any foreign invasion undertaken in his name. Marat reasoned that Louis had dethroned himself by his silence at the very instant of the Austrian and Prussian invasions. He had, therefore, to be brought to judgment as a citizen responsible for the subsequent massacre of thousands of the people at the Tuileries palace on 10 August 1791.

There was thus more than enough in the constitution, Marat would have told the deputies, to silence the defenders of the former monarch who would cite it as proof of his impunity. But his dismantling of the constitutional arguments had merely cleared the ground for a more fundamental indictment. "It's on the imprescriptible right of nations and the political laws of states that you will base your judgment of Louis Capet," he reasoned. In what free states would the laws not punish a ruler who had conspired against the homeland? It would be an outrage against the laws to invoke them in favor of "a liar, a traitor, a conspirator . . . a tyrant stained with every crime . . . a monster still reeking from the blood of the fellow citizens he has had slaughtered."[17]

It could not be forgotten, in Marat's view, that Louis had not worked alone to ruin the country. One benefit of placing him on trial was that he would incriminate his accomplices, all the ministers, faithless deputies, administrators, judges, and generals who had conspired with him against the public safety. Bringing him to judgment would thus be the surest means of saving the nation from its most dangerous enemies; it should therefore be carried out by the Convention on behalf of the nation, formally and with severity. There could be no talk that condemning an ex-king to live amid a free nation would be punishment enough. For as long as he breathed, Louis Capet would be the target of schemes to liberate him and destroy the liberty of the nation in scenes of bloody vengeance. To pardon him would be cowardice compounded by treason, perfidy, and villainy. "I conclude that the ex-monarch be judged promptly and that his punishment be capital."[18]

It's worth remarking that Condorcet, in his speech first published as an article in late November, also dismantled claims that the constitution protected the former king from further judgment. But there the similarity ended. Condorcet repudiated, as a violation of the first principles of jurisprudence, the notion of a trial procedure in which the assembly would be both accuser and judge. Instead, he offered an extensive proposal for the creation of a special national tribunal that would follow an elaborate procedure to allow a jury to reach a judgment by a plurality of votes.[19] The contrast was clear. Condorcet wanted a judicial showcase that would educate the world regarding the commitment of the Revolution to principles of universal justice. Marat wanted a trial that would purge the people of its enemies.

STARVE THE PEOPLE, SAVE THE KING?

By mid-November, it was clear that drawn-out deliberation on the matter of the king's trial was inevitable. Delay was ensured in any case by the press of other affairs. Among the most sensational was the discovery in the Tuileries palace of a secret strongbox (an *armoire de fer*) containing further evidence of Louis XVI's enduring hatred of the Revolution and his efforts to undermine the Legislative Assembly, suborn its members, encourage emigration, and conspire with counterrevolutionaries. The evidence of the papers shattered what was left of Mirabeau's reputation (vindicating Marat's attacks on him) by revealing the extent to which he had conspired with the court to restore royal authority. But the manner of the announcement on 20 November also inflicted collateral damage on Roland, who blithely informed the Convention that he had ordered the strongbox opened that morning and had quickly scanned its contents. That he had done so with no formal witnesses present, and without requiring an immediate inventory, opened him up to Montagnard suspicions that he could have tampered with the evidence for his own political purposes. Demands for a special committee to examine the papers, or for a special session to consider the issue, were complicated by arguments over the participation in them of potentially compromised former deputies.

Marat's efforts to intervene in this debate proved fruitless. When he mounted the tribune, deputies took their distance in response to a shout to "Clear the tribune!" His demand to speak was met with derision, the question was called, and the assembly decreed the formation of a committee of inquiry into the matter, to be chosen by lot. The People's Friend had to fall back on the *Journal de la République française* to lay out the ample possibilities for chicanery the opening of the strongbox might have allowed. The minister could have extracted documents inculpating Louis XVI or members of earlier legislatures corrupted by him; he could have forged and inserted materials incriminating the most patriotic friends of the people: he had, after all, insinuated that there would be new evidence regarding the revolution of 10 August.[20] Roland's dogged insistence on his integrity succeeded only in fueling the ongoing factional struggle.

A no less dramatic claim on the assembly's attention was presented by Dumouriez's striking success in invading Belgium, the high point of the series of French victories in the concluding months of 1792. Conquest brought its own, time-consuming problems. Were the conquered territories to be annexed to France or established as sister republics? Was Dumouriez's transparent plan to turn Belgium into a separate principality under his direction to be tolerated? What would be the status of such other conquered territories as the Swiss republics, Nice, Piedmont, the Rhineland? Enthusiastic when the French armies drove the Prussian and Austrian invaders from French soil, Marat became less so as they began to conquer. On 24 November, he was declaring the victories a sham faked by generals who would be returning with the enemy in the spring. The next day, mocking celebrations that republican France, victorious in destroying despotism at home, was now bringing liberty to its neighbors, he protested that its soldiers were being required to abandon their own homes to serve the conspiracies of the Revolution's enemies, the machinations of a hypocritical minister, and the plots of a criminal faction in the legislature tyrannizing the friends of liberty. Soon, he was denouncing Dumouriez's efforts to grab control of grain supply for his troops. The general's agents were scouring northern France for grain, reported the *Journal de la République française*, buying it up at outrageous prices and hoarding it for some nefarious purpose, perhaps in league with the ministers. It was certain, the journal went on to say, that Roland, the generals, and the capitalists were making famine their instrument of counterrevolution in the hope of provoking crises that would allow Louis XVI to be rescued from the Temple and restored to the throne. Dumouriez, Marat was sure, would go over to the enemy by the coming March.[21] Not a bad prediction: the general, frustrated in his ambitions, made that move in early April 1793.

Dumouriez was by no means the only general grabbing food supplies. Others were also putting pressure on the Convention to provide for their armies. Their needs simply aggravated the ever-present question of subsistence in the months following an uneven harvest in the summer of 1792. With shortages of grain and the rising cost of bread—trends increasingly burdensome for the population as assignats continued to lose value—reports of popular agitation began to reach the Convention from across the country. At the same time, anxiety about the prospect of future scarcity soared in the capital. Criticism of the system responsible for guaranteeing food supplies in Paris at customary prices had grown intense by mid-November, roiling debates in the Commune as the sections began to call for a maximum.

These demands took a radical turn on 16 November in a speech to the General Council of the Commune by Anaxagoras (formerly Pierre-Gaspard) Chaumette, who had by this time replaced Robespierre as the Commune's most visible figure. Future prosecutor of the Commune, Chaumette cited the language of Moses ("though we no longer believe in his relics") as evidence of the horror with which peoples had always regarded the despicable individuals who hoarded the subsistence that belonged to all. Dismissing the idea that provisioning the army had caused shortages, he instead blamed the entire sequence of depredations resulting from the war Louis XVI had unleashed. Not that he called for an end to the fighting. Shortages of all kinds would soon end, he seemed to say, once Europe in its entirety had been "Frenchified, municipalized, jacobinized," thereby becoming a zone in which necessities would circulate freely among members of the great human family.

This, at least, was the burden of Chaumette's speech as one journalist reported it. Another had heard something more menacing: a charge that the Constituent Assembly, leaving property undefined in the Declaration of the Rights of Man and of the Citizen, had omitted any mention of the right of individuals to a share in the common subsistence. It was time to tell the truth, Chaumette said, according to this account. It was time to distinguish the difference between *property* and *properties*: "the one is an offense against our person, our rights; the others, in a free state, are only relative." This meant that ownership of land, grain, and everything relating to subsistence was no more than conditional; the consumer was the true proprietor of such commodities; they belonged to the entire Republic. The possessor of these goods was only their guarantor and distributor; withholding the gifts of nature belonging to all was criminal.[22]

That same day, the Convention resumed discussion of a decree on subsistence drafted by its committees of agriculture and commerce. Preaching free trade while imposing controls in a bizarre concoction of regulations, the draft required all landed proprietors, farmers, or owners of grain supplies to report the quantities at their disposal and bring to market an amount to be mandated by the authorities; it prohibited export of grain and established controls over where it could be bought and sold domestically; it authorized funds for the minister of the interior to buy large quantities of grain from abroad. As before, the proposal led to sustained arguments for and against market freedom, with no agreement in sight. The assembly would be forced to debate the issue repeatedly over the coming weeks.

The pressure on the Convention to act was made abundantly clear on 19 November, when a petition from the electoral assembly of the department of Seine et Oise called for a maximum on the prices of necessities, controls on the grain trade, the preservation of small farms, and the elimination of "capitalists." "Liberty of the grain trade is incompatible with the existence of our republic," the petition insisted. "The law must ensure the provisioning of the republic and the subsistence of all." Shortly thereafter, the deputies heard a letter from Roland (written in his capacity as a citizen) urging free trade in grain and criticizing the Commune for its practice of subsidizing the price of bread in Paris. Resuming his official voice, the minister offered an extended lecture on the importance of the principle of freedom of trade, followed by a proclamation of the Executive Council to the same effect. In yet another communication, he reported convulsive agitations across the country, popular price-fixing, attacks on grain convoys, and competition among municipalities to keep control of local supplies. "It's time for the law to speak, and the law alone," the minister expostulated. Only "inexorable inflexibility" could bring calm to the Republic and give the entire world the example of the most perfect government to unite men.[23]

Marat offered his own analysis of the situation on 25 November, alleging in an issue of the *Journal de la République française* that counterrevolutionary ministers were in league with enemies of the homeland to starve the people into revolting against the Convention, demand restoration of the old regime, save Louis the Traitor from his punishment, and put him back on the throne. The scarcity of grain was artificial, he maintained. It was caused by the very fear of shortage spread by hoarders and enemies of the people to bring it about; by exportation of grain by speculators planning to reimport it at inflated prices; by Roland's own embezzlement and manipulation of funds granted him to buy foreign grain; by reluctance of producers to accept payment in uncertain bills of credit. The remedies were therefore obvious. The Convention had to relieve Roland of responsibility for provisioning departments short of grain and demand a full accounting from him. It had to make payments to producers more reliable. It had to open by force all the storehouses of merchants refusing to bring their grain to market.[24] Radical though these policies were, they fell far short of Chaumette's Enragé demands. The People's Friend was appealing to the supreme principle of public safety in a moment of emergency. He was far from preaching the agrarian law.

The "inexorable inflexibility" Roland wanted proved difficult to achieve. On 28 November, the minister was protesting again to the Convention about the disruptions the Commune was causing by caving to pressure to provide Paris markets with grain below the current market price. Two days later, he was communicating more "sad truths." Circulation of grain was being blocked everywhere; anyone trying to engage in the grain trade was being treated as a hoarder; armed mobs were marching on markets and farms, fixing prices, even seizing grain without paying. Thirty thousand armed men demanding to fix the price of foodstuffs had been pushed back from the gates of Chartres, swearing to return in greater numbers within two days. Armed bands were threatening Blois and Orléans. In and around Le Mans, officials had been forced at knife point to reduce prices. Anarchy was threatening Le Havre with famine. There had been disorders in Lyon. Paris was undeniably the source of these uprisings, Roland declared: disorders were being fomented throughout the country by agitators from the capital who were spreading rumors, preaching anarchy and civil war, and inciting counterrevolutionary sentiments wherever hatred of liberty and equality remained strong.

The capital itself, Roland warned, was also facing a subsistence crisis. Grain convoys heading toward it were being attacked and plundered. The Commune's policy of providing flour at below-market prices was attracting buyers from surrounding regions, their purchases further depleting supplies within the city walls. Rising demand and reduced prices were thus bringing the capital (and municipal finances) close to disaster. The only solution was for the Commune to reverse its dangerous policy and sell its flour stocks at market price, even in the face of pressure and threats of insurrection from the sections. Accordingly, the minister proposed a decree that would rigorously enforce freedom of commerce in grain and order the Commune to discontinue a policy that was "ruining the people and exposing it to famine out of cowardly considerations pushed by ill-intentioned men, contrary to the always good and just will of the people." His letter was met with considerable skepticism. Returning to the order of the day, the deputies had enough time to hear a single opinion regarding the king's trial before the session ended.[25]

Roland's attack on the Commune met a quick response. The next day, 29 November, the Convention received a deputation of representatives of the sections and the General Council demanding a very different remedy—in very different language—for the great misfortunes facing the capital. "The most numerous part of the people, the one that made the revolution and will maintain it, that knows how to love liberty and deserves your solicitude above all, is afflicted by the greatest disquiet and the cruelest misery," the deputation declared. Rich capitalists were conspiring to lay hold of all agricultural and industrial resources, it continued; they were maintaining high prices for grain, even as they were contaminating it by additives. A new aristocracy of wealth was striving to rise on the ruins of the old one. Institutions of commerce, banking, and welfare organizations were plotting with the tyrant in the Temple to starve the people back into despotism. "The revolution is over," they maintained. "In the name of public safety, we come to demand that you restore to the constituted authorities the right to fix the price of the most necessary commodities." In effect, the petitioners were invoking popular sovereignty in a call for a return to the market policies of the Old Regime.

Responding to these words as president of the Convention, Grégoire was firm. The people had paid too high a price for liberty to lose it now, he assured the deputation. A new aristocracy trying to mount the debris of the old one would meet the same fate; vampires trying to devour the people's subsistence would be punished. Heroic words, minimal action: the petition was referred to the committees on agriculture and commerce, and the deputies turned again to discussion of the decree these committees had long since proposed.[26]

In the debate that followed, Joseph Lequinio called for freedom of trade, importation of grain from overseas, no forced inventory of grain stocks. Another Montagnard, Joseph-Pierre-Marie Fayau, demanded the opposite. For his part, Saint-Just argued in a flamboyant speech that multiplication of assignats had produced a disproportion between signs and goods. In effect, he offered a caricature of commercial society in which too much money was chasing too few commodities, and assignats were driving out grain. Stop the increase in paper money, he advocated; reduce public expenses; let the farmer sell his grain; maintain government granaries for times of greatest misery. His heart, however, was not in the economics of the situation, though he discussed them at length. The more philosophical analysis he presented amounted to a profoundly Rousseauian nightmare in which an explosion of liberty had returned France to a sort of primordial chaos. "In the hideous state of anarchy where we find ourselves, man, falling back into a kind of savagery, no longer recognizes legitimate constraints. With individuals armed one against another in a struggle for mutual independence, there is no more law, there are no more judges, and all ideas of justice give birth to violence and crime for lack of a guarantee; isolated wills no longer oblige others; each individual acts naturally as legislator and magistrate and, in doing so, forms notions of order that produce general disorder." To end this horror, he pleaded, the foundation of the Republic had to be laid in virtue, without which liberty would disappear within six months. The first step was to execute the king. "All the abuses will live as long as the king does; we will never agree, we'll be at war one with another. The Republic doesn't win support with feebleness; let's do everything to make hatred of kings infuse the blood of the people. Then all eyes will turn toward the homeland."[27]

Saint-Just's words met with strong approval in the *Journal de la République française*. Marat declared him "the only orator yet to give me pleasure at the tribune." The young man's intervention, he added, "announced style, logic and ideas. When he is matured by reflections and renounces flash, he'll be a man, he's a thinker." Marat thought the speech had shown well that the French were still not free, that the source of the evils afflicting them was their egoism and their vices, that their liberty could still be just a bad dream ending in a hideous awakening. "I go much further," he commented. "For four years I haven't stopped repeating that our liberty is only a gross illusion, or rather that it exists only in words, that not only do we not have liberty but we can't have it because free men are not made with old slaves." The French were never as oppressed under despotism as they were now under the so-called reign of liberty, he continued, warming to a familiar theme. Roland was infecting the nation with antipatriotic propaganda, intercepting the mail of patriots, plotting with hoarders to starve the people, slaughtering it as it gathered to demand bread. All that was necessary was to open the granaries by force and make grain available at a controlled price. "When the people is abandoned to the horrors of misery and hunger is not the time to talk of upholding the laws, distributive justice, and the need to avoid harming commerce. The sole concern has to be public safety, preventing the people from dying of inanition and the state from the furies of civil war."[28]

Saint-Just's reflections about a state of war found some echoes, too, in the alarming news that greeted the Convention the following day. Deputies sent to investigate the disorders in Chartres on 28 November had returned abruptly to report that a large and aggressive crowd had attacked them, threatened them with death, and compelled them to endorse a series of price controls despite their insistence that they lacked authority to do so. The returnees noted the presence of priests in the crowd that had terrorized them; the priests had been the most unbridled in their behavior. Outrage at bread prices had been amplified by shouts for an agrarian law, anger at the alleged suppression of the Catholic Church, hatred of the rich, and hostility toward Paris.[29]

The deputies were shocked and incredulous at these events and the role of clergy in fanning the fury against the Revolution they revealed. In the debate that followed, Pétion was the first to demand forceful repression of the dangerous disorders for which grain shortage served as mere excuse. Men who had been misled had to be brought back to reason, he urged; those who had misled them had to be punished with severity. "Oh you who constantly debase the National Convention and the constituted authorities," he apostrophized, "how guilty you are! Tell me, what do you want?" Who was being blamed here? At least some members of his audience had little doubt. They had already interrupted the accounts of these events earlier with a cry of indignation against Marat. Now they reiterated their denunciation. "*It's Marat! It's the infamous Marat!*" they responded; applause followed.[30]

Danton's response was more measured. "We'll turn France upside down by too-hasty application of overly philosophical principles that I cherish but the people are not ready for, especially in the countryside," he warned. Leave the people the priests offering it lifelong consolation was his counsel; assure it grain; deploy the force of the nation against criminals aiming to create famine amid abundance. Above all, make a prompt decision regarding the judgment of the former king before uncertainty over his fate tore the nation apart. Robespierre soon reiterated this call. Take care of the issue of subsistence, he urged; lay the foundations of the constitution the following day. But first and foremost, "I demand that the last French tyrant, the leader and rallying point of the conspirators, be condemned to punishment for his crimes. So long as the Convention postpones the decision regarding this important trial, it will revivify factions and sustain the hope of the partisans of monarchy."[31]

As Buzot led the Girondins in clamoring for a repressive decree, The People's Friend mounted the tribune. "*Down with Marat*," came a cry. "As long as there are such men among you, don't be astonished that the people denies you respect," howled Kersaint to the deputies. For fifteen minutes, spasms of outrage from the extreme left of the hall competed with applause from the center. With order finally restored, Buzot returned to the factional fight. "You talk about judging the king. Ah! I can quickly see three men who'd like to succeed him.... These riots were not about the king or judging him . . . we're not here to address fresh sources of division." Over further objections, Marat insisted on the right to speak. "Citizens, you're told endlessly that the constituted authorities are not respected, but respect is inspired, not commanded. Let the authorities be worthy of respect and they will be respected," he scolded. "To confront unfortunates demanding bread with cannon and bayonets doesn't inspire confidence or restore calm, it's the method of tyrants." He insisted that blood had flowed around Chartres because the local administration was dominated by hoarders. The severity of the law had to be deployed against agitators who were the last hope of royalists and the henchmen of despotism, he acknowledged. "But let the public force be commanded by a patriot." *"Marat, for example?"* came the mocking reply.[32]

Not for the first time, there were appeals to end this factional squabbling. Marat's ally Louis Legendre protested that the people had no doubt that the current disorders were being fomented by desperate friends of Louis XVI in a last-ditch effort to save him; it wanted the matter decided. Legendre called for publication of all the speeches prepared for debate on the procedure to decide the former king's fate, leaving the Convention free to decide almost immediately whether there should be a trial or not. Mailhe trumped him by proposing that the trial begin instantly without waiting weeks for the speeches to be printed. "Who's talking about a trial?" countered the fervent Montagnard Jeanbon Saint-André to applause from the galleries. "There's no longer even a judgment to be declared. . . . The people pronounced it on 10 August. All that remains is to subject Louis the Traitor to the penalty he deserved. . . . If Louis XVI is innocent, Citizens, you are all rebels; if he is guilty, he must perish."[33]

Before the session ended, the Convention decreed the printing of speeches addressing whether and how Louis XVI should be judged, with debate on the matter to resume after their distribution. A second decree ordered an address to the nation explaining the advantages of free trade in foodstuffs and disavowing any intention on the part of the Convention to deny citizens the clergy promised them by the Civil Constitution of the Clergy. A third charged the executive power to take all measures necessary to punish the leaders of the mob that had attacked the deputies sent to Chartres. A fourth, passed after much argument, censured these same deputies for submitting to the demand for price controls rather than face death and declared that action null and void. In effect, the question of judging the king, still encumbered with many other issues, had barely advanced beyond square one.

Commentary from Paris radicals was not slow in coming. On 1 December, Marat's alienated former host Jacques Roux offered an enraged address to the Observatoire section under the title *Speech on the Judgment of Louis-the-Last, on the Prosecution of Speculators, Hoarders and Traitors.* It was quickly published for circulation to all the sections, the Commune, and popular societies of the capital. Roux's own Gravilliers section, one of the poorest of the city, found it compelling enough to urge its reading to the sections twice weekly for a month. "It's only by prompt and severe measures, in being always at the ready, that you will raise yourselves to the height of your destinies," Roux told his audience. Blasting the Convention, he too cited the example of the Romans, "our models in matters of revolution," who had made a terrifying example of senatorial usurpation, "the despotism as frightful as the scepter of kings because it enchains the people without its knowing." If the people had shown the courage to resist perfidious representatives earlier in the revolution, Roux contended, it would not be finding itself "starved, ruined, despairing, poisoned by venomous reptiles, parasitical speculators, and vampires, who, by a murderous monopolistic scheme, are taking over commerce in foodstuffs, devouring properties, manufactures and liberty, and bringing us by usurious trafficking to the point of counterrevolution." Would it now hesitate to "unleash the thunder of liberty when at the heart of the French senate virtue is barely safe, a perfidious faction is preparing mortal blows against public liberty, incorruptible defenders of the people are forced to keep silent, and impious legislators surround themselves with an armed force to stand in judgment with impunity and absolve Louis XVI, the executioner of the French?"

The future Enragé exhorted the people to show itself great, proud, inexorable, and terrifying, not only in declaring implacable war against hoarders and speculators but in confronting base and perverse representatives who begged the nation's indulgence on behalf of a constitutional tyrant. The assassin of the French people had to lose his head to the blade of the law at the earliest moment, along with the monsters who had served him in plotting to slaughter half the nation and enslave the other. It was time to teach the peoples of the earth that virtue alone makes a man inviolable and crime leads tyrants to the scaffold; time for the nation to tell its representatives that the people does not delegate its power to wipe away the crimes of kings; time for them to know that they would face the supreme tribunal of the nation if they failed to strike the tyrant in the midst of his crimes. "Kings deserve death from the moment they are born," Roux exclaimed, channeling Saint-Just. "Among the French, the freest of all peoples, the tyrant must not survive the tyranny. We have to crush pitilessly the hydra devouring us; and kings must exist henceforth only in the history recounting their crimes."[34]

"*Food, and to get it, force for the law!*" was Chaumette's demand on behalf of the sans-culottes nine months later in a famous session of the Convention on 5 September 1793 that is often seen as marking the onset of popular terror. *Bread, and to get it, the head of the king!* was Roux's implicit call on 1 December 1792. He put the Convention on notice that it would have to decide the king's fate under threat of insurrection by a hungry people.

A DECISION TO DECIDE

"We're amusing ourselves like children and the starving people is asking us for bread," Marat protested on 1 December as the Convention was busy discussing the placement in the Manège of war tribute from Tournai. It wasn't until the following day, after the Girondins had again fretted publicly about threats to their lives and liberty emanating from the city of Paris, that the deputies turned again to the proposed legislation regarding subsistence. This gave Robespierre the opportunity to speak on the question at some length. His principles were clearly stated. Society exists to maintain the imprescriptible rights of man, he stipulated, the first being the right to exist. The primary social law guarantees this right to all members of society. Subsistence necessary for all is therefore common to the entire society; only the excess is individual property available for commercial enterprise; speculation at the expense of the lives of others is no more than brigandage and fratricide. The task of legislation is thus to "guarantee all members of society enjoyment of that portion of the fruits of the earth necessary for their existence, assure the landowners or farmers the price of their industry, and turn over what's left to the liberty of commerce."

That freedom of commerce was essential to social welfare, Robespierre did not dispute. Circulation of goods was as crucial to society as the flow of blood was to the body, he acknowledged; it brought necessities within the reach of all, and abundance and life to the poorest hovel. But the flow of commerce had to be maintained against "obstacles imposed on circulation under the pretext of rendering it unlimited." To achieve this goal, the quantities of grain produced in each region and by every farmer had to be made known and merchants had to be forced to bring them to market openly. Monopolies, hoarding, and speculation had to be forbidden; the notion of indefinite liberty of commerce, which was their excuse, condition, and cause, had to be abandoned. "Laissez faire," Robespierre proclaimed, was "a system entirely contrary to society, entirely favorable to the grain merchants."

The people was naturally good and peaceable, Robespierre continued. Disorders were created by intrigue and ambition, by men arousing the people as an excuse to repress it. It followed that the first priority was to take measures to prevent the brigandage of monopoly by forcing men to be honest. "Rich egoists, know how to foresee and prevent the terrible results of the combat of pride and vile passions against justice and humanity. . . . And you, legislators, remember that you are not the representatives of a privileged caste but of the French people . . . , that justice is the source of order, the happiness of citizens the guarantee of public tranquility, and the long convulsions that tear states apart are only the struggle of prejudices against principles, egoism against the general interest, the pride and passions of powerful men against the rights and need of the feeble."[35] For Robespierre as for Saint-Just, the need for a reign of virtue in the service of social justice was coming into focus.

The Girondins did not appreciate the lofty lecture. "When the people are hungry, we'll give it Robespierre's speech," quipped Barbaroux. "The people's toadies give it words when it needs bread," taunted Birotteau. Robespierre's response to these barbs was less precise than his exposition of his principles. He wanted all proposals favoring unlimited commerce to be tabled. He wanted it recognized, "as an incontestable principle, that the sole means of alleviating the present ills is to adopt wise laws." Yes, wise laws! But what were they? "Let's vote, let's vote on Robespierre's proposal," came the derisive reply. The discussion was interrupted, and the assembly moved on to other matters.[36] This had not been among Robespierre's most impressive performances. His next would be more incisive.

A deputation on behalf of all forty-eight Paris sections was more forceful when it appeared before the Convention that same evening to represent the views of "a portion of the sovereign, this terrifying portion that has no fear of the power of bayonets, that has made the revolution and renewed it on its own responsibility." The people of Paris had "broken the constitutional yoke, overthrown the monstrous colossus of executive power, and freed the sovereign will from slavery," the deputies were reminded. It had stayed its hand to allow the vengeance of the entire body of the French people to be exercised more formally by its representatives. The Convention had been invested with sovereign power to lay the foundations of liberty and equality, and to execute the nation's vengeance against the monster who wanted to destroy them. Why was it delaying? "Agents of the national vengeance, what's holding back the arm you raised to swear to it? Why render useless this arm that was only awaiting a blade and has one today? Will it be paralyzed . . . ? Are the crimes of Louis the Perjurer not yet manifest? Has your hatred worn thin, believing it enough to vomit execrations against the civicidal Louis?" To ask whether the former king could be judged was political blasphemy, the sectionnaires insisted; it invited long discussions that compromised the will of the nation and risked its glory.

"Can't death relieve you of your victim . . . ?" they demanded. "To temporize is agreeing to prolong our ills. The people, patient as it is, can get tired of waiting. Dare to finish for us the story of the most horrible conspiracy. We swear, we're ready to ratify the judgment you owe us."

The message was clear: the assembly had to decide. The sectionnaires urged the deputies to devote four afternoon sessions a week to this purpose. Bertrand Barère, currently the assembly's president, was defensive in the face of implied threats of a new insurrection. The Convention had not waited for the Paris sections to express concern regarding judgment of the former king, he pleaded; it had decreed publication of speeches on the matter, pending a trial to be completed by a set date. He was firm, however, in asserting that the assembly would "never be preempted on matters of public safety by any section of the people," that it was impaired neither by torpor nor cowardice, that it would have the courage to snuff out all factions, "even the impious faction of *vilifiers* of the national power." The deputation was exercising the sacred right of petition, he acknowledged, but the Convention was accountable for its judgment of Louis the Traitor only to the entire Republic, one and indivisible.[37]

This starchy reprimand notwithstanding, pressure from the sections had its effect. The following day, 3 December, after still more fruitless debate over subsistence and a further report on the contents of the *armoire de fer* that proved embarrassing for some of the deputies, Barbaroux suddenly called for a trial to begin, carried out by the Convention itself. Supported in this by his Girondin allies, he was countered by Jeanbon Saint-André, who pressed the Jacobins' argument that either the king had been judged on 10 August or the insurrection that day was illegitimate. All that was necessary, Saint-André maintained, was to declare Louis XVI an enemy of the people. This call was taken up by Robespierre in one of his most celebrated speeches.

"There's no trial to be conducted here," the Incorruptible proclaimed. "Louis is not an accused person. You are not judges. You are and can only be men of state, the representatives of the nation. You don't have a verdict to give for or against an individual, but a measure of public safety to take, a measure to execute for the national welfare." A deposed king could be nothing but trouble in a republic, Robespierre continued; to treat Louis XVI's crime as problematic and his guilt as a matter of grave debate would render him even more dangerous to liberty. "Louis was King and the Republic is founded. The great question before you is answered simply in these words: Louis has been dethroned for his crimes." The former monarch had denounced the French people as rebellious; he had appealed to his fellow tyrants to punish his subjects. "Victory and the people decided that he alone was the rebel. Louis cannot be judged; he is already condemned, or the Republic is not absolved of guilt."

To put Louis XVI on trial, whatever the procedure, Robespierre thus contended, would bring the Revolution itself into court and throw into question the insurrection that had overthrown him. To invoke the constitution in Louis's favor was retrograde, a step back toward "constitutional despotism." There could be no "constitutional logic-chopping" in a Convention that was itself unconstitutional. "The Constitution forbade all that you have done . . . ," the Incorruptible reminded the deputies. "The Constitution condemns you." He did not follow Saint-Just in declaring kingship itself a crime against nature, but he insisted that the king's tyranny and the resulting insurrection had returned the nation to a state of nature in relation to its former monarch. The social contract thus destroyed, the people and its tyrant were now in a state of war; they no longer shared a common polity; they could not seek justice in a common court. "Peoples don't judge in the same way as courts of law. They don't deliver sentences, they hurl thunderbolts; they don't condemn kings, they plunge them back into the void." Robespierre saw only one possible conclusion. "Louis must die because the homeland must live. . . . I move that the Convention declare him, this very moment, a traitor to the French nation, a criminal toward humanity."[38]

To no avail. Robespierre's arguments went nowhere. In the tumult that followed, the Girondins carried the day. No one doubted Louis's guilt, Pétion now argued, but a punishment had to be declared, and for that a trial was necessary. At his instigation, the deputies finally decided by a large majority that Louis XVI would be judged, and by the Convention itself.[39]

Days of rancor followed. On 4 December, debate descended repeatedly into uproar. Deputies wrestled at the tribune to speak or struggled to do so over belligerent protests from the floor. The crowd in the galleries constantly erupted into applause or shouts of disapproval. Buzot, seizing the Girondin momentum from the previous day, proposed a law mandating the death penalty for anyone advocating the reestablishment of monarchy in France, under whatever title it might be. The move was understood as an implicit accusation that the Jacobins were conspiring to place Philippe Egalité, one of their number, on the throne. When Merlin blundered into calling for an exception to this law that would allow reinstatement of monarchy to be discussed within the primary assemblies, he triggered a violent reaction. Marat was convinced that Merlin had been duped into making this proposal, the more so because Guadet quickly exploited it to insinuate that some deputies were plotting to replace one despotism with another (the target replacement for Louis XVI presumably being Philippe Egalité or Maximilien Robespierre).

Passed without Merlin's amendment, Buzot's decree ordained death for anyone proposing or attempting to reestablish in France "either monarchy or any other power deleterious to the sovereignty of the people." The decision was too hasty in Robespierre's opinion, since the deputies missed an opportunity to proclaim in more solemn terms that "no nation can give itself a king." This axiom he characterized, remarkably, as "the only appropriate limit on the too unlimited and often misunderstood principle of the sovereignty of peoples."[40] The formulation was a telling one. The reach of the principle of popular sovereignty would remain a continuous critical issue until the king's trial was over, and well beyond.

The Jacobins, for their part, made several attempts to roll back or modify the 3 December decision that a trial before the Convention would decide the king's fate. Philippeaux, wanting a quick result, urged the assembly to go into permanent session until a judgment had been reached. In response, Pétion rejected that idea on the grounds that meeting nonstop would sooner or later winnow the majority and allow a minority to dominate. Marat declared, to the contrary, that it would allow the majority to starve the minority into submission. Robespierre warned against it on the grounds that it would lengthen debate and produce a bad result. Facing down shouts to dispatch him to the Abbaye prison, he observed that the assembly had decreed that Louis would be judged by the Convention without specifying a formal trial process. This omission allowed him to insist, one more time, that the former king should be condemned instantaneously in consequence of the insurrection of 10 August. Tumult followed. Eventually the assembly agreed to devote every day from eleven to six to a trial.[41]

Jacobin demands for a rapid outcome persisted nevertheless. On 6 December, claiming that "the people will have bread once the hoarder-in-chief has placed his head on the scaffold," a deputy called for judgment of the ex-king within five days. Bourbotte demanded a procedure that would bring the prisoner before the assembly immediately to confront his crimes, implicate others in them, and hear his death sentence within twenty-four hours. Billaud-Varenne, maintaining that Louis had already been judged on 10 August, proposed that he be brought before the assembly to hear his condemnation to death the following day. In the same spirit, François-Louis Bourdon, deputy of the Oise, demanded that the guilty monarch be confronted by the widows of the patriotic victims massacred on 10 August.

Marat, however, while predictably blasting almost everyone in authority as belonging to a criminal faction seeking to save the infamous tyrant from punishment, surprised the entire assembly by counseling against a rush to judgment. "There have been efforts to push the patriots in this assembly into ill-considered measures by demanding that they vote the death of the tyrant by acclamation," he warned. "Well, for my part, I call on them for the greatest calm; we must pronounce wisely. Let's not prepare for the enemies of liberty the atrocious calumnies they'll rain down on us if we abandon ourselves solely to sentiments of our force and indignation." Applause gave way to indignation, nonetheless, when The People's Friend went on to talk of traitors in the assembly ("*Name them!*") who could be identified infallibly by requiring publication of the opinions in a roll-call vote on the king's fate. He descended from the tribune to fervent cheers from the galleries. His call for the publication of individual votes in judgment of the former monarch raised the political stakes in a trial now deeply embedded in factional strife. Have a little patience, he was urging readers of the *Journal de la République française* on 6 December, "and we'll see if Capet's creatures don't hasten to poison the tyrant to prevent him from denouncing his accomplices."[42]

Before the stormy session ended on 6 December, the Convention finally decided on a trial procedure. A new committee would draw up an indictment of the former king, compile the evidence for each accusation of Louis's wrongdoing, and prepare a list of questions he would be compelled to answer in person. The dossier would be discussed by the deputies on 10 December, and Louis XVI would be brought before the Convention for trial beginning 11 December.[43]

"A NOVEL AND SUBLIME SPECTACLE"

By 9:30 that morning, when the Convention began its session, the galleries of the Manège were overflowing and the surrounding streets jammed. The entire route by which Louis had been brought from his prison to the assembly had been lined with crowds, almost all of them armed in a display of popular strength. The deputies, in fact, were not immediately ready to receive their former monarch at the appointed time. Jean-Baptiste-Robert Lindet, charged with drafting the act of accusation, had still been working to the point of utter exhaustion when he appeared before the assembly the previous evening. He had only been able to present part of his report, a long prefatory summary of the history of the Revolution showing that the former king, acting independently of his ministers, had constantly sought to "reconquer the scepter of despotism and destroy everything that would resist his efforts." Inciting the formation of a coalition of sovereigns, provoking foreign war, allowing the desolation of the colonies, and igniting internal dissension and civil war: these, Lindet charged, were the means Louis had employed in his effort to recover his throne or bury himself under its ruins.

No sooner had Lindet finished speaking than Marat had rushed to the tribune to list several other crimes to be added to the indictment of the former monarch, including mistreatment of patriotic volunteers, hoarding of specie and grain, "judicial massacres" carried out in the king's name, constraints on the administration of justice, "and so many other crimes of which Louis Capet is guilty." Once it had become clear that the act of accusation itself would not be ready that evening, the Convention had adjourned. Lindet had been left to work throughout the night to complete the indictment, leaving him prostrate the following morning. To the aggravation of the Jacobins, his belated final draft was read to the Convention on 11 December by none other than Barbaroux.[44]

The list of crimes Lindet had included in the act of accusation was extensive, though deputies had others to add, including Marat again, who emphasized the gravity of Louis's protection of refractory priests, hoarding of specie that had "reduced the people to the most profound misery," and hoarding of grain to "reduce the people to famine and thereby destroy liberty." While proliferating charges, The People's Friend also urged that the articles of accusation be limited to the king's actions after adoption of the constitution and reduced to a small number to avoid interminable discussions. Otherwise, he argued in the *Journal de la République française* (and attempted frequently to tell the Convention), the assembly would find itself trapped in a labyrinth of its own making.

The final version of the indictment the deputies agreed to present to Louis when he was eventually brought before them later that morning showed no such restraint. It accused the former monarch of a "multitude of crimes," from the closing of the Tennis Court on 20 June and many other acts of resistance to the Revolution in 1789 to the swearing of a false oath at the Festival of the Federation in 1790, attempting to flee the country in 1791, plotting with Lafayette at the time of the Champ de Mars Massacre, conspiring to undermine the constitution he had feigned to accept, intriguing with the émigrés and foreign rulers, undermining the war effort in defense of the nation, suborning the people's representatives, and inciting the massacre of patriots by the Swiss guard on 10 August 1792.[45]

Following this indictment, Barère, acting as president of the assembly, began a cross-examination that required Louis to respond to each clause of the act of accusation as it was read to him. Regarding various of his actions in 1789, the ex-king replied that they were within his power to take according to his best judgment. To the charge that he had used public monies for the purposes of corruption, he answered that he knew no greater pleasure than to give money to those in need of it but denied suborning any of the nation's representatives. Of other alleged infractions he claimed ignorance or lack of memory, that he was not accountable to the nation for his actions before he had accepted the constitution, that later ones were constitutionally permitted and taken by ministers in his name as required. On the matter of his travel to Varennes, he answered that explanations had already been given to the Constituent Assembly at the time. For the massacre on the Champ de Mars, or that of patriots at the Tuileries palace on 10 August 1792, he denied all responsibility. The list of questions exhausted after three hours, he was asked if there was anything he wished to add. He requested a copy of the questions presented to him, as well as the supporting documents, and asked for the right to choose a lawyer for his defense. But the proceedings were not yet over. He was then required to examine each supporting document leveled at him to verify its authenticity. "I don't recognize it," and "I have no knowledge of it," or plain "no," were his preferred answers. As he was ushered from the hall, he asked again for a lawyer.[46]

Louis's performance had impressed many of the deputies. He had accepted, at least formally, the right of the nation to put him on trial, while insisting that he could be judged only for actions he had taken since his acceptance of the constitution. He had maintained the constitutionality of those actions he acknowledged taking and his innocence or ignorance of the others with which he was charged. Demanding legal counsel, he had challenged his accusers to find him guilty under the law.[47] He had also blunted any inclination among the majority to proceed to an early verdict. The deputies' decision to return him to the Temple was followed immediately by a motion to allow him to choose one or more lawyers. This proposal was vigorously opposed by Marat and other Jacobins, whose shouts for an adjournment cast the assembly into prolonged uproar. Calm once restored, Marat was incensed anew by invocation of an article of the Civil Code allowing accused persons to choose defense counsel. "We're not dealing here with an ordinary trial," he expostulated, "we don't need the chicanery of the law courts." Tumult erupted yet again over Jacobin demands for a roll-call vote to decide this and any subsequent issues relating to the trial. Finally, by a massive majority, the Convention voted to allow Louis his choice of one or more legal counsel.[48] Selecting them and allowing them to pore over the act of accusation and the mass of supporting evidence would take time. The Jacobins had again been outmaneuvered in their campaign for a rapid judgment.

Marat had many criticisms of the procedure adopted on 11 December, especially provisions he anticipated would extend the length of the trial unnecessarily. Nonetheless, he celebrated the day. "It was a novel and sublime spectacle for the philanthropic thinker to see a despot, who was surrounded not long ago by the brilliance of his pomp and the formidable trappings of his power, now stripped of all the imposing signs of his past grandeur and brought like a criminal to the foot of a popular tribunal, to undergo its judgment and receive the punishment for his crimes," he wrote in the *Journal de la République française* a few days later. "Was the reign of servile prejudices finally over?" he asked. That this was irreversibly the case he had seen demonstrated by the attitude of the most oppressed classes of the people crowded that day into the public galleries of the Manège. They had witnessed the ex-monarch "with the most perfect indifference, I would have said, if they could have been indifferent to the judgment of a tyrant."[49]

Louis, on the other hand, struck The People's Friend as oblivious to his change in fortune and the precariousness of his position. Even so, he was accorded a measure of grudging respect. "We owe it to the truth to say that he presented and conducted himself at the bar with decency, however humiliating his position must have been, that he heard himself called *Louis Capet* a hundred times without showing the least annoyance, he who had never heard any name but *Majesty*," the *Journal de la République française* reported on 14 December; "he showed not the least impatience the whole time he was kept standing, he before whom no man had had the privilege to sit." There would have been grandeur in the ex-king's humiliation if he had been innocent and sensitive to it, Marat added, or if his apathetic calm had expressed the wise man's resignation to the harsh laws of necessity. His responses, assuming they had not been suggested to him, proved that he was less stupid than he had been thought. For the most part, however, they were evasive, impudent lies.[50]

What idea should one form, then, of Louis Capet? That of a soulless man never worthy of the throne, Marat answered, a despot perpetually forced by his counselors into conduct shifting with the circumstances, a tyrant pushed into every crime. "By turn haughty, insolent, vile, crawling, begging, he always showed himself harsh, barbarous, ferocious, false, deceitful, traitorous; he soaked his hands remorselessly in the blood of the people and, if he is not the author of the plots woven against public liberty, he agreed to them and is no less guilty of them in the eyes of justice."[51]

Over the next few days, Louis was allowed to choose a legal team for his defense. His first two choices were eminent lawyers of the Old Regime. The first, pleading infirmity, prudently declined to serve. The second,

François-Denis Tronchet, a former member of the Constituent Assembly and one of three designated to depose Louis XVI after the flight to Varenne, declared in accepting that he could not "as a man . . . refuse help to another over whose head the blade of justice is suspended." He was immediately joined in this sentiment by Guillaume-Chrétien de Lamoignon de Malesherbes, long honored as an enlightened former minister, protector of the philosophes, and one of the earliest critics of absolutism to call for a meeting of the Estates General. "I was called twice to counsel the man who was my master at a time when everyone aspired to this function. I owe him the same service when it is a function that many find dangerous," Malesherbes volunteered to the president of the Convention on 11 December (in an act of courage even Marat found admirable).[52] His offer, conveyed to his ex-king on 13 December, was instantly accepted. Four days later, after learning that the Convention had decided the trial would resume on 26 December, these two defenders requested the help of a third in dealing, within such a short time frame, with a mass of materials they had still barely received. Their choice was Raymond De Sèze, an astute lawyer from an ancient noble family, who had achieved prominence as a brilliant orator in some notable cases during the Revolution. His would be the voice pleading for the former king when the trial resumed.

ROLANDIN FOXES, PATRIOTIC TURKEYS

As Louis and his counsel hastily prepared their response to the mountain of evidence eventually placed before them, the Convention returned to its internecine feud between Jacobins and Girondins. Philippe Egalité was again the immediate target for the Girondins. Buzot, invoking the example of the expulsion of the Tarquins from a newly republican Rome, proposed on 16 December that the entire family of the Bourbons (save Louis XVI, his wife, and their children) be banished from republican France. That Egalité was the principal object of this proposal Buzot made entirely clear in arguing that the former prince's name, wealth, ambition, popular appeal in France, and intimate relations with the great in Britain exemplified the danger of resurgent royalism in a young republic. Enthusiastic applause for this speech from much of the assembly contrasted markedly with the angry agitation it incited on the part of the Mountain, which countered calls for an immediate vote on Buzot's proposal with a frantic motion to adjourn. When Louvet mounted the tribune to oppose adjournment, he went even further in channeling "the immortal founder of a famous republic, the father of Roman liberty, Brutus."[53] He meant the legendary consul Lucius Junius Brutus, whom the painter David had famously portrayed awaiting the bodies of the sons whose execution he had ordered for plotting the restoration of the ousted Tarquins.

"Yes, Brutus: the speech he pronounced more than two thousand years ago is so applicable to our current situation that one could believe I wrote it today," Louvet declaimed before reading the text (from Livy) in which the Roman consul had called for the exile of the last member of the Tarquin family. "Louvet mustn't crush us with the despotism of his talent," protested Duhem for the Jacobins, to no avail. The Girondin champion charged on to expatiate on the historical parallels between two young, vulnerable republics. He was soon followed by Lanjuinais who found no need for parallels with a distant past, instead bitterly recalling the more immediate history of Egalité's election to the Convention "under the axe of the new tyrants, on the orders of those who had to share the protectorate prepared for him." Without gaining much traction within the assembly, the Jacobins protested that Egalité was an elected representative of the people; that his expulsion would compromise judgment of Louis XVI and was perhaps even intended to do so; that any decision in his regard should be delayed until after the trial had been completed. Saint-Just was blunt: "Brutus chased out the Tarquins to assure Rome's liberty and I don't know whether, among us, the Tarquins aren't being pushed out to make room for other Tarquins."[54]

The confrontation between the factions abruptly shifted when Merlin not only urged expulsion of the Bourbons within three days but called for an end to divisions within the Convention between opposing parties favoring rival ministers. To applause from the Mountain and the galleries, Duhem seized on this opportunity to demand Roland's instant dismissal as interior minister. In response, applause from the Right and the Center supported a similar demand for the dismissal of Pache, the minister of war. Calls for the ostracism of one or other of the two ministers came next. Barère, supporting Merlin's proposal for the banishment of the royal family, bundled it with a motion to replace both ministers and to charge the Constitutional Committee to devise a mechanism allowing election of the executive power by the primary assemblies. Jacobins accused Roland of acting as the head of a party, using his immense power as minister to deploy government funds to control public opinion by subsidizing publications.

Barère had something more radical in mind. He was expressing dissatisfaction with a drift of the Convention toward a kind of party government, English-style, that he condemned as an affront to the sovereignty of the people. More significantly, he was looking toward a vote of the primary assemblies as a mechanism to halt that drift. An appeal to the people had already been bruited about as a potential check on the Convention's judgment of the king; Marat had reported on 15 December that Roland was circulating questions about that possibility among the deputies, preparing an infernal trap to get the tyrant absolved and himself named first minister. Now the idea had surfaced as offering a check on a dysfunctional representative assembly. Duhem saw the maneuver taking shape and tried to avert it. "They want to refer the judgment of the former king to the primary assemblies," he exclaimed. "I demand that we deliberate regarding Louis's fate without delay."[55]

By this time, though, the assembly was close to procedural meltdown. The discussion, increasingly tumultuous, had twice been declared closed; deputies were still clamoring to speak, even wrestling for possession of the tribune; the president had lost control. There were calls of "To the Abbaye!" The Jacobins, in an uproar, railed against the tyranny of a majority, the domination of Roland and his party, and the violation of the sovereignty of the people that would be implied in the banishment of one of its representatives. "This whole maneuver was planned," expostulated Choudieu on their behalf; "they wanted to present us as a faction attached to the Orléans party." Order was finally restored long enough for the assembly to decree the banishment of the Bourbons with the exception of the imprisoned royal family. The crucial decision regarding Philippe Egalité was postponed for two days. The session had lasted eight hours.[56]

On 19 December, returning to the issue of expelling Egalité and his extended family, the Convention endured yet another storm. The atmosphere was clouded, as ever, by fear of Paris extremism: the Girondins saw the danger represented by the presence in the galleries of "the turbulent portion of the people that arrogates national sovereignty to itself and tries to influence our deliberation by putting us under the knife," as well as by the noisy mass deputation outside, led by the mayor of Paris. This time, there was pushback against the "immoral" and "impolitic" decree against the Bourbons. There were protests that the Girondins had been so eager to deploy this law against their opponents that it had been improperly made public, communicated prematurely to the ministers before the minutes of the session had been circulated, and even sent to the army in Belgium (where the eldest son of Philippe Egalité was serving as a general under Dumouriez): all this before the definitive text had been read to the assembly for approval. The fact that this latter formality had been omitted (inexplicably!) the following day, and was still overdue, fed suspicion throughout the assembly. The Girondins had overreached, their attempts to expel Egalité threatening, by implication, the security of any representative chosen by the people. Marat himself had no doubt that action against Egalité was intended as a precedent for excluding the most energetic patriots from the Convention and even from the nation. Sensing defeat, the Girondins managed a strategic withdrawal. On Pétion's motion, the assembly suspended execution of the 16 December decree, postponing further discussion of it until after Louis XVI had been judged.[57]

As usual, Marat's effort to participate in these debates had been blocked. He had managed only a few shouts of protest from the floor. In frustration, and to mobilize support, he had turned to the Jacobin Club on 16 December, attending its meeting for the first time since 22 October. The *Journal des débats et de la correspondance de la Société des Jacobins* reported that he was welcomed with frenetic enthusiasm, even though the first order of business after his arrival was the reading of an address from the Jacobin Club of Châtellerault calling for his expulsion, and Robespierre's, from the society. One of many addresses to this effect the club had received from its affiliated societies around this time, it was noisily set aside, leaving Marat free to protest "the hideous plot to stifle liberty in the midst of the Convention and close the mouth of the true friends of the people." His voice had been silenced the previous day, he proclaimed, to exclamations of horror. "What a cruel insult to the people, because I, I myself, am the man of the people." His treatment was an affront to the friends of the people, he maintained; they had to form a holy coalition to counter the maneuvers of the Brissotins. Allowed to seize the podium again later (over the vehement protests of a member whose turn it was to speak), he took the opportunity to oppose Robespierre's support for the exile of Egalité and the Bourbon family. The Girondins wanted to banish all the enemies of the people, he observed, "and you, Robespierre, would be first in line. Let Egalité remain among us, let the patriots not abandon the field of battle; if we abandon him, liberty is lost irretrievably."[58]

There had to be an insurrection within the assembly, Marat told the Jacobin Club, "a holy insurrection of the minority against the majority." The Brissotins and Rolandins had to be prevented from monopolizing the presidency of the Convention and using its power to shut down those not of their party. This once done, it would be easy to crush the unworthy and vile men behind the machinations to attack his person, men who would destroy the body politic if the Jacobins allowed them to do so. This campaign for the Mountain to control the decision-making apparatus of the Convention was continued in the *Journal de la République française* the following morning. The criminal faction had used a thousand parliamentary tricks to silence him, Marat argued. "A deputy is a sentinel of the people. . . . His weapon is speech and the tribune his field of battle. Silencing him thus condemns him to incapacity to defend the people." By preventing patriotic deputies from speaking, he insisted, a handful of greedy intriguers devoted to an ambitious minister were effectively launching a counterrevolution. His subsequent call for patriotic deputies to support him and get themselves elected to the bureau of the assembly was a cry of despair. At the election of officers on 13 December, the Girondin Defermon had received 258 votes for the presidency to Marat's lone one.[59]

Over the next few days, the *Journal de la République française* mounted a series of attacks on Roland, the Girondins, their ally Dumouriez, and indeed the entire Convention. The issue of 21 December offered an extended diatribe against "The Rolandin Foxes and the Patriotic Turkeys." It indicted the Girondin foxes for their propaganda campaign to discredit Paris and its deputies (paid for by the minister of the interior), their scheme to move the Convention itself from the capital to the provinces, and their efforts to save Louis XVI by extending his trial indefinitely and referring his judgment eventually to the primary assemblies. It reproached the turkeys, the patriotic deputies on whom the Girondin foxes preyed, for their lack of unity, their petty jealousies, their readiness to abandon their fellow deputies most able to thwart conspiracies, their lack of knowledge, talent, judgment, virtue, and civic spirit. "I expect nothing good from them . . . ," Marat expostulated. "The disgust I feel among them would already have determined me to resign if I were not awaiting events that are inevitable, during which the true defenders of the people will be able to make their voices heard." The people had to recognize that the Convention could not fulfill its hopes as currently constituted, he warned. It had to recognize that the machine of government would not work until justice had been inflicted upon two hundred thousand criminals, all supporters of the old regime; that it had to invest its authority in men worthy of its confidence; that it had to reduce the number of its representatives by a quarter.[60] The bloodthirsty spirit of The People's Friend, the old urge to purge, was beginning to stir under the skin of the elected representative.

Pushback against him was already stirring at the Jacobin Club that same day when Deflers, the editor of the *Journal des débats . . . de la Société*, was unceremoniously expelled from the society for exaggerating the fervor with which The People's Friend had been received by the club on 16 December. Hostility toward him became more open a week later, when a letter from a corresponding society in praise of Robespierre and Marat, "these two incorruptible friends of the people," prompted Robert to insist on the need for patriots in the provinces to distinguish between them. Their conflation was the work of hostile propaganda in the departments, he countered, but what a difference there was between the two! Robespierre was wise and moderate, Marat a hothead. The provincial Jacobin societies had to be made aware of the contrast. This sentiment was soon amplified by another Montagnard, Bourdon. "We should have told the affiliated societies what we think of Marat long ago," he reiterated. "How could they ever have confused Marat and Robespierre? Robespierre is a truly virtuous man against whom we have had no reproach since the revolution began; Robespierre is moderate in his methods, whereas Marat is a violent writer who harms the Jacobins . . . and does much damage to us in the National Convention. The deputies imagine that we are Marat's partisans; we're even called Maratists." If it were once understood that the Jacobins knew how to assess this man, Bourdon continued, deputies would gravitate toward the Mountain, they would join the club, and the affiliated societies would rally anew to the cause of liberty. It was time for Marat to sacrifice himself to the cause of liberty, time for him to be thrown out of the club.

Applauded by some members, noisily rejected by others, and violently repudiated by the public in the galleries, this motion was vigorously opposed by Dufourny. Marat had been useful, serving the Revolution with courage, he pleaded to great applause. "Marat has been a necessary man; revolutions require forceful heads, capable of uniting states, and Marat is one of these rare men who are necessary for the overthrow of despotism." At this urging, the club voted against Marat's expulsion and in favor of a circular (never produced) to be sent to the affiliated societies detailing the similarities and differences between Robespierre and Marat in such a way that they would learn to "separate two names they wrongly believe must be eternally conjoined." A commentary in the *Journal des débats . . . de la Société* explained these attacks as motivated by a recent call of this "famous doctor" for a new bleeding of the body politic. Elsewhere, there was hostile speculation that Robespierre was behind these attacks, his nose out of joint at Marat's rapturous reception at the Jacobin Club on 16 December and the latter's open challenge to his position regarding the exile of Egalité.[61]

By 25 December, Marat was approaching a state of frenzy as he offered "a profession of faith" regarding Philippe Egalité "in response to the impostures of the Roland faction." His stance toward Egalité as an elected representative was clear: "the Convention has no right to strip a citizen of his status as a deputy and could not do so without infringing on national sovereignty, usurping absolute power, and making itself independent of the nation." But he insisted on a very different opinion in the face of Girondin charges that "the party of Marat and Robespierre, which never existed," was seeking the death of the dethroned despot in order to crown his cousin instead. "I declare, then, that I have always regarded Orléans as an unworthy favorite of fortune, without virtues, soul and guts, his only merit being the jargon of the alleys." This was a man without civic commitment, he continued, a man who lacked the intellect and courage to realize his ambitious projects despite his vast wealth, a man who was posturing as a patriot while secretly in league with the Roland faction. Whatever disasters might afflict the Revolution, The People's Friend asserted, Orléans would be the last man (other than conspirators and traitors) to whom he would turn. "And if I'm still among the living at that point, I'd rather suffer martyrdom than give him my voice."[62]

There was much more in this 25 December issue of the *Journal de la République française*. It overflowed with frustration. There were calls for the exclusion from public office of anyone who had served the Old Regime and failed to show active civic commitment since 14 July 1789; for reduction of the number of administrators weighing on the people; for greater severity against "the perturbers of society, the secret plotters, the clandestine corruptors and wrongdoers"; for an end to division in the Convention and its domination by "the gangrened members of the two legislatures, ex-nobles, ex-magistrates, ex priests, ex-financiers, ex-king's men." There were protests at the concerted efforts to prevent The People's Friend from speaking in the assembly and bitter complaints at the cowardice of patriots in failing to support "the only writer who has sanely judged all the characters who have appeared on the stage of the revolution, foreseen the direction taken by the two legislatures, revealed the vices of their liberticidal decrees, and uncovered the plots of the enemies of liberty and predicted long in advance the great events necessarily resulting from the clandestine maneuvers of the traitors at the helm of the state." Above all, there was defiance. "I can't hope then to do any good now, but I'll prevent evil and, despite the eternal denunciations and machinations of the henchmen of the Roland faction against me, I'll remain in the Convention to unmask the traitors and frustrate their plots because, as long as I have a drop of blood in my veins, I'll be the stalwart defender of the people."[63]

Marat did not have to wait long for an answer, but it came not from the Gironde but the Mountain, emphasizing his isolation within the Convention. That same day, Chabot invoked the decree imposing the death penalty on anyone proposing the reestablishment of monarchy or its equivalent in calling for a national head. He didn't need to mention a name. "It's Marat!" came the clamor. "Yes, it's Marat," Chabot replied to applause. One journalist reported that Marat merely smiled at the betrayal. Chabot proceeded to read the lines from the *Journal de la République française* on 25 December suggesting that it was inevitable that the nation would renounce democracy in favor of a leader. He continued by quoting the prediction in the 21 December issue that the Convention could not fulfill its goals as it was currently constituted and that the machine of government would not work until two hundred thousand criminals had been brought to justice. Concluding from these passages that Marat was calling for a dictator, Chabot demanded a decree of accusation against him. Calls of support for this action were heard from the floor.[64]

Marat faced them, addressing "the public enemies I've constantly pursued" and "the patriots without virtue, sodden with self-love, shocked that I called them turkeys." Constantly interrupted, he cited the record of his attacks on the monarchy, reiterated his disdain for Philippe Egalité, and signaled his contempt for the accusations that he wanted to put this Bourbon on the throne. He condemned the scandalous dissensions in an assembly without a spark of virtue and protested the indignities inflicted on him since becoming a deputy. To provoke the Convention and recall it to its duty, he acknowledged, he had declared that the people might end up giving itself a leader. For that opinion a false patriot had denounced him, even knowing the purity of his heart!

"You declare yourselves the protectors of liberty of opinion," he harangued the deputies, "and you're its cowardly tyrants. You're the ones demanding a decree of accusation against me; you're the ones putting the blade over my head. What fine legislators!" There was prolonged agitation and applause from the galleries before he could continue. He would brave the clamor of his enemies, he now told the Convention; it would not forget its wisdom enough to decree an act of accusation against him. But if it did so, he declared, "contempt would drive me from its midst, and I would appeal to the people. I call on my cowardly slanderers to take the trouble to refute me if they have the talent. March toward the public good in great steps, and don't waste your time in scandalous discussions."

At least some deputies heard him. A tussle pitted those wanting to return to the order of the day against those calling for the act of accusation against him or his assignment to the Abbaye for a few days. One deputy condemned the waste of time discussing "Maratic madness." But Jean-Baptiste Salle escalated the attack, demanding that the Committee on Legislation consider not just the day's charges but "all the crimes Marat may have committed since the beginning of the Convention." The assembly voted to refer the matter to committee, and the heated discussion was declared closed. But tempers flared again when Marat tried insistently to return to the tribune. There were more calls for him to be sent to the Abbaye or be publicly censured. "You won't put an end to me like that," he protested. Upbraided that "nothing degrades the Convention more than seeing a member fighting against the general will," he desisted for a while, haunting the tribune until a vote by a feeble majority allowed him to speak. He was ready to "retract sincerely the words that escaped me and that calumny could exploit to make people believe I'm not the best friend of order." But he complained, nonetheless, against Defermon's arbitrary move as president to get the denunciation against him referred to the Committee on Legislation.

Amid a tumult that prevented a great number of deputies from participating in the discussion, only one of the Montagnards, Camille Desmoulins, had attempted to speak in Marat's defense. The rest, one journalist reported, seemed divided in their opinions.[65] Some were apparently as ready to jettison The People's Friend as Robespierre had been to abandon Philippe Egalité.

WHO SHALL JUDGE?

With efforts to put Jean-Paul Marat on trial failing again, the Convention returned to the Manège the following day, 26 December, to hear the case for Louis Capet. From The People's Friend, back to Louis XVI. Was there still an uncanny gravitational effect between the two of them?

The former king and his three lawyers were summoned to enter the hall at precisely 9:46 a.m. Again, the public galleries were packed. De Sèze's speech had been keenly anticipated; Marat found it presented with a great deal of skill. Opening with an effort to stir compassion for an unfortunate prince now shorn of power and glory, he informed readers of his journal, Louis's defender then sought to save his client by pointing to the interest of the European powers in his fate. At this point, he reported, rhetorical dexterity gave way to the "sophistry and bad faith" of the familiar royalist arguments: that Louis could not be judged for his actions under a constitution that had both rendered him inviolable and limited to deposition the penalty for specific actions he might take against the nation (a summary that disregarded De Sèze's careful distinction, in the latter case, between deposition and the presumption of abdication). From this it followed, in Marat's acid interpretation, that the constitution had given the monarch the right to conspire with impunity against the state; annihilate liberty; pillage, assassinate, and poison citizens; and destroy the nation itself by fire and sword. As for De Sèze's plea that if, *per impossibile*, the ex-monarch could be judged, he would be entitled to claim the right of every citizen to due process, Marat deemed it absurd since "the tyrant must only be considered as a public enemy captured with weapons in his hand."

There could be no force, then, to the lawyer's protest that the Convention had improperly constituted itself as at once prosecutor, judge, and jury. Marat thought it indisputable that the assembly had been constituted by the nation with unlimited powers to punish the tyrant and secure the public good from danger; that the maxims of criminal jurisprudence could not apply to criminals against the state; that the entire nation was accusing Louis of conspiracies and atrocious attacks against the homeland; that the Convention had to judge him. As for De Sèze's responses to the lengthy series of accusations against the former monarch, Marat dismissed them as simply misrepresenting the facts. He could not resist the observation that the list of indictments had been too long and the Convention would have saved itself embarrassment by following his advice to limit the accusations against the monarch to the events of 10 August. "The supporters of the royalist or Rolandin faction made skillful use of them to drag out the procedure and gain time to save the tyrant."[66]

It is striking that Marat made no mention of De Sèze's peroration portraying Louis as blameless, pure, thrifty, just, severe, a monarch who had shown himself "the constant friend of the people" in responding to its pleas for relief and reform. "The people wanted liberty, he gave it to them" was included among the benefits of Louis's reign in the lawyer's encomium. The implication that freedom was something that could be given by a king to a people (rather than being its inalienable right) provoked an outburst of protest from the extreme left of the assembly and the galleries. De Sèze tried to strike the maladroit phrase from the manuscript before turning it over to the Convention, but the assembly insisted on its retention, allowing him only an apologetic note of explanation in the published version.[67]

More bitterly divisive, inevitably, was the fundamental issue facing the deputies as Louis was returned to prison after addressing them briefly, "for perhaps the last time," to attest the purity of his conscience. When Manuel proposed that further discussion be postponed until three days after De Sèze's speech had been printed and circulated, the Jacobin Duhem countered with a demand for an immediate roll-call vote to decide the ex-king's fate. "All the formalities have been completed, he's had his defenders, he's said he has nothing to add in his defense," Duhem argued. "It's time for the nation to know whether it has reason to want him freed or would see freeing him as a crime; whether Louis Capet is a traitor or an honest man. It's time for us to decide the question: will Louis Capet receive the death penalty, *yes* or *no?*"[68]

With this, battle was joined. Duhem was answered by Lanjuinais, who sought to explode the entire proceeding by denouncing as "insane and thoughtless" the Convention's momentary decision to judge the ex-king itself in the first place. Louis had to be judged according to the salutary legal processes applicable to all citizens, Lanjuinais maintained, not by "conspirators loudly declaring themselves the authors of the illustrious day of 10 August" and then constituting themselves as the prosecution, judge, and jury. This call to rescind the decision that the Convention would judge the king threw the assembly into an extended frenzy. Eventually, Amar found an opportunity, speaking for the Mountain, to reassert the need for an immediate judgment. The deputies were accused of being an interested party, he acknowledged, but was the nation itself any less interested in that it had borne the blows of the tyrant? "Where then to appeal? To the planets, no doubt!"—an apt reminder that this could only ever be a political rather than a judicial decision. The nation itself could not judge the tyrant in any case, Amar contended; twenty-five million people could not assemble to make any such judgment. "Who then will judge him? You have a Convention that must act in the judicial and political order, that must do for the people all that it would do for itself. I say, then, that it remains for us alone to proceed to a roll-call vote."[69]

In outraged response, the assembly erupted with calls for adjournment. Mounting the tribune to answer De Sèze's defense, Saint-Just could not make himself heard. Under pressure, the president finally allowed a vote on adjournment. The result was dubious, but the president's decision to declare it positive ignited the uprising in the Convention for which Marat had often called. A mass of deputies, perhaps four-score strong, descended from the Mountain, decrying infamy, threatening the president with the Abbaye, and demanding the roll-call vote.

The brouhaha continued for fifteen minutes, to noisy applause from the galleries and the shocked silence of the majority of the deputies. When it ended, Jullien rushed from the Mountain to the tribune to denounce the president, whose efforts to respond were shouted down by an angry group including Marat, Billaud Varenne, and Robespierre. "Citizens, they're aiming to dissolve the Republic," Jullien declaimed several times, stirring up agitated support from the left and from the galleries. "They're aiming to dissolve the republic by attacking the Convention at its very foundations.... And we, the imperturbable friends of the people, we, the fearless defenders of its rights, we'll laugh ... at your vain efforts and the storms you try to incite across the Republic's territory." "We've sworn to die, to die as free men saving the state," Jullien continued. "I occupy the heights ironically called the *Mountain*," he proclaimed as he climbed to the left of the hall, "but I do so without insolence. This path, if one dares attack it, will be the path of the Thermopolytes." "*Yes, yes, we'll die there*," chorused the Jacobin leaders and a host of the deputies on that side, Marat doubtless among them, as Jullien demanded that the president be stripped of his powers. The furor continued until Couthon finessed the demands for an immediate vote by proposing that discussion of the former monarch's culpability be opened and continue, exclusively of other matters, until a decision had been reached.[70]

This proposal had been accepted unanimously, and the debate declared closed, when Pétion ("the rearguard of the Brissotins") ignited a new storm by insisting on the right to speak. Marat, scrambling down from the Mountain, objected to yet another show of partiality and demanded that the president call for a vote on whether the former mayor should be allowed the floor. When that vote also proved favorable and the Jacobins continued to protest, the entire assembly erupted again. This time, deputies came to blows. Pétion was finally permitted to speak, only to insist successfully on the need to reopen the question of whether the Convention should indeed have declared itself the judge of the former monarch.[71] If not the Convention, who else? The ground was being laid for an appeal to the people. The campaign for it began in earnest the following morning.

Saint-Just was first at the podium that day, 27 December, when debate resumed. Reiterating his earlier claim that the very nature of kingship put monarchs beyond the reach of the law, he protested that giving Louis a trial was tantamount to putting the sovereign people in the dock with him. "If he is innocent, the people is guilty . . . , the homeland is accused by the very nature of the deliberation." He had ready a detailed response stripping away the whitewash of the king's defense, but he went on to head off a new threat to liberty. "I've heard talk of appealing to the people the judgment that the people itself is going to pronounce through your voice," he warned the deputies. In addition to throwing the accused's guilt into doubt, he reasoned, this move would separate the people from the legislative body, weaken representation, bring back monarchy, destroy liberty. Had the people not recused itself from judgment after 10 August? Had it not chosen the Convention to decide the culprit's fate? To talk now of humanity toward the guilty king was cruelty to the people; to suggest that he be pardoned was to decree the end of liberty. Proposing that the judgment be referred to the people could only be understood as a maneuver to save the king in the likelihood that foreign gold had already purchased the votes.[72]

"It will be said that the Revolution is over," Saint-Just cautioned; "that there is nothing more to be feared from the tyrant. . . . But Citizens, tyranny is a reed bent by the wind that rises back up." He reinforced this echo of the Aesop fable retold by La Fontaine with more scientific imagery. "The moral order is like the physical. Abuses disappear momentarily, the way humidity evaporates from the earth; they soon reappear, just as moisture falls again from the clouds. The revolution begins when the tyrant is finished." Speak the truth, the youngest deputy exhorted his elders. Disregard scary talk of seditious factions, a remnant of monarchy to be dissipated by the spirit of the Republic. Let each deputy declare Louis convicted or not, with the ultimate judgment decided by a roll-call vote.[73]

AN APPEAL TO THE PEOPLE? THE CRUCIAL QUESTION

Persuasive to the majority or not, Saint-Just could not fend off calls for the assembly's judgment regarding the fate of the king to be made subject to an ultimate appeal to the people. The Girondin campaign for this was about to kick into high gear. The initial case was promptly made by Salle, veteran of the Constituent Assembly, who had been one of the most influential speakers in 1789 to press for the suspensive royal veto as a device to appeal decisions of the representative body to the judgment of the sovereign nation. Now, three years later, he wanted an appeal to the people that would save the Convention from itself and the threat of Parisian radicalism (and perhaps the king from the guillotine). The issue, as he framed it, was political rather than judicial. His entire argument marked a crucial turning point in the debate, in that it rested on the assumption that the Convention would find Louis guilty. His declared aim was not to avert an erroneous judgment of the former king but to reduce the political risk to the Convention (and implicitly to the leadership of the Girondins within it) of fixing on a penalty for a guilty verdict. He proposed that the people be limited to a choice between only two punishments, death or imprisonment.

By Salle's calculations, execution of the former monarch would risk a backlash from the people, whose pity would be exploited by royalist factions portraying the members of the Convention as regicides; it would also provoke foreign powers to try imposing a new king in Louis's place (one popular with the people, implicitly Philippe Egalité). If, on the other hand, Louis was spared execution and sentenced to imprisonment, the people would condemn its representatives as cowardly or corrupt, there would be incitement to bloody insurrection by radicals dominating the populace of Paris, and the imprisoned former king would become the center, the target and the justification for endless agitation within and invasion from without. "The slightest reverse, the merest disturbance will throw agitated citizens into the arms of the factious; and the Convention, cursed, crushed, and annihilated, will hand its power over to the first tyrants who want to grab it." Salle offered only one way to avoid these evils: the political decision fixing the king's penalty had to be turned over to the people. "All the factions would fall silent before the sovereign, legitimate authority would not be placed at risk, the Republic would be safe from dissolution."[74]

Salle was followed to the tribune by Joseph Serre, who argued for

Louis's imprisonment for the duration of the war and his banishment thereafter but called in any case for the Convention's decision to be ratified by the people in the primary assemblies. For the stalwart Jacobin Lequinio, in response, the idea of an appeal to the people, though skillfully argued by Salle, was "the crudest trap set . . . by the enemies of liberty, fanatics and traitors to prolong this business forever and then incite trouble and division everywhere." He thought it obvious that such a measure would lead directly to civil war, "which is the goal of those who haven't been able to succeed by their other means." The people had given the Convention full power to act for its safety and liberty, Lequinio insisted. The tyrant had to be promptly judged, the people had to be saved from the precipice still prepared for it by the perfidious enemies teeming in Paris and spreading throughout the republic. These remarks drew applause from the Mountain and the public in the galleries, but they provoked the rest of the assembly to rise in indignation. The commotion came close to partisan battle before subsiding enough to allow the president to give a stern lecture on the principles of open debate and respect for the regulations established by the assembly's general will.[75]

The Girondins wanted more than a lecture, though. They pressed for sanctions, to be publicized throughout the departments, against anyone inciting disorders in the assembly that undermined respect for the principle of representation. In a sense this proposal was a variation on the notion of an appeal to the people. "We're not the Convention of Paris, nor of the tribunes, but of the entire Republic," Buzot protested; "we're responsible to that for our opinions and our conduct, and even for the insults we're feeble enough to suffer." He was interrupted by Duhem, demanding on behalf of the Jacobins that mention also be made of those members threatening deputies from the Mountain with assassination. ("Yesterday, Marat was insulted in the Tuileries," someone shouted, though that could scarcely be a winning argument!) In this debate, the Girondins carried the day. Henceforth, the assembly decreed at their instigation, offenders would be censured and their reproof reported throughout the departments in a kind of denunciation to the people. For the Jacobins, in the words of Jeanbon Saint-André, this was a manifesto for civil war.[76]

Allowed to complete his speech on the morning of 28 December, Lequinio brought it to a close with a horrifying picture of the likely results of an appeal to the people. In the scenario he predicted, remnants of the ancient idolatry of kings would be reactivated by men of ill will; the flames of fanaticism would be fanned by hypocrites in an ignorant population; discord would be fed by sinister interests and intrigue; false pity would dissolve the foundations of the republic and bring back monarchism. All this was inevitable, he maintained, if the deputies were unwilling or too feeble to accept their responsibility to decide for the people. He dismissed as disingenuous the argument that the Convention had not been empowered to judge the king when it had already decreed the end of the monarchy. Having overthrown the throne, why could it now not judge the tyrant? The people's charge to its deputies was clear: to have the courage to achieve the well-being of the Republic and punish the tyrant.[77]

Lequinio was immediately followed to the tribune by the Protestant minister Rabaut-Saint-Etienne, who denounced as profoundly misguided the Convention's abrupt decision to judge the ex-king itself, thus making it, tyrannically, "in the blink of an eye, a jury of accusation, a jury of judgment, a legislator, denouncer, accuser, judge, and interested party, which is to say the most despotic and frightening tribunal the world has ever seen." This decision was contrary to the first principles of jurisprudence, Rabaut argued (citing Condorcet) and a violation of the mandate the deputies had received from the nation. All they could do now, in effect, was to refer to it the penalty to be applied once the judgment regarding the ex-king's guilt had been made.

Rabaut was outbid in this view by the more obscure speaker succeeding him, Faure, who insisted that both the ex-king's judgment and the penalty against him be decided by the will of the people. "Perish the criminals who misunderstand the sovereignty of the people," Faure declaimed. "Representative despotism is their divinity. . . . It is useless to tell them that the commune of Paris and its sections are only a small part of the people and that insurrections, with which the city of Paris alone dares threaten us, are nothing but revolts against the law." These sentiments were reiterated at greater length and more sententiously by Buzot in a discourse invoking the authority of the general will, "legally expressed, and necessarily just," that would emanate from an appeal to the people. "Crazy demagogues, will you always talk to us about civil war when, to prevent it, we invoke national sovereignty?" he scolded the Jacobins. "This is how tyrants in all ages have slandered assemblies of the people they portray as the source of all divisions."[78]

It was time for Robespierre to do exactly that. This defender of the people now had to reverse his habitual stance by insisting on the reasons an appeal to it could not produce a democratic expression of the general will. In his definition of the situation, time was the enemy; each moment of delay brought new dangers, emboldening enemies of liberty, encouraging defiance and suspicion within the assembly, provoking civil war, offering foreign powers new opportunities for invasion. The longer the deputies delayed, he warned, the more vigor and wisdom they were losing, the further they were straying from the general will. "The glory of the National Convention consists in displaying a great character and sacrificing servile prejudices to the sublime principles of reason and philosophy; it consists in saving the homeland and consolidating liberty by giving the universe a great example," he proclaimed. "I see its dignity slipping away as we forget the energy of republican maxims to lose ourselves in a maze of useless and ridiculous chicanery, and as the speakers at this tribune prepare the nation for a new lesson in monarchy."[79]

This so-called appeal to the people would be an appeal against the people, Robespierre maintained, "an appeal away from what the people wanted, and from what it did, at the moment when its force was exerted, when it truly expressed its will, that is, at the time of the insurrection of 10 August." It would be impossible to restrict discussions of the primary assemblies to discussion of Louis's punishment, he argued; they would want to reopen the question of the former monarch's guilt; they would want to reexamine everything, including the founding of the Republic. Individually, they would become battle sites for and against the former monarch, for and against monarchy. As a multitude, they would never reach agreement. Interminable dissension would lead to civil war. One might as well open the whole Revolution to an appeal to the people to begin with.[80]

This was all the truer, the Incorruptible reasoned, because the greater part of the people would not in any case be found in the primary assemblies. Would the farmer be able to leave his plough, the artisan his bench? How would defenders of the nation who had rushed to the front be part of the discussion? They would be sacrificing their blood while the dregs of the nation who had stayed at home would be left to decide its fate. And who could guarantee that bad citizens, moderates, aristocrats, wily lawyers would be excluded? Why would royalists and enemies of liberty, intriguers and scoundrels of both the old and the new regimes, not flock to these gatherings to declaim and manipulate, proclaiming the sovereignty of the people to bring back monarchy and aristocracy? Was this the majority Salle was invoking?

"I trust the general will," Robespierre affirmed, "especially at moments when it is awakened by the pressing interest of public safety; I fear intrigue, especially during the troubles it brings and amid traps it has long prepared." The majority of the nation, he protested, the one including the most numerous, most unfortunate, and purest part of society on which all the crimes of egoism and tyranny weighed, had expressed its will when it threw off the yoke of the former king. "It must not be fatigued by continual or overlong assemblies in which an intriguing minority too often dominates; it cannot participate in your political assemblies from its workshops; it cannot judge Louis XVI when it nourishes with the sweat of its brow the robust citizens it gives the homeland."[81]

Was it not evident, Robespierre continued, that this appeal to the people would also be an appeal against the staunchest defenders of liberty, against the small number of oppressed patriots slandered everywhere as the result of an organized campaign of denigration financed by public funds, denounced as tyrants, attacked in the assembly with cries of vengeance and fury? There was a plot to debase the Convention and even dissolve it, he acknowledged. But this plot was not to be found among patriots who energetically invoked the principles of liberty, or the people who had sacrificed everything for it, or the majority within the Convention that was seeking the good and the true, or even among those who were merely the dupes of intrigue and the blind instruments of foreign passions. It belonged, instead, to "a score of scoundrels who control everything, who keep silent about the great interests of the homeland, who refrain above all from stating their opinion regarding the last king, but whose silent and pernicious activity causes all the disorders afflicting us and prepares all the ills that await us."[82]

To perpetuate discord and control debates, Robespierre charged, this sinister group had imagined a division of the assembly into a majority and a minority. This was their new way of attacking and silencing those assigned to the latter category. He saw no such division in the assembly. The majority, that of the good citizens, was not permanently fixed because it belonged to no party; it renewed itself at each free discussion according to the dictates of public good and eternal reason; when an error was recognized, the minority became the majority. "The general will is formed neither in secret gatherings nor around minister's tables. Everywhere the minority has the eternal right to give expression to the voice of virtue, or what it regards as such. Virtue has always been in a minority on the earth." This declaration sparked applause to the left of the assembly and in the galleries, but Marat could not contain his impatience at its rhetorical posturing. "All this is sheer charlatanism," he shouted.[83]

But Robespierre was in full flow. As examples of the virtuous minority, he invoked the seventeenth-century English martyrs to liberty, John Hampden (erroneously) and Algernon Sidney; Socrates "for he swallowed the hemlock"; Cato (the Younger) "for he ripped out his bowels." And he saw such men surrounding him in the Convention. "I know many men here who will serve liberty as Sidney did, if necessary; and even if there were only fifty. . . . This thought alone must discomfit the vile intriguers who want to mislead or corrupt the majority. Until then, I ask that we at least make the tyrant a priority." By this point, he was veering toward incoherence. Swearing on behalf of his fellow radicals to defend the people's cause, urging Parisians to keep guard around the Temple, he demanded yet again that the Convention declare Louis guilty and deserving of death.[84]

As the debate continued over the next few days, Birotteau offered a bitter condemnation of disorder in Paris and the conspiracies of its representatives in conjuring up the threat of civil war. Visceral hatred and distrust of the Jacobins oozed to the surface of his speech as he accused them of calling for the execution of Louis XVI while keeping Egalité waiting in the wings to replace him. His speech of 29 December was answered the following day by a massive deputation from the Paris sections that included patriots wounded on 10 August. It demanded the death of the royal traitor and assassin in the name of the supreme law of public safety and of all humanity. At its insistence, the wounded were allowed to parade through the Convention in a display of the tyrants' assault on the people.

The Girondins' most powerful speech in favor of an appeal to the people was still to come. It was made on 31 December by Vergniaud, who prefaced a bitter attack on Robespierre and the Jacobins by invoking the spirit of reason, principle, and openness to persuasion in the light of solid arguments.[85] In doing so, he addressed more explicitly than any other speakers the crucial theoretical issue entangled in this factional conflict: the problematic relationship between sovereignty and representation that had shaped the politics of the French Revolution from the start.

In Vergniaud's analysis, sovereignty was exercised by the people either directly or through a system of representation in which decisions of the representatives were presumed to express the general will. The people retained nonetheless the right to approve or improve any decision of the representative body once it was made known and found not to conform to the general will. "To wrest this right from the people would be to strip it of its sovereignty. It would be an act of criminal usurpation transferring sovereignty to the representatives the people had chosen, turning them into kings or tyrants." In this argument, the general will was not formed by the very procedure of representation as defenders of representative government had argued in the Constituent Assembly; the will of the nation was not made one only in the deliberations of the body of its deputies, as advocates of a strong theory of representation from Sieyès to Chapelier had claimed. Instead, the general will inhered in the body of the people prior to, and independently of, any decision of an assembly of its representatives and could always be invoked against it.

Striving to save the Convention from the populist attacks of the Jacobins in the Paris deputation, Vergniaud had in effect adopted their arguments and undermined the principle of representation in doing so. He failed to specify a precise criterion or mechanism beyond an appeal to the people by which the conformity of any decision of the representative body with the general will would be placed in question, hence subject to an appeal to the people. The absence of such a criterion or mechanism risked the absurd conclusion that an appeal to the people to determine whether a law was in conformity with the general will would require a prior appeal to the people to decide whether such an appeal was required.

By its decision to try Louis XVI itself, Vergniaud continued, the Convention had accumulated powers to indict, prosecute, judge, and punish in a way that had introduced a "terrifying monstrosity" into the political order. There could be no action more important for the people to ratify. The people, not the representatives, had guaranteed Louis inviolability under the constitution by taking an oath to maintain it. This was an expression of the general will that only the people could withdraw.

Robespierre's speech was moving, Vergniaud allowed, but the alarms it sounded were exaggerated. The process of consulting the people would be calm and orderly. Humankind was being defamed in the efforts to portray the majority of the deputies as intriguers, aristocrats, moderates, and so forth. "Virtue was always in the minority on earth" had been Robespierre's call. Vergniaud, citing examples, thought otherwise. Catiline, whose conspiracy could have destroyed liberty in Rome, had been in the minority in the Senate. Cazalès and Maury, the royalists whose support for religious and aristocratic resistance could have ended the Revolution, had been in the minority during the Constituent Assembly. Kings, for their part, were ever in the minority on earth. They, too, had asserted that virtue was in the minority and that the majority was composed of intriguers to be terrorized into silence to safeguard their empires. Now, Vergniaud argued, the purported friends of the people were saying that only they, and perhaps a hundred of their friends, were truly pure, truly virtuous, truly devoted to liberty and the people's cause! They would have to turn France into a desert to realize their sublime fantasies.

"We are accused," Vergniaud cried in response, by "men whose essential nature makes them turn every whisper into an imposture, just as it is the serpent's nature to exist only by distilling venom." "We are accused," he repeated in this ritual of mutual recrimination, "denounced as we were on 2 September in face of the assassin's sword." For his band, he swore, such a death held no terror. "Our blood is entirely the people's; in shedding it for the people we will have only one regret, that of not having more to offer." "We are accused," he continued, of wanting to incite civil war, in Paris if not in the departments. Why? Because "these true friends of liberty" were threatening with death the citizens unfortunate enough to disagree with them. There would be troubles in Paris, they were warning. But was it so difficult to anticipate fire in a house to which one was carrying the fuel to ignite it?[86]

By this time, Vergniaud was falling into paroxysms of denunciation. These were the men who wanted civil war, he attested, the ones who were preaching the assassination, as friends of tyranny, of all those they hated. These were the men calling for daggers against the nation's representatives and insurrection against the laws, demanding annihilation of the Convention, dissolution of the government, the substitution of the particular wills of a few insolent oppressors for the general will of the people. They were teaching maxims subversive of all social order from the very tribune of the Convention, in popular assemblies, in public squares. They were repudiating reason as perfidious Feuillantism, justice as dishonorable cowardice, and a sense of humanity as conspiracy. They were declaring a traitor every citizen falling short of the heights of brigandage and assassination. They were perverting every notion of morality and pushing the people to the most deplorable excesses with lying speeches and hypocritical fawning. "Civil war for proposing to pay homage to the sovereignty of the people! Do you see the sovereignty of peoples as such a calamity for the human race? I understand you; you want to rule."[87]

You want to rule! With this fateful charge, Vergniaud offered a scenario of war and anarchy that would follow Louis XVI's condemnation by the Convention if it were not validated by an appeal to the people. The continuing existence of the former monarch was being blamed for the shortage of bread. Who could guarantee that this blame would not then be shifted to the Convention by men calling for a new revolution, inciting one or another section to declare itself in a state of permanent insurrection, proclaiming the need to name a defender of the Republic (implicitly a Cromwell or dictator of the kind Marat had been accused of promoting) who would alone be capable of saving it? Who could guarantee that the September killers would not crawl from their holes to present the people with a liberator already covered with blood, "this *defender*, this leader said to have become so necessary?" When asked for bread, these men would offer the people of Paris more blood. In reaction, the capital would awaken from its stupor and the departments would rise up to avenge crimes against the most memorable of revolutions. Paris would be destroyed and the Republic dismembered into a federation.[88]

Would this happen? Vergniaud thought the madmen would recoil from the brink in the face of the departments. "But don't these disorders, as possible and more probable than the civil wars with which they threaten us, merit enough consideration to be put in the balance where you are weighing Louis's life?" He ended with a recapitulation of the principles regarding sovereignty and representation. The deputies would not be reproached, he assured them, if they respected these principles and the people decided on Louis's death. "If, on the contrary, you violate them, you will at least face the rebuke that you have deviated from your duty: and what terrifying responsibility this deviation would place on your heads! . . . I have nothing more to say."[89]

Vergniaud had run out of words; Robespierre had barely been able to stop. But the essential arguments had been made. The speeches continued into the new year, nonetheless. On 1 January, Dubois-Crancé argued for immediate judgment, condemnation, and execution; Saint-André called powerfully for an immediate vote on guilt; Michel-Edmé Petit for condemnation allowing the people to opt between penalties of death or perpetual imprisonment, as Salle had initially proposed; Brissot characterized an appeal to the people as an act of homage to the sovereignty that would reduce the threat of foreign invasion. By the time Pétion weighed in for the Girondins on 3 January, in support of a verdict of guilty to be ratified by the primary assemblies, the speeches on the matter were becoming less frequent. Squeezed from the agenda by the pressure of other business (despite the Convention's earlier decision to discuss the king's fate exclusively), they also gave way to another factional conflict in which Marat became deeply invested on behalf of the Jacobins: a fight ignited by revelations that the painter Boze had been a channel for negotiations between the Girondins and the king in the days preceding 10 August. It was time for discussion of the ex-king's fate to be done with, Barbaroux urged on 4 January in an effort to extricate the Girondins from this situation, interrupting the agenda to call for a decision regarding the king's guilt to be made the following day. The speeches could be published, as before, Thuriot added. Buzot's effort to speak in support of this proposal was challenged by Marat, and the assembly voted to return to the agenda without further decision.[90]

The order of the day finally brought Bertrand Barère to the tribune to deliver a decisive speech. Lasting several hours, and richly furbished with references to ancient and modern political experience, it amounted to a summation of the entire trial process to date, effectively bringing to a close the debate over an appeal to the people. Neither Jacobin nor Girondin, Barère talked from and to the center, bitterly denouncing the factional passions that had brought the Convention to the brink of disaster. "Calumnious insinuations and violent accusations have occupied our sessions too much," he fretted; "mutual hatreds have incited movements in popular opinion that are too unstable and dangerous. . . . It's not by the light of the torch of suspicious passions and personal vengeance that revolutionary convulsions are ended. Let's fulfill our arduous and imperious duty with calm. It's the parricide of public liberty to substitute egoism for love of the homeland and to add the hatreds of rivalry to the difficulties of an issue so important for the safety of the state."[91]

Barère found the evidence of the ex-king's guilt overwhelming, the assembly's trial procedure fair and just. There could be no question of reversing the Convention's decision to judge Louis itself, he insisted. "In revolutionary events, the paths taken are destroyed; the ships that have borne us are burned. There's no going back in a revolution." At issue in the disagreement over an appeal to the people, he argued, was how the will of the entire nation would be bound by the outcome of the assembly's judgment. In his analysis, the nation had already committed itself to that outcome by electing a Convention with unlimited powers and full exercise of its sovereignty. To appeal the decision to the people for ratification would be throwing back upon the nation the exercise of sovereignty it had expressly delegated to its deputies. An act of weakness and infidelity rather than of homage and duty, it would be subversive of the fundamental principles of representative government upon which the stability of great republics depended.[92]

With this reasoning, Barère ravaged Vergniaud's arguments for national sovereignty and the ex-king's inviolability, highlighted the inconsistencies in the various arguments for an appeal, and pilloried Salle on the basis of his own previous arguments (in a book on the subject published a year earlier) that it was of the essence of a national convention to exercise absolute and unlimited sovereignty. An appeal to the people would make it a judge in its own cause, Barère insisted. It would be politically disastrous; it would divide families; it would produce dissension and disorder. It would summon "from the cellars and underground of Paris the paid agitators preaching contempt for the laws and hatred of liberty, these perfidious men charged with the task of giving the republican state hideous forms that can incite desire for a leader or regret for monarchy."

There had been talk of insurrections, Barère added. That was legitimate and necessary when a throne and a conspiratorial court still existed. But now? "Insurrections! Against whom? Only the nation and its power remain. Thus there are only revolts and seditions: it's for the law to punish them, for the nation to repress them. Amid passions of all kinds that churn and crush one another, a single passion has the right to be heard, that of the public good, the national interest, and liberty. You're about to decide before the statue of Brutus [in the hall of the Manège], before your country, before the entire world. With the judgment of the last king of the French, the National Convention will enter the realm of posterity." With this peroration, Barère summoned the Convention to decide whether Louis was guilty of conspiracy against the state by a roll-call vote in which each deputy declared his verdict from the tribune, this judgment to be followed by application of the penalty established for such a crime by the criminal code. A decision regarding the fate of the Capet family would then take place.[93]

Powerful though it was, Barère's speech did little to calm the factional conflict he had condemned. It was reignited the very next day by a grim report on the situation in Paris. The city was in a state of fermentation, the mayor informed the deputies, not least owing to uncertainty over the fate of Louis Capet. The burden of the indigent, anxieties over subsistence, lack of employment, the fear of hidden enemies, the selfishness of the rich, the insecurity of the poor, the prevalence of theft and assassination: all these threatened the majority of the capital's citizens, good republicans all, burdened by their sacrifices to the Revolution, unsettled by agitators and conspirators, and neglected by the legislature. As the Girondins' ever-smoldering resentment of the capital was inflamed by this call for the Convention's attention, the Jacobins' distrust of the provinces was immediately activated, in turn, by a proclamation of the departmental administration of the Haute-Loire. Vilifying Paris for acting as if it were almost exclusively the sovereign of the Republic, for dictating decrees to the Convention at will, and for preventing the achievement of a good constitution, this declaration called for mobilization of volunteers to march on the capital "to disperse a horde of brigands threatening to usurp the fruits of a revolution that has cost all the citizens so much sacrifice." An address from the same administration urged the Convention to purge the troublemakers from its midst and leave Paris if necessary, promising aid in subjugating the city if it continued its rebellion against the law. In the bitter floor fight that followed, defenders of Paris hurled denunciations of federalism and counterrevolution against champions of the provinces indicting the despotism of the capital. Marat again failed in several attempts to speak from the tribune.[94]

Finally, on 7 January, the assembly decided to close the discussion and proceed to a vote regarding the king a week later. The vote was declared unanimous, but it left Marat furious. He became one of scores of deputies forced to publish their speech rather than presenting it directly from the tribune. In the *Journal de la République française*, he blamed Roland's faction for cutting off the debate just before it was his turn at the tribune, thus suppressing the speeches of patriots after permitting those of Capet's defenders. "*You see, it's Marat and Robespierre who don't want to close the discussion*," he quoted Barbaroux as shouting. "Foolish young man . . . ," he slashed back, "learn once and for all that Marat is a party of one, so alone that he couldn't even find one of his colleagues to defend him or support his views. If he had a party, no matter how small, France would long have been free and happy because it would be composed only of pure, disinterested, informed and farsighted men, burning with civic spirit, firm and unwavering like him."[95]

From Marat's perspective, the decision to close discussion on the appeal to the people before he could speak was consistent with the hostility he had encountered in the Convention throughout these debates. On 9 December, he was denounced for identifying himself as "The People's Friend" in the title of his published speech on whether Louis XVI should be tried. The Convention responded by forbidding the use of any such title on speeches published by its authority. In effect, he had been stripped of his public political persona. At the same session, his elimination from the Convention had clearly been a principal goal of an effort by Guadet to convoke the primary assemblies to purge deputies who had lost the people's confidence. His attempts to speak in the Convention had been blocked on numerous occasions and limited to frantic interjections from the floor. He had survived moves to indict him, to censure him publicly, to send him to the Abbaye. Doggedly resisting in the assembly, he had compensated by deploying his journal in a sustained guerrilla war against Roland and Mme Roland as well as Dumouriez, whom he denounced as their crony. His attacks against Mme Roland during this period had become particularly vituperative.[96]

Marat was in a bitter mood, then, when he published the repudiation of an appeal to the people that he had been unable to present to the Convention in person. It appeared in several parts in issues of *Journal de la République française* from 10 to 12 January before it was reorganized for publication mid-month as *Discours de Marat sur la défense de Louis XVI, la conduite de tenir par la Convention, et la marche allarmante que la faction royaliste s'efforce de lui faire suivre dans le jugement du tyran détroné*. Unlike Vergniaud, he had no reluctance about naming names. "The royalist faction" in the Convention he now pilloried was not an elusive conspiracy hiding in the shadows. Its principals were Salle, Rabaut, Buzot, Vergniaud, Brissot, Gensonné, the "anarchists" who had shown themselves to be the leading partisans of the appeal to the people, to say nothing of the cowards like Barbaroux who had kept their opinions to themselves.[97]

His charge against these men was direct: they had been working consistently since the beginning of the Convention to save the dethroned king from the punishment the people demanded and should have imposed, instantaneously, at the very moment of the revolution of 10 August. "It's a great shame in my eyes that the people didn't throw the tyrant and his cronies into the same ditch on 10 August," he bewailed. Instead, the Legislative Assembly had been allowed to defer the tyrant's judgment to the Convention along with reform of the vicious constitution it had abused to destroy liberty.[98]

By Marat's lengthy account of the process to date, electoral assemblies corrupted by counterrevolutionary gold had inflicted on the Convention a dominant faction determined to prolong judgment of the king until the moment arrived to save him. When it became clear that the argument for the king's inviolability would fail, this faction had come up with the notion of an appeal to the people. Its claim that the constitution accepted by the people had rendered Louis XVI inviolable was indefensible; its allegations that the Convention had arrogated to itself the functions of prosecutor, jury, and judge were ridiculous. To the contrary, he insisted, the deputies had been "invested by the French people with unlimited powers, to punish the tyrant as much as to save the state in a declared situation of peril."[99]

With this argument, Marat confronted the issue that Vergniaud had made most explicit: the relationship between sovereignty and representation. He had spent years preaching distrust of representation in the name of the sovereignty of the people. Now, in a remarkable volte-face, he became representation's strong defender. "They say that 'the sovereignty of the people is inalienable.' Who doubts it?" he would have told the assembly. "But do they call it usurping the *sovereignty of the people* to use the powers the people has delegated and fulfill the mission it has conferred?" he fumed. "They tell you that law is the expression of the general will and that will cannot be represented. From this they infer that it is up to the people to decide. All representative government thus becomes impossible." What were the deputies doing in the Manège, then? Were they just intruders without mission or standing, ceremoniously assembling to spend public funds and overthrow the state? Were they taking salaries for performing functions they could not exercise? Why had they not rejected their nomination on the grounds that sovereignty could not be represented? Why hadn't they told prospective constituents that the sovereignty of the people was inalienable, that they should go and exercise their rights themselves?[100]

By the logic of popular sovereignty now being offered by advocates of the appeal to the people, Marat reasoned, the participation of every citizen would be required for every public action. The gift of a sword, the creation of a bailiff's position, the sale of the meanest national property would depend on the convocation of the primary assemblies as much as the approval of constitutional laws. "Who doesn't see that these maxims are destructive of all representative government, that they can produce nothing but the most hideous anarchy in a state of any size? Accept them in a state such as France and the empire is dissolved instantaneously." The principle that the rights of the people were imprescriptible dictated that it delegate to representatives only what it could not do itself and that the laws made by these representatives be subject to the sanction of the nation. But to conclude from this that the nation had to sanction each decree and ratify each act of its representatives, he argued, would utterly destroy the only form of government that could create unity in a large state.[101]

The ridiculous spectacle of a great nation incessantly convoked to decide on the slightest actions of its representatives could scarcely be imagined, The People's Friend continued. "Hercules's club wielded to kill a fly would offer only a feeble image." More radically, the body of the people itself would be shattered by a kind of noxious individualism. "With each member of the political association being called upon to decide every matter regarding the whole association, each point of the state would become its center, each individual would be transformed into a legislator, a man of state, each primary assembly a national senate. Every father of a family, every merchant, every artisan, every farmer, every laborer would be forced to abandon his own affairs, his plough, his workshops, his occupation to occupy himself solely with political, economic and military discussions of which he understood nothing. . . . Implement the system of the appeal to the people for a few months and the uncultivated earth will be covered with brambles, the human race will perish of inanition, and the state will be reduced to a desert."[102]

It was time, Marat proclaimed, to cast away the political fantasies of inept schoolchildren or blundering scoundrels, time to send sound men to the nation's senate to govern its interests and guarantee its rights. How then to protect the people's sovereignty from these men? The only way was to declare all their decrees provisional, reserve the sanction of the people only for constitutional laws, and add to the Declaration of the Rights of Man that "*any decree infringing the constitutional laws is null and void, illegal, oppressive, and tyrannical, and that it is lawful to resist its execution by all possible means, even by force of arms.*" This, he maintained, was the indispensable clause always omitted by faithless legislators aiming to render illusory the rights of the citizens and the sovereignty of the people.[103] Against the appeal to the people, then, Marat cast the sacred right of resistance. By extension of this logic, legislation was never more than provisional, pending an insurrection against it. Conversely, in the face of an elected representative body claiming to exercise the general will, the sovereignty of the people could find expression only through violent negation.

FOUR STEPS TO AN EXECUTION

On 14 January 1793, opening its session to alarm at the prospect of disorder in the capital, the Convention spent its first tense hours debating whether to quash a decision of the Commune to close theaters in Paris in the interest of public security. The closure had been a response to protests from the sections against performances at the Théâtre de la Nation (the former Comédie française) of Jean-Louis Laya's *L'Ami des lois*, a powerful counterrevolutionary play directed against the tyranny exercised by the Jacobins in the name of the people (and, by implication, the arbitrary procedures imposed by them in the ex-king's trial) and notably vilifying Robespierre and Marat. For the Girondins, overruling the Commune and ordering the theaters to remain open offered a chance to assert the Convention's (dubious) authority over the city while ensuring the continuation of performances ridiculing their enemies. At the same time, the popular protests that had triggered the ban could be portrayed as evidence of continuing disorder in the capital and even of the threat of violence against the deputies themselves on the day marked for their fateful decision regarding the former king. The effort to assert the Convention's authority over the theaters failed, and the issue of authority was referred to the Executive Council.[104]

It took many more hours for the assembly, frequently collapsing into bitter disorder itself, to reach agreement on the voting procedure to decide Louis XVI's fate. Three questions had to be addressed. Was the king guilty of conspiracy against the nation? If so, what was the punishment? Would the Convention's verdicts be appealed to the people for a final decision? The questions themselves were scarcely in doubt. At the heart of the matter, though, was the order in which they would be presented for a roll-call vote. That the deputies would find Louis guilty by a substantial majority seemed inevitable; that they would also favor punishment by death much less so. Whether or not the assembly began by voting on an appeal to the people therefore assumed critical importance. If taken first, a decision in favor of appeal would give cover to deputies convinced of Louis's guilt but reluctant to vote for his death; they could find him guilty in the hope or expectation that a death sentence submitted to the people for ratification would be denied or reduced. As a result, the debate over the order of the questions, devolving as it did into an intense replay of the weeks of argument over the appeal to the people, became a battle between those ready to kill the king and those unwilling or hesitant to do so. Neither side secured a clear victory, though the outcome favored the latter. The Convention agreed that its members would vote first (for or against) on the question of Louis's guilt, but second on whether their judgment ("whatever that might be") would be submitted to the people for ratification. Only then would they proceed to a third vote on the penalty to be imposed. Crucially, they were not required to declare unambiguously for or against a sentence of death. There would be ample opportunity for improvisation and prevarication.

For Marat, writing in the *Journal de la République française*, this entire session had been a scene of utter madness. "Men obsessed by their stupid vanity, agitated by a thousand petty passions or animated by a zeal that is almost always blind" had insanely mocked, insulted, and threatened one another. "Base egoists, without enlightenment, virtue, civic commitment or shame" were being led by "a band of vile scoundrels devoured with ambition, busy effacing the traces of their crimes." To the outside observer, he reported, the Convention appeared divided into two. On one side was "a veritable faction" composed of the dregs of the old regime, "enemies of liberty by profession and principle," and "a handful of ambitious hypocrites, accomplices of the tyrant . . . , ceaselessly occupied to save their former master from the scaffold, hide their own treason, and seize on the authority of the people to tyrannize it after stripping it bare." On the other side, there were honest men lacking ideas, a plan, unity, and harmony; loving liberty but not knowing how to defend it; desiring the good but ignorant of how to achieve it. In a striking note, he called on the patriots of the Mountain to unite, sacrifice their egoism to the homeland, and choose eight or ten of their most enlightened to chart a common direction to be followed strictly and in unison.[105] He was offering the Jacobins a route to the future.

Voting began the following day, 15 January, with the question, "Is Louis Capet guilty of conspiracy against public liberty and attempts against the general security of the state?" The verdict, quickly reached, was overwhelmingly positive. Of the 719 deputies present to express their judgment, 693 voted yes, 26 qualified their decision in some way, none voiced an unambiguous no. The vote on the appeal to the people followed without delay but went on longer; many of the deputies took time to justify their decision. The Jacobins held firm. Danton and Collot d'Herbois were absent on Convention business, but 20 of the other 22 Paris deputies voted no. Marat exposed himself to ridicule in reiterating the arguments he had made in the published version of the speech on the matter; Camille Desmoulins offered an inflammatory remark denouncing corrupted deputies that sparked a mini-debate of its own; Billaud-Varenne invoked Brutus's act in sentencing his two royalist sons to death; David, the painter of that iconic republican scene, offered a simple no; Panis likened the appeal to a tool of despotism; Philippe Egalité declared himself bound by duty to oppose it. Among Jacobins from other departments, Couthon repudiated the appeal as a federalist assault on sovereignty; Saint-Just claimed his right to vote against the tyrant from nature if not from the people; Philippeaux declared himself ready to face death in doing so. The Girondin leaders also remained consistent. Vergniaud, Guadet, and Gensonné voted yes, though their fellow deputies from the Gironde disagreed. Brissot, Buzot, and Pétion voted yes, as did Salle while denouncing the Jacobins. Barbaroux and Louvet did the same, both railing against a faction ready to put Egalité on the throne. But Condorcet disappointed the Girondins by voting a reluctant no. When the votes were tallied, there were 283 votes in favor of an appeal to the people and 424 against. It followed that the decision on a penalty would be definitive.

Bizarrely, Marat declared this outcome a personal triumph. "My courage, my distance from every intrigue, my speeches at the tribune, my writings, my ardent civic commitment, succeeded in disabusing the Convention and drawing all hearts toward me," he claimed in his journal. "The hypocritical masks with which the supporters of the faction had covered themselves, the holy respect for the sovereignty of the people they advertised with such assurance the better to betray its cause, the tender interest with which they so jealously claimed to maintain their constituents in the exercise of their rights: all that was well calculated to sustain illusion and to win them votes, which would inevitably have occurred had I not long unmasked these perfidious men and exposed their plots, their designs, their projects. Known for what they were, they were betrayed even further by the hypocritical speeches that belied their criminal actions, while the force and conviction of the patriots' speeches explaining their opinions carried conviction."[106]

It was late on 16 January before voting began on the third and crucial question, the nature of the penalty to which the ex-king would be subject. The day had been spent in much fear and trembling as the Convention heard reports on the state of Rouen after a royalist insurrection; fought again over policing of the Paris theaters following riots at the Théâtre de la Nation demanding the performance of Laya's *L'Ami des lois*; confronted rumors of disorders in the capital. There was talk of impending prison massacres and invasion of the assembly by the mob. This time, Marat succeeded in mounting the tribunal to express his indignation. "I invite the Convention to respect itself and not be the dupe of fake terrors. The men affecting a panic attack today flaunted their *courage* three days ago and bragged in secret of *passing decrees*. They tell you that they are voting under the threat of the daggers," he taunted, laughing uproariously, "but none of them has suffered a scratch." The joke was poorly received, and there were sustained protests. Demanding silence, he continued. "Believe me, the men who complain of hearing threats of assassination are precisely the ones who have threatened me the same way a hundred times. . . . I hear it said that the departments are anxious, but what's the cause of their anxiety? The deputies who circulate these false alarms."

Offering a rumor of his own, Marat reported word in Paris that a great number of the deputies were desperate that the barriers to the city were being closed to prevent their flight. To follow up, he demanded that deputies not present in the assembly to fulfill their duty be declared *infâme* and those caught beyond the barriers arrested. Anxiety about the closure of the barriers was relieved by assurance from the mayor that they remained open. In the meantime, the Girondins called for forces to defend them and demanded that the Executive Council assume responsibility for maintaining order in the city. Marat interpreted this move as a ploy to make Roland dictator. It was blocked by the Montagnards.[107]

Fending off efforts to call for a two-thirds vote on the former monarch's sentence or modify the formulation of the question regarding it, the assembly finally began the roll call to determine his punishment at 8:00 p.m. It would continue for more than twenty-four hours as the deputies read out their often-lengthy justifications for their decisions. The first to vote was Mailhe, the author of the report that had set the trial process in motion two months earlier. There were charges that the voting order had been manipulated to achieve this result, particularly after Mailhe dropped a bombshell. Opting for death, he proposed that if this was the penalty adopted "it would be worthy of the National Convention to advance or delay the moment of execution." In effect, he had opened up the possibility of a fourth vote to determine the timing of the punishment, a move supported in turn by some of the most important Girondin leaders, including Vergniaud, Guadet, and Pétion. As the roll call continued, Louvet, Buzot, and Brissot each voted for death with delay of the sentence; Salle opted for imprisonment and banishment after the war. Gensonné, while voting for death, offered a different variation by calling for immediate discussion of the fate of the royal family and prosecution of "the assassins and brigands of 2 and 3 September." Barbaroux, also voting death, declared himself ready to decide within a few hours on the expulsion of the entire race of the Bourbons. Condorcet, opposed to the death penalty on principle, called for the next most severe penalty in the penal code, though he also favored Mailhe's proposal to discuss its timing.

The Jacobins were more solidary in their verdicts. All but two of the Paris deputation voting called for the death penalty, often with lengthy explanations. Among them, Robespierre needed time to reconcile his vote for the death of the despot with his earlier categorical opposition to capital punishment; Fabre d'Eglantine parsed Rousseau at some length, turning him into a partisan of the exercise of sovereign power through representation; Danton declared no truck for tyrants; Egalité simply declared death the appropriate penalty for all who had attacked the people's sovereignty. Marat, unusually brief, expressed his intimate conviction that "Louis is the principal author of the crimes that caused so much blood to flow on 10 August, and of all the massacres that have stained France since the revolution." He demanded execution of the sentence within twenty-four hours. Saint-Just, voting later with the deputation from the Aisne, was also uncharacteristically pithy: "Since Louis XVI was the enemy of the people, its liberty and its happiness, I conclude for death."

As the vote was being tallied, word spread that the majority would be razor thin. The atmosphere was electric, then, when an additional deputy was brought from his sickbed demanding to exercise his right to vote for the ex-king's banishment. His insistence threw the Mountain into a fury and the entire assembly into a turmoil that reached gale force when Manuel, serving as one of the secretaries, abruptly bolted from the hall, fighting his way from one blocked exit to another, perhaps in search of other late votes. (He returned a few minutes later.) Calm once restored, Vergniaud was ready as president to announce the results. There had been 361 votes for the death penalty without conditions, 23 for that penalty with support for Mailhe's proposal for further discussion of the timing of the execution, 11 for death with other provisos, mostly relating to the expulsion of the other Bourbons. The remaining 319 votes had been cast for imprisonment followed by banishment at the end of the war (votes Marat denounced in disgust as legalistically camouflaged efforts to keep Louis alive until he could perhaps remount the throne). The unconditional votes for death thus amounted, by one vote, to the barest majority of the total 721 cast. On this basis, Vergniaud solemnly declared "in the name of the National Convention, that the punishment it pronounces is death." There was silence in the hall, Marat reported to his readers. "Profound silence. Never was there a more imposing spectacle."[108]

Profound silence, that is, until the king's lawyers were allowed to address the assembly to present a communication, signed "Louis" in the absolutist monarchical style. It repudiated the Convention's judgment and appealed to the nation beyond it. De Sèze, glossing this demand as an expression of the natural right of every accused person to appeal a verdict of guilty, went on to invoke the text of the penal code that required a vote by three-quarters of the jurors for condemnation. Tronchet, in turn, challenged the procedure that had been followed initiating the final vote. But the Convention was unmoved, even by Malesherbes's tears. Its determination was symbolized by the unprecedented spectacle of Guadet and Robespierre in agreement as they declared the judgment irrevocable. The session ended at 11:00 p.m., after thirty-six hours, to renewed agitation in the galleries and among the deputies.[109]

In the meantime, the original three questions before the Convention had turned into four. The assembly still had to address Mailhe's proposal, which became, in effect, a call for a vote on reprieve offering yet another chance to spare Louis XVI from the guillotine. Before the issue was taken up on 19 January, the secretaries announced a revision of the vote count from the following day that reclassified as votes for death those also supporting Mailhe's position. The change yielded a final tally of 387 votes for death and 334 for a lesser penalty. It also brought the question of Mailhe's proposal to white heat. As the Jacobins demanded an immediate vote on a reprieve, confident that the result would send Louis directly to the scaffold, they were met by foot-dragging and arguments for further delay. Amid a storm of bitterness and incrimination, and as Marat, Panis, and the royalist Lanjuinais found themselves fighting for possession of the tribune, the president adjourned the session. The Mountain refused to leave the hall, noisily occupying it until Santerre, the commander of the National Guard, appeared. He was seen speaking with Marat and some other deputies before assuring the members of this rump assembly that the people would soon see the peaceful execution of justice. Fearing that they would be exhausted the following day when the supporters of the despot returned to the fray, Marat related, they took the wise course to retire.[110]

Marat was first to the podium the next morning as the debate over reprieve resumed. "It's with sadness and profound indignation that I see rekindled a question that has already been decided," he protested. "The discussion of reprieve is a battle of the minority against the majority. The tyrant is condemned to death and must meet it." Beginning to name names of the royalists supporting the tyrant, he was shouted down and threatened with censure. "I defy your censure," he retorted, going on to insist that a reprieve would throw the homeland back into misery. "The republic will be a chimera until the tyrant's head has been lopped off," he warned. Calling the question to end the debate, he reiterated his conviction that the king must face his penalty within the twenty-four hours laid down by the penal code.[111]

The debate continued, nonetheless, with mighty speeches on both sides that veered inevitably toward a replay of the arguments of the entire trial. The sequence was broken by a sentimental proposal on the part of Thomas Paine, lionized by the Convention, that Louis XVI be allowed to pass the remainder of his days exiled in the country his armies had done so much to liberate. Since Paine spoke no French, he simply stood at the tribune while his speech was read in translation by one of the secretaries. The performance was interrupted twice by Marat, initially to deny Paine's right to vote on the grounds that he was a Quaker opposed by his religious principles to the death penalty, then in support of other Jacobins unwilling to believe Paine responsible for what they were hearing in favor of a reprieve. Confident of his English, Marat mounted the tribune to consult with Paine. "I denounce the translation and I maintain that it's not the opinion of Thomas Paine," he shouted. "It's a malicious and misleading translation." Others disagreed, and the Convention allowed the reading of a lengthy published opinion Paine had previously prepared for presentation.[112]

It was time once again, though, for Barère to bring the reluctant deputies to the point of decision. Dissecting the various arguments for a reprieve and the conflicting proposals for its duration, he found it too dangerous to weigh the life of an individual against the good of the Republic. His call for a vote on the question, "Will there be a reprieve, yes or no?" was soon accepted and the roll call began, this time with the deputies allowed no opportunity to explain their vote. The tally reported by the *Moniteur* was 310 in favor of reprieve and 380 against (though Marat claimed that the majority against was 483 to 251). Among the Girondin leaders, Guadet voted yes with one other deputy of the Gironde; Vergniaud and Gensonné, ready to give up the fight, joined with the others in voting no. Barbaroux led most of the deputation from the Bouches du Rhône in making the same decision. Condorcet simply abstained, unable to say no on principle but refusing to say yes. Marat had no such qualms: he voted against reprieve along with all but two of the Paris deputies.[113]

It was 2:00 a.m. on 20 January when the tally was announced. Louis was informed of the judgment twelve hours later. As the news spread that afternoon, Louis-Michel Lepeletier de Saint-Fargeau, one of the deputies who had voted for execution, was assassinated. Louis Capet met his own fate at 10:00 a.m. the following day. To each side its martyr. "The head of the tyrant has fallen under the blade of the law," Marat wrote in the *Journal de la République française* two days later. "That same blow has overturned the foundations of the monarchy among us. I finally believe in the republic."[114]

TWENTY-FIVE

A PARTY OF ONE

On 14 January 1793, Jean-Paul Marat offered his readers a "Portrait of The People's Friend, Drawn by Himself." This was the day the Convention had scheduled to begin voting on Louis XVI's guilt, thus moving the trial into its climactic phase. Why a self-portrait at this critical juncture? It may well have been prompted by Laya's *L'Ami des lois*, the play opened at the Théâtre de la Nation on 2 January and closed by order of the Commune within days, following protests by clubs and sections denouncing it as counterrevolutionary. The title had been deployed against tyranny before, but there could be little doubt in the context of early 1793 that the play was directed against *L'Ami du peuple* and the Parisian radicals associated with Marat in the minds of moderates, Girondins, and supporters of the monarchy. There was logic in the fact that a deputy calling for the closure on 11 January was denounced in the Convention as talking like a Maratist. By this time, the Girondins had succeeded in making Marat one of the most hated men in France, turning his name into a term of opprobrium. "I'm not a disciple of Marat," Vadier expostulated on 7 January, repudiating "the ridiculous epithet, Maratist." The Girondins were discrediting patriots by "calling them Maratists, the name of a man covered with ignominy in the departments," protested another Montagnard, Nicolas Hentz, in a speech published around 15 January. The charge was repeated the following day by François Lamarque, another radical of the Mountain. "There's a man suspected in France who has pushed exaggerated ideas," he accused the Girondins of telling themselves. "Let's say all the patriots are under Marat's banner," they had realized, "and the hate incurred by a single individual will fall on all the patriots, whatever ideas they have adopted."[1] Marat was good to smear with.

In this inflammatory context, as the Convention ground its way toward a final judgment of Louis XVI, *L'Ami des lois* offered its audience two principal villains: the evil, grossly hypocritical *Nomophage*, or "Law Eater" (Robespierre), and his malicious, scheming sidekick, *Duricrâne*, or "Hardhead" (Marat). Duricrâne, "a brazen journalist whom no respect constrains," takes pride in being "a born denouncer," never happier than when revealing another plot (he boasts an average of four denunciations a week) and always ready to accelerate revolutionary justice by declaring the safety of the people the supreme law. Together with Nomophage, this madman denounces and misrepresents evidence to trick the people into condemning a moderate former noble. The latter's virtue and innocence are ultimately recognized by the people and the two intriguers are sent to jail to await the verdict of the law.[2] A fervent hope, it would appear, for fans of the play rioting for its performance.

"How can it be a crime to show myself as I am when the enemies of liberty endlessly denigrate me, portraying me as a scorched brain, a dreamer, a madman, or a cannibal, a tiger thirsty for blood, a monster who lives only for carnage, all to inspire fear at the sound of my name and prevent the good that I would and could do?" Marat pleaded in response. Against this caricature of himself as a monster he now set a very different portrait: a humanizing portrayal of a man "born with a sensitive soul, a fiery imagination, an exuberant, free and tenacious character, a clear mind, a heart open to all the exalted passions and especially to the love of glory." Protective parents had saved him from youthful excess, he recounted; a feeble constitution had rendered him a dutiful child and pupil. From his early years, love of humanity had inspired in him a moral sense; he could not stand the sight of cruelty, nor could he witness injustice without experiencing a sentiment of personal outrage. An unjust action by his schoolmaster, supported by his parents in what seemed to him an act of betrayal, had led him to attempt suicide at age eleven.[3]

Marat's earlier denial of the existence of pity as a natural human instinct was missing from this defense of his character, as was his emphasis on the natural state of humanity red in tooth and claw. Not so his thirst for glory. This latter had been his devouring passion throughout his life, he preened, its object changing through different phases of his existence but never for a moment abandoned. Surveying these phases, he made no mention of his experience in England or the radical *The Chains of Slavery* that had resulted from it (though he was soon to announce the publication of a French translation of that work). He preferred to emphasize "the eight volumes of metaphysical, anatomical and physiological research on man . . . , the twenty volumes of discoveries on different branches of phys-

FIGURE 25.1. Jean-François Garneray, *Portrait of Marat*, 1793. Musée Lambinet, Versailles. Christopher Fine Art/Getty Images.

ics . . . motivated by the sincere desire to be useful to humanity, a holy respect for the truth, the sentiment of the limits of human wisdom and my dominant passion of love for glory." His success in discovering great new and original truths, he informed his readers, had been confirmed by the shameful persecution he had experienced at the hands of the charlatans of the Academy of Sciences. "I had been groaning under this vile oppression for five years when the revolution was announced by the convocation of the Estates General," he recalled. "I quickly saw where things were going

FIGURE 25.2. Joseph Boze, *Portrait of Marat*, 1794. Musée Carnavalet, Paris. Bridgeman Images.

and began to breathe, in the hope of seeing humanity finally avenged, of participating in breaking its chains, and of achieving my place."[4] The latter motivation could scarcely be denied.

Adopting the mantle of The People's Friend, Marat recounted, he had soon recognized that it was imperative to purge the Constituent Assembly, "indignation having wrested from me this sad truth that there was no liberty, security or peace for us to hope for unless the vile schemers were removed from among the living . . . , a truth so well understood by all the peoples who have broken their chains that they have begun their revolutions by sacrificing the enemies of liberty." He was no less insistent on the persecution he had suffered in response. "I know my writings are not penned to reassure the enemies of the homeland," he boasted; "the scoundrels and traitors fear nothing so much as to be unmasked. The number of criminals who have sworn my death is prodigious. Forced to conceal their resentments, their base vengeance, their thirst for my blood under the mantle of love for humanity and respect for the laws, they emit a thousand atrocious and ridiculous lies against me from morning to night." The volley of self-justification continued. He'd been pilloried as "a scorched brain, an atrabiliar fool, or even a bloodthirsty monster, a paid criminal." "Is it so great a crime to have demanded five hundred criminal heads to spare five thousand innocent ones? Isn't this calculation a measure of wisdom and humanity?" he demanded. And yes, he'd been accused of taking bribes. Why, then, was he still living in poverty, having lost his profession and the rest of his fortune with the revolution, and been saddled with debts by swindlers thereafter?[5]

The self-portrait closed with an invitation. He had opened his heart to honest fellow deputies, he now declared. He was ready to work with them for the good of the people, a goal "too long forgotten in the cruel dissensions reigning in the assembly." They had only to say the word; he asked for nothing better than to "lay down the whip of censure for the measuring stick of the legislator." But he would not be duped. "If they abuse my trust, wanting only to control my pen, let them know that it will only be for a moment. I'll be quick to mark them with the sign of opprobrium and they will be my first victims, for I'll never agree to deceive the people."[6] It remained to be seen, in the following months of 1793, whether this menacing invitation would be taken up.

AT LAST, A REPUBLIC

Marat's account of the execution of Louis XVI was triumphant. "The punishment of Louis XVI is one of the memorable events that mark an epoch in the history of nations," the *Journal de la République française* proclaimed on 23 January 1793. "It will have a prodigious influence on the fate of Europe's despots and the peoples who have not yet broken their chains." Celebrating the Convention's greatness in taking this momentous action, the journal was careful nonetheless to stress that "it was the will of the nation, and the way in which the people has witnessed the punishment of its former master has raised it far above its representatives because, have no doubt, the same sentiments that have moved the citizens of Paris and the *fédérés* animate the citizens of all the departments."[7] There could be no implication, then, of regicide perpetrated by an act of parliamentary despotism.

Marat found proof of this claim in the people's conduct on the fateful day. "How empty were the fears the supporters of despotism had sought to spread," he assured his readers. Not a single voice had called for mercy as the monarch was taken from the Temple to the scaffold. A profound silence had reigned until the severed head was shown to the people, eliciting cries of *Vive la nation! Vive la République!* In this account, the rest of the day was perfectly calm. "For the first time since the [Festival of the] Federation, the people seemed animated by a serene joy, as if it had participated in a religious festival. Delivered of the weight of oppression that had so long burdened them, and penetrated with the sentiment of fraternity, all hearts were given over to the hope of a happier future."[8] This portrayal of a dignified, solemn people securing its liberty made no mention of the frenzy of the crowd to dip hands or clothing in the royal blood that featured in starker counterrevolutionary accounts.

For The People's Friend, the entire event had been marred only by the assassination of Michel Lepeletier, whose eulogy he now offered. Changing his mind about the Pantheon since its initiation in response to Mirabeau's death, he called for the remains of the new revolutionary martyr to be placed in "this glorious sanctuary for the mortal remains of the men who have merited most from the homeland," though he added the plea that it be "sullied no longer by the ashes of political charlatans." The martyr's death had put Marat in a sacramental mood. "In his blood have been washed away the numerous calumnies that have been spread so long against the defenders of liberty. Aghast at his fall, our despicable detractors are reduced to silence. . . . May there be placed on his coffin all the dissensions that have divided his colleagues. May his death revive in their hearts the love of the public good and cement liberty. . . . Cherished and holy shade, hover sometimes over the senate of the nation that you honor with your virtues, contemplate its work, see your brothers united, competing to achieve the happiness of the homeland, the happiness of humanity."[9] By this sacrificial victim's blood, the Revolution might be redeemed.

Far from troubling France, Marat now declared, the death of Louis XVI would serve only to strengthen it in "containing by terror not only the enemies within but those without." It would also give the nation "an energy and new force to repel the ferocious hordes of foreign satellites who will dare to bear arms against it, for we have no way of going back and we find ourselves today in the position that we have to conquer or perish." This, he proclaimed, was "the palpable truth that Cambon rendered in a sublime image when he said at the tribune two mornings ago, *We've finally reached the shores of the island of liberty and we've burned the vessels that brought us here."*

Conquer, then, or perish. Marat had not wanted the war, but with the tyrant extinguished he now saw its successful conduct as a principal goal. That, in turn, required political unity. "To defeat the innumerable legions of our enemies," he continued, "the first point is to be united among us." This unity would have been achieved in the Convention if it had purged the tyrant's accomplices, he continued. But Louis, convinced that denouncing his accomplices would not save himself, had kept silent and preferred to claim martyrdom.[10]

Such words offered little prospect of achieving the unity among the deputies for which they called. On 20 January, the Convention had learned that Kersaint had posted placards around the city to the effect that he could no longer serve as deputy "alongside men of ill will and the assassins of 2 September." His letter of resignation to the assembly was more specific: "It is impossible for me any longer to bear the shame of sitting with the men of blood while their opinion, preceded by terror, prevails over that of men of good will, and Marat's prevails over Pétion's. If love of country has made me endure the misfortune of being the colleague of the panegyrists and promoters of the assassinations of 2 September, I want at least to defend my memory from the reproach of being their accomplice. I have only this moment to do so; tomorrow will be too late." He meant, of course, that he had to resign before Louis XVI's execution was carried out.

These were belated scruples, Marat commented acidly. But Kersaint's language had alarmed the deputies: it raised the specter that colleagues would begin resigning in disavowal of the decision to punish the king while imputing to the entire assembly a shared responsibility for, or acquiescence in, the September Massacres. The effect, as Cambon had protested, was to discredit the condemnation of the former monarch as the act of "cannibals depraved by blood." Kersaint was ordered to return to the bar of the assembly two days later to explain his meaning. He did so by reiterating his longstanding aversion to serving in the assembly with the monstrous Marat and denying any intended offense to the deputies as a body.[11]

At the Girondins' instigation, nonetheless, the assembly passed a decree ordering the minister of justice to proceed with prosecution of "all the authors, accomplices and provocateurs of the assassinations and acts of brigandage committed in the first days of September." The Montagnards, for their part, insisted on including prosecution of the defenders of the Tuileries palace on 10 August. Marat, in turn, defended the September

Massacres in his journal as "a general insurrection provoked by indignation at seeing the courts protect the traitors of the nation, and fear at the prospect that the criminals detained in the cells would be released at the very moment the enemy armies were approaching our walls."[12] There could be little doubt that the factional conflict was fated to continue with increasing bitterness. Denunciation of the *septembriseurs* would remain a recurring theme of Girondin attacks on Marat and the Montagnards in the coming months. In response, The People's Friend would denounce as royalists all those who had voted for the appeal to the people and against the king's execution. Each side protested the need for unity; neither expected it to be achieved peaceably. A purge of some kind was inevitable.

In the meantime, Marat was capable of an occasional joke. "Last Monday, a day for ever memorable in the annals of our nascent Republic, all the crowned heads of Europe have been debased by the French, in the person of Louis XVI," he declared with pomposity on 26 January in celebration of the king's death. What then, he asked, of "the dictatorship to which the inhabitants of the Mountain have raised me?" Since the judgment of Louis XVI, he mocked (again suggesting his odd sense of identification with the former monarch), his own subjects on the Mountain had become unruly and uncivil, no longer wishing to hear of the duties of subordination and propriety. "O Heaven! Everything is turned upside down in my empire; there's no way to hang on to it; so here I am, ready to submit my dictatorial resignation, at least if the commissioner of my section who has received my complaint doesn't honor it in reestablishing my authority." Asking only for a loan to avoid the scandal of bankruptcy, he promised to spend it on a pair of boots if his faithful subjects returned to him. Almost in passing, the journal mentioned Roland's resignation as interior minister (offered to the Convention a day after the king's death and readily accepted on 23 January).[13]

The next day, with tongue still in cheek, Marat announced that with no loan forthcoming he was abandoning his dictatorship to the highest bidder, or to anyone interested in grabbing sovereign power. "And since the thirst for human greatness is not extinguished in my soul, I ask my people for the great favor of raising me to the dignity of moderator of the inflamed heads of the Mountain and igniter of the frozen heads of the Plain. I feel enough courage to fulfill this double task with glory, but it's important that these heads incline a little to their reform; if some are recalcitrant, I'll call for a decree of anathema against them, putting it in verse and setting it to music . . . , which will have a marvelous effect." As for the faction dead set against him, he jibed, "they can see that I'm of good enough disposition and it's no longer worth continuing to fill the departments with terror about the awful consequences of my dictatorial ambition."[14]

The joke about dictatorship was leaden, but it gave way to a new set of "Reflections on the Revolution and the Causes That Had Maintained It." From the razing of the Bastille to the destruction of the monarchy, this piece emphasized, the Revolution was a story no one could have predicted or even imagined without being treated as a visionary or a madman. A monarch adored for fifteen years had been brought to the scaffold as a tyrant, a republic had been proclaimed by acclamation, a Revolution constantly impeded by the classes it favored and defended by those it crushed. "These were events provoked successively by public opinion; foreseeing them from the outset was beyond the powers of the human mind."

In retrospect, though, Marat now saw a pattern. "The laborers, the workers, the artisans, the indigent, in a word the classes of society that lost everything to the revolution, and that the venal legislature had excluded from the rank of citizens, are the only ones that have constantly supported it and have finally consecrated it without ever opposing the artifices of their enemies with anything but the strength of their arms and the resources of their courage." Their ardor derived, he declared, from their penchant for spectacles, their indelible aversion to tyranny, and their hope for happiness. Had they been less numerous in the capital, always the seat of the Revolution, liberty would never have survived. Even so, its achievement had been far from assured. "When I imagine how little it would have taken, so many times, for despotism to be reestablished definitively, I regard the French revolution as a continual miracle, and I have difficulty fending off the idea that a tutelary deity has watched over the salvation of the friends of liberty."

Against all odds, Marat marveled, citizens without plans, perspectives, or wealth, and mostly without weapons, had triumphed against adroit criminals commanding all the positions of authority and disposing at will of the public treasury, the arsenals, and the army. It was striking that "in the last analysis, the people has triumphed only by its mass, the immense population of the capital, and the unforeseen strokes of chance." No less remarkable, though, was that "to reestablish his empire the despot lacked only an audacious leader, a man of genius." To prove the point, and to demonstrate his own political virtuosity, he laid out a devious strategy such a man might have followed. "While Louis XVI was still standing, I kept these ideas to myself. Now he is no more, I have no fear of making them public. They will serve to answer my calumniators who have represented me as a partisan of royalty and my detractors who have decried me as a hothead."[15]

A WAR EFFORT

The question of Louis XVI's fate had riven the politics of the Revolution for months. His death left war the most important issue on the deputies' agenda and even required attention to it as a means of reconstituting the sense of national embodiment. It is striking that the ex-monarch's final disappearance coincided with annexations of conquered territories to round out French territory to its "natural" boundaries. Physical geography, it seemed clear, could help make France one again.

Talk of war became urgent on 22 January, the day immediately following the king's execution. The Convention now hastened to hear from deputies dispatched to Belgium to investigate the state of Dumouriez's army there. Presented by Delacroix and Danton, the report was long, detailed, and damning. It revealed systemic maladministration compounded by malfeasance and financial peculation. It pointed to the inadequacies of inexperienced and untrustworthy officers who were replacing aristocratic holdovers from the Old Regime. It described desertions by volunteers approaching the end of their term of service as well as by regular troops. It criticized unreliable supplies of bread and acute shortages of fodder; lack of clothing, tents, and other equipment; inadequate means of transportation. It urged immediate attention to the reform of the army before new campaigns began.[16]

The Convention's response was to charge its committee on general defense to present a plan for the reorganization of the war ministry. Two days later, Sieyès was ready with a typically complicated report and proposed decrees, including the creation of an *Economat national*, a central financial agency responsible for all government purchases. Its discussion postponed, this plan was presented again on 28 January to mixed reviews. Saint-Just welcomed the idea of an *Economat national*; Fabre d'Eglantine considered it a potentially dangerous concentration of power. The idea found little favor in later discussions. Sieyès's proposal for reorganization of the war ministry scarcely fared better as deputies hurried to offer alternatives. The Montagnard Dubois-Crancé, in the meantime, had followed up with a report on the military strategy to be followed in the coming months. It prompted lengthy, ongoing debates over the reorganization of the army.[17]

In this heightened discussion of military matters, The People's Friend was eager to be heard. His powers of prediction failed him on 29 January when he imagined that Louis XVI's death might deter new enemies and "the punishment of the tyrant . . . will have better served the Republic than would a formidable army." He saw the Austrian forces close to exhaustion. He counseled holding back against Spain and Germany, "for why should we lavish our blood and treasure in bringing war beyond our borders to break the chains of other peoples . . . ? It will be enough to hold ourselves at the ready to support them as soon as they rise up against tyranny, and to consummate the revolution." England, he thought, was a different matter: he considered the country disinclined to war, but "if it arms against us, a descent of 100,000 Frenchmen onto that island and a visit to London would cover our war costs for the past eighteenth months." Two days later the French declared war on Britain, though no visit to London was forthcoming. In a bizarre contradiction, Marat opposed as useless the sending of an address across the Channel to explain that France was declaring war on England's government, not on a people he now deemed hostile.[18]

He would later accuse the French foreign minister of incompetence in not anticipating that the forced opening of the Scheldt waterway by the French in November would inevitably lead to tensions with Britain and in failing to recognize that nation's preparations for war. This consideration led him to reflect on the vices of political decision-making in democratic governments, placed by their processes of deliberation at a disadvantage in war against despotic states characterized by the speed and secrecy of their operations. "In a democracy, all men being equal and enjoying the same political rights are necessarily jealous one of another. The play of this petty passion in the national senate prevents the legislature from entrusting unlimited powers to any individual citizen, especially for secret operations, whatever precautions are taken to prevent abuses of authority and whatever penalty is laid down to punish them."

Compounded by the fantasies of antipatriotic deputies, Marat contended, this base democratic passion had prevented the Convention from creating a secret emergency committee to take measures for the public good. Intriguers swarming to become public functionaries, and thereby oppressors and vampires of the people, had spawned useless committees and multiplied the number and size of administrative bodies. The challenge of this "political epidemic"—difficult even for a people with settled civic habits—could only be worse in "a nation corrupted by thirteen centuries of despotism, liable to all the vices, and filled with intriguers, hypocrites, deceivers, shysters, scoundrels, traitors, and plotters covered by a mask of civic loyalty. We are still only seeing the first brambles from these seeds. Unless a fearless hand hastens to uproot them, they will soon cover the fields of liberty and stifle prematurely the happy fruits we can expect these fields to produce."[19] Despite his earlier protestations, Marat had not entirely given up the fantasy of a dictatorship.

He had, however, backed away from dreams of further conquest. Reasoning that the annexations of Nice and Savoy—and, above all, the anticipated acquisition of Belgium—were making French territory more defensible, he now argued that France should prepare for a standing war of engagement at the borders rather than the expansionist campaigns of corrupt generals. He thought it crucial, nonetheless, to transform the entire system of military administration by addressing issues of command, support, and supply that were undermining the fighting capacity of the army. "The majority of our soldiers have remained for a year without weapons, uniforms, shoes," he charged. "They have spent whole days without bread; even today, they are in the most hideous state of deprivation, the overpriced clothing sold to them are made of bad materials and their shoes are of a leather so detestable that the suppliers have had cardboard or metal put in the soles to give them a semblance of solidity. These criminal practices, without example in the weakest, most corrupt and disastrous reigns, have been committed with impunity under the new regime, under the republican regime."[20]

In Marat's analysis, despotism had never tolerated such problems. They resulted from choices made by corrupt revolutionary legislators with "the ineptness, or rather the perfidy, to organize the new regime with the instruments of the old one and, above all, to put the despot at the head of a free government." The army had been left to the dereliction of a counterrevolutionary monarch, the malfeasance of ministers, the embezzlement of generals. A principal error had been to authorize generals to find provisions for their armies, thus putting them into competition with the interior minister for the means of subsistence. The result had been price escalation, hoarding, unavailability of foodstuffs, and an artificial famine that could lead to a real one.[21]

Genius had been stifled by despotism before the Revolution, The People's Friend acknowledged, but since 1789 the remaining men of talent had everywhere been corrupted by the court. The army had been entrusted to counterrevolutionary generals and an officer corps composed of the dregs of the old regime. How then to proceed? He saw an example in the model army of Frederick the Great, whose relentless discipline had fashioned a mass of scoundrels and military deserters from all nations into an incomparable fighting machine. "He's been characterized as a tyrant: he was just, severe, inflexible. . . . Impunity alone multiplies crimes; inflexible justice is thus the sole means of suppressing disorders. His entire secret had been to find capable men and constrain them to their duty by inescapable punishments. And why should we not adopt, to make liberty triumph, the same measures despots use to destroy it?"[22] Despotism in the service of liberty? Why not? The rhetorical question was to echo throughout the following years.

The task of military reorganization required surveillance of ministerial agents, punishment of malefactors, honest tribunals, and an incorruptible master that "in a free state can only be the body that represents the sovereign." But Marat saw the succession of revolutionary legislatures as the continuing source of all the disorders in the military. The Convention's committees favored prevaricators, conspirators, faithless ministers, conniving generals, and traitors. A crowd of intriguers among the deputies were in cahoots with the interior minister, dining with him, disposing of all the places in his department and the funds at his disposition. "How can you claim to establish order in the ministry, in the armies, in all the branches of government, when it doesn't reign among you?" he demanded of his fellow deputies. "Have no doubt that unless the senate of the nation is composed of men who are pure, zealous for the public good, and inflexible in their severity toward the wrongdoers, it will be futile for you to make laws against malfeasance. They will be constantly eluded, the swindlers will continue to ruin the people, and the traitors will not stop plotting against liberty."[23]

It was with little hope then, puritanical republican that he was, that on 2 February Marat attempted to present to the Convention a bare-bones decree for the reorganization of the war ministry very different from that offered by Sieyès. Brutal in its simplicity, it proposed that the campaign on land be limited to defense of the Republic's borders; that the armies be nationalized by the integration of the regular army with the National Guard; that all soldiers receive the same pay. It made the war department completely independent of the Executive Council and its minister solely responsible for its operations and his choice of advisers, giving him the right to prosecute before the courts any suspected of malfeasance. Municipalities were to be charged with supply of all equipment for the men of the National Guard they would be sending to the front. Soldiers would have the right to bring claims against superiors or suppliers after the war, with oversight of the mails entrusted to municipal bodies to safeguard their complaints from interference. A committee of six would be established to receive denunciations of the minister or his agents, forwarding them to the Convention if warranted. Finally, a price would be put on the head of the fugitive Capets and a bounty offered to any enemy soldier joining the armies of France.[24]

Marat complained bitterly that he was improperly moved down the list of deputies waiting to speak on this matter until discussion was closed off. "The royalists of the Convention" still dominated the assembly's bureau and committees, he lamented; they would thus control all its business until patriotic deputies attended more sessions and voted more assiduously to replace them. As if to confirm this analysis, he was shouted down the following day when he protested appointment of a Girondin, Bernard-François Lidon, as a deputy *en mission* on the grounds that the candidate had voted in favor of the appeal to the people. The assembly dismissed this protest, expressing its "profound contempt" for the protester. The same faction, the *Journal de la République française* reported, had succeeded in forcing Pache's resignation as minister of war and replacing him by Beurnonville, a man to be watched carefully for his incompetence and lack of civic commitment. By now, the Girondins were acquiring new denominations in Marat's political lexicon: they were "the Roland faction, the royalists, the *hommes d'Etat*, the men of the appeal to the people . . . , the enemies of the homeland." *Hommes d'Etat* would become a favorite slur for the Montagnards against the enemies they viewed as a kind of political junta, men in place, politicos holding on to power.[25]

On 7 February, Dubois-Crancé introduced a draft decree on military organization that included Marat's proposals regarding the nationalization of the army through integration of professional and volunteer units and a common military pay scale. The resulting decree was adopted, after extended debate, on 21 February; it was explained to the nation in an expansive address approved for distribution two days later. The following day, the Convention decreed a levy of three hundred thousand men to bring the army up to strength. Local governments were required to fill quotas of unmarried men between eighteen and forty, supplementing their numbers of volunteers by other administrative means as necessary. Efforts to implement that recruitment, one of the Convention's most fateful measures, provoked massive resistance across the country. Within weeks, the west of France exploded into insurrection and civil war.

A THREAT FROM THE SECTIONS

Marat had emerged from the struggle to kill the king with enhanced popularity beyond the Convention. Letters offering him adulation, information, and calls for action—though also not a little contestation—had swelled in the pages of his journal. But the mood in the capital shifted and sharpened in February, and he found himself pushing back against popular radicalism. In the most activist sections, a generation of more radical militants was pushing to the fore, men from lower down the social scale no longer shackled by the distinction between active and passive citizens, veterans of the violent confrontations of 10 August and its sequel, insurgents eager to push aside more established popular leaders.[26] An anonymous letter ostensibly from a member of the Panthéon-Français section, published by Marat in the *Journal de la République française* in mid-February, offered a vivid account of the conflict in that section, along with a passing report that workers were denouncing Marat and Robespierre as scoundrels who had to be killed. These fresh political tensions erupted dramatically into more general view on 11 February when the deputies were presented with a petition demanding renewed action against escalating food prices.[27]

If the Convention wanted war, the people wanted bread. The assembly was still discussing military reorganization when its president, accepting that "hunger can't be adjourned," announced that a deputation from the Paris sections wished to present a petition regarding subsistence. Dismissively, the deputies referred the petitioners to the agricultural committee before returning to the business at hand. Minutes later, after the Paris deputation had engaged in a fraught discussion with the petitioners in an adjoining room, Marat reentered the assembly. Interrupting debate, he reported that despite his disapproval of some "ill-considered expressions that had escaped their patriotism," he had undertaken to demand on the petitioners' behalf that they be allowed to present their petition the following morning. "You're not friends of peace. . . . Do you want trouble?" he challenged deputies refusing to divert discussion from the order of the day. "Do you want to frighten us?" came the riposte as the assembly resumed its agenda. This negative response, conveyed by the Paris deputies to the waiting petitioners, provoked a bitter attack on their part against the Paris deputation. To defuse the situation, the Paris deputies brought the matter immediately to the committee on agriculture. At that body's urging, the Convention decided to receive the petitioners the following morning.[28]

The petition, when the assembly heard it the next day, was explosive. It asserted the will of the forty-eight sections as expressed by a committee of their delegates that had been meeting for several months at L'Evêché, the former palace of the archbishop of Paris.[29] "It's not enough to declare that we French are republicans," the speaker for the deputation began; "it's also necessary that the people be happy; there has to be bread, for where there is no bread there are no more laws, no more liberty, no more Republic." There followed a list of the deputies' errors in enforcing freedom of the grain trade in the face of "the hideous misery of an infinite number of families who cry in solitude and demand that you dry their tears." To put an end to that misery, the petitioners proposed severe measures: punishment of ten years in chains for administrators engaging in the grain trade; a uniform standard throughout the Republic for the measure of grain; a penalty of six years in chains for the first offense (and death for the second) against any farmer or merchant selling a 100-pound sack of grain for more than 25 livres; and the sole authority of the Convention to determine the maximum price.[30]

Demands for a maximum were shocking enough, but for the moment they paled in comparison to the language of a member of the deputation, one Claude Hendelet, who began to speak as "vice-president of the commission on subsistence . . . charged in the name of my constituents, in the name of all the brothers in the departments . . ." At this, he was interrupted by violent protests from the assembly and calls that he be immediately imprisoned as an imposter. "Are there two Conventions in France, two national representative bodies?" stormed Louvet. "And if the petitioner is the representative of the departments, who are we, then, and what are our powers?" The affront to the Convention was grievous. Claiming to represent the departments was tantamount to arrogating the authority of the deputies themselves. "No citizen can declare himself a delegate of his brothers in the departments unless he has received authorization," declared the president. "Recognize clearly that you are speaking here in front of the nation, and it hears you. Have you authorization from the departments, Yes or No, Reply."

Hendelet had clearly misspoken in a moment of self-aggrandizement and acknowledged that he had done so, but there were deputies in no mood for indulgence. Notable among them was Marat, who took the floor immediately to unleash a tirade against the petitioners. He declared the measures they proposed "so excessive, so outlandish, so subversive of all good order, tending so obviously to destroy the free circulation of grain and provoke troubles in the Republic, that I'm astonished that they have come from the mouths of men who purport to be rational beings, free citizens, friends of justice and peace." For their claim to represent the forty-eight sections of the capital to be legal, he stipulated, the petitioners had to be accompanied by the mayor. For one of them to speak in the name of the departments, he had to show authorization. "Don't be fooled, Citizens," he warned his fellow deputies, "this is a vile intrigue. I could identify known aristocrats here. . . . I demand that these men who have imposed on the Convention be prosecuted as disturbers of the public peace." Astonished to hear him speak in this antipopulist vein, a mass of the deputies shouted their support for his proposal.[31]

In a rare moment of apparent agreement between the two men, Buzot was among those seconding Marat's call. Declaring the suspicion that the petitioners were tools of a "hideous machiavellism," he cited a speech of Vergniaud's from the time when the escalating cost of grain had been blamed on failure to punish the imprisoned king. "Bread is expensive, they say; the cause is in the Temple! Well, one day they will say bread is expensive, the cause is in the National Convention." That day had come, Buzot told the assembly: the issue of subsistence was being used in the attempt to destroy public liberty; he feared a project to disorganize everything. "If the citizens attending the sections allow themselves to be deceived by the hypocrites of patriotism much longer," he warned, "Paris, which has been the cradle of liberty, will become its tomb."

Marat reported in his journal that he had warned the petitioners on 11 February that they were unwittingly serving the enemies of the homeland in "a criminal project to vilify their own representatives." But in Buzot's insinuation that the petition was the work of "the hypocrites of patriotism" he recognized a perfidious attempt to point the finger more directly at himself and the other Paris deputies. "Be on guard against any alien suggestion," he had already urged the sections in his journal. "Rely on the vigilance of your representatives whose pure civic commitment is not suspect and who are so jealous of your happiness. . . . Don't you know that it's only since the judgment of the dethroned despot that the patriotic deputies can work for the public good, that up to this time they had to defend themselves against the criminal faction that led the Convention? This is the accursed faction attempting to make you the instrument of its scaremongering views." For good measure, he also charged that Buzot had compared him to Cromwell in repudiating men whose actions he had incited, just as the English dictator had sacrificed the creatures who had served him in his seizure of absolute power. The attack had miscarried, he assured his readers: unlike Cromwell, he had no absolute power, nor was there a single deputy prepared to accept the comparison.[32]

What the deputies feared above all in this situation was the emergence of a body competing with the Convention to represent the nation. "In effect, a second Convention exists in Paris . . . ," one of them asserted, "an association not at all like the popular societies, but an assembly of citizens calling themselves defenders of the Republic with which the Paris sections communicate officially, by deliberations and delegates, and who believe themselves authorized to state the interests of the departments." "It's true," declaimed another, "there exists in this city a simulacrum of national representation composed of unknown men who say they are from the departments but aren't. . . . I demand that you pay attention to this monstrous grouping." These were Girondins doubtless eager to discomfit the Montagnard deputies by implying that the latter were losing their grasp on the politics of the Paris sections. But this more radical popular activism challenged both factions alike.

Before the lengthy session ended on 12 February, a repentant Hendelet acknowledged that he was a participant in an assembly of delegates from the sections that had been meeting for four months; that the petition had been submitted to the Commune and had received the support of *fédérés* from the eighty-five departments; that before it was presented to the Convention it had been discussed with several deputies, one of whom had urged them to demand a law on subsistence for the entire Republic. The deputy in question, it turned out, was Saint-Just; immediately summoned to account for his action, he explained it as an effort to fend off attacks of high living made against him. By this time, however, to Marat's fury, the delegates of the sections were already stealing away from the scene. Hendelet was arrested and sent to the Committee of General Security to answer for his "insolence in adopting the mask of a representative of the Republic, a deceitful mask that must be stripped away before the entire universe." At Marat's insistence, the petitioners' threatening letter to the Convention followed him.[33]

The explosive petition was disavowed by some sections in the next few days, but the Paris deputies had clearly been rattled by this challenge to their authority to represent the capital. They soon responded with an address, "The Deputies of the Paris Department to Their Constituents." Again, they denounced extremists among the petitioners they had confronted on 11 February, men who had falsely claimed to represent the entirety of the Paris sections and had gone so far as to threaten the elected representatives of the capital with a demand for their recall. Behind this conduct, they saw the hand of "disguised aristocrats attached to the old regime by ancient habits," plotters avid to find a new pretext for troubles, divisions, and calumnies. The duty of faithful representatives, the Paris deputies maintained, was "not to push the people to despair by exaggerated alarms in order to force arms upon them along with their bread, but to care for it with all the means in their power." It was not to give the people bread as if it were fodder for brute beasts. "Despots also give bread to their subjects," they lectured. "As representatives of the nation, our goal and duty are to assure it also the liberty, peace and abundance that are the fruit of just, wise and virtuous laws, the enjoyment of the sacred rights of man, and all the republican virtues that produce at once the happiness and adornment of human life."[34]

One imagines from this unguent language that the pen was Robespierre's. But the Paris deputies were at one in their anxiety that their political momentum might be disrupted, at the very moment of their success in dispatching the despot, by radical populists (or the reactionaries manipulating them) eager to exploit the economic despair of a mass of the people. "Is it the moment that the cause of patriotism begins to triumph within the National Convention that the attacks of the despots have to be repulsed, that the cause of liberty must be compromised by a fatal and senseless exaggeration?" they exhorted. Beware of enemies pushing discontent to the extreme to discredit the energy of patriots, they fumed. To destroy the capital was the goal of enemies of equality, whosoever they might be. "It's under the ruins of Paris that all the despots seek to bury the rights of humanity and the liberty of the world. . . . Citizens, remember that you have saved liberty so far by your patience even more than by your courage. Don't allow some intriguers to wrest from you in one day the prize of so many sacrifices and virtues."

At least for the moment, the Paris deputies were preaching against popular insurrection targeting treacherous representatives within the Convention. "A people worthy of liberty does not idolize its representatives," they allowed; "it keeps its eye on them and respects in them its own dignity. Its complaints are always imposing because they are marked by justice and reason. The blows it directs against tyranny are always sure because they are prepared by calm, directed by wisdom, and commanded by necessity. It is moderate because it is proud, calm because it is strong, patient because it is invincible. It endures the challenges of a great revolution." If abundance had not yet been achieved and the patriotism of the impoverished had been exhausted, the Paris deputies urged, these had to be restored by the wisdom of the laws, the zeal of good citizens, the defeat of tyrants, the downfall of the malevolent. Until that happy time there was compensation to be found in the achievement of liberty and equality, the triumph of principles of eternal justice, "the glory of having performed miracles that will change the face of the world and astonish posterity." With union, vigilance, action, courage, they held, the people could be assured that "the glorious destinies of our homeland will be accomplished."[35]

Published in both Marat's *Journal de la République française* and Robespierre's *Lettres à ses constituents*, this appeal to the Parisians failed to persuade. The desire for glory, it turned out, was less compelling than the need for commodities, which were now reaching outrageous prices. Over the following days, fears of popular agitation grew. They were evident on 23 February in a proclamation of the Commune drafted on its behalf by none other than the radical priest Jacques Roux. Published and posted around the city, the text appealed to the people to stay calm, resisting "the plots of those who want to make us accomplish our ruin through the disorders of license and the disorganization of the social body." These were "perverse men covered with the cloak of patriotism," it warned, "men who seek to dig the tomb of slavery by provoking you to take direct action." They were offering "the traps of expiring aristocracy." Assuring Parisians that "abundance and liberty will never be born amid agitations," the Commune promised that it would be presenting a petition to the Convention for action against hoarders of all kinds. From this body, "invested with the plenitude of your powers," had issued the fateful decree striking down the last king of France. From it would now burst "the thunderbolt that will annihilate forever the brigandage of hoarders [and] crush the speculation devouring manufactures, commerce and liberty."[36]

PREACHING PILLAGE?

The legislative thunderbolt the Commune promised was too slow in coming. The following day, 24 February, the Convention heard petitions from two groups of women. The first, a deputation of washerwomen complaining of high prices, particularly of soap, called for violent measures. "Legislators, you've felled the head of the tyrant under the blade of the laws. May the blade of the laws weigh on the heads of the public bloodsuckers, on these men who perpetually call themselves friends of the people and caress it the better to suffocate it." The second deputation of women, from a popular society meeting regularly in the same building as the Jacobin Club, expressed their fears of victimization by hoarders while their husbands were at the frontier. This on the day the Convention had decided on the levy of three hundred thousand men. The women were fended off, pending a report on subsistence conditions in Paris to be heard the next day. "We're adjourned to Tuesday," they were reported saying as they left the hall; "but we adjourn ourselves to Monday. When our children ask us for milk, we don't adjourn to the day after tomorrow!"[37]

Monday it was. On 25 February, the capital was rocked by massive riots as grocery stores and chandlers' shops were invaded across the city. The uprising spread rapidly outward from the center as crowds forcibly emptied the shops of sugar, coffee, tallow candles, and soap. As often in actions of this kind, prices were largely fixed by the mob, though some outright looting also occurred. The crowd, among whom women were conspicuous, included not only the indigent but also working people: laborers, artisans, market women, washerwomen, butchers' boys. Domestic servants were powerfully represented, too, apparently taking part not only on their own behalf but on that of their masters and mistresses. Some small merchants were also seen helping themselves at bargain prices. Even a National Guardsman or two.[38]

Pillaging continued in Paris on 26 February, though it was sparser, less intense, and more effectively suppressed by the National Guard under the authoritative leadership of Santerre, who had been otherwise engaged the previous day. There was more disorder in the Convention, though, as Marat faced a crowd of Girondin deputies howling for his indictment. His offense had been to publish, on the very morning of the riots, a scandalous issue of the *Journal de la République française*, number 133, that seemed in advance to justify if not to incite them. It began by associating "the capitalists, speculators, monopolists, [and] merchants of luxury" with the dregs of the old regime conspiring to destroy the reign of liberty and equality by forcing up the costs of subsistence. "Only the total destruction of this damned brood can restore the tranquility of the state . . . ," it declared. "Today they are redoubling their zeal to drive the people to despair through the exorbitant increase in the price of essential commodities and the fear of famine."

This much was familiar fare. But the journal continued in language deputies found more provocative. "Waiting for the nation fatigued by revolting disorders to take it upon itself to purge the land of liberty from this criminal race encouraged in its crimes by cowardly mandataries, one shouldn't find it strange that the people in each town, pushed to despair, imposes justice for itself," it argued. "In every country where the rights of the people are not empty expressions flamboyantly set down in a simple declaration, the pillage of a few shops at whose doors one would hang the hoarders would soon put an end to the derelictions that reduce five million people to despair and make thousands die of misery. Will the deputies of the people only ever know how to chatter about its ills without offering a remedy?"[39]

Marat had doubtless heard talk of pillage and was ready to exploit its occurrence for his own purposes when he wrote this minatory passage. Published the morning the pillage began, it is unlikely to have been intended as a direct incitement to popular violence and was probably too late to have had that effect to any significant degree. Directed toward the Convention rather than the people, it was more clearly part of an argument urging the deputies to take "revolutionary measures" before the populace did so and, more specifically, to create a state tribunal to convict the principal hoarders as traitors to the homeland. Another remedy was imaginable, in which the rich would band together to import essential commodities for the relief of the poor: Marat quickly set that aside as a nonstarter in a country lacking civic virtue. "Besides, these disorders cannot last long," he warned. "A little patience, and the people will finally recognize this great truth, that it must always save itself." As for the scoundrels trying to put it back in chains and punish it for getting rid of a handful of traitors in the September Days, "let them tremble to be included themselves among the number of putrid members it will judge necessary to amputate from the body politic." With this, the target of the article had been made abundantly clear. "Infamous hypocrites who strive to destroy the homeland under the pretext of assuring the rule of law, mount the tribune and denounce me with this issue in hand," Marat challenged. "I'm ready to confound you."[40]

The show of bravado was soon answered in a tumultuous debate unleashed when Barère took to the tribune to decry the riots as a breach of the sacred principle of property, an outrage against public morality, an abuse of the term "revolutionary" to indulge disorder, and a perversion of the sacred name of insurrection as a pretext for the pillage of luxuries. In Barère's analysis, the people, "good in itself," had been misled by false, extremist patriots and returning émigrés, on the one hand, while the authorities had been derelict in their duty, on the other. Disorders had been anticipated for days, he observed. "And if I wanted to dirty my mouth with the words of an atrocious and insane journalist, too well known among us for me to want to name him, you would see that, without being a sorcerer or prophet, one could anticipate what occurred. The thermometer in Paris had reached the point of *troubles*."[41] The reference to the unmentionable Marat was unmistakable.

No sooner had Barnave called for measures to investigate the riots and repress the rioters than Salle demanded a decree for Marat's arrest, citing number 133 of the *Journal de la République française* in evidence. With deputies rising in noisy support of this demand, The People's Friend mounted the tribune to equally rowdy applause from the galleries. Called upon to read the offending passages of the journal, the assembly secretary refused, leaving the task to an outraged volunteer among the deputies. Marat was ready to respond. As in the Jacobin Club the previous evening, he had sharpened his characterization of those inciting these disorders. He was no longer indicting a shadow conspiracy of counterrevolutionaries, but the "criminal faction" he now saw sitting to the right of the tribune.

Against them, he invoked his right to freedom of speech. "It's simple enough that the horde that is the enemy of liberty [illegible], seeing its own salvation only in a counterrevolution . . . , demands an indictment against me for using my freedom of opinion and proposing . . . to leave the people the sole means that can save it as the laws remain silent." Outrage surged through the assembly as he went on to indict "the criminal faction and its agents" sitting to his right. Guilty of fomenting disorder in response to the famine produced by Roland and his minions, he declared, they had incited misguided citizens to propose revolting measures. "These excesses are not my work but yours," he charged the deputies: "you've been awaiting its effects for five or six days; and because in my indignation I proposed, as an opinion, the sole means of stopping this execrable misconduct, this infernal faction has now called for an indictment against me." He descended from the tribune derisively muttering, "Pigs! . . . Imbeciles!"[42]

With the Montagnards led by Tallien and Thuriot rushing to defend him, The People's Friend swore he needed no such defenders and called for an indictment of his accusers as madmen to be sent to an asylum. Denounced for wanting to destroy property, he maintained that he had always defended it. Against Carra's charge that freedom of opinion did not protect provocation to pillage, and that he was perpetually misguided by a false idea of patriotism, "making monsters everywhere for himself . . . destroying the Republic in trying to save it," he asserted his right to an opinion the enemies of liberty were seizing on as an excuse to oppress patriots in the Paris deputation. "They've been enchanted to make you forget their fantasies and plots, to find in my journal a sentence to permit them to demand an indictment against me and trick the public. They're the mad ones, send them to the asylum, these *hommes d'Etat*." This last was one of many such calls. The favor was soon returned by shouts for Marat to be sent to the madhouse in Charenton until the Revolution was over (the premise, of course, for a celebrated play two hundred years later).[43]

Briefly, there was a voice for relative political sanity. Indictments could sometimes boomerang, Buzot intervened to argue. A Paris jury would exonerate Marat, what then? His indictment would be impolitic and dangerous: impolitic, because he would be acquitted on the ground of liberty of the press; dangerous, because it would give the image of importance to this man who was merely the instrument of perverse others. The problem Buzot saw was more general: it lay in the sentiment that the laws had to give way to revolutionary measures; it lay in the dark places from which Marat dredged up the maxims he retailed for 2 sous daily; it lay in the entire system of slander directed against pure patriots, in the maneuvers of men aiming for a reign of anarchy that would bring back monarchy. Return to the agenda, Buzot urged; "this man doesn't have the presence of mind necessary to organize his ideas." "I have enough to recognize your treasons," came the rejoinder. With this, the debate over an indictment ("*Yesterday Marat preached pillage . . . , there was pillage yesterday evening*") descended into tumult. It ended, in a partial victory for Marat and his defenders among the Montagnards, with a decision to refer his denunciation to the criminal courts and to charge the minister of justice to prosecute the authors and instigators of the riots. No one was sent to the madhouse.[44]

In the days that followed, Marat continued to stew over charges he saw as an insidious attack on the principle of freedom of opinion, "this great rampart of public liberty," and on the right of deputies to express their views without fear of being called before a tribunal. "Unlike you, I wasn't born to liberty yesterday," he carped in his journal, addressing the uncommitted deputies of the Plain. "I sucked it with my nurse's milk, and I was free for forty years while France was still peopled by slaves. My pen never had any constraint but the truth, and despite all the decrees in the world it will never have another, even if I must return today to my underground. I'll use it with you in broad daylight in all its plenitude."

He went on to argue for solutions to the people's misery that could be found in reducing inflation from the sheer volume of assignats, and by using the sale of *biens nationaux* to pay off the national debt. This latter, he maintained, could have "attached new proprietors to the homeland and cemented the revolution." In a second address, he preached to the Plain against "the party of the *hommes d'Etat*" that was now revealing itself to be in a state of open counterrevolution. "Any indulgence for these criminals becomes barbarity against the people. We must crush them or be crushed ourselves. Where will your system of moderatism lead if not to the ruin of the homeland? How do you not recognize that since the punishment of the tyrant your only safety lies in victory. Escape your apathy, then, join with ardor the patriots of the Mountain against the criminal faction, or you'll soon pay heavily with your ruin for your timid reasons for holding back."[45]

For all its craziness, then, the session of 26 February had marked a shift in political alignment. For the first time, Marat had received significant support from the Montagnards (though he scarcely found it adequate) and was expressing support for them in exchange. They shared the conviction that the subsistence crisis had to be addressed not by the imposition of a maximum but by stabilization of the value of the assignat and repression of hoarding and speculation. They shared a conviction, longstanding for Marat and growing stronger in the minds of the Montagnards, that the progress of the Revolution would require an eventual overthrow of the Girondins. More pressingly, they also shared a determination to protect the authority of the Convention from the threat of extremists in the sections and clubs.

In the face of that threat, Marat had become more useful to the Montagnards. One of them, René Levasseur, deputy of the Sarthe, later described him as representing "a kind of democratic *maximum*" that could not be outbid, thus serving them as a "sort of safeguard against the mercenary demagogues being paid from abroad." Camille Desmoulins later spelled out this logic more fully in his *Le Vieux Cordelier*. "Happily, we have Marat whose subterranean life and indefatigable writings have led to his being regarded as the maximum of patriotism . . . ," he recalled arguing at the time; "it will always seem to the people that beyond what Marat proposes there can be only madness and extravagance." It was as if Marat defined the extremes of what was thinkable in politics: Desmoulins compared describing what lay beyond it to the task of the geographers of Antiquity as they imagined the landscape at the limits of their maps, "where there were no more cities, no more dwellings, only deserts and savages, glaciers or volcanoes." Against radical petitions, he recalled, The People's Friend had shown his political genius, needing only a few words or a gesture to silence approval for them in the galleries. Herein lay "the immense service that he alone, perhaps, can render the Republic. He will always prevent the counterrevolution from being carried out in red bonnets [the liberty caps of the sans-culottes] and that's the only way it could possibly be achieved."[46] For the moment, The People's Friend served the Jacobins as a defense against the radicals they repudiated as instruments of counterrevolution.

In the Commune, Jacques Roux, having taken his part in the looting he had decried in advance, offered his own reading of Marat's views by remarking that the grocers had only given back to the people commodities for which it had long overpaid. "I'm called the little *Marat* of the Commune," he boasted; "I glory in professing the severe principles of this deputy, *the true friend of the people*."[47] He was duly censured. The municipal authorities, like the Convention, were holding firm against the Enragés. They were also risking a popular revolt.

INSURRECTION FEVER

"Citizens, I'm telling you that without an explosion of the people you will get nothing. If you turn the generals over to the courts, they won't be punished because imbeciles can't be punished as traitors. Your decrees of accusation will have no effect; treasons will multiply and escape the blade of the law. We're sleeping on luxurious beds while our brothers are shedding their blood at the frontiers. Revolutionary measures are what's necessary, not legalistic ones. The members of the Convention are more our enemies than was the tyrant. You can only save the republic by regenerating the Convention."[48]

So declared an anonymous member of the Jacobin Club at its meeting of 8 March 1793. He was giving voice to a powerful strain of radical opinion in the capital by that date. Popular agitation had not abated in the days following the 25 February riots. Economic anxieties continued to run high in early March. But the tone of popular discontent shifted as bad news began to filter back from the war zone in the north. Accounts circulated of ill-treatment of soldiers and incompetence of generals, along with word of military setbacks that were menacing both in themselves and in encouraging émigrés to return to the capital in anticipation of imminent French defeat. Suddenly, radicals in the sections and clubs were talking of a new insurrection to save the homeland.

Problems of military organization notwithstanding, the French had been buoyed by their astounding successes the previous fall as they readied their armies for a resumption of combat in the spring of 1793. The Convention had voted unanimously to declare war on Britain on 1 February and would do so against Spain on 7 March. "One more enemy for France," Barère had cheered; "that's just one more triumph for liberty." Belgium, overrun by Dumouriez in November, was by then being annexed to France piecemeal as its towns and districts voted to join the victorious revolutionary nation. From this base, Dumouriez had opened a new campaign on 16 February by heading north into the Dutch Republic to forestall a British move to defend its ally. At the same time his subaltern, General Francisco Miranda, was laying siege to the Dutch fortress of Maastricht to the east.

As early victories soon followed, Marat had waxed enthusiastic. "We have to consider the war we're carrying to neighboring countries as a veritable crusade, and never was war more sacred," he declared on 5 March. "Its object is the reestablishment of peoples in their rights and the triumph of liberty, no less than taking care for our own defense." He was sure that early decisions by Belgian communities to unite with France would quickly inspire others to follow suit. "Example is a terrible torrent, a hundred times more compelling than speeches, no matter how energetic they may be, because every people is naturally like a flock of sheep." The same consideration led him to caution the Convention against a policy in invading Holland that would favor entrenched elites at a time when the populace was devoted to the Stadtholder. In the meantime, "as a true Montagnard," he pressed for care of the wounded and admission of disabled and impoverished volunteers to the Hôtel des Invalides.[49]

The military situation changed dramatically on 1 March, however, when reinvigorated Austrian forces crossed the river Roer to reenter the Netherlands, defeated the French garrisoned at nearby Aldhoven, drove them from Aix-la-Chapelle, and marched against Miranda's troops besieging Maastricht. Within days, news was seeping into Paris that the siege had been lifted and Miranda's army driven into retreat. On 5 March, Billaud-Varenne demanded that a letter from deputies on mission in Belgium be disclosed to the entire Convention. (Marat, in his account, charged that it was being kept secret by the Committee of General Defense, "composed almost entirely of Girondins, *hommes d'Etat*, defenders of Louis Capet, these royalists in coalition with our generals who are almost all suspect and some of them recognized plotters.") Read to the Convention, the letter relayed news of the Austrian assault on Aix-la-Chapelle and Miranda's retreat from Maastricht, though the defeat was soon construed by the minister of war as the temporary interruption of an engagement to be resumed once Dumouriez was called back from Holland. The report immediately threw the assembly into angry debate. Montagnards called for *fédérés* daily reaching Paris to be rushed to defend the frontiers, while Girondins resisted that move on the grounds that these troops from the provinces were needed to remain in the capital to defend the Convention itself. "There's a committee in Paris called the *Insurrection Committee*," warned Lanjuinais, citing information that this "center of trouble and insurrection" was presided over by a member of the electoral assembly whose members were told, "Take care, if you're not pure, you'll be eliminated as you leave."[50]

Marat, for his part, called in the *Journal de la République française* on 9 March for a redoubling of surveillance, prompt judgment of the generals who had betrayed the homeland, dismissal of war minister Beurnonville for retaining these traitors at the head of the army, and a return to a more defensive military posture—unless the French could seize the dikes in Holland in "a blow that would soon put an end to this war that has begun so disastrously." The remaining pages of this issue of the journal were filled with letters from soldiers at the front detailing corruption in the management of supplies and the cowardice and betrayal of generals. One offered an estimate of at least three thousand casualties in the rout at Maastricht.[51]

A day earlier, Delacroix and Danton had returned urgently from their mission in Belgium to offer the Convention a more informed report on the military situation there. They were preceded at the tribune by Beurnonville, who glossed dispatches from the leading generals to assert optimistically that the defeated French armies were effectively regrouping for a counteroffensive for which they needed immediate reinforcements. Fresh from the front, Delacroix was more sober in offering "positive and certain facts" to counter the minister's "fine phrases." His account of the incompetence of the generals and the absenteeism of officers was incriminatory. He agreed with Beurnonville only in insisting on the urgency of the need to rush volunteers to battle. On his recommendation, the Convention canceled all officers' leaves, effective immediately, ordered their return to duty, and demanded an investigation into all absences, officially approved or not. It followed this action by revoking the leaves of its own members and summoning them back to the assembly. Marat later offered a more severe judgment, concluding from Delacroix's report that Miranda's lieutenants had betrayed the homeland and were being shamefully protected by Delacroix and Beurnonville. It was time for these generals to go, he admonished, time indeed for a law that would allow suspect generals to be immediately replaced at the will of their troops.[52]

This moment of crisis offered Robespierre an opportunity, in similar vein, to demand that the aristocratic spirit be purged from the officer corps along with the "traitors who will be crushed like insects by a great nation destined to punish all the tyrants of the world." The Convention, he expounded, had only to free the French from the obstacles facing them to achieve its divine mission to create liberty and direct its all-powerful force toward the fall of tyranny and the prosperity of peoples. "It will be enough for it to hold the blade of the law ceaselessly above the heads of the powerful conspirators and the perfidious generals, to trample underfoot the entire spirit of party and intrigue . . . , to sweep away all the traitors, extend protective hands to the friends of liberty, to the people that has made the revolution and whose prosperity can only rest on the basis of equality." Eloquent words. Danton, for his part, was more immediately practical, manifesting the difference in temperament between the two men that would become fatal for him a year later. "Citizens, you don't have a minute to lose . . . , war is only waged with enthusiasm," he proclaimed in a rousing call for Paris to jump-start lagging recruitment by acting on its burning commitment to defend the homeland. At his instigation, the Convention voted to send deputies to the sections that evening to describe the urgency of the military situation and incite volunteers to fly to the front in fulfillment of their vows to die for freedom and equality. The same message was ordered to be conveyed to the departments.[53]

While the deputies to be sent to the sections were being selected, the Montagnards launched an attack on the Girondin journalists who were campaigning against them, minimizing the extent of the military defeats, and defending the ministers and generals from charges of incompetence. These scribblers were "vile and despicable men . . . ," Duhem charged, "the libelous insects who are the sole and true obstacles to the progress of the Revolution . . . , the hack journalists whose sole occupation it is to corrupt public spirit, defame the National Convention . . . [and] slander patriots." "Polluted reptiles," they had to be silenced, he insisted; they had to be expelled from the assembly. "What confidence in the Convention do you want there to be when a Brissot slanders it daily?" demanded Bourdon. "Then let's also prohibit Marat's journal," came the rejoinder. But The People's Friend was not the target here. Duhem's insistence that "freedom of the press is not freedom to make the counterrevolution" became a theme in a lengthy speech by Jeanbon Saint-André targeting the journals of Brissot and Gorsas that Roland's slush fund had so handsomely supported to denigrate the Paris deputation.[54] Debate on the matter was closed for the moment, but its outcome was soon to be decided in the streets.

Attacks on the Girondin deputies and their press found their echo in calls for action that evening at a tumultuous meeting of the Jacobin Club. "Revolutionary measures are the only ones appropriate for us; the system of moderation compromises the safety of the republic," proclaimed Marat's ally, the deputy Pierre-Louis Bentabole, endorsing the call for insurrection that had opened the meeting. It was time to demand the recall of Lafayette's criminal cronies who were still commanding the armies, Hébert urged; time also to remove those still sitting in the Convention. "Remember that republics are maintained only by the force of opinion," declared the Montagnard Sylvain-Phalier Lejeune as he called for the indictment of Brissot and Gorsas; "the vile writer who saps public spirit at its foundations is a criminal guilty of *lèse nation*." A state tribunal was needed for the blade of the law to pass over the heads of all those who wanted to destroy liberty, he continued, in language Marat had long used; to save the republic, agents had to be sent throughout the country to strike pitilessly against all the traitors. Plans were apparently made, during or after the society's regular session, to prevent women from entering the public galleries of the Convention the following day in anticipation of a popular coup against the assembly. Radical members of the club, with support from ultra-radicals belonging to a group known as Defenders of the Republic One and Indivisible, also laid the groundwork for an insurrection that would include attacks on Girondin presses and the arrest, judgment, and execution of Girondin leaders.[55]

The session of the Convention that opened the following morning, 9 March, was momentous. Crowing that "the energy deployed by the patriots on this occasion and the public spirit manifested in the galleries triumphed over all the efforts of the *hommes d'Etat*," Marat later declared it "forever memorable in the annals of the French Republic." An agitated crowd had gathered on the terrace surrounding the Manège, brandishing pistols and copies of Marat's journal for the day denouncing the treasonous generals. There were reports that Pétion and Beurnonville were harassed and Marat raised up in triumph. Moves were made, and countered, to prevent women from entering the public galleries in anticipation of popular action against the Convention. Under the threat of insurrection, and in the face of repeated protests from their opponents that "We are not free," the Montagnards would seize the moment to push through their agenda, laying down some of the principal institutions of the state terror to come.[56]

The crucial discussion began as the deputies sent out to the sections returned to relate their encounters. They reported enthusiastic receptions in crowded meetings charged with hatred of tyrants and passion to fly to the defense of the homeland. They had found, though, that patriotic fervor to depart for the front was shadowed by concerns about the situation the volunteers would be leaving behind them. Resentment against the rich had provoked calls that they contribute to the war effort in cash if not in courage, by reimbursing those of their fellow citizens ready to shed their own blood. In response, following a similar demand by the Commune, the Convention soon decreed the establishment of a war tax on the wealthy. This measure was matched later in the session by decisions to abolish imprisonment for debt and free those currently incarcerated for it. These two decisions had been taken in accordance with "the great principles of philanthropy, philosophy and politics developed by Danton," Marat reported, acknowledging that they had been shrewdly presented at a moment when men were needed to defend the homeland.[57]

Misgivings about ministers and their generals had also prompted cries for vengeance against those responsible for military defeats, feeding into demands for what Bentabole now called "a counterrevolutionary tribunal" to punish traitors and conspirators. This body, he urged, was necessary and indispensable; not to establish it would "disgust all good citizens." An appeal by the Louvre section for the immediate creation of a "tribunal without appeal, to put an end to the audacity of major culprits and all the enemies of the public good," was eagerly seized upon by the future terrorist Jean-Baptiste Carrier. His motion that the Convention instantly decree the principle of the establishment of such a "revolutionary tribunal" (its mode of organization to be outlined by the Committee on Legislation within twenty-four hours) was adopted almost immediately. Opponents were left to push back against the use of the term "revolutionary" in the title of an institution whose dire effects they predicted. Established as an "extraordinary criminal tribunal to judge conspirators and counterrevolutionaries without appeal," but soon commonly feared as the Revolutionary Tribunal, it would become one of the central instruments of the Terror.[58]

A measure creating another such instrument soon followed, proposed by a future member of the Committee of Public Safety, the mathematician Lazare Carnot, destined to become legendary as the organizer of French victory in the years to come. It instituted the appointment of deputies *en mission*, to be sent from Paris to organize recruitment and oversee the war effort in departments throughout the country. At a subsequent session, Collot d'Herbois ignited a storm and invited threats of physical violence when he urged that only deputies who had voted against the *appel au peuple* be selected for this purpose. No formal decision to this effect was taken, but Montagnards proved much more willing than their opponents to take on a role allowing them to counter the successes of Girondin propaganda in the departments and advance their revolutionary policies. Soon dispatched as agents of the supreme power of the Convention, these deputies *en mission*—in effect, revolutionary commissars—were authorized to call local authorities to account, take any measures necessary to establish order, suspend officials, and arrest those found suspect.[59] They were eventually responsible for many of the worst excesses of the Revolution in the provinces.

That evening, at a session hastily improvised for the purpose, the Convention heard more from the sections. As newly formed contingents of volunteers paraded through the hall, proclamations of patriotic *élan* alternated with demands for radical political action. The latter came most notably in a clamorous petition from the Gravilliers section, the political home of Jacques Roux, whose program it largely presented. The deputies were "mandataries of the people," they were reminded; they were there to serve the interests of "the laborious and virtuous class of society" by legislating in accordance with principles of reason and eternal justice. For that class, the petition continued, liberty remained a phantom after four years of revolution; it was being exploited under the shadow of the law by the speculation, brigandage, and hoarding that were driving up the cost of subsistence and devouring the empire. "It is time to save the Republic," the deputies were told. "The enemies most avid for its failure are those who ruin, starve, and discourage the people . . . those who tolerate the crime share in it."

Were the wives and children of men fighting for the Republic to be left to suffer and die under the oppression of an aristocracy of the rich? the Gravilliers petitioners demanded. "There is no liberty without good laws; there is no equality as long as one class of men oppresses and betrays the other with impunity." A call for repression of monopolists, speculators, and hoarders followed, for fixing the value of the assignat, for taxing the rich, for rescuing the poor from their indigence. The people's mandataries had to purge the Republic of the monsters whose usurious calculations were constantly striking its death blow, to consult the wishes of the people, heal its ills, provide for its needs, do everything for its happiness. If they failed to do so, they were warned, they would "live in dishonor and die, like the last king of France, from the punishment reserved for traitors!"[60] It took a major act of diplomacy on the part of the Convention's president to acknowledge the petitioners' devotion before sending their demands to the financial committee for consideration.

As declarations followed from other sections fervently mobilizing volunteers to fight and die for *la patrie en danger*, they too were interspersed with demands for punitive action against internal enemies undermining their patriotic efforts. From Les Halles section, there were calls for elimination of formerly privileged persons from positions of command in the army, for suspension of legislation until the nation's defenders had returned to express their interests, for a revolutionary tribunal to try treasonous generals and other enemies of liberty and equality, taking punitive measures the people would not be obliged to take for itself. According to the Piques section, similar measures had to be extended to the provisional executive council.

This sequence of proclamations, patriotic or minatory, was abruptly interrupted, however, by news that a crowd of several hundred armed men had indeed invaded Gorsas's printshop, breaking the presses, destroying the fonts, and ransacking papers. Marat called for verification of the facts, but the assembly fell into chaos as the Mountain cheered and trumpets were sounded in celebration of the news. It later became clear that the printshop of Joseph Fievée, responsible for Condorcet's *Chronique de Paris*, had suffered the same fate. The premises of Charles-Joseph Panckoucke, publisher of the *Moniteur*, and Louis-Marie Prudhomme, editor of *Révolutions de Paris*, had apparently been better protected. Marat's were untouched. But without waiting for further information, the assembly decided that deputies who were also journalists would henceforth be required to opt for one or the other of the two occupations.[61]

For Marat, this decision was an outrage. "I've complained a hundred times . . . against the unworthy deputies who pass their time reporting the sessions in order to sell their manuscript to the journalists," he protested in his journal days later. Why should he be treated like these "vile mercenaries," he demanded; "I who have always freely consecrated my pen to the public good, whose writing has no other purpose than to unveil plots against liberty, unmask traitors, defend the oppressed and propose useful ideas; I who have taken time from my sleep to jot down my ideas, who grant myself only the bare necessities, who share my bread with the poor and have only my debts as the fruit of my labor." To evade this decision, he renamed his journal on 14 March, presenting it as the *Publiciste de la République française, ou Observations aux Français, par Marat, L'Ami du peuple, Député à la Convention nationale.* He retitled it again on 25 March as *Observations à mes commettants*, making it purportedly a publication intended for the constituents he served as a deputy. There were further variations until 9 April, when the title was stabilized as *Publiciste de la République française, par Marat L'Ami du Peuple, Député à la Convention, Auteur de plusieurs ouvrages patriotiques.*[62] With these changes, The People's Friend stayed ahead of a denunciation leveled against him on 26 March by the justice minister Garat for breaching the law against deputies' doubling as journalists. But he soon dropped the fiction that the journal was intended only for his constituents.

The attack on the Girondin presses, the work of a crowd led by the Defenders of the Republic One and Indivisible, signaled a moment for insurrection. Agitation was reported in Paris throughout the day on 10 March, turning more threatening as the evening approached. The Convention was surrounded by crowds, and many deputies from the right and center stayed away. The Montagnards, Marat among them, pushed the assembly to extend the powers of the deputies it was sending out to the departments, denounce the generals and the ministers, and order the arrest of those most suspect.

Crucially, steamrolling vehement objections from deputies within the assembly that they were instituting despotism, and conscious of the insurrectionary fervor of the throngs outside, the Montagnards pressed to establish the organization and political reach of the Revolutionary Tribunal. "Let's be terrible to dispense the people from being so," was Danton's memorable injunction. "Let's organize a tribunal, not well because that is impossible, but the least badly it can be, so that the blade of the law weighs on the head of all its enemies." For hours, in a passionate session interrupted by alarmed reports of popular insurrection, not least from the General Council of the Commune, the bitterly divided Convention hammered out the details of a tribunal that would punish every manifestation of counterrevolution. It was 4:30 a.m. before that task was completed.[63]

By that time, indeed hours before, the Jacobin Club had been invaded by volunteers from the section of Les Halles, as many as a thousand in one report, who pressed its members and the spectators in the galleries to join them in marching on the Convention to call the generals and ministers to account. After a half-hour of tumult, with some of the lights failing in the hall, and over the objection of the club's more moderate members, two crowds had headed out, one to the Convention, the other toward the Cordelier Club where an insurrectionary assembly was already in permanent session. In a chaotic scene there, radicals had enjoined the department of Paris, "integral part of the sovereign . . . , to seize sovereignty" and urged its electoral assembly to "replace members traitorous to the cause of the people." An address written by Jean-François Varlet in similar terms had also denounced the Girondin deputies, Dumouriez and other generals, indeed the entire government, as traitors responsible for the military defeats. Calling again upon the department of Paris, as "integral part of the sovereign, to exercise the sovereignty belonging to it," this address demanded a convocation of the sections to authorize the city's electoral assembly to "recall the faithless and unworthy mandataries as a matter of public right because they voted for the preservation of the tyrant and the appeal to the people."

Varlet's address was circulated during the night to all the sections, some of which welcomed it and declared themselves in a state of insurrection.

Even as they did so, however, the municipal authorities were mobilizing the forces of repression, Santerre at their head. The Cordelier Club, having initially decreed the closing of the barriers to the city and the sounding of the tocsin—the customary signals for a popular uprising—rescinded that decision in response to the pushback from the General Council of the Commune. Lacking that body's direction and support, indeed blocked by it, the efforts at insurrection fizzled out. "People, your magistrates prevented you from consummating the act into which you had been misled," jibed Isnard, celebrating the moment of relief to rapturous applause in the Convention on 12 March. "They issued a severe decree. The crowd was set straight, the project failed, and we're still alive for the salvation of the homeland, the triumph of liberty, and the destruction of tyrants."[64] Next time, he would discover, his faction would fare differently.

RECRIMINATIONS

Isnard's was the first of several speeches over the next few days that declaimed against the attempted insurrection. He identified the Jacobin Club as setting it in motion, though he blamed aristocrats disguised as patriots within it, or vile agents recruited by them, and William Pitt as its instigators. "Those who call themselves your most ardent friends are not always so," he warned the people in an obvious swipe at Marat. "And you, my colleagues, if you want to save the homeland, set aside mutual distrust. Let our discussions be free and calm. France needs wise laws, not empty clamors. Let's be fearful that in sowing only wind we'll harvest tempests. Let's abjure all hatreds in this moment, except that for crime." This effort to recover the initiative for the Girondins in the name of unity was rhapsodically received by a majority of the deputies and its publication was immediately decreed.

Marat was not among those applauding. He rushed to the tribune to reverse this action, "destroy its perfidious illusions [and] redirect indignation back upon the heads of the *hommes d'Etat*." Announcing that he had plots to reveal, he was immediately accused of complicity in conspiracy himself. He was quick to respond. "The intestine troubles aroused in the capital . . . have led to truly alarming excesses," he countered; former police agents acting on ministerial orders, or those of counterrevolutionary deputies, had been inciting assassinations of leading Girondins. "Yes. It's an atrocious crime, threatening to dissolve the Convention and destroy the homeland," he declared to doubtless astonished applause. "I myself went to these groups to preach peace; I betook myself to the patriotic society of the Cordeliers to confront some perfidious orators who could incite the people to this measure, and I today denounce the most suspect man in the world."[65]

The man Marat fingered for this distinction was one Fournier, sometimes identified as Fournier l'Américain, whom he accused of posturing with a gun aimed at Lafayette on the fatal day at the Champ de Mars, suspiciously remaining free while true patriots were being massacred, and later parading in the streets of Paris with those responsible for the bloodshed. "He's the criminal at the head of this sedition. I call for an indictment against him; he'll give us the key to this plot, whose authors I summon the Convention to turn over to the revolutionary tribunal." The denunciation was immediately reiterated by other Montagnards, Billaud-Varenne (who denounced Fournier again as an extremist to the Jacobin Club that same evening), and Bourdon de l'Oise, who accused him of incendiary talk outside the Convention on 10 March. Eventually arrested and ordered to appear before the Committee of General Security, Fournier insisted on answering the charge against him before the Convention the following day.[66]

In the meantime, Marat charged the *hommes d'Etat*, "the party of Roland," with the plot to destroy the Republic. Their appeal for unity was a charade, he maintained; they were awaiting the departure of the deputies *en mission* to incite an insurrection against the patriots in the Convention, provoke the assembly's dissolution, and move its seat to a counterrevolutionary city. "And I who have no love for the *hommes d'Etat* declare that I will make my body a rampart against attacks against them at the same time as I will defend [the Convention] from their machinations." The claim was ridiculed by Lasource, a former Montagnard now veering toward the Girondins, who caricatured Marat as a puppet duped by the true conspirators he identified as royalists. "We know where this man's head is; he's misled, he's manipulated; he's not the one who executes, the one who conceives, the one who thinks," Lasource declared. He wanted the nation to know, once and for all, that this troublesome journalist was merely "the instrument of perfidious men who play skillfully on his credulity, profiting from his natural aptitude to see everything in funereal colors, persuading him of everything they want and making him say everything that pleases them. Once they have filled his head, he rants and fantasizes as they wish."[67]

The deputies were still arguing a day later whether Isnard's speech should be published, or Marat's, or both—or neither. The Montagnard Thuriot argued forcefully for the latter option. He wanted to prevent evidence of division in the assembly circulating in the departments and to shift attention from still murky details of an attempted insurrection. But he was also keen to downplay Marat's influence and minimize the latter's association with the Mountain. "How could Marat influence a single member of the National Convention," he asked. "I'm far from believing that, as he persuades himself, he's the one who makes everything happen in the century in which we find ourselves. . . . A man who sees so much in black and so much in white, almost at the same moment, is not in a position to fix the general opinion."[68] Thuriot's speech was damning, but it was quickly overshadowed by an even more powerful one from Vergniaud, who mounted the tribune eager to report the results of his own investigation into the insurrectionary impulses of the previous days.

The Girondin leader was not in a mood to sweep an attempt at insurrection under the rug. To the contrary, he decried the degeneration of the Revolution to a point where respect for justice, humanity, and the rights of man was denounced as counterrevolutionary and provocation to murder and pillage was acclaimed as patriotic. The people, in his analysis, was now divided into two classes: "one, delirious from the excessive excitation to which it has been carried, works daily for its own ruin; the other, stupefied, endures a punishing existence in the anguish of terrors that know no end." A strange system had developed, he lamented, in which liberty had been turned into conformity of thought and action sanctioned by threats of popular vengeance. "And so, citizens, the fear has taken hold that the revolution, like Saturn devouring each of its children in turn, will finally give birth to despotism and the calamities that accompany it."[69]

These words have long been cherished by historians as epitomizing the dynamic of the French Revolution. In uttering them, Vergniaud was just hitting the rhetorical stride of one of his greatest speeches. He lamented the fissure that had been opened within the assembly, pitting those deputies who considered the Revolution completed by the declaration of the Republic against those who thought it vital to sustain "the effervescence of the revolution." He identified the passions unleashed by the refusal of the *appel au peuple* as inviting counterrevolutionaries to transform the Convention into a "burning crater emitting sulfurous expressions of conspiracies, treasons, and counterrevolution," and to redirect the people's anger against one side of the assembly toward the other. "Our rage will do the rest," he warned, obliquely suggesting the possibility of a purge. "And if some members of the Convention perish in the movement we will have incited, we will then present their colleagues to France as their assassins and executioners." At this, he predicted, public indignation would unleash a catastrophe that would destroy representation, and with it the revolution itself. Anarchy would reign, and despotism emerge from its midst. "The tyrant who is still hiding will arise from the debris of blood and carnage."

The creation of the Revolutionary Tribunal, he dared to imagine in the face of howls from the Mountain, might even become an instrument for the emergence of despotism from within the assembly.[70]

This said, Vergniaud unfolded a detailed narrative of the movement toward insurrection that had swept through the political societies and the clubs, identifying members of a shadowy "insurrection committee" whose arrest he demanded. One was Fournier, the others were François Desfieux, president of the Jacobin Club's correspondence committee, and Claude-François Lazowski, a hero of the revolution of 10 August and a sans-culotte activist in the sections. "Such, citizens, is the depth of the abyss that was dug beneath your feet," Vergniaud told the deputies. "Has the blindfold finally been lifted? Have you learned to recognize the usurpers of the title, *Friends of the People*? And you, hapless people, will you any longer be the dupes of hypocrites who like to get your applause more than earn it?" The royalists had wanted to oppress the people with the word *constitution*, he went on; the anarchists wanted to trick it with the word *sovereignty*. Now the counterrevolutionaries were abusing "liberty" and "equality." He saw a new politico-linguistic front opening and hastened to close it in the name of equality of rights, not that of possessions. Would the volunteers leaving their wives and children for the front be ready to shed their blood in defense of anarchy and brigandage, he demanded, provoking violent interruptions from the Mountain. "Citizens . . . , we want to overthrow thrones. Let's prove that we can be happy with a Republic."[71]

Vergniaud had barely left the tribune before there were enthusiastic demands that his speech be published—and a move by Marat to speak against any such measure. The Girondin had affected a scrupulous refusal to name names, but Marat's had been interjected from the floor more than once and he was ready to make the argument personal. (Robespierre, it is worth noting, remained stalwart in his silence.) "I don't present myself with embellished words and parasitical phrases to beg for applause," The People's Friend began. "I appear with luminous ideas meant to dissipate the empty nonsense you've just heard." No one was more disturbed than he by the scandalous scenes and baneful disagreements that had broken out in the assembly, he protested. "No one is more afflicted than I to see two parties, one that doesn't want to save the homeland and the other that doesn't know how to save it."[72]

It was beyond dispute, Marat contended, that the deputies voting for the *appel au peuple* wanted civil war and those voting to save the tyrant's life wanted to preserve tyranny. Public indignation, not his own, had indicted these men; the record of their own hypocrisy had condemned them. Guilty emissaries, perhaps even their own, had infiltrated groups of citizens to incite extremism. He later accused Pétion and Buzot of being "at the heart of the anarchic movements that have just occurred in Paris," complicit with soldiery ready to attack the Mountain. He, in contrast, had preached peace. "For the past several days, I have gone around the popular societies encouraging good citizens to watchfulness and moderation. I'm trying to put them on their guard against suggestions of the evildoers." He claimed the existence of witnesses to attest that he had made members of the Cordelier Club swear to shield with their bodies any deputies under threat of public indignation, and he announced that he had pledged to march at their head as they did so. The deputies on the right were calling for unity with the patriots of the Mountain now they saw that public opinion was against them, he charged. He urged them to do so. As for the publication of Vergniaud's speech, he opposed circulation of a text that would spread word in the departments of the assembly's divisions and alarms.[73]

In this fierce factional struggle, the assembly proceeded to tie itself in knots over whether to publish Vergniaud's speech and Marat's with it. First it decided that Vergniaud's would be published, then both, then neither. Then it battled again before voting in favor of Vergniaud's call for the arrest of Desfieux and Lazowski. Fournier, already indicted, soon presented himself for judgment, eager to confront his principal accuser, Marat, who had apparently left the hall. He, too, insisted that he had exerted himself to calm the situation at the Cordelier Club on the night of 10 March. He also repudiated suspicions that he had stolen valuables from prisoners (among them the former foreign minister Delessart) who had been notoriously slaughtered in Versailles at the time of the revolution of 10 August. He was declared innocent of all charges by the Convention and released. Lazowski, appearing before the assembly in turn, was dismissed after being resolutely defended by Marat as "an excellent patriot," indeed "a very revolutionary patriot" unjustly targeted by the Girondins. The charge against Desfieux simply evaporated.[74]

Denied a confrontation with his accuser in the Convention, Fournier retaliated in print. Claiming that he was a victim of mistaken identity, he sought to settle the score on 14 March by directing a blistering attack on Marat with a sideswipe at "the mass of insects" who had joined in accusing him. His broadside, *C. Fournier (Americain) à Marat*, in a fascinating detail suggesting a lineage from the sans-culottes to the socialist revolutionary tradition, was apparently drafted for him by none other than Gracchus Babeuf, later the instigator of the socialist Conspiracy of the Equals. "You denounce for the sake of denouncing, for the pleasure of slandering," the pamphlet blasted at The People's Friend. "Calumny is a compulsion for you. Your accusation on 12 March had exhausted the portion of your venomous spleen against me, so you had no more left to release on the thirteenth." You're not the Friend of the People you claim to be, this denunciation continued; friends of the people don't frivolously denounce the best patriots. Were you seen at the Bastille on 14 July, it taunted, at Versailles on the fifth and sixth of September, at the Champ de Mars that terrible day, at the Tuileries palace on 20 June or 10 August? "Where does the brave Marat hide in circumstances where his valor would be so useful? Alas, it's too well known, he's underground. But from there he launches his periodic oracles to fill the streets of Paris to tell the people that it has a friend. Let's take note that this so intimate friendship is sustained all the better because the numerous friends of this friend lend a hand to distribute it constantly for two sous a copy."[75]

Denunciations were scarcely unfamiliar to The People's Friend. There had been several from right-wing journalists within recent days. On 1 March, Carra's *Annales patriotiques et littéraires* had branded Marat's journal as a front for British agents. On 5 March, Gorsas's *Courrier des départements* had repeated this same charge, adding rumors that Marat had been accused of theft during his stay in England, that he was an agent of the former comte d'Artois, his employer under the Old Regime. These smears were taken up by the *Mercure français* the following day. It was not long before the story of the theft in England had been dramatized across the Channel by an article in *The Star*. (The fabrication was embroidered into English biographies of Marat for the best part of two centuries.)[76] But Marat's joy at the vandalization of the Girondin presses on 10 March was scarcely surprising.

Fournier's lambasting of Marat was more unusual, though, in that it came not from the Right but the radical revolutionary Left. His rage was understandable. The Cordeliers had claimed Marat as their own. A reading from the *Journal de la République française* had frequently opened earlier sessions of the Cordelier Club. The issue of 9 March had been touted that day, and The People's Friend himself raised up in acclamation by agitated crowds surrounding the Convention in anticipation of popular action against it. Moreover, the language of the radicals preaching insurrection had recapitulated incitements to retribution against traitors among the deputies, generals, and ministers that had punctuated *L'Ami du peuple* for months. Yet he was firm at the Jacobin Club on 13 March in repudiating talk of insurrection, for which he blamed the enemies of the people. "There are 500 or 600 scoundrels in Paris aiding them, they're circulating in the societies to lead them to their destruction by false measures. Nothing could be better than for the nation to rise up and strike down these scoundrels." It was time for the sections to post the names of dangerous citizens, he urged. With the departments still in the dark, "any partial insurrection, any sudden move" would prompt calumny from the antipatriotic faction. "Public opinion is the queen of the world," he reminded the Jacobins. It had to be mobilized. "Don't take any violent action against the faithless mandataries, brand them with infamy, overwhelm them with your contempt, unmask them in your publications, and that's the way to bring them down."[77]

The People's Friend had thus opted emphatically against insurrection, choosing to defend the representative body against those mobilizing for direct and immediate action against it in the name of an embodied sovereignty. Standing firm with the Montagnards, he was intent on eliminating the Girondins, but not at the risk of destroying the Convention and sabotaging the Revolution with it. However guilty the deputies who had betrayed the interests of the people might be, he wrote on 15 March, "any attack, any act of violence against them would be an atrocious crime that would lead to the dissolution of the Convention and the destruction of the Republic."[78] The Convention had to be purged, it seemed, but from within the Convention itself. It was ironic that the French translation of *The Chains of Slavery*, promised for many weeks in Marat's journal, would now soon appear in print on 28 March. Its warning against parliamentary despotism was wearing thin.

In panic at the threat of insurrection against them, the leaders of the Convention had called for a common front among the deputies. If Marat gave lip service to the idea in the assembly, he was franker in his journal on 19 March. Acknowledging that he himself was regarded as a stumbling block against unity, he offered yet another autobiographical defense against claims that he was an anarchist, desperate for power, a drinker of blood, a crazed mind. He had come to the Revolution with his ideas already formed, he declared. "The history of the different peoples of the world, the light of reason, and the principles of sound politics" had led him to the conclusion that "the only way to consolidate the revolution is for the party of liberty to crush that of its enemies." If this conviction had dictated calls for vigorous measures that supporters had called bloodthirsty, he pleaded, he would have preferred milder ones if they were effective. He had sometimes supported legal means of punishing prevaricators, oppressors, and schemers, but finding them counterproductive in practice he had returned to his initial views. He had appeared to be contradictory only because legislators and administrators had misled the people with false promises, derisory measures, prevarications, and violence. "My apparent contradictions are thus only the result of the perpetual snares of the enemies of the homeland."

Convinced that there could be no unity within the assembly until the *hommes d'Etat* were ready to vote with the Mountain to save the state, Marat was no less sure that this outcome was out of the question. "My conclusion is that it is impossible to count on the union of the *hommes d'Etat* and the patriots of the Mountain. Public safety will thus be endangered as long as these supporters of royalism who voted against the death of the tyrant are not recalled from the heart of the Convention."[79]

DISASTER IN BELGIUM

Insurrection threatened Paris on 10 March in response to developments that would prove critical in accelerating the revolutionary political dynamic. The collapse of French forces at Maastricht continued with routs at Neerwinden on 18 March and Louvain on 22 March. Culminating in a full-scale retreat from a country that had so recently been moving toward complete annexation, it revived fears of invasion by the now victorious Austrian and Prussian armies. At the same time, widespread provincial resistance to the war was provoked in France by the levy of three hundred thousand men ordered by the Convention on 24 February in a belated effort to replenish troop strength for a new campaigning season. In a dramatic episode on 15 March an antirecruitment riot in the city of Orléans left one of the deputies *en mission*, Léonard Bourdon, barely clinging to life. Beginning with a massacre of republicans in the more distant Loire-Atlantique town of Machecoul on 11 March, resistance to conscription rapidly escalated into royalist counterrevolution in the vast area of western France known as the Vendée. Within days, defeats of the Republic's forces there opened a civil war lasting months and feeding atrocities that eventually cost several hundred thousand lives.

For Marat, these developments could only be seen through the lens of his own escalating campaign against the *hommes d'Etat*. He was furious on 18 March when Lanjuinais demanded that the punishment for émigrés caught bearing arms—the death penalty without appeal—be extended to all those opposing recruitment or wearing the royalist white cocarde. This, he objected, was "the most insane measure, the most unworthy of a thinking being with good intentions toward the Republic." It would punish men who had been misled rather than their leaders, who themselves should be brought before courts-martial and punished by death. His opposition, with that of other deputies, blocked the proposed measure for the moment, and the assembly went on to adopt a range of other repressive policies urged by Barnave. But Lanjuinais's proposal was revived in more severe form the following day in a decree that condemned as outlaws, and hence deprived of their rights to legal process, all those caught engaged in counterrevolutionary revolts, antirecruitment riots, or other forms of rebellion. Individuals seized bearing arms were declared subject to summary execution and confiscation of property within twenty-four hours.[80]

Marat attributed the pattern of resistance emerging across the country to the actions, above all, of the vast mass of his political enemies who were entrenched in power. "The homeland has never been in greater danger," he thundered on 20 March.

> It's not only the enemy powers that plot the death of the French Republic but the leaders of the criminal faction of the *hommes d'Etat*, all supporters of monarchism, in league with our perfidious generals, the directories of districts and departments, the members of the courts, the aristocrats and the émigrés they openly protect.
>
> It's to their infernal plots that we must attribute the movements, troubles and disorders that have been exploding in Paris and most of the departments. It's the slanderous publications with which they have infected the entire Republic, and the lying letters they have been writing to their constituents directed against the most zealous defenders of liberty, that must be blamed for these intestine dissensions, assaults against the friends of the people, and assassinations of patriotic deputies.

The Montagnards could have foiled these plots, The People's Friend bewailed, had they been more united and more willing to back his efforts to confront the Convention. "May Heaven have pity on us if the nation doesn't rise up *en masse* to crush the implacable enemies of its peace both within and without."[81]

For the moment, however, Marat's immediate obsession was with General Dumouriez, whom he now made the fulcrum of his attacks on the entire political apparatus of the *hommes d'Etat*. He was helped in this regard by the actions of the general himself. On 12 March, Dumouriez had addressed a letter to the Convention from Louvain, his words the angry outburst of a vainglorious man now obliged to sacrifice the prospect of a decisive victory in Holland to direct the recovery of a defeated army in Belgium. The reverses the army had suffered had both practical and moral causes, he contended. He undertook to analyze them "with the frankness, now more necessary than ever, that would have constantly achieved the salvation of the Republic if all public agents had employed it in rendering their accounts, and if it had always been heard with more compliance than lying flattery." The general, like Marat, was ready to lay blame and had plenty to distribute.

Dumouriez censured previous war ministers for failure to address problems of supply, organization, and manpower he had identified in December in memoranda that had been ignored until Beurnonville became war minister. By that time, he charged, it was too late for the country to support both his own invasion of Holland (in his view, a necessary response to the too-hasty declaration of war against England) and Miranda's siege of Maastricht. Above all, he criticized the "avarice and injustice" motivating the occupation of Belgium that had been carried out by French officials oppressing religious freedom, looting religious institutions, forcing putatively voluntary unions with France, and imposing tyrannical requisitions. In his analysis, all this had brought inhabitants of the Belgian countryside to the point of inciting armed resistance. Terror and perhaps hatred had replaced the sweet fraternity of the initial liberation. Now there were enemies everywhere. "For them it's a holy war," he remonstrated; "for us it's criminal."[82]

This letter amounted to a wholesale attack on the policies of the Girondin leadership of the Convention with which Dumouriez had been so closely identified. There were thus strategic political reasons for keeping it under wraps. The president of the Convention took it to the Committee of General Defense for consideration immediately upon its receipt on 14 March without presenting it to the assembly. The deputies were still calling to hear it formally presented on 27 March, by which time it had been published in the Paris papers. Marat seems to have had it in mind as early as 19 March when he remarked in the retitled *Publiciste de la République française* that the general had removed his mask in attempting to usurp sovereignty in Belgium and Holland. Long Dumouriez's harshest critic, he had nevertheless opposed a demand for the general's dismissal and punishment brought to the Convention by a deputation of the Poissonnière section on 12 March. He was convinced at that juncture in the war that Dumouriez's leadership was essential if the French armies were to push back against the Austrians. But he soon changed his mind, seizing the opportunity to tar the *hommes d'Etat* with the brush of their association with the treacherous general. In his analysis, the Brissotins' disorientation at news of Dumouriez's suspected treasons soon offered, on 18 March, "the finest opportunity ever presented to assure the victory of the patriotic party." The Montagnards, he lamented, had failed to support his efforts to seize the moment. "It's impossible for the Convention ever to succeed unless the nation finally removes the enemies and the most gangrened members of the faction of *hommes d'Etat*," he swore. "Each day I'll put the mark of opprobrium on their forehead, until the nation imposes justice on them or public execration forces them to retire."[83]

On 20 March, claiming vindication of its earlier predictions of the treacherous ambitions of this "creature of the Brissotin faction," the *Publiciste de la République française* printed two of the general's proclamations, each dated 11 March. One invited expression of grievances from the occupied Belgian population against the tyranny of French administrators; a second forbade clubs and political societies from any engagement in politics. Commissioners had been sent to rein in the general, the journal reported, with powers to arrest him if he proved recalcitrant. This was an absurd response, Marat thought, placing these emissaries at risk of becoming its victims. He was wrong this time, but his apprehensions proved correct later. Delacroix and Danton had, in fact, been sent by the deeply divided Committee of General Defense to negotiate with Dumouriez after a stormy discussion of his 12 March letter. "He'll retract," Danton had vowed, "or I'll bring him back bound hand and foot."

Neither of these things happened. The only immediate success of this mission was to send General Miranda back to Paris to appear before the Convention. In the meantime, Marat's denunciation of the recalcitrant Dumouriez earned him harassment from a gang of *mouchards* as he left the Convention on 20 March. Their mood was reflected by the interim minister of justice Garat in a letter addressed to the assembly two days later. The minister condemned this same issue of the *Publiciste de la République française* for slandering the general and urged the assembly to put teeth into the law forbidding its members to double as journalists. The Committee on Legislation was charged on 26 March to report on these accusations.[84]

Marat was pilloried again as a public enemy on 21 March when a letter from Beurnonville informed the assembly of pillage by French troops in Belgium and another from Dumouriez described the rout at Neerwinden, blaming it on indiscipline among the troops. "Wrongdoing and disorganization are at their height," complained the general, expressing fear of "the disastrous consequences of this retreat in a country whose inhabitants we have incited against us through pillage and indiscipline." "Marat, Marat," came the cry from the hall; "this is the effect of your preaching." "It's the typical artifice of perfidious generals who have suffered a reverse to blame the patriotic soldiers and call for bloody laws against men whose burning zeal has motivated them to fly to the frontier," Marat countered, responding to calls for a more severe system of military discipline. "The soldiers aren't the thieves, it's some of their leaders, some of the conspirators infiltrating among them, who commit these disorders; it's on the leaders that the law should weigh. We've reached the moment to tear the veil and reveal everything. We don't have generals capable of facing the enemy; we don't have troops capable of battle." His comment was greeted by howls of indignation and cries that he was paid by the enemy. "Let Marat be heard," declared one of the Girondins, "let him vomit his calumnies and unmask himself." When he regained the tribune, it was to demand the right to present the Committee of General Defense with a plan for national defense. He was met with a call to declare him insane.[85]

The *Publiciste de la République française* had mentioned this defense plan on 20 March in offering a checklist of problems facing the nation. The latter included the eternal treasons of generals; French losses of life; outrages of the military leadership against National Guard troops, the most patriotic of whom had so many times been led to the slaughter; vengeance attacks by the population of the Low Countries against French forces; and, above all, a shortage of weapons resulting from ministerial incompetence. All these factors, Marat asserted, were reasons for the French to shift to the defensive strategy he had initially proposed months earlier, before the war had started. Within a week, on 26 March, he was reprinting material from December 1791 that had urged mass production of daggers to arm the population for guerrilla warfare. The following day, he was characterizing this method of arming the sans-culottes as "the one most advantageous and expeditious, the one most fitting the national character . . . , the only one that will strike our enemies with terror and dread in making them see their tomb on the battlefield." He would have pressed this plan on the Committee of General Defense, he told his readers, had that committee not been "almost entirely composed of *hommes d'Etat* and the leaders of the Brissot faction, in league with the ministers and generals to foment counterrevolution and hence monarchism." In any case, he added, the committee was already discredited by public opinion and had lost the confidence of moderate deputies; he was waiting for it be renewed as a Committee of Public Safety. Until then, he promised, he would appeal to the popular societies to launch a public subscription in support of his effort to arm the populace with his favorite weapon. In fact, he had already done so at the Jacobin Club on 25 March.[86] It was a crazy idea, perhaps, but was it less so than Danton's dramatic cry to arm the nation with pikes?

EXIT DUMOURIEZ

On 23 March, the day immediately following his army's defeat at Louvain, Dumouriez began negotiating with the Austrians for the peaceful withdrawal of French troops in return for surrender of Dutch and Belgian territories. By 25 March, he was proposing to march on Paris, overthrow the Convention, destroy the Jacobins, and restore the monarchy and the constitution of 1791. The Austrians agreed to halt their advance on France while he did so, on condition that his troops leave Belgian soil by 31 March.

Though he evaded meeting with Danton, Delacroix, and the Convention's other commissioners, Dumouriez made no secret of his plans. He shared them with members of his general staff among others and explained them at length to a group of three Jacobins (curiously sent by the foreign minister Le Brun) who met with him on 26 and 27 March. The conversations went so far as to touch on the possibility that the two sides might join in a conspiracy to dissolve the Convention, though the interest of either in doing so remained obscure. Each subsequently accused the other of raising the idea. Dumouriez reported the conversations to his friend, foreign minister Beurnonville. The Jacobins relayed their own account to Delacroix, by whom it was passed eventually to the Committee of General Defense. There it became a key element, along with Miranda's revelations of Dumouriez's plans and letters from the general himself, in the committee's agonized decision on 29 March to recommend that he be summoned to the Convention to account for his conduct. That recommendation, long deferred, was brought to the Convention and accepted almost unanimously by it the following morning. After some factional jostling, five deputies were named to accompany Beurnonville to deliver the summons to Dumouriez and arrest any generals, officers, or other public functionaries they deemed suspect. Marat, deeply suspicious of the minister's association with the treasonous general, was alone in opposition to sending him on a mission that would bring the two men together.[87]

Beurnonville and four of the commissioners were already on the road north when they encountered a courier bearing a defiant letter from Dumouriez to the minister, dated 29 March, together with a copy of his proclamation to the departments of the Nord and Pas-de-Calais the previous day. The proclamation announced his intention to march with his much-reduced army to confront "a monster more dangerous than external enemies" that was taking the forms and language of an exaggerated patriotism leading to license and crime. Swearing to defend the homeland with the same force against anarchy as against despotism, he promised a return to the rule of law. "I've often been threatened by death; have no fear: citizens, we will defend our heads because they are necessary to the Republic."[88]

Dumouriez's letter to Beurnonville was more intimate. A catalog of his grievances against the criminals within the Convention, it made clear his determination to "restore to the healthy and oppressed part of the assembly the force and authority whose deprivation debases them, even in the eyes of the departments." He was resolute in his refusal to meet with the Convention's commissioners sent earlier to return him to Paris. "I'm telling you, dear Beurnonville, that I consider my head too precious to hand it over to an arbitrary tribunal. I can only be judged in my lifetime by the entire nation, as I will be judged after my death by history." He sounded the same note of defiance in a second letter the following day. "You urge me not to lose courage, my friend, I assure you that will never happen to me; but I'm much more afraid of being pushed to the brink by the atrocities the Jacobins permit themselves against me."[89]

It was the evening of 1 April before Beurnonville and his party reached Dumouriez's headquarters at the spa town of Saint-Amand on the Franco-Belgian frontier. In a confrontation during which Marat was regularly invoked, the group met with the general's adamant refusal to return to Paris with them. He would not risk assassination en route to the capital, he insisted. He would not face condemnation by the Revolutionary Tribunal he was determined to destroy as a blight on a free nation. Nor would he appear at the bar of the Convention where Marat and the mob in the galleries dominated discussion. He would not submit to their fury; he would not allow himself to be condemned by them on sight. Would he not follow the example of obedience and civic abnegation set by the Roman generals, he was asked. Not in a moment of anarchy, was his reply. "The tigers want my head; I'm not giving it to them." But a state cannot subsist when a general places himself above the law, he was reminded, with evident reference to Roman history. "The Republic doesn't exist," was his rebuttal. "It's Marat and the Jacobin Club who are placing themselves above the law, not Dumouriez. I'm not trying to evade judgment. Let the nation have a solid government and I'll call for my own trial. Today, that would be an act of madness. I disobey, but I only disobey tyranny." Remember everything you've suffered from the anarchists, he urged the miserable Beurnonville. Aren't you Marat's designated victim?[90]

The exchange was concluded when Dumouriez summoned his hussars and placed the minister and four deputies under arrest. For the moment, he declared, they would be held in Tournai as hostages. They were soon turned over to the Austrians. The following day, 2 April, he began to mobilize his forces. It was time for the army to "purge France of its assassins and agitators and restore to our unhappy homeland the peace lost to it by the crimes of its representatives," he proclaimed to the troops, "my companions." He promised to lead them by example to live and die free. "We can only be free with good laws," he exhorted them; "otherwise, we will be the slaves of crime." A similar proclamation went to the department of the Nord. His letter of 12 March had provoked the Marats and the Robespierres to go for his head, the general told the administrators of this, his native department. He had detained the commissioners these criminals of the Convention had sent to arrest or eliminate him. He would no longer delay in marching to Paris to put an end to the bloody anarchy reigning there. He would restore the 1791 constitution, end civil and foreign war, and bring France peace, tranquility, and happiness. He swore by all that was sacred to him that, having no aspiration toward dictatorship, he intended to quit all public functions as soon as he had saved the homeland.[91]

An address to the nation sounded the same note. He had been slandered since October by "Marat, the most criminal of men and the shame of the French," Dumouriez proclaimed. He had been falsely accused of aiming at dictatorship in Belgium. He had retreated honorably from Neerwinden, and his battered army now wanted wise liberty and the rule of law. The Marats and the Robespierres, along with the entire Jacobin sect, were conspiring to destroy him and other generals already imprisoned; they wanted, in their word, to *septembrize* him. But the nation wanted the rule of law and the constitutional monarchy of 1791. Had it abolished the despotism of one man for that of seven hundred inflamed by the mob in the galleries under the sway of the Jacobin Club, an assembly that "groaned and legislated under the sword of the cronies of Marat and Robespierre"? Had it wanted the September Massacres, denunciations and proscriptions throughout the country, the immolation of Louis XVI without due process, the tyranny of a Revolutionary Tribunal, the absurdities of a chaotically maladministered war? Peace and the constitution of 1791 were to be the rallying point. His army, he declared, was ready to reestablish them.[92]

In fact, the army was less than resolute and profoundly divided in its response to the exhortations of its commander in chief. Its various units began to hold back in the face of a barrage of counter-propaganda carried to them by emissaries of the Convention. Within days, it became clear that Dumouriez would not be followed by enough of his troops to assure success. He barely escaped arrest by a battalion of volunteers on 4 April by fording a stream to reach the Austrian camp. Returning the following day, with an Austrian escort, he failed to rally his troops. Crossing the frontier a second time, he deserted with a handful of his officers, including Louis-Philippe, the son of Philippe Egalité and future king of France. The news reached the Convention on 6 April.

TO ARMS! TO ARMS!

Throughout this period, Marat was beside himself. His journal attacked Dumouriez and an ever-lengthening list of suspect generals almost daily, constantly placing responsibility for their treacheries on the criminal faction of the *hommes d'Etat*. The noisiest deputy in the Convention, he spoke, tried to speak, shouted, or otherwise intervened in the assembly more than twice as often as any of the leading orators (though far from exclusively in discussions of Dumouriez).[93] If his interventions were not the most substantial, they were the most constant. He was an increasingly active presence, too, at meetings of the Jacobins, where he began regularly sounding the alarm against treason.

In December, the Jacobin Club had been Robespierre's domain: its members had been eager to defend its political reputation by dissociating him from Marat, the evil twin with whom he had been yoked in the Girondin propaganda spread by Roland in the provinces. By late March, its mood was changing. According to one report, Marat was welcomed with joy at the meeting on 22 March: "he crosses the hall majestically, and the galleries shout 'Long Live our father and our liberator.'" On 25 March, responding to denunciations of the Mountain and the Jacobins in the provincial press as "Maratists" who "want to overthrow all property," Dubois-Crancé called for the club to circulate copies of Marat's journal in the departments. "Then Marat will be judged by his works," he argued; "the true friend of the people and of liberty will be recognized, and justice will be done to the Marat painted as a werewolf." To aid this effort, Marat himself offered the Montagnard deputies and fellow club members two hundred copies of his journal each to circulate. On 3 April, he was elected the club's president.[94]

In the meantime, on 24 March, he was urging the Jacobin Club to draw up lists of all those suspected of dubious patriotism to avoid their nomination to public functions. On 25 March, he was telling it that he had frustrated Dumouriez's projects by publicizing them. In league with the criminal faction, he charged, the general had aimed to grasp sovereignty over Belgium but had sold out to the enemy by contriving his defeat and withdrawing from the Low Countries once he saw that the Convention's commissioners opposed his treasons. On 27 March he called for all the Paris sections to join in demanding of the Convention whether it had the means of saving the homeland and in declaring that the people was ready to save itself if necessary. The same day, he launched a lengthy attack in his journal on the malversations of the Girondin leaders since the overthrow of the monarchy on 10 August, culminating in a particular denunciation of Beurnonville for his choice and support of suspect generals. This offensive was extended on 28 March in a wholesale denunciation of Dumouriez in the journal that morning and a personal confrontation with Beurnonville at the Committee of General Defense that evening. Urged there to suspend his denunciations, his reply was emphatic. "I will never bind myself; my pen will always be free, like my way of seeing things."[95]

Beurnonville left Paris as charged on 29 March to meet Dumouriez, accompanied by the Convention's second set of commissioners, whose fate at the general's hands he would share. Marat's journal welcomed that morning with yet another seething denunciation of the general and all his works. "What's most revolting in his conduct," it charged, "is that he blames all the reverses our armies have suffered on the indiscipline, cowardice, and brigandage of the soldiers of the homeland. An atrocious calumny, doubly so in his mouth." The general's subordinates had pillaged citizens in regions where the armies had been billeted; they had stolen, raped, and committed all kinds of depredation, creating disorder in the camps undermining morale on the day of battle. But Dumouriez had no right to complain about these criminals, the journal continued; he had recruited them and authorized their crimes. Consumed with ambition, he had dreamed of ruling an imaginary monarchy formed from Belgium and Holland. Frustrated in this by the defection of his troops, he had covered his treasons with the sham defeats he now imputed perfidiously to the indiscipline and misconduct of the soldiers of liberty. But the shame was his. "Europe can only see him as a vile intriguer who wanted to elevate himself at the expense of his homeland, and soon France will see him as a dastardly hypocrite, a base braggart, deserving the ultimate punishment. May he expiate his crimes under the avenging blade of the laws."[96]

Much more was to come. Tempers flared at the Convention on 29 March when Marat rose to denounce the criminal faction again—to applause from the crowd in the galleries and groans from the benches. "I demand that this man be heard," shouted Buzot; "since he only has calumnies to vomit up, it's good for him to reveal his base mind. . . . Go on, speak!" He was quick to return to the offensive after Marat had deplored the aggressions now directed against French troops in Belgium. "It's with profound indignation that I see a member of the Paris deputation constantly coming to occupy us with denunciations," he roared. "Would he like to transform the National Convention into a club?" The comment outraged the Montagnards with its federalist implication that the Paris deputies merely represented the capital, not the nation as a whole. But Buzot was not to be stopped. "If these men who dream only of revolutions and convulsions remember history, they will see that all free peoples have cemented their liberty in the face of reverses. In vain you're called upon to revolutionize and, in the expression of some men who are the execration of the Universe, to *septembrize* incessantly. Woe to us if such men can gain dominance here!"[97]

The attack precipitated yet another profession of faith from Marat, who offered a personal manifesto to the French people the following day. Amid a revolution against the oppressors and vampires of the people, he protested, he had felt it the most urgent duty of a good citizen to keep watch on the public functionaries so disposed to abuse their functions, to monitor the agents of authority so inclined to ally themselves with the despot, to unveil the maneuvers of the cabinet, frustrate its plots, and unmask the crooks. His success could be measured, he boasted, by the number of his enemies, by the attacks against him inundating France, pervading the national assembly, and filling the secret correspondence of the deputies. He was accused of "incessantly preaching murder and carnage," but he had demonstrated that sparing a few hundred criminal heads would cost the people thousands. "Only after five hundred thousand patriots have been seen slaughtered will it finally be recognized that the means I proposed was the only one that could save the homeland." He was accused of "preaching the agrarian law," this disastrous doctrine "destructive of all civil society," but he had "wailed a hundred times that the exaggerated principles of strict equality are not appropriate for a corrupt nation and would, without a doubt, soon lead us to this fatal outcome."

Finally, he was accused of "ambitious designs, aiming for dictatorship": as if, after a life lived underground the better to expose despotism, after four years of exposure to danger and suffering to assure the liberty of the people, he would expose himself to shame in aspiring to the power and dignities he despised. "I never made the slightest effort to obtain the position of deputy to the Convention. I accepted it because I hoped to be able to serve the homeland usefully. The little good I have done, the little good I anticipate still doing, the little good the Convention itself has done, have long made my hopes evaporate. I would have resigned if I hadn't been held back by expectation of some inevitable event that will necessitate great measures of public safety, the circumstances for the adoption of which will probably give weight to my charges." In the meantime, he declared, he was sighing only for a time when the people would be free and happy, and he could pass his remaining years in study and contemplation. "They only want to proscribe me to deprive me of the means of unmasking them and stopping their criminal projects. These are the secret motivations of their eternal calumnies."[98]

Egos collided, too, in the Jacobin Club on 31 March as the society awaited a report from its members who had met with Dumouriez a few days earlier. Marat, declaring the dangers threatening the homeland at their height, harangued fellow republicans to display their courage and energy. He was certain that Dumouriez had already emigrated, sure too that

Beurnonville had left Paris with the intention of conspiring with the general and perhaps even joining him in a march on the capital. Most dramatically, he appealed to Danton (as he had without success at the Convention two days earlier) to break the suspicious silence he had kept since his return from his mission to Dumouriez in company with Delacroix. The lion of the Mountain, fearing intimations of collusion with the general, was testy in responding that he had already given a report to the Committee of General Defense. He was nonetheless brutal in his judgment of Dumouriez, whose ambition he confessed to feeding for as long as it had served the homeland. The commissioners of the Convention, he attested, had found the general devastated by defeat and insolent in his rage against the people and its representatives. But they had hesitated to arrest a commander in chief at the head of his army.

It was time now for popular mobilization, Danton countered. The Jacobin Club had to take the lead with strong measures. It had to call on the popular societies to organize a central force of fifty thousand men to defend the capital, announcing to the universe that the city would always be the center of liberty or it would perish. "The enemies will only enter Paris through a mound of ashes; and with my own hand, seconded by all the good citizens, I will torch it rather than turn it over to the Austrians." The Convention was infected by Constituents and aristocrats, he maintained; it had to be purged of all those who had been too cowardly to vote for the death of the king. But there should be no attempt to dissolve the Convention, he insisted. "Let's try to get it to purge itself without tearing itself apart. . . . Let's try to make this central army numerous enough to extend Paris to the frontier. . . . Let's say to our enemies: we still want to show ourselves wise and calm, but if you raise your heads again you will all be annihilated."

Marat was not ready to see his thunder stolen. He responded by impugning Danton for his failure to arrest Dumouriez and prevent the latter's treason. At first the protégé and then the protector of the faction that had provoked the war, Marat charged, the general had remained in league with them. "I'm not content to talk, I need the facts, and I will never be satisfied until the heads of the traitors roll on the scaffold," he continued. "Danton, I summon you to mount the tribune and tear down the veil." Countering Danton's declaration that he would indeed fulfill his vow to do so, Marat urged upon him the noble abandon of the true patriot. "Take with me the vow to die to save the homeland," he cried as he brandished a dagger. "This is the weapon with which I swear to exterminate the traitors, the weapon I encourage you to fabricate for the citizens not acquainted with military developments," he admonished the club. His renewed call for a subscription for this purpose was adopted by acclamation as hats were thrown in the air in demonstration of universal assent. The performance had fulfilled its purpose in returning Jean-Paul Marat to the spotlight. The discussion that followed, beginning with Saint-Just's denunciation of Beurnonville, proved anticlimactic, though that speech prompted the newly appointed prosecutor for the Revolutionary Tribunal to appeal for more traitors to dispatch and ampler space in which to decide to do so. In turn, the relatively brief report of the three Jacobins who had met with Dumouriez roused the society to further indictments of the general.[99]

As uncertainty about Dumouriez's intentions grew, tensions mounted in the Paris streets. The *Publiciste de la République française* was reporting on 1 April that Montagnard deputies had been roughed up by hostile patrols; elsewhere, in the antipatriotic Feuillants section, patriots trying to arrest a group of counterrevolutionaries bad-mouthing the Convention were themselves detained. Efforts ordered by the assembly for the disarmament of ex-nobles and refractory priests, and the arrest of suspects more generally, were failing miserably in Marat's view. "What saddens me is that the Convention never passes decrees that appear revolutionary unless they are completely illusory, even derisory. One would think that the deputies of the people haven't the least ideas of politics, because it's absurd that the legislature directs a police operation only to make it fail." It was essential, he declared, that the Convention create a committee composed of six patriots with the power and the means to order the arrest of public enemies, seize their papers, and turn them over directly to the Revolutionary Tribunal.[100]

The need for truly revolutionary measures was also on Marat's mind as he sat in the Convention later that day. Anticipating the sentiment that would drive the Montagnards to the institution of revolutionary government months later, he was adamant that this was not the time to consider the constitution Condorcet had proposed on 15 February. "When the fire of sedition is burning in many parts of the Republic; when the exterior enemies press; when it's a question of suppressing civil war and halting the enemy, we only need revolutionary laws." The most immediate necessity was to rip the veil still shrouding Dumouriez's treasons and examine the conduct of the generals and the ministers denounced everywhere. "Strike the traitors wherever they may be found," he raged.

The Girondin response to this declamation was a masterpiece of political maneuver. "I support the proposal made by citizen Marat," was Birotteau's riposte. "At a moment when liberty is threatened from all sides, every kind of inviolability ceases. The people must not rest its confidence in a deputy against whom there have been numerous accusations. I demand that the Convention adopt a decree accusing the one of its members over whose head float so many violent suspicions."[101] No sooner said than done. The Convention immediately declared that in the interest of the supreme law of public safety, and without regard for the inviolability of any representative of the nation, it would decree the accusation of any of its members strongly suspected of complicity with the enemies of liberty, equality, and republican government on the basis of charges submitted to the Committee of General Defense. Marat, in effect, had been hoisted by his own petard. But so, in the end, would be his principal enemies among the *hommes d'Etat*. Parliamentary inviolability was abolished to target him, but the consequences were even graver for his enemies. Striking at Marat, they had also opened a way to their own eventual expulsion.

By this time on 1 April the Committee of General Defense had placed under house arrest, ostensibly for their personal safety, the three Jacobins who had met with Dumouriez. This action prompted The People's Friend to censure the committee as dominated by the Brissot, Guadet, Gensonné, Vergniaud faction, the *hommes d'Etat* leaving patriots in the minority. "Individual characteristics are facts when it's a matter of conspiracy," was his retort to calls to send him to the Abbaye as punishment for these personal attacks on fellow deputies. Nothing proved that adage true more than this session as Cambacérès, speaking on behalf of the Committees of General Defense and General Security, offered incriminating evidence of Dumouriez's recent conduct and convictions.

Cambacérès presented three documents. The first was the general's letter indicting the Convention on 12 March, now read publicly to the entire assembly for the first time. The second was a letter he had written to Beurnonville on 28 March hinting at the possibility of accommodation with the enemy. The third and most damning was the lengthy account submitted to the committee by the three Jacobins who had met with the general earlier that week. Substantially more detailed than the one they had offered the Jacobin Club the previous evening, it recounted a sequence of meetings in which Dumouriez, vacillating between violent agitation in public and shocking confidences in private, had displayed his fury at the Convention and the Jacobins. In this telling, the general had announced that he alone would save France despite the 745 tyrannical regicides in the assembly, and without regard for the fact that he would be maligned as a Caesar, a Cromwell, or a Monck. He had repudiated the Revolutionary Tribunal, mocked as stupid the proposed new constitution, and outlined his plans to make peace, bring his army to Paris to impose the constitution of 1791 and with it a monarchy, violently dismissing the suspicion that he would do so on behalf of Philippe Egalité. He had even entertained the idea that the Jacobins could conspire with him, redeeming the crimes of the 1789 and 1792 insurrections by inciting a third uprising that would disperse the tyrannical deputies as he marched on Paris and proclaimed a king. In the Jacobins' account, they had intimated this plan as a feint to draw the general out. The general, according to his letters, had taken them at their word. The ambiguity left the three Jacobins under a cloud of suspicion.[102]

Cambacérès's report provoked an acrid discussion of the way the disoriented and divided Committee of General Defense had kept Dumouriez's 12 March letter under wraps while it sent Danton and Delacroix to negotiate with him. It led, inevitably, to the question of why Danton had returned to Paris without having arrested Dumouriez, and why he had remained so suspiciously silent since returning from that mission. It was time for Danton to explain, which he now did. His insistence on the impossibility of arresting Dumouriez when the general was surrounded by his army, his call for a commission to investigate seditious writings that had inflamed Dumouriez's anger against Paris, his proposal for the creation of an armed camp to defend the capital: all these moves failed to satisfy the suspicions, spelled out by Lasource in response, that he was engaged with Delacroix in a conspiracy with Dumouriez to arouse the people, destroy the Convention, and reinstitute monarchy. "To prove to the nation that we will never capitulate to a tyrant," Lasource concluded, "let each of us vow to kill anyone who attempts to make himself king or dictator." Roused to a pitch of emotion, the entire assembly rose to repeat this vow.[103]

But Danton held on to the tribune. "You want to assassinate the patriots," he cried; "but the people will not be fooled; the Mountain will crush you." At this shout of defiance, the Montagnards and the audience in the galleries—with Marat at the forefront, in his account—applauded as one in support of this demand to continue speaking. "I propose to proclaim Danton a dictator," sounded a voice from the center, throwing the assembly again into tumult. "The galleries shared my indignation and public opinion, stronger than all the decrees in the world, recalled Danton to the tribune despite the efforts of the *hommes d'Etat* to push him aside," Marat later rejoiced. Finally allowed to resume speaking, Danton launched into an extended address, frequently interrupted, not least by Marat's barking in support. "There is no longer a truce between the Mountain, the patriots who wanted the death of the tyrant, and the scoundrels who, wanting to save him, have slandered us in France," he thundered as he packed months of grievances against the Girondins into a litany of defiance. "When Paris perishes, the Republic will be no more," he warned. "Paris is the established and natural center of free France. It's the center of enlightenment.

We're accused of being the agents of Parisian sedition. So be it, we've laid out our lives before the nation, the lives of men who have marched with firm step toward the Revolution. The criminal projects imputed to me, the charges of villainy, everything has been piled up against us, and now they hope to frighten us! Ah No!"[104]

Let a commission of inquiry begin its work, Danton declaimed; let it examine the conduct of every deputy since the opening of the Convention; let it investigate those who have maneuvered to destroy the Republic after its indivisibility had been decreed; let it examine those who in wanting to save a king have fed the hopes of monarchism. "You sound like Cromwell," someone shouted. "He was feared," Danton retorted, "because he was the strongest. Here those who have struck down the French tyrant will be feared too. They will be feared all the more in that liberty is fed by the blood of the tyrant. They will be feared because the nation is with them." Call on the people to unite in arms against the external enemy and crush the internal one, he exhorted the Montagnards. "Confound by the vigor and constancy of your character all the criminals, all the aristocrats, all the moderates, all those who have slandered you in the departments. No more truck with them. I'm marching toward the Republic; let's march there together. We'll see whether we or our detractors will reach our goal." For Marat, this speech was a masterpiece, an open and unambiguous declaration of the war between the Montagnards and the *hommes d'Etat* that was tearing the Convention apart. It was all the more crucial in that it sealed Danton's engagement. But there was perhaps a drop of acid in his pen when he wrote of this unpredictable ally that "much must be expected from the means of this celebrated patriot; the people has its eyes on him and awaits him in the field of honor."[105]

Tensions in the Convention, meanwhile, were finding their echo among the Parisian sections. At a session of the Jacobin Club that evening, members received an overture from a revolutionary "central committee of public safety meeting" at the Evêché and declaring itself sanctioned by the sections with "unlimited powers" to save the Republic and exterminate all the people's enemies. The approach, organized by a group of radicals led by Varlet, was received with suspicion of any popular action not directed by the club itself; at Marat's urging, the group's emissary to the Jacobins was thrown out and turned over to the Committee of General Security. The same invitation, repudiated by other sections as an incitement to insurrection usurping the power of the sections and threatening constituted authorities, was similarly denounced in the electoral assembly of Paris and referred to the general assembly of the Commune. As for Marat, he had already counseled the Jacobins against the pretensions of any one section to lay down the law for others. Preferring to invoke the threat of popular action to put pressure on the Convention, as he had on 27 March, he was not ready for an insurrection to overthrow it, least of all one that would occur without his direction. Proclaiming that "when it comes to public safety, I don't know any forms; the only form to follow is to make the heads of conspirators roll on the scaffold," he allowed himself yet another round of denunciation of Dumouriez.[106]

For the moment, though, he merely instigated the formation of a delegation to protest the imprisonment of the three Jacobin envoys to the general who had been arrested by order of the Committee of General Defense. With Marat as its principal spokesman, the group secured the envoys' release. Robespierre, in the meantime, counseled the society against any attempt to overthrow the Convention and secured its decision to exclude any member of the Bourbon family from membership.[107] The latter move was directed against Philippe Egalité, who was now suspected of collusion with Dumouriez, not least because of his son's desertion in company with the general.

Publishing his journal in the morning, scrabbling to speak in the Convention during the day, holding sway over the Jacobin Club in the evening: this remained the pattern of Marat's political existence over the following days as the spool of Dumouriez's betrayals unwound. On 2 April, he offered in the journal more details of the general's counterrevolutionary plans, not neglecting to implicate the *hommes d'Etat* in "this horrible system of dissolving the state after exhausting it with misery and upending it with anarchy." In the Convention, he called for all ex-nobles to be removed from their military commands lest they turn over strategic positions to the enemy. Demanding bread to relieve the popular misery that was "one of the principal causes that would perhaps force the people to demand servitude again," he fended off charges that this comment slandered the people with the claim that "no one knows the people better than I and appreciates its virtues better." And he confronted Barère's accusations of slander by invoking freedom of the press so effectively that the assembly abolished the 9 March law barring deputies from writing as journalists. Leaving the Manège for the Jacobin Club to predict again that Dumouriez would emigrate, he called for a price to be put on the traitor's head and a civic crown on that of the citizen who would deliver it.[108]

The lines of engagement within the Convention became all the sharper on 3 April after the assembly was presented with the evidence of Dumouriez's proclamations from 1 April to the departments of the north and the Pas-de-Calais, and to the French army. A gladiatorial combat followed as Robespierre called for Brissot's indictment in a passionate (and passionately self-justifying) speech alleging the latter's abiding complicity with Dumouriez since his instigation of the war that had served the general's ambitions, and in their shared animadversion toward the city of Paris. Tellingly, Brissot had to wait to respond while a deputation of the Commune reported its anxiety that it could maintain peace in the capital. But his reply was no less vigorous than his accuser's in its dismissal of the charge of personal responsibility for the declaration of war, of collusion with the general in promoting or conducting it, of sharing his hostility to Paris or embracing his desire to return France to monarchy.[109]

Marat's eventual intervention in the matter was blunter. "I have to say that part of the Convention doesn't deserve our confidence, since Dumouriez is coming to protect what he calls its healthy part against the one that must save the Republic. It's impossible for the Mountain to have the least confidence in the majority of the *hommes d'Etat*." The remark was incendiary. "Are we in permanent session to hear this man's insults?" one deputy shouted. A chorus followed: "He's the one who wants to dissolve the Convention. Down, down with Marat." Again, The People's Friend had thrown the Convention into uproar. Censured by the president, his remarks had gone too far, even for some of the Montagnards. Danton had to step in to offer the appeasing view that whatever the differences in opinions, the Convention still wanted the Republic. The session soon ended . . . at four o'clock in the morning.[110]

Danton may have talked the Convention away from a political precipice, but the mood in the Jacobin Club was approaching ground zero. At its meeting that same evening, 3 April, there were calls for an address appealing to the departments and popular societies to unite in demanding a purge of the Convention and to fly to the defense of revolutionary Paris against Dumouriez and his advancing army. Robespierre, for his part, called for the creation of a revolutionary army of patriots and sans-culottes to purify the sections and impose the popular will on the Convention.[111] On 5 April, coincidentally the day of Dumouriez's defection, the club published a circular address, "The Society of the Friends of Liberty in Paris to Their Brothers in the Departments." Signed by Marat, as president, along with other officers of the club, it was inflammatory in the extreme.

"*Friends, we're betrayed!*" it began:

> To Arms! To Arms! This is the terrible hour when the defenders of the homeland must conquer or be buried under the bloody rubble of the Republic. French people, your liberty has never been in such great peril! Our enemies have finally put the seal on their black perfidy, and to consummate it Dumouriez, their accomplice, is marching on Paris.

The manifest treasons of the generals in coalition with him leave no doubt that this plan of rebellion and this insolent audacity have been directed by the criminal faction that has supported and deified him, as it did Lafayette, and has misled us, up to the decisive moment, regarding the conduct, intrigues, failures and aggressions of this traitor, this wicked man who has just arrested four commissioners of the Convention and aims to dissolve it. . . .

But brothers, these are not your only perils. . . . Your greatest enemies are among you, they direct your undertakings: Oh Vengeance!!! They direct your defenses! . . . Yes, brothers and friends, yes, the senate is where parricidal hands rip out your entrails! Yes, the counterrevolution is in the government . . . in the National Convention! There, at the center of your security and hopes, criminal delegates are holding the threads of the plot they have hatched with the horde of despots who are coming to cut our throats . . . !

Let's rise up! Yes, let's all rise up. Let's arrest all the enemies of revolution and all suspect persons. Let's exterminate, pitilessly, all the conspirators unless we want to be exterminated ourselves. To restore its force and energy to the National Convention, let all the patriotic deputies on mission in the eighty-three departments be recalled and return as soon as possible . . . ; let new apostles of liberty chosen by and among you replace these commissioners; let them be sent into the towns and countryside to hasten recruitment or kindle civic enthusiasm and identify traitors.

Let departments, districts, municipalities, and all the popular societies unite and agree to protest to the Convention, to send and rain down on it petitions manifesting the formal demand for the instant recall of all the faithless members of the Convention who have betrayed their duty in not wanting the death of the tyrant, and especially those who have led astray such a great number of their colleagues. Such delegates are traitors, royalists, or inept. The Republic condemns the friends of kings! They fracture it, ruin it, and have sworn to annihilate it. Yes, citizens, they're the ones who have formed this criminal and disastrous faction. With them in place, your liberty is finished! By their prompt expulsion, the homeland is saved!!!

Let's all unite equally to demand that the thunderous decrees of accusation be hurled . . . against all the faithless agents of government. . . .

The center of their conspiracy is here: it's in Paris that our most perfidious enemies want to consummate their crime. Have no doubt that Paris, the cradle and the bastion of liberty, is where they have sworn to bury the holy cause of humanity under the corpses of patriots. It's

> against Paris that Dumouriez is directing his vengeance, rallying to his side all the royalists, Feuillants, moderates, and dastardly enemies of our liberty. It's in Paris that we have to defend it . . . ! And grasp well this truth, Paris can't save the republic without you.
>
> French people, the homeland is threatened by the greatest danger. Dumouriez is declaring war on the people and has suddenly become the vanguard of the ferocious enemies of France; a part of his army, seduced by this great criminal, is marching on Paris to reestablish monarchy and dissolve the National Convention.
>
> To Arms! REPUBLICANS! Fly to Paris; it's where France comes together. Paris must be the headquarters of the republic. To arms! To arms! . . . No debate, no delay, or liberty is lost! Every means to accelerate your march must be put to use. If we are attacked before you arrive, we'll know how to fight and die, and we will abandon Paris only when it has been reduced to ashes!!![112]

This call for an insurrection to defend Paris and force a purge of the Convention was explosive. Its appeal for mobilization in defense of the capital lost some of its urgency as it became clear that Dumouriez had abandoned his march on the city and deserted to the enemy. But its demand for a purge of the treacherous general's allies in the Convention would soon be invoked by the Girondins as grounds to send Marat to the Revolutionary Tribunal, one of the principal instruments of terror to emerge from the moment of the Dumouriez crisis. In the creation of this apparatus, The People's Friend played an active role.

INSTRUMENTS OF TERROR

The pattern of revelation, denunciation, recrimination, and polarization continued for several more days as Paris awaited a military putsch that never arrived and braved threats of a popular insurrection that never ripened. It was 6 April before the Convention learned that Dumouriez's efforts to march his troops toward Paris had fizzled and he had deserted to the Austrians. By that time, the climate of fear, suspicion, and betrayal was propelling the deputies to sharpen the apparatus of the Terror to come. Hostilities between Marat and the Girondins had already precipitated abandonment of the inviolability of the deputies on 31 March. Greater vulnerability loomed on 5 April when Danton led the Montagnards in urging a reorganization of the Revolutionary Tribunal that would allow its prosecutor to bring suspected persons directly before that court rather than requiring a prior decree of accusation by the Convention in each case.

A proposal followed to make an exception to this change in the case of deputies, ministers, generals, or other public functionaries. The idea was ridiculed by Marat, to violent reactions, in demanding that such exceptions be extended to members of all other professions indispensable for social organization, from tailors to bakers and butchers, from men capable of bearing arms, or involved in making them, to women producing children. Called to order by the president on the demand of outraged and insulted deputies, The People's Friend responded by recalling them to "common sense" and the recognition that "censure will never stop truth from being the truth." He was censured nonetheless. For the moment, the Convention reserved to itself the right to indict the highest public functionaries before they could be submitted to the judgment of the revolutionary court. That limitation was rendered moot before long by expansion of the powers of the second revolutionary body instituted during this brief period.[113]

This second body was the Committee of Public Safety, created to replace the Committee of General Defense. The latter committee had been large (extended to twenty-five members on 25 March) and its meetings had been open. Dominated by Dumouriez's supporters until the last minute, it had become increasingly discredited and dysfunctional. Marat played a significant part in shaping its replacement. "Only traitors can stifle my voice," he proclaimed on 3 April, fighting as usual to speak at the Convention. "If any man has the right to be heard, it is I who predicted to you eight months ago what would happen. Whatever the fate that threatens me, I tell you that you've acted since the Revolution like madmen escaped from the asylum." Bizarrely urging his listeners not to take his insults personally—"I only have love for the public safety. It will triumph over all"—he proceeded to call for the immediate naming of two committees, a committee of general security and a committee of general defense, each composed of twelve citizens of proven patriotism. They would meet in closed session and exercise "the most extensive and formidable powers" to pursue traitors, enemy agents, and suspected persons. They would be responsible to the Convention for the measures they would take. The already existing Committee of General Security, with renewed membership, would be charged with "all the measures of security against hidden internal enemies, including the arrest of persons and the seizure of papers" (as Marat elaborated in his journal). The reorganized Committee of General Defense, reduced in size and meeting in closed session, would "coordinate all the means of defense against the hidden internal and external enemies."[114]

The assembly moved on without discussing this proposal, but Marat reiterated it later in the session, threatening to give his resignation if it were not discussed. "Give it! Give it!" came the reply as he refused to leave the tribune and submit his views to the Committee of General Defense. "I won't go; a general can't deliberate amid his enemies," he responded, only to be reminded that "Marat, you're not a general!" Again, to Marat's frustration, the Convention moved on. At Thuriot's urging, Dumouriez was proclaimed a traitor and an outlaw. Any recognition of his authority as a general was declared treasonous; a reward of 300,000 livres and (at Marat's suggestion) a civic crown were offered for bringing him to Paris dead or alive.[115]

At the evening session that same day, however, Isnard presented a report on behalf of the Committee of General Defense that acknowledged prevailing public suspicions of the executive power and the Convention's committees. Recognizing that circumstances required more action, more energy, more unity, and more profound discussion, it advanced on Marat's proposal by advocating the creation of a nine-member executive committee composed of deputies deliberating in secret and reporting weekly to the assembly. This committee would be charged to fulfill all the functions previously attributed to the provisional executive council and to take all necessary measures of general defense; ministers would be reduced to its administrative agents. The nation had conferred the exercise of sovereignty and all powers on the Convention, Isnard reminded his colleagues. "Let's at last seize the reins of government with a bold, firm and pure hand," he urged. "It's no longer a question of debating forms but of defending the homeland. Before deciding on the practices owed to liberty, we must assure its triumph."

There were immediate objections to this proposal to combine the exercise of legislative and executive powers, the separation of which had been one of the fundamental principles of the Revolution. To these, Marat responded emphatically. "For the past six months, you've fought in vain against abuses; you still haven't taken the axe to the root. Common sense is all that's needed to save the homeland. You'll do nothing as long as you decide measures of public safety in public." He suggested his distrust of Isnard's proposal by declaring that the Convention could have no confidence in the part of its membership that Dumouriez had deemed "healthy" and was now marching to protect. "It's impossible for the Mountain to have the least confidence in the majority of the *hommes d'Etat*." This comment provoked loud applause from the left of the assembly and the galleries. From the right came the corresponding denunciation: "He's the one who wants to dissolve the Convention. Down with Marat! Down with Marat!" The uproar ended when the president called him to order and his views were disavowed (to his disgust at this sabotage) "in the name of the Mountain" by another of its members. Discussion of a new Committee of Public Safety was deferred at Danton's cooling suggestion until the following day.[116]

Marat later made clear in his journal that he had suspected Isnard's plan as an effort by the *hommes d'Etat* to grab direction of a new committee of general defense joined with the Committee of General Security into a "veritable state inquisition" that would be very different from the temporary exercise of executive power from within the Convention that he had proposed. He evidently saw this new body as a threat of the *hommes d'Etat* against the Mountain, combining mere oversight of the ministries of defense and of the navy with "unlimited searches for suspect citizens, under the guise of tracking down conspirators." By his account, he argued against it in a session of the Committee of General Defense that most probably occurred on 4 April. "This cumulation of the quite distinct functions of the two committees into a single one revolted me. I demonstrated that it would obviously lead to the establishment of tyranny without fulfilling the principal goal of defending the state." In response to his reasoning, he reported, it was decided that the new Committee of Public Safety was to be restricted to directing the activity of ministers charged with public defense, "with the simple power to require the cooperation of the committee of security for the arrest of evildoers or suspected persons."[117]

On 5 April, Isnard reopened the question in the Convention by observing that executive power no longer existed and could not be assumed by the Committee of General Defense when it was composed of twenty-five members and its deliberations were open to the entire assembly, hence impossible to keep secret. Observing that the committee itself demanded the creation of an alternative, he pushed for immediate discussion of the matter and opened it by announcing his own resignation from the dysfunctional committee. He was instantly followed in this action by Buzot, Barbaroux, and Bréard. Barère then followed, throwing behind Isnard's plan the weight of his now considerable authority over the Plain. Tellingly, he dismissed the fears of dictatorship the plan had elicited by declaring legitimate and necessary the dictatorship the nation already exercised over itself through the agency of the National Convention. The true dictatorship, the one to be repudiated, he added, was the dictatorship of calumny that was threatening the entire Revolution with destruction.[118] It was clear whom he had in mind. Before the session had ended, Marat had been denounced yet again—this time as an agent of Dumouriez—for his recurrent attacks on the *hommes d'Etat*.

The following morning, Isnard presented a fresh draft decree he had formulated in cooperation with Danton, Thuriot, Mathieu, and Barère. It provided for a nine-member Committee of Public Safety elected monthly from among the deputies and charged to report its activities to the assembly on a weekly basis along with its assessment of the situation of the Republic. Meeting in secret, this body would "oversee and accelerate the administrative action conferred upon the provisional executive committee," whose decrees it would have the power to suspend if it judged them contrary to the national interest and so informed the Convention without delay. It would also be authorized to order, by a majority vote of at least two-thirds, emergency measures of public safety to be immediately implemented by the executive committee. A budget would be provided to pay its agents. The draft was greeted with horror by Buzot as a blueprint for a dangerous dictatorship that would usurp the assembly's power to make laws and open the way to the despotism of a ruthlessly ambitious individual. His alarm was countered by Thuriot, who reversed his opposition to Isnard's earlier proposal in light of considerations that, in the event, proved shortsighted. "Citizens, you have nothing to fear from a committee depending on the Convention," he reasoned, "a committee that has only a precarious power, a committee that exists entirely to serve as intermediary between the executive power and this assembly. It's a mistake to believe it susceptible to doing evil; say rather that there are men vile enough to fear that it may do good."[119]

Whatever assurance Thuriot offered may well have been shaken in the face of the furious speech Marat now launched. The People's Friend declared himself adamant that circumstances left the Convention no choice but to create this new instrument of power. He saw it as forced upon the deputies by the treason of the generals, the threats of foreign powers, the need for emergency measures of public safety, and the loss of popular confidence in the Committee of General Defense. Political principles and constitutional laws were to be set aside in his view: "it's not a constituted authority you are establishing at this moment, it's a provisional authority destined solely to mobilize national forces and hurl them against internal and external enemies to crush them all at once." He saw no grounds for fear of dictatorship. "Those who present this objection know better than anyone that [a committee] provisionally granted supreme power will not, if it is tempted to abuse that power, escape the sovereign justice of the Convention before which all authorities disappear." There could be no question here of a dictatorship in which the plenitude of power was conferred upon an individual before whom the laws fell silent. The Convention retained sovereign authority and could dissolve the committee at will if it failed its purpose. "The sole objection to this committee is perhaps that it will not be invested with a power great enough to mobilize the national forces and crush the enemies. Liberty must be established by violence and the moment has come for us to organize the despotism of liberty by striking down the despotism of kings."[120]

The despotism of liberty: a phrase destined for a volcanic future in defense of Terror. Birotteau was surely not alone in sensing the menace of an ambitious individual behind it. What would become of liberty if such an individual had at his disposition the revolutionary tribunal, the powers of this committee, and command of an army, he demanded in response. He invoked the example of Dumouriez in demonstration that these fears were less chimerical than might be thought. The creation of the Committee of Public Safety was decreed on 6 April, nonetheless, though with the proviso (dropped on 28 July, when the committee was empowered to arrest any suspects) that its authority to summon or arrest individuals could be exercised only against agents of executive power. On 7 April deputies *en mission* were charged to report to the committee daily.[121]

"For five consecutive days," Marat related in his journal, "the leaders and principal supporters of the *hommes d'Etat* made every effort to prevent the formation of a committee of public safety destined to accelerate the concentration of our forces that must be opposed to the enemies. . . . It must be hoped that it will finally take the measures appropriate to the importance of the functions attributed to it. . . . It's time for the public safety to be no longer in the hands of the traitors the nation pays to defend and avenge it."[122]

It was telling that the Convention established the Committee of Public Safety the same day it heard of Dumouriez's desertion. Lafayette's treasonous exit had troubled the nascent Republic; Dumouriez's transformed it. This defining moment brought the conflict between Montagnards and Girondins to a point of no return. It sharpened future instruments of revolutionary oppression. It compromised the Girondins by their association with the treacherous general and confirmed Marat as the most hated and vociferous deputy in the assembly. The Girondins wanted their revenge.

TWENTY-SIX

THE MARAT MOMENT

With Dumouriez's departure the war within the Convention turned toward the nuclear. Battle flared on the evening of 8 April, fueled by popular interventions. A deputation from the Bonne-Nouvelle section was indirect in attacking Marat when it urged the nation's representatives to escape "the narrow circle traced around you by these men of small passions who see only the present moment, who spy out circumstances." The radical Bonconseil section was more forthright in identifying its own target. It denounced deputies whose constant clamors against the people, the city of Paris, and the popular societies had distracted the Convention from its most pressing task: organizing the army while the nation's enemies revived their forces and Dumouriez destroyed its own. "The voice of the public has long signaled to you the Brissots, the Gensonnés, the Vergniauds, the Barbaroux, the Buzots, the Louvets, the Guadets, etc. . . . , all the heads of the faction that have for so long fomented civil war with their accomplice Roland," the deputation declared before it was interrupted by wild cheers from the Mountain and the galleries, duly countered by calls from the rest of the assembly for its expulsion. Allowed to continue (with Marat's support and in terms straight from his journal), it addressed to the Mountain its call for action. "The responsibility for identifying the traitors rests on you . . . ," it declared; "it's time for you to strip of a liberticidal inviolability these perfidious men who, in league with our enemies, sit among you only to suppress your patriotism and paralyze your energy. Emerge, emerge from this sleep that is killing liberty. . . . Rise up, legislators, there's still time; turn over to the tribunals these monsters that public opinion has already proscribed. . . . Call down the blade of the law on these inviolable conspirators." In the storm that followed, the Convention called on its members to submit their denunciations of one another to the Committee of Public Safety within the week. An orgy of mutual destruction threatened.[1]

Yet another summons to the Mountain to take decisive action against its enemies was revealed to the assembly two days later by Pétion. This time it took the form of a draft address from the Halles-aux-Blés section that was being circulated among the others for approval. "Hear us, and hear us for the last time," it admonished the deputies on behalf of Paris and of the whole of France. It warned that the nation was tired of battling constant treasons, tired of seeing faithless mandataries abusing its confidence; that those representatives who had forgotten the people was their sovereign had to be recalled; that the nation wanted all traitors to fall under the blade of the laws. Blaming the Convention's indulgence in large part for the disasters facing the nation, it called again for a law against hoarders and financial manipulators. Economic necessity would not force the people to beg for support and a return to its chains, it swore; the people would perish only after witnessing the fall of those intriguers triumphing from its misery.

Why, this draft address demanded, had the Convention sent so many of its patriotic members on mission into the departments when the homeland was in danger? Was the fate of the republic to be left to a corrupt majority that had irretrievably lost the people's confidence? "Legislators, a great blow must be struck," it proclaimed; "punishment of the guilty must terrify the mandataries who might dare one day to renew crimes we have witnessed and suffered as victims." Among other measures, it called for a purge of the administration and the armies, indictments of deputies who had betrayed their constituents, and replacement of those lacking courage to defend the country. "Mountain of the Convention, patriotic deputies, it's you we address to save the Republic. If you don't feel strong enough to do so, dare to tell us frankly and we'll take charge of saving it. The crisis we are experiencing must be the last; the Republic must triumph, or France must be annihilated in its entirety."[2]

Pétion's report of this document was cheered by the Mountain and the galleries. His bitter response—"I'm not surprised that a petition aiming to dissolve the national representation has received applause"—triggered renewed chaos in the hall and a struggle, led by Danton, to replace him at the tribune. Danton's shouts against "Criminals!" were answered by cries of "Down with the Dictator!" Calm was finally restored after several minutes of agitation and a lecture from the assembly's president on the need for dignity among the nation's chosen representatives.[3]

Clinging to the tribune, nonetheless, Pétion launched into a lengthy tirade that was constantly interrupted but unwaveringly continued. He attacked the tiny subversive minority within the Paris sections he blamed for inciting anarchy, pillage, and the dissolution of the Republic in the name of all the sections and of the entire nation. He attacked deputies who were endorsing charges that the majority was corrupt, slandering the true friends of liberty, and tarnishing them by accusations of association with Dumouriez. Evoking fears of class warfare, he targeted agitators seeking to divide the nation and its assembly into *patriots* possessing something and *nonpatriots* possessing nothing, along with the dangerous men who talked unintelligibly about *an army of sans-culottes* fostering a "silent and intestine war spreading throughout the Republic." Nor did he omit secret committees that slandered defenders of liberty while mounting a "system of terror and threats that aims to influence the feeble-minded, obstruct deliberations, and produce those surprise votes that are so disastrous when it comes to palliating certain disorders or provoking revolutionary movements." Only "madmen or counterrevolutionary royalists" nostalgic for the old regime, he claimed, could be responsible for an address like this that threatened the Convention with dissolution.[4]

Demands for force and severity against these public enemies led Pétion in due course to the subject of Marat, the figure he saw as emblematic of all the threats facing the Convention. "You have among you a man covered with opprobrium, a man who has preached despotism to you in all its forms . . . ," he fulminated in the face of noisy interruption from the Mountain. "Yes, despotism, royalism, a triumvirate, murder, and pillage. Well, not only does he sit among us, but he certainly gets to speak more easily than a man known for his probity and morals. Remember what happened at the beginning of our sessions when scarcely any member wanted to sit next to him. Today, he constantly gets to speak, he alone is assured the right to denounce, to slander and, as he unerringly does, to denounce the best citizens every day." But Marat had denounced Dumouriez, a deputy objected. "Certainly, but it's not surprising that he hit on the truth," was Pétion's rejoinder. "When one denounces everyone, it's not impossible to find someone guilty. How would a man nourished on bile and slander, who sees only conspirators everywhere, not get it right one day and fall upon a traitor in the administration or the army? Besides, I suspect he had other motives, notably when I see him denounce Dumouriez and not Egalité."[5]

This move was key: Pétion was advancing the Girondins' strategy to deflect charges of their own collaboration with the treasonous general by tarring the former duc d'Orléans, now Philippe Egalité (and with him the

Mountain), with conspiracy. Moving toward his conclusion, he called for members of all the Paris sections to vote for what he expected to be their formal disapproval of the subversive address drafted by the Halles-aux-Blés section. He demanded that those responsible for it be condemned by the assembly and sent to the Revolutionary Tribunal. And he delivered a final goad at the deputies of the right and center: "And you, why are you still here? Is it to be witnesses to the end of the Republic and tranquil spectators of all the infamies and plots hatched around you?"[6]

With this cry, finally, it was time for the ever-impatient Danton to mount the tribune, to loud applause from the Mountain and the galleries as he did so. The fact that he had only heard the latter part of the address of the Halles-aux-Blés section had not inhibited him from calling for it to receive an honorable mention from the assembly. Nor did it now prevent his utter repudiation of Pétion's reaction. "Why should the people itself not have the right to erupt from an excess of patriotism that carries it to the point of frenzy when this tribune seems continually to be a gladiatorial arena, and when I myself am besieged and provoked by a great number of members of this assembly shouting their heads off at me that I wanted to be a dictator," he roared. To Pétion, the former mayor of the capital panicking in the face of an outburst of democratic energy, he offered a lecture on political realism in a populist moment. "[Pétion] knows well that when a monarchy is shattered and there's a desire to achieve a stable republic, the people, especially when it is threatened by external enemies, overreaches its goal by the force of its own *political propulsion*. Grasp these truths: they're eternal."

What, then, should the representatives of the nation do in the face of such popular energy? Stay calm and profit from it: this was Danton's prescription. Remember the experience of the Constituent Assembly, he urged. "Marat was no less terrifying to the aristocrats then, or less odious to the moderates. But he found defenders. He also said that the majority was bad, execrable, because it really was!" The deputies had a duty to respond to the people when it presented them with severe truths, Danton contended; they had to acknowledge that they had shown themselves unworthy of their mission to take great measures and save the homeland. "Since when have you deserved encomia? Are you at the end of your mission?" he chided. "Conquer the enemies, reestablish order at home and create a good constitution . . . , it will be all the better for being born amid the storms of liberty. This is the way a people of antiquity built its walls with a trowel in one hand and a sword in the other to repulse the enemies." Set aside fears of so-called calumny, he exhorted the assembly. "Let's do our duty, draw on the energy in the addresses the people send us, and above all let's not make war on ourselves in getting the sections to deliberate about calumnies and political opinion while we must concentrate their energy to direct it against the Austrians." To do otherwise Danton saw as an act of weakness. "Let's not have exaggerated denunciations brought before us as if we were afraid of dying."[7]

This speech did nothing to palliate the anger among Girondins, who continued to call for the Convention to defend itself from charges of corruption. They saw these attacks as emanating from a conspiracy to place Philippe Egalité on the throne, one that Guadet soon bundled for them into a single great plot combining Dumouriez's betrayals with the attempted popular insurrection of 10–11 March. Guadet wanted a grand inquisition to expose the threads of this great web, prosecute the guilty, and enlighten a people that was being constantly misled. "Make no mistake, citizens, they're trying to surround you with factitious opinions in order to disguise the true public opinion from you," he cautioned. Likening this fabricated opinion to "the croaking of toads . . . that for some savages expresses the will of their gods," he was caustically interrupted by Marat, who embraced the spirit of the metaphor by shouting, "Shut up, vile bird!" "As for me," Guadet continued, "I recognize the only truly imposing opinion for the virtuous man: that of the mass of the people."[8]

You won't save liberty, Guadet warned the deputies, if you allow criminals invoking the sacred name of the people to tell you that the majority among you is corrupt, that there are only a few men in this assembly who can save the Republic, that they are there to do it themselves if these men prove incapable to do so. "Citizens, you either represent the French nation or you are nothing. If you do represent the French nation, you owe it to its safety to punish such outrages; you owe it to the law that you yourselves have passed not to leave unpunished such an excess of audacity and crime." He demanded that the Convention send delegates to investigate the Halles-aux-Blés section and dispatch to the Revolutionary Tribunal all individuals found to be complicit in discussion of the offending address, if indeed such a discussion had occurred. Evoking a link to earlier events, he also urged that the public prosecutor be summoned to account for failure to prosecute those guilty of threatening the assembly on 9–10 March.[9]

In this extended combat, the moment now called for the two factions to send in their champions. Robespierre reached the tribune first, with Vergniaud at his heels. He was allowed to speak only on condition that the assembly would not adjourn before he had been answered. To declare the majority of the Convention corrupt was mad, he maintained, but to deny that the assembly could sometimes be misled by a profoundly corrupt coalition would be an imposture. "It erupts under your very eyes, this conspiracy that surrounds us. Everybody sees its nature and extent, it's a chain that stretches from London to all the courts of Europe, ending in this sacred space." Robespierre proclaimed himself ready now to offer "the history [*tableau*] of our revolution," the fruit of long reflection. "If the men I have to denounce are still supported in this assembly, if they remain in a position to dominate it . . . , then doubtless I will have made yet another vain effort. But at least I will have done my duty to the satisfaction of my conscience."[10]

His conscience thus brandished, Robespierre portrayed the powerful faction he decried as conspiring with the European powers to impose on France a monarch, an aristocratic constitution, and an illusory representative body with two chambers. Serving the purposes of the English government, this arrangement would suit "all the aristocratic bourgeois who have a horror of equality and have been scared for their property" and "the nobility all too happy to get back . . . the haughty distinctions they have lost." The Republic, he declared to the contrary, "suits only the people, the men of all conditions, who have a pure and elevated soul, the philosophical friends of humanity, the *Sans-Culottes*, which is to say the men of all estates who, in France, are proud to bear the title with which Lafayette and the Court wanted to brand them." He saw the deputies he was accusing of "aristocratic republicanism" as the political heirs of Lafayette, the Feuillants, the Moderates: the names had changed, but the goal had remained the same, and with more powerful support. "All the ambitious actors who have appeared so far in the theater of the Revolution have had this in common: they've defended the rights of the people as far as they thought was necessary. They've treated it as a stupid herd destined to be led by the strongest and most skillful. They've seen the representative assemblies as composed of greedy or credulous men that had to be corrupted or tricked into serving their criminal projects."[11]

Like their predecessors, Robespierre charged, the current masters of the national assembly had hidden their ambition under the mask of moderation and love of order while seeking to destroy the principles of liberty; they had used the popular societies against the court until they were ready to destroy them; they had dubbed friends of the homeland agitators and anarchists; they had scared citizens with the phantom of the agrarian law, separated the interests of the rich from those of the poor, presented themselves to the rich as their protectors from the sans-culottes and attracted all the enemies of equality to their side. Dominating the government and administration, they had used all their power to halt the progress of the public spirit, revive royalism, and resuscitate aristocracy. They had oppressed energetic patriots who had constantly defended the rights of the people. They had protected moderates under special pretexts. They had attempted to corrupt all those who had shown some talent in defending the interests of the homeland and persecuted the ones they couldn't seduce. "How could the Republic be born or survive when the public power exhausts itself to discourage virtue and reward lack of civic commitment and perfidy?"[12]

Throughout this speech, ominously, the enemy had remained unidentified. Now Robespierre was ready to name names in an extended history of a faction he portrayed as conspiring with the royal court before 10 August, striving to prevent the popular uprising of that day, struggling to halt and dishonor the revolution that resulted, and slandering the leadership of the Commune. "From these facts . . . you already recognize the persons I accuse and have the courage to denounce without thought of recompense or danger. . . . From these facts, I say . . . , you recognize the Brissots, the Guadets, the Vergniauds, the Gensonnés and other hypocritical agents of the same coalition." There followed a lengthy rehearsal of the betrayals of the Revolution committed by this group from the very beginning of the Convention.[13]

It was still some time before Robespierre reached the conclusion that "I've shown you a system, sustained from the revolution of 10 August to this moment, composed of clear, well-known facts, the result of which is the loss of the Republic." Tracing in detail the events culminating in Dumouriez's desertion, he reserved particular denunciations for Vergniaud, Gensonné, Pétion, and Brissot among the deputies and for the generals who had fled with Dumouriez, Valence and Egalité *fils*. ("And the father?" he was challenged. "The father? Hey! Why not?" was his answer regarding a popular rival he had long distrusted.) Along with these men he targeted Sillery, former comte de Genlis, whose wife (author of popular works on education) and sister had also fled with Dumouriez. Calling for this coterie to be denounced to the Revolutionary Tribunal, he renewed at the same time his demand for the same measure against Marie Antoinette. "I don't dare say that you must direct the same decree against patriots as distinguished as MM. Vergniaud, Brissot and others . . . ," he continued with heavy irony, greeted with laughter from the Mountain, "and it would be an act of sacrilege to demand Gensonné's indictment. Convinced as well of the powerlessness of my efforts in this regard, I rely on the wisdom of the Convention in everything concerning these illustrious members." With this challenge he left the tribune, to fervent applause from the Mountain and the galleries.[14]

It took some tense exchanges with a president sharing the assembly's profound agitation before Vergniaud could answer "the imposter who had distilled the poison" he saw now afflicting the representative body. "I shall dare to reply to M. Robespierre who by a perfidious fiction written in the silence of the study, and with snide irony, has just provoked new discord within the Convention," he declaimed. "I dare to reply to him without meditation. Unlike him, I don't need artifice. My soul is sufficient." He would speak dispassionately, Vergniaud vowed, not for himself but for the homeland, at a moment when denunciations as absurd as they were criminal had reduced the assembly to an obsession with miserable individual interests. He would speak in the knowledge that "in revolutions the dregs of nations churn and rise to the political surface, appearing at some moments to dominate the good men." He would speak to enlighten a France that was being led astray, in a voice that had many times launched terror against the palace of the tyrant, a voice that would now strike terror in the hearts of scoundrels who wanted to substitute their own tyranny for that of the monarchy.[15]

Lacking the time for meditation, Vergniaud claimed, he had nonetheless been able to reduce Robespierre's rambling denunciations to eighteen specific charges that he proceeded to address in the mode of full denial. Speaking for an undefined "we," he insisted that Robespierre's targets were neither leaders, nor intriguers, nor moderates following the line of the Feuillants. Repudiating the charge that they had slandered Paris, he decried the imputation of odious bloody scenes to the entire people: an indirect reference to the September Massacres that triggered Marat to interject that these were indeed "acts of national vengeance." His denial that they wanted to move the Convention from Paris was countered in its turn by Panis, as was his response to indictment of their failure in the Committee of General Defense to take decisive action against Dumouriez. It was a ridiculous absurdity, Vergniaud protested, to accuse his associates of complicity with the treasonous general. The traitor's true friends, he declared, were the conspirators who had threatened to overthrow the assembly on 10 March; those who had later formed a central committee of the sections with the same goal; the authors of the criminal address circulated by the Halles-aux-Blés section; and the false patriots who had been protecting them. "All these men, like Dumouriez, wanted the annihilation of the Convention; all these men, like Dumouriez, wanted a king."[16]

At this, Vergniaud's peroration lurched into pathos. He had hoped, he lamented, that Dumouriez's treason would bring the deputies together in recognition of a common danger and a spirit of commitment to save the homeland. What destiny had dictated petitions fomenting hatred and divisions among them, he pondered. What destiny had driven them to calumny and division? "You know I have swallowed in silence the bitterness showered upon me for the past six months, that I've sacrificed to my homeland my most just resentments. You know that under penalty of cowardice, of confessing culpability, of compromising the little good I am still permitted to hope to achieve, I could have spared myself from revealing Robespierre's impostures and ill will. May this day be the last we waste in scandalous debates."[17] At his suggestion, casting a veil over the Girondins' humiliation by association with Dumouriez, the Convention voted to summon to the bar of the assembly the signatories of the Halles-aux-Blés section's address and to confiscate its registers. A weak harvest for the Girondins from a session that had lasted almost ten hours, raised the hostility between the two factions to a searing pitch of intensity, and announced the Montagnards' commitment to the cause of the sans-culottes.

GUADET'S BOMB

Wounded on 10 April, the Girondins achieved a stunning comeback two days later. Battle had already been resumed by Pétion and Robespierre—and Marat had already been forcibly evicted from the tribune—by the time Guadet took a promised opportunity to respond to Robespierre's attack. His sense of the gravity of the moment was made clear as he invoked the classic political confrontation between Cicero and the conspirator Catiline. Cicero would have been received with indignation and contempt, Guadet scoffed, if he had accused Catiline on grounds as flimsy as those Robespierre had leveled against Guadet himself. Among a people that detested slander and knew how to punish it, the great Roman orator would have been hounded from the Senate if he had concluded such a speech with the kind of ironic mockery Robespierre had displayed. "But Cicero was a good man; he didn't accuse without proof; [he] hadn't speculated on the ignorance of the people; he wouldn't have seized on a popular reputation to make a grab for the Republic. . . . But I stop. . . . What can there be in common between Cicero and Robespierre, between Catiline and me!"[18]

Detailed and bitterly scornful, Guadet's self-defense was long and frequently interrupted, not least by brawling in the public galleries. He was adamant that his only crime was to put up with scoundrels and traitors for the sake of the public good, tolerating the infamous calumnies of a villainous faction that was targeting him as the head of a party. He denied membership of a Dumouriez faction or any other. "If I understand the meaning of terms, a faction is a group of men who work to overthrow legitimate authority and usurp power. Well, Robespierre, which of us, you or I, has operated in this way?" His was a group of individuals bound together by friendship, Guadet objected. "What! We're a faction, we your victims, we against whom you openly and publicly conspired on the night of 9–10 March? From what podium have we been seen trying to spread our factious and liberticidal principles? Have we approached the tribunes of your popular societies that have become the arsenal of slander, pillage, murder, and assassination . . . , of calls for attacks on the representative body of the nation? Do you see us in the Paris sections, swelling the number of those you yourselves call counterrevolutionaries when they have rendered you some reckless service? No, you don't see us anywhere; we live alone with our friends. Would you want to prohibit such relationships? Would you want to interject, into a deputation loosely bound by shared sentiments and principles, the division you introduce every day into the National Convention? No, you wouldn't succeed; liberty unites us, we are inseparable."[19]

What of the most serious accusation of all, the charge of responsibility for the war and its consequences? War had been forced on France by circumstances, Guadet retorted. "When we wanted war, all of France wanted it with us. Only Robespierre, in his pride, didn't want it because he never wants what others want." With what audacity had Robespierre asserted the existence of a chain of gold stretching from William Pitt into the heart of the Convention, the Girondin continued. With what infamy had he leveled the charge of corruption against the virtuous! "Public virtues spring from private virtues, and I know how much one must distrust those who speak to the people of *sans-culotterie* at the same time they display an insolent luxury. I know one must be wary of these men who call themselves exemplary patriots but could not bear an inquiry into their . . . their private actions." A chain of corruption extended from Pitt's London, he avowed. How else to explain the applause showered on Robespierre by his followers?

And how else, Guadet continued, would an agent of this criminal conspiracy have acted? He would have degraded public morale, making citizens in his hands resemble those once in the hands of priests; he would have thrown the national assembly into disrepute; he would have spread the love of pillage and murder throughout the Republic, and particularly within the city that was the assembly's seat. Having pushed into the Convention a man under his control with a voice calling for blood, a man execrated throughout France, he would have contrived ways to prevent the assembly from vomiting him from its midst. (No need for him, here, to name Marat!) He would have manipulated the electoral assembly of Paris to elect a man (Egalité) who could save the hopes of kings. He would have exacerbated division in the Convention with the aim of dissolving it, mobilizing for the same purpose the so-called patriotic societies and the sections in which he had placed his loyal friends. He would have empowered the atrocious system of slander to attack virtuous men and courageous men. "Did I do that? Have we done that?" Guadet demanded. The question was rhetorical. It was beyond doubt, he proclaimed, that this conspiracy existed and was intimately linked to Dumouriez's treason. "To everyone of good faith," he proclaimed over Marat's protest, "it's evident that Dumouriez was working for Egalité."[20]

In Guadet's analysis, two conspiracies had thus converged toward a common goal: the popular movement aiming at the dissolution of the Convention, and the treason of Dumouriez seeking the restoration of Bourbon rule under Philippe Egalité. At their juncture he located two men, Robespierre and Marat. Robespierre had revealed himself, he argued, when he belittled the grocery riots of 25 February by claiming that when the people rose up it had to be terrible in its vengeance, so many enemies were there to exterminate. "While this new Mahomed . . . enveloped in a mysterious designation the victims that had to be struck down, his Omar named them in his pages and others took responsibility to target them. It was the National Convention that had to be attacked." Do you think the danger is over? he roared at the assembly. "Wise up and listen."[21]

The bomb Guadet now had ready to drop on the assembly was the circular address published by the Jacobin Club on 5 April. The Convention exploded well before Guadet could finish his reading of its opening paragraphs denouncing treason within the assembly. "It's true," Marat managed to shout before the assembly was inundated by calls for his imprisonment and immediate indictment. Defiantly, boosted by applause from the galleries, he mounted the tribune. "Why this farce? What good does it serve?" he expostulated, dismissing Guadet's move as an effort to invoke the specter of a chimerical conspiracy to quash discussion of one that was all too real. He had offered unambiguous proof of his loyalty to France the previous day, he claimed, by calling for a price on the heads of Egalité *fils*, his father the would-be regent, the former comte d'Artois, and all the rebellious Bourbons. The idea, embraced by the Mountain, had been violently blocked by the enemy faction. "It's time for the conspirators to be unmasked and expire under the blade of the law. I renew my proposals and demand that they be put to the vote; we'll see which side Orléans supporters are on."[22]

For many in the assembly, to the contrary, it was time for other measures. They declared themselves ready to show themselves good republicans, ready to execute a law declaring no individual above the nation's representatives, ready for its blade to strike down a man convicted by his own admission of having provoked the disruption of the assembly. "Save the

Republic," came the cry; "it's lost if the Convention is dissolved. Strike! Pass the decree of accusation." Deputies proclaiming themselves resolved to face death were scarcely inclined to listen to Danton as he repudiated rash action that would determine the fate of one of their members without hearing his defense or considering the public interest. Marat recalled this speech as masterly, but there was little patience among the deputies for Danton's tactical argument for the priority of bringing the former duc d'Orléans (no longer dubbed Egalité!) before a revolutionary tribunal in Provence. They showed even less readiness to accept his contention that Marat could not justly be condemned without a formal inquiry into his actions by a committee that would also consider those of his accusers.[23]

"Many of our colleagues are absent," Danton argued, alluding to the fact that some one hundred deputies, mostly Montagnards, had been dispatched on mission to the provinces and armies. "Be careful," he warned. "Whether you want it or not, this great plot is getting complicated; it depends on public opinion more than ever. Marat has the right to be judged by the totality of his peers, and if you show partisanship to the point of sending him before the tribunals it will evidently be the result of your passions alone." There was no risk that Marat would flee, Danton added ("No," Marat shouted from the floor to confirm), and a representative could not be accused without a prior committee report. Such was the law or should be, Danton asserted, "especially now that I have shown that there is exasperation against the popular societies, against the people. . . ." His sentence was cut off by noisy indignation from the center and right of the assembly and lengthy applause from the galleries. "You're slandering us," came the retort; "we revere the people, you're the ones calling for daggers from yours."[24]

This was an opening for Boyer-Fonfrède, dogged fighter for the Girondins, to claim a people's voice as their own. He had no intention to "turn this awesome voice into an instrument of terror," he assured the Montagnards; he would not wrest from it, "through the horror to which I know your souls are immune," a decree favoring his own views. The people he had in mind was not the frightful radical populace of Paris but the citizens of France he portrayed as unanimous in demanding severe justice against Marat. "Is this man held in veneration or horror in the departments," he inquired. "Is his name blessed or execrated among your constituents? Are his writings destined for the press or for the fire? Is there one of you who has not been reproached for the existence of this man in the Convention? Haven't your fellow citizens implored you a hundred times to banish from the senate this evil genie whose handiwork is crimes, slanders, trouble, and discord . . . ?" It was the voice of this people that condemned Marat,

Boyer-Fonfrède insisted to applause. Ask your deputies on mission, none of them moderates, he urged the Montagnards. "Who among them has not disavowed his bloody doctrine? Who among them has dared boast of his relations with this man? How is it, then, that this man accused by all of France, whom no one acknowledges and of whom everyone is ashamed, finds defenders even here?"[25]

What need, then, for a committee report when the evidence was already so palpable? Deputies on mission were already promising republican societies that they would call for Marat's indictment when they returned, Fonfrède maintained as he amplified his charges. ("*To my honor and glory*," was the target's riposte!) "Haven't you passed laws against those provoking pillage? Well, Marat has provoked it. Haven't you passed laws against those provoking murder? Marat provokes it constantly." ("*Yes, against the royalists*," came the retort.) "Haven't you decreed pain of death against anyone demanding the reestablishment of arbitrary power? Well, Marat has called for a dictatorship. Haven't you passed laws against demanding dissolution of the Convention? Well, Marat demands that every day!" Danton had objected that the Convention would be both judge and party in this case, ironically echoing an argument the Girondins had deployed in defense of Louis XVI. But wasn't it up to the assembly to save the precious repository of national representation, Fonfrède countered. "France in its entirety accuses Marat; we're only his judges." Every day and everywhere, he charged, the Montagnards applauded the insolent addresses of misguided men bribed to demand the expulsion of three hundred members of the assembly. "If you had the power, you would not object that you're both judges and parties, you would banish them. And when the imperiled Republic summons you to banish your divisions with this man who designates even here the victims of his rage, this man who stirs the flames of discord among you, this is when, for him alone, you tell yourselves that you are incompetent to pronounce judgment."

Shouts of support, and calls for closure of the discussion, met Fonfrède's concluding call for Marat's indictment. Thuriot nonetheless intervened to counsel caution in this unprecedented situation. "The two extremes are very close to touching," he observed, warning the deputies of the Plain that both sides were doing everything they could to stir up popular agitation. Fearing that a rash decision in this factional conflict could reduce not only Paris but the entire country to flames, he pressed for a committee report to be heard before any action was taken. Seizing the moment, Marat leaped to the tribune to offer a response. He had not written the Jacobins' circular, he declared; he had signed it in his official capacity while presiding over the club for seven or eight minutes and in ignorance of its contents. Nonetheless, he avowed as his own the opinions in the text Guadet had read to the assembly.[26]

What was the situation here? The People's Friend asked the assembly. His accusers wanted a decree against him as he did against them. "Firm in my innocence and the purity of my civic commitment, I don't even challenge my known enemies. State your grievances against me; the ones I direct against you are contained in my writings if you're not already judged. As for my actions, I defy my most mortal enemy to say that I have ever been compromised with the enemies of the homeland or discovered among the conspirators in their night-time conclaves." His correspondence had been scrutinized by his enemies without their finding anything that could compromise him, he attested; he had turned over to the authorities anonymous letters meant to entrap him. "What outrages them against me is my extreme surveillance, my foresight, my courage in denouncing them. They want to cut my throat to rid themselves of an inconvenient watchdog."

Far from wanting to dissolve the Convention, Marat objected, he had done everything to prevent that. His accusers had merely used the pretext of saving the assembly to give the conspirators impunity. They had to be exposed, these conspirators, and authentically judged; their heads had to roll. "I declare for the rest that if I was a stumbling block in the assembly, if I was persuaded that public safety could only be preserved by my resignation, and if I would not compromise the reputation sustained by the confidence I inspire in the people, I would give my resignation; for I'm a friend of peace and if I knew I would be the occasion for a popular movement I would entomb myself today." In the meantime, he maintained, he would denounce incessantly the faction now striking against him, the men whom Dumouriez himself had indicted by claiming them as his allies against the Mountain.[27]

Calling for a decree to send Egalité to the Revolutionary Tribunal and set a price on the heads of the Capet family émigrés, Marat's voice was drowned out by contending demands from the Mountain for referral of the charges against him to a committee and from elsewhere in the assembly for an immediate vote of accusation against him. In his journal, he recounted a "hideous ruckus" in which Montagnards were threatened physically, a sword was drawn against them, and there were charges of a pistol being brandished in their defense. "I have to speak to avoid great unrest," he shouted, his implied threat of popular outrage on his behalf eliciting a rejoinder that any such movement would prove how dangerous he was. He asked to be taken to the Jacobin Club to preach peace, evoking a reproof from the president that it was an insult to the people of Paris to believe that they would not respect the law. Again, there were cries for an indictment, this time answered by a mass of Montagnards (led by Bentabole) shouting for a roll-call vote and advancing en masse toward the bureau to sign up for it.

At this, the assembly decreed that there would be a roll-call vote and that (as the Montagnards insisted) its results would be printed and circulated among the departments and the armies. Amid protests that the question to be decided had not been clearly posed, Delacroix intervened to invoke a law that an indictment had to be preceded by a committee report and to demand that Marat be placed under arrest until such a report had been presented. (It was reported to the Jacobin Club that evening that this proposal had earned Delacroix a punch in the face from a frenetic Gorsas.) Calls that this detention take the form of house arrest met noisy opposition before it was decided instead (as the result of an underhand maneuver by the assembly's secretaries) that he would be imprisoned in the Abbaye, pending a committee report the following day. "We'll go too, all of us, all of us!" came the cry from Montagnards concerned for his safety among convicted enemies of the Revolution.[28]

By Marat's own report, he was eventually left surrounded by a rump of some fifty deputies swearing to accompany him to the Abbaye prison, bolstered by a crowd flowing from the galleries to oppose his arrest. Challenging the validity of the order to restrain him (left unsigned, in the disorder of the moment, by the assembly's president), this cortège escorted him from the Manège, whence he disappeared once again into hiding. "They'll doubtless say I disobeyed the law," he later told his readers; "I declare that I don't recognize as a law the decisions taken by the faction of the *hommes d'Etat*" against the patriots of the Mountain, decisions taken in the tumult of passions and in the middle of an uproar. Laws must be made in silence and with dignity. If the nation witnessed the scandalous scenes in the Convention, it would soon expel some of its mandataries as traitors unworthy of its confidence, as escapees from the madhouse. "These are the sham legislators of France who can make my resistance to oppression a crime."[29]

THE MOVE TO INDICT

The Convention had returned to business on April 13 when it received a letter from Marat announcing his refusal to accept imprisonment in the Abbaye. Addressed to the assembly, it was also intended for a wider audience. Defiantly, it reiterated that Dumouriez had intended to march on Paris to support the criminal faction he had embraced as allies and accomplices, subdue the Montagnards he treated as anarchists, and use terror to deter them from supporting the cause of the people. It dismissed again, as a fantasy intended to divert attention from the Girondins' own support of émigrés and royalists, the claim that the Montagnards had been aiming to put Orléans on the throne. Desperate and furious men, Marat averred, they were hoodwinking the people by persecuting him as an incendiary writer. Seizing on the Jacobin Club circular, they were demanding his indictment for signing, as president of the club, a patriotic appeal for the people to take up arms to repel enemy armies and rebellious legions advancing to return it to chains. "Not daring to pronounce a decree of accusation against me without a prior report, they have decided I should be placed under arrest at the Abbaye. . . . I, the incorruptible defender of liberty, would be incarcerated by my most ferocious enemies for denouncing them as schemers, forcing them to confess themselves traitors, infamous supporters of monarchy. No, it won't happen. . . . I don't want to withhold my conduct from the examination of my judges, but neither will I expose myself to the fury of my enemies, all of them enemies of the homeland; I don't want to be slaughtered by their emissaries or poisoned in a prison." Succeeding in their criminal projects in his case, he warned, "they'll soon come for Robespierre, then Danton, then all the patriotic deputies who have shown some character."

"Before belonging to the Convention, I belonged to the homeland; I owe myself to the people; I am its eye," Marat's letter continued (its reading cheered from the public galleries). "I'm going to take cover from the attacks of paid criminals so that I can continue to unmask traitors and foil their plots until the nation knows their perfidious schemes and has done justice to them." Forty-seven departments, the letter claimed, had already called for expulsion of the deputies who had voted for the appeal to the people and imprisonment of the tyrant. "A little more patience and the nation will do justice to them. I don't want the Convention to be dissolved; I demand that it be purged of the traitors striving to destroy the nation by establishing despotism." Applauded from the Mountain and the galleries, this challenge was soon countered by presentation of the report on Marat the Convention had ordered the previous day. It was read on behalf of the Committee on Legislation by the centrist Pierre-Marie Delaunay, deputy of Maine-et-Loire.[30]

The report wasted no time in its indictment. "This hall has long resounded with complaints against Marat. Administrative bodies, popular societies, have long invoked the blade of the law against him," Delaunay began, provoking objections from Bentabole and Panis and growls from the Mountain as he proceeded to read the 5 April circular of the Jacobin Club. This overture provoked an immediate outburst from the Mountain. "If this address is culpable, decree an accusation against me because I approve it," declared Dubois-Crancé, inciting a throng of his fellow Montagnards to rise from their seats, shouting, "We all approve it! We're ready to sign it." Urged on by cries and applause from the galleries, David called for the address to be deposited at the bureau of the Convention so that patriots could add their signature to it. "Yes! Yes!" came the response as he launched himself toward the bureau accompanied by Thirion, Dubois-Crancé, and Camille Desmoulins. A hundred more Montagnards followed on their heels, shouting, "Decree accusations against us all!" Within minutes, the circular was endorsed by some ninety-eight signatures (a handful of which were not identifiably those of deputies). "Let eternal justice punish all the enemies of our liberty," wrote the last to sign, the mathematician Gilbert Romme, deputy of Puy-de-Dôme and soon to be champion of the revolutionary calendar.[31]

A proposal that the Jacobin address now be printed and circulated to the departments and the armies, quickly supported by both Robespierre and Vergniaud, threw the entire assembly into uproar. To do so would amount to acknowledgment that the assembly no longer had the confidence of its constituents, in which case it would be necessary to convoke the electoral assemblies, Delacroix asserted amid the cacophony that followed. "It's no longer possible to dissimulate after the fissure that has exploded in this assembly; everyone of good faith must acknowledge that all the bonds of mutual trust have been broken," proclaimed Gensonné. In his view, the Jacobin circular amounted to an appeal to the people against its representatives, for which he now called. It was time for the French to know whether the people was to make the law or a miserable faction, he declared. "In the state of division and hatred into which we have been thrown, we can have no other judge than the people. . . . It's up to the people in the primary assemblies to pronounce what opinion it adopts, what law it dictates to us, what law it dictates to all the minorities." There was a conspiracy to return France to the constitution of 1789, with a monarchy and regency, he avowed (*You know something about that!* interrupted Panis). It aimed to do so by spreading the sentiment of counterrevolution, he continued, by making the people believe that the form of government it had chosen produced nothing but disorder and anarchy, by calling for the dissolution of the National Assembly. It had done everything it could to prevent the Assembly from presenting a new constitution to the people, a democratic constitution it misrepresented as favoring the rich against the poor.

To withstand this conspiracy, Gensonné urged, the people needed to give itself new representatives invested with all the confidence necessary to defeat anarchy and maintain order. It needed the Convention to establish, and submit to popular vote, the basic constitutional principles of a democratic republic, one and indivisible. "Let's not wait a single moment to consult the people," he expostulated. "Wrest from the ambitious men who are our enemies the terrible weapon they can forge by a false public opinion. I supported the appeal to the people when the overthrow of Louis XVI was demanded, and I insist on the same idea." Interrupted by a Robespierre indignant at this blasphemy against liberty, he nevertheless continued to expound his reasons for demanding the election of the Convention after the revolution of 10 August and for now calling once more for the convocation of the primary assemblies to decide on constitutional principles and renew the mandates of deputies the people would judge worthy of its confidence.[32]

Meanwhile, some of the deputies who had rushed to add their signature to the Jacobin circular were beginning to reconsider the use to which the document might now be put. Not so Camille Desmoulins, glorying in having signed it, who went on to announce that the Paris sections and the departments would intervene the next day to demand that the Convention expel twenty-two "royalist" deputies allied with Dumouriez. These men knew what was coming to them, Desmoulins charged, and were ready to blow up everything before they perished. Consternation at this remark among the deputies was matched by a fracas in the galleries, followed by calls for the session to be suspended. But Buzot again brought clarity to the discussion by pressing for a return to the order of the day, more specifically the matter of Jean-Paul Marat. This session was far from over.

"It is inconceivable that this man is still interjecting division into the assembly," Buzot declaimed. "It is very strange that this man alone has the right to be above the law." His demand that Marat be indicted prompted new protest from the galleries, which he angrily dismissed as a challenge to his status as representative of the people and an affront to his virtue. "My entire life speaks for me," he attested before returning to his denunciation. "When you forbid journalists to sit among us, he makes himself one; when you order him to the Abbaye, he writes that he won't turn himself in there. Who is this species of homunculus who dares tell you he won't obey the law? And who are these base creatures who can associate their name with his? The Convention must finally repress a man who has degraded public morality, whose soul is nothing but slander, and whose whole life is a tissue of crimes. The departments will bless the day when you deliver the human species of a man who dishonors it. For the moment, he has to be transferred to the Abbaye. . . ." Interrupted by protests from the Mountain and shouts that Marat would not go to the Abbaye, Buzot nevertheless prevailed. "The assembly is all powerful," he adjured its president. "It's enough that it assume a character worthy of it, hear its committee spokesman in silence, then decree Marat's accusation." Convinced, the Convention finally allowed Delaunay to resume his report.[33]

Unsurprisingly, the report was zealous in its condemnation of writers abusing the press to foment murder and pillage, call for daggers against public officials, instigate the dissolution of the Convention, and place themselves above the law. Such men wanted counterrevolution, it insisted; they aimed to substitute anarchy and despotism for the reign of liberty and equality; they had to be sacrificed to public safety, whatever their position. In Marat's case, Delaunay reminded the deputies that they had already decided to suspend the inviolability of representatives accused of complicity with the enemies of liberty, equality, and republican government. It remained, then, to consider the particular charges against him.

Troubling the order of society and refusing to respect its laws; urging pillage without respect for property; demanding expropriation of the rich in favor of citizens duped into pillage or brigandage; exhorting to murder: a man guilty of such acts, Delaunay declared, was a scourge. He had to be purged. The committee report found no shortage of evidence of these offenses in Marat's writings. Citing his journal, it held him responsible for the pillage of the grocery riots of 25 February; for denigrating the Convention and attempting to dissolve it; for denouncing to the entire Republic those he called *hommes d'Etat*; for pillorying as royalists the deputies who had not voted for the tyrant's death and provoking the sections to call for their expulsion; for inciting the extermination of conspirators, among whom he counted those who had favored an appeal to the people and imprisonment or reprieve of the tyrant; for signing the circular that urged communes throughout the Republic to imitate the September Massacres; for demanding "in the name of *civic duty, philanthropy, and humanity, 250,000 heads, a dictator, a triumvirate or a military tribune*"; for declaring himself above the assembly's decrees in refusing to accept the one that prohibited deputies to serve also as journalists.

"The entire Republic is watching you . . . ," Delaunay warned the assembly in closing. "It's up to you to pronounce judgment." The committee had not been deterred by concern that Marat's arrest would trigger massive popular unrest in Paris, he guaranteed. The deputies would remain safe. The report, he assured them, "gives Paris the justice that is its due: the city is good, it loves you, and there are a host of its inhabitants that would throw themselves in front of any blows against you." With this conviction, he proposed Marat's indictment and referral to the Revolutionary Tribunal, for provocation to pillage, murder, and the dissolution of the Convention.[34]

This time, in a dramatic switch illuminating the underlying parallel between this debate and that over the judgment of Louis XVI—and exposing, indeed, the semiotic circle in which the Convention still found itself confined—it was a Montagnard, Charlier, who now called for a version of an appeal to the people. His proposal that the committee report be printed and circulated to the departments and the armies, and further discussion adjourned for three days, found some immediate support. But it elicited a powerful objection from one deputy who shouted, "I didn't vote for the appeal to the people for the death of Capet, I won't vote for the appeal to the people for the decree of accusation against Marat. This is the vicious circle in which we are being dragged." Charlier's rejoinder, that "I didn't talk at all about an appeal to the people, but I want to plead for national representation," seemed feeble in response. He received further support, however, from another Montagnard, Lecointe-Puyraveau. "Don't let it be said that you are afraid of movements by Marat's partisans," he exhorted. "Brave the daggers, brave too the assassins if they exist, and show that a representative of the people will not be treated less favorably than a tyrant." Declaring, to uproar from the galleries, his conviction that Marat was as culpable as the tyrant, he nevertheless demanded postponement of judgment until Delaunay's report had been printed and circulated.[35]

It was time, now, for Robespierre's attempt to walk on these increasingly muddied waters by postulating the dilemma the deputies now faced. "You find yourselves caught between a decree of accusation and adjournment," he reasoned. "You're unable to pass a decree of accusation because you haven't discussed it; nor can you adjourn because this representative of the people is under arrest, because you're sending to the departments an abusive report that is the fruit of passions and liberticidal plots." If this analysis was punctured by applause from the galleries, it also earned a snicker that Robespierre had spent too long at dinner to know that the discussion was over. To clamors for a vote to begin, abruptly leaving Robespierre in midsentence, the Convention came to a decision. It decreed publication and distribution of Delaunay's report, together with some additional evidence against Marat omitted from it, as well as Marat's letter of refusal to go to the Abbaye. More decisively, though, the decree also ordered the printing and circulation of the record of each deputy's opinion on whether Marat should be indicted. In effect, without explicitly doing so, the assembly had finally decided on a roll-call vote and was now eager to proceed to it.[36]

The deputies were frustrated in this, nonetheless, by Robespierre's continued demand for an addition to the decree he deemed "necessary to unmask traitors and demonstrate the true spirit of oppression" dominating the proceedings. "I know Marat's character; he has committed errors and faults of style," Robespierre now attested; "but there are conspirators and traitors on the other side." The remark was met by calls for an arrest decree against Robespierre himself, but he refused to be silenced. "Didn't you listen for three hours yesterday from other men? You can oppress and slaughter, but you won't stifle my voice," was his retort. "This is the man slaughtered by the assassins' blade," he gestured as he held aloft a portrait of the Montagnard martyr Lepeletier, thus provoking further violent objections from the assembly and matching applause from the galleries. The proposal he was offering would not be accepted, he asserted, but its refusal would expose to France and all of Europe the men who wanted civil war. "It's not against Marat alone that they want a decree of accusation . . . ," he warned; "it's rather against you, true Republicans, you who have offended by the passion of your souls; against me, perhaps, despite the fact that I seek constantly not to aggravate or offend anyone." He wanted, then, an addition to Delaunay's report stating that the Convention had "refused to hear an accused person who has never been my friend, whose errors travestied here as crimes I have never shared, but whom I regard as a good citizen, a zealous defender of the people's cause, and totally alien to the crimes imputed to him."[37]

This tortured and self-regarding defense of Marat was quickly set aside, and the vote was commenced by the deputies from the Meuse (the departmental deputation chosen by lot to do so). Immediately, there was confusion over whether they would be allowed to explain their vote. "Let's not have two weights and two measures," one of them expostulated. "In the discussion for the king at the moment of reprieve, we wanted to explain our opinions; this procedure was denied us." The analogy with the king's trial was ever in mind. This time, as in the initial vote over Louis XVI's guilt, justifications of individual votes were permitted (with copies to be submitted to the assembly's secretariat for later publication). The voting continued throughout the night until 7:00 the following morning, at which point the entire session had lasted twenty-one hours.[38]

A ROLL-CALL VOTE

Are there grounds for an accusation against Marat, member of the National Convention? Seven hundred forty-six deputies were named on the Convention's official report of the roll-call vote on this question. Almost exactly half that number, 372, were listed as absent. Of these, well over a hundred were away from the assembly as deputies *en mission* to the departments or armies. In pressing for an immediate vote in this situation, the Girondins had seized an opportunity that gave them an advantage over their opponents in the assembly, as Danton had anticipated. "Their absence has given the majority to that ambitious faction that tyrannizes us so cruelly," lamented Delacroix; "yes, since the departure of our patriotic colleagues, principles have been violated, the sovereignty of the people misunderstood, liberty persecuted and slaughtered." This sentiment was echoed by Guyardin, a Montagnard from the Haute-Marne. "To conquer us, they're seeking to divide us, and they're profiting from the moment when more than a hundred of our brothers in arms are dispersed across the republic," he declared; "but to continue resisting successfully we'll close ranks more tightly and form a formidable rampart."[39]

While the number of deputies away on mission undoubtedly affected the outcome of the vote, it is striking that roughly 250 other members of the Convention were also listed as not present. Fatigue and illness may have accounted for some of these absences, but it seems likely that many were motivated by growing aversion to the bitter factional fighting that had come to dominate the Convention's business. It also appears that some of the assembly's most prominent members may simply have decided to stay away. Notable among the absentees not on mission were Danton, Vergniaud, Brissot, Barère, and Marat's longtime ally Panis.

Of the 374 deputies the Convention did list as present, 220 voted in favor of Marat's indictment, 95 were against, and 34 abstained. Of the latter, 10 recused themselves as a matter of honor, most of them on the grounds that they had been personally slandered by Marat and could not therefore appear impartial. This group included several of his principal accusers. Guadet, Gensonné, and Louvet offered no further explanation for their recusal; Salle, surprising no one in expressing his conviction of Marat's guilt, doubtless spoke for others recusing themselves in emphasizing the "delicacy of not allowing the least doubt about my intentions." In a spirit of greater bravado, Lasource denounced Marat as "a man very dangerous for liberty, aiming to destroy it through disorder and bring back despotism through anarchy," but nevertheless refused to vote from "a sense of grandeur that my slanderers don't know, and only good men appreciate." Of deputies apparently less inclined to pretensions to grandeur, an additional 23 declared themselves not ready to vote for other reasons: 11 of them called explicitly for an adjournment to allow for further deliberation; Garran de Coulon, in doing so, added that the Convention was dysfunctional and should be dissolved. A lone wolf defied categorization by claiming that the assembly had not explicitly voted to allow deputies to explain their opinion.[40]

In fact, relatively few of the 220 deputies voting for Marat's indictment went beyond the one-word declaration of their opinion. Most of the 41 who did so (not quite 20 percent) were brief in offering variations on the charges that he had provoked pillage and murder, and had called for a dictatorship and dissolution of the Convention. A few went further to accuse him as "one of the most dangerous instruments" of "tyrants and the agents of tyranny" (Pierre-Charles-François Dupont); "the most radical counterrevolutionary" (Bernier); in league with and paid by Orléans in a conspiracy to restore monarchy (Delahaye, Boileau, Rivaud, Chambon); even "an accomplice of Dumouriez, agent of the Orléans faction" (Guyomar).[41]

Others voting for indictment declared their convictions at greater length. For Cazeneuve, Marat, by "perverting public opinion," could bring about "the dissolution of the state and the annihilation of liberty." Lanjuinais reached back to the time of the September Massacres to accuse him of provoking tyranny by preaching anarchy, pillage, and murder "after having soiled the cause of liberty by the hideous circular, with its message: *kill, we've killed*." Chiappé deemed him "unworthy of being a member of the National Convention . . . , more than any other cause of our reverses, because his morality makes French liberty appear odious to the nations." Féraud held that "a representative of the people must be more severely punished when he betrays his duties, and his inviolability disappears before his crimes in my eyes." Convinced of Marat's guilt in "provoking anarchy, assassination, contempt for the laws, pillage, violation of persons and property, dissolution of the national representation and the tyranny of a master or dictator," Souhait dismissed threats that an indictment would trigger "so-called popular movements." Having voted for the death of the tyrant without appeal, Boileau vowed, he could not view with indulgence the crimes of a man who had "set back liberty and public happiness by half a century." Several other deputies joined him in declaring themselves as convinced of Marat's guilt as they had been of Louis XVI's. Bernier, facing heckling as he pronounced Marat guilty, suggested it was time for each deputy to post an account of his own conduct before and during the Revolution to produce a list enabling the people to distinguish its true friends.[42] A proposal, ironically, that Marat would surely have supported.

In contrast, many more of the deputies opposing Marat's indictment felt compelled to justify their decision. Whether they voted no, abstained, declared themselves not ready to vote, or demanded adjournment, the overwhelming majority (77 percent) objected to a rush to judgment in which the report had not been circulated among the deputies prior to the vote, there had been no time for them to discuss it, the charges had not been communicated to the accused, and there had been no opportunity for him to respond or for anyone else to defend him. Among abstainers,

Thirion set a tone for many others when he declared that "in this strange affair, the most sacred principles and forms have been forgotten or violated." The jurist Jean-Jacques Régis de Cambacérès, destined for great authority under Napoleon and a principal author of the eventual Civil Code, deemed it "an error in politics and ethics to have rejected the adjournment demanded by many of our colleagues and to have put the draft decree to a roll-call vote without having submitted it for discussion." He withheld his vote, as did Philippe Antoine Merlin de Douai, another future collaborator in the writing of the Civil Code, who stated pithily that he would not vote before the charges against Marat had been published. Isnard, frank in declaring that he had been ready to vote for an indictment, nevertheless stated that "the violence of the effort to pass the decree before prior discussion, and the fear of being myself the victim of intrigue" had obliged him to withhold his vote.[43]

Deputies explicitly voting against Marat's indictment were also frequently vehement on the matter of procedure. They protested with Fabre d'Eglantine, for example, that "all forms have been set aside, all principles violated," or with Dubouchet that "the first principles of justice, reason and humanity have been violated . . . , the imprescriptible and sacred rights of man and of the citizen have been disregarded." They decried with Clauzel an act of "contempt for the eternal principles of the equality of rights," one characterized by Barbeau Dubarran as "a deliberation infringing on all the principles of justice and ethics." They repudiated with Nioche a violation of "the rules and principles that safeguard the security and liberty of citizens" (to an extent, he flamboyantly declared, that was "scarcely tolerated by the Inquisition in Goa").[44]

Negative votes on grounds of procedural violations also linked these infractions frequently to the extremes of factionalism they found evident in Delaunay's report. Dubois-Crancé, declaring the report false and slanderous, insisted that it was "manifestly the work of a faction that had already taken over the Legislative Assembly with its intrigues and has grown in the Convention . . . through the slanderous denunciations with which this tribune has resounded for the past six months, to the great scandal of the nation." For Vadier, too, the report was "the work of passion and vengeance, in an affair where an oppressive faction has refused all discussion, or any adjournment, without even being willing to hear the accused, and where the laws of justice and humanity have been scandalously violated." For Poultier, it was "manifestly dictated by the most atrocious vengeance and the most violent passion"; for Bar, it was marked by "the language of passion, prejudice and animosity"; for Pinet, it exhaled "passion, the spirit of vengeance and baseness" in the service of "partiality, injustice and tyranny."[45]

Pomme, deputy of Cayenne and Guyenne française, still fresh in his third day in the Convention, was shocked by the spectacle that had greeted him on his arrival. "I've seen a scandalous conflict between two parties bitterly opposed to one another," he maintained. "My mind stupefied, my memory overwhelmed, my heart saddened by all I have seen and heard in the last two sessions, I can't make anything out in a chaos of mutual denunciations."[46] He had, in fact, discerned one thing clearly. Hearing that enemies of Dumouriez could not fail to add their names to the Jacobin circular, he had rushed to the podium to endorse its republican principles. He had grasped how central the issue of Dumouriez's treachery remained to this entire proceeding.

For many deputies opposing it, the effort to secure Marat's indictment was indeed repudiated as a continuation of the conspiracy between Dumouriez and the Girondins that Marat had denounced so unflaggingly, earning Dumouriez's denunciation in return. They saw a vote against Marat as the equivalent of a vote in favor of Dumouriez, hence unthinkable. Anacharsis Cloots made this simple in stating that "I'm not an accomplice of Dumouriez, I say no." Thirion, for his part, rejected the "precipitation and passions unworthy of a legislature" as "a manifest continuation of the system of Dumouriez who has also accused Marat." Coupé similarly condemned "the work of passion and vengeance" that was "visibly a continuation of the conspiracy woven by Dumouriez." Poultier repudiated it as "the fruit of the hatred vowed against this representative by the accomplices of Dumouriez, whom he has constantly denounced." Meaulle objected that it would be "a remarkable epoch in the history of our revolution" if Marat were indicted at the very moment his dire prophecies had been realized. "Marat told you incessantly that Dumouriez would betray his homeland before the month of April; the treason has occurred at the time he indicated; and it's when his opinion must triumph that his loss seems more assured."[47]

Simple though it may have appeared, however, the motion before the assembly implicitly posed two questions rather than one. In addressing whether to indict "Marat, member of the National Convention," the deputies were also deciding on what grounds (and by what procedures) any member of the representative body might be accused. A number of those refusing to vote for indictment explicitly repudiated the procedure as an attack on the person of a deputy, hence a violation of the principle of representation itself. Osselin was blunt in this regard. "In Marat I see only a representative of the people," he maintained. "The national mandate invests someone charged with that role with a sacred character. A decree of accusation against a deputy is an attack (at least provisionally) on the exercise of the functions of a mandatary of the people. One must only go to such an extreme for powerful reasons, thoughtfully considered, clearly established, and strictly discussed."[48]

In this same spirit, Bonnet dismissed the committee report as "a bitter diatribe in which none of the great questions presented by a case that can compromise the whole national representation has been discussed, or even presented." Audoin protested "principles violated, liberty outraged, the homeland deprived of one of its representatives, brought before the tribunals by a base vengeance, what shall I say? by a continuation of the system of royalism and counterrevolution." Dubouchet similarly repudiated an action in which "the majesty of the people has been outraged in the person of one of its representatives." Romme feared an injustice toward a representative of the people that would amount to "a crime of lèse-nation." Barbeau Dubarran lamented that it was precisely when it came to "accusing a representative of the people, to depriving him of his liberty, to directly attacking the national representation," that judicial procedures were being set aside.[49]

Pinet went further, touching a Montagnard nerve as he contrasted the rushed attempt to condemn a "mandatary of the people" with "the baseness of discussing for four months whether the assassin of the people would be sent to the scaffold." Lebas objected that a representative of the people deserved at least the same procedural formalities as "a tyrant caught with his hand in the people's blood." Sergent expostulated that the absence in Marat's case of the procedures "observed with great care and slowness in consideration of the tyrant who had slaughtered thousands of the French" made a representative of the people "less sacred than a perjuring king." Lakanal, too, protested that "you wasted three months discussing the cause of a tyrant totally covered with the blood of many thousands of our brothers, and you refuse to grant three days to a representative of the people to enlighten your decision. Thus you've exhausted every measure of prudence to save the oppressors of the people, and you reject all those measures that could rescue its chosen mandataries from punishment." Champigny was even more direct in noting that Marat's accusers were the same men who had pleaded for months in favor of the tyrant, the men whom Dumouriez had designated as his friends. He pronounced his "*no* as affirmatively as I said *yes* when it was necessary to send the tyrant to the scaffold."[50]

Though some deputies who cited procedural grounds for voting no against Marat's indictment were careful to take their distance from him, it's possible that many were tacitly expressing their support. Relatively few others, only a rough one-third of them, did couple their no vote with an explicit defense of his conduct and campaigns. More than one did so on the grounds that Marat belonged in the madhouse. Others were more positive in praising him as "a martyr of the revolution . . . , a writer too often prophetic, to whom posterity will erect statues" (Desmoulins); "a true defender of liberty, who perhaps lacks only martyrdom to his glory" (Laignelot); "one of the firmest supports of the revolution" (Bentabole, Barbeau Dubarran); worthy of "a civic crown" (Ricord); "an intrepid defender of liberty and equality" (Martel, Dherbez-Latour); "the most vigilant sentinel of *patriotisme* . . . , a revolutionary man and sincere friend of liberty and equality" (Louchet); "the prophet of all our ills" (Milhaud); "a good patriot . . . , a friend of the republic," whose indictment would mark "the death of liberty" (Brival); "a fervent defender and friend of the people" (Reynaud); "a victim sacrificed to Dumouriez and the tyrants conspiring with him" (Meaulle); "a representative of the nation whose only crime has been to vomit insults and utter terrible truths against the enemies of the republic" (Drouet).[51]

Robespierre's opinion, however, one of the very longest, was carefully calibrated to defend Marat without actually praising him. It announced, characteristically, that "the Republic can only be founded on virtue, and virtue cannot permit neglect of the first principles of equity," insisting further that "the status of representative of the people must be respected by those whom the people has chosen to defend its cause, even if they don't respect that of men and citizens." Protesting that "all principles have been violated," it castigated as scandalous the contrast between the indulgence Marat's most violent accusers had accorded the former tyrant and their relentlessness against a fellow deputy—a contrast mirrored in their reluctance to act against Dumouriez and their haste to indict the man who had denounced him.

In answer to charges in Delaunay's report, Robespierre dismissed its condemnation of the Jacobin circular of 5 April as a mere pretext, given that—for all the "energy of expressions provoked by the extreme danger to the homeland and the shocking treasons of the military and civil agents of the Republic"—this address contained only "well-established facts and principles avowed by the friends the Republic." He blamed the grocery riots of 25 February not on "a writer's anathemas against hoarders" but on the instigation of agents of the aristocracy and foreign powers aiming to malign the people of Paris and provide Dumouriez with ammunition against it. As for Marat's assertion that liberty would only be established when the traitors and conspirators were exterminated, "however illegal it might appear," he maintained that this phrase "had never killed a single traitor or a single conspirator, and that the hypocritical enemies of the people have already caused the slaughter of three hundred thousand patriots and are conspiring to slaughter the rest."

Above all, Robespierre rejected this indictment as an effort to blacken the Montagnards by tarring Marat. In this entire deliberation, he saw "bias, vengeance, injustice, the spirit of party, and the continuation of a system . . . aiming to identify with Marat, whose exaggerations are reproached, all the friends of the Republic who are alien to him." If he rejected with contempt this "vile intrigue hatched to dishonor patriotism," Robespierre nevertheless left unclear whether the patriotism he was defending was Marat's or that of those being tarnished by association with him. His brother, also repudiating the entire procedure as a liberticidal effort to denigrate patriots, at least argued that Marat's accusers had portrayed him "not as he is but as they have wanted to make him." He judged Delaunay's charges as "a pretext to destroy an ardent patriot of the kind necessary in a time of revolution."[52]

Jean-Baptiste-Robert Lindet, in an opinion as lengthy as Robespierre's, adopted a very different tone. "Marat has served his country," he insisted; "he has served humanity; he has declared himself the friend of the people and the enemy of tyrants; he has disdained and rejected the favors of fortune; he has braved dangers; he has imperiled his liberty and his life to combat despotism and proclaim the rights of man. He has been constant in sustaining the same identity before and since the revolution." He continued with a full-throated defense of "the most ardent investigator of the crimes of traitors, counterrevolutionaries, and the enemies of liberty . . . , a representative of the people who has served his homeland, combatted despotism, and unmasked traitors." Marat's censure may sometimes have been unjust, Lindet acknowledged. "But is it in a time of revolution, in the unhappy times in which we find ourselves, amid the perils surrounding us, that one must examine coolly the ideas of a patriotic writer? Must we prohibit the impulses of liberty . . . ? Marat has wanted the Republic. . . . His crime thus consists only in the violence of his denunciations, in the impetuousness of his character, in the hate he has shown against traitors and the enemies of the homeland." How, he demanded, would posterity judge this vote when it "reads that surrounded by perils, pressed by enemies within and without, the National Convention has spent several sessions attacking the national representation and indicting one of its members instead of persecuting conspirators and counterrevolutionaries?"[53]

Finally, Dubois-Crancé's lengthy denunciation of the Girondins had a more direct and immediate answer to this question. Protesting their fabrication of a sect of Maratists to frighten the departments and discredit the Mountain, he declared it the height of absurdity to condemn Marat as a counterrevolutionary. "Marat will be absolved, declared innocent," he predicted, "and the people will bring him back to this hall in triumph." Seizing on Dubois-Crancé's justification of his vote, the Jacobin Club rapidly circulated it as a separate pamphlet.[54] Its prediction soon turned true.

BEFORE THE REVOLUTIONARY TRIBUNAL

At the session of the Jacobin Club on the evening of 12 April, the day Marat disappeared into hiding, a member had reported that The People's Friend had accused his enemies of planning to send him to the Abbaye as a way of inciting a popular uprising in Paris. Robespierre, returning from the Convention to praise Marat for the force, precision, and moderation of a speech that had "painted the crimes of our enemies in colors fit to bring a blush to the cheeks of any man susceptible to shame," elaborated on this same theme. The enemy faction had intended Marat's imprisonment to provoke a popular movement that would serve as a pretext for the repression of liberty in the capital while further blackening its reputation in the provinces, he charged. It had already recruited agents to incite such an uprising. He called for members of the club and its audience to fan out among the sections to expose these maneuvers, while the society prepared for an address calling for calm in response to them.[55]

Marat himself went further in this vein in his journal by claiming that the popular movement the Girondins wanted to incite was intended, in its effort to free him, to throw open the doors of the Abbaye to allow the escape of all the enemies of the Revolution imprisoned there. But he also offered a more intimate explanation for his refusal to pass through the prison's gates. "After two months, attacked by an inflammatory illness that demands care and disposes me to violence, I didn't want to expose myself in a dark place, amid dirt and vermin, to sad reflections on the lot of virtue in this world, to the emotions of indignation that arise in a generous soul at the sight of tyranny, to the exaggeration of character that is their necessary effect, and to the ills that can be the consequence of saintly conduct. I declare, in contempt of all the decrees of accusation in the world, that I will always regard myself as an innocent victim of the attacks of my dastardly enemies."[56] The illness that served as sign and symbol of his victimization over many years was becoming graver.

Ailing, the fugitive remained in hiding for eleven days, evading concerted efforts to discover him by a chain of command ranging from the Convention to the Committee of Public Safety, the minister of justice, the mayor of Paris, and the officers of his Marseille (formerly Théâtre-Français) section. A search party from the section dispatched to his residence at 4:00 a.m. the night of his disappearance returned empty-handed. Raiding his apartment in a second search three days later, officers of the section placed seals on his room after receiving assurance from Simonne Evrard that he had not returned home since 12 April. In the meantime, police charged to unearth him throughout Paris met with no success. The minister of justice was compelled to report these failures in a letter to the Convention dated 21 April and presented two days later. In doing so, he acknowledged that he had refused advice to arrest the hawkers of Marat's journal, on the grounds that such action would constitute an illegal infringement on the liberty of the press. Efforts to trace how copy for the journal was transmitted from editor to printer had proved fruitless.[57]

In fact, the *Publiciste de la République française* continued to appear almost daily during this period, its publication interrupted only on 13 and 15 April. Marat used it to rehearse the assembly's debates and contest the charges of 12–13 April against him and to escalate his indictment of his enemies. On 14 April, he enumerated a list of twenty-four leading conspirators (and alleged the existence of fifty unnamed others) among the *hommes d'Etat*. The Paris Commune and the sections followed suit the next day by denouncing to the Convention as traitors to their constituents a largely overlapping list of twenty-two deputies. On 18 April, publishing a letter to the Convention that the president had refused to read to the assembly, he rejected charges of disobedience to the law on the ground that "traitors and conspirators can never represent the people or decide on its rights and interests." Let the damnable *hommes d'Etat* be annihilated, he urged; once purged, the Convention could assure liberty and save the homeland until the traitors were replaced.

The following day, responding to his request, the Jacobin Club ordered a version of this letter printed and circulated as a poster. It had already published in its journal and sent to the Commune, on 15 April, a statement of "Marat's Profession of Faith" recycled from an earlier issue of his journal. On 17 April, it welcomed news that the Quinze-Vingts section had taken a vow to defend The People's Friend to the death. Two days later, it adopted a lengthy address to the nation in defense of "this austere philosopher shaped by misfortune and meditation, who joins to a soul on fire a great wisdom and a profound knowledge of the human heart that allows him to penetrate the traitors on their triumphant chariot at the moment the stupid vulgar idolizes them."[58]

The Jacobins were not alone in expressing their support. On 16 April, the Cordeliers responded enthusiastically to an invitation to endorse a circular from Marat's home section calling for his release. The crowd in the galleries swore vengeance against anyone laying sacrilegious hands upon him. "They've said he called for two hundred thousand heads," declared the club's president. "What Jacobin or Cordelier doesn't demand TWO MILLION? For there are more than two million counterrevolutionaries and their blood must flow." A week later, police spies were reporting that many sections had proclaimed The People's Friend under their protection, that the majority of the sections and citizens were vocal in his favor, that they were unlikely to tolerate any harm to his person or property. Some were described as awaiting a trial that would turn into an indictment of his accusers.[59]

Meanwhile, Marat elaborated in his journal on the theme of the righteousness of resistance to oppression through disobedience to the law. The formulation of the general will, he insisted, was achieved only by mature deliberation and peaceful, wise, and profound discussion. It could not be reached by "vile criminals, vicious conspirators and traitors to the homeland who have shamefully trafficked the interests and rights of the people with the enemies of the Republic," men who had voted for an appeal to the people to save the tyrant and ignite the torches of civil war, men who had conspired with the treacherous Dumouriez. Such individuals could not be considered representatives of the nation, nor could their decrees have the stamp of law. How could they be, when these edicts were contrived by force and deceit, without prior discussion, amid tumultuous passions and the commotion of insults and outrages? "Who doesn't know that the national senate most often offers the hideous spectacle of a gladiatorial arena, a smoke den, a dive where furious drunks abandon themselves to all the excesses of ferocity and madness . . . ? How then can the results of their altercations, their deadly passions, and perhaps their plots be laws . . . ? Judge whether I can regard as obligatory these acts of oppression and tyranny!" Liberty was done for, and the frontiers surrendered to the enemy, he wrote, "unless the whole people rises up to annihilate this execrable faction, to destroy this infernal horde under the blade of justice." All that was left for the patriots remaining in the Convention was to press the entire nation to "wipe out finally the criminal hordes of its base enemies, its unfaithful agents, its traitorous and conspiratorial mandataries."[60]

By 20 April, the *Publiciste de la République française* was launching a full-scale attack on the Convention for devoting extensive discussion that week to the draft constitution presented to the assembly by Condorcet in February. While Robespierre was campaigning for an opportunity to offer a more radical version of a declaration of rights, Marat repudiated the entire enterprise of constitution-making. In his analysis, the discussion was being pushed by the *hommes d'Etat* to advance their misguided constitutional project while so many patriotic deputies were away on mission; it was a gambit to divert public attention from their machinations. They were working to overthrow the state, destroy liberty, and reestablish despotism at the very moment they were claiming the high ground as the most fervent friends of law and order. If not perfidious and disastrous, he cried, their scheme was nonetheless ridiculous and ill-fated. "What! When the earth is being shaken by earthquakes, is it the moment one must work to lay the foundations of the temple of liberty? Who doesn't see, amid disorders, troubles, and convulsions that rack the state and tear it apart, that we need emergency laws, revolutionary measures to repress discontents, terrify internal enemies, punish evildoers, crush the corrupt, the speculators, the traitors, the conspirators?"[61]

In opposition to a constitution, Marat offered a program for revolutionary mobilization that amounted to a blueprint for the Terror. It required regulations to assure subsistence; measures to accelerate military recruitment, rearmament, and reorganization; a purge of suspect officers; a declaration of *la patrie en danger*; the entire nation galvanized. An army of sans-culottes, one million two hundred thousand strong, had to be mobilized under patriotic leaders to stand at the ready, assure subsistence, support unfortunate families of the defenders of liberty, get weapons forged, and annihilate internal and external enemies once and for all. "Only after crushing all the enemies of the homeland, after achieving the triumph of liberty, after assuring abundance, will it be permissible to work to give the government fixed bases and lay down the durable foundations of the Constitution." Evildoers would continuously foment new troubles, he warned, the henchmen of the old regime would relentlessly jam the wheels of the new, the political machine would seize up, and new laws, no matter how skillfully contrived, would serve only to compromise the authority of the legislature and strip it of all respect.[62]

In contrast to his own prescriptions, Marat proclaimed, the measures taken by the Convention to save France from disorder, anarchy, and civil war were more like those of escapees from the madhouse. But there was more than a touch of madness in the savagery of his own call for revolutionary laws he viewed as necessary to support a Committee of Public Safety composed of "the most zealous patriots of the Mountain." The first was to force all former nobles, magistrates, financiers, priests, and monks to wear the dress of their abolished orders in public, subject to the penalty of being declared outlaws if they failed to do so, a kind of collective expiation reminiscent of the exemplary punishments of the Old Regime. In addition, they were to be declared ineligible for all public employment, banned from participation in any popular assembly on pain of death, and prohibited from gathering together for any purpose in groups of more than three. A second such law was to order the execution of any public functionary scheming against the homeland. A third was to decree removal of the ear of any civil servant guilty of embezzlement and of both thumbs of any military person accused of a variety of infractions.[63]

As for the deputies in the Convention, the fugitive had another procedure in mind for them: a mandatory roll-call vote on his repeated demand that a price be put on the heads of the treasonous Capets in exile. This, he maintained, would be the ultimate test for monarchism: "the sole means left for patriotic deputies to know the true sentiments of the *hommes d'Etat*, and . . . for the *hommes d'Etat* to show their true dispositions." The enemy faction would resist such a vote, he was sure. They were living in fear that he would return to the assembly to force it upon them. "It's a cruel strait for them to pass through, I know. For us, it's the filter purging all the traitors that contaminate the Convention."[64]

Though Marat anticipated a less cruel strait for himself in appearing before the Revolutionary Tribunal, it was 24 April before he did so. In a tug-of-war with the Convention, he refused to leave his hiding place until a formal decree of accusation had been issued against him, while his enemies in the assembly refused to do this until he had presented himself before the court. On 16 April, when Bentabole called for the Committee on Legislation to formulate the accusation, Delaunay countered that no such action would be taken until the fugitive was under arrest. The younger Robespierre, in turn, charged the committee with a delaying tactic to deprive the people of an ardent defender in the certain knowledge that the Revolutionary Tribunal would quickly dismiss the charges against him. A similar standoff occurred on 18 April, when the deputies declined to hear a letter from Marat and a call was made to declare him an outlaw. Finally, pleading respect for the rule of law, Vergniaud secured a decision that the act of accusation be submitted for a vote the following day. Presented by Delaunay on 20 April, it was immediately adopted.[65]

Consistent with Delaunay's initial report, the act of accusation identified three broad offenses, each citing references to Marat's journal. For the first charge, provoking "pillage and murder," it attested to evidence in thirty issues, notably that of 25 February, which it accused of inciting the grocery riots that same day. It cited another eight issues in support of the second charge, advocating "a power in violation of the sovereignty of the people" to replace the Convention with an authority he designated variously as a leader, a tribune, a dictator, or a triumvirate. It pointed to an additional fifteen issues in laying out the third charge, "denigration and dissolution of the Convention" through attacks on a purported criminal faction within the assembly denounced as *hommes d'Etat*, royalists, conspirators, enemies of the homeland, and counterrevolutionaries, a group composed of "base and profoundly villainous men, atrocious men striving to ignite civil war, a faction foreign to the homeland, the enemy of all equality and liberty . . . , shameless men slaking their criminal passions, gorging on the remains of the people and tyrannizing the nation in the name of the law."[66]

At Bentabole's demand, the Convention ordered the indictment submitted to the Revolutionary Tribunal without delay, together with the accompanying evidence. Six copies were to be distributed to each deputy.[67]

TRIUMPH IN COURT

Notified that the act of accusation had at last reached the Revolutionary Tribunal, Marat announced on 23 April his readiness to appear before the court. "People! Your incorruptible defender will present himself to the revolutionary tribunal tomorrow," he promised. "He has only ever wished for your happiness and innocence to triumph. Your enemies will be confounded. He will emerge from this fight more worthy of you and will console himself for this new tribulation with hope for the advantages to be gained by the cause of liberty, the cause of the homeland." His hiding place, "in the Cordelier Club, under the protection of the Marseille section," had in any case been discovered by the police. He turned himself in at the Conciergerie prison that evening, accompanied by several fellow deputies of the Mountain and some military officers. In a preliminary hearing in which he repudiated the charges against him as based on "mutilated, truncated, and falsified passages of my writings," he demanded that the original texts be presented as evidence the following day and denied the need for any counsel beyond "the reading of my writings and public opinion." He then passed the night secure in the company of a police official. A later report to his readers was more dramatic in its description of efforts to protect him. "Scarcely had I entered the prison before several municipal officials and administrators appeared to guarantee my safety. They passed the night with me in a room they had had prepared for me. A good bed had been brought in and a supper prepared elsewhere was served. They pushed their precautions to the point of escorting the dishes themselves and having the carafes of water well sealed."[68]

By early morning, the hall of the Revolutionary Tribunal was packed with representatives from the sections and popular societies, their number swollen by a mass of sans-culottes spilling through the entire Palais de

Justice into the surrounding streets.[69] Marat recalled for his readers that the size of the "immense crowd of sans-culottes ready to avenge potential outrages to their faithful defender" was already a triumph for him, "the best response I could make to my dastardly slanderers." From the moment he entered the hall escorted by supporters to great applause, and before any formality could be initiated by the officials of the court, he turned the event into The Marat Show. He struck one observer as a bizarre figure. "His head was tied-up with a white handkerchief, knotted in the back. His chest was exposed, his gait was proud, and he might have appeared imposing if his short stature, wide chest, and delicate body had afforded him a little dignity."[70] Standing high on the step of the chair set out for the accused, he addressed his audience. "Citizens, this is not a culprit appearing before you, it's The People's Friend, the apostle and martyr of liberty," he cried, deriding the factious schemers who had brought the indictment against him and perhaps thanking them (as he claimed later) for this opportunity to "broadcast his innocence and cover them with opprobrium." Only then was he ready to acknowledge his formal identification before the tribunal and hear the act of accusation. According to Gorsas, whose attention to the details of the proceedings was doubtless sharpened in proportion to his hostility to Marat, the tone was set by the public prosecutor, the soon-to-be-notorious Fouquier-Tinville. More generously disposed toward an accused than he later became, Fouquier began by identifying this one as "a celebrated patriot who has always called himself the friend of the people and whom the people has always considered its friend and defender."[71]

The act of accusation once heard, Marat was asked by the prosecutor to confirm his authorship of the writings identified in the indictment. He demanded that the passages be read aloud in their entirety before doing so. By his account, Fouquier tipped his hand by supplementing his reading of the texts with "correct, judicious and salient observations regarding the difference between my completely conditional assertions and the positive ones contained in the act of accusation," in effect pointing out "the cunning and perfidy with which the passages denounced . . . had been truncated, mutilated, amplified and altered to transform simple hypothetical observations into positive advocacy, making the freedom of the philosopher a crime on my part." When efforts to drown out this reading of the evidence provoked noisy objections from the crowd, it was the accused who appealed for silence. "Citizens, my cause is yours, the cause of liberty," he reported saying. "I call on you to maintain the most perfect calm to avoid giving the enemies of the homeland persecuting me the pretext of slandering you, by accusing you of influencing the tribunal."[72]

From the very beginning, the interrogation of witnesses veered into an unexpected investigation that took on a life of its own. It concerned a recent squib in the Brissotin *Patriote français* to the effect that an English youth recently arrived in Paris had killed himself in despair upon discovering the loss of republican liberty there. "I came to France to enjoy liberty," read the note the victim had reportedly left for "a famous foreigner," "but Marat has assassinated it. Anarchy is even more cruel than despotism. I cannot resist the sad spectacle of the triumph of imbecility and inhumanity over talent and virtue." In response to a witness's report that the young man had been alarmed that Marat had called for all foreigners to be massacred, especially the English, The People's Friend dismissed this as an atrocious slander spread by the *hommes d'Etat* to make him appear odious in advance of the trial.

The witnesses soon revealed, however, that the troubled young man was still alive and nursing his wounds in the Paris residence of the "famous foreigner," none other than Tom Paine. This led to an inquisition into the character of the guests and conversations *chez* Paine, and to summonses to the editor of the *Patriote français*, Girey-Dupré, to Paine himself, and to Brissot, to testify regarding the way the suicide note had found its way to the press. Under questioning of the witnesses orchestrated by Marat, Girey-Dupré divulged that the report of the suicide had been handed to him by Brissot for publication. Paine, whom Marat charged with pretending not to understand French (the court appointed two translators for him), also admitted that he had received the death note from the would-be suicide and had shown it to Brissot before destroying it. As for Brissot, the call that he appear before the tribunal was set aside by the Convention.

Finally, the purported victim was summoned, only to tell the court that he had decided to end his life after reading not Marat but Gorsas (Marat's Girondist attacker) to whose journal Paine subscribed. He had feared for his American host's life, he said, in learning from that journal that Marat was preaching the massacre of all the deputies who had supported the appeal to the people during the trial of Louis XVI, Paine among them. The explosion of applause at this testimony to the Gorsas connection had to be hushed by Marat who appealed to the audience to remain silent lest it "harm the triumph of liberty." It was his conviction that this entire scheme had been contrived by Brissot and his allies to prejudice the court proceedings against him. Paine apparently believed the opposite. "We can see that in the debates brought up by this trial, no attention was paid to the facts stated in the indictment, no witness testified about them, and . . . [the whole object of the procedure] . . . was to compromise me and to provide Marat with the means to denounce me," he recalled. "During all the debates, Marat did not act like a defendant, but as though he was conducting the whole trial. For example, while the President questioned the witnesses . . . , [he bade?] them leave the chamber or enter; Marat spoke whenever he pleased, calling the galleries to order and forbidding them to applaud, as though he had been . . . [charged with] policing the hearing."[73]

Eventually the court's attention turned to the accusation at hand. Asked whether he had observations regarding the indictment or the depositions of the witnesses, Marat launched into a celebration of his political conduct, attesting to his publication in England, before the French Revolution, of "a work that contributed not a little to preparing it"; to his pamphlets reclaiming the rights of man at the time of the calling of the Estates General; to his continuing efforts, against all attempts to silence him, to unmask the traitors hiding behind the mask of popularity, shame the tyrant, and pursue him to his death. This affirmation of his commitment to defend the liberty and happiness of the entire human species was punctuated, almost as a matter of form, by questions on the part of the tribunal's president relating to the three charges in the indictment. Marat's responses, as he relayed them to the readers of his journal, could scarcely have been more disingenuous.[74]

Had he ever preached murder and pillage? This, The People's Friend replied, was "an absurd imputation by the infamous faction of *hommes d'Etat* . . . , the exercise of a revolting tyranny over thought in an effort to stifle even the desire to save the homeland, or rather a proof of stupidity."

Had he ever intended to propose the establishment of a head of state? This charge, the accused responded, "cannot be made seriously against me, the most mortal enemy of tyrants, despots, kings, and princes, the most ardent rebel against all arbitrary authority, the ceaseless avenger of the sovereignty of the people since the beginning of the revolution, insisting endlessly on the limits of powers and its agents."

Had he ever intended to provoke the degradation and dissolution of the Convention? "What slanderer could escape the cruel consequences of public indignation if he attacked a legislature showing itself worthy of the confidence and respects of the people?" he retorted. "Who more than I has lamented the scandalous scenes that have so often exploded in the midst of the Convention? Who more than I has strived to recall its members to the dignity of their functions."[75]

These protestations became a prelude to the lengthy rebuttal of the act of accusation Marat now offered. He denounced the efforts of the *hommes d'Etat* to discredit Paris and its patriotic municipal institutions and representatives in general, and to paint himself as a plotter, anarchist, and drinker of blood reaching for supreme power. He dismissed a decision reached by a minority of the assembly in a vote vitiated by procedural violations during a raucous session, initiated by a faction excoriated by patriotic deputies, and derided by the public in the galleries. Not only was the indictment baseless, a tissue of lies and fabrications, he charged, but it was illegal. Why? Because, by violating legal procedures proper to an accusation, the Convention had turned itself into a criminal court and his indictment into a conviction (a reworking of a charge directed at the assembly earlier by the defenders of Louis XVI). And because, more fundamentally, the opinions at issue had been expressed in the Convention before they had been published in his journal. They were therefore protected by the provision of the constitution of 1791 stipulating that "representatives of the nation are inviolable; they cannot be investigated, accused or judged at any time for what they have said, written or done in the exercise of their functions as representatives."

Bizarrely, having called countless times for a purge of the representative body, Marat thus invoked the principle of the inviolability of its members in his own defense. Without this essential right, he demanded, how could a small number of farsighted and determined patriots frustrate the plots of a numerous faction of conspirators? Once successful in punishing him, he warned, the *hommes d'Etat* could go on to destroy Robespierre, Danton, Collot d'Herbois, Panis, Lindet, Camille Desmoulins, David, Audouin, Leignelot, Meaulle, Dupuis, Javogues, Granet, and other courageous deputies, while constraining the rest by terror and usurping sovereignty.[76] With this honor roll of patriots, it appeared, inviolability could apply only to the virtuous.

The dénouement, when it came, was swift. Upon a summary from the prosecutor and brief instructions from the president of the Revolutionary Tribunal, the ten jurors withdrew to deliberate. They returned with a unanimous verdict within forty-five minutes. "I cannot imagine criminal and counterrevolutionary intentions on the part of the intrepid defender of the rights of the people," stated the leading juror. "It's difficult to contain one's just indignation when one sees one's country everywhere betrayed. I have found nothing in Marat's writings that appear to prove the offenses he is accused of." At the resulting judgment of *Not Guilty*, applause rocked the hall, resounding throughout the building and into the streets beyond. Crowned with oakleaves, Marat was hoisted to the shoulders of members of the crowd and marched in triumph through the streets back to the Convention. Contemporary representations of the march ranged from joyfully folkloric to bitterly satirical. The celebratory version of the scene rendered a year later by the painter Louis-Léopold Boilly showed Marat acclaimed by the crowd outside the Palais de Justice upon his acquittal.

FIGURE 26.1. Anonymous print, "Triomphe de Marat," 1793. Library of Congress, https://www.loc.gov/item/91480926/.

By Marat's account in the *Publiciste de la République française*, two hundred thousand people lined the route of his return from the Palais de Justice to the Convention shouting, "Long Live the Republic, Liberty, and Marat!" He claimed the procession itself was formed of more than one hundred thousand citizens, "almost all the sans-culottes of Paris." Other observers were skeptical of that number: Gorsas's estimate was closer to seven or eight hundred, a crowd he described as "looters and brigands."[77] Marat, in rejoinder, emphasized the peaceful orderliness of the throng that bore him back to the Manège. "Not a handkerchief was lost, not a punch thrown. But this was the good people so long slandered by the libelers paid by Roland and the *hommes d'Etat*, this good people that the Dulaures, the Gorsases, the Girey-Duprés, the Brissots, the Condorcets have incessantly depicted as a horde of brigands in retaliation for its clear-sightedness and for demanding the punishment of the traitors and plotters."[78]

The Convention had been discussing articles of a proposed constitution shortly before its business was disrupted by word that a crowd was approaching. "It's Marat," one deputy cried, eliciting calls from others to end the session immediately. When this proposal was defeated, and the assembly returned briefly to its agenda, some members thought it wise to

FIGURE 26.2. Lesueur Brothers, "Le Triomphe de Marat," 1793. Musée Carnavalet, Paris. Josse/Bridgeman Images.

make themselves scarce. The procession, when it appeared, was led in a moment of glory by one Durocher, a citizen who had volunteered for military service as a sapper. Igniting explosions of applause from the Mountain and in the galleries, he announced that the crowd was returning "the brave Marat" to the assembly. "Marat has always been the friend of the people," he declaimed, "and the people will always be for Marat. . . . If Marat's head falls, a sapper's will fall with it." A motion to allow the throng

FIGURE 26.3. Louis-Léopold Boilly, *Le Triomphe de Marat*, 1794. Palais des Beaux Arts, Lille/Ministry of Culture (France)/Bridgeman Images. Wikimedia Commons.

to file through the hall was approved, though not before Jacques Roux had expressed his regret that a representative of the people had been sent "on such frivolous pretexts before a tribunal he had contributed to creating." Flooding the floor and spilling over the benches, the mass of marchers shouted, "Long Live the Republic, Long Live the Nation, Long Live Marat, Long Live the People's Friend!" The hall rang with acclamation.

The din redoubled as Marat himself entered, escorted by citizens and representatives of the Commune. Embraced by deputies of the Mountain, he was swept to the tribune by the host surrounding him. It took a long time for him to impose enough silence to speak. "Legislators of the French people," he exulted, "these resounding expressions of civic spirit you have just seen among you have restored to the people one of its representatives whose rights have been violated in my person. I offer you at this moment a citizen who was accused and has now been completely vindicated. He offers you a pure heart. He will continue to defend, with all the energy of which he is capable, the rights of man, liberty, the rights of the people." His words incited renewed booms of applause; hats were waved, liberty bonnets thrown into the air. Resisting demands to say more, he stepped down from the tribune and left the hall. The Girondin Lasource, presiding, had neatly sidestepped a call to respond to the unwelcome returnee.

It remained for Danton to calm the continuing clamor and ease the departure of the crowd by celebrating the action of the people of Paris in turning into a festival the day an accused deputy had been restored to the assembly. The people, he preached, had shown its respect for the Convention and its satisfaction that the national representation had remained intact; it could now leave the assembly to its business. This was a shrewd move to clear the hall, perhaps, but scarcely one offering realistic hope for what was to come.[79]

True to form, The People's Friend was more vociferous when he returned to the Jacobin Club three days later. Rapturously received, with lavish ceremony, he set aside the civic crowns offered him and lost no time in calling for vengeance on his accusers. "They're humiliated, but they're not crushed yet," he warned. "Let's not concern ourselves with crowns. Let's beware of enthusiasm, leave all this childishness aside, and think only of crushing our enemies." Before long, he was denouncing corrupt ministers and calling for a list of their employees (and of potential patriotic replacements for them) to be drawn up for his review. A motion offered by Robespierre deflected this grasp for personal power by making the proposed purge the responsibility of the Committee of Public Safety.[80]

As for the Girondins, the stakes in Marat's triumph were no better described for them than by his former intellectual ally and now bitterly implacable enemy, Brissot, a few weeks later. Carried back to the very Convention he had so grievously abused, Brissot told his constituents, Marat reappeared as a conqueror. "And Danton declared a fine day this day of mourning for virtue and liberty . . . ! And this assembly remained mute in consternation, closing its eyes to the lies, to the violation of the law, to the outrage inflicted upon the national representation. Now, I ask every man of good faith, where then is now the supreme power? Is it in the Convention or in the revolutionary tribunal? Is it in the tribunal or in Marat? Is it in Marat or in the faction protecting him? Oh shame! Oh grief! Marat above the Convention! What enemy of France is not overwhelmed by this scandalous triumph? What republican has not been wounded to the soul, despairing of liberty?"[81]

TWENTY-SEVEN

PURGE

The Marat Moment electrified the Paris sections and popular societies and turbocharged the politics of the capital. It opened the period of Marat's greatest influence. The efforts of the *hommes d'Etat* to mislead the nation had succeeded only momentarily, The People's Friend exulted on 30 April. "But the clouds are dissipated, the veil is torn or about to be. . . . The moment of justice is approaching; it will be stupendous, you can be sure."[1] In the days and weeks that followed his triumphal return to the assembly, the conflict between the Girondins and the Montagnards metastasized throughout the city, intensified by the more radical interventions of the Commune and the sections.

The Convention had already received, on 15 April, a delegation from the Commune and a majority of the sections, led by the mayor. Insisting on the right of the Republic to purify its representation, the deputation declared revocability the essence of representation and the safeguard of the people. Its petition accused twenty-two Girondins of violating the trust of their constituents and demanded that its list of these criminal deputies be circulated to the departments to force their expulsion from the Convention. While doubtless already in preparation before Marat's indictment two days earlier (and preempted by his own denunciation of twenty-four Girondin deputies the previous day), this petition immediately took on significance in relation to it. When the Girondins' effort to purge him failed, their own elimination from the assembly became an obvious response.

The 15 April petition was cautious in several respects. Invoking the authority of a "portion of the public opinion of the Commune," it emphasized that Parisians were neither claiming exclusive exercise of sovereignty nor demanding "the terrifying dissolution of the Convention . . . , a truly anarchic idea imagined by traitors." It called only for the circulation to all departments of the "unanimous, considered and constant sentiments of the sections composing the Commune of Paris." But its talk of vengeance created panic among Girondins sensing the radical impulses that lay behind it. For Buzot, this was "no longer a question of a few individuals but of the Convention itself, attacked in its majority." For Gensonné, it was an "attack on liberty of opinion in the national representation," an "insurrection against the sovereignty of the people under the empty pretext that liberty is being threatened." A referendum like this was not what the Montagnards wanted. After the petitioners had been required to sign the document individually (as well as the mayor, though he had been reluctant to do so), Boyer-Fonfrède immediately urged that copies be circulated to the primary assemblies for a vote. The proposal, immediately opposed by the Montagnards as a prescription for civil war, was rendered even more alarming a day later. Lasource radically raised the stakes of this appeal to the people by moving that each primary assembly be required to render judgment on the entire body of the nation's representatives.[2]

Frustrated by the Convention's response on 15 April, the Commune decided the same day to submit another petition clarifying that its intention was to demand punishment of traitorous individuals, not the convocation of the primary assemblies. Keeping up the pressure, it required each Paris section to open registers for citizens to sign their adherence to the original petition, though ineffective execution of this plan eventually yielded disappointing results. On 18 April, at the instigation of its prosecutor Chaumette, invoking the oath taken by the revolutionary Commune of 10 August 1792, it declared itself once more in a state of insurrection. It thereupon proclaimed that it would take under its protection any presidents and secretaries of sections and popular societies, and indeed any individual citizens, menaced for their opinions. Twelve thousand copies of the petition were ordered for circulation in the departments. (The Jacobin Club received ten thousand copies the following day for that purpose and printed the text in its journal on 22 April.)[3]

These reactions provoked a furious debate in the Convention on 20 April when they were met by Gensonné's frantic proposal that sectional and communal assemblies throughout the Republic be placed in permanent session and all the communes of the Republic be declared in a state of revolution, ready to march on Paris if necessary to save the Convention from attack. Only after Vergniaud's devastating analysis of the risk of an action that would bring the country to civil war did the assembly retreat from the brink. It settled for censure of the 15 April petition as libelous of the twenty-two members denounced and the circulation of this judgment to all the departments.[4]

A striking feature of the 15 April petition targeting the twenty-two leading Girondins was that it had been adopted by a majority of thirty-five of the forty-eight Paris sections. The fact that the remaining thirteen sections had withheld support was indicative of considerable disagreement among activists in the capital. In the weeks that followed, tensions among and within the sections became acute. "Moderates" supporting the Girondins and "patriots" siding with the Montagnards battled for control of their general assemblies and their revolutionary committees. Fights and takeovers, partisan reverses, purges, contested elections, riots, arrests by revolutionary committees, class conflicts, and incursions of one section upon another became common.[5] Behind these struggles, and sharpening them, there loomed the presence of a newly reinvigorated group of revolutionary activists meeting in the Evêché, the former bishop's palace. Veterans of the abortive uprising of 10 March, perhaps, this group may well have been the initial source of the 15 April petition. It included the most radical of the so-called Enragés.

Aggravating these conflicts and exacerbating the tensions between Girondins and Montagnards, two issues continued to churn Parisian politics during this period. One was growing popular clamor for controls on grain prices, driven by escalating shortages and associated costs of subsistence. The other, closely connected, was conflict over the modes and burdens of military recruitment as citizens pressured to march against rebels in the Vendée demanded assurance that their families would not starve in their absence. On 18 April, while Marat was still in hiding, a deputation from the Paris department had appeared before the Convention to invoke "the general will of the poor class, the most numerous class, the most useful class, the class that is everything in a Republic, the one for which the legislature has done nothing while it has done everything." Dismissing the interests of commerce ("the useful and necessary relationship of every sociable being with his like . . . , no longer commerce when it becomes dangerous") and the principle of property (that "cannot be the right to starve the citizenry"), it declared the fruits of the earth "like air, belonging to all men." To end hoarding and speculation, it called for imposition of a maximum on the price of grain throughout the country, enforcement of a requirement that farmers bring their grain to market, and elimination of intermediaries between farmers and consumers other than millers and bakers. Strongly contested by Vergniaud and Buzot as ill-informed and potentially ruinous of commerce in grain, the petition was referred to the committees of agriculture and commerce for more expert review.[6]

The committees' joint report, submitted to the assembly on 25 April, made clear that their discussions had been long and intense. Opinions had differed; several were presented to the deputies for discussion. One, favored by the Paris departmental administration, laid out regulations for the draconian imposition of a maximum; another offered plans for grain to be held in public granaries and distributed according to a system of rationing; a third proposed alternative mechanisms to ensure that all grain be brought to market without the need for fixed prices. Other projects, and lengthy speeches, proliferated in the following days. In Marat's analysis, the *hommes d'Etat* were just spinning their wheels with one "long and fastidious dissertation" after another.

By 28 April, The People's Friend had had enough of this discussion. "You're passing your time listening to encyclopedists talk about subsistence, and we'll die of hunger in the midst of abundance," he castigated the deputies. He wanted more direct popular action of a kind that would later mark the Terror. "It's the embezzlement of hoarders that we must remedy; we need revolutionary laws. Force the merchants to bring grain to market; let the people, the sans-culottes, led by municipal officers, get the granaries open and provision the markets themselves. Abundance will soon revive in the Republic." To a racket from the galleries supporting this sentiment, the assembly moved promptly to postpone further discussion of the issue. When it was resumed two days later, the debate ended in a near-riot, spreading from the galleries throughout the hall. Galleries were forcibly emptied. In this context, Marat's call for a price on the head of the fugitive Capets went nowhere. It was to be repeated frequently over the coming weeks.[7]

Finally, on 2 May, under the watchful eyes of a deputation of women from Versailles demanding a fixed price on bread as the wives of volunteers who had already left for the front, and in the face of continued warnings from the Girondins that doing so would lead to economic disaster, the Convention decided in principle to institute a maximum on grain that would vary according to conditions in each department and decrease each month by 10 percent as more grain was forcibly brought to market. The definitive decree establishing the necessary mechanisms of control was adopted two days later. An additional proposal to forbid the wasteful use of flour for powdering hair was not taken up.[8]

Marat, for his part, had already moved on. No sooner was the maximum decreed than he was urging the passage of a decree (he claimed to have clawed it out of committee) that provided aid to needy families of men fighting at the front. "The nation has taken the property of the church . . . ; this property is the patrimony of the poor and it's not for you to deprive unfortunates of it," he maintained, expressing his long-held sentiment. Reservations about the cost of such aid were swept away by Vergniaud's insistence that it could be paid for by a war tax if necessary.[9]

In these conflicts, the interrelationship of the issues of subsistence and recruitment had been abundantly made clear. On 1 May, Chaumette had announced that the Commune was recruiting twelve thousand Parisians to defeat the rebels in the Vendée, hopefully within two days. Marat was quick to offer a motion celebrating the citizens of the capital for their civic commitment. The Parisians themselves were less ecstatic. Deputations from two of the sections quickly demanded that the regular troops stationed in the city be sent to the front in advance of any volunteers; at Marat's urging, their demand was sent to the Committee of Public Safety with a charge to report on the means of achieving this. That these paid troops had to include the guard of the Convention itself (though Marat had argued against this) was emphasized, in turn, by a delegation of the inhabitants of the faubourg Saint-Antoine claiming to speak for an immense crowd of nine thousand fellow citizens now encircling the Convention. The delegation's spokesman also made clear that imposition of a maximum on the necessities of life, long promised but never delivered, was now considered a condition of departure for the front. "The maximum, the termination of leases, and a war tax on the rich": these once decreed, he stipulated, the volunteers would leave, "*but not before.*" Failing that, the nine thousand men outside the doors stood ready to declare themselves in a state of insurrection. The ultimatum outraged the deputies and provoked calls for the Convention to prepare to move to Tours or Bourges, away from the anarchy in the capital, or for the arrest and prosecution of those responsible for it. Before any action had been taken, however, a second deputation from the faubourg Saint-Antoine appeared to disavow the language of the first, a reversal reflective of the battles going on in and among the sections and popular societies. Danton once again played the peacemaker in the assembly to bring the session to an end.[10]

Agitation over recruitment in Paris was also fueled by the mode of selection adopted by the Commune under the authority granted it by the Convention's initial order in February for the conscription of three hundred thousand men. The Commune had identified office workers and other employees of notaries, attorneys, bankers, and merchants as primary targets for enrollment. The reaction was noisy. For several days, the targeted groups and their supporters marched in protest on the streets and the Champs-Elysées, demanding that conscription be decided by lot. Arrests followed. Sections and popular societies were aboil. The Convention was showered with petitions.[11]

While the Montagnards held firm in support of the Commune's regulations in the hope of keeping more of the patriotic sans-culottes at home, they saw their enemies inciting this agitation to achieve the opposite result. "The leaders of the *hommes d'Etat*, covered with opprobrium, have become the object of public execration," Marat contended. "No longer having for them any more than a small, misguided part of the nation and the detritus of the supporters of the old regime . . . , [they] can save themselves only by a counterrevolution. They're doing everything they can to provoke it." To this end, he claimed, the Girondins had opposed measures to assure subsistence and were subverting recruitment efforts. They had incited the petition of citizens of the faubourg Saint-Antoine with its threat of insurrection and were now fomenting protests in the streets.[12]

The reaction in the streets was indeed bitter. They resounded with shouts of *Marat to the guillotine, To the devil with Marat, F**k the Jacobins*. Marat reported similar imprecations against Danton, Robespierre, the Mountain, the Republic, along with exclamations of *Long Live d'Orléans*. Defending the Commune's policy at his own section, he was booed and heckled. By one account, he threatened in response to have anyone who dared interrupt him sent to the Revolutionary Tribunal. *Down, down with this anarchist!* came the angry retort. Pressed by the president of the section to leave the tribune, he replied with a stream of vituperation. Outraged, the audience literally kicked him out of the hall and he had to be rescued from further attack by the National Guard. His own version of this event portrayed him remaining firm and escorted by a group of zealous patriots until he found the guard outside the Cordelier Club to accompany him home with sword drawn. He blamed his energetic rescuers for preventing him from getting the mutinous counterrevolutionaries arrested. But the following day, he was burned in effigy by a crowd in the Place du Carrousel.[13]

Rattled, The People's Friend reacted to this clamor by demanding that neither the rich nor members of the Commune's targeted group be allowed to enroll for service against the Vendée rebels without proof of their patriotism. "We only need devoted patriots in the cause of the Republic," he ranted somewhat incoherently at the Jacobin Club on 5 May. "We have a great method to reduce the rich to the class of the sans-culottes: by leaving them nothing to cover their behinds. . . . We'll level taxes for the costs of the war and make the sans-culottes the true proprietors."[14]

Recruitment was still lagging in Paris on 8 May when the Convention received alarming news that the Vendée rebels were making new advances and might eventually threaten the capital. The Montagnard Louis Legendre shouted for the tocsin to be sounded to announce a state of emergency. "Yes, yes, the *hommes d'Etat* are opposed," Marat shouted in support. "We, we'll rise up and then the worse for them." In panic, the deputies continued to argue over methods of increasing recruitment as well as the imposition of a war tax on the rich to cover the costs of mobilization and support for the families left at risk by the departure of men for the front. The *hommes d'Etat*, Marat charged, were aiming to enroll the flower of the patriots, the most active and energetic members of the sections, leaving the city at the mercy of the counterrevolutionaries who would remain. His solution was to increase the number of the city's defenders by emptying the prisons of all patriots incarcerated for offenses against public order. In a variation on this idea, he later proposed successfully that all soldiers detained for indiscipline be freed and returned to service. His further motion for a prisoner swap with the Austrians to bring veterans back into the service of their homeland was referred to committee.

On 9 May, the Convention put an end to the divisive debate on recruitment by decreeing that each section would decide on its own method of selection. The decision did not prevent a deputation from the Panthéon-Français section on 13 May from demanding an advance payment, funded by a war tax on its richest members, before its volunteers would leave for the front. Transformed into a motion by Marat, this demand was approved the same day. Many more were to follow until the Convention adopted on 20 May the principle of a forced loan on the rich to be repaid in the property of émigrés.[15]

By that time, talk of an insurrection forcing a purge or dissolution of the Convention was becoming widespread in the capital. A document circulated by the Cordelier Club on 1 May had declared that "the source of all our ills is within the National Convention: the monsters that tear us apart sit among the men we have sent to save us. Spread the word, Sans-Culottes, the avenging blade is ready to annihilate them." At the sound of an alarm, it urged, the friends of liberty had to unite and rise up. "Let all suspect persons be arrested; may a single blow annihilate our enemies wherever and whoever they may be, and France is saved at last."

Two weeks later, on 12 May, the police spy Dutard was telling Garat, the minister of the interior, that "this moment is terrible and seems a lot like those preceding 2 September." His report may have been exaggerated: recently employed, Dutard doubtless had an interest in providing Garat with striking information; he was also conscious that he might be heard with a measure of skepticism. The following day, however, his fellow spy

Terrasson reported that the agitators were redoubling their fury, while delegates of the sections meeting at the Echêvé seemed determined to press the Convention to arrest suspects within it. (Barère would tell the Convention, about the same time, that this group was planning a purge of the assembly.) The public was still making up its mind, Terrasson thought, but it would take a while to build enough public support for such action, and one could still hope that it would put pressure on the Convention without resorting to insurrection.

Nonetheless, Dutard continued over the following days to supply the minister with evidence of threats of insurrection, along with often lengthy suggestions of how they might be confronted. On 14 May, he reported the existence of the Evêché committee (mistakenly attributing its creation to the Jacobin faction) and relayed plans for the surveillance committees of the sections to arrest any persons appearing suspect ("which is to say, half of Paris"). The touchstone for imprisonment, he noted, would be failure to cry *Long Live Marat!* before speaking. The next day, he brought to the minister's attention the decrees of the Commune on 13 May that a paid revolutionary army would be created in Paris to defend citizens endangered by the departure of patriots to the front, and that disarmament and arrest of suspects would be assigned to the mayor and municipal police by methods to be discussed in secret.[16]

At the same time, though, Dutard was conveying the sense that the political temperature in the city had fallen. On 15 May, he reported that the crisis had passed; on 16 May, that Marat and the Jacobins were mentioned in his section with contempt. Present at the meeting of the Jacobin Club on 17 May, however, he encountered a remarkable scene that left him "cruelly electrified." Before the session started, he reported, the galleries were awash in talk of betrayals in the Convention and the need for a new insurrection along the lines of 10 August 1792. He saw passions exacerbated even more after Desfieux read out a letter Vergniaud had written to a popular society in Bordeaux lamenting the persecution of Girondin deputies, the fury of their enemies, the torrent of proscriptions and threats of assassination against them "from Marat and the men whose mannequin he merely is." (The letter had been echoed by a petition from citizens of Bordeaux, read to the Convention on 14 May, deploring the treatment of the city's deputies and threatening to march on the capital to avenge attacks upon them.) Indignant when Thuriot counseled prudence in the exercise of the people's power to impose its justice, the galleries of the club roared in approval, clapping and stomping, as Legendre took a more belligerent tone in calling on the people to act when the Mountain was proving powerless to do so. "What we used to call the holy enthusiasm of liberty and patriotism has changed into a fury of an enraged people that it is no longer possible to constrain or discipline except by force," Dutard observed. Derisively he saw the *peuple Bête* acting out its frustrations at the failure of the Revolution to satisfy its ignorant hopes.[17]

Within the membership of the Jacobin Club itself, Dutard saw a division between two parties: "the educated property owners thinking of their interests despite themselves—among them Santerre, Robespierre and a majority of the members of the Mountain—and the anarchists, Marat at their head, who rely partly on the Jacobins but principally on the Cordeliers." The first group, it now seemed to him, was moving toward moderation, hesitating at the prospect of an insurrection beyond its power to control. The second group, appearing more ready to follow the "anarchistic people" down the path to disorder, was also hostage to it as a result. "They love Marat, Robespierre, only as much as the latter will tell them 'Let's kill, let's despoil, let's assassinate.'" A lone member of the club "would be enough to lead this horde of bandits."[18]

The implications of the spy's analysis were clear: with the Jacobins and the Montagnards hesitating, the momentum toward insurrection was shifting elsewhere, to the Commune stirred up by Chaumette, to the more radical Cordeliers, and to the increasingly less secret committee that was meeting at the Evêché. On 16 May, the General Council of the Commune had decreed that each section send three delegates to a central revolutionary committee meeting at City Hall. Rumors soon circulated that summary executions of suspected deputies and counterrevolutionary leaders were being discussed at a meeting of this group. They were dismissed by the mayor, who maintained that a forced loan had been the topic of discussion, and at his insistence the group had left City Hall and begun meeting with the Enragés at the Evêché palace. But the mayor's denials were empty. Evidence soon surfaced to disprove them.

Matters took a dramatic turn on 18 May. By then, the possibility of a purge of the Convention was becoming a reality. This prospect pervaded the Convention's session the following day as a deputation from the Fraternité section, supported by others from the 1792 and Butte-des-Moulins, declared their commitment to defend every member of the "sacred seat of the national representation," not only against the Vendée rebels but against "those who ruin liberty with impunity under the perfidious mask of patriotism." "May the bloody scepter of anarchy be broken," this deputation proclaimed; "may the reign of the laws begin; may a constitution founded on liberty and equality achieve the triumph of the sovereignty of the people over the debris of all interests, all passions, all tyrannies." Guadet was no less defiant. It was not long before he raised the specter of Pride's Purge, the action that had winnowed the English Parliament in 1648, leaving a minority to force the execution of Charles I the following year.[19]

An incident creating disorder in the galleries, in turn, was immediately interpreted by Isnard as further evidence of a conspiracy to incite insurrection. It was being organized in clandestine committees, he warned. It would be started by women causing a commotion in the Convention. (Radical revolutionary women like Theroigne de Méricourt, denounced earlier in the session, were already assuming a more aggressive role in controlling access to the galleries. There was increasing anger against them among the Girondins.) In the disorder that would follow, Isnard predicted, men would rush to the women's aid; deputies would be proscribed or arrested; bloody conflict would break out in the chamber; misguided members themselves would be massacred; the national representation would be destroyed; civil war would break out; France would be devoured by anarchy; foreign powers would attack; aristocrats would appear; the counter-revolution would be accomplished. Imagining himself victimized in this slaughter while sitting in the president's chair, he had his last words ready. "God, save the liberty of my country," he would say, "and forgive its murderers, for they know not what they do." His prayer earned enthusiastic applause from much of the assembly, but it drove Marat into a paroxysm of fury. Shouting convulsively toward the president that the plot against the Revolution was coming from the faction of the *hommes d'Etat*, he had to be restrained by colleagues among the Montagnards. His repeated attempts to speak unleashed mutual recriminations.[20]

In his own bout of fury, Guadet charged that a so-called revolutionary committee meeting at City Hall on 16 May had plotted the dissolution of the Convention. This assembly, he claimed, had discussed arresting all suspected persons—"which is to say all those not distinguished by their participation in the honorable days of 2 September and 10 March"—then turning them over to the misguided multitude that had been inculcated with a love of blood. "How long, citizens, will you sleep like this on the edge of the abyss?" he demanded, appropriating his enemy's language. "How long will you leave the fate of liberty to chance?" The evil lay in anarchy, he continued, "in this sort of insurrection of the authorities against the Convention . . . , the Paris authorities, the anarchic authorities . . . avid for money and power." In retaliation, he proposed radical measures. One was suppression of the municipal government and its replacement by the presidents of the sections. The other was transfer of the Convention's alternate deputies to the city of Bourges, where they would stand ready to assume the functions of the Convention if it were to be dissolved.[21]

Over protests from the Mountain and the galleries, Guadet was answered immediately by Barère, now president of the Committee of Public Safety. Barère offered his own litany of plots emanating from the Commune under the direction of the "former monk" Chaumette; of conspiracies brewing among a group assembling in the Evêché; and of other machinations for a purge of the twenty-two deputies denounced by the Commune and the sections on 15 April. At the same time, rejecting Guadet's proposals as a recipe for certain anarchy, he offered as an alternative the creation of a committee with twelve members charged to take measures necessary to achieve public tranquility. The establishment of this Extraordinary Commission of Twelve was decreed almost immediately, with Marat's proposal that its power be shared by the (Montagnard-dominated) Committee of General Security swiftly set aside. Its brief was broad: to investigate the actions of the Commune and the sections for the past month; to discover all the plots against liberty within the Republic; to receive reports from the ministries of conspiracies threatening the national representation; and to "take all measures necessary to gather proofs of these conspiracies and secure the persons of the accused."[22] Its membership, announced three days later, was drawn entirely from among the Girondins. Its existence and actions became the burning focal point of the final conflict between Girondins and Montagnards over the following weeks. In defending representation, it pushed representation to its breaking point.

"A LIBERTICIDAL COMMISSION"

The Commission of Twelve lost little time in pursuing its mandate.[23] It immediately ordered the sections to turn over the minutes of their meetings for the past month (provoking strong resistance from the sections) and summoned Pache and Chaumette to appear before it. On 24 May, its members proposed the decree they deemed necessary to counter a plot against the assembly that they were sure could destroy liberty within days. The very first article sounded a general alert against the conspirators by placing the destiny of the public, the representative body, and the city of Paris "under the protection of the good citizens." A later provision held Parisians to their obligations in the National Guard. Another placed the guardsmen under the command of the most senior officer in each section. This latter move directly challenged the Commune's authority (also contested by the sections and the Convention) to name a provisional commander to replace Santerre, who was about to lead the Parisian contingent against the Vendée rebels. The concluding measures constrained activism in the sections by directing that their meetings end at 10:00 p.m., a clear effort to prevent the adoption of incendiary measures by the more radical members remaining as attendance dwindled into the night; by prohibiting outsiders from participating in these meetings; and by preventing unauthorized communications between the sections themselves.[24]

The proposed decree was immediately challenged by Marat as comprising measures against an imaginary plot, a project motivated by "fables in the air" that could only alarm the public. Other Montagnards weighed in with demands for proof of the plots against which the decree was directed. Powerfully defended by Vergniaud against Danton, the decree was passed. A letter from Pache, denying allegations of threats against the Convention and insisting that Paris had nothing to fear but fear itself, was read too late to affect the outcome of the vote and would probably not have done so in any case.[25] Much resented, the limit on sectional meetings was to be largely ignored, or evaded as the sections continued their deliberations after 10:00 p.m. in the guise of popular societies.

The same day, the commission also ordered the arrest of Hébert, assistant prosecutor of the Commune, and Varlet, the driving spirit of the revolutionary committee meeting at the Evêché. Hébert, long Marat's rival as editor of the radical journal *Père Duchêne*, was accused of publishing an inflammatory article denouncing the *hommes d'Etat* for creating disorder, inciting the grocery riots in February, and causing grain shortages. The other three were arrested for their alleged participation in discussions of assassination plots at the meetings at City Hall. These arrests, particularly those of Hébert and Varlet, proved utterly inflammatory. On 25 May, a deputation of the General Council of the Commune appeared before the Convention. Denouncing the Fraternité section for its charges that the delegates of the sections in City Hall had engaged in conspiratorial talk of purging the Convention—the charges upon which the Commission of Twelve had based its arrests of Varlet and the two police officials—it went on to protest the treatment of Hébert, "dragged from amid the general council while fulfilling his functions . . . and incarcerated in the Abbaye."

The sovereignty of the people was violated, the deputation insisted, when its magistrates were hauled arbitrarily from their functions without formal accusation or any proof of their offense. But Isnard's bitter response as president of the Convention was interrupted by shouts of protest every few words as its import became clear. His pronouncement was destined for infamy. "If ever the Convention were debased by one of these insurrections constantly renewed since the 10 March without its receiving any warning from the magistrates . . . If any of these constantly recurring insurrections end up harming the national representation, I declare to you in the name of the whole of France, Paris will be annihilated. . . . Soon they would be searching the banks of the Seine for evidence that Paris existed." Marat joined others in protest against this provocation. "Leave the chair, President. . . . You're dishonoring the assembly. . . . You're protecting the *hommes d'Etat*. . . ." But Isnard's declaration of war against the Commune was not to be stopped.[26]

His malediction rankled in an address offered the Convention the following day by a deputation representing sixteen Paris sections. Condemning Hébert's arrest as a violation of the law and an attack on freedom of opinion and the rights of man, the sectionnaires insisted that the Commission of Twelve had been given no mandate to arrest and imprison citizens. "Remember, Legislators, that we didn't break the scepter of tyranny to bend our neck under the yoke of this new despotism," they warned as they repudiated the charges being leveled at the city that was the cradle of the Revolution. Marat followed them by demanding that the Commission of Twelve be required to explain the grounds for Hébert's arrest. Billaud-Varenne demanded the journalist's release. Louis Legendre called for the commission's suppression. The session ended in confusion. In the meantime, the Commission of Twelve ordered the arrest of the president of the Cité section for refusing to hand over the minutes of its revolutionary committee for the commission's inspection. A riot over the same issue had occurred the same day in the Butte-aux-Moulins section.

There was greater clarity evident in the meeting of the Jacobin Club that evening. Words had been twisted, Marat insisted; it was important to reclaim the meaning of "republican" by uniting against the projects of the *hommes d'Etat*. "It's important to secure the annihilation of the counterrevolutionary Commission of Twelve, whose project is to put the most energetic friends of the people under the blade of the law. The entire Mountain must rise up against this shameful commission; it has to be condemned to public execration and annihilated without recourse." As news of the disorder at the Butte-aux-Moulins threw the meeting into a clamor, Robespierre responded even more decisively by calling explicitly for insurrection for the very first time. "When the people is oppressed, when it can rely only on itself, it would be base not to tell it to rise up," he declared. "It's when the laws are violated, when despotism is at its height, when good faith and decency are trampled underfoot, that the people must rebel. This moment has come: our enemies openly oppress patriots; in the name of the law, they want to plunge the people back into misery and servitude. . . . I call on the people to appear in insurrection against all the corrupt deputies. . . . I call on all Montagnard deputies to rally and combat aristocracy and I say that their only choice is to resist attempted plots with all their force and all their power or to resign."[27]

The offensive for which Robespierre and Marat now called with one voice was launched by the Montagnards the very next day. Marat led the charge. "The mass of the people is *patriote*," he declaimed against the *hommes d'Etat*; "it detests senatorial despotism as much as royal despotism. You talk constantly about the law, and you invoke it only to violate it in favor of members of your party. If the patriots rise in insurrection, it will be your work. I demand that this Commission of Twelve be suppressed as inimical to liberty and tending to provoke the insurrection of the people, which is only too close [*protests from the right and center*]; only too close, that is, because of the negligence with which you have allowed the price of foodstuffs to become excessive." Challenged, and in the face of further protests, he escalated his attack against "the faction of the *hommes d'Etat* upon whom I make war." His message was clear. "If the entire nation witnessed your prevarications and the care you take to cover up liberticidal plots, it would have you led to the scaffold. If you have any good faith left, if it is true that perfidy is not in your souls, join me, take the blindfold from your eyes, and let's call together for the suppression of the liberticidal Commission of Twelve." "I believe Marat has heard of the troubles that occurred last night," came a groan from the benches of the Gironde: "The Réunion section betook itself to the Temple section to discuss putting to death all the aristocrats and the twenty-two proscribed members tonight."[28]

There was bitter irony in the fact that, in this moment approaching ungovernability in the great city on the Seine, the Convention returned to its ongoing constitutional debates to consider the optimal size of municipalities. That discussion did not last long. It was soon interrupted by a deputation from the Cité section demanding that its president and secretary be freed and the members of the despotic Commission of Twelve sent before the Revolutionary Tribunal. The intervention provoked a blistering defense of liberty under law from Isnard, speaking as the assembly president: a reminder that liberty was more than words and symbols, that tyranny could find expression in the dark of a cellar or the light of a public square, on a throne or at the tribune of a club, gilded in its attire or sans a culotte, wearing a crown or sporting a bonnet. His contempt was met by fury, fanned by Marat first among others, into an explosion that brought the entire Mountain to its feet in an affirmation of resistance to oppression.

From the extended clamor that followed there emerged a call for a roll-call vote, initially from the Girondins to decide whether to convoke the primary assemblies and then, more successfully, from the Montagnards to decide whether to allow Robespierre to speak in advance of the presentation of a report from the Commission of Twelve. Voting on the latter question had barely begun before it was interrupted by word that the Convention was surrounded by a mass of citizens obstructing the avenues leading to it, and that several National Guard companies of the Butte-aux-Moulins section were blocking its doors. Challenged by Marat, pistol in hand, the commander of these companies flourished authorizations from the Commission of Twelve as the basis for his orders to protect the deputies. When these were accepted by the president, a furious Marat had to be forced amid yet another ruckus to leave the tribune.

In response to this situation, the minister of the interior and the mayor were summoned to account for the presence of troops surrounding the assembly and for the general situation in the capital. Garat's interminable report did little to reassure fearful Girondin deputies of their safety, while Pache's disingenuous words did much to fan Montagnard anger at the authorization of the Commission of Twelve to deploy the forces of order. Uncertain how to proceed, the assembly soon found its attention concentrated by the appearance of a deputation representing twenty-eight sections. Dramatically repudiating any possibility of unity between the "healthy, vigorous body" of the patriots and the "fetid and pestiferous cadaver" of their enemies—and swearing, *contra* Isnard, that the imposing monuments of Paris would stand forever in attestation to the city's vigor and pride—the deputation demanded the liberation of the "true republicans" under arrest and the destruction of the "tyrannical and odious commission" that had imprisoned them.[29]

The petition of the sections was welcomed with the promise of justice by Hérault de Séchelles, the Montagnard who had now taken over the chair. "The force of reason and the force of the people are the same thing," he declared. As if there were any doubt in the matter, a deputation of the Gravilliers section soon entered to offer its own address. Written by its spokesman, Jacques Roux, this was an incandescent denunciation of the betrayal of the people's mandate by an assembly corrupted from within by counterrevolution. "When the homeland is betrayed within and without, when speculation devours the land of equality, when a counterrevolutionary faction erects scaffolds for virtue and distributes crowns to crime, is there any other option than to resist oppression?" it demanded. "Woe to the traitors gorged with gold and greedy for power who want to give us a king and chains. The courage of the Sans-Culottes grows in the midst of storms. The hypocrites and the crooks, easy to identify because they are bound to the stake of public opinion, will be sorry that they have compelled the people of Paris to put its force to the test a third time. . . . Deputies of the Mountain, you've crushed the head of the tyrant, we adjure you to save the homeland. [*Yes! Yes! We'll save it!*] If you can and don't want to, you're cowards and traitors; if you want to and can't, say so, it's the goal of our mission. One hundred thousand arms are girded to defend you." To their demand for the liberation of the imprisoned patriots and the suppression of the Commission of Twelve, the Gravilliers deputation added a call for the infamous Roland to be put on trial. Its address was followed by yet another, from the Croix-Rouge section, repeating the same demands for the release of the arrested patriots and the suppression of a commission that had done nothing but attack the true friends of liberty.[30]

Without more ado, Delacroix turned these calls into a motion. It was almost instantly adopted. The resulting decree ordered the immediate liberation of the prisoners arrested by order of the Commission of Twelve, the suppression of the commission itself, and the investigation of its members by the Committee of General Security. Protests that the hour was late, that many of the deputies had already departed, that the decision had been taken illegally when the assembly was in a state of agitation were lost in a tsunami of shouts and applause from the galleries. In all likelihood, petitioners occupying seats vacated by deputies who had already left had also usurped their right to vote. In effect, the Montagnards had staged a midnight coup.[31]

Their triumph was short-lived. The Convention was plunged into utter disorder the next morning, 28 May, when the Montagnard Osselin read the decree for final passage. The Girondins protested violently that the decision, if indeed it had occurred, had been taken under the threat of popular violence while petitioners had invaded the vacated benches and participated in the vote. They were led in their charges by Lanjuinais, who launched into a denunciation of the tyranny exercised in the departments by Montagnard deputies *en mission*, leaving anarchists running free in Paris to "preach murder and anarchy at two sols a page." A motion in the Jacobin Club to massacre the Convention and the rich had been repeated by radicals meeting at the Evêché, Lanjuinais reported; the Montagnards were protecting "monsters greedy for blood and domination." Rejecting these claims and insisting on the legitimacy of the disputed decree, the Mountain called repeatedly for a vote to confirm its passage. The frenzy of mutual vituperation eventually gave way to a roll-call vote to decide the issue. While the vote was being counted, Robespierre found an opportunity to incriminate Brissot and lament, his voice failing, that "the most dastardly, vile and impure men on earth are triumphing and returning to slavery a nation of twenty-five million who wanted to be free."[32]

The vote, when it was announced, revealed a majority of 279 to 238 (with 244 abstentions) in favor of reversing the suppression of the Commission of Twelve. The numbers suggest that support for the Girondins, while still dominant in this case, was waning. A separate decree, intended by the Girondins to be conciliatory, subsequently upheld the liberation of the individuals the commission had imprisoned. But an attempt by Rabaut-Saint-Etienne to deliver a report on its behalf was drowned out by Montagnard interventions and clamors from the galleries incited by Marat. Rabaut's report had to be abandoned.[33]

Rejecting calls to end the session, the Convention prolonged the chaos of the day by hearing more deputations. One of them, from the Gardes françaises section, launched a vitriolic call for the elimination of the "troop of criminals hiding under the mask of patriotism" that was constantly responsible for "days of pillage." This address was revoked by another deputation from this section three days later as the work of a misguided criminal minority. But for the moment its words provoked deputies to the exchange of blows and threats of violence between left and right, and another noisy outburst of disorder. Declaring itself ready at any moment to reveal "the courage of good citizens" in defending the Convention against "the baseness and perfidy of a few brigands," the deputation decried the fact that the legislators had "left the instruments of revolution too long in the hands of the people." These instruments had to be removed, it insisted, to prevent the people from succumbing to misplaced passions, abandoning principles, and attaching itself to conspirators ready to divide the homeland for their own purposes. Isnard, from the chair, promised in response that a time would come when the agitated masses would turn against those inciting them to violence. "The representatives of the people know how to die," he assured the deputation; "their bodies will be trampled before they permit the reign of anarchy and the reestablishment of monarchy."[34]

In a blistering rejoinder, Danton declared it beyond the Convention's power to strip the people of its *instruments* of revolution, meaning its right to assemble to deliberate regarding public affairs. This instrument, he vowed, would be used to annihilate, in a single day, "men stupid enough to believe there is a distinction between the people and the citizens." It was time for the people to take the offensive once more against the enemies intent on destroying the Republic, he proclaimed, to applause from the Mountain and its supporting galleries. "Paris will not perish. . . . Paris will always create terror among the enemies of liberty; and the sections, in the great days when the people will unite *en masse*, will always wipe out these miserable *Feuillants*, these vile *moderates*, whose triumph is momentary."[35] With this promise of insurrection, the daylong session came to an end.

Before the evening was out, a secret insurrectionary committee was being formed by Varlet at the Evêché with support from a majority of the sections. By 30 May, joined by delegates from the Commune and the assembly of the department of Paris, this committee had been constituted as "the general and revolutionary assembly of the city of Paris." Eventually, it became known as "the Central Insurrectionary Committee." Claiming to derive unlimited powers from the sovereignty of the sections, it was ready that evening to declare the capital in a state of insurrection.[36]

Meanwhile Paris waited and watched as the Convention seemed to be attempting to exorcise the furies that had possessed it on 27–28 May. A lengthy report on the dire state of the republic presented by Barnave on behalf of the Committee of Public Safety took up much of the session on 29 May. Showing the committee's readiness to exercise executive authority, it called for unity among the deputies and an early draft of the elements of a constitution. Committee reports occupied the deputies for most of the session the following morning.

The evening session on 30 May, in contrast, intimated what was to follow. No sooner had the Montagnard Mallarmé defeated Lanjuinais in the vote for the presidency of the assembly (a significant loss for the Girondins) than Bourdon, the Montagnard deputy from the Oise, launched a renewed attack on the Commission of Twelve. He was answered by Lanjuinais, who insisted on the need to uphold the authority of the commission against the conspirators at the Evêché: "electors illegally named on 10 August, the most audacious leaders of the Jacobins and the sections, citizens most capable of promoting horrors, men most easily led into error." There, Hassenfratz had declared insurrection "a duty against the corrupt majority of the Convention," Lanjuinais reported, and a dictatorial committee had been created to carry it out. Furthermore, there had been talk of arresting deputies without killing them immediately, referring them instead to a court representing the departments.

Lanjuinais's motion for urgent action in response to this news was preempted, however, by the appearance of a deputation from twenty-two sections insisting that it was expressing the unanimous will of all forty-eight, even those previously misled. Likening themselves to Spartans facing a "Thermopylae of liberty," the petitioners declared their message brief and themselves ready to die. They called for the end of an "unjust, arbitrary commission," the indictment of its members before a tribunal of the eighty-six departments, and the celebration of a republican federation on 10 August (by which time, doubtless, they expected a repeat of the insurrection on that date in 1792). Admitted to the hall, they were joined almost immediately by two citizens from Rouen (dubbed "aristocrats" by Marat) bearing a vow of their city and department, on the contrary, to take all measures necessary to uphold the integrity of the Convention. It took a roll-call vote for the assembly to decide that this address would be published.[37]

Adjourning at 1:00 a.m. on the morning of 31 May, the Convention was summoned back into session five hours later by the sound of the tocsin and the general alarm. In the course of the night, the insurrectionary committee based in the Evêché, acting in the name of the sections, had suspended the Commune, taken it over, and declared it in a state of insurrection. The authorities of the department of Paris had thereupon decided to throw its support to the now insurrectionary Commune and to join the insurrectionary committee at the Evêché itself. The insurrectionary Commune then named Hanriot provisional commander-general of the Parisian National Guard and voted payment of 40 sous to the poor among the troops thus mobilized. Hanriot, in his new capacity, had ordered the sounding of the alarm. The insurrection had begun.[38]

Informed of these events, the deputies wavered between calling for the suppression of the Commission of Twelve, hearing a report from it, or summoning Hanriot to account for his actions. It helped little that, responding spontaneously to a proposal by Vergniaud, they rose as one to swear that they would die rather than betray the rights of the people. Danton, in an impassioned speech demanding the suppression of the Commission of Twelve and judgment of its members, urged justice for the people. "What people?" came the retort. "What people, you say?" he responded to applause. "The people of Paris. This people is immense, it's the advanced sentinel of the Republic. All the departments hate tyranny deeply. All the departments execrate this vile moderatism that is bringing back tyranny. All the departments, in a day of glory for Paris, will avow this great movement that will exterminate all the enemies of liberty. . . . I shall be the first to render effulgent justice to these courageous men who have made the air resound with . . ." "With violation of the law," came an interruption. "There is no violation of the law where the great will of the people manifests itself," Danton answered. "Not its will," was the retort, "but yours." The debate continued until, ignoring Danton's ultimate call for a roll-call vote to decide on suppression of the Commission of Twelve, the Convention decided to allow Rabaut-Saint-Etienne to present a report on its behalf. Once again, his attempt to do so was a disaster. A barrage of interruptions, including Marat's shouts for this counterrevolutionary's resignation, for suppression of the commission, and for immediate attention to a deputation from the Commune, finally brought Rabaut's hopeless efforts to a halt. Declaring the commission at an end, he stepped down from the tribune only to be forced back to it. The assembly descended once again into disorder.[39]

The deputation from the provisional General Council of the Commune, despite challenges to the legitimacy of its powers, was eventually permitted to present an address. Claiming a direct mandate from the sections, it announced that Paris had risen a third time to put an end to counterrevolutionary conspiracies. The Commune, it announced, had placed property under the protection of republican sans-culottes, who would in turn receive 40 sous daily to maintain order. The legality of these actions was immediately contested by Guadet, relentless against constant interruptions from the floor and unremitting protests from the galleries in denying the authority of such a body to legislate this way. Accusing the insurrectionary Commune of the criminal conspiracy against liberty it was claiming to repress, he attacked it as a radical threat to the Convention itself and to the very principle of representation. His calls for the Commission of Twelve (assuming it still existed) to investigate the responsibility for sounding the tocsin and the general alarm in the first place were repudiated by Couthon and the younger Robespierre. It took a further ten minutes of tumult for the assembly to refuse Marat the right to speak.[40]

Continuing debate did not serve the Convention well. Yet another deputation from the forty-eight sections now appeared to press for more radical demands anticipating much of the Terror. These included the creation of a paid revolutionary army of sans-culottes, spreading across the country to protect patriots from their enemies; indictment of the twenty-two deputies previously denounced, together with members of the Commission of Twelve; a maximum on the price of bread; the manufacture of weapons to arm all sans-culottes; dismissal of all former nobles from positions of military leadership; intervention against counterrevolutionary movements in Marseille and other cities in the south; a proclamation vindicating the city of Paris against the calumnies spread against it; arrest of ministers Clavière and Le Brun; and assured execution of the decrees for the provision of support of the families of soldiers who had sacrificed their lives in defense of liberty. The deputies ordered this address printed and circulated to the departments and its demands referred to the Committee of Public Safety. But before Barère, speaking for this committee, could present proposals for the maintenance of public order, he was interrupted by yet another deputation, this time from the department of Paris, the municipal authorities, and more delegates from the forty-eight sections.[41]

To constant applause from the Mountain, the spokesman for this delegation, the department's public prosecutor, declared the city's readiness to face utter destruction rather than accept tyranny. If Paris were to disappear from the face of the globe, he proclaimed, it would be for defending the indivisibility of the Republic. It would support the "worthy representatives of the people at the price of all its blood," taking pride in the fact that the city, nothing by itself, was the essence of all the departments, the mirror of opinion and the point of union of all free men. Denouncing Isnard for his sacrilege in threatening that Paris would disappear from the banks of the Seine, he added the members of the Commission of Twelve, the Brissots, the Guadets, the Vergniauds, the Gensonnés, the Buzots, the Barbaroux, the Rolands, the Lebruns to the call for the Convention's vengeance against conspirators. In response, swearing that Paris would not disappear from the globe, the acting president, Grégoire, invited the members of the deputation into the hall. With a crowd of citizens following them, they mingled with the Montagnards on the benches, making further deliberation by the Convention impossible. In response, it was decided that the Montagnard deputies would move to the other side of the hall. There could have been no more dramatic symbolism of this situation than that of the people represented on the right confronting the people now embodied on the right.[42]

With Barère attempting to resume his proposals for measures to maintain public order, Vergniaud declared further debate impossible and called for the deputies to leave the hall and seek protection from the guard outside. He left, followed by some others, to derisive applause from the galleries. When a majority refused to follow, he returned almost immediately, in time to hear Robespierre insisting on the need for the Convention to suppress the Commission of Twelve and take the more vigorous measures demanded by the earlier petitioners. Shouting at the Incorruptible to conclude, he received his answer. "Yes, I'm going to conclude," was Robespierre's retort, "and against you. Against you who, after the revolution of 10 August, wanted to send its authors to the scaffold; against you who have not ceased to provoke the destruction of Paris; against you who wanted to save the tyrant; against you who conspired with Dumouriez; against you who savagely persecuted the same patriots whose heads Dumouriez called for; against you whose criminal vengeances have provoked the very cries of indignation you want to turn into a crime on the part of your victims. Very well! My conclusion is the decree of accusation against all the accomplices of Dumouriez and against all those who have been named by the petitioners."[43]

At this decisive intervention, many of the Montagnards demanded an end to the discussion. But there remained an issue to be resolved: whether control of the Paris National Guard should be assumed by the Convention (as proposed by Barère) or retained by the Commune. This once settled by an empty compromise allowing the Convention's oversight of the Commune's use of force, the deputies finally adopted an amended version of the measures Barère had proposed on behalf of the Committee of Public Safety. The most important was the suppression of the Commission of

Twelve.[44] The Girondin leaders had fought to save it until this bitter final vote ("as if it wasn't enough," Marat commented later, "to dismiss traitorous and scheming public functionaries to have them caught red-handed and have the people rise up against them"), but their doing so provoked the escalation of other insurrectionary demands, not least for their own expulsion from the assembly. In effect, they had assured their own eventual destruction.

ENDGAME

The morning of 1 June found the deputies bitterly debating an address to the nation, presented by Barère on behalf of the Committee of Public Safety, that presented an anodyne and evasive account of the events of the previous day. Offering assurance that "in a nation worthy of exercising its sovereignty directly, the storms that threaten liberty make it purer and more indestructible, and that social order is perfected through the transitory infractions it receives," it described a day of momentary restlessness but happy results, "the astonishing spectacle of an insurrection in which life and property were protected as surely as in the best social order." The resulting discussion revealed profound differences over what had happened, and what—and how much—to say about it. "Let's not put revolutions on trial; let's seek to grasp their fruits," Barère urged. His prudence carried the day and his draft was adopted, but only after repeatedly contested votes. By Marat's account, he warned Barère that the calm in Paris his proclamation touted was only momentary and that the only way to restore tranquility in the capital was to bring the traitors within the Convention to justice. His comment, he reported, was dismissed "with a mocking smile."[45]

By this time, the revolutionary Commune and the insurrectional committee were readying their own joint address to the Convention. The extent of Marat's participation in this action remains disputed. By his own later account, he was recognized and followed by a crowd as he was returning from a temporary absence from the Convention and bombarded with denunciations of the Mountain's lack of energy and demands for the arrest of the criminal deputies. The streets, he claimed, resounded with cries of *Marat, save us!* Making it to the Committee of General Security, he was urged to return with the mayor to the Commune to prevent any disorganized collective action. There, assuring its members that the Committee of Public Safety was discussing measures to punish the traitors, he urged them "to remain in a state of uprising, deploy your forces, and lay down your arms only after you have obtained a striking justice and provided for your security."

Challenged by an objection that a betrayed people should rely on its magistrates and the rule of law, he answered that "when its mandataries continually abuse its confidence, when they traffic in its rights, betray its interests, despoil it, vex it and plot its destruction, the people must then resume its powers, deploy its force to make them return to their duty, punish the traitors and save itself." Assuring his fellow citizens that "you have no resource left but your energy," he exhorted them to "present an address demanding punishment of the faithless deputies of the nation; remain in a state of uprising, and lay down your arms only after you have obtained it." He nevertheless resisted invitations to join members of the Commune in their further deliberations with the insurrectionary committee at the Evêché. "I told them that my post was in the Convention and I would go to the Committee of Public Safety to render account of my mission."[46] He was ready, it seems, to counsel an insurrection, but not to engage in one.

Since the deputies had disbanded at 6:00 p.m., before the address of the Commune and the insurrectionary committee was ready, the insurgents again sounded the tocsin and the general alarm, bringing crowds into the streets and forcing the Convention back into session at 9:00 p.m. Failure of a majority of the Girondins to appear left the right side of the hall almost deserted and the Montagnards in control of the proceedings. Acting as president, Grégoire invited a deputation of the Commune to the bar, allowing Hassenfratz, its spokesman, to read its petition entitled *Municipality of Paris—Revolutionary General Council Established by the People of the Department of Paris*. The first paragraph made clear that Isnard's prediction of the city's disappearance from the banks of the Seine still rankled; later ones protested the constant defamation of the city in the provinces. But Paris was united, the petition insisted; it spoke with one voice through the present delegation. A third revolution would bring none of the bloodshed caused by division on 14 July and 10 August, Hassenfratz declared. Its purpose was evident: "Representatives of the people, the Revolution must end; tranquillity must reign; a liberticidal faction must be annihilated, a faction that defended Dumouriez and all the counterrevolutionaries, that declared war on all nations to arm all the tyrants of Europe and all their slaves against us." And its means were no less clear: "We demand a decree of accusation against Gensonné, Guadet, Brissot, Gorsas, Pétion, Vergniaud, Salle, Barbaroux, Birotteau, Ducos, Isnard, Lanjuinais, Lidon, Rabaut, Lasource, Louvet, Fonfrède, Lanthenas, Dusaulx, Fauchet, Grangeneuve, Lehardy and Lesage." An ultimatum warned the Montagnards, yet again, that if they could not save the homeland by indicting these criminals, the people was ready to do so, as it had done twice before.[47]

Marat had immediate thoughts to present about this list of the accused, one he had long contemplated. He had earlier offered a much longer list in his journal. Now he was eager to pare the number down. Dusaulx he excused as an "old dotard incapable of heading any party," Ducos as hardly among the counterrevolutionary leaders, Lanthenas as so weak-minded that he was not worth denouncing. Never could derision have been more welcome to its targets. Urging indictment of the others on the list, he nevertheless insisted on the principle (neglected earlier in his own case) that it be preceded by a report of the Committee of Public Safety the next day. "Tomorrow we have to purge the Convention," he insisted, "and the people must not lay down its weapons until after the act of purification." At Barnave's proposal, the assembly decreed that the Committee of Public Safety review the factual bases of the charges against individuals denounced within three days.[48] The people would not wait that long.

By the morning of 2 June, the Commune and the insurrectionary committee had ordered Hanriot to surround the Convention with enough troops to arrest the leading Girondins if that proved necessary. On this day, a Sunday, workers were free; a vast mass of armed men was thus at the ready by the time the deputies convened at 10:00 a.m. The routine morning review of communications brought the assembly bad news. Vendée rebels had made significant advances toward La Rochelle; counterrevolutionary sections had slaughtered eight hundred republicans in Lyon; civil war had broken out in the Lozère. The Montagnards demanded emergency measures to confront these threats, adding reports of others. The resulting decree also ordered local authorities throughout the Republic to arrest citizens suspected of aristocratic sentiments and lack of civic commitment.[49]

With a new deputation from the Commune waiting to address the assembly, Lanjuinais launched into a furious protestation against the tyranny and usurpation of the Convention's powers during the previous days, the way these actions had been laundered in the Convention's address to the nation, and the certainty that they would be continued. "A usurpatory assembly not only exists and deliberates," he cried; "but it acts, but it conspired Friday and Saturday; not the large assembly that seduces, misleads, and deceives the ignorant, but its directorial and executive committee. . . . This rebellious commune, illegally created, still exists. . . . When this rival and usurpatory authority has you surrounded by weapons and cannon, the petition dredged up from the muck of the streets of Paris has just been produced again." His words, constantly punctuated by Montagnard interventions and threats of personal violence, plunged the Convention into renewed turmoil. It had to be calmed before Lanjuinais could finally demand the suppression of the Evêché and the designation as outlaws, subject to immediate retribution at the hands of any citizen, of all those arrogating to themselves a new and illegal authority.[50]

Pressed by the Montagnards, a majority of the deputies chose instead to hear the deputation of the offending General Council of the Commune. As Lanjuinais had predicted, it demanded, one last time, the arrest of the deputies denounced earlier. When Mallarmé insisted as president that the facts of the charges had first to be established, Montagnards demanded an immediate report from the Committee of Public Safety. To this the assembly responded by referring the petition to the committee for review without further specification of a deadline for its report. At this point, the deputies were reminded that two more deputations, one from the forty-eight sections, another from a Society of Revolutionary Republicans, were waiting to present petitions. Disorder erupted again as the earlier petitioners from the Commune, admitted to the hall, now objected to further delay. Their abrupt departure to return to their sections to take immediate action incited a mass exodus of citizens from the galleries to do the same.[51]

Ignited by Levasseur's lengthy rehearsal of the history of Girondin crimes, demands for provisional detention of the Girondin leaders quickly escalated into a call for their more definitive arrest. These calls were interrupted by a report that deputies were being denied exit from the hall, provoking a dispute as to whether the doors were being blocked by a band of revolutionary women or armed guards. Marat joined Robespierre in shouting for an end to this argument, decrying it as "a mere stratagem to abuse the assembly and slander Paris." Eventually, the Committee of Public Safety was ready to report its decisions. Delacroix presented several measures on its behalf, including those securing the organization of an armed guard to protect the assembly. Barère then spoke to the crucial issue of action to be taken against the denounced Girondin leaders.[52]

His proposal was a compromise: a call on the potential victims to suspend their functions voluntarily for a given period. The suggestion was immediately accepted by Isnard, who resigned in a movingly patriotic speech. He was followed in doing so by Lanthenas, Fauchet, and eventually Dusaulx. Their colleagues proved recalcitrant. "Don't expect a resignation or suspension from me," Lanjuinais lashed out at the suggestion that he would sacrifice his powers as a representative. "What sacrifice!" he exclaimed. "What an abuse of words! Sacrifices must be free or they're not sacrifices. The Convention is besieged; cannon are positioned against it; we're forbidden to show ourselves at the window; the guns are loaded. I refuse to give an opinion and will remain silent at this moment." Barbaroux, in turn, vowed to die at his post, as he had sworn to do.[53]

Marat protested immediately. "So false a measure could only have embittered opinion and revolted the people in making it anticipate that it would have no satisfaction awaiting it," he reasoned later. In the moment, however, he also had a more personal response. The purge he had long demanded was not to be compromised by half-measures; his own civic virtue was not to be overshadowed by false shows of patriotic resignation. "One has to be pure to offer sacrifices to the homeland," he protested. "It's for me, a true martyr of liberty, to devote myself. Thus I will offer my own suspension the moment you have ordered the detention of the counterrevolutionaries." He demanded the addition of Louvet and Valazé to the number of those denounced (at which numerous deputies on the right clamored for the same honor) and called again for the removal of Ducos, Lanthenas, and Dusaulx, reiterating his conviction of the ridiculousness of the charges against them. Billaud-Varenne followed by declaring that the Convention had no right to provoke the suspension of any of its members, and demanding a roll-call vote on an indictment of thirty deputies now on the list.[54]

Before Billaud-Varenne could be answered, Delacroix shouted that he had been prevented by guards from leaving the assembly hall, inciting a mass of deputies to rush toward the blocked exit. A torrent of protest was unleashed before members of the assembly, passionately urged by Barnave to demonstrate its freedom, were led outside by the acting president, Hérault de Séchelles. With the troops yielding before them and offering salutations in their honor, the deputies marched around the Tuileries. By Marat's account, he remained in the hall with thirty or so Montagnards as the audience in the galleries became increasingly fretful. "I quieted them down. I flew after the Convention, found it at the swing bridge from which Barère was proposing to lead it to the Champ de Mars. Before reentering the hall, I urged it to return to its post; it came back and resumed its functions."[55] The entire walkout had been a futile gesture. The disabled Couthon, carried to the tribune, immediately demanded that the assembly, having demonstrated its liberty of action, decree the arrest of the twenty-two deputies denounced earlier, together with members of the Commission of Twelve and the ministers Clavière and Lebrun. Haggling over deletions and additions to the list yielded a final count of thirty-one names: eighteen deputies originally denounced, plus Rabaut-Saint-Etienne, the two ministers, and ten former members of the Commission of Twelve. With Rabaut named twice, a total of thirty individuals were placed under house arrest. As on the evening of 27 May, the benches on the right were largely empty and the crowd of citizens who had invaded the hall, embodying the people, participated indiscriminately in the vote. An experiment in representative democracy had come disastrously to an end.[56]

Marat saw things differently. "Without bloodshed, without horrors, without insult, without disorder, a day of alarms thus passed amid a hundred thousand armed citizens provoked by six months of machinations, assaults and atrocious slanders by their vile oppressors," he celebrated in his journal. "The exact narrative of facts is the sole response to be made against the infamous slanderers who will not fail to misrepresent it as a scene of brigandage in order to mislead the nation they have abused for so long."[57]

FINAL DAYS

True to his word, Marat submitted a letter to the Convention on 3 June declaring his suspension of his functions as a deputy until the representatives arrested the previous day had been brought to judgment. By doing so, he essentially identified himself as the totem of the people's purge of the Convention. Reiterating his opposition to Barnave's proposal to allow criminal representatives the honorable option of voluntary suspension, he again claimed the privilege for himself, "the eternal martyr of liberty, long ravaged by slander." He was "impatient to open the eyes of a nation deceived about me by so many paid hacks, wishing no longer to be a cause of discord," he declared, "and ready to sacrifice everything for a return to peace." "May the dolorous scenes that have so often afflicted the public no longer be repeated within the Convention," he exhorted. "May all its members sacrifice their passions to the love of their duties and march with great steps toward the goal of their mission; may my dear colleagues of the Mountain demonstrate to the nation that if they have not yet fulfilled its expectations it's because men of ill-will hampered their efforts; may they finally take the great measures to crush the enemies from without, fell the enemies from within, put an end to the ills that have desolated the homeland, restore peace and abundance, reinforce liberty with wise laws, establish the reign of justice, make the state flourish and cement the happiness of the French."[58]

The responses to his prayer were less pious. There were objections that he be required to remain at his post, that deputies choosing to suspend their functions be required to resign definitively or return to duty within twenty-four hours, that voluntary suspensions had not been anticipated by the constitution and should not be permitted. In response, Montagnards argued that his suspension would demonstrate that he was not the monster he had been made out to be, and that the liberticidal faction was to be found elsewhere. The Convention voted to insert his letter into its *Bulletin* and to proceed without further discussion.[59]

In fact, this suspension marked Marat's virtual withdrawal from activity as a deputy. He made few public appearances thereafter. He answered a summons to the Jacobin Club on 3 June to respond yet again to a charge that he had wanted a dictator, and he spoke before the Committee of Public Safety on 4 June to press for urgent action to support families of defenders of the homeland, imposition of the forced loan on the rich, and prohibition of permanent sessions of the sections, which he blamed for allowing counterrevolutionaries the opportunity to act while honest citizens were at work. He may also have made an appearance at the Bonconseil section on 9 June. On 13 June, he again attended a meeting of the Committee of Public Safety, speaking against the proposed appointment of the aristocratic Beauharnais as minister of war.[60]

On 4 June he addressed a letter to the Convention protesting the killing and incarceration of patriots by counterrevolutionaries in Marseilles, Lyon, and Grenoble, and demanding that the liberation of those imprisoned be decreed immediately. Read to the Convention two days later, the letter was referred to the Committee of Public Safety. No deputy took up Marat's request for a colleague to propose his demand on his behalf. On 14 June, announcing that he was now "kept abed by illness," he launched a similar appeal to fellow deputies to present a motion for him in his absence. Again, it met with no response. On 17 June, in a state of apparent frustration, he returned to the Convention to complain that his letters had not been read. Declaring that "the profound silence I have kept for fifteen days must be enough to dissipate the clouds cast over me," he announced his immediate resumption of his functions as a deputy. He was greeted with enthusiastic applause from the tribunes and the Mountain, and remained in the assembly to oppose a constitutional provision for mandatory arbitration in civil cases. "Ever the Cassandra of the Revolution," he reappeared the following day to offer a handful of denunciations and demands for decrees of accusation: against generals he held responsible for military defeat and provocation of rebellion in the Vendée, against deputies on mission he charged with fostering the same revolt, and against his old enemy Carra. His demands were not taken up.[61]

With this intervention, The People's Friend seems to have exhausted his capacity for public appearance. On 20 June he informed the Jacobin Club from his bed that he was "prey to an inflammatory malady, the fruit of the wakeful nights to which I have abandoned myself for the past four years in defense of liberty, and especially the torments I've given myself to fell the faction of the *hommes d'Etat*." On 21 June, he addressed a similar description of his condition to the Convention. Two days later, he informed his readers that he was still abed, "reduced to communicating my opinions in my writing instead of presenting them from the tribune of the Convention." "I'm not sleeping, citizen, but I'm in my bed, prey to a cruel malady," he wrote on 27 June in answer to a correspondent complaining of his inactivity. Volunteers being summoned to Paris by the enemies of liberty would meet Thuriot, Lindet, Saint-Just, all the good Montagnards, he promised on 5 July; they would see Danton, Robespierre, Panis, finding that men so often slandered were intrepid defenders of the people. But they might also confront a pitiful sight. "Perhaps, they'll come to see the dictator Marat, and they'll find in his bed a poor devil who would give all the dignities of the earth for a few days of health, but a hundred times more occupied with the ills of the people than with his own malady."[62]

On 3 July, insisting that there was not a moment to lose, he wrote again to the Convention accusing the Committee of Public Safety of negligence in responding to counterrevolutionary resistance in Lyon. Another letter followed on 4 July, calling at length for action against counterrevolutionary threats from princes in exile, Vendée rebels, and faithless generals. A missive written the same day castigated Thuriot for failing to get his letters read at the Convention. If this one met the same fate, Marat threatened, he would have himself carried to the assembly in his bed "to protest this violation of my rights as a deputy, awaken the concern of the deputies to the dangers facing the homeland and the means of countering them, and to prove to the people that it's not my fault if these means are not adopted after being proposed so many times."[63]

The letter at issue was presented to the Convention on 5 July, but its reading was abruptly discontinued on the grounds that a deputy could only make such demands in person. "I was not much surprised," Marat commented bitterly in his journal. "My letter had doubtless been communicated the evening before to the soporificers of the committee on public safety (or, as one says, the committee on public ruin) who got some of the weak-kneed in the Convention to call for the order of the day." The discarded letter was his last communication to the assembly. He complained to a visiting delegation from the Jacobins a week later that the Convention had consigned him to oblivion.[64] In effect, he had become the personification of the trauma of the purge of 2 June. The Convention was eager to move on without him.

In the meantime, "the poor devil" continued to labor on his journal, though he was forced to compensate for lack of energy to produce direct political commentary by filling his pages increasingly with the publication of letters from his abundant daily correspondence from the provinces.

There were letters reporting political and military developments, mostly decrying the explosion of counterrevolutionary movements. There were letters of adulation, support, and encouragement, letters urging political intervention and begging for personal help, letters of vilification, vituperation, and denunciation. He offered a brief selection of them on 19 June under the heading of "The For and Against," to show the "the extreme difference of the opinion of the French on my account." "Worthy defender of the homeland"; "infamous, twenty million times infamous, vilest of criminals"; "intrepid republican"; "dictator"; "perfidious accomplice of the enemies of my homeland"; "imperturbable Friend of the People, implacable enemy of tyranny"; "a man as respectable and simple as nature": these were among the salutations he received. His summation was perhaps among his few truly wise words: "To try to please the whole world is to play the fool; but to try to please the whole world in a time of revolution is to play the traitor."[65]

For the most part, the ebbing pages of the *Publiciste de la République française* played on familiar themes: denunciations of the stupidity of placing former nobles at the head of the armies, of perfidious generals, of faithless, conspiratorial deputies, of counterrevolutionary public servants and provincial administrators, of hoarders and greedy merchants. They frequently featured urgent reports of counterrevolutionary movements in Bordeaux and Marseille, but especially in Lyon, which had been further inflamed by reports of the 2 June purge. Marat's sense of exile and alienation found expression, too, in a vacillation between self-adulation and profound despair. "Without doubt my constant denunciations against the intrigues and plots of this criminal and traitorous faction, denunciations stamped with the purest civic conviction, will be finally recognized as unfortunately all too true," he proclaimed on 15 June in anticipation that the Girondin leaders would soon be brought to trial. "Whatever the results, I have fulfilled my duty and I will always applaud myself for being the first to rip off [their] mask and become the object of their atrocious persecutions. The nation will soon open its eyes and render justice to me at last."[66]

In the same self-justificatory tone, he was writing on 17 June to reassert the significance of his action throughout the entire Revolution. "The role I have played with energy since the taking of the Bastille will be a subject of profound reflections for posterity, and it will not astonish the reader less by the firmness of my courage and my imperturbable constancy than by the disastrous obstinacy with which men placed at the helm of affairs have eternally repudiated the means of public safety that I have ceaselessly proposed, means that are generally recognized today but have only ever been adopted in part and when it was too late."[67]

Self-justification alternated with expressions of profound disillusion. On 7 June he was warning that "if the assembly doesn't proceed with great steps to reform abuses, measures of public safety, and the strengthening of liberty, it will assuredly be its fault now that it is no longer prevented by a faction opposed to every good." The following day, he was decrying the feebleness of the Committee of Public Safety and the failure of successive revolutionary assemblies whose measures to establish liberty and consolidate the Revolution had been mindless, illusory, and to no avail, however well they might have been intended. "For the most part, they even appear intended to multiply abuses, perpetuate oppression, bring about anarchy, dearth, misery, and famine; to tire the people of its independence, to render liberty burdensome to them, to make them detest the revolution for its excessive disorders, to exhaust it with anxieties, fatigue, needs, inanition; to reduce it to despair by means of famine and return it to servitude through civil war." His judgment of the people was no less bitter. "This was the state of things four years ago. This is their state today. This is the state in which they will remain until it pleases Heaven to grant the French a grain of common sense, to strip the fools of the itch to reproduce themselves, to deprive the people of its fatal sense of security and give it the spirit of discernment, the courage to put an end to its ills, and determination to hold firm in its resolutions."[68]

There followed a total condemnation of the failure of the French to understand the fundamental nature of revolution, which must be total in the passion of its violence against its enemies. In effect Marat's final judgment on the French Revolution, it merits quotation at length:

> Among any people not tormented by the mania to be clever and the passion for distinctions, no sensible person has failed to understand that revolutions cannot be consolidated without one party crushing the other. It was reserved for the French to attempt to reverse all their political institutions and establish a new order of things solely by the force of philosophy, as if the most imperious passions were subject to the voice of reason! The revolution was made against the despotism of the prince, his courtiers, and the privileged orders. It was thus very simple for the people, when it had risen up, to begin by crushing the henchmen of despotism. Who would have thought that, far from taking the slightest precaution against them, it had allowed them to lead an insurrection against it! Who would have thought that, far from excluding the supporters of the old regime, it called upon them to organize the new one! From the earliest days of the revolution, it let them disguise themselves in civic ["bourgeois"] dress, to participate in all its

> assemblies, to make a show of love of liberty, talk equality, and share in all its deliberations.
>
> Still today, infamous courtiers are at the head of the armies of the Republic, former valets of the tyrant command the soldiers of liberty, former traffickers of the state head our administrations, former dealers in chicanery form our tribunals, creatures of the court sit in our senate. These declared enemies of the revolution, in coalition with the priests, the capitalists, the financiers, the speculators, the large landowners, the merchants of luxury, intriguers of every sort, the flunkeys and the thugs, are the ones who have not ceased for the longest time to plot against the homeland and engineer the destruction of its children.[69]

What was to be done? Marat's idea was now a tired one. He could only call on all the friends of liberty to convene the next day at the Champ de Mars to unite with the Mountain in a holy federation to maintain the unity and indivisibility of the Republic, joining with brothers in the departments to defend liberty to their last breath. He had urged this thought on the Jacobins in a letter discussed by the club the previous evening. There was no uptake. The discussion was adjourned. In despair on 21 June, he lamented a collapse of revolutionary government. "It's impossible that this state of things can last much longer. We are in a complete anarchy, a hideous chaos."[70]

There was still a moment, however, for the journal to offer thumbnail sketches of Marat's fellow accused "dictators," Robespierre ("so little suited to head a party that he avoids any group where there is tumult and pales at the sight of a naked saber") and Danton ("he has all the talents and energy of a party head, but his natural inclinations lead him so far from every idea of domination that he prefers a toilet seat to a throne"). As for himself, Marat added, he had neither the capacity nor the desire for party leadership. "If the entire nation put the crown on my head for a moment, I'd knock it off because such is the frivolity, the mobility of the people that I would not be sure that having crowned me in the morning it would not hang me that evening."[71] So much for frustrated hopes.

Marat saved more space and energy, though, to settle scores against enemies great and small. Against Brissot, for one: "the former police spy, henchman of Lafayette, Narbonne, Bailly, agent of Capet, accomplice of Dumouriez, damned soul of the faction of the *hommes d'Etat*." Having slipped away from Paris like other denounced Girondins, some of them heading for counterrevolutionary centers, Brissot had been arrested in Moulins. Marat mocked his pleading letter of 12 June to the Convention as the performance of a "vile intriguer." Against the duc d'Orléans for another, betrayed by the Girondins "after secret liaisons" with them while "contriving to sit with the Mountain," and still on trial in Marseille.[72]

Against the Enragés, Jacques Roux and his allies Jean-François Varlet and Théophile Leclerc, Marat grew particularly vitriolic. These were the radicals he saw as more dangerous than any aristocrats, royalists, or counterrevolutionaries, "the fanatical false patriots who use their mask of civic commitment to mislead good citizens and throw them into violent, risky, reckless and disastrous actions." These were the men (Marat disregarded the women) who had plotted popular insurrection for months, demanded an agrarian law, and constantly outbid him in speaking on behalf of the poor. Roux had created an uproar in the Convention on 25 June by presenting a petition on behalf of the Gravilliers section (and quickly disowned by it) that amounted to a manifesto for a new revolution on behalf of the poor. For him, his momentary host in a former time who had claimed the sobriquet "the little Marat" as a badge of honor, The People's Friend had saved some especially vicious calumny. His denunciation of Roux on 5 July had elicited an equally violent pamphlet in response, as well as a highly charged confrontation between the two men on the evening of 9 July as Roux burst into Marat's apartment to demand a retraction.[73] When Roux left, according to witnesses, he paused at the door in fury and indignation to throw "a vengeful look impossible to describe."[74]

There was time for one last denunciation, against Jean-Louis Carra, an old competitor of Marat's for scientific laurels under the Old Regime, turned rival patriotic journalist in 1789 and his acrimonious but unsuccessful contestant for election to the Convention (a failure compensated by remarkable electoral success in the provinces). Their mutual hostility had turned poisonous in 1793 as Carra had become a leading propagandist of the Girondins, deadly in his eviscerations of The People's Friend. Marat had responded in March with a venomous demolition and called in June for Carra's removal from the Convention for negligent conduct as a deputy on mission in the Vendée as the rebellion there took form.[75] On 13 July, a fateful day, he published a scathing "Two Words for Carra," promising more to come.[76]

On 12 July, hearing a report that Marat was very ill, the Jacobin Club had sent a deputation to visit him. "We found him in the bath, a table, inkpot, papers and books around him, occupied as usual with public affairs," the deputation reported. "This is not an illness, it's an indisposition that never attacks the deputies on the right; it's too much patriotism packed and concentrated in too small a body. The efforts this causes him are killing him. He complained to us of the oblivion to which the Convention was consigning him by neglecting to read many letters containing views regarding public safety. He thanks the Jacobins for their friendship and sends them fraternal greetings."[77] Remembering the details of this scene vividly, the painter Jacques-Louis David, Marat's friend and radical political ally, would soon transform them into an iconic representation of the prophet's death. With other members of the Jacobin deputation, he was among Marat's last visitors. Only Hébert, the assistant prosecutor of the Commune whose arrest by the Commission of Twelve had fired Marat's outrage, visited to speak with him that evening for the first (and last) time. "Exhausted by illness," he recounted, "Marat was working for the people; he was putting in order the authentic proofs of a conspiracy that had been denounced to him and it's probably this work that cost him his life."[78]

The next day, 13 July, The People's Friend, ailing and marginalized, received Charlotte Corday, a young noblewoman fresh from Caen in Normandy, a center of federalist resistance to the Convention since the purge of 2 June. Moved by the report of proscribed Girondins who had sought refuge there, she had set out for Paris to destroy the monster they held responsible for their fate. Pleading misfortune but intent on assassination, she plunged an unerring knife into his breast as he worked in his medicinal bath. A remarkable document surfaced much later, a page of his journal purportedly stained by the copious flow of his blood. It is now on display in the Musée de la Bibliothèque de France.[79]

(8)

tomber la pétition de la gendarmerie nationale, (1) qui venoit lui dénoncer les ordres traîtreux de leurs chefs et solliciter leur destitution. Voyez-le décréter de porter au complet le département de Paris, qui devroit être traîné sur un échafaud, au lieu d'être remis en activité. Voyez-le ne prendre aucune mesure pour faire transférer la famille Capet, toujours au manège, où les courtisans contre-révolutionnaires arrivent déguisés en gardes nationaux, pour l'enlever. Mais ce qui ne laisse le moindre doute sur ses perfides projets; ce sont ses efforts continuels pour dissoudre l'assemblée des commissaires patriotes des sections, et rétablir la municipalité contre-révolutionnaire. Elle voit avec désespoir que tant que ces dignes commissaires seront en activité, c'est en vain qu'elle se flatteroit de couronner ses attentats; que, pour les poursuivre sans obstacles, il lui faut un département, une municipalité et des juges de paix, tous suppôts du despotisme, qui, loin de permettre au peuple le déployement de ses forces et l'exercice de sa justice contre les traîtres conjurés à sa perte, le répriment et l'enchaînent pour le faire égorger.

O vous, dignes commissaires des sections de Paris, vrais représentans du peuple, gardez-vous des pièges que vous tendent ses infidèles députés, gardez-vous de leurs séductions; c'est à votre civisme éclairé et courageux que la capitale doit en partie les succès de ses habitans, et que la patrie devra son triomphe. Restez en place pour notre repos, pour votre gloire, pour le salut de l'empire. Ne quittez le timon de l'autorité publique, remis en vos mains, qu'après que la convention nationale nous aura débarrassé du despote et de sa race indigne; après qu'elle aura réformé les vices monstrueux de la constitution, source éternelle d'anarchie et de désastres, après qu'elle aura [illegible] liberté publique sur des bases inébranlables. [illegible] pour cela, faites révoquer le funeste décret [illegible] des députés appellés à la composer. [illegible] convoquez toutes les sections à ce [illegible] sa puissance, et qu'il fasse des[illegible] les scélérats qui osent machiner [illegible] s'opposer à son bonheur.

[illegible] montrée dans la journée du 10, [illegible] toutes les qualifications [illegible] son égarement antérieur. [illegible] de tous les bons citoyens [illegible] les gendarmes leurs frères, [illegible] plus.

[illegible] l'Ami du Peuple.

N°. 678.

L'AMI DU PEUPLE,

JOURNAL POLITIQUE ET IMPARTIAL;

Par J.-P. MARAT, Auteur de l'Offrande à la patrie, du Moniteur, du Plan de Constitution, et de plusieurs autres ouvrages patriotiques.

Vitam impendere vero.

Du Mardi 13 Août 1792.

Le Peuple abusé par ses Représentans, ou les nouvelles trahisons des peres conscrits depuis la prise du château des Tuilleries.

Le 9 août 1792, les deux tiers de l'assemblée nationale se montroient, non seulement archigangrénés, mais effrontément contre-révolutionaires: et le 10, ils se disent non seulement bons patriotes, mais brûlans de zèle pour la loi de l'égalité qui les désespère, mais intrépidément dévoués au salut de la patrie, dont ils machinoient la ruine. Que dis-je, le 10 à neuf heures du matin, ils se montroient effrontés oppresseurs (1) du

(1) Quand le lâche Louis va chercher un asyle avec les siens au milieu de ses complices; en leur annonçant qu'il fui, pour épargner au peuple qu'il alloit faire égorger, LE GRAND CRIME DE LE PUNIR DE SES FORFAITS et en les assurant qu'il se croit en sûreté parmi eux: le président lui répond fièrement, au nom de ses confrères; « Votre majesté peut compter sur la fermeté de l'assemblée nationale, ses membres ont juré de mourir à leur poste, en soutenant les autorités constituées. Et au premier bruit du canon, tous ses traîtres se lèvent pour s'échapper; retenus par les reproches sanglans des [illegible] vont chercher leur salut en se confondant [illegible] été une grande gaucherie du patriote [illegible] pêché ces scélérats de fuir; ils auroient [illegible] le peuple, et nous en serions [illegible]

FIGURE 27.1. Bloodstained page of *L'Ami du peuple*, 1793 or 1830s? Tallandier/Bridgeman Images.

Well before the murder, journals had been reporting that Marat was dangerously ill, even asking for extreme unction, perhaps already dead. He may or may not have been on his deathbed that day, but Corday's knife did offer a kind of political resurrection. He was returned to mythical life in an unprecedented cult of modern political martyrdom raising him to heights of quasi-religious adulation that would have exceeded his most fantastic dreams.

A MOMENT OF MARTYRDOM

A crowd of several thousand surged toward Marat's apartment on the rue des Cordeliers the evening of 13 July as news of his assassination spread. The heat in Paris was blistering, the political temperature already heightened in anticipation of the Festival of Unity and Indivisibility planned for the following day, the mood of the crowd unpredictable. Throughout the city, confusion over the details of the death was laced with tears of lamentation, shouts of indignation, rumors of an aristocratic plot, talk of a lynching, calls for insurrection, fears of an impending massacre. After an initial interrogation of Corday on the spot, adroit action by the police with support from deputations of the Committee of Public Security and the General Council of the Commune succeeded in getting her from the scene of the crime to the Abbaye prison, passing through the angry crowd without serious incident. But peace in the street was preserved only by the promise of vengeance. The message conveyed to the restless gathering that evening by a member of the Committee on General Security, Drouet de Varenne, was probably close to the one he presented the following day in a report to the Convention. "Citizens . . . , your indignation is at its height . . . ; you want to be avenged . . . ; you will be. . . . The immoderate desire to satisfy the shade of this zealous lover of liberty must not trouble the harmony that reigns in this city. . . . Consider, citizens, that this is exactly what our enemies are waiting for. Be calm but terrible, you will be avenged. Liberty will triumph, it doesn't hinge on the loss of one man."[80]

The fear Drouet was expressing—that Corday's action was the spearhead of a vast conspiracy aiming in part to provoke a popular uprising that would consume Paris, trigger a reaction in the provinces, and thus ignite civil war—was a real one for the Montagnards. It ran through Hébert's report to the General Council of the Commune the very night of Marat's murder. "The people will recognize that the day of vengeance has not yet arrived," he had maintained. "It will contain its indignation and suspend its anger until the moment comes. Marat recommended surveillance in his writings. Let his death not occasion any agitation. . . . The day of vengeance has not arrived; let's instruct the departments, let's prove to them that Paris is not inhabited by cannibals. Let's weep at Marat's tomb but be calm and peaceful, this is the way to exterminate our enemies." At Hébert's urging, the General Council voted to demand that the Convention confer on the martyr the "honors of apotheosis," to participate as a body in his funeral ceremonies, and to place his bust in its assembly hall. Celebration and commemoration were offered in response to the desire for popular vengeance.[81]

The same theme was taken up on 14 July when Jeanbon Saint-André, president of the Convention, speaking in hushed and emotional tones to the silent assembly, confirmed that "a great crime" had been committed against "one of our brothers, one of the founders of the Republic, a representative of the sovereign." Expressions of gratitude, grief, and outrage followed as successive deputations from the sections expressed their sentiments. Acknowledging that immediate transfer of Marat's remains to the Pantheon was precluded by a rule postponing any such action for at least twenty years after an individual's decease, the Panthéon-Français section proclaimed that the delay could only increase the glory of this illustrious martyr of liberty. "His memory will doubtless grow as it passes through the crucible of history. Calumny dies, truth remains, the just man returns to life entire; the shade of the French Cato will not be offended by this honorable deferral; the hearts of all republicans are, in advance, its most durable pantheon."[82]

The call for commemoration nevertheless remained constantly shadowed by the cry for vengeance, not only against the assassin and her immediate accomplices but against the vast counterrevolutionary conspiracy assumed to be behind her. In its address, the Contrat Social section wanted more immediate commemoration along with punishment of the parricidal act. "Marat is no more. People, you have lost your friend. Marat is no more," lamented its spokesman. Casting his eyes on David's painting of the martyred Lepeletier displayed in the assembly hall, he appealed to the artist. "Take up your brush, there's another painting to be done . . . ," he cried. "I won't forget!" was David's immediate response. "And you," the section's orator continued, now addressing the deputies at large, "you who cannot return Marat to us, give us a law, decree the most hideous punishment; there isn't one cruel enough to avenge our loss . . . ; annihilate federalism and crime forever; teach fanatics the value of life and, instead of cutting it like a thread, make the torments inflicted on Marat's assassins deflect forever the parricidal hands threatening the heads of our representatives." The Rights of Man section, abjuring spontaneous acts of popular vengeance in its turn, similarly expressed its hopes for early execution of national vengeance. Demands for unprecedented acts of retribution against enemies of the Revolution continued to reverberate in the weeks that followed, mutating eventually into the Terror. In the meantime, the Convention called for the Revolutionary Tribunal to deal with Corday and turned its attention to men she had implicated while in Paris, notably Bishop Fauchet and the deputy Claude-Romain Lauze de Perret.[83]

Corday's rushed trial three days later turned into an unprecedented media sensation. The public crowded into the courtroom to witness the criminal in person; the press luxuriated in the coverage it offered the massive audience at large. No effort had been spared by the authorities to find or fabricate proof that Corday had acted in the service of a conspiracy originating among the Girondins purged on 2 June. Dismissing any such charges, she remained unwavering in her insistence that she had been alone in conceiving and committing a deed that had delivered the Republic from the anarchist perverting it. Her unrepentant assertion, "I killed a man to save a hundred million," skillfully mirrored and outbid Marat's own calls for proactive bloodshed. As Guillaume Mazeau has noted, it also nullified the expiatory character of the legal mechanisms of prosecution and conviction. Punishment was immediate. After the painting of a portrait she requested to secure her fame, she was taken to the scaffold, standing erect and alone on the tumbril.[84] Before the theater of public opinion, Marat had met his match.

Repeated many times, the call for the pantheonization of The People's Friend was brought before the Jacobin Club as early as 14 July by his dear friend Bentabole. There it met with a powerful objection from Robespierre, who proclaimed in an apparent fit of jealousy (as Bentabole remarked) that mere chance had accorded Marat, sooner than himself, the honor of the assassin's dagger. Was the martyr to be placed in the Pantheon alongside the criminal intriguer Mirabeau, Robespierre sneered. "It's not today that we must give the people the spectacle of funereal pomp." To his mind, funereal ceremonies were dangerous; they had to wait until the Republic was victorious. "They make the people believe that the friends of liberty are compensating for the loss inflicted upon them and feel no further compulsion to avenge it. With the satisfaction of having honored the virtuous man, the desire to avenge him dies out in the heart, enthusiasm gives way to indifference, and his memory risks falling into oblivion." The murderers of Marat and Lepeletier had to expiate their crimes, Robespierre insisted; monstrous perpetrators of tyranny, treasonous deputies, all those resisting the Revolution had to pay with their blood; until then, the municipality had to set aside any idea of a funeral celebration. In effect, the Incorruptible was taking on Marat's mantle in calling for violence to avenge him, just as the Enragés they both so hated, Roux and Leclerc, were rushing to claim the legacy of The People's Friend for themselves by publishing competing continuations of his journal. With Robespierre's support, Simonne Evrard denounced the two radicals for daring to "usurp the memory of The People's Friend" when she appeared, as widow Marat, before the Convention on 8 August.[85]

Marat's corpse, meanwhile, could not remain unburied. Control of his remains had effectively been captured by the Cordelier Club as part of its own effort to claim his political legacy. On 15 July, the club announced its intention to separate the martyr's heart from the body (a practice not unusual at the death of the great) as a totem to be preserved in its meeting hall. The Jacobins, for their part, recognizing the Cordeliers' right to the heart, had to console themselves with a vow to perpetuate the martyr's spirit. The plan was to offer the embalmed corpse to the public in the church of the former Cordeliers before it was buried in a vault to be constructed for it in the adjoining garden. But the state of the cadaver presented challenges for such a public display, as David reported to the Convention that same morning. Parts of the body could not be shown uncovered because the victim "had leprosy and his skin had been burned." Though the artist still hoped to array his friend as the Jacobin delegation had witnessed him at work in his bathtub the day before the assassination, that no longer seemed possible. Still less imaginable was a proposal to parade the bath bearing the embalmed body throughout the departments, thus displaying to "the whole earth . . . the remains of this great man, this true republican." On the evening of 15 April, instead, the corpse was offered to view on an elevated platform in the Cordeliers church, with a side of the chest left uncovered to reveal the wound and a bare arm extended with pen in hand. An inscription bore the proclamation, "Marat, friend of the people, assassinated by its enemies. Moderate your joy, enemies of the homeland, there will be avengers." In the hours that followed, crowds of Parisians filed past to show their respects, but the cadaver had reached such a state of putrefaction in the infernal heat by midday on 16 April that the funeral had to be advanced a day and held that very evening.[86]

Hastily arranged, the ceremony was nonetheless a grandiose affair. By this time, the Revolution, and particularly its "pageant master" David, was adept at planning such commemorations. The funeral cortège left the Cordeliers church at 6:00 p.m., parading by torchlight and to the music of Gluck regularly interrupted by the sound of cannon. Passing through the streets of the Théâtre-Français section to the Pont-Neuf, it traversed the Seine, followed the quay to the Pont-au-Change and returned right across the river toward the Théâtre-Français itself and thence to the rue des Cor-

FIGURE 27.2. Unknown artist, Marat's corpse displayed at the Cordeliers church, 16 July 1793. Musée Carnavalet, Paris. Bridgeman Images.

Note: The Musée Carnavalet attributes this painting to Fougeat, an artist about whom nothing further is known. The attribution is based on identification of the painting with one on the same subject submitted for the *concours de l'an II* (the artistic competition organized by the Committee of Public Safety for 1793–94). Two lists of the submissions to this competition exist: that of the "Inspecteurs de la Salle" contains an entry for a "Marat exposé aux Cordeliers (Esquisse)" submitted by a Fougea; that of the Collection Desloynes includes an "Exposition du corps de Marat, tableau de 24 pouces sur 16." See Annie Jourdan, *Les monuments de la Révolution 1770–1804. Une histoire de representation* (Paris, 1997), 458, 474.

deliers. Halted every half-hour for speeches by representatives of the sections, the march took six hours. A contingent of gendarmes and veterans led the way, followed by deputations from the sections marching under their banners, members of popular societies, representatives of the Parisian authorities, and some eighty members of the Convention, most of them Montagnards. Citizens en masse followed in the rear. At the center of the procession, Marat's bathtub was shouldered by members of the Society of Revolutionary Women and his body borne on a litter carried by a dozen or so men. The corpse was shrouded by a cloth regularly dampened to delay putrefaction and bathed in the perfumed air of aromatics to disguise the smell of the decaying flesh. The assiduity of the revolutionary women in attending to the corpse, covering it with flowers, and collecting drops of its blood, was particularly notable.[87]

FIGURE 27.3. Marat funeral monument, 1793. Bibliothèque nationale de France, Gallica Digital Library.

At midnight, upon the return of the cortège to the garden of the Cordeliers, the corpse was committed to a vault prepared for it under the trees. The thousands of citizens who witnessed the interment were still dispersing at 2:00 a.m. An inscription attached to the coffin celebrated the return of the body to nature—rather than its conveyance to the corrupt splendor of the Pantheon—as the only inhumation appropriate to a sansculotte. The president of the Convention, still warning against hasty and ill-considered actions, assured the mourners that the time for vengeance would soon arrive. In the speeches of commemoration that followed, vows that vengeance would come were interwoven with those sustaining

FIGURE 27.4. Bust of Marat, polychrome stone, 1793. Bridgeman Images.

the theme of Marat's immortality. "Here lies Marat, assassinated by the enemies of the people, whose constant friend he was," read the epitaph. "Marat is not dead!" became the speakers' refrain.[88]

Interment brought no closure. Instead, it marked the beginning of an impassioned cult of Marat that would last for many months. One of the most remarkable expressions of this fever took form as a new cortège gathered in the Luxembourg Gardens on 28 July, this time to transport Marat's heart to an altar in the assembly hall of the Cordelier Club. To find a worthy receptacle for the relic, the Cordeliers had turned to the warehouse of treasures confiscated from the Tuileries palace after 10 August 1792, where they had found an urn fit for a king.[89] Among those attending the ceremony of installation, one member of the club rose to heights of oratorical fervor. "Oh heart of Jesus, Oh heart of Marat," he exclaimed; "sacred heart of Marat, sacred heart of Jesus, you have the same right to our homage." The analogy was extended as the enraptured disciple proceeded to identify the Jacobins and the Cordeliers with the apostles and the Pharisees with the aristocrats. "Jesus is a prophet, and Marat is a god," he continued, "and that is not all: I can say that Marat's companion is perfectly like Mary: one saved the infant Jesus in Egypt, the other snatched Marat from the blade of Lafayette, who like Herod would have put an end to him." The comparison was too much for Brochet, one of the organizers of the ceremony. "Marat is not made to be compared with Jesus," he objected. "This latter man gave birth to superstition, he defended kings, and Marat had the courage to crush them. Never talk to us about this Jesus, these are stupidities, germs of fanaticism, and all this nonsense has mutilated liberty in its cradle. Philosophy alone must be the guide of republicans and their only god is liberty."[90]

The exchange has echoed ever since in historiographical discussions of the meaning of the cult of Marat that followed. Was Marat sanctified as an object of devotion assimilated to Jesus in a broader appropriation of traditional religious observances for revolutionary purposes? Or was Jesus secularized: denigrated as the false god of kings and aristocrats, or sans-culottized with Marat as a hero of the people? The most careful analysis of the orations comparing Jesus and Marat during this period offers stronger evidence for the latter view.[91] Deification of The People's Friend (often in

FIGURE 27.5. "Inauguration du buste de Marat . . . , Place de la Réunion," 1793. Bibliothèque nationale de France, Gallica Digital Library.

analogy with the heroes among the Ancients) was one impulse here; desacralization of Jesus the other. They became two sides of the dechristianization movement that swept through France in the latter part of 1793. As Christian icons were ripped from the churches, they were replaced by memorials to Marat and other martyrs of the Revolution. Nor was the exercise of violence in memory of The People's Friend missing as an ingredient in these calls for what became the popular overture to the Terror. "Precious remains of a God," another Cordelier exclaimed as the heart of Marat (in an apparent change of plan) was suspended in its urn from the ceiling of the club's meeting hall a day or two later. "Will we perjure your shade with impunity; you call on us for vengeance, your assassins are beside us; we promised on Sunday to annihilate them . . . and they exist . . . what shall I say, they still triumph. . . . Awake Cordeliers . . . it's time, let's run to avenge Marat, let's run to dry the tears of a weeping France, its breast torn apart by criminals." At this speaker's instigation, the club swore to march to the Convention en masse the following day to obtain, with the shortest possible delay, the destitution and deportation of all the nobles.[92]

Over the following months, to improvise on a phrase of Albert Soboul's, the sans-culottes communed in the memory of the martyrs of liberty, Marat principal among them. They were stormy months. The Convention had been purged, hence undermined as a body representing the entire nation, provoking federalist revolts against the tyranny of the capital that were now added to the threat of the counterrevolutionary uprising in the Vendée. To the east the Prussians, and to the north the Austrians, now allied with the British, were resurgent on the battlefields, driving French forces back in disarray. The Jacobin constitution, sent to the departments for ratification the very day of Marat's death, remained in limbo, awaiting popular acceptance. After its overwhelming approval, its implementation was delayed indefinitely as the Montagnards perpetuated their grip on power in the Convention on 10 October, proclaiming their emergency government "revolutionary until the peace." During the intervening period of profound uncertainty, Marat came to symbolize unity in the popular resolve to mobilize in defense of the Republic against its enemies. As the Convention declared a *levée en masse* in August, and the sans-culottes pressed their demand that terror be made the order of the day in September, children across the country were named, and towns and sections renamed, in his honor. Souvenirs of various kinds—not only busts but prints, miniatures, plates, box lids, medallions, obelisks, brooches, rings—flooded the market. Monuments were erected; busts were paraded and installed in countless ceremonies; endless discourses were intoned. The Convention was constantly bombarded with requests from sections,

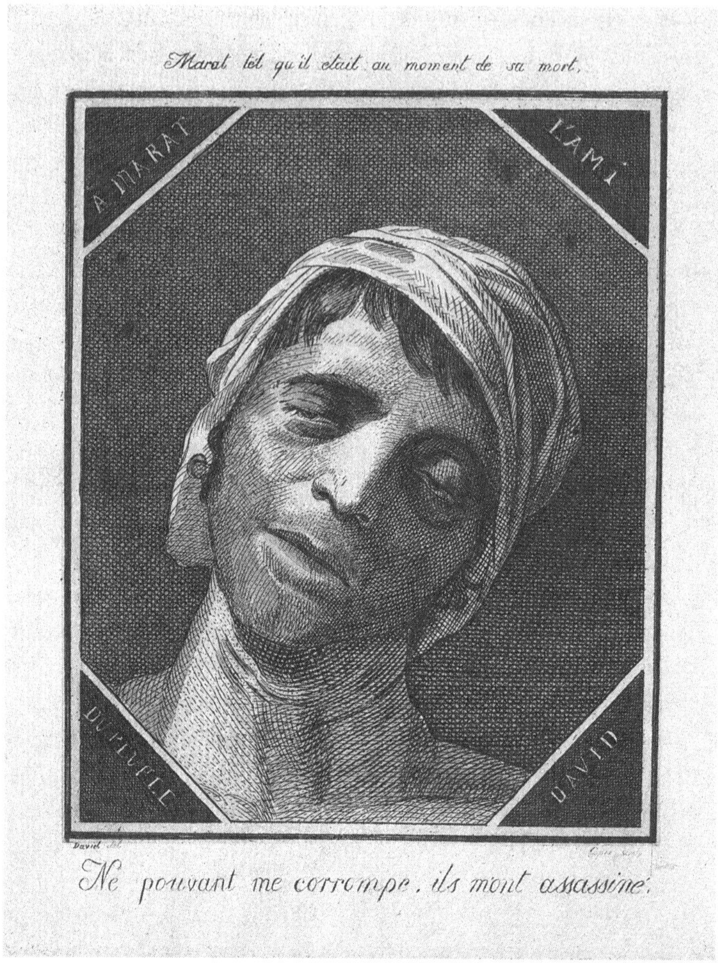

FIGURE 27.6. Jacques-Louis Copia, colored etching after Jacques-Louis David, "Marat tel qu'il était au moment de sa mort," 1793. Public domain mark. Wellcome Collection.

popular societies, and other groups for deputations to participate in these commemorations. More than fifty of them occurred in Paris between the beginning of September and the end of October, while many more were celebrated in the provinces.[93]

The rarest of all the artifacts memorializing Marat, floating above them all in its evocation of the sublime sacrifice of the martyr, was the painting David had promised the Convention on 14 July. Three (old-style) months later to the day, informing his fellow deputies that this work had been completed, the artist asked leave to lend it to the members of his own Musée section, to be paraded together with his painting of the martyred

FIGURE 27.7. Anonymous print, "Marat à l'immortalité," 1794. Bibliothèque nationale de France, Gallica Digital Library.

Lepeletier in a ceremony this section planned for two days later. The festival was notable not only for its rare totems but also for the fact that it had been preceded that morning by the execution of Marie Antoinette. The immense parade was headed by ten ranks of drummers and riflemen, followed by a detachment of the armed forces, popular societies with their standards, the sections with their banners, deputies of constituted bodies, and soldiers of the National Guard with flags and drums. Then followed the entire Musée section, a group of musicians leading the deputation from the Convention, conscripts carrying busts of Marat and Lepeletier, and female citizens of the section, dressed in white, leading their children by the hand and carrying flowers for Marat's tomb. Forces of the section brought up the rear. The marchers stopped at the Place de la Réunion, where they burned a copy of the indictment from Marat's trial in April. (A festival organized by the Society of Revolutionary Women on 18 August had also inaugurated a massive wooden obelisk there in his honor.) They then proceeded down the quay and into the great courtyard of the Louvre, where

David's paintings of Marat and Lepeletier had been mounted on two sarcophagi. Before these monuments, a funeral service was conducted, complete with music, hymns, and orations.[94]

Several weeks later, on 14 November, David's *Marat* was presented formally to the Convention. The artist's discourse was solemn in the extreme, a condensation of all the themes Marat had come to symbolize during these months. "The people demanded its friend back," David intoned:

> it made its voice heard; it provoked my art; it wanted to see the lineaments of its faithful friend again. David! Take up your brushes, it cried, avenge our enemy, avenge Marat! Let his vanquished enemies pale once more in seeing his disfigured traits, reduce them to envying the fate of the man whom, unable to corrupt, they had the baseness to get assassinated! I heard the voice of the people, I obeyed.[95]

David had inscribed two texts in his masterpiece. One was Corday's blazingly duplicitous claim to an audience that was her due as one of the unfortunates toward whom Marat had constantly shown his benevolence: her presence was not entirely erased from the painting. The other was the barely legible note left by the victim to accompany the gift of a 5 franc assignat to a mother of five children. Together, they evoked the virtuous Marat who had impoverished himself as the friend of the people and succorer of the poor, ready to shed his own blood and tears for their cause. Together, they distanced him from that other Marat, the figment of slanderous imaginations, the cannibal calling for the blood of others.

"Hasten all, mothers, widows, orphans, oppressed soldiers, all those he defended at the risk of his life!" David now implored on behalf of the martyr.

> Draw near, contemplate your friend. He who kept watch for us is no more. His pen, the terror of traitors, slips from his hand! Oh Despair! Your indefatigable friend is dead! He is dead, your friend, in giving you his last morsel of bread; he is dead, leaving nothing for his burial! Posterity, you will avenge him: you will tell his nephews how much wealth he could have amassed if he had not preferred virtue to a fortune! Humanity, you will tell those who call him a *drinker of blood* that your cherished child, Marat, never shed anything but tears!
>
> I invoke you, execrable calumny; yes, I will see you, one day not too distant, stifling desiccated serpents in your two hands, dying of rage as you swallow your own poisons. Then we will see aristocracy, exhausted and confused, no longer daring to show itself.

FIGURE 27.8. Jacques-Louis David, *La mort de Marat*, 1793. Musée royale des Beaux Arts de Belgique, Brussels. Bridgeman Images.

And you, Marat, from the depths of your tomb your cinders will rejoice, you will no longer regret your mortal remains; your glorious task will have been fulfilled and the people, crowning you a second time will bear you to the Pantheon.

To you, my colleagues, I offer the homage of my brushes. Gazing upon Marat's livid and bloodied traits, you will remember his virtues that must never cease to be your own.

Concluding this speech with its appeal for virtue among the deputies, David urged that the vice and imposture symbolized by the remains of Mirabeau now be swept from the Pantheon and replaced at the people's demand by those of the man who had never lied to them. On Romme's motion, this demand for Marat's pantheonization, frequently sounded since his death, was now immediately taken up and decreed by the Convention. For the moment, the removal of Mirabeau's remains was left undecided by the deputies. But the Convention ordered engravings of David's paintings of Marat and Lepeletier to be commissioned at the expense of the nation and a thousand prints to be made for distribution to the deputies and the departments. The paintings themselves were ordered to be placed permanently in the assembly hall of the Convention and legislative bodies succeeding it. There they joined the bust of Marat already installed on 5 November.[96]

Though these were high points in the celebrations of Marat's martyrdom, the power of the sans-culottes pressing for them began to fade as the Convention extended the power of revolutionary government to control popular activism and centralize Terror under the aegis of the Committee of Public Safety. Integrated into the cult of Reason, that of Marat and other revolutionary martyrs shared its fate. Robespierre's reluctance to see The People's Friend pantheonized held firm: it was not until 21 September 1794, weeks after the Incorruptible's overthrow as a tyrant on 9 Thermidor (27 July 1794), that Marat's remains were transferred to the temple of great men he had initially so despised. Less than six months later, on 8 February 1795, the wheel of fortune turned again. His remains were removed and transported across the street to be buried unmarked in the cemetery of the church of Saint-Etienne-du-Mont.

CONCLUSION

A REVOLUTIONARY DIPTYCH

"From the Mountain it's come," Marat declared in his journal at the moment of the Montagnards' rapid improvisation of a constitution. "Eight days was enough to complete it, and this plan is a monument of popularity and virtue." "This alone will serve to demonstrate finally to the eyes of the nation that, if the Convention has waited so long to give it good laws and lead it to liberty, peace, abundance and happiness, this is because at the heart of the assembly there was an anticivic, vile, criminal, atrocious faction that hid under the mask of hypocrisy to capture its confidence and conspire with the enemies of the homeland to achieve its destruction."[1]

Though he had played no part in its formulation, he printed this Jacobin constitution in his journal on 12–13 June. But he had less interest in discussing the new text than in railing anew against the one the Mountain had discarded, its authors, and its supporters. He had detested the Girondin constitution since Condorcet presented it to the Convention in February 1793 in what Marat mocked as his customary "reedy tone." He continued to do so in the following months. The heart of the issue between the two texts, ever the fundamental revolutionary problem of the relationship between sovereignty represented and sovereignty embodied, had become decisively evident in the debate over the trial of Louis XVI, and more specifically in the debate over the appeal to the primary assemblies. Until that moment the political stance inherited by the Girondins had held to a strong conception of the sovereign power delegated to the legislature, rejecting populist claims that the decisions of the representative body be constantly referred to the judgment of the public. Abruptly, faced with the clear prospect that the Convention would find Louis XVI guilty, the Girondins had reversed this position, calling for an appeal to the people on the grounds that a referendum was necessary to prevent the representatives from arrogating and distorting the expression of the general will. The Jacobins, Marat with them, had reacted by insisting on the power of the elected representative body to express the will of the people without any further need or obligation for a referendum. The condition of their claim was to achieve a unity of will within the legislative body that could mirror the unity of the general will of the people outside it. The circuit of will between the people and its representatives had to be closed.

Condorcet countered their challenge by imagining a new constitution that would free the practice of representation from factionalism, secure it from popular radicalism, and eliminate the constant threat of insurrection against it in the name of the general will. Marat responded by invoking the threat of popular insurrection, and eventually provoking it, in the service of an effort to purge the legislative body to give it the internal unity that would mirror and express the unitary will of the people. For one, the answer was in dispersing and rationalizing the exercise of power; for the other, the answer lay in concentrating power in the name of the people. For Condorcet, the key lay in organizing the deliberations of the primary assemblies in a way that would end further revolutions "by giving citizens the means to carry them out under a legal peaceful form." The questions submitted to them would be reduced to a set of propositions requiring a yes-or-no answer, to be decided in short meetings that would allow the introduction of no other business. Most important, any fifty citizens could convoke a primary assembly to initiate a demand for legislative action that, upon its approval, could be passed up the chain of assemblies from districts to departments to the National Assembly. If the National Assembly refused to consider the matter, its decision would be sent back to the primary assemblies for ratification, with new elections the consequence if the result was negative. This procedure, he argued, would ensure that "neither the voice of the representatives of the people, nor that of a portion of the citizens, could ever elude the empire of the general will."[2]

Marat had immediately recognized in February that the crucial element in Condorcet's project lay in the "many precautions to be taken in order to shackle the primary assemblies under the pretext of allowing no disorder to prevail and prevent them from lapsing into insurrection." The assemblies would be so constantly in movement for the least thing, he objected, that citizens would have no other occupation but assembling and deliberating. What madness, he expostulated, to set them in motion from one end of the state to the other to exercise the right of censure over acts of the legislature. Who could believe that to propose a new law or revise an old one, something a simple deputy could do, would tie up five million men for six weeks? In addition, he observed, the right of petition would be annihilated, and everything the popular societies had been doing so well voluntarily would instead be made obligatory for the primary assemblies. The criminal faction behind this constitution could not better have served the public good than by offering this monstrous proposal, he jibed; they would have done devastating harm with a mediocre text that might have passed. "In any case, it's from the Mountain that the Constitution will come. Despite this puerile and perfidious effort, the people's wait will not bring disappointment."

Five months later, The People's Friend could declare his prediction fulfilled. The Mountain, he proclaimed, had replaced a monstrous plan that would have rendered liberty a burden and filled the French with horror, "torn them from their personal occupations to pass their lives in their sections and, under the pretext of reestablishing them in their sovereignty, left them no time to cultivate their fields, or even eat and drink."[3]

Condorcet fought back. In the bitter analysis of the Montagnard scheme he soon published anonymously, he protested that electoral arrangements he had proposed to ensure accurate expression of the common reason had been replaced by procedures that would maximize the cacophony of competing wills. An executive council would no longer be elected directly by the people in the primary assemblies but would be selected by the legislature from nominees chosen by secondary assemblies. Those "who constantly flatter the people, who repeat that it is great and almost infallible when they hope to lead it to acts of violence," had become more cautious, he charged, when it was a matter of allowing it an independent choice of ministers. The right of referendum he had championed to approve or initiate legislation and constitutional change had been rendered meaningless. "Weigh these observations, Citizens, and you will see that one of these plans is made for the nation, the other to ensure the power of a particular association. One has as its object the most entire equality of influence: its aim has been to move from the fact of equality to a real equality of rights. The other gives the towns all the influence, because that same group hopes to retain most power there. You will judge which of the two projects has most scrupulously maintained for the citizens all the exercise of their political rights that it is useful for them to reserve for themselves. . . . You will perceive that everything that is good in the second is borrowed from the first; and that where the latter wishes to correct it only succeeds in perverting and corrupting."[4]

By the time Condorcet was indicted for this protest as a man "who imagines it is his duty to give laws to the French republic because he sat with some savants in the Academy," he had already fled into hiding to avoid arrest. He left behind him for publication a sketch of the vast conception of the generalized mathematization of social life he saw as the key to popular enlightenment and individual liberty. His social mathematics, ranging from the optimization of individual choices in everyday life to the rationalization of elections, political decision-making, and social choice, was meant to secure a democratic representative system from the despotism of ignorance and the tyranny of popular will.

Condorcet would die in an effort at final escape the following February, barely ten months after Marat had been assassinated. He was rehabilitated after the Terror by the Thermidorians who made his posthumous *Sketch for a Historical Picture of the Progress of the Human Mind* a chapbook for a renewed experiment in more liberal politics. They published it in March 1795, a month after they had cast Marat from the Pantheon into renewed infamy. Long at odds, these two figures were Saturn's children: each fell victim in his own way to revolutionary carnage. Their fates invite a brief concluding reflection on their divergent paths from Enlightenment into Revolution.

As far as I know, Condorcet and Marat never addressed one another face to face. Their very first encounter, in 1780, nevertheless set the fractious tone for their stance toward each other. Condorcet the aristocrat, established as a mathematician and political economist, spokesman for enlightenment and reform at the heart of the Old Regime, led the most powerful scientific body in Europe. Marat, the recent Swiss immigrant from England with no academic pedigree but immense scientific ambitions, was serving as doctor to the guardsmen of the comte d'Artois while sidelining his radical impulses and sacrificing his profitable medical practice in an effort to unseat Newton. Each was to deride the other as a charlatan.

Marat and Condorcet thus found themselves at odds from the start because Condorcet guarded the gates to the scientific fame and glory Marat desperately wanted and found himself denied. Marat carried his bitter resentment of the academicians into the French Revolution, blasting them as "vile henchmen of the despot, gutless champions of despotism." He despised Condorcet as the epitome of privileged beneficiaries of the Old Regime who penetrated the new political order, claiming enlightened leadership and reaping its rewards while undermining the Revolution from within.

There were also more profound intellectual differences between the two men. They were both Newtonians, but of very different stripes. Condorcet took his inspiration from the *Principia*. His early scientific work had been engaged in the great enterprise of continental mathematical physicists to translate the outdated mathematics of Newton's text into the modern calculus, to clarify its problems, iron out its obscurities, extend its theorems. That enterprise eventually yielded the system of the world laid out by Laplace that became what we now think of as the Newtonian system of the world. Its scientific model moved away from the search for ultimate physical causes of phenomena toward an epistemology of analytical abstraction. It aspired to a mathematization of the physical world in which "forces" and "fluids" became a figure of speech, a shorthand for the expression of a set of abstract, analytical relations expressing observed phenomena.

Marat, in contrast, was a Newtonian of the *Optics*, the founding text of a work of eighteenth-century empiricism, not only for its experiments with the prism but for its speculations about possible forces and fluids understood as real physical causes and effects. It was in the spirit of that work that he tried to show the actual matter of the fluid of fire, as well as the diffraction of light as an effect of the force of gravity. His misfortune as a scientist was to see his research on combustion swept aside by the paradigm shift in chemistry accomplished by Lavoisier at the very same time. Lavoisier had advanced by applying the combinatorial method of the mathematicians: his analytical method of investigation aimed to reduce phenomena to their elements through processes of decomposition and recomposition. Marat's approach, in contrast, was more essentialist: he wanted to grasp the very matter of fire, to display its very nature as a material entity. Above all, he wanted to show, to disclose, and to reveal. In comparison with the more modern mathematization that gave the Paris Academy its greatest prestige, his work appeared reactionary.

In moral philosophy and politics, as in science, Condorcet and Marat were radically opposed in their visions. Their differences in this regard were exposed early by their responses to the sensationist arguments for the primacy of self-interest they confronted in Helvétius's *De l'esprit*. "I am not of the opinion of Helvétius," Condorcet wrote to Turgot, "since I admit in man a sentiment the force of which he does not seem to have suspected." As a sensitive being, Condorcet reasoned, man seeks pleasure and avoids pain. But, as a sensitive being, he also finds that sympathy, or benevolence, forms spontaneously in his heart at the sight of the pain or pleasure of another being. This is the experience Condorcet sees as the origin of moral principles and the motivation for virtue.[5]

Marat, for his part, also found Helvétius's arguments wanting. But he refuted "the sophistical author of *De l'esprit*" by exalting love of glory as an ultimate motivating principle beyond the power of physical sensation to provoke. As for sympathy or benevolence, he was savage in repudiating the argument that pity is a natural sentiment humans share with animals. He found no wellspring of compassion native to the human breast. At bottom, his thinking was profoundly misanthropic. He saw violence as constitutive of society and the undergirding of liberty. He made it his constant theme that the French Revolution had failed radically in 1789 by not eliminating its enemies more ruthlessly from the very start. As the Revolution continued, his demands for slaughter of the enemies of the people escalated.

The People's Friend was no less dismissive of the notion of the progress of the human mind and the benefits of social transformation arising from it, the idea that became the principal element of Condorcet's legacy. "They repeat everywhere that this is the century of philosophy," he insisted in *Les Charlatans modernes*. "What a contrast between our ridiculous pretensions and our stupid credulity. . . . Despite the philosophers of our day . . . there is no progress for human reason. The experience of the fathers is lost for their sons and each individual, starting from the point of ignorance, instructs himself only by his own effort."[6]

For Condorcet, the philosopher of modernity, one might say, time is on the side of humankind. For Marat, the classical republican, time is its enemy. "Liberty has the fate of all other things," he had warned in England in 1774: "It yields to Time, which destroys every thing." This was the stark conclusion of *The Chains of Slavery*, the book upon which he drew for the rest of his political life. He was advertising its French adaptation in the very last issues of his journal in 1793. In the conception of politics upon which it drew, liberty would die without civic virtue, which in turn would die without social and institutional constraints against egotism and corruption, and in the absence of political invigoration by the constant engagement of the body of citizens. Lethargy and somnolence were the seedbed for tyranny in this political theory, vigilance and agitation were the condition of liberty. Marat made it his constant mission after 1789 to rouse the people from its political slumber, awakening it to the abyss that lay ever beneath its feet.

Marat's English experience left him with a book keenly attuned to the threat of parliamentary representation rendered dangerous and potentially despotic in a society where money corroded civic virtue and selfishness corrupted electors and elected alike. In England in 1774, he saw the threat to liberty embodied in the so-called placemen and pensioners within the House of Commons, the men whose loyalty to the crown and its ministers was assured by their dependence on the civil list of the monarchy. In France in 1789, he saw the same threat in the privileged members of the Old Regime who, like Condorcet, remained in place to threaten and corrupt the New Regime from within. Some of his earliest calls were for a purge of placemen and pensioners in the Constituent Assembly. "Let's take the ax to the root of the tree," he trumpeted in one of the earliest issues of his journal. "The political machine is only ever recharged by violent shocks, just as the air is only purified by storms."

Political purification also required insistence on the need to constrain the power of the representative body. In Marat's view, the sovereign power to declare the general will, absolute and unlimited, could only ever reside in the body of the people itself. Conversely, representation, unavoidable in a state as large and complex as France, could only ever be limited; representatives could only ever be held in distrust of their tendency toward corruption and self-interest, their potential to reduce the people to servitude in service to paymasters. The decrees of the representative body, he insisted, could have only provisional force pending their formal sanction by the people. He saw constant political vigilance, now in the form of daily surveillance by the press, as the only means of constraining the power of the representative body to distort or defy the popular will. Seizing a public identity as a journalist, he made himself the eye of the people, its sentinel against corrupt and misguided representatives.

That a new constitution should require that the decrees of a legislature be sanctioned by popular vote is, in fact, one of the few points of agreement between Marat and Condorcet early in the Revolution. Condorcet was also profoundly aware, if on other grounds than Marat's, of the risks inherent in representative government. His most ambitious mathematical work in the previous years had been dedicated to the proposition that the obligation of citizens to obey the laws rested on their assurance of the likelihood that the deliberations of a representative assembly would yield rational outcomes for the common good. His mathematics of decision-making aimed at methods of estimating that likelihood, depending as it must on such variables as the number of decision makers, their degree of enlightenment, the formulation of the questions they addressed, and their voting procedures. His purpose had been to show how the expression of individual wills and opinions could be transformed into the collective exercise of reason, but only under constrained voting systems.

In the course of the Revolution, Condorcet's fears and hesitations about the risks of representation were amplified as factionalism within the successive national assemblies fed, and were fed by, the radicalization of popular politics and the elaboration of claims to express the popular will from outside, and against, the representative body. This was the context in which the two men played out their most bitter political differences to the end.

As a deputy to the Convention, Marat shifted ground. Opposing the Girondin call for a referendum on the punishment of Louis XVI, he was obliged to insist with the Jacobins on the unrestrained power of the representative body to express the sovereign will of the people. But that will could only be construed as unitary. It followed that as conflict between Girondins and Jacobins intensified in 1793, so did Marat's calls for an insurrection by activists in the clubs and sections of Paris to purge the Convention and restore the unitary expression of the sovereign popular will.

To conclude, one might say that in politics, as in science, Condorcet wanted abstraction. He wanted to disperse the people and think of political and social life in terms of the freest possible choices for individuals. He wanted to avoid the concentration of power, the embodiment of will, the focalization of conflict. He wanted to make the exercise of political power a kind of rationalized background hum to everyday social life through the play of a multiplicity of elections, votes, pluralities. He wanted to abstract social life in the same way: to understand social action as the exercise of social choice among free and independent individuals rendered more rational through probabilistic reasoning. He embraced the model of the market in economic life. He imagined a better future.

Marat wanted quite the opposite. His science of disclosure devolved into a politics of suspicion and a search for hidden conspiratorial actors behind the apparent contingency of events. He wanted political will embodied in the people, even as he despaired of its democratic capacities. He wanted to sense its physicality and corporeality, to feel its embodied collective will. He feared the weakening of the people's vigor, its enervation through corruption, egotism, individualism. He wanted the goad of suspicion, vigilance, and denunciation, the power of repression, not the search for deliberation, consensus, and rational choice. He distrusted the logic of the market, and the power of money and self-interest to impoverish the people and pervert the public good.

From this perspective, Condorcet was the apostle of modern liberal society, Marat the classical republican martyr, the prophet of Terror, the first modern populist. Technologies of political communication and modes of political performance have changed in more than two hundred years. But together with other political actors in their eighteenth-century garb, these revolutionaries confronted dilemmas of constitutional restraint, transgressive leaders, and willful popular movements. Their crucial issue, the relationship between sovereignty represented and sovereignty embodied, still threatens democracy today.

ACKNOWLEDGMENTS

I have many friends and colleagues to thank for support and encouragement over the years it has taken to bring this book to fruition. I owe my deepest gratitude to Emma Rothschild and Dan Edelstein. True believers in the project from the outset, they have read and commented on its chapters as they were completed and sustained its progress by constant conversation. I've benefited, too, from the critical appraisals of often substantial parts of the manuscript by other generous readers, including Charles Walton, Andrew Jainchill, Bruno Belhoste, Kent Wright, Robert Morrissey, Jessica Riskin, Daniel Gordon, Ian Beacock, and David Bell, not to mention by name the legion of colleagues in seminars, workshops, and other events for which I made presentations of my work. James Sheehan generously weighed the work as a whole. Jeremy Popkin, François Zanetti, Laurent Cuvelier, Benoît Carré, and Damien Tricoire shared and discussed their unpublished work. Nicolas Rieucau has taken time from his unrelenting pursuit of Condorcet's correspondence to help with a variety of research issues in Paris. Katherine McDonough and Alvaro Santana-Acuña have also provided generous technical help. Colin Jones, Robert Darnton, David Como, Jonathan Gienapp, Dena Goodman, Peter Reill, Richard Saller, Dennis Sepper, Michel Biard, and Guillaume Mazeau also readily answered particular questions.

The book is also the continuation of a long conversation, now sadly one-sided, with my old friend, François Furet.

I am eager, too, to acknowledge the extensive institutional support from which I have benefited in my research and writing. The Stanford

Humanities Center granted me three annual fellowships over the years, supported by a gift from the Mericos Foundation, and the Institute for Advanced Research in Paris hosted me for another. I gained much from engagement with visitors and fellow scholars in residence in these centers during those years. At Stanford, the School of Humanities and Sciences and the Department of History have generously underwritten my research and publication and provided the company of remarkable colleagues and students. The Europe Center has also helped make possible the publication of this book.

Among crucial institutions, I also want to acknowledge the assistance of the often unheralded staffs of the Bibliothèque nationale de France, the British Library, and Stanford University Libraries. I owe a particular debt to Sarah Sussman, curator of French and Italian collections at Stanford, who has been an unfailing resource over the years. The Hathi Trust became a savior during the height of the pandemic.

I'm enormously grateful to the anonymous readers who took on the task of assessing the manuscript for the University of Chicago Press and offered helpful critiques and bracing suggestions for revision. My thanks, too, to the editors of the University of Chicago Press, first Mary Al-Sayed and then Dylan Montanari and Fabiola Enríquez Flores, who accepted a lengthy draft and have so skillfully guided it into print. Elizabeth Ellingboe has saved me from technical disaster. Lys Weiss of Post Hoc Academic Publishing Services has been a wonderful copyeditor.

This book, finally, would never have been completed without the warm encouragement of my family. My sons and grandchildren have cheered me on. My wife, Jennifer, has been as constant in her support as in her love. I owe more to her than I can say here.

NOTE ON SOURCES

My principal resource for this work has been Jean-Paul Marat, *Oeuvres politiques, 1789–1793: Texte et guide de lecture*, ed. Jacques De Cock and Charlotte Goëtz, 10 vols. (Brussels, 1989–95), which has aimed to take account of corrections of errata noted in the original text and includes revisions on other copies made by hand by Marat in preparation for a new edition of *L'Ami du peuple*. This approach has been criticized, notably by Olivier Coquard, *Jean-Paul Marat* (Paris, 1993), 490–91. My quotations from the edition have been verified against the digitized copy of *L'Ami du peuple* made available by the New York Public Library.

Jacques De Cock, *Marat avant 1789* (Lyon: Fantasques Editions, 2003), now offers the most comprehensive edition of Marat's prerevolutionary correspondence and related documents for the prerevolutionary period.

The Chèvremont Collection held in the British Library offers the fullest collection of Marat's publications and other materials relating to him up to the late nineteenth century. This is the primary collection I have consulted. (The Lacassagne Collection at the Bibliothèque municipale de Lyon offers another rich resource.) The two major collections of Marat manuscripts in the Bibliothèque nationale de France, the La Bédoyère Collection and the Roseby Collection, include copies of *L'Ami du peuple* containing autograph annotations and revisions prepared for a later edition. Their significance is discussed and debated in Olivier Coquard, "Les manuscrits de Marat à la BN," *Annales historiques de la Révolution française* (1987): 68–79; and Charlotte Goëtz and Jacques De Cock, *Marat corrigé par lui-même* (Brussels, 1990).

Charlotte Goëtz, *Plume de Marat. Pour une bibliographie générale, première partie* (Brussels: Pôle Nord, 2006), offers a comprehensive bibliography of Marat's writings. Charlotte Goëtz, *Plumes sur Marat. Pour une bibliographie générale, deuxième partie* (Brussels: Pôle Nord, 2006), provides a similar listing of secondary works on Marat to that date.

Unless stated otherwise, translations are my own.

ABBREVIATIONS

AP — *Archives parlementaires de 1787 à 1860, première série (1787–1799)*, ed. M. J. Mavidal and M. E. Laurent, 82 vols. (Paris, 1879–1913)

Appel — *Appel nominal qui a eu lieu dans la séance permanente du 13 au 14 avril 1793, l'an deuxième de la République française, à la suite du rapport du comité de Législation, sur la question:* Y a-t-il lieu à accusation contre MARAT, membre de la Convention nationale? (Paris, 1793)

CM — *La Correspondance de Marat*, ed. Charles Vellay (Paris, 1908)

CS — Jean-Paul Marat, *The Chains of Slavery, A Work Wherein the Clandestine and Villainous Attempts of Princes to Ruin Liberty are Pointed Out, and the Dreadful Scenes of Despotism Disclosed, To which is prefixed An Address to the Electors of Great Britain, in order to draw their Timely Attention to the Choice of Proper Representatives in the next Parliament* (London: J. Almon, T. Payne, Richardson & Urquhart, 1774)

EHS — Jean-Paul Marat, *An Essay on the Human Soul* (London, 1772)

MA — Jacques De Cock, *Marat avant 1789* (Lyon: Fantasques Editions, 2003)

Mon. — *Réimpression de l'ancien Moniteur*, 31 vols. (Paris, 1879–1913)

OP — Jean-Paul Marat, *Oeuvres politiques*, ed. Jacques De Cock and Charlotte Goëtz, 10 vols. (Brussels, 1989–95)

PEM — Jean-Paul Marat, *A Philosophical Essay on Man, being an Attempt to investigate the Principles and Laws of the Reciprocal Influence of the Soul on the Body*, 2 vols. (London, 1773)

NOTES

CHAPTER 1

1. Charlotte Goëtz, *Marat en famille. La Saga des Mara(t)*, 2 vols. (Brussels: Pôle Nord, 2001), 1:3. In the absence of real knowledge, or in some cases despite it, many legends have been spun about Marat's family background. Thanks above all to Goëtz's passion for gathering and sifting the available facts, the story that can now be told turns out to be even more interesting than the earlier speculations. The following discussion of Jean Mara and his family draws substantially on her work.
2. For this history, see Gillian Lee Weiss, *Captives and Corsairs: France and Slavery in the Early Modern Mediterranean* (Stanford: Stanford University Press, 2011).
3. Goëtz, *Marat en famille*, 1:54.
4. Goëtz, *Marat en famille*, 1:108.
5. Goëtz, *Marat en famille*, 1:125.
6. Goëtz, *Marat en famille*, 1:127.
7. Goëtz, *Marat en famille*, 1:131.
8. Goëtz, *Marat en famille*, 1:132.
9. The Société typographique de Neuchâtel (frequently cited as STN) has been at the center of explosive debates over printing and publishing in the Enlightenment since Robert Darnton famously brought it to scholarly attention in *The Business of Enlightenment: A Publishing History of the Encyclopédie, 1775–1800* (Cambridge, MA: Harvard University Press, 1979). For a brief discussion of the literature to date, see Matthew McDonald, "Provincial Cosmopolitanism and Swiss Sociability at the Société Typographique de Neuchâtel, 1769–1789," *Eighteenth-Century Studies* 55 (2022): 421–48.
10. Goëtz, *Marat en famille*, 1:193. In 1763, Jean Mara had sued a local butcher whose son had thrown the stone destroying Pierre's eye (1:177–78).
11. Goëtz, *Marat en famille*, 1:196–98.
12. Goëtz, *Marat en famille*, 1:198–99.
13. Goëtz, *Marat en famille*, 2:184.
14. Goëtz, *Marat en famille*, 2:185.
15. Jacques De Cock, *Marat avant 1789* (Lyon: Fantasques Editions, 2003), 330. Hereafter cited as *MA*.

16. Jean-Paul Marat, *An Essay on the Human Soul* (London: T. Becket and Co. 1772), 92–93. Hereafter cited as *EHS*.
17. Jean-Paul Marat, *Oeuvres politiques*, ed. Jacques De Cock and Charlotte Goëtz, 10 vols. (Brussels, 1989–1995), 8:5497. Further references to this work will be abbreviated as *OP* followed by the volume and page numbers. Page numbers with an asterisk refer to the "Guides de lecture" included in these volumes. For further information, see the Note on Sources.
18. *OP*, 8:5498–99.
19. For the following details, see Goëtz, *Marat en famille*, 2:67–119.
20. Goëtz, *Marat en famille*, 2:59.
21. A Mara was apparently named in connection with these events, but without mention of a first name. Goëtz, *Marat en famille*, 2:53.
22. S. Stelling-Michaud, ed., *Le livre du Recteur de l'Académie de Genève (1559–1878)*, 6 vols. (Geneva, 1959), 4:426.
23. *OP*, 8:5498.
24. Goëtz, *Marat en famille*, 1:128–30.

CHAPTER 2

1. A register of the marriages of Bordeaux Protestants dated 15 April 1789 (Archives municipales de Bordeaux, acte no. 13, cote GG 870) lists three children born between 1761 and 1765; Pierre Meller, *Essais généalogiques. La Famille Nairac* names another four (non-surviving?) children born between 1762 and 1769. I wish to thank Mme Agnès Vatican, conservateur des Archives municipales de Bordeaux, for supplying this information.
2. *OP*, 8:5498.
3. *La Correspondance de Marat*, ed. Charles Vellay (Paris: Eugène Fasquelle, 1908; repr. Paris: Elibron Classics, 2005), 25. Hereafter cited as *CM*.
4. *CM*, 25–26.
5. *EHS*, "Note to the Reader."
6. *EHS*, 7.
7. *EHS*, 8.
8. *EHS*, 3.
9. *EHS*, 3.
10. *EHS*, 4.
11. *EHS*, 4.
12. *EHS*, 5.
13. *EHS*, 7.
14. *EHS*, 8–9.
15. *EHS*, 9–10.
16. Bernard Mandeville, *The Fable of the Bees or Private Vices, Publick Benefits*, ed. F. B. Kaye (Oxford, 1924; repr. Indianapolis, 1988), 1:254–56. Why a sow? The image apparently goes back to Erasmus. On the theme of the ravenous sow and its punishment, see Paul Friedland, *Seeing Justice Done: The Age of Spectacular Capital Punishment in France* (Oxford: Oxford University Press, 2012), 1–11 and passim.
17. Jean-Jacques Rousseau, *A Discourse on Inequality*, trans. Maurice Cranston (London: Penguin Classics, 1984), 99–100.
18. *EHS*, 14.
19. *EHS*, 36–37.
20. *EHS*, 37–38.
21. *EHS*, 40–41.
22. *EHS*, 107.
23. *EHS*, 98.
24. *EHS*, 28, 45, 49.
25. *EHS*, 44.

CHAPTER 3

1. Roy Porter offers a vivid picture of this world in several books, most notably *Health for Sale: Quackery in England, 1660–1850* (Manchester, UK: Manchester University Press, 1989) and *Bodies Politic: Disease, Death and Doctors in Britain, 1650–1900* (London: Reaktion, 2001).
2. *The Art of Getting into Practice in Physick, Here at present in London. In a Letter to that very ingenious and most learned Physician (lately come to Town) Dr. Timothy Vanbustle, MD. ABC, &c* (London: Printed, and sold by J. Peele, at Lock's-head, in Pater-Noster-Row, 1722), 7–8. Satirical attacks on physicians were a familiar feature of Georgian England; for others, see Porter, *Bodies Politic*, 140–43.
3. [Oliver Goldsmith], *The Citizen of the World; or Letters from a Chinese Philosopher, Residing in London, to his Friends in the East*, 2 vols. (London, 1762), 2:10–11.
4. Richard Tames, *Soho Past* (London: Historical Publications, 1994), 35.
5. A certificate of Marat's admission to this affiliate of the Grand Lodge of London, last sold publicly in Paris on 2 April 1935, seems now to have disappeared from view. The text is reprinted in *MA*, 47–48.
6. *The Diary of Joseph Farington*, ed. Kenneth Garlick and Angus Macintyre, 16 vols. (New Haven: Yale University Press, 1978–98), 1:74 (27 October 1793). The description is Hamilton's, but Farington later reports that "Bonomi's description of Marat exactly corresponded with that given me by Hamilton," 1:109 (6 December 1793).
7. *The Diary of Joseph Farington*, 1:108. Marat gave his return address as "Old Slaughter Coffee House" in a letter to John Wilkes written in 1774 or 1775. See below, pp. 90–91.
8. *The Diary of Joseph Farington*, 1:109.
9. *The Diary of Joseph Farington*, 1:74.
10. J.-P. Brissot, *Mémoires (1754–1793)*, ed. Claude Perroud, 2 vols. (Paris: Alphonse Picard & fils, 1911), 1:196. Unless otherwise indicated, all references to Brissot's *Mémoires* are to this edition.
11. It is possible that Marat spent several years away from London, during the late 1760s and early 1770s, in his efforts to observe the practice of medicine in different localities, but there is little direct evidence in that regard. He did claim at one point that he had spent ten years in London and Edinburgh engaged in "research of all kinds" (Letter to Roume de Saint-Laurent, 20 November 1783, *CM*, 28) and wrote at another that he had spent "ten years in London, one in Dublin and Edinburgh, one in The Hague, Utrecht and Amsterdam" (*Publiciste de la République française*, 19 March 1793; *OP*, 9:5873). He was in Amsterdam in October 1774 and again in February 1775, and reported an important cure in Edinburgh in the summer of 1775, but he was probably back in London for the publication of his *Essay on Gleets* in November of that year.

    Claims that he spent several years in Newcastle as a physician and veterinarian (see *MA*, 15) have not been substantiated. Marat's sister is said to have told John Croker, who in the early nineteenth century formed the magnificent collection of French Revolutionary materials now in the British Library, that she possessed a certificate making Marat a freeman of the city of Newcastle (though Croker did not see it and no award of this kind is apparently mentioned in the city records [*MA*, 10]). Marat himself also maintained that he had been "given the keys to the city" during a brief visit to Newcastle in the fall of 1775 (perhaps as he was returning from Edinburgh to London). There is a story that he may also have formed a romantic attachment in the northern town of Warrington. The lady in question was Lucy Aikin, later celebrated as the poet and writer Anna Laetitia Barbaud, and also known for her role in the famous Blue Stocking Society of women intellectuals. She was the daughter of John Aikin, a Unitarian divine who taught at the noted Dissenters' school, Warrington Academy; her brother and occasional collaborator (also John Aikin) was a doctor and man of letters. A century later, one Andrew de Ternant recalled that his father had collected "in a Lancashire town" an edition of Marat's *Chaînes de l'Esclavage* published in Edinburgh in 1774 with two letters inserted; in these, he said, Marat had asked the recipient to serve as translator of his work, declared himself a suitor of the recipient's sister, and announced both his ambition to become a naturalized Englishman and his willingness, in marriage, to change his religion. However, since *The Chains of Slavery* did not appear in French until 1793, there was no need for a translator from that language in 1774; nor did Marat need to convert at marriage, since he had in fact been born and baptized a Protestant. There is little reason, then, to take the Ternant report seriously. See Andrew de Ternant, *Notes and Queries* 222 (15 July 1922): 53; reprinted in *MA*, 38–39.

12. *The Diary of Joseph Farington*, 1:74.
13. *The Art of Getting into Practice in Physick*, 10.
14. *An Essay on Gleets; Wherein the Defects of the Actual Method of treating those Complaints of the Urethra are pointed out and An Effectual Way of Curing them indicated (London, [1775])*, in *Reprint of Two Tracts, 1. An Essay on Gleets; 2. An Enquiry into the Nature, Cause and Cure of a Singular Disease of the Eyes. By Jean Paul Marat, M.D.*, ed. with an introduction by James Blake Bailey (London, 1891), 3.
15. *Reprint of Two Tracts*, 4.
16. On the mapping of venereal disease and conditions of the eye as easy territory for quacks, see *The Art of Getting into Practice in Physick*: "As to our venereal Merchants or Doctors, Oculists, Secret-mongers, &c. I have no great Occasion to take any great Notice of these to you; besides that, most of them do already pretty well know the most proper Way of introducing themselves into Practice. So that I shall leave them to their own Stock, their Gratis, or other Pamphlets, News, Books, Bills, Pills or Ballads &c.," 21.
17. *Reprint of Two Tracts*, 25–26, 44–45.
18. *The Critical Review, or Annals of Literature* (January 1777): 79; also (December 1775): 483; *The Monthly Review, or Literary Journal* (December 1776): 476.
19. The diploma, which remained in Marat's family until 1956, has been frequently reprinted in works on Marat. The final "t" in his name was added to the document subsequently. Since the diploma itself was dated 30 June 1775 and Marat's father informed Osterwald of the new spelling of his son's name on 15 November 1775, this gives a fairly precise indication of the moment at which Marat made this change.
20. Charles E. Rosenberg, "Medical Text and Social Context: Explaining William Buchan's *Domestic Medicine*," *Bulletin of the History of Medicine* 57 (1983): 22–42. Rosenberg identified at least 142 separate editions of *Domestic Medicine* in English between its initial publication in Edinburgh in 1769 and its last in Philadelphia in 1871; he concluded that "no health guide before the twentieth century enjoyed a greater popularity" (22). See also C. J. Lawrence, "William Buchan: Medicine Laid Open," *Medical History* 19 (1975): 20–35.
21. *The Diary of Joseph Farington*, 1:108.
22. *MA*, 48; Marat's presence at the Amsterdam Lodge was recorded on the back of his original certificate of membership in the King's Head Lodge. A letter of Isaac de Pinto dated 25 February 1775 showed him still in Holland. See Jeremy Popkin, "Marat en Hollande—Un témoignage inconnu," *Dix-huitième siècle* 22 (1990): 291–93. On the "La Bien-Aimée" Lodge and its lively history, see Margaret C. Jacob, *Living the Enlightenment. Freemasonry and Politics in 18th Century Europe* (Oxford: Oxford University Press, 1991).
23. Popkin, "Marat en Hollande," 291–92.
24. Popkin, "Marat en Hollande," 291–92.
25. *Reprint of Two Tracts*, 44.
26. *Observations Concerning the Prevention and Cure of the Venereal Disease* (London, 1796), xxvi–xxvii, quoted in Roy Porter, "Spreading Medical Enlightenment. The Popularization of Medicine in England and Its Consequences," in Porter, ed., *The Popularization of Medicine, 1650–1850* (London: Routledge, 1992), 219.
27. The text of the diploma is reprinted in *MA*, 49–51.

28. *EHS*, "Note to the Reader."
29. *Monthly Review* 46 (March 1772): 254, as in *MA*, 22–23.
30. The original title page listed its publishers as "F. Newbery at n° 20, the corner of Ludgate street, J. Ridley in St. James Street and T. Payne, at the Mews Gate." The work reappeared later that same year with the title slightly revised to refer to the influence of the soul "on the body," and with Newbery no longer included among the publishers. The same printing appeared again as a "Second Edition" published by "H. Setchel, Bookseller, King Street, Covent Garden, 1775."
31. *CM*, 45–46. On Roume and the context in which Marat prepared an extensive dossier for him in 1783, see below, chap. 12.
32. *CM*, 47.
33. *CM*, 26. This account suggests that Marat had initially written the book in French, entrusted the translation to someone else rather than attempting it himself, but "distrusted the exactness of the translation that had been made."
34. Quoted in *The Cambridge History of English and American Literature*, 18 vols. (Cambridge, UK: Cambridge University Press, 1907–21), 10: §13.
35. Marat later reported to Roume de Saint-Laurent that Lyttelton had "often spoken of me to the Russian minister: some months after the publication of my book I received proposals to move to Petersburg" (*CM*, 26). The dossier he submitted to Saint-Laurent included a letter from Lyttelton inviting him to call on the Russian minister to be informed of "something that can be very advantageous to you if you accept his propositions," adding that "I would be extremely gratified to have been able to be of service to you." Marat recalled that he had received this letter from Lyttelton "some months after the publication of my book." Since the book wasn't published until April 1773, this service to an unknown author would have been one of Lyttelton's last acts of patronage, since he died on 22 August of that year. The dating of the letter in *CM* is clearly erroneous ("27 December 1783" on page 49, a date taken over from the original publication of the Saint-Laurent dossier in the *Miscellanies of the Philobiblon Society* 8 [London, 1863–64], 41–97) and is changed in the table of contents, again implausibly, to 27 December 1773. A date of 27 December 1772 seems more likely.
36. On Collignon, see Arthur Rook, "Charles Collignon (1725–1785): Cambridge Physician, Anatomist and Moralist," *Medical History* 23 (1979): 339–45.
37. Charles Collignon, *An Enquiry into the Structure of the Human Body, Relative to its Supposed Influence on the Morals of Mankind* (Cambridge, 1764), 33–34. A third edition of this work appeared in 1771.
38. *CM*, 49.
39. *A Philosophical Essay on Man, being an Attempt to investigate the Principles and Laws of the Reciprocal Influence of the Soul on the Body*, 2 vols. (London: J. Ridley . . . and T. Payne, 1773), 1:iii. Hereafter cited as *PEM*.
40. *PEM*, 1:viii.
41. *PEM*, 1:viii.
42. *PEM*, 1:xii–xiv.
43. *PEM*, 1:xv–xvi.
44. *PEM*, 1:xx.
45. *PEM*, 1:xxvi.
46. *PEM*, 1:33.
47. *PEM*, 1:ii ("Introduction," second roman pagination).

CHAPTER 4

1. *PEM*, 1:33.
2. *PEM*, 1:xxiii.
3. Denis Diderot, "Eléments de physiologie," in *Oeuvres complètes de Diderot*, ed. J. Assezat

and M. Tourneux, 20 vols. (Paris, 1875–79), 9:270–71. This work remained unpublished in Diderot's lifetime.

4. According to a modern editor, Diderot drew more on Marat than on any other author with the exception of Haller. See Diderot, *Eléments de physiologie*, ed. Jean Mayer (Paris, 1964), xliii. This judgment has been amply confirmed by the digital analysis performed by Motoichi Terada in preparation for his new edition of the *Eléments de physiologie* (Paris, 2019), 13 and passim. Terada's research has made it possible to identify precise passages in Diderot's text that relate to Marat's.

5. *PEM*, 1:34; see also 1:xxiv. Compare Claude Nicolas Le Cat, *Traité des sensations et des passions en général, et des sens en particulier*, 3 vols. (Paris, 1767–68), 1:xix.

6. Haller's paper was read to the Royal Society of Sciences in Göttingen in 1752 and published (in Latin) in the proceedings of that society the following year. A French version, translated and with a preface by the eminent Swiss physician Simon André Tissot appeared in Lausanne in 1755. An English version of Tissot's edition, also published in 1755, is reprinted, with an introduction by Owsei Temkin, in Shirley A. Roe, ed., *The Natural Philosophy of Albrecht von Haller* (New York: Arno Press, 1981). Anne C. Vila, *Enlightenment and Pathology: Sensibility in the Literature and Medicine of Eighteenth-Century France* (Baltimore: Johns Hopkins University Press, 1998), 13–42, offers an illuminating discussion of the implications of Haller's paper in the context of eighteenth-century discussions of the soul-body relationship. For the general frame of eighteenth-century physiology, see Caroline Warman, *The Atheist's Bible* (Cambridge, UK: Open Book Publishers, 2021), especially chaps. 3–4.

7. "Dissertation on the Sensible and Irritable Parts of Animals," in Roe, ed., *The Natural Philosophy of Albrecht von Haller*, 695; Vila, *Enlightenment and Pathology*, 26–27. On La Mettrie, see also Kathleen Wellman, *La Mettrie. Medicine, Philosophy, and Enlightenment* (Durham, NC: Duke University Press, 1992).

8. Le Cat, *Traité des sensations*, 1:xxxvi, 60–61, 81–82, 114–21. For a more comprehensive understanding of vitalism in the Enlightenment, see the indispensable work of Peter Hanns Reill, *Vitalizing Nature in the Enlightenment* (Berkeley: University of California Press, 2005).

9. Le Cat, *Traité des sensations*, 1:85.

10. Le Cat, *Traité de l'existance, de la nature et des propriétés du fluide des nerfs, et principalement de son action dans le mouvement musculaire, ouvrage couronné en 1753 par l'Académie de Berlin, suivi des Dissertations sur la sensibilité des meninges, des tendons, etc., l'insensibilité du cerveau, la structure des nerfs, l'irritabilité Hallerienne, etc.* (Berlin, 1765), 314, 298–99.

11. Le Cat, *Traité de l'existance*, 126.

12. Le Cat, *Traité de l'existance*, 303–7.

13. *PEM*, 1:42.

14. *PEM*, 1:49–50.

15. Le Cat, *Traité des sensations*, 1:221.

16. *PEM*, 1:39.

17. *PEM*, 1:41.

18. *PEM*, 1:46–47.

19. *PEM*, 1:57.

20. *PEM*, 1:63.

21. *PEM*, 1:68.

22. Warman, *Atheist's Bible*, chap. 4, § 31.

23. *PEM*, 2:16.

24. *PEM*, 2:34.

25. *PEM*, 2:44. The physiology of terror is considered further at 2:82.

26. *PEM*, 2:38.

27. *Eléments de physiologie*, ed. Terada, 155. Haller, reading Marat from a very different per-

spective, was no less critical of his views. Reviewing *De l'homme* anonymously, the Swiss physiologist castigated Marat for lacking any understanding of the brain, for arrogantly dismissing earlier researchers, and, above all, for basing his work on Le Cat and contracting so many of the latter's errors in the process. See *Göttingische Anzeigen von gelehrten Sachen* (January 1778), 171–76, 181–84. I'm grateful to the late Hanns Peter Reill for help with this review.

28. *PEM*, 2:61.
29. *PEM*, 2:62.
30. *PEM*, 2:261. Marat is quick, though, to utilize the asterisk to note that "I pretend not to subject the *whole* to physical laws; I am well assured that the soul *partly* receives its character from moral causes."
31. *PEM*, 2:154–55.
32. *PEM*, 2:183.
33. *PEM*, 2:155.
34. On this possibility, see Warman, *Atheist's Bible*, part 2.
35. *CM*, 26; Jean Mara to Frédéric-Samuel Ostervald, 11 May 1776, in Goëtz, *Marat en famille*, 2:190–91.
36. *The Westminster Magazine* 1 (May 1773): 327. My thanks to Emma Rothschild for help in tracking down this review.
37. *The Gentleman's Magazine*, April 1773, 91, as in *MA*, 28.
38. *Journal encyclopédique*, 1 August 1773, vol. 5, part 3, 379–85, as in *MA*, 30–33.
39. *Journal encyclopédique*, February 1776, vol. 1, part 3, 379–96, and vol. 2, part 1, 36–45; as in *MA*, 62–73.
40. Jean Mara to Frédéric-Samuel Ostervald, 11 May 1776, in Goëtz, *Marat en famille*, 2:190–91.
41. Jean-Paul Marat to Frédéric-Samuel Ostervald, 14 May 1776, as in *MA*, 75–76; Robert Darnton, "Marat n'a pas été un voleur," *Annales historiques de la Révolution française* 38 (1966): 447–49.
42. *MA*, 75–76. I have been unable to track down the passage from an English journalist Marat apparently cites.
43. *CM*, 27. Marat also gave Roume to believe that the greater part of the edition found its way to Italy and Portugal, but the remainder sold out in a matter of days when it was finally allowed into Paris.
44. *Journal de politique et de littérature* 2, no. 13 (5 May 1777): 38–43, as in *MA*, 81–85.

CHAPTER 5

1. *St. James's Chronicle*, 3 March 1770, as quoted in John Brewer, *Party Ideology and Popular Politics at the Accession of George III* (Cambridge, UK: Cambridge University Press, 1976), 148.
2. In this account of Wilkes and the politics of parliamentary representation in London during Marat's stay, I rely principally on George Rudé, *Wilkes and Liberty: A Social Study of 1763 to 1774* (Oxford, UK: Lawrence Wishart Press, 1962); Brewer, *Party Ideology and Popular Politics*; and Ian R. Christie, *Wilkes, Wyvill, and Reform: The Parliamentary Reform Movement in British Politics, 1760–1785* (London: Macmillan, 1962). Arthur H. Cash, *John Wilkes: The Scandalous Father of Civil Liberty* (New Haven: Yale University Press, 2006), offers a lively biography of the flamboyant figure at the center of this critical moment in English politics.
3. In 1766 Parliament declared resort to such warrants illegal. See Rudé, *Wilkes and Liberty*, 23–30.
4. Rudé, *Wilkes and Liberty*, 39–40.
5. *The Annual Register, or a View of the History, Politicks, and Literature for the Year 1768* (London, 1769), 86; also quoted in Rudé, *Wilkes and Liberty*, 43.

6. *Ami du peuple* (22 October 1790), *OP* 3:1643.
7. *Ami du peuple* (22 October 1790), *OP* 3:1643.
8. Cash, *John Wilkes*, 223.
9. Rudé, *Wilkes and Liberty*, 105–34.
10. Brewer, *Party Ideology and Popular Politics*, 185. More generally, see Brewer, "Commercialization and Politics," in Neil McKendrick, John Brewer, and J. H. Plumb, *The Birth of a Consumer Society: The Commercialization of Eighteenth-Century England* (Bloomington: Indiana University Press, 1982), 197–262.
11. Christie, *Wilkes, Wyvil, and Reform*, 15–44.
12. Catharine Macaulay, *Observations on a pamphlet, entitled, Thoughts on the Cause of the Present Discontents* (London, 1770).
13. Catharine Macaulay, *History of England from the Accession of James I to that of the Brunswick Line*, 3rd ed., 4 vols. (London, 1769), 1:xi, xii, xix. The entire work was completed with its eighth volume in 1783.
14. Craggs Clare to Charles Jenkinson, 8 April 1771, as quoted in Rudé, *Wilkes and Liberty*, 164.
15. *The Chains of Slavery, A Work Wherein the Clandestine and Villainous Attempts of Princes to Ruin Liberty are Pointed Out, and the Dreadful Scenes of Despotism Disclosed, To which is prefixed An Address to the Electors of Great Britain, in order to draw their Timely Attention to the Choice of Proper Representatives in the next Parliament* (London: J. Almon, T. Payne, Richardson & Urquhart, 1774), v–vi. Hereafter cited as *CS*.
16. *CS*, x, vii, vi.
17. *CS*, ix, viii, x, ix–xii.
18. *CS*, 159.
19. *Les Chaînes de l'esclavage, OP*, 7:4167.
20. The first two of the four volumes were published prior to the 1774 election; see Carla H. Hay, *James Burgh, Spokesman for Reform in Hanoverian England* (Washington, DC: University Press of America, 1979), 122n55.
21. In fact, Marat's most concentrated discussion of the depredations of rulers in the years around 1770 was devoted to events in Warsaw rather than in Paris and took a rather different form than *The Chains of Slavery*. The epistolary novel left unpublished at his death, *Les Aventures du jeune comte Potowski*, offered a tale of love and treachery in a Poland torn apart by civil war and foreign invasion in the years 1769–71. The exact date of the novel's composition is unclear. For a fuller analysis, see Marat, *Les Aventures du jeune comte Potowski*, introduction and notes by Claire Nicolas-Lelièvre (Paris, 1989).

CHAPTER 6

1. G. G. Ramsay, trans., *Juvenal and Persius* (Cambridge, MA: Harvard University Press, 1969), 53. For the Roman context, see E. Courtney, *A Commentary on the Satires of Juvenal* (London: Athlone Press, 1980), 195–219; Gian Biagio Conte, *Latin Literature: A History* (Baltimore: Johns Hopkins University Press, 1994), 474–80. I'm grateful to Marcus Folch for his helpful advice on this poem.
2. Ramsay, trans., *Juvenal and Persius*, 54.
3. Jean-Jacques Rousseau, *Politics and the Arts: Letter to M. D'Alembert on the Theatre*, ed. Allan Bloom (Ithaca, NY: Cornell University Press, 1960), 132.
4. The latter work, generally cited as *Parliamentary History* by eighteenth-century British writers, appeared in twenty-four volumes (1751–61) with a second edition in 1761–63.
5. A list of Marat's references has been established by Goëtz and De Cock in Jean-Paul Marat, *Les Chaînes de l'esclavage 1793, The Chains of Slavery 1774*, ed. Charlotte Goëtz and Jacques De Cock (Brussels, 1995), xxxvii–xlii (also included in *OP*, vol. 7).
6. *CS*, 104–5.
7. *CS*, 107–9.

8. *CS*, 1–2.
9. *CS*, 22, 3, 4.
10. *CS*, 6, 15, 29, 23, 24, 25, 27, 29.
11. *CS*, 32, 56.
12. *CS*, 59, 60.
13. *CS*, 67–68.
14. *CS*, 70.
15. *CS*, 71, 73.
16. *CS*, 68.
17. *CS*, 74–75, 98–102.
18. *CS*, 114, 113.
19. Two notes were added to this extended denunciation of the political evils of Christianity, presumably to make it less offensive to English sensibilities. Remarking that Christian rulers alone seemed impervious to the gentler principles of the Gospel, one noted that such was particularly the case "in Catholic countries, where the priests grant dispensations to the rich for money, furnish them a thousand pretended means of atonement, and sometimes incite them to redeem, by new crimes, a whole life spent in iniquities. Now when the sinner may hope for Paradise without fearing Hell, religion has no more any empire." Extending consideration of the Pauline injunction to obey the powers that be, a second note asked rhetorically whether it was not "that fatal doctrine of passive obedience, which in the last century prevented our forefathers from shaking off their yoke? Fortunately for liberty, faith is no longer our weak side" (*CS*, 116–17).
20. *CS*, 115–19.
21. *CS*, 141.
22. *CS*, 165–66.
23. *CS*, 186, 189.
24. *CS*, 177. On the theme of the Franks on the Champ de Mars, see Elie Carcassonne, *Montesquieu et le problème de la constitution française au XVIIIe siècle* (Paris, 1927); Harold Ellis, *Boulainvilliers and the French Monarchy: Aristocratic Politics in Early Eighteenth-Century France* (Ithaca, NY: Cornell University Press, 1988); François Furet and Mona Ozouf, "Deux légitimations de la société française au XVIIIe siècle. Mably et Boulainvilliers," *Annales. Histoire, Sciences Sociales* 34 (1979): 438–50.
25. *CS*, 180.
26. *CS*, 181.
27. *CS*, 182.
28. *CS*, 195.
29. *CS*, 195–226. R. C. H. Catterall, "The Credibility of Marat," *American Historical Review* 16 (1910): 24–35, argued emphatically that the different style of this extended discussion and the higher quality of its English reveal that it was written by someone other than Marat. That may be so, though it is also possible that Marat had help with the language from a native English collaborator. Whatever the case, the work shows evidence of research in the sources of English history that Marat claimed to have consulted so frantically in 1774 and used in support of arguments he mobilized later in the course of the French Revolution.
30. *CS*, 198–99.
31. *CS*, 204, 202.
32. *CS*, 207–8.
33. *CS*, 209, 211.
34. *CS*, 211, 219.
35. *CS*, 259.
36. *MA*, 40–41.
37. *OP*, 4169.

38. *OP*, 4169–71.
39. *OP*, 4171–73.
40. *MA*, 38–46.
41. *MA*, 46–47.
42. *MA*, 39–40.
43. For details, see Rachel Hammersley, "Jean-Paul Marat's *The Chains of Slavery* in Britain and France, 1774–1833," *Historical Journal* 48 (2005): 641–60, especially 651.
44. Hammersley, "Jean-Paul Marat's *The Chains of Slavery* in Britain and France," 652.
45. Hammersley, "Jean-Paul Marat's *The Chains of Slavery* in Britain and France," 652–55.
46. *MA*.
47. On the quality and expensive price of the book, see Catterall, "The Credibility of Marat," 32. For its nineteenth-century fate, see *The Monthly Chronicle of North-Country Lore and Legend* (April 1887), as quoted in Hammersley, "Jean-Paul Marat's *The Chains of Slavery* in Britain and France," 652.

CHAPTER 7

1. *MA*, 74.
2. *MA*, 86.
3. Michel le Moël, "Les écuries du comte d'Artois," in Béatrice de Andia and Dominique Fernandès, eds., *La rue du Faubourg Saint Honoré* (Paris: Délégation à l'action artistique de la ville de Paris, 1994), 340–42.
4. Augustin Cabanès, *Marat inconnu. L'homme privé, le médecin, le savant*, 3rd ed. (Paris, 1920), 85, followed earlier accounts in giving the figure of 2,000 livres. It has generally been repeated, but Cabanès provided no documentary source for it. Olivier Coquard (*Jean-Paul Marat* [Paris: Fayard, 1993], 90, 441) found no record of a payment of that sum, or any other, in the household papers of the comte d'Artois. A reference work published in 1778 reported stipends of 1,200 livres (plus 273 livres for expenses) for *médecins ordinaires du Roi par quartier* and 300 livres (plus 120 livres for expenses) for the *médecin ordinaire* of the wife of the Dauphin. Marat's position is likely to have paid less. See N. F. J. Eloy, *Dictionnaire historique de la médecine ancienne et moderne*, 4 vols. (Mons, 1778), 3:252–53. My thanks to Colin Jones for help in clarifying the nature of this position.
5. See especially Laurence Brockliss and Colin Jones, *The Medical World of Early Modern France* (Oxford: Oxford University Press 1997), chap. 10; Colin Jones, "The Médecins du Roi at the end of the *Ancien Régime* and in the French Revolution," in Vivian Nutton, ed., *Medicine at the Courts of Europe, 1500–1837* (London: Routledge 1990), especially 232–38. For the "Great Chain of Buying," see Brockliss and Jones, *The Medical World of Early Modern France*, 643–58; and Colin Jones, "The Great Chain of Buying: Medical Advertisement, the Bourgeois Public Sphere and the Origins of the French Revolution," *American Historical Review* 101 (1996): 13–40.
6. The position was added to the *Almanach royal* for 1779. Marat was listed annually as its holder, and at this same address, until 1786. The position passed formally to a Dr. Enguehard on 23 April 1786 (see Cabanès, *Marat inconnu*, 97).
7. *MA*, 87–88.
8. *MA*, 89–90.
9. *CM*, 28.
10. *MA*, 90–93.
11. *MA*, 98–99.
12. *MA*, 94–95.
13. *MA*, 96–98.
14. *MA*, 99–101.

15. *MA*, 102.
16. *MA*, 106–8 (1 January 1778).
17. *MA*, 110–11 (8 January 1778).
18. *CM*, 52. This letter was included with others indicating Marat's success as a doctor in the dossier he submitted to Roume de Saint-Laurent in 1783. See chapter 12, below.
19. *MA*, 126–27, though possibly inauthentic. The market for Marat memorabilia has invited fraud. But Cabanès, *Marat inconnu*, 133, reproduces an autograph receipt from Marat in 1779 for two consultations, each at the cost of a louis d'or (24 livres).
20. Brissot, *Mémoires (1754–1793)*, ed. Claude Perroud, 2 vols. (Paris: Alphonse Picard et fils, 1911), 1:196.
21. *CM*, 91.
22. *MA*, 102–5, 112–13.
23. *CM*, 28–29.
24. This note was included in a series of extracts from secret police reports between 1781 and 1785 compiled later by Lenoir, as quoted in Robert Darnton, *The Literary Underground of the Old Regime* (Cambridge, MA: Harvard University Press, 1982), 26. I have made minor modifications to the translation. Since Marat had largely abandoned medical practice by 1785, the note probably dates from the earlier part of this period.
25. See Jones, "The Médecins du Roi," especially 232–38.
26. *CM*, 29.
27. For this work, and the broader context of the Berne prize, see the critical edition of *Le prix de la justice et de l'humanité* by Robert Granderoute in *Oeuvres complètes de Voltaire*, vol. 80B, *Writings of 1777–1778* (Oxford, UK: the Voltaire Foundation, 2009).
28. The *Eloge de Montesquieu* appeared in an edition published in 1883 by Arthur de Brézetz (Libourne, 1883). For Marat's pride in his plan for criminal legislation, see *OP*, 2:1061–62.
29. *Plan de législation en matière criminelle*, in Jacques Pierre Brissot, ed., *Bibliothèque philosophique, du législateur, du politique, du jurisconsulte, Ou Choix des meilleurs discours, dissertations, essais, fragments composés sur la législation criminelle par les plus célèbres écrivains en français, anglais, italien, allemand, espagnol, etc.* . . . , 10 vols. (Berlin and Paris, 1782–85), vol. 5 (1782): 113–14.
30. *Plan de législation en matière criminelle*, 115.
31. *Plan de législation en matière criminelle*, 115–16.
32. *Plan de législation en matière criminelle*, 127–28.
33. *Plan de législation en matière criminelle*, 123.
34. *Plan de législation en matière criminelle*, 122–25.
35. *Plan de législation en matière criminelle*, 141–42.
36. *Le Prix de la justice et de l'humanité*, as reprinted in Jacques Pierre Brissot, ed., *Bibliothèque philosophique*, 5:9.
37. *Plan de législation en matière criminelle*, 142–43.
38. *Plan de législation en matière criminelle*, 144–47.
39. *Plan de législation en matière criminelle*, 149–54.
40. *Plan de législation en matière criminelle*, 111.
41. *Plan de législation en matière criminelle*, 161–62.
42. *Plan de législation en matière criminelle*, 162–63.
43. *Plan de législation en matière criminelle*, 163–70.
44. *Plan de législation en matière criminelle*, 167–68.
45. Brissot, *Mémoires*, 1:205.

CHAPTER 8

1. Joseph Priestley, *History and Present State of Discoveries relating to Vision, Light, and Colours* (London, 1772), 270.

2. On this theme, see especially I. Bernard Cohen, *Franklin and Newton: An Inquiry into Speculative Newtonian Experimental Science and Franklin's Work in Electricity as an Example Thereof* (Philadelphia: American Philosophical Society, 1960); Robert E. Schofield, *Mechanism and Materialism: British Natural Philosophy in an Age of Reason* (Princeton: Princeton University Press, 1970).
3. Joseph Priestley, *The History and Present State of Electricity with Original Experiments*, 4th ed. (London, 1775), xi ("Preface to the First Edition, 1767"). A French translation appeared in 1771.
4. Peter Heering, "Analysing Experiments with Two Non-canonical Devices: Jean-Paul Marat's Helioscope and Perméomètre," *Bulletin of the Scientific Instrument Society* 74 (2002): 8–15.
5. Marat to Roume de Saint-Laurent, 20 November 1783, *CM*, 42. For the discussion of Marat's scientific writings that follows in this chapter, I have learned much from the analyses offered by Clifford Conner at www.maratscience.com, and from Charles Coulston Gillispie, *Science and Polity in France: The End of the Old Regime* (Princeton: Princeton University Press, 1980), 290–330.
6. *Découvertes de M. Marat, Docteur en Médecine & Médecin des Gardes-du-Corps de Monseigneur le comte d'Artois, sur le feu, l'électricité et la lumière, constatées par une suite d'expériences nouvelles qui viennent d'être vérifiés par MM. les commissaires de l'Académie des Sciences* (Paris, 1779), 3–4.
7. *Découvertes . . . sur le feu*, 1.
8. *Découvertes . . . sur le feu*, 29.
9. "Extrait des régistres de l'Académie royale des sciences, Rapport de MM. le comte de Maillebois, de Montigny, Le Roy et Sage, du 17 avril 1779," as printed in *Découvertes . . . sur le feu*.
10. Gillispie, *Science and Polity*, 305.
11. As quoted, Gillispie, *Science and Polity*, 304.
12. Marat to Franklin, shortly before 13 March 1779, *Benjamin Franklin Papers*, available online: http://franklinpapers.org.
13. Marat to Franklin, 29 March 1779, and also letters of 25, 30, 31 March 1779; Le Roy to Franklin, 17 March 1779, and also letter of 26 March 1779, *Benjamin Franklin Papers*, http://franklinpapers.org.
14. Balthasar-Georges Sage, *Analyse chimique et concordance des trois règnes*, 3 vols. (1786), 1:117, as quoted in *MA*, 131, 134–35.
15. Marat to Franklin, 12 April 1779, *Benjamin Franklin Papers*, http://franklinpapers.org.
16. *CM*, 52–53. Dated "Tuesday morning," this letter must have been sent on Tuesday, 20 April, three days after the committee had reported to the Academy. Le Roy promised Marat a copy of the report for the following Saturday.
17. The visiting researcher was the Genevan Jean-André Deluc, as quoted in Roger Hahn, *Pierre Simon Laplace, 1749–1827* (Cambridge, MA: Harvard University Press, 2005), 92. Lavoisier's own remark, recorded by Edmond Genêt in 1783, is cited by Jean-Pierre Poirier, *Lavoisier: Chemist, Biologist, Economist*, trans. Rebecca Balinski (Philadelphia: University of Pennsylvania Press, 1996), 81.
18. In this discussion of the development of Lavoisier's research, I draw largely on Henry Guerlac, "Chemistry as a Branch of Physics: Laplace's Collaboration with Lavoisier," *Historical Studies in the Physical Sciences* 7 (1976): 193–276; and Arthur Donovan, *Antoine Lavoisier: Science, Administration and Revolution* (Cambridge, UK: Cambridge University Press, 1993). Poirier's *Lavoisier* is the fullest biography to date. For a consideration of Mme Lavoisier's contributions to her husband's research, see "The Collaboration of Antoine and Marie-Anne Lavoisier and the First Measurements of Human Oxygen Consumption," *American Journal of Physiology—Lung Cellular and Molecular Physiology* 305, no. 11 (December 2013).

19. Macquer to Guyton de Morveau, 15 January 1778, as quoted by Guerlac, "Chemistry as a Branch of Physics," 218.
20. *Oeuvres de Lavoisier*, ed. J. B. Dumas and E. Grimaux, 6 vols. (Paris, 1864–93), 2:225. In an earlier expression of the mathematical ideal, Lavoisier had set out plans in 1778 for a second volume of *Opuscules physiques et chimiques* "following the method of the mathematicians [*géomètres*], a precious method that would constantly lead us to demonstrable knowledge [*évidence*] if we could always start in physics from sure and confirmed data." *Oeuvres de Lavoisier*, 5:267, as quoted in Guerlac, "Chemistry as a Branch of Physics," 215.
21. *Oeuvres de Lavoisier*, 2:228.
22. *Oeuvres de Lavoisier*, 2:233.
23. *Oeuvres de Lavoisier*, 2:228, 231.
24. "On the Combination of the Matter of Fire with Evaporable Fluids, and the Formation of Elastic Aeriform Fluids," *Oeuvres de Lavoisier*, 2:212–24.
25. *Recherches physiques sur le feu. Par M. Marat, Docteur en Médicine & Médecin des Gardes du Corps de Monseigneur le Comte d'Artois* (Paris, 1780), 193–94. The publisher, Claude Antoine Jombert, *fils aîné*, claimed the title of "The King's Bookseller for Engineering and Artillery."
26. *Recherches . . . sur le feu*, 1–2.
27. For the request, see *Procès verbaux de l'Académie royale des sciences*, 98 (1979), fol. 291 verso (17 November 1779). Sage, however, read the work as a Censor, approving it for publication as containing "new and interesting experiments," *Recherches . . . sur le feu*, 203.
28. *Journal de Paris*, 6 April 1780, as reprinted in *MA*, 164. Official publication permission was registered on 11 April.
29. *Journal de Paris*, 9 June 1780, as reprinted in *MA*, 179–80.
30. *Procès verbaux de l'Académie royale des sciences*, 99 (1780), fol. 148 (10 June 1780). Lavoisier's paper, "Considérations générales sur la nature des acides," was rushed into publication in the Academy's *Mémoires* for 1778 (appearing in 1781).
31. The relevant documents appear in *MA*, 180–83.
32. *Les charlatans modernes, ou Lettres sur le charlatanisme académique*, in *OP*, 3375–76.
33. *CM*, 29, 53–55, 68, 124–25, 145.
34. *MA*, 118.
35. *MA*, 138–39.
36. *MA*, 144–45.
37. *Journal encyclopédique de Bouillon* (1 October 1779), in *MA*, 146–49; Filassier, letter to the *Journal de Paris* (25 October 1779), in *MA*, 150–51.
38. *Année littéraire* (1779), 8:215–16.
39. *The London Review of English and Foreign Literature* (August 1779): 127–28.
40. *MA*, 151–53, 155, 159–62.
41. *The Monthly Review* 62 (January–June 1780): 546–48.
42. *The Critical Review, or, Annals of Literature* (October 1780): 313.
43. *CM*, 73–74, 81.
44. *MA*, 171–79. "Matran" may be a mistaken transcription of a reference to d'Ortous de Mairan, whose wide-ranging experimental research included variation on the heating effects of the sun of global temperatures. My thanks to Jessica Riskin for this suggestion.
45. *MA*, 207–8.
46. *Année littéraire* (1782), 1:283–88.
47. *MA*, 183, 207–8, 281–82.
48. *MA*, 252–54.
49. On Lavoisier's "balance-sheet" approach, see Jean-Pierre Poirier, "Lavoisier's Balance Sheet Method: Sources, Early Signs and Late Developments," in Marco Beretta, *Lavoisier in Perspective* (Munich: Deutsches Museum, 2005), 69–77. Among other essays in this fascinating volume, Peter Heering, "Weighing Heat: The Replication of the Experiments

with the Ice-Calorimeter of Lavoisier and Laplace," 27–41, offers a revealing perspective on these decisive experiments. On "compositionism" (as the key to Lavoisier's success) and its opposite, "principlism," see Hasok Chang, *Is Water H_2o? Evidence, Realism, and Pluralism* (Dordrecht: Springer, 2012), 37–42.

50. *Les charlatans modernes*, in *OP*, 3352.

CHAPTER 9

1. *MA*, 154.
2. *CM*, 3, where the letter is incorrectly dated.
3. Newton, *Opticks*, 4th ed. (1730), ed. Duane H. D. Roller (New York: Dover Books, 1952), 338–39. For an analysis of Newton's decision in this case and its broader context, see Alan E. Shapiro, "Newton's Optics and Atomism," in I. Bernard Cohen and George E. Smith, *The Cambridge Companion to Newton* (Cambridge, UK: Cambridge University Press, 2002), 227–55.
4. Charles Coulston Gillispie, *Science and Polity in France: The End of the Old Regime* (Princeton: Princeton University Press, 1980), 309. François Para de Phanjas, *Théorie des nouvelles découvertes en genre de physique et de chymie* (Paris, 1786), 527, offered a similar judgment rather more charitably, crediting Marat with the generation from "an ancient discovery . . . a host of small, curious and new phenomena that make evident much sagacity and industry but still remain dependent on Newton's own theory." For a more positive view, see Clifford Conner, at Maratscience.com. My thanks to Dennis Sepper for advice on this topic.
5. *Découvertes de M. Marat . . . Sur la lumière; constatées par une suite d'expériences nouvelles qui ont été faites un très-grand nombre de fois sous les yeux de MM. les Commissaires de l'Académie des Sciences* (London, "Et se trouve à Paris," 1780), 110.
6. *Procès verbaux de l'Académie royale des sciences*, 98 (1779), fol. 199 verso (19 June 1779); *CM*, 3–4, 56–58.
7. *CM*, 56–57; Marat to Franklin, 4 June, 22 August, 23 August 1779, *Benjamin Franklin Papers*, http://franklinpapers.org.
8. *CM*, 57–58, 5. Marat's boast that he had evicted the committee "à coups de pied au c . . . ," reported years later by an old friend of the 1780s, Dom Gourdin, is cited by Olivier Coquard, *Marat* (Paris: Fayard, 1993), 56.
9. *CM*, 58–64. Unless otherwise stated, quotations in the following paragraphs are drawn from these letters; phrases italicized are those emphasized by Marat. (This correspondence is also printed in *MA*.)
10. *CM*, 5–6.
11. *MA*, 167.
12. *CM*, 63.
13. I wish to express my appreciation to Mme Florence Greffe, former archivist of the Académie des sciences, for her help in providing a photocopy of the *plumitif* for Academy's session on 3 May 1780.
14. *CM*, 64.
15. *Procès verbaux de l'Académie royale des sciences*, 99 (1780), fol. 126–27 (10 May 1780); "Extrait des régistres de l'Académie royale des sciences, du 10 Mai 1780," as printed in *Découvertes . . . sur la lumière*, 3–4. There is some ambiguity in the record. According to the *plumitif*, the report on 10 May was presented by Maillebois, Le Roy, Sage, and Cousin, while the *PVAS*, 99:126–27, records it as given by Maillebois, Sage, and Cousin (omitting Trudaine and Le Roy) even though Maillebois was not actually listed among the attendees on 3 May or 10 May. This might mean that Maillebois had simply not signed the attendance sheet, though it seems odd that he would omit doing so twice. The report as published in the *Découvertes . . . sur la lumière* was signed only by Le Roy, Cousin, and

Sage. My thanks again to Mme Florence Greffe for a photocopy of the *plumitif* for the session of 10 May 1780. I am also grateful to Nicolas Rieucau for further discussion of this information.

16. *CM*, 66–67.
17. *Découvertes . . . sur la lumière*, 5–6.
18. Bibliothèque nationale de France, mss. nouv. acq. fr. 309 (MF 14042), fol. 3 recto. It appears that this revised edition was to be published anonymously; all reference to its author has been eliminated from the title page.

CHAPTER 10

1. Joseph Priestley, *The History and Present State of Electricity with Original Experiments*, 4th ed. (London, 1775), 87.
2. The standard account of the history of electricity in the eighteenth century is J. L. Heilbron, *Electricity in the 17th and 18th Centuries: A Study in Early Modern Physics* (Berkeley: University of California Press, 1979). On Franklin and his reception in France, see also I. Bernard Cohen, *Franklin and Newton: An Inquiry into Speculative Newtonian Experimental Science and Franklin's Work in Electricity as an Example Thereof* (Philadelphia: American Philosophical Society, 1960); Robert E. Schofield, *Mechanism and Materialism: British Natural Philosophy in an Age of Reason* (Princeton: Princeton University Press, 1970); and especially Jessica Riskin, *Science in the Age of Sensibility: The Sentimental Empiricists of the French Enlightenment* (Chicago: University of Chicago Press, 2002), chap. 3.
3. *Recherches physiques sur l'électricité; Par M. Marat, Docteur en Médecine, & Médecin des Gardes du Corps de Monseigneur le Comte d'Artois* (Paris, 1782), 12–13, 23.
4. Marat to Franklin, 18 November 1780, *Benjamin Franklin Papers*.
5. *Recherches . . . sur l'électricité*, 367.
6. Franklin to Marat, 24 November 1780, *Benjamin Franklin Papers*.
7. *Journal de littérature, des sciences et des arts* (November–December 1780), as printed in *MA*, 191–200.
8. As printed in *MA*, 191–205, 212–16, 221–28, 232–43, 252–53.
9. *MA*, 251–52, 256–57.
10. *MA*, 279–80, 282–97, 307–29.
11. *MA*, 287.
12. Marat to Franklin, 14 February and 1 March 1782; Franklin to Marat, 25 February 1782, *Benjamin Franklin Papers*, http://franklinpapers.org.
13. As established by Edwin Wolf II and Kevin J. Hayes, *The Library of Benjamin Franklin* (Philadelphia, 2006), Franklin possessed the *Recherches . . . sur le feu* and *Découvertes . . . sur la lumière*, bound together in a single volume, but not the *Recherches . . . sur l'électricité*. Nor does this latter appear in the catalog of The Library Company of Philadelphia, which did lend copies of Marat's other scientific works.
14. The fullest discussion is Clifford Conner, *Marat's Science 5: Marat's Investigations of Electricity*, www.maratscience.com.
15. *Recherches . . . sur l'électricité*, 10–11.
16. *Recherches . . . sur l'électricité*, 12.
17. Conner, *Marat's Science 5*:8, www.maratscience.com.
18. *Recherches . . . sur l'électricité*, 62–63, 13.
19. *Recherches . . . sur l'électricité*, 15.
20. *Recherches . . . sur l'électricité*, 15.
21. *Recherches . . . sur l'électricité*, 18–22.
22. *Recherches . . . sur l'électricité*, 150.
23. *Recherches . . . sur l'électricité*, 364.

24. *Recherches . . . sur l'électricité*, 406.
25. *Recherches . . . sur l'électricité*, 427.
26. Riskin, *Science in the Age of Sensibility*, chap. 5, offers the best discussion of this famous trial. Marat played no direct role in these proceedings, though his views on the lightning rod were known to some of the participants in the debate. He has often been confused with Hugues Maret, perpetual secretary of the Académie de Dijon, who was a member of the committee that judged in favor of the lightning rod.
27. *Recherches . . . sur l'électricité*, 423. Marat's views were restated in 1787 in a letter in the *Journal général de France* (26 and 28 July 1787); see *MA*, 498–502.
28. Bertholon to Antoine Buissart (15 December 1782), in *MA*, 303–5. For the charlatan Comus, see below, p. 158.
29. On Nollet, see Jean Torlais, *Un physicien au siècle des lumières, l'Abbé Nollet, 1700–1770* (Paris, 1954). This, and the following account, draws much on François Zanetti, "L'Électricité médicale dans la France des lumières. Histoire culturelle d'un nouveau remède," thèse de doctorat, Université de Paris Ouest, Nanterre/La Défense, 2013, now published in revised form as *L'Électricité médicale dans la France des lumières* (Oxford, UK, 2017). Note that citations of this work in what follows refer to the 2013 version. See also Paola Bertucci and Giuliano Pancaldi, eds., *Electric Bodies: Episodes in the History of Medical Electricity* (Bologna, 2001), especially Peter Heering, "Jean Paul Marat: Medical Electricity between Natural Philosophy and Revolutionary Politics," 91–136.
30. *Lettre de M. Mauduyt, Régent der la Faculté de Médicine de Paris sur les précautions nécessaires relativement aux maladies qu'on traite par l'électricité. Extrait du Journal de médicine du mois d'avril 1778.*
31. Zanetti, "L'Électricité médicale," 44–80.
32. Zanetti, "L'Électricité médicale," 93–100; Michael R. Lynn, "Experimental Physics in Enlightenment Paris: The Practice of Popularization in Urban Culture," in Bernadette Bensaude-Vincente and Christine Blondel, eds., *Science and Spectacle in the European Enlightenment* (London: Routledge, 2008), 65–74.
33. "Lettre de M. Le Dru, fils, sur quelques expériences de M. Marat," *Journal de physique* 18 (November 1781): 402–4, as reprinted in *MA*, 331–33.
34. *MA*, 331–33.
35. Zanetti, "L'Électricité médicale," 101–2.
36. See chapter 12, note 3.
37. *De l'électricité du corps humain dans l'état de santé et de maladie; Ouvrage couronné par l'Académie de Lyon, dans lequel on traite de l'Electricité de l'Atmosphère, de son influence & de ses effets sur l'économie animale. &c &c. Par M. l'Abbé Bertholon, de St. Lazare, des Académies royales des sciences de Montpellier, Béziers, Lyon, Marseille, Nîmes, Dijon, Rouen, Toulouse, Bordeaux, Rome, Hesse-Hombourg, &c. &c.* (Lyon, 1780), v. On Bertholon, see Jean-Paul Poirier, *L'abbé Bertholon. Un électricien des Lumières en province* (Paris: Hermann, 2008).
38. Charles de Robillard de Beaurepaire, *Extraits d'un manuscript de Dom Gourdin* (Rouen, 1867), 21–25; *MA*, 339–40, 344–45, 351, 353–57.
39. *Mémoire sur l'électricité médicale, couronné le 6 août 1783, par l'Académie des belles lettres, sciences et arts de Rouen* (Paris, 1784), 7.
40. *De l'électricité du corps humain dans l'état de santé et de maladie*, 5.
41. *Mémoire sur l'électricité médicale*, 6.
42. *Mémoire sur l'électricité médicale*, 10.
43. *Mémoire sur l'électricité médicale*, 4.
44. *Mémoire sur l'électricité médicale*, 47–48.
45. *Mémoire sur l'électricité médicale*, 34.
46. *Mémoire sur l'électricité médicale*, 34–37, 43.

47. *Mémoire sur l'électricité médicale*, 48.

48. Letter to William Daly, December [1782], *CM*, 12–14. Originally written in English, the letter is now known only in a French translation, which has been retranslated here.

49. *Mémoire sur l'électricité médicale*, 69–70.

50. *Mémoire sur l'électricité médicale*, 70–79.

51. François Masars de Cazeles, *Second Mémoire sur l'électricité médicale et histoire de quarante-deux maladies entièrement guéries, ou notablement soulagés par ce remède* (Paris, 1781). Marat reported that he carried out experiments to test the friction method in February 1782, achieving better results with a metal rod than one with a glass handle proposed by Masars.

52. *Mémoire sur l'électricité médicale*, 95.

53. *Mémoire sur l'électricité médicale*, 82–83.

54. Zanetti, "L'Électricité médicale," 80, describes Mauduyt's *Mémoire* as "in large part a translation of Cavallo."

55. "Lettre de M. l'Abbé Sans, à M. Marat, sur l'électricité négative et positive," *L'Année littéraire* (May 1785), 62–67, as reprinted in *MA*, 402–4.

56. *Observations de M. l'amateur Avec à M. l'Abbé Sans, sur la nécessité indispensable d'avoir une théorie solide et lumineuse, avant d'ouvrir boutique d'électricité médicale; en réponse à la Lettre de M. l'Abbé Sans à M. Marat, sur l'électricité positive & négative, publiée dans le N° 16 de l'Année Littéraire* ("A Epidaure et se trouve à Paris," 1785). The work was to be sold together with the *Mémoire sur l'électricité médicale*.

57. *Journal de médicine* (April 1785), republished in *Esprit des journaux* (June 1785), 157–68, and (with some variants) in *Journal encyclopédique de Bouillon* (July 1785), 12–22. *MA*, 408–19.

58. *MA*, 422–23. On the revisions to the *Découvertes . . . sur la lumière* Marat was making in preparation for this new *Traité d'optique*, see *MA*, 441–46, quotations at 423–24.

59. "Observations communiqués [aux auteurs de ce journal] par M. Bertholon, professeur de physique expérimentale des Etats-Généraux de Languedoc, & membre de plusieurs académies, sur plusieurs vérités fondamentales relatives à l'électricité du corps humain," (October 1785), 290–96; (November 1785), 493–501; in *MA*, 425–33; *Esprit des journaux* (November 1785), 343–58. On the reference to the Charles affair, see Bertholon's letters to Buissart quoted in *MA*, 446.

60. "Lettre de M. l'abbé Bertholon, professeur de physique expérimentale des Etats-Généraux de Languedoc, & membre de plusieurs académies, aux auteurs du *Journal encyclopédique*, sur un extrait inséré dans le 5e tome de cet ouvrage, année 1785," *Journal encyclopédique de Bouillon* (January 1786), 302–311, in *MA*, 441–46.

CHAPTER 11

1. *Découvertes . . . sur la lumière*, 5–6.

2. Brissot, *Mémoires (1754–1793)*, ed. Claude Perroud, 2 vols. (Paris: Alphonse Picard & fils, 1911), 1:225.

3. See below, chapter 12, p. 201.

4. Pilâtre's capacity to do so ended, however, when he died dramatically in the first fatal ballooning accident, in June 1785. Marat wrote an analysis of the "hideous catastrophe," claiming that he had warned Pilâtre of the danger of placing a hydrogen balloon above a hot air brazier. Critical of the hyper-enthusiasm of the ballooning craze, he argued nonetheless for the scientific, military, and public benefits of continuing the development of balloon flight. *Lettres de l'observateur Bon-Sens, à M. de ***, Sur la fatale catastrophe des infortunés Pilâtre de Rosier et Romain, les aéronautes & l'aérostation* (London, "Et se trouve à Paris," 1785). See also Mi Gyung Kim, *The Imagined Empire: Balloon Enlightenments in Revolutionary Europe* (Pittsburgh: University of Pittsburgh, 2016); Charles

Coulston Gillispie, *The Montgolfier Brothers and the Invention of Aviation, 1783–1784* (Princeton: Princeton University Press, 1983).

5. *MA*, 137, 161, 228, 259. On Pahin de la Blancherie's *salon de correspondance*, and the emergence of *musées* that followed its model, see Dena Goodman, *The Republic of Letters: A Cultural History of the French Enlightenment* (Ithaca, NY: Cornell University Press, 1994), 233–80; Michael R. Lynn, *Popular Science and Public Opinion in Eighteenth-Century France* (Manchester, UK: Manchester University Press, 2006), 72–96.

6. My thanks to Damien Tricoire for information about the Artois-Chartres network in his unpublished paper, "'Pour le bien du peuple, l'honneur de son prince, et pour la gloire et le sang de la maison d'Orléans.' Jacques-Pierre Brissot, de l'homme de lettres au révolutionnaire," and for further references in the Brissot papers showing the intimacy of Brissot and Marat within that group. See also Régis Coursin, *Jacques-Pierre Brissot. Sociologie historique d'une entrée en révolution* (Rennes: Presses Universitaires de Rennes, 2023).

7. *Nouvelles de la république des lettres et des arts* (21 November 1781), 71–72. My thanks to Robert Darnton for a reference to discussions of Marat in issues of this journal in 1781 and 1782.

8. *Nouvelles de la république des lettres et des arts* (12 December 1781), 1; (30 January 1782), 35–36; (20 March 1782), 91–93; (15 May 1782), 138–40. For the relationship between Pahin's assembly and the Academy of Sciences, see Goodman, *Republic of Letters*, 249–50.

9. Brissot, *Mémoires*, 1:185–96.

10. Brissot, *Mémoires*, 1:197.

11. *MA*, 258.

12. *Notions élémentaires d'optique* (Paris, 1784), iv. Funding for the publication was probably provided by the Montpellier naturalist, baron Philippe-Laurent de Joubert, on whom more below.

13. Brissot, *Mémoires*, 1:201. But Mercier was only in Paris in 1782 for a few months, having taken refuge in Neuchâtel against possible punishment for his work.

14. See *MA*, 461–92.

15. Brissot, *Mémoires*, 1:211.

16. Brissot, *Mémoires*, 1:198.

17. Brissot, *Mémoires*, 1:198–99.

18. Simon Burrows and Mark Curran, *The French Book Trade in Enlightenment Europe Database, 1769–1794*, fbtee.uws.edu.au/stn/interface/. The database lists 1,544 copies printed by the Société typographique de Neuchâtel and an additional 827 acquired by it, for a total of 2,260 copies sold or given (mostly in Paris). However, Robert Darnton notes in a review of this database (available online at https://reviews.history.ac.uk/review/1355) that the Société typographique de Neuchâtel faced restrictive French government policies that virtually closed the Paris market to it by June 1783.

19. Brissot, *De la vérité, ou Méditations sur les moyens de parvenir à la vérité dans toutes les connaissances humaines* (Neuchâtel, 1782), 346.

20. Brissot, *De la vérité*, 347–48.

21. Brissot, *De la vérité*, 109.

22. Brissot, *De la vérité*, 365, 135, 159.

23. Brissot, *De la vérité*, 359.

24. Brissot, *De la vérité*, 164.

25. Brissot, *De la vérité*, 165–66.

26. Brissot, *De la vérité*, 168.

27. Brissot, *De la vérité*, 172.

28. Brissot, *De la vérité*, 173–74.

29. *MA*, 375–76. My thanks to Nicolas Rieucau for confirming the authorship and establishing the date of this letter.

30. Brissot, *De la vérité*, 182.
31. Brissot, *De la vérité*, 187.
32. Brissot, *De la vérité*, 333–39.
33. *CM*, 9–10, as reprinted from Brissot's *Mémoires*; my thanks to Damien Tricoire for signaling the existence of the original in the Brissot papers, *AN* 446AP/7 (1587). Henry Maty published *The New Review*. Jean Guillaume Wirchaux was a bookseller and publisher in Hamburg. The London bookseller Peter Elmsley, a friend of John Wilkes, specialized in foreign books.
34. Brissot, *Mémoires*, ed. Mathurin François de Lescure (Paris, 1877), 181. See also Brissot, *Mémoires*, 1:200–201.
35. *MA*, 187–91.
36. *MA*, 201–5.
37. *MA*, 209–12.
38. *MA*, 282–86.
39. *MA*, 208–9.
40. *MA*, 215–17. This "Montigni" has not been identified; he could be the military officer, Louis-Joseph Méry de Montigny, vicomte de Dreux (1748–97).
41. *Année littéraire* (June 1781), 208–9.
42. *The Monthly Review* 67 (July–December 1782): 293–95. Also, *MA*, 298–303.
43. Marat, *Mémoires académiques ou Nouvelles Découvertes sur la lumière, relatives aux points les plus importants de l'Optique* (Paris, 1788), v.
44. Marat, *Mémoires académiques*, v–vi. This provincial campaign is discussed by Olivier Coquard, *Jean-Paul Marat* (Paris: Fayard, 1993), 164–79; and Olivier Coquard, "Marat et les académies de province," in Jean Bernard, Jean-François Lemaire, and Jean-Pierre Poirier, eds., *Marat, homme de science?* (Paris: Synthélabo, 1993), 65–93.
45. See *Eloge de Montesquieu présenté à l'Académie de Bordeaux le 28 mars 1785 par J.-P. Marat*, ed. Arthur de Brézetz (Libourne, 1883). The editor marshals persuasive arguments for attribution of this hitherto unpublished text to Marat. Fulsome in its praise, however, it lacks the critical edge common in Marat's work. The jurors rejected it as "cold and langorous, lacking flair in its style and energy in its analysis, and devoid as a whole of those philosophical perspectives for which the subject offers so vast a field and so many opportunities to be developed" (xx).
46. Charles de Robillard de Beaurepaire, *Extraits d'un manuscript de Dom Gourdin* (Rouen, 1867), 21–25.
47. *Mémoire sur l'électricité médicale, couronné le 6 août 1783, par l'Académie des belles lettres, sciences et arts de Rouen* (Paris, 1784), 7.
48. Robillard de Beaurepaire, *Extraits d'un manuscript de Dom Gourdin*, 29. Biographical details on Gourdin are taken from this account.
49. Marat, *Mémoires académiques*, 253–54.
50. Robillard de Beaurepaire, *Extraits d'un manuscript de Dom Gourdin*, 25–26.
51. Robillard de Beaurepaire, *Extraits d'un manuscript de Dom Gourdin*, 26–29.
52. Robillard de Beaurepaire, *Extraits d'un manuscript de Dom Gourdin*, 30–32.
53. Claudius Roux, *Marat et l'Académie de Lyon (d'après des documents inédits)* (Lyon, 1923), was the first to explore this episode in any detail. The relevant documents are now more easily available as reprinted in Jacques De Cock, *Marat et la lumière* (Brussels: Pôle Nord, 1991), 79–101 (for this quotation, see 79–80).
54. De Cock, *Marat et la lumière*, 80–81.
55. De Cock, *Marat et la lumière*, 81. For the speculations, see Roux, *Marat et l'Académie de Lyon* (unpaginated). On the source of the medal, see De Cock, *Marat et la lumière*, 88.
56. De Cock, *Marat et la lumière*, 82–83.
57. De Cock, *Marat et la lumière*, 85; Roux, *Marat et l'Académie de Lyon*.

58. De Cock, *Marat et la lumière*, 85.
59. De Cock, *Marat et la lumière*.
60. This was the conclusion drawn by Roux, a historian profoundly hostile to Marat. It has been challenged much more recently by one of Marat's defenders, Jacques De Cock, on the grounds that Gourdin's letter (which is undated) was recorded as received by the Lyon Academy on 14 September, well after the prize had been awarded, and that it bears the notation "answered 14 September." Whether this notation was actually made on the letter by La Tourette at the time, or by some later scholar or archivist, De Cock does not state. But there seem, in any case, to be two reasons for concluding that the letter from Gourdin recorded as received on 14 September is not the one at issue here but a second, entirely different one. First, this latter is described as reporting that the Rouen prize had been awarded "to the only anti-Newtonian mémoire," whereas the letter at issue (as printed by De Cock) offers no such report and promises only that Gourdin will send a copy of his committee report at some point in the future. Second, it is described as accompanied by Gourdin's "observations on grammar in general," whereas the letter at issue states that he will send the Lyon Academy this work "very shortly [dans peu de temps]." It seems clear, then, that (1) Gourdin did send the letter at issue before the Rouen prize committee reached its decision (which was publicly announced on 3 August 1786, but must actually have been made quite some time earlier); (2) he therefore did so before the Lyon prize committee arrived at its own judgment (which was presented to the Lyon Academy, and accepted by it, on 8 August 1786); (3) he followed up this first letter with a second one conveying the result of the Rouen competition, the letter reported in the Academy's registers as received on 14 September. It seems, then, that Gourdin's first letter was written before the Rouen and Lyon competitions had been decided and that it was indeed intended to influence the outcome of the Lyon prize contest. However, it may well have been received, or reported to the Lyon Academy by La Tourrette, after its prize had actually been awarded. That this was the case is suggested by entries in the Academy's register for 5 September 1786, which recorded that the academicians discussed two letters from Gourdin read to them by La Tourrette on that date. From these letters, it appeared that "Newton's color theory has just been attacked at Rouen." In them, "Dom Gourdin described a number of experiments he believed to be victorious against the system of the English philosopher." Formulating their response to Gourdin, the Lyon academicians decided (rather frostily) that it would be limited "to mentioning the prize recently awarded on the subject and promising to send a copy of the report once it is printed." Whether the Lyon academicians knew the outcome of the Rouen competition at this point is not clear. A note was added to the register, erroneously, to the effect that "the Academy of Rouen, like our Academy, awarded the prize to the mémoire that had adopted Newton's theory." A more careful search in the registers might throw additional light on the matter.
61. De Cock, *Marat et la lumière*, 91.
62. Marat remembered it later, offering an utterly trumped-up account, in his *Les charlatans modernes*.
63. Marat, *Mémoires académiques*, 5–8.
64. *MA*, 526–27. Père Louis Bertrand Castel had been a leading French critic of Newton's theories, and especially of his optics.
65. For what follows on the Montpellier prize essay contest, see Roux, *Marat et l'Académie de Lyon*; Coquard, *Marat et la lumière*, 177–79.

CHAPTER 12

1. *MA*, 542. On Breguet, see Emmanuel Breguet, *Breguet horloger depuis 1775. Vie et postérité d'Abraham-Louis Breguet (1747–1823)* (Paris: A. de Gourcuff, 1997). Breguet listed

Marat's watch as repaired in 1792 along with those belonging to Mme Condorcet, St. Just, Thomas Paine, and others.

2. On Roume de Saint-Laurent, see F. P. Renaut, "L'Odyssée d'un colonial sous l'Ancien Régime: Philippe-Rose Roume de Saint-Laurent (1776–1796)," *Revue de l'histoire des colonies françaises* 9 (1920): 329–48. This article, while informative, cites no sources.

3. *MA*, 336; incomplete in *CM*, 17–18. Roume must have asked Marat what he thought of Mesmer. "I'll occupy myself with M. Mesmer and give you a good account of him," he replied. "But this is not pressing business. You know how much I like to examine things and to examine them carefully before pronouncing on them." The promised analysis seems never to have been sent. Though, as Robert Darnton accurately notes, there is a parallel between Marat's repudiation by the Academy of Sciences (and Brissot's defense of them both) (see Darnton, *Mesmerism and the End of the Enlightenment in France* [Cambridge, MA: Harvard University Press, 1968], 92–95), Marat did not follow Brissot into a radical defense of Mesmerism, or the pamphleteering politics of the prerevolutionary period. There is little evidence to place him among the Grub Street literary proletariat, as suggested by Darnton in *The Literary Underground of the Old Regime* (Cambridge, MA: Harvard University Press, 1982), 20, 28, 38.

4. *MA*, 337; incomplete in *CM*, 18–19.

5. *MA*, 337–38; also *CM*, 19–20.

6. *MA*, 338; also *CM*, 20.

7. *MA*, 341; incomplete in *CM*, 21.

8. *MA*, 342.

9. *MA*, 342–43.

10. *MA*, 343. It is not clear whether this is a reference to the famous British maker of achromatic lenses, John Dolland, who had died in 1761.

11. *MA*, 343.

12. *MA*, 345–46.

13. *MA*, 346–48.

14. *MA*, 348.

15. *MA*, 349–50. Marat was in fact still giving demonstrations in his laboratory in 1782.

16. *MA*, 350.

17. *MA*, 352.

18. Aranda to Florida-Blanca, 21 September 1783, reprinted in José Barón Fernández, "Juan-Pablo Marat y la proyectada de ciencias de Madrid en 1783, según los documentos conservados en Simancas," *Medicina & Historia* 34 (1974): 7–26 (for this letter, see 19–24). My thanks to Alvaro Santana Acuña for translating this and the other Spanish documents published by Fernández.

19. Bernardo Belluga to Florida-Blanca, 21 September 1783, as reprinted in Fernandez, "Juan-Pablo Marat y la proyectada academia de ciencias de Madrid en 1783," 23.

20. Belluga to Florida-Blanca, 21 September 1783, as reprinted in Fernandez, "Juan-Pablo Marat y la proyectada academia de ciencias de Madrid en 1783," 23.

21. This was possibly Antonio Fernández Solano, a professor of physics in Madrid and a specialist in scientific instruments, who was visiting London and Paris in 1783. See *Diccionario biográfico electrónico* (Real Academia de la Historia, Madrid, 2011).

22. *MA*, 356; *CM*, 22–23.

23. Belluga to Florida Blanca, 10 October 1783, as reprinted in Fernández, "Juan-Pablo Marat y la proyectada academia de ciencias de Madrid en 1783."

24. Ponz to Eugenio, 24 November 1783, as reprinted in Fernández, "Juan-Pablo Marat y la proyectada academia de ciencias de Madrid en 1783."

25. *MA*, 355–56; *CM*, 22–23.

26. *MA*, 358; *CM*, 24–25.

27. *MA*, 372; *CM*, 44. Quotations in the following section are entirely from this letter, *MA*, 358–72; *CM*, 24–44.
28. *CM*, 44. To this notation, dated 10 February 1784, Roume de Saint-Laurent added, "I sent a certified copy to M. count Florida-Blanca three weeks ago."
29. *MA*, 405–6; *CM*, 89–90.
30. Brissot, *Mémoires (1754–1793)*, ed. Claude Perroud, 2 vols. (Paris: Alphonse Picard & fils, 1911), 1:203. On this question, see Olivier Coquard, *Jean-Paul Marat* (Paris: Fayard, 1993), 199–201.
31. *Mémoires académiques, ou Nouvelles découvertes sur la lumière, relatives aux points les plus importants de l'Optique* (Paris, 1788), 9.
32. Charles Coulston Gillispie, *Science and Polity in France: The End of the Old Regime* (Princeton: Princeton University Press, 1980), 321.
33. *MA*, 404–5.
34. *MA*, 405.
35. *Optique de Newton, traduction nouvelle, faite par M*** sur la dernière édition originale, ornée de vingt-une planches, & approuvée par l'Académie royale des sciences; Dédiée au Roi, par M. Beauzée, Éditeur de cet ouvrage, l'un des Quarante de l'Académie française, etc.*, 2 vols. (Paris, 1787), 1:v–vi.
36. *Optique de Newton*, 1:vii, ix–xi.
37. *L'Année littéraire* (1787), 2:317–20. An announcement in *L'Année littéraire* the previous year (1786, vol. 4) had invited subscriptions for this work, promising that the beauty and magnificence of its typography would match its intellectual importance, rendering it precious to all collectors of fine editions and justifying its place in every library.
38. *Journal encyclopédique de Bouillon* (March 1787), 200–206, reprinted in *MA*, 494–97.
39. *Journal des savants* (December 1787), 853–55, reprinted in *MA*, 517–19.
40. *Journal général de France*, 1 and 6 December 1787, 13 December 1787, 27 and 29 December 1787, 3 January 1788, reprinted in *MA*, 502–16, 523–24.
41. *Journal général de France* (3 January 1788), 6–7; *MA*, 523–24.
42. La Tourrette communicated Romé de Lisle's letter to the Lyon Academy on 29 January 1788, along with his response explaining why Marat's essay had not been published in 1785. The academicians urged the secretary to publish a statement of this kind, though no record of his doing so has been found. On 1 April one of the academicians, Le Camus, demanded to see the essays submitted and the committee report. La Tourrette responded by stating that the report was only given to him by Villers on condition that it not be communicated to anyone without the latter's consent. The Academy took the view that the report belonged to the body as a whole and its communication to one of its members could not be refused. The document was handed to Le Camus on condition that he read it and return it immediately. *MA*, 526–27, 532, 539.
43. *MA*, 525–26.
44. *Journal général de France* (22 January 1788), 37–38, reprinted in *MA*, 529–31.
45. *L'Année littéraire* (1788), 2:333–38.
46. Marat, letter dated 16 March 1788; *MA*, 537.
47. *Journal de physique* (February 1788), 140–42; *MA*, 532–35.
48. Marat to La Métherie, 10 March 1788; *MA*, 535–37.
49. Marat to La Métherie, 26 March 1788; *MA*, 538.
50. *MA*, 448–49; *CM*, 91–92.
51. Samuel Formey to Marat, 26 April 1788, in *MA*, 539–40.
52. Marat to Formey, 6 May 1788; *MA*, 540.
53. Marat to Formey, 23 June 1788 [?]; *MA*, 541.
54. *Advancing Knowledge: Selections from the Archives of the American Academy of Arts and Sciences* (Boston: American Academy of Arts and Sciences, 2015), 86–87.
55. Marat to Sir Joseph Banks, 27 March 1788, British Library, Add. Mss., 8097, fols. 93–94.

56. Marat to Sir Joseph Banks, 27 March 1788, British Library, Add. Mss., 8097, fol. 94 (undated draft reply appended to Marat's letter of 27 March 1788).
57. Marat to Banks, 20 April 1788, British Library, Add. Mss., 8097, fol. 95.

CHAPTER 13

1. *OP*, 2:718.
2. *OP*, 8:5499–5500.
3. Toni de Dios et al., "Metagenomic Analysis of a Blood Stain from the French Revolutionary Jean-Paul Marat (1743–1793)," https://doi.org/10.1101/825034; version posted January 27, 2020. On this issue, see Eric Walter, "Vies et maladies du docteur Marat. Le thème morbide dans le discours biographique," in Jean-Claude Bonnet et al., *La mort de Marat* (Paris, 1986), 335–72.
4. My thanks to Jonathan Giennap for helpful comments on this comparison.
5. *OP*, 1:1–5, 11–16.
6. *OP*, 1:2–3.
7. *OP*, 1:4–5.
8. *OP*, 1:5.
9. *OP*, 1:5–7.
10. *OP*, 1:10–11.
11. *OP*, 1:19–20, 24.
12. *OP*, 1:27–28.
13. *OP*, 1:29–33; Charles-Alexandre Calonne, *Lettre adressée au Roi par M. de Calonne, le 9 février 1789* (Paris, 1789), 23–24.
14. *OP*, 1:38.
15. *OP*, 1:32–33.
16. *OP*, 1:38–39.
17. *OP*, 1:39–40.
18. Joseph Antoine Joachim Cerutti, *Mémoire pour le peuple français*, 2nd ed. (n.p., 1788), 47, quoted in *OP*, 1:44–45.
19. *OP*, 1:30, 43.
20. *OP*, 1:53.
21. *OP*, 1:52, 33.
22. Olivier Coquard, *Jean-Paul Marat* (Paris: Fayard, 1993), 217, citing Archives nationales Y13319.
23. Robert H. Blackman, *1789: The French Revolution Begins* (Cambridge, UK: Cambridge University Press, 2019), offers a careful reconsideration of the creation of the National Assembly and its action during the summer and fall of 1789.
24. *OP* 1:55, 125; *Plan de legislation en matière criminelle*, in Brissot, ed., *Bibliothèque philosophique*, 5:118.
25. Mallet du Pan, *Mémoires et correspondance*, ed. A. [Pierre André] Sayous, 2 vols. (Paris, 1851), 1:126, dated this event to 1788, which seems unlikely. Jean Massin, *Marat* (Aix-en-Provence: Alinéa, 1988), 69, suggests 1789 as a possibility, but there seems no other evidence for its occurrence.
26. *OP*, 1:292. Brissot recounted the story in his journal, *Le Patriote français*, though he expressed doubts about its veracity in his *Mémoires*. See Coquard, *Marat*, 222–23.
27. Baker, "Revolutioning Revolution," in *Scripting Revolution: A Historical Approach to the Comparative Study of Revolutions*, ed. Keith Michael Baker and Dan Edelstein (Stanford, CA: Stanford University Press, 2015), 71–102; and see Dan Edelstein, *The Revolution to Come: A History of an Idea from Thucydides to Lenin* (Princeton, NJ: Princeton University Press, 2025), esp. 165–77.
28 *OP*, 1:617.
29. *OP*, 1:60.

30. *OP*, 1:56.
31. *OP*, 1:57–58.
32. See, most recently, Rafe Blaufarb, *The French Revolution and the Invention of Modern Property* (Oxford, UK: Oxford University Press, 2016).
33. *OP*, 1:62–63.
34. *OP*, 1:65.
35. *OP*, 1:20*–21*. Citations to starred pagination in this edition refer to the separately numerated "Guide de lecture" included in each volume.
36. *OP*, 1:21*; *Actes de la Commune de Paris pendant la Révolution, première série*, ed. Sigismond Lacroix, 7 vols. (Paris, 1894–98), 1:206.
37. For a fuller discussion of these debates, see my "The Idea of a Declaration of Rights," in Dale Van Kley, ed., *The French Idea of Freedom: The Old Regime and the Declaration of the Rights of 1789* (Stanford: Stanford University Press, 1994), 154–96.
38. *OP*, 1:69.
39. *OP*, 1:70.
40. *OP*, 1:73.
41. *OP*, 1:73–74.
42. *OP*, 1:74.
43. *OP*, 1:74–75.
44. *OP*, 1:75.
45. *OP*, 1:75–76.
46. *OP*, 1:77.
47. *OP*, 1:77.
48. *OP*, 1:77–78.
49. *Discours adressé aux Anglais le 15 avril 1774, sur les vices de leur Constitution, et les moyens d'y remédier*, *OP*, 7:4621–59. This French text is a revised and reorganized version of the section on the English constitution in *CS*, 195–226. In the French translation of 1793, it was separated from the body of the work and appeared (with a *Lettre au président des États-Généraux*, dated 23 August 1789) in an appendix entitled "*Tableau des vices de la Constitution anglaise*." There it is described as "presented to the Estates-General in August 1789 as a series of pitfalls to avoid in the government they wish to give France." However, no separate evidence has been found in support of this claim. The side-by-side comparison of the French and English texts offered in *OP* has also been published separately (with the same numeration) in Jean-Paul Marat, *Les Chaînes de l'esclavage 1793, The Chains of Slavery 1774*, ed. Charlotte Goëtz and Jacques De Cock (Brussels, 1995), 4621–59.
50. *OP*, 1:67–68, also *OP*, 7:4615–20. R. C. H. Catterall, "The Credibility of Marat," *American Historical Review* 16 (1910): 24–35, at 32–35, was rightly severe in his judgment of the claims in this letter for the influence of *The Chains of Slavery* in creating a "general fermentation," though less so in his indictment of the relatively minor variations in the wording of the reforms Marat added in August 1789. Marat's claim that his work inspired a subsequent Place Bill was also derided by Catterall on the grounds that no such bill was passed in 1775 or immediately thereafter. It could perhaps have been an inflated reference to Burke's Bill, Clerke's Contractors Bill, and Crewe's Revenue Officers Bill of 1782, each intended to reduce the political influence of the crown by eliminating places from the Civil List. See Earl A. Reitan, *Politics, Finance, and the People: Economical Reform in England in the Age of the American Revolution, 1770–92* (Basingstoke, UK: Palgrave Macmillan, 2007), 97–104. In aiming to reduce monarchical influence on Parliament, these acts expressed a common goal of reformers in Britain during the period; they were unlikely to have been influenced by Marat's work in particular.
51. *OP*, 1:71.
52. *OP*, 1:71–72.
53. *OP*, 1:72, 78.

54. *OP*, 1:79.
55. *OP*, 1:80–82.
56. *OP*, 1:79–80.
57. *OP*, 1:80.
58 *OP*, 1:83.
59. *OP*, 1:86.
60. *OP*, 1:86.
61. *OP*, 1:89, 93.
62. *OP*, 1:101.
63. *OP*, 1:103–4. Marat's memory was not quite precise. Mounier had spoken of "a vast society of 24 million," *Archives parlementaires de 1787 à 1860, première série (1787–1799)*, ed. M. J. Mavidal and M. E. Laurent, 82 vols. (Paris, 1879–1913), 8:215 (9 July 1789). The *Archives parlementaires* is hereafter cited as *AP*.
64. *OP*, 1:105. On this theme, see Patrice Rolland, "Marat, ou la politique du soupçon," *Le Débat*, no. 57 (1989): 129–48.

CHAPTER 14

1. In all, 140 new periodicals were created in 1789; 34 survived at least a year. Others included its future competition: Brissot's *Patriote français*; Condorcet's *Chronique de Paris*; Elysée Loustalot's *Révolutions de Paris*; Camille Desmoulins's *Révolutions de France et de Brabant*; the *Annales patriotiques* of a former scientific rival, Jean-Louis Carra, and the prolific writer Louis-Sébastien Mercier. See Jeremy D. Popkin, *Revolutionary News: The Press in France, 1789–1799* (Durham, NC: Duke University Press, 1990), 32–33, for these figures, and throughout for the revolutionary press.
2. *OP*, 1:113.
3. On the declaration of the National Assembly as a "performative," see Paul Friedland, *Political Actors: Representative Bodies and Theatricality in the Age of the French Revolution* (Ithaca, NY: Cornell University Press, 2002), chap. 4.
4. *OP*, 1:113–15.
5. For a fuller discussion of these debates, see my *Inventing the French Revolution* (Cambridge, UK: Cambridge University Press, 1990), 252–305. For a critical response, see Barry M. Shapiro, *Traumatic Politics: The Deputies and the King in the Early French Revolution* (University Park: Pennsylvania State University Press, 2009), chap. 9; and Shapiro, "Opting for the Terror? A Critique of Keith Baker's Analysis of the Suspensive Veto of 1789," *Proceedings of the Western Society for French History* 26 (2000): 324–34. See also Robert H. Blackman, *1789: The French Revolution Begins* (Cambridge, UK: Cambridge University Press, 2019).
6. Baker, *Inventing*, 273.
7. *OP*, 1:133, 139–40.
8. *OP*, 1:141.
9. *OP*, 1:144.
10. *OP*, 1:142. For an illuminating discussion of the evolution of the notion of public opinion in relationship to the practice of representation in the French Revolution, see Jon Cowans, *To Speak for the People: Public Opinion and the Problem of Legitimacy in the French Revolution* (New York: Routledge, 2001).
11. Colin Lucas, "The Theory and Practice of Denunciation in the French Revolution," *Journal of Modern History* 68 (1996): 768–85.
12. *OP*, 1:153–54.
13. *OP*, 1:156, 161–62.
14. *OP*, 1:162.
15. *OP*, 1:162–63, 167, 180.
16. *OP*, 1:179–81.
17. *OP*, 1:150, 187.

18. The classic study is Steven L. Kaplan, *The Famine Plot Persuasion in Eighteenth-Century France*, in *Transactions of the American Philosophical Society* 72, part 3 (Philadelphia: American Philosophical Society, 1982).
19. Camille Desmoulins, *Révolutions de France et de Brabant* 47 (October 1790), as quoted in *OP*, 1:44*.
20. *OP*, 1:263.
21. *OP*, 1:239.
22. *OP*, 1:221–24.
23. *OP*, 1:224, 57*.
24. *OP*, 1:183–85.
25. *OP*, 1:185.
26. *OP*, 1:188.
27. *OP*, 1:189–90, 192–94.
28. *OP*, 1:200.
29. *OP*, 1:210–13. The municipality recorded a rather less contentious display on Marat's part. See *Actes de la Commune de Paris pendant la Révolution, première série*, ed. Sigismond Lacroix, 7 vols. (Paris, 1894–98), 2:103–5.
30. *OP*, 1:213, 224.
31. *OP*, 1:33, 40*–43*; *Actes de la Commune de Paris pendant la Révolution, première série*, ed. 2:157–58.
32. *OP*, 6:3827, 1:46*–60*.
33. *OP*, 6:1024*.
34. *OP*, 6:3828, 1:254–55.
35. *OP*, 1:260, 583.
36. *OP*, 1:260, 584.
37. *OP*, 1:589. On Loustalot, see Pierre Rétat, "Forme et discours d'un journal révolutionnaire. Les *Révolutions de Paris* en 1789," in Claude Labrosse, Pierre Rétat, and Henri Duranton, *L'Instrument périodique. La fonction de la presse au XVIIIe siècle* (Lyon: Presses universitaires de Lyon, 1986), 139–78; Baker, *Inventing*, 218–23.
38. *OP*, 1:584–85.
39. *OP*, 1:585–88.
40. *OP*, 1:590–91.
41. *OP*, 1:593–94.
42. *OP*, 1:588–89, 596.
43. *OP*, 1:599–600.
44. *OP*, 1:614.
45. *OP*, 1:615.
46. *OP*, 1:616.
47. *OP*, 1:617–18.
48. *Justification de M. Necker, Premier Ministre des Finances: ou Réponse à la dénonciation du sieur Marat. Par un citoyen du district de Saint-André des Arts.*
49. *OP*, 1:582, 70*.
50. *OP*, 1:262–65.
51. These revisions, announced on 10 October (*OP*, 1:31), are apparently reprinted in *OP*, 1:311–428, from a manuscript collection in the BnF, nouv. acq. fr., 310; see also *OP*, 1:82*. The editors argue that Marat worked on them in the last weeks of 1789. However, Olivier Coquard, "Note sur les manuscrits de Marat à la BN," *Annales historiques de la Révolution française* 267 (1987): 68–79, suggests that the revisions may date to 1792, when Marat was working on preparing a collection of his writings under the title "L'Ecole du citoyen." For the latter, see below, pp. 509–10.
52. *OP*, 1:284.
53. *OP*, 1:285.

54. *OP*, 1:284, 287–88.
55. *OP*, 1:288–89.
56. *OP*, 1:297–98.
57. See *OP*, 1:86*–92*.
58. *OP*, 1:435–39.
59. On this period, see Timothy Tackett, "Nobles and Third Estate in the Revolutionary Dynamic of the National Assembly, 1789–1790," *American Historical Review* 94 (1989): 271–301; Barry M. Shapiro, "Revolutionary Justice in 1789–90: The Comité des Recherches, the Châtelet, and the Fayettist Coalition," *French Historical Studies* 17 (1992): 656–69.
60. *OP*, 1:486, 491–92, 534.
61. *OP*, 1:490–91.
62. *OP*, 1:474, 499, 478.
63. *OP*, 1:468.
64. *OP*, 1:506, 526–27.
65. *OP*, 1:499, 510–15, 518–19, 532–33, 540–41.
66. *OP*, 1:531.
67. *OP*, 1:534–35.
68. *OP*, 1:542–45.
69. *OP*, 1:547–51, 117*–18*; *Actes de la Commune de Paris pendant la Révolution, première série*, 3:522.
70. *AP*, 11:259–64; Alma Söderhjelm, *Le régime de la presse pendant la Révolution française* (Helsingfors, 1900–1901), 1:117–27. See Charles Walton, *Policing Public Opinion in the French Revolution: The Culture of Calumny and the Problem of Free Speech* (Oxford, UK: Oxford University Press, 2009), 104–6, for the Sieyès proposal and throughout for discussion of recurring legislative battles over the policing of slander considered in the following chapters.
71. *OP*, 1:633–35.
72. *OP*, 1:116*–17*, 560.
73. *OP*, 1:118*–23*.
74. *OP*, 1:124*–26*; *Actes de la Commune de Paris pendant la Révolution, première série*, 3:458–59, 462–63, 465.
75. *OP*, 1:579–81, 621–22.
76. Jacques De Cock, *Les Cordeliers dans la Révolution française. Textes et documents* (Lyon: Fantasques Éditions, 2002): 307–8; *OP*, 1:127*–28*.
77. This account of the events of 22 January is drawn from E. Babut, "Une journée au district des Cordeliers. Le 22 janvier 1790," *Revue historique* (1903): 279–300; *OP*, 1:130*–78*; and De Cock, *Cordeliers*, 313–83. For the district's address to the National Assembly, see *OP*, 1:145*–46*, 337–38; De Cock, *Cordeliers*, 337–38.
78. For a discussion of these papers and the light they throw on the daily business of publishing *L'Ami du peuple*, see Olivier Coquard, Jean-Paul *Marat* (Paris: Fayard, 1993), 255–62.

CHAPTER 15

1. *Pamphlets de Jean-Paul Marat*, ed. Charles Vellay (Paris: Charpentier et Fasquelle, 1911), 122.
2. Vellay, ed., *Pamphlets de Jean-Paul Marat*, 122.
3. Vellay, ed., *Pamphlets de Jean-Paul Marat*, 153–54.
4. Vellay, ed., *Pamphlets de Jean-Paul Marat*, 154.
5. Vellay, ed., *Pamphlets de Jean-Paul Marat*, 155.
6. See Marc de Wilde, "Roman Dictatorship in the French Revolution," *History of European Ideas* 47 (2021): 140–57; Christian Bruschi, "La dictature romaine dans l'histoire des idées politiques de Machiavel à la Révolution française," in Michel Ganzin, *L'Influence de*

l'Antiquité sur la pensée politique Européenne (XVI–XXème siècles), 195–218. I have also learned much on this topic from a still unpublished paper by Adam Lebovitz, "Dictatorship in the American Founding."

7. Vellay, ed., *Pamphlets de Jean-Paul Marat*, 155.
8. Vellay, ed., *Pamphlets de Jean-Paul Marat*, 160–61.
9. Vellay, ed., *Pamphlets de Jean-Paul Marat*, 161.
10. *OP*, 2:719, 732.
11. *OP*, 2:686–90.
12. See Jean-Paul Marat, *Plan de législation criminelle. Texte conforme à l'édition de 1790*, ed. Daniel Hamiche (Paris: Aubier, 1974). *MA*, 899–1377, offers both the 1782 and 1790 texts and a guide to comparing them.
13. *OP*, 2:717, 840.
14. *OP*, 2:795–96.
15. *OP*, 1:113–14, 145, 469–70.
16. *OP*, 3:1969.
17. *OP*, 7:3964.
18. On the shifting patterns of correspondence in *L'Ami du peuple* and its successors, see Olivier Coquard, "La Correspondance de Marat dans les journaux de Marat," *Annales historiques de la Révolution française* 267 (1987): 58–67.
19. For brilliant evocations of Marat's invention of the persona of "The People's Friend," see especially Philippe Roger, "L'homme de sang. L'invention sémiotique de Marat," in Jean-Claude Bonnet et al., *La mort de Marat* (Paris: Flammarion, 1986), 141–66; and Mona Ozouf, "Marat," in *A Critical Dictionary of the French Revolution*, ed. François Furet and Mona Ozouf, trans. Arthur Goldhammer (Cambridge, MA: Harvard University Press, 1989), 244–50.
20. As quoted by Marat, *OP*, 5:2826.
21. *OP*, 5:2826.
22. *OP*, 2:749, 726, 746–57.
23. *OP*, 2:749.
24. *OP*, 2:808.
25. *OP*, 2:790–91.
26. *OP*, 2:791.
27. *OP*, 2:881–85.
28. *OP*, 2:944–45.
29. *OP*, 2:945.
30. *OP*, 2:949.
31. My thanks to Richard Saller for clarification of this point.
32. *OP*, 2:952.
33. *OP*, 2:954.
34. *OP*, 2:986–88.
35. *OP*, 2:1023–24, 1027.
36. *OP*, 2:1039–40.
37. *OP*, 2:976, 1040.
38. *OP*, 2:976.
39. *OP*, 2:1004.
40. *OP*, 2:1040.
41. *OP*, 2:1040, 1041, 1043.
42. Louis-Sébastien Mercier, *Le nouveau Paris*, ed. Jean-Claude Bonnet et al. (Paris, 1994), 78. On the Festival of Federation, see Mona Ozouf, *Festivals and the French Revolution*, trans. Alan Sheridan (Cambridge, MA: Harvard University Press, 1988), 33–60.
43. *OP*, 2, 745–46.
44. *AP*, 16:139 (8 June 1790).

45. *OP*, 2:773, 856–57.
46. *OP*, 2:872–75, 881–85.
47. *OP*, 2:1021.
48. *OP*, 2:1022–23.
49. *OP*, 2:1035, 1037.
50. Vellay, *Pamphlets de Jean-Paul Marat*, 197–200.
51. *OP*, 2:1059, 1078.

CHAPTER 16

1. *PM*, 201.
2. *OP*, 2:1102–5, 1127, 1136.
3. *OP*, 2:1136.
4. *PM*, 209.
5. *OP*, 2:379*.
6. *AP*, 17:450.
7. *AP*, 17:451.
8. *AP*, 17:485–86.
9. *AP*, 17:506.
10. *AP*, 17:509–10.
11. *AP*, 17:456.
12. *AP*, 17:456–57.
13. *AP*, 17:457.
14. *OP*, 2:1151.
15. *PM*, 211–17.
16. For a lengthy account of the reaction to *C'en est fait de nous*, see *OP*, 2:340*–404*. The Assembly debate is also discussed in Alma Söderhjelm, *Le régime de la presse pendant la Révolution française* (Helsingfors, 1900–1901), 1:128–40; and Charles Walton, *Policing Public Opinion in the French Revolution: The Culture of Calumny and the Problem of Free Speech* (Oxford, UK: Oxford University Press, 2009), 106–9.
17. Samuel F. Scott, *The Response of the Royal Army to the French Revolution* (Oxford, UK: Oxford University Press, 1978), 91–95.
18. *OP*, 3:1349.
19. *OP*, 2:1152, 1212–13, 1225.
20. *OP*, 3:1438.
21. *OP*, 3:1919.
22. *OP*, 3:1926–27.
23. *OP*, 5:2814, 2843, 2937.
24. *OP*, 6:3339.
25. Walter Markov and Albert Soboul, eds., *Die Sansculotten von Paris. Dokumenten zur Geschichte des Volksbewegung, 1793–1794* (Berlin, 1957), 219, as translated in Baker, *The Old Regime and the French Revolution* (Chicago: University of Chicago Press, 1987), 340.
26. *OP*, 2:1267–68; *OP*, 4:639*–42*.
27. See discussion above, chap. 6.

CHAPTER 17

1. *AP*, 18:494; *OP*, 3:1358.
2. *AP*, 18:530; *OP*, 3:1372.
3. *OP*, 3:1376–77.
4. *OP*, 3:1441.
5. *OP*, 3:1393, 1395, 1475–77.
6. *OP*, 3:1532, 1540, 1558, 1559, 1579, 1590, 1592, 1601, 1624, 1658.
7. *OP*, 3:1737, 1777, 1815; *AP*, 20:522–23, 592–98.

8. *AP*, 21:235–38.
9. *OP*, 3:1873–74.
10. *OP*, 3:1873–75.
11. *OP*, 3:1876–77.
12. *OP*, 3:1439–40.
13. *OP*, 3:1931.
14. They are discussed in detail in *OP*, 3:525*–66*.
15. *OP*, 3:1932–33, 1942, 1969.
16. On Mandar and his ideological allies, see Rachel Hammersley, "English Republicanism in Revolutionary France: The Case of the Cordelier Club," *Journal of British Studies* 43 (2004): 464–91.
17. *OP*, 4:2239–40.
18. *OP*, 3:1381–33.
19. *OP*, 3:1718.
20. "All, even our best authors, have ever expressed the *amor patriae* by the love of one's country, two things that ought to be carefully distinguished," Marat had lamented (using his English voice) in *The Chains of Slavery*. "The one is but the love of one's native land; the other, is the affection or tie of a country where one enjoys all the privileges a freeman is entitled to. Turks have no patria, though they do not want [i.e., lack] a name for it: The English have a patria, and no word to express it." *CS*, 15.
21. *OP*, 3:1723–25.
22. *OP*, 2:1191; *OP*, 3:1442.
23. *OP*, 3:1707–8.
24. *OP*, 3:1727.
25. *OP*, 3:1708.
26. *OP*, 3:1384, 1386, 1756.
27. *OP*, 3:1572–73.
28. *OP*, 3:1596–97.
29. *OP*, 3:1574, 1653–54.
30. *OP*, 3:1651–54, 1679–80.
31. *OP*, 3:1751.
32. *OP*, 3:1845.
33. *OP*, 3:1881.
34. *OP*, 3:1912, 1915.
35. *OP*, 3:1902–3.
36. *OP*, 3:1983–84.
37. *OP*, 3:1984.
38. *OP*, 3:1985–86.
39. *OP*, 3:1986.
40. *OP*, 3:1987.
41. *OP*, 3:1948–49.
42. *OP*, 3:1949, 1954.
43. *OP*, 3:1960.

CHAPTER 18

1. *OP*, 4:1999.
2. On other radical journals during this period, see Jack R. Censer, *Prelude to Power: The Parisian Radical Press, 1789–1791* (Baltimore: Johns Hopkins University Press, 1976).
3. On Paris in 1790, see David Andress, *Massacre at the Champ de Mars: Popular Dissent and Political Culture in the French Revolution* (Woodbridge, UK: Boydell and Brewer, 2000).

4. Olivier Coquard, "La Correspondance de Marat dans les journaux de Marat," *Annales historiques de la Révolution française* 267 (1987): 58–67.
5. *OP*, 4:1999, 2025, 2178, 2212.
6. *OP*, 4:1999–2000.
7. *OP*, 4:2050, 2084–85.
8. *OP*, 4:2119, 2221. See Isabelle Bourdin, *Les sociétés populaires à Paris pendant la Révolution* (Paris, 1937), 53–56, on Marat as father of the popular societies of 1791, and 57–282 for a fuller history of the societies themselves.
9. *OP*, 4:2338–41.
10. Jacques De Cock, *Les Cordeliers dans la Révolution française. Textes et documents* (Lyon: Fantasques éditions, 2002), 672.
11. *OP*, 4:2264.
12. *OP*, 4:2429, 2357, 2471, 2495.
13. *OP*, 4:2506.
14. Andress, *Massacre*, 41–42.
15. *AP*, 22:516. Marat had frequently included Kabers in lists of Lafayette's spies, most recently on 26 January (*OP*, 4:2141–43). He gave an account of Kabers's beating on 28 January (*OP*, 4:2164) and of Bailly's letter to the Assembly on 31 January (*OP*, 4:2176–77). See also Andress, *Massacre*, 50–51.
16. *AP*, 22:531, 537.
17. *AP*, 22:538.
18. *OP*, 4:2283.
19. *AP*, 22:544.
20. *AP*, 22:545.
21. *OP*, 4:2283–89.
22. *OP*, 4:2406–10.
23. *AP*, 23:558–60.
24. *AP*, 23:564.
25. *OP*, 4:2414–15.
26. *OP*, 4:2419.
27. *OP*, 4:2420.
28. *OP*, 5:2721.
29. *OP*, 5:2720, 2795.
30. *OP*, 5:2722.
31. *OP*, 5:2721.
32. *OP*, 5:2650.
33. *OP*, 5:2656–57.
34. *OP*, 5:2661.
35. *OP*, 5:2662–63, 2722.
36. *OP*, 5:2820, 4:713*.
37. *OP*, 5:2821–23.
38. *OP*, 5:2826–27.
39. *OP*, 5:2827–29.
40. De Cock, *Cordeliers*, 737–38.
41. *OP*, 5:2737.
42. *OP*, 5:2744.
43. *OP*, 5:2802, 2765, 2787.
44. *OP*, 5:2749.
45. *OP*, 5:2762–63.
46. *OP*, 5:2788–95, 2971, 2795.
47. Andress, *Massacres*, 109–22. For a fuller discussion, see Laurent Cuvelier, *La ville captivée. Affichage et publicité au XVIIIe siècle* (Paris: Flammarion, 2024).

48. *AP*, 25:352.
49. *AP*, 25:678.
50. *AP*, 25:679.
51. *AP*, 25:680–81.
52. *AP*, 25:681–701.
53. *OP*, 5:2854–56.
54. *OP*, 5:2869–70, 2872–73.
55. *OP*, 4:2520–21.
56. See William H. Sewell Jr., *Work and Revolution in France: The Language of Labor from the Old Regime to the French Revolution* (Cambridge, UK: Cambridge University Press, 1980); Michael Sonenscher, *Work and Wages: Natural Law, Politics, and the Eighteenth-Century French Trades* (Cambridge, UK: Cambridge University Press, 1989); Steven L. Kaplan, *La fin de corporations* (Paris: Fayard, 2001).
57. *OP*, 5:3014–15.
58. *AP*, 27:210.
59. See Andrew Paul Schupanitz, "Revolutionary Competition: Coalitions, Labor, and the Birth of Modern French Antitrust, 1791–1864," PhD diss., Stanford University, 2020.
60. *AP*, 27:210–12.
61. *OP*, 5:3049.

CHAPTER 19

1. *OP*, 5:2907, 2979–80, 2985, 2987.
2. *OP*, 5:2843, 2937.
3. *OP*, 3:1955.
4. *OP*, 5:2958, 3033, 3039.
5. *OP*, 5:3065.
6. *OP*, 5:3066–68.
7. *OP*, 5:3068.
8. *OP*, 5:3068–69.
9. *OP*, 5:3069, 3074.
10. *OP*, 5:3083.
11. *OP*, 5:3086, 3089.
12. *OP*, 5:3086–87, 3091.
13. *OP*, 5:3094–96.
14. David Andress, *Massacre at the Champ de Mars: Popular Dissent and Political Culture in the French Revolution* (Woodbridge, UK: Boydell and Brewer, 2000), 157, 181, 187; *Lettres de Mme. Roland, 1780–1793*, ed. Claude Perroud, 2 vols. (Paris, 1913), 2:313.
15. *OP*, 5:3155, 3159.
16. *OP*, 5:3175–76.
17. *Lettres de Mme. Roland*, 2:329.
18. *OP*, 5:892*–93*.
19. Jacques De Cock, *Les Cordeliers dans la Révolution française. Textes et documents* (Lyon: Fantasques éditions, 2002), 867–68.
20. De Cock, *Cordeliers*, 870–75; *Journal du Club des Cordeliers*, reprinted in *Aux origines de la République, 1789–1792*, 6 vols. (Paris: EDHIS, 1791), vol. 4.
21. *Journal des débats de la Société des amis de la Constitution*, undated issue, no. 14 (1791), 2–3 (probably 23 June).
22. *Journal du Club des Cordeliers*, undated issue, no. 14 (1791), 32–33; Billaud de Varenne, *Acéphrocratie* (Paris, 1791), 58, 61.
23. *Le Républicain, ou Le Défenseur du gouvernement représentatif, par une société des républicains*, reprinted in *Aux origines de la République, 1789–1792*, 3:11, 52–53; Thomas Paine, *The Rights of Man. Part the Second. Combining Principle and Practice* (London, 1792), 25.

On the *Cercle social*, see Gary Kates, *The Cercle Social, the Girondins, and the French Revolution* (Princeton: Princeton University Press, 1985).

24. Brissot, "Discours sur la question de savoir si le roi peut être jugé . . . ," in *La Société des Jacobins: Recueil de documents pour l'histoire du club des Jacobins de Paris*, ed. F.-A. Aulard, 6 vols. (Paris, 1889–97), 2:608–26 (quotation at 626).
25. Brissot, "Discours sur la question de savoir si le roi peut être jugé . . ."; Aulard, *Jacobins*, 2:610.
26. De Cock, *Cordeliers*, 885–88.
27. De Cock, *Cordeliers*, 968, 972–75.
28. *OP*, 5:3184, 3190.
29. *AP*, 28:231–42.
30. *AP*, 28:237.
31. *AP*, 28:237, 235.
32. *AP*, 28:235.
33. *AP*, 28:242.
34. *OP*, 5:3186–87.
35. *OP*, 5:3187–88.
36. *OP*, 5:3189.
37. *AP*, 28:244, 247.
38. *AP*, 28:248, 274, 277.
39. *AP*, 28:250, 251.
40. *OP*, 5:3190.
41. *OP*, 5:3192; *AP*, 28:255–57, 264. Salle would change his mind about the feasibility of referring decisions of the legislative body to the primary assemblies for ratification when it came to the question of deciding on Louis XVI's punishment. See below, p. 651.
42. *AP*, 28:261–63.
43. *AP*, 28:267–68.
44. *AP*, 28:269–70.
45. *AP*, 28:258–59.
46. *AP*, 28:259.
47. *OP*, 5:3192, 3207.
48. *OP*, 5:3207, 3210–11; *AP*, 28:365.
49. *OP*, 5:3211.
50. *AP*, 28:312; De Cock, *Cordeliers*, 984–85.
51. *OP*, 5:3196–97.
52. *AP*, 28:316–18.
53. *OP*, 5:3197.
54. *AP*, 28:319–20; *OP*, 5:3197.
55. *AP*, 28:320–24; *OP*, 5:3199.
56. *AP*, 28:324–26.
57. *OP*, 5:3198; *AP*, 28:326.
58. *AP*, 28:328.
59. *AP*, 28:327.
60. *AP*, 28:328–29.
61. *OP*, 5:3198–99.
62. *AP*, 28:329.
63. *AP*, 28:329–30.
64. *AP*, 28:330, 376–78.
65. *OP*, 5:3199.
66. *OP*, 5:3199–3200.
67. *OP*, 5:3201.
68. *OP*, 5:3205–6.

69. De Cock, *Cordeliers*, 997.
70. *OP*, 5:3211, 3215.
71. *OP*, 5:3211–16.
72. *AP*, 28:404; *OP*, 5:3216.
73. *OP*, 5:960*–61*, 6:1019*–23*.

CHAPTER 20

1. This, and the following account, is based on police reports printed in full in *OP*, 5:935*–53*. On the repression that followed the Champ de Mars Massacre more generally, see Albert Mathiez, *Le Club des Cordeliers pendant la crise de Varennes et le massacre du Champ de Mars* (Paris, 1910), 191–337.
2. *OP*, 5:942*–46*.
3. *OP*, 6:3500–3501. The editors note, however, that the entire passage devoted to Colombe was crossed out in the version of *L'Ami du peuple* Marat prepared for a later edition. As for Verrières, he escaped punishment, led veterans from Paris in the invasion of Belgium, and became military governor of occupied Anvers in November 1792. He died in Brussels in January 1793. See http://www.menouetsesvoisinsdargonne.fr/sphp?article1216.
4. An announcement of the Paris municipality to this effect, posted on 27 July, is reprinted in *OP*, 5:960*. See also Mathiez, *Le Club des Cordeliers*, 209–10, 258–59, 297–302, 317, 360–61, 370, for the questioning of specific prisoners regarding Marat and his accomplices.
5. *OP*, 6:3263, 3275.
6. *Lettres de Mme. Roland, 1780–1793*, ed. Claude Perroud, 2 vols. (Paris, 1913), 2:312.
7. *OP*, 5:953*–61*.
8. *OP*, 5:3219–23. See *OP*, 5:967*–78* for a discussion of the interruption, and counterfeit issues, of *L'Ami du peuple* during these weeks. For the issue dated 7 August, the name of the author was changed from "M. Marat" to "M. P. Marat," perhaps in an effort to outflank the counterfeiters.
9. *OP*, 6:3231. For the "illusion of politics," see François Furet, *Interpreting the French Revolution*, trans. Elborg Forster (Cambridge, UK: Cambridge University Press, 1981), 24–28.
10. *OP*, 6:3231–32.
11. *OP*, 6:3232.
12. *OP*, 6:3231–38.
13. *OP*, 5:3219.
14. *AP*, 29:264.
15. *AP*, 29:264, 275.
16. *AP*, 29:265, 276.
17. *AP*, 29:276.
18. *OP*, 6:3241.
19. *OP*, 6:3243.
20. *AP*, 29:411–12; *OP*, 6:3243.
21. Mona Ozouf offers a brilliant analysis of this debate in *Varennes. La mort de la royauté (21 juin 1791)* (Paris: Gallimard, 2005), 378–86.
22. *AP*, 29:329, 331–32.
23. *AP*, 29:331.
24. *AP*, 29:323, 327.
25. *AP*, 29:329.
26. *AP*, 29:329–30.
27. Ozouf, *Varennes. La mort de la royauté*, 182–83.
28. *AP*, 29:331, 412–13, 659–61.
29. *OP*, 6:3242, 3251–52, 3284, 3245, 3293.
30. *OP*, 6:3272, 3333.

31. *OP*, 6:3252, 3242.
32. *OP*, 6:3270.
33. *OP*, 6:3270–74.
34. *AP*, 29:631–39.
35. *AP*, 29:646.
36. *AP*, 29:647.
37. *AP*, 29:648–49.
38. *AP*, 29:650–51.
39. *AP*, 29:659.
40. *OP*, 6:3274–76.
41. *OP*, 6:3278.
42. *OP*, 6:3279.
43. *OP*, 6:3279–80, 3282–83, 3287.
44. *AP*, 30:35–38.
45. *OP*, 6:3304, 3309–11.
46. *OP*, 6:3311–12.
47. *AP*, 30:41, 38–39.
48. *AP*, 30:38–44.
49. *AP*, 30:44; *OP*, 6:3303, 3308.
50. *AP*, 30:44–54.
51. *OP*, 6:3309.
52. *AP*, 30:61–62.
53. *AP*, 30:62.
54. *AP*, 30:68, 70, 71.
55. *OP*, 6:3304–5.
56. *AP*, 30:93–95.
57. *AP*, 30:95–96.
58. *AP*, 30:99, 100.
59. *AP*, 30:100, 102.
60. *OP*, 6:3314–15.
61. *AP*, 30:108, 111.
62. *OP*, 6:3315.
63. *AP*, 30:108, 111–14.
64. *OP*, 6:3316–17.
65. *AP*, 30:117–18, 132–35.
66. *AP*, 30:168, 187, 189.
67. *OP*, 6:3319, 3333, 3415.
68. *OP*, 6:3319, 3328–29, 3336–38.
69. *OP*, 6:3338–39.
70. *OP*, 6:3340, 3391.
71. *OP*, 6:3379.
72. *OP*, 6:3399–3403.
73. See Olivier Coquard, *Jean-Paul Marat* (Paris: Fayard, 1993), 292.
74. *OP*, 6:3405–8, 3419, 3432; *PM*, 331.
75. *OP*, 6:3409–12.
76. *OP*, 6:3413–14.
77. *OP*, 6:3413.
78. *OP*, 6:3415–18.
79. *OP*, 6:3422–23.
80. *OP*, 6:3424–25.
81. *OP*, 6:3425.
82. *OP*, 6:3427.

83. *OP*, 6:3429.
84. *OP*, 6:3430–31.
85. *OP*, 6:3432.
86. *OP*, 6:3435–36.
87. *OP*, 6:3440–41.
88. On this issue, see *OP*, 6:1085*–86*.
89. *OP*, 6:3436–37.
90. *OP*, 6:3437.

CHAPTER 21

1. *AP*, 31:617–23, partially translated in Keith Michael Baker, ed., *The Old Regime and the French Revolution* (Chicago: University of Chicago Press, 1987), 278–86. The decree was adopted, but never implemented.
2. *OP*, 6:3462–3466.
3. *OP*, 6:3387–91, 3472.
4. *Réimpression de l'Ancien Moniteur*, 31 vols. (Paris, 1879–1913), 10:87. Hereafter cited as *Mon.*, with volume and page number. On this, and the Legislative Assembly more generally, see C. J. Mitchell, *The French Legislative Assembly of 1791* (Leiden, 1988).
5. *OP*, 6:3472, 3484–85.
6. *OP*, 6:3473.
7. *OP*, 6:3496–98. My thanks to David Como for pointing out that Cromwell rarely needed this kind of direct military intervention to get his way.
8. *OP*, 6:3476–77.
9. *OP*, 6:3482–83.
10. *OP*, 6:3483–86.
11. *OP*, 6:3487, 3492, 3493–94.
12. *OP*, 6:3488–89.
13. *OP*, 6:3489–90, 3498.
14. *OP*, 6:3516, 3474–76, 3527–28.
15. *OP*, 6:3505, 3620–21.
16. *OP*, 6:3497, 3517, 3519–20.
17. *OP*, 6:3553–54, 3560, 3596–97.
18. *OP*, 6:3521.
19. *OP*, 6:3522, 3391, 3664.
20. *OP*, 6:3621.
21. *OP*, 6:3506, 3621–22.
22. Jacques Godechot, *La Contre-Révolution, doctrine et action 1789–1804* (Paris, 1961), 160–73.
23. *OP*, 6:3481.
24. *OP*, 6:3455.
25. *AP*, 34:236–39; *OP*, 6:3540–43; *Mon.*, 10:119, 126; *Choix de rapports, opinions et discours. Prononcés à la Tribune Nationale depuis 1789 jusqu'à ce jour*, 21 vols. (Paris, 1818–22), 8:234–35.
26. *AP*, 34:248–54.
27. *OP*, 6:3540–42.
28. *OP*, 6:3542–45, 3549.
29. *AP*, 34:309, 311.
30. *AP*, 34:313, 316. On this theme, see François Furet, "Les Girondins et la guerre. Les débuts de l'Assemblée législative," in François Furet and Mona Ozouf, eds., *La Gironde et les Girondins* (Paris, 1991), 189–203.
31. *AP*, 34:317–18.
32. *OP*, 6:3557–59.

33. *OP*, 6:3559–62.
34. *OP*, 6:3562–64.
35. *AP*, 34:397–98.
36. *AP*, 34:403–5.
37. *AP*, 34:470–74.
38. *OP*, 6:3598–99.
39. *OP*, 6:3600–3601.
40. *OP*, 6:3632–34.
41. *OP*, 6:3630, 3640, 3634–36.
42. *OP*, 6:3636–39.
43. *OP*, 6:3636–37.
44. *OP*, 6:3640–41.
45. *OP*, 6:3656–60.
46. *OP*, 6:3661; *Mon.*, 10:362–63.
47. *OP*, 6:3663–64.
48. *OP*, 6:3664, 3692–93, 3714–15, 3793–95.
49. *OP*, 6:3479.
50. *OP*, 6:3490–91, 7:3904.
51. *OP*, 6:3550.
52. *AP*, 34:329–39.
53. *OP*, 6:3564–69.
54. *OP*, 6:3570.
55. *OP*, 6:3572; *AP*, 34:420–23.
56. *AP*, 34:425, 443–49, 611–13.
57. *OP*, 6:3573–74.
58. *OP*, 6:3581–83; *AP*, 34:433–35, 631–38.
59. *OP*, 6:3610–11, 3658–59.
60. *OP*, 6:3659–10.
61. *OP*, 6:3673–75, 3680–86. The case lingered on, with further protests by Rovère and the appointment of a commission of inquiry.
62. *AP*, 35:31–33, 42–44.
63. *AP*, 35:64–69.
64. *OP*, 6:3668–69; compare *AP*, 35:66–68; *Mon.*, 10:375; *Choix de rapports*, 8:122.
65. *AP*, 35:427–33.
66. *AP*, 35:435–37.
67. See Laurent Dubois, *Avengers of the New World: The Story of the Haitian Revolution* (Cambridge, MA: Harvard University Press, 2004), chap. 1.
68. Instructions issued on 18 March 1790 for the creation of the colonial assemblies in accordance with the 8 March decree had in fact defined active citizens as adult men owning property in the colony, or resident there for at least two years, stating further that parish assemblies would comprise "all persons" fulfilling the property and tax conditions for active citizenship. This language left uncertain the inclusion of free persons of color under these criteria, leading to considerable dispute and acrimony in subsequent debates (*AP*, 31:728–34).
69. *AP*, 26:62.
70. *OP*, 5:2891.
71. *AP*, 29:623–28. On the debates, see Lauren R. Clay, "Liberty, Equality, Slavery: Debating the Slave Trade in Revolutionary France," *American Historical Review* 128 (2023): 89–119.
72. *AP*, 29:706–7; 30:118–25. Communications received and published by the committees dealing with the colonies by 12 September were largely in favor of suspension or revocation of the decree, though the list may not have been complete (*AP*, 30:592–60).
73. *OP*, 6:3381–84; *AP*, 30:235–39, *Mon.*, 9:604–6, 612–15.

74. *AP*, 31:252–58.
75. *AP*, 31:258–59, 438–39.
76. *OP*, 6:3437–38.
77. *OP*, 6:3439.
78. *OP*, 6:3584–85.
79. *OP*, 6:3591–95.
80. *OP*, 6:3592, 3594, 3601.
81. *OP*, 6:3687–88.
82. *AP*, 35:471–72.
83. *OP*, 6:3753–54; *AP*, 35:475, 541–42.
84. *OP*, 6:3788–89.
85. *OP*, 6:3730.
86. *AP*, 35:290–92, 397–401; *OP*, 6:3701–2, 3728–29.
87. *OP*, 6:3741–42; *AP*, 35:441–42.
88. *OP*, 6:3741–42.
89. *AP*, 35:439–40, 453; *OP*, 6:3743. The ultimatum to the German princes, when Louis XVI made it, was enough to trigger threats of retaliation by the Austrian emperor, followed in turn by counter-threats from Paris. By late January, the French were heading toward war. On this entire episode, see T. W. C. Blanning, *The Origins of the French Revolutionary Wars* (London: Routledge, 1986), 96–104.
90. *OP*, 6:3721–22, 3736.
91. *OP*, 6:3724.
92. *OP*, 6:3724, 3784, 3762.
93. These passages are as quoted in *OP*, 6:1131*–32*.
94. *OP*, 6:3790–91.
95. *OP*, 6:3795–96.
96. *OP*, 6:3797–3802.

CHAPTER 22

1. This quotation is punctuated as it appeared in the inventory of Marat's papers after his death (*Archives de la Seine*, D[11] U[1]18). A version with somewhat less coherent punctuation appeared in *Journal de la Montagne* 53 (23 July 1793): 325. Both are reprinted in *OP*, 6:3811, 1213*–14*.
2. *Journal de la Montagne* 53 (23 July 1793): 325, as quoted in *OP*, 6:1214*.
3. *Réponse aux détracteurs de L'Ami du Peuple, par Albertine Marat* [Paris, 1793], 6.
4. The information in the preceding paragraphs is drawn from the discussion of Simonne Evrard by Jacques De Cock and Charlotte Goëtz in *OP*, 6:1198*–1235*.
5. The document, sold at Sotheby's in London in 1990, is printed in *OP*, 6:3813–14.
6. In a pamphlet published in July 1793 castigating Marat for a calumny he blamed for his recent expulsion from the Cordelier Club, Roux was insistent on the services he had rendered his former idol. Among them he recalled being summoned to Marat's lodging with the Evrard sisters in March or April 1792. There he had been charged with delivery of one letter to the Cordeliers urging the club to subscribe to a printing of the earlier issues of *L'Ami du peuple* and another to Robespierre requesting that he interest the Jacobins in an edition of Marat's writings. He also recollected days of asylum he had afforded The People's Friend shortly thereafter.
7. *OP*, 6:3815–16. Marat addressed another letter on the same subject, also dated 3 March, to a certain Delisle, apparently a potential editor of the work. It mentioned the possibility of opposition to his proposal within the club, the potential profit-sharing for philanthropic purposes, and his insistence that the Cordeliers' support imply no censorship of his work on their part. *OP*, 6:3813–14.

8. *OP*, 6:3817–21.
9. For the details of this account, see *OP*, 6:1183*–86*. There is some dispute concerning the fate of the manuscript. Goëtz and De Cock believe that no trace of it has yet been found. Coquard suggests that some of it may be part of the "La Bédoyère" collection now held at the Bibliothèque nationale de France. See Olivier Coquard, *Jean-Paul Marat* (Paris: Fayard, 1993), 473n5; and Coquard, "Notes sur les manuscrits de J. P. Marat au fonds 'La Bédoyère' à la Bibliothèque Nationale," *AHRF* 267 (1987): 68–73.
10. *OP*, 7:3847, 3853.
11. The following discussion owes much to the analysis offered by T. W. C. Blanning, *The Origins of the French Revolutionary Wars* (London: Routledge, 1986), 96–130.
12. *AP*, 36:352–55.
13. *AP*, 36:600–612.
14. *AP*, 36:612–16.
15. *AP*, 36:616–19.
16. *AP*, 36:698.
17. *AP*, 36:698–99; Blanning, *Origins*, 104.
18. *AP*, 37:410–13.
19. *AP*, 37:413–14.
20. *AP*, 37:414–16, 423.
21. *AP*, 37:464–71.
22. *AP*, 37:657, 717.
23. *AP*, 39:248.
24. *AP*, 39:250.
25. *AP*, 39:253.
26. *AP*, 39:254.
27. Marat later offered a fanciful explanation of Delessart's abrupt dismissal, and the sudden declaration of war that followed, as the first move in an extensive and insanely wide-ranging plot initiated by Narbonne but taken over by Lafayette, to name first one, then the other, as a dictator under a Protectorate. *OP*, 7:3929–33.
28. The news was reported in the *Moniteur* on 13 March, on the basis of a copy of an official bulletin forwarded from Luxembourg on the ninth. See *Mon.*, 11:606.
29. *OP*, 7:3848.
30. Reversing the Constituent Assembly's decision of 24 August, a decree of 4 April granted equality of rights to free persons in the colonies.
31. *OP*, 7:3856, 3852, 3901.
32. *OP*, 7:3856–58, 3888.
33. *OP*, 7:3885–86. See David A. Bell, *The First Total War: Napoleon's Europe and the Birth of Warfare As We Know It* (Boston: Houghton Mifflin, 2007), 7; and Bell, *Men on Horseback: The Power of Charisma in the Age of Revolution* (New York: Farrar, Straus & Giroux, 2020).
34. *OP*, 7:3886–87.
35. *OP*, 7:3911–12.
36. *OP*, 7:3915. Blanning, *Origins*, 118. The charge that Brissot had been a police spy under the Old Regime was destined for a long life. See, most notably, Robert Darnton, "The Grub Street Style of Revolution: J.-P. Brissot, Police Spy," *Journal of Modern History* 40 (1968): 301–27.
37. *OP*, 7:3915–16.
38. *OP*, 7:3917.
39. *OP*, 7:3920.
40. *OP*, 7:3945, 3923–24, 3945, 3928.
41. *OP*, 6:3794–95.

42. *OP*, 7:3905, 3909; see Maurice Genty, *Paris 1789–1795. L'apprentissage de la citoyenneté* (Paris, 1987), 108–11.
43. R. B. Rose, *The Making of the Sans-Culottes: Democratic Ideas and Institutions in Paris, 1789–92* (Manchester, UK: Manchester University Press, 1983), 146–51.
44. *Mon.*, 12:139.
45. *OP*, 7:3881–82, 3901–5.
46. *Mon.*, 11:573.
47. *OP*, 7:3864–69.
48. *OP*, 7:3869.
49. *OP*, 7:3947–49, 3955–59, 4019–20. Robespierre, *Le Défenseur de la Constitution* 4 (7 June 1792), as quoted in Mona Ozouf, *La fête révolutionnaire, 1789–1799* (Paris, 1976), 89. Ozouf offers a classic analysis of these two competing festivals, presenting a strong argument for their underlying similarities.
50. *La Société des Jacobins: Recueil de documents pour l'histoire du club des Jacobins de Paris*, ed. F.-A. Aulard, 6 vols. (Paris, 1889–97), 3:512–20, 524–42 (sessions of 20, 25, 27, 29 April 1792).
51. *OP*, 7:1250*–54*.
52. *OP*, 7:3964–65, 3967.
53. *OP*, 7:3949.
54. *OP*, 7:3968–70.
55. *AP*, 42:706–7.
56. *AP*, 42:707–14.
57. *Jacques Roux à Marat* (July 1793), 3. An editorial note attested that the pamphlet had already been published before Marat's death (on 13 July 1793).
58. *OP*, 7:3980–81.
59. *AP*, 43:622–23, 629–31; *OP*, 7:1270*–86*.
60. *AP*, 43:631.
61. *AP*, 45:106–7, 117–19; *OP*, 7:3984, 4086–87.
62. *OP*, 7:4040–56, 3922. For press responses, see *OP*, 7:1264*–69*.
63. *OP*, 7:4082, 4003, 4161.
64. *OP*, 7:3995, 3997–99.
65. *OP*, 7:3987, 4001, 4012–13.
66. *OP*, 7:4028; *AP*, 44:33–43. For the Austrian Committee and its genealogy, see Thomas E. Kaiser, "Who's Afraid of Marie-Antoinette? Diplomacy, Austrophobia, and the Queen," *French History* 14 (2000): 241–71; and Kaiser, "La fin du renversement des alliances. La France, l'Autriche et la Déclaration de Guerre du 20 avril 1792," *AHRF* 351 (2008): 77–98.
67. *OP*, 7:4066–67.
68. *OP*, 7:4068–69.
69. On this theme, see Marisa Linton, *Choosing Terror: Virtue, Friendship, and Authenticity in the French Revolution* (Oxford, UK: Oxford University Press, 2013).
70. *OP*, 7:4075–76.
71. *OP*, 7:4076–87.
72. *OP*, 7:4064, 4081–82.
73. *OP*, 7:4082–85.
74. *AP*, 45:163–64. Roland's speech is partially translated in Baker, *Old Regime and French Revolution*, 286–90.
75. *AP*, 45:411–32, passim; Rose, *The Making of the Sans-Culottes*, 154–55; Micah Alpaugh, "The Making of the Parisian Political Demonstration: A Case Study of 20 June 1792," *Proceedings of the Western Society for French History* 34 (2006): 115–33; Timothy Tackett, *The Coming of the Terror in the French Revolution* (Cambridge, MA: Harvard University Press, 2015), 176–80.

76. *AP*, 45:509, 653–58. Marcel Reinhard, *La chute de la royauté* (Paris: Gallimard, 1969), 342–46; Tackett, *The Coming of the Terror*, 180.
77. *OP*, 7:4128–29.
78. *OP*, 7:4131–33.
79. *OP*, 7:4088, 4101–2.
80. *OP*, 7:4088–89, 4101.
81. *OP*, 7:4089–90.
82. *OP*, 7:4116–17.
83. *OP*, 7:4090–91.
84. As noted by Jean Massin, *Marat* (Aix: Alinéa, 1988), 160.
85. *OP*, 7:4092–93, 4099.
86. *OP*, 7:4093–94.
87. *OP*, 7:4095–99.
88. *OP*, 7:4099–4100.
89. *OP*, 7:4100.
90. *OP*, 7:4134–46.
91. *OP*, 7:4147–48.
92. *OP*, 7:4151.
93. Massin, *Marat*, 202.
94. The intensity of the activity of the sections during this moment, and the divisions among and within them, is made clear by Frédéric Braesch, *La commune du dix août 1792. Etude sur l'histoire de Paris du 20 janvier au 2 décembre 1792* (Paris, 1911), 134–73.
95. Jacques De Cock, *Les Cordeliers dans la Révolution française. Textes et documents* (Lyon: Fantasques éditions, 2002), 867–68, 1101–2; Billaud-Varenne, "Discours . . . dans la séance du dimanche 15 juillet," *Journal des débats . . . de la Société des Amis de la Constitution* 233 (18 July 1792): 3–4; Robespierre, *Discours . . .* (29 July 1792), in P. J. B. Buchez and P. C. Roux, *Histoire parlementaire de la Révolution française*, 16:220–35; *AP*, 47:457–58, 475–76, partially translated in Baker, *Old Regime and French Revolution*, 286–89.
96. *AP*, 47:372–73, 423, 425–27.
97. *AP*, 47:524–25.
98. *OP*, 7:4156–57.
99. Charles Barbaroux, *Mémoires de Barbaroux*, ed. Alfred Chabaud (Paris, 1936), 45, 138–43.
100. On Panis during this moment, see Braesch, *La commune du dix août 1792*, 39, 49, 60, 184–85, 295, 337, and for his activities during the September Massacres, 364–66. On d'Aubigny, see the same work, 175, 263, 374, 553–54. Rovère, the radical from Avignon with whom Marat had been in touch for several months, also mentioned in this context by Barbaroux, is not mentioned by Braesch. On the special seat for Marat in the Insurrectionary Commune, and his appointment to its surveillance committee, see Braesch, *La commune du dix août 1792*, 291, 366–68.
101. *OP*, 8:5023, 5067.
102. *AP*, 47:560–79, 613, 615–16. The Commission report was published, on the basis of Condorcet's manuscript, in the 1804 edition of his collected works. See A. Condorcet O'Connor and François Arago, eds., *Oeuvres de Condorcet*, 12 vols. (Paris, 1847–49), 10:523–30.
103. *AP*, 47:634.
104. This account of the events of 10 August draws principally on Braesch, *La commune du dix août* 1792, 173–233; Marcel Reinhard, *La chute de la royauté*, 389–410; Tackett, *The Coming of the Terror*, 186–91.
105. *AP*, 47:644–46.
106. *OP*, 7:4161. The decree of accusation that had driven Marat into hiding was not formally lifted until 3 September when the Legislative Assembly responded to petitions for this action from his section and other citizens. The latter may have been members of the Jaco-

bin Club, who discussed such a petition on 3 September. *OP*, 10:1350*–51*; *AP*, 48:429, 49:277; *Jacobins*, 4:254–55.

107. *OP*, 7:4161–63.

CHAPTER 23

1. Frédéric Braesch, *La commune du dix août 1792. Etude sur l'histoire de Paris du 20 janvier au 2 décembre 1792* (Paris, 1911), 340. Braesch offers the most detailed account of this period of intense conflict between the Legislative Assembly and the Insurrectionary Commune lasting from 10 August until the Convention began meeting on 21 September. For a more concise discussion, see Timothy Tackett, *The Coming of the Terror in the French Revolution* (Cambridge, MA: Harvard University Press, 2015), 192–216.
2. *AP*, 48:79–80, 78, 99.
3. Braesch, *La commune du dix août 1792*, 350–55; *AP*, 48:369, 667–69; 49:8–9.
4. *OP*, 8:4678.
5. *OP*, 8:4680.
6. *OP*, 8:4680.
7. *OP*, 8:4684–85.
8. Braesch, *La commune du dix août 1792*, 350.
9. *AP*, 48:180–81.
10. *AP*, 48:297–99.
11. *OP*, 8:4691.
12. *OP*, 10:1338*–49*, 8:4708–11. Dated 2 September by Marat's first biographer, Chèvremont, this appeal to the duc d'Orléans has been convincingly redated to 10 September by Paul Matouchet in Etienne Charavay, *L'Assemblée électorale de Paris, 2 septembre–17 frimaire an II* (Paris, 1905), 606n1. The lengthy preface to this volume, written after Charavay's death, appeared initially as Matouchet, "Le mouvement électoral à Paris en août–septembre 1792," *La Révolution française* 44 (1903): 137–64, 223–48, 296–320 (dating at 158n4).
13. *OP*, 8:4693; 10:1353*–54*.
14. *OP*, 8:4699–4700.
15. *AP*, 49:78, 83, 90; Tackett, *The Coming of the Terror*, 209.
16. *AP*, 49:112–13, 141–42.
17. *AP*, 49:118.
18. *AP*, 49:144–45.
19. *AP*, 49:200, 212, 209–10.
20. Almost every detail of the massacres that began in Paris on 2 September and continued there into the fifth and sixth has been contested along with the reams of claims, counterclaims, and rumor accumulating in narratives of the French Revolution over more than two centuries. Historians have tended to turn for information to three principal investigations of unequal quality and uneven political coloration. The earliest, by Mortimer Ternaux, *Histoire de la terreur, 1792–1794 d'après des documents authentiques et inédits*, vol. 3 (Paris, 1868), was crucial in bringing to light documents that were subsequently lost to fire in 1871; it was also extravagant in its reactionary assumptions and indictments. The next, Braesch's immensely detailed account of the history of the Insurrectionary Committee (Braesch, *La commune du dix août 1792*), paid more attention to causes and consequences of the massacres than to the events themselves. Characterizing the slaughter in the prisons as an expression of popular fury beyond the power of any authorities to stop, he nonetheless indicted the Commune's surveillance committee, and Marat more specifically within it, for complicity in encouraging and celebrating it. The third essential resource, by Pierre Caron, *Les massacres de septembre* (Paris, 1935), elaborated more fully on the collective character of this overwhelming eruption of popular sentiment, assigned somewhat more active complicity to the Commune's General Council and less to its

surveillance committee. Frédéric Bluche, *Septembre 1792. Logiques d'un massacre* (Paris, 1986), in a conservative reinterpretation, moved from consideration of individual responsibilities to the conclusion that the massacres expressed a logic of violence inherent in the French Revolution from the very start.

21. Braesch, *La commune du dix-août 1792*, 484–85.
22. The actual document, identified by Mortimer Ternaux, was lost in a fire in 1871, but a facsimile was preserved. It is reprinted in *OP*, 10:1374*–75*, and in Caron, *Les massacres de septembre*, 296n3. Brought up before the Commune on 14 November, Duffort, one of the adjuncts named to the new surveillance committee, claimed that their appointments had been approved by the General Council. Veterans of the Commune denied this vociferously, insisting that the committee was illegal and that action it had taken (in this case, to seize counterfeit assignats) had been "null, arbitrary and abusive."
23. *OP*, 10:1377*.
24. *OP*, 8:4712–13.
25. *OP*, 8:4713.
26. Caron, *Les massacres de septembre*, 253–62.
27. Caron, *Les massacres de septembre*, 296–302.
28. Braesch, *La commune du dix août 1792*, 518–19.
29. On the nature of the Girondins as a group, or congeries of groups, see Marisa Linton, *Choosing Terror: Virtue, Friendship, and Authenticity in the French Revolution* (Oxford, UK: Oxford University Press, 2013), chaps. 4–5. For the classic analyses, see M. J. Sydenham, *The Girondins* (London: Greenwood Press, 1961); and Alison Patrick, *The Men of the First French Republic* (Baltimore: Johns Hopkins University Press, 1972). For other lists of members of the two groups, see also Jacqueline Chaumié, "Les Girondins," in Albert Soboul, ed., *Actes du Colloque Girondins et Montagnards (Sorbonne, 14 décembre 1975)* (Paris: Société de Etudes Robespierristes, 1980), 19–60; "Les députés montagnards en juin 1793," 346–58. A table comparing the various lists is offered in Michel Biard et al., *Dictionnaire des Conventionnels, 1792–1795*, 2 vols. (Ferney-Voltaire: Centre internationale d'étude du XVIIIe siècle, 2022), 2:1192–1219.
30. *OP*, 8:4704–6, 4710. Dated 30 September by Chèvremont, Marat's first placard discussing lists of potential candidates for the Convention has been redated to 5 September by Matouchet in Charavay, *L'Assemblée électorale*, xix n3. Matouchet also pointed to evidence that the second list, retracting some names and adding others, must have appeared on 10 September, not 2 September as Chèvremont suggested (see above, note 4).
31. *OP*, 8:4706.
32. *OP*, 10:1403*–4*. The journal offered a less positive assessment after Marat had been elected.
33. This account of the electoral assembly follows Charavay, *L'Assemblée électorale*, xi–ci.
34. *OP*, 10:1405*–6*, 1402*.
35. *OP*, 8:4722–25; 10:1406*–1412*.
36. *OP*, 10:1412*–14*; 8:4735, 4787.
37. *OP*, 8:4717–20.
38. *AP*, 50:69, 87.
39. *AP*, 50:74, 94.
40. Braesch, *La commune du dix août 1792*, 553–54, quoting the account of this session in Condorcet's *Chronique de Paris*, hardly an objective source but the fullest available.
41. *AP*, 50:121–22, 123–25.
42. *OP*, 8:4744–47.
43. *Révolutions de Paris* 167 (15–22 September 1792): 522, as cited in *OP*, 10:1418*.
44. John Moore, *Journal of a Residence in France, from the beginning of August to the middle of September, 1792. To which is added an account of the most remarkable events that happened at Paris at that time to the death of the late King of France*, 2 vols. (London; reprinted New

York, 1793–94), 1:260. For views of Marat's "new direction" and the path he took through the Convention as a result, see Jean Massin, *Marat* (Aix-en-Provence: Alinea, 1988), 224–26; Lorenzo Gianni, "Le réalisme politique de Jean-Paul Marat, député à la Convention," *AHRF*, 306 (1996): 675–92.

45. "A crowd of denouncers, including Cambon, Goupilleau, Rebecquy, surrounded me with menacing gestures; they pushed me, they shouldered me, putting their fist under my nose, to keep me from the tribune" (*OP*, 8:4789).

46. This discussion of the Convention's session of 25 September draws on the *Moniteur*, 14:40–44, 46–52, and *AP*, 52:128–43, together with supplementary notes offered in *OP*, 8:4754–73, 10:1420*–31*. For Brissot, see *Le Patriote français* (26 September 1792), 351. For Gorsas, see *Courrier de départements* (26 September 1792), 79–80; (27 September 1792), 93. For applause from the galleries, see *Thermomètre du jour* (27 September 1792), 707; *Journal des débats et décrets* (25 September 1792), 94. Marat gave additional versions of the debates and a fuller text of his speech (redacted from memory) in *OP*, 8:4785–97.

47. *OP*, 8:4797–98.

48. *OP*, 10:1434*–37*.

49. *OP*, 10:2004*–5*, lists thirty-three occasions on which Marat attempted to speak at the Convention between 21 September 1792 and 21 January 1793, the day of the king's execution, but that accounting seems to have omitted several other unsuccessful efforts mentioned at 10:1546* (and there may be others).

50. *OP*, 10:1495*.

51. *OP*, 8:4820, 4810–12, 4820–21; *AP*, 52:263–69.

52. *AP*, 52:306–12; *OP*, 8:4830–48, 4852–53, 4855–60, 4882–88; *AP*, 52:453–55; *OP*, 8:4925–26, 4886.

53. *La Société des Jacobins. Recueil de documents pour l'histoire du club des Jacobins de Paris*, ed. F.-A. Aulard, 6 vols. (Paris, 1889–97), 4:376–78, 380–81, 383–84; *OP*, 8:4898–99, 4918–22. For this session, and Marat's relationship to the Jacobin Club, see especially 10:1475*–1510*. The club addressed a lengthy denunciation of Brissot to its affiliated societies on 15 October; see Aulard, *La Société des Jacobins*, 4:394–99.

54. *OP*, 8:4905–7.

55. *OP*, 8:4848, 4846.

56. *OP*, 8:4846–48.

57. *AP*, 52:434, 444–45; *OP*, 8:4902–3, 4917.

58. *OP*, 8:4936–41, 4960–62, 4990–92; Aulard, *La Société des Jacobins*, 4:399–403.

59. *OP*, 8:4963–64, 4978.

60. *OP*, 8:4969; *AP*, 55:145–48; *OP*, 8:5318–21.

61. *OP*, 8:4974, 4987, 5097–98.

62. *OP*, 8:4967.

63. *AP*, 52:605, 657–58.

64. *AP*, 52:658–59; *OP*, 8:4994–5009, 5020–25.

65. Archives nationales de France, Peyrefitte, F/7/4590, plaq. 3. The flyer is small, 21.5 × 15.5 cm (approximately 8.5 × 6 in.). My thanks to Nicolas Rieucau and Françoise Launay for their help in deciphering these captions:

> Marat Lou fourat Lanterna per loou recompense = Marat il lui faudra la lanterne comme recompense
> Que loou Le veras peendu Ceras = Celui qui l'enlevera sera pendu
> Marat Lenemi du peuple = Marat, L'ennemi du peuple
> Qui mautera pandu Seras = Qui m'ôtera sera pendu

An English translation would read as follows:

Marat has to be strung up in recompense
Whoever removes him will be hanged
Marat, the enemy of the people
Whoever takes me down will be hanged

66. *OP*, 10:1524*–27*; *AP*, 53:12–13, 42–43.
67. *AP*, 53:50–51.
68. *AP*, 53:52–55.
69. *AP*, 53:52, 56.
70. *AP*, 53:52, 56–58.
71. *AP*, 53:99, 148–50; *OP*, 10:1535*–43*.
72. *AP*, 53:161, 158–59, 167.
73. *OP*, 10:1541*.
74. *OP*, 10:1546*.

CHAPTER 24

1. *OP*, 8:5144.
2. For this paragraph and much of what follows in this chapter regarding the politics of the king's trial, see the indispensable account by David P. Jordan, *The King's Trial: The French Revolution vs. Louis XVI* (Berkeley, CA: University of California Press, 1979). The principal speeches have been analyzed, and translated, in Michael Walzer, ed., *Regicide and Revolution: Speeches at the Trial of Louis XVI* (Cambridge, UK: Cambridge University Press, 1974). Crucial understanding of the most radical arguments for execution, grounded on principles of natural law, has been added by Dan Edelstein, *The Terror of Natural Right: Republicanism, the Cult of Nature, and the French Revolution* (Chicago: University of Chicago Press, 2009), 146–58.
3. Albert Soboul, ed., *Le procès de Louis XVI* (Paris, 1966), 50–55; *La Société des Jacobins. Recueil de documents pour l'histoire du club des Jacobins de Paris*, ed. F.-A. Aulard, 6 vols. (Paris, 1889–97), 4:429–30.
4. *AP*, 53:210–17, 219–24.
5. *AP*, 52:525–26; 53:115–16.
6. *AP*, 53:276–78, 278, 279, 281.
7. *AP*, 53:281.
8. *OP*, 8:5074.
9. *AP*, 53:386, 389.
10. *AP*, 53:391.
11. *AP*, 53:390, 392.
12. Edelstein, *Terror of Natural Right*, 148–52.
13. *AP*, 53:393–94, 398–401, 394–97.
14. *AP*, 53:385, 420, 421–27.
15. *OP*, 8:5200; *Opinion de Marat, Député à la Convention nationale, Sur le jugement de l'ex-monarque. Imprimé par ordre de la Convention*, *OP*, 8:5200–5209; also printed, with minor variations in phrasing, in *Journal de la République française* (5 December 1792), *OP*, 8:5193–98. The text is translated in Walzer, *Regicide and Revolution*, 158–66.
16. *OP*, 8:5209.
17. *OP*, 8:5206–7.
18. *OP*, 8:5209.
19. Condorcet's speech (*AP*, 54:146–53) is also translated in Walzer, *Regicide and Revolution*, 139–58.
20. *AP*, 53:493–95; *OP*, 8:5129–33, 5141.
21. *OP*, 8:5159–61.

22. Frédéric Braesch, *La commune du dix août 1792. Etude sur l'histoire de Paris du 20 janvier au 2 décembre 1792* (Paris, 1911), 840–41, citing *Chronique de Paris* (16 November) and *La Feuille de Paris* (17 November).
23. *AP*, 53:457–82.
24. *OP*, 8:5127–41.
25. *AP*, 53:607–9, 640–43.
26. *AP*, 53:654.
27. *AP*, 53:657–66.
28. *OP*, 8:5173–75.
29. *AP*, 53:676–78.
30. *AP*, 53:674, 677.
31. *AP*, 53:678, 679–80.
32. *AP*, 53:681–82.
33. *OP*, 53:682–83.
34. *Discours sur le jugement de Louis-le-dernier, sur la poursuite des agioteurs, des accapareurs et des traîtres; prononcé dans l'Assemblée générale de la Section de l'Observatoire . . . par Jacques Roux*, 4, 5, 7, 8, 9 (available in Gallica).
35. *AP*, 54:45–47.
36. *AP*, 54:47–48.
37. *AP*, 54:53.
38. *AP*, 54:74–77.
39. *AP*, 54:77–78.
40. *AP*, 54:349–54; *OP*, 8:5211–19.
41. *AP*, 54:350–53; *OP*, 8:5218–19.
42. *AP*, 54:394, 396–97, 398–99; *Mon.*, 14:668; *OP*, 8:5221–27, 5219.
43. *AP*, 54:400.
44. *AP*, 54:740–47.
45. *AP*, 55:2–5; *OP*, 8:5303, 5365–66.
46. *AP*, 55:7–15.
47. Jordan, *The King's Trial*, 106–16.
48. *AP*, 55:15.
49. *OP*, 8:5280.
50. *OP*, 8:5281.
51. *OP*, 8:5281–82.
52. *AP*, 55:43, 38, 90; *OP*, 8:5340.
53. *OP*, 8:5285; *AP*, 55:79–80.
54. *AP*, 55:80–84.
55. *AP*, 55:84–88; *OP*, 8:5285–86.
56. *AP*, 55:88–89.
57. *AP*, 55:148–49, 160–64, 165–69; *OP*, 8:5317, 5326.
58. *OP*, 8:5296–5300.
59. *AP*, 55:160; *OP*, 8:5317, 5296–5300, 5301–5; *AP*, 55:43.
60. *OP*, 8:5324–27.
61. *OP*, 10:1501*–6*; *Journal des débats et de la correspondance de la Société des Jacobins* 323 (23 December 1792) and 325 (25 December 1792).
62. *OP*, 8:5347–48.
63. *OP*, 8:5348–52.
64. *AP*, 55:427.
65. *AP*, 55:427–28, 435; *OP*, 8:5355–63.
66. *OP*, 8:5372–73.
67. *AP*, 55:633–34, 637.

68. *AP*, 55:634.
69. *AP*, 55:634.
70. *AP*, 55:638–39, 640–41.
71. *AP*, 55:641–43; *OP*, 8:5374.
72. *AP*, 55:706–10.
73. *AP*, 55:710.
74. *AP*, 55:713–16.
75. *AP*, 55:716–24.
76. *AP*, 55:724–26.
77. *AP*, 56:7.
78. *AP*, 56:7–10, 10–12, 12–16.
79. *AP*, 56:17.
80. *AP*, 56:18.
81. *AP*, 56:20.
82. *AP*, 56:22.
83. *AP*, 56:22.
84. *AP*, 56:22.
85. *AP*, 56:90–95.
86. *AP*, 56:92.
87. *AP*, 56:93.
88. *AP*, 56:94.
89. *AP*, 56:95.
90. *AP*, 56:198–99.
91. *AP*, 56:199.
92. *AP*, 56:200.
93. *AP*, 56:214.
94. *AP*, 56:232.
95. *OP*, 8:5434–35.
96. *AP*, 54:717, 714; *OP*, 8:5395–96, 5405–9.
97. *OP*, 8:5435, 5449, 5459, 5482.
98. *OP*, 8:5450, 5474.
99. *OP*, 8:5455, 5479.
100. *OP*, 8:5436–37, 5488.
101. *OP*, 8:5437, 5489.
102. *OP*, 8:5438, 5489–90.
103. *OP*, 8:5438–39, 5490.
104. *AP*, 57:43–47; *OP*, 8:5516–17. The executive council allowed the theaters to remain open but banned performances of troublesome plays such as *L'Ami des lois*. On the play, and the political storm it ignited, see especially Jean-Louis Laya, *L'Ami des Lois*, ed. Mark Darlow and Yann Robert (London: Modern Humanities Research Association, 2011).
105. *OP*, 8:5515–19. This session and the following ones leading to Louis XVI's execution are vividly described in Jordan, *The King's Trial*.
106. *OP*, 8:5529–30.
107. *AP*, 57:336–38; *OP*, 8:5532–36.
108. *AP*, 57:411; *OP*, 8:5536–37, 5545.
109. *AP*, 57:411–15; *OP*, 8:5546.
110. *AP*, 57:432–34; *OP*, 8:5547, 5531.
111. *AP*, 57:439; *OP*, 8:5550–51.
112. *AP*, 57:454; *OP*, 8:5551–52.
113. *AP*, 57:457–67; *OP*, 8:5552.
114. *OP*, 9:5557.

CHAPTER 25

1. *AP*, 56:723, 585; 57:208, 351.
2. Jean-Louis Laya, *L'Ami des Lois*, ed. Mark Darlow and Yann Robert (London: Modern Humanities Research Association, 2011).
3. *OP*, 8:5497–98.
4. *OP*, 8:5549–50.
5. *OP*, 8:5502.
6. *OP*, 8:5502–3.
7. *OP*, 9:5558.
8. *OP*, 9:5557. For more graphic descriptions, see Daniel Arasse, *The Guillotine and The Terror* (London: Penguin, 1989).
9. *OP*, 9:5560–61.
10. *OP*, 9:5558.
11. *AP*, 57:428, 507–13, 539–40; *OP*, 9:5559.
12. *AP*, 57:509–11, 539; *OP*, 9:5559.
13. *OP*, 8:5367–69.
14. *OP*, 9:5572–73.
15. *OP*, 9:5573–77.
16. *AP*, 57:547, 601, 606–31.
17. *AP*, 57:674–49, 644–53, 737–44; 58:34–46, 97–100; 57:674–49.
18. *OP*, 9:5587–88, 5601.
19. *OP*, 9:5630–31.
20. *OP*, 9:5613, 5609, 5593, 5610.
21. *OP*, 9:5595, 5614, 5612.
22. *OP*, 9:5596–97.
23. *OP*, 9:5597–98, 5612, 5614.
24. *OP*, 9:5612, 5615.
25. *OP*, 9:5618–20, 5623; 10:1597*; *AP*, 58:180.
26. For these developments, see especially Haim Burstin, *Une révolution à l'oeuvre. Le faubourg Saint-Marcel (1789–1794)* (Seyssel, 2005), 512–41; Paolo Viola, "Le mouvement populaire parisien de février–mars 1793," *AHRF* 214 (1973): 503–18, and "Luttes pour l'hégémonie au printemps," in Albert Soboul, ed., *Actes du Colloque et montagnards (Sorbonne, 14 décembre 1975)* (Paris, 1980), 121–48.
27. *OP*, 9:5695–96.
28. *AP*, 58:453, 456, 463; *OP*, 9:5648–51, 5664–66.
29. Henri Calvet, "Les origines du Comité de l'Evêché," *AHRF* 37 (1930): 12–23.
30. *AP*, 58:475–76.
31. *AP*, 58:476.
32. *AP*, 48:477; *OP*, 9:5659, 5667–68, 5676.
33. *AP*, 58:477–81.
34. *OP*, 9:5712–14.
35. *OP*, 9:5714–17.
36. Suzanne Petersen, "Jacques Roux et le pillage des épiciers (25 février 1793)," *AHRF* 245 (1981): 449–51.
37. *AP*, 59:151; Albert Mathiez, *La vie chère et le mouvement social sous la terreur* (Paris, 1927), 146; *Les Révolutions de Paris* 190 (23 February–2 March 1793): 390.
38. George Rudé, *The Crowd in the French Revolution* (Oxford, UK: Clarendon Press, 1959), 114–17; and Rudé, "Les émeutes des 25, 26 février 1793 à Paris. D'après les procès-verbaux des commissaires de police des sections parisiennes," *AHRF* 130 (1953): 33–57.
39. *OP*, 9:5740–41.
40. *OP*, 9:5740–41.

41. *AP*, 59:273.
42. *AP*, 59:275.
43. *AP*, 59:275–76.
44. *AP*, 59:276–79; OP, 9:5767–72.
45. *OP*, 9:5775, 5781–82.
46. René Levasseur, *Mémoires*, as quoted by Jean Massin, *Marat* (Aix: Alinéa, 1988), 251; Camille Desmoulins, *Le Vieux Cordelier* 2 (10 December 1793), ed. Pierre Pachet (Paris, 1987), 42–43.
47. Petersen, "Jacques Roux et le pillage des épiciers," 451.
48. *Journal des débats . . . de la Société des Jacobins* 369 (11 March 1793): 1.
49. *OP*, 9:5798, 5785, 5799, 5803–4, 5809.
50. *AP*, 59:615–16; *OP*, 9:5812.
51. *OP*, 9:5812–16.
52. *AP*, 59:716–18; *OP*, 9:5820–21.
53. *AP*, 59:718–20.
54. *AP*, 59:720–21.
55. *Journal des débats . . . de la Société des Jacobins* 368 (10 March 1793): 2–4; 369 (11 March 1793): 1–2; A.-M. Boursier, "L'Emeute Parisienne du 10 mars 1793," *AHRF* 208 (1972): 210–11. Further details regarding the events of 9–10 March are drawn from Boursier's account.
56. *OP*, 9:5851–52; *AP*, 60:5.
57. *AP*, 60:1–2, 8, 13–14; *OP*, 9:5851.
58. *AP*, 60:1–5; *OP*, 9:5853–4.
59. *AP*, 60:9–10. On the deputies *en mission*, see Michel Biard, *Missionnaires de la République. Les représentants du peuple en mission (1793–5)* (Paris: Vendémiaire, 2015).
60. *AP*, 60:17–18.
61. *AP*, 60:20–24, 54.
62. *OP*, 9:5851, 5853; *AP*, 60:54, 560.
63. *AP*, 60:63.
64. *AP*, 60:124; Boursier, "L'Emeute Parisienne," 216–23; Jacques De Cock, *Les Cordeliers dans la Révolution française. Textes et documents* (Lyon: Fantasques éditions, 2002), 1152–59.
65. *Logotachygraphe* (16 March 1793), as quoted in De Cock, *Cordeliers*, 1154; also *OP*, 9:5829–30, 5859–61. A slightly different version appears in *AP*, 60:124–25. Marat's reports of his speeches in issues of his journal also reworked them in relatively minor ways. In the following discussion, as elsewhere, I have cited debates in the Convention as they appear in the *Archives parlementaires* unless there are particular reasons to do otherwise.
66. *AP*, 60:125, 132.
67. *AP*, 60:130–31, 5385–87.
68. *AP*, 60:160.
69. *AP*, 60:161, 162.
70. *AP*, 60:162–63.
71. *AP*, 60:165.
72. *AP*, 60:166; *OP*, 9:5839–41.
73. *AP*, 60:167; *OP*, 9:5645, 5884.
74. *AP*, 60:174–75, 204.
75. *OP*, 10:1614*–17*.
76. For these articles, see *OP*, 10:1619*–21*.
77. *OP*, 9:5846–47.
78. *OP*, 9:5860, 5931.
79. *OP*, 9:5876–77.
80. *OP*, 9:5884; *AP*, 60:284–85, 331–32; *OP*, 9:5870–71.

81. *OP*, 9:5882.
82. *AP*, 60:528–30.
83. *AP*, 60:125; *OP*, 9:5827, 5883–84.
84. *OP*, 9:5879–81, 5891–92; *AP*, 60:560.
85. *AP*, 60:390–93; *OP*, 9:5888–89.
86. *OP*, 9:5886–87, 5911–18, 5909.
87. *AP*, 60:707; *OP*, 9:5935; Arthur Chuquet, *Dumouriez* (Paris, 1914), 187–94.
88. *AP*, 61:266–67.
89. *AP*, 61:98–99.
90. Chuquet, *Dumouriez*, 197–201. Carnot, the fifth of the deputies named to the delegation, had failed to meet the others as arranged.
91. *AP*, 61:267. Several versions of the proclamation to the department of the Nord are reported in *AP*, 61:136, 139, 142, 200.
92. This account of Dumouriez's address to the nation draws on Chuquet, *Dumouriez*, 201–3.
93. A search of speaker tabs in the digitized version of the *Archives parlementaires* in the French Revolution Digital Archive at Stanford (frda.stanford.edu) displayed the following hits for the two periods 9–30 March (vol. 60) and 31 March–12 April (vol. 61): Marat 71/122, Robespierre 32/66, Danton 30/76, Vergniaud 21/25, Buzot 20/19, Guadet 18/28. Marat's score for 31 March to 12 April may be skewed by the fact that his arrest was ordered after an intense debate on 12 April. See below, chapter 26.
94. *OP*, 9:5896–97, 5906–9, 6008.
95. *OP*, 9:5899, 5909, 5918–21, 5925, 5926–31, 5935, 5984–85.
96. *OP*, 9:5938–41.
97. *AP*, 60:694–95.
98. *OP*, 9:5951–59.
99. *Journal des débats . . . de la Société des Jacobins* 385 (2 April 1793).
100. *OP*, 9:5967, 5969.
101. *AP*, 61:63–64.
102. *AP*, 61:39–46.
103. *AP*, 61:49–53.
104. *AP*, 61:54–57; *OP*, 9:5996.
105. *AP*, 61:57–59; *OP*, 9:5996–97.
106. *Journal des débats . . . de la Société des Jacobins* 386 (3 April): 2–4; 387 (4 April): 1–4; 383 (29 March): 1. Etienne Charavay, *Assemblée électorale de Paris, 2 septembre 1792–17 frimaire an II* (Paris, 1905), 465–67; *OP*, 9:5924.
107. *Journal des débats . . . de la Société des Jacobins* 386 (3 April): 2–4; 387 (4 April): 1–4.
108. *OP*, 9:5983; *AP*, 61:91, 96–97; *OP*, 9:5993–94.
109. *AP*, 61:271–77.
110. *AP*, 61:278–79.
111. *Journal des débats . . . de la Société des Jacobins* 388 (5 April): 2–3. The resulting address, published on 5 April, was also printed in the *Journal (Correspondance)* 184.
112. *AP*, 61:695–96; *OP*, 9:6024–26.
113. *AP*, 61:334–37.
114. *OP*, 9:6005; *AP*, 61:127–28.
115. *AP*, 61:128, 129, 132; *OP*, 9:6001–7, 6016–17.
116. *AP*, 61:277–79; *OP*, 9:6048–49.
117. *OP*, 9:6045–46.
118. *AP*, 61:341–43, 345.
119. *AP*, 61:373–77.
120. *AP*, 61:377.

121. *AP*, 61:377.

122. *OP*, 9:6063–64.

CHAPTER 26

1. *AP*, 61:452–54.
2. *AP*, 61:522–23.
3. *AP*, 61:523.
4. *AP*, 61:523–24.
5. *AP*, 61:525.
6. *AP*, 61:525.
7. *AP*, 61:525–28.
8. *AP*, 61:529–30.
9. *AP*, 61:530–31.
10. *AP*, 61:531.
11. *AP*, 61:532.
12. *AP*, 61:532.
13. *AP*, 61:532–39.
14. *AP*, 61:541.
15. *AP*, 61:542.
16. *AP*, 61:549.
17. *AP*, 61:549–50.
18. *AP*, 61:630.
19. *AP*, 61:633–34.
20. *AP*, 61:634–35.
21. *AP*, 61:637.
22. *AP*, 61:637–38. For Marat's account of this session, see *OP*, 9:6089–6102.
23. *AP*, 61:638–39.
24. *AP*, 61:639.
25. *AP*, 61:640.
26. *AP*, 61:641.
27. *AP*, 61:641–42.
28. *AP*, 61:642–44; *OP*, 9:6106–7, 6110–11.
29. *OP*, 9:6097, 6111.
30. *OP*, 9:6098–6102.
31. *AP*, 62:26–27.
32. *AP*, 61:27–29.
33. *AP*, 62:30–31.
34. *AP*, 62:31–33.
35. *AP*, 62:34.
36. *AP*, 62:35.
37. *AP*, 62:35.
38. *AP*, 62:35.
39. *Appel nominal qui a eu lieu dans la séance permanente du 13 au 14 avril 1793, l'an deuxième de la République française, à la suite du rapport du comité de Législation, sur la question:* Y a-t-il lieu à accusation contre MARAT, membre de la Convention nationale? (Paris, 1793), 54, 76. Hereafter cited as *Appel.*
40. *Appel*, 77, 22. These numbers are based on an analysis of the *Appel*. They differ very slightly from those offered by the standard account of Alison Patrick, *The Men of the First French Republic: Political Alignments in the National Convention of 1792* (Baltimore: Johns Hopkins University Press, 1972), 111. Patrick's figure for the number of deputies *en mission* is 128 (of whom 96 came from the Mountain). Michel Biard, *Missionnaires de la*

République. Les représentants du peuple en mission (1793–5) (Paris: Vendémiaire, 2015), 41, 45, gives a total of 115 (plus 6 alternates). My thanks to Katherine McDonough for help in setting up a database for this analysis and in generating the results.

41. *Appel*, 11, 20, 48.
42. *Appel*, 12, 61, 12, 26, 27, 21.
43. *Appel*, 2, 60, 23.
44. *Appel*, 8, 15, 36, 57, 62.
45. *Appel*, 31–32, 34, 3, 2, 49, 43.
46. *Appel*, 43.
47. *Appel*, 4, 33, 4, 3, 67.
48. *Appel*, 8.
49. *Appel*, 37, 18, 15, 11, 58.
50. *Appel*, 49, 10, 8, 36, 63.
51. *Appel*, 7, 9, 14, 59, 23, 29, 30, 38, 42, 46, 67, 69, 74–75.
52. *Appel*, 5–7.
53. *Appel*, 51–54.
54. *Appel*, 34.
55. *Journal des débats . . . des Jacobins* 393 (14 April 1793): 3–4.
56. *OP*, 9:6114, 6119.
57. The documents regarding these searches are reprinted in *OP*, 10:1668*–78*.
58. *OP*, 9:6104, 6124, 6130–34; *Journal des débats . . . des Jacobins* (19, 21 April 1793).
59. Jacques De Cock, *Les Cordeliers dans la Révolution française. Textes et documents* (Lyon: Fantasques éditions, 2002), 1177–79.
60. *OP*, 9:6127–29.
61. *OP*, 9:6135–36.
62. *OP*, 9:6136–37.
63. *OP*, 9:6137–38.
64. *OP*, 9:6142–43.
65. *OP*, 9:6119, 6157; *AP*, 62:177, 617; 63:29–30.
66. *AP*, 63:29–31; *OP*, 10:1679*–83*.
67. *AP*, 63:30.
68. *OP*, 9:6158, 6167–69, 6197. For some details on this and what follows, see Olivier Coquard, *Jean-Paul Marat* (Paris: Fayard, 1993), 395–99.
69. The official minutes of the trial, *Procès-verbal de séance du tribunal criminel révolutionnaire établi à Paris par la loi du 10 mars 1793, et en vertu des pouvoirs à lui délégués par la Loi du 5 avril de la même année, du mardi 24 avril 1793*, are reprinted in *OP*, 10:1684*–87*. The *Moniteur* reported on it at length on 3 May 1793 (*Mon.*, 16:275–80). For Marat's own account, see *OP*, 9:6204–10, 6186–91, 6170–83. The accounts are not entirely consistent in relaying the precise sequence of the proceedings. Gorsas's acid description, in *Le Courrier des départements* (26 April 1793), 404–13, offered much additional detail.
70. The observer was Thomas Paine, as recorded in an account of the Marat trial in a manuscript recently discovered by Carine Lounissi and Adam Lebovitz independently. The text has been established by Lebovitz for publication, with notes and an introduction, and translated by Deborah Furet. The authenticity of the piece, written in 1825 purportedly on the basis of notes apparently made by Paine earlier but also incorporating material by the 1825 editor, is disputed by Lounissi, "Thomas Paine's Reflections on the Revolution in France: Inventing a Reactionary Paine in 1825," *French History* 36 (2022): 317–33. The precise source and date of the description cited here are unclear.
71. *OP*, 9:6171–72, 6198, 6204. Gorsas, *Courrier des départements* (26 April 1793), 404–5.
72. *OP*, 9:6205. The reporter for the *Moniteur* offered a slightly different version; see *Mon.*, 16:277.

73. Gorsas offered a similar observation that Marat had acted more as the accuser than the accused; see *Courrier des départements* (26 April 1793), 412.
74. *Mon.*, 16:277.
75. *OP*, 9:6205–27.
76. *OP*, 9:6186–91; *Mon.*, 16:278–79.
77. Gorsas, *Courrier des départements* (27 April 1793), 422.
78. *OP*, 9:6214.
79. *AP*, 62:216–18.
80. *Journal des débats . . . de la Société des Jacobins* (28 April 1793): 2.
81. *Adresse de Brissot à ses commettants*, cited in *OP*, 10:1696*–97*.

CHAPTER 27

1. *OP*, 9:6221.
2. *AP*, 62:132–38, 187, 193–96; 63:17–18.
3. *Mon.*, 16:163, 170, 177, 209; *Journal des débats . . . des Jacobins* (22 April 1793).
4. *AP*, 63:16, 18, 29.
5. Morris Slavin, *The Making of an Insurrection: Parisian Sections and the Gironde* (Cambridge, MA: Harvard University Press, 1960), 61, 23–65.
6. *AP*, 62:620–22, 777–78.
7. *AP*, 63:314–19, 427–34, 507–27, 644–46; *OP*, 9:6232–33.
8. *AP*, 64:11–17, 35, 54.
9. *AP*, 64:58; *OP*, 9:6251.
10. *AP*, 63:681–82.
11. *OP*, 10:1699*; also, *OP*, 9:6257.
12. *OP*, 9:6267.
13. *OP*, 9:6268; *OP*, 10:1699*–1702*. See Adolphe Schmidt, *Tableaux de la Révolution française. Publiés sur les papiers inédits du département et de la police secrète de Paris*, 3 vols. (Leipzig, 1867–70), 1:185, for the report of Dutard, police spy, to Garat, 5 May 1793.
14. *OP*, 9:6259.
15. *OP*, 9:6304; *AP*, 64:308, 314, 555, 571, 363, 625, 629; 65:130.
16. Schmidt, *Tableaux*, 1:212, 217, 225, 228, 220, 229.
17. Schmidt, *Tableaux*, 1:242–44, 245–46; *Journal des débats . . . de la Société des Jacobins* (20 May 1793); *AP*, 65:668–69.
18. Schmidt, *Tableaux*, 1:2[illegible]6
19. *AP*, 65:23, 36–39.
20. *AP*, 65:43–44.
21. *AP*, 65:46–47.
22. *AP*, 65:47.
23. For what follows on the Commission of Twelve and its suppression, see also Jacques Balossier, *La Commission extraordinaire des Douze (18 mai 1793–31 mai 1793)* (Paris: Presses Universitaires de France, 1986).
24. *AP*, 65:279–80.
25. *AP*, 65:280, 282–87.
26. *AP*, 65:319–20.
27. *Journal des débats . . . de la Société des Jacobins* (28 May 1793): 1; (29 May 1793): 2.
28. *AP*, 65:370–71.
29. *AP*, 65:388.
30. *AP*, 65:389–90.
31. *AP*, 65:391.
32. *AP*, 65:489–95; *OP*, 10:6457.
33. *AP*, 65:496–97.

34. *AP*, 65:498–99.
35. *AP*, 65:499.
36. Slavin, *Insurrection*, 72–75; Henri Wallon, *La révolution du 31 mai et le fédéralisme en 1793* (Paris, 1886), 481–83.
37. *AP*, 65:628–34.
38. Slavin, *Insurrection*, 90–109.
39. *AP*, 65:638–45.
40. *AP*, 65:645–51.
41. *AP*, 65:651–52.
42. *AP*, 65:652–54.
43. *AP*, 65:655.
44. *AP*, 65:656.
45. *AP*, 65:676–79; *OP*, 10:6458. For the events of 1–2 June, see Slavin, *Insurrection*, 110–26; Wallon, *31 mai*, 270–88, 484–88.
46. *OP*, 10:6458–59.
47. *AP*, 65:688.
48. *AP*, 65:689–90.
49. *AP*, 65:697–98.
50. *AP*, 65:698–700.
51. *AP*, 65:700–701.
52. *AP*, 65:701–4.
53. *AP*, 65:705.
54. *OP*, 10:6465; *AP*, 65:705–6.
55. Marat's account is confirmed by that of Serre, deputy of Hautes-Alpes; see Wallon, *31 mai*, 486.
56. *AP*, 65:706–8; *OP*, 10:6466.
57. *OP*, 10:6467.
58. *AP*, 66:8–9; *OP*, 10:6445–46, 6466–67.
59. *AP*, 66:9.
60. *OP*, 10:6499, 6481, 6503.
61. *OP*, 10:6455, 6459, 6535, 6560–65; *AP*, 66:92, 599, 672.
62. *OP*, 10:6550, 6558, 6561, 6580, 6626.
63. *OP*, 10:6605, 6618, 6621–24, 6630–33.
64. *OP*, 10:6637–38, 6660.
65. *OP*, 10:6537–43.
66. *OP*, 10:6513.
67. *OP*, 10:6519.
68. *OP*, 10:6468, 6474.
69. *OP*, 10:6474–75.
70. *OP*, 10:6475, 6473, 6555.
71. *OP*, 10:6538.
72. *OP*, 10:6504, 6506.
73. For this confrontation and its context, see Jacques De Cock, *Les Cordeliers dans la Révolution française. Textes et documents* (Lyon: Fantasques éditions, 2002), 1199–1203, 1219–57. Jean Massin, *Marat* (Aix: Alinéa, 1988), 282–87, also offers a passionate analysis.
74. *OP*, 10:6612–14, 1717*–20*.
75. For a sketch of this rivalry, see Serge Bianchi, *Marat* (Paris: Éditions Belin, 2017), 154–61.
76. *OP*, 10:6661–62.
77. *Journal de la Montagne* (15 July 1793), 248, as cited in *OP*, 10:1721*.
78. Jacques-René Hébert, speech to the General Council of the Commune, 13 July 1793,

reconstituted by Jacques Guilhaumou from newspaper reports, in Jean-Claude Bonnet et al., *La mort de Marat* (Paris: Fayard, 1986), 444–46.

79. The issue, dramatically bearing the date 13 August 1792, had been the first to reappear after the popular insurrection overthrowing the monarchy three days earlier. An annotation on the document by the collector, Maurin, dated 24 May 1837, claims that he received it from Marat's sister, Albertine. However, there is a possibility that the bloodstain was fabricated around this time. Guillaume Mazeau, *Corday contre Marat. Deux siècles d'images* (Versailles: Art Lys Editions, 2009), 29, suggests a possible dating of 1834; my thanks to him for further discussion of this point. Authentic or not, the blood on the document has been used as the basis for a metagenomic analysis. Toni de Dios et al., "Metagenomic Analysis of a Blood Stain from the French Revolutionary Jean-Paul Marat (1743–1793)," https://doi.org/10.1101/825034.

80. *AP*, 68:722. Drouet was dubbed "de Varenne" in acknowledgment that his recognition of Louis XVI in that town put an end to the king's flight to the frontier in 1791. On the situation in Paris on 13 July and Drouet's action on 13–14 July, see Guillaume Mazeau, *Le bain de l'histoire. Charlotte Corday et l'attentat contre Marat, 1793–2009* (Seyssel: Champ Vallon, 2009), especially 80–81. Other accounts of the assassination and the events that followed include Jacques Guilhaumou, "La mort de Marat à Paris (13 juillet–16 juillet 1793)," in Bonnet, *La mort de Marat*, 39–80; Eugène de France, *Charlotte Corday et la mort de Marat*, 3rd ed. (Paris: Mercure de France, 1909); Ian Germani, *Jean-Paul Marat: Hero and Anti-Hero of the French Revolution* (Lewiston, NY: Edward Mellen Press, 1992).

81. Hébert's speech is cited here as reconstructed by Jacques Guilhaumou from newspaper accounts; see Bonnet, *La mort de Marat*, 444–46. He struck a very different tone in his journal, *Le père Duchesne*, a few days later; see Mazeau, *Le bain de l'histoire*, 108–9.

82. *AP*, 68:709–10.

83. *AP*, 68:710–11. Fauchet and De Perret were arrested and eventually executed with other Girondins on 31 October 1793.

84. For this account, I have drawn on Mazeau, *Le bain de l'histoire*, 143–55.

85. Robespierre's speech is reprinted in Bonnet, *La mort de Marat*, 448–51.

86. De Cock, *Jacobins*, 1267.

87. Accounts of the procession vary in detail. I have largely followed Mazeau, *Le bain de l'histoire*, 140–43.

88. Guilhaumou, "La mort de Marat," 72–78. De Cock, *Jacobins*, 1267, quotes the *Courrier français* as estimating the size of the crowd at the funeral assembly as more than fifty thousand.

89. For the reaction of *Les Révolutions de Paris* to this extravagance reeking of royalism, see Franck Paul Bowman, "Le 'Sacré Coeur de Marat,'" in Jean Ehrard and Paul Vialleix, eds., *Les fêtes de la Révolution* (Paris: Sociétés des Études Robespierristes, 1977), 158.

90. De Cock, *Cordeliers*, 1277–78.

91. See Bowman, "Le 'Sacré Coeur de Marat'" 159; also Bonnet, "Les formes de célébration," in Bonnet, *La mort de Marat*, 122–23; Albert Soboul, "Sentiments religieux et cultes populaires pendant la Revolution. Saintes patriotes et martyrs de la liberté," *AHRF* 148 (1957): 193–213.

92. De Cock, *Cordeliers*, 1279.

93. Bonnet, "Les formes de célébration," 102; Germani, *Jean-Paul Marat: Hero and Anti-Hero of the French Revolution*. The uncertainty of the situation in the months following Marat's death has been emphasized by Soboul, "Sentiments religieux." See also T. J. Clark, "Painting in the Year Two," in his *Farewell to an Idea: Episodes from a History of Modernism* (New Haven: Yale University Press, 1999); and Mazeau, *Le bain de l'histoire*.

94. Clark, "Painting in the Year Two," 16–18, following Soboul, *Les sans-culottes parisiens en l'an II* (Paris: Clavreuil, 1958), 304.

95. *Mon.*, 18:429 (16 November; report on session of 24 brumaire/14 November).
96. *Mon.*, 18:429 (16 November; report on session of 24 brumaire/14 November).

CONCLUSION

1. *OP*, 10:6493.
2. *AP*, 58:587; Keith Michael Baker, *Condorcet: From Natural Philosophy to Social Mathematics* (Chicago: University of Chicago Press, 1975), 322–23.
3. *OP*, 10:6492.
4. Baker, *Condorcet*, 328–29.
5. Baker, *Condorcet*, 215–18.
6. *OP*, 6:3350.

INDEX

Page numbers in italics refer to figures.